The Conscious Reader

The Conscious Reader
Reader *fourth edition*

◆◆◆◆

Caroline Shrodes
San Francisco State University

Harry Finestone
California State University, Northridge

Michael Shugrue
*The College of Staten Island
of the City University of New York*

Macmillan Publishing Company
New York

Macmillan Publishing Company
866 Third Avenue, New York, New York 10022
Collier Macmillan Canada, Inc.

Library of Congress Cataloging-in-Publication Data
The Conscious reader

   Includes index.
    1. College readers.   I. Shrodes, Caroline.
II. Finestone, Harry.   III. Shugrue, Michael Francis.
PE1122.C586 1988   808'.0427   87-7050
ISBN 0-02-410361-6

Printing: 4 5 6 7   Year: 9 0 1 2 3 4

Acknowledgments

Copyright works, listed in the order of appearance, are printed by permission of the
following.

Joan Didion,"On Keeping a Notebook." Reprinted with the permission of Farrar, Straus & Giroux Inc., from *Slouching Towards Bethlehem* by Joan Didion, copyright © 1966 by Joan Didion.

Vladimir Nabokov, "The Beginning of Consciousness," from *Speak, Memory.* Copyright 1950 by Vladimir Nabokov, © 1960, 1966 by Vladimir Nabokov. Reprinted by permission of the estate of Vladimir Nabokov. This material was first published in *The New Yorker.*

Peter Werner, "Both Sides Now," excerpted from the book *Stories Parents Seldom Hear: College Students Write About Their Lives and Families* by Harriet Harvey. Copyright © 1983 by Harriet Harvey. Reprinted by permission of Delacorte Press/Seymour Lawrence. A Merloyd Lawrence Book.

Jorge Luis Borges, "Borges and Myself." From the book *The Aleph and Other Stories 1933–1969* by Jorge Luis Borges. Ed. and trans. by Norman Thomas di Giovanni. Eng. trans. copyright © 1968, 1969, 1970 by Emece Editores, S. A. and Norman Thomas di Giovanni; copyright © 1970 by Jorge Luis Borges. Published by E. P. Dutton & Co., Inc., and used with their permission.

A. Alvarez, "Sylvia Plath: A Memoir," from *The Savage God.* Copyright © 1971 by A. Alvarez. Reprinted from *The Savage God*, by A. Alvarez, by permission of Weidenfeld & Nicolson Ltd.

Quotation within Alvarez selection by Sylvia Plath, from "Daddy." From *Ariel* by Sylvia Plath. Copyright © 1963 by Ted Hughes. Reprinted by permission of Harper & Row, Publishers, Inc.

Quotation within Alvarez selection by Sylvia Plath, from "Kindness." Reprinted by permission of Harper & Row, Publishers, Inc.

Maxine Hong Kingston, "No Name Woman," from *The Woman Warrior: Memoirs of a Girlhood Among Ghosts.* Copyright © 1975, 1976 by Maxine Hong Kingston. Originally published by Alfred A. Knopf, Inc., 1976. Published in the U.S. by Random House, Inc. Reprinted by permission of Random House.

Russell Baker, "My Lack of Gumption." From *Growing Up* by Russell Baker. Copyright © 1982 by Russell Baker. Reprinted by permission of Congdon & Weed, Inc.

Maya Angelou, "Finishing School," from *I Know Why the Caged Bird Sings.* Copyright © 1969 by Maya Angelou. Reprinted by permission of Random House.

Lillian Hellman, "An Unfinished Woman," from *An Unfinished Woman.* Copyright © 1969 by Lillian Hellman. By permission of Little, Brown and Company.

Alice Walker, "When the Other Dancer Is the Self." Copyright © 1983 by Alice Walker. Reprinted from her volume *In Search of Our Mothers' Gardens* by permission of Harcourt Brace Jovanovich, Inc.

James E. Miller, Jr., "Discovering the Self," from *Word, Self, Reality: The Rhetoric of Imagination* by James E. Miller, Jr. (Dodd, Mead & Company, Inc.). Copyright © 1972 by Harper & Row, Publishers, Inc. Reprinted by permission of Harper & Row, Publishers, Inc.

Theodore Roethke, "Some Self-Analysis." From *On the Poet and His Craft: Selected Prose of Theodore Roethke,* ed. Ralph J. Mills, copyright © 1965 by Beatrice Roethke as administratrix of the estate of Theodore Roethke. Reprinted by permission of the University of Washington Press.

Carson McCullers, "Loneliness . . . An American Malady," from *The Mortgaged Heart.* Copyright 1940, 1941, 1942, 1945, 1948, 1949, 1953, © 1956, 1963, 1967, 1971 by Floria V. Lasky, Executrix of Estate of Carson McCullers. Copyright 1936, 1952, © 1955, 1957, 1963 by Carson McCullers. Reprinted by permission of Houghton Mifflin Company.

Bruno Bettelheim, "The Child's Need for Magic," from *The Uses of Enchantment: The Meaning and Importance of Fairy Tales.* Copyright © 1976 by Bruno Bettelheim. Reprinted by permission of Alfred A. Knopf, Inc.

Lance Morrow, "Daydreams of What You'd Rather Be," from *Time* magazine, June 28, 1982, p. 78. Copyright © 1982 by Time Inc. All rights reserved. Reprinted by permission from *Time.*

Ellen Goodman, "The Company Man," from *At Large.* Copyright © 1981 by The Washington Post Company. Reprinted by permission of Summit Books, a division of Simon & Schuster, Inc.

Robert N. Bellah, Richard Madsen, William M. Sullivan, Ann Swindler, and Stephen M. Tipton, "Love and the Self," from *Habits of the Heart* by Robert Bellah et alia. Copyright © 1985 The Regents of the University of California. Reprinted by permission of the University of California Press.

William Faulkner, "The Bear." Copyright 1942 and renewed 1970 by Estelle Faulkner and Jill Faulkner Summers. Reprinted by permission of Random House, Inc. An expanded version of this story appears in *Go Down Moses,* by William Faulkner.

Ernest Hemingway, "Indian Camp." "Indian Camp" is reprinted by permission of Charles Scribner's Sons from *In Our Time* by Ernest Hemingway. Copyright 1925 Charles Scribner's Sons; renewal copyright 1953 Ernest Hemingway.

Elizabeth Taylor, "Girl Reading," from *A Dedicated Man and Other Stories.* Copyright © by Elizabeth Taylor. Reprinted by permission of the estate of Elizabeth Taylor. This material was first published in *The New Yorker.*

Lionel Trilling, "Of This Time, Of That Place," from *Of This Time, Of That Place,* copyright 1943, 1971 by Lionel Trilling. Reprinted by permission of Harcourt Brace Jovanovich, Inc.

T. S. Eliot, "The Love Song of J. Alfred Prufrock." From *Collected Poems 1909–1962* by T. S. Eliot, copyright 1936 by Harcourt Brace Jovanovich, Inc.; copyright © 1963, 1964 by T. S. Eliot.

Child Is Simple, and Is Good." From *The World of Gwendolyn Brooks* by Gwendolyn Brooks. Copyright 1949 by Gwendolyn Brooks Blakely. By permission of Harper & Row, Publishers, Inc.

Randall Jarrell, "The Player Piano." Reprinted with the permission of Farrar, Straus & Giroux, Inc., from *The Complete Poems* by Randall Jarrell, copyright © 1967 by Mrs. Randall Jarrell.

James Wright, "Mutterings over the Crib of a Deaf Child." Copyright © 1971 by James Wright. Reprinted from *Collected Poems* by permission of Wesleyan University Press.

Nancy Willard, "Questions My Son Asked Me, Answers I Never Gave Him," from *The Longman Anthology of Contemporary American Poetry 1950–1980*, edited by Friebert and Young. Copyright by Nancy Willard. Reprinted by permission of Nancy Willard.

D. H. Lawrence, "Give Her a Pattern." From *Phoenix II: Uncollected Papers of D. H. Lawrence,* ed. by Warren Roberts and Harry T. Moore. All rights reserved. Reprinted by permission of The Viking Press, Inc.

Virginia Woolf, "The Angel in the House." From *The Death of the Moth and Other Essays* by Virginia Woolf, copyright 1942 by Harcourt Brace Jovanovich, Inc.; renewed 1970 by Marjorie T. Parsons, Executrix. Reprinted by permission of the publisher.

Katherine Anne Porter, "The Necessary Enemy," © 1948 by Katherine Anne Porter. First appeared as "Love and Hate" in *Mademoiselle*. Reprinted from the book *The Collected Essays and Occasional Writings of Katherine Anne Porter* by permission of Delacorte Press/Seymour Lawrence.

Cynthia Ozick, "We Are the Crazy Lady," *Ms.* Magazine, Spring 1973, copyright 1973 by Cynthia Ozick. Reprinted by permission of the author.

Germaine Greer, "The Stereotype." From *The Female Eunuch* by Germaine Greer. Copyright © 1970, 1971 by Germaine Greer. Used with permission of McGraw-Hill Book Company.

Norman Mailer, "Who Would Finally Do the Dishes?" an excerpt from *The Prisoner of Sex.* Copyright 1971 by Norman Mailer. Reprinted by permission of the author and the author's agent, Scott Meredith Literary Agency, Inc., 845 Third Avenue, New York, New York 10022.

Calvin Trillin, "Incompatible, with One L." Copyright © 1982 by Calvin Trillin. From *Uncivil Liberties*, published by Ticknor & Fields. Reprinted by permission of Lescher & Lescher, Ltd.

Carolyn Heilbrun, "Androgyny," from *Toward a Recognition of Androgyny*, Alfred A. Knopf Publishers, 1973. Reprinted by permission of Curtis Brown Associates, Ltd. Copyright © 1964, 1965, 1968, 1971, 1972, 1973 by Carolyn Heilbrun.

Noel Perrin, "The Androgynous Man," from *The New York Times Magazine*, February 5, 1984. Copyright © 1984 by the New York Times Company. Reprinted by permission.

Mark Gerzon, "Manhood: The Elusive Goal," from *A Choice of Heroes: The Changing Faces of America's Manhood* by Mark Gerzon. Copyright © 1982 by Mark Gerzon. Reprinted by permission of Houghton Mifflin Company.

Carol Gilligan, "Women's Rights and Women's Judgment." Excerpted by permission of the publishers of *In a Different Voice* by Carol Gilligan, Cambridge, Mass.: Harvard University Press, copyright © 1982 by Carol Gilligan.

Ellen Goodman, "The Tapestry of Friendships," from *Close to Home.* Copyright © 1979 by The Washington Post Company. Reprinted by permission of Simon & Schuster, Inc.

Margaret Atwood, "Fiction: Happy Endings." Reprinted by permission of Margaret Atwood from *Murder in the Dark,* published by Coach House Press, copyright © 1983.

Jill Tweedie, "The Future of Love," from *In The Name of Love* by Jill Tweedie. Copyright © 1979 by Jill Tweedie. Reprinted by permission of Pantheon Books, a Division of Random House, Inc.

James Thurber, "The Unicorn in the Garden." Copyright © 1940 James Thurber. Copyright © 1968 Helen Thurber. From *Fables for Our Time*, published by Harper & Row. Originally printed in *The New Yorker*.

John Steinbeck, "The Chrysanthemums." From *The Long Valley* by John Steinbeck. Copyright 1938 by John Steinbeck. Copyright renewed © 1966 by John Steinbeck. Reprinted by permission of Viking Penguin Inc.

Carson McCullers, "The Sojourner," from *The Ballad of the Sad Cafe and Collected Short Stories* by Carson McCullers. Copyright 1936, 1941, 1942, 1943, 1950, 1951, 1955 by Carson McCullers. Copyright renewed by Flora V. Lasky. Reprinted by permission of Houghton Mifflin Company.

James Thurber, "The Catbird Seat." Copyright © 1945 James Thurber. Copyright © 1973 Helen W. Thurber and Rosemary T. Sauers. From *The Thurber Carnival,* published by Harper & Row Publishers, Inc.

Raymond Carver, "What We Talk About When We Talk About Love." Copyright © 1981 by Raymond Carver. Reprinted from *What We Talk About When We Talk About Love* by Raymond Carver, by permission of Alfred A. Knopf, Inc.

Katherine Anne Porter, "Rope." From *Flowering Judas and Other Stories,* copyright 1930, 1958 by Katherine Anne Porter. Reprinted by permission of Harcourt Brace Jovanovich, Inc.

W. H. Auden, "Lay Your Sleeping Head, My Love." Copyright 1940 and renewed 1968 by W. H. Auden. Reprinted from *Collected Shorter Poems 1927–1957,* by W. H. Auden, by permission of Random House, Inc.

Edna St. Vincent Millay, "Love Is Not All." From *Collected Poems,* Harper & Row. Copyright 1931, 1958 by Edna St. Vincent Millay and Norma Millay Ellis. Reprinted by permission of Norma Millay Ellis.

Denise Levertov, "The Third Dimension." Copyright © 1957 by Denise Levertov. Reprinted by permission of the author.

E. E. Cummings, "I Like My Body When It Is with Your." Copyright 1925, by E. E. Cummings. From *Complete Poems 1913–1962.* By permission of Harcourt Brace Jovanovich, Inc.

Adrienne Rich, "Living in Sin." From *The Diamond Cutters,* published by Harper & Row, New York, 1955.

Reprinted by permission of Adrienne Rich.

May Swenson, "Women Should Be Pedestals." "Women" by May Swenson (copyright © 1968 May Swenson), which first appeared in the *New American Review #3,* is reprinted by permission of Charles Scribner's Sons from *Iconographs.*

Studs Terkel, "Miss U.S.A," from *American Dreams: Lost and Found.* Copyright © 1980 by Studs Terkel. Reprinted by permission of Random House, Inc.

Bobbie Ann Mason, "Reaching the Stars: My Life as a Fifties Groupie." Reprinted by permission; © 1986 Bobbie Ann Mason. Originally in *The New Yorker,* May 26, 1986.

Art Buchwald, "Leisure Will Kill You." Reprinted by permission of G. P. Putnam's Sons from *Laid Back in Washington* by Art Buchwald. Copyright © 1978, 1979, 1980, 1981 by Art Buchwald.

Roger Angell, "Reflections: The Cheers for Keith." Reprinted by permission; © 1986 Roger Angell. Originally in *The New Yorker,* May 5, 1986.

Marie Winn, "The Plug-In Drug: TV and the American Family." Originally titled "Family Life." From *The Plug-In Drug* by Marie Winn. Copyright © 1977 by Marie Winn Miller. Reprinted by permission of Viking Penguin Inc.

S. J. Perelman, "Meanness Rising from the Suds," from *The Last Laugh.* Copyright © 1981 by James Mathias, as executor of the estate of S. J. Perelman. Reprinted by permission of Simon & Schuster, Inc. This material was first published in *The New Yorker.*

George Grella, "James Bond: Culture Hero," from *The New Republic,* 1964. Copyright 1964 by George Grella. Reprinted by permission of George Grella.

Robert Palmer, "What Pop Lyrics Say to Us Today," from *The New York Times,* February 24, 1985. Copyright © 1985 by the New York Times Company. Reprinted by permission.

E. J. Hobsbawm, "The Jazz Comeback." Reprinted with permission from The New York Review of Books. Copyright 1987, New York Review, Inc.

John Cheever, "The Enormous Radio," from *The Enormous Radio and Other Stories*. Reprinted by permission of International Creative Management. Copyright © 1953 by John Cheever. Copyright renewed 1981 by John Cheever.

Alice Walker, "Nineteen Fifty-five." Copyright © 1981 by Alice Walker. Reprinted from her volume *You Can't Keep a Good Woman Down* by permission of Harcourt Brace Jovanovich, Inc.

Rainer Maria Rilke, "Letter to a Young Poet." Reprinted from *Letters to a Young Poet* by Rainer Maria Rilke, translated by M. D. Herter Norton, by permission of W. W. Norton & Company, Inc. Copyright 1934 by W. W. Norton & Company, Inc. Copyright renewed 1962 by M. D. Herter Norton. Revised Edition copyright 1954 by W. W. Norton & Company, Inc. Copyright 1982 by M. D. Herter Norton.

Hermann Hesse, "To a Cabinet Minister, August 1917." From *If the War Goes On* by Hermann Hesse, translation copyright © 1970, 1971 by Farrar, Straus & Giroux, Inc.

John Gardner, "Learning from Disney and Dickens," from *The New York Times*, January 30, 1983, Book Review. Copyright © 1983 by the New York Times Company. Reprinted by permission.

Aaron Copland, "Listening to Music," from *What to Listen for in Music*. Copyright © 1957 McGraw-Hill Book Company. Reprinted by permission.

Northrop Frye, "The Keys to Dreamland," from *The Educated Imagination*. Reprinted by permission of Indiana University Press and CBC Enterprises/Les Entreprises Radio-Canada.

Mike Royko, "The Virtue of Prurience," April 17, 1983. © with permission the *Chicago Sun-Times*, Inc., 1987.

E. M. Forster, "Art for Art's Sake." Copyright 1949 by E. M. Forster; renewed 1977 by Donald Parry. Reprinted from *Two Cheers for Democracy* by E. M. Forster by permission of Harcourt Brace Jovanovich, Inc.

Oscar Mandel, "Dissonant Music Sixty Years After," from *South Atlantic Quarterly*, 72(1). Copyright © 1973 Duke University Press.

Anne Tyler, "Still Just Writing." Reprinted from *The Writer on Her Work*, edited by Janet Sternberg, by permission of W. W. Norton & Company, Inc. Copyright © 1980 by Janet Sternberg.

Marya Mannes, "How Do You Know It's Good?" Reprinted from *But Will It Sell* by permission of Harold Ober Associates.

Christopher Lasch, "The Degradation of Work." Copyright © 1984 *Harper's Magazine*. All rights reserved. Reprinted from the February issue by special permission.

Muriel Rukeyser, "The Backside of the Academy," from *The Speed of Darkness*. Reprinted by permission of International Creative Management. Copyright © 1968 by Muriel Rukeyser.

Archibald MacLeish, "Invocation to the Social Muse." From *Collected Poems 1917–1952*. Copyright © 1962 by Archibald MacLeish. Reprinted by permission of Houghton Mifflin Company.

Marianne Moore, "Poetry." Reprinted with permission of Macmillan Publishing Co., Inc., from *Collected Poems* by Marianne Moore. Copyright 1935 by Marianne Moore, renewed 1963 by Marianne Moore and T. S. Eliot.

Bertrand Russell, "If We Are to Survive This Dark Time," from *The Basic Writings of Bertrand Russell*, edited by Robert F. Egner and Lester E. Denonn. Copyright © 1961 by Allen & Unwin Ltd. Reprinted by permission of Simon & Schuster, Inc.

Karl Jaspers, "Is Science Evil?" Reprinted from *Commentary*, by permission; copyright © 1950 by the American Jewish Committee. Reprinted by permission of the publisher.

Jacob Bronowski, "The Reach of the Imagination." *American Scholar*, Spring 1967. Reprinted by permission of the author.

Joseph Weizenbaum, "On the Impact of the Computer on Society," from *Science, 176:* 609–614, May 1972. © 1972 by The American Association for the Advancement of Science. Reprinted by permission of the American Association for the Advancement of Science and by permission of Joseph Weizenbaum.

Lewis Thomas, "A Trip Abroad," from *The Medusa and the Snail* by Lewis

Schell. Reprinted by permission of Random House, Inc. This excerpt appeared in *Lifestudies*, by David Cavitch, under the title, "The Choice."

George Orwell, "The Principles of Newspeak." From *Nineteen Eighty-Four* by George Orwell, copyright 1939 by Harcourt Brace Jovanovich, Inc.; renewed 1977 by Sonia Brownell Orwell. Reprinted by permission of the publisher.

Rebecca West, "The Meaning of Treason," from *Harper's*, October 1947. Reprinted by permission of A D Peters & Co Ltd.

Carol Tavris, "Anger in an Unjust World," from *Anger: The Misunderstood Emotion*. Copyright © 1983 by Carol Tavris. Reprinted by permission of Simon & Schuster, Inc.

Jean-Paul Sartre, "The Passion of the Anti-Semite." Reprinted by permission of Schocken Books Inc. From *Anti-Semite and Jew* by Jean-Paul Sartre, translated by George J. Becker. Copyright © 1948 by Schocken Books Inc. Copyright renewed © 1976 by Schocken Books Inc.

James Baldwin, "Fifth Avenue Uptown: A Letter from Harlem." Copyright © 1960 by James Baldwin, from the book *Nobody Knows My Name*. Reprinted by permission of Doubleday & Company.

Ryszard Kapuscinski, "Fire on the Road," trans. William Brand, copyright by Ryszard Kapuscinski. Reprinted by permission of Harper & Row, Publishers, Inc.

Franz Kafka, "A Report to an Academy." Reprinted by permission of Schocken Books Inc. from *The Penal Colony* by Franz Kafka. Copyright © 1948, 1976 by Schocken Books, Inc.

William Faulkner, "Dry September," from *Collected Stories of William Faulkner*. Reprinted by permission of Random House, Inc.

Ray Bradbury, "Perhaps We Are Going Away," from *The Machineries of Joy*. Reprinted by permission of Don Congdon Associates, Inc. Copyright © 1962 by Ray Bradbury.

Wilfred Owen, "Dulce et Decorum Est." Wilfred Owen, *The Collected Poems of Wilfred Owen*. Copyright © 1963 by Chatto & Windus, Ltd. Reprinted by permission of New Directions Publishing Corporation.

William Stafford, "Freedom." *New American Review 2*, 1968. Copyright © 1968. Reprinted by permission of the author.

W. H. Auden, "The Unknown Citizen." Copyright 1940 and renewed 1968 by W. H. Auden. Reprinted from *Collected Shorter Poems 1927–1957*, by W. H. Auden, by permission of Random House, Inc.

Robert Frost, "Departmental." From *The Poetry of Robert Frost*, edited by Edward Connery Lathem. Copyright 1936 by Robert Frost. Copyright © 1964 by Lesley Frost Ballantine. Copyright © 1969 by Holt, Rinehart and Winston. Reprinted by permission of Henry Holt and Company, Inc.

Sophocles, from *The Antigone of Sophocles: An English Version* by Dudley Fitts and Robert Fitzgerald, copyright 1939 by Harcourt Brace Jovanovich, Inc.; renewed 1967 by Dudley Fitts and Robert Fitzgerald. Reprinted by permission of the publisher. *Caution:* All rights, including professional, amateur, motion picture, recitation, lecturing, performance, public reading, radio broadcasting, and television are strictly reserved. Inquiries on all rights should be addressed to Harcourt Brace Jovanovich, Inc., 111 Fifth Avenue, New York, NY 10003.

Lincoln Steffens, "I Go to College," Parts I and II from *The Autobiography of Lincoln Steffens* by Lincoln Steffens, copyright 1931 by Harcourt Brace Jovanovich, Inc.; renewed 1959 by Peter Steffens. Reprinted by permission of the publisher.

Maya Angelou, "Graduation," from *I Know Why the Caged Bird Sings* by Maya Angelou. Copyright © 1969 by Maya Angelou. Reprinted by permission of Random House, Inc.

Lewis Thomas, "Humanities and Science." from *Late Night Thoughts on Listening to Mahler's Ninth Symphony* by Lewis Thomas. Copyright © 1983 by Lewis Thomas. Reprinted by permission of Viking Penguin Inc.

Woody Allen, "My Speech to the Graduates," from *The New York Times*, August 10, 1979 (Op-Ed). Copyright © 1979 by The New York Times Company. Reprinted by permission.

Anna Tuttle Villegas, "The Teacher

as Dragon," from *California Living Magazine*, January 23, 1983. Reprinted with permission from California Living Magazine of the San Francisco Sunday Examiner and Chronicle, copyright © 1984, San Francisco Examiner.

Howard Gardner, "Human Intelligence Isn't What We Think It Is." Copyright, 1984, *U.S. News & World Report*. Reprinted from issue of March 19, 1984.

Harold Brodkey, "Reading: The Most Dangerous Game." From *The New York Times*, November 24, 1985. Copyright © 1985 by The New York Times Company. Reprinted by permission.

Loren Eiseley, "The Hidden Teacher." From "The Hidden Teacher" in *The Unexpected Universe*, copyright © 1964, 1969 by Loren Eiseley. Reprinted by permission of Harcourt Brace Jovanovich, Inc.

"What Should Michael Do?" Symposium, *The New Republic*, June 30, 1986. Reprinted by permission of *The New Republic*, copyright © 1986, The New Republic, Inc.

John Cheever, "Expelled." Reprinted by permission of International Creative Management. Copyright 1930 by John Cheever. This story first appeared in *The New Republic*, October 1, 1930, and again in July 19 and 26, 1982.

Max Shulman, "Love Is a Fallacy," from *Reading for Rhetoric* (previously published by Doubleday). Copyright 1951, renewed 1979 by Max Shulman. Reprinted by permission of Harold Matson Company, Inc.

Langston Hughes, "Theme for English B," from *Montage of a Dream Deferred*. Reprinted by permission of Harold Ober Associates Incorporated. Copyright 1951 by Langston Hughes. Copyright renewed 1979 by George Houston Bass.

Theodore Roethke, "Elegy for Jane: My Student Thrown by a Horse," copyright © 1950 by Theodore Roethke from the book *The Collected Poems of Theodore Roethke* by Theodore Roethke. Reprinted by permission of Doubleday & Company, Inc.

Marianne Moore, "The Student," from *What Are Years?* Reprinted with permission of Macmillan Publishing Company. Copyright 1941, and renewed 1969, Marianne Moore.

Eudora Welty, "Finding a Voice." Reprinted by permission of the publishers from *One Writer's Beginnings* by Eudora Welty. Cambridge, Mass.: Harvard University Press, Copyright © 1983, 1984 by Eudora Welty.

Ralph Ellison, "On Becoming a Writer." Copyright © 1964 by Ralph Ellison. Reprinted from *Shadow and Act* by Ralph Ellison, by permission of Random House, Inc.

Jules Olitski, "Wonder Is Sacred," from *The Courage of Convictions*. Reprinted by permission by Dodd, Mead & Company, Inc. from *The Courage of Conviction*, edited by Phillip L. Berman. Copyright © 1985 by the Center for the Study of Contemporary Belief.

Saul Bellow and Adrienne Rich, From the National Book Award acceptance speech, "Three Cheers for Good Marks: Writers on Their Prizes," from *The New York Times*, November 16, 1986. Copyright © 1986 by The New York Times Company. Reprinted by permission.

Gerald Weissmann, "Foucault and the Bag Lady," from *The Woods Hole Cantata* by Gerald Weissmann. Reprinted by permission of Dodd, Mead & Company, Inc. Copyright © 1985 by Gerald Weissmann, M.D.

Studs Terkel, "Carl Murray Bates, Mason," from *Working: People Talk About What They Do All Day and How They Feel About What They Do* by Studs Terkel. Copyright © 1972, 1974 by Studs Terkel. Reprinted by permission of Pantheon Books, a Division of Random House, Inc.

Raymond Firth, "God and Anthropology," from *The Times Literary Supplement*, May 23, 1986. Copyright © 1986 Times Newspapers Limited.

Brian Pippard, "God the Physical Scientist," from *The Times Literary Supplement*, May 23, 1986. Copyright © 1986 Times Newspapers Limited.

Annie Dillard, "Sight into Insight," from *Harper's Magazine*, February 1974. Reprinted by permission of the author and her agent Blanche C. Gregory, Inc. Copyright © 1974 by Annie Dillard.

John Reed, "Almost Thirty," from *The New Republic,* April 15, 1936. Reprinted by permission of *The New Republic.*

Lewis Thomas, "Seven Wonders." From *Late Night Thoughts on Listening to Mahler's Ninth Symphony* by Lewis Thomas. Copyright © 1983 by Lewis Thomas. Reprinted by permission of Viking Penguin Inc.

Rollo May, "The Man Who Was Put in a Cage," from *Psychology and the Human Dilemma.* Reprinted by permission of Van Nostrand Reinhold Co.

Helen Keller, "Three Days to See." Reprinted by permission of the American Foundation for the Blind, Inc.

Loren Eiseley, "Man in the Autumn Light," in *The Invisible Pyramid.* Copyright © 1970 Loren Eiseley. Reprinted with the permission of Charles Scribner's Sons.

Ellen Goodman, "It's Failure, Not Success," from *Close to Home.* Copyright © 1979 by The Washington Post Company. Reprinted by permission of Simon & Schuster, Inc.

Tom Wolfe, "Mauve Gloves & Madmen, Clutter & Vine," from *Mauve Gloves & Madmen, Clutter & Vine* by Tom Wolfe. Copyright © 1975, 1976 by Tom Wolfe. Reprinted by permission of Farrar, Straus & Giroux, Inc.

May Sarton, "The Rewards of Living a Solitary Life," from *The New York Times,* April 8, 1974 (Op-Ed). Copyright © 1974 by The New York Times Company. Reprinted by permission.

E. M. Forster, "What I Believe." From *Three Cheers for Democracy,* copyright 1939, 1967 by E. M. Forster. Reprinted by permission of Harcourt Brace Jovanovich, Inc.

Jeffrey H. Goldstein, "The Healing Power of Laughter." This article reprinted by permission of *The Sciences* and is from the August/September 1982 issue. Individual subscriptions are $13.50 per year. Write to The Sciences, 2 East 63rd Street, New York, NY 10021 or call 1-800-THE NYAS.

Stuart Chase, "A Very Private Utopia," from *The Nation, 126,* May 16, 1928. Reprinted by permission of the publisher.

Joyce Carol Oates, "New Heaven and Earth," from *Saturday Review Magazine,* November 4, 1972. Reprinted by permission of the author and her agent Blanche C. Gregory, Inc. Copyright © 1972 by Joyce Carol Oates.

Anton Chekhov, "The Bet," from *The Schoolmistress and Other Stories* by Anton Chekhov, translated from the Russian by Constance Garnett. Reprinted with permission of Macmillan Publishing Company. Copyright © 1979 by Macmillan Publishing Co., Inc.

Walter Van Tilburg Clark, "The Portable Phonograph." Reprinted by permission of International Famous Agency. Copyright © 1941, 1969 by Walter Van Tilburg Clark.

E. B. White, "The Second Tree from the Corner," from *The Second Tree from the Corner* by E. B. White. Copyright 1947 by E. B. White. Originally appeared in *The New Yorker* and is reprinted by permission of Harper & Row, Publishers, Inc.

Marianne Moore, "The Mind Is an Enchanting Thing." Reprinted with permission of Macmillan Publishing Co., Inc., from *Collected Poems* by Marianne Moore. Copyright 1944 by Marianne Moore, renewed 1972 by Marianne Moore.

Theodore Roethke, "The Waking." Copyright 1948 by Theodore Roethke. From *The Collected Poems of Theodore Roethke.* Reprinted by permission of Doubleday & Company, Inc.

Jorge Luis Borges, "The Web," from *The New Yorker,* June 2, 1986. Translated by Alastair Reid. Reprinted by permission; © 1986 Alastair Reid. Originally in *The New Yorker.*

Credits for Art Insert

Gauguin, Paul: *Self-Portrait* (1889), National Gallery of Art, Washington; Chester Dale Collection.

Cassatt, Mary: *The Boating Party* (1983–1984), National Gallery of Art, Washington; Chester Dale Collection.

Renoir, Pierre Auguste: *The Luncheon of the Boating Party*, The Phillips Collection, Washington, D.C.

Legér, Fernand: *The Great Parade* (1954), Collection, Solomon R. Guggenheim Museum, New York.

Delaunay, Robert-Victor-Félix: *Red Eiffel Tower* (1911–1912), Collection, Solomon R. Guggenheim Museum, New York. Photo: David Heald.

Daumier, Honoré: *The Uprising*, The Phillips Collection, Washington, D.C.

Grosz, George: *Student*, The Cleveland Museum of Art, Purchase, General Reserve Fund.

Beckmann, Max: *Departure* (1932–33), Oil on Canvas; tryptych, center panel 7' 3/4″ × 45 3/8″; side panels each 7' 3/4″ × 39 1/4″. Collection, The Museum of Modern Art, New York. Given anonymously (by exchange).

Preface

—◆◆◆—

. . . the unexamined life is not worth living.
—Plato, The Apology

Some years ago Alvin Toffler deplored the fact that students can finish twelve years of schooling without once asking themselves such basic questions as "What's life about? What am I here for? What's better than something else? What's worth dying for?"

Believing that the development of writing skills depends on the heightening of consciousness, the editors of *The Conscious Reader* invite students to examine and to respond to the basic questions that writers since Plato have posed. The selections included engage our interests by their style and by their focus on issues of universal concern. They reflect the continuity between past and present, serve as a catalyst to self-expression, sharpen our perceptions, and widen our sympathies. Consciousness heightened through reading develops effective writing, and the act of writing fosters self-definition. As we extend awareness by reading, we become increasingly conscious of the reservoir of memories and experiences from which to draw and the variety of forms and techniques that give shape to our writing.

Over two-thirds of the readings in this book are nonfiction prose, primarily exposition or argument. Some of the essays are personal and readily comprehensible and provide models for early writing assignments. Others, more complex, should help students develop the ability to reason abstractly. Although most of the authors included are accomplished literary stylists, others are primarily distinguished for their contributions to popular culture, science, philosophy, and psychology.

We have also included twenty-eight stories and thirty-six poems. The inclusion of imaginative literature in a composition course needs no special justification. It serves a number of important goals: to enhance the pleasure of reading, to educate the emotions as well as the mind, to stimulate original creative efforts, and to provide vicarious experience with which to test the ideas expressed in essays. The dramatic situations, vivid character portrayals, and the verbal compression of fiction and poetry also suggest techniques to enliven student writing. We are convinced more than ever that the most stimulating as well as most economical means of helping students to develop conceptual literacy is to expose them to literate essays and imaginative literature, both of which will arrest their interest and challenge their thinking.

This Fourth Edition of *The Conscious Reader* includes three significant additions that enrich the central themes presented and enlarge the humanistic scope of the collection. The first addition extends our representation of genres to include drama. *Antigone* by Sophocles and Ibsen's *Ghosts* add depth to the discussion of themes such as "Men and Women" and "Freedom and Human Dignity." A new thematic section, "Professional Values," is the second addition. The personal meaning of work and career are almost as central to our culture as are personal values. The new section provides the opportunity to explore what people write about what they do and what they think about what they do. Our third innovation in this edition allows students to approach the themes through the art of painting. In choosing works to reproduce, we determined that they should be lively and colorful, that they should relate to certain themes in *The Conscious Reader,* and that they should elicit interesting discussions and compositions. These three extensions of the collection's scope should increase the book's versatility and its capacity to engage the reader deeply.

Each selection has a head note and suggestions for discussion and writing to help students explore multiple levels of understanding. The suggestions invite students to pay careful attention to thought and structure and to compare their experience with the vision of life expressed in the selections. Exploring cultural patterns both similar and alien to one's own should encourage a continuing dialectic in classroom discussion as well as in writing. Also to encourage discussion we have included selections that represent a wide range of academic disciplines and interests—from psychology to biology and computer science.

The thematic groupings represent a convenient division of the book. The readings begin with the search for self and move to consideration of the self in relation to others—parents, friends, and lovers. The next section focuses on culture, including discussions of both popular culture and art and society. The next section explores many facets of the world of science and technology. The readings continue with a variety of statements about our aspirations and failures to ensure a sense of freedom and human dignity for all. The book concludes with several sections on the examined life. The selections mediate between problems of education and human concerns and then return full cycle to the individual's search for meaning and value.

If there is a dominant theme in these readings, it is that neither understanding of the past nor projections of the future can eliminate conflict from our lives and that opposing forces in the self and society are a part of the human condition. Indeed, it is vital that they contend. For it is primarily through conscious recognition and expression of these conflicting forces that we may find our way to a tolerance of ambiguity and to an increased freedom of choice.

Acknowledgments

Jennifer S. Banks
Michigan State University

Janet Boyle
Wheeling College

George R. Bozzini
George Washington University

Esther P. Burgess
Walla Walla Community College

Patricia Burns
University of Maine-Orono

Nancy Frey Dillard
The University of Alabama-Huntsville

Judi Doumas
Old Dominion University

Anita Gandolfo
West Virginia University

Franklin Hamilton
C. S. Mott Community College

Maureen Hoag
Wichita State University

Frederick Kiley
Trenton State University

Harvey Lillywhite
Towson State University

Samuel E. Longmire
University of Evansville

James Maxfield
Whitman College

William McKim
Northern Kentucky University

Terry Otten
Wittenberg University

C. Ruth Sabol
West Chester University

Jenny S. Spencer
Vanderbilt University

John W. Taylor
South Dakota State University

Dorothy C. Whitley
Campbell University

Terri Whitney
North Shore Community College

We also want to thank the following individuals for their continued commitment and concern: Mary Catherine Farley, Robert E. Jackson, Carl Barth, Charles Dolan, and, particularly for her help with the paintings, Eve Finestone. Finally, for his valuable assistance and patience, we wish to thank our editor at Macmillan, D. Anthony English.

C. S.
H. F.
M. S.

CONTENTS

——— ◆◆◆◆ ———

The Search for Self

Personal Reminiscences

Essays

Poetry

Personal Relationships: Men and Women

Essays

Fiction

Drama

Poetry

The Cultural Tradition: Popular Culture

Personal Reminiscences

Essays

Fiction

The Cultural Tradition: Art and Society

Letters and Personal Reminiscences

Essays

Fiction

Poetry

Science, Technology, and the Future

Essays

Fiction

Poetry

Freedom and Human Dignity

Personal Reminiscences

Essays

Fiction

Poetry

Drama

The Examined Life: Education

Personal Reminiscences

Essays

Fiction

Poetry

The Examined Life: Professional Values

Personal Reminiscences

Essays and Addresses

The Examined Life: Personal Values

Personal Reminiscences

Essays

Fiction

Poetry

Rhetorical Contents

◆◆◆

The following arrangement of expository essays will suggest ways in which readers can approach the selections. The classifications are not, of course, rigid, and many selections might fit as easily into one category as another.

Identification

Comparison/Contrast

Definition

Analysis _____

Illustration

Argument and Persuasion _____

Diction and Tone

Narration

Argument and Persuasion

Diction and Tone

Narration

The Search for Self

◆◆◆

Love, then, creates a dilemma for Americans. In some ways, love is the quintessential expression of individuality and freedom. At the same time, it offers intimacy, mutuality, and sharing. In the ideal love relationship, these two aspects of love are perfectly joined—love is both absolutely free and completely shared. Such moments of perfect harmony among free individuals are rare, however. The sharing and commitment in a love relationship can seem, for some, to swallow up the individual, making her (more often than him) lose sight of her own interests, opinions, and desires. Paradoxically, since love is supposed to be a spontaneous choice by free individuals, someone who has "lost" herself cannot really love, or cannot contribute to a real love relationship. Losing a sense of one's self may also lead to being exploited, or even abandoned, by the person one loves.

> —**Robert N. Bellah, et al.,** "Love and the Self" from
> *Habits of the Heart*

As I dance, whirling and joyous, happier than I've ever been in my life, another bright faced dancer joins me. . . . The other dancer has obviously come through all right, as I have done. She is beautiful, whole, and free. And she is also me.

> —**Alice Walker,** "When the Other Dancer Is the Self"

I think we are well advised to keep on nodding terms with the people we used to be, whether we find them attractive company or not. Otherwise they turn up unannounced and surprise us, come hammering on the mind's door at 4 A.M. of a bad night and demand to know who deserted them,

who betrayed them, who is going to make amends. . . .
We forget the loves and the betrayals alike, forget what we
whispered and what we screamed, forget who we were.

—**Joan Didion,** "On Keeping a Notebook"

Whether in the pastoral joys of country life or in the labyrinthine city, we Americans are always seeking. We wander,
question. But the answer waits in each separate heart—the
answer of our own identity and the way by which we can
master loneliness and feel that at last we belong.

—**Carson McCullers,** "Loneliness . . . An American
Malady"

For writing *is* discovery. The language that never leaves our
head is like colorful yarn, endlessly spun out multicolored
threads dropping into a void, momentarily compacted, entangled, fascinating, elusive . . . writing that is discovery
forces the capturing, the retrieving, the bringing into focus
these stray and random thoughts. Sifting through them, we
make decisions that are as much about the self as about language.

—**James E. Miller,** "Discovering the Self"

All of our lives we are accompanied vaguely by the selves
we might be. Man is the only creature that can imagine
being someone else. The fantasy of being someone else is
the basis of sympathy, of humanity. . . . The past twenty
years have stimulated the anti-self. They have encouraged
the notion of continuous self-renewal. . . .

—**Lance Morrow,** "Daydreams of What You'd Rather Be"

Personal Reminiscences
◆◆◆

Jack London
What Life Means to Me

Jack London (1876–1916), American novelist and short-story writer, drew upon his extensive travels in such works as *The Call of the Wild* (1903) and his South Sea tales and developed social themes in such works as *The Iron Heel* (1907). Although London experienced the loss of many illusions about man's goodness and integrity, he retained his belief in human nobility and excellence.

I was born in the working-class. Early I discovered enthusiasm, ambition, and ideals; and to satisfy these became the problem of my child-life. My environment was crude and rough and raw. I had no outlook, but an uplook rather. My place in society was at the bottom. Here life offered nothing but sordidness and wretchedness, both of the flesh and the spirit; for here flesh and spirit were alike starved and tormented.

Above me towered the colossal edifice of society, and to my mind the only way out was up. Into this edifice I early resolved to climb. Up above, men wore black clothes and boiled shirts, and women dressed in beautiful gowns. Also, there were good things to eat, and there was plenty to eat. This much for the flesh. Then there were the things of the spirit. Up above me, I knew, were unselfishnesses of the spirit, clean and noble thinking, keen intellectual living. I knew all this because I read "Seaside Library" novels, in which, with the exception of the villains and adventuresses, all men and women thought beautiful thoughts, spoke a beautiful tongue, and performed glorious deeds. In short, as I accepted the rising of the sun, I accepted that up above me was all that was fine and noble and gracious, all that gave decency and dignity to life, all that made life worth living and that remunerated one for his travail and misery.

But it is not particularly easy for one to climb up out of the working-class—especially if he is handicapped by the possession of ideals and illusions. I lived on a ranch in California, and I was hard put to find the ladder whereby to climb. I early inquired the rate of interest on invested money, and worried my child's brain into an understanding of the virtues and excellencies of that remarkable invention of man, compound interest. Further, I ascertained the current rates of wages for workers of all ages, and the cost of living. From all this data I concluded that if I began immediately and worked and saved until I was fifty years of age, I could then stop working and enter into participation in a fair portion of the delights and goodnesses that would then be open to me higher up in society. Of course, I resolutely determined not to marry, while I quite forgot to consider at all that great rock of disaster in the working-class world—sickness.

But the life that was in me demanded more than a meagre existence of scraping and scrimping. Also, at ten years of age, I became a newsboy on the streets of a city, and found myself with a changed uplook. All about me were still the same sordidness and wretchedness, and up above me was still the same paradise waiting to be gained; but the ladder whereby to climb was a different one. It was now the ladder of business. Why save my earnings and invest in government bonds, when, by buying two newspapers for five cents, with a turn of the wrist I could sell them for ten cents and double my capital? The business ladder was the ladder for me, and I had a vision of myself becoming a baldheaded and successful merchant prince.

Alas for visions! When I was sixteen I had already earned the title of "prince." But this title was given me by a gang of cut-throats and thieves, by whom I was called "The Prince of the Oyster Pirates." And at that time I had climbed the first rung of the business ladder. I was a capitalist. I owned a boat and a complete oyster-pirating outfit. I had begun to exploit my fellow-creatures. I had a crew of one man. As captain and owner I took two-thirds of the spoils, and gave the crew one-third, though the crew worked just as hard as I did and risked just as much his life and liberty.

This one rung was the height I climbed up the business ladder. One night I went on a raid amongst the Chinese fishermen. Ropes and nets were worth dollars and cents. It was robbery, I grant, but it was precisely the spirit of capitalism. The capitalist takes away the possessions of his fellow-creatures by means of a rebate, or of a betrayal of trust, or by the purchase of senators and supreme-court judges. I was merely crude. That was the only difference. I used a gun.

But my crew that night was one of those inefficients against whom the capitalist is wont to fulminate, because, forsooth, such inefficients increase expenses and reduce dividends. My crew did both. What of his carelessness: he set fire to the big mainsail and totally destroyed it. There weren't any dividends that night, and the Chinese fishermen were richer by the nets and ropes we did not get. I was bankrupt, unable just then to pay sixty-five dollars for a new mainsail. I left my boat at anchor and went off on a bay-pirate boat on a raid up the Sacramento River. While away on this trip, another gang of bay pirates raided my boat. They stole everything, even the anchors; and later on, when I recovered the drifting hulk, I sold it for twenty dollars. I had slipped back the one rung I had climbed, and never again did I attempt the business ladder.

From then on I was mercilessly exploited by other capitalists. I had the muscle, and they made money out of it while I made but a very indifferent living out of it. I was a sailor before the mast, a longshoreman, a roustabout;

I worked in canneries, and factories, and laundries; I mowed lawns, and cleaned carpets, and washed windows. And I never got the full product of my toil. I looked at the daughter of the cannery owner, in her carriage, and knew that it was my muscle, in part, that helped drag along that carriage on its rubber tires. I looked at the son of the factory owner, going to college, and knew that it was my muscle that helped, in part, to pay for the wine and good fellowship he enjoyed.

But I did not resent this. It was all in the game. They were the strong. Very well, I was strong. I would carve my way to a place amongst them and make money out of the muscles of other men. I was not afraid of work. I loved hard work. I would pitch in and work harder than ever and eventually become a pillar of society.

And just then, as luck would have it, I found an employer that was of the same mind. I was willing to work, and he was more than willing that I should work. I thought I was learning a trade. In reality, I had displaced two men. I thought he was making an electrician out of me; as a matter of fact, he was making fifty dollars per month out of me. The two men I had displaced had received forty dollars each per month; I was doing the work of both for thirty dollars per month.

This employer worked me nearly to death. A man may love oysters, but too many oysters will disincline him toward that particular diet. And so with me. Too much work sickened me. I did not wish ever to see work again. I fled from work. I became a tramp, begging my way from door to door, wandering over the United States and sweating bloody sweats in slums and prisons.

I had been born in the working-class, and I was now, at the age of eighteen, beneath the point at which I had started. I was down in the cellar of society, down in the subterranean depths of misery about which it is neither nice nor proper to speak. I was in the pit, the abyss, the human cesspool, the shambles and charnel-house of our civilization. This is the part of the edifice of society that society chooses to ignore. Lack of space compels me here to ignore it, and I shall say only that the things I there saw gave me a terrible scare.

I was scared into thinking. I saw the naked simplicities of the complicated civilization in which I lived. Life was a matter of food and shelter. In order to get food and shelter men sold things. The merchant sold shoes, the politician sold his manhood, and the representative of the people, with exceptions, of course, sold his trust; while nearly all sold their honor. Women, too, whether on the street or in the holy bond of wedlock, were prone to sell their flesh. All things were commodities, all people bought and sold. The one commodity that labor had to sell was muscle. The honor of labor had no price in the market-place. Labor had muscle, and muscle alone, to sell.

But there was a difference, a vital difference. Shoes and trust and honor had a way of renewing themselves. They were imperishable stocks. Muscle, on the other hand, did not renew. As the shoe merchant sold shoes, he continued to replenish his stock. But there was no way of replenishing the laborer's stock of muscle. The more he sold of his muscle, the less of it remained to him. It was his one commodity, and each day his stock of it diminished. In the end, if he did not die before, he sold out and put up his shutters. He was a muscle bankrupt, and nothing remained to him but to go down into the cellar of society and perish miserably.

I learned, further, that brain was likewise a commodity. It, too, was different from muscle. A brain seller was only at his prime when he was fifty or sixty years old, and his wares were fetching higher prices than ever. But a laborer was worked out or broken down at forty-five or fifty. I had been in the cellar of society, and I did not like the place as a habitation. The pipes and drains were unsanitary, and the air was bad to breathe. If I could not live on the parlor floor of society, I could, at any rate, have a try at the attic. It was true, the diet there was slim, but the air at least was pure. So I resolved to sell no more muscle, and to become a vender of brains.

Then began a frantic pursuit of knowledge. I returned to California and opened the books. While thus equipping myself to become a brain merchant, it was inevitable that I should delve into sociology. There I found, in a certain class of books, scientifically formulated, the simple sociological concepts I had already worked out for myself. Other and greater minds, before I was born, had worked out all that I had thought and a vast deal more. I discovered that I was a socialist.

The socialists were revolutionists, inasmuch as they struggled to overthrow the society of the present, and out of the material to build the society of the future. I, too, was a socialist and a revolutionist. I joined the groups of working-class and intellectual revolutionists, and for the first time came into intellectual living. Here I found keen-flashing intellects and brilliant wits; for here I met strong and alert-brained, withal horny-handed, members of the working-class; unfrocked preachers too wide in their Christianity for any congregation of Mammon-worshippers; professors broken on the wheel of university subservience to the ruling class and flung out because they were quick with knowledge which they strove to apply to the affairs of mankind.

Here I found, also, warm faith in the human, glowing idealism, sweetnesses of unselfishness, renunciation, and martyrdom—all the splendid, stinging things of the spirit. Here life was clean, noble, and alive. Here life rehabilitated itself, became wonderful and glorious; and I was glad to be alive. I was in touch with great souls who exalted flesh and spirit over dollars and cents, and to whom the thin wail of the starved slum child meant more than all the pomp and circumstance of commerical expansion and world empire. All about me were nobleness of purpose and heroism of effort, and my days and nights were sunshine and starshine, all fire and dew, with before my eyes, ever burning and blazing, the Holy Grail, Christ's own Grail, the warm human, long-suffering and maltreated, but to be rescued and saved at the last.

And I, poor foolish I, deemed all this to be a mere foretaste of the delights of living I should find higher above me in society. I had lost many illusions since the day I read "Seaside Library" novels on the California ranch. I was destined to lose many of the illusions I still retained.

As a brain merchant I was a success. Society opened its portals to me. I entered right in on the parlor floor, and my disillusionment proceeded rapidly. I sat down to dinner with the masters of society, and with the wives and daughters of the masters of society. The women were gowned beautifully, I admit; but to my naïve surprise I discovered that they were of the same clay as all the rest of the women I had known down below in the cellar. "The colonel's lady and Judy O'Grady were sisters under their skins"—and gowns.

It was not this, however, so much as their materialism, that shocked me. It is true, these beautifully gowned, beautiful women prattled sweet little ideals and dear little moralities; but in spite of their prattle the dominant key of the life they lived was materialistic. And they were so sentimentally selfish! They assisted in all kinds of sweet little charities, and informed one of the fact, while all the time the food they ate and the beautiful clothes they wore were bought out of dividends stained with the blood of child labor, and sweated labor, and of prostitution itself. When I mentioned such facts, expecting in my innocence that these sisters of Judy O'Grady would at once strip off their blood-dyed silks and jewels, they became excited and angry, and read me preachments about the lack of thrift, the drink, and the innate depravity that caused all the misery in society's cellar. When I mentioned that I couldn't quite see that it was the lack of thrift, the intemperance, and the depravity of a half-starved child of six that made it work twelve hours every night in a Southern cotton mill, these sisters of Judy O'Grady attacked my private life and called me an "agitator"—as though that, forsooth, settled the argument.

Nor did I fare better with the masters themselves. I had expected to find men who were clean, noble, and alive, whose ideals were clean, noble, and alive. I went about amongst the men who sat in the high places—the preachers, the politicians, the business men, the professors, and the editors. I ate meat with them, drank wine with them, automobiled with them, and studied them. It is true, I found many that were clean and noble; but with rare exceptions, they were not *alive*. I do verily believe I could count the exceptions on the fingers of my two hands. Where they were not alive with rottenness, quick with unclean life, they were merely the unburied dead—clean and noble, like well-preserved mummies, but not alive. In this connection I may especially mention the professors I met, the men who live up to that decadent university ideal, "the passionless pursuit of passionless intelligence."

I met men who invoked the name of the Prince of Peace in their diatribes against war, and who put rifles in the hands of Pinkertons with which to shoot down strikers in their own factories. I met men incoherent with indignation at the brutality of prize-fighting, and who, at the same time, were parties to the adulteration of food that killed each year more babies than even red-handed Herod had killed.

I talked in hotels and clubs and homes and Pullmans and steamer-chairs with captains of industry, and marvelled at how little travelled they were in the realm of intellect. On the other hand, I discovered that their intellect, in the business sense, was abnormally developed. Also, I discovered that their morality, where business was concerned, was nil.

This delicate, aristocratic-featured gentleman, was a dummy director and a tool of corporations that secretly robbed widows and orphans. This gentleman, who collected fine editions and was an especial patron of literature, paid blackmail to a heavy-jowled, black-browed boss of a municipal machine. This editor, who published patent medicine advertisements and did not dare print the truth in his paper about said patent medicines for fear of losing the advertising, called me a scoundrelly demagogue because I told him that his political economy was antiquated and that his biology was contemporaneous with Pliny.

This senator was the tool and the slave, the little puppet of a gross, uneducated machine boss; so was this governor and this supreme-court judge; and all three rode on railroad passes. This man, talking soberly and earnestly about the beauties of idealism and the goodness of God, had just betrayed his comrades in a business deal. This man, a pillar of the church and heavy contributor to foreign missions, worked his shop girls ten hours a day on a starvation wage and thereby directly encouraged prostitution. This man, who endowed chairs in universities, perjured himself in courts of law over a matter of dollars and cents. And this railroad magnate broke his word as a gentleman and a Christian when he granted a secret rebate to one of two captains of industry locked together in a struggle to the death.

It was the same everywhere, crime and betrayal, betrayal and crime—men who were alive, but who were neither clean nor noble, men who were clean and noble but who were not alive. Then there was a great, hopeless mass, neither noble nor alive, but merely clean. It did not sin positively nor deliberately; but it did sin passively and ignorantly by acquiescing in the current immorality and profiting by it. Had it been noble and alive it would not have been ignorant, and it would have refused to share in the profits of betrayal and crime.

I discovered that I did not like to live on the parlor floor of society. Intellectually I was bored. Morally and spiritually I was sickened. I remembered my intellectuals and idealists, my unfrocked preachers, broken professors, and clean-minded, class-conscious workingmen. I remembered my days and nights of sunshine and starshine, where life was all a wild sweet wonder, a spiritual paradise of unselfish adventure and ethical romance. And I saw before me, ever blazing and burning the Holy Grail.

So I went back to the working-class, in which I had been born and where I belonged. I care no longer to climb. The imposing edifice of society above my head holds no delights for me. It is the foundation of the edifice that interests me. There I am content to labor, crowbar in hand, shoulder to shoulder with intellectuals, idealists, and class-conscious workingmen, getting a solid pry now and again and setting the whole edifice rocking. Some day, when we get a few more hands and crowbars to work, we'll topple it over, along with all its rotten life and unburied dead, its monstrous selfishness and sodden materialism. Then we'll cleanse the cellar and build a new habitation for mankind, in which there will be no parlor floor, in which all the rooms will be bright and airy, and where the air that is breathed will be clean, noble, and alive.

Such is my outlook. I look forward to a time when man shall progress upon something worthier and higher than his stomach, when there will be a finer incentive to impel men to action than the incentive of today, which is the incentive of the stomach. I retain my belief in the nobility and excellence of the human. I believe that spiritual sweetness and unselfishness will conquer the gross gluttony of today. And last of all, my faith is in the working-class. As some Frenchman has said, "The stairway of time is ever echoing with the wooden shoe going up, the polished boot descending."

Suggestions for Discussion

1. Discuss the adequacy of London's metaphor of "the colossal edifice of society" in present-day America.

2. Describe the several ways in which London attempted to attain "all that gave decency and dignity to life."

3. Compare eighteen-year-old London's perception of "the naked simplicities of the complicated civilization" in which he lived with that of your classmates.

Suggestions for Writing

1. London has called this piece "What Life Means to Me." Describe in you own words what that is.

2. In a short paper recall an illusion you formerly had and describe the events which destroyed that illusion.

Joan Didion

On Keeping a Notebook

Joan Didion (b. 1934), California-born, began her career when she won Vogue's Prix de Paris award in her senior year of college. She later became an associate editor of *Vogue* and has written columns for *The Saturday Evening Post* and *Life.* Her novels *Run River* (1963) and *Play It as It Lays* (1971) and her collection of essays *Slouching Towards Bethlehem* (1969) have established her as an important American writer. She and her husband, writer John Gregory Dunne, have collaborated on several screenplays. In keeping her notebook, as recounted in *Slouching Towards Bethlehem,* the author recounts not facts but feelings, "an indiscriminate and erratic assemblage with meaning only for its maker" and sometimes not for her.

" 'That woman Estelle,' " the note reads, " 'is partly the reason why George Sharp and I are separated today.' *Dirty crepe-de-Chine wrapper, hotel bar, Wilmington RR, 9:45 a.m. August Monday morning.*"

Since the note is in my notebook, it presumably has some meaning to me. I study it for a long while. At first I have only the most general notion of what I was doing on an August Monday morning in the bar of the hotel across from the Pennsylvania Railroad station in Wilmington, Delaware (waiting for a train? missing one? 1960? 1961? why Wilmington?), but I do remember being there. The woman in the dirty crepe-de-Chine wrapper had come down from her room for a beer, and the bartender had heard before the reason why George Sharp and she were separated today. "Sure," he said, and went on mopping the floor. "You told me." At the other end of the bar is a girl. She is talking, pointedly, not to the man beside her but to a cat lying in the triangle of sunlight cast through the open door. She is wearing a plaid silk dress from Peck & Peck, and the hem is coming down.

Here is what it is: the girl has been on the Eastern Shore, and now she is going back to the city, leaving the man beside her, and all she can see ahead are the viscous summer sidewalks and the 3 A.M. long-distance calls that will make her lie awake and then sleep drugged through all the steaming mornings left in August (1960? 1961?). Because she must go directly from the train to lunch in New York, she wishes that she had a safety pin for the hem of the plaid silk dress, and she also wishes that she could forget about the hem and the lunch and stay in the cool bar that smells of disinfectant and malt and make friends with the woman in the crepe-de-Chine wrapper. She is afflicted by a little self-pity, and she wants to compare Estelles. That is what that was all about.

Why did I write it down? In order to remember, of course, but exactly what was it I wanted to remember? How much of it actually happened? Did any of it? Why do I keep a notebook at all? It is easy to deceive oneself on all those scores. The impulse to write things down is a peculiarly compulsive one, inexplicable to those who do not share it, useful only accidentally, only secondarily, in the way that any compulsion tries to justify itself. I suppose that it begins or does not begin in the cradle. Although I have felt compelled to write things down since I was five years old, I doubt that my daughter ever will, for she is a singularly blessed and accepting child, delighted with life exactly as life presents itself to her, unafraid to go to sleep and unafraid to wake up. Keepers of private notebooks are a different breed altogether, lonely and resistant rearrangers of things, anxious malcontents, children afflicted apparently at birth with some presentiment of loss.

My first notebook was a Big Five tablet, given to me by my mother with the sensible suggestion that I stop whining and learn to amuse myself by writing down my thoughts. She returned the tablet to me a few years ago; the first entry is an account of a woman who believed herself to be freezing to death in the Arctic night, only to find, when day broke, that she had stumbled onto the Sahara Desert, where she would die of the heat before lunch. I have no idea what turn of a five-year-old's mind could have prompted so insistently "ironic" and exotic a story, but it does reveal a certain predilection for the extreme which has dogged me into adult life; perhaps if I were analytically inclined I would find it a truer story than any I might have told about Donald Johnson's birthday party or the day my cousin Brenda put Kitty Litter in the aquarium.

So the point of my keeping a notebook has never been, nor is it now, to have an accurate factual record of what I have been doing or thinking. That would be a different impulse entirely, an instinct for reality which I sometimes envy but do not possess. At no point have I ever been able successfully to keep a diary; my approach to daily life ranges from the grossly negligent to the merely absent, and on those few occasions when I have tried dutifully to record a day's events, boredom has so overcome me that the results are mysterious at best. What is this business about "shopping, typing piece, dinner with E, depressed"? Shopping for what? Typing what piece? Who is E? Was this "E" depressed, or was I depressed? Who cares?

In fact I have abandoned altogether that kind of pointless entry; instead I tell what some would call lies. "That's simply not true," the members of my family frequently tell me when they come up against my memory of a shared event. "The party was *not* for you, the spider was *not* a black widow, *it wasn't that way at all.*" Very likely they are right, for not only have I always had trouble distinguishing between what happened and what merely might have happened, but I remain unconvinced that the distinction, for my purposes, matters. The cracked crab that I recall having for lunch the day my father came home from Detroit in 1945 must certainly be embroidery, worked into the day's pattern to lend verisimilitude; I was ten years old and would not now remember the cracked crab. The day's events did not turn on cracked crab. And yet it is precisely that fictitious crab that makes me see the afternoon all over again, a home movie run all too often, the father bearing gifts, the child weeping, an exercise in family love and guilt. Or that is what it was to me. Similarly, perhaps it never did snow that August in Vermont; perhaps there never were flurries in the night wind, and maybe no one else felt the ground hardening and summer already dead even as we pretended to bask in it, but that was how it felt to me, and it might as well have snowed, could have snowed, did snow.

How it felt to me: that is getting closer to the truth about a notebook. I sometimes delude myself about why I keep a notebook, imagine that some thrifty virtue derives from preserving everything observed. See enough and write it down, I tell myself, and then some morning when the world seems drained of wonder, some day when I am only going through the motions of doing what I am supposed to do, which is write—on that bankrupt morning I will simply open my notebook and there it will all be, a forgotten account with accumulated interest, paid passage back to the world out there: dialogue overheard in hotels and elevators and at the hat-check counter in Pavillon (one middle-aged man shows his hat-check to another and says, "That's my old football number"); impressions of Bettina Aptheker and Benjamin Sonnenberg and Teddy ("Mr. Acapulco") Stauffer; careful *aperçus* about tennis bums and failed fashion models and Greek shipping heiresses, one of whom taught me a significant lesson (a lesson I could have learned from F. Scott Fitzgerald, but perhaps we all must meet the very rich for ourselves) by asking, when I arrived to interview her in her orchid-filled sitting room on the second day of a paralyzing New York blizzard, whether it was snowing outside.

I imagine, in other words, that the notebook is about other people. But of course it is not. I have no real business with what one stranger said to another at the hat-check counter in Pavillon; in fact I suspect that the line "That's my old football number" touched not my own imagination at all, but merely some memory of something once read, probably "The Eighty-Yard Run." Nor is my concern with a woman in a dirty crepe-de-Chine wrapper in a Wilmington bar. My stake is always, of course, in the unmentioned girl in the plaid silk dress. *Remember what it was to be me:* that is always the point.

It is a difficult point to admit. We are brought up in the ethic that others, any others, all others, are by definition more interesting than ourselves; taught to be diffident, just this side of self-effacing. ("You're the least important person in the room and don't forget it," Jessica Mitford's governess would hiss in her ear on the advent of any social occasion; I copied that into my notebook because it is only recently that I have been able to enter a room without hearing some such phrase in my inner ear.) Only the very young and the very old may recount their dreams at breakfast, dwell upon self, interrupt with memories of beach picnics and favorite Liberty lawn dresses and the rainbow trout in a creek near Colorado Springs. The rest of us are expected, rightly, to affect absorption in other people's favorite dresses, other people's trout.

And so we do. But our notebooks give us away, for however dutifully we record what we see around us, the common denominator of all we see is always, transparently, shamelessly, the implacable "I." We are not talking here about the kind of notebook that is patently for public consumption, a structural conceit for binding together a series of graceful *pensées;* we are talking about something private, about bits of the mind's string too short to use, an indiscriminate and erratic assemblage with meaning only for its maker.

And sometimes even the maker has difficulty with the meaning. There does not seem to be, for example, any point in my knowing for the rest of my life that, during 1964, 720 tons of soot fell on every square mile of New York City, yet there it is in my notebook, labeled "FACT." Nor do I really need to remember that Ambrose Bierce liked to spell Leland Stanford's name "£eland $tanford" or that "smart women almost always wear black in Cuba," a fashion hint without much potential for practical application. And does not the relevance of these notes seem marginal at best?:

> In the basement museum of the Inyo County Courthouse in Independence, California, sign pinned to a mandarin coat: "This MANDARIN COAT was often worn by Mrs. Minnie S. Brooks when giving lectures on her TEAPOT COLLECTION."

> Redhead getting out of car in front of Beverly Wilshire Hotel, chinchilla stole, Vuitton bags with tags reading:
>
> > MRS LOU FOX
> > HOTEL SAHARA
> > VEGAS

Well, perhaps not entirely marginal. As a matter of fact, Mrs. Minnie S. Brooks and her MANDARIN COAT pull me back into my own childhood, for although I never knew Mrs. Brooks and did not visit Inyo County until I was thirty, I grew up in just such a world, in houses cluttered with Indian relics and bits of gold ore and ambergris and the souvenirs my Aunt Mercy Farnsworth brought back from the Orient. It is a long way from that world to Mrs. Lou Fox's world, where we all live now, and is it not just as well to remember that? Might not Mrs. Minnie S. Brooks help me to remember what I am? Might not Mrs. Lou Fox help me to remember what I am not?

But sometimes the point is harder to discern. What exactly did I have in mind when I noted down that it cost the father of someone I know $650 a month to light the place on the Hudson in which he lived before the Crash? What use was I planning to make of this line by Jimmy Hoffa: "I may have my faults, but being wrong ain't one of them"? And although I think it interesting to know where the girls who travel with the Syndicate have their hair done when they find themselves on the West Coast, will I ever make suitable use of it? Might I not be better off just passing it on to John O'Hara? What is a recipe for sauerkraut doing in my notebook? What kind of magpie keeps this notebook? *"He was born the night the Titanic went down."* That seems a nice enough line, and I even recall who said it, but is it not really a better line in life than it could ever be in fiction?

But of course that is exactly it: not that I should ever use the line, but that I should remember the woman who said it and the afternoon I heard it. We were on her terrace by the sea, and we were finishing the wine left from lunch, trying to get what sun there was, a California winter sun. The woman whose husband was born the night the *Titanic* went down wanted to rent her house, wanted to go back to her children in Paris. I remember wishing that I could afford the house, which cost $1,000 a month. "Someday you will," she said lazily. "Someday it all comes." There in the sun on her terrace it seemed easy to believe in someday, but later I had a low-grade afternoon hangover and ran over a black snake on the way to the supermarket and was flooded with inexplicable fear when I heard the checkout clerk explaining to the man ahead of me why she was finally divorcing her husband. "He left me no choice," she said over and over as she punched the register. "He has a little seven-month-old baby by her, he left me no choice." I would like to believe that my dread then was for the human condition, but of course it was for me, because I wanted a baby and did not then have one and because I wanted to own the house that cost $1,000 a month to rent and because I had a hangover.

It all comes back. Perhaps it is difficult to see the value in having one's self back in that kind of mood, but I do see it; I think we are well advised to keep on nodding terms with the people we used to be, whether we find them attractive company or not. Otherwise they turn up unannounced and surprise us, come hammering on the mind's door at 4 A.M. of a bad night and demand to know who deserted them, who betrayed them, who is going to make amends. We forget all too soon the things we thought we could never forget. We forget the loves and the betrayals alike, forget what we whispered and what we screamed, forget who we were. I have already lost touch with a couple of people I used to be; one of them, a seventeen-year-old, presents little threat, although it would be of some interest to me to know again what it feels like to sit on a river levee drinking vodka-and-orange-juice and listening to Les Paul and Mary Ford and their echoes sing "How High the Moon" on the car radio. (You see I still have the scenes, but I no longer perceive myself among those present, no longer could even improvise the dialogue.) The other one, a twenty-three-year-old, bothers me more. She was always a good deal of trouble, and I suspect she will reappear when I least want to see her, skirts too long, shy to the point of aggravation, always the injured party, full of recriminations and little hurts and stories I do not want to hear again, at once saddening me and angering me with her vulnerability and ignorance, an apparition all the more insistent for being so long banished.

It is a good idea, then, to keep in touch, and I suppose that keeping in touch is what notebooks are all about. And we are all on our own when it comes to keeping those lines open to ourselves: your notebook will never help me, nor mine you. *"So what's new in the whiskey business?"* What could that possibly mean to you? To me it means a blonde in a Pucci bathing suit sitting with a couple of fat men by the pool at the Beverly Hills Hotel. Another man approaches, and they all regard one another in silence for a while. "So what's new in the whiskey business?" one of the fat men finally says by way of welcome, and the blonde stands up, arches one foot and dips it in the pool, looking all the while at the cabaña where Baby Pignatari is talking on the telephone. That is all there is to that, except that several years later I saw the blonde coming out of Saks Fifth Avenue in New York with her California complexion and a voluminous mink coat. In the harsh wind that day she looked old and irrevocably tired to me, and even the skins in the mink coat were not worked the way they were doing them that year, not the way she would have wanted them done, and there is the point of the story. For a while after that I did not like to look in the mirror, and my eyes would skim the newspapers and pick out only the deaths, the cancer victims, the premature coronaries, the suicides, and I stopped riding the Lexington Avenue IRT because I noticed for the first time that all the strangers I had seen for years—the man with the seeing-eye dog, the spinster who read the classified pages every day, the fat girl who always got off with me at Grand Central—looked older than they once had.

It all comes back. Even that recipe for sauerkraut: even that brings it back. I was on Fire Island when I first made that sauerkraut, and it was raining, and we drank a lot of bourbon and ate the sauerkraut and went to bed at ten, and I listened to the rain and the Atlantic and felt safe. I made the sauerkraut again last night and it did not make me feel any safer, but that is, as they say, another story.

Suggestions for Discussion

1. What rhetorical devices does the author use to bring her subject into focus? For example, she compares and contrasts two women in the bar and her daughter and herself.

2. What kinds of details are employed to explain the varied purposes of keeping a notebook?

3. How does the author explain the paradox "I imagine . . . that the notebook is about other people. But of course it is not."

4. Account for the adverbs and adjectives used in the statement "the common denominator of all we see is always, transparently, shamelessly, the implacable 'I.' "

5. How do the citations in the notebook contribute to the central thesis? to the tone? to the author's sense of self? to her writing?

6. Explain: "I have already lost touch with a couple of people I used to be. . . ."

7. T. S. Eliot uses the term *objective correlative* to describe the artist's faculty of achieving emotional impact "by finding a set of objects, a situation, a chain of events, which shall be the formula of that particular emotion such that when the external facts are given, the emotion is immediately evoked." How do the items in the notebook illustrate this theory?

Suggestions for Writing

1. Keep a journal in which you record the events or thoughts of each day. What does it tell you about other people? about yourself?

2. Write an essay on question 4 or 6 above.

3. Write an essay in which you interweave excerpts from your journal with commentary on them.

Vladimir Nabokov

The Beginning of Consciousness

Vladimir Nabokov (1899–1977) was born in Russia and educated at Trinity College, Cambridge. He was a professor at Cornell University and a regular contributor to popular magazines. Among his works written in English are *The Real Life of Sebastian Knight* (1941); *Pnin* (1957); *Lolita* (1958); *Pale Fire* (1962); two collections of short stories, *Nabokov's Dozen* (1958) and *Nabokov's Quartet* (1966); *King, Queen, Knave* (1968); *Ada* (1969); and an autobiography, *Speak, Memory* (1951). Nabokov describes the awakening of his consciousness as a series of "spaced flashes with intervals between them gradually diminishing until bright blocks of perception are formed, affording memory a slippery hold." His sense of self and his awareness that his parents were his parents came after he had learned numbers and speech.

The cradle rocks above an abyss, and common sense tells us that our existence is but a brief crack of light between two eternities of darkness. Although the two are identical twins, man, as a rule, views the prenatal abyss with more calm than the one he is heading for (at some forty-five hundred heartbeats an hour). I know, however, of a young chronophobiac who experienced something like panic when looking for the first time at homemade movies that had been taken a few weeks before his birth. He saw a world that was practically unchanged—the same house, the same people—and then realized that he did not exist there at all and that nobody mourned his absence. He caught a glimpse of his mother waving from an upstairs window, and that unfamiliar gesture disturbed him, as if it were some mysterious farewell. But what particularly frightened him was the sight of a brand new baby carriage standing there on the porch, with the smug, encroaching air of a coffin; even that was empty, as if, in the reverse course of events, his very bones had disintegrated.

Such fancies are not foreign to young lives. Or, to put it otherwise, first and last things often tend to have an adolescent note—unless, possibly, they are directed by some venerable and rigid religion. Nature expects a full-grown man to accept the two black voids, fore and aft, as stolidly as he accepts the extraordinary visions in between. Imagination, the supreme delight of the immortal and the immature, should be limited. In order to enjoy life, we should not enjoy it too much.

I rebel against this state of affairs. I feel the urge to take my rebellion outside and picket nature. Over and over again, my mind has made colossal efforts to distinguish the faintest of personal glimmers in the impersonal darkness on both sides of my life. That this darkness is caused merely by the walls of time separating me and by bruised fists from the free world of timelessness is a belief I gladly share with the most gaudily painted savage. I have journeyed back in thought—with thought hopelessly tapering off as I went—to remote regions where I groped for some secret outlet only to discover that the prison of time is spherical and without exits. Short of suicide, I have tried everything. I have doffed my identity in order to pass for a conventional spook and steal into realms that existed before I was conceived. I have mentally endured the degrading company of Victorian lady novelists and retired colonels who remembered having, in former lives, been slave messengers on a Roman road or sages under the willows of Lhasa. I have ransacked my oldest dreams for keys and clues—and let me say at once that I reject completely the vulgar, shabby, fundamentally medieval world of Freud, with its crankish quest for sexual symbols (something like searching for Baconian acrostics in Shakespeare's works) and its bitter little embryos spying, from their natural nooks, upon the love life of their parents.

Initially, I was unaware that time, so boundless at first blush, was a prison. In probing my childhood (which is the next best to probing one's eternity) I see the awakening of consciousness as a series of spaced flashes, with the intervals between them gradually diminishing until bright blocks of perception are formed, affording memory a slippery hold. I had learned numbers and speech more or less simultaneously at a very early date, but the inner knowledge that I was I and that my parents were my parents seems to have been established only later, when it was directly associated with my discovering their age in relation to mine. Judging by the strong sunlight that, when I think of that revelation, immediately invades my memory with lobed sun flecks through overlapping patterns of greenery, the occasion may have been my mother's birthday, in late summer, in the country, and I had asked questions and had assessed the answers I received. All this is as it should be according to the theory of recapitulation; the beginning of reflexive consciousness in the brain of our remotest ancestor must surely have coincided with the dawning of the sense of time.

Thus, when the newly disclosed, fresh and trim formula of my own age, four, was confronted with the parental formulas, thirty-three and twenty-seven, something happened to me. I was given a tremendously invigorating shock. As if subjected to a second baptism, on more divine lines than the Greek Catholic ducking undergone fifty months earlier by a howling, half-drowned half-Victor (my mother, through the half-closed door, behind which an old custom bade parents retreat, managed to correct the bungling arch-presbyter, Father Konstantin Vetvenitski), I felt myself plunged abruptly into a radiant and mobile medium that was none other than the pure element of time. One shared it—just as excited bathers share shining seawater—with creatures that were not oneself but that were joined to one by time's common flow, an environment quite different from the spatial world, which not only man but apes and butterflies can perceive. At that instant, I became acutely aware that the twenty-seven-year-old being, in soft white and pink, holding my left hand, was my mother, and that the thirty-three-year-old being, in hard white and gold, holding my right hand, was my father. Between them, as they evenly progressed, I strutted, and trotted, and strutted again, from sun fleck to sun fleck, along the middle of a path, which I easily identify today with an alley of ornamental oaklings in the park of our country estate, Vyra, in the former Province of St. Petersburg, Russia. Indeed, from my present ridge or remote, isolated, almost uninhabited time, I see my diminutive self as celebrating, on that August day 1903, the birth of sentient life. If my left-hand-holder and my right-hand-holder had both been present before in my vague infant world, they had been so under the mask of a tender incognito; but now my father's attire, the resplendent uniform of the Horse Guards, with that smooth golden swell of cuirass burning upon his chest and back, came out like the sun, and for several years afterward I remained keenly interested in the age of my parents and kept myself informed about it, like a nervous passenger asking the time in order to check a new watch.

My father, let it be noted, had served his term of military training long before I was born, so I suppose he had that day put on the trappings of his old regiment as a festive joke. To a joke, then, I owe my first gleam of complete consciousness—which again has recapitulatory implications, since the first creatures on earth to become aware of time were also the first creatures to smile.

Suggestions for Discussion

1. How does the author convey the tone of the panic that can be aroused by contemplating the "prenatal abyss"?

2. By specific reference to the text, explain the author's statement that "first and last things often tend to have an adolescent note."

3. Identify all the phrases in this selection that grow out of the image of existence as a "brief crack of light between two eternities of darkness." How literal is this image intended to be? What overtones of experience and myth are there in the image?

4. At the end of the fourth paragraph Nabokov writes, "the beginning of reflexive consciousness in the brain of our remotest ancestor must surely have coincided with the dawning of the sense of time." By what logical process does he arrive at this conclusion? Is the process defensible? Is the conclusion trustworthy?

Suggestions for Writing

1. Recall an incident in your childhood that marked a dramatic change in your concept of yourself or your parents, or your concept of the passage of time.

2. Discuss this paradox in relation to its context: "In order to enjoy life, we should not enjoy it too much."

Peter Werner

Both Sides Now

Peter Werner (pseudonym) as a Yale freshman was one of a small number permitted to enroll in a writing course in the 1970s. He grew up in a large, devout
Roman Catholic family in East Meadow, Long Island. After receiving his degree
at Yale he studied playwriting in graduate school, and after working in a bank
he took a job teaching English in the New York public schools. Werner portrays
some of the conflicts and ironies in his experience with "both sides" of the
economic structure.

When I was in high school, I don't know how many afternoons I spent
upstairs in my bedroom, listening to the neighborhood kids playing roller
hockey in the street while I struggled to play the guitar. I was trying to teach
myself, and from a huge book of music titled something like *Greatest Hits of
the Sixties with Simplified Chords,* I had chosen Joni Mitchell's "Both Sides
Now."

The chords were simple, and the song seemed to demand a voice that
wasn't too good. As with so many of the folk songs of that era, the lyrics
seemed so much more earnest when sung poorly, as if the words demanded
to be heard no matter what the quality of the singer's voice. I finally managed
to learn the song, and a few more after that, before deciding that as bad as
my voice was, it would never sound as earnest as Bob Dylan's, so there was
not much point in going on.

And yet to this day I still remember the chords and lyrics to "Both Sides
Now," for over the years the song took on an ironic significance as circumstances in my own life changed. What I should have learned from the song
was how multifaceted and deeply layered these two sides can be.

When I was living at home, I thought I already had seen both sides. I grew
up rather comfortably on suburban Long Island in a family that gradually
grew to include eight children. My father supported us all with his job as a
space engineer under government contract to NASA.

Then the United States landed a man on the moon, and my father was laid
off along with thousands of other space engineers on Long Island. Suddenly
we had no money and I saw the "other side." According to government statistics, we were living in poverty, but things weren't much different than
before. They were just a bit more strained. For me, the two sides then were
simply "richer" and "poorer."

Since coming to Yale I have had a chance to see more of these two sides.
Here I learned that in many cases "richer" and "poorer" also define the distinction between "superior" and "inferior." Money, education, and family
background all play their part in determining human value. Some people are
meant to serve others; others to be served.

As a bursary student, I find myself in a strange position. One minute I'll
be on one side, sipping sherry at a reception, while men and women in
starched white uniforms offer me hors d'oeuvres from silver platters. The next

minute I'll be on the other side, washing dishes in a hot kitchen of one of Yale's dining halls, or wearing a red jacket and serving my fellow classmates a French dinner. I meet students whose fathers are millionaires, then talk to dining hall workers who try to support a family on seven thousand dollars a year. When I joined the Duke's Men, an informal singing group at Yale, our spring concert tour took us through a series of posh resorts and hotels, a world of servants and masters, another world with two sides.

Here are some glimpses of the two sides:

A Phone Call Home

Tom is one of my three roommates, a blond surfer from a Los Angeles suburb. Although our relationship was rather cool early in the year, as the months have progressed we've become close friends. When we're drunk, we call each other by the names of characters taken from a Lawrence novel on our freshman reading list.

I can tell that Tom's family is well off, not by any of Tom's possessions but by his general demeanor and the fact that he's well traveled. I know that Tom thinks my family is comfortable enough, if not abundantly wealthy, and God knows I haven't done anything to make him think otherwise. We're among the last to be able to take advantage of an already slipping fashion dictate that demands that rich and poor alike wear nothing but jeans and cotton T-shirts, and so it's been difficult for me to guess just how much money Tom is used to, and impossible for Tom to realize how poor my own family has become.

We weren't always poor, but we were never wealthy. When my father still had his job as a space engineer, our family of ten lived in a barn-red colonial home in a suburban neighborhood and had a beige Chrysler Town and Country station wagon parked in the driveway. After my father lost his job, he couldn't find other work as an engineer. He tried his hand at real estate and lost money. There were no savings to draw from, and the family had a desperate struggle hanging on to the house and the car. When relatives had no more money to lend us, government assistance became a necessity, and my mother started training as a nurse in order to bring money into the household.

Tonight I find myself chiding Tom for his upper-class prejudices and social naïveté. This always confuses Tom, because he has no way of knowing where I'm coming from and no reason to suspect the personal vindictiveness that creeps into these "consciousness raising" sessions. Tom is trying to convince me that the reason he didn't have any friends among the Chicanos who attended his high school is not because they were poor but because they lived so far away. In fact he does, he insists, have white friends who are really quite poor.

"Listen to this," he says. "I have this friend. There are four kids in his family, and his father makes twenty thousand dollars a year."

I can't quite figure out the moral to this story, although I'm afraid of what's coming. In the best days, my father supported ten people on twenty-three thousand a year.

"Well . . .?" I say, waiting for a conclusion.

Tom says nothing.

"Is that poor? Is twenty thousand dollars a year poor?" I ask, and my voice is angry and condescending.

Tom is annoyed that his humanitarianism in unappreciated. His head cocks back and his eyes go cold.

"Well . . . my old man makes a hundred grand a year."

Those words, that number, affect me as if I had just been drenched with a bucket of ice water. I want to shout back, "Well, my 'old man' is unemployed and we get six thousand dollars a year from welfare. So how do you like that?" Instead I say nothing.

Tom tries to press his point. He thinks I don't understand.

"Well, how much does your father make?"

"Fuck you," I reply.

Tom shakes his head in disgust and goes into his room to study. He's learned that there's no point in talking to me when I get into one of my moods. And like I've said, he's seen no sign of my family's financial state. When my parents visited on parents' day, the Chrysler was in good condition. My father still had his fine cashmere coat, and my mother's "simple black dress" did not betray its age. So he can't understand my anger.

I think about that number and I realize that there are some who would consider it pocket money, but still it's more than four times what my father ever made, and I resent it. I resent the way Tom takes the money for granted and I resent the way he takes it for granted that my own family is well off. I wish I had the courage to tell him the truth.

How much easier it would be if I were black or Puerto Rican. Then I would be expected to be poor. They could look at me and marvel at how I was advancing. "Look! He goes to Yale!" But to be white and poor. The white rich really don't want to know about it. It upsets them; they think it's disgusting. You're upsetting the order of things. Blacks are poor. Puerto Ricans are poor. They can't help it. They're not smart enough to handle money. But whites aren't handicapped. If they're not rich, it's their own fault. They're not living up to their race. They're a disgrace.

The noise from the stereo is beginning to annoy me. That weirdo David Bowie. It is Tom's record, not mine (which makes it all the more annoying). But the stereo is mine. None of us brought a stereo in September, so the kid who's on welfare had to go home to bring one back. The same thing with the typewriter. The kid whose dad earns a hundred grand a year shows up at Yale without a typewriter. I spend half my summer earnings to buy a decent machine, half that summer slaving in a department store. And Tom just uses it whenever he wants.

Typical, I think. That's why his people are rich and my people aren't.

Bowie keeps whining. It is the same record that was playing when my brother Michael visited in December. Hearing the record, the first thing he said when he came in the door was, "What's going on here? Have you gone gay?"

Michael sat down without taking off his coat, and we tried to catch up with each other on the past few months. After about ten minutes he stood up to remove his coat.

"Boy, it's hot in here."

"Well, you should have taken your coat off."

"I just got sort of used to wearing it around the house. We haven't had any heat this past week."

"What?" I shouted, and broke into laughter. I pictured my family seated around the big oak table in the dining room, eating dinner in their winter coats, my sister Ann trying to avoid dipping her fur cuffs into her food.

"Dad wasn't able to pay the oil bill, so they stopped delivering." Michael was laughing too. He fell back onto the couch and the two of us sat there laughing until tears came to our eyes.

Remembering the laughter, I realize that it would take a great effort to make myself upset about the incident. My family isn't miserable in their predicament; they are able to laugh about it. They're as happy as ever. Then my anger returns when I realize that Tom is happy too.

It's easy not to mind being poor if you think the wealthy are miserable. It's easy to go to see a play or a movie or read a book where the rich are at each other's throats and they're lonely and unhappy and their lives are empty and half of them end up committing suicide. The rich are different and they get their just desserts in the end.

But Tom is really not so different from me. That is one of the reasons we're so close. I can easily see myself in Tom's position through a simple quirk of fate called parentage. I might not have been happier but things would have been much more . . . convenient. Tom is no different, and yet he has so much more. Not only has he money, but he has the ability to enjoy it.

But now it's easy to let the heating incident upset me, and tears of anger burn in my eyes. I remember going home two weeks later for Christmas vacation to discover that, for financial reasons, my family had learned to make do without lunch. My stomach, conditioned to Yale's twenty-one meal plan, was not pleased with this. In the afternoon I would rummage around the kitchen, looking for a quick snack to tide me over until dinner. But there was nothing that could be called "quick." There were no convenience foods that could be taken from a package. They were too expensive. Everything had to be washed or peeled and cooked, and a simple snack would entail a major production. There wasn't even a loaf of bread. My father made fresh rolls before each meal. It was cheaper.

On New Year's Eve, I was particularly hungry. My stomach nagged me all day and I looked forward to supper. But when supper came there was nothing but soup. Soup and the fresh hot rolls I had grown sick of—three to a person. I wanted to cry, but I held back the tears.

I don't now. I pick up my books and go into my room so that no one will see me. I'd like to hate Tom. I'd like so much to hate him but I cannot, and that makes me feel guilty. I am consorting with the enemy.

I try to hate, but the closest I can come to hate is jealousy. I want to have money also. Realizing this, the guilt presses against my lungs like stones. I want to travel. I want to have a swimming pool. I might enjoy a boat. Someday I might be able to have these things, but how could I enjoy them while others were miserable? How do the wealthy do it?

I try to escape to my books. I pick up my Religious Studies assignment. *The Documents of Vatican II.* The words become blurred as I read, the tears swelling in my eyes.

In His goodness and wisdom, God chose to reveal Himself and to make known to us the hidden purpose of His will by which through Christ, the Word made Flesh, man has access to the Father in the Holy Spirit and comes to share in His divine nature. Through His revelation, therefore, the invisible God, out of

> the abundance of His love, speaks to men as friends and lives among them so that He may invite them and take them into fellowship with Himself.

The book lands in a pile of dust underneath the bed, for in my present state it seems more than likely that Christ was sent forth by Herod. Something had to be done to keep the starving masses from revolting.

My thoughts return to my family at home. My father has taken to going to our church each weekday morning and praying for guidance.

"Just trust in God," he always said. "Don't worry about tomorrow. Everything will work out according to God's will."

I had stopped worrying about tomorrow, but I'd never really trusted in God. And yet things had worked out. For me. But the rest of the family were still at home.

My mother had joined the charismatic movement of our church. She was going to be rebaptized in the Holy Spirit. Born again. But still she was able to say to my father, "Why don't you spend less time in church and more time looking for a job?"

My father laughed and called her a Holy Roller.

My sadness increases, and I want to talk to my parents. I want to call home and hear the voices of my family. They always sound happy. Mary will talk about her school play, *Oklahoma!* And in the background I might hear Paul practicing his French horn. That will cheer me up.

I wait until I've calmed down enough so that my voice will sound normal over the phone. I check my face in the mirror so that my roommates won't see I've been crying.

I go to the phone in the living room and dial my number. It takes a while for the connection to go through. The phone starts ringing, and then there is a click followed by a white fuzzy sound.

A nasal tape-recorded voice speaks.

"The number you have reached, five-five-five, four-eight-nine-five, has been disconnected. Please check the number you are calling to make sure that you have dialed correctly."

I let the receiver fall and the voice starts to repeat itself from the floor. I have dialed correctly. My parents haven't paid the phone bill again. Tears come, and then sobs, and there is nothing I can do to stop them.

In the next room, I can see Tom at his desk, concentrating on his chemistry.

Kevin

Kevin is a full-time dishwasher at Timothy Dwight College. I work with him five days a week. He is twenty-five years old and mentally retarded.

"Peter, are you going home for Thanksgiving?"

"Yes."

"Where do you live?"

"Long Island."

"Are you taking a plane?"

"Kevin, I live on Long Island."

"I know. Are you taking a plane?"

I tell him where Long Island is. I tell him that it's two hours away by car. The next day, Kevin starts again.

"Peter, are you going home for Thanksgiving?"

"Yes."

"Are you taking a plane . . .?"

This goes on every day for two weeks until Thanksgiving arrives.

His affliction is not severe. His speech is normal and he is physically healthy and coordinated, though he is barely five feet tall. He wears the same brown corduroy jeans and tan shoes to work every day, topped by a blue work shirt and a black rubber apron. I remember the pants and shoes when they were new.

"Peter, look what I got for my birthday."

Kevin has a thing about his birthday. He keeps track of it as if it might become lost if he didn't.

"In eight months and ten days I'll be twenty-six years old. Last year the students surprised me on my birthday. They came in and decorated the whole dish machine. The whole place. They didn't do it this year though. Maybe they'll do it again next year. I don't know. Maybe they will. . . .

"In four years I'll be thirty . . . In five years I'll be thirty-one . . . In six years I'll be . . . I'll be . . . How old will I be?"

He's obsessed with rules and instructions. They must not be transgressed. Everything must follow a certain order. There is no room for change.

"Peter, take some trays over there. They need trays. . . .No, not those trays, those are for the coffee cups. Did you hear me? Hey! Where are you going? Bring those back! Those are for the coffee cups!"

Kevin might have the mind of a child, but physically he is a man, and his mind doesn't quite know how to handle this:

"I know about sex. I read those magazines. *Playboy. Playgirl.* I go to the movies. The filthiest movie I every saw, *Superfly.* Oh, boy, you should have seen it. . . .

"If I had a girl in bed you know what I'd do? You know what I'd do? I'd suck her titties. That's what I'd do. . . .

"I got my back pay today. Almost a hundred dollars. Maybe I won't give it to my mother. Maybe I'll get a girlfriend with it. Put on my fancy clothes and get a girlfriend. Go dancing. Maybe she'll let me play sex with her. . . .

"Is that your girlfriend, Peter? Ahhhh. I know you. I bet you're a big lady's man. I bet you've even kissed her. You'll see. I'm gonna kiss a girl some day. . . .

"I'm twenty-five years old and I've never even kissed a girl. Really. Never. I ain't lyin'. Never."

He's proud of his job. He's proud of his salary. Thursday comes and it's payday.

"Whad'ja get, Peter? Lemmee see. I made a hundred and sixty-four dollars this week. Sunday I worked overtime. I'm a good worker. Juan's a good worker too. I make more than he does."

His parents are separated.

"My father's down in Milford. He's married again. I make more than he does."

Thinking about him, I realize now that I've never once seen Kevin do anything to hurt anyone. He's never been selfish, never cruel. His virtues are rather amazing considering the home life that he tells me about.

"My mother takes all my money. She gives me ten dollars a week. I can't do nothin'. If I don't give it to her she'll throw me out of the house. . . .

"My brother's in trouble with the police. He's been stealin' cars and pushin' dope. He got in an accident and the doctor found out they were carryin' drugs in their underwear. The car was stolen. He's sixteen years old. He has to go to a special school now. . . .

"I saw my mother playing sex with one of her boyfriends. I did. I went in her room to get something and there they were, playin' sex. Boy, she was mad. She said, 'Get the hell out of this room!' That was last year."

Due to the recent decision to lay off forty-three dining hall employees, Kevin faces the prospect of losing his job.

"Why does Yale want to do this to me? They have work. I'm a good worker. I never take a break. I'm workin' all day. Who's gonna load the machine if I'm gone? You? You, Peter? You don't know how. You're not fast. You'll be here all night. . . .

"I don't even know how to collect unemployment. I never did it before. I don't want to. They don't mail it to you. You have to go and pick it up. . . .

"They need me here. Who's gonna do all these things? . . . What's gonna happen when I'm gone?"

The Bank Collector

During our spring break, the Duke's Men made a concert tour to Washington and some of the southern states. We spent one night late in our tour at the summer estate of one of the Dukes' girlfriends in Baltimore. Her father is a lung surgeon in Washington.

The estate was on a river leading into Chesapeake Bay. Bolstered by four white pillars, the house stood on a hill about two hundred yards from the private docks, where two sailboats and a motor boat were moored. Inside the house, the floors were covered with Persian rugs and the rooms were filled with antiques.

On one side of the house was a closed-in porch that had a lovely view of the river. It was pleasantly furnished with a green rug and white wicker furniture set against green walls. The large plants that hung from the ceiling thrived in the sun that poured in through the glass windows and doors.

Against one wall was a long shelf holding a collection of antique small mechanical banks. Little metal clowns, acrobats, hunters, and Uncle Sams stood poised, ready to spring into action upon being fed a coin. The amusing figures, painted in bright but now aging colors, created a carnival atmosphere that contrasted with the formality of the rest of the house.

What is it that is so alluring about a carnival? Is it that seductively evil force that always seems to be running through a noisy, crowded, rundown fairground on a hot summer night? Is it the false and deceptive smile of the Kewpie doll?

I looked down at the shelf of antique banks and that same force seemed to be present. The metal figures all wore unchanging smiles that seemed to say they had a secret. They were doing something wrong and getting away with it.

"I see you've found my banks," a voice behind me spoke.

I turned to face the doctor.

"Yes. They're very interesting."

"It's not a big collection," he said, sitting down, "but several of them are fine specimens. Quite rare."

I sat down in a chair across from him.

"It's a great hobby," he continued, "but it's expensive. That's why I've only got twenty-three."

I sympathized with him. I bet myself that some of his banks could have cost more than two hundred dollars.

"It used to be you could buy a whole collection for the same amount that just one bank costs today," he said nostalgically. "But now it seems like everybody's got their own collection. The banks are just about all bought up now. You won't find one just sitting around in an antique shop anymore.

"Every now and then someone will put an ad in the classified section of a magazine that he has one for sale, and he'll get offers from all over the country. I had a friend who answered one of them. He recognized that the bank in question was a very rare one, but the guy selling it didn't know it. It turned out there were only two of them left in the whole country. Well, he bought it from this guy for only two thousand dollars.

"The next thing he did was take it to a well-known collector, who was going to give him ten thousand dollars for it. But this guy got a better offer from the Shorelys—you know, the banking Shorelys. Oh, well. Anyway, he sold it to them for twenty-two thousand dollars.

"The collector thought he had it all wrapped up for ten thousand, and it was swept from right under his feet," the doctor chuckled. "Twenty-two thousand dollars. That's a twenty-thousand-dollar profit in just a few days. Not bad."

I was too dumbfounded to say anything. The doctor continued his monologue.

"Here, let me show you one of mine." He went over to the shelf, took down one of the banks, and set it on the table in front of us. The base of the bank was a blue circus pedestal, one of those round structures that trainers train elephants to stand on. In the top of the base was a slot for coins. At the back of the base stood a vertical bar that became a curved fork above the pedestal. A cast-iron acrobat balanced between the sides of the fork on a metal bar which he held on to.

The figure was dressed in a white clown's suit that had been painted on and had now turned creamy with age. He had red buttons and trim, a pair of red pointed slippers, and a red stocking cap. His black face was frozen in a leering grin.

"This one's a prize," the doctor said, giving it a pat. "Look at him. Not a scratch on him. That's all the original paint and there's not a scratch on him. He cost me seven thousand dollars just a few years back. I don't know how much he's worth now. At least twelve. Watch this," he said, reaching into his pocket. He pulled out a nickel and fitted it into the clown's cap. The metal figure bent slowly forward until his head was quite close to the base. The coin fell into the slot in the blue drum, and the figure swung back up again, grinning proudly.

The doctor's face fell. "He's supposed to do a flip, but he needs adjusting. Maybe with something heavier . . ."

He reached into his pocket for a quarter. This time he gave the clown a little push as he fitted the coin into the cap. The clown performed a full flip and he resurfaced with that same evil grin.

"There!" the doctor said proudly. "With something heavier, like a half-dollar, he'll do two flips."

The little metal acrobat swung back and forth on his stand, basking in glory with his huge, gloating grin. I began to understand what evil secret that hunk of metal possessed. He held the power to keep a person fed and alive for several years. That was the power that ran through those atoms of iron. That was the force that give the metal man life.

The doctor was still speaking.

"You know, if you get your hands on some money these days and you want to invest it, you've got a problem. Look at the stock market. This country's ecomony is a mess." He smiled at his shelves of banks. "That's what's so great about these things. They're good investments. They're safe. People are taking an interest in these things again. Anything from the early days of America. That's where you should put your money these days, in anything American."

Anything American.

Breakfast at Timothy's

In my job as a dishwasher at Timothy Dwight College I usually worked dinners, but one of the workers had asked me to fill in for him at breakfast one day when he would be away. I needed the money so I agreed, expecting to wash dishes. When I reported to work, though, it turned out that I was expected to work on the serving line.

At all of Yale's dining halls, a hot breakfast is served until nine o'clock. After nine, only continental breakfast is available; students serve themselves cold cereal, toast, or Danish. When nine o'clock rolled around, I still had some scrambled eggs, one piece of French toast, and one piece of regular toast. I decided to finish serving them, rather than bring them back to the kitchen, where they would just be thrown out.

At about ten after nine, a resident fellow of Timothy Dwight showed up for breakfast. He was a tall man, about forty-five years old, with stumpy gray hair and a pair of wire-rimmed glasses. He mumbled something and pointed in the direction of the French toast. I put the toast on a plate and served it to him.

"Okay," he growled, "would you like to give me some eggs? I asked for eggs."

I took another plate and gave him some eggs. He was angry.

"Now would you like to give me some toast to eat with the eggs?" I reached for the last piece of toast and put it on his plate.

"Now," he exploded, "would you like to give me two pieces of toast instead of one piece of toast?"

"That was the last piece," I told him as I put two more pieces of bread in the toaster. Then I remembered that it was after nine o'clock and that I didn't have to be making more toast.

"If you want breakfast," I said, "you should get down here before nine o'clock."

He looked at me, his eyes filled with contempt. He spoke through clenched teeth and the words fell from his lips like bird droppings.

"Tomorrow," he snarled, "you can come and serve me breakfast in my room before nine o'clock."

"Don't count on it," I said. I reached behind me to the toaster and pushed up the slices of bread, half toasted. If he wanted toast, he could make it himself. He stalked out of the kitchen.

When he left, I realized I was shaking. My eyes were burning and it was hard for me to swallow. If I had been alone in my room, I probably would have cried. It hurt to be treated as if I were inferior. I felt a hate for that man stronger than any hate I had ever felt before, and the strength of that hate scared me. I would have liked to see him dead.

In Our Nation's Capital

I sat at a table in the Crystal Room of the Sheraton Carlton Hotel in Washington, D.C. The Duke's Men had been hired to sing at a Saint Patrick's Day luncheon in honor of the Irish ambassador to the United States and of the hotel's manager, who was retiring.

People had gathered an hour earlier to sip cocktails in the Mount Vernon Room, and the Duke's Men hadn't passed up the opportunity either. We were among the first ones there, and we watched the room fill around us with Washington VIPs. The only one that most of us could recognize was J. W. Fulbright. Danny, one of the Duke's Men, whose father is a Washington lawyer, was able to point out important congressmen, aides, consultants, etc. They didn't look like much to me.

More interesting than these stale Washington politicians were the wives they brought with them. Their identities were concealed behind layers of face powder, and most of them were dressed all in green for the occasion. Each of them was responsible for maintaining and advancing the social status of her family, and they were all trying to engage in friendly conversation with women a step ahead of them on the social ladder, in hope that room might be made for them on that step. Their behavior reminded me of the tigers in "Little Black Sambo" who chased each other's tails around a tree in a continuous circle until they turned to butter. Lunch was called, and the women were saved from a similar fate.

I vowed not to sit with any Duke's Men, to force myself to eat and talk with some of these people. I saw it as an educational experience. I sat alone at a table and chased away any of the Duke's Men that tried to join me. Two unassuming men in clerical collars sat down and introduced themselves as monsignors with Irish-sounding names, and that was as far as our conversation went. I began to despair and was unconsoled by the chlorine smell of the hot tuna crepes on my plate. Then a woman who introduced herself as "Grosvenor" sat down and announced that the rest of the seats at the table were reserved for an important congressman, his wife, and an admiral. She greeted the two monsignors, whom she didn't seem very interested in, and started a conversation with me.

She asked me what I was studying, and I told her I was interested in writing. Her eyes lit up, and she told me that she, too, was a writer. She had been an editor for *Business Week,* and a Washington columnist. She was retired, and was now writing a book of amusing anecdotes about "all the famous people" in Washington. I listened intently as she rattled off a story about Prince Charles's visit to Washington.

". . . Well, he was standing on the reception line, and everybody had been carefully screened, you know, and there was a man there and nobody knew who he was or how he got in. . . ."

She was quite tickled by the tale she was telling, and her breath came in short little pants, like that of an overexcited toy poodle.

"Well, finally he reached up to the prince, and he shook his hand and the prince asked, 'And what is your connection?' And do you know what he said?" she gasped. "Do you know what he said? . . . 'Western Union'!"

She repeated "Western Union!" and I realized that I was supposed to laugh. So I laughed politely, trying to figure out the punchline.

The congressman, his wife, and the admiral arrived, and a waiter appeared and filled our wineglasses. Danny later informed me that the congressman was one of the five most powerful men in Washington, along with Ford and Kissinger. His wife was a huge woman with a beaked nose, an elaborate hairdo, and a double chin that danced when she turned her head. She was dressed in pink. The congressman was also fat, and both he and the admiral were bald, roundheaded men whose faces were distorted by thick lenses set in jet-black frames. All of them appeared to be well into their seventies.

Mrs. Grosvenor introduced us, and I remembered to stand up as I shook their hands.

"This young man," Mrs. Grosvenor informed them, "has been most delightful to talk to. He's interested in becoming a writer."

"Awhh," the admiral guffawed, "you'd better tell him to find another field. There's no money in writing. He won't make a cent." He turned to me and looked at me as a father would. "Really, you'd better study something else. Why, you'd be better off in the army!"

"Listen to him," the congressman's wife advised me. "He knows what he's talking about. Why, since the admiral retired, he's simply been raking it in!" The table burst into laughter, and even the two monsignors, who had been totally uninvolved in the conversation, smiled sheepishly.

"He's been . . . He's been . . ." the woman tried to speak through her uncontrollable laughter. "He's been . . . working as a . . . 'consultant'!" And the table was overcome by renewed fits of laughter.

The admiral sat with a huge grin on his face, quite proud of himself.

"You've got to have money, son," he continued, suddenly turning quite somber, "because without money, you're nothing. You don't go anywhere without money."

"He's right, you know." Mrs. Grosvenor frowned. "Money talks."

I waited for more laughter. I waited for them to acknowledge their joke. But there was no laughter, no acknowledgment. These people were serious.

Special People

Mary is a full-time worker at the dining hall where I work part-time as a dishwasher. She's one of those women who can be big and fat but somehow you never notice their size. Although she must be close to sixty, she has a spirited personality that might belong to a sixteen-year-old girl. There is something dry and clean about her; she is the definition of "baby powder fresh." Her hair is dyed dark black; her skin is white with a thin dusting of powder, and her lips bright red with lipstick. She always has a kind word for everyone, and all of the students love her.

One Saturday night, just as we were ready to close the serving line, a busload of Yale alumni appeared with their wives, ready to be served dinner. They were members of the Yale Club of Hartford and had been expected two hours earlier in the evening. But they hadn't arrived, and nobody was ready for them now. General havoc took place in the kitchen as the workers tried to whip up a last-minute meal for the Old Blues and their wives.

I became increasingly annoyed. It especially pained me to see Mary running around excitedly as the Yale Club sat there coolly, waiting to be served. She ran by me in a huff and shouted.

"Quick, Peter! Get some coffee cups! They need coffee cups!"

I walked up to the stack of clean cups with deliberate slowness and started counting them out onto a tray, one by one.

"Hurry up, for Christ's sake," Mary whined. "These people are waiting."

"All right! Don't worry about it. They'll get their goddamn coffee cups," I shouted at her, loud enough for the Yale Club to hear. They looked on in disapproval and Mary walked by them shaking her head.

"Boy, these student workers," she said. "They're so slow!"

I felt terrible.

I had taken my anger out on Mary when she was the one I was angry *for*. I hated to see her so subservient, and yet it was I who put her down further, and in front of them. So much so that she'd had to defend herself. I couldn't understand how everything had gotten so twisted.

She approached me afterward, when we were cleaning up.

"You know, Peter, You'd better watch it. You were wrong to wise off in front of those people."

"I know, Mary." I tried to apologize. "I'm sorry."

"Those were special people," she said, her face set in earnest, "and you had to go and get wise. They don't like that, you know."

"Oh, Mary," I said, exasperated, "those were not special people."

"Yes they were. The manager made a special trip down here to tell us to make sure that they were well taken care of. You'd better be careful, you know. They might report you. You might lose your job."

She turned to the counter and started shoving cottage cheese into a container.

I almost cried for her. I wanted to take her in my arms and try to convince her that there weren't any "special people," that she was as special as anyone else in the world.

I put my arm on her shoulder.

"Mary, there's no such thing as special people. People are people. That's all."

She stood there, shaking her head and shoveling the cottage cheese.

"Peter, you're wrong. Those were special people and you had to open your big mouth."

"Mary, look at them," I said, pointing toward the dining room. "What's so special about them?"

"Peter. Shush. They'll hear you."

"Mary," I pleaded, "can't you see that you're more special to me than any of those people? That's why I got so mad. I hated seeing you run around for them."

Her eyes suddenly glazed with tears and she hurried to the refrigerator with the cottage cheese.

"Peter, what am I going to do with you?" she called back. "You're gonna give me gray hairs. You're gonna get yourself in trouble too. You don't know your place. Those were special people."

Suggestions for Discussion

1. With what details does Werner describe the ironic significance of the song, "Both Sides Now"? How does he portray the multifaceted and deep-layered character of the two sides?

2. Account for the tone of the section "A Phone Call Home."

3. How can the heating incident both amuse and upset him?

4. How is irony expressed in the juxtaposition of the sketches of Kevin and the bank collector?

5. What does the narrative of "In Our Nation's Capital" tell you about the author's, the admiral's, and Mrs. Grosvenor's values?

6. Compare Mary's and Peter's implicit definition of "special people."

7. What do you infer is Peter's sense of self at the stage of life he portrays in "Both Sides Now"?

Suggestions for Writing

1. Describe one or more of your experiences with "both sides" of the economic structure.

2. On the basis of his descriptions of the people he encountered at Yale and his reactions to them, write a character study of Peter.

Jorge Luís Borges

Borges and Myself

Translated by Norman Thomas di Giovanni

Jorge Luís Borges (1899–1986), Argentine poet, short-story writer, essayist, critic, and university professor, was best known for his esoteric short fiction. He received little recognition in America until the publication in 1968 of English translations of *Ficciónes, Labyrinths,* and *The Aleph and Other Stories.* In this very short piece the writer speaks of his dual nature, the self who surrenders everything to the creative Borges so that he can weave his tales and poems.

It's to the other man, to Borges, that things happen. I walk along the streets of Buenos Aires, stopping now and then—perhaps out of habit—to look at the arch of an old entranceway or a grillwork gate; of Borges I get news through the mail and glimpse his name among a committee of professors or in a dictionary of biography. I have a taste for hourglasses, maps, eighteenth-century typography, the roots of words, the smell of coffee, and Stevenson's prose; the other man shares these likes, but in a showy way that turns them into stagy mannerisms. It would be an exaggeration to say that we are on bad terms; I live, I let myself live, so that Borges can weave his tales and poems, and those tales and poems are my justification. It is not hard for me to admit that he has managed to write a few worthwhile pages, but these pages cannot save me, perhaps because what is good no longer belongs to anyone—not even the other man—but rather to speech or tradition. In any case, I am fated to become lost once and for all, and only some moment of myself will survive in the other man. Little by little, I have been surrendering everything to him, even though I have evidence of his stubborn habit of falsification and exaggerating. Spinoza held that all things try to keep on being themselves; a stone wants to be a stone and the tiger, a tiger. I shall remain in Borges, not in myself (if it is so that I am someone), but I recognize myself less in his books than in those of others or than in the laborious tuning of a guitar. Years ago, I tried ridding myself of him and I went from myths of the outlying slums of the city to games with time and infinity, but those games are now part of Borges and I will have to turn to other things. And so, my life is a running away, and I lose everything and everything is left to oblivion or to the other man.

Which of us is writing this page I don't know.

Suggestions for Discussion

1. Who is the speaker?

2. What is his relationship to and attitude toward Borges, the writer?

3. With what details are the dual aspects of his personality made clear? Define them.

4. How does he substantiate his belief that he is "fated to become lost once and for all"?

5. On the basis of this brief sketch, what conclusions are you invited to draw about the creative process and about the sources and subject matter of Borges' art?

Suggestions for Writing

1. Read a number of Borges's short stories and analyze the basis of their appeal.

2. The concept of the double appears frequently in literature. Write a sketch of a character in literature (Conrad's "The Secret Sharer," Melville's "Bartleby the Scrivener," Dostoevsky's "The Double," Poe's "William Wilson") who might be described as having a double.

3. Record your daily activities and thoughts for a week, paying no attention to mechanics or organization. Then select one of the journal items for full and logical development.

A. Alvarez

Sylvia Plath: A Memoir

Alfred Alvarez (b. 1929), English critic and teacher, has been the poetry editor and poetry critic for *The Observer* since 1956. He is the author of *Stewards of Excellence* and *The School of Donne* and is a regular contributor to *The Spectator*. His memoir of Sylvia Plath, which appeared first in *New American Review*, was later included in his book *The Savage God* (1971), a study of suicide. Although Plath was often able to turn her "anger, implacability, and her roused, needle-sharp sense of trouble" into her creativity, even into a kind of celebration, she succumbed to depression and everything, according to Alvarez who knew her well, finally conspired to destroy her.

They were living in a tiny flat not far from the Regent's Park Zoo. Their windows faced onto a run-down square: peeling houses around a scrappy wilderness of garden. Closer to the Hill, gentility was advancing fast: smart Sunday newspaper house-agents had their boards up, the front doors were all fashionable colors—"Cantaloupe," "Tangerine," "Blueberry," "Thames Green"—and everywhere was a sense of gleaming white interiors, the old houses writ large and rich with new conversions.

Their square, however, had not yet been taken over. It was dirty, cracked, and racketty with children. The rows of houses that led off it were still occupied by the same kind of working-class families they had been built for eighty years before. No one, as yet, had made them chic and quadrupled their price—though that was to come soon enough. The Hughes' flat was one floor up a bedraggled staircase, past a pram in the hall and a bicycle. It was so small that everything seemed sideways on. You inserted yourself into a hallway so narrow and jammed that you could scarcely take off your coat. The kitchen seemed to fit one person at a time, who could span it with arms outstretched. In the living room you sat side by side, longways on, between a wall of books and a wall of pictures. The bedroom off it, with its flowered wallpaper, seemed to have room for nothing except a double bed. But the colors were cheerful, the bits and pieces pretty, and the whole place had a sense of liveliness about it, of things being done. A typewriter stood on a little table by the window, and they took turns at it, each working shifts while the other minded the baby. At night they cleared it away to make room for the child's cot. Later, they borrowed a room from another American poet, W. S. Merwin, where Sylvia worked the morning shift, Ted the afternoon.

This was Ted's time. He was on the edge of a considerable reputation. His first book had been well received and won all sorts of prizes in the States, which usually means that the second book will be an anticlimax. Instead, *Lupercal* effortlessly fulfilled and surpassed all the promises of *The Hawk in the Rain*. A figure had emerged on the drab scene of British poetry, powerful and undeniable. Whatever his natural hesitations and distrust of his own work, he must have had some sense of his own strength and achievement. God alone knew how far he was eventually going, but in one essential way he had already arrived. He was a tall, strong-looking man in a black corduroy jacket, black trousers, black shoes; his dark hair hung untidily forward; he had a long, witty mouth. He was in command.

In those days Sylvia seemed effaced; the poet taking a back seat to the young mother and housewife. She had a long, rather flat body, a longish face, not pretty but alert and full of feeling, with a lively mouth and fine brown eyes. Her brownish hair was scraped severely into a bun. She wore jeans and a neat shirt, briskly American: bright, clean, competent, like a young woman in a cookery advertisement, friendly and yet rather distant.

Her background, of which I knew nothing then, belied her housewifely air: she had been a child prodigy—her first poem was published when she was eight—and then a brilliant student, winning every prize to be had, first at Wellesley High School, then at Smith College: scholarships all the way, straight A's, Phi Beta Kappa, president of this and that college society, and prizes for everything. A New York glossy magazine, *Mademoiselle,* had picked her as an outstanding possibility and wined her, dined her, and photographed her all over Manhattan. Then, almost inevitably, she had won a Fulbright to Cambridge, where she met Ted Hughes. They were married in 1956, on Bloomsday. Behind Sylvia was a self-sacrificing, widowed mother, a schoolteacher who had worked herself into the ground so that her two children might flourish. Sylvia's father—ornithologist, entomologist, ichthyologist, international authority on bumblebees, and professor of biology at Boston University—had died when she was nine. Both parents were of German stock and were German-speaking, academic, and intellectual. When she and Ted went to the States after Cambridge, a glittering university career seemed both natural and assured.

On the surface it was a typical success story: the brilliant examination-passer driving forward so fast and relentlessly that nothing could ever catch up with her. And it can last a lifetime, provided nothing checks the momentum, and the vehicle of all those triumphs doesn't disintegrate into sharp fragments from sheer speed and pressure. But already her progress had twice lurched to a halt. Between her month on *Mademoiselle* and her last year in college she had had the nervous breakdown and suicide attempt which became the theme of her novel, *The Bell Jar*. Then, once reestablished at Smith—"an outstanding teacher," said her colleagues—the academic prizes no longer seemed worth the effort. So in 1958 she had thrown over university life—Ted had never seriously contemplated it—and gone free-lance, trusting her luck and talent as a poet. All this I learned much later. Now Sylvia had simply slowed down; she was subdued, absorbed in her new baby daughter, and friendly only in that rather formal, shallow, transatlantic way that keeps you at your distance.

Ted went downstairs to get the pram ready while she dressed the baby. I stayed behind a minute, zipping up my son's coat. Sylvia turned to me, suddenly without gush:

"I'm so glad you picked *that* poem," she said. "It's one of my favorites but no one else seemed to like it."

For a moment I went completely blank; I didn't know what she was talking about. She noticed and helped me out.

"The one you put in *The Observer* a year ago. About the factory at night."

"For Christ's sake, Sylvia *Plath*." It was my turn to gush. "I'm sorry. It was a lovely poem."

"Lovely" wasn't the right word, but what else do you say to a bright young housewife? I had picked it from a sheaf of poems which had arrived from America, immaculately typed, with self-addressed envelope and international reply coupon efficiently supplied. All of them were stylish and talented but that in itself was not rare in those days. The late fifties was a period of particularly high style in American verse, when every campus worth its name had its own "brilliant" poetic technician in residence. But at least one of these poems had more going for it than rhetorical elegance. It had no title, though later, in *The Colossus*, she called it "Night Shift." It was one of those poems which starts by saying what it is *not* about so strongly that you don't believe the explanations that follow:

> It was not a heart, beating,
> That muted boom, that clangor
> Far off, not blood in the ears
> Drumming up any fever
>
> To impose on the evening.
> The noise came from outside:
> A metal detonating
> Native, evidently, to
>
> These stilled suburbs: nobody
> Startled at it, though the sound
> Shook the ground with its pounding.
> It took root at my coming . . .

It seemed to me more than a piece of good description, to be used and moralized upon as the fashion of that decade dictated. The note was aroused and all the details of the scene seemed continually to be turning inward. It is a poem, I suppose, about fear, and although in the course of it the fear is rationalized and explained (that pounding in the night is caused by machines turning), it ends by reasserting precisely the threatening masculine forces there were to be afraid of. It had its moments of awkwardness—for example, the prissy, pausing flourish in the manner of Wallace Stevens: "Native, evidently, to . . . ." But compared with most of the stuff that thudded unsolicited through my letterbox every morning, it was that rare thing: the always unexpected, wholly genuine article.

I was embarrassed not to have known who she was. She seemed embarrassed to have reminded me, and also depressed.

After that I saw Ted occasionally, Sylvia more rarely. He and I would meet for a beer in one of the pubs near Primrose Hill or the Heath, and sometimes we would walk our children together. We almost never talked shop; without mentioning it, we wanted to keep things unprofessional. At some point during the summer Ted and I did a broadcast together. Afterward we collected Sylvia from the flat and went across to their local. The recording had been a success and we stood outside the pub, around the baby's pram, drinking our beers and pleased with ourselves. Sylvia, too, seemed easier, wittier, less constrained than I had seen her before. For the first time I understood something of the real charm and speed of the girl.

About that time my wife and I moved from our flat near Swiss Cottage to a house higher up in Hampstead, near the Heath. A couple of days before we were due to move I broke my leg in a climbing accident, and that put out everything and everyone, since the house had to be decorated, broken leg or not. I remember sticking black and white tiles to floor after endless floor, a filthy dark brown glue coating my fingers and clothes and gumming up my hair, the great, inert plaster cast dragging behind me like a coffin as I crawled. There wasn't much time for friends. Ted occasionally dropped in and I would hobble with him briefly to the pub. But I saw Sylvia not at all. In the autumn I went to teach for a term in the States.

While I was there *The Observer* sent me her first book of poems to review. It seemed to fit the image I had of her: serious, gifted, withheld, and still partly under the massive shadow of her husband. There were poems that had been influenced by him, others which echoed Theodore Roethke or Wallace Stevens; clearly, she was still casting about for her own style. Yet the technical ability was great, and beneath most of the poems was a sense of resources and disturbances not yet tapped. "Her poems," I wrote, "rest secure in a mass of experience that is never quite brought out into the daylight. . . . It is this sense of threat, as though she were continually menaced by something she could see only out of the corners of her eyes, that gives her work its distinction."

Throughout this time the evidence of the poems and the evidence of the person were utterly different. There was no trace of the poetry's despair and unforgiving destructiveness in her social manner. She remained remorselessly bright and energetic: busy with her children and her beekeeping in Devon, busy flat-hunting in London, busy seeing *The Bell Jar* through the press, busy typing and sending off her poems to largely unreceptive editors (just before she died she sent a sheaf of her best poems, most of them now classics, to one of the national British weeklies; none was accepted). She had also taken up horse-riding again, teaching herself to ride on a powerful stallion called Ariel, and was elated by this new excitement.

Cross-legged on the red floor, after reading her poems, she would talk about her riding in her twanging New England voice. And perhaps because I was also a member of the club, she talked, too, about suicide in much the same way: about her attempt ten years before which, I suppose, must have been very much on her mind as she corrected the proofs of her novel, and about her recent car crash. It had been no accident; she had gone off the road deliberately, seriously, wanting to die. But she hadn't, and all that was now in the past. For this reason I am convinced that at this time she was not contemplating suicide. On the contrary, she was able to write about the act so freely because it was already behind her. The car crash was a death she had survived, the death she sardonically felt herself fated to undergo once every decade:

> I have done it again.
> One year in every ten
> I manage it—
>
> A sort of walking miracle . . .
> I am only thirty.
> And like the cat I have nine times to die.
>
> This is Number Three . . .

In life, as in the poem, there was neither hysteria in her voice, nor any appeal for sympathy. She talked about suicide in much the same tone as she talked about any other risky, testing activity: urgently, even fiercely, but altogether without self-pity. She seemed to view death as a physical challenge she had, once again, overcome. It was an experience of much the same quality as riding Ariel or mastering a bolting horse—which she had done as a Cambridge undergraduate—or careening down a dangerous snow slope without properly knowing how to ski—an incident, also from life, which is one of the best things in *The Bell Jar*. Suicide, in short, was not a swoon into death, an attempt "to cease upon the midnight with no pain"; it was something to be felt in the nerve-ends and fought against, an initiation rite qualifying her for a *life* of her own.

God knows what wound the death of her father had inflicted on her in her childhood, but over the years this had been transformed into the conviction that to be an adult meant to be a survivor. So, for her, death was a debt to be met once every decade: in order to stay alive as a grown woman, a mother, and a poet, she had to pay—in some partial, magical way—with her life. But because this impossible payment involved also the fantasy of joining or regaining her beloved dead father, it was a passionate act, instinct as much with love as with hatred and despair. Thus in that strange, upsetting poem "The Bee Meeting," the detailed, doubtless accurate description of a gathering of local beekeepers in her Devon village gradually becomes an invocation of some deadly ritual in which she is sacrificial virgin whose coffin, finally, waits in the sacred grove. Why this should happen becomes, perhaps, slightly less mysterious when you remember that her father was an authority on bees; so her beekeeping becomes a way of symbolically allying herself to him, and reclaiming him from the dead.

The tone of all these late poems is hard, factual and, despite the intensity, understated. In some strange way, I suspect she thought of herself as a realist: the deaths and resurrections of "Lady Lazarus," the nightmares of "Daddy," and the rest had all been proved on her pulses. That she brought to them an extraordinary inner wealth of imagery and associations was almost beside the point, however essential it is for the poetry itself. Because she felt she was simply describing the facts as they had happened, she was able to tap in the coolest possible way all her large reserves of skill: those subtle rhymes and half-rhymes, the flexible, echoing rhythms and offhand colloquialism by which she preserved, even in her most anguished probing, complete artistic control. Her internal horrors were as factual and precisely sensed as the barely controllable stallion on which she was learning to ride or the car she had smashed up.

So she spoke of suicide with a wry detachment, and without any mention of the suffering or drama of the act. It was obviously a matter of self-respect that her first attempt had been serious and nearly successful, instead of a mere hysterical gesture. That seemed to entitle her to speak of suicide as a subject, not as an obsession. It was an act she felt she had a right to as a grown woman and a free agent, in the same way as she felt it to be necessary to her development, given her queer conception of the adult as a survivor, an imaginary Jew from the concentration camps of the mind. Because of this there was never any question of motives: you do it because you do it, just as an artist always knows what he knows.

Perhaps this is why she scarcely mentioned her father, however clearly and deeply her fantasies of death were involved with him. The autobiographical heroine of *The Bell Jar* goes to weep at her father's grave immediately before she holes up in a cellar and swallows fifty sleeping pills. In "Daddy," describing the same episode, she hammers home her reasons with repetitions:

> At twenty I tried to die
> And get back, back, back to you.
> I thought even the bones would do.

I suspect that finding herself alone again now, however temporarily and voluntarily, all the anguish she had experienced at her father's death was reactivated: despite herself, she felt abandoned, injured, enraged, and bereaved as purely and defenselessly as she had as a child twenty years before. As a result, the pain that had built up steadily inside her all that time came flooding out. There was no need to discuss motives because the poems did that for her.

These months were an amazingly creative period, comparable, I think, to the "marvellous year" in which Keats produced nearly all the poetry on which his reputation finally rests. Earlier she had written carefully, more or less painfully, with much rewriting and, according to her husband, with constant recourse to *Roget's Thesaurus*. Now, although she abandoned none of her hard-earned skills and discipline, and still rewrote and rewrote, the poems flowed effortlessly, until, at the end, she occasionally produced as many as three a day. She also told me that she was deep into a new novel. *The Bell Jar* was finished, proofread and with her publishers; she spoke of it with some embarrassment as an autobiographical apprentice-work which she had to write in order to free herself from the past. But this new book, she implied, was the genuine article.

Considering the conditions in which she worked, her productivity was phenomenal. She was a full-time mother with a two-year-old daughter, a baby of ten months, and a house to look after. By the time the children were in bed at night she was too tired for anything more strenuous than "music and brandy and water." So she got up very early each morning and worked until the children woke. "These new poems of mine have one thing in common," she wrote in a note for a reading she prepared, but never broadcast, for the BBC, "they were all written at about four in the morning—that still blue, almost eternal hour before the baby's cry, before the glassy music of the milkman, settling his bottles." In those dead hours between night and day, she was able to gather herself into herself in silence and isolation, almost as though she were reclaiming some past innocence and freedom before life got a grip on her. Then she could write. For the rest of the day she was shared among the children, the housework, the shopping, efficient, bustling, harassed, like every other housewife.

Yet lonely she was, touchingly and without much disguise, despite her buoyant manner. Despite, too, the energy of her poems, which are, by any standards, subtly ambiguous performances. In them she faced her private horrors steadily and without looking aside, but the effort and risk involved in doing so acted on her like a stimulant; the worse things got and the more directly she wrote about them, the more fertile her imagination became. Just as disaster, when it finally arrives, is never as bad as it seems in expectation, so she now wrote almost with relief, swiftly as though to forestall further horrors. In a way, this is what she had been waiting for all her life, and now it had come she knew she must use it. "The passion for destruction is also a creative passion," said Michael Bakunin, and for Sylvia also this was true. She turned anger, implacability, and her roused, needle-sharp sense of trouble into a kind of celebration.

I have suggested that her cool tone depends a great deal on her realism, her sense of fact. As the months went by and her poetry became progressively more extreme, this gift of transforming every detail grew steadily until, in the last weeks, each trivial event became the occasion for poetry: a cut finger, a fever, a bruise. Her drab domestic life fused with her imagination richly and without hesitation. Around this time, for example, her husband produced a strange radio play in which the hero, driving to town, runs over a hare, sells the dead animal for five shillings, and with the blood money buys two roses. Sylvia pounced on this, isolating its core, interpreting and adjusting it according to her own needs. The result was the poem "Kindness," which ends:

> The blood jet is poetry,
> There is no stopping it.
> You hand me two children, two roses.

There was, indeed, no stopping it. Her poetry acted as a strange, powerful lens through which her ordinary life was filtered and refigured with extraordinary intensity. Perhaps the elation that comes of writing well and often helped her to preserve that bright American façade she unfailingly presented to the world. In common with her other friends of that period, I chose to believe in this cheerfulness against all the evidence of the poems. Or rather, I believed in it, and I didn't believe. But what could one do? I felt sorry for her but she clearly didn't want that. Her jauntiness forestalled all sympathy, and, if only by her blank refusal to discuss them otherwise, she insisted that her poems were purely poems, autonomous. If attempted suicide is, as some psychiatrists believe, a cry for help, then Sylvia at this time was not suicidal. What she wanted was not help but confirmation: she needed someone to acknowledge that she was coping exceptionally well with her difficult routine life of children, nappies, shopping, and writing. She needed, even more, to know that the poems worked and were good, for although she had gone through a gate Lowell had opened, she was now far along a peculiarly solitary road on which not many would risk following her. So it was important for her to know that her messages were coming back clear and strong. Yet not even her determinedly bright self-reliance could disguise the loneliness that came from her almost palpably, like a heat haze. She asked for neither sympathy nor help but, like a bereaved widow at a wake, she simply wanted company in her mourning. I suppose it provided confirmation that, despite the odds and the internal evidence, she still existed.

It was an unspeakable winter, the worst, they said, in a hundred and fifty years. The snow began just after Christmas and would not let up. By New Year the whole country had ground to a halt. The trains froze on the tracks, the abandoned trucks froze on the roads. The power stations, overloaded by million upon pathetic million of hopeless electric fires, broke down continually; not that the fires mattered, since the electricians were mostly out on strike. Water pipes froze solid; for a bath you had to scheme and cajole those rare friends with centrally heated houses, who became rarer and less friendly as the weeks dragged on. Doing the dishes became a major operation. The gastric rumble of water in outdated plumbing was sweeter than the sound of mandolins. Weight for weight, plumbers were as expensive as smoked salmon, and harder to find. The gas failed and Sunday joints went raw. The lights failed and candles, of course, were unobtainable. Nerves failed and marriages crumbled. Finally, the heart failed. It seemed the cold would never end. Nag, nag, nag.

In December *The Observer* had published a still uncollected poem by Sylvia called "Event"; in mid-January they published another, "Winter Trees." Sylvia wrote me a note about it, adding that maybe we should take our children to the zoo and she would show me "the nude verdigris of the condor." But she no longer dropped into my studio with poems. Later that month I met the literary editor of one of the big weeklies. He asked me if I had seen Sylvia recently.

"No. Why?"

"I was just wondering. She sent us some poems. Very strange."

"Did you like them?"

"No," he replied. "Too extreme for my taste. I sent them all back. But she sounds in a bad state. I think she needs help."

Her doctor, a sensitive, overworked man, thought the same. He prescribed sedatives and arranged for her to see a psychotherapist. Having been bitten once by American psychiatry, she hesitated for some time before writing for an appointment. But her depression did not lift, and finally the letter was sent. It did no good. Either her letter or that of the therapist arranging a consultation went astray; apparently the postman delivered it to the wrong address. The therapist's reply arrived a day or two after she died. This was one of several links in the chain of accidents, coincidences, and mistakes that ended in her death.

I am convinced by what I know of the facts that this time she did not intend to die. Her suicide attempt ten years before had been, in every sense, deadly serious. She had carefully disguised the theft of the sleeping pills, left a misleading note to cover her tracks, and hidden herself in the darkest, most unused corner of a cellar, rearranging behind her the old firelogs she had disturbed, burying herself away like a skeleton in the nethermost family closet. Then she had swallowed a bottle of fifty sleeping pills. She was found late and by accident, and survived only by a miracle. The flow of life in her was too strong even for the violence she had done it. This, anyway, is her description of the act in *The Bell Jar;* there is no reason to believe it false. So she had learned the hard way the odds against successful suicide; she had learned that despair must be counterpoised by an almost obsessional attention to detail and disguise.

By these lights she seemed, in her last attempt, to be taking care not to succeed. But this time everything conspired to destroy her. An employment agency had found her an *au pair* girl to help with the children and housework while Sylvia got on with her writing. The girl, an Australian, was due to arrive at nine o'clock on the morning of Monday, February 11th. Meanwhile, a recurrent trouble, Sylvia's sinuses were bad; the pipes in her newly converted flat froze solid; there was still no telephone, and no word from the psychotherapist; the weather continued monstrous. Illness, loneliness, depression, and cold, combined with the demands of two small children, were too much for her. So when the weekend came she went off with the babies to stay with friends in another part of London. The plan was, I think, that she would leave early enough on Monday morning to be back in time to welcome the Australian girl. Instead, she decided to go back on the Sunday. The friends were against it but she was insistent, made a great show of her old competence and seemed more cheerful than she had been for some time. So they let her go. About eleven o'clock that night she knocked on the door of the elderly painter who lived below her, asking to borrow some stamps. But she lingered in the doorway, drawing out the conversation until he told her that he got up well before nine in the morning. Then she said goodnight and went back upstairs.

Around six A.M. she went up to the children's room and left a plate of bread and butter and two mugs of milk, in case they should wake hungry before the *au pair* girl arrived. Then she went back down to the kitchen, sealed the door and window as best she could with towels, opened the oven, laid her head in it, and turned on the gas.

The Australian girl arrived punctually at nine A.M. She rang and knocked a long time but could get no answer. So she went off to search for a telephone kiosk in order to phone the agency and make sure she had the right address. Sylvia's name, incidentally, was not on either of the doorbells. Had everything been normal, the neighbor below would have been up by then; even if he had overslept, the girl's knocking should have aroused him. But as it happened, the neighbor was very deaf and slept without his hearing aid. More important, his bedroom was immediately below Sylvia's kitchen. The gas seeped down and knocked him out cold. So he slept on through all the noise. The girl returned and tried again, still without success. Again she went off to telephone the agency and ask what to do; they told her to go back. It was now about eleven o'clock. This time she was lucky: some builders had arrived to work in the frozen-up house, and they let her in. When she knocked on Sylvia's door there was no answer and the smell of gas was overpowering. The builders forced the lock and found Sylvia sprawled in the kitchen. She was still warm. She had left a note saying, "Please call Dr.—" and giving his telephone number. But it was too late.

Had everything worked out as it should—had the gas not drugged the man downstairs, preventing him from opening the front door to the *au pair* girl— there is no doubt she would have been saved. I think she wanted to be; why else leave her doctor's telephone number? This time, unlike the occasion ten years before, there was too much holding her to life. Above all, there were the children: she was too passionate a mother to want to lose them or them to lose her. There were also the extraordinary creative powers she now unequivocally knew she possessed: the poems came daily, unbidden and unstoppable, and she was again working on a novel about which, at last, she had no reservations.

Why, then, did she kill herself? In part, I suppose, it was "a cry for help" which fatally misfired. But it was also a last, desperate attempt to exorcise the death she had summoned up in her poems. I have already suggested that perhaps she had begun to write obsessively about death for two reasons. First, when she and her husband separated, however mutual the arrangement, she went through again the same piercing grief and bereavement she had felt as a child when her father, by his death, seemed to abandon her. Second, I believe she thought her car crash the previous summer had set her free; she had paid her dues, qualified as a survivor, and could now write about it. But, as I have written elsewhere, for the artist himself art is not necessarily therapeutic; he is not automatically relieved of his fantasies by expressing them. Instead, by some perverse logic of creation, the act of formal expression may simply make the dredged-up material more readily available to him. The result of handling it in his work may well be that he finds himself living it out. For the artist, in short, nature often imitates art. Or, to restate the cliché, when an artist holds a mirror up to nature he finds out who and what he is; but the knowledge may change him irredeemably so that he becomes that image.

I think Sylvia, in one way or another, sensed this. In an introductory note she wrote to "Daddy" for the BBC, she said of the poem's narrator, "she has to act out the awful little allegory once over before she is free of it." The allegory in question was, as she saw it, the struggle in her between a fantasy Nazi father and a Jewish mother. But perhaps it was also a fantasy of containing in herself her own dead father, like a woman possessed by a demon (in the poem she actually calls him a vampire). In order for her to be free of him, he has to be released like a genie from a bottle. And this is precisely what the poems did: they bodied forth the death within her. But they also did so in an intensely living and creative way. The more she wrote about death, the stronger and more fertile her imaginative world became. And this gave her everything to live for.

I suspect that in the end she wanted to have done with the theme once and for all. But the only way she could find was "to act out the awful little allegory once over." She had always been a bit of a gambler, used to taking risks. The authority of her poetry was in part due to her brave persistence in following the thread of her inspiration right down to the Minotaur's lair. And this psychic courage had its parallel in her physical arrogance and carelessness. Risks didn't frighten her; on the contrary, she found them stimulating. Freud has written, "Life loses in interest, when the highest stake in the game of living, life itself, may not be risked." Finally, Sylvia took that risk. She gambled for the last time, having worked out that the odds were in her favor, but perhaps, in her depression, not much caring whether she won or lost. Her calculations went wrong and she lost.

It was a mistake, then, and out of it a whole myth has grown. I don't think she would have found it much to her taste, since it is a myth of the poet as a sacrificial victim, offering herself up for the sake of her art, having been dragged by the Muses to that final altar through every kind of distress. In these terms, her suicide becomes the whole point of the story, the act which validates her poems, gives them their interest, and proves her seriousness. So people are drawn to her work in much the same spirit as *Time* featured her at length: not for the poetry but for the gossipy, extra-literary "human interest." Yet just as the suicide adds nothing at all to the poetry, so the myth of Sylvia as a passive victim is a total perversion of the woman she was. It misses altogether her liveliness, her intellectual appetite and harsh wit, her great imaginative resourcefulness and vehemence of feeling, her control. Above all, it misses the courage with which she was able to turn disaster into art. The pity is not that there is a myth of Sylvia Plath but that the myth is not simply that of an enormously gifted poet whose death came recklessly, by mistake, and too soon.

I used to think of her brightness as a façade, as though she were able, in a rather schizoid way, to turn her back on her suffering for the sake of appearances, and pretend it didn't exist. But maybe she was also able to keep her unhappiness in check because she could write about it, because she knew she was salvaging from all those horrors something rather marvelous. The end came when she felt she could stand the subject no longer. She had written it out and was ready for something new.

> The blood-jet is poetry,
> There is no stopping it.

The only method of stopping it she could see, her vision by then blinkered by depression and illness, was that last gamble. So having, as she thought, arranged to be saved, she lay down in front of the gas oven almost hopefully, almost with relief, as though she were saying, "Perhaps this will set me free."

On Friday, February 15th, there was an inquest in the drab, damp coroner's court behind Camden Town: muttered evidence, long silences, the Australian girl in tears. Earlier that morning I had gone with Ted to the undertakers in Mornington Crescent. The coffin was at the far end of a bare, draped room. She lay stiffly, a ludicrous ruff at her neck. Only her face showed. It was gray and slightly transparent, like wax. I had never before seen a dead person and I hardly recognized her; her features seemed too thin and sharp. The room smelled of apples, faint, sweet but somehow unclean, as though the apples were beginning to rot. I was glad to get out into the cold and noise of the dingy streets. It seemed impossible that she was dead.

Even now I find it hard to believe. There was too much life in her long, flat, strongly boned body, and her longish face with its fine brown eyes, shrewd and full of feeling. She was practical and candid, passionate and compassionate. I believe she was a genius. I sometimes catch myself childishly thinking I'll run into her walking on Primrose Hill or the Heath, and we'll pick up the conversation where we left off. But perhaps that is because her poems still speak so distinctly in her accents: quick, sardonic, unpredictable, effortlessly inventive, a bit angry, and always utterly her own.

Suggestions for Discussion

1. What complications do you discern in the author's picture of Sylvia Plath's earlier background, her parents, her domestic life, and her early successes?

2. How does the author relate Sylvia Plath's poetry to her experience, especially in the case of "Daddy"?

3. What details and theories give support to Alvarez's views about the meaning of suicide for Sylvia Plath, the precipitating events leading to her last attempt, and her lack of intention to succeed in it.

4. Explain the statement in context, "For the artist, in short, nature often imitates art."

5. Study the organization of the memoir. How are earlier events in Plath's life related to the chronologically narrated incidents of the author's association with her? How does the author use his narrative to illuminate the poems he quotes?

6. Toward the end of the memoir, Alvarez objects to readers' being "drawn to her work . . . not for the poetry but for the gossipy, extraliterary 'human interest.' Yet the suicide adds nothing at all to the poetry. . . ." How can this statement be reconciled with his clarification of the poetry noted in question 5?

Suggestion for Writing

Read the poetry of Sylvia Plath or her early novel *The Bell Jar*. Attempt to account for the enormous impact her writing has on college students.

Maxine Hong Kingston

No Name Woman

Maxine Hong Kingston (b. 1940) was born in Stockton, California, and graduated from the University of California. Her two books, *The Woman Warrior* (1976) from which this excerpt has been taken and *China Men* (1980), both focus on her experiences as a Chinese American. "No Name Woman" graphically portrays the complex problems of cultural identity and implicitly suggests the author's sense of self.

"You must not tell anyone," my mother said, "what I am about to tell you. In China your father had a sister who killed herself. She jumped into the family well. We say that your father has all brothers because it is as if she had never been born.

"In 1924 just a few days after our village celebrated seventeen hurry-up weddings—to make sure that every young man who went 'out on the road' would responsibly come home—your father and his brothers and your grandfather and his brothers and your aunt's new husband sailed for America, the Gold Mountain. It was your grandfather's last trip. Those lucky enough to get contracts waved good-bye from the decks. They fed and guarded the stowaways and helped them off in Cuba, New York, Bali, Hawaii. 'We'll meet in California next year,' they said. All of them sent money home.

"I remember looking at your aunt one day when she and I were dressing; I had not noticed before that she had such a protruding melon of a stomach. But I did not think, 'She's pregnant,' until she began to look like other pregnant women, her shirt pulling and the white tops of her black pants showing. She could not have been pregnant, you see, because her husband had been gone for years. No one said anything. We did not discuss it. In early summer she was ready to have the child, long after the time when it could have been possible.

"The village had also been counting. On the night the baby was to be born the villagers raided our house. Some were crying. Like a great saw, teeth strung with lights, files of people walked zigzag across our land, tearing the rice. Their lanterns doubled in the disturbed black water, which drained away through the broken bunds. As the villagers closed in, we could see that some of them, probably men and women we knew well, wore white masks. The people with long hair hung it over their faces. Women with short hair made it stand up on end. Some had tied white bands around their foreheads, arms, and legs.

"At first they threw mud and rocks at the house. Then they threw eggs and began slaughtering our stock. We could hear the animals scream their deaths—the roosters, the pigs, a last great roar from the ox. Familiar wild heads flared in our night windows; the villagers encircled us. Some of the faces stopped to peer at us, their eyes rushing like searchlights. The hands flattened against the panes, framed heads, and left red prints.

"The villagers broke in the front and the back doors at the same time, even though we had not locked the doors against them. Their knives dripped with the blood of our animals. They smeared blood on the doors and walls. One woman swung a chicken, whose throat she had slit, splattering blood in red arcs about her. We stood together in the middle of our house, in the family hall with the pictures and tables of the ancestors around us, and looked straight ahead.

"At that time the house had only two wings. When the men came back, we would build two more to enclose our courtyard and a third one to begin a second courtyard. The villagers rushed through both wings, even your grandparents' rooms, to find your aunt's, which was also mine until the men returned. From this room a new wing for one of the younger families would grow. They ripped up her clothes and shoes and broke her combs, grinding them underfoot. They tore her work from the loom. They scattered the cooking fire and rolled the new weaving in it. We could hear them in the kitchen breaking our bowls and banging the pots. They overturned the great waist-high earthenware jugs; duck eggs, pickled fruits, vegetables burst out and mixed in acrid torrents. The old woman from the next field swept a broom through the air and loosed the spirits-of-the-broom over our heads. 'Pig.' 'Ghost.' 'Pig,' they sobbed and scolded while they ruined our house.

"When they left, they took sugar and oranges to bless themselves. They cut pieces from the dead animals. Some of them took bowls that were not broken and clothes that were not torn. Afterward we swept up the rice and sewed it back up into sacks. But the smells from the spilled preserves lasted. Your aunt gave birth in the pigsty that night. The next morning when I went for the water, I found her and the baby plugging up the family well.

"Don't let your father know that I told you. He denies her. Now that you have started to menstruate, what happened to her could happen to you. Don't humiliate us. You wouldn't like to be forgotten as if you had never been born. The villagers are watchful."

Whenever she had to warn us about life, my mother told stories that ran like this one, a story to grow up on. She tested our strength to establish realities. Those in the emigrant generations who could not reassert brute survival died young and far from home. Those of us in the first American generations have had to figure out how the invisible world the emigrants built around our childhoods fit in solid America.

The emigrants confused the gods by diverting their curses, misleading them with crooked streets and false names. They must try to confuse their offspring as well, who, I suppose, threaten them in similar ways—always trying to get things straight, always trying to name the unspeakable. The Chinese I know hide their names; sojourners take new names when their lives change and guard their real names with silence.

Chinese-Americans, when you try to understand what things in you are Chinese, how do you separate what is peculiar to childhood, to poverty, insanities, one family, your mother who marked your growing with stories, from what is Chinese? What is Chinese tradition and what is the movies?

If I want to learn what clothes my aunt wore, whether flashy or ordinary, I would have to begin, "Remember Father's drowned-in-the-well sister?" I cannot ask that. My mother has told me once and for all the useful parts. She will add nothing unless powered by Necessity, a riverbank that guides her life. She plants vegetable gardens rather than lawns; she carries the odd-shaped tomatoes home from the fields and eats food left for the gods.

Whenever we did frivolous things, we used up energy; we flew high kites. We children came up off the ground over the melting cones our parents brought home from work and the American movie on New Year's Day—*Oh, You Beautiful Doll* with Betty Grable one year, and *She Wore a Yellow Ribbon* with John Wayne another year. After the one carnival ride each, we paid in guilt; our tired father counted his change on the dark walk home.

Adultery is extravagance. Could people who hatch their own chicks and eat the embryos and the heads for delicacies and boil the feet in vinegar for party food, leaving only the gravel, eating even the gizzard lining—could such people engender a prodigal aunt? To be a woman, to have a daughter in starvation time was a waste enough. My aunt could not have been the lone romantic who gave up everything for sex. Women in the old China did not choose. Some man had commanded her to lie with him and be his secret evil. I wonder whether he masked himself when he joined the raid on her family.

Perhaps she encountered him in the fields or on the mountain where the daughters-in-law collected fuel. Or perhaps he first noticed her in the marketplace. He was not a stranger because the village housed no strangers. She had to have dealings with him other than sex. Perhaps he worked an adjoining field, or he sold her the cloth for the dress she sewed and wore. His demand must have surprised, then terrified her. She obeyed him; she always did as she was told.

When the family found a young man in the next village to be her husband, she stood tractably beside the best rooster, his proxy, and promised before they met that she would be his forever. She was lucky that he was her age and she would be the first wife, an advantage secure now. The night she first saw him, he had sex with her. Then he left for America. She had almost forgotten what he looked like. When she tried to envision him, she only saw the black and white face in the group photograph the men had had taken before leaving.

The other man was not, after all, much different from her husband. They both gave orders: she followed. "If you tell your family, I'll beat you. I'll kill you. Be here again next week." No one talked sex, ever. And she might have separated the rapes from the rest of living if only she did not have to buy her oil from him or gather wood in the same forest. I want her fear to have lasted just as long as rape lasted so that the fear could have been contained. No drawn-out fear. But women at sex hazarded birth and hence lifetimes. The fear did not stop but permeated everywhere. She told the man, "I think I'm pregnant." He organized the raid against her.

On nights when my mother and father talked about their life back home, sometimes they mentioned an "outcast table" whose business they still seemed to be settling, their voices tight. In a commensal tradition, where food is precious, the powerful older people made wrongdoers eat alone. Instead of letting them start separate new lives like the Japanese, who could become samurais and geishas, the Chinese family, faces averted but eyes glowering sideways, hung on to the offenders and fed them leftovers. My aunt must have lived in the same house as my parents and eaten at an outcast table. My mother spoke about the raid as if she had seen it, when she and my aunt, a daughter-in-law to a different household, should not have been living together at all. Daughters-in-law lived with their husbands' parents, not their own; a synonym for marriage in Chinese is "taking a daughter-in-law." Her husband's parents could have sold her, mortgaged her, stoned her. But they had sent her back to her own mother and father, a mysterious act hinting at disgraces not told me. Perhaps they had thrown her out to deflect the avengers.

She was the only daughter; her four brothers went with her father, husband, and uncles "out on the road" and for some years became western men. When the goods were divided among the family, three of the brothers took land, and the youngest, my father, chose an education. After my grandparents gave their daughter away to her husband's family, they had dispensed all the adventure and all the property. They expected her alone to keep the traditional ways, which her brothers, now among the barbarians, could fumble without detection. The heavy, deep-rooted women were to maintain the past against the flood, safe for returning. But the rare urge west had fixed upon our family, and so my aunt crossed boundaries not delineated in space.

The work of preservation demands that the feelings playing about in one's guts not be turned into action. Just watch their passing like cherry blossoms. But perhaps my aunt, my forerunner, caught in a slow life, let dreams grow and fade and after some months or years went toward what persisted. Fear at the enormities of the forbidden kept her desires delicate, wire and bone. She looked at a man because she liked the way the hair was tucked behind his ears, or she liked the question-mark line of a long torso curving at the shoulder and straight at the hip. For warm eyes or a soft voice or a slow walk—that's all—a few hairs, a line, a brightness, a sound, a pace, she gave up family. She offered us up for a charm that vanished with tiredness, a pigtail that didn't toss when the wind died. Why, the wrong lighting could erase the dearest thing about him.

It could very well have been, however, that my aunt did not take subtle enjoyment of her friend, but, a wild woman, kept rollicking company. Imagining her free with sex doesn't fit, though. I don't know any women like that, or men either. Unless I see her life branching into mine, she gives me no ancestral help.

To sustain her being in love, she often worked at herself in the mirror, guessing at the colors and shapes that would interest him, changing them frequently in order to hit on the right combination. She wanted him to look back.

On a farm near the sea, a woman who tended her appearance reaped a reputation for eccentricity. All the married women blunt-cut their hair in flaps about their ears or pulled it back in tight buns. No nonsense. Neither style blew easily into heart-catching tangles. And at their weddings they displayed themselves in their long hair for the last time. "It brushed the backs of my knees," my mother tells me. "It was braided, and even so, it brushed the backs of my knees."

At the mirror my aunt combed individuality into her bob. A bun could have been contrived to escape into black streamers blowing in the wind or in quiet wisps about her face, but only the older women in our picture album wear buns. She brushed her hair back from her forehead, tucking the flaps behind her ears. She looped a piece of thread, knotted into a circle between her index fingers and thumbs, and ran the double strand across her forehead. When she closed her fingers as if she were making a pair of shadow geese bite, the string twisted together catching the little hairs. Then she pulled the thread away from her skin, ripping the hairs out neatly, her eyes watering from the needles of pain. Opening her fingers, she cleaned the thread, then rolled it along her hairline and the tops of her eyebrows. My mother did the same to me and my sisters and herself. I used to believe that the expression "caught by the short hairs" meant a captive held with a depilatory string. It especially hurt at the temples, but my mother said we were lucky we didn't have to have our feet bound when we were seven. Sisters used to sit on their beds and cry together, she said, as their mothers or their slave removed the bandages for a few minutes each night and let the blood gush back into their veins. I hope that the man my aunt loved appreciated a smooth brow, that he wasn't just a tits-and-ass man.

Once my aunt found a freckle on her chin, at a spot that the almanac said predestined her for unhappiness. She dug it out with a hot needle and washed the wound with peroxide.

More attention to her looks than these pullings of hairs and pickings at spots would have caused gossip among the villagers. They owned work clothes and good clothes, and they wore good clothes for feasting the new seasons. But since a woman combing her hair hexes beginnings, my aunt rarely found an occasion to look her best. Women looked like great sea snails—the corded wood, babies, and laundry they carried were the whorls on their backs. The Chinese did not admire a bent back; goddesses and warriors stood straight. Still there must have been a marvelous freeing of beauty when a worker laid down her burden and stretched and arched.

Such commonplace loveliness, however, was not enough for my aunt. She dreamed of a lover for the fifteen days of New Year's, the time for families to exchange visits, money, and food. She plied her secret comb. And sure enough she cursed the year, the family, the village, and herself.

Even as her hair lured her imminent lover, many other men looked at her. Uncles, cousins, nephews, brothers would have looked, too, had they been home between journeys. Perhaps they had already been restraining their curiosity, and they left, fearful that their glances, like a field of nesting birds, might be startled and caught. Poverty hurt, and that was their first reason for leaving. But another, final reason for leaving the crowded house was the never-said.

She may have been unusually beloved, the precious only daughter, spoiled and mirror gazing because of the affection the family lavished on her. When her husband left, they welcomed the chance to take her back from the in-laws; she could live like the little daughter for just a while longer. There are stories that my grandfather was different from other people, "crazy ever since the little Jap bayoneted him in the head." He used to put his naked penis on the dinner table, laughing. And one day he brought home a baby girl, wrapped up inside his brown western-style greatcoat. He had traded one of his sons, probably my father, the youngest, for her. My grandmother made him trade back. When he finally got a daughter of his own, he doted on her. They must have all loved her, except perhaps my father, the only brother who never went back to China, having once been traded for a girl.

Brothers and sisters, newly men and women, had to efface their sexual color and present plain miens. Disturbing hair and eyes, a smile like no other, threatened the ideal of five generations living under one roof. To focus blurs, people shouted face to face and yelled from room to room. The immigrants I know have loud voices, unmodulated to American tones even after years away from the village where they called their friendships out across the fields. I have not been able to stop my mother's screams in public libraries or over telephones. Walking erect (knees straight, toes pointed forward, not pigeon-toed, which is Chinese-feminine) and speaking in an inaudible voice, I have tried to turn myself American-feminine. Chinese communication was loud, public. Only sick people had to whisper. But at the dinner table, where the family members came nearest one another, no one could talk, not the outcasts nor any eaters. Every word that falls from the mouth is a coin lost. Silently they gave and accepted food with both hands. A preoccupied child who took his bowl with one hand got a sideways glare. A complete moment of total attention is due everyone alike. Children and lovers have no singularity here, but my aunt used a secret voice, a separate attentiveness.

She kept the man's name to herself throughout her labor and dying; she did not accuse him that he be punished with her. To save her inseminator's name she gave silent birth.

He may have been somebody in her own household, but intercourse with a man outside the family would have been no less abhorrent. All the village were kinsmen, and the titles shouted in loud country voices never let kinship be forgotten. Any man within visiting distance would have been neutralized as a lover—"brother," "younger brother," "older brother"—one hundred and fifteen relationship titles. Parents researched birth charts probably not so much to assure good fortune as to circumvent incest in a population that has but one hundred surnames. Everybody has eight million relatives. How use-less then sexual mannerisms, how dangerous.

As if it came from an atavism deeper than fear, I used to add "brother" silently to boys' names. It hexed the boys, who would or would not ask me to dance, and made them less scary and as familiar and deserving of benevolence as girls.

But, of course, I hexed myself also—no dates. I should have stood up, both arms waving, and shouted out across libraries, "Hey, you! Love me back." I had no idea, though, how to make attraction selective, how to control its direction and magnitude. If I made myself American-pretty so that the five or six Chinese boys in the class fell in love with me, everyone else—the Caucasian, Negro, and Japanese boys—would too. Sisterliness, dignified and honorable, made much more sense.

Attraction eludes control so stubbornly that whole societies designed to organize relationships among people cannot keep order, not even when they bind people to one another from childhood and raise them together. Among the very poor and the wealthy, brothers married their adopted sisters, like doves. Our family allowed some romance, paying adult brides' prices and providing dowries so that their sons and daughters could marry strangers. Marriage promises to turn strangers into friendly relatives—a nation of sib-lings.

In the village structure, spirits shimmered among the live creatures, bal-anced and held in equilibrium by time and land. But one human being flaring up into violence could open up a black hole, a maelstrom that pulled in the sky. The frightened villagers, who depended on one another to maintain the real, went to my aunt to show her a personal, physical representation of the break she had made in the "roundness." Misallying couples snapped off the future, which was to be embodied in true offspring. The villagers punished her for acting as if she could have a private life, secret and apart from them.

If my aunt had betrayed the family at a time of large grain yields and peace, when many boys were born, and wings were being built on many houses, perhaps she might have escaped such severe punishment. But the men—hungry, greedy, tired of planting in dry soil, cuckolded—had had to leave the village in order to send food-money home. There were ghost plagues, bandit plagues, wars with the Japanese, floods. My Chinese brother and sister had died of an unknown sickness. Adultery, perhaps only a mistake during good times, became a crime when the village needed food.

The round moon cakes and round doorways, the round tables of graduated size that fit one roundness inside another, round windows and rice bowls— these talismans had lost their power to warn this family of the law: a family must be whole, faithfully keeping the descent line by having sons to feed the old and the dead, who in turn look after the family. The villagers came to show my aunt and her lover-in-hiding a broken house. The villagers were speeding up the circling of events because she was too shortsighted to see that her infidelity had already harmed the village, that waves of consequences would return unpredictably, sometimes in disguise, as now, to hurt her. This roundness had to be made coin-sized so that she would see its circumference: punish her at the birth of her baby. Awaken her to the inexorable. People who refused fatalism because they could invent small resources insisted on culpability. Deny accidents and wrest fault from the stars.

After the villagers left, their lanterns now scattering in various directions toward home, the family broke their silence and cursed her. "Aiaa, we're going to die. Death is coming. Death is coming. Look what you've done. You've killed us. Ghost! Dead ghost! Ghost! You've never been born." She ran out into the fields, far enough from the house so that she could no longer hear their voices, and pressed herself against the earth, her own land no more. When she felt the birth coming, she thought that she had been hurt. Her body seized together. "They've hurt me too much," she thought. "This is gall, and it will kill me." With forehead and knees against the earth, her body convulsed and then relaxed. She turned on her back, lay on the ground. The black well of sky and stars went out and out and out forever; her body and her complexity seemed to disappear, without home, without a companion, in eternal cold and silence. An agoraphobia rose in her, speeding higher and higher, bigger and bigger; she would not be able to contain it; there would be no end to fear.

Flayed, unprotected against space, she felt pain return, focusing her body. This pain chilled her—a cold, steady kind of surface pain. Inside, spasmodically, the other pain, the pain of the child, heated her. For hours she lay on the ground, alternately body and space. Sometimes a vision of normal comfort obliterated reality: she saw the family in the evening gambling at the dinner table, the young people massaging their elders' backs. She saw them congratulating one another, high joy on the mornings the rice shoots came up. When these pictures burst, the stars drew yet further apart. Black space opened.

She got to her feet to fight better and remembered that old-fashioned women gave birth in their pigsties to fool the jealous, pain-dealing gods, who do not snatch piglets. Before the next spasms could stop her, she ran to the pigsty, each step a rushing out into emptiness. She climbed over the fence and knelt in the dirt. It was good to have a fence enclosing her, a tribal person alone.

Laboring, this woman who had carried her child as a foreign growth that sickened her every day, expelled it at last. She reached down to touch the hot, wet, moving mass, surely smaller than anything human, and could feel that it was human after all—fingers, toes, nails, nose. She pulled it up on to her belly, and it lay curled there, butt in the air, feet precisely tucked one under the other. She opened her loose shirt and buttoned the child inside. After resting, it squirmed and thrashed and she pushed it up to her breast. It turned its head this way and that until it found her nipple. There, it made little snuffling noises. She clenched her teeth at its preciousness, lovely as a young calf, a piglet, a little dog.

She may have gone to the pigsty as a last act of responsibility: she would protect this child as she had protected its father. It would look after her soul, leaving supplies on her grave. But how would this tiny child without family find her grave when there would be no marker for her anywhere, neither in the earth nor the family hall? No one would give her a family hall name. She had taken the child with her into the wastes. At its birth the two of them had felt the same raw pain of separation, a wound that only the family pressing tight could close. A child with no descent line would not soften her life but only trail after her, ghost-like, begging her to give it purpose. At dawn the villagers on their way to the fields would stand around the fence and look.

Full of milk, the little ghost slept. When it awoke, she hardened her breasts against the milk that crying loosens. Toward morning she picked up the baby and walked to the well.

Carrying the baby to the well shows loving. Otherwise abandon it. Turn its face into the mud. Mothers who love their children take them along. It was probably a girl; there is some hope of forgiveness for boys.

"Don't tell anyone you had an aunt. Your father does not want to hear her name. She has never been born." I have believed that sex was unspeakable and words so strong and fathers so frail that "aunt" would do my father mysterious harm. I have thought that my family, having settled among immigrants who had also been their neighbors in the ancestral land, needed to clean their name, and a wrong word would incite the kinspeople even here. But there is more to this silence: they want me to participate in her punishment. And I have.

In the twenty years since I heard this story I have not asked for details nor said my aunt's name; I do not know it. People who can comfort the dead can also chase after them to hurt them further—a reverse ancestor worship. The real punishment was not the raid swiftly inflicted by the villagers, but the family's deliberately forgetting her. Her betrayal so maddened them, they saw to it that she would suffer forever, even after death. Always hungry, always needing, she would have to beg food from other ghosts, snatch and steal it from those whose living descendants give them gifts. She would have to fight the ghosts massed at crossroads for the buns a few thoughtful citizens leave to decoy her away from village and home so that the ancestral spirits could feast unharassed. At peace, they could act like gods, not ghosts, their descent lines providing them with paper suits and dresses, spirit money, paper houses, paper automobiles, chicken, meat, and rice into eternity—essences delivered up in smoke and flames, steam and incense rising from each rice bowl. In an attempt to make the Chinese care for people outside the family, Chairman Mao encourages us now to give our paper replicas to the spirits of outstanding soldiers and workers, no matter whose ancestors they may be. My aunt remains forever hungry. Goods are not distributed evenly among the dead.

My aunt haunts me—her ghost drawn to me because now, after fifty years of neglect, I alone devote pages of paper to her, though not origamied into houses and clothes. I do not think she always means me well. I am telling on her, and she was a spite suicide, drowning herself in the drinking water. The Chinese are always very frightened of the drowned one, whose weeping ghost, wet hair hanging and skin bloated, waits silently by the water to pull down a substitute.

Suggestions for Discussion

1. What is the tone of the author's address to Chinese Americans? In what sense does this paragraph logically follow her mother's story?

2. Why must Chinese emigrants try to confuse their offspring as well as "the gods"?

3. How did the author piece together the reasons for her aunt's adultery?

4. With what details does the reader get a picture of the lives of daughters in old China?

5. What does the phrase "taking a daughter-in-law" as a synonym for marriage tell the reader about men–women relationships in old China?

6. With what details do you learn about differing attitudes toward boys and girls?

7. Compare the conjectured and real behavior of the aunt's lover with hers after her ostracism.

8. How did the economy, plagues, floods, and wars affect attitudes toward adultery?

9. Trace the organization of the aunt's story. Compare the way in which it is narrated in the mother's words and in those of the author? What purpose is served by the author's intervening introspections?

10. How does the author account for the aunt's suicide?

11. How does Kingston convey that the story of her aunt was a story "to grow up on"? Kingston speaks of being haunted by the ghost of her aunt. What do her introspections tell you implicitly of her sense of self?

Suggestions for Writing

1. Narrate a story "to grow up on" that tested your "strength to establish realities."

2. The critic, John Leonard, called the book, in which this is the first chapter, "a poem turned into a sword." Justify this assessment by analyzing the writer's diction and tone.

◇ ◇ ◇ ◇

Russell Baker

My Lack of Gumption

Russell Baker (b. 1925) has been a journalist throughout his professional career. After graduating from Johns Hopkins University, he worked as a reporter and in 1954 served as a correspondent for the *New York Times* in Washington, D.C., where he was variously assigned to the White House, the State Department, national politics, and the activities of Congress. He subsequently became a columnist for the *New York Times* and won a Pulitzer Prize in 1979. He won a second Pulitzer Prize in 1983 for his autobiography, entitled *Growing Up*. Although Baker writes about his boyhood with a light touch and an irreverent humor, there is an overtone of pathos and seriousness in his description of the people and forces that lead to a young boy's development of a sense of self.

I began working in journalism when I was eight years old. It was my mother's idea. She wanted me to "make something" of myself and, after a level-headed appraisal of my strengths, decided I had better start young if I was to have any chance of keeping up with the competition.

The flaw in my character which she had already spotted was lack of "gumption." My idea of a perfect afternoon was lying in front of the radio re-reading my favorite Big Little Book, *Dick Tracy Meets Stooge Viller*. My mother despised inactivity. Seeing me having a good time in repose, she was powerless to hide her disgust. "You've got no more gumption than a bump on a log," she said. "Get out in the kitchen and help Doris do those dirty dishes."

My sister Doris, though two years younger than I, had enough gumption for a dozen people. She positively enjoyed washing dishes, making beds, and cleaning the house. When she was only seven she could carry a piece of short-weighted cheese back to the A&P, threaten the manager with legal action, and come back triumphantly with the full quarter-pound we'd paid for and a few ounces extra thrown in for forgiveness. Doris could have made something of herself if she hadn't been a girl. Because of this defect, however, the best she could hope for was a career as a nurse or schoolteacher, the only work that capable females were considered up to in those days.

This must have saddened my mother, this twist of fate that had allocated all the gumption to the daughter and left her with a son who was content with Dick Tracy and Stooge Viller. If disappointed, though, she wasted no energy on self-pity. She would make me make something of myself whether I wanted to or not. "The Lord helps those who help themselves," she said. That was the way her mind worked.

She was realistic about the difficulty. Having sized up the material the Lord had given her to mold, she didn't overestimate what she could do with it. She didn't insist that I grow up to be President of the United States.

Fifty years ago parents still asked boys if they wanted to grow up to be President, and asked it not jokingly but seriously. Many parents who were hardly more than paupers still believed their sons could do it. Abraham Lincoln had done it. We were only sixty-five years from Lincoln. Many a grandfather who walked among us could remember Lincoln's time. Men of grandfatherly age were the worst for asking if you wanted to grow up to be President. A surprising number of little boys said yes and meant it.

I was asked many times myself. No, I would say, I didn't want to grow up to be President. My mother was present during one of these interrogations. An elderly uncle, having posed the usual question and exposed my lack of interest in the Presidency, asked, "Well, what *do* you want to be when you grow up?"

I loved to pick through trash piles and collect empty bottles, tin cans with pretty labels, and discarded magazines. The most desirable job on earth sprang instantly to mind. "I want to be a garbage man," I said.

My uncle smiled, but my mother had seen the first distressing evidence of a bump budding on a log. "Have a little gumption, Russell," she said. Her calling me Russell was a signal of unhappiness. When she approved of me I was always "Buddy."

When I turned eight years old she decided that the job of starting me on the road toward making something of myself could no longer be safely delayed. "Buddy," she said one day, "I want you to come home right after school this afternoon. Somebody's coming and I want you to meet him."

When I burst in that afternoon she was in conference in the parlor with an executive of the Curtis Publishing Company. She introduced me. He bent low from the waist and shook my hand. Was it true as my mother had told him, he asked, that I longed for the opportunity to conquer the world of business?

My mother replied that I was blessed with a rare determination to make something of myself.

"That's right," I whispered.

"But have you got the grit, the character, the never-say-quit spirit it takes to succeed in business?"

My mother said I certainly did.

"That's right," I said.

He eyed me silently for a long pause, as though weighing whether I could be trusted to his confidence, then spoke man-to-man. Before taking a crucial step, he said, he wanted to advise me that working for the Curtis Publishing Company placed enormous responsibility on a young man. It was one of the great companies of America. Perhaps the greatest publishing house in the world. I had heard, no doubt, of the *Saturday Evening Post?*

Heard of it? My mother said that everyone in our house had heard of the *Saturday Post* and that I, in fact, read it with religious devotion.

Then doubtless, he said, we were also familiar with those two monthly pillars of the magazine world, the *Ladies Home Journal* and the *Country Gentlemen.*

Indeed we were familiar with them, said my mother.

Representing the *Saturday Evening Post* was one of the weightiest honors that could be bestowed in the world of business, he said. He was personally proud of being a part of that great corporation.

My mother said he had every right to be.

Again he studied me as though debating whether I was worthy of a knighthood. Finally: "Are you trustworthy?"

My mother said I was the soul of honesty.

"That's right," I said.

The caller smiled for the first time. He told me I was a lucky young man. He admired my spunk. Too many young men thought life was all play. Those young men would not go far in this world. Only a young man willing to work and save and keep his face washed and his hair neatly combed could hope to come out on top in a world such as ours. Did I truly and sincerely believe that I was such a young man?

"He certainly does," said my mother.

"That's right," I said.

He said he had been so impressed by what he had seen of me that he was going to make me a representative of the Curtis Publishing Company. On the following Tuesday, he said, thirty freshly printed copies of the *Saturday Evening Post* would be delivered at our door. I would place these magazines, still damp with the ink of the presses, in a handsome canvas bag, sling it over my shoulder, and set forth through the streets to bring the best in journalism, fiction, and cartoons to the American public.

He had brought the canvas bag with him. He presented it with reverence fit for a chasuble. He showed me how to drape the sling over my left shoulder and across the chest so that the pouch lay easily accessible to my right hand, allowing the best in journalism, fiction, and cartoons to be swiftly extracted and sold to a citizenry whose happiness and security depended upon us soldiers of the free press.

The following Tuesday I raced home from school, put the canvas bag over my shoulder, dumped the magazines in, and, tilting to the left to balance their weight on my right hip, embarked on the highway of journalism.

We lived in Belleville, New Jersey, a commuter town at the northern fringe of Newark. It was 1932, the bleakest year of the Depression. My father had died two years before, leaving us with a few pieces of Sears, Roebuck furniture and not much else, and my mother had taken Doris and me to live with one of her younger brothers. This was my Uncle Allen. Uncle Allen had made something of himself by 1932. As salesman for a soft-drink bottler in Newark, he had an income of $30 a week; wore pearl-gray spats, detachable collars, and a three-piece suit; was happily married; and took in threadbare relatives.

With my load of magazines I headed toward Belleville Avenue. That's where the people were. There were two filling stations at the intersection with Union Avenue, as well as an A&P, a fruit stand, a bakery, a barber shop, Zuccarelli's drugstore, and a diner shaped like a railroad car. For several hours I made myself highly visible, shifting position now and then from corner to corner, from shop window to shop window, to make sure everyone could see the heavy black lettering on the canvas bag that said the *Saturday Evening Post*. When the angle of the light indicated it was suppertime, I walked back to the house.

"How many did you sell, Buddy?" my mother asked.

"None."

"Where did you go?"

"The corner of Belleville and Union Avenues."

"What did you do?"

"Stood on the corner waiting for somebody to buy a *Saturday Evening Post.*"

"You just stood there?"

"Didn't sell a single one."

"For God's sake, Russell!"

Uncle Allen intervened. "I've been thinking about it for some time," he said, "and I've about decided to take the *Post* regularly. Put me down as a regular customer." I handed him a magazine and he paid me a nickel. It was the first nickel I earned.

Afterwards my mother instructed me in salesmanship. I would have to ring doorbells, address adults with charming self-confidence, and break down resistance with a sales talk pointing out that no one, no matter how poor, could afford to be without the *Saturday Evening Post* in the home.

I told my mother I'd changed my mind about wanting to succeed in the magazine business.

"If you think I'm going to raise a good-for-nothing," she replied, "you've got another think coming." She told me to hit the streets with the canvas bag and start ringing doorbells the instant school was out next day. When I objected that I didn't feel any aptitude for salesmanship, she asked how I'd like to lend her my leather belt so she could whack some sense into me. I bowed to superior will and entered journalism with a heavy heart.

My mother and I had fought this battle almost as long as I could remember. It probably started even before memory began, when I was a country child in northern Virginia and my mother, dissatisfied with my father's plain workman's life, determined that I would not grow up like him and his people, with calluses on their hands, overalls on their backs, and fourth-grade educations in their heads. She had fancier ideas of life's possibilities. Introducing me to the *Saturday Evening Post,* she was trying to wean me as early as possible from my father's world where men left with their lunch pails at sunup, worked with their hands until the grime ate into the pores, and died with a few sticks of mail-order furniture as their legacy. In my mother's vision of the better life there were desks and white collars, well-pressed suits, evenings of reading and lively talk, and perhaps—if a man were very, very lucky and hit the jackpot, really made something important of himself—perhaps there might be a fantastic salary of $5,000 a year to support a big house and a Buick with a rumble seat and a vacation in Atlantic City.

And so I set forth with my sack of magazines. I was afraid of the dogs that snarled behind the doors of potential buyers. I was timid about ringing the doorbells of strangers, relieved when no one came to the door, and scared when someone did. Despite my mother's instructions, I could not deliver an engaging sales pitch. When a door opened I simply asked, "Want to buy a *Saturday Evening Post?*" In Belleville few persons did. It was a town of 30,000 people, and most weeks I rang a fair majority of its doorbells. But I rarely sold my thirty copies. Some weeks I canvassed the entire town for six days and still had four or five unsold magazines on Monday evening; then I dreaded the coming of Tuesday morning, when a batch of thirty fresh *Saturday Evening Posts* was due at the front door.

"Better get out there and sell the rest of those magazines tonight," my mother would say.

I usually posted myself then at a busy intersection where a traffic light controlled commuter flow from Newark. When the light turned red I stood on the curb and shouted my sales pitch at the motorists.

"Want to buy a *Saturday Evening Post?*"

One rainy night when car windows were sealed against me I came back soaked and with not a single sale to report. My mother beckoned to Doris.

"Go back down there with Buddy and show him how to sell those magazines," she said.

Brimming with zest, Doris, who was then seven years old, returned with me to the corner. She took a magazine from the bag, and when the light turned red she strode to the nearest car and banged her small fist against the closed window. The driver, probably startled at what he took to be a midget assaulting his car, lowered the window to stare and Doris thrust a *Saturday Evening Post* at him.

"You need this magazine," she piped, "and it only costs a nickel."

Her salesmanship was irresistible. Before the light changed half a dozen times she disposed of the entire batch. I didn't feel humiliated. To the contrary. I was so happy I decided to give her a treat. Leading her to the vegetable store on Belleville Avenue, I bought three apples, which cost a nickel, and gave her one.

"You shouldn't waste money," she said.

"Eat your apple." I bit into mine.

"You shouldn't eat before supper," she said. "It'll spoil your appetite."

Back at the house that evening, she dutifully reported me for wasting a nickel. Instead of a scolding, I was rewarded with a pat on the back for having the good sense to buy fruit instead of candy. My mother reached into her bottomless supply of maxims and told Doris, "An apple a day keeps the doctor away."

By the time I was ten I had learned all my mother's maxims by heart. Asking to stay up past normal bedtime, I knew that a refusal would be explained with, "Early to bed and early to rise, makes a man healthy, wealthy, and wise." If I whimpered about having to get up early in the morning, I could depend on her to say, "The early bird gets the worm."

The one I most despised was, "If at first you don't succeed, try, try again." This was the battle cry with which she constantly sent me back into the hopeless struggle whenever I moaned that I had rung every doorbell in town and knew there wasn't a single potential buyer left in Belleville that week. After listening to my explanation, she handed me the canvas bag and said, "If at first you don't succeed . . ."

Three years in that job, which I would gladly have quit after the first day except for her insistence, produced at least one valuable result. My mother finally concluded that I would never make something of myself by pursuing a life in business and started considering careers that demanded less competitive zeal.

One evening when I was eleven I brought home a short "composition" on my summer vacation which the teacher had graded with an A. Reading it with her own schoolteacher's eye, my mother agreed that it was top-drawer seventh grade prose and complimented me. Nothing more was said about it immediately, but a new idea had taken life in her mind. Halfway through supper she suddenly interrupted the conversation.

"Buddy," she said, "maybe you could be a writer."

I clasped the idea to my heart. I had never met a writer, had shown no previous urge to write, and hadn't a notion how to become a writer, but I loved stories and thought that making up stories must surely be almost as much fun as reading them. Best of all, though, and what really gladdened my heart, was the ease of the writer's life. Writers did not have to trudge through the town peddling from canvas bags, defending themselves against angry dogs, being rejected by surly strangers. Writers did not have to ring doorbells. So far as I could make out, what writers did couldn't even be classified as work.

I was enchanted. Writers didn't have to have any gumption at all. I did not dare tell anybody for fear of being laughed at in the schoolyard, but secretly I decided that what I'd like to be when I grew up was a writer.

Suggestions for Discussion

1. What do the details of Baker's reminiscence suggest to you about the sense of self of an eight- and eleven-year-old boy?

2. What do the mother's responses to the executive of the Curtis Publishing Company tell you about Baker's view of his mother? What does his listing of his mother's maxims convey of his attitude toward his mother? What other devices does Baker use to acquaint the reader with his mother's character?

3. By what means does Baker make his sister, Doris, come to life?

4. Relate the title to the author's sense of self; to his mother's sense of him as a person.

5. With what details does Baker achieve a humorous tone?

Suggestions for Writing

1. Describe your childhood and/or adolescent views of what you might like to do when you were "grown up." You might present the changes that may have occurred in the form of a diary, a monologue, a dialogue, or a narrative in which you reminisce about your early years as Baker does.

2. Baker obviously scoffs at his mother's maxims. Why? Why are these maxims still repeated? What is their value? Their limitation?

Maya Angelou
Finishing School

Maya Angelou (b. 1928) has had careers as dancer, poet, television writer and producer, actress, and writer. She has served as coordinator of the Martin Luther King Southern Christian Leadership Conference. Her books include *I Know Why the Caged Bird Sings* (1970), from which this selection is taken, and a memoir, *The Heart of a Woman* (1981). The irony of the title is immediately apparent to the reader of this graphic portrait of Angelou's racist employer.

Recently a white woman from Texas, who would quickly describe herself as a liberal, asked me about my hometown. When I told her that in Stamps my grandmother had owned the only Negro general merchandise store since the turn of the century, she exclaimed, "Why, you were a debutante." Ridiculous and even ludicrous. But Negro girls in small Southern towns, whether poverty-stricken or just munching along on a few of life's necessities, were given as extensive and irrelevant preparations for adulthood as rich white girls shown in magazines. Admittedly the training was not the same. While white girls learned to waltz and sit gracefully with a tea cup balanced on their knees, we were lagging behind, learning the mid-Victorian values with very little money to indulge them. . . .

We were required to embroider and I had trunkfuls of colorful dishtowels, pillowcases, runners and handkerchiefs to my credit. I mastered the art of crocheting and tatting, and there was a life-time's supply of dainty doilies that would never be used in sacheted dresser drawers. It went without saying that all girls could iron and wash, but the finer touches around the home, like setting a table with real silver, baking roasts, and cooking vegetables without meat, had to be learned elsewhere. Usually at the source of those habits. During my tenth year, a white woman's kitchen became my finishing school.

Mrs. Viola Cullinan was a plump woman who lived in a three-bedroom house somewhere behind the post office. She was singularly unattractive until she smiled, and then the lines around her eyes and mouth which made her look perpetually dirty disappeared, and her face looked like the mask of an impish elf. She usually rested her smile until late afternoon when her women friends dropped in and Miss Glory, the cook, served them cold drinks on the closed-in porch.

The exactness of her house was inhuman. This glass went here and only here. That cup had its place and it was an act of impudent rebellion to place it anywhere else. At twelve-o'clock the table was set. At 12:15 Mrs. Cullinan sat down to dinner (whether her husband had arrived or not). At 12:16 Miss Glory brought out the food.

It took me a week to learn the difference between a salad plate, a bread plate, and a dessert plate.

Mrs. Cullinan kept up the tradition of her wealthy parents. She was from Virginia. Miss Glory, who was a descendant of slaves that had worked for the Cullinans, told me her history. She had married beneath her (according to

Miss Glory). Her husband's family hadn't had their money very long and what they had "didn't 'mount to much."

As ugly as she was, I thought privately, she was lucky to get a husband above or beneath her station. But Miss Glory wouldn't let me say a thing against her mistress. She was very patient with me, however, over the housework. She explained the dishware, silverware, and servants' bells. The large round bowl in which soup was served wasn't a soup bowl, it was a tureen. There were goblets, sherbet glasses, ice-cream glasses, wine glasses, green glass coffee cups with matching saucers, and water glasses. I had a glass to drink from, and it sat with Miss Glory's on a separate shelf from the others. Soup spoons, gravy boat, butter knives, salad forks, and carving platter were additions to my vocabulary and in fact almost represented a new language. I was fascinated with the novelty, with the fluttering Mrs. Cullinan and her Alice-in-Wonderland house.

Her husband remains, in my memory, undefined. I lumped him with all the other white men that I had ever seen and tried not to see.

On our way home one evening, Miss Glory told me that Mrs. Cullinan couldn't have children. She said that she was too delicate-boned. It was hard to imagine bones at all under those layers of fat. Miss Glory went on to say that the doctor had taken out all her lady organs. I reasoned that a pig's organs included the lungs, heart and liver, so if Mrs. Cullinan was walking around without those essentials, it explained why she drank alcohol out of unmarked bottles. She was keeping herself embalmed.

When I spoke to Bailey about it, he agreed that I was right, but he also informed me that Mr. Cullinan had two daughters by a colored lady and that I knew them very well. He added that the girls were the spitting image of their father. I was unable to remember what he looked like, although I had just left him a few hours before, but I thought of the Coleman girls. They were very light-skinned and certainly didn't look very much like their mother (no one ever mentioned Mr. Coleman).

My pity for Mrs. Cullinan preceded me the next morning like the Cheshire cat's smile. Those girls, who could have been her daughters, were beautiful. They didn't have to straighten their hair. Even when they were caught in the rain, their braids still hung down straight like tamed snakes. Their mouths were pouty little cupid's bows. Mrs. Cullinan didn't know what she missed. Or maybe she did. Poor Mrs. Cullinan.

For weeks after, I arrived early, left late and tried very hard to make up for her barrenness. If she had had her own children, she wouldn't have had to ask me to run a thousand errands from her back door to the back door of her friends. Poor old Mrs. Cullinan.

Then one evening Miss Glory told me to serve the ladies on the porch. After I set the tray down and turned toward the kitchen, one of the women asked, "What's your name, girl?" It was the speckled-face one. Mrs. Cullinan said, "She doesn't talk much. Her name's Margaret."

"Is she dumb?"

"No. As I understand it, she can talk when she wants to but she's usually quiet as a little mouse. Aren't you, Margaret?"

I smiled at her. Poor thing. No organs and couldn't even pronounce my name correctly.

"She's a sweet little thing, though."

"Well, that may be, but the name's too long. I'd never bother myself. I'd call her Mary if I was you."

I fumed into the kitchen. That horrible woman would never have the chance to call me Mary because if I was starving I'd never work for her. . . .

That evening I decided to write a poem on being white, fat, old and without children. It was going to be a tragic ballad. I would have to watch her carefully to capture the essence of her loneliness and pain.

The very next day, she called me by the wrong name. Miss Glory and I were washing up the lunch dishes when Mrs. Cullinan came to the doorway. "Mary?"

Miss Glory asked, "Who?"

Mrs. Cullinan, sagging a little, knew and I knew. "I want Mary to go down to Mrs. Randall's and take her some soup. She's not been feeling well for a few days."

Miss Glory's face was a wonder to see. "You mean Margaret, ma'am. Her name's Margaret."

"That's too long. She's Mary from now on. Heat that soup from last night and put it in the china tureen and, Mary, I want you to carry it carefully."

Every person I knew had a hellish horror of being "called out of his name." It was a dangerous practice to call a Negro anything that could be loosely construed as insulting because of the centuries of their having been called niggers, jigs, dinges, blackbirds, crows, boots and spooks.

Miss Glory had a fleeting second of feeling sorry for me. Then as she handed me the hot tureen she said, "Don't mind, don't pay that no mind. Sticks and stones may break your bones, but words . . . You know, I been working for her for twenty years."

She held the back door open for me. "Twenty years. I wasn't much older than you. My name used to be Hallelujah. That's what Ma named me, but my mistress give me 'Glory,' and it stuck. I likes it better too."

I was in the little path that ran behind the houses when Miss Glory shouted. "It's shorter too."

For a few seconds it was a tossup over whether I would laugh (imagine being named Hallelujah) or cry (imagine letting some white woman rename you for her convenience). My anger saved me from either outburst. I had to quit the job, but the problem was going to be how to do it. Momma wouldn't allow me to quit for just any reason.

"She's a peach. That woman is a real peach." Mrs. Randall's maid was talking as she took the soup from me, and I wondered what her name used to be and what she answered to now.

For a week I looked into Mrs. Cullinan's face as she called me Mary. She ignored my coming late and leaving early. Miss Glory was a little annoyed because I had begun to leave egg yolk on the dishes and wasn't putting much heart in polishing the silver. I hoped that she would complain to our boss, but she didn't.

Then Bailey solved my dilemma. He had me describe the contents of the cupboard and the particular plates she liked best. Her favorite piece was a casserole shaped like a fish and the green glass coffee cups. I kept his instructions in mind, so on the next day when Miss Glory was hanging out clothes and I had again been told to serve the old biddies on the porch, I dropped the empty serving tray. When I heard Mrs. Cullinan scream, "Mary!" I picked up the casserole and two of the green glass cups in readiness. As she rounded the kitchen door I let them fall on the tiled floor.

I could never absolutely describe to Bailey what happened next, because each time I got to the part where she fell on the floor and screwed up her ugly face to cry, we burst out laughing. She actually wobbled around on the floor and picked up shards of the cups and cried, "Oh, Momma. Oh, dear Gawd. It's Momma's china from Virginia. Oh, Momma, I sorry."

Miss Glory came running in from the yard and the women from the porch crowded around. Miss Glory was almost as broken up as her mistress. "You mean to say she broke our Virginia dishes? What we gone do?"

Mrs. Cullinan cried louder, "That clumsy nigger. Clumsy little black nigger."

Old speckled-face leaned down and asked, "Who did it, Viola? Was it Mary? Who did it?"

Everything was happening so fast I can't remember whether her action preceded her words, but I know that Mrs. Cullinan said, "Her name's Margaret, goddamn it, her name's Margaret." And she threw a wedge of the broken plate at me. It could have been the hysteria which put her aim off, but the flying crockery caught Miss Glory right over her ear and she started screaming.

I left the front door wide open so all the neighbors could hear.

Mrs. Cullinan was right about one thing. My name wasn't Mary.

Suggestions for Discussion

1. With what details does Angelou bring the Cullinan household to life?

2. Angelou's changed views of Mrs. Cullinan are very marked. Characterize the contrasting portraits and suggest the means by which each is made graphic.

3. What is the significance of the name changes? How do they contribute to Angelou's view of Mrs. Cullinan?

4. Angelou uses fresh and surprising language on occasion; how does the phrase (par. 1) "munching along on a few of life's necessities" contribute to her reminiscence? She states that Mrs. Viola Cullinan usually "rested her smile until late afternoon." What does that description tell you about her employer?

5. What does the enumeration of each type of glass and silverware contribute to Angelou's thesis?

6. What is Angelou's central thesis? Relate the title to her experiences? To whom does it appear to be addressed?

7. How would you describe the tone of the piece? Cite examples in which the diction contributes to the tone. Cite examples of irony.

Suggestions for Writing

1. Describe a person or situation in which your initial impressions were reversed or changed. By means of setting, characterization, dialogue, figurative language, and simple narrative account for your shifts in attitude.

2. Write a narrative in which you or a person you know are the victim of discrimination or injustice.

Lillian Hellman

An Unfinished Woman

Lillian Hellman (1905–1984) was an American playwright who focused on psychological and social themes in such works as *The Children's Hour* (1934), *The Little Foxes* (1939), *Watch on the Rhine* (1941), *Another Part of the Forest* (1946), and *The Autumn Garden* (1951). She also worked as a professional play reader and a book reviewer for the *New York Herald Tribune,* and in 1966 she edited *The Short Novels of Dashiell Hammett.* She published three memoirs, *An Unfinished Woman* (1969), *Pentimento* (1973), and *Scoundrel Time* (1976). In this memoir the adolescent Hellman makes some significant and rather terrifying discoveries about herself.

I was, they told me, turning into a handful. Mrs. Stillman said I was wild, Mr. Stillman said that I would, of course, bring pain to my mother and father, and Fizzy said I was just plain disgusting mean. It had been a bad month for me. I had, one night, fallen asleep in the fig tree and, coming down in the morning, refused to tell my mother where I had been. James Denery the Third had hit me very hard in a tug-of-war and I had waited until the next day to hit him over the head with a porcelain coffee pot and then his mother complained to my mother. I had also refused to go back to dancing class.

And I was now spending most of my time with a group from an orphanage down the block. I guess the orphan group was no more attractive than any other, but to be an orphan seemed to me desirable and a self-made piece of independence. In any case, the orphans were more interesting to me than my schoolmates, and if they played rougher they complained less. Frances, a dark beauty of my age, queened it over the others because her father had been killed by the Mafia. Miriam, small and wiry, regularly stole my allowance from the red purse my aunt had given me, and the one time I protested she beat me up. Louis Calda was religious and spoke to me about it. Pancho was dark, sad, and to me, a poet, because once he said, *"Yo te amo."* I could not sleep a full night after this declaration, and it set up in me forever after both sympathy and irritability with the first sexual stirrings of little girls, so masked, so complex, so foolish as compared with the sex of little boys. It was Louis Calda who took Pancho and me to a Catholic Mass that could have made me a fourteen-year-old convert. But Louis explained that he did not think me worthy, and Pancho, to stop my tears, cut off a piece of his hair with a knife, gave it to me as a gift from royalty, and then shoved me into the gutter. I don't know why I thought this an act of affection, but I did, and went home to open the back of a new wristwatch my father had given me for my birthday and to put the lock of hair in the back. A day later when the watched stopped, my father insisted I give it to him immediately, declaring that the jeweler was unreliable.

It was that night that I disappeared, and that night that Fizzy said I was disgusting mean, and Mr. Stillman said I would forever pain my mother and father, and my father turned on both of them and said he would handle his family affairs himself without comments from strangers. But he said it too late. He had come home very angry with me: the jeweler, after my father's complaints about his unreliability, had found the lock of hair in the back of the watch. What started out to be a mild reproof on my father's part soon turned angry when I wouldn't explain about the hair. (My father was often angry when I was most like him.) He was so angry that he forgot that he was attacking me in front of the Stillmans, my old rival Fizzy, and the delighted Mrs. Dreyfus, a new, rich boarder who only that afternoon had complained about my bad manners. My mother left the room when my father grew angry with me. Hannah, passing through, put up her hand as if to stop my father and then, frightened of the look he gave her, went out to the porch. I sat on the couch, astonished at the pain in my head. I tried to get up from the couch, but one ankle turned and I sat down again, knowing for the first time the rampage that could be caused in me by anger. The room began to have other forms, the people were no longer men and women, my head was not my own. I told myself that my head had gone somewhere and I have little memory of anything after my Aunt Jenny came into the room and said to my father, "Don't you remember?" I have never known what she meant, but I knew that soon after I was moving up the staircase, that I slipped and fell a few steps, that when I woke up hours later in my bed, I found a piece of angel cake— an old love, an old custom—left by my mother on my pillow. The headache was worse and I vomited out of the window. Then I dressed, took my red purse, and walked a long way down St. Charles Avenue. A St. Charles Avenue mansion had on its back lawn a famous doll's-house, an elaborate copy of the mansion itself, built years before for the small daughter of the house. As I passed this showpiece, I saw a policeman and moved swiftly back to the doll palace and crawled inside. If I had known about the fantasies of the frightened, that ridiculous small house would not have been so terrible for me. I was surrounded by ornate, carved reproductions of the mansion furniture, scaled for children, bisque figurines in miniature, a working toilet seat of gold leaf in suitable size, small draperies of damask with a sign that said "From the damask of Marie Antoinette," a miniature samovar with small bronze cups, and a tiny Madame Récamier couch on which I spent the night, my legs on the floor. I must have slept, because I woke from a nightmare and knocked over a bisque figurine. The noise frightened me, and since it was now almost light, in one of those lovely mist mornings of late spring when every flower in New Orleans seems to melt and mix with the air, I crawled out. Most of that day I spent walking, although I had a long session in the ladies' room of the railroad station. I had four dollars and two bits, but that wasn't much when you meant it to last forever and when you knew it would not be easy for a fourteen-year-old girl to find work in a city where too many people knew her. Three times I stood in line at the railroad ticket windows to ask where I could go for four dollars, but each time the question seemed too dangerous and I knew no other way of asking it.

Toward evening, I moved to the French Quarter, feeling sad and envious as people went home to dinner. I bought a few Tootsie Rolls and a half loaf of bread and went to the St. Louis Cathedral in Jackson Square. (It was that night that I composed the prayer that was to become, in the next five years, an obsession, mumbled over and over through the days and nights: "God forgive me, Papa forgive me, Mama forgive me, Sophronia, Jenny, Hannah, and all others, through this time and that time, in life and in death." When I was nineteen, my father, who had made several attempts through the years to find out what my lip movements meant as I repeated the prayer, said, "How much would you take to stop that? Name it and you've got it." I suppose I was sick of the nonsense by that time because I said, "A leather coat and a feather fan," and the next day he bought them for me.) After my loaf of bread, I went looking for a bottle of soda pop and discovered, for the first time, the whorehouse section around Bourbon Street. The women were ranged in the doorways of the cribs, making the first early evening offers to sailors, who were the only men in the streets. I wanted to stick around and see how things like that worked, but the second or third time I circled the block, one of the girls called out to me. I couldn't understand the words, but the voice was angry enough to make me run toward the French Market.

The Market was empty except for two old men. One of them called to me as I went past, and I turned to see that he had opened his pants and was shaking what my circle called "his thing." I flew across the street into the coffee stand, forgetting that the owner had known me since I was a small child when my Aunt Jenny would rest from her marketing tour with a cup of fine, strong coffee.

He said, in the patois, "*Que faites, ma 'fant? Je suis fermé.*"

I said, "*Rien. Ma tante attend*—Could I have a doughnut?"

He brought me two doughnuts, saying one was *lagniappe*, but I took my doughnuts outside when he said "*Mais où est vo' tante à c'heure?*"

I fell asleep with my doughnuts behind a shrub in Jackson Square. The night was damp and hot and through the sleep there were many voices and, much later, there was music from somewhere near the river. When all sounds had ended, I woke, turned my head, and knew I was being watched. Two rats were sitting a few feet from me. I urinated on my dress, crawled backwards to stand up, screamed as I ran up the steps of St. Louis Cathedral and pounded on the doors. I don't know when I stopped screaming or how I got to the railroad station, but I stood against the wall trying to tear off my dress and only knew I was doing it when two women stopped to stare at me. I began to have cramps in my stomach of a kind I had never known before. I went into the ladies' room and sat bent in a chair, whimpering with pain. After a while the cramps stopped, but I had an intimation, when I looked into the mirror, of something happening to me: my face was blotched, and there seemed to be circles and twirls I had never seen before, the straight blonde hair was damp with sweat, and a paste of green from the shrub had made lines on my jaw. I had gotten older.

Sometime during that early morning I half washed my dress, threw away my pants, put cold water on my hair. Later in the morning a cleaning woman appeared, and after a while began to ask questions that frightened me. When she put down her mop and went out of the room, I ran out of the station. I walked, I guess, for many hours, but when I saw a man on Canal Street who worked in Hannah's office, I realized that the sections of New Orleans that were known to me were dangerous for me.

Years before, when I was a small child, Sophronia and I would go to pick up, or try on, pretty embroidered dresses that were made for me by a colored dressmaker called Bibettera. A block up from Bibettera's there had been a large ruin of a house with a sign, ROOMS—CLEAN—CHEAP, and cheerful people seemed always to be moving in and out of the house. The door of the house was painted a bright pink. I liked that and would discuss with Sophronia why we didn't live in a house with a pink door.

Bibettera was long since dead, so I knew I was safe in this Negro neighborhood. I went up and down the block several times, praying that things would work and I could take my cramps to bed. I knocked on the pink door. It was answered immediately by a small young man.

I said, "Hello." He said nothing.

I said, "I would like to rent a room, please."

He closed the door but I waited, thinking he had gone to get the lady of the house. After a long time, a middle-aged woman put her head out of a second-floor-window and said, "What you at?"

I said, "I would like to rent a room, please. My mama is a widow and has gone to work across the river. She gave me money and said to come here until she called for me."

"Who your mama?"

"Er. My mama."

"What you at? Speak out."

"I told you. I have money . . ." But as I tried to open my purse, the voice grew angry.

"This is a nigger house. Get you off. *Vite*."

I said, in a whisper, "I know. I'm part nigger."

The small young man opened the front door. He was laughing. "You part mischief. Get the hell out of here."

I said, "Please"—and then, "I'm related to Sophronia Mason. She told me to come. Ask her."

Sophronia and her family were respected figures in New Orleans Negro circles, and because I had some vague memory of her stately bow to somebody as she passed this house, I believed they knew her. If they told her about me I would be in trouble, but phones were not usual then in poor neighborhoods, and I had no other place to go.

The woman opened the door. Slowly I went into the hall.

I said, "I won't stay long. I have four dollars and Sophronia will give more if . . ."

The woman pointed up the stairs. She opened the door of a small room. "Washbasin place down the hall. Toilet place behind the kitchen. Two-fifty and no fuss, no bother."

I said, "Yes ma'am, yes ma'am," but as she started to close the door, the young man appeared.

"Where your bag?"

"Bag?"

"Nobody put up here without no bag."

"Oh. You mean the bag with my clothes? It's at the station. I'll go and get it later . . ." I stopped because I knew I was about to say I'm sick, I'm in pain, I'm frightened.

He said, "I say you lie. I say you trouble. I say you get out."

I said, "And I say you shut up."

Years later, I was to understand why the command worked, and to be sorry that it did, but that day I was very happy when he turned and closed the door. I was asleep within minutes.

Toward evening, I went down the stairs, saw nobody, walked a few blocks and bought myself an oyster loaf. But the first bite made me feel sick, so I took my loaf back to the house. This time, as I climbed the steps, there were three women in the parlor, and they stopped talking when they saw me. I went back to sleep immediately, dizzy and nauseated.

I woke to a high, hot sun and my father standing at the foot of the bed staring at the oyster loaf.

He said, "Get up now and get dressed."

I was crying as I said, "Thank you, Papa, but I can't."

From the hall, Sophronia said, "Get along up now. *Vite*. The morning is late."

My father left the room. I dressed and came into the hall carrying my oyster loaf. Sophronia was standing at the head of the stairs. She pointed out, meaning my father was on the street.

I said, "He humiliated me. He did. I won't . . ."

She said, "Get you going or I will never see you whenever again."

I ran past her to the street. I stood with my father until Sophronia joined us, and then we walked slowly, without speaking, to the streetcar line. Sophronia bowed to us, but she refused my father's hand when he attempted to help her into the car. I ran to the car meaning to ask her to take me with her, but the car moved and she raised her hand as if to stop me. My father and I walked again for a long time.

He pointed to a trash can sitting in front of a house. "Please put that oyster loaf in the can."

At Vanalli's restaurant, he took my arm. "Hungry?"

I said, "No, thank you, Papa."

But we went through the door. It was, in those days, a New Orleans custom to have an early black coffee, go to the office, and after a few hours have a large breakfast at a restaurant. Vanalli's was crowded, the headwaiter was so sorry, but after my father took him aside, a very small table was put up for us—too small for my large father, who was accommodating himself to it in a manner most unlike him.

He said, "Jack, my rumpled daughter would like cold crayfish, a nice piece of pompano, a separate bowl of Béarnaise sauce, don't ask me why, French fried potatoes . . ."

I said, "Thank you, Papa, but I am not hungry. I don't want to be here."

My father waved the waiter away and we sat in silence until the crayfish came. My hand reached out instinctively and then drew back.

My father said, "Your mother and I have had an awful time."

I said, "I'm sorry about that. But I don't want to go home, Papa."

He said, angrily, "Yes, you do. But you want me to apologize first. I do apologize but you should not have made me say it."

After a while I mumbled, "God forgive me, Papa forgive me, Mama forgive me, Sophronia, Jenny, Hannah . . ."

"Eat your crayfish."

I ate everything he had ordered and then a small steak. I suppose I had been mumbling throughout my breakfast.

My father said, "You're talking to yourself. I can't hear you. What are you saying?"

"God forgive me, Papa forgive me, Mama forgive me, Sophronia, Jenny . . ."

My father said, "Where do we start your training as the first Jewish nun on Prytania Street?"

When I finished laughing, I liked him again. I said, "Papa, I'll tell you a secret. I've had very bad cramps and I am beginning to bleed. I'm changing life."

He stared at me for a while. Then he said, "Well, it's not the way it's usually described, but it's accurate, I guess. Let's go home now to your mother."

We were never, as long as my mother and father lived, to mention that time again. But it was of great importance to them and I've thought about it all my life. From that day on I knew my power over my parents. That was not to be too important: I was ashamed of it and did not abuse it too much. But I found out something more useful and more dangerous: if you are willing to take the punishment, you are halfway through the battle. That the issue may be trivial, the battle ugly, is another point.

Suggestions for Discussion

1. What do the details describing Hellman's "bad month" tell you about her personality? How are you led to account for her behavior?

2. What is conveyed about Hellman's relationship to Sophronia? What is Sophronia's attitude toward Hellman's escapade? What is the attitude toward Hellman of the people in the household with the pink door?

3. In what sense is this a narrative of initiation?

4. How are Hellman's feelings about her mother and father conveyed?

5. What did the author's running away from home tell her about herself?

6. What is the significance of Hellman's prayer? Account for her father's attitude toward it.

7. In the last paragraph the author makes a distinction between the two lessons she learned. What is it?

Suggestions for Writing

1. Write a narrative in which you recall an episode in your early adolescence and suggest its significance to your life.

2. Did you ever exercise your "power" over your parents? Describe an episode in which you took advantage of their concern and caring for you.

Alice Walker

When the Other Dancer Is the Self

Alice Walker (b. 1944) has received numerous awards for her fiction: *The Color Purple* (1982), a best-selling novel, was nominated for the Book Critics' Circle Award and received the American Book Award, the Candace Award of the National Coalition of 100 Black Women, and a Pulitzer Prize. She has also published two collections of short stories, *You Can't Keep a Good Woman Down* (1981) and *In Love and Trouble.* Her recent book, *In Search of Our Mothers' Gardens: Womanist Prose* (1983), includes this reminiscence of the effect of a traumatic injury to her eye on her self image.

It is a bright summer day in 1947. My father, a fat, funny man with beautiful eyes and a subversive wit, is trying to decide which of his eight children he will take with him to the county fair. My mother, of course, will not go. She is knocked out from getting most of us ready: I hold my neck stiff against the pressure of her knuckles as she hastily completes the braiding and then be-ribboning of my hair.

My father is the driver for the rich old white lady up the road. Her name is Miss Mey. She owns all the land for miles around, as well as the house in which we live. All I remember about her is that she once offered to pay my mother thirty-five cents for cleaning her house, raking up piles of her magnolia leaves, and washing her family's clothes, and that my mother—she of no money, eight children, and a chronic earache—refused it. But I do not think of this in 1947. I am two and a half years old. I want to go everywhere my daddy goes. I am excited at the prospect of riding in a car. Someone has told me fairs are fun. That there is room in the car for only three of us doesn't faze me at all. Whirling happily in my starchy frock, showing off my biscuit-polished patent-leather shoes and lavender socks, tossing my head in a way that makes my ribbons bounce, I stand, hands on hips, before my father. "Take me, Daddy," I say with assurance; "I'm the prettiest!"

Later, it does not surprise me to find myself in Miss Mey's shiny black car, sharing the back seat with the other lucky ones. Does not surprise me that I thoroughly enjoy the fair. At home that night I tell the unlucky ones all I can remember about the merry-go-round, the man who eats live chickens, and the teddy bears, until they say: that's enough, baby Alice. Shut up now, and go to sleep.

It is Easter Sunday, 1950. I am dressed in a green, flocked, scalloped-hem dress (handmade by my adoring sister, Ruth) that has its own smooth satin petticoat and tiny hot-pink roses tucked into each scallop. My shoes, new T-strap patent leather, again highly biscuit-polished. I am six years old and have learned one of the longest Easter speeches to be heard that day, totally unlike the speech I said when I was two: "Easter lilies/pure and white/blossom in/ the morning light." When I rise to give my speech I do so on a great wave of love and pride and expectation. People in the church stop rustling their new crinolines. They seem to hold their breath. I can tell they admire my dress, but it is my spirit, bordering on sassiness (womanishness), they secretly applaud.

"That girl's a little *mess*," they whisper to each other, pleased.

Naturally I say my speech without stammer or pause, unlike those who stutter, stammer, or, worst of all, forget. This is before the word "beautiful" exists in people's vocabulary, but "Oh, isn't she the *cutest* thing!" frequently floats my way. "And got so much sense!" they gratefully add . . . for which thoughtful addition I thank them to this day.

It was great fun being cute. But then, one day, it ended.

I am eight years old and a tomboy. I have a cowboy hat, cowboy boots, checkered shirt and pants, all red. My playmates are my brothers, two and four years older than I. Their colors are black and green, the only difference in the way we are dressed. On Saturday nights we all go the picture show, even my mother; Westerns are her favorite kind of movie. Back home, "on the ranch," we pretend we are Tom Mix, Hopalong Cassidy, Lash LaRue (we've even named one of our dogs Lash LaRue); we chase each other for hours rustling cattle, being outlaws, delivering damsels from distress. Then my parents decide to buy my brothers guns. These are not "real" guns. They shoot "BBs," copper pellets my brothers say will kill birds. Because I am a girl, I do not get a gun. Instantly I am relegated to the position of Indian. Now there appears a great distance between us. They shoot and shoot at everything with their new guns. I try to keep up with my bow and arrows.

One day while I am standing on top of our makeshift "garage"—pieces of tin nailed across some poles—holding my bow and arrow and looking out toward the fields, I feel an incredible blow in my right eye. I look down just in time to see my brother lower his gun.

Both brothers rush to my side. My eye stings, and I cover it with my hand. "If you tell," they say, "we will get a whipping. You don't want that to happen, do you?" I do not. "Here is a piece of wire." says the older brother, picking it up from the roof; "say you stepped on one end of it and the other flew up and hit you." The pain is beginning to start. "Yes," I say. "Yes, I will say that is what happened." If I do not say this is what happened, I know my brothers will find ways to make me wish I had. But now I will say anything that gets me to my mother.

Confronted by our parents we stick to the lie agreed upon. They place me on a bench on the porch and I close my left eye while they examine the right. There is a tree growing from underneath the porch that climbs past the railing to the roof. It is the last thing my right eye sees. I watch as its trunk, its branches, and then its leaves are blotted out by the rising blood.

I am in shock. First there is intense fever, which my father tries to break using lily leaves bound around my head. Then there are chills: my mother tries to get me to eat soup. Eventually, I do not know how, my parents learn what has happened. A week after the "accident" they take me to see a doctor. "Why did you wait so long to come?" he asks, looking into my eye and shaking his head. "Eyes are sympathetic," he says. "If one is blind, the other will likely become blind too."

This comment of the doctor's terrifies me. But it is really how I look that bothers me most. Where the BB pellet struck there is a glob of whitish scar tissue, a hideous cataract, on my eye. Now when I stare at people—a favorite pastime, up to now—they will stare back. Not at the "cute" little girl, but at her scar. For six years I do not stare at anyone, because I do not raise my head.

Years later, in the throes of a mid-life crisis, I ask my mother and sister whether I changed after the "accident." "No," they say, puzzled. "What do you mean?"

What do I mean?

I am eight, and, for the first time, doing poorly in school, where I have been something of a whiz since I was four. We have just moved to the place where the "accident" occurred. We do not know any of the people around us because this is a different county. The only time I see the friends I knew is when we go back to our old church. The new school is the former state penitentiary. It is a large stone building, cold and drafty, crammed to overflowing with boisterous, ill-disciplined children. On the third floor there is a huge circular imprint of some partition that has been torn out.

"What used to be here?" I ask a sullen girl next to me on our way past it to lunch.

"The electric chair," says she.

At night I have nightmares about the electric chair, and about all the people reputedly "fried" in it. I am afraid of the school, where all the students seem to be budding criminals.

"What's the matter with your eye?" they ask, critically.

When I don't answer (I cannot decide whether it was an "accident" or not), they shove me, insist on a fight.

My brother, the one who created the story about the wire, comes to my rescue. But then brags so much about "protecting" me, I become sick.

After months of torture at the school, my parents decide to send me back to our old community, to my old school. I live with my grandparents and the teacher they board. But there is no room for Phoebe, my cat. By the time my grandparents decide there *is* room, and I ask for my cat, she cannot be found. Miss Yarborough, the boarding teacher, takes me under her wing, and begins to teach me to play the piano. But soon she marries an African—a "prince," she says—and is whisked away to his continent.

At my old school there is at least one teacher who loves me. She is the teacher who "knew me before I was born" and bought my first baby clothes. It is she who makes life bearable. It is her presence that finally helps me turn on the one child at the school who continually calls me "one-eyed bitch." One day I simply grab him by his coat and beat him until I am satisfied. It is my teacher who tells me my mother is ill.

My mother is lying in bed in the middle of the day, something I have never seen. She is in too much pain to speak. She has an abscess in her ear. I stand looking down on her, knowing that if she dies, I cannot live. She is being treated with warm oils and hot bricks held against her cheek. Finally a doctor comes. But I must go back to my grandparents' house. The weeks pass but I am hardly aware of it. All I know is that my mother might die, my father is not so jolly, my brothers still have their guns, and I am the one sent away from home.

"You did not change," they say.

Did I imagine the anguish of never looking up?

I am twelve. When relatives come to visit I hide in my room. My cousin Brenda, just my age, whose father works in the post office and whose mother is a nurse, comes to find me. "Hello," she says. And then she asks, looking at my recent school picture, which I did not want taken, and on which the "glob," as I think of it, is clearly visible, "You still can't see out of that eye?"

"No," I say, and flop back on the bed over my book.

That night, as I do almost every night, I abuse my eye. I rant and rave at it, in front of the mirror. I plead with it to clear up before morning. I tell it I hate and despise it. I do not pray for sight. I pray for beauty.

"You did not change," they say.

I am fourteen and baby-sitting for my brother Bill, who lives in Boston. He is my favorite brother and there is a strong bond between us. Understanding my feelings of shame and ugliness he and his wife take me to a local hospital, where the "glob" is removed by a doctor named O. Henry. There is still a small bluish crater where the scar tissue was, but the ugly white stuff is gone. Almost immediately I become a different person from the girl who does not raise her head. Or so I think. Now that I've raised my head I win the boy-friend of my dreams. Now that I've raised my head I have plenty of friends. Now that I've raised my head classwork comes from my lips as faultlessly as Easter speeches did, and I leave high school as valedictorian, most popular student, and *queen*, hardly believing my luck. Ironically, the girl who was voted most beautiful in our class (and was) was later shot twice through the chest by a male companion, using a "real" gun, while she was pregnant. But that's another story in itself. Or is it?

"You did not change," they say.

It is now thirty years since the "accident." A beautiful journalist comes to visit and to interview me. She is going to write a cover story for her magazine that focuses on my latest book. "Decide how you want to look on the cover," she says. "Glamorous, or whatever."

Never mind "glamorous," it is the "whatever" that I hear. Suddenly all I can think of is whether I will get enough sleep the night before the photography session: if I don't, my eye will be tired and wander, as blind eyes will.

At night in bed with my lover I think up reasons why I should not appear on the cover of a magazine. "My meanest critics will say I've sold out," I say. "My family will now realize I write scandalous books."

"But what's the real reason you don't want to do this?" he asks.

"Because in all probability," I say in a rush, "my eye won't be straight."

"It will be straight enough," he says. Then, "Besides, I thought you'd made your peace with that."

And I suddenly remember that I have.

I remember:

I am talking to my brother Jimmy, asking if he remembers anything unusual about the day I was shot. He does not know I consider that day the last time my father, with his sweet home remedy of cool lily leaves, chose me, and that I suffered and raged inside because of this. "Well," he says, "all I remember is standing by the side of the highway with Daddy, trying to flag down a car. A white man stopped, but when Daddy said he needed somebody to take his little girl to the doctor, he drove off."

I remember:

I am in the desert for the first time. I fall totally in love with it. I am so overwhelmed by its beauty, I confront for the first time, consciously, the meaning of the doctor's words years ago: "Eyes are sympathetic. If one is blind, the other will likely become blind too." I realize I have dashed about the world madly, looking at this, looking at that, storing up images against the fading of the light. *But I might have missed seeing the desert!* The shock of that possibility—and gratitude for over twenty-five years of sight—sends me literally to my knees. Poem after poem comes—which is perhaps how poets pray.

On Sight

I am so thankful I have seen
The Desert
And the creatures in the desert
And the desert Itself.

The desert has its own moon
Which I have seen
With my own eye.

There is no flag on it.

Trees of the desert have arms
All of which are always up
That is because the moon is up
The sun is up
Also the sky
The stars
Clouds
None with flags.

If there *were* flags, I doubt
the trees would point.
Would you?

But mostly, I remember this:

I am twenty-seven, and my baby daughter is almost three. Since her birth I have worried about her discovery that her mother's eyes are different from other people's. Will she be embarrassed? I think. What will she say? Every day she watches a television program called "Big Blue Marble." It begins with a picture of the earth as it appears from the moon. It is bluish, a little battered-looking, but full of light, with whitish clouds swirling around it. Every time I see it I weep with love, as if it is a picture of Grandma's house. One day when I am putting Rebecca down for her nap, she suddenly focuses on my eye. Something inside me cringes, gets ready to try to protect myself. All children are cruel about physical differences, I know from experience, and that they don't always mean to be is another matter. I assume Rebecca will be the same.

But no-o-o-o. She studies my face intently as we stand, her inside and me outside her crib. She even holds my face maternally between her dimpled little hands. Then, looking every bit as serious and lawyerlike as her father, she says, as if it may just possibly have slipped my attention: "Mommy, there's a *world* in your eye." (As in, "Don't be alarmed, or do anything crazy.") And then, gently, but with great interest: "Mommy, where did you *get* that world in your eye?"

For the most part, the pain left then. (So what, if my brothers grew up to buy even more powerful pellet guns for their sons and to carry real guns themselves. So what, if a young "Morehouse man" once nearly fell off the steps of Trevor Arnett Library because he thought my eyes were blue.) Crying and laughing I ran to the bathroom, while Rebecca mumbled and sang herself off to sleep. Yes indeed, I realized, looking into the mirror. There *was* a world in my eye. And I saw that it was possible to love it: that in fact, for all it had taught me of shame and anger and inner vision, I *did* love it. Even to see it drifting out of orbit in boredom, or rolling up out of fatigue, not to mention floating back at attention in excitement (bearing witness, a friend has called it), deeply suitable to my personality, and even characteristic of me.

That night I dream I am dancing to Stevie Wonder's song "Always" (the name of the song is really "As," but I hear it as "Always"). As I dance, whirling and joyous, happier than I've ever been in my life, another bright-faced dancer joins me. We dance and kiss each other and hold each other through the night. The other dancer has obviously come through all right, as I have done. She is beautiful, whole and free. And she is also me.

Suggestions for Discussion

1. How does the author use detail to portray herself at various ages? To portray her mother?

2. What changes in her personality and view of herself take place in the several age periods that Walker describes?

3. The line "you did not change" recurs. What is its relation to the narrative in the several scenes?

4. What is the significance of the repeated reference to raising her head at various stages of the author's development?

5. How does Walker equate prayer with poetry?

6. How does her daughter's comment on her eye affect her attitude?

7. What does the title signify?

Suggestions for Writing

1. Write a series of short vignettes illustrating how you viewed yourself and/or others viewed you at various stages of your development.

2. Describe the ways in which a traumatic episode in your childhood or that of a person close to you has affected your attitudes or behavior.

Essays

James E. Miller, Jr.
Discovering the Self

James E. Miller (b. 1920), American educator and author, has served as a professor of English at the University of Chicago since 1962. The editor of *College English* from 1960 to 1966, he is the author of several scholarly works on Fitzgerald, Whitman, and Melville. In this excerpt from his book *Word, Self, Reality* (1972) Miller develops his thesis that by means of language we "proclaim our identities, shape our lives, and leave our impress on the world."

"I speak; therefore I am."

Though this declaration may seem a little strange at first, it can be supported by considerable evidence. The individual establishes his individuality, his distinction as a human being, through language. He *becomes*—through language. Not only does he proclaim his existence, his being, through speech, but also his identity—the special and particular nature that makes him *him*. The declaration may then be rewritten: "I speak; *thus*, I am."

The creation of the self must, by its very nature, be a cooperative affair. The potentiality for language acquisition and language-use appears to be granted as a birthright. But the accident of birth will determine whether the language acquired will be Chinese, Swahili, Spanish, or English. And the

> . . . the mentality of mankind and the language of mankind created each other. If we like to assume the rise of language as a given fact, then it is not going too far to say that the souls of men are the gift from language to mankind.
>
> The account of the sixth day should be written, He gave them speech, and they became souls.
>
> —Alfred North Whitehead, *Modes of Thought*, 1938

same accident will determine the nature of the dialect acquired within the language. These "accidents" assume the presence of people and a culture that together bring the language to the individual.

If, then, the individual creates himself through language, it is only with the help provided by a sympathetic environment; a mother who encourages him to babble, to distinguish sounds and consequences, and then to utter sentences; and a host of other people who act and react linguistically around him. Gradually as the individual develops, he acquires not only language but what might be called a "linguistic personality," a set of language behavior patterns that make up a substantial part of his identity as a person different from other persons.

This *creation of the self*—in the sense of the self's development into a distinctive person with distinctions that are in large part linguistic (or asserted or fulfilled through language)—is a creation of the self in a kind of gross or obvious sense. Few would quarrel with the rough outline sketched above, though some might want to express it in a different set of terms. But there is another, more subtle sense in which we can speak of the creation of the self implied in "I speak; therefore I am." This profounder sense is implied in Alfred North Whitehead's assertion that "it is not going too far to say that the souls of men are the gift from language to mankind." Where a nineteenth-century divine, or a twentieth-century philosopher, might refer to "souls," the modern psychologist might refer to the sense of an enduring self. This sense is generated, sustained, and preserved in language.

One way through which the sense of self is generated appears in the basic human impulse to sort through one's thoughts, or to think through the day's (or a lifetime's) experiences. To follow this impulse throws the individual back on his language resources. The experiences and thoughts that make up one's life are, in some sense, the essence of the individual, the things that are uniquely his and that make him what he is. In the process of sorting through his thoughts, or of disentangling and examining his tangled experiences, he is in effect defining himself, outlining himself, asserting and proclaiming himself. There can be no more vital activity for the individual: the results and the actions (new thoughts and new experiences) proceeding from it will further define his identity, not only for him but for the world he inhabits. In the old

> . . . the fundamental human capacity is the capacity and the need for creative self-expression, for free control of all aspects of one's life and thought. One particularly crucial realization of this capacity is the creative use of language as a free instrument of thought and expression. Now having this view of human nature and human needs, one tries to think about the modes of social organization that would permit the freest and fullest development of the individual, of each individual's potentialities in whatever direction they might take, that would permit him to be fully human in the sense of having the greatest possible scope for his freedom and initiative.
>
> —**Noam Chomsky,** "Linguistics and Politics—Interview," 1969.

> It is language . . . that really reveals to man that world which is closer to him than any world of natural objects and touches his weal and woe more directly than physical nature. For it is language that makes his existence in a community possible; and only in society, in relation to a "Thee," can his subjectivity assert itself as a "Me."
>
> —Ernst Cassirer, *Language and Myth,* 1946.

vocabulary, he is in this process revitalizing, reconstituting, refreshing, renewing his soul.

To live an aware life, the individual must begin with an awareness of self. He must conduct a running examination and periodic reexaminations of the self—in language, the medium of furthest reaches, deepest diving, most labyrinthine windings. The sorting through might well begin with the ordinary, everyday experiences of life. A diary or journal enables one to sift through and evaluate experiences, as well as to come to understand them and their significance—or insignificance. Most of us do this sifting and evaluation in moments of reverie or in that state of mental vagabondage just before sleep. There is some (even great) advantage, however, in subjecting ourselves to the discipline of written language, in which the vague and the mushy and the muddled must give way to the specific, the firm, the clearly formulated.

For writing *is* discovery. The language that never leaves our head is like colorful yarn, endlessly spun out multicolored threads dropping into a void, momentarily compacted, entangled, fascinating, elusive. We have glimpses that seem brilliant but quickly fade; we catch sight of images that tease us with connections and patterns that too-soon flow on; we hold in momentary view a comprehensive arrangement (insight) that dissolves rapidly and disappears.

Writing that is discovery forces the capturing, the retrieving, the bringing into focus these stray and random thoughts. Sifting through them, we make decisions that are as much about the self as about language. Indeed, writing is largely a process of choosing among alternatives from the images and thoughts of the endless flow, and this choosing is a matter of making up one's mind, and this making up one's mind becomes in effect the making up of one's self. In this way writing that is honest and genuine and serious (though

> I did not exist to write poems, to preach or to paint, neither I nor anyone else. All of that was incidental. Each man had only one genuine vocation—to find the way to himself. He might end up as poet or madman, as prophet or criminal—that was not his affair, ultimately it was of no concern. His task was to discover his own destiny—not an arbitrary one—and live it out wholly and resolutely within himself. Everything else was only a would-be existence, an attempt at evasion, a flight back to the ideas of the masses, conformity and fear of one's own inwardness.
>
> —Hermann Hesse, *Demian,* 1925.

not necessarily without humor or wit) constitutes the discovery of the self. It is not uncommon, before the choices are made, before the words are fixed on paper, to be quite unsure of which way the choices will go. Most people have experienced the phenomenon of their opinions or feelings changing, sometimes markedly, in the process of writing a paper which forces confrontations with language and choices among expressions. All people have experienced the clarification of their views and perspectives as they have worked through the process of placing them on paper. It is not at all unusual to find an individual who is uncertain and unclear about his feelings on a subject or an issue, but who, on discovering his attitude in the process of writing, becomes committed, often dedicated, and sometimes even fanatical: he has come to know himself. When this happens the individual is not being insincere, but is simply experiencing the discoveries of writing—discoveries that are often surprising and frequently exhilarating.

As suggested earlier, in setting forth on this voyage of self-discovery, it is best to begin, not with the problems of the universe, but with what appear to be the trivia of everyday events. Indeed, it might turn out ultimately that the big is somehow indirectly connected with the little. The self-examination which requires simply the writing of an account of one's life for a single day might bring unexpected illumination. Such an account would necessitate reviewing in detail and reliving imaginatively moments of pain and fun, joy and sobriety. A list of the events of that day (or week, month) would require consideration as to what, for an individual, constitutes events. Presumably they left some kind of mark—intellectual, emotional, imaginative. What kind of mark, how deep, how long-lasting? There might be public events and private events—events for which there were some, perhaps many, witnesses, and events that had no witnesses at all.

The list of a day's events in an individual's life might be posed against a list of the general public events and happenings—in the community, town, state, country, or world. Where do the two lists intersect, if at all? Did any of the world's events leave any mark on the individual, or did they reach him remotely or impersonally through the mass media, newspapers, radio-TV, and then fade into the distance? A third list might be composed of a close friend's perspective on the personal events on the first list, some of which he will have witnessed (but only externally), and others of which he will be totally unaware. Compilation of these lists, either in fact or imagination, may enable the individual to see the narrative of his life as marking a circle around him, with him—absolutely alone—at the center.

This circle marks the individual's personal turf, material for his intellectual and imaginative use or growth that is his and his alone, impossible to share

---

YEE-AH! I feel like part of the shadows that make company for me in this warm *amigo* darkness.
I am "My Majesty Piri Thomas," with a high on anything and like a stoned king, I gotta survive my kingdom.
I'm a skinny, dark-face, curly-haired, intense Porty-Ree-can—
Unsatisfied, hoping, and always reaching.

—**Piri Thomas,** *Down These Mean Streets,* 1967.

> *Interviewer:* Is there anything else you can say to beginning writers?
>
> *Simenon:* Writing is considered a profession, and I don't think it is a profession. I think that everyone who does not *need* to be a writer, who thinks he can do something else, ought to do something else. Writing is not a profession but a vocation of unhappiness. I don't think an artist can ever be happy.
>
> *Interviewer:* Why?
>
> *Simenon:* Because, first, I think that if a man has the urge to be an artist, it is because he needs to find himself. Every writer tries to find himself through his characters, through all his writing.
>
> *Interviewer:* He is writing for himself?
>
> *Simenon:* Yes. Certainly.
>
> —**Georges Simenon,** *Writers at Work: The Paris Review Interviews,* 1958.

totally with anyone, no matter how close. One who begins to feel a sense of the preciousness of this material, this segment of life that is his and no one else's, is in fact feeling a sense of the self. If he begins to discover sequence and sense—a kind of unified narrative—in the events of his life for a day, he is making the discovery of self that the process of writing brings about: the unification must come from the indivdual's unique sensibility and identity.

Henry James had something of all this in mind in some advice he gave to young writers: "Oh, do something from your point of view; an ounce of example is worth a ton of generalities . . . do something with life. Any point of view is interesting that is a direct impression of life. You each have an impression colored by your individual conditions; make that into a picture, a picture framed by your own personal wisdom, your glimpse of the American world. The field is vast for freedom, for study, for observation, for satire, for truth."

Suggestions for Discussion

1. In earlier sections of his book *Word, Self, Reality,* Miller defines language as a form of creation whereby we create both our world and ourselves. With what details does Miller support his belief that it is through language that we create ourselves and our world?

2. What role does environment play in enabling the individual to create himself or herself through language?

3. How does sorting through one's thoughts or thinking through one's experiences relate to self-definition? What role does choice play in this process?

4. How do the quotations from Whitehead, Chomsky, Cassirer, Hesse, Thomas, and Simenon relate to the author's central thesis?

5. Miller maintains the continuity of his thought by careful linking of his paragraphs. Identify the transitional devices that bind each of the paragraphs to the preceding and the following one. Identify the logic that justifies the division of the essay into its constituent paragraphs.

6. Examine the ninth paragraph ("Writing that is discovery . . .") to determine (a) what subject matter is in it, (b) what transitional devices give it internal coherence, (c) what stages of development the discussion undergoes.

7. The eighth paragraph ("For writing *is* discovery.") includes an ingenious simile: language is like yarn. Test whether this simile is merely ornamental, useful in conveying the thought, or essential to the thought by rewriting the paragraph in abstract, nonfigurative language and comparing your version with Miller's original.

Suggestions for Writing

1. Keep a journal recording your fleeting impressions, daydreams, night dreams, feelings, and random thoughts as well as your more considered reflections over a period of two weeks. Include your thoughts about your own immediate activities, memories evoked of past events, and reflections on what is going on in the world. Be concerned with getting down on paper as much as possible of what you are feeling and what has gone through your mind and don't concern yourself with the usual mechanics of writing or with the possibly repetitive nature of some of your feelings. At the end of this two-week period, reread your journal and attempt to discover what recurrent patterns of feeling and thought have emerged. Write a brief analysis of the nature of your own thoughts, what experiences seem to precipitate them, what patterns seem to repeat themselves. What do you make of such repetitions?

2. Select one of the journal entries that most interests you and elaborate on it in the form of a short essay or narrative in which you attempt to give shape and unity to the earlier expression.

3. Make the lists suggested in Miller's essay and write a commentary on your discoveries.

Theodore Roethke
Some Self-Analysis

Theodore Roethke (1908–1963), American poet, taught during the last years of his life at the University of Washington. *The Waking: Poems, 1933–1953* was the winner of the Pulitzer Prize for Poetry in 1953. He received the Bollingen Award for Poetry in 1958. A collected volume, *Words for the Wind,* appeared in 1958, and *The Far Field* was published posthumously in 1964. In this statement, written when he was an undergraduate, Roethke recounts his hopes for the writing course he is taking, assesses his strengths and limitations as a writer, and expresses his faith in himself.

I expect this course to open my eyes to story material, to unleash my too dormant imagination, to develop that quality utterly lacking in my nature—a sense of form. I do not expect to acquire much technique. I expect to be able to seize upon the significant, reject the trivial. I hope to acquire a greater love for humanity in all its forms.

I have long wondered just what my strength was as a writer. I am often filled with tremendous enthusiasm for a subject, yet my writing about it will seem a sorry attempt. Above all, I possess a driving sincerity,—that prime virtue of any creative worker. I write only what I believe to be the absolute truth,—even if I must ruin the theme in so doing. In this respect I feel far superior to those glib people in my classes who often garner better grades than I do. They are so often pitiful frauds,—artificial—insincere. They have a line that works. They do not write from the depths of their hearts. Nothing of theirs was ever born of pain. Many an incoherent yet sincere piece of writing has outlived the polished product.

I write only about people and things that I know thoroughly. Perhaps I have become a mere reporter, not a writer. Yet I feel that this is all my present abilities permit. I will open my eyes in my youth and store this raw, living material. Age may bring the fire that molds experience into artistry.

I have a genuine love of nature. It is not the least bit affected, but an integral and powerful part of my life. I know that Cooper is a fraud—that he doesn't give a true sense of the sublimity of American scenery. I know that Muir and Thoreau and Burroughs speak the truth.

I can sense the moods of nature almost instinctively. Ever since I could walk, I have spent as much time as I could in the open. A perception of nature—no matter how delicate, how subtle, how evanescent,—remains with me forever.

I am influenced too much, perhaps, by natural objects. I seem bound by the very room I'm in. I've associated so long with prosaic people that I've dwarfed myself spiritually. When I get alone under an open sky where man isn't too evident—then I'm tremendously exalted and a thousand vivid ideas and sweet visions flood my consciousness.

I think that I possess story material in abundance. I have had an unusual upbringing. I was let alone, thank God! My mother insisted upon two things,—that I strive for perfection in whatever I did and that I always try to be a gentleman. I played with Italians, with Russians, Poles, and the "sissies" on Michigan Avenue. I was carefully watched, yet allowed to follow my own inclinations. I have seen a good deal of life that would never have been revealed to an older person. Up to the time I came to college then I had seen humanity in diverse forms. Now I'm cramped and unhappy. I don't feel that these idiotic adolescents are worth writing about. In the summer, I turn animal and work for a few weeks in a factory. Then I'm happy.

My literary achievements have been insignificant. At fourteen, I made a speech which was translated into twenty-six languages and used as Red Cross propaganda. When I was younger, it seemed that everything I wrote was eminently successful. I always won a prize when I entered an essay contest. In college, I've been able to get only one "A" in four rhetoric courses. I feel this keenly. If I can't write, what can I do? I wonder.

When I was a freshman, I told Carleton Wells that I knew I could write whether he thought so or not. On my next theme he wrote "You can Write!" How I have cherished that praise!

It is bad form to talk about grades, I know. If I don't get an "A" in this course, it wouldn't be because I haven't tried. I've made a slow start. I'm going to spend Christmas vacation writing. A "B" symbolizes defeat to me. I've been beaten too often.

I do wish that we were allowed to keep our stories until we felt that we had worked them into the best possible form.

I do not have the divine urge to write. There seems to be something surging within,—a profound undercurrent of emotion. Yet there is none of that fertility of creation which distinguishes the real writer.

Nevertheless, I have faith in myself. I'm either going to be a good writer or a poor fool.

Suggestions for Discussion

1. There are a number of paradoxical statements in Roethke's self-analysis, written when he was an undergraduate. Identify and explain.

2. Contrast Roethke's image of himself with what you imagine would be the view of his parents, his instructors, his contemporaries.

Suggestions for Writing

1. Write a statement of your expectations in a course in composition following the format of Roethke's statement. Include an analysis of your strengths and weaknesses, formative influences, sense of present accomplishment, and hopes for the future.

2. In the light of his self-analysis, comment on a selection of Roethke's published poems.

Carson McCullers
Loneliness . . . An American Malady

Carson McCullers (1917–1967), a Southern writer, was awarded Guggenheim Fellowships in 1942 and in 1946. Her published works include *The Heart Is a Lonely Hunter* (1940), *Reflections in a Golden Eye* (1941), *The Member of the Wedding* (1946), *The Ballad of the Sad Cafe* (1951), and *Clock Without Hands* (1961). This excerpt from *The Mortgaged Heart* (1971) suggests that the way by which we master loneliness is "to belong to something larger and more powerful than the weak, lonely self".

This city, New York—consider the people in it, the eight million of us. An English friend of mine, when asked why he lived in New York City, said that he liked it here because he could be so alone. While it was my friend's desire to be alone, the aloneness of many Americans who live in cities is an involuntary and fearful thing. It has been said that loneliness is the great American malady. What is the nature of this loneliness? It would seem essentially to be a quest for identity.

To the spectator, the amateur philosopher, no motive among the complex ricochets of our desires and rejections seems stronger or more enduring than the will of the individual to claim his identity and belong. From infancy to death, the human being is obsessed by these dual motives. During our first weeks of life, the question of identity shares urgency with the need for milk. The baby reaches for his toes, then explores the bars of his crib; again and again he compares the difference between his own body and the objects around him, and in the wavering, infant eyes there comes a pristine wonder.

Consciousness of self is the first abstract problem that the human being solves. Indeed, it is this self-consciousness that removes us from lower animals. This primitive grasp of identity develops with constantly shifting emphasis through all our years. Perhaps maturity is simply the history of those mutations that reveal to the individual the relation between himself and the world in which he finds himself.

After the first establishment of identity there comes the imperative need to lose this new-found sense of separateness and to belong to something larger and more powerful than the weak, lonely self. The sense of moral isolation is intolerable to us.

In *The Member of the Wedding* the lonely 12-year-old girl, Frankie Addams, articulates this universal need: "The trouble with me is that for a long time I have just been an *I* person. All people belong to a *We* except me. Not to belong to a *We* makes you too lonesome."

Love is the bridge that leads from the *I* sense to the *We*, and there is a paradox about personal love. Love of another individual opens a new relation between the personality and the world. The lover responds in a new way to nature and may even write poetry. Love is affirmation; it motivates the *yes* responses and the sense of wider communication. Love casts out fear, and in the security of this togetherness we find contentment, courage. We no longer fear the age-old haunting questions: "Who am I?" "Why am I?" "Where am I going?"—and having cast out fear, we can be honest and charitable.

For fear is a primary source of evil. And when the question "Who am I?" recurs and is unanswered, then fear and frustration project a negative attitude. The bewildered soul can answer only: "Since I do not understand 'Who I am,' I only know what I am *not*." The corollary of this emotional incertitude is snobbism, intolerance, and racial hate. The xenophobic individual can only reject and destroy, as the xenophobic nation inevitably makes war.

The loneliness of Americans does not have its source in xenophobia; as a nation we are an outgoing people, reaching always for immediate contacts, further experience. But we tend to seek out things as individuals, alone. The European, secure in his family ties and rigid class loyalties, knows little of the moral loneliness that is native to us Americans. While the European artists tend to form groups or aesthetic schools, the American artist is the eternal maverick—not only from society in the way of all creative minds, but within the orbit of his own art.

Thoreau took to the woods to seek the ultimate meaning of his life. His creed was simplicity and his *modus vivendi* the deliberate stripping of external life to the Spartan necessities in order that his inward life could freely flourish. His objective, as he put it, was to back the world into a corner. And in that way did he discover "What a man thinks of himself, that it is which determines, or rather indicates, his fate."

On the other hand, Thomas Wolfe turned to the city, and in his wanderings around New York he continued his frenetic and lifelong search for the lost brother, the magic door. He too backed the world into a corner, and as he passed among the city's millions, returning their stares, he experienced "That silent meeting [that] is the summary of all the meetings of men's lives."

Whether in the pastoral joys of country life or in the labyrinthine city, we Americans are always seeking. We wander, question. But the answer waits in each separate heart—the answer of our own identity and the way by which we can master loneliness and feel that at last we belong.

Suggestion for Discussion

How does the author establish the connections between loneliness and identity? between *I* and *We*? between lack of a sense of identity and fear? between fear and hatred or destruction? between Thoreau's search and that of Thomas Wolfe?

Suggestions for Writing

1. Develop or challenge Thoreau's belief, "What a man thinks of himself, that it is which determines, or rather indicates, his fate."

2. Develop an essay in which you argue that country life is or is not more conducive to the development of a sense of self than city life.

Bruno Bettelheim

The Child's Need for Magic

Bruno Bettelheim (b. 1903) was born in Vienna and educated at the University of Vienna. Having survived the Nazi holocaust, he became an American psychoanalyst and educator and was director of the remarkable University of Chicago Sonia Shankman Orthogenic School from 1944 to 1973. He has written many penetrating works on parents and children and the significance of the holocaust. In this excerpt from *The Uses of Enchantment* (1976) the author believes that fairy tales provide answers to the child's pressing questions about his identity and his world.

Myths and fairy stories both answer the eternal questions: What is the world really like? How am I to live my life in it? How can I truly be myself? The answers given by myths are definite, while the fairy tale is suggestive; its messages may imply solutions, but it never spells them out. Fairy tales leave to the child's fantasizing whether and how to apply to himself what the story reveals about life and human nature.

The fairy tale proceeds in a manner which conforms to the way a child thinks and experiences the world; this is why the fairy tale is so convincing to him. He can gain much better solace from a fairy tale than he can from an effort to comfort him based on adult reasoning and viewpoints. A child trusts what the fairy story tells, because its world view accords with his own.

Whatever our age, only a story conforming to the principles underlying our thought processes carries conviction for us. If this is so for adults, who have learned to accept that there is more than one frame of reference for comprehending the world—although we find it difficult if not impossible truly to think in any but our own—it is exclusively true for the child. His thinking is animistic.

Like all preliterate and many literate people, "the child assumes that his relations to the inanimate world are of one pattern with those to the animate world of people: he fondles as he would his mother the pretty thing that pleased him; he strikes the door that has slammed on him." It should be added that he does the first because he is convinced that this pretty thing loves to be petted as much as he does; and he punishes the door because he is certain that the door slammed deliberately, out of evil intention.

As Piaget has shown, the child's thinking remains animistic until the age of puberty. His parents and teachers tell him that things cannot feel and act; and as much as he may pretend to believe this to please these adults, or not to be ridiculed, deep down the child knows better. Subjected to the rational teachings of others, the child only buries his "true knowledge" deeper in his soul and it remains untouched by rationality; but it can be formed and informed by what fairy tales have to say.

To the eight-year-old (to quote Piaget's examples), the sun is alive because it gives light (and, one may add, it does that because it wants to). To the child's animistic mind, the stone is alive because it can move, as it rolls down a hill. Even a twelve-and-a-half-year-old is convinced that a stream is alive and has a will, because its water is flowing. The sun, the stone, and the water are believed to be inhabited by spirits very much like people, so they feel and act like people.

To the child, there is no clear line separating objects from living things; and whatever has life has life very much like our own. If we do not understand what rocks and trees and animals have to tell us, the reason is that we are not sufficiently attuned to them. To the child trying to understand the world, it seems reasonable to expect answers from those objects which arouse his curiosity. And since the child is self-centered, he expects the animal to talk about the things which are really significant to him, as animals do in fairy tales, and as the child himself talks to his real or toy animals. A child is convinced that the animal understands and feels with him, even though it does not show it openly.

Since animals roam freely and widely in the world, how natural that in fairy tales these animals are able to guide the hero in his search which takes him into distant places. Since all that moves is alive, the child can believe that the wind can talk and carry the hero to where he needs to go, as in "East of the Sun and West of the Moon." In animistic thinking, not only animals feel and think as we do, but even stones are alive; so to be turned into stone simply means that the being has to remain silent and unmoving for a time. By the same reasoning, it is entirely believable when previously silent objects begin to talk, give advice, and join the hero on his wanderings. And since everything is inhabited by a spirit similar to all other spirits (namely, that of the child who has projected his spirit into all these things), because of this inherent sameness it is believable that man can change into animal, or the other way around, as in "Beauty and the Beast" or "The Frog King." Since there is no sharp line drawn between living and dead things, the latter, too, can come to life.

When, like the great philosophers, children are searching for the solutions to the first and last questions—"Who am I? How ought I to deal with life's problems? What must I become?"—they do so on the basis of their animistic thinking. But since the child is so uncertain of what his existence consists, first and foremost comes the question "Who am I?"

As soon as a child begins to move about and explore, he begins to ponder the problem of his identity. When he spies his mirror image, he wonders whether what he sees is really he, or a child just like him standing behind this glassy wall. He tries to find out by exploring whether this other child is really, in all ways, like him. He makes faces, turns this way or that, walks away from the mirror and jumps back in front of it to ascertain whether this other one has moved away or is still there. Though only three years old, the child is already up against the difficult problem of personal identity.

The child asks himself: "Who am I? Where did I come from? How did the world come into being? Who created man and all the animals? What is the purpose of life?" True, he ponders these vital questions not in the abstract, but mainly as they pertain to him. He worries not whether there is justice for individual man, but whether *he* will be treated justly. He wonders who or what projects him into adversity, and what can prevent this from happening to him. Are there benevolent powers in addition to his parents? Are his parents benevolent powers? How should he form himself, and why? Is there hope for him, though he may have done wrong? Why has all this happened to him? What will it mean for his future? Fairy tales provide answers to these pressing questions, many of which the child becomes aware of only as he follows the stories.

From an adult point of view and in terms of modern science, the answers which fairy stories offer are fantastic rather than true. As a matter of fact, these solutions seem so incorrect to many adults—who have become estranged from the ways in which young people experience the world—that they object to exposing children to such "false" information. However, realistic explanations are usually incomprehensible to children, because they lack the abstract understanding required to make sense of them. While giving a scientifically correct answer makes adults think they have clarified things for the child, such explanations leave the young child confused, overpowered, and intellectually defeated. A child can derive security only from the conviction that he understands now what baffled him before—never from being given facts which create *new* uncertainties. Even as the child accepts such an answer, he comes to doubt that he has asked the right question. Since the explanation fails to make sense to him, it must apply to some unknown problem—not the one he asked about.

It is therefore important to remember that only statements which are intelligible in terms of the child's existing knowledge and emotional preoccupations carry conviction for him. To tell a child that the earth floats in space, attracted by gravity into circling around the sun, but that the earth doesn't fall to the sun as the child falls to the ground, seems very confusing to him. The child knows from his experience that everything has to rest on something, or be held up by something. Only an explanation based on that knowledge can make him feel he understands better about the earth in space. More important, to feel secure on earth, the child needs to believe that this world is held firmly in place. Therefore he finds a better explanation in a myth that tells him that the earth rests on a turtle, or is held up by a giant.

If a child accepts as true what his parents tell him—that the earth is a planet held securely on its path by gravity—then the child can only imagine that gravity is a string. Thus the parents' explanation has led to no better understanding or feeling of security. It requires considerable intellectual maturity to believe that there can be stability to one's life when the ground on which one walks (the firmest thing around, on which everything rests) spins with incredible speed on an invisible axis; that in addition it rotates around the sun; and furthermore hurtles through space with the entire solar system. I have never yet encountered a prepubertal youngster who could comprehend all these combined movements, although I have known many who could repeat this information. Such children parrot explanations which according to their own experience of the world are lies, but which they must believe to be true because some adult has said so. The consequence is that children come to distrust their own experience, and therefore themselves and what their minds can do for them.

In the fall of 1973, the comet Kohoutek was in the news. At that time a competent science teacher explained the comet to a small group of highly intelligent second- and third-graders. Each child had carefully cut out a paper circle and had drawn on it the course of the planets around the sun; a paper ellipse, attached by a slit to the paper circle, represented the course of the comet. The children showed me the comet moving along at an angle to the planets. When I asked them, the children told me that they were holding the comet in their hands, showing me the ellipse. When I asked how the comet which they were holding in their hands could also be in the sky, they were all nonplussed.

In their confusion, they turned to their teacher, who carefully explained to them that what they were holding in their hands, and had so diligently created, was only a model of the planets and the comet. The children all agreed that they understood this, and would have repeated it if questioned further. But whereas before they had regarded proudly this circle-cum-ellipse in their hands, they now lost all interest. Some crumpled the paper up, others dropped the model in the wastepaper basket. When the pieces of paper had been the comet to them, they had all planned to take the model home to show their parents, but now it no longer had meaning for them.

In trying to get a child to accept scientifically correct explanations, parents all too frequently discount scientific findings of how a child's mind works. Research on the child's mental processes, especially Piaget's, convincingly demonstrates that the young child is not able to comprehend the two vital abstract concepts of the permanence of quantity, and of reversibility—for instance, that the same quantity of water rises high in a narrow receptacle and remains low in a wide one; and that subtraction reverses the process of addition. Until he can understand abstract concepts such as these, the child can experience the world only subjectively.

Scientific explanations require objective thinking. Both theoretical research and experimental exploration have shown that no child below school age is truly able to grasp these two concepts, without which abstract understanding is impossible. In his early years, until age eight or ten, the child can develop only highly personalized concepts about what he experiences. Therefore it seems natural to him, since the plants which grow on this earth nourish him as his mother did from her breast, to see the earth as a mother or a female god, or at least as her abode.

Even a young child somehow knows that he was created by his parents; so it makes good sense to him that, like himself, all men and where they live were created by a superhuman figure not very different from his parents— some male or female god. Since his parents watch over the child and provide him with his needs in his home, then naturally he also believes that something like them, only much more powerful, intelligent, and reliable—a guardian angel—will do so out in the world.

A child thus experiences the world order in the image of his parents and of what goes on within the family. The ancient Egyptians, as a child does, saw heaven and the sky as a motherly figure (Nut) who protectively bent over the earth, enveloping it and them serenely. Far from preventing man from later developing a more rational explanation of the world, such a view offers security where and when it is most needed—a security which, when the time is ripe, allows for a truly rational world view. Life on a small planet surrounded by limitless space seems awfully lonely and cold to a child—just the opposite of what he knows life ought to be. This is why the ancients needed to feel sheltered and warmed by an enveloping mother figure. To depreciate protective imagery like this as mere childish projections of an immature mind is to rob the young child of one aspect of the prolonged safety and comfort he needs.

True, the notion of a sheltering sky-mother can be limiting to the mind if clung to for too long. Neither infantile projections nor dependence on imaginary protectors—such as a guardian angel who watches out for one when one is asleep, or during Mother's absence—offers true security; but as long as one cannot provide complete security for oneself, imaginings and projections are far preferable to no security. It is such (partly imagined) security which, when experienced for a sufficient length of time, permits the child to develop that feeling of confidence in life which he needs in order to trust himself—a trust necessary for his learning to solve life's problems through his own growing rational abilities. Eventually the child recognizes that what he has taken as literally true—the earth as a mother—is only a symbol.

A child, for example, who has learned from fairy stories to believe that what at first seemed a repulsive, threatening figure can magically change into a most helpful friend is ready to believe that a strange child whom he meets and fears may also be changed from a menace into a desirable companion. Belief in the "truth" of the fairy tale gives him courage not to withdraw because of the way this stranger appears to him at first. Recalling how the hero of many a fairy tale succeeded in life because he dared to befriend a seemingly unpleasant figure, the child believes he may work the same magic.

I have known many examples where, particularly in late adolescence, years of belief in magic are called upon to compensate for the person's having been deprived of it prematurely in childhood, through stark reality having been forced on him. It is as if these young people feel that now is their last chance to make up for a severe deficiency in their life experience; or that without having had a period of belief in magic, they will be unable to meet the rigors of adult life. Many young people who today suddenly seek escape in drug-induced dreams, apprentice themselves to some guru, believe in astrology, engage in practicing "black magic," or who in some other fashion escape from reality into daydreams about magic experiences which are to change their life for the better, were prematurely pressed to view reality in an adult way. Trying to evade reality in such ways has its deeper cause in early formative experiences which prevented the development of the conviction that life can be mastered in realistic ways.

What seems desirable for the individual is to repeat in his life span the process involved historically in the genesis of scientific thought. For a long time in his history man used emotional projections—such as gods—born of his immature hopes and anxieties to explain man, his society, and the universe; these explanations gave him a feeling of security. Then slowly, by his own social, scientific, and technological progress, man freed himself of the constant fear for his very existence. Feeling more secure in the world, and also within himself, man could now begin to question the validity of the images he had used in the past as explanatory tools. From there man's "childish" projections dissolved and more rational explanations took their place. This process, however, is by no means without vagaries. In intervening periods of stress and scarcity, man seeks for comfort again in the "childish" notion that he and his place of abode are the center of the universe.

Translated in terms of human behavior, the more secure a person feels within the world, the less he will need to hold on to "infantile" projections—mythical explanations or fairy-tale solutions to life's eternal problems—and the more he can afford to seek rational explanations. The more secure a man is within himself, the more he can afford to accept an explanation which says his world is of minor significance in the cosmos. Once man feels truly significant in his human environment, he cares little about the importance of his planet within the universe. On the other hand, the more insecure a man is in himself and his place in the immediate world, the more he withdraws into himself because of fear, or else moves outward to conquer for conquest's sake. This is the opposite of exploring out of a security which frees our curiosity.

For these same reasons a child, as long as he is not sure his immediate human environment will protect him, needs to believe that superior powers, such as a guardian angel, watch over him, and that the world and his place within it are of paramount importance. Here is one connection between a family's ability to provide basic security and the child's readiness to engage in rational investigations as he grows up.

As long as parents fully believed that Biblical stories solved the riddle of our existence and its purpose, it was easy to make a child feel secure. The Bible was felt to contain the answers to all pressing questions: the Bible told man all he needed to know to understand the world, how it came into being, and how to behave in it. In the Western world the Bible also provided prototypes for man's imagination. But rich as the Bible is in stories, not even during the most religious of times were these stories sufficient for meeting all the psychic needs of man.

Part of the reason for this is that while the Old and New Testaments and the histories of the saints provided answers to the crucial questions of how to live the good life, they did not offer solutions for the problems posed by the dark sides of our personalities. The Biblical stories suggest essentially only one solution for the asocial aspects of the unconscious: repression of these (unacceptable) strivings. But children, not having their ids in conscious control, need stories which permit at least fantasy satisfaction of these "bad" tendencies, and specific models for their sublimation.

Explicitly and implicitly, the Bible tells of God's demands on man. While we are told that there is greater rejoicing about a sinner who reformed than about the man who never erred, the message is still that we ought to live the good life, and not, for example, take cruel revenge on those whom we hate. As the story of Cain and Abel shows, there is no sympathy in the Bible for the agonies of sibling rivalry—only a warning that acting upon it has devastating consequences.

But what a child needs most, when beset by jealousy of his sibling, is the permission to feel that what he experiences is justified by the situation he is in. To bear up under the pangs of his envy, the child needs to be encouraged to engage in fantasies of getting even someday; then he will be able to manage at the moment, because of the conviction that the future will set things aright. Most of all, the child wants support for his still very tenuous belief that through growing up, working hard, and maturing he will one day be the victorious one. If his present sufferings will be rewarded in the future, he need not act on his jealousy of the moment, the way Cain did.

Like Biblical stories and myths, fairy tales were the literature which edified everybody—children and adults alike—for nearly all of man's existence. Except that God is central, many Bible stories can be recognized as very similar to fairy tales. In the story of Jonah and the whale, for example, Jonah is trying to run away from his superego's (conscience's) demand that he fight against the wickedness of the people of Nineveh. The ordeal which tests his moral fiber is, as in so many fairy tales, a perilous voyage in which he has to prove himself.

Jonah's trip across the sea lands him in the belly of a great fish. There, in great danger, Jonah discovers his higher morality, his higher self, and is wondrously reborn, now ready to meet the rigorous demands of his superego. But the rebirth alone does not achieve true humanity for him: to be a slave neither to the id and the pleasure principle (avoiding arduous tasks by trying to escape from them) nor to the superego (wishing destruction upon the wicked city) means true freedom and higher selfhood. Jonah attains his full humanity only when he is no longer subservient to either institution of his mind, but relinquishes blind obedience to both id and superego and is able to recognize God's wisdom in judging the people of Nineveh not according to the rigid structures of Jonah's superego, but in terms of their human frailty.

Suggestions for Discussion

1. How does Bettelheim distinguish myths from fairy tales? the Bible from fairy tales?

2. Who is Piaget? How has he influenced current thought regarding the way children think and learn?

3. Explain Bettelheim's reference to children as "animistic thinkers." How does this description of them relate to their need for fairy tales?

4. What similarities does the author see between the child and the philosopher? How do they differ?

5. Explain why Bettelheim believes it mistaken to deprive children of fairy tales. How does he relate their need for fairy tales to the difficulties they have in comprehending scientific ideas?

Suggestions for Writing

1. Using one or more fairy tales with which you are familiar, write an essay explaining how magical elements might serve to explain the universe to a child.

2. Write a comparison between a fairy tale and one of the popular children's stories about ordinary life.

Lance Morrow

Daydreams of What You'd Rather Be

Lance Morrow (b. 1939), who was educated at Harvard, has been a contributor to *Time* since 1976. The author speculates on the relationship between the self and the antiself, which may sometimes be a monster and at others the basis of our humanity.

Kierkegaard once confided to his journal that he would have been much happier if he had become a police spy rather than a philosopher. Richard Nixon always wanted to be a sportswriter. If one considers these fantasies together, they seem to have got weirdly crossed. It is Nixon who should have been the police spy. On the other hand, Kierkegaard would probably have made an extraordinarily depressing sportswriter (*Fear and Trembling: The Angst of Bucky Dent*).

We have these half-secret old ambitions—to be something else, to be someone else, to leap out of the interminable self and into another skin, another life. It is usually a brief out-of-body phenomenon, the sort of thing that we think when our gaze drifts away in the middle of a conversation. Goodbye. The imagination floats through a window into the conjectural and finds there a kind of bright blue antiself. The spirit stars itself in a brief hypothesis, an alternative, a private myth. What we imagine at such moments can suggest peculiar truths of character.

One rummages in closets for these revelations. Kierkegaard's fancy about being a police spy is a dark, shiny little item: a melancholic's impulse toward sneaking omnipotence, the intellectual furtively collaborating with state power, committing sins of betrayal in police stations in the middle of the night. It is not far from another intellectual's fantasy: Norman Mailer once proposed that Eugene McCarthy, the dreamboat of the late '60s moderate left, might have made an ideal director of the FBI. McCarthy agreed. But of course, McCarthy had a sardonic genius for doubling back upon his public self and making it vanish. He did magic tricks of self-annihilation. Nixon's imaginary career—wholesome, all-American, unimpeachable—may suggest both a yearning for blamelessness (what could possibly be tainted in his writing about baseball?) and an oblique, pre-emptive identification with an old enemy: the press.

The daydream of an alternative self is a strange, flitting thing. This wistful speculation often occurs in summer, when a vacation loosens the knot of one's vocational identity. Why, dammit, says the refugee from middle management on his 13th day on the lake, why not just stay here all year? Set up as a fishing guide. Open a lodge. We'll take the savings and . . . The soul at odd moments (the third trout, the fourth beer) will make woozy rushes at the pipe dream. Like a gangster who has cooperated with the district attorney, we want a new name and a new career and a new house in a different city—and maybe a new nose from the D.A.'s cosmetic surgeon.

Usually, the impulse passes. The car gets packed and pointed back toward the old reality. The moment dissolves, like one of those instants when one falls irrevocably in love with the face of a stranger through the window as the bus pulls away.

Sometimes, the urge does not vanish. The results are alarming. This month Ferdinand Waldo Demara Jr. died. That was his final career change. His obituary listed nearly as many metamorphoses as Ovid did. Demara, "the Great Imposter," spent years of his life being successfully and utterly some-one else: a Trappist monk, a doctor of psychology, a dean of philosophy at a small Pennsylvania college, a law student, a surgeon in the Royal Canadian Navy, a deputy warden at a prison in Texas. Demara took the protean itch and amateur's gusto, old American traits, to new frontiers of pathology and fraud.

Usually, it is only from the safety of retrospect and an established self that we entertain ourselves with visions of an alternative life. The daydreams are an amusement, a release from the monotony of what we are, from the life sentence of the mirror. The imagination's pageant of an alternative self is a kind of vacation from one's fate. Kierkegaard did not really mean he should have been a police spy, or Nixon that he should have been a sportswriter. The whole mechanism of daydreams of the antiself usually depends upon the fantasy remaining fantasy. Hell is answered prayers. God help us if we had actually married that girl when we were 21.

In weak, incoherent minds, the yearning antiself rises up and breaks through a wall into actuality. That seems to have happened with John W. Hinckley Jr., the young man who shot Ronald Reagan last year. Since no strong self disciplined his vagrant aches and needs, it was his antiself that pulled the trigger. It was his nonentity. The antiself is a monster sometimes, a cancer, a gnawing hypothesis.

All of our lives we are accompanied vaguely by the selves we might be. Man is the only creature that can imagine being someone else. The fantasy of being someone else is the basis of sympathy, of humanity. Daydreams of pos-sibility enlarge the mind. They are also haunting. Around every active mind there always hovers an aura of hypothesis and the subjunctive: almost every conscious intellect is continuously wandering elsewhere in time and space.

The past 20 years have stimulated the antiself. They have encouraged the notion of continuous self-renewal—as if the self were destined to be an end-less series of selves. Each one would be better than the last, or at least differ-ent, which was the point: a miracle of transformations, dreams popping into reality on fast-forward, life as a hectic multiple exposure.

For some reason, the more frivolous agitations of the collective antiself seem to have calmed down a little. Still, we walk around enveloped in it, like figures in the nimbus of their own ghosts on a television screen. Everything that we are not has a kind of evanescent being within us. We dream, and the dream is much of the definition of the true self. Last week Lena Horne said that she has always imagined herself being a teacher. Norman Vincent Peale says fervently that he wanted to be a salesman—and of course that is, in a sense, what he has always been. Opera singer Grace Bumbry wants to be a professional race-car driver. Bill Veeck, former owner of the Chicago White Sox, confides the alternate Veeck: a newspaperman. In a "nonfiction short story," Truman Capote wrote that he wanted to be a girl. Andy Warhol con-fesses without hesitation: "I've always wanted to be an airplane. Nothing more, nothing less. Even when I found out that they could crash, I still wanted to be an airplane."

The antiself has a shadowy, ideal life of its own. It is always blessed (the antiself is the Grecian Urn of our personality) and yet it subtly matures as it runs a course parallel to our actual aging. The Hindu might think that the antiself is a premonition of the soul's next life. Perhaps. But in the last moment of this life, self and antiself may coalesce. It should be their parting duet to mutter together: "On the whole, I'd rather be in Philadelphia."

Suggestions for Discussion

1. Why does Morrow think the Kierkegaard-Nixon fantasies seem to have got weirdly crossed? In his third paragraph he suggests the validity of the fantasies. How?

2. What are the symptoms, dangers, and values of dreaming of an alternative self?

3. What is the significance of the last sentence?

Suggestions for Writing

1. Describe the alternative self or selves which you have aspired to be.

2. Select one of the following statements and develop it in several paragraphs: A vacation loosens the knot of one's vocational identity; the daydreams are an amusement, a release . . . from the life sentence of the mirror; hell is answered prayers; the antiself is a monster sometimes, a cancer, a gnawing hypothesis; all of our lives we are accompanied vaguely by the selves we might be; the fantasy of being someone else is the basis of sympathy, of humanity; the past twenty years have stimulated the antiself; we dream, and the dream is much of the definition of the true self.

Ellen Goodman

The Company Man

Ellen Goodman (b. 1942) was educated at Radcliffe College and pursued a career as a journalist. She was a researcher and reporter for *Newsweek,* a feature writer for the *Boston Globe,* and a syndicated columnist with Washington Post Writers Group. She has been a Nieman fellow at Harvard University and named columnist of the year by the New England Women's Press Association. In 1980 she won a Pulitzer Prize for distinguished commentary. Her books include *Turning Points* (1979) and *At Large* (1981), a collection of newspaper columns. In this essay she portrays a workaholic whose sense of self is totally based upon his identification with his company.

He worked himself to death, finally and precisely, at 3:00 A.M. Sunday morning.

The obituary didn't say that, of course. It said that he died of a coronary thrombosis—I think that was it—but everyone among his friends and acquaintances knew it instantly. He was a perfect Type A, a workaholic, a classic, they said to each other and shook their heads—and thought for five or ten minutes about the way they lived.

This man who worked himself to death finally and precisely at 3:00 A.M. Sunday morning—on his day off—was fifty-one years old and a vice-president. He was, however, one of six vice-presidents, and one of three who might conceivably—if the president died or retired soon enough—have moved to the top spot. Phil knew that.

He worked six days a week, five of them until eight or nine at night, during a time when his own company had begun the four-day week for everyone but the executives. He worked like the Important People. He had no outside "extracurricular interests," unless, of course, you think about a monthly golf game that way. To Phil, it was work. He always ate egg salad sandwiches at his desk. He was, of course, overweight, by 20 or 25 pounds. He thought it was okay, though, because he didn't smoke.

On Saturdays, Phil wore a sports jacket to the office instead of a suit, because it was the weekend.

He had a lot of people working for him, maybe sixty, and most of them liked him most of the time. Three of them will be seriously considered for his job. The obituary didn't mention that.

But it did list his "survivors" quite accurately. He is survived by his wife, Helen, forty-eight years old, a good woman of no particular marketable skills, who worked in an office before marrying and mothering. She had, according to her daughter, given up trying to compete with his work years ago, when the children were small. A company friend said, "I know how much you will miss him." And she answered, "I already have."

"Missing him all these years," she must have given up part of herself which had cared too much for the man. She would be "well taken care of."

His "dearly beloved" eldest of the "dearly beloved" children is a hardworking executive in a manufacturing firm down South. In the day and a half before the funeral, he went around the neighborhood researching his father, asking the neighbors what he was like. They were embarrassed.

His second child is a girl, who is twenty-four and newly married. She lives near her mother and they are close, but whenever she was alone with her father, in a car driving somewhere, they had nothing to say to each other.

The youngest is twenty, a boy, a high-school graduate who has spent the last couple of years, like a lot of his friends, doing enough odd jobs to stay in grass and food. He was the one who tried to grab at his father, and tried to mean enough to him to keep the man at home. He was his father's favorite. Over the last two years, Phil stayed up nights worrying about the boy.

The boy once said, "My father and I only board here."

At the funeral, the sixty-year-old company president told the forty-eight-year old widow that the fifty-one-year-old deceased had meant much to the company and would be missed and would be hard to replace. The widow didn't look him in the eye. She was afraid he would read her bitterness and, after all, she would need him to straighten out the finances—the stock options and all that.

Phil was overweight and nervous and worked too hard. If he wasn't at the office, he was worried about it. Phil was a Type A, a heart-attack natural. You could have picked him out in a minute from a lineup.

So when he finally worked himself to death, at precisely 3:00 A.M. Sunday morning, no one was really surprised.

By 5:00 P.M. the afternoon of the funeral, the company president had begun, discreetly of course, with care and taste, to make inquiries about his replacement. One of three men. He asked around: "Who's been working the hardest?"

Suggestions for Discussion

1. What does the clause "and thought for five or ten minutes about the way they lived" tell the reader about the author's point of view? About her tone?

2. What is the significance of the statement that the man who died was one of six vice-presidents and one of three who might . . . have moved to the top spot?

3. Why doesn't the author identify the man by name until the end of the third paragraph?

4. Goodman makes statements about Phil, then qualifies them. Cite instances. What is the nature of the qualification? How does this technique add to the characterization? To the tone?

5. What does the brief item on each family member and the company president tell readers about Phil? About themselves?

6. Account for the repetition of Phil's age and the hour of his death.

7. What is the significance of the president's question after the funeral?

8. What is the implicit statement that Goodman makes about workaholics? About large companies?

9. Speculate upon Phil's sense of self.

Suggestions for Writing

1. Make a study of a person you know whose sense of self is based on his or her identification with an institution, a business, a school, or a character in fiction.

2. If you know a workaholic, write a description using incidents and dialogue that illuminate his or her character.

Robert N. Bellah, Richard Madsen, William M. Sullivan, Ann Swidler, and Steven M. Tipton

Love and the Self

from *Habits of the Heart*

Robert N. Bellah is Ford Professor of Sociology and Comparative Studies, University of California at Berkeley. He is the author of several books, including *The New Religious Consciousness* (with Charles Y. Glock). Richard Madsen is Associate Professor of Sociology, University of California at San Diego. His most recent book is *Morality and Power in a Chinese Village*. William M. Sullivan is Associate Professor of Philosophy, La Salle College, Philadelphia. He is the author of *Reconstructing Public Philosophy*. Ann Swidler is Assistant Professor of Sociology, Stanford University. She is the author of *Organization Without Authority: Dilemmas of Social Control in Free Schools*. Steven M. Tipton is Associate Professor, Candler School of Theology, Emory University. He is the author of *Getting Saved from the Sixties: Moral Meaning in Conversion and Cultural Change*. The writers began their examination of the American culture by posing the questions: How ought we to live? How do we think about how to live? Who are we, as Americans? What is our character? The brief section that follows from their longer work, *Habits of the Heart* (1986), explores the paradoxical nature of love.

Americans believe in love as the basis for enduring relationships. A 1970 survey found that 96 percent of all Americans held to the ideal of two people sharing a life and a home together. When the same question was asked in 1980, the same percentage agreed. Yet when a national sample was asked in 1978 whether "most couples getting married today expect to remain married for the rest of their lives," 60 percent said no. Love and commitment, it appears, are desirable, but not easy. For, in addition to believing in love, we Americans believe in the self. Indeed, . . . there are few criteria for action outside the self. The love that must hold us together is rooted in the vicissitudes of our subjectivity. No wonder we don't believe marriage is easy today.

Yet when things go well, love seems so natural it hardly requires explanation. A love relationship is good because it works, because it "feels right," because it is where one feels most at home. Marge and Fred Rowan have been married for twelve years and have two children. They were high school sweethearts. When asked to say how they decided to marry, Fred says "there wasn't a lot of discussion." Marge was always "the kind of girl I wanted to marry" and "somewhere along the line" he just assumed "that's where our relationship was headed." There may be reasons, both practical and romantic, for marrying the person one does, but they are almost afterthoughts. What matters is the growing sense that the relationship is natural, right. One does not so much choose as simply accept what already is. Marge, Fred's wife, describes having the sense, before she married, that Fred was the "right person." "It was, like he said, very unspoken, but absolutely that's exactly how we felt. Fred was always 'my guy.' He was just 'mine.'" They were "right on ever since high school," and even when she tried to date someone else in college, "I felt stupid about it because I knew I was in love with Fred. I didn't want to be with anybody else."

Searching for a definition of "real love" becomes pointless if one "feels good" enough about one's relationship. After all, what one is looking for is the "right place" for oneself. As Fred says, "It just felt right, and it was like being caught in the flow. That's just the way it was. It wasn't a matter of deciding, so there could be no uncertainty." A relationship of the kind Fred and Marge describe seems so natural, so spontaneous that it carries a powerful sense of inevitability. For them, their relationship embodies a deep sense of their own identity, and thus a sense that the self has found its right place in the world. Love embodies one's real self. In such a spontaneous, natural relationship, the self can be both grounded and free.

Not every couple finds the easy certainty of love that Fred and Marge convey. But most couples want a similar combination of spontaneity and solidity, freedom and intimacy. Many speak of sharing—thoughts, feelings, tasks, values, or life goals—as the greatest virtue in a relationship. Nan Pfautz, a divorced secretary in her mid-forties, describes how, after being alone for many years, she fell deeply in love. "I think it was the sharing, the real sharing of feelings. I don't think I've ever done that with another man." Nan knew that she loved Bill because "I let all my barriers down. I really was able to be myself with him—very, very comfortable. I could be as gross as I wanted or I could be as funny as I wanted, as silly as I wanted. I didn't worry about, or have to worry—or didn't anyway—about what his reaction was going to be. I was just me. I was free to be me." The natural sharing of one's real self is, then, the essence of love.

But the very sharing that promises to be the fulfillment of love can also threaten the self. The danger is that one will, in sharing too completely with another, "lose oneself." Nan struggled with this problem during her marriage, and afterward still found difficulty achieving the right balance between sharing and being separate. "Before my relationship with Bill, seven, eight years ago now, I seemed to want to hang on to people too much. It was almost as though I devoured them. I wanted them totally to be mine, and I wanted to be totally theirs, with no individuality. Melding . . . I lost all of myself that way and had nothing of *me* left."

How is it that one can "lose" oneself in love, and what are the consequences of that loss? Nan says she lost herself when she lost her "own goals." At first, her marriage was "very good. It was very give and take in those days, It really was. We went skiing the first time together, and I didn't like skiing. From then on, he went skiing on his own, and I did something I wanted to do." Thus not losing yourself has something to do with having a sense of your own interests. What can be lost are a set of independent preferences and the will to pursue them. With the birth of her son, Nan became absorbed in the mother role, and stopped asserting herself. She became "someone to walk on. Very dull and uninteresting, not enthused about anything. Oh, I was terrible. I wouldn't have wanted to be around me at all." The ironic consequence of passively adapting to others' needs is that one becomes less valuable, less interesting, less desirable. Nan's story is particularly interesting because her behavior conformed fairly well to the early ideology of "woman's sphere," where unselfish devotion was the ideal of wifely behavior. But giving up one's self, a subtle shift in emphasis from "unselfishness," may, in the contemporary middle class, as in Nan's case, lead to losing precisely the self that was loved—and perhaps losing one's husband.

A younger woman, Melinda Da Silva, married only a few years, has a similar way of describing her difficulties in the first years of her marriage. She acted out the role of the good wife, trying continually to please her husband. "The only way I knew to be was how my mother was a wife. You love your husband and this was the belief that I had, you do all these things for him. This is the way you show him that you love him—to be a good wife, and the fear that if you don't do all these things, you're not a good wife, and maybe you don't love your husband." Trying so hard to be a good wife, Melinda failed to put her *self* into the relationship. In trying so hard to "show Thomas that I loved him," she "was putting aside anything that I thought in trying to figure out what he thought. Everything was just all put aside." What Melinda had "put aside" was her willingness to express her own opinions and act on her own judgment, even about how best to please her husband.

Melinda sought help from a marriage counselor, and came to feel that the problem with her marriage was less her husband than the loss of her self. "That's all I thought about, was what he wanted, thinking that he would love me more if I did what he wanted. I began to realize when Thomas and I went in for counseling I wouldn't voice my opinion, and I was doing things just for him and ignoring things for myself. The very things I was doing to get his approval were causing him to view me less favorably." Thus losing a sense of who one is and what one wants can make one less attractive and less interesting. To be a person worth loving, one must assert one's individuality. Melinda could "give a lot to our marriage" only when she "felt better" about herself. Having an independent self is a necessary precondition to joining fully in a relationship.

Love, then, creates a dilemma for Americans. In some ways, love is the quintessential expression of individuality and freedom. At the same time, it offers intimacy, mutuality, and sharing. In the ideal love relationship, these two aspects of love are perfectly joined—love is both absolutely free and completely shared. Such moments of perfect harmony among free individuals are rare, however. The sharing and commitment in a love relationship can seem, for some, to swallow up the individual, making her (more often than him) lose sight of her own interests, opinions, and desires. Paradoxically, since love is supposed to be a spontaneous choice by free individuals, someone who has "lost" herself cannot really love, or cannot contribute to a real love relationship. Losing a sense of one's self may also lead to being exploited, or even abandoned, by the person one loves.

Suggestions for Discussion

1. How do the authors relate the belief in love and the rightness of a given relationship to a deep sense of self?

2. Under what circumstances is the fulfillment of love a threat to the self? How do the examples show that "having an independent self is a necessary precondition to joining fully in a relationship"?

3. Define the paradox explored in the essay.

Suggestions for Writing

1. Drawing upon your experience and observation discuss the paradox explored in the essay.

2. Explore possible differences between women's and men's expectations concerning a lasting relationship and suggest how you would account for them, if indeed you believe differences exist.

Fiction
—◆◆◆—

William Faulkner
The Bear

William Faulkner (1897–1962) lived most of his life in Oxford, Mississippi. After a year at the University of Mississippi, he joined the Royal Canadian Air Force, out of eagerness to fight in World War I. His novels, set in his imaginary Yoknapatawpha County, include *The Sound and the Fury* (1929), *Light in August* (1932), *Absalom, Absalom!* (1936), and *The Hamlet* (1940). In 1949 he won the Nobel Prize for Literature. In this story of initiation the boy learns that "what the heart holds to becomes truth, as far as we know the truth."

He was ten. But it had already begun, long before that day when at last he wrote his age in two figures and he saw for the first time the camp where his father and Major de Spain and old General Compson and the others spent two weeks each November and two weeks again each June. He had already inherited then, without ever having seen it, the tremendous bear with one trap-ruined foot which, in an area almost a hundred miles deep, had earned itself a name, a definite designation like a living man.

He had listened to it for years: the long legend of corncribs rifled, of shoats and grown pigs and even calves carried boldly into the woods and devoured, of traps and deadfalls overthrown and dogs mangled and slain, and shotgun and even rifle charges delivered at point-blank range and with no more effect than so many peas blown through a tube by a boy—a corridor of wreckage and destruction beginning back before he was born, through which sped, not fast but rather with the ruthless and irresistible deliberation of a locomotive, the shaggy tremendous shape.

It ran in his knowledge before he ever saw it. It looked and towered in his dreams before he even saw the unaxed woods where it left its crooked print, shaggy, huge red-eyed, not malevolent but just big—too big for the dogs which tried to bay it, for the horses which tried to ride it down, for the men and bullets they fired into it, too big for the very country which was its constricting scope. He seemed to see it entire with a child's complete divination before he ever laid eyes on either—the doomed wilderness whose edges were being constantly and punily gnawed at by men with axes and plows who feared it because it was wilderness, men myriad and nameless even to one another in the land where the old bear had earned a name, through which ran not even a mortal animal but an anachronism, indomitable and invincible, out of an old dead time, a phantom, epitome and apotheosis of the old wild life at which the puny humans swarmed and hacked in a fury of abhorrence and fear, like pygmies about the ankles of a drowsing elephant: the old bear solitary, indomitable and alone, widowered, childless, and absolved of mortality—old Priam reft of his old wife and having outlived all his sons.

Until he was ten, each November he would watch the wagon containing the dogs and the bedding and food and guns and his father and Tennie's Jim, the Negro, and Sam Fathers, the Indian, son of a slave woman and a Chickasaw chief, depart on the road to town, to Jefferson, where Major de Spain and the others would join them. To the boy, at seven, eight, and nine, they were not going into the Big Bottom to hunt bear and deer, but to keep yearly rendezvous with the bear which they did not even intend to kill. Two weeks later they would return, with no trophy, no head and skin. He had not expected it. He had not even been afraid it would be in the wagon. He believed that even after he was ten and his father would let him go too, for those two weeks in November, he would merely make another one, along with his father and Major de Spain and General Compson and the others, the dogs which feared to bay at it and the rifles and shotguns which failed even to bleed it, in the yearly pageant of the old bear's furious immortality.

Then he heard the dogs. It was in the second week of his first time in the camp. He stood with Sam Fathers against a big oak beside the faint crossing where they had stood each dawn for nine days now, hearing the dogs. He had heard them once before, one morning last week—a murmur, sourceless, echoing through the wet woods, swelling presently into separate voices which he could recognize and call by name. He had raised and cocked the gun as Sam told him and stood motionless again while the uproar, the invisible course, swept up and past and faded; it seemed to him that he could actually see the deer, the buck, blond, smoke-colored, elongated with speed, fleeing, vanishing, the woods, the gray solitude, still ringing even when the cries of the dogs had died away.

"Now let the hammers down," Sam said.

"You knew they were not coming here too," he said.

"Yes," Sam said. "I want you to learn how to do when you didn't shoot. It's after the chance for the bear or the deer has done already come and gone that men and dogs get killed."

"Anyway," he said, "it was just a deer."

Then on the tenth morning he heard the dogs again. And he readied the too-long, too-heavy gun as Sam had taught him, before Sam even spoke. But this time it was no deer, no ringing chorus of dogs running strong on a free scent, but a moiling yapping an octave too high, with something more than indecision and even abjectness in it, not even moving very fast, taking a long time to pass completely out of hearing, leaving then somewhere in the air that echo, thin, slightly hysterical, abject, almost grieving, with no sense of a fleeing, unseen, smoke-colored, grass-eating shape ahead of it, and Sam, who had taught him first of all to cock the gun and take position where he could see everywhere and then never move again, had himself moved up beside him; he could hear Sam breathing at his shoulder, and he could see the arched curve of the old man's inhaling nostrils.

"Hah," Sam said. "Not even running. Walking."

"Old Ben!" the boy said. "But up here!" he cried. "Way up here!"

"He do it every year," Sam said. "Once. Maybe to see who in camp this time, if he can shoot or not. Whether we got the dog yet that can bay and hold him. He'll take them to the river, and then he'll send them back home. We may as well go back too; see how they look when they come back to camp."

When they reached the camp the hounds were already there, ten of them crouching back under the kitchen, the boy and Sam squatting to peer back into the obscurity where they had huddled, quiet, the eyes luminous glowing at them and vanishing, and no sound, only that effluvium of something more than dog, stronger than dog and not just animal, just beast, because still there had been nothing in front of that abject and almost painful yapping save the solitude, the wilderness, so that when the eleventh hound came in at noon and with all the others watching—even old Uncle Ash, who called himself first a cook—Sam daubed the tattered ear and the raked shoulder with turpentine and axle grease, to the boy it was still no living creature, but the wilderness which, leaning for the moment down, had patted lightly once the hound's temerity.

"Just like a man," Sam said. "Just like folks. Put off as long as she could having to be brave, knowing all the time that sooner or later she would have to be brave to keep on living with herself, and knowing all the time before hand what was going to happen to her when she done it."

That afternoon, himself on the one-eyed wagon mule which did not mind the smell of blood nor, as they told him, of bear, and with Sam on the other one, they rode for more than three hours through the rapid, shortening winter day. They followed no path, no trail even that he could see; almost at once they were in a country which he had never seen before. Then he knew why Sam had made him ride the mule which would not spook. The sound one stopped short and tried to whirl and bolt even as Sam got down, blowing its breath, jerking and wrenching at the rein, while Sam held it, coaxing it forward with his voice, since he could not risk tying it, drawing it forward while the boy got down from the marred one.

Then, standing beside Sam in the gloom of the dying afternoon, he looked down at the routed over-turned log, gutted and scored with claw marks and, in the wet earth beside it, the print of the enormous warped two-toed foot. He knew now what he had smelled when he peered under the kitchen where the dogs huddled. He realized for the first time that the bear which had run in his listening and loomed in his dreams since before he could remember to the contrary, and which, therefore, must have existed in the listening and dreams of his father and Major de Spain and even old General Compson, too, before they began to remember in their turn, was a mortal animal, and that if they had departed for the camp each November without any actual hope of bringing its trophy back, it was not because it could not be slain, but because so far they had had no actual hope to.

"Tomorrow," he said.

"We'll try tomorrow," Sam said. "We ain't got the dog yet."

"We've got eleven. They ran him this morning."

"It won't need but one," Sam said. "He ain't here. Maybe he ain't nowhere. The only other way will be for him to run by accident over somebody that has a gun."

"That wouldn't be me," the boy said. "It will be Walter or Major or—"

"It might," Sam said. "You watch close in the morning. Because he's smart. That's how come he has lived this long. If he gets hemmed up and has to pick out somebody to run over, he will pick out you."

"How?" the boy said. "How will he know—" He ceased. "You mean he already knows me, that I ain't never been here before, ain't had time to find out yet whether I—" He ceased again, looking at Sam, the old man whose face revealed nothing until it smiled. He said humbly, not even amazed, "It was me he was watching. I don't reckon he did need to come but once."

The next morning they left the camp three hours before daylight. They rode this time because it was too far to walk, even the dogs in the wagon; again the first gray light found him in a place which he had never seen before, where Sam had placed him and told him to stay and then departed. With the gun which was too big for him, which did not even belong to him, but to Major de Spain, and which he had fired only once—at a stump on the first day, to learn the recoil and how to reload it—he stood against a gun tree beside a little bayou whose black still water crept without movement out of a canebrake and crossed a small clearing and into cane again, where, invisible, a bird—the big woodpecker called Lord-to-God by Negroes—clattered at a dead limb.

It was a stand like any other, dissimilar only in incidentals to the one where he had stood each morning for ten days; a territory new to him, yet no less familiar than that other one which, after almost two weeks, he had come to believe he knew a little—the same solitude, the same loneliness through which human beings had merely passed without altering it, leaving no mark, no scar, which looked exactly as it must have looked when the first ancestor of Sam Father's Chickasaw predecessors crept into it and looked about, club or stone ax or bone arrow drawn and poised; different only because, squatting at the edge of the kitchen, he smelled the hounds huddled and cringing beneath it and saw the raked ear and shoulder of the one who, Sam said, had had to be brave once in order to live with herself, and saw yesterday in the earth beside the gutted log the print of the living foot.

He heard no dogs at all. He never did hear them. He only heard the drumming of the woodpecker stop short off and knew that the bear was looking at him. He never saw it. He did not know whether it was in front of him or behind him. He did not move, holding the useless gun, which he had not even had warning to cock and which even now he did not cock, tasting in his saliva that taint as of brass which he knew now because he had smelled it when he peered under the kitchen at the huddled dogs.

Then it was gone. As abruptly as it had ceased, the woodpecker's dry, monotonous clatter set up again, and after a while he even believed he could hear the dogs—a murmur, scarce a sound even, which he had probably been hearing for some time before he even remarked it, drifting into hearing and then out again, dying away. They came nowhere near him. If it was a bear they ran, it was another bear. It was Sam himself who came out of the cane and crossed the bayou, followed by the injured bitch of yesterday. She was almost at heel, like a bird dog, making no sound. She came and crouched against his leg, trembling, staring off into the cane.

"I didn't see him," he said. "I didn't, Sam!"

"I know it," Sam said. "He done the looking. You didn't hear him neither, did you?"

"No," the boy said. "I—"

"He's smart," Sam said. "Too smart." He looked down at the hound, trembling faintly and steadily against the boy's knee. From the raked shoulder a few drops of fresh blood oozed and clung. "Too big. We ain't got the dog yet. But maybe someday. Maybe not next time. But someday."

So I must see him, he thought. *I must look at him.* Otherwise, it seemed to him that it would go on like this forever, as it had gone on with his father and Major de Spain, who was older than his father, and even with old General Compson, who had been old enough to be a brigade commander in 1865. Otherwise, it would go on forever, next time and next time, after and after and after. It seemed to him that he could never see the two of them, himself and the bear, shadowy in the limbo from which time emerged, becoming time; the old bear absolved of mortality and himself partaking, sharing a little of it, enough of it. And he knew now what he had smelled in the huddled dogs and tasted in his saliva. He recognized fear. *So I will have to see him,* he thought, without dread or even hope. *I will have to look at him.*

It was June of the next year. He was eleven. They were in camp again, celebrating Major de Spain's and General Compson's birthdays. Although the one had been born in September and the other in the depth of winter and in another decade, they had met for two weeks to fish and shoot squirrels and turkey and run coons and wildcats with the dogs at night. That is, he and Boon Hoggenbeck and the Negroes fished and shot squirrels and ran the coons and cats, because the proved hunters, not only Major de Spain and old General Compson, who spent those two weeks sitting in a rocking chair before a tremendous iron pot of Brunswick stew, stirring and tasting, with old Ash to quarrel with about how he was making it and Tennie's Jim to pour whiskey from the demijohn into the tin dipper from which he drank it, but even the boy's father and Walter Ewell, who were still young enough, scorned such, other than shooting the wild gobblers with pistols for wagers on their marksmanship.

Or, that is, his father and the others believed he was hunting squirrels. Until the third day, he thought that Sam Fathers believed that too. Each morning he would leave the camp right after breakfast. He had his own gun now, a Christmas present. He went back to the tree beside the bayou where he had stood that morning. Using the compass which old General Compson had given him, he ranged from that point; he was teaching himself to be a better-than-fair woodsman without knowing he was doing it. On the second day he found the gutted log where he had first seen the crooked print. It was almost completely crumbled now, healing with unbelievable speed, a passionate and almost visible relinquishment, back into the earth from which the tree had grown.

He ranged the summer woods now, green with gloom; if anything, actually dimmer than in November's gray dissolution, where, even at noon, the sun fell only in intermittent dappling upon the earth, which never completely dried out and which crawled with snakes—moccasins and water snakes and rattlers, themselves the color of the dappling gloom, so that he would not always see them until they moved, returning later and later, first day, second day, passing in the twilight of the third evening the little log pen enclosing the log stable where Sam was putting up the horses for the night.

"You ain't looked right yet," Sam said.

He stopped. For a moment he didn't answer. Then he said peacefully, in a peaceful rushing burst as when a boy's miniature dam in a little brook gives way, "All right. But how? I went to the bayou. I even found that log again. I—"

"I reckon that was all right. Likely he's been watching you. You never saw his foot?"

"I," the boy said—"I didn't—I never thought—"

"It's the gun," Sam said. He stood beside the fence motionless—the old man, the Indian, in the battered faded overalls and the five-cent straw hat which in the Negro's race had been the badge of its enslavement and was now the regalia of his freedom. The camp—the clearing, the house, the barn and its tiny lot with which Major de Spain in his turn had scratched punily and evanescently at the wilderness—faded in the dusk, back into the immemorial darkness of the woods. *The gun*, the boy thought. *The gun.*

"Be scared," Sam said. "You can't help that. But don't be afraid. Ain't nothing in the woods going to hurt you unless you corner it, or it smells that you are afraid. A bear or a deer, too, has got to be scared of a coward the same as a brave man has got to be."

The gun, the boy thought.

"You will have to choose," Sam said.

He left the camp before daylight, long before Uncle Ash would wake in his quilts on the kitchen floor and start the fire for breakfast. He had only the compass and a stick for snakes. He could go almost a mile before he would begin to need the compass. He sat on a log, the invisible compass in his invisible hand, while the secret night sounds, fallen still at his movements, scurried again and then ceased for good, and the owls ceased and gave over to the waking of day birds, and he could see the compass. Then he went fast yet still quietly; he was becoming better and better as a woodsman, still without having yet realized it.

He jumped a doe and a fawn at sunrise, walked them out of the bed, close enough to see them—the crash of undergrowth, the white scut, the fawn scudding behind her faster than he had believed it could run. He was hunting right, upwind, as Sam had taught him; not that it mattered now. He had left the gun; of his own will and relinquishment he had accepted not a gambit, not a choice, but a condition in which not only the bear's heretofore inviolable anonymity but all the old rules and balances of hunter and hunted had been abrogated. He would not even be afraid, not even in the moment when the fear would take him completely—blood, skin, bowels, bones, memory from the long time before it became his memory—all save that thin, clear, immortal lucidity which alone differed him from this bear and from all the other bear and deer he would ever kill in the humility and pride of his skill and endurance, to which Sam had spoken when he leaned in the twilight on the lot fence yesterday.

By noon he was far beyond the little bayou, farther into the new and alien country than he had ever been. He was traveling now not only by the old, heavy, biscuit-thick silver watch which had belonged to his grandfather. When he stopped at last, it was for the first time since he had risen from the log at dawn when he could see the compass. It was far enough. He had left the camp nine hours ago; nine hours from now, dark would have already been an hour old. But he didn't think that. He thought, *All right. Yes. But what?* and stood for a moment, alien and small in the green and topless solitude, answering his own question before it had formed and ceased. It was the watch, the compass, the stick—the three lifeless mechanicals with which for nine hours he had fended the wilderness off; he hung the watch and compass carefully on a bush and leaned the stick beside them and relinquished completely to it.

He had not been going very fast for the last two or three hours. He went no faster now, since distance would not matter even if he could have gone fast. And he was trying to keep a bearing on the tree where he had left the compass, trying to complete a circle which would bring him back to it or at least intersect itself, since direction would not matter now either. But the tree was not there, and he did as Sam had schooled him—made the next circle in the opposite direction, so that the two patterns would bisect somewhere, but crossing no print of his own feet, finding the tree at last, but in the wrong place—no bush, no compass, no watch—and the tree not even the tree, because there was a down log beside it and he did what Sam Fathers had told him was the next thing and the last.

As he sat down on the log he saw the crooked print—the warped, tremendous, two-toed indentation which, even as he watched it, filled with water. As he looked up, the wilderness coalesced, solidified—the glade, the tree he sought, the bush, the watch and the compass glinting where a ray of sunshine touched them. Then he saw the bear. It did not emerge, appear; it was just there, immobile, solid, fixed in the hot dappling of the green and windless noon, not as big as he had dreamed it, but as big as he had expected it, bigger, dimensionless, against the dappled obscurity, looking at him where he sat quietly on the log and looked back at it.

Then it moved. It made no sound. It did not hurry. It crossed the glade, walking for an instant into the full glare of the sun; when it reached the other side it stopped again and looked back at him across one shoulder while his quiet breathing inhaled and exhaled three times.

Then it was gone. It didn't walk into the woods, the under-growth. It faded, sank back into the wilderness as he had watched a fish, a huge old bass, sink and vanish into the dark depths of its pool without even any movements of its fins.

He thought, *It will be next fall.* But it was not next fall, nor the next nor the next. He was fourteen then. He had killed his buck, and Sam Fathers had marked his face with the hot blood, and in the next year he killed a bear. But even before that accolade he had become as competent in the woods as many grown men with the same experience; by his fourteenth year he was a better woodsman than most grown men with more. There was no territory within thirty miles of the camp that he did not know—bayou, ridge, brake, landmark, tree and path. He could have led anyone to any point in it without deviation, and brought them out again. He knew the game trails that even Sam Fathers did not know; in his thirteenth year he found a buck's bedding place, and unbeknown to his father he borrowed Walter Ewell's rifle and lay in wait at dawn and killed the buck when it walked back to the bed, as Sam had told him how the old Chickasaw fathers did.

But not the old bear, although by now he knew its footprints better than he did his own, and not only the crooked one. He could see any one of the three sound ones and distinguish it from any other, and not only by its size. There were other bears within these thirty miles which left tracks almost as large, but this was more than that. If Sam Fathers had been his mentor and the back-yard rabbits and squirrels at home his kindergarten, then the wilderness the old bear ran was his college, the old male bear itself, so long unwifed and childless as to have become its own ungendered progenitor, was his alma mater. But he never saw it.

He could find the crooked print now almost whenever he liked, fifteen or ten or five miles, or sometimes nearer the camp than that. Twice while on stand during the three years he heard the dogs strike its trail by accident; on the second time they jumped it seemingly, the voices high, abject, almost human in hysteria, as on that first morning two years ago. But not the bear itself. He would remember that noon three years ago, the glade, himself and the bear fixed during that moment in the windless and dappled blaze, and it would seem to him that it had never happened, that he had dreamed that too. But it had happened. They had looked at each other, they had emerged from the wilderness old as earth, synchronized to the instant by something more than the blood that moved the flesh and bones which bore them, and touched, pledged something, affirmed something more lasting than the frail web of bones and flesh which any accident could obliterate.

Then he saw it again. Because of the very fact that he thought of nothing else, he had forgotten to look for it. He was still hunting with Walter Ewell's rifle. He saw it cross the end of a long blow-down, a corridor where a tornado had swept, rushing through rather than over the tangle of trunks and branches as a locomotive would have, faster than he had ever believed it could move, almost as fast as a deer even, because a deer would have spent most of that time in the air, faster than he could bring the rifle sights up with it. And now he knew what had been wrong during all the three years. He sat on a log, shaking and trembling as if he had never seen the woods before nor anything that ran them, wondering with incredulous amazement how he could have forgotten the very thing which Sam Fathers had told him and which the bear itself had proved the next day and had now returned after three years to reaffirm.

And now he knew what Sam Fathers had meant about the right dog, a dog in which size would mean less than nothing. So when he returned alone in April—school was out then, so that the sons of farmers could help with the land's planting, and at last his father had granted him permission, on his promise to be back in four days—he had the dog. It was his own, a mongrel of the sort called by Negroes a fyce, a ratter, itself not much bigger than a rat and possessing that bravery which had long since stopped being courage and had become foolhardiness.

It did not take four days. Alone again, he found the trail on the first morning. It was not a stalk; it was an ambush. He timed the meeting almost as if it were an appointment with a human being. Himself holding the fyce muffled in a feed sack and Sam Fathers with two of the hounds on a piece of a plow-line rope, they lay down wind of the trail at dawn of the second morning. They were so close that the bear turned without even running, as if in surprised amazement at the shrill and frantic uproar of the released fyce, turning at bay against the trunk of a tree, on its hind feet; it seemed to the boy that it would never stop rising, taller and taller, and even the two hounds seemed to take a desperate and despairing courage from the fyce, following it as it went in.

Then he realized that the fyce was actually not going to stop. He flung, threw the gun away, and ran; when he overtook and grasped the frantically pin-wheeling little dog, it seemed to him that he was directly under the bear.

He could smell it, strong and hot and rank. Sprawling, he looked up to where it loomed and towered over him like a cloudburst and colored like a thunderclap, quite familiar, peacefully and even lucidly familiar, until he remembered: This was the way he had used to dream about it. Then it was gone. He didn't see it go. He knelt, holding the frantic fyce with both hands, hearing the abashed wailing of the hounds drawing farther and farther away, until Sam came up. He carried the gun. He laid it down quietly beside the boy and stood looking down at him.

"You've done seed him twice now with a gun in your hands," he said. "This time you couldn't have missed him."

The boy rose. He still held the fyce. Even in his arms and clear of the ground, it yapped frantically, straining and surging after the fading uproar of the two hounds like a tangle of wire springs. He was panting a little, but he was neither shaking nor trembling now.

"Neither could you!" he said. "You had the gun! Neither did you!"

"And you didn't shoot," his father said. "How close were you?"

"I don't know, sir," he said. "There was a big wood tick inside his right hind leg. But I didn't have the gun then."

"But you didn't shoot when you had the gun," his father said. "Why?"

But he didn't answer, and his father didn't wait for him to, rising and crossing the room, across the pelt of the bear which the boy had killed two years ago and the larger one which his father had killed before he was born, to the bookcase beneath the mounted head of the boy's first buck. It was the room which his father called the office, from which all the plantation business was transacted; in it for the fourteen years of his life he had heard the best of all talking. Major de Spain would be there and sometimes old General Compson, and Walter Ewell and Boon Hoggenbeck and Sam Fathers and Tennie's Jim, too, were hunters, knew the woods and what ran them.

He would hear it, not talking himself but listening—the wilderness, the big woods, bigger and older than any recorded document of white man fatuous enough to believe he had bought any fragment of it or Indian ruthless enough to pretend that any fragment of it had been his to convey. It was of the men, not white nor black nor red, but men, hunters with the will and hardihood to endure and the humility and skill to survive, and the dogs and the bear and deer juxtaposed and reliefed against it, ordered and compelled by and within the wilderness in the ancient and unremitting contest by the ancient and immitigable rules which voided all regrets and brooked no quarter, the voices quiet and weighty and deliberate for retrospection and recollection and exact remembering, while he squatted in the blazing firelight as Tennie's Jim squatted, who stirred only to put more wood on the fire and to pass the bottle from one glass to another. Because the bottle was always present, so that after a while it seemed to him that those fierce instants of heart and brain and courage and wiliness and speed were concentrated and distilled into that brown liquor which not women, not boys and children, but only hunters drank, drinking not of the blood they had spilled but some condensation of the wild immortal spirit, drinking it moderately, humbly even, not with the pagan's base hope of acquiring the virtues of cunning and strength and speed, but in salute to them.

His father returned with the book and sat down again and opened it: "Listen," he said. He read the five stanzas aloud, his voice quiet and deliberate in the room where there was no fire now because it was already spring. Then he looked up. The boy watched him. "All right," his father said. "Listen." He read again, but only the second stanza this time, to the end of it, the last two lines, and closed the book and put it on the table beside him. "She cannot fade, though thou hast not thy bliss, forever wilt thou love, and she be fair," he said.

"He's talking about a girl," the boy said.

"He had to talk about something," his father said. Then he said, "He was talking about truth. Truth doesn't change. Truth is one thing. It covers all things which touch the heart—honor and pride and pity and justice and courage and love. Do you see now?"

He didn't know. Somehow it was simpler than that. There was an old bear, fierce and ruthless, not merely just to stay alive, but with the fierce pride of liberty and freedom, proud enough of the liberty and freedom to see it threatened without fear or even alarm; nay, who at times even seemed deliberately to put that freedom and liberty in jeopardy in order to savor them, to remind his old strong bones and flesh to keep supple and quick to defend and preserve them. There was an old man, son of a Negro slave and an Indian king, inheritor on the one side of the long chronicle of a people who had learned humility through suffering, and pride through the endurance which survived the suffering and injustice, and on the other side, the chronicle of a people even longer in the land than the first, yet who no longer existed in the land at all save in the solitary brotherhood of an old Negro's alien blood and the wild and invincible spirit of an old bear. There was a boy who wished to learn humility and pride in order to become skillful and worthy in the woods, who suddenly found himself becoming so skillful so rapidly that he feared he would never become worthy because he had not learned humility and pride, although he had tried to, until one day and as suddenly he discovered that an old man who could not have defined either had led him, as though by the hand, to that point where an old bear and a little mongrel of a dog showed him that, by possessing one thing other, he would possess them both.

And a little dog, nameless and mongrel and many-fathered, grown, yet weighing less than six pounds, saying as if to itself, "I can't be dangerous, because there's nothing much smaller than I am; I can't be fierce, because they would call it just a noise; I can't be humble, because I'm already too close to the ground to genuflect; I can't be proud, because I wouldn't be near enough to it for anyone to know who was casting the shadow, and I don't even know that I'm not going to heaven, because they have already decided that I don't possess an immortal soul. So all I can be is brave. But it's all right. I can be that, even if they still call it just noise."

That was all. It was simple, much simpler than somebody talking in a book about youth and a girl he would never need to grieve over, because he could never approach any nearer her and would never have to get any farther away. He had heard about a bear, and finally got big enough to trail it, he trailed it four years and at last met it with a gun in his hands and he didn't shoot. Because a little dog—But he could have shot long before the little dog covered the twenty yards to where the bear waited, and Sam Fathers could have shot at any time during that interminable minute while Old Ben stood on his hind feet over them. He stopped. His father was watching him gravely across the spring-rife twilight of the room; when he spoke, his words were as quiet as the twilight, too, not loud, because they did not need to be because they would last. "Courage, and honor, and pride," his father said, "and pity, and love of justice and of liberty. They all touch the heart, and what the heart holds to becomes truth, as far as we know the truth. Do you see now?"

Sam, and Old Ben, and Nip, he thought. And himself too. He had been all right too. His father had said so. "Yes, sir," he said.

Suggestions for Discussion

1. What do the details in the first three paragraphs contribute to the meaning and tone of the story?

2. By what means are you made aware that the bear has a symbolic and mystical meaning?

3. Trace the steps by which the boy conquers his fear. What role does Sam Fathers play? the mongrel dog? the boy's father? How does his father's reading of Keats' "Ode on a Grecian Urn" help the boy to interpret his experience? What do his father's concluding words enable him to see?

4. From what point of view is the story told? How does the use of interior monologue and dialogue contribute to the reader's sense of immediacy?

Suggestions for Writing

1. Compare the manner in which Faulkner develops his narrative with that of Hemingway in the next selection. What do these two stories have in common? In what respects do they differ? Compare the point of view, diction and tone, and characterization. Compare them as stories of initiation. Compare the nature of the protagonist's anxiety or fear in each story. How is it manifested and how resolved?

2. Relate the boy's fears and resolution of them to the concept of identity.

3. Record an experience in which you describe an early fear and the ways in which you overcame it.

◊◊◊◊

Ernest Hemingway

Indian Camp

Ernest Hemingway (1898–1961), novelist and short-story writer, began his career as a reporter and during World War I served with an ambulance unit in France and Italy. After the war he lived in Paris as a correspondent for the Hearst papers. During the Spanish Civil War he went to Spain as a war correspondent. His works include the collections of short stories *In Our Time* (1925), *Men Without Women* (1927), *The Fifth Column and the First 49 Stories* (1938); and the novels *The Sun Also Rises* (1926), *A Farewell to Arms* (1929), *For Whom the Bell Tolls* (1940), and *The Old Man and the Sea* (1952), which was awarded a Pulitzer Prize. In 1954 he received the Nobel Prize for Literature. This is a story of initiation, from the collection *In Our Time,* in which the boy is exposed to a violent birth and death.

At the lake shore there was another rowboat drawn up. The two Indians stood waiting.

Nick and his father got in the stern of the boat and the Indians shoved it off and one of them got in to row. Uncle George sat in the stern of the camp rowboat. The young Indian shoved the camp boat off and got in to row Uncle George.

The two boats started off in the dark. Nick heard the oarlocks of the other boat quite a way ahead of them in the mist. The Indians rowed with quick choppy strokes. Nick lay back with his father's arm around him. It was cold on the water. The Indian who was rowing them was working very hard, but the other boat moved further ahead in the mist all the time.

"Where are we going, Dad?" Nick asked.

"Over to the Indian camp. There is an Indian lady very sick."

"Oh," said Nick.

Across the bay they found the other boat beached. Uncle George was smoking a cigar in the dark. The young Indian pulled the boat way up on the beach. Uncle George gave both the Indians cigars.

They walked up from the beach through a meadow that was soaking wet with dew, following the young Indian who carried a lantern. Then they went into the woods and followed a trail that led to the logging road that ran back into the hills. It was much lighter on the logging road as the timber was cut away on both sides. The young Indian stopped and blew out his lantern and they all walked on along the road.

They came around a bend and a dog came out barking. Ahead were the lights of the shanties where the Indian bark-peelers lived. More dogs rushed out at them. The two Indians sent them back to the shanties. In the shanty nearest the road there was a light in the window. An old woman stood in the doorway holding a lamp.

Inside on a wooden bunk lay a young Indian woman. She had been trying to have her baby for two days. All the old women in the camp had been helping her. The men had moved off up the road to sit in the dark and smoke out of range of the noise she made. She screamed just as Nick and the two

Indians followed his father and Uncle George into the shanty. She lay in the lower bunk, very big under a quilt. Her head was turned to one side. In the upper bunk was her husband. He had cut his foot very badly with an ax three days before. He was smoking a pipe. The room smelled very bad.

Nick's father ordered some water to be put on the stove, and while it was heating he spoke to Nick.

"This lady is going to have a baby, Nick," he said.

"I know," said Nick.

"You don't know," said his father. "Listen to me. What she is going through is called being in labor. The baby wants to be born and she wants it to be born. All her muscles are trying to get the baby born. That is what is happening when she screams."

"I see," Nick said.

Just then the woman cried out.

"Oh, Daddy, can't you give her something to make her stop screaming?" asked Nick.

"No. I haven't any anaesthetic," his father said. "But her screams are not important. I don't hear them because they are not important."

The husband in the upper bunk rolled over against the wall.

The woman in the kitchen motioned to the doctor that the water was hot. Nick's father went into the kitchen and poured about half of the water out of the big kettle into a basin. Into the water left in the kettle he put several things he unwrapped from a handkerchief.

"Those must boil," he said, and began to scrub his hands in the basin of hot water with a cake of soap he had brought from the camp. Nick watched his father's hands scrubbing each other with the soap. While his father washed his hands very carefully and thoroughly, he talked.

"You see, Nick, babies are supposed to be born head first but sometimes they're not. When they're not they make a lot of trouble for everybody. Maybe I'll have to operate on this lady. We'll know in a little while."

When he was satisfied with his hands he went in and went to work.

"Pull back that quilt, will you, George?" he said. "I'd rather not touch it."

Later when he started to operate Uncle George and three Indian men held the woman still. She bit Uncle George on the arm and Uncle George said, "Damn squaw bitch!" and the young Indian who had rowed Uncle George over laughed at him. Nick held the basin for his father. It all took a long time.

His father picked the baby up and slapped it to make it breathe and handed it to the old woman.

"See, it's a boy, Nick," he said. "How do you like being an interne?"

Nick said, "All right." He was looking away so as not to see what his father was doing.

"There. That gets it," said his father and put something into the basin.

Nick didn't look at it.

"Now," his father said, "there's some stitches to put in. You can watch this or not, Nick, just as you like. I'm going to sew up the incision I made."

Nick did not watch. His curiosity had been gone for a long time.

His father finished and stood up. Uncle George and the three Indian men stood up. Nick put the basin out in the kitchen.

Uncle George looked at his arm. The young Indian smiled reminiscently.

"I'll put some peroxide on that, George," the doctor said.

He bent over the Indian woman. She was quiet now and her eyes were closed. She looked very pale. She did not know what had become of the baby or anything.

"I'll be back in the morning," the doctor said, standing up. "The nurse should be here from St. Ignace by noon and she'll bring everything we need."

He was feeling exalted and talkative as football players are in the dressing room after a game.

"That's one for the medical journal, George," he said. "Doing a Caesarean with a jack-knife and sewing it up with nine-foot, tapered gut leaders."

Uncle George was standing against the wall, looking at his arm.

"Oh, you're a great man, all right," he said.

"Ought to have a look at the proud father. They're usually the worst sufferers in these little affairs," the doctor said. "I must say he took it all pretty quietly."

He pulled back the blanket from the Indian's head. His hand came away wet. He mounted on the edge of the lower bunk with the lamp in one hand and looked in. The Indian lay with his face toward the wall. His throat had been cut from ear to ear. The blood had flowed down into a pool where his body sagged the bunk. His head rested on his left arm. The open razor lay, edge up, in the blankets.

"Take Nick out of the shanty, George," the doctor said.

There was no need of that. Nick, standing in the door of the kitchen, had a good view of the upper bunk when his father, the lamp in one hand, tipped the Indian's head back.

It was just beginning to be daylight when they walked along the logging road back toward the lake.

"I'm terribly sorry I brought you along, Nickie," said his father, all his post-operative exhilaration gone. "It was an awful mess to put you through."

"Do ladies always have such a hard time having babies?" Nick asked.

"No, that was very, very exceptional."

"Why did he kill himself, Daddy?"

"I don't know, Nick. He couldn't stand things, I guess."

"Do many men kill themselves, Daddy?"

"Not very many, Nick."

"Do many women?"

"Hardly ever."

"Don't they ever?"

"Oh, yes. They do sometimes."

"Daddy?"

"Yes."

"Where did Uncle George go?"

"He'll turn up all right."

"Is dying hard, Daddy?"

"No, I think it's pretty easy, Nick. It all depends."

They were seated in the boat, Nick in the stern, his father rowing. The sun was coming up over the hills. A bass jumped, making a circle in the water. Nick trailed his hand in the water. It felt warm in the sharp chill of the morning.

In the early morning on the lake sitting in the stern of the boat with his father rowing, he felt quite sure that he would never die.

Suggestions for Discussion

1. How is the emotional tension of the story built up by the descriptive details of the journey to the Indian camp and the arrival at the shanties?

2. Inside the hut, what images of sight, sound, and smell take you into the heart of the scene?

3. What is the effect of the rather cold, scientific attitude of the doctor-father? of his laconic explanations to his son interspersed with details of action? Note the verbs he uses.

4. What do Uncle George and the young Indian observers contribute to the reader's rising sense of horror?

5. How are you prepared for the suicide of the husband?

6. Comment on the irony of the concluding conversation and the significance of the experience in Nick's emotional growth and awareness of life and death.

7. Explain the final sentence.

8. By specific reference to the text, support the view that this is primarily a story of Nick's initiation.

Suggestions for Writing

1. Discuss the story as a commentary on the condition of Indians in rural areas or on reservations today.

2. Write about an early experience in which you learned about birth or death, death or violence.

3. Compare and contrast "Indian Camp" and "The Bear" as stories of initiation. Consider the boys' fears, their fathers' attitudes, and the resolution of the action.

Elizabeth Taylor

Girl Reading

Elizabeth Taylor (1912–1975) was born in England and is distinguished for her short stories. Among her publications are *In a Summer Season* (1961), *The Wedding Group* (1968), and *The Devastating Boys and Other Stories* (1972). She was a frequent contributor to *The New Yorker*. "Girl Reading," from *A Dedicated Man and Other Stories* (1965), is a story of Ettas's evolving experience from initial insecurity to a sense of power.

Etta's desire was to belong. Sometimes she felt on the fringe of the family, at other times drawn headily into its very center. At mealtimes—those occasions of argument and hilarity, of thrust and counterstroke, bewildering to her at first—she was especially on her mettle, turning her head alertly from one to another as if watching a fast tennis match. She hoped soon to learn the art of riposte and already used, sometimes unthinkingly, family words and phrases; and had one or two privately treasured memories of even having made them laugh. They delighted in laughing and often did so scoffingly—"at the expense of those less fortunate" as Etta's mother would sententiously have put it.

Etta and Sarah were school friends. It was not the first time that Etta had stayed with the Lippmanns in the holidays. Everyone understood that the hospitality would not be returned, for Etta's mother, who was widowed, went out to work each day. Sarah had seen only the outside of the drab terrace house where her friend lived. She had persuaded her elder brother, David, to take her spying there one evening. They drove fifteen miles to Market Swanford and Sarah, with great curiosity, studied the street names until at last she discovered the house itself. No one was about. The street was quite deserted and the two rows of houses facing one another were blank and silent as if waiting for a hearse to appear. "Do hurry!" Sarah urged her brother. It had been a most dangerous outing and she was thoroughly depressed by it. Curiosity now seemed a trivial sensation compared with the pity she was feeling for her friend's drab life and her shame at having confirmed her own suspicions of it. She was threatened by tears. "Aren't you going in?" her brother asked in great surprise. "Hurry, hurry," she begged him. There had never been any question of her calling at that house.

"She must be very lonely there all through the holidays, poor Etta," she thought, and could imagine hour after hour in the dark house. Bickerings with the daily help she had already heard of and—Etta trying to put on a brave face and make much of nothing—trips to the public library the highlight of the day, it seemed. No wonder that her holiday reading was always so carefully done, thought Sarah, whereas she herself could never snatch a moment for it except at night in bed.

Sarah had a lively conscience about the seriousness of her friend's private world. Having led her more than once into trouble, at school, she had always afterwards felt a disturbing sense of shame; for Etta's work was more important than her own could ever be, too important to be interrupted by escapades. Sacrifices had been made and scholarships must be won. Once—it was a year ago when they were fifteen and had less sense—Sarah had thought up some rough tomfoolery and Etta's blazer had been torn. She was still haunted by her friend's look of consternation. She had remembered too late, as always—the sacrifices that had been made, the widowed mother sitting year after year at her office desk, the holidays that were never taken and the contriving that had to be done.

Her own mother was so warm and worldly. If she had anxieties she kept them to herself, setting the pace of gaiety, up to date and party-loving. She was popular with her friends' husbands who, in their English way, thought of her comfortably as nearly as good company as a man and full of bright ways as well. Etta felt safer with her than with Mr. Lippmann, whose enquiries were often too probing; he touched nerves, his jocularity could be an embarrassment. The boys—Sarah's elder brothers—had their own means of communication which their mother unflaggingly strove to interpret and, on Etta's first visit, she had tried to do so for her, too.

She *was* motherly, although she looked otherwise, the girl decided. Lying in bed at night, in the room she shared with Sarah, Etta would listen to guests driving noisily away or to the Lippmanns returning, full of laughter, from some neighbor's house. Late night door-slamming in the country disturbed only the house's occupants, who all contributed to it. Etta imagined them pottering about downstairs—husband and wife—would hear bottles clinking, laughter, voices raised from room to room, goodnight endearments to cats and dogs and at last Mrs. Lippmann's running footsteps on the stairs and the sound of her jingling bracelets coming nearer. Outside their door she would pause, listening, wondering if they were asleep already. They never were. "Come in!" Sarah would shout, hoisting herself up out of the bed clothes on one elbow, her face turned expectantly towards the door, ready for laughter— for something amusing would surely have happened. Mrs. Lippmann, sitting on one of the beds, never failed them. When they were children, Sarah said, she brought back *petits fours* from parties; now she brought back *faux pas*. She specialised in little stories against herself—Mummy's Humiliations, Sarah named them—tactless things she had said, never-to-be-remedied remarks which sprang fatally from her lips. Mistakes in identity was her particular line, for she never remembered a face, she declared. Having kissed Sarah, she would bend over Etta to do the same. She smelt of scent and gin and cigarette smoke. After this they would go to sleep. The house would be completely quiet for several hours.

Etta's mother had always had doubts about the suitability of this *ménage*. She knew it only at second hand from her daughter, and Etta said very little about her visits and that little was only in reply to obviously resented questions. But she had a way of looking about her with boredom when she returned, as if she had made the transition unwillingly and incompletely. She hurt her mother—who wished only to do everything in the world for her, having no one else to please or protect.

"I should feel differently if we were able to return the hospitality," she told Etta. The Lippmanns' generosity depressed her. She knew that it was despicable to feel jealous, left out, kept in the dark, but she tried to rationalize her feelings before Etta. "I could take a few days off and invite Sarah here," she suggested.

Etta was unable to hide her consternation and her expression deeply wounded her mother. "I shouldn't know what to do with her," she said.

"Couldn't you go for walks? There are the Public Gardens. And take her to the cinema one evening. What do you do at *her* home?"

"Oh, just fool about. Nothing much." Some afternoons they just lay on their beds and ate sweets, keeping all the windows shut and the wireless on loud, and no one ever disturbed them or told them they ought to be out in the fresh air. Then they had to plan parties and make walnut fudge and de-flea the dogs. Making fudge was the only one of these things she could imagine them doing in her own home and they could not do it all the time. As for the dreary Public Gardens, she could not herself endure the asphalt paths and the bandstand and the beds of salvias. She could imagine vividly how dejected Sarah would feel.

Early in these summer holidays, the usual letter had come from Mrs. Lippmann. Etta, returning from the library, found that the charwoman had gone early and locked her out. She rang the bell, but the sound died away and left an ever more forbidding silence. All the street, where elderly people dozed in stuffy rooms, was quiet. She lifted the flap of the letter-box and called through it. No one stirred or came. She could just glimpse an envelope, lying face up on the doormat, addressed in Mrs. Lippmann's large, loopy, confident handwriting. The house-stuffiness wafted through the letter-box. She imagined the kitchen floor slowly drying, for there was a smell of soapy water. A tap was steadily dripping.

She leaned against the door, waiting for her mother's return, in a sickness of impatience at the thought of the letter lying there inside. Once or twice, she lifted the flap and had another look at it.

Her mother came home at last, very tired. With an anxious air, she set about cooking supper, which Etta had promised to have ready. The letter was left among her parcels on the kitchen table, and not until they had finished their stewed rhubarb did she send Etta to fetch it. She opened it carefully with the bread knife and deepened the frown on her forehead in preparation for reading it. When she had, she gave Etta a summary of its contents and put forward her objections, her unnerving proposal.

"She wouldn't come," Etta said. "She wouldn't leave her dog."

"But, my dear, she has to leave him when she goes back to school."

"I know. That's the trouble. In the holidays she likes to be with him as much as possible, to make up for it."

Mrs. Salkeld, who had similar wishes about her daughter, looked sad. "It is too one-sided," she gently explained. "You must try to understand how I feel about it."

"They're only too glad to have me. I keep Sarah company when they go out."

They obviously went out a great deal and Mrs. Salkeld suspected that they were frivolous. She did not condemn them for that—they must lead their own lives, but those were in a world which Etta would never be able to afford the time or money to inhabit. "Very well, Musetta," she said, removing the girl further from her by using her full name—used only on formal and usually menacing occasions.

That night she wept a little from tiredness and depression—from disappointment, too, at the thought of returning in the evenings to the dark and empty house, just as she usually did, but when she had hoped for company. They were not healing tears she shed and they did nothing but add self-contempt to her other distresses.

A week later, Etta went the short distance by train to stay with the Lippmanns. Her happiness soon lost its edge of guilt, and once the train had rattled over the iron bridge that spanned the broad river, she felt safe in a different country. There seemed to be even a different weather, coming from a wider sky, and a riverside glare—for the curves of the railway line brought it close to the even more winding course of the river, whose silver loops could be glimpsed through the trees. There were islands and backwaters and a pale heron standing on a patch of mud.

Sarah was waiting at the little station and Etta stepped down onto the platform as if taking a footing into promised land. Over the station and the gravelly lane outside hung a noonday quiet. On one side were grazing meadows, on the other side the drive gateways of expensive houses. The Gables was indeed gabled and so was its boathouse. It was also turreted and balconied. There was a great deal of woodwork painted glossy white, and a huge-leaved Virginia creeper covered much of the red brick walls—in the front beds were the salvias and lobelias Etta had thought she hated. Towels and swim-suits hung over balcony rails and a pair of tennis shoes had been put out on a window-sill to dry. Even though Mr. Lippmann and his son, David, went to London every day, the house always had—for Etta—a holiday atmosphere.

The hall door stood open and on the big round table were the stacks of new magazines which seemed to her the symbol of extravagance and luxury. At the back of the house, on the terrace overlooking the river, Mrs. Lippmann, wearing tight, lavender pants and a purple shirt, was drinking vodka with a neighbour who had called for a subscription to some charity. Etta was briefly enfolded in scented silk and tinkling bracelets and then released and introduced. Sarah gave her a red, syrupy drink and they sat down on the warm steps among the faded clumps of aubretia and rocked the ice cubes to and fro in their glasses, keeping their eyes narrowed to the sun.

Mrs. Lippmann gossiped, leaning back under a fringed chair-umbrella. She enjoyed exposing the frailties of her friends and family, although she would have been the first to hurry to their aid in trouble. Roger, who was seventeen, had been worse for drink the previous evening, she was saying. Faced with breakfast, his face had been a study of disgust which she now tried to mimic. And David could not eat, either; but from being in love. She raised her eyes to heaven most dramatically, to convey that great patience was demanded to her.

"He eats like a horse," said Sarah. "Etta, let's go upstairs." She took Etta's empty glass and led her back across the lawn, seeming not to care that her mother would without doubt begin to talk about her the moment she had gone.

Rich and vinegary smells of food came from the kitchen as they crossed the hall. (There was a Hungarian cook to whom Mrs. Lippmann spoke in German and a Portuguese "temporary" to whom she spoke in Spanish.) The food was an important part of the holiday to Etta, who had nowhere else eaten *Sauerkraut* or *Apfelstrudel* or cold fried fish, and she went into the dining-room each day with a sense of adventure and anticipation.

On this visit she was also looking forward to the opportunity of making a study of people in love—an opportunity she had not had before. While she unpacked, she questioned Sarah about David's Nora, as she thought of her; but Sarah would only say that she was quite a good sort with dark eyes and an enormous bust, and that as she was coming to dinner that evening, as she nearly always did, Etta would be able to judge for herself.

While they were out on the river all the afternoon—Sarah rowing her in a dinghy along the reedy backwater—Etta's head was full of love in books, even in those holiday set books Sarah never had time for—*Sense and Sensibility* this summer. She felt that she knew what to expect, and her perceptions were sharpened by the change of air and scene, and the disturbing smell of the river, which she snuffed up deeply as if she might be able to store it up in her lungs. "Mother thinks it is polluted," Sarah said when Etta lifted a streaming hand from trailing in the water and brought up some slippery weeds and held them to her nose. They laughed at the idea.

Etta, for dinner, put on the Liberty silk they wore on Sunday evenings at school and Sarah at once brought out her own hated garment from the back of the cupboard where she had pushed it out of sight on the first day of the holidays. When they appeared downstairs, they looked unbelievably dowdy, Mrs. Lippmann thought, turning away for a moment because her eyes had suddenly pricked with tears at the sight of her kind daughter.

Mr. Lippmann and David returned from Lloyd's at half-past six and with them brought Nora—a large, calm girl with an air of brittle indifference towards her fiancé which disappointed but did not deceive Etta, who knew enough to remain undeceived by banter. To interpret from it the private tendernesses it hid was part of the mental exercise she was to be engaged in. After all, David would know better than to have his heart on his sleeve, especially in this *dégagé* family where nothing seemed half so funny as falling in love.

After dinner, Etta telephoned her mother, who had perhaps been waiting for the call, as the receiver was lifted immediately. Etta imagined her standing in the dark and narrow hall with its smell of umbrellas and furniture polish.

"I thought you would like to know I arrived safely."

"What have you been doing?"

"Sarah and I went to the river. We have just finished dinner." Spicy smells still hung about the house. Etta guessed that her mother would have had half a tin of sardines and put the other half by for her breakfast. She felt sad for her and guilty herself. Most of her thoughts about her mother were deformed by guilt.

"What have you been doing?" she asked.

"Oh, the usual," her mother said brightly. "I am just turning the collars and cuffs of your winter blouses. By the way, don't forget to pay Mrs. Lippmann for the telephone call."

"No. I shall have to go now. I just thought . . ."

"Yes, of course, dear. Well, have a lovely time."

"We are going for a swim when our dinner has gone down."

"Be careful of cramp, won't you? But I mustn't fuss from this distance. I know you are in good hands. Give my kind regards to Mrs. Lippmann and Sarah, will you, please. I must get back to your blouses."

"I wish you wouldn't bother. You must be tired."

"I am perfectly happy doing it," Mrs. Salkeld said. But if that were so, it was unnecessary, Etta thought, for her to add, as she did: "And someone has to do it."

She went dully back to the others. Roger was strumming on a guitar, but he blushed and put it away when Etta came into the room.

As the days went quickly by, Etta thought that she was belonging more this time than ever before. Mr. Lippmann, a genial patriarch, often patted her head when passing, in confirmation of her existence, and Mrs. Lippmann let her run errands. Roger almost wistfully sought her company, while Sarah disdainfully discouraged him; for they had their own employments, she implied; her friend—"my best friend," as she introduced Etta to lesser ones or adults—could hardly be expected to want the society of schoolboys. Although he was a year older than themselves, being a boy he was less sophisticated, she explained. She and Etta considered themselves to be rather worldly-wise—Etta having learnt from literature and Sarah from putting two and two together, her favourite pastime. Her parents seemed to her to behave with the innocence of children, unconscious of their motives, so continually betraying themselves to her experienced eye, when knowing more would have made them guarded. She had similarly put two and two together about Roger's behaviour to Etta, but she kept these conclusions to herself—partly from not wanting to make her friend feel self-conscious and partly—for she scorned self-deception—from what she recognised to be jealousy. She and Etta were very well as they were, she thought.

Etta herself was too much absorbed by the idea of love to ever think of being loved. In this house, she had her first chance of seeing it at first hand and she studied David and Nora with such passionate speculation that their loving seemed less their own than hers. At first, she admitted to herself that she was disappointed. Their behaviour fell short of what she required of them; they lacked a romantic attitude to one another and Nora was neither touching nor glorious—neither Viola nor Rosalind. In Etta's mind to be either was satisfactory; to be boisterous and complacent was not. Nora was simply a plump and genial girl with a large bust and a faint moustache. She could not be expected to inspire David with much gallantry and, in spite of all the red roses he brought her from London, he was not above telling her that she was getting fat. Gaily retaliatory, she would threaten him with the bouquet, waving it about his head, her huge engagement ring catching the light, flashing with different colours, her eyes flashing too.

Sometimes, there was what Etta's mother would have called "horseplay," and Etta herself deplored the noise, the dishevelled romping. "We know quite well what it's instead of," said Sarah. "But I sometimes wonder if *they* do. They would surely cut it out if they did."

As intent as a bird-watcher, Etta observed them, but was puzzled that they behaved like birds, making such a display of their courtship, an absurd-looking frolic out of a serious matter. She waited in vain for a sigh or secret glance. At night, in the room she shared with Sarah, she wanted to talk about them more than Sarah, who felt that her own family was the last possible source of glamour or enlightenment. Discussing her bridesmaid's dress was the most she would be drawn into and that subject Etta felt was devoid of romance. She was not much interested in mere weddings and thought them rather banal and public celebrations. "With an overskirt of embroidered net," said Sarah in her decisive voice. "How nice if you could be a bridesmaid, too; but she has all those awful Greenbaum cousins. As ugly as sin, but not to be left out." Etta was inattentive to her. With all her studious nature she had set herself to study love and study it she would. She made the most of what the holiday offered and when the exponents were absent she fell back on the textbooks—*Tess of the D'Urbervilles* and *Wuthering Heights* at that time.

To Roger she seemed to fall constantly into the same pose, as she sat on the river bank, bare feet tucked sideways, one arm cradling a book, the other outstretched to pluck—as if to aid her concentration—at blades of grass. Her face remained pale, for it was always in shadow, bent over her book. Beside her, glistening with oil, Sarah spread out her body to the sun. She was content to lie for hour after hour with no object but to change the colour of her skin and with thoughts crossing her mind as seldom as clouds passed over-head—and in as desultory a way when they did so. Sometimes, she took a book out with her, but nothing happened to it except that it became smoth-ered with oil. Etta, who found sunbathing boring and enervating, read stead-ily on—her straight, pale hair hanging forward as if to seclude her, to screen her from the curious eyes of passers-by—shaken by passions of the imagina-tion as she was. Voices from boats came clearly across the water, but she did not heed them. People going languidly by in punts shaded their eyes and admired the scarlet geraniums and the greenness of the grass. When motor-cruisers passed, their wash jogged against the mooring stage and swayed into the boathouse, whose lacy fretwork trimmings had just been repainted glossy white.

Sitting there, alone by the boathouse at the end of the grass bank, Roger read, too; but less diligently than Etta. Each time a boat went by, he looked up and watched it out of sight. A swan borne towards him on a wake, sitting neatly on top of its reflection, held his attention. Then his place on the page was lost. Anyhow, the sun fell too blindingly upon it. He would glance again at Etta and briefly, with distaste, at his indolent, spread-eagled sister, who had rolled over on to her stomach to give her shiny back, crisscrossed from the grass, its share of sunlight. So the afternoons passed, and they would never have such long ones in their lives again.

Evenings were more social. The terrace with its fringed umbrellas—sym-bols of gaiety to Etta—became the gathering place. Etta, listening intently, continued her study of love and as intently Roger studied her and the very emotion which in those others so engrossed her.

"You look still too pale," Mr. Lippmann told her one evening. He put his hands to her face and tilted it to the sun.

"You shan't leave us until there are roses in those cheeks." He implied that only in his garden did sun and air give their full benefit. The thought was there and Etta shared it. "Too much of a bookworm, I'm afraid," he added and took one of her textbooks which she carried everywhere for safety, lest she should be left on her own for a few moments. *Tess of the D'Urbervilles*," read out Mr. Lippmann. "Isn't it deep? Isn't it on the morbid side?" Roger was kicking rhythmically at a table leg in glum embarrassment. "This won't do you any good at all, my dear little girl. This won't put the roses in your cheeks."

"You are doing that," his daughter told him—for Etta was blushing as she always did when Mr. Lippmann spoke to her.

"What's a nice book, Babs?" he asked his wife, as she came out on to the terrace. "Can't you find a nice story for this child?" The house must be full, he was sure, of wonderfully therapeutic novels if only he knew where to lay hands on them. "Roger, you're our bookworm. Look out a nice storybook for your guest. This one won't do her eyes any good." Buying books with small print was a false economy, he thought, and bound to land one in large bills from an eye specialist before long. "A very short-sighted policy," he explained genially when he had given them a little lecture to which no one listened.

His wife was trying to separate some slippery cubes of ice and Sarah sprawled in a cane chair with her eyes shut. She was making the most of the setting sun, as Etta was making the most of romance.

"We like the same books," Roger said to his father. "So she can choose as well as I could."

Etta was just beginning to feel a sense of surprised gratitude, had half turned to look in his direction when the betrothed came through the french windows and claimed her attention.

"In time for a lovely drink," Mrs. Lippmann said to Nora.

"She is too fat already," said David.

Nora swung round and caught his wrists and held them threateningly. "If you say that once more, I'll . . . I'll just . . ." He freed himself and pulled her close. She gasped and panted, but leant heavily against him. "Promise!" she said again.

"Promise what?"

"You won't ever say it again?"

He laughed at her mockingly.

They were less the centre of attention than they thought—Mr. Lippmann was smiling, but rather at the lovely evening and that the day in London was over; Mrs. Lippmann, impeded by the cardigan hanging over her shoulders, was mixing something in a glass jug and Sarah had her eyes closed against the evening sun. Only Etta, in some bewilderment, heeded them. Roger who had his own ideas about love, turned his head scornfully.

Sarah opened her eyes for a moment and stared at Nora, in her mind measuring against her the wedding dress she had been designing. She is too fat for satin, she decided, shutting her eyes again and disregarding the bridal gown for the time being. She returned to thoughts of her own dress, adding a little of what she called "back interest" (though lesser bridesmaids would no doubt obscure it from the congregation—or audience) in the form of long velvet ribbons in turquoise . . . or rose? She drew her brows together and with her eyes still shut said, "All the colours of the rainbow aren't very many, are they?"

"Now, Etta dear, what will you have to drink?" asked Mrs. Lippmann.

Just as she was beginning to ask for some tomato juice, Mr. Lippmann interrupted. He interrupted a great deal, for there were a great many things to be put right, it seemed to him. "Now, Mommy, you should give her a glass of sherry with an egg beaten up in it. Roger, run and fetch a nice egg and a whisk, too . . . all right Babsie dear, I shall do it myself . . . don't worry child," he said, turning to Etta and seeing her look of alarm. "It is no trouble to me. I shall do this for you every evening that you are here. We shall watch the roses growing in your cheeks, shan't we, Mommy?"

He prepared the drink with a great deal of clumsy fuss and sat back to watch her drinking it, smiling to himself, as if the roses were already blossoming. "Good, good!" he murmured, nodding at her as she drained the glass. Every evening, she thought, hoping that he would forget; but horrible though the drink had been, it was also reassuring; their concern for her was reassuring. She preferred it to the cold anxiety of her mother hovering with pills and thermometer.

"Yes," said Mr. Lippmann, "we shall see. We shall see. I think your parents won't know you." He puffed out his cheeks and sketched with a curving gesture the bosom she would soon have. He always forgot that her father was dead. It was quite fixed in his mind that he was simply a fellow who had obviously not made the grade; not everybody could. Roger bit his tongue hard, as if by doing so he could curb his father's. I must remind him again, Sarah and her mother were both thinking.

The last day of the visit had an unexpected hazard as well as its own sadness, for Mrs. Salkeld had written to say that her employer would lend her his car for the afternoon. When she had made a business call for him in the neighbourhood she would arrive to fetch Etta at about four o'clock.

"She is really to leave us, Mommy?" asked Mr. Lippmann at breakfast, folding his newspaper and turning his attention on his family before hurrying to the station. He examined Etta's face and nodded. "Next time you stay longer and we make rosy apples of these." He patted her cheeks and ruffled her hair. "You tell your Mommy and Dadda next time you stay a whole week."

"She *has* stayed a whole week," said Sarah.

"Then a fortnight, a month."

He kissed his wife, made a gesture as if blessing them all, with his newspaper raised above his head, and went from the room at a trot. "Thank goodness," thought Sarah, "that he won't be here this afternoon to make kind enquiries about *her* husband."

When she was alone with Etta, she said, "I'm sorry about that mistake he keeps making."

"I don't mind," Etta said truthfully, "I am only embarrassed because I know that you are." That's *nothing*, she thought; but the day ahead was a different matter.

As time passed, Mrs. Lippmann also appeared to be suffering from tension. She went upstairs and changed her matador pants for a linen skirt. She tidied up the terrace and told Roger to take his bathing things off his window-sill. As soon as she had stubbed out a cigarette, she emptied and dusted the ashtray. She was conscious that Sarah was trying to see her with another's eyes.

"Oh, do stop taking photographs," Sarah said tetchily to Roger, who had been clicking away with his camera all morning. He obeyed her only because he feared to draw attention to his activities. He had just taken what he hoped would be a very beautiful study of Etta in a typical pose—sitting on the river bank with a book in her lap. She had lifted her eyes and was gazing across the water as if she were pondering whatever she had been reading. In fact, she had been arrested by thoughts of David and Nora and, although her eyes followed the print, the scene she saw did not correspond with the lines she read. She turned her head and looked at the willow trees on the far bank, the clumps of borage from which moorhens launched themselves. "Perhaps next time that I see them, they'll be married and it will all be over," she thought. The evening before, there had been a great deal of high-spirited sparring about between them. Offence meant and offence taken they assured one another. "If you do that once more . . . I am absolutely serious," cried Nora. "You are trying not to laugh," David said. "I'm not. I am absolutely serious." "It will end in tears," Roger had muttered contemptuously. Even good-tempered Mrs. Lippmann had looked down her long nose disapprovingly. And that was the last, Etta supposed, that she would see of love for a long time. She was left once again with books. She returned to the one she was reading.

Roger had flung himself on to the grass near by, appearing to trip over a tussock of grass and collapse. He tried to think of some opening remark which might lead to a discussion of the book. In the end, he asked abruptly, "Do you like that?" She sat brooding over it, chewing the side of her finger. She nodded without looking up and, with a similar automatic gesture, she waved away a persistent wasp. He leaned forward and clapped his hands together smartly and was relieved to see the wasp drop dead into the grass, although he would rather it had stung him first. Etta, however, had not noticed this brave deed.

The day passed wretchedly for him; each hour was more filled with the doom of her departure than the last. He worked hard to conceal his feelings, in which no one took an interest. He knew that it was all he could do, although no good could come from his succeeding. He took a few more secret photographs from his bedroom window, and then he sat down and wrote a short letter to her, explaining his love.

At four o'clock, her mother came. He saw at once that Etta was nervous and he guessed that she tried to conceal her nervousness behind a much jauntier manner to her mother than was customary. It would be a bad hour, Roger decided.

His own mother, in spite of her linen skirt, was gaudy and exotic beside Mrs. Salkeld, who wore a navy-blue suit which looked as if it had been sponged and pressed a hundred times—a depressing process unknown to Mrs. Lippmann. The pink-rimmed spectacles that Mrs. Salkeld wore seemed to reflect a little colour on to her cheekbones, with the result that she looked slightly indignant about something or other. However, she smiled a great deal, and only Etta guessed what an effort it was to her to do so. Mrs. Lippmann gave her a chair where she might have a view of the river and she sat down, making a point of not looking round the room, and smoothed her gloves. Her jewellery was real but very small.

"If we have tea in the garden, the wasps get into Anna's rose-petal jam," said Mrs. Lippmann. Etta was not at her best, she felt—not helping at all. She was aligning herself too staunchly with the Lippmanns, so that her mother seemed a stranger to her, as well. "You see, I am at home here," she implied, as she jumped up to fetch things or hand things round. She was a little daring in her familiarity.

Mrs. Salkeld had contrived the visit because she wanted to understand and hoped to approve of her daughter's friends. Seeing the lawns, the light reflected from the water, later this large, bright room, and the beautiful poppy-seed cake the Hungarian cook had made for tea, she understood completely and felt pained. She could see then, with Etta's eyes, their own dark, narrow house, and she thought of the lonely hours she spent there reading on days of imprisoning rain. The Lippmanns would even have better weather, she thought bitterly. The bitterness affected her enjoyment of the poppy-seed cake. She had, as puritanical people often have, a sweet tooth. She ate the cake with a casual air, determined not to praise.

"You are so kind to spare Etta to us," said Mrs. Lippmann.

"*You* are kind to invite her," Mrs. Salkeld replied, and then for Etta's sake, added: "She loves to come to you."

Etta looked self-consciously down at her feet.

"No, I don't smoke," her mother said primly. "Thank you."

Mrs. Lippmann seemed to decide not to, either, but very soon her hand stole out and took a cigarette—while she was not looking, thought Roger, who was having some amusement from watching his mother on her best behavior.

Wherever she was, the shagreen cigarette case and the gold lighter were near by. Ashtrays never were. He got up and fetched one before Etta could do so.

The girls' school was being discussed—one of the few topics the two mothers had in common. Mrs. Lippmann had never taken it seriously. She laughed at the uniform and despised the staff—an attitude she might at least have hidden from her daughter, Mrs. Salkeld felt. The tea-trolley was being wheeled away and her eyes followed the remains of the poppy-seed cake. She had planned a special supper for Etta to return to, but she felt now that it was no use. The things of the mind had left room for an echo. It sounded with every footstep or spoken word in that house where not enough was going on. She began to wonder if there were things of the heart and not the mind that Etta fastened upon so desperately when she was reading. Or was her desire to be in a different place? Lowood was a worse one—she could raise her eyes and look round her own room in relief; Pemberley was better and she would benefit from the change. But how can I help her? she asked herself in anguish. What possible change—and radical it must be—can I ever find the strength to effect? People had thought her wonderful to have made her own life and brought up her child alone. She had kept their heads above water and it had taken all her resources to do so.

Her lips began to refuse the sherry Mrs. Lippmann suggested and then, to her surprise and Etta's astonishment, she said "yes" instead.

It was very early to have suggested it, Mrs. Lippmann thought, but it would seem to put an end to the afternoon. Conversation had been as hard work as she had anticipated and she longed for a dry martini to stop her from yawning, as she was sure it would; but something about Mrs. Salkeld seemed to discourage gin drinking.

"Mother, it isn't half-past five yet," said Sarah.

"Darling, don't be rude to your Mummy. I know perfectly well what the time is." (Who better? she wondered.) "And this isn't a public house, you know."

She had flushed a little and was lighting another cigarette. Her bracelets jangled against the decanter as she handed Mrs. Salkeld her glass of sherry, saying, "Young people are so stuffy," with an air of complicity.

Etta, who had never seen her mother drinking sherry before, watched nervously, as if she might not know how to do it. Mrs. Salkeld—remembering the flavor from Christmas mornings many years ago and—more faintly—from her mother's party trifle—sipped cautiously. In an obscure way she was doing this for Etta's sake. "It may speed her on her way," thought Mrs. Lippmann, playing idly with her charm bracelet, having run out of conversation.

When Mrs. Salkeld rose to go, she looked round the room once more as if to fix it in her memory—the setting where she would imagine her daughter on future occasions.

"And come again soon, there's a darling girl," said Mrs. Lippmann, putting her arm round Etta's shoulder as they walked towards the car. Etta, unused to but not ungrateful for embraces, leaned awkwardly against her. Roger, staring at the gravel, came behind carrying the suitcase.

"I have wasted my return ticket," Etta said.

"Well, that's not the end of the world," her mother said briskly. She thought, but did not say, that perhaps they could claim the amount if they wrote to British Railways and explained.

Mrs. Lippmann's easy affection meant so much less than her own stiff endearments, but she resented it all the same and when she was begged, with enormous warmth, to visit them all again soon her smile was a prim twisting of her lips.

The air was bright with summer sounds, voices across the water and rooks up in the elm trees. Roger stood back listening in a dream to the good-byes and thank-yous. Nor was *this* the end of the world, he told himself. Etta would come again and, better than that, they would also grow older and so be less at the mercy of circumstances. He would be in a position to command his life and turn occasions to his own advantage. Meanwhile, he had done what he could. None the less, he felt such dejection, such an overwhelming conviction that it *was* the end of the world after all, that he could not watch the car go down the drive, and he turned and walked quickly—rudely, off-handedly, his mother thought—back to the house.

Mrs. Salkeld, driving homewards in the lowering sun, knew that Etta had tears in her eyes. "I'm glad you enjoyed yourself," she said. Without waiting for an answer, she added: "They are very charming people." She had always suspected charm and rarely spoke of it, but in this case the adjective seemed called for.

Mr. Lippmann would be coming back from London about now, Etta was thinking. And David will bring Nora. They will all be on the terrace having drinks—dry martinis, not sherry.

She was grateful to her mother about the sherry and understood that it had been an effort towards meeting Mrs. Lippmann's world half-way, and on the way back, she had not murmured one word of criticism—for their worldliness or extravagance or the vulgar opulence of their furnishings. She had even made a kind remark about them.

I might buy her a new dress, Mrs. Salkeld thought—something like the one Sarah was wearing. Though it does seem a criminal waste when she has all her good school clothes to wear out.

They had come onto the main road, and evening traffic streamed by. In the distance the gas holder looked pearl grey and the smoke from factories was pink in the sunset. They were nearly home. Etta, who had blinked her tears back from her eyes, took a sharp breath, almost a sigh.

Their own street with its tall houses was in shadow. "I wish we had a cat," said Etta, as she got out of the car and saw the next door tabby looking through the garden railings. She imagined burying her face in its warm fur, it loving only her. To her surprise, her mother said: "Why not?" Briskly, she went up the steps and turned the key with its familiar grating sound in the lock. The house with its smell—familiar, too—of floor polish and stuffiness, looked secretive. Mrs. Salkeld, hardly noticing this, hurried to the kitchen to put the casserole of chicken in the oven.

Etta carried her suitcase upstairs. On the dressing-table was a jar of marigolds. She was touched by this—just when she did not want to be touched. She turned her back on them and opened her case. On the top was the book she had left on the terrace. Roger had brought it to her at the last moment. Taking it now, she found a letter inside. Simply "Etta" was written on the envelope.

Roger had felt that he had done all he was capable of and that was to write in the letter those things he could not have brought himself to say, even if he had had an opportunity. No love letter could have been less anticipated and Etta read it twice before she could realise that it was neither a joke nor a mistake. It was the most extraordinary happening of her life, the most incredible.

Her breathing grew slower and deeper as she sat staring before her, pondering her mounting sense of power. It was as if the whole Lippmann family—Nora as well—had proposed to her. To marry Roger—a long, long time ahead though she must wait to do so—would be the best possible way of belonging.

She got up stiffly—for her limbs now seemed too clumsy a part of her body with its fly-away heart and giddy head—she went over to the dressing-table and stared at herself in the glass. "I am I," she thought, but she could not believe it. She stared and stared, but could not take in the tantalising idea.

After a while, she began to unpack. The room was a place of transit, her temporary residence. When she had made it tidy, she went downstairs to thank her mother for the marigolds.

Suggestions for Discussion

1. What does the metaphor of Etta watching a tennis match tell you about Sarah's family?

2. With what details does the reader learn about Sarah and her relationship to Etta? By what means does one learn about Sarah's mother and other members of the family?

3. Why did Etta resent questions from her mother about her visits to the Lippmanns? Why are "Etta's thoughts about her mother deformed by guilt"? How is the guilt conveyed?

4. What do the activities and conversations of Mrs. Lippmann tell you about her attitudes and values?

5. The story is written from the omniscient author point of view, and the focus shifts back and forth from Sarah and Etta to both mothers and to members of Sarah's family. How does the story achieve a singleness of purpose?

6. "Etta's desire was to belong" we are told in the first sentence. With what incidents and commentary is her concern validated? How successful is she in achieving her desire? How is her success communicated?

7. On what are Etta's reflections on love based? How do you account for her disappointment in her observations of David and Nora?

8. Relate the contrasting phrases "things of the mind" and "things of the heart" to Etta's evolving experience.

9. Account for Etta's awareness of a "mounting sense of power." What is the significance of the disbelief that "I am I"?

10. Relate the title to the theme of the story.

Suggestions for Writing

1. Describe a friend, relative, or yourself in a state of being in love.

2. Compare and contrast your family with that of a friend.

3. Develop your own definition and comparison of "things of the mind" and "things of the heart."

4. Drawing upon specific incidents in the story, write a character study of Etta.

Lionel Trilling
Of This Time, Of That Place

Lionel Trilling (1905–1975) was born in New York City and received his doctorate from Columbia University, where he was a professor of literature. His works include two critical biographies, *Matthew Arnold* (1939) and *E. M. Forster* (1943); a novel, *The Middle of the Journey* (1949); and literary criticism and social commentary in his collections of essays, *The Liberal Imagination* (1950), *The Opposing Self* (1955), and *Beyond Culture* (1965). In this story of initiation, in which Joseph Howe discovers "the possibility of the corruption and seduction in academic life" and his own susceptibility to them, the central questions of identity and moral responsibility are posed.

I

It was a fine September day. By noon it would be summer again but now it was true autumn with a touch of chill in the air. As Joseph Howe stood on the porch of the house in which he lodged, ready to leave for his first class of the year, he thought with pleasure of the long indoor days that were coming. It was a moment when he could feel glad of his profession.

On the lawn the peach tree was still in fruit and young Hilda Aiken was taking a picture of it. She held the camera tight against her chest. She wanted the sun behind her but she did not want her own long morning shadow in the foreground. She raised the camera but that did not help, and she lowered it but that made things worse. She twisted her body to the left, then to the right. In the end she had to step out of the direct line of the sun. At last she snapped the shutter and wound the film with intense care.

Howe, watching her from the porch, waited for her to finish and called good morning. She turned, startled, and almost sullenly lowered her glance. In the year Howe had lived at the Aikens', Hilda had accepted him as one of her family, but since his absence of the summer she had grown shy. Then suddenly she lifted her head and smiled at him, and the humorous smile confirmed his pleasure in the day. She picked up her bookbag and set off for school.

The handsome houses on the streets to the college were not yet fully awake but they looked very friendly. Howe went by the Bradby house where he would be a guest this evening at the first dinner-party of the year. When he had gone the length of the picket fence, the whitest in town, he turned back. Along the path there was a fine row of asters and he went through the gate and picked one for his buttonhole. The Bradbys would be pleased if they happened to see him invading their lawn and the knowledge of this made him even more comfortable.

He reached the campus as the hour was striking. The students were hurrying to their classes. He himself was in no hurry. He stopped at his dim cubicle of an office and lit a cigarette. The prospect of facing his class had suddenly presented itself to him and his hands were cold, the lawful seizure of power he was about to make seemed momentous. Waiting did not help. He put out his cigarette, picked up a pad of theme paper and went to his classroom.

As he entered, the rattle of voices ceased and the twenty-odd freshmen settled themselves and looked at him appraisingly. Their faces seemed gross, his heart sank at their massed impassivity, but he spoke briskly.

"My name is Howe," he said and turned and wrote it on the blackboard. The carelessness of the scrawl confirmed his authority. He went on, "My office is 412 Slemp Hall and my office hours are Monday, Wednesday, and Friday from eleven-thirty to twelve-thirty."

He wrote, "M., W., F., 11:30 – 12:30." He said, "I'll be very glad to see any of you at that time. Or if you can't come then, you can arrange with me for some other time."

He turned again to the blackboard and spoke over his shoulder. "The text for the course is Jarman's *Modern Plays*, revised edition. The Co-op has it in stock." He wrote the name, underlined "revised edition" and waited for it to be taken down in the new notebooks.

When the bent heads were raised again he began his speech of prospectus. "It is hard to explain—," he said, and paused as they composed themselves. "It is hard to explain what a course like this is intended to do. We are going to try to learn something about modern literature and something about prose composition.

As he spoke, his hands warmed and he was able to look directly at the class. Last year on the first day the faces had seemed just as cloddish, but as the term wore on they became gradually alive and quite likable. It did not seem possible that the same thing could happen again.

"I shall not lecture in this course," he continued. "Our work will be carried on by discussion and we will try to learn by an exchange of opinion. But you will soon recognize that my opinion is worth more than anyone else's here."

He remained grave as he said it, but two boys understood and laughed. The rest took permission from them and laughed too. All Howe's private ironies protested the vulgarity of the joke but the laughter made him feel benign and powerful.

When the little speech was finished, Howe picked up the pad of paper he had brought. He announced that they would write an extemporaneous theme. Its subject was traditional, "Who I am and why I came to Dwight College." By now the class was more at ease and it gave a ritualistic groan of protest.

Then there was a stir as fountain-pens were brought out and the writing arms of the chairs were cleared and the paper was passed about. At last all the heads bent to work and the room became still.

Howe sat idly at his desk. The sun shone through the tall clumsy windows. The cool of the morning was already passing. There was a scent of autumn and of varnish, and the stillness of the room was deep and oddly touching. Now and then a student's head was raised and scratched in the old elaborate students' pantomime that calls the teacher to witness honest intellectual effort.

Suddenly a tall boy stood within the frame of the open door. "Is this," he said, and thrust a large nose into a college catalogue, "is this the meeting place of English 1A? The section instructed by Dr. Joseph Howe?"

He stood on the very sill of the door, as if refusing to enter until he was perfectly sure of all his rights. The class looked up from work, found him absurd and gave a low mocking cheer.

The teacher and the new student, with equal pointedness, ignored the disturbance. Howe nodded to the boy, who pushed his head forward and then jerked it back in a wide elaborate arc to clear his brow of a heavy lock of hair. He advanced into the room and halted before Howe, almost at attention. In a loud clear voice he announced, "I am Tertan, Ferdinand R., reporting at the direction of Head of Department Vincent."

The heraldic formality of this statement brought forth another cheer. Howe looked at the class with a sternness he could not really feel, for there was indeed something ridiculous about this boy. Under his displeased regard the rows of heads dropped to work again. Then he touched Tertan's elbow, led him up to the desk and stood so as to shield their conversation from the class.

"We are writing an extemporaneous theme," he said. "The subject is, 'Who I am and why I came to Dwight College.' "

He stripped a few sheets from the pad and offered them to the boy. Tertan hesitated and then took the paper but he held it only tentatively. As if with the effort of making something clear, he gulped, and a slow smile fixed itself on his face. It was at once knowing and shy.

"Professor," he said, "to be perfectly fair to my classmates"—he made a large gesture over the room—"and to you"—he inclined his head to Howe—"this would not be for me an extemporaneous subject."

Howe tried to understand. "You mean you've already thought about it—you've heard we always give the same subject? That doesn't matter."

Again the boy ducked his head and gulped. It was the gesture of one who wishes to make a difficult explanation with perfect candor. "Sir," he said, and made the distinction with great care, "the topic I did not expect but I have given much ratiocination to the subject."

Howe smiled and said, "I don't think that's an unfair advantage. Just go ahead and write."

Tertan narrowed his eyes and glanced sidewise at Howe. His strange mouth smiled. Then in quizzical acceptance, he ducked his head, threw back the heavy dank lock, dropped into a seat with a great loose noise and began to write rapidly.

The room fell silent again and Howe resumed his idleness. When the bell rang, the students who had groaned when the task had been set now groaned again because they had not finished. Howe took up the papers and held the class while he made the first assignment. When he dismissed it, Tertan bore down on him, his slack mouth held ready for speech.

"Some professors," he said, "are pedants. They are Dryasdusts. However, some professors are free souls and creative spirits. Kant, Hegel, and Nietzsche* were all professors." With this pronouncement he paused. "It is my opinion," he continued, "that you occupy the second category."

Howe looked at the boy in surprise and said with good-natured irony, "With Kant, Hegel, and Nietzsche?"

Not only Tertan's hand and head but his whole awkward body waved away the stupidity. "It is the kind and not the quantity of the kind," he said sternly.

Rebuked, Howe said as simply and seriously as he could, "It would be nice to think so." He added, "Of course I am not a professor."

This was clearly a disappointment but Tertan met it. "In the French sense," he said with composure. "Generically, a teacher."

Suddenly he bowed. It was such a bow, Howe fancied, as a stage-director might teach an actor playing a medieval student who takes leave of Abelard†—stiff, solemn, with elbows close to the body and feet together. Then, quite as suddenly, he turned and left.

A queer fish, and as soon as Howe reached his office he sifted through the batch of themes and drew out Tertan's. The boy had filled many sheets with his unformed headlong scrawl. "Who am I?" he had begun. "Here, in a mundane, not to say commercialized academe, is asked the question which from time long immemorably out of mind has accreted doubts and thoughts in the psyche of man to pester him as a nuisance. Whether in St. Augustine (or Austin as sometimes called) or Miss Bashkirtsieff or Frederic Amiel or Empedocles,‡ or in less lights of the intellect than these, this posed question has been ineluctable."

Howe took out his pencil. He circled "academe" and wrote "vocab," in the margin. He underlined "time long immemorably out of mind" and wrote "Diction!" But this seemed inadequate for what was wrong. He put down his pencil and read ahead to discover the principle of error in the theme. "Today as ever, in spite of gloomy prophets of the dismal science (economics) the question is uninvalidated. Out of the starry depths of heaven hurtles this spear of query demanding to be caught on the shield of the mind ere it pierces the skull and the limbs be unstrung."

Baffled but quite caught, Howe read on. "Materialism, by which is meant the philosophic concept and not the moral idea, provides no aegis against the question which lies beyond the tangible (metaphysics). Existence without alloy is the question presented. Environment and heredity relegated aside, the rags and old clothes of practical life discarded, the name and the instrumen-

---

*Kant, Hegel, and Nietzsche: influential German philosophers and teachers.

†Abelard: Peter Abelard (1079–1142), French philosopher, theologian, and teacher. Abelard's romance with his student, the beautiful and learned Heloise, led to his being castrated and temporarily imprisoned. He later built a monastery called the Paraclete and gave it to Heloise, who became abbess of a sisterhood there.

‡St. Augustine, Miss Bashkirtsieff, Frederick Amiel, Ampedocles: St. Augustine (354–430), an early Christian church father and theologian: Maria Constantinowna Bashkirtsieff (1860–1884), a minor Russian writer; Frederic Amiel (1821–1881), Swiss poet, philosopher, and scholar; and Empedocles (495?–435 B.C.), Greek poet and philosopher who taught that the four indestructible elements were earth, water, air, and fire.

tality of livelihood do not, as the prophets of the dismal science insist on in this connection, give solution to the interrogation which not from the professor merely but veritably from the cosmos is given. I think, therefore I am (cogito etc.) but who am I? Tertan I am, but what is Tertan? Of this time, of that place, of some parentage, what does it matter?"

Existence without alloy: the phrase established itself. Howe put aside Tertan's paper and at random picked up another. "I am Arthur J. Casebeer Jr." he read. "My father is Arthur J. Casebeer and my grandfather was Arthur J. Casebeer before him. My mother is Nina Wimble Casebeer. Both of them are college graduates and my father is in insurance. I was born in St. Louis eighteen years ago and we still make our residence there."

Arthur J. Casebeer, who knew who he was, was less interesting than Tertan, but more coherent. Howe picked up Tertan's paper again. It was clear that none of the routine marginal comments, no "sent. str." or "punct." or "vocab." could cope with this torrential rhetoric. He read ahead, contenting himself with underscoring the errors against the time when he should have the necessary "conference" with Tertan.

It was a busy and official day of cards and sheets, arrangements and small decisions, and it gave Howe pleasure. Even when it was time to attend the first of the weekly Convocations he felt the charm of the beginning of things when intention is still innocent and uncorrupted by effort. He sat among the young instructors on the platform and joined in their humorous complaints at having to assist at the ceremony, but actually he got a clear satisfaction from the ritual of prayer and prosy speech and even from wearing his academic gown. And when the Convocation was over the pleasure continued as he crossed the campus, exchanging greetings with men he had not seen since the spring. They were people who did not yet, and perhaps never would, mean much to him, but in a year they had grown amiably to be part of his life. They were his fellow townsmen.

The day had cooled again at sunset and there was a bright chill in the September twilight. Howe carried his voluminous gown over his arm, he swung his doctoral hood by its purple neckpiece and on his head he wore his mortarboard with its heavy gold tassel bobbing just over his eye. These were the weighty and absurd symbols of his new profession and they pleased him. At twenty-six Joseph Howe had discovered that he was neither so well off nor so bohemian as he had once thought. A small income, adequate when supplemented by a sizable cash legacy, was genteel poverty when the cash was all spent. And the literary life—the room at the Lafayette or the small apartment without a lease, the long summers on the Cape, the long afternoons and the social evenings—began to weary him. His writing filled his mornings and should perhaps have filled his life, yet it did not. To the amusement of his friends and with a certain sense that he was betraying his own freedom, he had used the last of his legacy for a year at Harvard. The small but respectable reputation of his two volumes of verse had proved useful—he continued at Harvard on a fellowship and when he emerged as Dr. Howe he received an excellent appointment, with prospects, at Dwight.

He had his moments of fear when all that had ever been said of the dangers of the academic life had occurred to him. But after a year in which he had tested every possibility of corruption and seduction he was ready to rest easy.

His third volume of verse, most of it written in his first year of teaching, was not only ampler but, he thought, better than its predecessors.

There was a clear hour before the Bradby dinner-party and Howe looked forward to it. But he was not to enjoy it, for lying with his mail on the hall table was a copy of this quarter's issue of *Life and Letters,* to which his land-lord subscribed. Its severe cover announced that its editor, Frederic Woolley, had this month contributed an essay called "Two Poets," and Howe, picking it up, curious to see who the two poets might be, felt his own name start out at him with cabalistic power—Joseph Howe. As he continued to turn the pages his hand trembled.

Standing in the dark hall, holding the neat little magazine, Howe knew that his literary contempt for Frederic Woolley meant nothing, for he sud-denly understood how he respected Woolley in the way of the world. He knew this by the trembling of his hand. And of the little world as well as the great, for although the literary groups of New York might dismiss Woolley, his name carried high authority in the academic world. At Dwight it was even a revered name, for it had been here at the college that Frederic Woolley had made the distinguished scholarly career from which he had gone on to literary journalism. In middle life he had been induced to take the editorship of *Life and Letters,* a literary monthly not widely read but heavily endowed and in its pages he had carried on the defense of what he sometimes called the older values. He was not without wit, he had great knowledge and con-siderable taste and even in the full movement of the "new" literature he had won a certain respect for his refusal to accept it. In France, even in England, he would have been connected with a more robust tradition of conservatism, but America gave him an audience not much better than genteel. It was known in the college that to the subsidy of *Life and Letters* the Bradbys contributed a great part.

As Howe read, he saw that he was involved in nothing less than an event. When the Fifth Series of *Studies in Order and Value* came to be collected, this latest of Frederic Woolley's essays would not be merely another step in the old direction. Clearly and unmistakably, it was a turning point. All his literary life Woolley had been concerned with the relation of literature to morality, religion, and the private and delicate pieties, and he had been un-alterably opposed to all that he had called "inhuman humanitarianism." But here, suddenly, dramatically late, he had made an about-face, turning to the public life and to the humanitarian politics he had so long despised. This was the kind of incident the histories of literature make much of. Frederic Wool-ley was opening for himself a new career and winning a kind of new youth. He contrasted the two poets, Thomas Wormser who was admirable, Joseph Howe who was almost dangerous. He spoke of the "precious subjectivism" of Howe's verse. "In times like ours," he wrote, "with millions facing penury and want, one feels that the qualities of the *tour d'ivoire* are well-nigh inhu-man, nearly insulting. The *tour d'ivoire* becomes the *tour d'ivresse** and it is

---

*tour d'ivoire and *tour d'ivresse: tour d'ivoire* is an ivory tower, a place of mental withdrawal from reality and action, a symbol of escapism; *tour d'ivresse* is a tower of drunkenness or intoxi-cation.

not self-intoxicated poets that our people need." The essay said more: "The problem is one of meaning. I am not ignorant that the creed of the esoteric poets declares that a poem does not and should not *mean* anything, that it *is* something. But poetry is what the poet makes it, and if he is a true poet he makes what his society needs. And what is needed now is the tradition in which Mr. Wormser writes, the true tradition of poetry. The Howes do no harm, but they do no good when positive good is demanded of all responsible men. Or do the Howes indeed do no harm? Perhaps Plato would have said they do, that in some ways theirs is the Phrygian music that turns men's minds from the struggle. Certainly it is true that Thomas Wormser writes in the lucid Dorian* mode which sends men into battle with evil."

It was easy to understand why Woolley had chosen to praise Thomas Wormser. The long, lilting lines of *Corn Under Willows* hymned, as Woolley put it, the struggle for wheat in the Iowa fields and expressed the real lives of real people. But why out of the dozen more notable examples he had chosen Howe's little volume as the example of "precious subjectivism" was hard to guess. In a way it was funny, this multiplication of himself into "the Howes." And yet this becoming the multiform political symbol by whose creation Frederic Woolley gave the sign of a sudden new life, this use of him as a sacrifice whose blood was necessary for the rites of rejuvenation, made him feel oddly unclean.

Nor could Howe get rid of a certain practical resentment. As a poet he had a special and respectable place in the college life. But it might be another thing to be marked as the poet of a willful and selfish obscurity.

As he walked to the Bradby's Howe was a little tense and defensive. It seemed to him that all the world knew of the "attack" and agreed with it. And indeed the Bradbys had read the essay but Professor Bradby, a kind and pretentious man, said, "I see my old friend knocked you about a bit, my boy," and his wife Eugenia looked at Howe with her childlike blue eyes and said, "I shall *scold* Frederic for the untrue things he wrote about you. You aren't the least obscure." They beamed at him. In their genial snobbery they seemed to feel that he had distinguished himself. He was the leader of Howe-ism. He enjoyed the dinner-party as much as he had thought he would.

And in the following days, as he was more preoccupied with his duties, the incident was forgotten. His classes had ceased to be mere groups. Student after student detached himself from the mass and required or claimed a place in Howe's awareness. Of them all it was Tertan who first and most violently signaled his separate existence. A week after classes had begun Howe saw his silhouette on the frosted glass of his office door. It was motionless for a long time, perhaps stopped by the problem of whether or not to knock before entering. Howe called, "Come in!" and Tertan entered with his shambling stride.

He stood beside the desk, silent and at attention. When Howe asked him to sit down, he responded with a gesture of head and hand as if to say that such amenities were beside the point. Nevertheless he did take the chair. He put his ragged crammed briefcase between his legs. His face, which Howe

---

*Phrygian, Dorian: Phrygian is an ancient Greek mode in music characterized by its boldness and assertiveness; by contrast, Dorian is an ancient Greek mode in music characterized by its clarity and simplicity.

now observed fully for the first time, was confusing, for it was made up of florid curves, the nose arched in the bone and voluted in the nostril, the mouth loose and soft and rather moist. Yet the face was so thin and narrow as to seem the very type of asceticism. Lashes of unusual length veiled the eyes and, indeed, it seemed as if there were a veil over the whole countenance. Before the words actually came, the face screwed itself into an attitude of preparation for them.

"You can confer with me now?" Tertan said.

"Yes, I'd be glad to. There are several things in your two themes I want to talk to you about." Howe reached for the packet of themes on his desk and sought for Tertan's. But the boy was waving them away.

"These are done perforce," he said. "Under the pressure of your requirement. They are not significant, mere duties." Again his great hand flapped vaguely to dismiss his themes. He leaned forward and gazed at his teacher.

"You are," he said, "a man of letters? You are a poet?" It was more declaration than question.

"I should like to think so," Howe said.

At first Tertan accepted the answer with a show of appreciation, as though the understatement made a secret between himself and Howe. Then he chose to misunderstand. With his shrewd and disconcerting control of expression, he presented to Howe a puzzled grimace. "What does that mean?" he said.

Howe retracted the irony. "Yes. I am a poet." It sounded strange to say.

"That," Tertan said, "is a wonder." He corrected himself with his ducking head. "I mean that is wonderful."

Suddenly he dived at the miserable briefcase between his legs, put it on his knees and began to fumble with the catch, all intent on the difficulty it presented. Howe noted that his suit was worn thin, his shirt almost unclean. He became aware, even, of a vague and musty odor of garments worn too long in unaired rooms. Tertan conquered the lock and began to concentrate upon a search into the interior. At last he held in his hand what he was after, a torn and crumpled copy of *Life and Letters*.

"I learned it from here," he said, holding it out.

Howe looked at him sharply, his hackles a little up. But the boy's face was not only perfectly innocent, it even shone with a conscious admiration. Apparently nothing of the import of the essay had touched him except the wonderful fact that his teacher was a "man of letters." Yet this seemed too stupid and Howe, to test it, said, "The man who wrote that doesn't think it's wonderful."

Tertan made a moist hissing sound as he cleared his mouth of saliva. His head, oddly loose on his neck, wove a pattern of contempt in the air. "A critic," he said, "who admits *prima facie* that he does not understand." Then he said grandly, "It is the inevitable fate."

It was absurd, yet Howe was not only aware of the absurdity but of a tension suddenly and wonderfully relaxed. Now that the "attack" was on the table between himself and this strange boy and subject to the boy's funny and absolutely certain contempt, the hidden force of his feeling was revealed to him in the very moment that it vanished. All unsuspected, there had been a film over the world, a transparent but discoloring haze of danger. But he had no time to stop over the brightened aspect of things. Tertan was going on. "I also am a man of letters. Putative."

"You have written a good deal?" Howe meant to be no more than polite and he was surprised at the tenderness he heard in his words.

Solemnly the boy nodded, threw back the dank lock and sucked in a deep anticipatory breath. "First, a work of homiletics, which is a defense of the principles of religious optimism against the pessimism of Schopenhauer and the humanism of Nietzsche."

"Humanism? Why do you call it humanism?"

"It is my nomenclature for making a deity of man," Tertan replied negligently. "Then three fictional works, novels. And numerous essays in science, combating materialism. Is it your duty to read these if I bring them to you?"

Howe answered simply, "No, it isn't exactly my duty, but I shall be happy to read them."

Tertan stood up and remained silent. He rested his bag on the chair. With a certain compunction—for it did not seem entirely proper that, of two men of letters, one should have the right to blue-pencil the other, to grade him or to question the quality of his "sentence structure"—Howe reached for Tertan's papers. But before he could take them up, the boy suddenly made his bow-to-Abelard, the stiff inclination of the body with the hands seeming to emerge from the scholar's gown. Then he was gone.

But after his departure something was still left of him. The timbre of his curious sentences, the downright finality of so quaint a phrase as "It is the inevitable fate" still rang in the air. Howe gave the warmth of his feeling to the new visitor who stood at the door announcing himself with a genteel clearing of the throat.

"Dr. Howe, I believe?" the student said. A large hand advanced into the room and grasped Howe's hand. "Blackburn, sir, Theodore Blackburn, vice-president of the Student Council. A great pleasure, sir."

Out of a pair of ruddy cheeks a pair of small eyes twinkled good-naturedly. The large face, the large body were not so much fat as beefy and suggested something "typical," monk, politician, or innkeeper.

Blackburn took the seat beside Howe's desk. "I may have seemed to introduce myself in my public capacity, sir," he said. "But it is really as an individual that I came to see you. That is to say, as one of your students to be."

He spoke with an "English" intonation and he went on, "I was once an English major, sir."

For a moment Howe was startled, for the roast-beef look of the boy and the manner of his speech gave a second's credibility to one sense of his statement. Then the collegiate meaning of the phrase asserted itself, but some perversity made Howe say what was not really in good taste even with so forward a student, "Indeed? What regiment?"

Blackburn stared and then gave a little pouf-pouf of laughter. He waved the misapprehension away. "*Very* good, sir. It certainly is am ambiguous term." He chuckled in appreciation of Howe's joke, then cleared his throat to put it aside. "I look forward to taking your course in the romantic poets, sir," he said earnestly. "To me the romantic poets are the very crown of English literature."

Howe made a dry sound, and the boy, catching some meaning in it, said, "Little as I know them, of course. But even Shakespeare who is so dear to us of the Anglo-Saxon tradition is in a sense but the preparation for Shelley, Keats and Byron. And Wadsworth."

Almost sorry for him, Howe dropped his eyes. With some embarrassment, for the boy was not actually his student, he said softly, "Wordsworth."

"Sir?"

"Wordsworth, not Wadsworth. You said Wadsworth."

"Did I, sir?" Gravely he shook his head to rebuke himself for the error. "Wordsworth, of course—slip of the tongue." Then, quite in command again, he went on. "I have a favor to ask of you, Dr. Howe. You see, I began my college course as an English major,"—he smiled—"as I said."

"Yes?"

"But after my first year I shifted. I shifted to the social sciences. Sociology and government—I find them stimulating and very *real*." He paused, out of respect for reality. "But now I find that perhaps I have neglected the other side."

"The other side?" Howe said.

"Imagination, fancy, culture. A well-rounded man." He trailed off as if there were perfect understanding between them. "And so, sir, I have decided to end my senior year with your course in the romantic poets."

His voice was filled with an indulgence which Howe ignored as he said flatly and gravely, "But that course isn't given until the spring term."

"Yes, sir, and that is where the favor comes in. Would you let me take your romantic prose course? I can't take it for credit, sir, my program is full, but just for background it seems to me that I ought to take it. I do hope," he concluded in a manly way, "that you will consent."

"Well, it's no great favor, Mr. Blackburn. You can come if you wish, though there's not much point in it if you don't do the reading."

The bell rang for the hour and Howe got up.

"May I begin with this class, sir?" Blackburn's smile was candid and boyish.

Howe nodded carelessly and together, silently, they walked to the classroom down the hall. When they reached the door Howe stood back to let his student enter, but Blackburn moved adroitly behind him and grasped him by the arm to urge him over the threshold. They entered together with Blackburn's hand firmly on Howe's bicep, the student inducting the teacher into his own room. Howe felt a surge of temper rise in him and almost violently he disengaged his arm and walked to the desk, while Blackburn found a seat in the front row and smiled at him.

II

The question was, At whose door must the tragedy be laid?*

All night the snow had fallen heavily and only now was abating in sparse little flurries. The windows were valanced high with white. It was very quiet, something of the quiet of the world had reached the class and Howe found that everyone was glad to talk or listen. In the room there was a comfortable sense of pleasure in being human.

---

*the tragedy: the play discussed in Howe's class is *Ghosts* by the Norwegian dramatist Henrik Ibsen (1828–1906).

Casebeer believed that the blame for the tragedy rested with heredity. Picking up the book he read, "The sins of the fathers are visited on their children." This opinion was received with general favor. Nevertheless Johnson ventured to say that the fault was all Pastor Manders' because the Pastor had made Mrs. Alving go back to her husband and was always hiding the truth. To this Hibbard objected with logic enough, "Well then, it was really all her husband's fault. He *did* all the bad things." De Witt, his face bright with an impatient idea, said that the fault was all society's. "By society I don't mean upper-crust society," he said. He looked around a little defiantly, taking in any members of the class who might be members of upper-crust society. "Not in that sense. I mean the social unit."

Howe nodded and said, "Yes, of course."

"If the society of the time had progressed far enough in science," De Witt went on, "then there would be no problem for Mr. Ibsen to write about. Captain Alving plays around a little, gives way to perfectly natural biological urges, and he gets a social disease, a venereal disease. If the disease is cured, no problem. Invent salvarsan and the disease is cured. The problem of heredity disappears and li'l Oswald just doesn't get paresis. No paresis, no problem—no problem, no play."

This was carrying the ark into battle and the class looked at De Witt with respectful curiosity. It was his usual way and on the whole they were sympathetic with his struggle to prove to Howe that science was better than literature. Still, there was something in his reckless manner that alienated them a little.

"Or take birth control, for instance," De Witt went on. "If Mrs. Alving had had some knowledge of contraception, she wouldn't have had to have li'l Oswald at all. No li'l Oswald, no play."

The class was suddenly quieter. In the back row Stettenhover swung his great football shoulders in a righteous sulking gesture, first to the right, then to the left. He puckered his mouth ostentatiously. Intellect was always ending up by talking dirty.

Tertan's hand went up and Howe said, "Mr. Tertan." The boy shambled to his feet and began his long characteristic gulp. Howe made a motion with his fingers, as small as possible, and Tertan ducked his head and smiled in apology. He sat down. The class laughed. With more than half the term gone, Tertan had not been able to remember that one did not rise to speak. He seemed unable to carry on the life of the intellect without this mark of respect for it. To Howe the boy's habit of rising seemed to accord with the formal shabbiness of his dress. He never wore the casual sweaters and jackets of his classmates. Into the free and comfortable air of the college classroom he brought the stuffy sordid strictness of some crowded metropolitan high school.

"Speaking from one sense," Tertan began slowly, "there is no blame ascribable. From the sense of determinism, who can say where the blame lies? The preordained is the preordained and it cannot be said without rebellion against the universe, a palpable absurdity."

In the back row Stettenhover slumped suddenly in his seat, his heels held out before him, making a loud dry disgusted sound. His body sank until his neck rested on the back of his chair. He folded his hands across his belly and looked significantly out of the window, exasperated not only with Tertan but with Howe, with the class, with the whole system designed to encourage this kind of thing. There was a certain insolence in the movement and Howe flushed. As Tertan continued to speak, Howe walked casually toward the window and placed himself in the line of Stettenhover's vision. He stared at the great fellow, who pretended not to see him. There was so much power in the big body, so much contempt in the Greek-athlete face under the crisp Greek-athlete curls, that Howe felt almost physical fear. But at last Stettenhover admitted him to focus and under his disapproving gaze sat up with slow indifference. His eyebrows raised high in resignation, he begun to examine his hands. Howe relaxed and turned his attention back to Tertan.

"Flux of existence," Tertan was saying, "produces all things, so that judgment wavers. Beyond the phenomena, what? But phenomena are adumbrated and to them we are limited."

Howe saw it for a moment as perhaps it existed in the boy's mind—the world of shadows which are cast by a great light upon a hidden reality as in the old myth of the Cave. But the little brush with Stettenhover had tired him and he said irritably, "But come to the point, Mr. Tertan."

He said it so sharply that some of the class looked at him curiously. For three months he had gently carried Tertan through his verbosities, to the vaguely respectful surprise of the other students, who seemed to conceive that there existed between this strange classmate and their teacher some special understanding from which they were content to be excluded. Tertan looked at him mildly and at once came brilliantly to the point. "This is the summation of the play," he said and took up his book and read, " 'Your poor father never found any outlet for the overmastering joy of life that was in him. And I brought no holiday into his home, either. Everything seemed to turn upon duty and I am afraid I made your poor father's home unbearable to him, Oswald.' Spoken by Mrs. Alving."

Yes, that was surely the "summation" of the play and Tertan had hit it, as he hit, deviously and eventually, the literary point of almost everything. But now, as always, he was wrapping it away from sight. "For most mortals," he said, "there are only joys of biological urgings, gross and crass, such as the sensuous Captain Alving. For certain few there are the transmutations beyond these to a contemplation of the utter whole."

Oh, the boy was mad. And suddenly the word, used in hyperbole, intended almost for the expression of exasperated admiration, became literal. Now that the word was used, it became simply apparent to Howe that Tertan was mad.

It was a monstrous word and stood like a bestial thing in the room. Yet it so completely comprehended everything that had puzzled Howe, it so arranged and explained what for three months had been perplexing him that almost at once its horror became domesticated. With this word Howe was able to understand why he had never been able to communicate to Tertan the value of a single criticism or correction of his wild, verbose themes. Their conferences had been frequent and long but had done nothing to reduce to order the splendid confusion of the boy's ideas. Yet, impossible though its expression was, Tertan's incandescent mind could always strike for a moment into some dark corner of thought.

And now it was suddenly apparent that it was not a faulty rhetoric that Howe had to contend with. With his new knowledge he looked at Tertan's face and wondered how he could have so long deceived himself. Tertan was still talking and the class had lapsed into a kind of patient unconsciousness, a coma of respect for words which, for all that most of them knew, might be profound. Almost with a suffusion of shame, Howe believed that in some dim way the class had long ago had some intimation of Tertan's madness. He reached out as decisively as he could to seize the thread of Tertan's discourse before it should be entangled further.

"Mr. Tertan says that the blame must be put upon whoever kills the joy of living in another. We have been assuming that Captain Alving was a wholly bad man, but what if we assume that he became bad only because Mrs. Alving, when they were first married, acted toward him in the prudish way she says she did?"

It was a ticklish idea to advance to freshmen and perhaps not profitable. Not all of them were following.

"That would put the blame on Mrs. Alving herself, whom most of you admire. And she herself seems to think so." He glanced at his watch. The hour was nearly over. "What do you think, Mr. De Witt?"

De Witt rose to the idea, wanted to know if society couldn't be blamed for educating Mrs. Alving's temperament in the wrong way. Casebeer was puzzled, Stettenhover continued to look at his hands until the bell rang.

Tertan, his brows louring in thought, was making as always for a private word. Howe gathered his books and papers to leave quickly. At this moment of his discovery and with the knowledge still raw, he could not engage himself with Tertan. Tertan sucked in his breath to prepare for speech and Howe made ready for the pain and confusion. But at that moment Casebeer detached himself from the group with which he had been conferring and which he seemed to represent. His constituency remained at a tactful distance. The mission involved the time of an assigned essay. Casebeer's presentation of the plea—it was based on the freshmen's heavy duties at the fraternities during Carnival Week—cut across Tertan's preparations for speech. "And so some of us fellows thought," Casebeer concluded with heavy solemnity, "that we could do a better job, give our minds to it more, if we had more time."

Tertan regarded Casebeer with mingled curiosity and revulsion. Howe not only said that he would postpone the assignment but went on to talk about the Carnival and even drew the waiting constituency into the conversation. He was conscious of Tertan's stern and astonished stare, then of his sudden departure.

Now that the fact was clear, Howe knew that he must act on it. His course was simple enough. He must lay the case before the Dean. Yet he hesitated. His feeling for Tertan must now, certainly, be in some way invalidated. Yet could he, because of a word, hurry to assign to official and reasonable solicitude what had been, until this moment, so various and warm? He could at least delay and, by moving slowly, lend a poor grace to the necessary, ugly act of making his report.

It was with some notion of keeping the matter in his own hands that he went to the Dean's office to look up Tertan's records. In the outer office the Dean's secretary greeted him brightly and at his request brought him the manila folder with the small identifying photograph pasted in the corner. She laughed. "He was looking for the birdie in the wrong place," she said.

Howe leaned over her shoulder to look at the picture. It was as bad as all the Dean's-office photographs were, but it differed from all that Howe had ever seen. Tertan, instead of looking into the camera, as no doubt he had been bidden, had, at the moment of exposure, turned his eyes upward. His mouth, as though conscious of the trick played on the photographer, had the sly superior look that Howe knew.

The secretary was fascinated by the picture. "What a funny boy," she said. "He looks like Tartuffe!"*

And so he did, with the absurd piety of the eyes and the conscious slyness of the mouth and the whole face bloated by the bad lens.

"Is he *like* that?" the secretary said.

"Like Tartuffe? No."

From the photograph there was little enough comfort to be had. The records themselves gave no clue to madness, though they suggested sadness enough. Howe read of a father, Stanislaus Tertan, born in Budapest and trained in engineering in Berlin, once employed by the Hercules Chemical Corporation—this was one of the factories that dominated the south end of the town—but now without employment. He read of a mother Erminie (Youngfellow) Tertan, born in Manchester, educated at a Normal School at Leeds, now housewife by profession. The family lived on Greenbriar Street, which Howe knew as a row of once elegant homes near what was now the factory district. The old mansions had long ago been divided into small and primitive apartments. Of Ferdinand himself there was little to learn. He lived with his parents, had attended a Detroit high school and had transferred to the local school in his last year. His rating for intelligence, as expressed in numbers, was high, his scholastic record was remarkable, he held a college scholarship for his tuition.

Howe laid the folder on the secretary's desk. "Did you find what you wanted to know?" she asked.

The phrases from Tertan's momentous first theme came back to him. "Tertan I am, but what is Tertan? Of this time, of that place, of some parentage, what does it matter?"

"No, I didn't find it," he said.

Now that he had consulted the sad half-meaningless record he knew all the more firmly that he must not give the matter out of his own hands. He must not release Tertan to authority. Not that he anticipated from the Dean anything but the greatest kindness for Tertan. The Dean would have the experience and skill which he himself could not have. One way or another the Dean could answer the question, "What is Tertan?" Yet this was precisely what he feared. He alone could keep alive—not forever but for a somehow important time—the question, "What is Tertan?" He alone could keep it still a question. Some sure instinct told him that he must not surrender the question to a clean official desk in a clear official light to be dealt with, settled and closed.

He heard himself saying, "Is the Dean busy at the moment? I'd like to see him."

His request came thus unbidden, even forbidden, and it was one of the surprising and startling incidents of his life. Later, when he reviewed the events, so disconnected in themselves or so merely odd, of the story that

*Tartuffe: hypocritical central character in the comedy *Tartuffe or the Imposter,* by the French dramatist Molière (1622–1673).

unfolded for him that year, it was over this moment, on its face the least notable, that he paused longest. It was frequently to be with fear and never without a certainty of its meaning in his own knowledge of himself that he would recall this simple, routine request and the feeling of shame and freedom it gave him as he sent everything down the official chute. In the end, of course, no matter what he did to "protect" Tertan, he would have had to make the same request and lay the matter on the Dean's clean desk. But it would always be a landmark of his life that, at the very moment when he was rejecting the official way, he had been, without will or intention, so gladly drawn to it.

After the storm's last delicate flurry, the sun had come out. Reflected by the new snow, it filled the office with a golden light which was almost musical in the way it made all the commonplace objects of efficiency shine with a sudden sad and noble significance. And the light, now that he noticed it, made the utterance of his perverse and unwanted request even more momentous.

The secretary consulted the engagement pad. "He'll be free any minute. Don't you want to wait in the parlor?"

She threw open the door of the large and pleasant room in which the Dean held his Committee meetings and in which his visitors waited. It was designed with a homely elegance on the masculine side of the eighteenth-century manner. There was a small coal fire in the grate and the handsome mahogany table was strewn with books and magazines. The large windows gave on the snowy lawn and there was such a fine width of window that the white casements and walls seemed at this moment but a continuation of the snow, the snow but an extension of casement and walls. The outdoors seemed taken in and made safe, the indoors seemed luxuriously freshened and expanded.

Howe sat down by the fire and lighted a cigarette. The room had its intended effect upon him. He felt comfortable and relaxed, yet nicely organized, some young diplomatic agent of the eighteenth century, the newly fledged Swift carrying out Sir William Temple's business.* The rawness of Tertan's case quite vanished. He crossed his legs and reached for a magazine.

It was that famous issue of *Life and Letters* that his idle hand had found and his blood raced as he sifted through it and the shape of his own name, Joseph Howe, sprang out at him, still cabalistic in its power. He tossed the magazine back on the table as the door of the Dean's office opened and the Dean ushered out Theodore Blackburn.

"Ah, Joseph!" the Dean said.

Blackburn said, "Good morning, Doctor." Howe winced at the title and caught the flicker of amusement over the Dean's face. The Dean stood with his hand high on the doorjamb and Blackburn, still in the doorway, remained standing almost under his long arm.

Howe nodded briefly to Blackburn, snubbing his eager deference. "Can you give me a few minutes?" he said to the Dean.

"All the time you want. Come in." Before the two men could enter the

---

*Swift, Sir William Temple: Jonathan Swift (1667–1745), English satirist and author of *Gulliver's Travels*, served early in his career as secretary to Sir William Temple (1628–1699), a diplomat and writer.

office, Blackburn claimed their attention with a long full "Er." As they turned to him, Blackburn said, "Can *you* give *me* a few minutes, Dr. Howe?" His eyes sparkled at the little audacity he had committed, the slightly impudent play with hierarchy. Of the three of them Blackburn kept himself the lowest, but he reminded Howe of his subaltern relation to the Dean.

"I mean, of course," Blackburn went on easily, "when you've finished with the Dean."

"I'll be in my office shortly," Howe said, turned his back on the ready "Thank you, sir," and followed the Dean into the inner room.

"Energetic boy," said the Dean. "A bit beyond himself but very energetic. Sit down."

The Dean lighted a cigarette, leaned back in his chair, sat easy and silent for a moment, giving Howe no signal to go ahead with business. He was a young Dean, not much beyond forty, a tall handsome man with sad, ambitious eyes. He had been a Rhodes scholar. His friends looked for great things from him and it was generally said that he had notions of education which he was not yet ready to try to put into practice.

His relaxed silence was meant as a compliment to Howe. He smiled and said, "What's the business, Joseph?"

"Do you know Tertan—Ferdinand Tertan, a freshman?"

The Dean's cigarette was in his mouth and his hands were clasped behind his head. He did not seem to search his memory for the name. He said, "What about him?"

Clearly the Dean knew something and he was waiting for Howe to tell him more. Howe moved only tentatively. Now that he was doing what he resolved not to do, he felt more guilty at having been so long deceived by Tertan and more need to be loyal to his error.

"He's a strange fellow," he ventured. He said stubbornly, "In a strange way he's very brilliant." He concluded, "But very strange."

The springs of the Dean's swivel chair creaked as he came out of his sprawl and leaned forward to Howe. "Do you mean he's so strange that it's something you could give a name to?"

Howe looked at him stupidly. "What do you mean?" he said.

"What's his trouble?" the Dean said more neutrally.

"He's very brilliant, in a way. I looked him up and he has a top intelligence rating. But somehow, and it's hard to explain just how, what he says is always on the edge of sense and doesn't quite make it."

The Dean looked at him and Howe flushed up. The Dean had surely read Woolley on the subject of "the Howes" and the *tour d'ivresse*. Was that quick glance ironical?

The Dean picked up some papers from his desk and Howe could see that they were in Tertan's impatient scrawl. Perhaps the little gleam in the Dean's glance had come only from putting facts together.

"He sent me this yesterday," the Dean said. "After an interview I had with him. I haven't been able to do more than glance at it. When you said what you did, I realized there was something wrong."

Twisting his mouth, the Dean looked over the letter. "You seem to be involved," he said without looking up. "By the way, what did you give him at midterm?"

Flushing, setting his shoulders, Howe said firmly, "I gave him A-minus."

The Dean chuckled. "Might be a good idea if some of our boys went crazy—just a little." He said, "Well," to conclude the matter and handed the papers to Howe. "See if this is the same thing you've been finding. Then we can go into the matter again."

Before the fire in the parlor, in the chair that Howe had been occupying, sat Blackburn. He sprang to his feet as Howe entered.

"I said my office, Mr. Blackburn." Howe's voice was sharp. Then he was almost sorry for the rebuke, so clearly and naively did Blackburn seem to relish his stay in the parlor, close to authority.

"I'm in a bit of a hurry, sir," he said, "and I did want to be sure to speak to you, sir."

He was really absurd, yet fifteen years from now he would have grown up to himself, to the assurance and mature beefiness. In banks, in consular offices, in brokerage firms, on the bench, more seriously affable, a little sterner, he would make use of his ability to be administered by his job. It was almost reassuring. Now he was exercising his too-great skill on Howe. "I owe you an apology, sir," he said.

Howe knew that he did but he showed surprise.

"I mean, Doctor, after your having been so kind about letting me attend your class, I stopped coming." He smiled in deprecation. "Extra-curricular activities take up so much of my time. I'm afraid I undertook more than I could perform."

Howe had noticed the absence and had been a little irritated by it after Blackburn's elaborate plea. It was an absence that might be interpreted as a comment on the teacher. But there was only one way for him to answer. "You've no need to apologize," he said. "It's wholly your affair."

Blackburn beamed. "I'm so glad you feel that way about it, sir. I was worried you might think I had stayed away because I was influenced by—" He stopped and lowered his eyes.

Astonished, Howe said, "Influenced by what?"

"Well, by—" Blackburn hesitated and for answer pointed to the table on which lay the copy of *Life and Letters*. Without looking at it, he knew where to direct his hand. "By the unfavorable publicity, sir." He hurried on. "And that brings me to another point, sir. I am secretary of Quill and Scroll, sir, the student literary society, and I wonder if you would address us. You could read your own poetry, sir, and defend your own point of view. It would be very interesting."

It was truly amazing. Howe looked long and cruelly into Blackburn's face, trying to catch the secret of the mind that could have conceived this way of manipulating him, this way so daring and inept—but not entirely inept—with its malice so without malignity. The face did not yield its secret. Howe smiled broadly and said, "Of course I don't think you were influenced by the unfavorable publicity."

"I'm still going to take—regularly, for credit—your romantic poets course next term," Blackburn said.

"Don't worry, my dear fellow, don't worry about it."

Howe started to leave and Blackburn stopped him with, "But about Quill, sir?"

"Suppose we wait until next term? I'll be less busy then."

And Blackburn said, "Very good, sir, and thank you."

In his office the little encounter seemed less funny to Howe, was even in some indeterminate way disturbing. He made an effort to put it from his mind by turning to what was sure to disturb him more, the Tertan letter read in the new interpretation. He found what he had always found, the same florid leaps beyond fact and meaning, the same headlong certainty. But as his eye passed over the familiar scrawl it caught his own name and for the second time that hour he felt the race of his blood.

"The Paraclete," Tertan had written to the Dean, "from a Greek word meaning to stand in place of, but going beyond the primitive idea to mean traditionally the helper, the one who comforts and assists, cannot without fundamental loss be jettisoned. Even if taken no longer in the supernatural case, the concept remains deeply in the human consciousness inevitably. Humanitarianism is no reply, for not every man stands in the place of every other man for this other's comrade comfort. But certain are chosen out of the human race to be the consoler of some other. Of these, for example, is Joseph Barker Howe, Ph.D. Of intellects not the first yet of true intellect and lambent instructions, given to that which is intuitive and irrational, not to what is logical in the strict word, what is judged by him is of the heart and not the head. Here is one chosen, in that he chooses himself to stand in the place of another for comfort and consolation. To him more than another I give my gratitude, with all respect to our Dean who reads this, a noble man, but merely dedicated, not consecrated. But not in the aspect of the Paraclete only is Dr. Joseph Barker Howe established, for he must be the Paraclete to another aspect of himself, that which is driven and persecuted by the lack of understanding in the world at large, so that he in himself embodies the full history of man's tribulations and, overflowing upon others, notably the present writer, is the ultimate end."

This was love. There was no escape from it. Try as Howe might to remember that Tertan was mad and all his emotions invalidated, he could not destroy the effect upon him of his student's stern, affectionate regard. He had betrayed not only a power of mind but a power of love. And however firmly he held before his attention the fact of Tertan's madness, he could do nothing to banish the physical sensation of gratitude he felt. He had never thought of himself as "driven and persecuted" and he did not now. But still he could not make meaningless his sensation of gratitude. The pitiable Tertan sternly pitied him, and comfort came from Tertan's never-to-be comforted mind.

III

In an academic community, even an efficient one, official matters move slowly. The term drew to a close with no action in the case of Tertan, and Joseph Howe had to confront a curious problem. How should he grade his strange student, Tertan?

Tertan's final examination had been no different from all his other writing, and what did one "give" such a student? De Witt must have his A, that was clear. Johnson would get a B. With Casebeer it was a question of a B-minus or a C-plus, and Stettenhover, who had been crammed by the team tutor to fill half a blue-book with his thin feminine scrawl, would have his C-minus which he would accept with mingled indifference and resentment. But with Tertan it was not so easy.

The boy was still in the college process and his name could not be omitted from the grade sheet. Yet what should a mind under suspicion of madness be graded? Until the medical verdict was given, it was for Howe to continue as Tertan's teacher and to keep his judgment pedagogical. Impossible to give him an F: he had not failed. B was for Johnson's stolid mediocrity. He could not be put on the edge of passing with Stettenhover, for he exactly did not pass. In energy and richness of intellect he was perhaps even De Witt's superior, and Howe toyed grimly with the notion of giving him an A, but that would lower the value of the A De Witt had won with his beautiful and clear, if still arrogant, mind. There was a notation which the Registrar recognized—Inc. for Incomplete and in the horrible comedy of the situation, Howe considered that. But really only a mark of M for Mad would serve.

In his perplexity, Howe sought the Dean, but the Dean was out of town. In the end, he decided to maintain the A-minus he had given Tertan at mid-term. After all, there had been no falling away from that quality. He entered it on the grade sheet with something like bravado.

Academic time moves quickly. A college year is not really a year, lacking as it does three months. And it is endlessly divided into units which, at their beginning, appear larger than they are—terms, half-terms, months, weeks. And the ultimate unit, the hour, is not really an hour, lacking as it does ten minutes. And so the new term advanced rapidly and one day the fields about the town were all brown, cleared of even the few thin patches of snow which had lingered so long.

Howe, as he lectured on the romantic poets, became conscious of Black-burn emanating wrath. Blackburn did it well, did it with enormous dignity. He did not stir in his seat, he kept his eyes fixed on Howe in perfect attention, but he abstained from using his notebook, there was no mistaking what he proposed to himself as an attitude. His elbow on the writing-wing of the chair, his chin on the curled fingers of his hand, he was the embodiment of intellectual indignation. He was thinking his own thoughts, would give no public offense, yet would claim his due, was not to be intimidated. Howe knew that he would present himself at the end of the hour.

Blackburn entered the office without invitation. He did not smile, there was no cajolery about him. Without invitation he sat down beside Howe's desk. He did not speak until he had taken the blue-book from his pocket. He said, "What does this mean, sir?"

It was a sound and conservative student tactic. Said in the usual way it meant, "How could you have so misunderstood me?" or "What does this mean for my future in the course?" But there were none of the humbler tones in Blackburn's way of saying it.

Howe made the established reply, "I think that's for you to tell me."

Blackburn continued icy. "I'm sure I can't, sir."

There was a silence between them. Both dropped their eyes to the blue-book on the desk. On its cover Howe had penciled: "F. This is very poor work."

Howe picked up the blue-book. There was always the possibility of injustice. The teacher may be bored by the mass of papers and not wholly attentive. A phrase, even the student's handwriting, may irritate him unreasonably. "Well," said Howe, "let's go through it."

He opened the first page. "Now here: you write, 'In *The Ancient Mariner*, Coleridge lives in and transports us to a honey-sweet world where all is rich and strange, a world of charm to which we can escape from the humdrum existence of our daily lives, the world of romance. Here, in this warm and honey-sweet land of charming dreams we can relax and enjoy ourselves.' "

Howe lowered the paper and waited with a neutral look for Blackburn to speak. Blackburn returned the look boldly, did not speak, sat stolid and lofty. At last Howe said, speaking gently, "Did you mean that, or were you just at a loss for something to say?"

"You imply that I was just 'bluffing'?" The quotation marks hung palpable in the air about the word.

"I'd like to know. I'd prefer believing that you were bluffing to believing that you really thought this."

Blackburn's eyebrows went up. From the height of a great and firm-based idea he looked at his teacher. He clasped the crags for a moment and then pounced, craftily, suavely. "Do you mean, Dr. Howe, that there aren't two opinions possible?"

It was superbly done in its air of putting all of Howe's intellectual life into the balance. Howe remained patient and simple. "Yes, many opinions are possible, but not this one. Whatever anyone believes of *The Ancient Mariner*, no one can in reason believe that it represents a—a honey-sweet world in which we can relax."

"But that is what I *feel*, sir."

This was well done too. Howe said, "Look, Mr. Blackburn. Do you really relax with hunger and thirst, the heat and the sea-serpents, the dead men with staring eyes, Life in Death and the skeletons? Come now, Mr. Blackburn."

Blackburn made no answer and Howe pressed forward. "Now you say of Wordsworth, 'Of peasant stock himself, he turned from the effete life of the salons and found in the peasant the hope of a flaming revolution which would sweep away all the old ideas. This is the subject of his best poems.' "

Beaming at his teacher with youthful eagerness, Blackburn said, "Yes, sir, a rebel, a bringer of light to suffering mankind. I see him as a kind of Prothemeus."

"A kind of what?"

"Prothemeus, sir."

"Think, Mr. Blackburn. We were talking about him only today and I mentioned his name a dozen times. You don't mean Prothemeus. You mean—" Howe waited but there was no response.

"You mean Prometheus."

Blackburn gave no assent and Howe took the reins. "You've done a bad job here, Mr. Blackburn, about as bad as could be done." He saw Blackburn stiffen and his genial face harden again. "It shows either a lack of preparation or a complete lack of understanding." He saw Blackburn's face begin to go to pieces and he stopped.

"Oh, sir," Blackburn burst out, "I've never had a mark like this before, never anything below a B, never. A thing like this has never happened to me before."

It must be true, it was a statement too easily verified. Could it be that other instructors accepted such flaunting nonsense? Howe wanted to end the interview. "I'll set it down to lack of preparation." he said. "I know you're busy. That's not an excuse but it's an explanation. Now suppose you really prepare and then take another quiz in two weeks. We'll forget this one and count the other."

Blackburn squirmed with pleasure and gratitude. "Thank you, sir. You're really very kind, very kind."

Howe rose to conclude the visit. "All right then—in two weeks."

It was that day that the Dean imparted to Howe the conclusion of the case of Tertan. It was simple and a little anticlimactic. A physician had been called in, and had said the word, given the name.

"A classic case, he called it," the Dean said. "Not a doubt in the world," he said. His eyes were full of miserable pity and he clutched at a word. "A classic case, a classic case." To his aid and to Howe's there came the Parthenon* and the form of the Greek drama, the Aristotelian logic,† Racine‡ and the Well-Tempered Clavichord,§ the blueness of the Aegean# and its clear sky. Classic—that is to say, without a doubt, perfect in its way, a veritable model, and, as the Dean had been told, sure to take a perfectly predictable and inevitable course to a foreknown conclusion.

It was not only pity that stood in the Dean's eyes. For a moment there was fear too. "Terrible," he said, "it is simply terrible."

Then he went on briskly. "Naturally we've told the boy nothing. And naturally we won't. His tuition's paid by his scholarship and we'll continue him on the rolls until the end of the year. That will be kindest. After that the matter will be out of our control. We'll see, of course, that he gets into the proper hands. I'm told there will be no change, he'll go on like this, be as good as this, for four to six months. And so we'll just go along as usual."

So Tertan continued to sit in Section 5 of English 1A, to his classmates still a figure of curiously dignified fun, symbol to most of them of the respectable but absurd intellectual life. But to his teacher he was now very different. He had not changed—he was still the greyhound casting for the scent of ideas and Howe could see that he was still the same Tertan, but he could not feel it. What he felt as he looked at the boy sitting in his accustomed place was the hard blank of a fact. The fact itself was formidable and depressing. But what Howe was chiefly aware of was that he had permitted the metamorphosis of Tertan from person to fact.

As much as possible he avoided seeing Tertan's upraised hand and eager eye. But the fact did not know of its mere factuality, it continued its existence

*Parthenon: most famous Greek temple, built 447–438 B.C. on the Acropolis in Athens and often considered the height of classical achievement.
†Aristotelian logic: the formal system of deductive reasoning developed and taught by the classical Greek philosopher Aristotle (384–322 B.C.).
‡Racine: Jean Racine (1639–1699), French neoclassical poet and dramatist whose tragedies are noted for their dignity, elegance, and control.
§the Well-Tempered Clavichord: forty-eight sets of preludes and fugues in all keys by the neoclassical English composer Johann Sebastian Bach (1685–1750).
#Aegean: the Aegean Sea, an arm of the Mediterranean Sea that borders Greece and that was important to the development of classical Greek civilization.

as if it were Tertan, hand up and eye questioning, and one day it appeared in Howe's office with a document.

"Even the spirit who lives egregiously, above the herd, must have its relations with the fellowman," Tertan declared. He laid the document on Howe's desk. It was headed "Quill and Scroll Society of Dwight College. Application for Membership."

"In most ways these are crass minds," Tertan said, touching the paper. "Yet as a whole, bound together in their common love of letters, they transcend their intellectual lacks, since it is not a paradox that the whole is greater than the sum of its parts."

"When are the elections?" Howe asked.

"They take place tomorrow."

"I certainly hope you will be successful."

"Thank you. Would you wish to implement that hope?" A rather dirty finger pointed to the bottom of the sheet. "A faculty recommender is necessary," Tertan said stiffly, and waited.

"And you wish me to recommend you?"

"It would be an honor."

"You may use my name."

Tertan's finger pointed again. "It must be a written sponsorship, signed by the sponsor." There was a large blank space on the form under the heading, "Opinion of Faculty Sponsor."

This was almost another thing and Howe hesitated. Yet there was nothing else to do and he took out his fountain pen. He wrote, "Mr. Ferdinand Tertan is marked by his intense devotion to letters and by his exceptional love of all things of the mind." To this he signed his name which looked bold and assertive on the white page. It disturbed him, the strange affirming power of a name. With a businesslike air, Tertan whipped up the paper, folded it with decision and put it into his pocket. He bowed and took his departure, leaving Howe with the sense of having done something oddly momentous.

And so much now seemed odd and momentous to Howe that should not have seemed so. It was odd and momentous, he felt, when he sat with Blackburn's second quiz before him and wrote in an excessively firm hand the grade of C-minus. The paper was a clear, an indisputable failure. He was carefully and consciously committing a cowardice. Blackburn had told the truth when he had pleaded his past record. Howe had consulted it in the Dean's office. It showed no grade lower than a B-minus. A canvass of some of Blackburn's previous instructors had brought vague attestations to the adequate powers of a student imperfectly remembered and sometimes surprise that his abilities could be questioned at all.

As he wrote the grade, Howe told himself that this cowardice sprang from an unwillingness to have more dealings with a student he disliked. He knew it was simpler than that. He knew he feared Blackburn: that was the absurd truth. And cowardice did not solve the matter after all. Blackburn, flushed with a first success, attacked at once. The minimal passing grade had not assuaged his feelings and he sat at Howe's desk and again the blue-book lay between them. Blackburn said nothing. With an enormous impudence, he was waiting for Howe to speak and explain himself.

At last Howe said sharply and rudely, "Well?" His throat was tense and the blood was hammering in his head. His mouth was tight with anger at himself for his disturbance.

Blackburn's glance was almost baleful. "This is impossible, sir."

"But there it is," Howe answered.

"Sir?" Blackburn had not caught the meaning but his tone was still haughty.

Impatiently Howe said, "There it is, plain as day. Are you here to complain again?"

"Indeed I am, sir." There was surprise in Blackburn's voice that Howe should ask the question.

"I shouldn't complain if I were you. You did a thoroughly bad job on your first quiz. This one is a little, only a very little, better." This was not true. If anything, it was worse.

"That might be a matter of opinion, sir."

"It is a matter of opinion. Of my opinion."

"Another opinion might be different, sir."

"You really believe that?" Howe said.

"Yes." The omission of the "sir" was monumental.

"Whose, for example?"

"The Dean's, for example." Then the fleshy jaw came forward a little. "Or a certain literary critic's, for example."

It was colossal and almost too much for Blackburn himself to handle. The solidity of his face almost crumpled under it. But he withstood his own audacity and went on. "And the Dean's opinion might be guided by the knowledge that the person who gave me this mark is the man whom a famous critic, the most eminent judge of literature in this country, called a drunken man. The Dean might think twice about whether such a man is fit to teach Dwight students."

Howe said in quiet admonition, "Blackburn, you're mad," meaning no more than to check the boy's extravagance.

But Blackburn paid no heed. He had another shot in the locker. "And the Dean might be guided by the information, of which I have evidence, documentary evidence,"—he slapped his breast pocket twice—"that this same person personally recommended to the college literary society, the oldest in the country, that he personally recommended a student who is crazy, who threw the meeting into an uproar, a psychiatric case. The Dean might take that into account."

Howe was never to learn the details of that "uproar." He had always to content himself with the dim but passionate picture which at that moment sprang into his mind, of Tertan standing on some abstract height and madly denouncing the multitude of Quill and Scroll who howled him down.

He sat quiet a moment and looked at Blackburn. The ferocity had entirely gone from the student's face. He sat regarding his teacher almost benevolently. He had played a good card and now, scarcely at all unfriendly, he was waiting to see the effect. Howe took up the blue-book and negligently sifted through it. He read a page, closed the book, struck out the C-minus and wrote an F.

"Now you may take the paper to the Dean," he said. "You may tell him that after reconsidering it, I lowered the grade."

The gasp was audible. "Oh sir!" Blackburn cried. "Please!" His face was agonized. "It means my graduation, my livelihood, my future. Don't do this to me."

"It's done already."

Blackburn stood up. "I spoke rashly, sir, hastily. I had no intention, no real intention, of seeing the Dean. It rests with you—entirely, entirely. I *hope* you will restore the first mark."

"Take the matter to the Dean or not, just as you choose. The grade is what you deserve and it stands."

Blackburn's head dropped. "And will I be failed at midterm, sir?"

"Of course."

From deep out of Blackburn's great chest rose a cry of anguish. "Oh sir, if you want me to go down on my knees to you, I will, I will."

Howe looked at him in amazement.

"I will, I will. On my knees, sir. This mustn't, mustn't happen."

He spoke so literally, meaning so very truly that his knees and exactly his knees were involved and seeming to think that he was offering something of tangible value to his teacher, that Howe, whose head had become icy clear in the nonsensical drama, thought, "The boy is mad," and began to speculate fantastically whether something in himself attracted or developed aberration. He could see himself standing absurdly before the Dean and saying, "I've found another. This time it's the vice-president of the Council, the manager of the debating team, and secretary of Quill and Scroll."

One more such discovery, he thought, and he himself would be discovered! And there, suddenly, Blackburn was on his knees with a thump, his huge thighs straining his trousers, his hands outstretched in a great gesture of supplication.

With a cry, Howe shoved back his swivel chair and it rolled away on its casters half across the little room. Blackburn knelt for a moment to nothing at all, then got to his feet.

Howe rose abruptly. He said, "Blackburn, you will stop acting like an idiot. Dust your knees off, take your paper and get out. You've behaved like a fool and a malicious person. You have half a term to do a decent job. Keep your silly mouth shut and try to do it. Now get out."

Blackburn's head was low. He raised it and there was a pious light in his eyes. "Will you shake hands, sir?" he said. He thrust out his hand.

"I will not," Howe said.

Head and hand sank together. Blackburn picked up his blue-book and walked to the door. He turned and said, "Thank you, sir." His back, as he departed, was heavy with tragedy and stateliness.

IV

After years of bad luck with the weather, the College had a perfect day for Commencement. It was wonderfully bright, the air so transparent, the wind so brisk that no one could resist talking about it.

As Howe set out for the campus he heard Hilda calling from the back yard. She called, "Professor, professor," and came running to him.

Howe said, "What's this 'professor' business?"

"Mother told me," Hilda said. "You've been promoted. And I want to take your picture."

"Next year," said Howe. "I won't be a professor until next year. And you know better than to call anybody 'professor.' "

"It was just in fun," Hilda said. She seemed disappointed.

"But you can take my picture if you want. I won't look much different next year." Still, it was frightening. It might mean that he was to stay in this town all his life.

Hilda brightened. "Can I take it in this?" she said, and touched the gown he carried over his arm.

Howe laughed. "Yes, you can take it in this."

"I'll get my things and meet you in front of Otis," Hilda said. "I have the background all picked out."

On the campus the Commencement crowd was already large. It stood about in eager, nervous little family groups. As he crossed, Howe was greeted by a student, capped and gowned, glad of the chance to make an event for his parents by introducing one of his teachers. It was while Howe stood there chatting that he saw Tertan.

He had never seen anyone quite so alone, as though a circle had been woven about him to separate him from the gay crowd on the campus. Not that Tertan was not gay, he was the gayest of all. Three weeks had passed since Howe had last seen him, the weeks of examination, the lazy week before Commencement, and this was now a different Tertan. On his head he wore a panama hat, broadbrimmed and fine, of the shape associated with South American planters. He wore a suit of raw silk, luxurious but yellowed with age and much too tight, and he sported a whangee cane. He walked sedately, the hat tilted at a devastating angle, the stick coming up and down in time to his measured tread. He had, Howe guessed, outfitted himself to greet the day in the clothes of that ruined father whose existence was on record in the Dean's office. Gravely and arrogantly he surveyed the scene—in it, his whole bearing seemed to say, but not of it. With his haughty step, with his flashing eye, Tertan was coming nearer. Howe did not wish to be seen. He shifted his position slightly. When he looked again, Tertan was not in sight.

The chapel clock struck the quarter hour. Howe detached himself from his chat and hurried to Otis Hall at the far end of the campus. Hilda had not yet come. He went up into the high portico and, using the glass of the door for a mirror, put on his gown, adjusted the hood on his shoulders and set the mortarboard on his head. When he came down the steps Hilda had arrived.

Nothing could have told him more forcibly that a year had passed than the development of Hilda's photographic possessions from the box camera of the previous fall. By a strap about her neck was hung a leather case, so thick and strong, so carefully stitched and so molded to its contents that it could only hold a costly camera. The appearance was deceptive, Howe knew, for he had been present at the Aikens' pre-Christmas conference about its purchase. It was only a fairly good domestic camera. Still, it looked very impressive. Hilda carried another leather case from which she drew a collapsible tripod. Decisively she extended each of its gleaming legs and set it up on the path. She removed the camera from its case and fixed it to the tripod. In its compact efficiency the camera almost had a life of its own, but Hilda treated it with easy familiarity, looked into its eye, glanced casually at its gauges. Then from a pocket she took still another leather case and drew from it a small instrument through which she looked first at Howe, who began to feel inanimate and lost, and then at the sky. She made some adjustment on the instrument, then some adjustment on the camera. She swept the scene with her eye, found a spot and pointed the camera in its direction. She walked to the spot, stood on it and beckoned to Howe. With each new leather case, with each new instrument and with each new adjustment she had grown in ease and now she said, "Joe, will you stand here?"

Obediently Howe stood where he was bidden. She had yet another instrument. She took out a tape-measure on a mechanical spool. Kneeling down before Howe, she put the little metal ring of the tape under the tip of his shoe. At her request, Howe pressed it with his toe. When she had measured her distance, she nodded to Howe who released the tape. At a touch, it sprang back into the spool. "You have to be careful if you're going to get what you want," Hilda said. "I don't believe in all this snap-snap-snapping," she remarked loftily. Howe nodded in agreement, although he was beginning to think Hilda's care excessive.

Now at last the moment had come. Hilda squinted into the camera, moved the tripod slightly. She stood to the side, holding the plunger of the shutter-cable. "Ready," she said. "Will you relax, Joseph, please?" Howe realized that he was standing frozen. Hilda stood poised and precise as a setter, one hand holding the little cable, the other extended with curled dainty fingers like a dancer's as if expressing to her subject the precarious delicacy of the moment. She pressed the plunger and there was the click. At once she stirred to action, got behind the camera, turned a new exposure. "Thank you," she said. "Would you stand under that tree and let me do a character study with light and shade?"

The childish absurdity of the remark restored Howe's ease. He went to the little tree. The pattern the leaves made on his gown was what Hilda was after. He had just taken a satisfactory position when he heard in the unmistakable voice, "Ah, Doctor! Having your picture taken?"

Howe gave up the pose and turned to Blackburn who stood on the walk, his hands behind his back, a little too large for his bachelor's gown. Annoyed that Blackburn should see him posing for a character study in light and shade, Howe said irritably, "Yes, having my picture taken."

Blackburn beamed at Hilda. "And the little photographer," he said. Hilda fixed her eyes on the ground and stood closer to her brilliant and aggressive camera. Blackburn, teetering on his heels, his hands behind his back, wholly prelatical and benignly patient, was not abashed at the silence. At last Howe said, "If you'll excuse us, Mr. Blackburn, we'll go on with the picture."

"Go right ahead, sir. I'm running along." But he only came closer. "Dr. Howe," he said fervently, "I want to tell you how glad I am that I was able to satisfy your standards at last."

Howe was surprised at the hard insulting brightness of his own voice and even Hilda looked up curiously as he said, "Nothing you have ever done has satisfied me and nothing you could ever do would satisfy me, Blackburn."

With a glance at Hilda, Blackburn made a gesture as if to hush Howe—as though all his former bold malice had taken for granted a kind of understanding between himself and his teacher, a secret which must not be betrayed to a third person. "I only meant, sir," he said, "that I was able to pass your course after all."

Howe said, "You didn't pass my course. I passed you out of my course. I passed you without even reading your paper. I wanted to be sure the college would be rid of you. And when all the grades were in and I did read your paper, I saw I was right not to have read it first."

Blackburn presented a stricken face. "It was very bad, sir?"

But Howe had turned away. The paper had been fantastic. The paper had been, if he wished to see it so, mad. It was at this moment that the Dean came up behind Howe and caught him arm. "Hello, Joseph," he said. "We'd better be getting along, it's almost late."

He was not a familiar man, but when he saw Blackburn, who approached to greet him, he took Blackburn's arm, too. "Hello, Theodore," he said. Leaning forward on Howe's arm and on Blackburn's, he said, "Hello, Hilda dear." Hilda replied quietly, "Hello, Uncle George."

Still clinging to their arms, still linking Howe and Blackburn, the Dean said, "Another year gone, Joe, and we've turned out another crop. After you've been here a few years, you'll find it reasonably upsetting—you wonder how there can be so many graduating classes while you stay the same. But of course you don't stay the same." Then he said, "Well," sharply, to dismiss the thought. He pulled Blackburn's arm and swung him around to Howe. "Have you heard about Teddy Blackburn?" he asked. "He has a job already, before graduation, the first man of his class to be placed." Expectant of congratulations, Blackburn beamed at Howe. Howe remained silent.

"Isn't that good?" the Dean said. Still Howe did not answer and the Dean, puzzled and put out, turned to Hilda. "That's a very fine-looking camera, Hilda." She touched it with affectionate pride.

"Instruments of precision," said a voice. "Instruments of precision." Of the three with joined arms, Howe was the nearest to Tertan, whose gaze took in all the scene except the smile and the nod which Howe gave him. The boy leaned on his cane. The broad-brimmed hat, canting jauntily over his eye, confused the image of his face that Howe had established, suppressed the rigid lines of the ascetic and brought out the baroque curves. It made an effect of perverse majesty.

"Instruments of precision," said Tertan for the last time, addressing no one, making a casual comment to the universe. And it occurred to Howe that Tertan might not be referring to Hilda's equipment. The sense of the thrice-woven circle of the boy's loneliness smote him fiercely. Tertan stood in majestic jauntiness, superior to all the scene, but his isolation made Howe ache with a pity of which Tertan was more the cause than the object, so general and indiscriminate was it.

Whether in his sorrow he made some unintended movement toward Tertan which the Dean checked or whether the suddenly tightened grip on his arm was the Dean's own sorrow and fear, he did not know. Tertan watched them in the incurious way people watch a photograph being taken and suddenly the thought that, to the boy, it must seem that the three were posing for a picture together made Howe detach himself almost rudely from the Dean's grasp.

"I promised Hilda another picture," he announced—needlessly, for Tertan was no longer there, he had vanished in the last sudden flux of visitors who, now that the band had struck up, were rushing nervously to find seats.

"You'd better hurry," the Dean said. "I'll go along, it's getting late for me." He departed and Blackburn walked stately by his side.

Howe again took his position under the little tree which cast its shadow over his face and gown. "Just hurry, Hilda, won't you?" he said. Hilda held the cable at arm's length, her other arm crooked and her fingers crisped. She rose on her toes and said "Ready," and pressed the release. "Thank you," she said gravely and began to dismantle her camera as he hurried off to join the procession.

Suggestions for Discussion

1. How does each section contribute to the developing action? Trace Howe's relationship to Tertan through rising action, climax, recognition, and resolution. By what other means is Howe's character unfolded? Analyze the changes in it. Why is it easier for Howe to come to terms with Blackburn than with Tertan? Since Howe's recognition takes place in the second section, how is tension maintained until the end?

2. Show how the point of view permits the action to encompass both past and present. Is the action always rendered dramatically, or is there some authorial intervention? Specify. Can you account for the curious shift in point of view in the second section, which interrupts the continuity of the climactic scene and describes the self-knowledge that Howe later acquires?

3. How are setting and the two camera scenes related to action, tone, and theme? What is the function of Hilda and her cameras? Why is the discussion of *Ghosts* especially relevant to theme and tone?

4. How does the use of irony contribute to theme and tone? Consider especially the following instances: Tertan's madness and Blackburn's "sanity"; Woolley's review; Howe as Paraclete; the first theme assignment; Tertan's remark, "instruments of precision."

5. Discuss Howe's relationship to Blackburn, Stettenhover, and the Dean as each advances the action and our understanding of Howe.

6. Trilling states that he conceived of Tertan as in some sense heroic. Does Tertan achieve tragic stature? Is it Tertan's story or Howe's? Is Howe a tragic character?

7. In Trilling's commentary upon the story, he acknowledged that many readers felt that he had not clarified the matter of Tertan's insanity. Do you think he has?

Suggestions for Writing

1. Attempt a "character study in light and shade" of one of your teachers and/or one of your peers.

2. What was Tertan's view of himself? What did he mean by "existence without alloy"?

3. Trace the development of Howe's sense of self?

Poetry

T. S. Eliot
The Love Song of J. Alfred Prufrock

Thomas Stearns Eliot (1888–1965) was born in St. Louis, was educated at Harvard University, and studied in Paris and Oxford. He settled in England in 1914 and became a British subject in 1927. His most influential poem, *The Waste Land,* was published in 1922, followed by *The Hollow Men* (1925), *Poems: 1909–1925* (1925), and *Poems: 1909–1935* (1936). His criticism includes *The Use of Poetry and the Use of Criticism* (1933), *Essays Ancient and Modern* (1936), *Notes Toward the Definition of Culture* (1948), and *To Criticize the Critic* (1965). His best-known poetic dramas are *Murder in the Cathedral* (1935), *The Family Reunion* (1939), and *The Cocktail Party* (1950). Prufrock's opposed selves in this dramatic monologue are separated from each other, the one exploring the idea of human involvement and the other observing it in comfortable isolation.

> *S'io credesse che mia risposta fosse*
> *A persona che mai tornasse al mondo,*
> *Questa fiamma staria senza piu scosse.*
> *Ma perciocche giammai di questo fondo*
> *Non torno vivo alcun, s'i'odo il vero,*
> *Senza tema d'infamia ti rispondo.*

> ["If I believed that my answer would be to one who
> would ever return to the world, this flame would
> shake no more; but since no one ever returns alive
> from this depth, if what I hear is true, I answer you
> without fear of infamy."—Dante's *Inferno,* XXVII, 61–66]

Let us go then, you and I,
When the evening is spread out against the sky
Like a patient etherised upon a table;

Let us go, through certain half-deserted streets,
The muttering retreats
Of restless nights in one-night cheap hotels
And sawdust restaurants with oyster-shells:
Streets that follow like a tedious argument
Of insidious intent
To lead you to an overwhelming question . . .
Oh, do not ask, "What is it?"
Let us go and make our visit.

In the room the women come and go
Talking of Michelangelo.

The yellow fog that rubs its back upon the window-panes,
The yellow smoke that rubs its muzzle on the window-panes
Licked its tongue into the corners of the evening,
Lingered upon the pools that stand in drains,
Let fall upon its back the soot that falls from chimneys,
Slipped by the terrace, made a sudden leap,
And seeing that it was a soft October night,
Curled once about the house, and fell asleep.

And indeed there will be time
For the yellow smoke that slides along the street,
Rubbing its back upon the window-panes;
There will be time, there will be time
To prepare a face to meet the faces that you meet;
There will be time to murder and create,
And time for all the works and days of hands
That lift and drop a question on your plate;
Time for you and time for me,
And time yet for a hundred indecisions,
And for a hundred visions and revisions,
Before the taking of a toast and tea.

In the room the women come and go
Talking of Michelangelo.

And indeed there will be time
To wonder, "Do I dare?" and, "Do I dare?"
Time to turn back and descend the stair,
With a bald spot in the middle of my hair—
[They will say: "How his hair is growing thin!]
My morning coat, my collar mounting firmly to the chin,
My necktie rich and modest, but asserted by a simple pin—
[They will say: "But how his arms and legs are thin!"]
Do I dare
Disturb the universe?
In a minute there is time
For decisions and revisions which a minute will reverse.

For I have known them all already, known them all:—
Have known the evenings, mornings, afternoons,

I have measured out my life with coffee spoons;
I know the voices dying with a dying fall
Beneath the music from a farther room.
  So how should I presume?

  And I have known the eyes already, known them all—
The eyes that fix you in a formulated phrase,
And when I am formulated, sprawling on a pin,
When I am pinned and wriggling on the wall,
Then how should I begin
To spit out all the butt-ends of my days and ways?
  And how should I presume?

  And I have known the arms already, known them all—
Arms that are braceleted and white and bare
[But in the lamplight, downed with light brown hair!]
Is it perfume from a dress
That makes me so digress?
Arms that lie along a table, or wrap about a shawl.
  And should I then presume?
  And how should I begin?

Shall I say, I have gone at dusk through narrow streets
And watched the smoke that rises from the pipes
Of lonely men in shirt-sleeves, leaning out of windows? . . .
  I should have been a pair of ragged claws
Scuttling across the floors of silent seas.

And the afternoon, the evening, sleeps so peacefully!
Smoothed by long fingers,
Asleep . . . tired . . . or it malingers,
Stretched on the floor, here beside you and me.
Should I, after tea and cakes and ices,
Have the strength to force the moment to its crisis?
But though I have wept and fasted, wept and prayed,
Though I have seen my head [grown slightly bald] brought in upon a platter,
I am no prophet—and here's no great matter;
I have seen the moment of my greatness flicker,
And I have seen the eternal Footman hold my coat, and snicker,
And in short, I was afraid.

And would it have been worth it, after all,
After the cups, the marmalade, the tea,
Among the porcelain, among some talk of you and me,
Would it have been worth while,
To have bitten off the matter with a smile,
To have squeezed the universe into a ball
To roll it toward some overwhelming question,
To say: "I am Lazarus, come from the dead.
Come back to tell you all, I shall tell you all"—
If one, settling a pillow by her head,

Should say: "That is not what I meant at all.
That is not it, at all."

And would it have been worth it, after all,
Would it have been worth while,
After the sunsets and the dooryards and the sprinkled streets,
After the novels, after the teacups, after the skirts that trail along the floor—
And this, and so much more?—
It is impossible to say just what I mean!
But as if a magic lantern threw the nerves in patterns on a screen:
Would it have been worth while
If one, settling a pillow or throwing off a shawl,
And turning toward the window, should say:
    "That is not it at all,
    That is not what I meant, at all."

No! I am not Prince Hamlet, nor was meant to be;
Am an attendant lord, one that will do
To swell a progress, start a scene or two,
Advise the prince; no doubt, an easy tool,
Deferential, glad to be of use,
Politic, cautious, and meticulous;
Full of high sentence, but a bit obtuse;
At times, indeed, almost ridiculous—
Almost, at times, the Fool.

    I grow old . . . I grow old . . .
I shall wear the bottoms of my trousers rolled.

    Shall I part my hair behind? Do I dare to eat a peach?
I shall wear white flannel trousers, and walk upon the beach.
I have heard the mermaids singing, each to each.

    I do not think that they will sing to me.

    I have seen them riding seaward on the waves
Combing the white hair of the waves blown back
When the wind blows the water white and black.

    We have lingered in the chambers of the sea
By sea-girls wreathed with seaweed red and brown
Till human voices wake us, and we drown.

Suggestions for Discussion

1. Who are "you and I"?

2. What evidence can you find in the structural development of the poem to support the view that one self in the dramatic monologue acts out the conflict and the other assumes the role of observer? Cite lines from the poem in which shifts in mood and tone occur. How does the poem achieve dramatic unity?

3. Contrast the images of Prufrock's interior world with those of the external world. How does their recurring juxtaposition illuminate the doubleness of the speaker and contribute to tone? How is sensory experience used to convey the circularity of the dialogue with self? Why are the images of the etherized patient, the staircase, winding streets, cat, and fog especially appropriate dramatic symbols of the speaker's state of mind? Trace the use of sea imagery. How does it function differently in the metaphor of the crab and the vision of the mermaids? How do both relate to theme and tone? What do the allusions to John the Baptist, Lazarus, and Hamlet have in common?

4. Distinguish between the dramatic and the lyric elements. How is the mock heroic used to satirize both speaker and society? Study the effects of repetition on rhythm, tone, and meaning. How do the stanzas and the typographical breaks mark the shifts in tone? Discuss the relationship of tone to syntax, refrain, internal rhyme, diction, tempo, and melody. Comment on the irony in the title.

5. How does time function in the poem? How does the shift in tense from present to present perfect and future provide a key to the poem's resolution? What form does the speaker's recognition take? By what means does the poet evoke sympathy for Prufrock, who is psychically impotent to establish an intimate human relationship? To what do you attribute Prufrock's rejection of human encounter? What part does his self-mockery play in our response to him? Does the poem move beyond pathos and self-mockery?

6. In what respect may the poem be viewed as an expression of a search for self?

Suggestions for Writing

1. Write a character study of Prufrock in which you refer directly to the poem.

2. Write a dialogue in which your interior self is counterpointed against your social self or *persona*.

Dylan Thomas

The Force That Through the Green Fuse Drives the Flower

Dylan Thomas (1914–1953) was born in Wales. He was a newspaper reporter for a time and worked for the BBC during World War II. He gained recognition as a lyric poet in his twenties and grew in popularity until his death while on a lecture tour in the United States. His *Collected Poems* appeared in 1953. A collection of his stories, sketches, and essays, *Quite Early One Morning*, was published in 1954; a group of stories and and essays, *A Prospect of the Sea*, in 1955;

and a verse play, *Under Milk Wood,* in 1954. The poet views natural forces as both destructive and life giving; the poem is an expression of his sense of the energy, both creative and destructive, that runs through all things.

The force that through the green fuse drives the flower
Drives my green age; that blasts the roots of trees
Is my destroyer.
And I am dumb to tell the crooked rose
My youth is bent by the same wintry fever.

The force that drives the water through the rocks
Drives my red blood; that dries the mouthing streams
Turns mine to wax.
And I am dumb to mouth unto my veins
How at the mountain spring the same mouth sucks.

The hand that whirls the water in the pool
Stirs the quicksand; that ropes the blowing wind
Hauls my shroud sail.
And I am dumb to tell the hanging man
How of my clay is made the hangman's lime.

The lips of time leech to the fountain head;
Love drips and gathers, but the fallen blood
Shall calm her sores.
And I am dumb to tell a weather's wind
How time has ticked a heaven round the stars.

And I am dumb to tell the lover's tomb
How at my sheet goes the same crooked worm.

Suggestions for Discussion

1. What images suggest the relationship the poet sees between the world of nature and that of human passions?

2. How does the poet express the sense that the energy that runs through all things is both creator and destroyer? How does the two-line refrain at the end of each stanza relate this theme to the voice of the poet?

3. What images depict contrasting forces of life and death? How does the diction convey the sense of sexual energy?

Personal Relationships: Parents and Children

◆◆◆◆

When I was your age I lived with a great dream. The dream grew and I learned how to speak of it and make people listen. Then the dream divided one day when I decided to marry your mother after all, even though I knew she was spoiled and meant no good to me. I was sorry immediately I had married her but, being patient in those days, made the best of it and got to love her in another way. You came along and for a long time we made quite a lot of happiness out of our lives. But I was a man divided—she wanted me to work too much for *her* and not enough for my dream. She realized too late that work was dignity, and the only dignity, and tried to atone for it by working herself, but it was too late and she broke and is broken forever.

—**F. Scott Fitzgerald,** *Dearest Scottie*

Sometimes my mother or father would come up with an image, or a fragment of a story, and we would all weave imaginary plots around it. Sometimes we talked about books or movies or the poetry we recited to each other on Sunday afternoons. Often we talked and speculated about other people, our neighbors and friends. No one ever hesitated to be mean—although the insults were usually also pretty funny. We were so mean to each other, in fact, that guests were often astonished and shocked. They didn't catch the undertone of humor in our quick sarcasms, and there were times when we didn't catch it either. Explosions and tears and sudden departures were not at all uncommon. My brothers called our dinner table "the bear garden."

—**Susan Cheever,** "Portrait of My Father" from *Home Before Dark*

I will never total it all. I will never come in to say: She was a child seldom smiled at. Her father left me before she was a year old. I had to work her first six years when there was work, or I sent her home and to his relatives. There were years she had care she hated. She was dark and thin and foreign-looking in a world where the prestige went to blondness and curly hair and dimples, she was slow where glibness was prized. She was a child of anxious, not proud, love. We were poor and could not afford for her the soil of easy growth. I was a young mother, I was a distracted mother. There were the other children pushing up, demanding. Her younger sister seemed all that she was not. There were years she did not want me to touch her. She kept too much in herself, her life was such she had to keep too much in herself. My wisdom came too late. She has much to her and probably little will come of it. She is a child of her age, of depression, of war; of fear.

Let her be. So all that is in her will not bloom—but in how many does it? There is still enough left to live by. Only help her to know—help make it so there is cause for her to know—that she is more than this dress on the ironing board, helpless before the iron.

—**Tillie Olsen**, "I Stand Here Ironing" from *Tell Me a Riddle*

A boy wants something very special from his father. You hear it said that fathers want their sons to be what they feel they cannot themselves be, but I tell you it also works the other way. I know that as a small boy I wanted my father to be a certain thing he was not. I wanted him to be a proud, silent, dignified father. When I was with other boys and he passed along the street, I wanted to feel a glow of pride: "There he is. That is my father."

—**Sherwood Anderson**, "Discovery of a Father"

My father . . . believed that he (or rather, his wife) could raise children according to his unique moral and intellectual plan, thus proving to the world the values of enlightened, unorthodox child-rearing. I believe that my mother . . . at first genuinely and enthusiastically embraced the experiment, and only later found that in carrying out my father's intense, perfectionist program, she was in conflict with her deep instincts as a mother.

—**Adrienne Rich**, "The Anger of a Child"

Behind the newspaper Julian was withdrawing into the inner compartment of his mind where he spent most of his time. This was a kind of mental bubble in which he established himself when he could not bear to be a part of what was going on around him. From it he could see out and judge but in it he was safe from any kind of penetration from without. It was the only place where he felt free of the general idiocy of his fellows. His mother had never entered it but from it he could see her with absolute clarity.

. . . She might as well be made to understand what had happened to her. "Don't think that was just an uppity Negro woman," he said. "That was the whole colored race which will no longer take your condescending pennies. That was your black double. She can wear the same hat as you, and to be sure," he added gratuitously (because he thought it was funny), "it looked better on her than it did on you. What all this means," he said, "is that the old world is gone. The old manners are absolute. . . . You aren't who you thing you are." . . .

> —**Flannery O'Connor,** "Everything That Rises Must Converge"

Letters and Personal Reminiscences

◆◆◆

Sherwood Anderson

Discovery of a Father

Sherwood Anderson (1876–1941) was an American short-story writer, essayist, and novelist whose writing often reflected his own confusion about man in the modern world of the machine, but whose keen insights into human beings continue to illuminate life for readers of his collection of short stories, *Winesburg, Ohio* 1919, his novels, *Many Marriages* (1922) and *Dark Laughter* (1925), and his semiautobiographical *A Story Teller's Story* (1924). In "Discovery of a Father," from Anderson's *Memoirs* (1939), the boy's negative, even contemptuous, attitude toward his father undergoes a radical change: his earlier wish that his father would be someone else gives way to the secure knowledge that he would never again want another father.

One of the strangest relationships in the world is that between father and son. I know it now from having sons of my own.

A boy wants something very special from his father. You hear it said that fathers want their sons to be what they feel they cannot themselves be, but I tell you it also works the other way. I know that as a small boy I wanted my father to be a certain thing he was not. I wanted him to be a proud, silent, dignified father. When I was with other boys and he passed along the street, I wanted to feel a glow of pride: "There he is. That is my father."

But he wasn't such a one. He couldn't be. It seemed to me then that he was always showing off. Let's say someone in our town had got up a show. They were always doing it. The druggist would be in it, the shoe-store clerk, the horse doctor, and a lot of women and girls. My father would manage to get the chief comedy part. It was, let's say, a Civil War play and he was a comic Irish soldier. He had to do the most absurd things. They thought he was funny, but I didn't.

I thought he was terrible. I didn't see how Mother could stand it. She even laughed with the others. Maybe I would have laughed if it hadn't been my father.

Or there was a parade, the Fourth of July or Decoration Day. He'd be in that, too, right at the front of it, as Grand Marshal or something, on a white horse hired from a livery stable.

He couldn't ride for shucks. He fell off the horse and everyone hooted with laughter, but he didn't care. He even seemed to like it. I remember once when he had done something ridiculous, and right out on Main Street, too. I was with some other boys and they were laughing and shouting at him and he was shouting back and having as good a time as they were. I ran down an alley back of some stores and there in the Presbyterian Church sheds I had a good long cry.

Or I would be in bed at night and Father would come home a little lit up and bring some men with him. He was a man who was never alone. Before he went broke, running a harness shop, there were always a lot of men loafing in the shop. He went broke, of course, because he gave too much credit. He couldn't refuse it and I thought he was a fool. I had got to hating him.

There'd be men I didn't think would want to be fooling around with him. There might even be the superintendent of our schools and a quiet man who ran the hardware store. Once, I remember, there was a white-haired man who was a cashier of the bank. It was a wonder to me they'd want to be seen with such a windbag. That's what I thought he was. I know now what it was that attracted them. It was because life in our town, as in all small towns, was at times pretty dull and he livened it up. He made them laugh. He could tell stories. He'd even get them to singing.

If they didn't come to our house they'd go off, say at night, to where there was a grassy place by a creek. They'd cook food there and drink beer and sit about listening to his stories.

He was always telling stories about himself. He'd say this or that wonderful thing happened to him. It might be something that made him look like a fool. He didn't care.

If an Irishman came to our house, right away father would say he was Irish. He'd tell what county in Ireland he was born in. He'd tell things that happened there when he was a boy. He'd make it seem so real that, if I hadn't known he was born in southern Ohio, I'd have believed him myself.

If it was a Scotchman, the same thing happened. He'd get a burr into his speech. Or he was a German or a Swede. He'd be anything the other man was. I think they all knew he was lying, but they seemed to like him just the same. As a boy that was what I couldn't understand.

And there was Mother. How could she stand it? I wanted to ask but never did. She was not the kind you asked such questions.

I'd be upstairs in my bed, in my room above the porch, and Father would be telling some of his tales. A lot of Father's stories were about the Civil War. To hear him tell it he'd been in about every battle. He'd known Grant, Sherman, Sheridan, and I don't know how many others. He'd been particularly intimate with General Grant so that when Grant went East, to take charge of all the armies, he took Father along.

"I was an orderly at headquarters and Sam Grant said to me, 'Irve,' he said, 'I'm going to take you along with me.' "

It seems he and Grant used to slip off sometimes and have a quiet drink together. That's what my father said. He'd tell about the day Lee surrendered and how, when the great moment came, they couldn't find Grant.

"You know," my father said, "about General Grant's book, his memoirs. You've read of how he said he had a headache and how, when he got word that Lee was ready to call it quits, he was suddenly and miraculously cured.

"Huh," said Father. "He was in the woods with me.

"I was in there with my back against a tree. I was pretty well corned. I had got hold of a bottle of pretty good stuff.

"They were looking for Grant. He had got off his horse and come into the woods. He found me. He was covered with mud.

"I had the bottle in my hand. What'd I care? The war was over. I knew we had them licked."

My father said that he was the one who told Grant about Lee. An orderly riding by had told him, because the orderly knew how thick he was with Grant. Grant was embarrassed.

"But, Irve, look at me. I'm all covered with mud," he said to Father.

And then, my father said, he and Grant decided to have a drink together. They took a couple of shots and then, because he didn't want Grant to show up potted before the immaculate Lee, he smashed the bottle against the tree.

"Sam Grant's dead now and I wouldn't want it to get out on him," my father said.

That's just one of the kind of things he'd tell. Of course, the men knew he was lying, but they seemed to like it just the same.

When we got broke, down and out, do you think he ever brought anything home? Not he. If there wasn't anything to eat in the house, he'd go off visiting around at farm houses. They all wanted him. Sometimes he'd stay away for weeks, Mother working to keep us fed, and then home he'd come bringing, let's say, a ham. He'd got it from some farmer friend. He'd slap it on the table in the kitchen. "You bet I'm going to see that my kids have something to eat," he'd say, and Mother would just stand smiling at him. She'd never say a word about all the weeks and months he'd been away, not leaving us a cent for food. Once I heard her speaking to a woman in our street. Maybe the woman had dared to sympathize with her. "Oh," she said "it's all right. He isn't ever dull like most of the men in this street. Life is never dull when my man is about."

But often I was filled with bitterness, and sometimes I wished he wasn't my father. I'd even invent another man as my father. To protect my mother I'd make up stories of a secret marriage that for some strange reason never got known. As though some man, say the president of a railroad company or maybe a Congressman, had married my mother, thinking his wife was dead and then it turned out she wasn't.

So they had to hush it up but I got born just the same. I wasn't really the son of my father. Somewhere in the world there was a very dignified, quite wonderful man who was really my father. I even made myself half believe these fancies.

And then there came a certain night. Mother was away from home. Maybe there was church that night. Father came in. He'd been off somewhere for two or three weeks. He found me alone in the house, reading by the kitchen table.

It had been raining and he was very wet. He sat and looked at me for a long time, not saying a word. I was startled, for there was on his face the saddest look I had ever seen. He sat for a time, his clothes dripping. Then he got up.

"Come on with me," he said.

I got up and went with him out of the house. I was filled with wonder but I wasn't afraid. We went along a dirt road that led down into a valley, about a mile out of town, where there was a pond. We walked in silence. The man who was always talking had stopped his talking.

I didn't know what was up and had the queer feeling that I was with a stranger. I didn't know whether my father intended it so. I don't think he did.

The pond was quite large. It was still raining hard and there were flashes of lightning followed by thunder. We were on a grassy bank at the pond's edge when my father spoke, and in the darkness and rain his voice sounded strange.

"Take off your clothes," he said. Still filled with wonder, I began to undress. There was a flash of lightning and I saw that he was already naked.

Naked, we went into the pond. Taking my hand, he pulled me in. It may be that I was too frightened, too full of a feeling of strangeness, to speak. Before that night my father had never seemed to pay any attention to me.

"And what is he up to now?" I kept asking myself. I did not swim very well, but he put my hand on his shoulder and struck out into the darkness.

He was a man with big shoulders, a powerful swimmer. In the darkness I could feel the movements of his muscles. We swam to the far edge of the pond and then back to where we had left our clothes. The rain continued and the wind blew. Sometimes my father swam on his back, and when he did he took my hand in his large powerful one and moved it over so that it rested always on his shoulder. Sometimes there would be a flash of lightning and I could see his face quite clearly.

It was as it was earlier, in the kitchen, a face filled with sadness. There would be the momentary glimpse of his face, and then again the darkness, the wind and the rain. In me there was a feeling I had never known before.

It was a feeling of closeness. It was something strange. It was as though there were only we two in the world. It was as though I had been jerked suddenly out of myself, out of my world of the schoolboy, out of a world in which I was ashamed of my father.

He had become blood of my blood; he the strong swimmer and I the boy clinging to him in the darkness. We swam in silence, and in silence we dressed in our wet clothes and went home.

There was a lamp lighted in the kitchen, and when we came in, the water dripping from us, there was my mother. She smiled at us. I remember that she called us "boys." "What have you boys been up to?" she asked, but my father did not answer. As he had begun the evening's experience with me in silence, so he ended it. He turned and looked at me. Then he went, I thought, with a new and strange dignity, out of the room.

I climbed the stairs to my room, undressed in darkness and got into bed. I couldn't sleep and did not want to sleep. For the first time I knew that I was the son of my father. He was a storyteller as I was to be. It may be that I even laughed a little softly there in the darkness. If I did, I laughed knowing that I would never again be wanting another father.

Suggestions for Discussion

1. How does the author bring the subject into focus?

2. Account for the feelings the narrator had toward his father's public behavior.

3. How do the sentence structure and diction contribute to purpose and tone?

4. How do you explain the father's action in taking the boy swimming? How do you account for the boy's changed view of his father?

Suggestions for Writing

1. Write on one of these topics: a portrait of my father; imaginary parents.

2. Write a narrative in which a seemingly simple event effects a change in attitude.

Franz Kafka

Letter to His Father

Translated by Ernest Kaiser and Eithene Wilkins

Franz Kafka (1883–1924), the German novelist who portrays alienated characters in an absurd world, made little mark during his life but is now considered a major modern writer. Many of his novels have been published posthumously, including *The Trial, The Castle,* and *Amerika.* In the letter, also published posthumously, the author in a legalistic manner indicts himself as well as his father in assessing responsibility for his, Kakfa's, insecurity as a person.

Dearest Father:

You asked me recently why I maintain that I am afraid of you. As usual, I was unable to think of any answer to your question, partly for the very reason that I am afraid of you, and partly because an explanation of the grounds for this fear would mean going into far more details than I could even approximately keep in mind while talking. And if I now try to give you an answer in writing, it will still be very incomplete, because even in writing this fear and its consequences hamper me in relation to you and because [anyway] the magnitude of the subject goes far beyond the scope of my memory and power of reasoning. . . .

Compare the two of us: I, to put it in a very much abbreviated form, a Löwy with a certain basis of Kafka, which, however, is not set in motion by the Kafka will to life, business, and conquest, but by a Löwyish spur that urges more secretly, more diffidently, and in another direction, and which often fails to work entirely. You, on the other hand, a true Kafka in strength, health, appetite, loudness of voice, eloquence, self-satisfaction, worldly dominance, endurance, presence of mind, knowledge of human nature, a certain way of doing things on a grand scale, of course with all the defects and weaknesses that go with all these advantages and into which your temperament and sometimes your hot temper drive you. . . .

However it was, we were so different and in our difference so dangerous to each other that, if anyone had tried to calculate in advance how I, the slowly developing child, and you, the full-grown man, would stand to each other, he could have assumed that you would simply trample me underfoot so that nothing was left of me. Well, that didn't happen. Nothing alive can be calculated. But perhaps something worse happened. And in saying this I would all the time beg of you not to forget that I never, and not even for a single moment, believe any guilt to be on your side. The effect you had on me was the effect you could not help having. But you should stop considering it some particular malice on my part that I succumbed to that effect.

I was a timid child. For all that, I am sure I was also obstinate, as children are. I am sure that Mother spoilt me too, but I cannot believe I was particularly difficult to manage; I cannot believe that a kindly word, a quiet taking of me by the hand, a friendly look, could not have got me to do anything that was wanted of me. Now you are after all at bottom a kindly and softhearted person (what follows will not be in contradiction to this, I am speaking only of the impression you made on the child), but not every child has the endurance and fearlessness to go on searching until it comes to the kindliness that lies beneath the surface. You can only treat a child in the way you yourself are constituted, with vigor, noise, and hot temper, and in this case this seemed to you, into the bargain, extremely suitable, because you wanted to bring me up to be a strong brave boy. . . .

There is only one episode in the early years of which I have a direct memory. You may remember it, too. Once in the night I kept on whimpering for water, not, I am certain, because I was thirsty, but probably partly to be annoying, partly to amuse myself. After several vigorous threats had failed to have any effect, you took me out of bed, carried me out onto the *pavlatche* and left me there alone for a while in my nightshirt, outside the shut door. I am not going to say that this was wrong—perhaps at that time there was really no other way of getting peace and quiet that night—but I mention it as typical of your methods of bringing up a child and their effect on me. I dare say I was quite obedient afterwards at that period, but it did me inner harm. What was for me a matter of course, that senseless asking for water, and the extraordinary terror of being carried outside were two things that I, my nature being what it was, could never properly connect with each other. Even years afterwards I suffered from the tormenting fancy that the huge man, my father, the ultimate authority, would come almost for no reason at all and take me out of bed in the night and carry me out onto the *pavlatche*, and that therefore I was such a mere nothing for him.

That then was only a small beginning, but this sense of nothingness that often dominates me (a feeling that is in another respect, admittedly, also a noble and fruitful one) comes largely from your influence. What I would have needed was a little encouragement, a little friendliness, a little keeping open of my road, instead of which you blocked it for me, though of course with the good intention of making me go another road. But I was not fit for that. You encouraged me, for instance, when I saluted and marched smartly, but I was no future soldier, or you encouraged me when I was able to eat heartily or even drink beer with my meals, or when I was able to repeat songs, singing what I had not understood, or prattle to you using your own favorite expressions, imitating you, but nothing of this had anything to do with my future. And it is characteristic that even today you really only encourage me in anything when you yourself are involved in it, when what is at stake is your sense of self-importance.

At that time, and at that time everywhere, I would have needed encouragement. I was, after all, depressed even by your mere physical presence. I remember, for instance, how we often undressed together in the same bathing hut. There was I, skinny, weakly, slight; you strong, tall, broad. Even inside the hut I felt myself a miserable specimen, and what's more, not only in your eyes but in the eyes of the whole world, for you were for me the measure of all things. But then when we went out of the bathing hut before the people, I with you holding my hand, a little skeleton, unsteady, barefoot on the boards, frightened of the water, incapable of copying your swimming strokes, which you, with the best of intentions, but actually to my profound humiliation, always kept on showing me, then I was frantic with desperation and all my bad experiences in all spheres at such moments fitted magnificently together. . . .

In keeping with that, furthermore, was your intellectual domination. You had worked your way up so far alone, by your own energies, and as a result you had unbounded confidence in your opinion. For me as a child that was not yet so dazzling as later for the boy growing up. From your armchair you ruled the world. Your opinion was correct, every other was mad, wild, *meshugge*, not normal. With all this your self-confidence was so great that you had no need to be consistent at all and yet never ceased to be in the right. It did sometimes happen that you had no opinion whatsoever about a matter and as a result all opinions that were at all possible with respect to the matter were necessarily wrong, without exception. You were capable, for instance, of running down the Czechs, and then the Germans, and then the Jews, and what is more, not only selectively but in every respect, and finally nobody was left except yourself. For me you took on the enigmatic quality that all tyrants have whose rights are based on their person and not on reason. At least so it seemed to me.

Now where I was concerned you were in fact astonishingly often in the right, which was a matter of course in talk, for there was hardly ever any talk between us, but also in reality. Yet this too was nothing particularly incomprehensible; in all my thinking I was, after all, under the heavy pressure of your personality, even in that part of it—and particularly in that—which was not in accord with yours. All these thoughts, seemingly independent of you, were from the beginning loaded with the burden of your harsh and dogmatic judgments; it was almost impossible to endure this, and yet to work out one's thoughts with any measure of completeness and permanence. I am not here speaking of any sublime thoughts, but of every little enterprise in childhood. It was only necessary to be happy about something or other, to be filled with the thought of it, to come home and speak of it, and the answer was an ironical sigh, a shaking of the head, a tapping of the table with one finger: "Is that all you're so worked up about?" or "I wish I had your worries!" or "The things some people have time to think about!" or "What can you buy yourself with that?" or "What a song and dance about nothing!" Of course, you couldn't be expected to be enthusiastic about every childish triviality, toiling and moiling as you used to. But that wasn't the point. The point was, rather, that you could not help always and on principle causing the child such disappointments, by virtue of your antagonistic nature, and further that this antagonism was ceaselessly intensified through accumulation of its material, that it finally became a matter of established habit even when for once you were of the same opinion as myself, and that finally these disappointments of the child's were not disappointments in ordinary life but, since what it concerned was your person, which was the measure of all things, struck to the very core. Courage, resolution, confidence, delight in this and that, did not endure to the end when you were against whatever it was or even if your opposition was merely to be assumed; and it was to be assumed in almost everything I did. . . .

You have, I think, a gift for bringing up children: you could, I am sure, have been of use to a human being of your own kind with your methods; such a person would have seen the reasonableness of what you told him, would not have troubled about anything else, and would quietly have done things the way he was told. But for me a child everything you shouted at me was positively a heavenly commandment, I never forgot it, it remained for me the most important means of forming a judgment of the world, above all of forming a judgment of you yourself, and there you failed entirely. Since as a child I was together with you chiefly at meals, your teaching was to a large extent teaching about proper behavior at table. What was brought to the table had to be eaten up, there could be no discussion of the goodness of the food— but you yourself often found the food uneatable, called it "this swill," said "that brute" (the cook) had ruined it. Because in accordance with your strong appetite and your particular habit you ate everything fast, hot and in big mouthfuls, the child had to hurry, there was a somber silence at table, interrupted by admonitions: "Eat first, talk afterwards," or "faster, faster, faster," or "there you are, you see, I finished ages ago." Bones mustn't be cracked with the teeth, but you could. Vinegar must not be sipped noisily, but you could. The main thing was that the bread should be cut straight. But it didn't matter that you did it with a knife dripping with gravy. One had to take care that no scraps fell on the floor. In the end it was under your chair that there were most scraps. At table one wasn't allowed to do anything but eat, but you cleaned and cut your fingernails, sharpened pencils, cleaned your ears with the toothpick. Please, Father, understand me rightly: these would in themselves have been utterly insignificant details, they only became depressing for me because you, the man who was so tremendously the measure of all things for me, yourself did not keep the commandments you imposed on me. Hence the world was for me divided into three parts: into one in which I, the slave, lived under laws that had been invented only for me and which I could, I did not know why, never completely comply with; then into a second world, which was infinitely remote from mine, in which you lived, concerned with government, with the issuing of orders and with annoyance about their not being obeyed; and finally into a third world where everybody else lived happily and free from orders and from having to obey. I was continually in disgrace, either I obeyed your orders, and that was a disgrace, for they applied, after all, only to me, or I was defiant, and that was a disgrace too, for how could I presume to defy you, or I could not obey because, for instance, I had not your strength, your appetite, your skill, in spite of which you expected it of me as a matter of course; this was the greatest disgrace of all. What moved in this way was not the child's reflections, but his feelings. . . .

It was true that Mother was illimitably good to me, but all that was for me in relation to you, that is to say, is no good relation. Mother unconsciously played the part of a beater during a hunt. Even if your method of upbringing might in some unlikely case have set me on my own feet by means of producing defiance, dislike, or even hate in me, Mother canceled that out again by kindness, by talking sensibly (in the maze and chaos of my childhood she was the very pattern of good sense and reasonableness), by pleading for me, and I was again driven back into your orbit, which I might perhaps otherwise have broken out of, to your advantage and to my own. Or it was so that no real reconciliation ever came about, that Mother merely shielded me from you in secret, secretly gave me something, or allowed me to do something, and then where you were concerned I was again the furtive creature, the cheat, the guilty one, who in his worthlessness could only pursue backstairs methods even to get the things he regarded as his right. Of course, I then became used to taking such courses also in quest of things to which, even in my own view, I had no right. This again meant an increase in the sense of guilt.

It is also true that you hardly ever really gave me a whipping. But the shouting, the way your face got red, the hasty undoing of the braces and the laying of them ready over the back of the chair, all that was almost worse for me. It is like when someone is going to be hanged. If he is really hanged, then he's dead and it's all over. But if he has to go through all the preliminaries to being hanged and only when the noose is dangling before his face is told of his reprieve, then he may suffer from it all his life long. Besides, from so many occasions when I had, as you clearly showed you thought, deserved to be beaten, when you were however gracious enough to let me off at the last moment, here again what accumulated was only a huge sense of guilt. On every side I was to blame, I was in debt to you.

You have always reproached me (and what is more either alone or in front of others, you having no feeling for the humiliation of this latter, your children's affairs always being public affairs) for living in peace and quiet, warmth, and abundance, lack for nothing, thanks to your hard work. I think here of remarks that must positively have worn grooves in my brain, like: "When I was only seven I had to push the barrow from village to village." "We all had to sleep in one room." "We were glad when we got potatoes." "For years I had open sores on my legs from not having enough clothes to wear in winter." "I was only a little boy when I was sent away to Pisek to go into business." "I got nothing from home, not even when I was in the army, even then I was sending money home." "But for all that, for all that—Father was always Father to me. Ah, nobody knows what that means these days! What do these children know of things? Nobody's been through that! Is there any child that understands such things today?" Under other conditions such stories might have been very educational, they might have been a way of encouraging one and strengthening one to endure similar torments and deprivations to those one's father had undergone. But that wasn't what you wanted at all; the situation had, after all, become quite different as a result of all your efforts, and there was no opportunity to distinguish oneself in the world as you had done. Such an opportunity would first of all have had to be created by violence and revolution, it would have meant breaking away from home (assuming one had had the resolution and strength to do so and that Mother wouldn't have worked against it, for her part, with other means). But all that was not what you wanted at all, that you termed ingratitude, extravagance, disobedience, treachery, madness. And so, while on the one hand you tempted me to it by means of example, story, and humiliation, on the other hand you forbade it with the utmost severity. . . .

(Up to this point there is in this letter relatively little I have intentionally passed over in silence, but now and later I shall have to be silent on certain matters that it is still too hard for me to confess—to you and to myself. I say this in order that, if the picture as a whole should be somewhat blurred here and there, you should not believe that what is to blame is any lack of evidence; on the contrary, there is evidence that might well make the picture unbearably stark. It is not easy to strike a median position.) Here, it is enough to remind you of early days. I had lost my self-confidence where you were concerned, and in its place had developed a boundless sense of guilt. (In recollection of this boundlessness I once wrote of someone, accurately: "He is afraid the shame will outlive him, even.") I could not suddenly undergo a transformation when I came into the company of other people; on the contrary, with them I came to feel an even deeper sense of guilt, for, as I have already said, in their case I had to make good the wrongs done them by you in the business, wrongs in which I too had my share of responsibility. Besides, you always, of course, had some objection to make, frankly or covertly, to everyone I associated with, and for this too I had to beg his pardon. The mistrust that you tried to instill into me, at business and at home, towards most people (tell me of any single person who was of importance to me in my childhood whom you didn't at least once tear to shreds with your criticism), this mistrust, which oddly enough was no particular burden to you (the fact was that you were strong enough to bear it, and besides, it was in reality perhaps only a token of the autocrat), this mistrust, which for me as a little boy was nowhere confirmed in my own eyes, since I everywhere saw only people excellent beyond all hope of emulation, in me turned into mistrust of myself and into perpetual anxiety in relation to everything else. There, then, I was in general certain of not being able to escape from you.

Suggestions for Discussion

Kafka gave this letter (from which you have only excerpts) to his mother, asking her to give it to his father. Understandably she never did so, but it was found among Kafka's unpublished manuscripts after his death. Although Kafka had asked his friend Max Brod to destroy all unpublished material, Brod did not comply with this request.

1. Study the legalistic manner in which Kafka indicts himself as well as his father. Assuming you were on a jury, evaluate the points for prosecution and defense of both father and son. What would be your final judgment as to responsibility for the boy's insecurity as a person?

2. Study the scenes through which Kafka dramatizes certain moments of special significance in his childhood. In spite of his attempt to be fair, by what means does he enlist sympathy with the child?

3. What seems to be the role of the mother? Why does the boy more closely identify with her and her family than with his father?

Suggestions for Writing

1. Write about a significant moment in your childhood relationship with your parents. What effect may it have had on your self-image?

2. Write on the parents' image versus the child's.

3. Contrast this father with the one portrayed in E.E. Cummings's poem "My Father Moved Through Dooms of Love."

Russell Baker

In My Day . . .

Russell Baker (b. 1925) has been a journalist throughout his professional career. After graduating from Johns Hopkins University he worked as a reporter, and in 1954 served as a correspondent for the *New York Times* in Washington, D.C., where he was variously assigned to the White House, the State Department, national politics, and the activities of Congress. He subsequently became a columnist for the *New York Times* and won a Pulitzer Prize in 1979. He won a second Pulitzer Prize in 1983 for his autobiography, entitled *Growing Up.* In this section from *Growing Up,* he movingly describes his mother's shifting behavior from rage at "the weakness, the boredom, and the absence of love" in her late seventies to happiness in her last years in "free-wheeling excursions back through time."

At the age of eighty my mother had her last bad fall, and after that her mind wandered free through time. Some days she went to weddings and funerals that had taken place half a century earlier. On others she presided over family dinners cooked on Sunday afternoons for children who were now gray with age. Through all this she lay in bed but moved across time, traveling among the dead decades with a speed and ease beyond the gift of physical science.

"Where's Russell?" she asked one day when I came to visit at the nursing home.

"I'm Russell," I said.

She gazed at this improbably overgrown figure out of an inconceivable future and promptly dismissed it.

"Russell's only this big," she said, holding her hand, palm down, two feet from the floor. That day she was a young country wife with chickens in the backyard and a view of hazy blue Virginia mountains behind the apple orchard, and I was a stranger old enough to be her father.

Early one morning she phoned me in New York. "Are you coming to my funeral today?" she asked.

It was an awkward question with which to be awakened. "What are you talking about, for God's sake?" was the best reply I could manage.

"I'm being buried today," she declared briskly, as though announcing an important social event.

"I'll phone you back," I said and hung up, and when I did phone back she was all right, although she wasn't all right, of course, and we all knew she wasn't.

She had always been a small woman—short, light-boned, delicately structured—but now, under the white hospital sheet, she was becoming tiny. I thought of a doll with huge, fierce eyes. There had always been a fierceness in her. It showed in that angry, challenging thrust of the chin when she issued an opinion, and a great one she had always been for issuing opinions.

"I tell people exactly what's on my mind," she had been fond of boasting. "I tell them what I think, whether they like it or not." Often they had not liked it. She could be sarcastic to people in whom she detected evidence of the ignoramus or the fool.

"It's not always good policy to tell people exactly what's on your mind," I used to caution her.

"If they don't like it, that's too bad," was her customary reply, "because that's the way I am."

And so she was. A formidable woman. Determined to speak her mind, determined to have her way, determined to bend those who opposed her. In that time when I had known her best, my mother had hurled herself at life with chin thrust forward, eyes blazing, and an energy that made her seem always on the run.

She ran after squawking chickens, an axe in her hand, determined on a beheading that would put dinner in the pot. She ran when she made the beds, ran when she set the table. One Thanksgiving she burned herself badly when, running up from the cellar oven with the ceremonial turkey, she tripped on the stairs and tumbled back down, ending at the bottom in the debris of giblets, hot gravy, and battered turkey. Life was combat, and victory was not to the lazy, the timid, the slugabed, the drugstore cowboy, the libertine, the mushmouth afraid to tell people exactly what was on his mind whether people liked it or not. She ran.

But now the running was over. For a time I could not accept the inevitable. As I sat by her bed, my impulse was to argue her back to reality. On my first visit to the hospital in Baltimore, she asked who I was.

"Russell," I said.

"Russell's way out west," she advised me.

"No, I'm right here."

"Guess where I came from today?" was her response.

"Where?"

"All the way from New Jersey."

"When?"

"Tonight."

"No. You've been in the hospital for three days," I insisted.

"I suggest the thing to do is calm down a little bit," she replied. "Go over to the house and shut the door."

Now she was years deep into the past, living in the neighborhood where she had settled forty years earlier, and she had just been talking with Mrs. Hoffman, a neighbor across the street.

"It's like Mrs. Hoffman said today: The children always wander back to where they come from," she remarked.

"Mrs. Hoffman has been dead for fifteen years."

"Russ got married today," she replied.

"I got married in 1950," I said, which was the fact.

"The house is unlocked," she said.

So it went until a doctor came by to give one of those oral quizzes that medical men apply in such cases. She failed catastrophically, giving wrong answers or none at all to "What day is this?" "Do you know where you are?" "How old are you?" and so on. Then, a surprise.

"When is your birthday?" he asked.

"November 5, 1897," she said. Correct. Absolutely correct.

"How do you remember that?" the doctor asked.

"Because I was born on Guy Fawkes Day," she said.

"Guy Fawkes?" asked the doctor. "Who is Guy Fawkes?"

She replied with a rhyme I had heard her recite time and again over the years when the subject of her birth date arose:

> Please to remember the Fifth of November,
> Gunpowder treason and plot.
> I see no reason why gunpowder treason
> Should ever be forgot.

Then she glared at this young doctor so ill informed about Guy Fawkes' failed scheme to blow King James off his throne with barrels of gunpowder in 1605. She had been a schoolteacher, after all, and knew how to glare at a dolt. "You may know a lot about medicine, but you obviously don't know any history," she said. Having told him exactly what was on her mind, she left us again.

The doctors diagnosed a hopeless senility. Not unusual, they said. "Hardening of the arteries" was the explanation for laymen. I thought it was more complicated than that. For ten years or more the ferocity with which she had once attacked life had been turning to a rage against the weakness, the boredom, and the absence of love that too much age had brought her. Now, after the last bad fall, she seemed to have broken chains that imprisoned her in a life she had come to hate and to return to a time inhabited by people who loved her, a time in which she was needed. Gradually I understood. It was the first time in years I had seen her happy.

She had written a letter three years earlier which explained more than "hardening of the arteries." I had gone down from New York to Baltimore, where she lived, for one of my infrequent visits and, afterwards, had written her with some banal advice to look for the silver lining, to count her blessings instead of burdening others with her miseries. I suppose what it really amounted to was a threat that if she was not more cheerful during my visits I would not come to see her very often. Sons are capable of such letters. This one was written out of a childish faith in the eternal strength of parents, a naive belief that age and wear could be overcome by an effort of will, that all she needed was a good pep talk to recharge a flagging spirit. It was such a foolish, innocent idea, but one thinks of parents differently from other people. Other people can become frail and break, but not parents.

She wrote back in an unusually cheery vein intended to demonstrate, I suppose, that she was mending her ways. She was never a woman to apologize, but for one moment with the pen in her hand she came very close. Referring to my visit, she wrote: "If I seemed unhappy to you at times—" Here she drew back, reconsidered, and said something quite different:

"If I seemed unhappy to you at times, I am, but there's really nothing anyone can do about it, because I'm just so very tired and lonely that I'll just go to sleep and forget it." She was then seventy-eight.

Now, three years later, after the last bad fall, she had managed to forget the fatigue and loneliness and, in these free-wheeling excursions back through time, to recapture happiness. I soon stopped trying to wrest her back to what I considered the real world and tried to travel along with her on those fantastic swoops into the past. One day when I arrived at her bedside she was radiant.

"Feeling good today," I said.

"Why shouldn't I feel good?" she asked. "Papa's going to take me up to Baltimore on the boat today."

At that moment she was a young girl standing on a wharf at Merry Point, Virginia, waiting for the Chesapeake Bay steamer with her father, who had been dead sixty-one years. William Howard Taft was in the White House, Europe still drowsed in the dusk of the great century of peace, America was a young country, and the future stretched before it in beams of crystal sunlight. "The greatest country on God's green earth," her father might have said, if I had been able to step into my mother's time machine and join him on the wharf with the satchels packed for Baltimore.

I could imagine her there quite clearly. She was wearing a blue dress with big puffy sleeves and long black stockings. There was a ribbon in her hair and a big bow tied on the side of her head. There had been a childhood photograph in her bedroom which showed all this, although the colors of course had been added years later by a restorer who tinted the picture.

About her father, my grandather, I could only guess, and indeed, about the girl on the wharf with the bow in her hair, I was merely sentimentalizing. Of my mother's childhood and her people, of their time and place, I knew very little. A world had lived and died, and though it was part of my blood and bone I knew little more about it than I knew of the world of the pharaohs. It was useless now to ask for help from my mother. The orbits of her mind rarely touched present interrogators for more than a moment.

Sitting at her bedside, forever out of touch with her, I wondered about my own children, and their children, and children in general, and about the disconnections between children and parents that prevent them from knowing each other. Children rarely want to know what their parents were before they were parents, and when age finally stirs their curiosity there is no parent left to tell them. If a parent does lift the curtain a bit, it is often only to stun the young with some exemplary tale of how much harder life was in the old days.

I had been guilty of this when my children were small in the early 1960s and living the affluent life. It galled me that their childhoods should be, as I thought, so easy when my own had been, as I thought, so hard. I had developed the habit, when they complained about the steak being overcooked or the television being cut off, of lecturing them on the harshness of life in my day.

"In my day all we got for dinner was macaroni and cheese, and we were glad to get it."

"In my day we didn't have any television."

"In my day . . . ."

"In my day . . . ."

At dinner one evening a son had offended me with an inadequate report card, and as I leaned back and cleared my throat to lecture, he gazed at me with an expression of unutterable resignation and said, "Tell me how it was in your day, Dad."

I was angry with him for that, but angrier with myself for having become one of those ancient bores whose highly selective memories of the past become transparently dishonest even to small children. I tried to break the habit, but must have failed. A few years later my son was referring to me when I was out of earshot as "the old-timer." Between us there was a dispute about time. He looked upon the time that had been my future in a disturbing way. My future was his past, and being young, he was indifferent to the past.

As I hovered over my mother's bed listening for muffled signals from her childhood, I realized that this same dispute had existed between her and me. When she was young, with life ahead of her, I had been her future and resented it. Instinctively, I wanted to break free, cease being a creature defined by her time, consign her future to the past, and create my own. Well, I had finally done that, and then with my own children I had seen my exciting future become their boring past.

These hopeless end-of-the-line visits with my mother made me wish I had not thrown off my own past so carelessly. We all come from the past, and children ought to know what it was that went into their making, to know that life is a braided cord of humanity stretching up from time long gone, and that it cannot be defined by the span of a single journey from diaper to shroud.

I thought that someday my own children would understand that. I thought that, when I am beyond explaining, they would want to know what the world was like when my mother was young and I was younger, and we two relics passed together through strange times. I thought I should try to tell them how it was to be young in the time before jet planes, superhighways, H-bombs, and the global village of television. I realized I would have to start with my mother and her passion for improving the male of the species, which in my case took the form of forcing me to "make something of myself."

Lord, how I hated those words. . . .

Suggestions for Discussion

1. Note the change in Baker's attitude toward his mother's senility. How does he account for it?

2. Baker moves from his narrative that describes his mother's movement "across time" to his reminiscences about her personality. Why is this an effective device?

3. With what details do you learn of his mother's character?

4. Why does Baker dismiss the doctor's diagnosis of "hardening of the arteries" as a simplistic explanation of his mother's behavior? How does he interpret her living in the past? Against what was she rebelling?

5. How does the dialogue enliven and illuminate Baker's relationship to his mother?

6. In his reflections about the seeming indifference of children toward their heritage, Baker both laughs and expresses anger at himself. What prompts this dual response? How do you know that he is in part laughing at himself?

7. How was Baker's youthful relationship to his mother reflected in his son's life?

8. Baker concludes with a didactic message in the last two paragraphs. What is it?

Suggestions for Writing

1. What is your interpretation of Baker's statement that "children ought to know what it was that went into their making, to know that life is a braided cord of humanity stretching up from time long gone, and that it cannot be defined by the span of a single journey from diaper to shroud"?

2. Baker wonders about the "disconnections between children and parents that prevent them from knowing each other." Drawing upon your observations and experience, comment upon this statement.

3. Support or challenge by the use of concrete examples Baker's view that "one thinks of parents differently from other people," that they are invulnerable.

Adrienne Rich

The Anger of a Child

Adrienne Rich (b.1929) has been an activist in the women's movement, and her attitudes are reflected in her poetry, literary criticism, and essays on patriarchy in our culture. Her publications include *A Change of World* (1951), *Snapshots of a Daughter-in-Law* (1963), and *The Will to Change* (1971). The following excerpt appears in her book *Of Woman Born* (1976). It reflects her ambivalence toward her parents and "old, smoldering patches of deep-burning anger."

It is hard to write about my mother. Whatever I do write, it is my story I am telling, my version of the past. If she were to tell her own story other landscapes would be revealed. But in my landscape or hers, there would be old, smoldering patches of deep-burning anger. Before her marriage, she had trained seriously for years both as a concert pianist and a composer. Born in a southern town, mothered by a strong, frustrated woman, she had won a scholarship to study with the director at the Peabody Conservatory in Baltimore, and by teaching at girls' schools had earned her way to further study in New York, Paris, and Vienna. From the age of sixteen, she had been a young belle, who could have married at any time, but she also possessed unusual talent, determination, and independence for her time and place. She read—and reads—widely and wrote—as her journals from my childhood and her letters of today reveal—with grace and pungency.

She married my father after a ten years' engagement during which he finished his medical training and began to establish himself in academic medicine. Once married, she gave up the possibility of a concert career, though for some years she went on composing, and she is still a skilled and dedicated pianist. My father, brilliant, ambitious, possessed by his own drive, assumed that she would give her life over to the enhancement of his. She would manage his household with the formality and grace becoming to a medical professor's wife, though on a limited budget; she would "keep up" her music, though there was no question of letting her composing and practice conflict with her duties as a wife and mother. She was supposed to bear him two children, a boy and a girl. She had to keep her household books to the last penny—I still can see the big blue-gray ledgers, inscribed in her clear, strong hand; she marketed by streetcar, and later, when they could afford a car, she drove my father to and from his laboratory or lectures, often awaiting him for hours. She raised two children, and taught us all our lessons, including music. (Neither of us was sent to school until the fourth grade.) I am sure that she was made to feel responsible for all our imperfections.

My father, like the transcendentalist Bronson Alcott, believed that he (or rather, his wife) could raise children according to his unique moral and intellectual plan, thus proving to the world the values of enlightened, unorthodox child-rearing. I believe that my mother, like Abigail Alcott, at first genuinely and enthusiastically embraced the experiment, and only later found that in carrying out my father's intense, perfectionist program, she was in conflict with her deep instincts as a mother. Like Abigail Alcott, too, she must have found that while ideas might be unfolded by her husband, their daily, hourly practice was going to be up to her. ("'Mr. A. aids me in general principles, but nobody can aid me in the detail,' she mourned. . . . Moreover her husband's views kept her constantly wondering if she were doing a good job. 'Am I doing what is right? Am I doing enough? Am I doing too much?'" The appearance of "temper" and "will" in Louisa, the second Alcott daughter, was blamed by her father on her inheritance from her mother.) Under the institution of motherhood, the mother is the first to blame if theory proves unworkable in practice, or if anything whatsoever goes wrong. But even earlier, my mother had failed at one part of the plan: she had not produced a son.

For years, I felt my mother had chosen my father over me, had sacrificed me to his needs and theories. When my first child was born, I was barely in communication with my parents. I had been fighting my father for my right to an emotional life and a selfhood beyond his needs and theories. We were all at a draw. Emerging from the fear, exhaustion, and alienation of my first childbirth, I could not admit even to myself that I wanted my mother, let alone tell her how much I wanted her. When she visited me in the hospital neither of us could uncoil the obscure lashings of feeling that darkened the room, the tangled thread running backward to where she had labored for three days to give birth to me, and I was not a son. Now, twenty-six years later, I lay in a contagious hospital with my allergy, my skin covered with a mysterious rash, my lips and eyelids swollen, my body bruised and sutured, and, in a cot beside my bed, slept the perfect, golden, male child I had brought forth. How could I have interpreted her feelings when I could not begin to decipher my own? My body had spoken all too eloquently, but it was, medically, just my body. I wanted her to mother me again, to hold my baby in her arms as she had once held me; but that baby was also a gauntlet flung down: *my son.* Part of me longed to offer him for her blessing; part of me wanted to hold him up as a badge of victory in our tragic, unnecessary rivalry as women.

But I was only at the beginning. I know now as I could not possibly know then, that among the tangle of feelings between us, in that crucial yet unreal meeting, was her guilt. Soon I would begin to understand the full weight and burden of maternal guilt, that daily, nightly, hourly, *Am I doing what is right? Am I doing enough? Am I doing too much?* The institution of motherhood finds all mothers more or less guilty of having failed their children; and my mother, in particular, had been expected to help create, according to my father's plan, a perfect daughter. This "perfect" daughter, though gratifyingly precocious, had early been given to tics and tantrums, had become permanently lame from arthritis at twenty-two; she had finally resisted her father's Victorian paternalism, his seductive charm and controlling cruelty, had married a divorced graduate student, had begun to write "modern," "obscure," "pessimistic" poetry, lacking the fluent sweetness of Tennyson, had had the final temerity to get pregnant and bring a living baby into the world. She had ceased to be the demure and precocious child or the poetic, seducible adolescent. Something, in my father's view, had gone terribly wrong. I can imagine that whatever else my mother felt (and I know that part of her *was* mutely on my side) she also was made to feel blame. Beneath the "numbness" that she has since told me she experienced at that time, I can imagine the guilt of Everymother, because I have known it myself.

But I did not know it yet. And it is difficult for me to write of my mother now, because I have known it too well. I struggle to describe what it felt like to be her daughter, but I find myself divided, slipping under her skin; a part of me identified too much with her. I know deep reservoirs of anger toward her still exist: the anger of a four-year-old locked in the closet (my father's orders, but my mother carried them out) for childish misbehavior; the anger of a six-year-old kept too long at piano practice (again, at his insistence, but it was she who gave the lessons) till I developed a series of facial tics. (As a mother I know what a child's facial tic is—a lancet of guilt and pain running through one's own body.) And I still feel the anger of a daughter, pregnant, wanting my mother desperately and feeling she had gone over to the enemy.

And I know there must be deep reservoirs of anger in her; every mother has known overwhelming, unacceptable anger at her children. When I think of the conditions under which my mother became a mother, the impossible expectations, my father's distaste for pregnant women, his hatred of all that he could not control, my anger at her dissolves into grief and anger *for* her, and then dissolves back again into anger at her: the ancient, unpurged anger of the child.

My mother lives today as an independent woman, which she was always meant to be. She is a much-loved, much-admired grandmother, an explorer in new realms; she lives in the present and future, not the past. I no longer have fantasies—they are the unhealed child's fantasies, I think—of some infinitely healing conversation with her, in which we could show all our wounds, transcend the pain we have shared as mother and daughter, say everything at last. But in writing these pages, I am admitting, at least, how important her existence is and has been for me.

Suggestions for Discussion

1. What is the tone of Rich's portrait of her father? With what details does it become apparent?

2. With what details does the author convey her anger at her mother?

3. How does the author feel about the relationship of her father and mother?

4. How did Rich recognize her mother's guilt?

5. Account for the author's ambivalence toward her mother.

6. The author concedes that she is writing her "version of the past" and that her mother might tell her story differently. Provide some of the details in the mother's story if told by her.

Suggestions for Writing

1. Write on your views of enlightened child rearing.

2. Recall an episode in your childhood in which you felt anger at your parents.

3. Develop your version of the mother's story.

F. Scott Fitzgerald
Dearest Scottie

F. Scott Fitzgerald (1896–1940) attended Princeton University but did not graduate. He was commissioned in the army and when stationed at Camp Sheridan he met his future wife, Zelda, about whom he writes in this letter. He wrote copy in an advertising agency in New York while trying to succeed as a novelist. His best known books are *This Side of Paradise* (1920), which draws upon his experiences at college; *The Beautiful and the Damned* (1922), *Tales of the Jazz Age* (1922), *The Great Gatsby* (1925), and *Tender is the Night* (1934). The letter that follows reflects not only his disappointment in his daughter and his feeling of bitterness about his marriage but also conveys his sadness that his dream was aborted.

Dearest Scottie:

I don't think I will be writing letters many more years and I wish you would read this letter twice—bitter as it may seem. You will reject it now, but at a later period some of it may come back to you as truth. When I'm talking to you, you think of me as an older person, an "authority," and when I speak of my own youth what I say becomes unreal to you—for the young can't believe in the youth of their fathers. But perhaps this little bit will be understandable if I put it in writing.

When I was your age I lived with a great dream. The dream grew and I learned how to speak of it and make people listen. Then the dream divided one day when I decided to marry your mother after all, even though I knew she was spoiled and meant no good to me. I was sorry immediately I had married her but, being patient in those days, made the best of it and got to love her in another way. You came along and for a long time we made quite a lot of happiness out of our lives. But I was a man divided—she wanted me to work too much for *her* and not enough for my dream. She realized too late that work was dignity, and the only dignity, and tried to atone for it by working herself, but it was too late and she broke and is broken forever.

It was too late also for me to recoup the damage—I had spent most of my resources, spiritual and material, on her, but I struggled on for five years till my health collapsed, and all I cared about was drink and forgetting.

The mistake I made was in marrying her. We belonged to different worlds—she might have been happy with a kind simple man in a southern garden. She didn't have the strength for the big stage—sometimes she pretended, and pretended beautifully, but she didn't have it. She was soft when she should have been hard, and hard when she should have been yielding. She never knew how to use her energy—she's passed that failing on to you.

For a long time I hated *her* mother for giving her nothing in the line of good habit—nothing but "getting by" and conceit. I never wanted to see again in this world women who were brought up as idlers. And one of my chief desires in life was to keep you from being that kind of person, one who brings ruin to themselves and others. When you began to show disturbing signs at about fourteen, I comforted myself with the idea that you were too precocious socially and a strict school would fix things. But sometimes I think that idlers seem to be a special class for whom nothing can be planned, plead as one will with them—their only contribution to the human family is to warm a seat at the common table.

My reforming days are over, and if you are that way I don't want to change you. But I don't want to be upset by idlers inside my family or out. I want my energies and my earnings for people who talk my language.

I have begun to fear that you don't. You don't realize that what I am doing here is the last tired effort of a man who once did something finer and better. There is not enough energy, or call it money, to carry anyone who is dead weight and I am angry and resentful in my soul when I feel that I am doing this. People like _____ _____ and your mother must be carried because their illness makes then useless. But it is a different story that *you* have spent two years doing no useful work at all, improving neither your body nor your mind, but only writing reams and reams of dreary letters to dreary people, with no possible object except obtaining invitations which you could not accept. Those letters go on, even in your sleep, so that I know your whole trip now is one long waiting for the post. It is like an old gossip who cannot still her tongue.

You have reached the age when one is of interest to an adult only insofar as one seems to have a future. The mind of a little child is fascinating, for it looks on old things with new eyes—but at about twelve this changes. The adolescent offers nothing, can do nothing, say nothing that the adult cannot do better. Living with you in Baltimore (and you have told Harold that I alternated between strictness and neglect, by which I suppose you mean the times I was so inconsiderate as to have T.B., or to retire into myself to write, for I had little social life apart from you) represented a rather too domestic duty forced on me by your mother's illness. But I endured your Top Hats and Telephones until the day you snubbed me at dancing school, less willingly after that. . . .

To sum up: What you have done to please me or make me proud is practically negligible since the time you made yourself a good diver at camp (and now you are softer than you have ever been). In your career as a "wild society girl," vintage of 1925, I'm not interested. I don't want any of it—it would bore me, like dining with the Ritz Brothers. When I do not feel you are "going somewhere," your company tends to depress me for the silly waste and triviality involved. On the other hand, when occasionally I see signs of life and intention in you, there is no company in the world I prefer. For there is no doubt that you have something in your belly, some real gusto for life—a real dream of your own—and my idea was to wed it to something solid before it was too late—as it was too late for your mother to learn anything when she got around to it. Once when you spoke French as a child it was enchanting with your odd bits of knowledge—now your conversation is as commonplace as if you'd spent the last two years in the Corn Hollow High School—what you saw in *Life* and read in *Sexy Romances.*

I shall come East in September to meet your boat—but this letter is a declaration that I am no longer interested in your promissory notes but only in what I see. I love you always but I am only interested by people who think and work as I do and it isn't likely that *I* shall change at my age. Whether you will—or want to—remains to be seen.

Daddy

P.S. If you keep the diary, please don't let it be the dry stuff I could buy in a ten-franc guide book. I'm not interested in dates and places, even the Battle of New Orleans, unless you have some unusual reaction to them. Don't try to be witty in the writing, unless it's natural—just true and real.

P.P.S. Will you please read this letter a second time? I wrote it over twice.

Suggestions for Discussion

1. How would you describe the philosophical differences between Fitzgerald and Scottie's mother?

2. What do you infer was Fitzgerald's dream?

3. How valid do you think is Fitzgerald's comparison of the mind of a child with that of an adolescent?

4. Partly by inference the writer provides a picture of Scottie's recent life. What details do you learn of it?

Suggestions for Writing

1. Write the letter that your mother or father might write to you.

2. Imagine you have received a critical letter from your mother or father. How would you answer it?

3. Is it true that the young can't believe in the youth of their fathers (or mothers)?

Susan Cheever

Portrait of My Father
from *Home Before Dark*

Susan Cheever (b. 1943) was educated at Brown University. She wrote as a professional journalist before she began writing novels. She also taught creative writing at Hofstra University. Her novels are *Looking For Work* (1980) and *A Handsome Man* (1981). Her recent biography of her father, famous novelist, John Cheever, is entitled *Home Before Dark*. By a variety of means—quotations from his journal, statements regarding his philosophy, his contradictions and confusions, his fantasies, and his intimidating qualities—Susan Cheever presents a moving portrait of her father, whom she deeply reveres.

Susan calls me," my father wrote in his journal in 1952. "It is four or five in the morning. 'I have such awful thoughts, Daddy,' she says. 'I think there is a tiger in the hall and that he will eat me.' She laughs, but she is frightened. It is the hour before light. The dark is troubled for us both. There are no ghosts of men or tigers in the hall, but the dark is hard to bear. There will be great pain and labor before we see this obscurity transformed into sweet morning."

On a cold sunny Monday, about two months before my father died, I checked into New York Hospital and had my own first child, a daughter, Sara. From the instant I saw her, a tiny red creature bathed in the weird underwater light of the hospital operating room, I loved her with an intensity that life had not prepared me for. As I had grown more pregnant, my father had become sicker. He lost a little every day, and that loss seemed to cast a shadow over all of us. The birth of the baby didn't take away that loss, but it changed everything for me.

My parents drove in to visit me at the hospital the day after she was born. My mother brought a calico mobile, I drank a glass of champagne, and my father's gaunt unbalanced face beamed in at Sarah's plastic bassinet through the transparent wall of the nursery. Her birth seemed to revitalize him. He called the next morning and told me that he felt much better. It was early, but the hospital was already awake. My room was filled with flowers. The cancer was finished, my father had decided. "I've kicked it, Susie," he said. "It's over."

It' a measure of human optimism that we all believed him. For a few weeks it even seemed to be true. He would never be well, of course, but the weakened, wasted father that was left seemed infinitely precious. My first post-pregnancy outing was to see him receive the National Medal for Literature at Carnegie Hall. He looked frail, but he spoke with great strength. Afterward my husband and I went backstage. He wasn't there; we found him and the rest of the family ensconced on the banquettes of the Russian Tea Room next door, laughing and eating and ordering more. But early in May, when we took the month-old baby out to visit my parents in Ossining, he looked weaker.

"Make your famous baby noise, John," my mother urged him, and he curled up his lip in a comic high-pitched squeal. Then suddenly he seemed very tired. "Thank you for remembering, dear," he said. That's when I knew he was worse again. As the baby awakened to the world around her that first and last spring, my father waned and faded and grew more absent. The weather stayed warm and sunny. The cherry trees blossomed and shed their pink flowers like a snowfall on the paths in Central Park. The trees turned lush and green. Babies keep odd hours, and often as I watched the sunrise colors well up from the East Side while I fed my daughter, I thought of my father who might be lying awake in his bed in Ossining. In the evening when the baby slept, I called him. By that time, he rarely answered the telephone.

"He won't eat anything," my mother said. Her voice sounded ragged. "Here, Susie, you tell him he has to eat something."

"Hello," my father said in the normal voice that he still managed for telephone hellos and one-word answers.

"Hi, Daddy," I said. "I think you should eat something."

"Yes." His voice had subsided to a grating whisper, and the words were slow and drawn out. Sickness seemed to heighten his sense of social propriety. As his thinking became more chaotic, his manners became more impeccable.

"Shall I call you after dinner?" he said.

"Yes, Daddy." The receiver banged against the telephone as he dropped it.

I remember my father at the head of our family dinner table. First, when there were only three of us, he sat at the end of the plain pine table in the hallway that was the dining room of our apartment on Fifty-ninth Street in New York City.

Later, after we had moved out to Scarborough, he sat at the black modern table next to the window that looked out over the lawns toward Beechwood and the green metal garbage pails behind the estate's big garage. My brother Ben and I sat on opposite sides of the table. At breakfast, before we went to school, Ben would hold a napkin up to his face, slipping food under the bottom edge so that he wouldn't have to look at me. At dinner, nothing like that was allowed. I set the table and my mother cooked and brought the food out in serving dishes and we all sat down and my father said grace.

"Dear Lord, we thank Thee for Thy bounty," he would say while Ben looked longingly at the protection of his napkin. If we children were fighting, as we often were, my father would add a pointed, "And bless this table with peace." And if the dogs were grumbling for scraps under the table, he would also add, "both top and bottom." Then he would say "Amen." My father always said grace. Sometimes he stayed with the short and traditional, sometimes he improvised. Later on, for special occasions, he would base the grace on his favorite quotation, a paraphrase of a line from Jowett's translation of Plato: "Let us consider that the soul of man is immortal, able to endure every sort of good and every sort of evil." Then he would add a paraphrase of the words of the prophet Micah: "So let us live humbly and give thanks unto Our Lord God. Amen."

In the house at Ossining there was a long cherry dining room table with Italian wood and wicker chairs. I always sat on my father's left, with my back to the wall, facing the fireplace with the wing chair in front of it and the long bench next to it that was piled precariously high with galleys of new books and newspapers and magazines: that day's *New York Times*, the local *Ossining Citizen Register*, *The New Yorker*, *The New York Review of Books*, *Newsweek* (when I was working there), *Antaeus*, and sometimes *The Smithsonian* or the *Brown Alumni Monthly*—or anything else that had come in the mail recently enough to have avoided being thrown out. Sometimes at the table my head bumped against the frame of the Piranesi etching that hung on the wall behind me.

I went away to school in 1960, the year my parents bought the house, and Ben went off soon afterward. We three children were rarely there at the same time. When we were, my two brothers sat across from me on the same side of the table. The dogs warmed our feet, sometimes raising themselves for a halfhearted sally after one of the cats. At Christmas vacation, the porch outside would be piled high with snow. In the summer, delicious smells from my mother's flower garden wafted through the open top half of the Dutch door at the end of the room.

The family meal was always served onto our plates by my father from serving platters, and when everyone had said grace and we had all concluded "Amen," my mother would say, "Oh, John, you haven't left yourself anything but the carcass" (if it was a chicken), or "the head" (if it was a fish), or "the tail" (if it was a steak), or "the gristle" (if it was a roast). She was often right. My mother always felt that there wouldn't be enough for her family to eat. Food was so rich and so abundant in our house that even the pets were all overweight. My father, on the other hand, was convinced that somehow he would go hungry—that he would be left out, overlooked, not provided for. He usually managed to make *his* fears seem legitimate, even if it meant heaping our plates to the edges so that there wouldn't be quite enough left for him. "Oh don't worry about me, dear," he would answer my mother. "This is plenty for me." We used to call him Eeyore.

The food, however, was not the main event at our dinner table. Conversation was the main event. Sometimes there was a general discussion of one person's problem: What would I do if Roddy Butler asked me to the dance at the country club? Should Ben major in English at school? Could Fred bring his friend Brad to New Hampshire? Advice, comments, and suggestions came from all quarters. Sometimes it was funny, sometimes it was friendly, sometimes it was harsh or sarcastic. Someone would certainly point out that Roddy had no intention of asking me anywhere, that Ben would be lucky to *pass* English, and that Fred might have trouble keeping his friends if he didn't learn to keep his elbows off the table. There was a lot of joking and very little serious counsel. We learned to make real decisions privately, on our own. My parents' problems were rarely discussed, because that usually ended in tears from my mother or recriminations and sarcasm from my father—and nobody got dessert.

Sometimes my mother or father would come up with an image, or a fragment of a story, and we would all weave imaginary plots around it. Sometimes we talked about books or movies or the poetry we recited to each other on Sunday afternoons. Often we talked and speculated about other people, our neighbors and friends. No one ever hesitated to be mean—although the insults were usually also pretty funny. We were so mean to each other, in fact, that guests were often astonished and shocked. They didn't catch the undertone of humor in our quick sarcasms, and there were times when we didn't catch it either. Explosions and tears and sudden departures were not at all uncommon. My brothers called our dinner table "the bear garden."

"My daughter says that our dinner table is like a shark tank," my father wrote in his journal one day in 1970, between a drunken lunch in honor of his friend Yevtushenko and an evening spent brooding over a bad review of *Bullet Park*. "I go into a spin. I am not a shark, I am a dolphin. Mary is the shark, etc. . . . But what we stumble on is the banality of family situations. Thinking of Susan, she makes the error of daring not to have been invented by me, of laughing at the wrong time and speaking lines I have not written. Does this prove that I am incapable of love or can only love myself? Scotch for breakfast and I do not like these mornings."

By Thanksgiving of 1981, my father was already too sick to eat much. Of course we didn't know how sick. He had had a kidney removed in June, and all summer he had seemed to get better, but in the autumn, as the air cooled and the leaves changed color, he seemed to be weaker again. When Richard Avedon took a picture of him for the cover of *The Dial*, the photograph looked stark and strange. He couldn't ride his bicycle anymore, and so the doctor sent him to a chiropractor. He went twice a week and installed a primitive traction device on Ben's bed upstairs, where he was working then. He wasn't working much, though. *Paradise* had been finished in the spring, and he spent most of his time answering mail and keeping the journal.

My father never quite trusted medicine. On the one hand, he always thought he was fine; at the same time, he always knew he was dying. His perception of physical reality was tenuous at best. Maybe his mother's Christian Science had something to do with it, too. His solution was to stick to small-town doctors and small-town hospitals, where at least he was known and felt comfortable and where it seemed they often told him what he wanted to hear. As a result, when he needed sophisticated diagnosis and expert medical care, he seemed to prefer jolly talk and home remedies. As the pains in his ribs and legs got worse, he was often depressed.

It was the beginning of December by the time he went back into the hospital for some X-rays. The shadows on those heavy plastic sheets showed that cancer had spread from his kidney up to his lungs and down into his legs; and that was why he felt, as he put it, "so lousy." After they saw the X-rays, the doctors told him there was nothing they could do. There was no treatment. The cancer was too far along.

My husband and I were in La Jolla, California, visiting my husband's daughter that week. "It's very bad," my mother said when I called home to see how the X-rays had come out. "It's very bad." Her voice sounded strange. I was sitting on a bed in a hotel room in Southern California. There was a bureau with a few books on it, and my maternity clothes were thrown over a chair. The main street of La Jolla was outside heavily curtained windows.

"They say I'm a dying man," my father said. His voice was still strong, but the laugh in it seemed to fade as I listened. "They say that my bones look moth-eaten." There was an edge of irony to his voice, as if he were talking about someone else. The hotel room had been decorated in Spanish mission style, and the walls and the bedspread were orange. It was the end of the day. Downstairs, people were waiting to meet us for drinks in the Patio Bar. My father told me that my brother Fred would be flying home for the holidays. "Some people will do almost anything to get their children home for Christmas," he said. I leaned back against the headboard, and the ridges of molded wood dug into my spine. A painting of a cowboy hung on the wall. In the distance, I could hear the sound of the sea. . . .

Suggestions for Discussion

1. How does the quotation from her father's journal set the tone for the chapter?

2. What is gained by the juxtaposition of the author's feelings about the birth of her daughter and the declining days of her father? What details sharpen the contrast between the beginning and end of life?

3. In what different contexts are food and the dinner table the subject of discussion? What do these descriptions tell the reader about the writer's father? about the family relationship?

4. What contradictions does the writer see in her father, especially in regard to his attitude toward appearances?

5. Compare the expectations of Fitzgerald and Cheever for their daughters. How does Cheever's response to his daughter's dating reflect his own conflicts?

6. What was the nature of the father–daughter relationship when the latter became a writer?

7. What does the author's description of the setting in the last paragraph contribute to the tone? How does she make the reader know how deeply she cared for her father?

Suggestions for Writing

1. Discuss the banality of family situations.

2. Write a description of someone whose appearance makes a statement about him or her meeting the world. Or write a description of someone whose appearance is very deceptive.

3. Discuss the role that parental expectations play in fostering or inhibiting their children's growth and development.

Essays

John Gregory Dunne

Quintana

John Gregory Dunne (b. 1932) was educated at Princeton University. He has written a number of film scripts with his wife, Joan Didion: *The Panic in Needle Park* (1971), *Play It As It Lays* (1972), and *True Confessions* (1982). His publications include *Delano: The Story of the California Grape Strike* (1967), *The Studio* (1969), and *Vegas: A Memoir of a Dark Season* (1974). In this excerpt from *Quintana and Friends* (1978) Dunne acknowledges that if it is important for Quintana to know her parentage, she is free to make the decision and her adoptive parents will respect it.

Quintana will be eleven this week. She approaches adolescence with what I can only describe as panache, but then watching her journey from infancy has always been like watching Sandy Koufax pitch or Bill Russell play basketball. There is the same casual arrogance, the implicit sense that no one has ever done it any better. And yet it is difficult for a father to watch a daughter grow up. With each birthday she becomes more like us, an adult, and what we cling to is the memory of the child. I remember the first time I saw her in the nursery at Saint John's Hospital. It was after visiting hours and my wife and I stood staring through the soundproof glass partition at the infants in their cribs, wondering which was ours. Then a nurse in a surgical mask appeared from a back room carrying a fierce, black-haired baby with a bow in her hair. She was just seventeen hours old and her face was still wrinkled and red and the identification beads on her wrist had not our name but only the letters "NI." "NI" stood for "No Information," the hospital's code for an infant to be placed for adoption. Quintana is adopted.

It has never been an effort to say those three words, even when they occasion the well-meaning but insensitive compliment, "You couldn't love her more if she were your own." At moments like that, my wife and I say nothing and smile through gritted teeth. And yet we are not unaware that sometime

195

in the not too distant future we face a moment that only those of us who are adoptive parents will ever have to face—our daughter's decision to search or not to search for her natural parents.

I remember that when I was growing up a staple of radio drama was the show built around adoption. Usually the dilemma involved a child who had just learned by accident that it was adopted. This information could only come accidentally, because in those days it was considered a radical departure from the norm to inform your son or daughter that he or she was not your own flesh and blood. If such information had to be revealed, it was often followed by the specious addendum that the natural parents had died when the child was an infant. An automobile accident was viewed as the most expeditious and efficient way to get rid of both parents at once. One of my contemporaries, then a young actress, was not told that she was adopted until she was twenty-two and the beneficiary of a small inheritance from her natural father's will. Her adoptive mother could not bring herself to tell her daughter the reason behind the bequest and entrusted the task to an agent from the William Morris office.

Today we are more enlightened, aware of the psychological evidence that such barbaric secrecy can only inflict hurt. When Quintana was born, she was offered to us privately by the gynecologist who delivered her. In California, such private adoptions are not only legal but in the mid-sixties, before legalized abortion and before the sexual revolution made it acceptable for an unwed mother to keep her child, were quite common. The night we went to see Quintana for the first time at Saint John's, there was a tacit agreement between us that "No Information" was only a bracelet. It was quite easy to congratulate ourselves for agreeing to be so open when the only information we had about her mother was her age, where she was from and a certified record of her good health. What we did not realize was that through one bureaucratic slipup we would learn her mother's name and that through another she would learn ours, and Quintana's.

From the day we brought Quintana home from the hospital, we tried never to equivocate. When she was little, we always had Spanish-speaking help and one of the first words she learned, long before she understood its import, was *adoptada*. As she grew older, she never tired of asking us how we happened to adopt her. We told her that we went to the hospital and were given our choice of any baby in the nursery. "No, not that baby," we had said, "not that baby, not that baby . . ." All this with full gestures of inspection, until finally: "That baby!" Her face would always light up and she would say: "Quintana." When she asked a question about her adoption, we answered, never volunteering more than she requested, convinced that as she grew her questions would become more searching and complicated. In terms I hoped she would understand, I tried to explain that adoption offered to a parent the possibility of escaping the prison of genes, that no matter how perfect the natural child, the parent could not help acknowledging in black moments that some of his or her bad blood was bubbling around in the offspring; with an *adoptada*, we were innocent of any knowledge of bad blood.

In time Quintana began to intuit that our simple parable of free choice in the hospital nursery was somewhat more complex than we had indicated. She now knew that being adopted meant being born of another mother, and that person she began referring to as "my other mommy." How old, she asked, was my other mommy when I was born? Eighteen, we answered, and on her stubby little fingers she added on her own age, and with each birthday her other mommy became twenty-three, then twenty-five and twenty-eight. There was no obsessive interest, just occasional queries, some more difficult to answer than others. Why had her other mother given her up? We said that we did not know—which was true—and could only assume that it was because she was little more than a child herself, alone and without the resources to bring up a baby. The answer seemed to satisfy, at least until we became close friends with a young woman, unmarried, with a small child of her own. The contradiction was, of course, apparent to Quintana, and yet she seemed to understand, in the way that children do, that there had been a millennium's worth of social change in the years since her birth, that the pressures on a young unmarried mother were far more in 1966 than they were in 1973. (She did, after all, invariably refer to the man in the White House as President Nixon Vietnam Watergate, almost as if he had a three-tiered name like John Quincy Adams.) We were sure that she viewed her status with equanimity, but how much so we did not realize until her eighth birthday party. There were twenty little girls at the party, and as little girls do, they were discussing things gynecological, specifically the orifice in their mothers' bodies from which they had emerged at birth. "I didn't," Quintana said matter-of-factly. She was sitting in a large wicker fan chair and her pronouncement impelled the other children to silence. "I was adopted." We had often wondered how she would handle this moment with her peers, and we froze, but she pulled it off with such élan and aplomb that in moments the other children were bemoaning their own misfortune in not being adopted, one even claiming, "Well, I was almost adopted."

Because my wife and I both work at home, Quintana has never had any confusion about how we make our living. Our mindless staring at our respective typewriters means food on the table in a way the mysterious phrase "going to the office" never can. From the time she could walk, we have taken her to meetings whenever we were without help, and she has been a quick study on the nuances of our life. "She's remarkably well adjusted," my brother once said about her. "Considering that every time I see her she's in a different city." I think she could pick an agent out of a police lineup, and out of the blue one night at dinner she offered that all young movie directors were short and had frizzy hair and wore Ditto pants and wire glasses and shirts with three buttons opened. (As far as I know, she had never laid eyes on Bogdanovich, Spielberg or Scorsese.) Not long ago an actress received an award for a picture we had written for her. The actress's acceptance speech at the televised award ceremony drove Quintana into an absolute fury. "She never," Quintana reported, "thanked *us.*" Since she not only identifies with our work but at times even considers herself an equal partner, I of course discussed this piece with her before I began working on it. I told her what it was about and said I would drop it if she would be embarrassed or if she thought that subject was too private. She gave it some thought and finally said she wanted me to write it.

I must, however, try to explain and perhaps even try to justify my own motives. The week after *Roots* was televised, each child in Quintana's fifth-grade class was asked to trace a family tree. On my side Quintana went back to her great-grandfather Burns, who arrived from Ireland shortly after the

Civil War, a ten-year-old refugee from the potato famine, and on her mother's side to her great-great-great-great-grandmother Cornwall, who came west in a wagon train in 1846. As it happens, I have little interest in family beyond my immediate living relatives. (I can never remember the given names of my paternal grandparents and have never known my paternal grandmother's maiden name. This lack of interest mystifies my wife.) Yet I wanted Quintana to understand that if she wished, there were blood choices other than Dominick Burns and Nancy Hardin Cornwall. Over the past few years, there has been a growing body of literature about adoptees seeking their own roots. I am in general sympathetic to this quest, although not always to the dogged absolutism of the more militant seekers. But I would be remiss if I did not say that I am more than a little sensitive to the way the literature presents adoptive parents. We are usually shown as frozen in the postures of radio drama, untouched by the changes in attitudes of the last several generations. In point of fact we accept that our children might seek out their roots, even encourage it; we accept it as an adventure like life itself—perhaps painful, one hopes enriching. I know not one adoptive parent who does not feel this way. Yet in the literature there is the implicit assumption that we are threatened by the possibility of search, that we would consider it an act of disloyalty on the part of our children. The patronizing nature of this assumption is never noted in the literature. It is as if we were Hudson and Mrs. Bridges, belowstairs surrogates taking care of the wee one, and I don't like it one damn bit.

Often these days I find myself thinking of Quintana's natural mother. Both my wife and I admit more than a passing interest in the woman who produced this extraordinary child. (As far as we know, she never named the father, and even more interesting, Quintana has never asked about him.) When Quintana was small, and before the legalities of adoption were complete, we imagined her mother everywhere, a wraith-like presence staring through the chain-link fence at the blond infant sunbathing in the crib. Occasionally today we see a photograph of a young woman in a magazine—the mother as we imagine her to look—and we pass it to each other without comment. Once we even checked the name of a model in *Vogue* through her modeling agency; she turned out to be a Finn. I often wonder if she thinks of Quintana, or of us. (Remember, we know each other's names.) There is the possibility that having endured the twin traumas of birth and the giving up of a child, she blocked out the names the caseworker gave her, but I don't really believe it. I consider it more likely that she has followed the fairly well-documented passage of Quintana through childhood into adolescence. Writers are at least semipublic figures, and in the interest of commerce or selling a book or a movie, or even out of simple vanity, we allow interviews and photo layouts and look into television cameras; we even write about ourselves, and our children. I recall wondering how this sentient young woman of our imagination had reacted to four pages in *People*. It is possible, even likely, that she will read this piece. I know that it is an almost intolerable invasion of her privacy. I think it probable, however, that in the dark reaches of night she has considered the possibility of a further incursion, of opening a door one day and seeing a young woman who says, "Hello, Mother, I am your daughter."

Perhaps this is romantic fantasy. We know none of the circumstances of the woman's life, or even if she is still alive. We once suggested to our lawyer that we make a discreet inquiry and he quite firmly said that this was a quest that belonged only to Quintana, if she wished to make it, and not to us. What is not fantasy is that for the past year, Quintana has known the name of her natural mother. It was at dinner and she said that she would like to meet her one day, but that it would be hard, not knowing her name. There finally was the moment: we had never equivocated; did we begin now? We took a deep breath and told Quintana, then age ten, her mother's name. We also said that if she decided to search her out, we would help her in any way we could. (I must allow, however, that we would prefer she wait to make this decision until the Sturm and Drang of adolescence is past.) We then considered the possibility that her mother, for whatever good or circumstantial reasons of her own, might prefer not to see her. I am personally troubled by the militant contention that the natural mother has no right of choice in this matter. "I did not ask to be born," an adoptee once was quoted in a news story I read. "She has to see me." If only life were so simple, if only pain did not hurt. Yet we would never try to influence Quintana on this point. How important it is to know her parentage is a question only she can answer; it is her decision to make.

All parents realize, or should realize, that children are not possessions, but are only lent to us, angel boarders, as it were. Adoptive parents realize this earlier and perhaps more poignantly than others. I do not know the end of this story. It is possible that Quintana will find more reality in family commitment and cousins across the continent and heirloom orange spoons and pictures in an album and faded letters from Dominick Burns and diary entries from Nancy Hardin Cornwall than in the uncertainties of blood. It is equally possible that she will venture into the unknown. I once asked her what she would do if she met her natural mother. "I'd put one arm around Mom," she said, "and one arm around my other mommy, and I'd say, 'Hello, Mommies.'"

If that's the way it turns out, that is what she will do.

Suggestions for Discussion

1. Justify the use of the word *panache* in the description of Quintana.

2. How have attitudes toward adoption changed?

3. How did Quintana's parents learn that she viewed her adoption with equanimity?

4. How does the author feel about the possibility of Quintana's meeting her natural mother?

5. What does the reader learn about the character of Quintana's adoptive father?

Suggestions for Writing

1. Characterize a parent or parents who regard children as possessions.

2. Defend the point of view that adopted children should be aided in seeking their natural parents.

Bruno Bettelheim
Joey: A "Mechanical Boy"

Bruno Bettelheim (b. 1903) was born in Vienna and educated at the University of Vienna. Having survived the Nazi holocaust, he became an American psychoanalyst and educator and was director of the remarkable University of Chicago Sonia Shankman Orthogenic School from 1944 to 1973. He has written many penetrating works on parents and children and the significance of the holocaust. Bettelheim clarifies the concept of emotional development in a machine age by drawing upon the experiences of a single individual, Joey. The illustration is developed by taking an extreme and atypical example of a boy who "froze himself" in the image of the machine.

Joey, when we began our work with him, was a mechanical boy. He functioned as if by remote control, run by machines of his own powerfully creative fantasy. Not only did he himself believe that he was a machine but, more remarkably, he created this impression in others. Even while he performed actions that are intrinsically human, they never appeared to be other than machine-started and executed. On the other hand, when the machine was not working he had to concentrate on recollecting his presence, for he seemed not to exist. A human body that functions as if it were a machine and a machine that duplicates human functions are equally fascinating and frightening. Perhaps they are so uncanny because they remind us that the human body can operate without a human spirit, that body can exist without soul. And Joey was a child who had been robbed of his humanity.

Not every child who possesses a fantasy world is possessed by it. Normal children may retreat into realms of imaginary glory or magic powers, but they are easily recalled from these excursions. Disturbed children are not always able to make the return trip; they remain withdrawn, prisoners of the inner world of delusion and fantasy. In many ways Joey presented a classic example of this state of infantile autism. In any age, when the individual has escaped into a delusional world, he has usually fashioned it from bits and pieces of the world at hand. Joey, in his time and world, chose the machine and froze himself in its image. His story has a general relevance to the understanding of emotional development in a machine age.

Joey's delusion is not uncommon among schizophrenic children today. He wanted to be rid of his unbearable humanity, to become completely automatic. He so nearly succeeded in attaining this goal that he could almost convince others, as well as himself, of his mechanical character. The descriptions of autistic children in the literature take for their point of departure and comparison the normal or abnormal human being. To do justice to Joey I would have to compare him simultaneously to a most inept infant and a highly complex piece of machinery. Often we had to force ourselves by a conscious act of will to realize that Joey was a child. Again and again his acting-out of his delusions froze our own ability to respond as human beings.

During Joey's first weeks with us we would watch absorbedly as this at once fragile-looking and imperious nine-year-old went about his mechanical existence. Entering the dining room, for example, he would string an imaginary wire from his "energy source"—an imaginary electric outlet—to the table. There he "insulted" himself with paper napkins and finally plugged himself in. Only then could Joey eat, for he firmly believed that the "current" ran his ingestive apparatus. So skillful was the pantomime that one had to look twice to be sure there was neither wire nor outlet nor plug. Children and members of our staff spontaneously avoided stepping on the "wires" for fear of interrupting what seemed the source of his very life.

For long periods of time, when his "machinery" was idle, he would sit so quietly that he would disappear from the focus of the most conscientious observation. Yet in the next moment he might be "working" and the center of our captivated attention. Many times a day he would turn himself on and shift noisily through a sequence of higher and higher gears until he "exploded," screaming "crash, crash!" and hurling items from his ever present apparatus— radio tubes, light bulbs, even motors or, lacking these, any handy breakable object. (Joey had an astonishing knack for snatching bulbs and tubes unobserved.) As soon as the object thrown had shattered, he would cease his screaming and wild jumping and retire to mute, motionless nonexistence.

Our maids, inured to difficult children, were exceptionally attentive to Joey; they were apparently moved by his extreme infantile fragility, so strangely coupled with megalomaniacal superiority. Occasionally some of the apparatus he fixed to his bed to "live him" during his sleep would fall down in disarray. This machinery he contrived from masking tape, cardboard, wire and other paraphernalia. Usually the maids would pick up such things and leave them on a table for the children to find, or disregard them entirely. But Joey's machine they carefully restored: "Joey must have the carburetor so he can breathe." Similarly they were on the alert to pick up and preserve the motors that ran him during the day and the exhaust pipes through which he exhaled.

How had Joey become a human machine? From intensive interviews with his parents we learned that the process had begun even before birth. Schizophrenia often results from parental rejection, sometimes combined ambivalently with love. Joey, on the other hand, had been completely ignored.

"I never knew I was pregnant," his mother said, meaning that she had already excluded Joey from her consciousness. His birth, she said, "did not make any difference." Joey's father, a rootless draftee in the wartime civilian army, was equally unready for parenthood. So, of course, are many young couples. Fortunately most such parents lose their indifference upon the baby's birth. But not Joey's parents. "I did not want to see or nurse him," his mother declared. "I had no feeling of actual dislike—I simply didn't want to take care of him." For the first three months of his life Joey "cried most of the time." A colicky baby, he was kept on a rigid four-hour feeding schedule, was not touched unless necessary and was never cuddled or played with. The mother, preoccupied with herself, usually left Joey alone in the crib or playpen during the day. The father discharged his frustrations by punishing Joey when the child cried at night.

Soon the father left for overseas duty, and the mother took Joey, now a year and a half old, to live with her at her parents' home. On his arrival the grandparents noticed that ominous changes had occurred in the child. Strong and healthy at birth, he had become frail and irritable; a responsive baby, he had become remote and inaccessible. When he began to master speech, he talked only to himself. At an early date he became preoccupied with machinery, including an old electric fan which he could take apart and put together again with surprising deftness.

Joey's mother impressed us with a fey quality that expressed her insecurity, her detachment from the world and her low physical vitality. We were struck especially by her total indifference as she talked about Joey. This seemed much more remarkable than the actual mistakes she made in handling him. Certainly he was left to cry for hours when hungry, because she fed him on a rigid schedule; he was toilet-trained with great rigidity so that he would give no trouble. These things happen to many children. But Joey's existence never registered with his mother. In her recollections he was fused at one moment with one event or person; at another, with something or somebody else. When she told us about his birth and infancy, it was as if she were talking about some vague acquaintance, and soon her thoughts would wander off to another person or to herself.

When Joey was not yet four, his nursery school suggested that he enter a special school for disturbed children. At the new school his autism was immediately recognized. During his three years there he experienced a slow improvement. Unfortunately a subsequent two years in a parochial school destroyed this progress. He began to develop compulsive defenses, which he called his "preventions." He could not drink, for example, except through elaborate piping systems built of straws. Liquids had to be "pumped" into him, in his fantasy, or he could not suck. Eventually his behavior became so upsetting that he could not be kept in the parochial school. At home things did not improve. Three months before entering the Orthogenic School he made a serious attempt at suicide.

To us Joey's pathological behavior seemed the external expression of an overwhelming effort to remain almost nonexistent as a person. For weeks Joey's only reply when addressed was "Bam." Unless he thus neutralized whatever we said, there would be an explosion, for Joey plainly wished to close off every form of contact not mediated by machinery. Even when he was bathed he rocked back and forth with mute, engine-like regularity, flooding the bathroom. If he stopped rocking, he did this like a machine too; suddenly he went completely rigid. Only once, after months of being lifted from his bath and carried to bed, did a small expression of puzzled pleasure appear on his face as he said very softly: "They even carry you to bed here."

For a long time after he began to talk he would never refer to anyone by name, but only as "that person" or "the little person" or "the big person." He was unable to designate by its true name anything to which he attached feelings. Nor could he name his anxieties except through neologisms or word contaminations. For a long time he spoke about "master paintings" and "a master painting room" (*i.e.*, masturbating and masturbating room). One of his machines, the "criticizer," prevented him from "saying words which have unpleasant feelings." Yet he gave personal names to the tubes and motors in his collection of machinery. Moreover, these dead things had feelings; the tubes bled when hurt and sometimes got sick. He consistently maintained this reversal between animate and inanimate objects.

In Joey's machine world everything, on pain of instant destruction, obeyed inhibitory laws much more stringent than those of physics. When we came to know him better, it was plain that in his momemts of silent withdrawal, with his machine switched off, Joey was absorbed in pondering the compulsive laws of his private universe. His preoccupation with machinery made it difficult to establish even practical contacts with him. If he wanted to do something with a counselor, such as play with a toy that had caught his vague attention, he could not do so: "I'd like this very much, but first I have to turn off the machine." But by the time he had fulfilled all the requirements of his preventions, he had lost interest. When a toy was offered to him, he could not touch it because his motors and his tubes did not leave him a hand free. Even certain colors were dangerous and had to be strictly avoided in toys and clothing, because "some colors turn off the current, and I can't touch them because I can't live without the current."

Joey was convinced that machines were better than people. Once when he bumped into one of the pipes on our jungle gym he kicked it so violently that his teacher had to restrain him to keep him from injuring himself. When she explained that the pipe was much harder than his foot, Joey replied: "That proves it. Machines are better than the body. They don't break; they're much harder and stronger." If he lost or forgot something, it merely proved that his brain ought to be thrown away and replaced by machinery. If he spilled something his arm should be broken and twisted off because it did not work properly. When his head or arm failed to work as it should, he tried to punish it by hitting it. Even Joey's feelings were mechanical. Much later in his therapy, when he had formed a timid attachment to another child and had been rebuffed, Joey cried: "He broke my feelings."

Gradually we began to understand what had seemed to be contradictory in Joey's behavior—why he held on to the motors and tubes, then suddenly destroyed them in a fury, then set out immediately and urgently to equip himself with new and larger tubes. Joey had created these machines to run his body and mind because it was too painful to be human. But again and again he became dissatisfied with their failure to meet his need and rebellious at the way they frustrated his will. In a recurrent frenzy he "exploded" his light bulbs and tubes, and for a moment became a human being—for one crowning instant he came alive. But as soon as he had asserted his dominance through the self-created explosion, he felt his life ebbing away. To keep on existing he had immediately to restore his machines and replenish the electricity that supplied his life energy.

What deep-seated fears and needs underlay Joey's delusional system? We were long in finding out, for Joey's preventions effectively concealed the secret of his autistic behavior. In the meantime we dealt with his peripheral problems one by one.

During his first year with us Joey's most trying problem was toilet behavior. This surprised us, for Joey's personality was not "anal" in the Freudian sense; his original personality damage had antedated the period of his toilet-training. Rigid and early toilet-training, however, had certainly contributed to his anxieties. It was our effort to help Joey with this problem that led to his first recognition of us as human beings.

Going to the toilet, like everything else in Joey's life, was surrounded by elaborate preventions. We had to accompany him; he had to take off all his clothes; he could only squat, not sit, on the toilet seat; he had to touch the wall with one hand, in which he also clutched frantically the vacuum tubes that powered his elimination. He was terrified lest his whole body be sucked down.

To counteract this fear we gave him a metal wastebasket in lieu of a toilet. Eventually, when eliminating into the wastebasket, he no longer needed to take off all his clothes, nor to hold on to the wall. He still needed the tubes and motors which, he believed, moved his bowels for him. But here again the all-important machinery was itself a source of new terrors. In Joey's world the gadgets had to move their bowels, too. He was terribly concerned that they should, but since they were so much more powerful than men, he was also terrified that if his tubes moved their bowels, their feces would fill all of space and leave him no room to live. He was thus always caught in some fearful contradiction.

Our readiness to accept his toilet habits, which obviously entailed some hardship for his counselors, gave Joey the confidence to express his obsessions in drawings. Drawing these fantasies was the first step toward letting us in, however distantly, to what concerned him most deeply. It was the first step in a year-long process of externalizing his anal preoccupations. As a result he began seeing feces everywhere; the whole world became to him a mire of excrement. At the same time he began to eliminate freely wherever he happend to be. But with this release from his infantile imprisonment in compulsive rules, the toilet and the whole process of elimination became less dangerous. Thus far it had been beyond Joey's comprehension that anybody could possibly move his bowels without mechanical aid. Now Joey took a further step forward; defecation became the first physiological process he could perform without the help of vacuum tubes. It must not be thought that he was proud of this ability. Taking pride in his achievement presupposes that one accomplished it of one's own free will. He still did not feel himself an autonomous person who could do things on his own. To Joey defecation still seemed enslaved to some incomprehensible but utterly binding cosmic law, perhaps the law his parents had imposed on him when he was being toilet-trained.

It was not simply that his parents had subjected him to rigid, early training. Many children are so trained. But in most cases the parents have a deep emotional investment in the child's performance. The child's response in turn makes training an occasion for interaction between them and for the building of genuine relationships. Joey's parents had no emotional investment in him. His obedience gave them no satisfaction and won him no affection or approval. As a toilet-trained child he saved his mother labor, just as household machines saved her labor. As a machine he was not loved for his performance, nor could he love himself.

So it had been with all other aspects of Joey's existence with his parents. Their reactions to his eating or noneating, sleeping or wakening, urinating or defecating, being dressed or undressed, washed or bathed did not flow from any unitary interest in him, deeply embedded in their personalities. By treating him mechanically his parents made him a machine. The various functions of life—even the parts of his body—bore no integrating relationship to one another or to any sense of self that was acknowledged and confirmed by others. Though he had acquired mastery over some functions, such as toilet-training and speech, he had acquired them separately and kept them isolated from each other. Toilet-training had thus not gained him a pleasant feeling of body mastery; speech had not led to communication of thought or feeling. On the contrary, each achievement only steered him away from self-mastery and integration. Toilet-training had enslaved him. Speech left him talking in neologisms that obstructed his and our ability to relate to each other. In Joey's development the normal process of growth had been made to run backward. Whatever he had learned put him not at the end of his infantile development toward integration but, on the contrary, farther behind than he was at its very beginning. Had we understood this sooner, his first years with us would have been less baffling.

It is unlikely that Joey's calamity could befall a child in any time and culture but our own. He suffered no physical deprivation; he starved for human contact. Just to be taken care of is not enough for relating. It is a necessary but not a sufficient condition. At the extreme where utter scarcity reigns, the forming of relationships is certainly hampered. But our society of mechanized plenty often makes for equal difficulties in a child's learning to relate. Where parents can provide the simple creature-comforts for their children only at the cost of significant effort, it is likely that they will feel pleasure in being able to provide for them; it is this, the parents' pleasure, that gives children a sense of personal worth and sets the process of relation in motion. But if comfort is so readily available that the parents feel no particular pleasure in winning it for their children, then the children cannot develop the feeling of being worthwhile around the satisfaction of their basic needs. Of course parents and children can and do develop relationships around other situations. But matters are then no longer so simple and direct. The child must be on the receiving end of care and concern given with pleasure and without the exaction of return if he is to feel loved and worthy of respect and consideration. This feeling gives him the ability to trust; he can entrust his well-being to persons to whom he is so important. Out of such trust the child learns to form close and stable relationships.

For Joey relationship with his parents was empty of pleasure in comfort-giving as in all other situations. His was an extreme instance of a plight that sends many schizophrenic children to our clinics and hospitals. Many months passed before he could relate to us; his despair that anybody could like him made contact impossible.

When Joey could finally trust us enough to let himself become more infantile, he began to play at being a papoose. There was a corresponding change in his fantasies. He drew endless pictures of himself as an electrical papoose. Totally enclosed, suspended in empty space, he is run by unknown, unseen powers through wireless electricity.

As we eventually came to understand, the heart of Joey's delusional system was the artificial, mechanical womb he had created and into which he had locked himself. In his papoose fantasies lay the wish to be entirely reborn in a womb. His new experiences in the school suggested that life, after all, might be worth living. Now he was searching for a way to be reborn in a better way. Since machines were better than men, what was more natural than to try rebirth through them? This was the deeper meaning of his electrical papoose.

As Joey made progress, his pictures of himself became more dominant in his drawings. Though still machine-operated, he has grown in self-importance. Another great step forward is represented in a picture in which he has acquired hands that do something, and he has had the courage to make a picture of the machine that runs him. Later still the papoose became a person, rather than a robot encased in glass.

Eventually Joey began to create an imaginary family at the school: the "Carr" family. Why the Carr family? In the car he was enclosed as he had been in his papoose, but at least the car was not stationary; it could move. More important, in a car one was not only driven but also could drive. The Carr family was Joey's way of exploring the possibility of leaving the school, of living with a good family in a safe, protecting car.

Joey at last broke through his prison. In this brief account it has not been possible to trace the painfully slow process of his first true relations with other human beings, Suffice it to say that he ceased to be a mechanical boy and become a human child. This newborn child was, however, nearly 12 years old. To recover the lost time is a tremendous task. That work has occupied Joey and us ever since. Sometimes he sets to it with a will; at other times the difficulty of real life makes him regret that he ever came out of his shell. But he has never wanted to return to his mechanical life.

One last detail and this fragment of Joey's story has been told. When Joey was 12, he made a float for our Memorial Day parade. It carried the slogan: "Feelings are more important than anything under the sun." Feelings, Joey had learned, are what make for humanity; their absence, for a mechanical existence. With this knowledge Joey entered the human condition.

Suggestions for Discussion

1. What is meant by "mechanical boy"? How does the author account for Joey's behavior? How does the author develop his analogy?

2. What cause–effect relationships are discussed and how are they illustrated and supported?

3. How does the author illustrate his statement that "in Joey's development the normal process of growth had been made to run backward"?

4. How does the analogy of labor-saving devices contribute to your understanding of Joey's problem? How does the succeeding paragraph further illuminate the analogy?

5. What is the relationship of Joey's Memorial Day slogan to the concluding sentence? To the author's central purpose?

6. With what concrete illustrations does the author make clear each of the following dualities: human–mechanical; fragile–imperious; internalize–externalize; explosions–preventions?

7. How does the diction, appropriate to the vocabulary of a machine, contribute to the tone? Provide emphasis? Refer both to the author's descriptions and to Joey's own choice of words.

8. What is Bettelheim's attitude toward Joey? toward his mother? How do you know?

9. From what point of view does Bettelheim narrate the story of Joey? Is he speaking solely as a psychiatrist? Is he also passing judgment upon society? Discuss.

Suggestions for Writing

1. Formulate your own definition of childhood schizophrenia by referring to specific details in the text.

2. Describe a sensitive or rebellious child or adolescent by providing concrete illustrations of his behavior and by showing your subject interacting with family, friends, or teachers.

3. Clarify a general concept by drawing upon the experiences of a single individual. Beginning with an observation about the family, the university, an occupation, a leisure activity, attempt to illustrate your concept by narrating the experiences of a single individual.

4. Analyze the means by which the author transforms what might have been a medical case history into a moving portrait of Joey. Examine a number of case histories in psychiatric texts. What are the differences in intention, tone, perspective, and diction in the two modes of writing?

Richard Rodriguez

Mr. Secrets

Richard Rodriguez (b. 1944) was born in San Francisco and attended Stanford University, Columbia University, and the University of California at Berkeley. He has written about his experiences as a scholarship and minority student in *College English* and *American Scholar.* This excerpt from his autobiography, *Hunger of Memory* (1982), reflects his loneliness as a writer and his sensitivity to his parents' reluctance to have their privacy violated.

I am writing about those very things my mother has asked me not to reveal. Shortly after I published my first autobiographical essay seven years ago, my mother wrote me a letter pleading with me never again to write about our family life. "Write about something else in the future. Our family life is private." And besides: "Why do you need to tell the *gringos* about how 'divided' you feel from the family?"

I sit at my desk now, surrounded by versions of paragraphs and pages of this book, considering that question.

When I decided to compose this intellectual autobiography, a New York editor told me that I would embark on a lonely journey. Over the noise of voices and dishes in an East Side restaurant, he said. "There will be times when you will think the entire world has forgotten you. Some mornings you will yearn for a phone call or a letter to assure you that you still are connected to the world." There *have* been mornings when I've dreaded the isolation this writing requires. Mornings spent listless in silence and in fear of confronting the blank sheet of paper. There have been times I've rushed away from my papers to answer the phone; gladly gotten up from my chair, hearing the mailman outside. Times I have been frustrated by the slowness of words, the way even a single paragraph never seemed done.

I had known a writer's loneliness before, working on my dissertation in the British Museum. But that experience did not prepare me for the task of writing these pages where my own life is the subject. Many days I feared I had stopped living by committing myself to remember the past. I feared that my absorption with events in the past amounted to an immature refusal to live in the present. Adulthood seemed consumed by memory. I would tell myself otherwise. I would tell myself that the act of remembering is an act of the present. (In writing this autobiography, I am actually describing the man I have become—the man in the present.)

Times when the money ran out, I left writing for temporary jobs. Once I had a job for over six months. I resumed something like a conventional social life. But then I have turned away, come back to my San Francisco apartment to closet myself in the silence I both need and fear.

I stay away from late-night parties. (To be clearheaded in the morning.) I disconnect my phone for much of the day. I must avoid complex relationships—a troublesome lover or a troubled friend. The person who knows me best scolds me for escaping from life. (*Am* I evading adulthood?) People I know get promotions at jobs. Friends move away. Friends get married. Friends divorce. One friend tells me she is pregnant. Then she has a baby. Then the baby has the formed face of a child. Can walk. Talk. And still I sit at this desk laying my words like jigsaw pieces, a fellow with ladies in housecoats and old men in slippers who watch TV. Neighbors in my apartment house rush off to work about nine. I hear their steps on the stairs. (They will be back at six o'clock.) Somewhere planes are flying. The door slams behind them.

"Why?" My mother's question hangs in the still air of memory.

The loneliness I have felt many mornings, however, has not made me forget that I am engaged in a highly public activity. I sit here in silence writing this small volume of words, and it seems to me the most public thing I ever have done. My mother's letter has served to remind me: I am making my personal life public. Probably I will never try to explain my motives to my mother and father. My mother's question will go unanswered to her face. Like everything else on these pages, my reasons for writing will be revealed instead to public readers I expect never to meet.

It is to those whom my mother refers to as the *gringos* that I write. The *gringos*. The expression reminds me that she and my father have not followed their children all the way down the path to full Americanization. They were changed—became more easy in public, less withdrawn and uncertain—by the public success of their children. But something remained unchanged in their lives. With excessive care they continue today to note the difference between private and public life. And their private society remains only their family. No matter how friendly they are in public, no matter how firm their smiles, my parents never forget when they are in public. My mother must use a high-pitched tone of voice when she addresses people who are not relatives. It is a tone of voice I have all my life heard her use away from the house. Coming home from grammar school with new friends, I would hear it, its reminder: My new intimates were strangers to her. Like my sisters and brother, over the years, I've grown used to hearing that voice. Expected to hear it. Though I suspect that voice has played deep in my soul, sounding a lyre, to recall my "betrayal," my movement away from our family's intimate past. It is the voice I hear even now when my mother addresses her son- or daughter-in-law. (They remain public people to her.) She speaks to them, sounding the way she does when talking over the fence to a neighbor.

It was, in fact, the lady next door to my parents—a librarian—who first mentioned seeing my essay seven years ago. My mother was embarrassed because she hadn't any idea what the lady was talking about. But she had heard enough to go to a library with my father to find the article. They read what I wrote. And then she wrote her letter.

It is addressed to me in Spanish, but the body of the letter is in English. Almost mechanically she speaks of her pride at the start. ("Your dad and I are very proud of the brilliant manner you have to express yourself.") Then the matter of most concern comes to the fore. "Your dad and I have only one objection to what you write. You say too much about the family . . . Why do you have to do that? . . . Why do you need to tell the *gringos*? . . . Why do you think we're so separated as a family? Do you really think this, Richard?"

A new paragraph changes the tone. Soft, maternal. Worried for me she adds, "Do not punish yourself for having to give up our culture in order to 'make it' as you say. Think of all the wonderful achievements you have obtained. You should be proud. Learn Spanish better. Practice it with your dad and me. Don't worry so much. Don't get the idea that I am mad at you either.

"Just keep one thing in mind. Writing is one thing, the family is another. I don't want *tus hermanos* hurt by your writings. And what do you think the cousins will say when they read where you talk about how the aunts were maids? Especially I don't want the *gringos* knowing about our private affairs. Why should they? Please give this some thought. Please write about something else in the future. Do me this favor."

Please.

To the adult I am today, my mother needs to say what she would never have needed to say to her child: the boy who faithfully kept family secrets. When my fourth-grade teacher made our class write a paper about a typical evening at home, it never occurred to me actually to do so. "Describe what you do with your family," she told us. And automatically I produced a fictionalized account. I wrote that I had six brothers and sisters; I described watching my mother get dressed up in a red-sequined dress before she went with my father to a party; I even related how the imaginary baby sitter ("a high school student") taught my brother and sisters and me to make popcorn and how, later, I fell asleep before my parents returned. The nun who read what I wrote would have known that what I had written was completely imagined. But she never said anything about my contrivance. And I never expected her to either. I never thought she *really* wanted me to write about my family life. In any case, I would have been unable to do so.

I was very much the son of parents who regarded the most innocuous piece of information about the family to be secret. Although I had, by that time, grown easy in public, I felt that my family life was strictly private, not to be revealed to unfamiliar ears or eyes. Around the age of ten, I was held by surprise listening to my best friend tell me one day that he "hated" his father. In a furious whisper he said that when he attempted to kiss his father before going to bed, his father had laughed: "Don't you think you're getting too old for that sort of thing, son?" I was intrigued not so much by the incident as by the fact that the boy would relate it to *me*.

In those years I was exposed to the sliding-glass-door informality of middle-class California family life. Ringing the doorbell of a friend's house, I would hear someone inside yell out, "Come on in, Richie; door's not locked." And in I would go to discover my friend's family undisturbed by my presence. The father was in the kitchen in his underwear. The mother was in her bathrobe. Voices gathered in familiarity. A parent scolded a child in front of me; voices quarreled, then laughed; the mother told me something about her son after he had stepped out of the room and she was sure he couldn't overhear; the father would speak to his children and to me in the same tone of voice. I was one of the family, the parents of several good friends would assure me. (Richie.)

My mother sometimes invited my grammar school friends to stay for dinner or even to stay overnight. But my parents never treated such visitors as part of the family, never told them they were. When a school friend ate at our table, my father spoke less than usual. (Stray, distant words.) My mother was careful to use her "visitor's voice." Sometimes, listening to her, I would feel annoyed because she wouldn't be more herself. Sometimes I'd feel embarrassed that I couldn't give to a friend at my house what I freely accepted at his.

I remained, nevertheless, my parents' child. At school, in sixth grade, my teacher suggested that I start keeping a diary. ("You should write down your personal experiences and reflections.") But I shied away from the idea. It was the one suggestion that the scholarship boy couldn't follow. I would not have wanted to write about the minor daily events of my life; I would never have been able to write about what most deeply, daily, concerned me during those years: I was growing away from my parents. Even if I could have been certain that no one would find my diary, even if I could have destroyed each page after I had written it, I would have felt uncomfortable writing about my home life. There seemed to me something intrinsically public about written words.

Writing, at any rate, was a skill I didn't regard highly. It was a grammar school skill I acquired with comparative ease. I do not remember struggling to write the way I struggled to learn how to read. The nuns would praise student papers for being neat—the handwritten letters easy for others to read; they promised that my writing style would improve as I read more and more. But that wasn't the reason I became a reader. Reading was for me the key to "knowledge"; I swallowed facts and dates and names and themes. Writing, by contrast, was an activity I thought of as a kind of report, evidence of learning. I wrote down what I heard teachers say. I wrote down things from my books. I wrote down all I knew when I was examined at the end of the school year. Writing was performed after the fact; it was not the exciting experience of learning itself. In eighth grade I read several hundred books, the titles of which I still can recall. But I cannot remember a single essay I wrote. I only remember that the most frequent kind of essay I wrote was the book report.

In high school there were more "creative" writing assignments. English teachers assigned the composition of short stories and poems. One sophomore story I wrote was a romance set in the Civil War South. I remember that it earned me a good enough grade, but my teacher suggested with quiet tact that next time I try writing about "something you know more about—something closer to home." Home? I wrote a short story about an old man who lived all by himself in a house down the block. That was as close as my writing ever got to my house. Still, I won prizes. When teachers suggested I contribute articles to the school literary magazine, I did so. And when I was asked to join the school newspaper, I said yes. I did not feel any great pride in my writings, however. (My mother was the one who collected my prize-winning essays in a box she kept in her closet.) Though I remember seeing my by-line in print for the first time, and dwelling on the printing press letters with fascination: RICHARD RODRIGUEZ. The letters furnished evidence of a vast public identity writing made possible.

When I was a freshman in college, I began typing all my assignments. My writing speed decreased. Writing became a struggle. In high school I had been able to handwrite ten- and twenty-page papers in little more than an hour—and I never revised what I wrote. A college essay took me several nights to prepare. Suddenly everything I wrote seemed in need of revision. I became a self-conscious writer. A stylist. The change, I suspect, was the result of seeing my words ordered by the even, impersonal, anonymous typewriter print. As arranged by a machine, the words that I typed no longer seemed mine. I was able to see them with a new appreciation for how my reader would see them.

From grammar school to graduate school I could always name my reader. I wrote for my teacher. I could consult him or her before writing, and after. I suppose that I knew other readers could make sense of what I wrote—that, therefore, I addressed a general reader. But I didn't think very much about it. Only toward the end of my schooling and only because political issues pressed upon me did I write, and have published in magazines, essays intended for readers I never expected to meet. Now I am struck by the opportunity. I write today for a reader who exists in my mind only phantasmagorically. Someone with a face erased; someone of no particular race or sex or age or weather. A gray presence. Unknown, unfamiliar. All that I know about him is that he has had a long education and that his society, like mine, is often public *(un gringo)*.

Suggestions for Discussion

1. With what details does Rodriguez convey his sense of the isolation and frustration of the writer?

2. What are the nagging concerns and questions that afflict the author?

3. In what sense is Rodriguez's autobiography both private and public?

4. Account for the differences in his parents' public and private lives. How does the mother's letter illuminate them?

5. How does the author clarify his childhood and youthful attitudes toward his family life and that of his friends?

6. Why couldn't the young Rodriguez write about his early life in a diary?

7. Account for his differing view of reading and writing when he was in the eighth grade.

8. How does Rodriguez account for his changed view of writing when he was a college freshman and subsequently? How does his sense of audience shift?

Suggestions for Writing

1. Compare and contrast your childhood views of your family with those you currently have.

2. Describe an episode in which the setting is the family dining room and the characters are you and your parents.

Fiction

William Carlos Williams
The Use of Force

William Carlos Williams (1883–1963) practiced medicine in Rutherford, New Jersey, the factory town in which he was born. *Selected Poems* appeared in 1949, *Collected Later Poetry* (1950), and *Collected Poems* (1951). His long epic poem, *Paterson,* won the National Book Award for Poetry in 1950. *Desert Music* appeared in 1954, *Journey to Love* in 1955. He has also written novels, *White Mule* (1937) and *In the Money* (1940); short stories, *Life Along the Passaic* (1938), *Selected Essays* (1954); and an *Autobiography* (1951). He received the Bollingen Award for poetry in 1953. The simple and direct language in this short story heightens the intensity of the feelings of the doctor, parents, and child.

They were new patients to me, all I had was the name, Olson.

Please come down as soon as you can, my daughter is very sick.

When I arrived I was met by the mother, a big startled looking woman, very clean and apologetic who merely said, Is this the doctor? and let me in. In the back, she added. You must excuse us, doctor, we have her in the kitchen where it is warm. It is very damp here sometimes.

The child was fully dressed and sitting on her father's lap near the kitchen table. He tried to get up, but I motioned for him not to bother, took off my overcoat and started to look things over. I could see that they were all very nervous, eyeing me up and down distrustfully. As often, in such cases, they weren't telling me more than they had to, it was up to me to tell them; that's why they were spending three dollars on me.

The child was fairly eating me up with her cold, steady eyes, and no expression to her face whatever. She did not move and seemed, inwardly, quiet; an unusually attractive little thing, and as strong as a heifer in appearance. But her face was flushed, she was breathing rapidly, and I realized that she had a high fever. She had magnificent blonde hair, in profusion. One of those picture children often reproduced in advertising leaflets and the photogravure sections of the Sunday papers.

She's had a fever for three days, began the father and we don't know what it comes from. My wife has given her things, you know, like people do, but it don't do no good. And there's been a lot of sickness around. So we tho't you'd better look her over and tell us what is the matter.

As doctors often do I took a trial shot at it as a point of departure. Has she had a sore throat?

Both parents answered me together, No. . . No, she says her throat don't hurt her.

Does your throat hurt you? added the mother to the child. But the little girl's expression didn't change nor did she move her eyes from my face.

Have you looked?

I tried to, said the mother, but I couldn't see.

As it happens we had been having a number of cases of diphtheria in the school to which this child went during that month and we were all, quite apparently, thinking of that, though no one had as yet spoken of the thing.

Well, I said, suppose we take a look at the throat first. I smiled in my best professional manner and asking for the child's first name I said, come on, Mathilda, open your mouth and let's take a look at your throat.

Nothing doing.

Aw, come on, I coaxed, just open your mouth wide and let me take a look. Look, I said opening both hands wide, I haven't anything in my hands. Just open up and let me see.

Such a nice man, put in the mother. Look how kind he is to you. Come on, do what he tells you to. He won't hurt you.

At that I ground my teeth in disgust. If only they wouldn't use the word "hurt" I might be able to get somewhere. But I did not allow myself to be hurried or disturbed but speaking quietly and slowly I approached the child again.

As I moved my chair a little nearer suddenly with one catlike movement both her hands clawed instinctively for my eyes and she almost reached them too. In fact she knocked my glasses flying and they fell, though unbroken, several feet away from me on the kitchen floor.

Both the mother and father almost turned themselves inside out in embarrassment and apology. You bad girl, said the mother, taking her and shaking her by one arm. Look what you've done. The nice man . . .

For heaven's sake, I broke in. Don't call me a nice man to her. I'm here to look at her throat on the chance that she might have diphtheria and possibly die of it. But that's nothing to her. Look here, I said to the child, we're going to look at your throat. You're old enough to understand what I'm saying. Will you open it now by yourself or shall we have to open it for you?

Not a move. Even her expression hadn't changed. Her breaths however were coming faster and faster. Then the battle began. I had to do it. I had to have a throat culture for her own protection. But first I told the parents that it was entirely up to them. I explained the danger but said that I would not insist on a throat examination so long as they would take the responsibility.

If you don't do what the doctor says you'll have to go to the hospital, the mother admonished her severely.

Oh yeah? I had to smile to myself. After all, I had already fallen in love with the savage brat, the parents were contemptible to me. In the ensuing struggle they grew more and more abject, crushed, exhausted while she surely rose to magnificent heights of insane fury of effort bred of her terror of me.

The father tried his best, and he was a big man but the fact that she was his daughter, his shame at her behavior, and his dread of hurting her made him release her just at the critical times when I had almost achieved success, till I wanted to kill him. But his dread also that she might have diphtheria made him tell me to go on, go on though he himself was almost fainting, while the mother moved back and forth behind us raising and lowering her hands in an agony of apprehension.

Put her in front of you on your lap, I ordered, and hold both her wrists.

But as soon as he did the child let out a scream. Don't, you're hurting me. Let go of my hands. Let them go I tell you. Then she shrieked terrifyingly, hysterically. Stop it! Stop it! You're killing me!

Do you think she can stand it, doctor! said the mother.

You get out, said the husband to his wife. Do you want her to die of diphtheria?

Come on now, hold her, I said.

Then I grasped the child's head with my left hand and tried to get the wooden tongue depressor between her teeth. She fought, with clenched teeth, desperately! But now I also had grown furious—at a child. I tried to hold myself down but I couldn't. I know how to expose a throat for inspection. And I did my best. When finally I got the wooden spatula behind the last teeth and just the point of it into the mouth cavity, she opened up for an instant but before I could see anything she came down again and gripped the wooden blade between her molars she reduced it to splinters before I could get it out again.

Aren't you ashamed, the mother yelled at her. Aren't you ashamed to act like that in front of the doctor?

Get me a smooth-handled spoon of some sort, I told the mother. We're going through with this. The child's mouth was already bleeding. Her tongue was cut and she was screaming in wild hysterical shrieks. Perhaps I should have desisted and come back in an hour or more. No doubt it would have been better. But I have seen at least two children lying dead in bed of neglect in such cases, and feeling that I must get a diagnosis now or never I went at it again. But the worst of it was that I too had got beyond reason. I could have torn the child apart in my own fury and enjoyed it. It was a pleasure to attack her. My face was burning with it.

The damned little brat must be protected against her own idiocy, one says to one's self at such times. Others must be protected against her. It is a social necessity. And all these things are true. But a blind fury, a feeling of adult shame, bred of a longing for muscular release are the operatives. One goes on to the end.

In the final unreasoning assault I overpowered the child's neck and jaws. I forced the heavy silver spoon back of her teeth and down her throat till she gagged. And there it was—both tonsils covered with membrane. She had fought valiantly to keep me from knowing her secret. She had been hiding that sore throat for three days at least and lying to her parents in order to escape just such an outcome as this.

Now truly she was furious. She had been on the defensive before but now she attacked. Tried to get off her father's lap and fly at me while tears of defeat blinded her eyes.

Suggestions for Discussion

1. How do you explain the child's resistance to the doctor?
2. Account for the doctor's statement: "I had already fallen in love with the savage brat; the parents were contemptible to me."
3. How are the doctor's feelings reflected during the struggle? How does he rationalize them?
4. Attempt to recreate the child's relationship with each of her parents.
5. Comment on the use of force. What alternatives did the doctor have?

Suggestion for Writing

Create a scene in which there is interaction between the child and her parents.

Flannery O'Connor

Everything That Rises Must Converge

Flannery O'Connor (1925–1965), born in Georgia, was educated in Georgia schools and the University of Iowa. She received the O. Henry Award in 1957 and a Ford Foundation grant in 1959. Her books include the novels *Wise Blood* (1952) and *The Violent Bear It Away* (1960). Her collection of short stories, *Everything That Rises Must Converge*, was published posthumously in 1965. The tension between mother and son is aggravated by the racial conflict and leads to a tragic resolution in which the internal conflict merges with the climax of the racial incident.

Her doctor had told Julian's mother that she must lose twenty pounds on account of her blood pressure, so on Wednesday nights Julian had to take her downtown on the bus for a reducing class at the Y. The reducing class was designed for working girls over fifty, who weighed from 165 to 200 pounds. His mother was one of the slimmer ones, but she said ladies did not tell their age or weight. She would not ride the buses by herself at night since they had been integrated, and because the reducing class was one of her few pleasures, necessary for her health, and *free*, she said Julian could at least put himself out to take her, considering all she did for him. Julian did not like to consider all she did for him, but every Wednesday night he braced himself and took her.

She was almost ready to go, standing before the hall mirror, putting on her hat, while he, his hands behind him, appeared pinned to the door frame, waiting like Saint Sebastian for the arrows to begin piercing him. The hat was new and had cost her seven dollars and a half. She kept saying, "Maybe I shouldn't have paid that for it. No, I shouldn't have. I'll take it off and return it tomorrow. I shouldn't have bought it."

Julian raised his eyes to heaven. "Yes, you should have bought it," he said. "Put it on and let's go." It was a hideous hat. A purple velvet flap came down on one side of it and stood up on the other; the rest of it was green and looked like a cushion with the stuffing out. He decided it was less comical than jaunty and pathetic. Everything that gave her pleasure was small and depressed him.

She lifted the hat one more time and set it down slowly on top of her head. Two wings of gray hair protruded on either side of her florid face, but her eyes, sky-blue, were as innocent and untouched by experience as they must have been when she was ten. Were it not that she was a widow who had struggled fiercely to feed and clothe and put him through school and who was supporting him still, "until he got on his feet," she might have been a little girl that he had to take to town.

"It's all right, it's all right," he said. "Let's go." He opened the door himself and started down the walk to get her going. The sky was a dying violet and the houses stood out darkly against it, bulbous liver-colored monstrosities of a uniform ugliness though no two were alike. Since this had been a fashionable neighborhood forty years ago, his mother persisted in thinking they did well to have an apartment in it. Each house had a narrow collar of dirt around it in which sat, usually, a grubby child. Julian walked with his hands in his pockets, his head down and thrust forward and his eyes glazed with the determination to make himself completely numb during the time he would be sacrificed to her pleasure.

The door closed and he turned to find the dumpy figure, surmounted by the atrocious hat, coming toward him. "Well," she said, "you only live once and paying a little more for it, I at least won't meet myself coming and going."

"Some day I'll start making money," Julian said gloomily—he knew he never would—"and you can have one of those jokes whenever you take the fit." But first they would move. He visualized a place where the nearest neighbors would be three miles away on either side.

"I think you're doing fine," she said, drawing on her gloves. "You've only been out of school a year. Rome wasn't built in a day."

She was one of the few members of the Y reducing class who arrived in hat and gloves and who had a son who had been to college. "It takes time," she said, "and the world is in such a mess. This hat looked better on me than any of the others, though when she brought it out I said, 'Take that thing back. I wouldn't have it on my head,' and she said, 'Now wait till you see it on,' and when she put it on me, I said, 'We-ull,' and she said, 'If you ask me, that hat does something for you and you do something for the hat, and besides,' she said 'with that hat, you won't meet yourself coming and going.' "

Julian thought he could have stood his lot better if she had been selfish, if she had been an old hag who drank and screamed at him. He walked along, saturated in depression, as if in the midst of his martyrdom he had lost his faith. Catching sight of his long, hopeless, irritated face, she stopped suddenly with a grief-stricken look, and pulled back on his arm. "Wait on me," she said. "I'm going back to the house and take this thing off and tomorrow I'm going to return it. I was out of my head. I can pay the gas bill with that seven-fifty."

He caught her arm in a vicious grip. "You are not going to take it back," he said. "I like it."

"Well," she said, "I don't think I ought . . ."

"Shut up and enjoy it," he muttered, more depressed than ever.

"With the world in the mess it's in," she said, "it's a wonder we can enjoy anything. I tell you, the bottom rail is on the top."

Julian sighed.

"Of course," she said, "if you know who you are, you can go anywhere." She said this every time he took her to the reducing class. "Most of them in it are not our kind of people," she said, "but I can be gracious to anybody. I know who I am."

"They don't give a damn for your graciousness," Julian said savagely. "Knowing who you are is good for one generation only. You haven't the foggiest idea where you stand now or who you are."

She stopped and allowed her eyes to flash at him. "I most certainly do know who I am," she said, "and if you don't know who you are, I'm ashamed of you."

"Oh hell," Julian said.

"Your great-grandfather was a former governor of this state," she said. "Your grandfather was a prosperous landowner. Your grandmother was a God-high."

"Will you look around you," he said tensely, "and see where you are now?" and he swept his arm jerkily out to indicate the neighborhood, which the growing darkness at least made less dingy.

"You remain what you are," she said. "Your great-grandfather had a plantation and two hundred slaves."

"There are no more slaves," he said irritably.

"They were better off when they were," she said. He groaned to see that she was off on that topic. She rolled onto it every few days like a train on an open track. He knew every stop, every junction, every swamp along the way, and knew the exact point at which her conclusion would roll majestically into the station: "It's ridiculous. It's simply not realistic. They should rise, yes, but on their own side of the fence."

"Let's skip it," Julian said.

"The ones I feel sorry for," she said, "are the ones that are half white. They're tragic."

"Will you skip it?"

"Suppose we were half white. We would certainly have mixed feelings."

"I have mixed feelings now," he groaned.

"Well let's talk about something pleasant," she said. "I remember going to Grandpa's when I was a little girl. Then the house had double stairways that went up to what was really the second floor—all the cooking was done on the first. I used to like to stay down in the kitchen on account of the way the walls smelled. I would sit with my nose pressed against the plaster and take deep breaths. Actually the place belonged to the Godhighs but your grandfather Chestny paid the mortgage and saved it for them. They were in reduced circumstances," she said, "but reduced or not, they never forgot who they were."

"Doubtless that decayed mansion reminded them," Julian muttered. He never spoke of it without contempt or thought of it without longing. He had seen it once when he was a child before it had been sold. The double stairways had rotted and been torn down. Negroes were living in it. But it remained in his mind as his mother had known it. It appeared in his dreams regularly. He would stand on the wide porch, listening to the rustle of oak leaves, then wander through the high-ceilinged hall into the parlor that opened onto it and gaze at the worn rugs and faded draperies. It occurred to him that it was he, not she, who could have appreciated it. He preferred its threadbare elegance to anything he could name and it was because of it that all the neighborhoods they had lived in had been a torment to him—whereas she had hardly known the difference. She called her insensitivity "being adjustable."

"And I remember the old darky who was my nurse, Caroline. There was no better person in the world. I've always had a great respect for my colored friends," she said. "I'd do anything in the world for them and they'd . . ."

"Will you for God's sake get off that subject?" Julian said. When he got on a bus by himself, he made it a point to sit down beside a Negro, in reparation as it were for his mother's sins.

"You're mighty touchy tonight," she said. "Do you feel all right?"

"Yes I feel all right," he said. "Now lay off."

She pursed her lips. "Well, you certainly are in a vile humor," she observed. "I just won't speak to you at all."

They had reached the bus stop. There was no bus in sight and Julian, his hands still jammed in his pockets and his head thrust forward, scowled down the empty street. The frustration of having to wait on the bus as well as ride on it began to creep up his neck like a hot hand. The presence of his mother was borne in upon him as she gave a pained sigh. He looked at her bleakly. She was holding herself very erect under the preposterous hat, wearing it like a banner of her imaginary dignity. There was in him an evil urge to break her spirit. He suddenly unloosened his tie and pulled it off and put it in his pocket.

She stiffened. "Why must you look like *that* when you take me to town?" she said. "Why must you deliberately embarrass me?"

"If you'll never learn where you are," he said, "you can at least learn where I am."

"You look like a—thug," she said.

"Then I must be one," he murmured.

"I'll just go home," she said. "I will not bother you. If you can't do a little thing like that for me . . ."

Rolling his eyes upward, he put his tie back on. "Restored to my class," he muttered. He thrust his face toward her and hissed, "True culture is in the mind, the *mind*," he said, and tapped his head, "the mind."

"It's in the heart," she said, "and in how you do things and how you do things is because of who you *are*."

"Nobody in the damn bus cares who you are."

"I care who I am," she said icily.

The lighted bus appeared on top of the next hill and as it approached, they moved out into the street to meet it. He put his hand under her elbow and hoisted her up on the creaking step. She entered with a little smile, as if she were going into a drawing room where everyone had been waiting for her. While he put in the tokens, she sat down on one of the broad front seats for three which faced the aisle. A thin woman with protruding teeth and long yellow hair was sitting on the end of it. His mother moved up beside her and left room for Julian beside herself. He sat down and looked at the floor across the aisle where a pair of thin feet in red and white canvas sandals were planted.

His mother immediately began a general conversation meant to attract anyone who felt like talking. "Can it get any hotter?" she said and removed from her purse a folding fan, black with a Japanese scene on it, which she began to flutter before her.

"I reckon it might could," the woman with the protruding teeth said, "but I know for a fact my apartment couldn't get no hotter."

"It must get the afternoon sun," his mother said. She sat forward and looked up and down the bus. It was half filled. Everybody was white. "I see we have the bus to ourselves," she said. Julian cringed.

"For a change," said the woman across the aisle, the owner of the red and white canvas sandals. "I come on one the other day and they were thick as fleas—up front and all through."

"The world is in a mess everywhere," his mother said. "I don't know how we've let it get in this fix."

"What gets my goat is all those boys from good families stealing automobile tires," the woman with the protruding teeth said. "I told my boy, I said you may not be rich but you been raised right and if I ever catch you in any such mess, they can send you on to the reformatory. Be exactly where you belong."

"Training tells," his mother said. "Is your boy in high school?"

"Ninth grade," the woman said.

"My son just finished college last year. He wants to write but he's selling typewriters until he gets started," his mother said.

The woman leaned forward and peered at Julian. He threw her such a malevolent look that she subsided against the seat. On the floor across the aisle there was an abandoned newspaper. He got up and got it and opened it out in front of him. His mother discreetly continued the conversation in a lower tone but the woman across the aisle said in a loud voice, "Well that's nice. Selling typewriters is close to writing. He can go right from one to the other."

"I tell him," his mother said, "that Rome wasn't built in a day."

Behind the newspaper Julian was withdrawing into the inner compartment of his mind where he spent most of his time. This was a kind of mental bubble in which he established himself when he could not bear to be a part of what was going on around him. From it he could see out and judge but in it he was safe from any kind of penetration from without. It was the only place where he felt free of the general idiocy of his fellows. His mother had never entered it but from it he could see her with absolute clarity.

The old lady was clever enough and he thought that if she had started from any of the right premises, more might have been expected of her. She lived according to the laws of her own fantasy world, outside of which he had never seen her set foot. The law of it was to sacrifice herself for him after she had first created the necessity to do so by making a mess of things. If he had permitted her sacrifices, it was only because her lack of foresight had made them necessary. All of her life had been a struggle to act like a Chestny without the Chestny goods, and to give him everything she thought a Chestny ought to have; but since, said she, it was fun to struggle, why complain? And when you had won, as she had won, what fun to look back on the hard times! He could not forgive her that she had enjoyed the struggle and that she thought *she* had won.

What she meant when she said she had won was that she had brought him up successfully and had sent him to college and that he had turned out so well—good looking (her teeth had gone unfilled so that his could be straightened), intelligent (he realized he was too intelligent to be a success), and with a future ahead of him (there was of course no future ahead of him). She excused his gloominess on the grounds that he was still growing up and his radical ideas on his lack of practical experience. She said he didn't yet know a thing about "life," that he hadn't even entered the real world—when already he was as disenchanted with it as a man of fifty.

The further irony of all this was that in spite of her, he had turned out so well. In spite of going to only a third-rate college, he had, on his own initiative, come out with a first-rate education; in spite of growing up dominated by a small mind, he had ended up with a large one; in spite of all her foolish views, he was free of prejudice and unafraid to face facts. Most miraculous of all, instead of being blinded by love for her as she was for him, he had cut himself emotionally free of her and could see her with complete objectivity. He was not dominated by his mother.

The bus stopped with a sudden jerk and shook him from his meditation. A woman from the back lurched forward with little steps and barely escaped falling in his newspaper as she righted herself. She got off and a large Negro got on. Julian kept his paper lowered to watch. It gave him a certain satisfaction to see injustice in daily operation. It confirmed his view that with a few exceptions there was no one worth knowing within a radius of three hundred miles. The Negro was well dressed and carried a briefcase. He looked around and then sat down on the other end of the seat where the woman with the red and white canvas sandals was sitting. He immediately unfolded a newspaper and obscured himself behind it. Julian's mother's elbow at once prodded insistently into his rib. "Now you see why I won't ride on these buses by myself," she whispered.

The woman with the red and white canvas sandals had risen at the same time the Negro sat down and had gone further back in the bus and taken the seat of the woman who had got off. His mother leaned forward and cast her an approving look.

Julian rose, crossed the aisle, and sat down in the place of the woman with the canvas sandals. From this position, he looked serenely across at his mother. Her face had turned an angry red. He stared at her, making his eyes the eyes of a stranger. He felt his tension suddenly lift as if he had openly declared war on her.

He would have liked to get in conversation with the Negro and to talk with him about art or politics or any subject that would be above the comprehension of those around them, but the man remained entrenched behind his paper. He was either ignoring the change of seating or had never noticed it. There was no way for Julian to convey his sympathy.

His mother kept her eyes fixed reproachfully on his face. The woman with the protruding teeth was looking at him avidly as if he were a type of monster new to her.

"Do you have a light?" he asked the Negro.

Without looking away from his paper, the man reached in his pocket and handed him a packet of matches.

"Thanks," Julian said. For a moment he held the matches foolishly. A NO SMOKING sign looked down upon him from over the door. This alone would not have deterred him; he had no cigarettes. He had quit smoking some months before because he could not afford it. "Sorry," he muttered and handed back the matches. The Negro lowered the paper and gave him an annoyed look. He took the matches and raised the paper again.

His mother continued to gaze at him but she did not take advantage of his momentary discomfort. Her eyes retained their battered look. Her face seemed to be unnaturally red, as if her blood pressure had risen. Julian allowed no glimmer of sympathy to show on his face. Having got the advantage, he wanted desperately to keep it and carry it through. He would have liked to teach her a lesson that would last her a while, but there seemed no way to continue the point. The Negro refused to come out from behind his paper.

Julian folded his arms and looked stolidly before him, facing her but as if he did not see her, as if he had ceased to recognize her existence. He visualized a scene in which, the bus having reached their stop, he would remain in his seat and when she said, "Aren't you going to get off?" he would look at her as at a stranger who had rashly addressed him. The corner they got off on was usually deserted, but it was well lighted and it would not hurt her to walk by herself the four blocks to the Y. He decided to wait until the time came and then decide whether or not he would let her get off by herself. He would have to be at the Y at ten to bring her back, but he could leave her wondering if he was going to show up. There was no reason for her to think she could always depend on him.

He retired again into the high-ceilinged room sparsely settled with large pieces of antique furniture. His soul expanded momentarily but then he became aware of his mother across from him and the vision shriveled. He studied her coldly. Her feet in little pumps dangled like a child's and did not quite reach the floor. She was training on him an exaggerated look of reproach. He felt completely detached from her. At that moment he could with pleasure have slapped her as he would have slapped a particularly obnoxious child in his charge.

He began to imagine various unlikely ways by which he could teach her a lesson. He might make friends with some distinguished Negro professor or lawyer and bring him home to spend the evening. He would be entirely justified but her blood pressure would rise to 300. He could not push her to the extent of making her have a stroke, and moreover, he had never been successful at making any Negro friends. He had tried to strike up an acquaintance on the bus with some of the better types, with ones that looked like professors or ministers or lawyers. One morning he had sat down next to a distinguished-looking dark brown man who had answered his questions with a sonorous solemnity but who had turned out to be an undertaker. Another day he had sat down beside a cigar-smoking Negro with a diamond ring on his finger, but after a few stilted pleasantries, the Negro had rung the buzzer and risen, slipping two lottery tickets into Julian's hand as he climbed over him to leave.

He imagined his mother lying desperately ill and his being able to secure only a Negro doctor for her. He toyed with that idea for a few minutes and then dropped it for a momentary vision of himself participating as a sympathizer in a sit-in demonstration. This was possible but he did not linger with it. Instead, he approached the ultimate horror. He brought home a beautiful suspiciously Negroid woman. Prepare yourself, he said. There is nothing you can do about it. This is the woman I've chosen. She's intelligent, dignified, even good, and she's suffered and she hasn't thought it *fun*. Now persecute us, go ahead and persecute us. Drive her out of here, but remember, you're driving me too. His eyes were narrowed and through the indignation he had generated, he saw his mother across the aisle, purple-faced, shrunken to the dwarf-like proportions of her moral nature, sitting like a mummy beneath the ridiculous banner of her hat.

He was tilted out of his fantasy again as the bus stopped. The door opened with a sucking hiss and out of the dark a large, gaily dressed, sullenlooking colored woman got on with a little boy. The child, who might have been four, had on a short plaid suit and a Tyrolean hat with a blue feather in it. Julian hoped that he would sit down beside him and that the woman would push in beside his mother. He could think of no better arrangement.

As she waited for her tokens, the woman was surveying the seating possibilities—he hoped with the idea of sitting where she was least wanted. There was something familiar-looking about her but Julian could not place what it was. She was a giant of a woman. Her face was set not only to meet opposition but to seek it out. The downward tilt of her large lower lip was like a warning sign: DON'T TAMPER WITH ME. Her bulging figure was encased in a green crepe dress and her feet overflowed in red shoes. She had on a hideous hat. A purple velvet flap came down on one side of it and stood up on the other; the rest of it was green and looked like a cushion with the stuffing out. She carried a mammoth red pocketbook that bulged throughout as if it were stuffed with rocks.

To Julian's disappointment, the little boy climbed up on the empty seat beside his mother. His mother lumped all children, black and white, into the common category, "cute," and she thought little Negroes were on the whole cuter than little white children. She smiled at the little boy as he climbed on the seat.

Meanwhile the woman was bearing down upon the empty seat beside Julian. To his annoyance, she squeezed herself into it. He saw his mother's face change as the woman settled herself next to him and he realized with satisfaction that this was more objectionable to her than it was to him. Her face seemed almost gray and there was a look of dull recognition in her eyes, as if suddenly she had sickened at some awful confrontation. Julian saw that it was because she and the woman had, in a sense, swapped sons. Though his mother would not realize the symbolic significance of this, she would feel it. His amusement showed plainly on his face.

The woman next to him muttered something unintelligible to herself. He was conscious of a kind of bristling next to him, a muted growling like that of an angry cat. He could not see anything but the red pocketbook upright on the bulging green thighs. He visualized the woman as she had stood waiting for her tokens—the ponderous figure, rising from the red shoes upward over the solid hips, the mammoth bosom, the haughty face, to the green and purple hat.

His eyes widened.

The vision of the two hats, identical, broke upon him with the radiance of a brilliant sunrise. His face was suddenly lit with joy. He could not believe that Fate had thrust upon his mother such a lesson. He gave a loud chuckle so that she would look at him and see that he saw. She turned her eyes on him slowly. The blue in them seemed to have turned a bruised purple. For a moment he had an uncomfortable sense of her innocence, but it lasted only a second before principle rescued him. Justice entitled him to laugh. His grin hardened until it said to her as plainly as if he were saying aloud: Your punishment exactly fits your pettiness. This should teach you a permanent lesson.

Her eyes shifted to the woman. She seemed unable to bear looking at him and to find the woman preferable. He became conscious again of the bristling presence at his side. The woman was rumbling like a volcano about to become active. His mother's mouth began to twitch slightly at one corner. With a sinking heart, he saw incipient signs of recovery on her face and realized that this was going to strike her suddenly as funny and was going to be no lesson at all. She kept her eyes on the woman and an amused smile came over her face as if the woman were a monkey that had stolen her hat. The little Negro was looking up at her with large fascinated eyes. He had been trying to attract her attention for some time.

"Carver!" the woman said suddenly. "Come heah!"

When he saw that the spotlight was on him at last, Carver drew his feet up and turned himself toward Julian's mother and giggled.

"Carver!" the woman said. "You heah me? Come heah!"

Carver slid down from the seat but remained squatting with his back against the base of it, his head turned slyly around toward Julian's mother, who was smiling at him. The woman reached a hand across the aisle and snatched him to her. He righted himself and hung backwards on her knees, grinning at Julian's mother. "Isn't he cute?" Julian's mother said to the woman with the protruding teeth.

"I reckon he is," the woman said without conviction.

The Negress yanked him upright but he eased out of her grip and shot across the aisle and scrambled, giggling wildly, onto the seat beside his love.

"I think he likes me," Julian's mother said, and smiled at the woman. It was the smile she used when she was being particularly gracious to an inferior. Julian saw everything lost. The lesson had rolled off her like rain on a roof.

The woman stood up and yanked the little boy off the seat as if she were snatching him from contagion. Julian could feel the rage in her at having no weapon like his mother's smile. She gave the child a sharp slap across his leg.

He howled once and then thrust his head into her stomach and kicked his feet against her shins. "Be-have," she said vehemently.

The bus stopped and the Negro who had been reading the newspaper got off. The woman moved over and set the little boy down with a thump between herself and Julian. She held him firmly by the knee. In a moment he put his hands in front of his face and peeped at Julian's mother through his fingers.

"I see yoooooooo!" she said and put her hand in front of her face and peeped at him.

The woman slapped his hand down. "Quit yo' foolishness," she said, "before I knock the living Jesus out of you!"

Julian was thankful that the next stop was theirs. He reached up and pulled the cord. The woman reached up and pulled it at the same time. Oh my God, he thought. He had the terrible intuition that when they got off the bus together, his mother would open her purse and give the little boy a nickel. The gesture would be as natural to her as breathing. The bus stopped and the woman got up and lunged to the front, dragging the child, who wished to stay on, after her. Julian and his mother got up and followed. As they neared the door, Julian tried to relieve her of her pocketbook.

"No," she murmured, "I want to give the little boy a nickel."

"No!" Julian hissed. "No!"

She smiled down at the child and opened her bag. The bus door opened and the woman picked him up by the arm and descended with him, hanging at her hip. Once in the street she set him down and shook him.

Julian's mother had to close her purse while she got down the bus step but as soon as her feet were on the ground, she opened it again and began to rummage inside. "I can't find but a penny," she whispered, "but it looks like a new one."

"Don't do it!" Julian said fiercely between his teeth. There was a streetlight on the corner and she hurried to get under it so that she could better see into her pocketbook. The woman was heading off rapidly down the street with the child still hanging backward on her hand.

"Oh little boy!" Julian's mother called and took a few quick steps and caught up with them just beyond the lamppost. "Here's a bright new penny for you," and she held out the coin, which shone bronze in the dim light.

The huge woman turned and for a moment stood, her shoulders lifted and her face frozen with frustrated rage, and stared at Julian's mother. Then all at once she seemed to explode like a piece of machinery that had been given one ounce of pressure too much. Julian saw the black fist swing out with the red pocketbook. He shut his eyes and cringed as he heard the woman shout, "He don't take nobody's pennies!" When he opened his eyes, the woman was disappearing down the street with the little boy staring wide-eyed over her shoulder. Julian's mother was sitting on the sidewalk.

"I told you not to do that," Julian said angrily. "I told you not to do that!"

He stood over her for a minute, gritting his teeth. Her legs were stretched out in front of her and her hat was on her lap. He squatted down and looked her in the face. It was totally expressionless. "You got exactly what you deserved," he said. "Now get up."

He picked up her pocketbook and put what had fallen out back in it. He picked the hat up off her lap. The penny caught his eye on the sidewalk and he picked that up and let it drop before her eyes into the purse. Then he stood up and leaned over and held his hands out to pull her up. She remained immobile. He sighed. Rising above them on either side were black apartment buildings, marked with irregular rectangles of light. At the end of the block a man came out of a door and walked off in the opposite direction. "All right," he said, "suppose somebody happens by and wants to know why you're sitting on the sidewalk?"

She took the hand and, breathing hard, pulled heavily up on it and then stood for a moment, swaying slightly as if the spots of light in the darkness were circling around her. Her eyes, shadowed and confused, finally settled on his face. He did not try to conceal his irritation. "I hope this teaches you a lesson," he said. She leaned forward and her eyes raked his face. She seemed trying to determine his identity. Then, as if she found nothing familiar about him, she started off with a headlong movement in the wrong direction.

"Aren't you going on to the Y?" he asked.

"Home," she muttered.

"Well, are we walking?"

For answer she kept going. Julian followed along, his hands behind him. He saw no reason to let the lesson she had had go without backing it up with an explanation of its meaning. She might as well be made to understand what had happened to her. "Don't think that was just an uppity Negro woman," he said. "That was the whole colored race which will no longer take your condescending pennies. That was your black double. She can wear the same hat as you, and to be sure," he added gratuitously (because he thought it was funny), "it looked better on her than it did on you. What all this means," he said, "is that the old world is gone. The old manners are obsolete and your graciousness is not worth a damn." He thought bitterly of the house that had been lost for him. "You aren't who you think you are," he said.

She continued to plow ahead, paying no attention to him. Her hair had come undone on one side. She dropped her pocketbook and took no notice. He stooped and picked it up and handed it to her but she did not take it.

"You needn't act as if the world had come to an end," he said, "because it hasn't. From now on you've got to live in a new world and face a few realities for a change. Buck up," he said, "it won't kill you."

She was breathing fast.

"Let's wait on the bus," he said.

"Home," she said thickly.

"I hate to see you behave like this," he said. "Just like a child. I should be able to expect more of you." He decided to stop where he was and make her stop and wait for a bus. "I'm not going any farther," he said, stopping. "We're going on the bus."

She continued to go on as if she had not heard him. He took a few steps and caught her arm and stopped her. He looked into her face and caught his breath. He was looking into a face he had never seen before. "Tell Grandpa to come get me," she said.

He stared, stricken.

"Tell Caroline to come get me," she said.

Stunned, he let her go and she lurched forward again, walking as if one leg were shorter than the other. A tide of darkness seemed to be sweeping her from him. "Mother!" he cried. "Darling, sweetheart, wait!" Crumpling, she fell to the pavement. He dashed forward and fell at her side, crying, "Mamma, Mamma!" He turned her over. Her face was fiercely distorted. One eye, large and staring, moved slightly to the left as if it had become unmoored. The other remained fixed on him, raked his face again, found nothing and closed.

"Wait here, wait here!" he cried and jumped up and began to run for help toward a cluster of lights he saw in the distance ahead of him. "Help, help!" he shouted, but his voice was thin, scarcely a thread of sound. The lights drifted farther away the faster he ran and his feet moved numbly as if they carried him nowhere. The tide of darkness seemed to sweep him back to her, postponing from moment to moment his entry into the world of guilt and sorrow.

Suggestions for Discussion

1. Trace the steps in the rising action of the story, noting shifts between internal and external action. Study the transitions from one narrative mode to another. How are they effected? What point of view is adopted? What is gained or lost by this device?

2. Characterize the son, distinguishing between his apparent self-image and the individual as you see him.

3. What is the central conflict? What details of setting define the conflict? How is it extended into a larger social area? Comment on the way in which each scene heightens the tension and prepares for the climax.

4. How is your impression of the mother's character created? What is your reaction to the Negro woman's striking of the mother, the son's behavior, and the resulting amnesia? Do you assume that the mother will die? Has the author prepared you for acceptance of the climax, or does it seem contrived? If so, why?

5. What is the central symbol of identity and status in the story? What symbolic elements are used in the description of scene?

6. Find examples of irony and relate them to the controlling purpose of the story.

7. Relate the title to the central theme(s) of the story.

Suggestions for Writing

1. Select one of the above questions for development.

2. The relationship between experience and insight is a central theme of the story. Support this statement by specific references.

3. Compare your view of personal identity with that of your mother and/or father.

Delmore Schwartz

In Dreams Begin Responsibilities

Delmore Schwartz (1913–1966), American poet and critic, was a teacher of English at Harvard University from 1940 to 1947. He is best known for *In Dreams Begin Responsibilities* (1938), which consists of a story, poems, and verse-drama, and for a collection of poems, *Summer Knowledge: New and Selected Poems 1938–1958* (1959). He was an editor of *Partisan Review* and poetry editor of *The New Republic.* The six sections of the narrative "In Dreams Begin Responsibilities" follow a logical time sequence determined by the movie framework of the son's dream. This convention permits the narrator-son to imagine events in the premarital lives of his parents and enter into their emotional states in scenes filtered through his own perceptions and feelings.

I

I think it is the year 1909. I feel as if I were in a moving-picture theater, the long arm of light crossing the darkness and spinning, my eyes fixed upon the screen. It is a silent picture, as if an old Biograph one, in which the actors are dressed in ridiculously old-fashioned clothes, and one flash succeeds another with sudden jumps, and the actors, too, seem to jump about, walking too fast. The shots are full of rays and dots, as if it had been raining when the picture was photographed. The light is bad.

It is Sunday afternoon, June 12th, 1909, and my father is walking down the quiet streets of Brooklyn on his way to visit my mother. His clothes are newly pressed, and his tie is too tight in his high collar. He jingles the coins in his pocket, thinking of the witty things he will say. I feel as if I had by now relaxed entirely in the soft darkness of the theater; the organist peals out the obvious approximate emotions on which the audience rocks unknowingly. I am anonymous. I have forgotten myself: it is always so when one goes to a movie, it is, as they say, a drug.

My father walks from street to street of trees, lawns and houses, once in a while coming to an avenue on which a street-car skates and gnaws, progressing slowly. The motorman, who has a handle-bar mustache, helps a young lady wearing a hat like a feathered bowl onto the car. He leisurely makes change and rings his bell as the passengers mount the car. It is obviously Sunday, for everyone is wearing Sunday clothes and the street-car's noises emphasize the quiet of the holiday (Brooklyn is said to be the city of churches). The shops are closed and their shades drawn but for an occasional stationery store or drugstore with great green balls in the window.

My father has chosen to take this long walk because he likes to walk and think. He thinks about himself in the future and so arrives at the place he is to visit in a mild state of exaltation. He pays no attention to the houses he is passing, in which the Sunday dinner is being eaten, nor to the many trees which line each street, now coming to their full green and the time when they will enclose the whole street in leafy shadow. An occasional carriage passes, the horses' hooves falling like stones in the quiet afternoon, and once in a while an automobile, looking like an enormous upholstered sofa, puffs and passes.

My father thinks of my mother, of how lady-like she is, and of the pride which will be his when he introduces her to his family. They are not yet engaged and he is not yet sure that he loves my mother, so that, once in a while, he becomes panicky about the bond already established. But then he reassures himself by thinking of the big men he admires who are married: William Randolph Hearst and William Howard Taft, who has just become the President of the United States.

My father arrives at my mother's house. He has come too early and so is suddenly embarrassed. My aunt, my mother's younger sister, answers the loud bell with her napkin in her hand, for the family is still at dinner. As my father enters, my grandfather rises from the table and shakes hands with him. My mother has run upstairs to tidy herself. My grandmother asks my father if he has had his dinner and tells him that my mother will be down soon. My grandfather opens the conversation by remarking about the mild June weather. My father sits uncomfortably near the table, holding his hat in his hand. My grandmother tells my aunt to take my father's hat. My uncle, twelve years old, runs into the house, his hair tousled. He shouts a greeting to my father, who has often given him nickels, and then runs upstairs, as my grandmother shouts after him. It is evident that the respect in which my father is held in this house is tempered by a good deal of mirth. He is impressive, but also very awkward.

II

Finally my mother comes downstairs and my father, being at the moment engaged in conversation with my grandfather, is made uneasy by her entrance, for he does not know whether to greet my mother or to continue the conversation. He gets up from his chair clumsily and says "Hello" gruffly. My grandfather watches this, examining their congruence, such as it is, with a critical eye, and meanwhile rubbing his bearded cheek roughly, as he always does when he reasons. He is worried; he is afraid that my father will not make a good husband for his oldest daughter. At this point something happens to the film, just as my father says something funny to my mother: I am awakened to myself and my unhappiness just as my interest has become most intense. The audience begins to clap impatiently. Then the trouble is attended to, but the film has been returned to a portion just shown, and once more I see my grandfather rubbing his bearded cheek, pondering my father's character. It is difficult to get back into the picture once more and forget myself, but as my mother giggles at my father's words, the darkness drowns me.

My father and mother depart from the house, my father shaking hands with my grandfather once more, out of some unknown uneasiness. I stir uneasily also, slouched in the hard chair of the theater. Where is the older uncle, my mother's older brother? He is studying in his bedroom upstairs, studying for his final examinations at the College of the City of New York, having been dead of double pneumonia for the last twenty-one years. My mother and father walk down the same quiet streets once more. My mother is holding my father's arm and telling him of the novel she has been reading and my father utters judgments of the characters as the plot is made clear to him. This is a habit which he very much enjoys, for he feels the utmost superiority and confidence when he is approving or condemning the behavior of other people. At times he feels moved to utter a brief "Ugh" whenever the story becomes what he would call sugary. This tribute is the assertion of his manliness. My mother feels satisfied by the interest she has awakened; and she is showing my father how intelligent she is and how interesting.

They reach the avenue, and the street-car leisurely arrives. They are going to Coney Island this afternoon, although my mother really considers such pleasures inferior. She has made up her mind to indulge only in a walk on the boardwalk and a pleasant dinner, avoiding the riotous amusements as being beneath the dignity of so dignified a couple.

My father tells my mother how much money he has made in the week just past, exaggerating an amount which need not have been exaggerated. But my father has always felt that actualities somehow fall short, no matter how fine they are. Suddenly I begin to weep. The determined old lady who sits next to me in the theater is annoyed and looks at me with an angry face, and being intimidated, I stop. I drag out my handkerchief and dry my face, licking the drop which has fallen near my lips. Meanwhile I have missed something, for here are my father and mother alighting from the street-car at the last stop, Coney Island.

III

They walk toward the boardwalk and my mother commands my father to inhale the pungent air from the sea. They both breathe in deeply, both of them laughing as they do so. They have in common a great interest in health, although my father is strong and husky, and my mother is frail. They are both full of theories about what is good to eat and not good to eat, and sometimes have heated discussions about it, the whole matter ending in my father's announcement, made with a scornful bluster, that you have to die sooner or later anyway. On the boardwalk's flagpole, the American flag is pulsing in an intermittent wind from the sea.

My father and mother go to the rail of the boardwalk and look down on the beach where a good many bathers are casually walking about. A few are in the surf. A peanut whistle pierces the air with its pleasant and active whine, and my father goes to buy peanuts. My mother remains at the rail and stares at the ocean. The ocean seems merry to her; it pointedly sparkles and again and again the pony waves are released. She notices the children digging in the wet sand, and the bathing costumes of the girls who are her own age. My father returns with the peanuts. Overhead the sun's lightning strikes and strikes, but neither of them are at all aware of it. The boardwalk is full of people dressed in their Sunday clothes and casually strolling. The tide does not reach as far as the boardwalk, and the strollers would feel no danger if it did. My father and mother lean on the rail of the boardwalk and absently stare at the ocean. The ocean is becoming rough; the waves come in slowly, tugging strength from far back. The moment before they somersault, the moment when they arch their backs so beautifully, showing white veins in the green and black, that moment is intolerable. They finally crack, dashing fiercely upon the sand, actually driving, full force downward, against it, bouncing upward and forward, and at last petering out into a small stream of bubbles which slides up the beach and then is recalled. The sun overhead does not disturb my father and my mother. They gaze idly at the ocean, scarcely interested in its harshness. But I stare at the terrible sun which breaks up sight, and the fatal merciless passionate ocean. I forget my parents. I stare fascinated, and finally, shocked by their indifference, I burst out weeping once more. The old lady next to me pats my shoulder and says: "There, there, young man, all of this is only a movie, only a movie," but I look up once more at the terrifying sun and the terrifying ocean, and being unable to control my tears I get up and go to the men's room, stumbling over the feet of the other people seated in my row.

IV

When I return, feeling as if I had just awakened in the morning sick for lack of sleep, several hours have apparently passed and my parents are riding on the merry-go-round. My father is on a black horse, my mother on a white one, and they seem to be making an eternal circuit for the single purpose of snatching the nickel rings which are attached to an arm of one of the posts. A hand organ is playing: it is inseparable from the ceaseless circling of the merry-go-round.

For a moment it seems that they will never stop, and I feel as if I were looking down from the fiftieth story of a building. But at length they do get off; even the hand organ has ceased for a moment. There is a sudden and sweet stillness, as if the achievement of so much motion. My mother has acquired only two rings, my father, however, ten of them, although it was my mother who really wanted them.

They walk on along the boardwalk as the afternoon descends by imperceptible degrees into the incredible violet of dusk. Everything fades into a relaxed glow, even the ceaseless murmuring from the beach. They look for a place to have dinner. My father suggests the best restaurant on the boardwalk and my mother demurs, according to her principles of economy and housewifeliness.

However they do go to the best place, asking for a table near the window so that they can look out upon the boardwalk and the mobile ocean. My father feels omnipotent as he places a quarter in the waiter's hand in asking for a table. The place is crowded and here too there is music, this time from a kind of string trio. My father orders with a fine confidence.

As their dinner goes on, my father tells of his plans for the future and my mother shows with expressive face how interested she is, and how impressed. My father becomes exultant, lifted up by the waltz that is being played and his own future begins to intoxicate him. My father tells my mother that he is going to expand his business, for there is a great deal of money to be made. He wants to settle down. After all, he is twenty-nine, he has lived by himself since his thirteenth year, he is making more and more money, and he is envious of his friends when he visits them in the security of their homes, surrounded, it seems, by the calm domestic pleasures, and by delightful children, and then as the waltz reaches the moment when the dancers all swing madly, then, then with awful daring, then he asks my mother to marry him, although awkwardly enough and puzzled as to how he had arrived at the question, and she, to make the whole business worse, begins to cry, and my father looks nervously about, not knowing at all what to do now, and my mother says: "It's all I've wanted from the first moment I saw you," sobbing, and he finds all of this very difficult, scarcely to his taste, scarcely as he thought it would be, on his long walks over Brooklyn Bridge in the revery of a fine cigar, and it was then, at that point, that I stood up in the theater and shouted: "Don't do it! It's not too late to change your minds, both of you. Nothing good will come of it, only remorse, hatred, scandal, and two children whose characters are monstrous." The whole audience turned to look at me, annoyed, the usher came hurrying down the aisle flashing his searchlight, and the old lady next to me tugged me down into my seat, saying: "Be quiet. You'll be put out, and you paid thirty-five cents to come in." And so I shut my eyes because I could not bear to see what was happening. I sat there quietly.

V

But after a while I begin to take brief glimpses and at length I watch again with thirsty interest, like a child who tries to maintain his sulk when he is offered the bribe of candy. My parents are now having their picture taken in a photographer's booth along the boardwalk. The place is shadowed in the mauve light which is apparently necessary. The camera is set to the side on its tripod and looks like a Martian man. The photographer is instructing my parents in how to pose. My father has his arm over my mother's shoulder, and both of them smile emphatically. The photographer brings my mother a bouquet of flowers to hold in her hand, but she holds it at the wrong angle. Then the photographer covers himself with the black cloth which drapes the camera and all that one sees of him is one protruding arm and his hand with which he holds tightly to the rubber ball which he squeezes when the picture is taken. But he is not satisfied with their appearance. He feels that somehow there is something wrong in their pose. Again and again he comes out from his hiding place with new directions. Each suggestion merely makes matters worse. My father is becoming impatient. They try a seated pose. The photographer explains that he has his pride, he wants to make beautiful pictures, he is not merely interested in all of this for the money. My father says: "Hurry up, will you? We haven't got all night." But the photographer only scurries about apologetically, issuing new directions. The photographer charms me, and I approve of him with all my heart, for I know exactly how he feels, and as he criticizes each revised pose according to some obscure idea of rightness, I become quite hopeful. But then my father says angrily: "Come on, you've had enough time, we're not going to wait any longer." And the photographer, sighing unhappily, goes back into the black covering, and holds out his hand, saying: "One, two, three, Now!", and the picture is taken, with my father's smile turned to a grimace and my mother's bright and false. It takes a few minutes for the picture to be developed and as my parents sit in the curious light they become depressed.

VI

They have passed a fortune-teller's booth and my mother wishes to go in, but my father does not. They begin to argue about it. My mother becomes stubborn, my father once more impatient. What my father would like to do now is walk off and leave my mother there, but he knows that that would never do. My mother refuses to budge. She is near tears, but she feels an uncontrollable desire to hear what the palm-reader will say. My father consents angrily and they both go into the booth which is, in a way, like the photographer's, since it is draped in black cloth and its light is colored and shadowed. The place is too warm, and my father keeps saying that this is all nonsense, pointing to the crystal ball on the table. The fortune-teller, a short, fat woman garbed in robes supposedly exotic, comes into the room and greets them, speaking with an accent, but suddenly my father feels that the whole thing is intolerable; he tugs at my mother's arm but my mother refuses to budge. And then, in terrible anger, my father lets go of my mother's arm and strides out, leaving my mother stunned. She makes a movement as if to go after him, but the fortune-teller holds her and begs her not to do so, and I in my seat in the darkness am shocked and horrified. I feel as if I were walking a tight-rope one hundred feet over a circus audience and suddenly the rope is showing signs of breaking, and I get up from my seat and begin to shout once more the first words I can think of to communicate my terrible fear, and once more the usher comes hurrying down the aisle flashing his searchlight, and the old lady pleads with me, and the shocked audience has turned to stare at me, and I keep shouting: "What are they doing? Don't they know what they are doing? Why doesn't my mother go after my father and beg him not to be angry? If she does not do that, what will she do? Doesn't my father know what he is doing?" But the usher has seized my arm, and is dragging me away, and as he does so, he says: "What are *you* doing? Don't you know you can't do things like this, you can't do whatever you want to do, even if other people aren't about? You will be sorry if you do not do what you should do. You can't carry on like this, it is not right, you will find that out soon enough, everything you do matters too much," and as he said that, dragging me through the lobby of the theater, into the cold light, I woke up into the bleak winter morning of my twenty-first birthday, the window-sill shining with its lip of snow, and the morning already begun.

Suggestions for Discussion

1. Trace the development of the narrative in the six sections that follow the time sequence of the movie framework of the son's dream. How does the use of the son as narrator provide a double vision?

2. Relate the title to the action and theme of the story.

3. Describe the son's emotional state. How does it relate to the events of each episode?

4. Analyze the relationship of the parents to each other and that of the son to the parents.

5. Is there a resolution to the conflict? What do you assume will be the son's future?

6. Relate the following images to the theme of the story: the movie audience, the usher, the old lady, the Coney Island scene, the turbulent ocean, the photographer, the fortune teller.

Suggestion for Writing

Draw a portrait of your parents by means of an imaginary dialogue or a narrative.

Tillie Olsen

I Stand Here Ironing

Tillie Olsen (b. 1913) was born in Omaha, Nebraska, but has lived most of her adult life in the San Francisco Bay Area. She worked for a time in manual and clerical jobs but in later years received a number of literary awards: a Stanford University Creative Writing Fellowship, a Ford Foundation Grant in Literature, and a Radcliffe Institute for Independent Study fellowship. She is best known for her collection of stories, *Tell Me a Riddle* (1956), from which this story was selected, and her latest book, *Silences* (1979). The tension of the story lies in the writer's conception of the distance between what might have been and what is.

I stand here ironing, and what you asked me moves tormented back and forth with the iron.

"I wish you would manage the time to come in and talk with me about your daughter. I'm sure you can help me understand her. She's a youngster who needs help and whom I'm deeply interested in helping."

"Who needs help." . . . Even if I came, what good would it do? You think because I am her mother I have a key, or that in some way you could use me as a key? She has lived for nineteen years. There is all that life that has happened outside of me, beyond me.

And when is there time to remember, to sift, to weigh, to estimate, to total? I will start and there will be an interruption and I will have to gather it all together again. Or I will become engulfed with all I did or did not do, with what should have been and what cannot be helped.

She was a beautiful baby. The first and only one of our five that was beautiful at birth. You do not guess how new and uneasy her tenancy in her now-loveliness. You did not know her all those years she was thought homely, or see her poring over her baby pictures, making me tell her over and over how beautiful she had been—and would be, I would tell her—and was now, to the seeing eye. But the seeing eyes were few or nonexistent. Including mine.

I nursed her. They feel that's important nowadays. I nursed all the children, but with her, with all the fierce rigidity of first motherhood, I did like the books then said. Though her cries battered me to trembling and my breasts ached with swollenness, I waited till the clock decreed.

Why do I put that first? I do not even know if it matters, or if it explains anything.

She was a beautiful baby. She blew shining bubbles of sound. She loved motion, loved light, loved color and music and textures. She would lie on the floor in her blue overalls patting the surface so hard in ecstasy her hands and feet would blur. She was a miracle to me, but when she was eight months old I had to leave her daytimes with the woman downstairs to whom she was no miracle at all, for I worked or looked for work and for Emily's father, who "could no longer endure" (he wrote in his good-bye note) "sharing want with us."

I was nineteen. It was the pre-relief, pre-WPA world of the depression. I would start running as soon as I got off the streetcar, running up the stairs, the place smelling sour, and awake or asleep to startle awake, when she saw me she would break into a clogged weeping that could not be comforted, a weeping I can hear yet.

After a while I found a job hashing at night so I could be with her days, and it was better. But it came to where I had to bring her to this family and leave her.

It took a long time to raise the money for her fare back. Then she got chicken pox and I had to wait longer. When she finally came, I hardly knew her, walking quick and nervous like her father, looking like her father, thin, and dressed in a shoddy red that yellowed her skin and glared at the pockmarks. All the baby loveliness gone.

She was two. Old enough for nursery school they said, and I did not know then what I know now—the fatigue of the long day, and the lacerations of group life in the kinds of nurseries that are only parking places for children.

Except that it would have made no difference if I had known. It was the only place there was. It was the only way we could be together, the only way I could hold a job.

And even without knowing, I knew. I knew the teacher that was evil because all these years it has curdled into my memory, the little boy hunched in the corner, her rasp, "why aren't you outside, because Alvin hits you? that's no reason, go out, scaredy." I knew Emily hated it even if she did not clutch and implore "don't go Mommy" like the other children, mornings.

She always had a reason why we should stay home. Momma, you look sick. Momma, I feel sick. Momma, the teachers aren't there today, they're sick. Momma, we can't go, there was a fire there last night. Momma, it's a holiday today, no school, they told me.

But never a direct protest, never rebellion. I think of our others in their three-, four-year-oldness—the explosions, the tempers, the denunciations, the demands—and I feel suddenly ill. I put the iron down. What in me demanded that goodness in her? And what was the cost, the cost to her of such goodness?

The old man living in the back once said in his gentle way: "You should smile at Emily more when you look at her." What *was* in my face when I looked at her? I loved her. There were all the acts of love.

It was only with the others I remembered what he said, and it was the face of joy, and not of care or tightness or worry I turned to them—too late for Emily. She does not smile easily, let alone almost always as her brothers and sisters do. Her face is closed and sombre, but when she wants, how fluid. You must have seen it in her pantomimes, you spoke of her rare gift for comedy on the stage that rouses a laughter out of the audience so dear they applaud and applaud and do not want to let her go.

Where does it come from, that comedy? There was none of it in her when she came back to me that second time, after I had had to send her away again. She had a new daddy now to learn to love, and I think perhaps it was a better time.

Except when we left her alone nights, telling ourselves she was old enough.

"Can't you go some other time, Mommy, like tomorrow?" she would ask. "Will it be just a little while you'll be gone? Do you promise?"

The time we came back, the front door open, the clock on the floor in the hall. She rigid awake. "It wasn't just a little while. I didn't cry. Three times I called you, just three times, and then I ran downstairs to open the door so you could come faster. The clock talked loud. I threw it away, it scared me what it talked."

She said the clock talked loud again that night I went to the hospital to have Susan. She was delirious with the fever that comes before red measles, but she was fully conscious all the week I was gone and the week after we were home when she could not come near the new baby or me.

She did not get well. She stayed skeleton thin, not wanting to eat, and night after night she had nightmares. She would call for me, and I would rouse from exhaustion to sleepily call back: "You're all right, darling, go to sleep, it's just a dream," and if she still called, in a sterner voice, "now go to sleep, Emily, there's nothing to hurt you." Twice, only twice, when I had to get up for Susan anyhow, I went in to sit with her.

Now when it is too late (as if she would let me hold and comfort her like I do the others) I get up and go to her at once at her moan or restless stirring. "Are you awake, Emily? Can I get you something?" And the answer is always the same: "No, I'm all right, go back to sleep, Mother."

They persuaded me at the clinic to send her away to a convalescent home in the country where "she can have the kind of food and care you can't manage for her, and you'll be free to concentrate on the new baby." They still send children to that place. I see pictures on the society page of sleek young women planning affairs to raise money for it, or dancing at the affairs, or decorating Easter eggs or filling Christmas stockings for the children.

They never have a picture of the children so I do not know if the girls still wear those gigantic red bows and the ravaged looks on the every other Sunday when parents can come to visit "unless otherwise notified"—as we were notified the first six weeks.

Oh it is a handsome place, green lawns and tall trees and fluted flower beds. High up on the balconies of each cottage the children stand, the girls in their red bows and white dresses, the boys in white suits and giant red ties. The parents stand below shrieking up to be heard and the children shriek down to be heard, and between them the invisible wall "Not To Be Contaminated by Parental Germs or Physical Affection."

There was a tiny girl who always stood hand in hand with Emily. Her parents never came. One visit she was gone. "They moved her to Rose Cottage" Emily shouted in explanation. "They don't like you to love anybody here."

She wrote once a week, the labored writing of a seven-year-old. "I am fine. How is the baby. If I write my leter nicly I will have a star. Love" There never was a star. We wrote every other day, letters she could never hold or keep but only hear read—once. "We simply do not have room for children to keep any personal possessions," they patiently explained when we pieced one Sunday's shrieking together to plead how much it would mean to Emily, who loved so to keep things, to be allowed to keep her letters and cards.

Each visit she looked frailer, "She isn't eating," they told us.

(They had runny eggs for breakfast or mush with lumps, Emily said later, I'd hold it in my mouth and not swallow. Nothing ever tasted good, just when they had chicken.)

It took us eight months to get her released home, and only the fact that she gained back so little of her seven lost pounds convinced the social worker.

I used to try to hold and love her after she came back, but her body would stay stiff, and after a while she'd push away. She ate little. Food sickened her, and I think much of life too. Oh she had physical lightness and brightness, twinkling by on skates, bouncing like a ball up and down up and down over the jump rope, skimming over the hill; but these were momentary.

She fretted about her appearance, thin and dark and foreign-looking at a time when every little girl was supposed to look or thought she should look a chubby blonde replica of Shirley Temple. The doorbell sometimes rang for her, but no one seemed to come and play in the house or be a best friend. Maybe because we moved so much.

There was a boy she loved painfully through two school semesters. Months later she told me how she had taken pennies from my purse to buy him candy. "Licorice was his favorite and I brought him some every day, but he still liked Jennifer better'n me. Why, Mommy?" The kind of question for which there is no answer.

School was a worry to her. She was not glib or quick in a world where glibness and quickness were easily confused with ability to learn. To her overworked and exasperated teachers she was an overconscientious "slow learner" who kept trying to catch up and was absent entirely too often.

I let her be absent, though sometimes the illness was imaginary. How different from my now-strictness about attendance with the others. I wasn't working. We had a new baby, I was home anyhow. Sometimes, after Susan grew old enough, I would keep her home from school, too, to have them all together.

Mostly Emily had asthma, and her breathing, harsh and labored, would fill the house with a curiously tranquil sound. I would bring the two old dresser mirrors and her boxes of collections to her bed. She would select beads and single earrings, bottle tops and shells, dried flowers and pebbles, old postcards and scraps, all sorts of oddments; then she and Susan would play Kingdom, setting up landscapes and furniture, peopling them with action.

Those were the only times of peaceful companionship between her and Susan. I have edged away from it, that poisonous feeling between them, that terrible balancing of hurts and needs I had to do between the two, and did so badly, those earlier years.

Oh there are conflicts between the others too, each one human, needing, demanding, hurting, taking—but only between Emily and Susan, no, Emily toward Susan that corroding resentment. It seems so obvious on the surface, yet it is not obvious. Susan, the second child, Susan, golden- and curly-haired and chubby, quick and articulate and assured, everything in appearance and manner Emily was not; Susan, not able to resist Emily's precious things, losing or sometimes clumsily breaking them; Susan telling jokes and riddles to company for applause while Emily sat silent (to say to me later: that was *my* riddle, Mother, I told it to Susan); Susan, who for all the five years' difference in age was just a year behind Emily in developing physically.

I am glad for that slow physical development that widened the difference between her and her contemporaries, though she suffered over it. She was too vulnerable for that terrible world of youthful competition, of preening and parading, of constant measuring of yourself against every other, of envy, "If I had that copper hair," "If I had that skin. . . ." She tormented herself enough about not looking like the others, there was enough of the unsureness, the having to be conscious of words before you speak, the constant caring—what are they thinking of me? without having it all magnified by the merciless physical drives.

Ronnie is calling. He is wet and I change him. It is rare there is such a cry now. That time of motherhood is almost behind me when the ear is not one's own but must always be racked and listening for the child cry, the child call. We sit for a while and I hold him, looking out over the city spread in charcoal with its soft aisles of light. "*Shoogily,*" he breathes and curls closer. I carry him back to bed, asleep. *Shoogily.* A funny word, a family word, inherited from Emily, invented by her to say: *comfort.*

In this and other ways she leaves her seal, I say aloud. And startle at my saying it. What do I mean? What did I start to gather together, to try and make coherent? I was at the terrible, growing years. War years. I do not remember them well. I was working, there were four smaller ones now, there was not time for her. She had to help be a mother, and housekeeper, and shopper. She had to set her seal. Mornings of crisis and near hysteria trying to get lunches packed, hair combed, coats and shoes found, everyone to school or Child Care on time, the baby ready for transportation. And always the paper scribbled on by a smaller one, the book looked at by Susan then mislaid, the homework not done. Running out to that huge school where she was one, she was lost, she was a drop; suffering over the unpreparedness, stammering and unsure of her classes.

There was so little time left at night after the kids were bedded down. She would struggle over books, always eating (it was in those years she developed her enormous appetite that is legendary in our family) and I would be ironing, or preparing food for the next day, or writing V-mail to Bill, or tending the baby. Sometimes, to make me laugh, or out of her despair, she would imitate happenings or types at school.

I think I said once: "Why don't you do something like this in the school amateur show?" One morning she phoned me at work, hardly understandable through the weeping: "Mother, I did it. I won, I won; they gave me first prize; they clapped and clapped and wouldn't let me go."

Now suddenly she was Somebody, and as imprisoned in her difference as she had been in anonymity.

She began to be asked to perform at other high schools, even in colleges, then at city and statewide affairs. The first one we went to, I only recognized her that first moment when thin, shy, she almost drowned herself into the curtains. Then: Was this Emily? The control, the command, the convulsing and deadly clowning, the spell, then the roaring, stamping audience, unwilling to let this rare and precious laughter out of their lives.

Afterwards: You ought to do something about her with a gift like that—but without money or knowing how, what does one do? We have left it all to her, and the gift has as often eddied inside, clogged and clotted, as been used and growing.

She is coming. She runs up the stairs two at a time with her light graceful step, and I know she is happy tonight. Whatever it was that occasioned your call did not happen today.

"Aren't you ever going to finish the ironing, Mother? Whistler painted his mother in a rocker. I'd have to paint mine standing over an ironing board." This is one of her communicative nights and she tells me everything and nothing as she fixes herself a plate of food out of the icebox.

She is so lovely. Why did you want me to come in at all? Why were you concerned? She will find her way.

She starts up the stairs to bed. "Don't get me up with the rest in the morning." "But I thought you were having midterms." "Oh, those," she comes back in, kisses me, and say quite lightly, "in a couple of years when we'll all be atom-dead they won't matter a bit."

She has said it before. She *believes* it. But because I have been dredging the past, and all that compounds a human being is so heavy and meaningful in me, I cannot endure it tonight.

I will never total it all. I will never come in to say: She was a child seldom smiled at. Her father left me before she was a year old. I had to work her first six years when there was work, or I sent her home and to his relatives. There were years she had care she hated. She was dark and thin and foreign-looking in a world where the prestige went to blondeness and curly hair and dimples, she was slow where glibness was prized. She was a child of anxious, not proud, love. We were poor and could not afford for her the soil of easy growth. I was a young mother, I was a distracted mother. There were the other children pushing up, demanding. Her younger sister seemed all that she was not. There were years she did not want me to touch her. She kept too much in herself, her life was such she had to keep too much in herself. My wisdom came too late. She has much to her and probably little will come of it. She is a child of her age, of depression, of war, of fear.

Let her be. So all that is in her will not bloom—but in how many does it? There is still enough left to live by. Only help her to know—help make it so there is cause for her to know—that she is more than this dress on the ironing board, helpless before the iron.

Suggestions for Discussion

1. In this story in which the mother speaks of her daughter, who is the listener? What evidence is there that she is speaking to herself as well as to the unnamed listener? How does this technique affect the emotional impact of the story?

2. What is the symbolic and real significance of the title and the opening and concluding allusions to ironing?

3. As you review the chronology of events in the lives of the mother and Emily, how would you characterize the changes in their attitudes, feelings, and behavior?

4. In what respects might it be said that the author portrays two lives that move beyond the personal and reflect a universal phenomenon?

5. What attitude toward life is expressed in the final paragraph?

Suggestions for Writing

1. After stating in your own words the attitude toward life expressed in the last paragraph, discuss your view of it by making reference to your own experience or your observation of others (real or fictional).

2. Rewrite the story of Emily chronologically. What is lost of the author's artistry?

3. Write a monologue in which Emily is the speaker.

Poetry

E. E. Cummings
My Father Moved Through Dooms of Love

Edward Estlin Cummings (1894–1963) was an American whose novel *The Enormous Room* (1922) and whose books of poetry *&* and *XLI Poems* (1925) established his reputation as an avant-garde writer interested in experimenting with stylistic techniques. Awarded several important prizes for poetry, he also was Charles Eliot Norton Lecturer at Harvard University in 1952 and published *i: six nonlectures* (1953). The theme of wholeness and reconciliation of opposites in the father's character is implictly expressed in this poem in which images of death, hate, and decay are counterpointed against images that celebrate life and growth.

> my father moved through dooms of love
> through sames of am through haves of give,
> singing each morning out of each night
> my father moved through depths of height
>
> this motionless forgetful where
> turned at his glance to shining here;
> that if (so timid air is firm)
> under his eyes would stir and squirm
>
> newly as from unburied which
> floats the first who, his april touch
> drove sleeping selves to swarm their fates
> woke dreamers to their ghostly roots
>
> and should some why completely weep
> my father's fingers brought her sleep:
> vainly no smallest voice might cry
> for he could feel the mountains grow.

Lifting the valleys of the sea
my father moved through griefs of joy;
praising a forehead called the moon
singing desire into begin

joy was his song and joy so pure
a heart of star by him could steer
and pure so now and now so yes
the wrists of twilight would rejoice

keen as midsummer's keen beyond
conceiving mind of sun will stand,
so strictly (over utmost him
so hugely) stood my father's dream

his flesh was flesh his blood was blood:
no hungry man but wished him food;
no cripple wouldn't creep one mile
uphill to only see him smile.

Scorning the pomp of must and shall
my father moved through dooms of feel;
his anger was as right as rain
his pity was as green as grain

septembering arms of year extend
less humbly wealth to foe and friend
than he to foolish and to wise
offered immeasurable is

proudly and (by octobering flame
beckoned) as earth will downward climb,
so naked for immortal work
his shoulders marched against the dark

his sorrow was as true as bread:
no liar looked him in the head;
if every friend became his foe
he'd laugh and build a world with snow.

My father moved through theys of we,
singing each new leaf out of each tree
(and every child was sure that spring
danced when she heard my father sing)

then let men kill which cannot share,
let blood and flesh be mud and mire,
scheming imagine, passion willed,
freedom a drug that's bought and sold

giving to steal and cruel kind,
a heart to fear, to doubt a mind,
to differ a disease of same,
conform the pinnacle of am

though dull were all we taste as bright,
bitter all utterly things sweet,
maggoty minus and dumb death
all we inherit, all bequeath

and nothing quite so least as truth
—i say though hate were why men breathe—
because my father lived his soul
love is the whole and more than all

Suggestions for Discussion

1. Study the verbal juxtapositions that seem antithetical: "dooms of love"; "depths of height"; "griefs of joy." How is the theme of wholeness and reconciliation of opposites in the character of the father implicitly expressed?

2. Cite passages in which the natural imagery of life, love, birth, and rebirth is counterpointed against images of death, hate, and decay.

3. Compare the images of celebration of life and growth with the imagery in Whitman's "Out of the Cradle Endlessly Rocking." Contrast this father with Kafka's in "Letter to His Father."

Sylvia Plath

Daddy

Sylvia Plath (1932–1963) began her career while still a college student by serving as guest editor of *Mademoiselle*. She studied in both the United States and England, taught at Smith College, and then settled in England, where she lived until her suicide. Her poetry is collected in *The Colossus* (1960), *Ariel* (1965), *Crossing the Water* (1971), and *Winter Trees* (1972), and she contributed to such magazines as *Seventeen*, *Atlantic*, and *The Nation*. *The Bell Jar*, her only novel, was written about her late-adolescent attempt at suicide and was published posthumously in 1963 under the pseudonym Victoria Lucas. In "Daddy," the poet as child recalls the past and reinvokes her brutal image of her father.

You do not do, you do not do
Any more, black shoe
In which I have lived like a foot
For thirty years, poor and white,
Barely daring to breath or Achoo.

Daddy, I have had to kill you.
You died before I had time—
Marble-heavy, a bag full of God,
Ghastly statue with one grey toe
Big as a Frisco seal

And a head in the freakish Atlantic
Where it pours bean green over blue
In the waters off beautiful Nauset.
I used to pray to recover you.
Ach, du.

In the German tongue, in the Polish town
Scraped flat by the roller
Of wars, wars, wars.
But the name of the town is common.
My Polack friend

Says there are a dozen or two.
So I never could tell where you
Put your foot, your root,
I never could talk to you.
The tongue stuck in my jaw.

It stuck in a barb wire snare.
Ich, ich, ich, ich
I could hardly speak.
I thought every German was you.
And the language obscene

An engine, an engine
Chuffing me off like a Jew.
A Jew to Dachau, Auschwitz, Belsen.
I began to talk like a Jew.
I think I may well be a Jew.

The snows of the Tyrol, the clear beer of Vienna
Are not very pure or true.
With my gypsy ancestress and my weird luck
And my Taroc pack and my Taroc pack
I may be a bit of a Jew.

I have always been scared of *you*,
With your Luftwaffe, your gobbledygoo.
And your neat moustache
And your Aryan eye, bright blue.
Panzer-man, panzer-man, O You—

Not God but a swastika
So black no sky could squeak through.
Every woman adores a Fascist,
The boot in the face, the brute
Brute heart of a brute like you.

You stand at the blackboard, daddy,
In the picture I have of you,
A cleft in your chin instead of your foot
But no less a devil for that, no not
Any less the black man who

Bit my pretty red heart in two.
I was ten when they buried you.
At twenty I tried to die
And get back, back, back to you.
I thought even the bones would do.

But they pulled me out of the sack,
And they stuck me together with glue.
And then I knew what to do.
I made a model of you,
A man in black with a Meinkampf look

And a love of the rack and the screw.
And I said I do, I do.
So daddy, I'm finally through.
The black telephone's off at the root,
The voice just can't worm through.

If I've killed one man, I've killed two—
The vampire who said he was you
And drank my blood for a year,
Seven years, if you want to know.
Daddy, you can lie back now.

There's a stake in your fat black heart
And the villagers never liked you.
They are dancing and stamping on you.
They always *knew* it was you.
Daddy, daddy, you bastard, I'm through.

Suggestions for Discussion

1. Discuss the theme and mood of the poem. Comment on the relative maturity or insight the narrator has achieved through the distance of time.

2. What may Sylvia Plath's father have had in common with Kafka's father?

3. To what extent does your reading of A. Alvarez's "Sylvia Plath: A Memoir" illuminate your reading of the poem?

Theodore Roethke

My Papa's Waltz

Theodore Roethke (1908–1963), American poet, taught during the last years of his life at the University of Washington. *The Waking: Poems, 1933–1953* was the winner of the Pulitzer Prize for Poetry in 1953. He received the Bollingen Award for Poetry in 1958. A collected volume, *Words for the Wind,* appeared in 1958, and *The Far Field* was published posthumously in 1964. The poet remembers his antic father and his own difficult childhood.

> The whiskey on your breath
> Could make a small boy dizzy;
> But I hung on like death:
> Such waltzing was not easy.
>
> We romped until the pans
> Slid from the kitchen shelf;
> My mother's countenance
> Could not unfrown itself.
>
> The hand that held my wrist
> Was battered on one knuckle;
> At every step I missed
> My right ear scraped a buckle.
>
> You beat time on my head
> With a palm caked hard by dirt,
> Then waltzed me off to bed
> Still clinging to your shirt.

Suggestion for Discussion

Compare the relationship of father and son in this poem with that in Anderson's "Discovery of a Father." Contrast the two mothers.

William Butler Yeats
A Prayer for My Daughter

William Butler Yeats (1865–1939), the leading poet of the Irish literary revival and a playwright, was born near Dublin and educated in London and Dublin. He wrote plays for the Irish National Theatre Society (later called the Abbey Theatre). For a number of years he served as a senator of the Irish Free State. His volumes of poetry range from *The Wanderings of Oisin* (1889) to *The Last Poems* (1939). *The Collected Poems of W. B. Yeats* appeared in 1933, 1950, and 1956; *The Collected Plays of W. B. Yeats* were published in 1934 and 1952. From his view of a chaotic, threatening world, the poet prays for the harmony and order he considers requisite to the growth of his daughter.

Once more the storm is howling, and half hid
Under this cradle-hood and coverlid
My child sleeps on. There is no obstacle
But Gregory's wood and one bare hill
Whereby the haystack- and roof-levelling wind,
Bred on the Atlantic, can be stayed;
And for an hour I have walked and prayed
Because of the great gloom that is in my mind.

I have walked and prayed for this young child an hour
And heard the sea-wind scream upon the tower,
And under the arches of the bridge, and scream
In the elms above the flooded stream;
Imagining in excited reverie
That the future years had come,
Dancing to a frenzied drum,
Out of the murderous innocence of the sea.

May she be granted beauty and yet not
Beauty to make a stranger's eye distraught,
Or hers before a looking-glass, for such,
Being made beautiful overmuch,
Consider beauty a sufficient end,
Lose natural kindness and maybe
The heart-revealing intimacy
That chooses right, and never find a friend.

Helen, being chosen, found life flat and dull
And later had much trouble from a fool,
While that great Queen, that rose out of the spray,
Being fatherless, could have her way
Yet chose a bandy-leggèd smith for man.
It's certain that fine women eat
A crazy salad with their meat
Whereby the Horn of Plenty is undone.

In courtesy I'd have her chiefly learned;
Hearts are not had as a gift but hearts are earned
By those that are not entirely beautiful;
Yet many, that have played the fool
For beauty's very self, has charm made wise,
And many a poor man that has roved,
Loved and thought himself beloved,
From a glad kindness cannot take his eyes.

May she become a flourishing hidden tree
That all her thoughts may like the linnet be,
And have no business but dispensing round
Their magnanimities of sound.
Nor but in merriment began a chase,
Nor but in merriment a quarrel.
O may she live like some green laurel
Rooted in one dear perpetual place.

My mind, because the minds that I have loved,
The sort of beauty that I have approved,
Prosper but little, has dried up of late,
Yet knows that to be choked with hate
May well be of all evil chances chief.
If there's no hatred in a mind
Assault and battery of the wind
Can never tear the linnet from the leaf.

An intellectual hatred is the worst,
So let her think opinions are accursed.
Have I not seen the loveliest woman born
Out of the mouth of Plenty's horn,
Because of her opinionated mind
Barter that horn and every good
By quiet natures understood
For an old bellows full of angry wind?

Considering that, all hatred driven hence,
The soul recovers radical innocence
And learns at last that it is self-delighting,
Self-appeasing, self-affrighting,
And that its own sweet will is Heaven's will;
She can, though every face should scowl
And every windy quarter howl
Or every bellows burst, be happy still.

And may her bridegroom bring her to a house
Where all's accustomed, ceremonious;
For arrogance and hatred are the wares
Peddled in the thoroughfares.
How but in custom and in ceremony
Are innocence and beauty born?
Ceremony's a name for the rich horn,
And custom for the spreading laurel tree.

Suggestions for Discussion

1. Is he imposing on her a conservative ideal of womanhood?

2. What words or images suggest that he might quarrel with the ideas of feminists today?

3. Discuss: "How but in custom and in ceremony/Are innocence and beauty born?"

4. What seems to be the poet's concept of happiness for a woman?

Gwendolyn Brooks

Life for My Child Is Simple, and Is Good

Gwendolyn Brooks (b.1917) is an American poet who grew up in Chicago's slums. Her works, which focus on contemporary Black life in the United States, include *A Street in Bronzeville* (1949); *Annie Allen* (1949), which won a Pulitzer Prize; and *The Bean Eaters* (1960). She also has written a novel and a book for children. In this brief poem the writer sets forth her hopes for her son's joy and growth.

Life for my child is simple, and is good.
He knows his wish. Yes, but that is not all.
Because I know mine too.
And we both want joy of undeep and unabiding things,
Like kicking over a chair or throwing blocks out of a window
Or tipping over an icebox pan
Or snatching down curtains or fingering an electric outlet
Or a journey or a friend or an illegal kiss.
No. There is more to it than that.
It is that he has never been afraid.
Rather, he reaches out and lo the chair falls with a beautiful crash,
And the blocks fall, down on the people's heads,
And the water comes slooshing sloopily out across the floor.
And so forth.
Not that success, for him, is sure, infallible.
But never has he been afraid to reach.
His lesions are legion.
But reaching is his rule.

Suggestions for Discussion

1. Compare Brooks's hopes for her child with those of Yeats for his daughter.

2. What do the joys of "unabiding things" have in common?

3. What oppositions are posed in the poem, and how are they resolved?

Randall Jarrell

The Player Piano

Born in Nashville, Tennessee, and educated at Vanderbilt University, Randall Jarrell (1914–1965) taught for most of his life. A poet and critic, he won two Guggenheim Fellowships and served as Poetry Consultant at the Library of Congress. He was a careful craftsman who drew often on his imagination rather than his personal experience as the source for his poems.

I ate pancakes one night in a Pancake House
Run by a lady my age. She was gay.
When I told her that I came from Pasadena
She laughed and said, "I lived in Pasadena
When Fatty Arbuckle drove the El Mólino bus."

I felt that I had met someone from home.
No, not Pasadena, Fatty Arbuckle.
Who's that? Oh, something that we had in common
Like—like—the false armistice. Piano rolls.
She told me her house was the first Pancake House

East of the Mississippi, and I showed her
A picture of my grandson. Going home—
Home to the hotel—I began to hum,
"Smile a while, I bid you sad adieu,
When the clouds roll back I'll come to you."

Let's brush our hair before we go to bed,
I say to the old friend who lives in my mirror.
I remember how I'd brush my mother's hair
Before she bobbed it. How long has it been
Since I hit my funnybone? had a scab on my knee?

Here are Mother and Father in a photograph,
Father's holding me. . . . They both look so *young*.
I'm so much older than they are. Look at them,
Two babies with their baby. I don't blame you,
You weren't old enough to know any better;

If I could I'd go back, sit down by you both,
And sign our true armistice: you weren't to blame.
I shut my eyes and there's our living room.
The piano's playing something by Chopin,
And Mother and Father and their little girl

Listen. Look, the keys go down by themselves!
I go over, hold my hands out, play I play—
If only, somehow, I had learned to live!
The three of us sit watching, as my waltz
Plays itself out a half-inch from my fingers.

Suggestions for Discussion

1. What is the significance of the title of the poem?

2. Characterize the speaker in the poem.

3. Describe the occurrence which leads the speaker to reminisce about her childhood.

4. What regrets does the speaker express?

Suggestion for Writing

Describe a scene from your childhood that evokes poignant memories.

James Wright

Mutterings over the Crib of a Deaf Child

James Wright (1927–1980) was educated at Kenyon College and the University of Washington. He taught at Hunter College, served as a Fulbright fellow, and won the Yale Series of Younger Poets award (1957). In 1972 he won the Pulitzer Prize for *Collected Poems.* Other books are *Two Citizens* (1973), *Moments of the Italian Summer* (1976), and *To a Blossoming Pear Tree* (1978). The poet laments the fact that his deaf child will be denied both commonplace pleasures and special delights of natural sounds.

"How will he hear the bell at school
Arrange the broken afternoon,
And know to run across the cool
Grasses where the starlings cry,
Or understand the day is gone?"

Well, someone lifting curious brows
Will take the measure of the clock.
And he will see the birchen boughs
Outside sagging dark from the sky,
And the shade crawling upon the rock.

"And how will he know to rise at morning?
His mother has other sons to waken,
She has the stove she must build to burning
Before the coals of the nighttime die;
And he never stirs when he is shaken."

I take it the air affects the skin,
And you remember, when you were young,
Sometimes you could feel the dawn begin,
And the fire would call you, by and by,
Out of the bed and bring you along.

"Well, good enough. To serve his needs
All kinds of arrangements can be made.
But what will you do if his finger bleeds?
Or a bobwhite whistles invisibly
And flutes like an angel off in the shade?"

He will learn pain. And, as for the bird,
It is always darkening when that comes out.
I will putter as though I had not heard,
And lift him into my arms and sing
Whether he hears my song or not.

Suggestions for Discussion

1. Who is the speaker? What are his feelings about the child?

2. What compensations does the deaf child have? How are they conveyed?

3. Justify the use of the word *mutterings* in the title.

Nancy Willard

Questions My Son Asked Me, Answers I Never Gave Him

Nancy Willard (b. 1936) received her Ph.D. from the University of Michigan. She has won the Hopwood Award, a Woodrow Wilson Fellowship, and an O. Henry Award for the best short story in 1970. Her publications include *In His Country: Poems* (1966), *Skin of Grace* (1967), and *The Carpenter of the Sun: Poems* (1974). In this poem Willard responds to her child's questions concerning the nature of his universe with tenderness and whimsy.

1. Do gorillas have birthdays?
   Yes. Like the rainbow they happen,
   like the air they are not observed.

2. Do butterflies make a noise?
   The wire in the butterfly's tongue
   hums gold.
   Some men hear butterflies
   even in winter.

3. Are they part of our family?
   They forgot us, who forgot how to fly.

4. Who tied my navel? Did God tie it?
   God made the thread: O man, live forever!
   Man made the knot: enough is enough.

5. If I drop my tooth in the telephone
   will it go through the wires and bite someone's ear?
   I have seen earlobes pierced by a tooth of steel.
   It loves what lasts.
   It does not love flesh.
   It leaves a ring of gold in the wound.

6. If I stand on my head
   will the sleep in my eye roll up into my head?
   Does the dream know its own father?
   Can bread go back to the field of its birth?

7. Can I eat a star?
   Yes, with the mouth of time
   that enjoys everything.

8. Could we xerox the moon?
   This is the first commandment:
   I am the moon, thy moon.
   Thou shalt have no other moons before thee.

9. Who invented water?
   The hands of the air, that wanted to wash each other.

10. What happens at the end of numbers?
    I see three men running toward a field.
    At the edge of the tall grass, they turn into light.

11. Do the years ever run out?
    God said, I will break time's heart.
    Time ran down like an old phonograph.
    It lay flat as a carpet.
    At rest on its threads I am learning to fly.

Suggestions for Discussion

1. Since each question is answered, why does the author suggest in her title that she did not answer it?

2. What do the son's questions tell you about him? Note the range of his questions.

3. What do the writer's answers tell you about her? How would you characterize the answers?

4. How does figurative language affect the tone? Describe the tone of the answers. In No. 3 Willard says we "forgot how to fly." What does she mean? The figure of flying is repeated in the last stanza. What is its significance? How does it relate to the question?

5. On the basis of the questions and answers, how would you describe the relationship of mother and son?

Suggestion for Writing

Write your own answer(s) to a hypothetical question you are either asking yourself or someone is asking you.

Personal Relationships: Men and Women

◆◆◆◆

Thus changes in women's rights change women's moral judgments, seasoning mercy with justice by enabling women to consider it moral to care not only for others but for themselves. The issue of inclusion first raised by the feminists in the public domain reverberates through the psychology of women as they begin to notice their own exclusion of themselves. When the concern with care extends from an injunction not to hurt others to an ideal of responsibility in social relationships, women begin to see their understanding of relationships as a source of moral strength. But the concept of rights also changes women's moral judgments by adding a second perspective to the consideration of moral problems, with the result that judgment becomes more tolerant and less absolute.

> —**Carol Gilligan,** "Women's Rights and Women's Judgment," from *In A Different Voice*

If it is not perfect, it is not love, and if it is not love, it is bound to be hate sooner or later. This is perhaps a not too exaggerated statement of the extreme position of Romantic Love, more especially in America, where we are all brought up on it, whether we know it or not. Romantic Love is changeless, faithful, passionate, and its sole end is to render the two lovers happy. It has no obstacles save those provided by the hazards of fate (that is to say, society), and such sufferings as the lovers may cause each other are only another word for delight: exciting jealousies, thrilling uncertainties, the ritual dance of courtship within the charmed closed circle of their secret alliance; all *real* troubles come from without, they face them unitedly in perfect confidence. Marriage is not the end but only the beginning of true happiness, cloudless, changeless to the end. That the candidates for this blissful condition have never seen an example of it, nor every knew anyone who had, makes no difference. That is the ideal and they will achieve it.

—**Katherine Anne Porter**, "The Necessary Enemy"

Love cannot thrive in inequality or extreme poverty. It requires enough leisure for introspection and enough introspection for empathy. It demands that the individual feel a certain control over his life because, in too great a storm, we tend to seek any refuge. It thrives on honesty and therefore must do away with great need, since need drives out honesty. It is rational, it knows its own roots, it is moral and controllable because it stems from the head and not the heart. Any resemblance it bears to love as we know it today is purely fictional.

And true love is still in embryo, fragile compared to other ties because it derives no strength from more ancient needs. Its roots are not in the past but in the future. It is a beginning, a new survival mechanism slowly evolving to suit new circumstances.

—**Jill Tweedie**, "The Future of Love"

That the test did reveal something other than the superficiality of its makers I realized only many years later. What it revealed was that there is a large class of men and women both, to which I belong, who are essentially androgynous. That doesn't mean we're gay, or low in the appropriate hormones, or uncomfortable performing the jobs traditionally assigned our sexes. (A few years after that summer, I was leading troops in combat and, unfashionable as it now is to admit this, having a very good time. War is exciting. What a pity the 20th century went and spoiled it with high-tech weapons.)

—**Noel Perrin**, "The Androgynous Man"

Strange how things change. The image of manhood against which I am measured has changed so much that now, almost twenty years later, I am told I am not sensitive *enough*. When tensions build in our relationship, Shelley will admonish me for being out of touch with my feelings.

How can I explain it to her? How can any man explain it to any woman? Women are not raised to abort all tears. They are not measured by their toughness. They are not expected to bang against each other on hockey rinks and football fields and basketball courts. They do not go out into the woods to play soldiers. They do not settle disagreements by punching each other. For them, tears are a badge of femininity. For us, they are a masculine demerit.

—**Mark Gerzon,** "Manhood: The Elusive Goal" from *A Choice of Heroes*

Her mind only vaguely grasped what he was saying. Her physical being was for the moment predominant. She was not thinking of his words, only drinking in the tones of his voice. She wanted to reach out her hand in the darkness and touch him with the sensitive tips of her fingers upon the face or the lips. She wanted to draw close to him and whisper against his cheek—she did not care what—as she might have done if she had not been a respectable woman.

—**Kate Chopin,** "A Respectable Woman"

Essays

Mary Wollstonecraft
A Vindication of the Rights of Woman

Mary Wollstonecraft (1759–1797), whose husband was the radical William Godwin and whose daughter became Mrs. Percy Bysshe Shelley, was a schoolteacher, governess, and a member of a publishing firm. Her *Vindication of the Rights of Woman* (1792) was an extraordinary defense of the rights of eighteenth-century women. This eighteenth-century diatribe against those who would keep women enslaved was written with the wish to persuade women to acquire strength of mind and body.

My own sex, I hope, will excuse me, if I treat them like rational creatures, instead of flattering their *fascinating* graces, and viewing them as if they were in a state of perpetual childhood, unable to stand alone. I earnestly wish to point out in what true dignity and human happiness consists—I wish to persuade women to endeavor to acquire strength, both of mind and body, and to convince them that the soft phrases, susceptibility of heart, delicacy of sentiment, and refinement of taste, are almost synonymous with epithets of weakness, and that those beings who are only the objects of pity and that kind of love, which has been termed its sister, will soon become objects of contempt.

Dismissing, then, those pretty feminine phrases, which the men condescendingly use to soften our slavish dependence, and despising that weak elegancy of mind, exquisite sensibility, and sweet docility of manners, supposed to be the sexual characteristics of the weaker vessel, I wish to show that elegance is inferior to virtue, that the first object of laudable ambition is to obtain a character as a human being, regardless of the distinction of sex; and that secondary views should be brought to this simple touchstone.

This is a rough sketch of my plan; and should I express my conviction with the energetic emotions that I feel whenever I think of the subject, the dictates of experience and reflection will be felt by some of my readers. Animated by this important object, I shall disdain to cull my phrases or polish my style; I aim at being useful, and sincerity will render me unaffected; for, wishing rather to persuade by the force of my arguments, than dazzle by the elegance of my language, I shall not waste my time in rounding periods, or in fabricating the turgid bombast of artificial feelings, which, coming from the head, never reach the heart. I shall be employed about things, not words! and, anxious to render my sex more respectable members of society, I shall try to avoid that flowery diction which has slided from essays into novels, and from novels into familiar letters and conversation.

These pretty superlatives, dropping glibly from the tongue, vitiate the taste, and create a kind of sickly delicacy that runs away from simple unadorned truth; and a deluge of false sentiments and overstretched feelings, stifling the natural emotions of the heart, render the domestic pleasures insipid, that ought to sweeten the exercise of those severe duties, which educate a rational and immortal being for a nobler field of action.

The education of women has, of late, been more attended to than formerly; yet they are still reckoned a frivolous sex, and ridiculed or pitied by the writers who endeavor by satire or instruction to improve them. It is acknowledged that they spend many of the first years of their lives in acquiring a smattering of accomplishments; meanwhile strength of body and mind are sacrificed to libertine notions of beauty, to the desire of establishing themselves—the only way women can rise in the world—by marriage. And this desire making mere animals of them, when they marry they act as such children may be expected to act—they dress; they paint, and nickname God's creatures. Surely these weak beings are only fit for a seraglio!—Can they be expected to govern a family with judgment, or take care of the poor babes whom they bring into the world?

If then it can be fairly deduced from the present conduct of the sex, from the prevalent fondness for pleasure which takes place of ambition, and those nobler passions that open and enlarge the soul; that the instruction which women have hitherto received has only tended, with the constitution of civil society, to render them insignificant objects of desire—mere propagators of fools!—if it can be proved that in aiming to accomplish them, without cultivating their understandings, they are taken out of their sphere of duties, and made ridiculous and useless when the short-lived bloom of beauty is over,[1] I presume that *rational* men will excuse me for endeavoring to persuade them to become more masculine and respectable.

Indeed the word masculine is only a bugbear: there is little reason to fear that women will acquire too much courage or fortitude; for their apparent inferiority with respect to bodily strength, must render them, in some degree, dependent on men in the various relations of life; but why should it be increased by prejudices that give a sex to virtue, and confound simple truths with sensual reveries?

Women are, in fact, so much degraded by mistaken notions of female excellence, that I do not mean to add a paradox when I assert, that this artificial weakness produces a propensity to tyrannize, and gives birth to cunning, the natural opponent of strength, which leads them to play off those contemptible infantine airs that undermine esteem even whilst they excite desire. Let men

---

[1]A lively writer, I cannot recollect his name, asks what business women turned of forty have to do in the world?

become more chaste and modest, and if women do not grow wiser in the same ratio, it will be clear that they have weaker understandings. It seems scarcely necessary to say, that I now speak of the sex in general. Many individuals have more sense than their male relatives; and, as nothing preponderates where there is a constant struggle for an equilibrium, without it has naturally more gravity, some women govern their husbands without degrading themselves, because intellect will always govern.

Suggestions for Discussion

1. Why does the author urge women to reject their conventional image of weakness?

2. How does she relate diction and style to the cause of women's rights? The author acknowledges that her feelings are "energetic." How are you made aware of the strength of her conviction? Why is *fascinating* italicized?

3. How does her own use of language affect her purpose and tone?

4. With what details does she convey her view of marriage? How would you characterize her attitude toward members of her own sex?

5. What evidence is there in this brief excerpt that the author is detached from her subject? deeply involved?

6. According to Wollstonecraft, how does the education of women both reflect and foster the concept of their frivolity and weakness? What does she see as its effect on the family?

7. What causal relationship is established in the last paragraph?

8. How does the concept of self function in the author's argument?

9. What rhetorical devices are used to persuade the reader?

Suggestions for Writing

1. Imagine a dialogue between Mary Wollstonecraft and D. H. Lawrence, whose essay follows. Focus on points of agreement and disagreement.

2. ". . . the first object of laudable ambition is to obtain a character as a human being, regardless of the distinction of sex." Discuss this statement in the light of your reading on the search for self.

3. Defend or refute the comment that the word *masculine,* as applied to women, is "only a bugbear."

D. H. Lawrence
Give Her a Pattern

D. H. Lawrence (1885–1930) was a schoolteacher before he turned to writing and became one of the great English novelists of the twentieth century. His best-known novels, which focus on relationships between men and women, include *Sons and Lovers* (1913), *Women in Love* (1920), and *Lady Chatterley's Lover* (1928). He also wrote short stories, essays, poetry, and literary criticism. In "Give Her a Pattern," Lawrence castigates men for not accepting women as real human beings of the feminine sex.

The real trouble about women is that they must always go on trying to adapt themselves to men's theories of women, as they always have done. When a woman is thoroughly herself, she is being what her type of man wants her to be. When a woman is hysterical it's because she doesn't quite know what to be, which pattern to follow, which man's picture of woman to live up to.

For, of course, just as there are many men in the world, there are many masculine theories of what women should be. But men run to type, and it is the type, not the individual, that produces the theory, or "ideal" of woman. Those very grasping gentry, the Romans, produced a theory or ideal of the matron, which fitted in very nicely with the Roman property lust. "Caesar's wife should be above suspicion."—So Caesar's wife kindly proceeded to be above it, no matter how far below it the Caesar fell. Later gentlemen like Nero produced the "fast" theory of woman, and later ladies were fast enough for everybody. Dante arrived with a chaste and untouched Beatrice, and chaste and untouched Beatrices began to march self-importantly through the centuries. The Renaissances discovered the learned woman, and learned women buzzed mildly into verse and prose. Dickens invented the child-wife, so child-wives have swarmed ever since. He also fished out his version of the chaste Beatrice, a chaste but marriageable Agnes. George Eliot imitated this pattern, and it became confirmed. The noble woman, the pure spouse, the devoted mother took the field, and was simply worked to death. Our own poor mothers were this sort. So we younger men, having been a bit frightened of our noble mothers, tended to revert to the child-wife. We weren't very inventive. Only the child-wife must be a boyish little thing—that was the new touch we added. Because young men are definitely frightened of the real female. She's too risky a quantity. She is too untidy, like David's Dora. No, let her be a boyish little thing, it's safer. So a boyish little thing she is.

There are, of course, other types. Capable men produce the capable woman ideal. Doctors produce the capable nurse. Business men produce the capable secretary. And so you get all sorts. You can produce the masculine sense of honor (whatever that highly mysterious quantity may be) in women, if you want to.

There is, also, the eternal secret ideal of men—the prostitute. Lots of women live up to this idea: just because men want them to.

And so, poor woman, destiny makes away with her. It isn't that she hasn't got a mind—she has. She's got everything that man has. The only difference is that she asks for a pattern. Give me a pattern to follow! That will always be woman's cry. Unless of course she has already chosen her pattern quite young, then she will declare she is herself absolutely, and no man's idea of women has any influence over her.

Now the real tragedy is not that women ask and must ask for a pattern of womanhood. The tragedy is not, even, that men give them such abominable patterns, child-wives, little-boy-baby-face girls, perfect secretaries, noble spouses, self-sacrificing mothers, pure women who bring forth children in virgin coldness, prostitutes who just make themselves low, to please the men; all the atrocious patterns of womanhood that men have supplied to woman; patterns all perverted from any real natural fullness of a human being. Man is willing to accept woman as an equal, as man in skirts, as an angel, a devil, a baby-face, a machine, an instrument, a bosom, a womb, a pair of legs, a servant, an encyclopaedia, an ideal, or an obscenity; the one thing he won't accept her as, is a human being, a real human being of the feminine sex.

And, of course, women love living up to strange patterns, weird patterns—the more uncanny the better. What could be more uncanny than the present pattern of the Eton-boy girl with flower-like artificial complexion? It is just weird. And for its very weirdness women like living up to it. What can be more gruesome than the little-boy-baby-face pattern? Yet the girls take it on with avidity.

But even that isn't the real root of the tragedy. The absurdity, and often, as in the Dante–Beatrice business, the inhuman nastiness of the pattern—for Beatrice had to go on being chaste and untouched all her life, according to Dante's pattern, while Dante had a cozy wife and kids at home—even that isn't the worst of it. The worst of it is, as soon as a woman has really lived up to the man's pattern, the man dislikes her for it. There is intense secret dislike for the Eton-young-man girl, among the boys, now that she is actually produced. Of course, she's very nice to show in public, absolutely the thing. But the very young men who have brought about her production detest her in private and in their private hearts are appalled by her.

When it comes to marrying, the pattern goes all to pieces. The boy marries the Eton-boy girl, and instantly he hates the *type*. Instantly his mind begins to play hysterically with all the other types, noble Agneses, chaste Beatrices, clinging Doras, and lurid *filles de joie*. He is in a wild welter of confusion. Whatever pattern the poor woman tries to live up to, he'll want another. And that's the condition of modern marriage.

Modern woman isn't really a fool. But modern man is. That seems to me the only plain way of putting it. The modern man is a fool, and the modern young man a prize fool. He makes a greater mess of his women than men have ever made. Because he absolutely doesn't know *what* he wants her to be. We shall see the changes in the woman-pattern follow one another fast and furious now, because the young men hysterically don't know what they want. Two years hence women may be in crinolines—there was a pattern for you!—or a bead flap, like naked negresses in mid-Africa—or they may be wearing brass armor, or the uniform of the Horse Guards. They may be anything. Because the young men are off their heads, and don't know what they want.

The women aren't fools, but they *must* live up to some pattern or other. They *know* the men are fools. They don't really respect the pattern. Yet a pattern they must have, or they can't exist.

Women are not fools. They have their own logic, even if it's not the masculine sort. Women have the logic of emotion, men have the logic of reason. The two are complementary and mostly in opposition. But the woman's logic of emotion is no less real and inexorable than the man's logic of reason. It only works differently.

And the woman never really loses it. She may spend years living up to a masculine pattern. But in the end, the strange and terrible logic of emotion will work out the smashing of that pattern, if it has not been emotionally satisfactory. This is the partial explanation of the astonishing changes in women. For years they go on being chaste Beatrices or child-wives. Then on a sudden—bash! The chaste Beatrice becomes something quite different, the child-wife becomes a roaring lioness! The pattern didn't suffice, emotionally.

Whereas men are fools. They are based on a logic of reason, or are supposed to be. And then they go and behave, especially with regard to women, in a more-than-feminine unreasonableness. They spend years training up the little-boy-baby-face type, till they've got her perfect. Then the moment they marry her, they want something else. Oh, beware, young women, of the young men who adore you! The moment they've got you they'll want something utterly different. The moment they marry the little-boy-baby-face, instantly they begin to pine for the noble Agnes, pure and majestic, or the infinite mother with deep bosom of consolation, or the perfect business woman, or the lurid prostitute on black silk sheets; or, most idiotic of all, a combination of all the lot of them at once. And that is the logic of reason! When it comes to women, modern men are idiots. They don't know what they want, and so they never want, permanently, what they get. They want a cream cake that is at the same time ham and eggs and at the same time porridge. They are fools. If only women weren't bound by fate to play up to them!

For the fact of life is that women *must* play up to man's pattern. And she only gives her best to a man when he gives her a satisfactory pattern to play up to. But today, with a stock of ready-made, worn-out idiotic patterns to live up to, what can women give to men but the trashy side of their emotions? What could a woman possibly give to a man who wanted her to be a boy-baby-face? What could she possibly give him but the dribblings of an idiot?— And, because women aren't fools, and aren't fooled even for very long at a time, she gives him some nasty cruel digs with her claws, and makes him cry for mother dear!—abruptly changing his pattern.

Bah! men are fools. If they want anything from women, let them give women a decent, satisfying idea of womanhood—not these trick patterns of washed-out idiots.

Suggestions for Discussion

1. Consider the title "Give Her a Pattern" in the light of Lawrence's attitude toward women. As he sketches some of the patterns imposed on women by men through the ages, whom does he regard as villain? Is there any evidence that he regards both men and women as victims of their culture?

2. What details provide the basis for the statement that the one thing man "won't accept her as, is a human being, a real human being of the feminine sex"?

3. Observe the repetition of the charge that modern men are fools. What does Lawrence mean by the statement that women are bound by fate to play up to men? How does he suggest that women are not as great "fools" as men?

4. What is the basis for his fatalistic attitude toward the possibility of real change in relationships between men and women?

5. What relationship does he make between art and nature?

6. How does he lead up to a definition of woman's tragedy?

7. How are comparison and contrast employed to develop his thesis?

8. How do structure, diction, exclamatory sentences, and metaphor contribute to tone and purpose?

9. What rhetorical devices are used to persuade the reader?

Suggestions for Writing

1. Write on modern female stereotypes and the mass media.

2. ". . . women love living up to strange patterns." What are some of these patterns today?

3. "When it comes to marrying, the pattern goes all to pieces." Can you illustrate?

4. Discuss and illustrate the "terrible logic of emotion" from your own experience.

Virginia Woolf

The Angel in the House

Virginia Woolf (1882–1941) was an English novelist and critic known for her experimentation with the form of the novel. Her works include *The Voyage Out* (1915), *Night and Day* (1919), *Jacob's Room* (1922), *Mrs. Dalloway* (1925), *To the Lighthouse* (1927), *Orlando: A Biography* (1928), *The Waves* (1931), *The Years* (1937), *Between the Acts* (1941), and several collections of essays. With her husband, Leonard Woolf, she founded the Hogarth Press. Although Mrs. Woolf was able to overcome certain obstacles to honest writing, she states that women still have "many ghosts to fight, many prejudices to overcome."

When your secretary invited me to come here, she told me that your Society is concerned with the employment of women and she suggested that I might tell you something about my own professional experiences. It is true I am a woman; it is true I am employed; but what professional experiences have I had? It is difficult to say. My profession is literature; and in that profession there are fewer experiences for women than in any other, with the exception of the stage—fewer, I mean, that are peculiar to women. For the road was cut many years ago—by Fanny Burney, by Aphra Behn, by Harriet Martineau, by Jane Austen, by George Eliot—many famous women, and many more unknown and forgotten, have been before me, making the path smooth, and regulating my steps. Thus, when I came to write, there were very few material obstacles in my way. Writing was a reputable and harmless occupation. The family peace was not broken by the scratching of a pen. No demand was made upon the family purse. For ten and sixpence one can buy paper enough to write all the plays of Shakespeare—if one has a mind that way. Pianos and models, Paris, Vienna, and Berlin, masters and mistresses, are not needed by a writer. The cheapness of writing paper is, of course, the reason why women have succeeded as writers before they have succeeded in the other professions.

But to tell you my story—it is a simple one. You have only got to figure to yourselves a girl in a bedroom with a pen in her hand. She had only to move that pen from left to right—from ten o'clock to one. Then it occurred to her to do what is simple and cheap enough after all—to slip a few of those pages into an envelope, fix a penny stamp in the corner, and drop the envelope into the red box at the corner. It was thus that I became a journalist; and my effort was rewarded on the first day of the following month—a very glorious day it was for me—by a letter from an editor containing a cheque for one pound ten shillings and sixpence. But to show you how little I deserve to be called a professional woman, how little I know of the struggles and difficulties of such lives, I have to admit that instead of spending that sum upon bread and butter, rent, shoes and stockings, or butcher's bills, I went out and bought a cat—a beautiful cat, a Persian cat, which very soon involved me in bitter disputes with my neighbours.

What could be easier than to write articles and to buy Persian cats with the profits? But wait a moment. Articles have to be about something. Mine, I seem to remember, was about a novel by a famous man. And while I was writing this review, I discovered that if I were going to review books I should need to do battle with a certain phantom. And the phantom was a woman, and when I came to know her better I called her after the heroine of a famous poem. The Angel in the House. It was she who used to come between me and my paper when I was writing reviews. It was she who bothered me and wasted my time and so tormented me that at last I killed her. You who come of a younger and happier generation may not have heard of her—you may not know what I mean by the Angel in the House. I will describe her as shortly as I can. She was intensely sympathetic. She was immensely charming. She was utterly unselfish. She excelled in the difficult arts of family life. She sacrificed herself daily. If there was chicken, she took the leg; if there was a draught she sat in it—in short she was so constituted that she never had a mind or 'a wish of her own, but preferred to sympathize always with the minds and wishes of others. Above all—I need not say it—she was pure. Her purity was supposed to be her chief beauty—her blushes, her great grace. In those days—the last of Queen Victoria—every house had its Angel. And when I came to write I encountered her with the very first words. The shadow of her wings fell on my page; I heard the rustling of her skirts in the room. Directly, that is to say, I took my pen in hand to review that novel by a famous man, she slipped behind me and whispered: "My dear, you are a young woman. You are writing about a book that has been written by a man. Be sympathetic; be tender; flatter; deceive; use all the arts and wiles of our sex. Never let anybody guess that you have a mind of your own. Above all, be pure." And she made as if to guide my pen. I now record the one act for which I take some credit to myself, though the credit rightly belongs to some excellent ancestors of mine who left me a certain sum of money—shall we say five hundred pounds a year?—so that it was not necessary for me to depend solely on charm for my living. I turned upon her and caught her by the throat. I did my best to kill her. My excuse, if I were to be had up in a court of law, would be that I acted in self-defense. Had I not killed her she would have killed me. She would have plucked the heart out of my writing. For, as I found, directly I put pen to paper, you cannot review even a novel without having a mind of your own, without expressing what you think to be the truth about human relations, morality, sex. And all these questions, according to the Angel in the House, cannot be dealt with freely and openly by women; they must charm, they must conciliate, they must—to put it bluntly—tell lies if they are to succeed. Thus, whenever I felt the shadow of her wing or the radiance of her halo upon my page, I took up the inkpot and flung it at her. She died hard. Her fictitious nature was of great assistance to her. It is far harder to kill a phantom than a reality. She was always creeping back when I thought I had despatched her. Though I flatter myself that I killed her in the end, the struggle was severe; it took much time that had better have been spent upon learning Greek grammar; or in roaming the world in search of adventures. But it was a real experience; it was an experience that was bound to befall all women writers at that time. Killing the Angel in the House was part of the occupation of a woman writer.

But to continue my story. The Angel was dead; what then remained? You may say that what remained was a simple and common object—a young woman in a bedroom with an inkpot. In other words, now that she had rid herself of falsehood, that young woman had only to be herself. Ah, but what is "herself"? I mean, what is a woman? I assure you, I do not know. I do not believe that you know. I do not believe that anybody can know until she has expressed herself in all the arts and professions open to human skill. That indeed is one of the reasons why I have come here—out of respect for you, who are in process of showing us by your experiments what a woman is, who are in process of providing us, by your failures and successes, with that extremely important piece of information.

But to continue the story of my professional experiences. I made one pound ten and six by my first review; and I bought a Persian cat with the proceeds. Then I grew ambitious. A Persian cat is all very well, I said; but a Persian cat is not enough. I must have a motor car. And it was thus that I became a novelist—for it is a very strange thing that people will give you a motor car if you will tell them a story. It is a still stranger thing that there is nothing so delightful in the world as telling stories. It is far pleasanter than writing reviews of famous novels. And yet, if I am to obey your secretary and tell you my professional experiences as a novelist, I must tell you about a very strange experience that befell me as a novelist. And to understand it you must try first to imagine a novelist's state of mind. I hope I am not giving away professional secrets if I say that a novelist's chief desire is to be as unconscious as possible. He has to induce in himself a state of perpetual lethargy. He wants life to proceed with the utmost quiet and regularity. He wants to see the same faces, to read the same books, to do the same things day after day, month after month, while he is writing, so that nothing may break the illusion in which he is living—so that nothing may disturb or disquiet the mysterious nosings about, feelings round, darts, dashes and sudden discoveries of that very shy and illusive spirit, the imagination. I suspect that this state is the same both for men and women. Be that as it may, I want you to imagine me writing a novel in a state of trance. I want you to figure to yourselves a girl sitting with a pen in her hand, which for minutes, and indeed for hours, she never dips into the inkpot. The image that comes to my mind when I think of this girl is the image of a fisherman lying sunk in dreams on the verge of a deep lake with a rod held out over the water. She was letting her imagination sweep unchecked round every rock and cranny of the world that lies sub-merged in the depths of our unconscious being. Now came the experience, the experience that I believe to be far commoner with women writers than with men. The line raced through the girl's fingers. Her imagination had rushed away. It had sought the pools, the depths, the dark places where the largest fish slumber. And then there was a smash. There was an explosion. There was foam and confusion. The imagination had dashed itself against something hard. The girl was roused from her dream. She was indeed in a state of the most acute and difficult distress. To speak without figure she had thought of something, something about the body, about the passions which it was unfitting for her as a woman to say. Men, her reason told her, would be shocked. The consciousness of what men will say of a woman who speaks the truth about her passions had roused her from her artist's state of unconsciousness. She could write no more. The trance was over. Her imagination could work no longer. This I believe to be a very common experience with women writers—they are impeded by the extreme conventionality of the other sex. For though men sensibly allow themselves great freedom in these respects, I doubt that they realize or can control the extreme severity with which they condemn such freedom in women.

These then were two very genuine experiences of my own. These were two of the adventures of my professional life. The first—killing the Angel in the House—I think I solved. She died. But the second, telling the truth about my own experiences as a body, I do not think I solved. I doubt that any woman has solved it yet. The obstacles against her are still immensely powerful—and yet they are very difficult to define. Outwardly, what is sim-pler than to write books? Outwardly, what obstacles are there for a woman rather than for a man? Inwardly, I think, the case is very different; she has still many ghosts to fight, many prejudices to overcome. Indeed it will be a long time still, I think, before a woman can sit down to write a book without finding a phantom to be slain, a rock to be dashed against. And if this is so in literature, the freest of all professions for women, how is it in the new profes-sions which you are now for the first time entering?

Those are the questions that I should like, had I time, to ask you. And indeed, if I have laid stress upon these professional experiences of mine, it is because I believe that they are, though in different forms, yours also. Even when the path is nominally open—when there is nothing to prevent a woman from being a doctor, a lawyer, a civil servant—there are many phantoms and obstacles, as I believe, looming in her way. To discuss and define them is I think of great value and importance; for thus only can the labor be shared, the difficulties be solved. But besides this, it is necessary also to discuss the ends and the aims for which we are fighting, for which we are doing battle with these formidable obstacles. Those aims cannot be taken for granted; they must be perpetually questioned and examined. The whole position, as I see it—here in this hall surrounded by women practising for the first time in history I know not how many different professions—is one of extraordinary interest and importance. You have won rooms of your own in the house hitherto exclusively owned by men. You are able, though not without great labor and effort, to pay the rent. You are earning your five hundred pounds a year. But this freedom is only a beginning; the room is your own, but it is still bare. It has to be furnished; it has to be decorated; it has to be shared. How are you going to furnish it, how are you going to decorate it? With whom are you going to share it, and upon what terms? These, I think are questions of the utmost importance and interest. For the first time in history you are able to ask them; for the first time you are able to decide for yourselves what the answers should be. Willingly would I stay and discuss those questions and answers—but not tonight. My time is up; and I must cease.

Suggestions for Discussion

1. What are the characteristics of this phantom, the Angel in the House? Do they persist today?

2. Why does the author say she had to kill the Angel?

3. What remaining obstacles to truth did she find? In what ways may women still encounter these obstacles?

4. What are the implications in the concluding paragraph concerning relationships with men?

5. "Ah, but what is 'herself'? I mean, what is a woman?" Discuss these rhetorical questions in relation to purpose and tone.

6. What points of agreement or disagreement might Woolf have with Lawrence?

7. What rhetorical devices are employed to persuade the reader?

Suggestions for Writing

1. Describe an Angel in the House you know.

2. Does this phantom of the Angel still haunt contemporary drama, movies, fiction, advertising?

3. Apply one or more of Woolf's generalizations to a woman poet or writer of fiction.

◇◇◇

Katherine Anne Porter
The Necessary Enemy

Katherine Anne Porter (1890–1980) worked in Chicago as a newspaper reporter, as a traveling singer of Scottish ballads in Texas, and again as a journalist in Texas and in Denver. After several years as a free-lance writer for such publications as *Century Magazine, The Nation,* and the *New Republic,* she began to write and publish short stories. Among her books are *Flowering Judas* (1930), which resulted in a Guggenheim Fellowship, *Noon Wine* (1937), *Pale Horse, Pale Rider* (1939), *The Leaning Tower* (1944), and her allegorical novel, *Ship of Fools* (1962). If our view of love is subjected to ideals impossible of fulfillment, its growth is impaired, and one fails "to recognize its human limitations and come to grips with them."

She is a frank, charming, fresh-hearted young woman who married for love. She and her husband are one of those gay, good-looking young pairs who ornament this modern scene rather more in profusion perhaps than ever before in our history. They are handsome, with a talent for finding their way in their world, they work at things that interest them, their tastes agree and their hopes. They intend in all good faith to spend their lives together, to have children and do well by them and each other—to be happy, in fact, which for them is the whole point of their marriage. And all in stride, keeping their wits about them. Nothing romantic, mind you; their feet are on the ground.

Unless they were this sort of person, there would be not much point to what I wish to say; for they would seem to be an example of the high-spirited, right-minded young whom the critics are always invoking to come forth and do their duty and practice all those sterling old-fashioned virtues which in every generation seem to be falling into disrepair. As for virtues, these young people are more or less on their own, like most of their kind; they get very little moral or other aid from their society; but after three years of marriage this very contemporary young woman finds herself facing the oldest and ugliest dilemma of marriage.

She is dismayed, horrified, full of guilt and forebodings because she is finding out little by little that she is capable of hating her husband, whom she loves faithfully. She can hate him at times as fiercely and mysteriously, indeed in terribly much the same way, as often she hated her parents, her brothers and sisters, whom she loves, when she was a child. Even then it had seemed to her a kind of black treacherousness in her, her private wickedness that, just the same, gave her her only private life. That was one thing her parents never knew about her, never seemed to suspect. For it was never given a name. They did and said hateful things to her and to each other as if by right, as if in them it was a kind of virtue. But when they said to her, "Control your feelings," it was never when she was amiable and obedient, only in the black times of her hate. So it was her secret, a shameful one. When they punished her, sometimes for the strangest reasons, it was, they said, only because they loved her—it was for her good. She did not believe this, but she thought herself guilty of something worse than ever they had punished her for. None of this really frightened her: the real fright came when she discovered that at times her father and mother hated each other; this was like standing on the doorsill of a familiar room and seeing in a lightning flash that the floor was gone, you were on the edge of a bottomless pit. Sometimes she felt that both of them hated her, but that passed, it was simply not a thing to be thought of, much less believed. She thought she had outgrown all this, but here it was again, an element in her own nature she could not control, or feared she could not. She would have to hide from her husband, if she could, the same spot in her feelings she had hidden from her parents, and for the same no doubt disreputable, selfish reason: she wants to keep his love.

Above all, she wants him to be absolutely confident that she loves him, for that is the real truth, no matter how unreasonable it sounds, and no matter how her own feelings betray them both at times. She depends recklessly on his love; yet while she is hating him, he might very well be hating her as much or even more, and it would serve her right. But she does not want to be served right, she wants to be loved and forgiven—that is, to be sure he would forgive her anything, if he had any notion of what she had done. But best of all she would like not to have anything in her love that should ask for forgiveness. She doesn't mean about their quarrels—they are not so bad. Her feelings are out of proportion, perhaps. She knows it is perfectly natural for people to disagree, have fits of temper, fight it out; they learn quite a lot about each other that way, and not all of it disappointing either. When it passes, her hatred seems quite unreal. It always did.

Love. We are early taught to say it. I love you. We are trained to the thought of it as if there were nothing else, or nothing else worth having without it, or nothing worth having which it could not bring with it. Love is taught, always by precept, sometimes by example. Then hate, which no one meant to teach us, comes of itself. It is true that if we say I love you, it may be received with doubt, for there are times when it is hard to believe. Say I hate you, and the one spoken to believes it instantly, once for all.

Say I love you a thousand times to that person afterward and mean it every time, and still it does not change the fact that once we said I hate you, and meant that too. It leaves a mark on that surface love had worn so smooth with its eternal caresses. Love must be learned, and learned again and again; there is no end to it. Hate needs no instruction, but waits only to be provoked . . . hate, the unspoken word, the unacknowledged presence in the house, that faint smell of brimstone among the roses, that invisible tongue-tripper, that unkempt finger in every pie, that sudden oh-so-curiously *chilling* look—could it be boredom?—on your dear one's features, making them quite ugly. Be careful: love, perfect love, is in danger.

If it is not perfect, it is not love, and if it is not love, it is bound to be hate sooner or later. This is perhaps a not too exaggerated statement of the extreme position of Romantic Love, more especially in America, where we are all brought up on it, whether we know it or not. Romantic Love is changeless, faithful, passionate, and its sole end is to render the two lovers happy. It has no obstacles save those provided by the hazards of fate (that is to say, society), and such sufferings as the lovers may cause each other are only another word for delight: exciting jealousies, thrilling uncertainties, the ritual dance of courtship within the charmed closed circle of their secret alliance; all *real* troubles come from without, they face them unitedly in perfect confidence. Marriage is not the end but only the beginning of true happiness, cloudless, changeless to the end. That the candidates for this blissful condition have never seen an example of it, nor ever knew anyone who had, makes no difference. That is the ideal and they will achieve it.

How did Romantic Love manage to get into marriage at last, where it was most certainly never intended to be? At its highest it was tragic; the love of Héloïse and Abélard. At its most graceful, it was the homage of the trouvère for his lady. In its most popular form, the adulterous strayings of solidly married couples who meant to stray for their own good reasons, but at the same time do nothing to upset the property settlements or the line of legitimacy; at its most trivial, the pretty trifling of shepherd and the shepherdess.

This was generally condemned by church and state and a word of fear to honest wives whose mortal enemy it was. Love within the sober, sacred realities of marriage was a matter of personal luck, but in any case, private feelings were strictly a private affair having, at least in theory, no bearing whatever on the fixed practice of the rules of an institution never intended as a recreation ground for either sex. If the couple discharged their religious and social obligations, furnished forth a copious progeny, kept their troubles to themselves, maintained public civility and died under the same roof, even if not always on speaking terms, it was rightly regarded as a successful marriage. Apparently this testing ground was too severe for all but the stoutest spirits; it too was based on an ideal, as impossible in its way as the ideal Romantic Love. One good thing to be said for it is that society took responsibility for the conditions of marriage, and the sufferers within its bonds could always blame the system, not themselves. But Romantic Love crept into the marriage bed, very stealthily, by centuries, bringing its absurd notions about love as eternal springtime and marriage as a personal adventure meant to provide personal happiness. To a Western romantic such as I, though my views have been much modified by painful experience, it still seems to me a charming work of the human imagination, and it is a pity its central notion has been taken too literally and has hardened into a convention as cramping and enslaving as the older one. The refusal to acknowledge the evils in ourselves which therefore are implicit in any human situation is as extreme and unworkable a proposition as the doctrine of total depravity; but somewhere between them, or maybe beyond them, there does exist a possibility for reconciliation between our desires for impossible satisfactions and the simple unalterable fact that we also desire to be unhappy and that we create our own sufferings; and out of these sufferings we salvage our fragments of happiness.

Our young woman who has been taught that an important part of her human nature is not real because it makes trouble and interferes with her peace of mind and shakes her self-love, has been very badly taught; but she has arrived at a most important stage of her re-education. She is afraid her marriage is going to fail because she has not love enough to face its difficulties; and this because at times she feels a painful hostility toward her husband, and cannot admit its reality because such an admission would damage in her own eyes her view of what love should be, an absurd view, based on her vanity of power. Her hatred is real as her love is real, but her hatred has the advantage at present because it works on a blind instinctual level, it is lawless; and her love is subjected to a code of ideal conditions, impossible by their very nature of fulfillment, which prevents its free growth and deprives it of its right to recognize its human limitations and come to grips with them. Hatred is natural in a sense that love, as she conceives it, a young person brought up in the tradition of Romantic Love, is not natural at all. Yet it did not come by hazard, it is the very imperfect expression of the need of the human imagination to create beauty and harmony out of chaos, no matter how mistaken its notion of these things may be, nor how clumsy its methods. It has conjured love out of the air, and seeks to preserve it by incantations; when she spoke a vow to love and honor her husband until death, she did a very reckless thing, for it is not possible by an act of the will to fulfill such an engagement. But it was the necessary act of faith performed in defense of a mode of feeling, the statement of honorable intention to practice as well as she is able the noble, acquired faculty of love, that very mysterious overtone to sex which is the best thing in it. Her hatred is part of it, the necessary enemy and ally.

Suggestions for Discussion

1. What is the "necessary enemy" of love? In what sense is it also an ally? What are its causes and effects?

2. This essay is written from the perspective of a woman. Examine the introspective thoughts in the first section and determine their universality for women; for both sexes.

3. "Love is taught, always by precept, sometimes by example." Interpret this statement in the light of your personal experience, or with specific reference to your reading of fiction.

4. Why is learning to love an endless process?

5. To what extent are the hazards and failures of romantic love functions of fate (i.e., society)? Of the character of the individuals concerned? Of the institution of marriage? Comment on each.

6. What are some of the implications of the women's liberation movement for romantic love? What bearing does it have upon Porter's views?

Suggestions for Writing

1. Discuss repetitive patterns in parent–child and man–woman relationships.

2. What are the values and dangers of free expression of feeling in intimate relationships?

3. Write on question 3, 5, or 6 above.

Cynthia Ozick

We Are the Crazy Lady

Cynthia Ozick (b. 1928) is an American novelist who has written fiction, essays, poetry, and translations in various magazines and reviews. She is the author of *Trust* (1966); *The Pagan Rabbi and Other Stories* (1971); *Bloodshed and Three Novellas* (1976); *Levitation: Five Fictions* (1981); and *The Cannibal Galaxy* (1983). A series of episodes in the 1950s and 1960s in which the writer experiences sexual discrimination are ironically narrated.

I. The Crazy Lady Double

A long, long time ago, in another century—1951, in fact—when you, dear younger readers, were most likely still in your nuclear-family playpen (where, if female, you cuddled a rag-baby to your potential titties, or, if male, let down virile drool over your plastic bulldozer), Lionel Trilling told me never, never to use a parenthesis in the very first sentence. This was in a graduate English seminar at Columbia University. To get into this seminar, you had to submit to a grilling wherein you renounced all former allegiance to the then-current literary religion, New Criticism, which considered that only the text existed, not the world. I passed the interview by lying, cunningly, and against my real convictions. I said that probably the world *did* exist—and walked triumphantly into the seminar room.

There were four big tables arranged in a square, with everyone's feet sticking out into the open middle of the square. You could tell who was nervous, and how much, by watching the pairs of feet twist around each other. Professor Trilling presided awesomely from the high bar of the square. His head was a majestic granite-gray, like a centurion in command; he *looked* famous. His clean shoes twitched only slightly, and only when he was angry.

It turned out he was angry at me a lot of the time. He was angry because he thought me a disrupter, a rioter, a provocateur, and a fool; also crazy. And this was twenty years ago, before these things were *de rigueur* in the universities. Everything was very quiet in those days. There were only the Cold War and Korea and Joe McCarthy and the Old Old Nixon, and the only revolutionaries around were in Henry James's *The Princess Casamassima.*

Habit governed the seminar. Where you sat the first day was where you settled forever. So, to avoid the stigmatization of the ghetto, I was careful not to sit next to the other woman in the class: the Crazy Lady.

At first the Crazy Lady appeared to be remarkably intelligent. She was older than the rest of us, somewhere in her thirties (which was why we thought of her as a Lady), with wild tan hair, a noticeably breathing bosom, eccentric gold-rimmed old-pensioner glasses, and a tooth-crowded wild mouth that seemed to get wilder the more she talked. She talked like a motorcycle, fast and urgent. Everything she said was almost brilliant, only not actually on point, and frenetic with hostility. She was tough and negative. She volunteered a lot and she stood up and wobbled with rage, pulling at her hair and mouth. She fought Trilling point for point, piecemeal and wholesale, mixing up queerly-angled literary insights with all sorts of private and public fury. After the first meetings, he was fed up with her. The rest of us accepted that she probably wasn't all there, but in a room where everyone was on the make for recognition—you talked to save your life, and the only way to save your life was to be the smartest one that day—she was a nuisance, a distraction, a pain in the ass. The class became a bunch of Good Germans, determinedly indifferent onlookers to a vindictive match between Trilling and the Crazy Lady, until finally he subdued her by shutting his eyes, and, when that didn't always work, by cutting her dead and lecturing right across the sound of her strong, strange voice.

All this was before R. D. Laing had invented the superiority of madness, of course, and, cowards all, no one liked the thought of being tarred with the Crazy Lady's brush. Ignored by the boss, in the middle of everything she would suddenly begin to mutter to herself. She mentioned certain institutions she'd been in, and said we all belonged there. The people who sat on either side of her shifted chairs. If the Great Man ostracized the Crazy Lady, we had to do it too. But one day the Crazy Lady came in late and sat down in the seat next to mine, and stayed there the rest of the semester.

Then an odd thing happened. There, right next to me, was the noisy Crazy Lady, tall, with that sticking-out sighing chest of hers, orangey curls dripping over her nose, snuffling furiously for attention. And there was I, a brownish runt, a dozen years younger and flatter and shyer than the Crazy Lady, in no way her twin, physically or psychologically. In those days I was bone-skinny, small, sallow and myopic, and so scared I could trigger diarrhea at one glance from the Great Man. All this stress on looks is important. The Crazy Lady and I had our separate bodies, our separate brains. We handed in our separate papers.

But the Great Man never turned toward me, never at all, and if ambition broke feverishly through shyness so that I dared to push an idea audibly out of me, he shut his eyes when I put up my hand. This went on for a long time. I never got to speak, and I began to have the depressing feeling that Lionel Trilling hated me. It was no small thing to be hated by the man who had written "Wordsworth and the Rabbis" and *Matthew Arnold*, after all. What in hell was going on? I was in trouble, because, like everyone else in that demented contest, I wanted to excel. Then, one slow afternoon, wearily, the Great Man let his eyes fall on me. He called me by name, but it was not my name—it was the Crazy Lady's. The next week the papers came back—and there, right at the top of mine, in the Great Man's own handwriting, was a rebuke to the Crazy Lady for starting an essay with a parenthesis in the first sentence, a habit he took to be a continuing sign of that unruly and unfocused mentality so often exhibited in class. And then a Singular Revelation crept coldly through me. Because the Crazy Lady and I sat side by side, because we were a connected blur of Woman, Lionel Trilling, master of ultimate distinctions, couldn't tell us apart. The Crazy Lady and I! He couldn't tell us apart! It didn't matter that the Crazy Lady was crazy! *He couldn't tell us apart!*

Moral 1: All cats are gray at night,
        all darkies look alike.

Moral 2: Even among intellectual humanists, every woman has a *Doppel-gänger*—every other woman.

II. The Lecture, 1

I was invited by a women's group to be guest speaker at a Book-Author Luncheon. The women themselves had not really chosen me: the speaker had been selected by a male leader and imposed on them. The plan was that I would autograph copies of my book, eat a good meal and then lecture. The woman in charge of the programming phoned to ask me what my topic would be. This was a matter of some concern, since they had never had a woman author before, and no one knew how the idea would be received. I offered as my subject "The Contemporary Poem."

When the day came, everything went as scheduled—the autographing, the food, the welcoming addresses. Then it was time to go to the lectern. I aimed at the microphone and began to speak of poetry. A peculiar rustling sound flew up from the audience. All the women were lifting their programs to the light, like hundreds of wings. Confused murmurs ran along the walls. I began to feel very uncomfortable. Then I too took up the program. It read, "Topic: The Contemporary Home."

Moral: Even our ears practice the caste system.

III. The Lecture, 2

I was in another country, the only woman at a philosophical seminar lasting three days. On the third day, I was to read a paper. I had accepted the invitation with a certain foreknowledge. I knew, for instance, that I could not dare to be the equal of any other speaker. To be an equal would be to be less. I understood that mine had to be the most original and powerful paper of all. I had no choice; I had to toil beyond my most extreme possibilities. This was not ambition, but only fear of disgrace.

For the first two days, I was invisible. When I spoke, people tapped impatiently, waiting for the interruption to be over with. No one took either my presence or my words seriously. At meals, I sat with my colleagues' wives.

The third day arrived, and I read my paper. It was successful beyond my remotest imaginings. I was interviewed, and my remarks appeared in newspapers in a language I could not understand. The Foreign Minister invited me to his home. I hobnobbed with famous poets.

Now my colleagues noticed me. But they did not notice me as a colleague. They teased and kissed me. I had become their mascot.

Moral: There is no route out of caste which does not instantly lead back into it.

IV. Propaganda

For many years, I had noticed that no book of poetry by a woman was ever reviewed without reference to the poet's sex. The curious thing was that, in the two decades of my scrutiny, there were *no* exceptions whatever. It did not matter whether the reviewer was a man or woman: in every case the question of the "feminine sensibility" of the poet was at the center of the reviewer's response. The maleness of male poets, on the other hand, hardly ever seemed to matter.

Determined to ridicule this convention, I wrote a tract, a piece of purely tendentious mockery, in the form of a short story. I called it "Virility."

The plot was, briefly, as follows: A very bad poet, lustful for fame, is despised for his pitiful lucubrations and remains unpublished. But luckily, he comes into possession of a cache of letters written by his elderly spinster aunt, who lives an obscure and secluded working-class life in a remote corner of England. The letters contain a large number of remarkable poems; the aunt, it turns out, is a genius. The bad poet publishes his find under his own name, and instantly attains world-wide adulation. Under the title *Virility*, the poems become immediate classics. They are translated into dozens of languages and are praised and revered for their unmistakably masculine qualities: their strength, passion, wisdom, energy, boldness, brutality, worldliness, robustness, authenticity, sensuality, compassion. A big, handsome sweating man, the poet swaggers from country to country, courted everywhere, pursued by admirers, yet respected by the most demanding critics.

Meanwhile, the old aunt dies. The supply of genius runs out. Bravely and contritely the poor poet confesses his ruse, and, in a burst of honesty, publishes the last batch under the real poet's name. The book is entitled *Flowers from Liverpool*. But the poems are at once found negligible and dismissed: "Thin feminine art," say the reviews, "a lovely girlish voice." Also: "Choked with female inwardness," and "The fine womanly intuition of a competent poetess." The poems are utterly forgotten.

I included this fable in a collection of short stories. In every review, the salvo went unnoticed. Not one reviewer recognized that the story was a sly tract. Not one reviewer saw the smirk or the point. There was one delicious comment, though. "I have some reservations," a man in Washington, D.C., wrote, "about the credibility of some of her male characters when they are chosen as narrators."

Moral: In saying what is obvious, never choose cunning. Yelling works better.

V. Hormones

During a certain period of my life, I was reading all the time, and fairly obsessively. Sometimes, though, sunk in a book of criticism or philosophy, I would be brought up short. Consider: here is a paragraph that excites the intellect. Inwardly, one assents passionately to its premises; the writer's idea is an exact diagram of one's own deepest psychology or conviction; one feels oneself seized as for a portrait. Then the disclaimer: "It is, however, otherwise with the female sex. . . ." A rebuke from the World of Thinking. *I didn't mean you, lady.* In the instant one is in possession of one's humanity most intensely, it is ripped away.

These moments I discounted. What is wrong—intrinsically, psychologically, culturally, morally—can be dismissed.

But to dismiss in this manner is to falsify one's most genuine actuality. A Jew reading of the aesthetic glories of European civilization without taking notice of his victimization during, say, the era of the building of the great cathedrals, is self-forgetful in the most dangerous way. So would be a black who read of King Cotton with an economist's objectivity.

I am not offering any strict analogy between the situation of women and the history of Jews or colonialized blacks, as many politically radical women do (though the analogy with blacks is much the more frequent one). It seems to me to be abusive of language in the extreme when some women speak, in the generation after Auschwitz, in the very hour of the Bengali horror, of the "oppression" of women. Language makes culture, and we make a rotten culture when we abuse words. We raise up rotten heroines. I use "rotten" with particular attention to its precise meanings: foul, putrid, tainted, stinking. I am thinking now especially of a radical women's publication, *Off Our Backs*, which not long ago presented Leila Khaled, terrorist and foiled murderer, as a model for the political conduct of women.

But if I would not support the extreme analogy (and am never surprised when black women, who have a more historical comprehension of actual, not figurative, oppression, refuse to support the analogy), it is anyhow curious to see what happens to the general culture when any enforced class in any historical or social condition is compelled to doubt its own self-understanding, when identity is extremely defined, when individual humanity is called into question as being different from "standard" humanity. What happens is that the general culture, along with the object of its debasement, is also debased. If you laugh at women, you play Beethoven in vain. If you laugh at women, your laboratory will lie.

We can read in Charlotte Perkins Gilman's 1912 essay, "Are Women Human Beings?", an account of an opinion current sixty years ago. Women, said one scientist, are not only "not the human race—they are not even half the human race, but a sub-species set apart for purposes of reproduction merely."

Though we are accustomed to the idea of "progress" in science, if not in civilization generally, the fact is that more information has led to something very like regression.

I talked with an intelligent physician, the Commissioner of Health of a middle-sized city in Connecticut, a man who sees medicine not discretely but as part of the social complex. He treated me to a long list of all the objective differences between men and women, including particularly an account of current endocrinal studies relating to female hormones. Aren't all of these facts? he asked. How can you distrust facts? Very good, I said, I'm willing to take your medically-educated word for it. I'm not afraid of facts, I welcome facts—*but a congeries of facts is not equivalent to an idea.* This is the essential fallacy of the so-called "scientific" mind. People who mistake facts for ideas are incomplete thinkers; they are gossips.

You tell me, I said, that my sense of my own humanity as being "standard" humanity—which is, after all, a subjective idea—is refuted by hormonal research. My psychology, you tell me, which in your view is the source of my ideas, is the result of my physiology. It is not I who express myself, it is my hormones which express me. A part is equal to the whole, you say. Worse yet, the whole is simply the issue of the part: my "I" is a flash of chemicals. You are willing to define all my humanity by hormonal investigation under a microscope. This you call "objective irrefutable fact," as if tissue-culture were equivalent to culture. But each scientist can assemble his own (subjective) constellation of "objective irrefutable fact," just as each social thinker can assemble his own (subjective) selection of traits that define "humanity." Who can prove what is "standard" humanity, and which sex, class, or race is to be exempted from whole participation in it? On what basis do you regard female hormones as causing a modification from normative humanity? And what better right do you have to define normative humanity by what males have traditionally apperceived than by what females have traditionally apperceived— assuming (as I, lacking presumptuousness, do not) that their apperceptions have not been the same? Only Tiresias—that mythological character who was both man and woman consecutively—is in a position to make the comparison and present the proof. And then not even Tiresias, because to be a hermaphrodite is to be a monster, and not human.

"Why are you so emotional about all this?" said the Commissioner of Health. "You see how it is? Those are your female hormones working on you right now."

Moral: Defamation is only applied research.

VI. Ambition

After thirteen years, I at last finished a novel. The first seven years were spent in a kind of apprenticeship—the book that came out of that time was abandoned without much regret. A second one was finished in six weeks and buried. It took six years to write the third novel, and this one was finally published.

How I lived through those years is impossible to recount in a short space. I was a recluse, a priest of Art. I read seas of books. I believed in the idea of masterpieces. I was scornful of the world of journalism, jobs, everydayness. I did not live like any woman I knew. I lived like some men I had read about— Flaubert, or Proust, or James—the subjects of those literary biographies I endlessly drank in. I did not think of them as men, but as writers. I read the diaries of Virginia Woolf, and biographies of George Eliot, but I did not think of them as women. I thought of them as writers. I thought of myself as a writer.

It goes without saying that all this time my relatives regarded me as abnormal. I accepted this. It seemed to me, from what I had read, that most writers were abnormal. Yet on the surface, I could easily have passed for normal. The husband goes to work, the wife stays home—that is what is normal. Well, I was married. My husband went to his job every day. His job paid the rent and bought the groceries. I stayed home, reading and writing, and felt myself to be an economic parasite. To cover guilt, I joked that I had been given a grant from a very private, very poor, foundation—my husband.

But my relatives never thought of me as a parasite. The very thing I was doubtful about—my economic dependence—they considered my due as a woman. They saw me not as a failed writer without an income, but as a childless housewife, a failed woman. They did not think me abnormal because I was a writer, but because I was not properly living my life as a woman. In one respect we were in agreement utterly—my life was failing terribly, ter ribly. For me it was because, already deep into my thirties, I had not yet published a book. For them, it was because I had not yet borne a child.

I was a pariah, not only because I was a deviant, but because I was not recognized as the kind of deviant I meant to be. A failed woman is not the same as a failed writer. Even as a pariah I was the wrong kind of pariah.

Still, relations are only relations. What I aspired to, what I was in thrall to, was Art, was Literature, not familial contentment. I knew how to distinguish the trivial from the sublime. In Literature and in Art, I saw, my notions were not pariah notions. There, I inhabited the mainstream. So I went on reading and writing. I went on believing in Art, and my intention was to write a masterpiece. Not a saucer of well-polished craft (the sort of thing "women writers" are always accused of being accomplished at), but something huge, contemplative, Tolstoyan. My ambition was a craw.

I called the book *Trust*. I began it in the summer of 1957 and finished it in November of 1963, on the day President John Kennedy was assassinated. In manuscript, it was 801 pages divided into four parts: "America," "Europe," "Birth," and "Death." The title was meant to be ironic. In reality, it was about distrust. It seemed to me I had touched on distrust in every order or form of civilization. It seemed to me I had left nothing out. It was (though I did not know this then) a very hating book. What it hated above all was the whole—the whole—of Western Civilization. It told how America had withered into another Europe. It dreamed dark and murderous pagan dreams, and hated what it dreamed.

In style, the book was what has come to be called "mandarin": a difficult, aristocratic, unrelenting virtuoso prose. It was, in short, unreadable. I think I knew this. I was sardonic enough to say, echoing Joyce about *Finnegan's Wake*, "I expect you to spend your life at this." In any case, I had spent a decade-and-a-half of my own life at it. Though I did not imagine the world would fall asunder at its appearance, I thought—at the very least—the ambition, the all-swallowingness, the wild insatiability of the writer would be plain to everyone who read it. I had, after all, taken History for my subject: not merely History as an aggregate of events, but History as a judgment on events. No one could say my theme was flighty. Of all the novelists I read (and in those days I read them all, broiling in the envy of the unpublished, which is like no envy on earth), who else had dared so vastly?

During that period, Françoise Sagan's first novel was published. I held the thin little thing and laughed. Women's pulp!

My own novel, I believed, contained everything—the whole world.

But there was one element I had consciously left out. Though on principle I did not like to characterize it or think about it much, the truth is I was thinking about it all the time. It was only a fiction-technicality, but I was considerably afraid of it. It was the question of the narrator's "sensibility." The narrator, as it happened, was a young woman; I had chosen her to be the eye—and the "I"—of the novel because all the other characters in some way focused on her. She was the one most useful to my scheme. Nevertheless, I wanted her not to live. Everything I was reading in reviews of other people's books made me fearful: I would have to be very cautious; I would have to drain my narrator of emotive value of any kind, because I was afraid to be pegged as having written a "woman's" novel. Nothing was more certain to lead to that than a point-of-view seemingly lodged in a woman, and no one takes a woman's novel seriously. I was in terror, above all, of sentiment and feelings, those telltale taints. I kept the fury and the passion for other, safer, characters.

So what I left out of my narrator entirely, sweepingly, with exquisite consciousness of what exactly I *was* leaving out, was any shred of "sensibility." I stripped her of everything, even a name. I crafted and carpentered her. She was for me a bloodless device, fulcrum or pivot, a recording voice, a language-machine. She confronted moment or event, took it in, gave it out. And what to me was all the more wonderful about this nameless fiction-machine I had invented was that the machine itself, though never alive, was a character in the story, without ever influencing the story. My machine-narrator was there for efficiency only, for flexibility, for craftiness, for subtlety, but never, never, as a "woman." I wiped the "woman" out of her. And I did it out of fear, out of vicarious vindictive critical imagination, out of the terror of my ambition, out of, maybe, paranoia. I meant my novel to be taken for what it really was. I meant to make it impossible for it to be mistaken for something else.

Publication. Review in *The New York Times* Sunday Book Review.

Review is accompanied by a picture of a naked woman seen from the back. Her bottom is covered by some sort of drapery.

Title of review: "Daughter's Reprieve."

Excerpts from review: "These events, interesting in themselves, exist to reveal the sensibility of the narrator." "She longs to play some easy feminine role." "She has been unable to define herself as a woman." "The main body of the novel, then, is a revelation of the narrator's inner, turbulent, psychic drama."

O rabid rotten Western Civilization, where are you? O judging History, O foul Trust and fouler Distrust, where?

O Soap Opera, where did you come from?

(Meanwhile the review in *Time* was calling me a "housewife.")

Pause.

All right, let us take up the rebuttals.

Q. Maybe you *did* write a soap opera without knowing it. Maybe you only *thought* you were writing about Western Civilization when you were really only rewriting Stella Dallas.

A. A writer may be unsure of everything—trust the tale not the teller is a good rule—but not of his obsessions; of these he is certain. If I were rewriting Stella Dallas, I would turn her into the Second Crusade and demobilize her.

Q. Maybe you're like the blind Jew who wants to be a pilot, and when they won't give him the job he says they're anti-Semitic. Look, the book was lousy, you deserved a lousy review.

A. You mistake me, I never said it was a bad review. It was in fact an extremely favorable review, full of gratifying adjectives.

Q. Then what's eating you?

A. I don't know. Maybe the question of language. By language I mean literacy. See the next section, please.

Q. No Moral for *this* section?

A. Of course. If you look for it, there will always be a decent solution for female ambition. For instance, it is still not too late to enroll in a good secretarial school.

Q. Bitter, bitter! You mean your novel failed?

A. Perished, is dead and buried. I sometimes see it exhumed on the shelf in the public library. It's always there. No one ever borrows it.

Q. Dummy! You should've written a soap opera. Women are good at that.

A. Thank you. You almost remind me of a Second Moral: In conceptual life, junk prevails. Even if you do not produce junk, it will be taken for junk.

Q. What does that have to do with women?

A. The products of women are frequently taken for junk.

Q. And if a woman *does* produce junk . . . ?

A. Glory—they will treat her almost like a man who produces junk. They will say her name on television. Do please go on to the next section. Thank you.

VII. Conclusion, and a Peek

Actually I had two more stories to tell you. One was about Mr. Machismo, a very angry, well-groomed, *clean man* (what a pity he isn't a woman—ah, deprived of vaginal spray) who defines as irresponsible all those who do not obey him, especially his mother and sister. A highly morbid and titillating Gothic tale. The other story was about Mr. Littletable, the Petty Politician, at the Bankers' Feast—how he gathered up the wives in a pretty garland, threw them a topic to chatter over. A Bronx neighborhood where you can buy good lox, I think it was. Having set them all up so nicely, he went off to lick the nearest Vice-President-of-Morgan-Guaranty.

But these are long stories, Ladies and Gentlemen. No room up there for another Woman's Novel.

Suggestions for Discussion

1. How does the author establish tone? What are its components? Cite examples.

2. Find examples of effective metaphoric language and show how they contribute to purpose and tone.

3. What is the causal relationship between the experiences and the "morals"? State each "moral" in your own words. How does the phrasing of the "morals" contribute to tone?

4. How does the author develop the paradox that more information leads to repression?

5. Cite examples of irony.

6. What generalization does each incident illustrate?

Suggestions for Writing

1. Out of your own experience and observation develop the thesis underlying one of the author's "morals."

2. Write a sketch or narrative recounting an experience in which your sexual identity made a difference in the outcome.

3. Develop or refute the following statements of the author: "If you laugh at women, you play Beethoven in vain. If you laugh at women, your laboratory will lie."

Germaine Greer

The Stereotype

Germaine Greer (b. 1939) is an Australian-born writer and educator, best known as a standard bearer of the women's liberation movement and as the author of the best-selling *The Female Eunuch* (1971), from which this selection is taken, and of *Sex and Destiny: The Politics of Human Fertility* (1984). The stereotype—the Eternal Feminine—sought by women as well as by men, reduces a woman to a cipher and castrates her.

In that mysterious dimension where the body meets the soul the stereotype is born and has her being. She is more body than soul, more soul than mind. To her belongs all that is beautiful, even the very word beauty itself. All that exists, exists to beautify her. The sun shines only to burnish her skin and gild her hair; the wind blows only to whip up the color in her cheeks; the sea strives to bathe her; flowers die gladly so that her skin may luxuriate in their essence. She is the crown of creation, the masterpiece. The depths of the sea are ransacked for pearl and coral to deck her; the bowels of the earth are laid open that she might wear gold, sapphires, diamonds, and rubies. Baby seals are battered with staves, unborn lambs ripped from their mothers' wombs, millions of moles, muskrats, squirrels, minks, ermines, foxes, beavers, chinchillas, ocelots, lynxes, and other small and lovely creatures die untimely deaths that she might have furs. Egrets, ostriches, and peacocks, butterflies and beetles yield her their plumage. Men risk their lives hunting leopards for her coats, and crocodiles for her handbags and shoes. Millions of silkworms offer her their yellow labors; even the seamstresses roll seams and whip lace by hand, so that she might be clad in the best that money can buy.

The men of our civilization have stripped themselves of the fineries of the earth so that they might work more freely to plunder the universe for trea-

> Taught from infancy that beauty is woman's scepter, the mind shapes itself to the body, and roaming round its gilt cage, only seeks to adorn its prison.
>
> —Mary Wollstonecraft, *A Vindication of the Rights of Woman*, 1792, p. 90.

sures to deck my lady in. New raw materials, new processes, new machines are all brought into her service. My lady must therefore be the chief spender as well as the chief symbol of spending ability and monetary success. While her mate toils in his factory, she totters about the smartest streets and plushiest hotels with his fortune upon her back and bosom, fingers, and wrists, continuing that essential expenditure in his house which is her frame and her setting, enjoying that silken idleness which is the necessary condition of maintaining her mate's prestige and her qualification to demonstrate it. Once upon a time only the aristocratic lady could lay claim to the title of crown of creation: only her hands were white enough, her feet tiny enough, her waist narrow enough, her hair long and golden enough; but every well-to-do burgher's wife set herself up to ape my lady and to follow fashion, until my lady was forced to set herself out like a gilded doll overlaid with monstrous rubies and pearls like pigeon's eggs. Nowadays the Queen of England still considers it part of her royal female role to sport as much of the family jewelry as she can manage at any one time on all public occasions, although the male monarchs have escaped such showcase duty, which develops exclusively upon their wives.

At the same time as woman was becoming the showcase for wealth and caste, while men were slipping into relative anonymity and "handsome is as handsome does," she was emerging as the central emblem of western art. For the Greeks the male and female body had beauty of a human, not necessarily a sexual, kind; indeed they may have marginally favored the young male form as the most powerful and perfectly proportioned. Likewise the Romans showed no bias towards the depiction of femininity in their predominantly monumental art. In the Renaissance the female form began to predominate, not only as the mother in the predominant emblem of *madonna con bambino*, but as an aesthetic study in herself. At first naked female forms took their chances in crowd scenes or diptychs of Adam and Eve, but gradually Venus claims ascendancy, Mary Magdalene ceases to be wizened and emaciated, and becomes nubile and ecstatic, portraits of anonymous young women, chosen only for their prettiness, begin to appear, are gradually disrobed, and renamed Flora or Primavera. Painters begin to paint their own wives and mistresses and royal consorts as voluptuous beauties, divesting them of their clothes if desirable, but not of their jewelry. Susanna keeps her bracelets on in the bath, and Hélène Fourment keeps ahold of her fur as well!

What happened to women in painting happened to her in poetry as well. Her beauty was celebrated in terms of the riches which clustered around her: her hair was gold wires, her brow ivory, her lips ruby, her teeth gates of pearl, her breasts alabaster veined with lapis lazuli, her eyes as black as jet. The fragility of her loveliness was emphasized by the inevitable comparisons with the rose, and she was urged to employ her beauty in love-making before it withered on the stem. She was for consumption; other sorts of imagery spoke of her in terms of cherries and cream, lips as sweet as honey and skin white as milk, breasts like cream uncurdled, hard as apples. Some celebrations yearned over her finery as well, her lawn more transparent than morning mist, her lace as delicate as gossamer, the baubles that she toyed with and the favors that she gave. Even now we find the thriller hero describing his classy dames' elegant suits, cheeky hats, well-chosen accessories and footwear; the imagery no longer dwells on jewels and flowers but the consumer emphasis is the same. The mousy secretary blossoms into the feminine stereo-type when she reddens her lips, lets down her hair, and puts on something frilly.

Nowadays women are not expected, unless they are Paola di Liegi or Jackie Onassis, and then only on gala occasions, to appear with a king's ransom de-ployed upon their bodies, but they are required to look expensive, fashion-able, well-groomed, and not to be seen in the same dress twice. If the duty of the few may have become less onerous, it has also become the duty of the many. The stereotype marshals an army of servants. She is supplied with cosmetics, underwear, foundation garments, stockings, wigs, postiches, and hairdressing as well as her outer garments, her jewels, and furs. The effect is to be built up layer by layer, and it is expensive. Splendor has given way to fit, line, and cut. The spirit of competition must be kept up, as more and more women struggle toward the top drawer, so that the fashion industry can rely upon an expanding market. Poorer women fake it, ape it, pick up on the fashions a season too late, use crude effects, mistaking the line, the sheen, the gloss of the high-class article for a garish simulacrum. The business is so complex that it must be handled by an expert. The paragons of the stereotype must be dressed, coifed, and painted by the experts and the style-setters, although they may be encouraged to give heart to the housewives studying their lives in pulp magazines by claiming a lifelong fidelity to their own hair and soap and water. The boast is more usually discouraging than otherwise, unfortunately.

As long as she is young and personable, every woman may cherish the dream that she may leap up the social ladder and dim the sheen of luxury by sheer natural loveliness; the few examples of such a feat are kept before the eye of the public. Fired with hope, optimism, and ambition, young women study the latest forms of the stereotype, set out in *Vogue, Nova, Queen,* and other glossies, where the mannequins stare from among the advertisements for fabulous real estate, furs, and jewels. Nowadays the uniformity of the year's fashions is severely affected by the emergence of the pert female de-signers who direct their appeal to the working girl, emphasizing variety, com-fort, and simple, striking effects. There is no longer a single face of the year: even Twiggy has had to withdraw into marketing and rationed personal ap-pearances, while the Shrimp works mostly in New York. Nevertheless the stereotype is still supreme. She has simply allowed herself a little more varia-tion.

The stereotype is the Eternal Feminine. She is the Sexual Object sought by all men, and by all women. She is of neither sex, for she has herself no sex at all. Her value is solely attested by the demand she excites in others. All she must contribute is her existence. She need achieve nothing, for she is the reward of achievement. She need never give positive evidence of her moral character because virtue is assumed from her loveliness, and her pas-sivity. If any man who has no right to her be found with her she will not be punished, for she is morally neuter. The matter is solely one of male rivalry. Innocently she may drive men to madness and war. The more trouble she can cause, the more her stocks go up, for possession of her means more the more demand she excites. Nobody wants a girl whose beauty is imperceptible to all but him; and so men welcome the stereotype because it directs their taste into the most commonly recognized areas of value, although they may

> The myth of the strong black woman is the other side of the coin of the myth of the beautiful dumb blonde. The white man turned the white woman into a weak-minded, weak-bodied, delicate freak, a sex pot, and placed her on a pedestal; he turned the black woman into a strong self-reliant Amazon and deposited her in his kitchen. . . . The white man turned himself into the Omnipotent Administrator and established himself in the Front Office.
>
> —**Eldridge Cleaver,** "The Allegory of the Black Eunuchs," *Soul on Ice,* 1968, p. 162

protest because some aspects of it do not tally with their fetishes. There is scope in the stereotype's variety for most fetishes. The leg man may follow miniskirts, the tit man can encourage see-through blouses and plunging necklines, although the man who likes fat women may feel constrained to enjoy them in secret. There are stringent limits to the variations on the stereotype, for nothing must interfere with her function as sex object. She may wear leather, as long as she cannot actually handle a motorbike: she may wear rubber, but it ought not to indicate that she is an expert diver or waterskier. If she wears athletic clothes the purpose is to underline her unathleticism. She may sit astride a horse, looking soft and curvy, but she must not crouch over its neck with her rump in the air.

Because she is the emblem of spending ability and the chief spender, she is also the most effective seller of this world's goods. Every survey ever held has shown that the image of an attractive woman is the most effective advertising gimmick. She may sit astride the mudguard of a new car, or step into it ablaze with jewels; she may lie at a man's feet stroking his new socks; she may hold the petrol pump in a challenging pose, or dance through woodland glades in slow motion in all the glory of a new shampoo; whatever she does her image sells. The gynolatry of our civilization is written large upon its face, upon hoardings, cinema screens, television, newspapers, magazines, tins, packets, cartons, bottles, all consecrated to the reigning deity, the female fetish. Her dominion must not be thought to entail the rule of women, for she is not a woman. Her glossy lips and mat complexion, her unfocused eyes and flawless fingers, her extraordinary hair all floating and shining, curling, and gleaming, reveal the inhuman triumph of cosmetics, lighting, focusing, and printing, cropping and composition. She sleeps unruffled, her lips red and juicy and closed, her eyes as crisp and black as if new painted, and her false lashes immaculately curled. Even when she washes her face with a new and creamier toilet soap her expression is as tranquil and vacant and her paint as flawless as ever. If ever she should appear tousled and troubled, her features are miraculously smoothed to their proper veneer by a new washing powder or a bouillon cube. For she is a doll: weeping, pouting, or smiling, running or reclining, she is a doll. She is an idol, formed of the concatenation of lines and masses, signifying the lineaments of satisfied impotence.

Her essential quality is castratedness. She absolutely must be young, her body hairless, her flesh buoyant, and *she must not have a sexual organ.* No

> She was created to be the toy of man, his rattle, and it must
> jingle in his ears whenever, dismissing reason, he chooses to
> be amused.
>
> —Mary Wollstonecraft, *A Vindication of the Rights of
> Woman*, 1792, p. 66

musculature must distort the smoothness of the lines of her body, although
she may be painfully slender or warmly cuddly. Her expression must betray
no hint of humor, curiosity, or intelligence, although it may signify hauteur
to an extent that is actually absurd, or smoldering lust, very feebly signified
by drooping eyes and a sullen mouth (for the stereotype's lust equals irrational
submission), or, most commonly, vivacity and idiot happiness. Seeing that the
world despoils itself for this creature's benefit, she must be happy; the entire
structure would topple if she were not. So the image of woman appears plas-
tered on every surface imaginable, smiling interminably. An apple pie evokes
a glance of tender beatitude, a washing machine causes hilarity, a cheap box
of chocolates brings forth meltingly joyous gratitude, a Coke is the cause of a
rictus of unutterable brilliance, even a new stick-on bandage is saluted by a
smirk of satisfaction. A real woman licks her lips and opens her mouth and
flashes her teeth when photographers appear: *she* must arrive at the premiere
of her husband's film in a paroxysm of delight, or his success might be murmured about. The occupational hazard of being a Playboy Bunny is the aching
facial muscles brought on by the obligatory smiles.

So what is the beef? Maybe I couldn't make it. Maybe I don't have a pretty
smile, good teeth, nice tits, long legs, a cheeky ass, a sexy voice. Maybe I
don't know how to handle men and increase my market value, so that the
rewards due to the feminine will accrue to me. Then again, maybe I'm sick
of the masquerade. I'm sick of pretending eternal youth. I'm sick of belying
my own intelligence, my own will, my own sex. I'm sick of peering at the
world through false eyelashes, so everything I see is mixed with a shadow of
bought hairs; I'm sick of weighting my head with a dead mane, unable to
move my neck freely, terrified of rain, of wind, of dancing too vigorously in
case I sweat into my lacquered curls. I'm sick of the Powder Room. I'm sick
of pretending that some fatuous male's self-important pronouncements are the
objects of my undivided attention, I'm sick of going to films and plays when
someone else wants to, and sick of having no opinions of my own about either.
I'm sick of being a transvestite. I refuse to be a female impersonator. I am a
woman, not a castrate.

April Ashley was born male. All the information supplied by genes, chromosomes, internal and external sexual organs added up to the same thing.
April was a man. But he longed to be a woman. He longed for the stereotype,
not to embrace, but to be. He wanted soft fabrics, jewels, furs, makeup, the
love and protection of men. So he was impotent. He couldn't fancy women at
all, although he did not particularly welcome homosexual addresses. He did
not think of himself as a pervert, or even as a transvestite, but as a woman
cruelly transmogrified into manhood. He tried to die, became a female im-

> Discretion is the better part of Valerie
> though all of her is nice
> lips as warm as strawberries
> eyes as cold as ice
> the very best of everything
> only will suffice
> not for her potatoes
> and puddings made of rice
>
> —**Roger McGough,** *Discretion*

personator, but eventually found a doctor in Casablanca who came up with a more acceptable alternative. He was to be castrated, and his penis used as the lining of a surgically constructed cleft, which would be a vagina. He would be infertile, but that has never affected the attribution of femininity. April returned to England, resplendent. Massive hormone treatment had eradicated his beard, and formed tiny breasts: he had grown his hair and bought feminine clothes during the time he had worked as an impersonator. He became a model, and began to illustrate the feminine stereotype as he was perfectly qualified to do, for he was elegant, voluptuous, beautifully groomed, and in love with his own image. On an ill-fated day he married the heir to a peerage, the Hon. Arthur Corbett, acting out the highest achievement of the feminine dream, and went to live with him in a villa in Marbella. The marriage was never consummated. April's incompetence as a woman is what we must expect from a castrate, but it is not so very different after all from the impotence of feminine women, who submit to sex without desire, with only the infantile pleasure of cuddling and affection, which is their favorite reward. As long as the feminine stereotype remains the definition of the female sex, April Ashley is a woman, regardless of the legal decision ensuing from her divorce. She is as much a casualty of the polarity of the sexes as we all are. Disgraced, unsexed April Ashley is our sister and our symbol.

> To what end is the laying out of the embroidered Hair, embared Breasts; vermilion Cheeks, alluring looks, Fashion gates, and artful Countenances, effeminate intangling and insnaring Gestures, their Curls and Purls of proclaiming Petulancies, boulstered and laid out with such example and authority in these our days, as with Allowance and beseeming Conveniency?
>
> Doth the world wax barren through decrease of Generations, and become, like the Earth, less fruitful heretofore? Doth the Blood lose his Heat or do the Sunbeams become waterish and less fervent, than formerly they have been, that men should be thus inflamed and persuaded on to lust?
>
> —**Alex. Niccholes,** *A Discourse of Marriage and Wiving,*
> 1615, pp. 143–152

Suggestions for Discussion

1. How does the author develop the concept that "beauty is woman's scepter"? How does the long series of examples in the first paragraph contribute to purpose and tone?

2. What does the author mean by the stereotype? How does she develop and support her extended definition?

3. In what context does the author invoke the first person? How does its intrusion affect purpose and tone?

4. What purpose is served by the introduction of April Ashley? Do the last two sentences constitute an appropriate summation of what has gone before? Explain.

Suggestion for Writing

Drawing on your own experience and observation, write an essay on stereotypes.

◇◇◇◇

Norman Mailer
Who Would Finally Do the Dishes?

Norman Mailer (b. 1923) grew up in Brooklyn and was educated at Harvard University, where he wrote many short stories. He has written *The Naked and the Dead* (1948), *Barbary Shore* (1951), and *An American Dream* (1965). From 1953 to 1963 he edited *Dissent,* and in 1956 he cofounded *The Village Voice.* He is a public personality and columnist and a contributor to many major periodicals, such as the *New York Post, Partisan Review,* and *Esquire.* He received the National Institute of Arts and Letters Grant in literature in 1960. More recent books are *Armies of the Night* (1968), *Of a Fire on the Moon* (1971), *The Prisoner of Sex* (1971), *The Fight* (1975), and *Ancient Evenings* (1983). This excerpt from *The Prisoner of Sex* (1971), in which the author refers to himself as "he" and "the prisoner," moves from the question of who finally would do the dishes to the issue of the ultimate responsibility of women to select the fathers of their children.

Still he had not answered the question with which he began. Who finally would do the dishes? And in his reading through an Agreement drawn between husband and wife where every piece of housework was divided, and duty-shifts to baby-sit were divided, and weekends where the man worked to compensate the wife for chores of weekday transportation. Shopping was balanced, cooking was split, so was the transportation of children. It was a crystal of a contract bound to serve as model for many another, and began on this high and fundamental premise:

> We reject the notion that the work which brings in more money is more valuable. The ability to earn more money is already a privilege which must not be compounded by enabling the larger earner to buy out his/her duties and put the burden on the one who earns less, or on someone hired from outside.
>
> We believe that each member of the family has an equal right to his/her own time, work, value, choices. As long as all duties are performed, each person may use his/her extra time any way he/she chooses. If he/she wants to use it making money, fine. If he/she wants to spend it with spouse, fine. If not, fine.
>
> As parents we believe we must share all responsibility for taking care of our children and home—not only the work, but the responsibility. At least during the first year of this agreement, *sharing responsibility* shall mean:
>
>   1. Dividing the *jobs* (see "Job Breakdown" below); and
>   2. Dividing the *time* (see "Schedule" below) for which each parent is responsible.

There were details which stung:

>   10. Cleaning: Husband does all the house-cleaning, in exchange for wife's extra childcare (3:00 to 6:30 daily) and sick care.
>   11. Laundry: Wife does most home laundry. Husband does all dry cleaning delivery and pick up. Wife strips beds, husband remakes them.

No, he would not be married to such a woman. If he were obliged to have a roommate, he would pick a man. The question had been answered. He could love a woman and she might even sprain her back before a hundred sinks of dishes in a month, but he would not be happy to help her if his work should suffer, no, not unless her work was as valuable as his own. But he was complacent with the importance of respecting his work—what an agony for a man if work were meaningless: then all such rights were lost before a woman. So it was another corollary of Liberation that as technique reduced labor to activities which were often absurd, like punching the buttons on an automatic machine, so did the housework of women take on magnitude, for their work was directed at least to a basic end. And thinking of that Marriage Agreement which was nearly the equal of a legal code, he was reminded of his old campaign for mayor when Breslin and himself had called for New York City to become the fifty-first state and had preached Power to the Neighborhoods and offered the idea that a modern man would do well to live in a small society of his own choosing, in a legally constituted village within the city, or a corporate zone, in a traditional religious park or a revolutionary commune— the value would be to discover which of one's social ideas were able to work. For nothing was more difficult to learn in the modern world. Of course, it had been a scheme with all the profound naïveté of assuming that people voted as an expression of their desire when he had yet to learn the electorate obtained satisfaction by venting their hate. Still he wondered if it was not likely that the politics of government and property would yet begin to alter into the politics of sex. Perhaps he had been living with the subject too closely, but he saw no major reason why one could not await a world—assuming there would be a world—where people would found their politics on the fundamental demands they would make of sex. So might there yet be towns within the city which were homosexual, and whole blocks legally organized for married couples who thought the orgy was ground for the progressive action of the day. And there would be mournful areas of the city deserted on Sunday, all suitable for the mood of masturbators who liked the open air and the street, perhaps even pseudo-Victorian quarters where brothels could again be found. There could be city turfs steaming with the nuances of bisexuals living on top of bisexuals, and funky tracts for old-fashioned lovers where the man was the rock of the home; there would always be horizons blocked by housing projects vast as the legislation which had gone into the division of household duties between women and men. There would be every kind of world in the city, but their laws would be founded on sex. It was, he supposed, the rationalized end of that violence which had once existed between men and women as the crossed potential of their love, violence which was part perhaps of the force to achieve and the force to scourge, it had been that violence which entered into all the irrationality of love, "the rooting out of the old bodily shame" of which Lawrence had spoke, and the rooting out of the fear in women that they were more violent than their men, and would betray them, or destroy them in the transcendence of sex; yes, the play of violence had been the drama of love between a man and a woman, for too little, and they were friends never to be gripped by any attraction which could send them far; too much, and they were ruined, or love was ruined, or they must degenerate to bully and victim, become no better than a transmission belt to bring in the violence and injustice of the world outside, bring it in to poison the cowardice of their home. But the violence of lovers was on its way to disappear in all the other deaths of the primitive which one could anticipate as the human became the human unit—human violence would go to some place outside (like the smog) where it could return to kill them by slow degree—and equally. But he had made his determination on beginning his piece that he would not write of sex and violence too long, for that would oblige him to end in the unnatural position of explaining what he had attempted in other work. So he would step aside by remarking that a look at sex and violence was the proper ground of a novel and he would rather try it there. And content himself now with one last look at his remark that "the prime responsibility of a woman probably is to be on earth long enough to find the best mate for herself, and conceive children who will improve the species." Was it too late now to suggest that in the search for the best mate was concealed the bravery of a woman, and to find the best mate, whatever ugly or brutal or tyrannical or unbalanced or heart-searing son of misery he might appear, his values nonetheless, mysterious fellow of values, would inevitably present themselves in those twenty-three chromsomes able to cut through fashion, tradition, and class.

There is a famous study of neurotics which shows that patients who received psychoanalysis had an improvement rate of 44 percent; psychotherapy was more effective—a rate of 64 percent; and 72 percent was the unhappiest improvement, for that was the rate of cure of patients who had never been treated at all. The Eysenck study it is called, and later studies confirm its results. It was, the prisoner decided, a way of telling us that the taste in the mouth of explaining too much is the seating of the next disease. One cannot improve the human condition through comfort and security, or through generalized sympathy and support—it is possible the untreated patients got better because the violence of their neurosis was not drained. The cure of the human was in his leap.

But now he could comprehend why woman bridled at the thought she must "find the best mate for herself and . . . improve the species." How full of death was the idea if one looked at any scheme which brought people who were fundamentally unattracted to each other down marriage aisles, their qualifications superb, their qualities neuter. So he was grateful to a writer who wrote a book, *The Lady*, published in 1910, Emily James Putnam, first dean of Barnard. She was a writer with a whip of the loveliest wit. He would give the last quotation to her for she had given the hint of a way.

> Apart from the crude economic question, the things that most women mean when they speak of "happiness," that is, love and children and the little republic of the home, depend upon the favour of men, and the qualities that win this favour are not in general those that are most useful for other purposes. A girl should not be too intelligent or too good or too highly differentiated in any direction. Like a ready-made garment she should be designed to fit the average man. She should have "just about as much religion as my William likes." The age-long operation of this rule, by which the least strongly individualised women are the most likely to have a chance to transmit their qualities, has given it the air of a natural law.

It was finally obvious. Women must have their rights to a life which would allow them to look for a mate. And there would be no free search until they were liberated. So let woman be what she would, and what she could. Let her cohabit on elephants if she had to, and fuck with Borzoi hounds, let her bed with eight pricks and a whistle, yes, give her freedom and let her burn it, or blow it, or build it to triumph, or collapse. Let her conceive her children, and kill them in the womb if she thought they did not have it, let her travel to the moon, write the great American novel, and allow her husband to send her off to work with her lunch pail and a cigar; she could kiss the cooze of forty-one Rockettes in Macy's store window; she could legislate, incarcerate, and wear a uniform; she could die of every male disease, and years of burden was the first, for she might learn that women worked at onerous duties and men worked for egos which were worse than onerous and often insane. So women could have the right to die of men's diseases, yes, and might try to live with men's egos in their own skull case and he would cheer them on their way—would he? Yes, he thought that perhaps they may as well do what they desired if the anger of the centuries was having its say. Finally, he would agree with everything they asked but to quit the womb, for finally a day had to come when women shattered the pearl of their love for pristine and feminine will and found the man, yes that man in the million who could become the point of the seed which would give an egg back to nature, and let the woman return with a babe who came from the root of God's desire to go all the way, wherever was that way. And who was there to know that God was not the greatest lover of them all? The idiocy was to assume the oyster and the clam knew more than the trees and the grass. (Unless dear God was black and half-Jewish and a woman, and small and mean as mother-wit. We will never know until we take the trip. And so saying realized he had been able to end a portentous piece in the soft sweet flesh of parentheses.)

Suggestions for Discussion

1. How does the author finally resolve the question he poses in the opening lines of this excerpt? How does the question serve both a rhetorical and substantive function in the development of Mailer's ideas?

2. Describe the change in tone between the first paragraph and the paragraphs following item 11 of the contract.

3. How does Mailer relate his mayoral campaign to women's liberation?

4. What is Mailer's view of the prime responsibility of women? Of men? What does it tell you about Mailer? What is your reaction?

5. How does the Eysenck study relate to the status of women? What is the meaning of the statement: "The cure of the human was in his leap"?

6. Explain the last paragraph in this selection. What concessions has Mailer made, if any?

Suggestions for Writing

1. Write a marriage contract with which you could happily live and introduce it with the premises on which it is based.

2. Discuss your views of the prime responsibility of women or of men.

3. Write a description of a truly liberated woman; of a truly liberated man.

Calvin Trillin

Incompatible, with One L

Calvin Trillin (b.1935) writes regularly for *The Nation* and *The New Yorker.* In addition he is the author of the following books: *U.S. Journal* (1971), *An Education in Georgia* (1971), *American Fried* (1974), *Runestruck* (1977), *Alice, Let's Eat* (1978), and *Killings* (1984). The essay that follows was published in a collection, *Uncivil Liberties* (1982). With wit and understatement he portrays a relationship in which the partners appear to be both compatible and committed.

September 16, 1978

I married Alice under the assumption that she could spell "occurred." She now insists that nothing specific was mentioned about "occurred" in prenuptial discussions. It seems to me, though, that implicit in someone's making a living as a college English teacher is the representation that she is a speller with a repertoire adequate to any occasion. She must have known that the only person in her line of work I had any experience being related to, my Cousin Keith from Salina, once reached the finals of the Kansas State Spelling Bee. She now says Cousin Keith's spelling triumph was never spoken of between us. I distinctly remember, though, that I listed for Alice the highlights of our family's history, as any prospective bridegroom might for his future wife, and Cousin Keith has always been part of my standard Family History recitation—along with my Cousin Neil, who was once the head drum major of the University of Nebraska marching band, and my Uncle Benny Daynofsky, who in his early eighties was knocked down by a car while planting tomatoes in his own backyard in St. Jo. It is significant that she does not deny knowing about Uncle Benny.

Is spelling the sort of thing that modern young couples get straightened out beforehand in marriage contracts? I wouldn't bring it up after all of these years, except that, as it happens, I can't spell "occurred" either. I was forced to look it up twice in order to write the first paragraph, and once more to get this far in the second. Somehow, I had expected to marry someone whose spelling would be, if not perfect, at least complementary to mine. We would face the future with heads held high, and maybe a short song on our lips—confident that together we could spell anything they dished out. Before we had been married a month, the real world started to eat away at that fantasy: It turned out that Alice was not very good on "commitment." I don't mean she didn't have any; she couldn't spell it. I have never been able to spell "commitment" myself.

I know how to spell "embarrass"—usually considered by double-letter specialists to be a much more difficult word. I have been able to spell it for years. I planted "embarrass" in my mind at an early age through a rather brilliant mnemonic device having to do with barstools. In fact, not to make a lot out of it, I had always thought of my ability to spell "embarrass" as a nice little facility to bring to a marriage—the sort of minor bonus that is sometimes found in a husband's ability to rewire lamps. (I don't mean it was the only facility I was able to contribute: Although I can't rewire a lamp, I can bark like a dog and I can blow a hard-boiled egg out of its shell seven times out of ten.) We have now been married thirteen years, and Alice still has not asked me how to spell "embarrass." Apparently, she has a mnemonic device of her own. I have never inquired. That sort of thing doesn't interest me.

For a while, our reformist friends used to urge us to make a list of the words that troubled both of us—their theory being that some wretched consistency in the American educational system would be further documented by the fact that a husband and wife who went to public schools 1,300 miles apart were left without the ability to spell precisely the same words. Not long ago, an analytically inclined Easterner who came over for a drink when Alice happened to be out of town tried to establish some psychological significance in which words Alice and I were able to spell and which ones we weren't. "Is it really an accident that neither of you can spell 'commitment' but both of you can spell 'embarrass'?" he said. It has been my experience that when analytically inclined Easterners ask a question that begins "Is it really an accident . . ." the answer is always yes. I wanted to write Alice to describe the psychological analysis of our spelling problem, but, as it happens, the one word she can spell and I can't is "cockamamie."

Converts to the new politics of lowered expectations have told me that I should simply accept Alice's spelling limitations and comfort myself with thoughts of the many splendid qualities she does have—the way Americans are now supposed to settle for only two gigantic automobiles, reminding themselves that some people in Chad have none at all. I have tried that. I have reminded myself that Alice can explain foreign movies and decipher road maps. I suspect that in a pinch she might be able to rewire a lamp. But, having come of drinking age in the 1950s, I may be culturally immune to the politics of lowered expectations. I can't get over the suspicion that a politician who preaches that doctrine is really arguing that we ought to settle for him. I still find myself thinking back on the old-fashioned scenes I had envisioned for our marriage: We are sitting peacefully in the parlor—after having kissed the little ones goodnight—and I glance up from the desk, where I have been polishing off a letter to the *Times* on our policy in the Far East, and say, "Alice, how do you spell 'referred'?" Alice tells me. Or, on another evening, Alice looks over from her side of the desk (in this version of our marriage, the custodian of an abandoned courthouse in Pennsylvania had sold us an 18th-century double-desk for $85 including delivery to New York in his brother's pickup), where she has been composing a letter to her parents saying how sublimely happy she is. She asks me how to spell "embarrass." I tell her.

Suggestions for Discussion

1. What is the source of Trillin's humor? What does the spelling of *occurred* or *embarrass* have to do with this description of a marriage?

2. Relate the title to the theme of this sketch.

3. Are the author and Alice compatible? How do you know?

4. How serious is Trillin about his immunity to "the politics of lowered expectations"?

Suggestions for Writing

1. Discuss the values of, and obstacles to, marriage contracts or write a marriage contract which reflects your feelings about a satisfying relationship.

2. Discuss your diminished expectations in a relationship.

3. What is the meaning and significance of commitment in a relationship?

Carolyn Heilbrun

Androgyny

Carolyn Heilbrun is a professor of English literature at Columbia University. She has written *Toward a Recognition of Androgyny* (1973), from which the following selection is taken; a number of articles and reviews; a history of the Garnetts (a literary family); and a study of Christopher Isherwood. Androgyny defines a condition in which there are no assigned roles for men and women but rather a full range of experience open to both sexes.

"When a subject is highly controversial," Virginia Woolf observed to an audience forty-five years ago, "and any question about sex is that, one cannot hope to tell the truth. One can only show how one came to hold whatever opinion one does hold." My opinion is easily enough expressed: I believe that our future salvation lies in a movement away from sexual polarization and the prison of gender toward a world in which individual roles and the modes of personal behavior can be freely chosen. The ideal toward which I believe we should move is best described by the term "androgyny." This ancient Greek word—from *andro* (male) and *gyn* (female)—defines a condition under which the characteristics of the sexes, and the human impulses expressed by men and women, are not rigidly assigned. Androgyny seeks to liberate the individual from the confines of the appropriate.

There will always be those to whom a clear demarcation between proper behavior for one sex and the other will seem fundamental, as though it had been laid down at the creation. Probably both the traditionalist and the revolutionary are to some extent deluded in this, as in other matters. Thinking about profound social change, conservatives always expect disaster, while revolutionaries confidently anticipate utopia. Both are wrong. But in the end, I am convinced, the future lies with those who believe salvation likelier to spring from the imagination of possibility than from the delineation of the historical.

Yet recognition, not revolution, is the object of this essay. My method is to use the vast world of myth and literature as a universe in which to seek out the sometimes obscure signs of androgyny. My hope is that the occasional interpretation I bring to the literature of the past will suggest new ways of responding to the circumstances of our own lives and the literature of our own times. Once the name of androgyny has been spoken and some of its past appearances identified, the reader to whom the idea is not viscerally unbearable will begin to see this largely undefined phenomenon in many places. The idea of androgyny, at first startling, rapidly becomes less so. If this essay succeeds in its purpose, the reader returning to it later will be struck by the familiarity and simplicity of its central idea. . . .

Androgyny suggests a spirit of reconciliation between the sexes; it suggests, further, a full range of experience open to individuals who may, as women, be aggressive, as men, tender; it suggests a spectrum upon which human beings choose their places without regard to propriety or custom. The unbounded and hence fundamentally indefinable nature of androgyny is best evoked by borrowing a description of Dionysus from the critic Thomas Rosen-meyer's discussion of the *Bacchae* of Euripides: "Dionysus, who is Euripides' embodiment of universal vitality, is described variously by chorus, herdsman, commoners, and princes. The descriptions do not tally, for the god cannot be defined. He can perhaps be totaled but the sum is never definitive; further inspection adds new features to the old. If a definition is at all possible it is a definition by negation or cancelation. For one thing, Dionysus appears to be neither woman nor man; or, better, he presents himself as woman-in-man, or man-in-woman, the unlimited personality. . . . In the person of the god strength mingles with softness, majestic terror with coquettish glances. To follow him or to comprehend him we must ourselves give up our precariously controlled, socially desirable sexual limitations." A better description of the difficulties of defining androgyny could not be hoped for, although we have perhaps reached the stage where the social desirability of sexual limitations is in question. Such, at least, is my hope.

Unfortunately, it is easier to know what we fear from androgyny than what we may hope from it. The question of who will go through doorways first, or who will care for young children, is immediate and practical; the rewards to men from sharing their professional haunts with highly trained women are at best unclear. Change which threatens our established institutions and habits threatens our individual security, regardless of whether those institutions serve us individually well or ill. When Simone de Beauvoir remarked that men have found in women more complicity than the oppressor usually finds in the oppressed, she expressed an understanding of this fear of lost security, palpable to women as to men.

Androgyny appears to threaten men and women even more profoundly in their sexual than in their social roles. There has been a fear, not only of homosexuality or the appearance of homosexuality, but of impotence and fri-gidity as the consequence of less rigid patterns of sexual behavior. That we already have more than enough impotence and frigidity is apparently blamed more comfortably on the changing of roles than on strict adherence to them. If the man does not pursue, assuming aggressive attitudes, if the woman does not limit her response to consent or refusal, assuming passive attitudes, may we not lose altogether our skill at sexual performance? Women, terrified of "unmanning" men or making themselves less "feminine" and compliant, have failed to explore with men the possibilities inherent in heterosexual love freed from ritualized attitudes. Yet the complicity of women and the insistence of men on maintaining the old sexual order is daily less to be relied on. More and more women, many men, are coming to realize that the delight inherent in male-female relationships, whether in conversation or passion, is capable only of enhancement as the androgynous ideal is approached.

Those youths so often seen almost anywhere in the world today—their long hair and costumes making uneasy, in both senses of the word, the immediate identification of gender—suggest a new homage to androgyny. Indeed, the androgynous ideal is gaining acceptance faster than I had dared hope when I began this book. Then the danger I felt in suggesting so startling an idea was palpable. In the first introduction that I wrote my remarks were hedged about with protestations, defenses, caveats, for I much feared that I would be mis-understood. But ideas move rapidly when their time comes. Today one may speak of androgyny without assuming a defensive tone. One danger perhaps remains: that androgyny, an ideal, might be confused with hermaphroditism, an anomalous physical condition.

Homosexuality and bisexuality have seemed to occur very often in those societies and among those artists who have produced androgynous works. Readers of my own generation may find themselves at first uncomfortable, as I did, in the recognition of widespread homosexuality. Yet I have come to realize that today's youth are less threatened than were we by this subject and, in all likelihood, future generations will be still less concerned.

I made, in this connection, an interesting discovery when I returned in the *Symposium* to Plato's actual story of the circular beings who existed before the split of humans into male and female halves. As Aristophanes, the character in the *Symposium* who presents this myth of sexuality tells the tale; there were originally three wholes: all male, all female, male and female; each person seeking his other, original half might be in search with equal likelihood for someone of the same or of the other sex. I did one of those instant surveys among my friends and acquaintances which are the delight of the pedagogical profession, to discover that I was not alone in having blocked out the homosexual wholes of Plato's parable. Perhaps we all need to be reminded of the necessity of remaining open to new, or newly recovered, ways of being.

In a certain sense this book* is a tribute to the persistence of Victorianism. Most of us nowadays regard the Victorian age as part of the very remote past. Its major ideas, no longer thought to be the imprisoning conventions of our youth, are now consigned to the museum of antique beliefs, where we study them with a certain condescension and amusement. How quaint and implausible they were; how remote their power now seems. Or so we believe. Yet in the matter of sexual polarization and the rejection of androgyny we still accept the convictions of Victorianism; we view everything, from our study of animal habits to our reading of literature, through the paternalistic eyes of the Victorian era.

Masculine domination of life accompanied by extreme sexual polarization was not, of course, unique to the nineteenth century. Patriarchy reached its apotheosis in the years of Victoria's reign, but it is a habit thousands of years old, its roots deep in the Judaeo-Christian tradition. Whether or not patriarchy arose as a reaction to matriarchy is not readily established, and has not easily been accepted at any time by those considered the proper authorities. The opinions of J. J. Bachofen, for example, the chief expounder in the nineteenth century of the belief in an early matriarchy, are not now in academic fashion. For any purposes, however, the verification of theories of prehistoric matriarchy, even were that possible, is not important. Nor is it particularly important to decide whether the male principle at one time ruled the world well. Indeed, one might sensibly argue that the patriarchy, whether or not it supplanted a matriarchy, was necessary to human development and has brought many blessings. Yet I believe that it has also brought many curses to our almost dying earth. What is important now is that we free ourselves from the prison of gender and, before it is too late, deliver the world from the almost exclusive control of the masculine impulse.

*This essay is an introduction to a book of critical pieces on Victorian writers.

If we are still, in our definition of sexual roles, the heirs of the Victorian age, we must also recognize that our definitions of the terms "masculine" and "feminine" are themselves little more than unexamined, received ideas. According to the conventional view, "masculine" equals forceful, competent, competitive, controlling, vigorous, unsentimental, and occasionally violent; "feminine" equals tender, genteel, intuitive rather than rational, passive, unaggressive, readily given to submission. The "masculine" individual is popularly seen as a maker, the "feminine" as a nourisher. Qualities which the Victorians considered admirable in men they thought perverted in women, an attitude which Freud did much to sanctify. The confident assurance that directing traffic or driving trucks somehow disqualifies women for their "feminine" roles, that the care of young children or the working of crewels disqualifies men for their masculine roles, is indicative of the rigidity with which human beings have been divided, not by talent, inclination, or attribute, but by gender. Recently, for example, *The New York Times* related the story of a young girl who, for lack of enough good boy players, had been drafted onto a Little League baseball team. The ensuing ruckus might have been justified had someone been caught practicing medicine without training or license, though the response where this does happen is less hysterical. The girl was thrown off the team together with the manager who had been unpolitical enough to let her play. There followed long discussions about the weakness and physical vulnerability of girls, the wisdom of their partaking in sports, and so forth. But the obvious points were nowhere mentioned: she had qualified for the team by being able to play better than any available boy, and whatever physical disabilities her sex may be thought to have endowed her with, so wide is the extent of individual variation that she was clearly better able to cope with the rigors of competitive contact sports than many boys. What she had outraged were preconceived ideas of the "feminine" role and the "masculine" rights to certain activities. If in fact a graph showing the frequency distribution of athletic ability in girls is superimposed upon one for boys, the upper end of the graph, signifying highest ability, will perhaps be all male, the lower end perhaps all female, but a wide intermediate range will comprise both sexes. This pattern (or its reverse, with females at the upper end) recurs for almost every human attribute that is thought to be associated with sex, apart from primary sex characteristics.

Yet so wedded are we to the conventional definitions of "masculine" and "feminine" that it is impossible to write about androgyny without using these terms in their accepted, received sense. I have done so throughout this essay, and have placed the terms in quotation marks to make my usage clear. What is more, the term "masculine" is often used pejoratively in what follows. My reason for so using it must be carefully explained.

Because "masculine" traits are now and have for so many years been the dominant ones, we have ample evidence of the danger the free play of such traits brings in its wake. By developing in men the ideal "masculine" characteristics of competitiveness, aggressiveness, and defensiveness, and by placing in power those men who most embody these traits, we have, I believe, gravely endangered our own survival. Unless we can effectively check the power of manly men and the women who willingly support them, we will experience new Vietnams, My Lais, Kent States. Even the animal world is now threatened by the aggression of man, the hunter. So long as we continue to believe the "feminine" qualities of gentleness, lovingness, and the counting of cost in human rather than national or property terms are out of place among rulers, we can look forward to continued self-brutalization and perhaps even to self-destruction.

In appearing to exalt feminine traits, I mean to suggest that these, since they have been so drastically undervalued, must now gain respect, so that a sort of balance is achieved among those in power, and within individuals. Obviously, not all women embody "feminine" characteristics: the parent who said that the National Guard at Kent State should have shot all the students was a mother. Such women are described by Simone de Beauvoir as "the poetesses of the bourgeoisie since they represent the most conservative element in this threatened class. . . . they orchestrate the grand mystification intended to persuade women to 'stay womanly.' " But for the most part, and especially for literary artists, the "feminine" impulses are most frequently embodied in women. The cry within literary works for more balanced human experience, from *The Trojan Women* to *Saint Joan*, has largely been the cry of women.

If the argument on behalf of androgyny sounds, more often than not, like a feminist or "women's lib" cry, that is because of the power men now hold, and because of the political weakness of women. If "feminine" resounds throughout this essay with the echoes of lost virtue, while "masculine" thuds with the accusation of misused power, this is a reflection on our current values, not on the intrinsic virtues of either "masculine" or "feminine" impulses. Humanity requires both.

So typical a Victorian as Leslie Stephen may, in his opinions on androgyny, be seen as equally typical of our own day. Creator of the *Dictionary of National Biography* and father, in a certain sense, of the Bloomsbury group, Leslie Stephen found the condition of androgyny to be evil. He used the words "masculine" and "manly" to indicate the highest praise; for purposes of denigration, "effeminate" and "morbid" were synonymous. His biographer Noel Annan summed up Stephen's views on the sexes in the statement that "men must be manly and women womanly; and the slightest androgynous taint must be condemned."

Yet the androgynous ideal, as Norman O. Brown has shown, persists in all the dreams of mysticism even through the nineteenth century:

> In the West, cabalistic mysticism has interpreted Genesis 1:27—"God created man in his own image . . . male and female created he them"—as implying the androgynous nature of God and of human perfection before the Fall. From cabalism this notion passed into the Christian mysticism of Boehme, where it is fused with the Pauline mysticism of Galatians 3:28 —"There can be no male and female; for ye are all one man in Christ Jesus." In neglecting Boehme, or this side of Boehme, later Protestantism only keeps its head in the sand; for, as Berdyaev writes: "The great anthropological myth which alone can be the basis of an anthropological metaphysic is the myth about the androgyne. . . . According to his Idea, to God's conception of him, man is a complete, masculinely feminine being, solar and telluric, logoic and cosmic at the same time. . . . Original sin is connected in the first instance with division into two sexes and the Fall of the androgyne, i.e., of man as a complete being."

In the East, Taoist mysticism, as Needham shows, seeks to recover the androgynous self: one of the famous texts of the Tao Te Ching says:

> He who knows the male, yet cleaves to what is female,
> Becomes like a ravine, receiving all things under heaven.
> [Thence] the eternal virtue never leaks away.
> This is returning to the state of infancy.

And since poetry, as well as psychoanalysis, is the modern heir of the mystical tradition, the hermaphroditic ideal is central, for example, in the message of Rilke. In *Letters to a Young Poet* he writes: "And perhaps the sexes are more related than we think, and the great renewal of the world will perhaps consist in this, that man and maid, freed from all false feeling and aversion, will seek each other not as opposites, but as brother and sister, as neighbors, and will come together as *human beings.*" But deeper than the problem of the relation between the sexes is the problem of the reunification of the sexes in the self. In Rilke as artist, according to his friend Lou Andreas Salome, "both sexes unite into an entity." And Rilke, in his call to God to perfect him as an artist, calls on God to make him a hermaphrodite.

What poets understood, psychologists discovered. Donald W. MacKinnon, director of the Institute of Personality Assessment and Research at the University of California in Berkeley, wrote in 1962: "[Openness to experience] may be observed, for example, in the realm of sexual identifications and interests, where creative males give more expression to the feminine side of their nature than do less creative men. On a number of tests of masculinity–femininity, creative men score relatively high on femininity, and this despite the fact that, as a group, they do not present an effeminate appearance or give evidence of increased homosexual interests or experiences. Their elevated scores on femininity indicate rather an openness to their feelings and emotions, a sensitive intellect and understanding self-awareness and wide ranging interests including many which in the American culture are thought of as more feminine, and these traits are observed and confirmed by other techniques of assessment. If one were to use the language of the Swiss psychiatrist C. G. Jung, it might be said that creative persons are not so completely identified with their masculine *persona* roles as to blind themselves to or deny expression to the more feminine traits of the *anima.*"

Joseph Campbell in *The Masks of God*, his comprehensive and incisive account of world mythology, tells us that the patriarchal, anti-androgynous view is distinguished "by its setting apart of all pairs of opposites—male and female, life and death, true and false, good and evil." Though Campbell identifies the androgynous ideal as the "archaic view," which predated the patriarchal, we must not therefore suppose that his ideal is to be encountered only "in the dark backward and abysm of time. . . ."

Suggestions for Discussion

1. To what extent is androgyny, as defined by Heilbrun, a liberating mode of personal behavior? To what extent do you feel that human impulses expressed by men and women are rigidly assigned?

2. How valid is the concern that androgyny is a threat to the sexual roles of men and women?

3. How valid is the author's view that the androgynous ideal is rapidly gaining acceptance? If true, to what do you attribute such a shift in attitude?

4. Defend or challenge the author's statement that we ought to free ourselves from the "prison of gender" and, before it is too late, deliver the world from the almost exclusive control of the masculine impulse.

5. In what sense do the author's views transcend the personal and embrace political and societal concerns?

Suggestions for Writing

1. Discuss your sense of the possibilities inherent in heterosexual love freed from ritualized attitudes.

2. Write on any of the above questions for discussion.

3. Discuss the author's statement: "deeper than the problem of the relation between the sexes is the problem of the reunification of the sexes in the self."

4. Write on one of the following topics: the prison of gender; sexual polarization; a spirit of reconciliation between the sexes; the unlimited personality; the imprisoning conventions of youth; the patriarchy as a bringer of blessings or of curses.

Noel Perrin

The Androgynous Man

Noel Perrin (b. 1927), a professor of English at Dartmouth College, is a contributor to *The New Yorker*. Among his published works are a book of essays, *A Passport Secretly Green* (1961), *Vermont: In All Weathers* (1973), *First Person Rural: Essays of a Sometime Farmer* (1980), and *Third Person Rural: More Essays of a Sometime Farmer* (1981). The writer cites a number of examples to support his view that the androgynous man has a range of choices denied the macho man.

The summer I was 16, I took a train from New York to Steamboat Springs, Colo., where I was going to be assistant horse wrangler at a camp. The trip took three days, and since I was much too shy to talk to strangers, I had quite a lot of time for reading. I read all of "Gone With the Wind." I read all the interesting articles in a couple of magazines I had, and then I went back and read all the dull stuff. I also took all the quizzes, a thing of which magazines were even fuller then than now.

The one that held my undivided attention was called "How Masculine/Feminine Are You?" It consisted of a large number of inkblots. The reader was supposed to decide which of four objects each blot most resembled. The choices might be a cloud, a steam engine, a caterpillar and a sofa.

When I finished the test, I was shocked to find that I was barely masculine at all. On a scale of 1 to 10, I was about 1.2. Me, the horse wrangler? (And not just wrangler, either. That summer, I had to skin a couple of horses that died—the camp owner wanted the hides.)

The results of that test were so terrifying to me that for the first time in my life I did a piece of original analysis. Having unlimited time on the train, I looked at the "masculine" answers over and over, trying to find what it was that distinguished real men from people like me—and eventually I discovered two very simple patterns. It was "masculine" to think the blots looked like man-made objects, and "feminine" to think they looked like natural objects. It was masculine to think they looked like things capable of causing harm, and feminine to think of innocent things.

Even at 16, I had the sense to see that the compilers of the test were using rather limited criteria—maleness and femaleness are both more complicated than *that*—and I breathed a huge sigh of relief. I wasn't necessarily a wimp, after all.

That the test did reveal something other than the superficiality of its makers I realized only many years later. What it revealed was that there is a large class of men and women both, to which I belong, who are essentially androgynous. That doesn't mean we're gay, or low in the appropriate hormones, or uncomfortable performing the jobs traditionally assigned our sexes. (A few years after that summer, I was leading troops in combat and, unfashionable as it now is to admit this, having a very good time. War is exciting. What a pity the 20th century went and spoiled it with high-tech weapons.)

What it does mean to be spiritually androgynous is a kind of freedom. Men who are all-male, or he-man, or 100 percent red-blooded Americans, have a little biological set tht causes them to be attracted to physical power, and probably also to dominance. Maybe even to watching football. I don't say this to criticize them. Completely masculine men are quite often wonderful people: good husbands, good (though sometimes overwhelming) fathers, good members of society. Furthermore, they are often so unself-consciously at ease in the world that other men seek to imitate them. They just aren't as free as us androgynes. They pretty nearly have to be what they are; we have a range of choices open.

The sad part is that many of us never discover that. Men who are not 100 percent red-blooded Americans—say, those who are only 75 percent red-blooded—often fail to notice their freedom. They are too busy trying to copy the he-men ever to realize that men, like women, come in a wide variety of acceptable types. Why this frantic imitation? My answer is mere speculation, but not casual. I have speculated on this for a long time.

Partly they're just envious of the he-man's unconscious ease. Mostly they're terrified of finding that there may be something wrong with them deep down, some weakness at the heart. To avoid discovering that, they spend their lives acting out the role that the he-man naturally lives. Sad.

One thing that men owe to the women's movement is that this kind of failure is less common than it used to be. In releasing themselves from the single ideal of the dependent woman, women have more or less incidentally released a lot of men from the single ideal of the dominant male. The one mistake the feminists have made, I think, is in supposing that *all* men need this release, or that the world would be a better place if all men achieved it. It wouldn't. It would just be duller.

So far I have been pretty vague about just what the freedom of the androgynous man is. Obviously it varies with the case. In the case I know best, my own, I can be quite specific. It has freed me most as a parent. I am, among other things, a fairly good natural mother. I like the nurturing role. It makes me feel good to see a child eat—and it turns me to mush to see a 4-year-old holding a glass with both small hands, in order to drink. I even enjoyed sewing patches on the knees of my daughter Amy's Dr. Dentons when she was at the crawling stage. All that pleasure I would have lost if I had made myself stick to the notion of the paternal role that I started with.

Or take a smaller and rather ridiculous example. I feel free to kiss cats. Until recently it never occurred to me that I would want to, though my daughters have been doing it all their lives. But my elder daughter is now 22, and in London. Of course, I get to look after her cat while she is gone. He's a big, handsome farm cat named Petrushka, very unsentimental, though used from kittenhood to being kissed on the top of the head by Elizabeth. I've gotten very fond of him (he's the adventurous kind of cat who likes to climb hills with you), and one night I simply felt like kissing him on the top of the head, and did. Why did no one tell me sooner how silky cat fur is?

Then there's my relation to cars. I am completely unembarrassed by my inability to diagnose even minor problems in whatever object I happen to be driving, and don't have to make some insider's remark to mechanics to try to establish that I, too, am a "Man With His Machine."

The same ease extends to household maintenance. I do it, of course. Service people are expensive. But for the last decade my house has functioned better than it used to because I've had the aid of a volume called "Home Repairs Any Woman Can Do," which is pitched just right for people at my technical level. As a youth, I'd as soon have touched such a book as I would have become a transvestite. Even though common sense says there is really nothing sexual whatsoever about fixing sinks.

Or take public emotion. All my life I have easily been moved by certain kinds of voices. The actress Siobhan McKenna's, to take a notable case. Give her an emotional scene in a play, and within 10 words my eyes are full of tears. In boyhood, my great dread was that someone might notice. I struggled manfully, you might say, to suppress this weakness. Now, of course, I don't see it as a weakness at all, but as a kind of fulfillment. I even suspect that the true he-men feel the same way, or one kind of them does, at least, and it's only the poor imitators who have to struggle to repress themselves.

Let me come back to the inkblots, with their assumption that masculine equates with machinery and science, and feminine with art and nature. I have no idea whether the right pronoun for God is He, She or It. But this I'm pretty sure of. If God could somehow be induced to take that test, God would not come out macho, and not feminismo, either, but right in the middle. Fellow androgynes, it's a nice thought.

Suggestions for Discussion

1. In what ways does the magazine test reflect society's stereotypes of masculine and feminine?

2. What is Perrin's definition of androgyny and why does he believe it to be liberating?

3. What is the writer's view of the strengths and limitations of the completely masculine man? Why are what he calls the "75 percent red-blooded" Americans sad to contemplate?

4. What elements of androgyny discussed by Carolyn Heilbron does Perrin leave out?

Suggestions for Writing

1. Support or challenge the assumption that "masculine equates with machinery and science, and feminine with art and nature."

2. Drawing upon your own life or your observation of a friend, describe what might be called androgynous experiences.

Mark Gerzon

Manhood:
The Elusive Goal

Mark Gerzon is the author of *The Whole World is Watching: A Young Man Looks at Youth's Dissent* (1969); *A Childhood for Every Child: The Politics of Parenthood* (1973); and *A Choice of Heroes* (1982) from which this chapter was selected. Manhood is an elusive goal because our culture does not provide an appropriate rite of passage for young men who are "caught between the competing ideals of chauvinism and liberation."

> *There is no steady unretracing progress in this life*
> *. . . Once gone through, we trace the round again;*
> *and are infants, boys, and men, and Ifs eternally.*
> —Melville, *Moby-Dick*

It was not coincidence that when love entered my life, so did violence. I fell in love for the first time with a high school classmate, Diana. She was a cheerleader, the most feminine of all roles. Even now, almost twenty years later, I think of her when I see cheerleaders practicing. In one cheer, they would shout each letter of each member of the starting line-up's name as they ran onto the basketball court, heralding them as if they were heroes. They had mastered the art of feminine support: they remained on the sidelines while acclaiming the men who played the game.

In this, Diana was wholehearted. In winter, her face would glow when the ball swished through the hoop; she would look crestfallen when it fell short. In autumn, chanting "Hit 'em again, hit 'em again, harder, harder," her body pulsed to the rhythm of her words. Even if she was not the most beautiful cheerleader, she was certainly the most magnetic. She made us feel like men.

Before she and I started dating, she went with a fellow two years my senior, a leading figure in one of the male clubs known for its toughness. Since he and Diana had broken up (or so she said), I felt no qualms when our study dates became romantic. Soon she and I were together almost constantly. When she invited me to a party sponsored by her club, I accepted. After all, she was "mine."

Midway through the evening, however, her former beau arrived with several of his hefty club brothers behind him. "They want you," a friend warned me, then quickly disappeared. My strategy, which was to pretend that I had not noticed their arrival, became impractical when three of them had me cornered. And I had no club brothers to back me up.

"Let's go outside," said Diana's old beau.

"What for?" I was still playing dumb.

The purpose of our outing was to settle with our fists who Diana belonged to. He obviously felt that he had staked his claim first and that I was trespassing on his territory. I believed that she had the right to choose for herself to whom she wanted to belong. Neither of us, perhaps not even Diana herself, considered it odd that at the age of sixteen she should belong to anyone.

As it turned out, the other boy friend and I didn't fight, at least not that night. "Why'd you let him talk you out of it?" one of his buddies asked him. He was outraged at being deprived of what was to be the high point of his evening.

A few weeks later, after a basketball game, my adversary and I passed each other under the bleachers. Without warning, he punched me hard in my right eye. My fist was raised to return the blow when several arms pressed me back against the wall.

"Whatsa matter?" he shouted at me contemptuously. "Are you gonna cry?"

The impatient crowd pushed us in opposite directions. Stunned, I felt my eye to check if it was bleeding. Only then did I feel the tell-tale moistness. Although no tears trickled down my cheeks, they were still evidence against my manliness. First, I had weaseled out of a fight. Next, I let him hit me without ever returning the blow. But the most damaging evidence of all were my barely averted tears. To be hit and to cry was the ultimate violation of the code of masculine conduct.

That happened half a lifetime ago. I no longer see my unwillingness to fight as an indictment of my character. Had I been as old and as tough as my adversary, perhaps I would have handled our conflict differently. Perhaps I would have fought. Perhaps I even might have won. Instead, aware of my relative weakness and inexperience, I chose not to. I wanted to protect my eyes, my mouth, my groin. I thought I might need them in the future. But the deeper reason had nothing to do with self-protection but with love. I could not understand what the winner of a fight would gain. Would Diana accept the verdict of our brawl? Like a Kewpie doll at the fairgrounds, would she let herself be claimed by whichever contestant came out on top? If her love could be won by violence, I was not sure I wanted it. I wanted her to love me for who I was, not for how I fought.

My problem, my friends told me then, was that I was too sensitive.

Strange how things change. The image of manhood against which I am measured has changed so much that now, almost twenty years later, I am told I am not sensitive *enough*. When tensions build in our relationship, Shelley will admonish me for being out of touch with my feelings. "You are always so defensive, always trying to protect yourself," she will say. "Why can't you be more open to your feelings?"

How can I explain it to her? How can any man explain it to any woman? Women are not raised to abort all tears. They are not measured by their toughness. They are not expected to bang against each other on hockey rinks and football fields and basketball courts. They do not go out into the woods to play soldiers. They do not settle disagreements by punching each other. For them, tears are a badge of femininity. For us, they are a masculine demerit.

Nothing has made me see this more clearly than talking with Richard Ryan, a former alcoholic. Sitting in the sun one afternoon by a lake near his home, Richard reminded me of a masculine rite of passage I had almost forgotten.

"After I gave this rap about alcoholism at the high school, this kid came up to me and said, 'Can I talk with you privately, Mr. Ryan?' Usually that means that either the kid's parents are alcoholic or he is. But not this kid. He said to me, 'Mr. Ryan, I've never been drunk, never smoked a joint. What's wrong with me?'

"So I said to him, 'Nothing's wrong with you, man. You're doin' fine.'

" 'But why do I feel I have to lie to my friends about it?' he asked. 'If they knew I didn't drink or smoke they'd make fun of me.' "

Richard Ryan rolled over onto his stomach as he finished the story. Either the sun or his emotions made him hide his face.

"I always felt like I had to lie as a kid," Ryan told me. "I liked to bake cookies. I liked to watch my kid brothers and sisters. I liked to write poetry. But my dad made me feel that was wrong somehow. So I started to pretend I *didn't* want to do it."

I had heard the lament so often now that I pushed him for specifics. "But what did your dad do? Did he walk in and say, 'Get out of the kitchen' or 'That's women's work'?"

"No, no. Nothing like that. It was more subtle." He thought for a moment. "For example, when my mother's mother died, I wanted to be her pallbearer. Grandma had been very special to me. I felt like she'd carried me all my life. When she died, I wanted to carry her once. So I asked my dad if I could be a pallbearer. He said, 'Only if you promise not to cry. Pallbearers can't cry!' I knew if I lied and said I wouldn't, he'd let me. But I felt like that'd be betraying her. How could I go to her funeral and not cry? Since I wouldn't promise, my dad refused to let me do it."

Now in his mid-thirties, Ryan runs a project called Creative Drug Education. He visits high schools and talks about alcohol and drug abuse. But he doesn't preach. He tells his own story:

"When I used to go out and get bombed, guys would say, 'He drinks like a man' or 'He holds it like a man.' Being drunk, I really felt like I was something great. The other guys and I, we were like a pack, and drinking was our bond. We'd get together and, because we drank, we'd say stuff and hug each other and do all sorts of things we'd never let ourselves do if we were sober."

Only after reaching the age of thirty did Richard realize he was an alcoholic. "I've only recently felt I can be who I am," he continues. "All those years I felt I had to blot out a whole side of myself. I used alcohol to make myself feel good about myself. After I quit drinking, I thought I was free. But then I realized I was addicted to smoking. And I mean *addicted.* My withdrawal from nicotine was almost as bad as from booze—the shakes, sweating, couldn't sleep. I found it hard to be around people without a cigarette in my hand. It was the whole Marlboro man thing—it made me look cool, made me feel like a man. When a friend told me I should stop, I told him, 'Anybody can quit smoking. It takes a real man to face cancer.' I said it as a joke, but I meant it. That's how sick I was."

Richard no longer looks sick. He is big and muscular. We swam out to the middle of the lake and back and, when we dried off, he wasn't even out of breath. He is respected by the people with whom he works. Teachers tell me he is more effective with young people who use drugs than anyone they've ever met.

As we walked back to the car, I saw a sadness in him, a wound that had not yet healed.

"What you thinking about?" I asked, not knowing a better way to probe.

He laughed. "Oh, I was just thinking about Grandma's funeral. You know what? Every one of those pallbearers cried."

In Western societies, there are clearly no longer any rites of passage. The very existence of terms such as teenager (the German word is *Halbwüchsiger,* half-grown) shows that the absence of this social institution results in an in-between stage. All too often adult society avoids this whole question by regarding those in their teens in terms of the high school health book definition. Adolescence, it says, is the period when the person is no longer a child, but not yet an adult. This is defining the concept of adolescence by avoiding it altogether. This is why we have a youth culture. It is where adolescents go (and sometimes stay) before they become grownups.

Despite the absence of any established initiation rite, young men need one. By default, other institutions take the place of these missing rites. Some commentators on growing up in America point to sports or fraternities, for example, to demonstrate that our culture does have various kinds of initiation rites. But they are wrong.

Sports, for instance, can hardly serve as the means for gaining manhood. Sports are games. Except for the professionals who make their living from them, these games have little connection with real life. Moreover, only a small minority of males in American high schools and colleges can participate in athletics. As dozens of articles document, sports play a key role in enabling boys and young men to test their physical prowess, but they do not alone make a boy a man.

Fraternities, too, are a painfully inadequate means for gaining manhood. Except for token community service projects once a year, most fraternities are disconnected from society. How can they provide a socially recognized initiation rite when they involve only members of the younger generation? Frat members do not go off into seclusion with the adults of the "tribe." They go off into seclusion with themselves. They are initiated into youth culture, perhaps, but not into the world of adults.

The young man facing adulthood cannot reach across this great divide. He has only rites of impasse. There is no ritual—not sexual, economic, military, or generational—that can confirm his masculinity. Maturity eludes him. Our culture is famous for its male adolescent pain. From James Dean in *Rebel Without a Cause* and Dustin Hoffman in *The Graduate* to the more recent box office hits *Breaking Away, My Bodyguard,* and *Ordinary People,* young men try to prove they are grown men. But to no avail. None of the surrogate initiation rites—car duels, college diplomas, after-work drinking rituals, first paychecks, sports trophies—answers their deepest needs. None has proven to· be what William James called the "moral equivalent of war."

The only rituals that confirm manhood now are imitations of war. The military academies, for example, like boot camp itself, involve many of the ingredients of primitive rites of passage. Young men are secluded with older men. They must endure tests of psychological or physical endurance.

Pat Conroy's novel *The Lords of Discipline,* which depicts life in a southern military academy, and Lucian K. Truscott IV's *Dress Gray,* which portrays West Point, showed how boys are turned into men—the kind of men the military needs. But, as we have recognized, the Soldier is no longer the hero. The Vietnam war was "billed on the marquee as a John Wayne shoot-'em-up test of manhood," wrote Mark Baker in *Nam,* but it ended up "a warped version of *Peter Pan* . . . a brutal Never Never Land where little boys didn't have to grow up. They just grew old before their time." Similarly, the heroes of Conroy's and Truscott's tales are not the brave soldier but the dissenter. Nevertheless, because military service is the only rite of passage available, men are drawn to it like moths to light. We need to prove our manhood and will take whatever paths our culture offers.

With the option of going to war foreclosed, young men seek to prove themselves by performing other manly deeds. The most obvious surrogates for war often involve violence too. It is not directed at the enemy, but at each other and ourselves.

Each week, the news media overflow with accounts of young men between the ages of fifteen and twenty-five who have committed acts of violence. Too old to be boys, too young to have proven themselves men, they are finding their own rites of passage. Here are three, culled from the newspapers:

A Boy Scout leader smashes his new car on a country road at 100 miles per hour: he is "showing off" to the four scouts who were riding with him. Now they are all dead.

A 16-year-old who lives in a comfortable suburb throws a large rock from a freeway overpass through the windshield of a car. The victim, a 31-year-old housewife, suffers a concussion but survives. "You do it for the thrill," the boy says. "It's a boring town," says one of his classmates.

A teenage boy is so upset that his girl friend has jilted him that he threatens to kill himself. Talking to her on the phone, he says he will drive over to her house and smash his car into the tree in her front yard if she will not go out with him. She refuses. So he does it, killing himself.

Many movies are made as surrogate rites of passage for young men. They are designed for the guy who, in actor Clint Eastwood's words, "sits alone in the theater. He's young and he's scared. He doesn't know what he's going to do with his life. He wishes he could be self-sufficient, like the man he sees up there on the screen, somebody who can look out for himself, solve his own problems." The heroes of these films are men who are tough and hard, quick to use violence, wary of women. Whether cowboys, cops, or superheroes, they dominate everything—women, nature, and other men. Young men cannot outmaneuver the Nazis as Indiana Jones did in *Raiders of the Lost Ark*, or battle Darth Vader, or outsmart Dr. No with James Bond's derring-do. To feel like heroes they turn to the other sex. They ask young women for more than companionship, or sex, or marriage. They ask women to give them what their culture could not—their manhood.

Half the nation's teenagers have had sex before they graduate from high school. The easiest way to prove oneself a man today is to make it with a girl. First we make out or put the make on her. Then we make it. We are not, like our "primitive" forebears, joining together with a woman as adults. We are coming together in order to become adults, if not in society's eyes, then in our own.

"You in her pants yet?" one of the high school jocks asks his classmate in *Ordinary People*, the Academy Award–winning movie directed by Robert Redford. We prove our manhood on the football field or the basketball court by scoring points against other men. We prove our manhood in sex by scoring with women.

The young man, armed with lines like "Don't you love me?" is always ready for action. He wants to forge ahead, explore new territory. After all, he has nothing to lose. He has no hymen, no uterus. He is free to play the role of bold adventurer, coaxing the reluctant girl to let him sow his wild oats in her still virgin land. "I love you, but I don't feel ready," she may say. She may be afraid that her refusal may jeopardize her relationship with her young explorer, but she is even more afraid to get pregnant. She may feel less mature than her sex-hungry companion. But the emotional reality may be precisely the opposite. Certain of her femininity and of her pregnability, she dares to wait until the time is right. Insecure about his masculinity and obsessed with proving it—to himself and his buddies, if not to her—he needs to score in order to feel that he has made the team.

Sonny Burns, the sexually insecure hero of Dan Wakefield's *Going All the Way*, finds himself engaged in an amorous overture on a double date. But he admits to himself, and to a generation of readers, that he is doing so not because he finds his date exciting. On the contrary, she bores him. He does so because he wants to impress his buddy in the front seat. He must prove he is a man, and a man takes whatever "pussy" he can get. Pretending to be passionate, he thinks about the high school rating system, according to which boys reported their sexual scores: "The next day, when the guys asked you what you got the night before, you could say you got finger action inside the pants. That wasn't as good as really fucking but it rated right along with dry-humping and was much better than just the necking stuff like frenching and getting covered-tit or bare-tit. It was really pretty much of a failure if you parked with a girl and got only covered-tit."

Even if he wins, the victory is private. There are no fans in the bleachers as he crosses home plate and scores. He has not proved himself a man to adult males, as did young men in traditional rites of passage. His sexual conquest is a rite of passage only in his own mind. If adult society were to pass judgment on these back-seat gymnastics, it would probably be negative. The responsible adult would ask him if he was ready for marriage. Could he support her if he had to? And of course the answers are no. He has become an adult sexually, not socially. He has proved his virility in the dark of night. By the light of day, the proof has vanished.

As Margaret Mead pointed out in *Male and Female,* our culture leaves adolescents in a quandary. We give them extraordinary freedom but tell them not to use it. "We permit and encourage situations in which young people can indulge in any sort of sex behavior that they elect," wrote Mead a generation ago. "We actually place our young people in a virtually intolerable situation, giving them the entire setting for behaviour for which we then punish them when it occurs." It is a cultural arrangement for which some young women pay an awful price.

Whether veiled in fiction or revealed in autobiography, women recall the ritual of modern courtship with caustic humor at best, more often with bitterness. So objectified do they feel that they develop a detached attitude toward their bodies. Reports the cheerleader heroine in Lisa Alther's *Kinflicks:* "Joe Bob would dutifully knead my breasts through my uniform jacket and padded bra, as though he were a housewife poking plums to determine their ripeness." Later, she would observe him sucking "at my nipples while I tried to decide what to do with my hands to indicate my continuing involvement in the project."

But Alther's good-natured response is not typical. Other sagas of car-seat courtships and apartment affairs leave their heroines harboring a deep distaste for men. Some declare themselves feminists or lesbians. Some become depressed. Others, as in Judith Rossner's *Looking for Mr. Goodbar,* are killed by their lovers. And a few, after great turmoil, find a man who will treat them gently, with genuine care.

The movie theater, that public living room for a nation of young lovers, reflects this yearning too. For those who have grown weary of the macho hero whose physical prowess is enough, Hollywood has provided a countertype. For those who are not infatuated with the Soldier, there are now movies about the anti-soldier. "In what may be an emerging genre in the movies," wrote Paul Starr in his review of *Coming Home, An Unmarried Woman,* and *Alice Doesn't Live Here Anymore,* "there appears a character who expresses in his personality and in his relations with the heroine a new idea of masculinity. He might be described as the emotionally competent hero . . . He is the man to whom women turn as they try to change their own lives: someone who is strong and affectionate, capable of intimacy . . . masculine without being dominating." The new hero, though perhaps not rugged and tough in the familiar mold, can be intimate. He can feel. "The new softer image of masculinity seems to represent what is distinctive and significant in recent films, and I expect we will see more of the post-feminist hero because the old, strong, silent type no longer seems adequate as lover—or as person."

Who, then, is to be the young man's hero? The gentle, post-feminist figure extolled by the new genre of films and by the roughly five thousand men's consciousness-raising groups across America? Or the self-sufficient, hard-hitting tough that Eastwood tries to embody and that the military breeds? Faced with such polarized and politicized choices, how does a boy become a man? By being hard or by being soft?

From the sensible to the absurd, we have answers. We have so many shifting, contradictory criteria for manhood that they confuse rather than inspire.

American boys coming of age encounter sexual chaos. A chorus of liberation advocates, now with bass as well as soprano voices, encourages them to free themselves from the oppressive male role, to become softer, and to consider themselves women's equals. But another vociferous group beckons them in another direction. For every pro-feminist man, there is his counterpart, who denounces those "fuzzy-headed housemales, purporting to represent 'men's liberation,' but sponsored by NOW." One Minnesota men's rights leader argued, for example, that men who support women's liberation are "eunuchs," motivated by an "urge to slip into a pair of panties." According to him and his followers: "Men's liberation means establishing the right of males to be men, not to liberate them from being men."

The hard-liners and soft-liners both have their respective magazines, organizations, and conferences. Repulsed by the cacophony, most young men try to ignore it. But the questions gnaw at them anyway. Although the pro- and anti-feminist activists irritate them, young men cannot deny their own uncertainty. They are caught between the competing ideals of chauvinism and liberation. The old archetypes do not work; the new ones remain vague and incomplete. If we are not to be John Wayne, then who?

Into the vacuum created by the demise of the old archetypes rush myriad images. Each hopes to inspire a following. Masculinity becomes the target for everyone from toothpaste advertisers to Hollywood superstars. These salesmen of self-help all have their diagnoses for the young man struggling to find his own identity. Some take the pose of proud aging lions, defending the traditional masculine role as Western civilization enters a precipitous, psychosexual decline. In *Sexual Suicide*, George Gilder warned of the imminent feminization of man and masculinization of woman and called on men to reassert their superiority.

Others do not oppose liberation but rather seem to exploit it. Cynically catering to masculine insecurity, they describe the world of white-collar commuters as a stark and brutal asphalt jungle in which men must constantly flex their aggressive personalities in order to survive. According to Michael Korda, author of *Power!* and *Success!*, life is nothing more than a series of encounters in which one dominates or is dominated, intimidates or is intimidated, achieves power over or is oneself overpowered. "Your gain is inevitably someone else's loss," philosophizes this latter-day Nietzsche, "your failure someone else's victory."

There are also the advocates of liberation who seek to free us from the manacles of machismo. Although they are constructive in intent, they too increase the confusion. In their attempt to free us from one-sidedness, they double our load. They now want us to be "assertive *and* yielding, independent *and* dependent, job *and* people oriented, strong *and* gentle, in short, both masculine *and* feminine." The prescriptions are not wrong, just overwhelming. Their lists of do's and don'ts, like Gail Sheehy's *Passages*, seem too neat, too tidy. They write of "masculinity in crisis" with such certainty. They encourage us to cry with such stoicism. They advise us to "be personal, be intimate with men" with such authority. It is all too much.

Whichever model young men choose, they know the traditional expectation of their culture. At least until the seventies, Americans of all ages and of all educational and income levels were in wide agreement about what traits are masculine. According to one study, based on more than a thousand interviews, men are expected to be very aggressive, not at all emotional, very dominant, not excitable, very competitive, rough, and unaware of others' feelings. And women are expected to be more of less the opposite.

If this is what maleness is, then a young man must find ways to demonstrate those traits. Without a rite of passage, he can only prove what he is *not*. Not a faggot, a pussy, a queer. Not a pushover, a loser, or a lightweight. Not a dimwit or a dunce. Not a jerk or a nobody. Not a prick or a pansy. Not, above all, anything that is feminine. Indeed, without clear rites of passage, the only way to be a man is essentially negative: to not be a woman.

If we are to be masculine, then they must be feminine. We convince ourselves that women are yielding, that they are more interested in our careers than in their own, that they are interested in sex whenever we are, that they are fulfilled by raising children. That, we assume, is who they are. Should one of them act differently, then something is wrong, not with our assumptions, but with her.

Having entered physical manhood, we are nevertheless emotionally unsure of ourselves. The more unsure we are, the more we stress that we are not "feminine" and the more we are threatened when women act "masculine." We try to rid ourselves of any soft, effeminate qualities. We gravitate toward all-male cliques in the form of sports teams, social clubs, or professional groups. When we are with a woman, it is virtually always in a sexually charged atmosphere. To be merely friends is nearly impossible because it suggests that we have something in common. We are trying, after all, to prove precisely the opposite, which is why so many marriages fail.

Suggestions for Discussion

1. How did the author's adolescent confrontation with the cheerleader affect him? How does he view it from his adult perspective?

2. With what details from the text can you explain the circumstances that led Gerzon's friends to call him too sensitive when he was an adolescent and almost twenty years later to regard him as not sensitive enough?

3. How does the author's talk with a former alcoholic confirm his feeling that societal forces make it difficult if not impossible for men always to be in touch with their feelings and not defensive about them?

4. What reasons does Gerzon offer for an appropriate rite of passage or initiation rite for young men? Why does he regard sports and fraternities as inadequate in helping a boy achieve manhood?

5. How do recent fiction and films support the author's statement that none of the surrogate initiation rites have provided what William James called the "moral equivalent of war"?

6. What does Gerzon mean when he says that many movies are made as "surrogate rites of passage for young men"?

7. What are some of the differences in attitude expressed by male and female novelists?

8. With what details does the author describe what appears to be an emerging genre in the movies?

9. The author believes that young men are "caught between the competing ideals of chauvinism and liberation." Restate this point of view in your own words and provide examples in defending or challenging it.

10. To what does the author attribute the failure of many marriages?

Suggestions for Writing

1. What do you see as the primary difficulties for boys in achieving manhood?

2. What do you see as the primary difficulties that girls experience in achieving adulthood?

3. Discuss question 9 above.

Carol Gilligan

Women's Rights and Women's Judgment

from *In a Different Voice*

Carol Gilligan (b. 1936) is associate professor of education at Harvard University. Her book *In a Different Voice* (1982) presents a fresh view of women's moral development and the female life cycle. In this chapter the author illustrates how the concept of equal rights has changed women's moral judgments in the direction of greater tolerance and an imperative to act responsively toward both themselves and others.

The century marked by the movement for women's rights is spanned roughly by the publication of two novels, both written by women and posing the same moral dilemma, a heroine in love with her cousin Lucy's man. In their parallel triangles these novels provide an historical frame in which to consider the effects of women's rights on women's moral judgments and thus offer a way of addressing the centennial question as to what has changed and what has stayed the same.

In George Eliot's novel *The Mill on the Floss* (1860), Maggie Tulliver "clings to the right." Caught between her love for her cousin Lucy and her "stronger feeling" for Stephen, Lucy's fiancée, Maggie is unswerving in her judgment that, "I must not, cannot, seek my own happiness by sacrificing others." When Stephen says that their love, natural and unsought, makes it "right that we should marry each other," Maggie replies that while "love is natural, surely pity and faithfulness and memory are natural too." Even after "it was too late already not to have caused misery," Maggie refuses to "take a good for myself that has been wrung out of [others'] misery," choosing instead to renounce Stephen and return alone to St. Oggs.

While the minister, Mr. Kenn, considers "the principle upon which she acted as a safer guide than any balancing of consequences," the narrator's judgment is less clear. George Eliot, having placed her heroine in a dilemma that admits no viable resolution, ends the novel by drowning Maggie, but not without first cautioning the reader that "the shifting relation between passion and duty is clear to no man who is capable of apprehending it." Since "the mysterious complexity of our life" cannot be "laced up in formulas," moral judgment cannot be bound by "general rules" but must instead be informed "by a life vivid and intense enough to have created a wide, fellow-feeling with all that is human."

Yet given that in this novel the "eyes of intense life" that were Maggie's look out in the end from a "weary, beaten face," it is not surprising that Margaret Drabble, steeped in the tradition of nineteenth century fiction but engaged in the issues of twentieth century feminism, should choose to return to Eliot's story and explore the possibility of an alternative resolution. In *The Waterfall* (1969) she recreates Maggie's dilemma in *The Mill on the Floss* but, as the title implies, with the difference that the societal impediment has been removed. Thus Drabble's heroine, Jane Grey, clings not to the right but to Lucy's husband, renouncing the renunciations and instead "drowning in the first chapter." Immersed in a sea of self-discovery, "not caring who should drown so long as I should reach the land," Jane is caught by the problem of judgment as she seeks to apprehend the miracle of her survival and to find a way to tell that story. Her love for James, Lucy's husband, is narrated by two different voices, a first and a third person who battle constantly over the issues of judgment and truth, engaging and disengaging the moral questions of responsibility and choice.

Though the balance between passion and duty has shifted between 1860 and 1969, the moral problem remains in both novels the same. Across the intervening century, the verdict of selfishness impales both heroines. The same accusation that compels Maggie's renunciation orchestrates Jane's elaborate plea of helplessness and excuse: "I was merely trying to defend myself against an accusation of selfishness, judge me leniently, I said, I am not as others are, I am sad, I am mad, so I have to have what I want." But the problem with activity and desire that the accusation of selfishness implies not only leads Jane into familiar strategies of evasion and disguise but also impels her to confront the underlying premise on which this accusation is based. Taking apart the moral judgment of the past that had made it seem, "in a sense, better to renounce myself than them," Jane seeks to reconstitute it in a way that could "admit me and encompass me." Thus she strives to create "a new ladder, a new virtue," one that could include activity, sexuality, and survival without abandoning the old virtues of responsibility and care: "If I need to understand what I am doing, if I cannot act without my own approbation—and I must act, I have changed, I am no longer capable of inaction— then I will invent a morality that condones me. Though by doing so, I risk condemning all that I have been."

These novels thus demonstrate the continuing power for women of the judgment of selfishness and the morality of self-abnegation that it implies. This is the judgment that regularly appears at the fulcrum of novels of female adolescence, the turning point of the *Bildungsroman* that separates the invulnerability of childhood innocence from the responsibility of adult participation and choice. The notion that virtue for women lies in self-sacrifice has complicated the course of women's development by pitting the moral issue of goodness against the adult questions of responsibility and choice. In addition, the ethic of self-sacrifice is directly in conflict with the concept of rights that has, in this past century, supported women's claim to a fair share of social justice.

But a further problem arises from the tension between a morality of rights that dissolves "natural bonds" in support of individual claims and a morality of responsibility that knits such claims into a fabric of relationship, blurring the distinction between self and other through the representation of their interdependence. This problem was the concern of Wollstonecraft and Stanton, of Eliot and Drabble. This concern emerged as well in interviews with college women in the 1970s. All of these women talked about the same conflict, all revealed the enormous power of the judgment of selfishness in women's thought. But the appearance of this judgment in the moral conflicts described by contemporary women brings into focus the role that the concept of rights plays in women's moral development. These conflicts demonstrate the continuation through time of an ethic of responsibility as the center of women's moral concern, anchoring the self in a world of relationships and giving rise to activities of care, but also indicate how this ethic is transformed by the recognition of the justice of the rights approach.

The senior year interview with Nan, one of the women in the college student study, illustrates some of the dimensions of women's moral concern in 1973, the year that the Supreme Court decided that abortion is legal and that women have the right to choose whether or not to continue a pregnancy. Two years before, Nan chose to take a course on moral and political choice because she was "looking for different ways of thinking about things" and was interested "in arguments that protect individual freedom." Claiming to "suffer from a low self-image," she reports, in her senior year, a sense of moral progress and growth which she attributes to having had "to review a lot of what I thought about myself" as a result of having become pregnant and deciding to have an abortion. Attributing the pregnancy to "a lapse of self-control, decision-making, and very much stupidity," she considered abortion to be a desperate and life-saving solution ("I felt very much to save my own life that I had to do it"), but one which she viewed as, "at least in the eyes of society, if not my own, a moral sin."

Given her "personal feeling of being very evil," her discovery that "people would help me out anyway did great things for my feelings toward them and myself." In the month that she spent waiting and thinking about the abortion, she thought "a lot about decision-making, and for the first time I wanted to take control of and responsibility for my own decisions in life." As a result, her self-image changed:

> Because now that you are going to take control of your life, you don't feel like you are a pawn in other people's hands. You have to accept the fact that you have done something wrong, and it also gives you a little more integrity, because you are not fighting off these things in yourself all the time. A lot of

conflicts are resolved, and you have a sense of a new beginning, based on a kind of conviction that you can act in a situation.

Thus she "came out basically supporting myself, not as a good or bad human being, but simply as a human being who had a lot to learn either way." Seeing herself in the present as capable of choice, she feels responsible for herself in a new way. But while the experience of choice has led Nan to a greater sense of personal integrity, her judgment of these choices stays remarkably the same. Although she has come to a more inclusive and tolerant understanding of herself and a new conception of relationships that will, she believes, allow her to be "more obvious with myself and more independent," the moral issue remains one of responsibility.

In this sense, she considers the pregnancy to have "come to my aid" in illuminating her previous failure to take responsibility:

> It was so serious that it brought to light things in myself, like feelings about myself, my feelings about the world. What I had done, I felt, was so wrong that it came to light to me that I was not taking responsibility where I could have, and I could have gone on like I was, not taking responsibility. So the seriousness of the situation brings the questions right up in front of your face. You see them very clearly, and then the answers are there for you.

Seeing her own irresponsibility as having led to a situation in which she could envision no way of acting that would not cause hurt, she begins "getting rid of old ideas" about morality that now seem an impediment to her goal of living in a way that will not "cause human suffering." In doing so, she calls into question the opposition of selfishness and morality, discerning that "the word *selfish* is tricky." Recognizing that "individual freedom" is not "all that incompatible with morality," she expands her conception of morality, defining it as "the sense of concern for another human being and your sense of concern for yourself." While the moral questions remain, "How much suffering are you going to cause?" and "Why do you have the right to cause human suffering?" these questions apply not only to others but also to herself. Responsibility, separated from self-sacrifice, becomes tied instead to the understanding of the causes of suffering and the ability to anticipate which actions are likely to eventuate in hurt.

The right to include oneself in the compass of a morality of responsibility was a critical question for college women in the 1970s. This question, which arose in differing contexts, posed a problem of inclusion that could be resolved through the logic of justice, the fairness of equating other and self. But it also posed a problem of relationships, whose solution required a new understanding of responsibility and care. Hilary, explaining at age twenty-seven how her thinking about morality has changed, describes her understanding of morality at the time she entered college:

> I was much more simple-minded then. I went through a period in which I thought there were fairly simple answers to questions of right and wrong in life. I even went through a period that now strikes me as so simplistic: I thought that as long as I didn't hurt anybody, everything would be fine. And I soon figured out, or eventually figured out, that things were not that simple, that you were bound to hurt people, they were bound to hurt you, and life is full of tension and conflict. People are bound to hurt each other's feelings, intentionally, unintentionally, but just in the very way things are. So I abandoned that idea.

This abandonment occurred in her first years of college:

> I became involved in a love affair with a guy who wanted to settle down and get married, and I could not imagine a worse fate, but I was really quite fond of him. And we broke up, and he was so upset by it that he left school for a year, and I realized that I had hurt him very badly and that I hadn't meant to, and I had violated my first principle of moral behavior, but I had made the right decision.

Explaining that she "could not have possibly married him," Hilary felt that there was, in that sense, an "easy answer" to the dilemma she faced. Yet, in another sense, given her moral injunction against hurting, the situation presented an insoluble problem, allowing no course of action that would not eventuate in hurt. This realization led her to question her former absolute moral injunction and to "figure that this principle [of not hurting] was not all there was to it." The limitation she saw pertained directly to the issue of personal integrity; "What that principle was not even attempting to achieve was, 'To thine own self be true.'" Indicating that she had started to think more about maintaining her personal integrity, she says that this experience led her to conclude that, "You can't worry about not hurting other people; just do what is right for you."

Yet, in view of her continuing equation of morality with caring for others and her continuing belief that "acts that are self-sacrificing and that are done for other people or for the good of humanity are good acts," her abandonment of the principle of not hurting others was tantamount to an abandonment of moral concern. Recognizing the rightness of her decision but also realizing its painful consequences, she can see no way to maintain her integrity while adhering to an ethic of care in relationships. Seeking to avoid conflict and compromise in choice by "just doing what is right for you," she is in fact left with a feeling of compromise about herself.

This feeling is apparent as she recounts the dilemma that she faced in her work as a lawyer when opposing counsel in a trial overlooked a document that provided critical support for his client's "meritorious claim." Deliberating whether or not to tell her opponent of the document that would help his client's case, Hilary realized that the adversary system of justice impedes not only "the supposed search for truth" but also the expression of concern for the person on the other side. Choosing in the end to adhere to the system, in part because of the vulnerability of her own professional position, she sees herself as having failed to live up to her standard of personal integrity as well as to her moral ideal of self-sacrifice. Thus her description of herself contrasts both with her depiction of her husband as "a person of absolute integrity who would never do anything he didn't feel was right" and with her view of her mother as "a very caring person" who is "selfless" in giving to others.

On her own behalf, Hilary says somewhat apologetically that she has become, since college, more tolerant and more understanding, less ready to blame people whom formerly she would have condemned, more capable of seeing the integrity of different perspectives. Though she has access, as a lawyer, to the language of rights and recognizes clearly the importance of self-determination and respect, the concept of rights remains in tension with an ethic of care. The continuing opposition of selfishness and responsibility, however, leaves her no way to reconcile the injunction to be true to herself with the ideal of responsibility in relationships.

The clash between a morality of rights and an ethic of responsibility erupted in a moral crisis described by Jenny, another student in the college study. She also articulates a morality of selflessness and self-sacrificing behavior, exemplified by her mother who represents her ideal.

> If I could grow up to be like anyone in the world, it would be my mother, because I've just never met such a selfless person. She would do anything for anybody, up to a point that she has hurt herself a lot because she just gives so much to other people and asks nothing in return. So, ideally, that's what you'd like to be, a person who is selfless and giving.

In contrast, Jenny describes herself as "much more selfish in a lot of ways." But seeing the limitation of self-sacrifice in its potential to hurt others who are close to the self, she seeks to resolve the tension between selfishness and care, revising her definition of "the best person you could possibly be" by adding to its basic component, "doing the most good for other people," the qualification "while fulfilling your own potentialities."

Two years earlier, in the course on moral and political choice, Jenny had set out to examine morality in terms of the questions, "How much do you owe yourself?" and "How much do you owe other people?" Defining morality as a problem of obligation, she attempted, through the equation of self and others, to challenge the premises underlying self-sacrifice and to align her conception of responsibility with an understanding of rights. But a crisis that occurred in her family at that time called into question the logic of this endeavor by demonstrating the inadequacy of the rights terminology to deal with the issues of responsibility in relationships. The crisis was caused by the suicide of a relative at a time when the resources of the family already were strained by the illness of her grandfather, who was in need of continual care. Although the morality of suicide had been discussed in the course from the perspective of individual rights, this suicide appeared instead to Jenny as an act of consummate irresponsibility, increasing the burden of care for others and adding further suffering and hurt.

Trying to bring her feelings of rage into connection with her logic of reason, she reached an impasse in the discovery that her old way of thinking did not work anymore:

> The whole semester we had been discussing what's right and what's wrong, what's good, and how much do you owe yourself and how much do you owe other people, and then my [relative] killed himself, right then, and that's a moral crisis, right? And I didn't know how to handle it because I really ended up hating him for having done that, and I knew I really couldn't do this. I mean, that was wrong, but how could he do this to his family? And I really had to seriously reevaluate that whole course because it just didn't work anymore. All these nice little things that we had been discussing are fine when you talk about it. I remember, we had little stories, like, if you were on a mission and were leading a patrol and somebody had to go and throw a hand grenade or something. Well, that's fine, but when it's something like this that's close to you, it just doesn't work anymore. And I had to seriously reevaluate everything I had said in that course and why, if I believed all that, I could end up with such an intense hatred?

Given the awesome dimensions of this problem, the underlying logic of the equation of how much is owed to oneself versus others began to unravel and then fall apart.

> All of a sudden, all the definitions and all the terminology just fell apart. It became the type of thing that you could not place any value on it to say, "Yes, it was moral," or "No, it was not." It's one of those things that is just irrational and undefinable.

Jenny realized that whatever the judgment, the action itself was irreversible and had consequences that affected the lives of others as well. Since rights and responsibilities, selfishness and self-sacrifice, were so inextricably confounded in this situation, she could find no way of thinking about it except to say that, while in one sense it seemed a moral crisis, in another it appeared "just irrational and undefinable."

Five years later, when interviewed again, Jenny says that these events changed her life by bringing into focus for her "the whole thing about responsibility." When the opposition between selfishness and morality prevailed, she was responsive neither to others nor to herself; not wanting "to take responsibility for her grandfather," she also did not want to take responsibility for herself. Having been, in this sense, both selfish and selfless, she saw the limitation of the opposition itself. Realizing that "it was too easy to go through life the way I had done, letting someone else take responsibility for the direction of my life," she challenged herself to take control and "changed the direction of my life."

The underlying construction of morality as a problem of responsibility and the struggle for women in taking responsibility for their own lives are evident in the dilemmas described by other college students who took part in the rights and responsibilities study.

. . .

The image of drifting along or riding it out recurs throughout the interviews to denote the experience of women caught in the opposition between selfishness and responsibility. Describing a life lived in response, guided by the perception of others' needs, they can see no way of exercising control without risking an assertion that seems selfish and hence morally dangerous. Like the heroine of *The Waterfall*, who begins the novel by saying, "If I were drowning I couldn't reach out a hand to save myself, so unwilling am I to set myself up against fate," without even thinking "that it might be the truth," these women are drawn unthinkingly by the image of passivity, the appeal of avoiding responsibility by sinking, like Jane, into an "ice age of inactivity," so that "providence could deal with her without her own assistance."

But the image of drifting, while seeming to offer safety from the onus of responsibility, carries with it the danger of landing in a more painful confrontation with choice, as in the stark alternatives of an abortion decision, or in Maggie Tulliver's realization that she had unwittingly done the thing she most feared. Then in the recognition of consequence, the issue of responsibility returns, bringing with it the related questions of choice and of truth.

Maggie, giving in to her feelings for Stephen by momentarily ceasing her resistance to him,

> felt that she was being led down the garden among the roses, being helped with firm tender care into the boat, having the cushion and cloak arranged for her feet and her parasol opened for her (which she had forgotten)—all by this stronger presence that seemed to bear her along without any act of her own will.

But when she realized how far they had gone, "a terrible alarm took possession of her," and her "yearning after that belief that the tide was doing it all" quickly gave way, first to "feelings of angry resistance toward Stephen," whom she accused of having wanted to deprive her of choice and having taken advantage of her thoughtlessness, but then to the realization of her own participation. No longer "paralyzed," she recognized that "the feelings of a few short weeks had hurried her into the sins that her nature had most recoiled from: breach of faith and cruel selfishness." Then Maggie, "longing after perfect goodness," chooses "to be true to my calmer affections and live without the joy of love."

However, while Maggie longs for goodness, her counterpart Jane searches for truth. Discovering in her desire for James "such depths of selfishness" that she considers drowning herself "in an effort to reclaim lost renunciations like Maggie Tulliver," Jane chooses instead to question the renunciations and in the end to "identify myself with love." Observing that although "Maggie Tulliver never slept with her man, she did all the damage there was to be done, to Lucy, to herself, to the two men who loved her, and then, like a woman of another age she refrained," Jane confronts "an event seen from angles where there used to be one event and one way only of enduring it." Consequently she "wonders, in this age, what is to be done?"

The moral distinction between selfish and selfless behavior, which became increasingly clear to Maggie, thus becomes for Jane increasingly blurred. Having "sought virtue" only to find that she "could not ascend by the steps that others seemed to take," she then sought innocence "in abnegation, in denial, in renunciation," thinking that,

> if I could deny myself enough I would achieve some kind of innocence, despite those intermittent nightmare promptings of my true nature. I thought I could negate myself and wipe myself out.

Yet she discovers that, no matter which way she tells the story, whether in the first or the third person, in the end she confronts the truth that despite all the renunciations, she has "drowned in a willing sea."

It is against the pull of such renunciations, the vision of an innocence attained by the denial of self, that women begin to search for the truth of their own experience and to talk of taking control.

.   .   .

In one sense, then, not much has changed. George Eliot, observing that "we have no master-key that will fit all cases" of moral decision, returns to the casuists in whose "perverted spirit of minute discrimination" she sees "the shadow of a truth to which eyes and hearts are too often fatally sealed—the truth that moral judgments must remain false and hollow unless they are checked and enlightened by a perpetual reference to the special circumstances that mark the individual lot." Thus moral judgment must be informed by "growing insight and sympathy," tempered by the knowledge gained through experience that "general rules" will not lead people "to justice by a ready-made patent method, without the trouble of exerting patience, discrimination, impartiality, without any care to assure whether they have the insight that comes from a hardly-earned estimate of temptation or from a life vivid and intense enough to have created a wide, fellow feeling with all that is human."

And yet, for Eliot, at least in this novel, the moral problem remains one of renunciation, a question of "whether the moment has come in which a man has fallen below the possibility of a renunciation that will carry any efficacy, and must accept the sway of a passion against which he had struggled as a trespass." The opposition of passion and duty thus binds morality to an ideal of selflessness, the "perfect goodness" toward which Maggie Tulliver aspired.

Both this opposition and this ideal are called into question by the concept of rights, by the assumption underlying the idea of justice that self and other are equal. Among college students in the 1970s, the concept of rights entered into their thinking to challenge a morality of self-sacrifice and self-abnegation. Questioning the stoicism of self-denial and replacing the illusion of innocence with an awareness of choice, they struggled to grasp the essential notion of rights, that the interests of the self can be considered legitimate. In this sense, the concept of rights changes women's conceptions of self, allowing them to see themselves as stronger and to consider directly their own needs. When assertion no longer seems dangerous, the concept of relationships changes from a bond of continuing dependence to a dynamic of interdependence. Then the notion of care expands from the paralyzing injunction not to hurt others to an injunction to act responsively toward self and others and thus to sustain connection. A consciousness of the dynamics of human relationships then becomes central to moral understanding, joining the heart and the eye in an ethic that ties the activity of thought to the activity of care.

Thus changes in women's rights change women's moral judgments, seasoning mercy with justice by enabling women to consider it moral to care not only for others but for themselves. The issue of inclusion first raised by the feminists in the public domain reverberates through the psychology of women as they begin to notice their own exclusion of themselves. When the concern with care extends from an injunction not to hurt others to an ideal of responsibility in social relationships, women begin to see their understanding of relationships as a source of moral strength. But the concept of rights also changes women's moral judgments by adding a second perspective to the consideration of moral problems, with the result that judgment becomes more tolerant and less absolute.

As selfishness and self-sacrifice become matters of interpretation and responsibilities live in tension with rights, moral truth is complicated by psychological truth, and the matter of judgment becomes more complex. Drabble's heroine, who sought to write "a poem as round and hard as a stone," only to find that words and thoughts obtrude, concludes that "a poem so round and smooth would say nothing" and sets out to describe the variegated edges of an event seen from angles, finding in the end no unified truth. Instead, through a final shift in perspective, she relegates her suspicions to "that removed, third person" and, no longer fending off the accusation of selfishness, identifies herself with the first person voice.

Suggestions for Discussion

1. How do the two novels that span roughly a century illustrate Gilligan's thesis? What is the thesis?

2. How do George Eliot's comments about Maggie suggest that she may have a different viewpoint from that of her heroine?

3. How does Drabble's heroine differ from Maggie?

4. How do contemporary women's conflicts demonstrate that an ethic of responsibility is the center of women's moral concern, an ethic transformed by the recognition of the justice of the equal rights movement? How are the conflicts resolved in each of the case studies?

5. On what basis does Gilligan conclude that in one sense not much has changed since Eliot wrote *The Mill on the Floss*? In what ways have women's rights changed women's moral judgments?

6. What does the author mean when she says that "moral truth is complicated by psychological truth"?

Suggestions for Writing

1. Drawing upon your observation, experience, or your reading of fiction, discuss the author's thesis. Illustrate your point of view by citing concrete illustrations. If you disagree with her point of view, justify and illustrate an opposing position.

2. Examine one of the quotations from the Eliot or Drabble novel and discuss its implications for men–women relationships.

Ellen Goodman

The Tapestry of Friendships

Ellen Goodman (b. 1941) is a journalist whose columns for the *Boston Globe* are syndicated in over two hundred newspapers in the United States. She graduated from Radcliffe College and was a Nieman Fellow at Harvard University. Among her publications are *Turning Points* (1979) and a collection of essays, *Close to Home* (1978), in which "The Tapestry of Friendships" appears. Goodman is encouraged by her observation that the female version of friendship as she defines it is becoming the ideal.

It was, in many ways, a slight movie. Nothing actually happened. There was no big-budget chase scene, no bloody shoot-out. The story ended without any cosmic conclusions.

Yet she found Claudia Weill's film *Girlfriends* gentle and affecting. Slowly, it panned across the tapestry of friendship—showing its fragility, its resiliency, its role as the connecting tissue between the lives of two young women.

When it was over, she thought about the movies she'd seen this year—

Julia, The Turning Point and now *Girlfriends*. It seemed that the peculiar eye, the social lens of the cinema, had drastically shifted its focus. Suddenly the Male Buddy movies had been replaced by the Female Friendship flicks.

This wasn't just another binge of trendiness, but a kind of *cinéma vérité*. For once the movies were reflecting a shift, not just from men to women but from one definition of friendship to another.

Across millions of miles of celluloid, the ideal of friendship had always been male—a world of sidekicks and "pardners," of Butch Cassidys and Sundance Kids. There had been something almost atavistic about these visions of attachments—as if producers culled their plots from some pop anthropology book on male bonding. Movies portrayed the idea that only men, those direct descendants of hunters and Hemingways, inherited a primal capacity for friendship. In contrast, they portrayed women picking on each other, the way they once picked berries.

Well, that duality must have been mortally wounded in some shootout at the You're OK, I'm OK Corral. Now, on the screen, they were at least aware of the subtle distinction between men and women as buddies and friends.

About 150 years ago, Coleridge had written, "A woman's friendship borders more closely on love than man's. Men affect each other in the reflection of noble or friendly acts, whilst women ask fewer proofs and more signs and expressions of attachment."

Well, she thought, on the whole, men had buddies, while women had friends. Buddies bonded, but friends loved. Buddies faced adversity together, but friends faced each other. There was something palpably different in the way they spent their time. Buddies seemed to "do" things together; friends simply "were" together.

Buddies came linked, like accessories, to one activity or another. People have golf buddies and business buddies, college buddies and club buddies. Men often keep their buddies in these categories, while women keep a special category for friends.

A man once told her that men weren't real buddies until they'd been "through the wars" together—corporate or athletic or military. They had to soldier together, he said. Women, on the other hand, didn't count themselves as friends until they'd shared three loathsome confidences.

Buddies hang tough together; friends hang onto each other.

It probably had something to do with pride. You don't show off to a friend; you show need. Buddies try to keep the worst from each other; friends confess it.

A friend of hers once telephoned her lover, just to find out if he were home. She hung up without a hello when he picked up the phone. Later, wretched with embarrassment, the friend moaned, "Can you believe me? A thirty-five-year-old lawyer, making a chicken call?" Together they laughed and made it better.

Buddies seek approval. But friends seek acceptance.

She knew so many men who had been trained in restraint, afraid of each other's judgment or awkward with each other's affection. She wasn't sure which. Like buddies in the movies, they would die for each other, but never hug each other.

She'd reread *Babbitt* recently, that extraordinary catalogue of male grievances. The only relationship that gave meaning to the claustrophobic life of

George Babbitt had been with Paul Riesling. But not once in the tragedy of their lives had one been able to say to the other: You make a difference.

Even now men shocked her at times with their description of friendship. Does this one have a best friend? "Why, of course, we see each other every February." Does that one call his most intimate pal long distance? "Why, certainly, whenever there's a real reason." Do those two old chums ever have dinner together? "You mean alone? Without our wives?"

Yet, things were changing. The ideal of intimacy wasn't this parallel play-mate, this teammate, this trenchmate. Not even in Hollywood. In the double standard of friendship, for once the female version was becoming accepted as the general ideal.

After all, a buddy is a fine life-companion. But one's friends, as Santayana once wrote, "are that part of the race with which one can be human."

Suggestions for Discussion

1. With what details does Goodman describe male views of friendship?

2. How does she develop and support the Coleridge quotation on woman's friendship? Discuss each antithesis that follows and evaluate it in the light of your observation and experience.

3. How does her view of friendship illustrate Santayana's definition of friends?

4. What is the relationship of the alllusion to Babbitt to the author's view of friend-ship?

5. How do the rhetorical questions Goodman asks and the answers that follow illus-trate her point of view?

6. What do the initial paragraphs on changing views of friendship in film add to her analysis?

Suggestions for Writing

1. Drawing upon your observations and experience discuss what Goodman refers to as "the tapestry of friendship . . . its fragility, its resiliency, its role as the con-necting tissue" between two lives.

2. Write an essay on one of Goodman's antithetical statements comparing men's and women's friendships. Defend or challenge her point of view.

3. Analyze the nature of a female or male friendship in a movie you have seen or a book you have read.

Margaret Atwood
Fiction: Happy Endings

Margaret Atwood (b. 1939) has lived both in the United States and Europe, but her home is in Toronto. She is best known as the author of the novels *The Edible Woman* (1976); *Surfacing* (1981); *Life Before Man* (1980); *Bodily Harm* (1982); and most recently the powerful political thriller, *The Handmaid's Tale* (1986). She also has written short stories, television plays, children's books, criticism, and poetry. She did graduate work at Harvard on a Woodrow Wilson Fellowship and has taught at a number of Canadian and American universities. In this understated critique of happy endings, the author comments bitterly upon the relationships of men and women and the vicissitudes of life.

> *John and Mary meet. What happens next? If you want a happy ending, try A.*

A

John and Mary fall in love and get married. They both have worthwhile and remunerative jobs which they find stimulating and challenging. They buy a charming house. Real estate values go up. Eventually, when they can afford live-in help, they have two children, to whom they are devoted. The children turn out well. John and Mary have a stimulating and challenging sex life and worthwhile friends. They go on fun vacations together. They retire. They both have hobbies which they find stimulating and challenging. Eventually they die. This is the end of the story.

B

Mary falls in love with John but John doesn't fall in love with Mary. He merely uses her body for selfish pleasure and ego gratification of a tepid kind. He comes to her apartment twice a week and she cooks him dinner, you'll notice that he doesn't even consider her worth the price of a dinner out, and after he's eaten the dinner he fucks her and after that he falls asleep, while she does the dishes so he won't think she's untidy, having all those dirty dishes lying around, and puts on fresh lipstick so she'll look good when he wakes up, but when he wakes up he doesn't even notice, he puts on his socks and his shorts and his pants and his shirt and his tie and his shoes, the reverse order from the one in which he took them off. He doesn't take off Mary's clothes, she takes them off herself, she acts as if she's dying for it every time, not because she likes sex exactly, she doesn't but she wants John to think she does because if they do it often enough surely he'll get used to her, he'll come to depend on her and they will get married, but John goes out the door with hardly so much as a good-night and three days later he turns up at six o'clock and they do the whole thing over again.

Mary gets run down. Crying is bad for your face, everyone knows that and so does Mary but she can't stop. People at work notice. Her friends tell her John is a rat, a pig, a dog, he isn't good enough for her, but she can't believe it. Inside John, she thinks, is another John, who is much nicer. This other John will emerge like a butterfly from a cocoon, a Jack from a box, a pit from a prune, if the first John is only squeezed enough.

One evening John complains about the food. He has never complained about the food before. Mary is hurt.

Her friends tell her they've seen him in a restaurant with another woman, whose name is Madge. It's not even Madge that finally gets to Mary: it's the restaurant. John has never taken Mary to a restaurant. Mary collects all the sleeping pills and aspirins she can find, and takes them and half a bottle of sherry. You can see what kind of a woman she is by the fact that it's not even whiskey. She leaves a note for John. She hopes he'll discover her and get her to the hospital in time and repent and then they can get married, but this fails to happen and she dies.

John marries Madge and everything continues as in A.

C

John, who is an older man, falls in love with Mary, and Mary, who is only twenty-two, feels sorry for him because he's worried about his hair falling out. She sleeps with him even though she's not in love with him. She met him at work. She's in love with someone called James, who is twenty-two also and not yet ready to settle down.

John on the contrary settled down long ago: this is what is bothering him. John has a steady respectable job and is getting ahead in his field, but Mary isn't impressed by him, she's impressed by James, who has a motorcycle, being free. Freedom isn't the same for girls, so in the meantime Mary spends Thursday evenings with John. Thursdays are the only days John can get away.

John is married to a woman called Madge and they have two children, a charming house which they bought just before the real estate values went up, and hobbies which they find stimulating and challenging, when they have the time. John tells Mary how important she is to him, but of course he can't leave his wife because a commitment is a commitment. He goes on about this more than is necessary and Mary finds it boring, but older men can keep it up longer so on the whole she has a fairly good time.

One day James breezes in on his motorcycle with some top-grade California hybrid and James and Mary get higher than you'd believe possible and and they climb into bed. Everything becomes very underwater, but along comes John, who has a key to Mary's apartment. He finds them stoned and entwined. He's hardly in any position to be jealous, considering Madge, but nevertheless he's overcome with despair. Finally he's middle-aged, in two years he'll be bald as an egg and he can't stand it. He purchases a handgun, saying he needs it for target practice—this is the thin part of the plot, but it can be dealt with later—and shoots the two of them and himself.

Madge, after a suitable period of mourning, marries an understanding man called Fred and everything continues as in A, but under different names.

D

Fred and Madge have no problems. They get along exceptionally well and are good at working out any little difficulties that may arise. But their charming house is by the seashore and one day a giant tidal wave approaches. Real estate values go down. The rest of the story is about what caused the tidal wave and how they escape from it. They do, though thousands drown. Some of the story is about how the thousands drown, but Fred and Madge are virtuous and lucky. Finally on high ground they clasp each other, wet and dripping and grateful, and continue as in A.

E

Yes, but Fred has a bad heart. The rest of the story is about how kind and understanding they both are until Fred dies. Then Madge devotes herself to charity work until the end of A. If you like, it can be "Madge," "cancer," "guilty and confused," and "birdwatching."

F

If you think this is all too bourgeois, make John a revolutionary and Mary a counterespionage agent and see how far that gets you. You'll still end up with A, though in between you may get a lustful brawling saga of passionate involvement, a chronicle of our times, sort of.

You'll have to face it, the endings are the same however you slice it. Don't be deluded by any other endings, they're all fake, either deliberately fake, with malicious intent to deceive, or just motivated by excessive optimism if not by downright sentimentality.

The only authentic ending is the one provided here:

John and Mary die. John and Mary die. John and Mary die.

So much for endings. Beginnings are always more fun. True connoisseurs, however, are known to favor the stretch in between, since it's the hardest to do anything with.

That's about all that can be said for plots, which anyway are just one thing after another, a what and a what and a what.

Now try How and Why.

Suggestions for Discussion

1. In the spare language of A there are simple undeveloped declarative sentences. What is the effect on substance and tone?

2. What is the author saying about men–women relationships in B and C? What is the significance of the ending in B and C in which everything continues as in A?

3. Why does A provide the only authentic ending?

4. What does Atwood mean when she says that plots are "just one thing after another, a what and a what and a what"?

5. In her last sentence the author says "Now try How and Why." What is she saying about plots, about fiction, and about relationships?

Suggestions for Writing

1. In her discussion of Mary and John the author poses a number of problems in men–women relationships. Discuss them drawing on illustrations from your observation or experience.

2. Discuss what you believe to be the major areas of disagreement in marriage.

3. Review a book in which you find an illogical happy ending.

Jill Tweedie

The Future of Love

Jill Tweedie (b. 1936) is a London journalist for *The Guardian.* The essay that follows appears in her book *In the Name of Love* (1979). She finds that the stereotypes of men and women that still prevail make it impossible for true love to exist. However, she foresees a time when love "comes into its own as an evolutionary tool" which will help men and women grow.

Love, it seems, is as much a part of the unique equipment of homo sapiens as language or laughter and far more celebrated. If all the words that have been written about it since mankind first put stick to clay were laid end to end, they would rocket past Venus and vanish into deep space. Histories of love, philosophies of love, psychologies of love, guidebooks to love, love letters, love hymns, love stories, love poems, love songs have covered tablets and papyrus, parchment and paper and walls, filled theatres across time and lands from Epidaurus to Radio City, and been declaimed by gods and goddesses of love from Sappho to Warren Beatty. Love has been, is now, and ever shall be our scourge and balm, our wound and salve, source of our finest and most bestial actions, the emotion that passeth all understanding. It is a heavenly body out of our orbit, beyond man-made laws, ethics, or control, a magical splendour that descends upon us like the gift of tongues and possesses us whether we will or no. Love transforms us into something strange and rare, it ignites our lives and, dying, takes all meaning away.

> The mind has a thousand eyes
> And the heart but one
> Yet the light of a whole life dies
> When love is done.

We die of love and die without it, our hearts beat for it and break for it. Love built the Taj Mahal, wrote the Song of Solomon and cooks a billion meals every day, across the world. Love is the only thing that matters at all, after all.

Or so they say. And in my opinion what they say, give or take an epigram or two, is rubbish. Take off the rose-coloured glasses and what does a close examination of the facts reveal to the naked eye? That love, true love, is the rarest of all the emotions and one that has been conspicuous only by its absence ever since mankind dropped from the trees. If we condense the earth's history into one calendar year, homo sapiens appeared in the late evening of December 31st and love, his much-vaunted race-long companion, is still merely a glimmer on the midnight horizon of the coming New Year. Love, in other words, inhabits the future, a kind of reverse star whose light reaches us before it is born instead of after it has died. Certainly, intimations of love's coming have touched an individual here and there through time and its prophets have started new religions, composed great symphonies, made beautiful sculpture, and painted exquisite canvases. But for the wide river of humanity, the ordinary mass of men and women who have peopled our planet and reproduced our race, love was not necessary, not possible, and not there.

Why, then, the stories, the poems, and the songs, the jubilations and the suicides? How can you argue that love does not exist when human beings deliberately end their own existence for love? Surely nothing is as indisputable as that love and mankind go hand in hand. I love, therefore I am. But is it love they feel? I think not. The word is a vast umbrella that covers a multitude of virtues and sins and because we are perfectly familiar with all of love's precursors and understudies, we imagine that we have pinned down love itself when we have merely trapped its shadow. Co-operation, for instance, midwife to that most ancient of drives, survival. You scratch my back and I'll scratch yours. Sex, a powerhouse so overwhelming in its assault upon us that, trying to domesticate it, we have given it the prettier name of love. We know about affection and friendship. We feel liking, duty, deference, greed, lust, ambition, attraction, protectiveness, ingratiation, and the desire to conform. We are gripped by infatuation, obsession, adoration, vanity, addiction, jealousy, fear, and the dread of being alone. Very deeply we know about need. I need you. He needs me. Needs must.

But love is somewhere else and all those other drives and needs and feelings are like the gases that swirl about in space, inwardly spiralling through the centuries to centre at last on a small hard core, gases that are only hot air in themselves but essential for the eventual formation of a new world, a world of real love. We may arrive at it one day, given time, but we are not there yet. . . .

The interesting thing is that the slow emergence of true love does not predicate some higher version of morality. No sudden conversions, no lights upon the road to Damascus are in any way necessary. A new generation with new standards of loving will not come about as a result of some mystical mutation or spiritual growth, though these may well follow. The facts are more practical. As equality becomes commonplace between men and women, they themselves will perforce change from stereotypes, however successful or unsuccessful, into ordinary human beings, each one rather different from the next. Standard sexual roles—the breadwinner, the housewife and mother—already blurred, will eventually disappear and with them will go the suppression or exaggeration of parts of the individual character made necessary by those roles. And as these masks, stylised as the masks of Japanese Kabuki, slip to reveal the human face behind, romantic love, so heavily dependent upon an artificial facade and predictable masculine or feminine behaviour, will die from starvation. Already it is showing the first signs of incipient malnutrition. When, added to that, children are raised in equality and mothers, secure in their own identity, no longer pass their fears and inferiorities on to their daughters or too great an admiration on to their sons; when both parents are equally concerned with the upbringing of children and therefore ensure that those children cannot divide their own emotions between the sexes and discard one whole area, we will have bred a race of human beings differentiated by their own personalities rather than their genitalia. The old war-cry of sexists—*vive la différence*—actually implied exactly the opposite; the rigid division of an infinite variety of people into just two categories, male and female. *Vive la similarité*. Variety will replace conformity and variety, apart from being an evolutionary must, forces each potential lover to take stock of an individual rather than search for the stereotyped ideal of a whole sex.

Nor is this change dependent solely on a conscious wish for change. Evolution has always had a voracious appetite for variety, it is literally the spice of life, offering as it does a wide menu for natural selection. And it is becoming clear to many of us that the old stereotypes of male and female are increasingly a positive threat to the well-being of the race and the earth. Women, confined to a domestic and biological cage, produce unwanted children to crowd an already overpopulated world, while their own abilities wither on the hearth. Men, driven by out-dated standards of virility, continue to denude the planet and threaten each other with uncontemplatable war. Love between such men and such women serves only their own artificial needs and seals them off in their *folie à deux* from the rest of the world instead of involving them more deeply, as real love would do. Our planetary problems are rapidly becoming too serious to permit the net-curtain mentality of the average self-satisfied couple as they peep out at trouble and hastily withdraw, safe in the certainty that God himself blesses their cosy twosome and demands nothing more than its continuation, properly seeded with kiddies.

That is not to say that monogamy is on its way out, only that monogamy as we know it today—sacrosanct, heterosexual, reproductive, lifelong, and almost always a retreat from life, no longer adequately fulfills either the individuals concerned or society. All research done recently, whether anthropological, paediatric, psychiatric, criminal, or social, arrives at the same conclusion: human beings develop most fully and happily if they can feel loved as children by one or two constantly present adults and, as adults themselves, reproduce the same closeness with one other adult. But there is nothing to prove that years of monogamy with the *same* adult are necessarily beneficial. Lifelong monogamy may be nice for the Church and useful for the tax-collector but it has many drawbacks for the individual, who is a learning as well as an imprinted being. As we change and learn, from youth to old age, we must give ourselves room for that change. Like snakes, we need occasionally to shed our old skins and often we cannot do that if we are tied by bonds of guilt to an outgrown love. None of us grows at the same speed or in the same way and the chances of a parallel development with one other human being are not great. But nor does this imply a lack of love or some pervasive shame. Each of us may give another person love and help in inner growth for a while. But in a changing world, with changing people, why should we expect that love to last forever or denigrate it if it does not? Why should love, once a mansion, be made into a cage through false expectations of what love is?

Lifelong monogamy has other drawbacks, even when it works, perhaps *especially* when it works. In a cold and problematic world it is all too easy to withdraw into the cosiness of a familiar love, leaving those problems for others to solve. We have a genetic need for other people; monogamous love, in attempting to assuage that need with one other person, may not only sour into neuroses or a mutual flattery that reduces both partners, making them fear the outside world, but may also isolate us from our fellows and allow us to care less about their fate. When my husband is away from home, I turn in need to my friends, even to strangers. I become vulnerable once again to their larger opinion of me. I see myself as others, more coldly, see me. On his return my instinct is to warm myself at his me-centred love, to soothe my slightly bruised ego. Luckily for me, he does not need to build me up for his own ego and so he is not all *that* warm, just warm enough. He leaves place in me for others, because he himself has place for others.

All this—changing women, the danger of stereotypes, and intractable monogamy, the needs of our race and our planet in the future—implies one imperative. We must leave adolescence behind and grow up. It is absolutely vital, if we are to continue to exist in some comfort upon our earth, that we take a giant step into true adulthood, learn to filter the emotions through our reasoning capacities and learn that survival itself rests on knowing who we are, respecting others' space, and endeavouring justly to balance our own and others' needs.

And this is where love truly comes into its own as an evolutionary tool. Parental love teaches children one vital fact: that they are loved and lovable and therefore can themselves love. But the love between adults differs in one absolute from parental love: it is conditional, or should be. We find out who we are by feeling our outlines against other people, by finding out who we are not. In loving but honest eyes we see prisms of our own vague face, slowly we put the prisms together and distinguish certain unchanging features, form certain principles. Inside, a centre begins to form and once it is firmly established, roots well grown, blossoms flourishing, we can turn from it towards others with a real sense of where we differ and where we are the same. And once we know that, once we respect ourselves, it becomes impossible to accept another who violates our beliefs and ourselves. A weak ego, a weak hold on reality, opens the doors to any passing stranger who flatters us enough and makes us feel real. A strong ego, a firm knowledge of who we are, demands conditions of that stranger, demands a similarity of belief and behaviour and can discard what it does not respect, even at the price of rejecting easy flattery.

And that is what true love is there to help us do. Properly informed, lovingly detached, centred respectfully in itself, it provides us with a real reflection of ourselves, to help us grow. Principles do not need to be suppressed for fear of displeasing, for fear of loss, because when the crunch comes, we can cope alone.

Love cannot thrive in inequality or extreme poverty. It requires enough leisure for introspection and enough introspection for empathy. It demands that the individual feel a certain control over his life because, in too great a storm, we tend to seek any refuge. It thrives on honesty and therefore must do away with great need, since need drives out honesty. It is rational, it knows its own roots, it is moral and controllable because it stems from the head and not the heart. Any resemblance it bears to love as we know it today is purely fictional.

And true love is still in embryo, fragile compared to other ties because it derives no strength from more ancient needs. Its roots are not in the past but in the future. It is a beginning, a new survival mechanism slowly evolving to suit new circumstances.

Suggestions for Discussion

1. After the author's panegyric to love in the opening paragraph, the reader is startled by her statement that what has been said, "give or take an epigram or two, is rubbish." To what extent does she mean this disclaimer?

2. Love for Tweedie is "a vast umbrella that covers a multitude of virtues and sins." What are they?

3. Under what circumstances does the author believe that there will be an emergence of true love?

4. With what details does Tweedie express her negative feelings about the old stereotypes of male and female?

5. Why does she believe that monogamy is on its way out?

6. Why does true love require a strong ego in the lover? What are other requisites of true love?

7. How does Tweedie's use of figurative language contribute to her point of view? to the tone of her essay?

Suggestions for Writing

1. "Variety will replace conformity and variety apart from being an evolutionary must, forces each potential lover to take stock of an individual rather than search for the stereotyped ideal of a whole sex." Discuss.

2. The author believes that romantic love leads to self-deceptive fantasies that are not compatible with reality. Defend or challenge her point of view.

3. Bring to bear your experience and observation in your discussion of what true love means to you. Or defend or challenge Tweedie's views.

4. Reexamine the stories by McCullers and Carver. Discuss some of Tweedie's ideas in relation to one or both of these stories.

Fiction

Nathaniel Hawthorne

The Birthmark

Nathaniel Hawthorne (1804–1864) was born of New England Puritan stock in Salem, Massachusetts. His first publication, *Twice-Told Tales* (1837), was followed by the novels *The Scarlet Letter* (1850), *The House of the Seven Gables* (1851), and *The Marble Faun* (1860). Other short fiction includes a second series of *Twice-Told Tales* (1842), *Mosses from an Old Manse* (1846), and *The Snow Image and Other Twice-Told Tales* (1851). In "The Birthmark," Aylmer's love for Georgiana deteriorates into self-love and an obsessive sense of his own omnipotence; his faith in science is reduced to an unconscious belief in the possibility of magical exorcism. The opposed forces in his personality become completely separated, and when they cease to contend there is no possibility of a reconciliation between them.

In the latter part of the last century there lived a man of science, an eminent proficient in every branch of natural philosophy, who not long before our story opens had made experience of a spiritual affinity more attractive than any chemical one. He had left his laboratory to the care of an assistant, cleared his fine countenance from the furnace smoke, washed the stain of acids from his fingers, and persuaded a beautiful woman to become his wife. In those days, when the comparatively recent discovery of electricity and other kindred mysteries of Nature seemed to open paths into the region of miracle, it was not unusual for the love of science to rival the love of woman in its depth and absorbing energy. The higher intellect, the imagination, the spirit, and even the heart might all find their congenial aliment in pursuits which, as some of their ardent votaries believed, would ascend from one step of powerful intelligence to another, until the philosopher should lay his hand on the secret of creative force and perhaps make new worlds for himself. We know not whether Aylmer possessed this degree of faith in man's ultimate control over Nature. He had devoted himself, however, too unreservedly to

333

scientific studies ever to be weaned from them by any second passion. His love for his young wife might prove the stronger of the two; but it could only be by intertwining itself with his love of science and uniting the strength of the latter to his own.

Such a union accordingly took place, and was attended with truly remarkable consequences and a deeply impressive moral. One day, very soon after their marriage, Aylmer sat gazing at his wife with a trouble in his countenance that grew stronger until he spoke.

"Georgiana," said he, "has it never occurred to you that the mark upon your cheek might be removed?"

"No, indeed," said she, smiling; but, perceiving the seriousness of his manner, she blushed deeply. "To tell you the truth, it has been so often called a charm that I was simple enough to imagine it might be so."

"Ah, upon another face perhaps it might," replied her husband; "but never on yours. No, dearest Georgiana, you came so nearly perfect from the hand of Nature that this slightest possible defect, which we hesitate whether to term a defect or a beauty, shocks me, as being the visible mark of earthly imperfection."

"Shocks you, my husband!" cried Georgiana, deeply hurt; at first reddening with momentary anger, but then bursting into tears. "Then why did you take me from my mother's side? You cannot love what shocks you!"

To explain this conversation, it must be mentioned that in the centre of Georgiana's left cheek there was a singular mark, deeply interwoven, as it were, with the texture and substance of her face. In the usual state of her complexion—a healthy though delicate bloom—the mark wore a tint of deeper crimson, which imperfectly defined its shape amid the surrounding rosiness. When she blushed it gradually became more indistinct, and finally vanished amid the triumphant rush of blood that bathed the whole cheek with its brilliant glow. But if any shifting motion caused her to turn pale there was the mark again, a crimson stain upon the snow, in what Aylmer sometimes deemed an almost fearful distinctness. Its shape bore not a little similarity to the human hand, though of the smallest pygmy size. Georgiana's lovers were wont to say that some fairy at her birth hour had laid her tiny hand upon the infant's cheek, and left this impress there in token of the magic endowments that were to give her such sway over all hearts. Many a desperate swain would have risked life for the privilege of pressing his lips to the mysterious hand. It must not be concealed, however, that the impression wrought by this fairy sign manual varied exceedingly according to the difference of temperament in the beholders. Some fastidious persons—but they were exclusively of her own sex—affirmed that the bloody hand, as they chose to call it, quite destroyed the effect of Georgiana's beauty and rendered her countenance even hideous. But it would be as reasonable to say that one of those small blue stains which sometimes occur in the purest statuary marble would convert the Eve of Powers to a monster. Masculine observers, if the birthmark did not heighten their admiration, contented themselves with wishing it away, that the world might possess one living specimen of ideal loveliness without the semblance of a flaw. After his marriage,—for he thought little or nothing of the matter before,—Aylmer discovered that this was the case with himself.

Had she been less beautiful,—if Envy's self could have found aught else to sneer at,—he might have felt his affection heightened by the prettiness of this mimic hand, now vaguely portrayed, now lost, now stealing forth again and glimmering to and fro with every pulse of emotion that throbbed within her heart; but, seeing her otherwise so perfect, he found this one defect grow more and more intolerable with every moment of their united lives. It was the fatal flaw of humanity which Nature, in one shape or another, stamps ineffaceably on all her productions, either to imply that they are temporary and finite, or that their perfection must be wrought by toil and pain. The crimson hand expressed the ineludible gripe in which mortality clutches the highest and purest of earthly mould, degrading them into kindred with the lowest, and even with the very brutes, like whom their visible frames return to dust. In this manner, selecting it as the symbol of his wife's liability to sin, sorrow, decay, and death, Aylmer's sombre imagination was not long in rendering the birthmark a frightful object, causing him more trouble and horror than ever Georgiana's beauty, whether of soul or sense, had given him delight.

At all the seasons which should have been their happiest he invariably, and without intending it, nay, in spite of a purpose to the contrary, reverted to this one disastrous topic. Trifling as it at first appeared, it so connected itself with innumerable trains of thought and modes of feeling that it became the central point of all. With the morning twilight Aylmer opened his eyes upon his wife's face and recognized the symbol of imperfection; and when they sat together at the evening hearth his eyes wandered stealthily to her cheek, and beheld, flickering with the blaze of the wood fire, the spectral hand that wrote mortality where he would fain have worshipped. Georgiana soon learned to shudder at his gaze. It needed but a glance with the peculiar expression that his face often wore to change the roses of her cheek into a deathlike paleness, amid which the crimson hand was brought strongly out, like a bas relief of ruby on the whitest marble.

Late one night, when the lights were growing dim so as hardly to betray the stain on the poor wife's cheek, she herself, for the first time, voluntarily took up the subject.

"Do you remember, my dear Aylmer," said she, with a feeble attempt at a smile, "have you any recollection, of a dream last night about this odious hand?"

"None! none whatever!" replied Aylmer, starting; but then he added, in a dry, cold tone, affected for the sake of concealing the real depth of his emotion, "I might well dream of it; for, before I fell asleep, it had taken a pretty firm hold of my fancy."

"And you did dream of it?" continued Georgiana, hastily; for she dreaded lest a gush of tears should interrupt what she had to say. "A terrible dream! I wonder that you can forget it. Is it possible to forget this one expression?— 'It is in her heart now; we must have it out!' Reflect, my husband; for by all means I would have you recall that dream."

The mind is in a sad state when Sleep, the all-involving, cannot confine her spectres within the dim region of her sway, but suffers them to break forth, affrighting this actual life with secrets that perchance belong to a deeper one. Aylmer now remembered his dream. He had fancied himself with his servant Aminadab, attempting an operation for the removal of the birthmark; but the deeper went the knife, the deeper sank the hand, until at length its tiny grasp appeared to have caught hold of Georgiana's heart; whence, however, her husband was inexorably resolved to cut or wrench it away.

When the dream had shaped itself perfectly in his memory Aylmer sat in his wife's presence with a guilty feeling. Truth often finds its way to the mind close muffled in robes of sleep, and then speaks with uncompromising directness of matters in regard to which we practise an unconscious self-deception during our waking moments. Until now he had not been aware of the tyrannizing influence acquired by one idea over his mind, and of the lengths which he might find in his heart to go for the sake of giving himself peace.

"Aylmer," resumed Georgiana, solemnly, "I know not what may be the cost to both of us to rid me of this fatal birthmark. Perhaps its removal may cause cureless deformity; or it may be the stain goes as deep as life itself. Again: do we know that there is a possibility, on any terms, of unclasping the firm grip of this little hand which was laid upon me before I came into the world?"

"Dearest Georgiana, I have spent much thought upon the subject," hastily interrupted Aylmer. "I am convinced of the perfect practicability of its removal."

"If there be the remotest possibility of it," continued Georgiana, "let the attempt be made, at whatever risk. Danger is nothing to me; for life, while this hateful mark makes me the object of your horror and disgust—life is a burden which I would fling down with joy. Either remove this dreadful hand, or take my wretched life! You have deep science. All the world bears witness of it. You have achieved great wonders. Cannot you remove this little, little mark, which I cover with the tips of two small fingers? Is this beyond your power, for the sake of your own peace, and to save your poor wife from madness?"

"Noblest, dearest, tenderest wife," cried Aylmer, rapturously, "doubt not my power. I have already given this matter the deepest thought—thought which might almost have enlightened me to create a being less perfect than yourself. Georgiana, you have led me deeper than ever into the heart of science. I feel myself fully competent to render this dear cheek as faultless as its fellow; and then, most beloved, what will be my triumph when I shall have corrected what Nature left imperfect in her fairest work! Even Pygmalion, when his sculptured woman assumed life, felt not greater ecstasy than mine will be."

"It is resolved, then," said Georgiana, faintly smiling. "And, Aylmer, spare me not, though you should find the birthmark take refuge in my heart at last."

Her husband tenderly kissed her cheek—her right cheek—not that which bore the impress of the crimson hand.

The next day Aylmer apprised his wife of a plan that he had formed whereby he might have opportunity for the intense thought and constant watchfulness which the proposed operation would require; while Georgiana, likewise, would enjoy the perfect repose essential to its success. They were to seclude themselves in the extensive apartments occupied by Aylmer as a laboratory, and where, during his toilsome youth, he had made discoveries in the elemental powers of Nature that had roused the admiration of all the learned societies in Europe. Seated calmly in this laboratory, the pale philosopher had investigated the secrets of the highest cloud region and of the profoundest mines; he had satisfied himself of the causes that kindled and kept alive the fires of the volcano; and had explained the mystery of fountains, and how it is that they gush forth; some so bright and pure, and others with such rich medicinal virtues, from the dark bosom of the earth. Here, too, at an earlier period, he had studied the wonders of the human frame, and attempted to fathom the very process by which Nature assimilates all her precious influences from earth and air, and from the spiritual world, to create and foster man, her masterpiece. The latter pursuit, however, Aylmer had long laid aside in unwilling recognition of the truth—against which all seekers sooner or later stumble—that our great creative Mother, while she amuses us with apparently working in the broadest sunshine, is yet severely careful to keep her own secrets, and, in spite of her pretended openness, shows us nothing but results. She permits us, indeed, to mar, but seldom to mend, and, like a jealous patentee, on no account to make. Now, however, Aylmer resumed these half-forgotten investigations; not, of course, with such hopes or wishes as first suggested them; but because they involved much physiological truth and lay in the path of his proposed scheme for the treatment of Georgiana.

As he led her over the threshold of the laboratory, Georgiana was cold and tremulous. Aylmer looked cheerfully into her face, with intent to reassure her, but was so startled with the intense glow of the birthmark upon the whiteness of her cheek that he could not restrain a strong convulsive shudder. His wife fainted.

"Aminadab! Aminadab!" shouted Aylmer, stamping violently on the floor.

Forthwith there issued from an inner apartment a man of low stature, but bulky frame, with shaggy hair hanging about his visage, which was grimed with the vapors of the furnace. This personage had been Aylmer's underworker during his whole scientific career, and was admirably fitted for that office by his great mechanical readiness, and the skill with which, while incapable of comprehending a single principle, he executed all the details of his master's experiments. With his vast strength, his shaggy hair, his smoky aspect, and the indescribable earthiness that incrusted him, he seemed to represent man's physical nature; while Aylmer's slender figure, and pale, intellectual face, were no less apt a type of the spiritual element.

"Throw open the door of the boudoir, Aminadab," said Aylmer, "and burn a pastil."

"Yes, master," answered Aminadab, looking intently at the lifeless form of Georgiana; and then he muttered to himself, "If she were my wife, I'd never part with that birthmark."

When Georgiana recovered consciousness she found herself breathing an atmosphere of penetrating fragrance, the gentle potency of which had recalled her from her deathlike faintness. The scene around her looked like enchantment. Aylmer had converted those smoky, dingy, sombre rooms, where he had spent his brightest years in recondite pursuits, into a series of beautiful apartments not unfit to be the secluded abode of a lovely woman. The walls were hung with gorgeous curtains, which imparted the combination of grandeur and grace that no other species of adornment can achieve; and, as they fell from the ceiling to the floor, their rich and ponderous folds, concealing all angles and straight lines, appeared to shut in the scene from infinite space. For aught Georgiana knew, it might be a pavilion among the clouds. And Aylmer, excluding the sunshine, which would have interfered with his chemical processes, had supplied its place with perfumed lamps, emitting flames of various hue, but all uniting in a soft, impurpled radiance. He now knelt by his wife's side, watching her earnestly, but without alarm; for he was confident in his science, and felt that he could draw a magic circle round her within which no evil might intrude.

"Where am I? Ah, I remember," said Georgiana, faintly; and she placed her hand over her cheek to hide the terrible mark from her husband's eyes.

"Fear not, dearest!" exclaimed he. "Do not shrink from me! Believe me, Georgiana, I even rejoice in this single imperfection, since it will be such a rapture to remove it."

"O, spare me!" sadly replied his wife. "Pray do not look at it again. I never can forget that convulsive shudder."

In order to soothe Georgiana, and, as it were, to release her mind from the burden of actual things, Aylmer now put in practice some of the light and playful secrets which science had taught him among its profounder lore. Airy figures, absolutely bodiless ideas, and forms of unsubstantial beauty came and danced before her, imprinting their momentary footsteps on beams of light. Though she had some indistinct idea of the method of these optical phenomena, still the illusion was almost perfect enough to warrant the belief that her husband possessed sway over the spiritual world. Then again, when she felt a wish to look forth from her seclusion, immediately, as if her thoughts were answered, the procession of external existence flitted across a screen. The scenery and the figures of actual life were perfectly represented, but with that bewitching yet indescribable difference which always makes a picture, an image, or a shadow so much more attractive than the original. When wearied of this, Aylmer bade her cast her eyes upon a vessel containing a quantity of earth. She did so, with little interest at first; but was soon startled to perceive the germ of a plant shooting upward from the soil. Then came the slender stalk; the leaves gradually unfolded themselves; and amid them was a perfect and lovely flower.

"It is magical!" cried Georgiana. "I dare not touch it."

"Nay, pluck it," answered Aylmer,—"pluck it, and inhale its brief perfume while you may. The flower will wither in a few moments and leave nothing save its brown seed vessels; but thence may be perpetuated a race as ephemeral as itself."

But Georgiana had no sooner touched the flower than the whole plant suffered a blight, its leaves turning coal-black as if by the agency of fire.

"There was too powerful a stimulus," said Aylmer, thoughtfully.

To make up for this abortive experiment, he proposed to take her portrait by a scientific process of his own invention. It was to be effected by rays of light striking upon a polished plate of metal. Georgiana assented; but, on looking at the result, was affrighted to find the features of the portrait blurred and indefinable; while the minute figure of a hand appeared where the cheek should have been. Aylmer snatched the metallic plate and threw it into a jar of corrosive acid.

Soon, however, he forgot these mortifying failures. In the intervals of study and chemical experiment he came to her flushed and exhausted, but seemed invigorated by her presence, and spoke in glowing language of the resources of his art. He gave a history of the long dynasty of the alchemists, who spent so many ages in quest of the universal solvent by which the golden principle might be elicited from all things vile and base. Aylmer appeared to believe that, by the plainest scientific logic, it was altogether within the limits of possibility to discover this long-sought medium; "but," he added, "a philosopher who should go deep enough to acquire the power would attain too lofty a wisdom to stoop to the exercise of it." Not less singular were his opinions in regard to the elixir vitae. He more than intimated that it was at his option to concoct a liquid that should prolong life for years, perhaps interminably; but that it would produce a discord in Nature which all the world, and chiefly the quaffer of the immortal nostrum, would find cause to curse.

"Aylmer, are you in earnest?" asked Georgiana, looking at him with amazement and fear. "It is terrible to possess such power, or even to dream of possessing it."

"O, do not tremble, my love," said her husband. "I would not wrong either you or myself by working such inharmonious effects upon our lives; but I would have you consider how trifling, in comparison, is the skill requisite to remove this little hand."

At the mention of the birthmark, Georgiana, as usual, shrank as if a red-hot iron had touched her cheek.

Again Aylmer applied himself to his labors. She could hear his voice in the distant furnace room giving directions to Aminadab, whose harsh, uncouth, misshapen tones were audible in response, more like the grunt or growl of a brute than human speech. After hours of absence, Aylmer reappeared and proposed that she should now examine his cabinet of chemical products and natural treasures of the earth. Among the former he showed her a small vial, in which, he remarked, was contained a gentle yet most powerful fragrance, capable of impregnating all the breezes that blow across a kingdom. They were of inestimable value, the contents of that little vial; and, as he said so, he threw some of the perfume into the air and filled the room with piercing and invigorating delight.

"And what is this?" asked Georgiana, pointing to a small crystal globe containing a gold-colored liquid. "It is so beautiful to the eye that I could imagine it the elixir of life."

"In one sense it is," replied Aylmer; "or rather, the elixir of immortality. It is the most precious poison that ever was concocted in this world. By its aid I could apportion the lifetime of any mortal at whom you might point your finger. The strength of the dose would determine whether he were to linger out years, or drop dead in the midst of a breath. No king on his guarded throne could keep his life if I, in my private station, should deem that the welfare of millions justified me in depriving him of it."

"Why do you keep such a terrific drug?" inquired Georgiana in horror.

"Do not mistrust me, dearest," said her husband, smiling; "its virtuous potency is yet greater than its harmful one. But see! here is a powerful cosmetic. With a few drops of this in a vase of water, freckles may be washed away as easily as the hands are cleansed. A stronger infusion would take the blood out of the cheek, and leave the rosiest beauty a pale ghost."

"Is it with this lotion that you intend to bathe my cheek?" asked Georgiana, anxiously.

"O, no," hastily replied her husband; "this is merely superficial. Your case demands a remedy that shall go deeper."

In his interviews with Georgiana, Aylmer generally made minute inquiries as to her sensations, and whether the confinement of the rooms and the temperature of the atmosphere agreed with her. These questions had such a particular drift that Georgiana began to conjecture that she was already subjected to certain physical influences, either breathed in with the fragrant air or taken with her food. She fancied likewise, but it might be altogether fancy, that there was a stirring up of her system—a strange, indefinite sensation creeping through her veins, and tingling, half painfully, half pleasurably, at her heart. Still, whenever she dared to look into the mirror, there she beheld herself pale as a white rose and with the crimson birthmark stamped upon her cheek. Not even Aylmer now hated it so much as she.

To dispel the tedium of the hours which her husband found it necessary to devote to the processes of combination and analysis, Georgiana turned over the volumes of his scientific library. In many dark old tomes she met with chapters full of romance and poetry. They were the works of the philosophers of the middle ages, such as Albertus Magnus, Cornelius Agrippa, Paracelsus, and the famous friar who created the prophetic Brazen Head. All these antique naturalists stood in advance of their centuries, yet were imbued with some of their credulity, and therefore were believed, and perhaps imagined themselves to have acquired from the investigation of Nature a power above Nature, and from physics a sway over the spiritual world. Hardly less curious and imaginative were the early volumes of the Transactions of the Royal Society, in which the members, knowing little of the limits of natural possibility, were continually recording wonders or proposing methods whereby wonders might be wrought.

But to Georgiana, the most engrossing volume was a large folio from her husband's own hand, in which he had recorded every experiment of his scientific career, its original aim, the methods adopted for its development, and its final success or failure, with the circumstances to which either event was attributable. The book, in truth, was both the history and emblem of his ardent, ambitious, imaginative, yet practical and laborious life. He handled physical details as if there were nothing beyond them; yet spiritualized them all and redeemed himself from materialism by his strong and eager aspiration towards the infinite. In his grasp the veriest clod of earth assumed a soul. Georgiana, as she read, reverenced Aylmer and loved him more profoundly than ever, but with a less entire dependence on his judgment than heretofore. Much as he had accomplished, she could not but observe that his most splendid successes were almost invariably failures, if compared with the ideal at which he aimed. His brightest diamonds were the merest pebbles, and felt to be so by himself, in comparison with the inestimable gems which lay hidden beyond his reach. The volume, rich with achievements that had won renown for its author, was yet as melancholy a record as ever mortal hand had penned. It was the sad confession and continual exemplification of the shortcomings of the composite man, the spirit burdened with clay and working in matter, and of the despair that assails the higher nature at finding itself so miserably thwarted by the earthly part. Perhaps every man of genius, in whatever sphere, might recognize the image of his own experience in Aylmer's journal.

So deeply did these reflections affect Georgiana that she laid her face upon the open volume and burst into tears. In this situation she was found by her husband.

"It is dangerous to read in a sorcerer's books," said he with a smile, though his countenance was uneasy and displeased. "Georgiana, there are pages in that volume which I can scarcely glance over and keep my senses. Take heed lest it prove detrimental to you."

"It has made me worship you more than ever," said she.

"Ah, wait for this one success," rejoined he, "then worship me if you will. I shall deem myself hardly unworthy of it. But come, I have sought you for the luxury of your voice. Sing to me, dearest."

So she poured out the liquid music of her voice to quench the thirst of his spirit. He then took his leave with a boyish exuberance of gayety, assuring her that her seclusion would endure but a little longer, and that the result was already certain. Scarcely had he departed when Georgiana felt irresistibly impelled to follow him. She had forgotten to inform Aylmer of a symptom which for two or three hours past had begun to excite her attention. It was a sensation in the fatal birthmark, not painful, but which induced a restlessness throughout her system. Hastening after her husband, she intruded for the first time into the laboratory.

The first thing that struck her eye was the furnace, that hot and feverish worker, with the intense glow of its fire, which by the quantities of soot clustered above it seemed to have been burning for ages. There was a distilling apparatus in full operation. Around the room were retorts, tubes, cylinders, crucibles, and other apparatus of chemical research. An electrical machine stood ready for immediate use. The atmosphere felt oppressively close, and was tainted with gaseous odors which had been tormented forth by the process of science. The severe and homely simplicity of the apartment, with its naked walls and brick pavement, looked strange, accustomed as Georgiana had become to the fantastic elegance of her boudoir. But what chiefly, indeed almost solely, drew her attention, was the aspect of Aylmer himself.

He was pale as death, anxious and absorbed, and hung over the furnace as if it depended upon his utmost watchfulness whether the liquid which it was distilling should be the draught of immortal happiness or misery. How different from the sanguine and joyous mien that he had assumed for Georgiana's encouragement!

"Carefully now, Aminadab; carefully, thou human machine; carefully, thou man of clay," muttered Aylmer, more to himself than his assistant. "Now, if there be a thought too much or too little, it is all over."

"Ho! ho!" mumbled Aminadab. "Look, master! look!"

Aylmer raised his eyes hastily, and at first reddened, then grew paler than ever, on beholding Georgiana. He rushed towards her and seized her arm with a gripe that left the print of his fingers upon it.

"Why do you come hither? Have you no trust in your husband?" cried he, impetuously. "Would you throw the blight of that fatal birthmark over my labors? It is not well done. Go, prying woman! go!"

"Nay, Aylmer," said Georgiana with the firmness of which she possessed no stinted endowment, "it is not you that have a right to complain. You mistrust your wife; you have concealed the anxiety with which you watch the development of this experiment. Think not so unworthily of me, my husband. Tell me all the risk we run, and fear not that I shall shrink; for my share in it is far less than your own."

"No, no, Georgiana!" said Aylmer, impatiently; "it must not be."

"I submit," replied she, calmly. "And, Aylmer, I shall quaff whatever draught you bring me; but it will be on the same principle that would induce me to take a dose of poison if offered by your hand."

"My noble wife," said Aylmer, deeply moved, "I knew not the height and depth of your nature until now. Nothing shall be concealed. Know, then, that this crimson hand, superficial as it seems, has clutched its grasp into your being with a strength of which I had no previous conception. I have already administered agents powerful enough to do aught except to change your entire physical system. Only one thing remains to be tried. If that fail us we are ruined."

"Why did you hesitate to tell me this?" asked she.

"Because, Georgiana," said Aylmer, in a low voice, "there is danger."

"Danger? There is but one danger—that this horrible stigma shall be left upon my cheek!" cried Georgiana. "Remove it, remove it, whatever be the cost, or we shall both go mad!"

"Heaven knows your words are too true," said Aylmer, sadly. "And now, dearest, return to your boudoir. In a little while all will be tested."

He conducted her back and took leave of her with a solemn tenderness which spoke far more than his words how much was now at stake. After his departure Georgiana became rapt in musings. She considered the character of Aylmer and did it completer justice than at any previous moment. Her heart exulted, while it trembled, at his honorable love—so pure and lofty that it would accept nothing less than perfection nor miserably make itself contented with an earthlier nature than he had dreamed of. She felt how much more precious was such a sentiment than that meaner kind which would have borne with the imperfection for her sake, and have been guilty of treason to holy love by degrading its perfect idea to the level of the actual; and with her whole spirit she prayed that, for a single moment, she might satisfy his highest and deepest conception. Longer than one moment she well knew it could not be; for his spirit was ever on the march, ever ascending, and each instant required something that was beyond the scope of the instant before.

The sound of her husband's footsteps aroused her. He bore a crystal goblet containing a liquor colorless as water, but bright enough to be the draught of immortality. Aylmer was pale; but it seemed rather the consequence of a highly-wrought state of mind and tension of spirit than of fear or doubt.

"The concoction of the draught has been perfect," said he, in answer to Georgiana's look. "Unless all my science have deceived me, it cannot fail."

"Save on your account, my dearest Aylmer," observed his wife, "I might wish to put off this birthmark of mortality by relinquishing mortality itself in preference to any other mode. Life is but a sad possession to those who have attained precisely the degree of moral advancement at which I stand. Were I weaker and blinder, it might be happiness. Were I stronger, it might be endured hopefully. But, being what I find myself, methinks I am of all mortals the most fit to die."

"You are fit for heaven without tasting death!" replied her husband. "But why do we speak of dying? The draught cannot fail. Behold its effect upon this plant."

On the window seat there stood a geranium diseased with yellow blotches which had overspread all its leaves. Aylmer poured a small quantity of the liquid upon the soil in which it grew. In a little time, when the roots of the plant had taken up the moisture, the unsightly blotches began to be extinguished in a living verdure.

"There needed no proof," said Georgiana, quietly. "Give me the goblet. I joyfully stake all upon your word."

"Drink, then, thou lofty creature!" exclaimed Aylmer, with fervid admiration. "There is no taint of imperfection on thy spirit. Thy sensible frame, too, shall soon be all perfect."

She quaffed the liquid and returned the goblet to his hand.

"It is grateful," said she, with a placid smile. "Methinks it is like water from a heavenly fountain; for it contains I know not what of unobtrusive fragrance and deliciousness. It allays a feverish thirst that had parched me for many days. Now, dearest, let me sleep. My earthly senses are closing over my spirit like the leaves around the heart of a rose at sunset."

She spoke the last words with a gentle reluctance, as if it required almost more energy than she could command to pronounce the faint and lingering syllables. Scarcely had they loitered through her lips ere she was lost in slumber. Aylmer sat by her side, watching her aspect with the emotions proper to a man the whole value of whose existence was involved in the process now to be tested. Mingled with this mood, however, was the philosophic investigation characteristic of the man of science. Not the minutest symptom escaped him. A heightened flush of the cheek, a slight irregularity of breath, a quiver of the eyelid, a hardly perceptible tremor through the frame,—such were the details which, as the moments passed, he wrote down in his folio volume. Intense thought had set its stamp upon every previous page of that volume; but the thoughts of years were all concentrated upon the last.

While thus employed, he failed not to gaze often at the fatal hand, and not without a shudder. Yet once, by a strange and unaccountable impulse, he pressed it with his lips. His spirit recoiled, however, in the very act; and Georgiana, out of the midst of her deep sleep, moved uneasily and murmured as if in remonstrance. Again Aylmer resumed his watch. Nor was it without avail. The crimson hand, which at first had been strongly visible upon the marble paleness of Georgiana's cheek, now grew more faintly outlined. She remained not less pale than ever; but the birthmark, with every breath that came and went lost somewhat of its former distinctness. Its presence had been awful; its departure was more awful still. Watch the stain of the rainbow fading out of the sky, and you will know how that mysterious symbol passed away.

"By Heaven! it is well nigh gone!" said Aylmer to himself, in almost irrepressible ecstasy. "I can scarcely trace it now. Success! success! And now it is like the faintest rose color. The lightest flush of blood across her cheek would overcome it. But she is so pale!"

He drew aside the window curtain and suffered the light of natural day to fall into the room and rest upon her cheek. At the same time he heard a gross, hoarse chuckle, which he had long known as his servant Aminadab's expression of delight.

"Ah, clod! ah, earthly mass!" cried Aylmer, laughing in a sort of frenzy, "you have served me well! Matter and spirit—earth and heaven—have both done their part in this! Laugh, thing of the senses! You have earned the right to laugh."

These exclamations broke Georgiana's sleep. She slowly unclosed her eyes and gazed into the mirror which her husband had arranged for that purpose. A faint smile flitted over her lips when she recognized how barely perceptible was now that crimson hand which had once blazed forth with such disastrous brilliancy as to scare away all their happiness. But then her eyes sought Aylmer's face with a trouble and anxiety that he could by no means account for.

"My poor Aylmer!" murmured she.

"Poor? Nay, richest, happiest, most favored!" exclaimed he. "My peerless bride, it is successful! You are perfect!"

"My poor Aylmer," she repeated, with a more than human tenderness, "you have aimed loftily; you have done nobly. Do not repent that, with so high and pure a feeling, you have rejected the best the earth could offer. Aylmer, dearest Aylmer, I am dying!"

Alas! it was too true! The fatal hand had grappled with the mystery of life, and was the bond by which an angelic spirit kept itself in union with a mortal frame. As the last crimson tint of the birth-mark—that sole token of human imperfection—faded from her cheek, the parting breath of the now perfect woman passed into the atmosphere, and her soul, lingering a moment near her husband, took its heavenward flight. Then a hoarse, chuckling laugh was heard again! Thus ever does the gross fatality of earth exult in its invariable triumph over the immortal essence which, in this dim sphere of half development, demands the completeness of a higher state. Yet, had Aylmer reached a profounder wisdom, he need not thus have flung away the happiness which would have woven his mortal life of the selfsame texture with the celestial. The momentary circumstance was too strong for him; he failed to look beyond the shadowy scope of time, and, living once for all in eternity, to find the perfect future in the present.

Suggestions for Discussion

1. What do you regard as the forces motivating Aylmer's attitude and behavior?

2. Discuss the multiple ways in which the dream advances the story's development. Justify or challenge the statement that Aylmer's dream marks the climax of the story.

3. Examine the language and imagery with special reference to the birthmark and the varied responses to it. How does the juxtaposition of religious and sexual imagery contribute to characterization, meaning, and tone? What is the function of the animistic detail? How does the contrasting imagery describing Georgiana's chambers and Aylmer's laboratory advance the action?

4. By what means are the polarities between the earthly and the spiritual developed? How are they reflected in the descriptions of Aylmer and Aminadab? What support can you find for the idea that Aminadab is presented as Aylmer's double, representing the submerged aspect of Aylmer's personality (note the significance of Aminadab spelled backward)? How would you define the opposing forces in Aylmer? At what point do they cease to contend? In responding to this question, identify the rising action, climax, falling action, and resolution.

5. What has been gained and lost by the use of the omniscient author point of view? How necessary are the author's interpolations to the reader's understanding of the story's latent meaning? Note especially the author's comments upon the dream; the expository first paragraph; the passage beginning, "It was the fatal flaw of human-

ity," and the later one on "the shortcomings of the composite man." (Cf. *Hamlet,* I, iv, 11. 23–38.)

6. Trace the changes that take place in Georgiana's consciousness in the course of the action. If her last words to Aylmer reflect a tragic recognition of what Aylmer has rejected, to what does she remain blind? Discuss the irony in her becoming the instrument of her own fate.

7. Find the examples of the skillful use of foreshadowing. How is suspense maintained? While the reader experiences a mounting sense of impending doom, does he completely surrender his disbelief in the possibility that a miracle might be wrought?

Suggestions for Writing

1. Define the relationship of Aylmer and Georgiana. To what extent is the story dated? Under what circumstances could the action of the story take place today?

2. Discuss "The Birthmark" as a story of moral flaw or of psychological determination. Bring to bear what evidence you can for either point of view by specific allusion to the imagery, setting, and characterizations.

Kate Chopin

A Respectable Woman

Kate Chopin (1851–1904) was an early feminist who did not begin to write until her late thirties. Her first novel, *At Fault* (1890), was followed by two volumes of short stories, *Bayou Folk* (1894) and *A Night in Acadie* (1897), and her masterpiece, the novel *The Awakening* (1899). The "respectable woman" undergoes a metamorphosis after her earlier indifference to her husband's friend.

Mrs. Baroda was a little provoked to learn that her husband expected his friend, Gouvernail, up to spend a week or two on the plantation.

They had entertained a good deal during the winter; much of the time had also been passed in New Orleans in various forms of mild dissipation. She was looking forward to a period of unbroken rest, now, and undisturbed tête-à-tête with her husband, when he informed her that Gouvernail was coming up to stay a week or two.

This was a man she had heard much of but never seen. He had been her husband's college friend; was now a journalist, and in no sense a society man or "a man about town," which were, perhaps, some of the reasons she had never met him. But she had unconsciously formed an image of him in her mind. She pictured him tall, slim, cynical; with eye-glasses, and his hands in his pockets; and she did not like him. Gouvernail was slim enough, but he wasn't very tall nor very cynical; neither did he wear eye-glasses nor carry his hands in his pockets. And she rather liked him when he first presented himself.

But why she liked him she could not explain satisfactorily to herself when she partly attempted to do so. She could discover in him none of those brilliant and promising traits which Gaston, her husband, had often assured her that he possessed. On the contrary, he sat rather mute and receptive before her chatty eagerness to make him feel at home and in face of Gaston's frank and wordy hospitality. His manner was as courteous toward her as the most exacting woman could require; but he made no direct appeal to her approval or even esteem.

Once settled at the plantation he seemed to like to sit upon the wide portico in the shade of one of the big Corinthian pillars, smoking his cigar lazily and listening attentively to Gaston's experience as a sugar planter.

"This is what I call living," he would utter with deep satisfaction, as the air that swept across the sugar field caressed him with its warm and scented velvety touch. It pleased him also to get on familiar terms with the big dogs that came about him, rubbing themselves sociably against his legs. He did not care to fish, and displayed no eagerness to go out and kill grosbecs when Gaston proposed doing so.

Gouvernail's personality puzzled Mrs. Baroda, but she liked him. Indeed, he was a lovable, inoffensive fellow. After a few days, when she could understand him no better than at first, she gave over being puzzled and remained piqued. In this mood she left her husband and her guest, for the most part, alone together. Then finding that Gouvernail took no manner of exception to her action, she imposed her society upon him, accompanying him in his idle strolls to the mill and walks along the batture. She persistently sought to penetrate the reserve in which he had unconsciously enveloped himself.

"When is he going—your friend?" she one day asked her husband. "For my part, he tires me frightfully."

"Not for a week yet, dear. I can't understand; he gives you no trouble."

"No. I should like him better if he did; if he were more like others, and I had to plan somewhat for his comfort and enjoyment."

Gaston took his wife's pretty face between his hands and looked tenderly and laughingly into her troubled eyes. They were making a bit of toilet sociably together in Mrs. Baroda's dressing-room.

"You are full of surprises, ma belle," he said to her. "Even I can never count upon how you are going to act under given conditions." He kissed her and turned to fasten his cravat before the mirror.

"Here you are," he went on, "taking poor Gouvernail seriously and making a commotion over him, the last thing he would desire or expect."

"Commotion!" she hotly resented. "Nonsense! How can you say such a thing? Commotion, indeed! But, you know, you said he was clever."

"So he is. But the poor fellow is run down by overwork now. That's why I asked him here to take a rest."

"You used to say he was a man of ideas," she retorted, unconciliated. "I expected him to be interesting, at least. I'm going to the city in the morning to have my spring gowns fitted. Let me know when Mr. Gouvernail is gone; I shall be at my Aunt Octavie's."

That night she went and sat alone upon a bench that stood beneath a live oak tree at the edge of the gravel walk.

She had never known her thoughts or her intentions to be so confused. She could gather nothing from them but the feeling of a distinct necessity to quit her home in the morning.

Mrs. Baroda heard footsteps crunching the gravel; but could discern in the darkness only the approaching red point of a lighted cigar. She knew it was Gouvernail, for her husband did not smoke. She hoped to remain unnoticed, but her white gown revealed her to him. He threw away his cigar and seated himself upon the bench beside her; without a suspicion that she might object to his presence.

"Your husband told me to bring this to you, Mrs. Baroda," he said, handing her a filmy, white scarf with which she sometimes enveloped her head and shoulders. She accepted the scarf from him with a murmur of thanks, and let it lie in her lap.

He made some commonplace observation upon the baneful effect of the night air at that season. Then as his gaze reached out into the darkness, he murmured, half to himself:

"'Night of south winds—night of the large few stars!
Still nodding night—'"

She made no reply to this apostrophe to the night, which indeed, was not addressed to her.

Gouvernail was in no sense a diffident man, for he was not a self-conscious one. His periods of reserve were not constitutional, but the result of moods. Sitting there beside Mrs. Baroda, his silence melted for the time.

He talked freely and intimately in a low, hesitating drawl that was not unpleasant to hear. He talked of the old college days when he and Gaston had been a good deal to each other; of the days of keen and blind ambitions and large intentions. Now there was left with him, at least, a philosophic acquiescence to the existing order—only a desire to be permitted to exist, with now and then a little whiff of genuine life, such as he was breathing now.

Her mind only vaguely grasped what he was saying. Her physical being was for the moment predominant. She was not thinking of his words, only drinking in the tones of his voice. She wanted to reach out her hand in the darkness and touch him with the sensitive tips of her fingers upon the face or the lips. She wanted to draw close to him and whisper against his cheek—she did not care what—as she might have done if she had not been a respectable woman.

The stronger the impulse grew to bring herself near him, the further, in fact, did she draw away from him. As soon as she could do so without an appearance of too great rudeness, she rose and left him there alone.

Before she reached the house, Gouvernail had lighted a fresh cigar and ended his apostrophe to the night.

Mrs. Baroda was greatly tempted that night to tell her husband—who was also her friend—of this folly that had seized her. But she did not yield to the temptation. Beside being a respectable woman she was a very sensible one;

and she knew there are some battles in life which a human being must fight alone.

When Gaston arose in the morning, his wife had already departed. She had taken an early train to the city. She did not return till Gouvernail was gone from under her roof.

There was some talk of having him back during the summer that followed. That is, Gaston greatly desired it; but this desire yielded to his wife's strenuous opposition.

However, before the year ended, she proposed, wholly from herself, to have Gouvernail visit them again. Her husband was surprised and delighted with the suggestion coming from her.

"I am glad, chère amie, to know that you have finally overcome your dislike for him; truly he did not deserve it."

"Oh," she told him, laughingly, after pressing a long, tender kiss upon his lips, "I have overcome everything! you will see. This time I shall be very nice to him."

Suggestions for Discussion

1. How do you learn that Mrs. Baroda is ambivalent about Gouvernail?

2. Why do you think Mrs. Baroda left for the city? What precipitated the move?

3. What details suggest to you that this story was written in an earlier era?

4. What is the significance of the title? Relate it to the theme of the story. Is it used ironically?

5. What are you led to surmise is the relationship of Mrs. Baroda to her husband?

6. What do you think will happen on Gouvernail's next visit? How are you prepared for it?

Suggestion for Writing

Write an essay on question 4 or 6 above.

James Thurber

The Unicorn in the Garden

James Thurber (1894–1961), American humorist and artist, began contributing in 1927 to *The New Yorker*, in which most of his work first appeared. His humorous essays and short stories are collected in such books as *The Owl in the Attic* (1931), *My Life and Hard Times* (1933), *The Thurber Carnival* (1945), *The Beast in Me* (1948), and *Lanterns and Lances* (1961). He also wrote the short story "The Secret Life of Walter Mitty," several fantasies for children, and with Elliot Nugent, a comedy called *The Male Animal* (1940). "The Unicorn in the Garden," a fable of hostile feelings between husband and wife, ends with a surprise twist.

Once upon a sunny morning a man who sat in a breakfast nook looked up from his scrambled eggs to see a white unicorn with a gold horn quietly cropping the roses in the garden. The man went up to the bedroom where his wife was still asleep and woke her. "There's a unicorn in the garden," he said. "Eating roses." She opened one unfriendly eye and looked at him. "The unicorn is a mythical beast," she said, and turned her back to him. The man walked slowly downstairs and out into the garden. The unicorn was still there; he was now browsing among the tulips. "Here, unicorn," said the man, and he pulled up a lily and gave it to him. The unicorn ate it gravely. With a high heart, because there was a unicorn in his garden, the man went upstairs and roused his wife again. "The unicorn," he said, "ate a lily." His wife sat up in bed and looked at him, coldly. "You are a booby," she said, "and I am going to have you put in the booby-hatch." The man, who had never liked the words "booby" and "booby-hatch," and who liked them even less on a shining morning when there was a unicorn in the garden, thought for a moment. "We'll see about that," he said. He walked over to the door. "He has a golden horn in the middle of his forehead," he told her. Then he went back to the garden to watch the unicorn; but the unicorn had gone away. The man sat down among the roses and went to sleep.

As soon as the husband had gone out of the house, the wife got up and dressed as fast as she could. She was very excited and there was a gloat in her eye. She telephoned the police and she telephoned a psychiatrist; she told them to hurry to her house and bring a strait-jacket. When the police and the psychiatrist arrived they sat down in chairs and looked at her, with great interest. "My husband," she said, "saw a unicorn this morning." The police looked at the psychiatrist and the psychiatrist looked at the police. "He told me it ate a lily," she said. The psychiatrist looked at the police and the police looked at the psychiatrist. "He told me it had a golden horn in the middle of its forehead," she said. At a solemn signal from the psychiatrist, the police leaped from their chairs and seized the wife. They had a hard time subduing her, for she put up a terrific struggle, but they finally subdued her. Just as they got her into the strait-jacket, the husband came back into the house.

"Did you tell your wife you saw a unicorn?" asked the police. "Of course not," said the husband. "The unicorn is a mythical beast." "That's all I wanted to know," said the psychiatrist. "Take her away. I'm sorry, sir, but your wife is as crazy as a jay bird." So they took her away, cursing and screaming, and shut her up in an institution. The husband lived happily ever after.

Moral: Don't count your boobies until they are hatched.

Suggestions for Discussion

1. From what details do you become aware of the hostile feelings between husband and wife?

2. What is Thurber's attitude toward his characters, including the psychiatrist? Refer to the diction, the role of the unicorn, the setting, the details of the action, the twist at the end, the moral, and the drawing.

3. What other "moral" might be appropriate to append to this fable?

4. What evidence can you find that the author is (or is not) detached from his subject?

Suggestions for Writing

1. Write an imaginary description of the events leading up to the situation at the beginning of the fable.

2. Read "The Secret Life of Walter Mitty" and compare situation, tone, and resolution with those of the fable of the unicorn.

3. Write a fable depicting a domestic relationship.

John Steinbeck
The Chrysanthemums

John Steinbeck (1902–1968) wrote novels, short stories, travel sketches, and essays. Born in Salinas, California, he studied at Stanford University. Before he achieved success as a writer, he worked as ranch hand, laborer, and newspaperman. Among his novels are *Tortilla Flat* (1935), *Of Mice and Men* (1937), *The Grapes of Wrath* (1939), which was awarded a Pulitzer Prize, and *East of Eden* (1952). In 1962 he was awarded the Nobel Prize for Literature. Although Elisa's encounter with the tinker in "The Chrysanthemums" leads to her awareness of herself as a woman and of formerly submerged feelings, nothing in her external world has been significantly altered. Her isolation, vitality, and creative energy leave her unfulfilled as a woman.

The high grey-flannel fog of winter closed off the Salinas Valley from the sky and from all the rest of the world. On every side it sat like a lid on the mountains and made of the great valley a closed pot. On the broad, level land floor the gang plows bit deep and left the black earth shining like metal where the shares had cut. On the foothill ranches across the Salinas River, the yellow stubble fields seemed to be bathed in pale cold sunshine, but there was no sunshine in the valley now in December. The thick willow scrub along the river flamed with sharp and positive yellow leaves.

It was a time of quiet and of waiting. The air was cold and tender. A light wind blew up from the southwest so that the farmers were mildly hopeful of a good rain before long; but fog and rain do not go together.

Across the river, on Henry Allen's foothill ranch there was little work to be done, for the hay was cut and stored and the orchards were plowed up to receive the rain deeply when it should come. The cattle on the higher slopes were becoming shaggy and rough-coated.

Elisa Allen, working in her flower garden, looked down across the yard and saw Henry, her husband, talking to two men in business suits. The three of them stood by the tractor shed, each man with one foot on the side of the little Fordson. They smoked cigarettes and studied the machine as they talked.

Elisa watched them for a moment and then went back to her work. She was thirty-five. Her face was lean and strong and her eyes were as clear as water. Her figure looked blocked and heavy in her gardening costume, a man's black hat pulled low down over her eyes, clodhopper shoes, a figured print dress almost completely covered by a big corduroy apron with four big pockets to hold the snips, the trowel and scratcher, the seeds and the knife she worked with. She wore heavy leather gloves to protect her hands while she worked.

She was cutting down the old year's chrysanthemum stalks with a pair of short and powerful scissors. She looked down toward the men by the tractor shed now and then. Her face was eager and mature and handsome; even her work with the scissors was over-eager, over-powerful. The chrysanthemum stems seemed too small and easy for her energy.

She brushed a cloud of hair out of her eyes with the back of her glove, and left a smudge of earth on the cheek in doing it. Behind her stood the neat white farm house with red geraniums close-banked around it as high as the windows. It was a hard-swept looking little house, with hard-polished windows, and a clean mud-mat on the front steps.

Elisa cast another glance toward the tractor shed. The strangers were getting into their Ford coupe. She took off a glove and put her strong fingers down into the forest of new green crysanthemum sprouts that were growing around the old roots. She spread the leaves and looked down among the close-growing stems. No aphids were there, no sowbugs or snails or cutworms. Her terrier fingers destroyed such pests before they could get started.

Elisa started at the sound of her husband's voice. He had come near quietly, and he leaned over the wire fence that protected her flower garden from cattle and dogs and chickens.

"At it again," he said. "You've got a strong new crop coming."

Elisa straightened her back and pulled on the gardening glove again. "Yes. They'll be strong this coming year." In her tone and on her face there was a little smugness.

"You've got a gift with things," Henry observed. "Some of those yellow chrysanthemums you had this year were ten inches across. I wish you'd work out in the orchard and raise some apples that big."

Her eyes sharpened. "Maybe I could do it, too. I've a gift with things, all right. My mother had it. She could stick anything in the ground and make it grow. She said it was having planters' hands that knew how to do it."

"Well, it sure works with flowers," he said.

"Henry, who were those men you were talking to?"

"Why, sure, that's what I came to tell you. They were from the Western Meat Company. I sold those thirty head of three-year-old steers. Got nearly my own price, too."

"Good," she said. "Good for you."

"And I thought," he continued, "I thought how it's Saturday afternoon, and we might go into Salinas for dinner at a restaurant, and then to a picture show—to celebrate, you see."

"Good," she repeated. "Oh, yes. That will be good."

Henry put on his joking tone. "There's fights tonight. How'd you like to go to the fights?"

"Oh, no," she said breathlessly. "No, I wouldn't like fights."

"Just fooling, Elisa. We'll go to a movie. Let's see. It's two now. I'm going to take Scotty and bring down those steers from the hill. It'll take us maybe two hours. We'll go in town about five and have dinner at the Cominos Hotel. Like that?"

"Of course I'll like it. It's good to eat away from home."

"All right, then. I'll go get up a couple of horses."

She said, "I'll have plenty of time to transplant some of these sets, I guess."

She heard her husband calling Scotty down by the barn. And a little later she saw the two men ride up the pale yellow hillside in search of the steers.

There was a little square sandy bed kept for rooting the chrysanthemums. With her trowel she turned the soil over and over, and smoothed it and patted it firm. Then she dug ten parallel trenches to receive the sets. Back at the chrysanthemum bed she pulled out the little crisp shoots, trimmed off the leaves of each one with her scissors and laid it on a small orderly pile.

A squeak of wheels and plod of hoofs came from the road. Elisa looked up. The country road ran along the dense bank of willows and cottonwoods that bordered the river, and up this road came a curious vehicle, curiously drawn. It was an old spring-wagon, with a round canvas top on it like the cover of a prairie schooner. It was drawn by an old bay horse and a little grey-and-white burro. A big stubble-bearded man sat between the cover flaps and drove the crawling team. Underneath the wagon, between the hind wheels, a lean and rangy mongrel dog walked sedately. Words were painted on the canvas in clumsy, crooked letters. "Pots, pans, knives, sisors, lawn mores. Fixed." Two rows of articles and the triumphantly definitive "Fixed" below. The black paint had run down in little sharp points beneath each letter.

Elisa, squatting on the ground, watched to see the crazy, loose-jointed wagon pass by. But it didn't pass. It turned into the farm road in front of her house, crooked old wheels skirling and squeaking. The rangy dog darted from between the wheels and ran ahead. Instantly the two ranch shepherds flew out at him. Then all three stopped, and with stiff and quivering tails, with taut straight legs, with ambassadorial dignity, they slowly circled, sniffing daintily. The caravan pulled up to Elisa's wire fence and stopped. Now the newcomer dog, feeling out-numbered, lowered his tail and retired under the wagon with raised hackles and bared teeth.

The man on the wagon seat called out. "That's a bad dog in a fight when he gets started."

Elisa laughed. "I see he is. How soon does he generally get started?"

The man caught up her laughter and echoed it heartily. "Sometimes not for weeks and weeks," he said. He climbed stiffly down, over the wheel. The horse and the donkey drooped like unwatered flowers.

Elisa saw that he was a very big man. Although his hair and beard were greying, he did not look old. His worn black suit was wrinkled and spotted with grease. The laughter had disappeared from his face and eyes the moment his laughing voice ceased. His eyes were dark, and they were full of the brooding that gets in the eyes of teamsters and of sailors. The calloused hands he rested on the wire fence were cracked, and every crack was a black line. He took off his battered hat.

"I'm off my general road, ma'am," he said. "Does this dirt road cut over across the river to the Los Angeles highway?"

Elisa stood up and shoved the thick scissors in her apron pocket. "Well, yes, it does, but it winds around and then fords the river. I don't think your team could pull through the sand."

He replied with some asperity, "It might surprise you what them beasts can pull through."

"When they get started?" she asked.

He smiled for a second. "Yes. When they get started."

"Well," said Elisa, "I think you'll save time if you go back to the Salinas road and pick up the highway there."

He drew a big finger down the chicken wire and made it sing. "I ain't in any hurry, ma'am. I go from Seattle to San Diego and back every year. Takes all my time. About six months each way. I aim to follow nice weather."

Elisa took off her gloves and stuffed them in the apron pocket with the scissors. She touched the under edge of her man's hat, searching for fugitive hairs. "That sounds like a nice kind of a way to live," she said.

He leaned confidentially over the fence. "Maybe you noticed the writing on my wagon. I mend pots and sharpen knives and scissors. You got any of them things to do?"

"Oh, no," she said quickly. "Nothing like that." Her eyes hardened with resistance.

"Scissors is the worst thing," he explained. "Most people just ruin scissors trying to sharpen 'em but I know how. I got a special tool. It's a little bobbit kind of thing, and patented. But is sure does the trick."

"No. My scissors are all sharp."

"All right, then. Take a pot," he continued earnestly, "a bent pot, or a pot with a hole. I can make it like new so you don't have to buy no new ones. That's a saving for you."

"No," she said shortly. "I tell you I have nothing like that for you to do."

His face fell to an exaggerated sadness. His voice took on a whining undertone. "I ain't had a thing to do today. Maybe I won't have no supper tonight. You see I'm off my regular road. I know folks on the highway clear from Seattle to San Diego. They save their things for me to sharpen up because they know I do it so good and save them money."

"I'm sorry," Elisa said irritably. "I haven't anything for you to do."

His eyes left her face and fell to searching the ground. They roamed about until they came to the chrysanthemum bed where she had been working. "What's them plants, ma'am?"

The irritation and resistance melted from Elisa's face. "Oh, those are chrysanthemums, giant whites and yellows. I raise them every year, bigger than anybody around here."

"Kind of a long-stemmed flower? Looks like a quick puff of colored smoke?" he asked.

"That's it. What a nice way to describe them."

"They smell kind of nasty till you get used to them," he said.

"It's a good bitter smell," she retorted, "not nasty at all."

He changed his tone quickly. "I like the smell myself."

"I had ten-inch blooms this year," she said.

The man leaned farther over the fence. "Look. I know a lady down the road a piece, has got the nicest garden you ever seen. Got nearly every kind of flower but no chrysanthemums. Last time I was mending a copper-bottom washtub for her (that's a hard job but I do it good), she said to me, 'If you ever run acrost some nice chrysanthemums I wish you'd try to get me a few seeds.' That's what she told me."

Elisa's eyes grew alert and eager. "She couldn't have known much about chrysanthemums. You can raise them from seed, but it's much easier to root the little sprouts you see there."

"Oh," he said. "I s'pose I can't take none to her, then."

"Why yes you can," Elisa cried. "I can put some in damp sand, and you can carry them right along with you. They'll take root in the pot if you keep them damp. And then she can transplant them."

"She'd sure like to have some, ma'am. You say they're nice ones?"

"Beautiful," she said. "Oh, beautiful." Her eyes shone. She tore off the battered hat and shook out her dark pretty hair. "I'll put them in a flower pot, and you can take them right with you. Come into the yard."

While the man came through the picket gate Elisa ran excitedly along the geranium-bordered path to the back of the house. And she returned carrying a big red flower pot. The gloves were forgotten now. She kneeled on the ground by the starting bed and dug up the sandy soil with her fingers and scooped it into the bright new flower pot. Then she picked up the little pile of shoots she had prepared. With her strong fingers she pressed them into the sand and tamped around them with her knuckles. The man stood over her. "I'll tell you what to do," she said. "You remember so you can tell the lady."

"Yes, I'll try to remember."

"Well, look. These will take root in about a month. Then she must set them out, about a foot apart in good rich earth like this, see?" She lifted a handful of dark soil for him to look at. "They'll grow fast and tall. Now remember this. In July tell her to cut them down, about eight inches from the ground."

"Before they bloom?" he asked.

"Yes, before they bloom." Her face was tight with eagerness. "They'll come right up again. About the last of September the buds will start."

She stopped and seemed perplexed. "It's the budding that takes the most care," she said hesitantly. "I don't know how to tell you." She looked deep into his eyes, searchingly. Her mouth opened a little, and she seemed to be listening. "I'll try to tell you," she said. "Did you ever hear of planting hands?"

"Can't say I have, ma'am."

"Well, I can only tell you what it feels like. It's when you're picking off the buds you don't want. Everything goes right down into your fingertips. You watch your fingers work. They do it themselves. You can feel how it is. They pick and pick the buds. They never make a mistake. They're with the plant. Do you see? Your fingers and the plant. You can feel that, right up your arm. They know. They never make a mistake. You can feel it. When you're like that you can't do anything wrong. Do you see that? Can you understand that?"

She was kneeling on the ground looking up at him. Her breast swelled passionately.

The man's eyes narrowed. He looked away, self-consciously. "Maybe I know," he said. "Sometimes in the night in the wagon there—"

Elisa's voice grew husky. She broke in on him. "I've never lived as you do, but I know what you mean. When the night is dark—why, the stars are sharp-pointed, and there's quiet. Why, you rise up and up! Every pointed star gets driven into your body. It's like that. Hot and sharp and—lovely."

Kneeling there, her hand went out toward his legs in the greasy black trousers. Her hesitant fingers almost touched the cloth. Then her hand dropped to the ground. She crouched low like a fawning dog.

He said, "It's nice, just like you say. Only when you don't have no dinner, it ain't."

She stood up then, very straight, and her face was ashamed. She held the flower pot out to him and placed it gently in his arms. "Here. Put it in your wagon, on the seat, where you can watch it. Maybe I can find something for you to do."

At the back of the house she dug in the can pile and found two old and battered aluminum saucepans. She carried them back and gave them to him. "Here, maybe you can fix these."

His manner changed. He became professional. "Good as new I can fix them." At the back of his wagon he set a little anvil, and out of an oily tool box dug a small machine hammer. Elisa came through the gate to watch him while he pounded out the dents in the kettles. His mouth grew sure and knowing. At a difficult part of the work he sucked his under-lip.

"You sleep right in the wagon?" Elisa asked.

"Right in the wagon, ma'am. Rain or shine I'm dry as a cow in there."

"It must be nice," she said. "It must be very nice. I wish women could do such things."

"It ain't the right kind of a life for a woman."

Her upper lip raised a little, showing her teeth. "How do you know? How can you tell?" she said.

"I don't know ma'am," he protested. "Of course I don't know. Now here's your kettles, done. You don't have to buy no new ones."

"How much?"

"Oh, fifty cents'll do. I keep my prices down and my work good. That's why I have all them satisfied customers up and down the highway."

Elisa brought him a fifty-cent piece from the house and dropped it in his hand. "You might be surprised to have a rival some time. I can sharpen scissors, too. And I can beat the dents out of little pots. I could show you what a woman might do."

He put his hammer back in the oily box and shoved the little anvil out of sight. "It would be a lonely life for a woman, ma'am, and a scarey life, too, with animals creeping under the wagon all night." He climbed over the singletree, steadying himself with a hand on the burro's white rump. He settled himself in the seat, picked up the lines. "Thank you kindly, ma'am," he said. "I'll do like you told me; I'll go back and catch the Salinas road."

"Mind," she called, "if you're long in getting there, keep the sand damp."

"Sand, ma'am? . . . Sand? Oh, sure. You mean round the chrysanthemums. Sure I will." He clucked his tongue. The beasts leaned luxuriously into their collars. The mongrel dog took his place between the back wheels. The wagon turned and crawled out the entrance road and back the way it had come, along the river.

Elisa stood in front of her wire fence watching the slow progress of the caravan. Her shoulders were straight, her head thrown back, her eyes half-closed, so that the scene came vaguely into them. Her lips moved silently, forming the words "Good-bye—good-bye." Then she whispered. "That's a bright direction. There's a glowing there." The sound of her whisper startled her. She shook herself free and looked about to see whether anyone had been listening. Only the dogs had heard. They lifted their heads toward her from their sleeping in the dust, and then stretched out their chins and settled asleep again. Elisa turned and ran hurriedly into the house.

In the kitchen she reached behind the stove and felt the water tank. It was full of hot water from the noonday cooking. In the bathroom she tore off her soiled clothes and flung them into the corner. And then she scrubbed herself with a little block of pumice, legs and thighs, loins and chest and arms, until her skin was scratched and red. When she had dried herself she stood in front of a mirror in her bedroom and looked at her body. She tightened her stomach and threw out her chest. She turned and looked over her shoulder at her back.

After a while she began to dress, slowly. She put on her newest underclothing and her nicest stockings and the dress which was the symbol of her prettiness. She worked carefully on her hair, pencilled her eyebrows and rouged her lips.

Before she was finished she heard the little thunder of hoofs and the shouts of Henry and his helper as they drove the red steers into the corral. She heard the gate bang shut and set herself for Henry's arrival.

His step sounded on the porch. He entered the house calling "Elisa, where are you?"

"In my room, dressing. I'm not ready. There's hot water for your bath. Hurry up. It's getting late."

When she heard him splashing in the tub, Elisa laid his dark suit on the bed, and shirt and socks and tie beside it. She stood his polished shoes on the floor beside the bed. Then she went to the porch and sat primly and stiffly down. She looked toward the river road where the willow-line was still yellow with frosted leaves so that under the high grey fog they seemed a thin band of sunshine. This was the only color in the grey afternoon. She sat unmoving for a long time. Her eyes blinked rarely.

Henry came banging out of the door, shoving his tie inside his vest as he came. Elisa stiffened and her face grew tight. Henry stopped short and looked at her. "Why—why, Elisa. You look so nice!"

"Nice? You think I look nice? What do you mean by 'nice'?"

Henry blundered on. "I don't know. I mean you look different, strong and happy."

"I am strong? Yes, strong. What do you mean 'strong'?"

He looked bewildered. "You're playing some kind of a game," he said helplessly. "It's a kind of a play. You look strong enough to break a calf over your knee, happy enough to eat it like a watermelon."

For a second she lost her rigidity. "Henry! Don't talk like that. You didn't know what you said." She grew complete again. "I'm strong," she boasted. "I never knew before how strong."

Henry looked down toward the tractor shed, and when he brought his eyes back to her, they were his own again. "I'll get out the car. You can put on your coat while I'm starting."

Elisa went into the house. She heard him drive to the gate and idle down his motor, and then she took a long time to put on her hat. She pulled it here and pressed it there. When Henry turned the motor off she slipped into her coat and went out.

The little roadster bounced along on the dirt road by the river, raising the birds and driving the rabbits into the brush. Two cranes flapped heavily over the willow-line and dropped into the river-bed.

Far ahead on the road Elisa saw a dark speck. She knew.

She tried not to look as they passed it, but her eyes would not obey. She whispered to herself sadly. "He might have thrown them off the road. That wouldn't have been much trouble, not very much. But he kept the pot," she explained. "He had to keep the pot. That's why he couldn't get them off the road."

The roadster turned a bend and she saw the caravan ahead. She swung full around toward her husband so she could not see the little covered wagon and the mismatched team as the car passed them.

In a moment they had left behind them the man who had not known or needed to know what she said, the bargainer. She did not look back.

To Henry, she said loudly, to be heard above the motor, "It will be good, to-night, a good dinner."

"Now you're changed again," Henry complained. He took one hand from the wheel and patted her knee. "I ought to take you in to dinner oftener. It would be good for both of us. We get so heavy out on the ranch."

"Henry," she asked, "could we have wine at dinner?"

"Sure. Say! That will be fine."

She was silent for a while; then she said, "Henry, at those prize fights do the men hurt each other very much?"

"Sometimes a little, not often. Why?"

"Well, I've read how they break noses, and blood runs down their chests. I've read how the fighting gloves get heavy and soggy with blood."

He looked round at her. "What's the matter, Elisa? I didn't know you read things like that." He brought the car to a stop, then turned to the right over the Salinas River bridge.

"Do any women ever go to the fights?" she asked.

"Oh, sure, some. What's the matter, Elisa? Do you want to go? I don't think you'd like it, but I'll take you if you really want to go."

She relaxed limply in the seat. "Oh, no. I don't want to go. I'm sure I don't." Her face was turned away from him. "It will be enough if we can have wine. It will be plenty." She turned up her coat collar so he could not see that she was crying weakly—like an old woman.

Suggestions for Discussion

1. What descriptive details prepare you for Elisa's emotional isolation?

2. The action, rising in emotional intensity to its climax, is developed in four scenes. Describe Elisa's feelings in each scene and attempt to account for them.

3. Discuss the possible symbolic functions of the scissors, the chrysanthemum shoots, the wine, and the fights. How are they related to the complication and resolution of the action?

4. How is the tinker's deception foreshadowed?

5. By what means are we made aware of the change in Elisa's image of herself? How adequately does the story account for Elisa's frustration? Explain the fluctuations in her appearance and mood. By what means are we made aware that her relationship with Henry is not satisfying?

Suggestions for Writing

1. Relate the story to the essay by Greer (p. 282).

2. Write a character study of Elisa.

3. Portray in narrative form a marital relationship in which there is a failure in communication.

Carson McCullers

The Sojourner

Carson McCullers (1917–1967), a Southern writer, was awarded Guggenheim Fellowships in 1942 and in 1946. Her published works include *The Heart Is a Lonely Hunter* (1940), *Reflections in a Golden Eye* (1941), *The Member of the Wedding* (1946), *The Ballad of the Sad Cafe* (1951), and *Clock Without Hands* (1961). After a rootless man relives and revisits his past, the experience enables him to acknowledge the waste of his years, the brevity of life, and his need to reorder his relationships with those close to him.

The twilight border between sleep and waking was a Roman one this morning: splashing fountains and arched, narrow streets, the golden lavish city of blossoms and age-soft stone. Sometimes in this semiconsciousness he sojourned again in Paris, or German war rubble, or a Swiss skiing and a snow hotel. Sometimes, also, in a fallow Georgia field at hunting dawn. Rome it was this morning in the yearless region of dreams.

John Ferris awoke in a room in a New York hotel. He had the feeling that something unpleasant was awaiting him—what it was, he did not know. The feeling, submerged by matinal necessities, lingered even after he had dressed and gone downstairs. It was a cloudless autumn day and the pale sunlight sliced between the pastel skyscrapers. Ferris went into the next-door drugstore and sat at the end booth next to the window glass that overlooked the sidewalk. He ordered an American breakfast with scrambled eggs and sausage.

Ferris had come from Paris to his father's funeral which had taken place the week before in his home town in Georgia. The shock of death had made him aware of youth already passed. His hair was receding and the veins in his now naked temples were pulsing and prominent and his body was spare except for an incipient belly bulge. Ferris had loved his father and the bond between them had once been extraordinarily close—but the years had somehow unraveled this filial devotion; the death, expected for a long time, had left him with an unforeseen dismay. He had stayed as long as possible to be near his mother and brothers at home. His plane for Paris was to leave the next morning.

Ferris pulled out his address book to verify a number. He turned the pages with growing attentiveness. Names and addresses from New York, the capitals of Europe, a few faint ones from his home state in the South. Faded, printed names, sprawled drunken ones. Betty Wills: a random love, married now. Charlie Williams: wounded in the Hürtgen Forest, unheard of since. Grand old Williams—did he live or die? Don Walker: a B.T.O. in television, getting rich. Henry Green: hit the skids after the war, in a sanitarium now, they say. Cozie Hall: he had heard that she was dead. Heedless, laughing Cozie—it was strange to think that she too, silly girl, could die. As Ferris closed the address book, he suffered a sense of hazard, transience, almost of fear.

It was then that his body jerked suddenly. He was staring out of the window when there, on the sidewalk, passing by, was his ex-wife. Elizabeth passed quite close to him, walking slowly. He could not understand the wild quiver of his heart, nor the following sense of recklessness and grace that lingered after she was gone.

Quickly Ferris paid his check and rushed out to the sidewalk. Elizabeth stood on the corner waiting to cross Fifth Avenue. He hurried toward her meaning to speak, but the lights changed and she crossed the street before he reached her. Ferris followed. On the other side he could easily have overtaken her, but he found himself lagging unaccountably. Her fair hair was plainly rolled, and as he watched her Ferris recalled that once his father had remarked that Elizabeth had a "beautiful carriage." She turned at the next corner and Ferris followed, although by now his intention to overtake her had disappeared. Ferris questioned the bodily disturbance that the sight of Elizabeth aroused in him, the dampness of his hands, the hard heartstrokes.

It was eight years since Ferris had last seen his ex-wife. He knew that long ago she had married again. And there were children. During recent years he had seldom thought of her. But at first, after the divorce, the loss had almost destroyed him. Then after the anodyne of time, he had loved again, and then again. Jeannine, she was now. Certainly his love for his ex-wife was long since past. So why the unhinged body, the shaken mind? He knew only that his clouded heart was oddly dissonant with the sunny, candid autumn day. Ferris wheeled suddenly and, walking with long strides, almost running, hurried back to the hotel.

Ferris poured himself a drink, although it was not yet eleven o'clock. He sprawled out in an armchair like a man exhausted, nursing his glass of bourbon and water. He had a full day ahead of him as he was leaving by plane the next morning for Paris. He checked over his obligations: take luggage to Air France, lunch with his boss, buy shoes and an overcoat. And something— wasn't there something else? Ferris finished his drink and opened the telephone directory.

His decision to call his ex-wife was impulsive. The number was under Bailey, the husband's name, and he called before he had much time for self-debate. He and Elizabeth had exchanged cards at Christmastime, and Ferris had sent a carving set when he received the announcement of her wedding. There was no reason *not* to call. But as he waited, listening to the ring at the other end, misgiving fretted him.

Elizabeth answered; her familiar voice was a fresh shock to him. Twice he had to repeat his name, but when he was identified, she sounded glad. He explained he was only in town for that day. They had a theater engagement, she said—but she wondered if he would come by for an early dinner. Ferris said he would be delighted.

As he went from one engagement to another, he was still bothered at odd moments by the feeling that something necessary was forgotten. Ferris bathed and changed in the late afternoon, often thinking about Jeannine: he would be with her the following night. "Jeannine," he would say, "I happened to run into my ex-wife when I was in New York. Had dinner with her. And her husband, of course. It was strange seeing her after all these years."

Elizabeth lived in the East Fifties, and as Ferris taxied uptown he glimpsed at intersections the lingering sunset, but by the time he reached his destination it was already autumn dark. The place was a building with a marquee and a doorman, and the apartment was on the seventh floor.

"Come in, Mr. Ferris."

Braced for Elizabeth or even the unimagined husband, Ferris was astonished by the freckled red-haired child; he had known of the children, but his mind had failed somehow to acknowledge them. Surprise made him step back awkwardly.

"This is our apartment," the child said politely. "Aren't you Mr. Ferris? I'm Billy. Come in."

In the living room beyond the hall, the husband provided another surprise; he too had not been acknowledged emotionally. Bailey was a lumbering red-haired man with a deliberate manner. He rose and extended a welcoming hand.

"I'm Bill Bailey. Glad to see you. Elizabeth will be in, in a minute. She's finishing dressing."

The last words struck a gliding series of vibrations, memories of the other years. Fair Elizabeth, rosy and naked before her bath. Half-dressed before the mirror of her dressing table, brushing her fine, chestnut hair. Sweet, casual intimacy, the soft-fleshed loveliness indisputably possessed. Ferris shrank from the unbidden memories and compelled himself to meet Bill Bailey's gaze.

"Billy, will you please bring that tray of drinks from the kitchen table?"

The child obeyed promptly, and when he was gone Ferris remarked conversationally, "Fine boy you have there."

"We think so."

Flat silence until the child returned with a tray of glasses and a cocktail shaker of Martinis. With the priming drinks they pumped up conversation: Russia, they spoke of, and the New York rain-making, and the apartment situation in Manhattan and Paris.

"Mr. Ferris is flying all the way across the ocean tomorrow," Bailey said to the little boy who was perched on the arm of his chair, quiet and well behaved. "I bet you would like to be a stowaway in his suitcase."

Billy pushed back his limp bangs. "I want to fly in an airplane and be a newspaperman like Mr. Ferris." He added with sudden assurance, "That's what I would like to do when I am big."

Bailey said, "I thought you wanted to be a doctor."

"I do!" said Billy. "I would like to be both. I want to be a atom-bomb scientist too."

Elizabeth came in carrying in her arms a baby girl.

"Oh, John!" she said. She settled the baby in the father's lap. "It's grand to see you. I'm awfully glad you could come."

The little girl sat demurely on Bailey's knees. She wore a pale pink crepe de Chine frock, smocked around the yoke with rose, and a matching silk hair ribbon tying back her pale soft curls. Her skin was summer tanned and her brown eyes flecked with gold and laughing. When she reached up and fingered her father's horn-rimmed glasses, he took them off and let her look through them a moment. "How's my old Candy?"

Elizabeth was very beautiful, more beautiful perhaps than he had ever realized. Her straight clean hair was shining. Her face was softer, glowing and serene. It was a madonna loveliness, dependent on the family ambiance.

"You've hardly changed at all," Elizabeth said, "but it has been a long time."

"Eight years." His hand touched his thinning hair self-consciously while further amenities were exchanged.

Ferris felt himself suddenly a spectator—an interloper among these Baileys. Why had he come? He suffered. His own life seemed so solitary, a fragile column supporting nothing amidst the wreckage of the years. He felt he could not bear much longer to stay in the family room.

He glanced at his watch. "You're going to the theater?"

"It's a shame," Elizabeth said, "but we've had this engagement for more than a month. But surely, John, you'll be staying home one of these days before long. You're not going to be an expatriate, are you?"

"Expatriate," Ferris repeated. "I don't much like the word."

"What's a better word?" she asked.

He thought for a moment. "Sojourner might do."

Ferris glanced again at his watch, and again Elizabeth apologized. "If only we had known ahead of time—"

"I just had this day in town. I came home unexpectedly. You see, Papa died last week."

"Papa Ferris is dead?"

"Yes, at Johns Hopkins. He had been sick there nearly a year. The funeral was down home in Georgia."

"Oh, I'm so sorry, John. Papa Ferris was always one of my favorite people."

The little boy moved from behind the chair so that he could look into his mother's face. He asked, "Who is dead?"

Ferris was oblivious to apprehension; he was thinking of his father's death. He saw again the outstretched body on the quilted silk within the coffin. The corpse flesh was bizarrely rouged and the familiar hands lay massive and joined above a spread of funeral roses. The memory closed and Ferris awakened to Elizabeth's calm voice.

"Mr. Ferris's father, Billy. A really grand person. Somebody you didn't know."

"But why did you call him *Papa* Ferris?"

Bailey and Elizabeth exchanged a trapped look. It was Bailey who answered the questioning child. "A long time ago," he said, "your mother and Mr. Ferris were once married. Before you were born—a long time ago."

"Mr. Ferris?"

The little boy stared at Ferris, amazed and unbelieving. And Ferris's eyes, as he returned the gaze, were somehow unbelieving too. Was it indeed true that at one time he had called this stranger, Elizabeth, Little Butterduck during nights of love, that they had lived together, shared perhaps a thousand days and nights and—finally—endured in the misery of sudden solitude the fiber by fiber (jealousy, alcohol and money quarrels) destruction of the fabric of married love?

Bailey said to the children, "It's somebody's suppertime. Come on now."

"But Daddy! Mama and Mr. Ferris—I—"

Billy's everlasting eyes—perplexed and with a glimmer of hostility—reminded Ferris of the gaze of another child. It was the young son of Jeannine—a boy of seven with a shadowed little face and knobby knees whom Ferris avoided and usually forgot.

"Quick march!" Bailey gently turned Billy toward the door. "Say good night now, son."

"Good night, Mr. Ferris." He added resentfully, "I thought I was staying up for the cake."

"You can come in afterward for the cake," Elizabeth said. "Run along now with Daddy for your supper."

Ferris and Elizabeth were alone. The weight of the situation descended on those first moments of silence. Ferris asked permission to pour himself another drink and Elizabeth set the cocktail shaker on the table at his side. He looked at the grand piano and noticed the music on the rack.

"Do you still play as beautifully as you used to?"

"I still enjoy it."

"Please play, Elizabeth."

Elizabeth rose immediately. Her readiness to perform when asked had always been one of her amiabilities; she never hung back, apologized. Now as she approached the piano there was the added readiness of relief.

She began with a Bach prelude and fugue. The prelude was as gaily iridescent as a prism in a morning room. The first voice of the fugue, an announcement pure and solitary, was repeated intermingling with a second voice, and again repeated within an elaborated frame, the multiple music, horizontal and serene, flowed with unhurried majesty. The principal melody was woven with two other voices, embellished with countless ingenuities—now dominant, again submerged, it had the sublimity of a single thing that does not fear surrender to the whole. Toward the end, the density of the material gathered for the last enriched insistence on the dominant first motif and with a chorded final statement the fugue ended. Ferris rested his head on the chair back and closed his eyes. In the following silence a clear, high voice came from the room down the hall.

"Daddy, how *could* Mama and Mr. Ferris—" A door was closed.

The piano began again—what was this music? Unplaced, familiar, the limpid melody had lain a long while dormant in his heart. Now it spoke to him of another time, another place—it was the music Elizabeth used to play. The delicate air summoned a wilderness of memory. Ferris was lost in the riot of past longings, conflicts, ambivalent desires. Strange that the music, catalyst for this tumultuous anarchy, was so serene and clear. The singing melody was broken off by the appearance of the maid.

"Miz Bailey, dinner is out on the table now."

Even after Ferris was seated at the table between his host and hostess, the unfinished music still overcast his mood. He was a little drunk.

"*L'improvisation de la vie humaine,*" he said. "There's nothing that makes you so aware of the improvisation of human existence as a song unfinished. Or an old address book."

"Address book?" repeated Bailey. Then he stopped, noncommittal and polite.

"You're still the same old boy, Johnny," Elizabeth said with a trace of the old tenderness.

It was a Southern dinner that evening, and the dishes were his old favorites. They had fried chicken and corn pudding and rich, glazed candied sweet potatoes. During the meal Elizabeth kept alive a conversation when the silences were overlong. And it came about that Ferris was led to speak of Jeannine.

"I first knew Jeannine last autumn—about this time of the year—in Italy. She's a singer and she had an engagement in Rome. I expect we will be married soon."

The words seemed so true, inevitable, that Ferris did not at first acknowledge to himself the lie. He and Jeannine had never in that year spoken of marriage. And indeed, she was still married—to a White Russian moneychanger in Paris from whom she had been separated for five years. But it was too late to correct the lie. Already Elizabeth was saying: "This really makes me glad to know. Congratulations, Johnny."

He tried to make amends with truth. "The Roman autumn is so beautiful. Balmy and blossoming." He added, "Jeannine has a little boy of six. A curious trilingual little fellow. We go to the Tuileries sometimes."

A lie again. He had taken the boy once to the gardens. The sallow foreign child in shorts that bared his spindly legs had sailed his boat in the concrete pond and ridden the pony. The child had wanted to go in to the puppet show. But there was not time, for Ferris had an engagement at the Scribe Hotel. He had promised they would go to the guignol another afternoon. Only once had he taken Valentin to the Tuileries.

There was a stir. The maid brought in a white-frosted cake with pink candles. The children entered in their night clothes. Ferris still did not understand.

"Happy birthday, John," Elizabeth said. "Blow out the candles."

Ferris recognized his birthday date. The candles blew out lingeringly and there was the smell of burning wax. Ferris was thirty-eight years old. The veins in his temples darkened and pulsed visibly.

"It's time you started for the theater."

Ferris thanked Elizabeth for the birthday dinner and said the appropriate good-byes. The whole family saw him to the door.

A high, thin moon shone above the jagged, dark skyscrapers. The streets were windy, cold. Ferris hurried to Third Avenue and hailed a cab. He gazed at the nocturnal city with the deliberate attentiveness of departure and perhaps farewell. He was alone. He longed for flight-time and the coming journey.

The next day he looked down on the city from the air, burnished in sunlight, toylike, precise. Then America was left behind and there was only the Atlantic and the distant European shore. The ocean was milky pale and placid

beneath the clouds. Ferris dozed most of the day. Toward dark he was thinking of Elizabeth and the visit of the previous evening. He thought of Elizabeth among her family with longing, gentle envy and inexplicable regret. He
sought the melody, the unfinished air, that had so moved him. The cadence,
some unrelated tones, were all that remained; the melody itself evaded him.
He had found instead the first voice of the fugue that Elizabeth had played—
it came to him, inverted mockingly and in a minor key. Suspended above the
ocean the anxieties of transience and solitude no longer troubled him and he
thought of his father's death with equanimity. During the dinner hour the
plane reached the shore of France.

At midnight Ferris was in a taxi crossing Paris. It was a clouded night and
mist wreathed the lights of the Place de la Concorde. The midnight bistros
gleamed on the wet pavements. As always after a transocean flight the change
of continents was too sudden. New York at morning, this midnight Paris.
Ferris glimpsed the disorder of his life: the succession of cities, of transitory
loves; and time, the sinister glissando of the years, time always.

"*Vite! Vite!*" he called in terror. "*Dépêchez-vous.*"

Valentin opened the door to him. The little boy wore pajamas and an outgrown red robe. His grey eyes were shadowed and, as Ferris passed into the
flat, they flickered momentarily.

"*J'attends Maman.*"

Jeannine was singing in a night club. She would not be home before another hour. Valentin returned to a drawing, squatting with his crayons over
the paper on the floor. Ferris looked down at the drawing—it was a banjo
player with notes and wavy lines inside a comicstrip balloon.

"We will go again to the Tuileries."

The child looked up and Ferris drew him closer to his knees. The melody,
the unfinished music that Elizabeth had played came to him suddenly. Unsought, the load of memory jettisoned—this time bringing only recognition
and sudden joy.

"Monsieur Jean," the child said, "did you see him?"

Confused, Ferris thought only of another child—the freckled, family-loved
boy. "See who, Valentin?"

"Your dead papa in Georgia." The child added, "Was he okay?"

Ferris spoke with rapid urgency: "We will go often to the Tuileries. Ride
the pony and we will go into the guignol. We will see the puppet show and
never be in a hurry any more."

"Monsieur Jean," Valentin said. "The guignol is now closed."

Again, the terror, the acknowledgment of wasted years and death. Valentin, responsive and confident, still nestled in his arms. His cheek touched the
soft cheek and felt the brush of the delicate eyelashes. With inner desperation
he pressed the child close—as though an emotion as protean as his love could
dominate the pulse of time.

Suggestions for Discussion

1. In *The Mortgaged Heart* McCullers suggests that the way by which we master
   loneliness is "to belong to something larger and more powerful than the weak,
   lonely self." How is this belief developed in her short story?

2. What do the descriptions in the opening four paragraphs tell you about Ferris? In particular, try to account for his emotional response to the names in his address book.

3. From the moment Ferris catches a glimpse of Elizabeth on the sidewalk outside the restaurant to his flight to Paris and his taxi ride across the city, the reader gains an understanding of Elizabeth and of their relationship. What details clarify your knowledge of Elizabeth? Of Ferris?

4. What is Ferris' response to his evening at the Baileys? How does the playing of the fugue and the second piece he couldn't identify affect Ferris?

5. Why does Ferris lie to Elizabeth about his relationship with Jeannine and Valentin?

6. How are you prepared for Ferris' new relationship with Valentin?

7. What is the meaning of the last sentence? Relate it to what has gone before in Ferris' life.

Suggestions for Writing

1. Discuss the McCullers quotation in question 1.

2. Write a narrative growing out of your observation or experience about the effects of divorce on the former mates and/or the children.

James Thurber
The Catbird Seat

James Thurber (1894–1961), American humorist and artist, began contributing in 1927 to *The New Yorker,* in which most of his work first appeared. His humorous essays and short stories are collected in such books as *The Owl in the Attic* (1931), *My Life and Hard Times* (1933), *The Thurber Carnival* (1945), *The Beast in Me* (1948), and *Lanterns and Lances* (1961). He also wrote the short story "The Secret Life of Walter Mitty," several fantasies for children, and with Elliot Nugent, a comedy called *The Male Animal* (1961). "The Catbird Seat" invites the reader to enter a world of fantasy in which the satiric commentary upon human frailty is subordinate to the spirit of fun and the ironic reversals of character and situation.

Mr. Martin bought the pack of Camels on Monday night in the most crowded cigar store on Broadway. It was theater time and seven or eight men were buying cigarettes. The clerk didn't even glance at Mr. Martin, who put the pack in his overcoat pocket and went out. If any of the staff at F & S had seen him buy the cigarettes, they would have been astonished, for it was generally known that Mr. Martin did not smoke, and never had. No one saw him.

It was just a week to the day since Mr. Martin had decided to rub out Mrs. Ulgine Barrows. The term "rub out" pleased him because it suggested nothing more than the correction of an error—in this case an error of Mr. Fitweiler. Mr. Martin had spent each night of the past week working out his plan and examining it. As he walked home now he went over it again. For the hundredth time he resented the element of imprecision, the margin of guesswork that entered into the business. The project as he had worked it out was casual and bold, the risks were considerable. Something might go wrong anywhere along the line. And therein lay the cunning of his scheme. No one would ever see in it the cautious, painstaking hand of Erwin Martin, head of the filing department at F & S of whom Mr. Fitweiler had once said, "Man is fallible but Martin isn't." No one would see his hand, that is, unless it were caught in the act.

Sitting in his apartment, drinking a glass of milk, Mr. Martin reviewed his case against Mrs. Ulgine Barrows, as he had every night for seven nights. He began at the beginning. Her quaking voice and braying laugh had first profaned the halls of F & S on March 7, 1941 (Mr. Martin had a head for dates). Old Roberts, the personnel chief, had introduced her as the newly appointed special adviser to the president of the firm, Mr. Fitweiler. The woman had appalled Mr. Martin instantly, but he hadn't shown it. He had given her his dry hand, a look of studious concentration, and a faint smile. "Well," she had said, looking at the papers on his desk, "are you lifting the oxcart out of the ditch?" As Mr. Martin recalled the moment, over his milk, he squirmed slightly. He must keep his mind on her crimes as a special adviser, not on her peccadillos as a personality. This he found difficult to do, in spite of entering an objection and sustaining it. The faults of the woman as a woman kept chattering on in his mind like an unruly witness. She had, for almost two years now, baited him. In the halls, in the elevator, even in his own office, into which she romped now and then like a circus horse, she was constantly shouting these silly questions at him. "Are you lifting the oxcart out of the ditch? Are you tearing up the pea patch? Are you hollering down the rain barrel? Are you scraping around the bottom of the pickle barrel? Are you sitting in the catbird seat?"

It was Joey Hart, one of Mr. Martin's two assistants, who had explained what the gibberish meant. "She must be a Dodger fan," he had said. "Red Barber announces the Dodger games over the radio and he uses those expressions—picked 'em up down South." Joey had gone on to explain one or two. "Tearing up the pea patch" meant going on a rampage; "sitting in the catbird seat" meant sitting pretty, like a batter with three balls and no strikes on him. Mr. Martin dismissed all this with an effort. It had been annoying, it had driven him near to distraction, but he was too solid a man to be moved to murder by anything so childish. It was fortunate, he reflected as he passed on to the important charges against Mrs. Barrows, that he had stood up under it so well. He had maintained always an outward appearance of polite tolerance. "Why, I even believe you like the woman," Miss Paird, his other assistant, had once said to him. He had simply smiled.

A gavel rapped in Mr. Martin's mind and the case was resumed. Mrs. Ulgine Barrows stood charged with willful, blatant, and persistent attempts to destroy the efficiency and system of F & S. It was competent, material, and relevant to review her advent and rise to power. Mr. Martin had got the story from Miss Paird, who seemed always able to find things out. According to her, Mrs. Barrows had met Mr. Fitweiler at a party, where she had rescued him from the embraces of a powerfully built drunken man who had mistaken the president of F & S for a famous retired Middle Western football coach. She had led him to a sofa and somehow worked upon him a monstrous magic. The aging gentleman had jumped to the conclusion there and then that this was a woman of singular attainments, equipped to bring out the best in him and the firm. A week later he had introduced her into F & S as his special adviser. On that day confusion got its foot in the door. After Miss Tyson, Mr. Brundage, and Mr. Bartlett had been fired and Mr. Munson had taken his hat and stalked out, mailing in his resignation later, old Roberts had been emboldened to speak to Mr. Fitweiler. He mentioned that Mr. Munson's department had been "a little disrupted" and hadn't they perhaps better resume the old system there? Mr. Fitweiler had said certainly not. He had the greatest faith in Mrs. Barrows' ideas. "They require a little seasoning, a little seasoning, is all," he had added. Mr. Roberts had given it up. Mr. Martin reviewed in detail all the changes wrought by Mrs. Barrows. She had begun chipping at the cornices of the firm's edifice and now she was swinging at the foundation with a pickaxe.

Mr. Martin came now, in his summing up, to the afternoon of Monday, November 2, 1942—just one week ago. On that day, at 3 P.M., Mrs. Barrows had bounced into his office. "Boo!" she had yelled. "Are you scraping around the bottom of the pickle barrel?" Mr. Martin had looked at her from under his green eyeshade, saying nothing. She had begun to wander about the office, taking it in with her great, popping eyes. "Do you really need *all* these filing cabinets?" she had demanded suddenly. Mr. Martin's heart had jumped. "Each of these files," he had said, keeping his voice even, "plays an indispensable part in the system of F & S." She had brayed at him, "Well, don't tear up the pea patch!" and gone to the door. From there she had bawled, "But you sure have got a lot of fine scrap in here!" Mr. Martin could no longer doubt that the finger was on his beloved department. Her pickaxe was on the upswing, poised for the first blow. It had not come yet; he had received no blue memo from the enchanted Mr. Fitweiler bearing nonsensical instructions deriving from the obscene woman. But there was no doubt in Mr. Martin's mind that one would be forthcoming. He must act quickly. Already a precious week had gone by. Mr. Martin stood up in his living room, still holding his milk glass. "Gentlemen of the jury," he said to himself, "I demand the death penalty for this horrible person."

The next day Mr. Martin followed his routine, as usual. He polished his glasses more often and once sharpened an already sharp pencil, but not even Miss Paird noticed. Only once did he catch sight of his victim; she swept past him in the hall with a patronizing "Hi!" At five-thirty he walked home, as usual, and had a glass of milk, as usual. He had never drunk anything stronger in his life—unless you could count ginger ale. The late Sam Schlosser, the S of F & S, had praised Mr. Martin at a staff meeting several years before for his temperate habits. "Our most efficient worker neither drinks nor smokes," he had said. "The results speak for themselves." Mr. Fitweiler had sat by, nodding approval.

Mr. Martin was still thinking about that red-letter day as he walked over to the Schrafft's on Fifth Avenue near Forty-sixth Street. He got there, as he always did, at eight o'clock. He finished his dinner and the financial page of the *Sun* at a quarter to nine, as he always did. It was his custom after dinner to take a walk. This time he walked down Fifth Avenue at a casual pace. His gloved hands felt moist and warm, his forehead cold. He transferred the Camels from his overcoat to a jacket pocket. He wondered, as he did so, if they did not represent an unnecessary note of strain. Mrs. Barrows smoked only Luckies. It was his idea to puff a few puffs on a Camel (after the rubbing-out), stub it out in the ashtray holding her lipstick-stained Luckies, and thus drag a small red herring across the trail. Perhaps it was not a good idea. It would take time. He might even choke, too loudly.

Mr. Martin had never seen the house on West Twelfth Street where Mrs. Barrows lived, but he had a clear enough picture of it. Fortunately, she had bragged to everybody about her ducky first-floor apartment in the perfectly darling three-story red-brick. There would be no doorman or other attendants; just the tenants of the second and third floors. As he walked along, Mr. Martin realized that he would get there before nine-thirty. He had considered walking north on Fifth Avenue from Schrafft's to a point from which it would take him until ten o'clock to reach the house. At that hour people were less likely to be coming in or going out. But the procedure would have made an awkward loop in the straight thread of his casualness, and he had abandoned it. It was impossible to figure when people would be entering or leaving the house, anyway. There was a great risk at any hour. If he ran into anybody, he would simply have to place the rubbing-out of Ulgine Barrows in the inactive file forever. The same thing would hold true if there were someone in her apartment. In that case he would just say that he had been passing by, recognized her charming house, and thought to drop in.

It was eighteen minutes after nine when Mr. Martin turned into Twelfth Street. A man passed him, and a man and a woman, talking. There was no one within fifty paces when he came to the house, halfway down the block. He was up the steps and in the small vestibule in no time, pressing the bell under the card that said "Mrs. Ulgine Barrows." When the clicking in the lock started he jumped forward against the door. He got inside fast, closing the door behind him. A bulb in a lantern hung from the hall ceiling on a chain seemed to give a monstrously bright light. There was nobody on the stair, which went up ahead of him along the left wall. A door opened down the hall in the wall on the right. He went toward it swiftly, on tiptoe.

"Well, for God's sake, look who's here!" bawled Mrs. Barrows, and her braying laugh rang out like the report of a shotgun. He rushed past her like a football tackle, bumping her. "Hey, quit shoving!" she said, closing the door behind them. They were in her living room, which seemed to Mr. Martin to be lighted by a hundred lamps. "What's after you?" she said. "You're as jumpy as a goat." He found he was unable to speak. His heart was wheezing in his throat. "I—yes," he finally brought out. She was jabbering and laughing as she started to help him off with his coat. "No, no," he said. "I'll put it here." He took it off and put it on a chair near the door. "Your hat and gloves, too," she said. "You're in a lady's house." He put his hat on top of the coat.

Mrs. Barrows seemed larger than he had thought. He kept his gloves on. "I was passing by," he said. "I recognized—is there anyone here?" She laughed louder than ever. "No," she said, "we're all alone. You're as white as a sheet, you funny man. Whatever *has* come over you? I'll mix you a toddy." She started toward a door across the room. "Scotch-and-soda be all right? But say, you don't drink, do you?" She turned and gave him her amused look. Mr. Martin pulled himself together. "Scotch-and-soda will be all right," he heard himself say. He could hear her laughing in the kitchen.

Mr. Martin looked quickly around the living room for the weapon. He had counted on finding one there. There were andirons and a poker and something in a corner that looked like an Indian club. None of them would do. It couldn't be that way. He began to pace around. He came to a desk. On it lay a metal paper knife with an ornate handle. Would it be sharp enough? He reached for it and knocked over a small brass jar. Stamps spilled out of it and it fell to the floor with a clatter. "Hey," Mrs. Barrows yelled from the kitchen, "are you tearing up the pea patch?" Mr. Martin gave a strange laugh. Picking up the knife, he tried its point against his left wrist. It was blunt. It wouldn't do.

When Mrs. Barrows reappeared, carrying two highballs, Mr. Martin, standing there with his gloves on, became acutely conscious of the fantasy he had wrought. Cigarettes in his pocket, a drink prepared for him—it was all too grossly improbable. It was more than that; it was impossible. Somewhere in the back of his mind a vague idea stirred, sprouted. "For heaven's sake, take off those gloves," said Mrs. Barrows. "I always wear them in the house," said Mr. Martin. The idea began to bloom, strange and wonderful. She put the glasses on a coffee table in front of a sofa and sat on the sofa. "Come over here, you odd little man," she said. Mr. Martin went over and sat beside her. It was difficult getting a cigarette out of the pack of Camels, but he managed it. She held a match for him, laughing. "Well," she said, handing him his drink, "this is perfectly marvelous. You with a drink and a cigarette."

Mr. Martin puffed, not too awkwardly, and took of gulp of the highball. "I drink and smoke all the time," he said. He clinked his glass against hers. "Here's nuts to that old windbag, Fitweiler," he said, and gulped again. The stuff tasted awful, but he made no grimace. "Really, Mr. Martin," she said, her voice and posture changing, "you are insulting our employer." Mrs. Barrows was now all special adviser to the president. "I am preparing a bomb," said Mr. Martin, "which will blow the old goat higher than hell." He had only had a little of the drink, which was not strong. It couldn't be that. "Do you take dope or something?" Mrs. Barrows asked coldly. "Heroin," said Mr. Martin. "I'll be coked to the gills when I bump the old buzzard off." "Mr. Martin!" she shouted, getting to her feet. "That will be all of that. You must go at once." Mr. Martin took another swallow of his drink. He tapped his cigarette out in the ashtray and put the pack of Camels on the coffee table. Then he got up. She stood glaring at him. He walked over and put on his hat and coat. "Not a word about this," he said, and laid an index finger against his lips. All Mrs. Barrows could bring out was "Really!" Mr. Martin put his hand on the doorknob. "I'm sitting in the catbird seat," he said. He stuck his tongue out at her and left. Nobody saw him go.

Mr. Martin got to his apartment, walking, well before eleven. No one saw him go in. He had two glasses of milk after brushing his teeth, and he felt elated. It wasn't tipsiness, because he hadn't been tipsy. Anyway, the walk had worn off all effects of the whiskey. He got in bed and read a magazine for a while. He was asleep before midnight.

Mr. Martin got to the office at eight-thirty the next morning, as usual. At a quarter to nine, Ulgine Barrows, who had never before arrived at work before ten, swept into his office. "I'm reporting to Mr. Fitweiler now!" she shouted. "If he turns you over to the police, it's no more than you deserve!" Mr. Martin gave her a look of shocked surprise. "I beg your pardon?" he said. Mrs. Barrows snorted and bounced out of the room, leaving Miss Paird and Joey Hart staring after her. "What's the matter with that old devil now?" asked Miss Paird. "I have no idea," said Mr. Martin, resuming his work. The other two looked at him and then at each other. Miss Paird got up and went out. She walked slowly past the closed door of Mr. Fitweiler's office. Mrs. Barrows was yelling inside, but she was not braying. Miss Paird could not hear what the woman was saying. She went back to her desk.

Forty-five minutes later, Mrs. Barrows left the president's office and went into her own, shutting the door. It wasn't until half an hour later that Mr. Fitweiler sent for Mr. Martin. The head of the filing department, neat, quiet, attentive, stood in front of the old man's desk. Mr. Fitweiler was pale and nervous. He took his glasses off and twiddled them. He made a small, bruffing sound in his throat. "Martin," he said, "you have been with us more than twenty years." "Twenty-two, sir," said Mr. Martin. "In that time," pursued the president, "your work and your—uh—manner have been exemplary." "I trust so, sir," said Mr. Martin. "I have understood, Martin," said Mr. Fitweiler, "that you have never taken a drink or smoked." "That is correct, sir," said Mr. Martin. "Ah, yes." Mr. Fitweiler polished his glasses. "You may describe what you did after leaving the office yesterday, Martin," he said. Mr. Martin allowed less than a second for his bewildered pause. "Certainly, sir," he said. "I walked home. Then I went to Schrafft's for dinner. Afterward I walked home again. I went to bed early, sir, and read a magazine for a while. I was asleep before eleven." "Ah, yes," said Mr. Fitweiler again. He was silent for a moment, searching for the proper words to say to the head of the filing department. "Mrs. Barrows," he said finally, "Mrs. Barrows has worked hard, Martin, very hard. It grieves me to report that she has suffered a severe breakdown. It has taken the form of a persecution complex accompanied by distressing hallucinations." "I am very sorry, sir," said Mr. Martin. "Mrs. Barrows is under the delusion," continued Mr. Fitweiler, "that you visited her last evening and behaved yourself in an—uh—unseemly manner." He raised his hand to silence Mr. Martin's little pained outcry. "It is the nature of these psychological diseases," Mr. Fitweiler said, "to fix upon the least likely and most innocent party as the—uh—source of persecution. These matters are not for the lay mind to grasp, Martin. I've just had my psychiatrist, Dr. Fitch, on the phone. He would not, of course, commit himself, but he made enough generalizations to substantiate my suspicions. I suggested to Mrs. Barrows, when she had completed her—uh—story to me this morning, that she visit Dr. Fitch, for I suspected a condition at once. She flew, I regret to say, into a rage, and demanded—uh—requested that I call you on the carpet. You may not know, Martin, but Mrs. Barrows had planned a reorganization of your department—subject to my approval, of course, subject to my approval. This brought you, rather than anyone else, to her mind—

but again that is a phenomenon for Dr. Fitch and not for us. So, Martin, I am afraid Mrs. Barrows' usefulness here is at an end." "I am dreadfully sorry, sir," said Mr. Martin.

It was at this point that the door to the office blew open with the suddenness of a gas-main explosion and Mrs. Barrows catapulted through it. "Is the little rat denying it?" she screamed. "He can't get away with that!" Mr. Martin got up and moved discreetly to a point beside Mr. Fitweiler's chair. "You drank and smoked at my apartment," she bawled at Mr. Martin, "and you know it! You called Mr. Fitweiler an old windbag and said you were going to blow him up when you got coked to the gills on your heroin!" She stopped yelling to catch her breath and a new glint came into her popping eyes. "If you weren't such a drab, ordinary little man," she said, "I'd think you'd planned it all. Sticking your tongue out, saying you were sitting in the catbird seat, because you thought no one would believe me when I told it! My God, it's really too perfect!" She brayed loudly and hysterically, and the fury was on her again. She glared at Mr. Fitweiler. "Can't you see how he has tricked us, you old fool? Can't you see his little game?" But Mr. Fitweiler had been surreptitiously pressing all the buttons under the top of his desk and employees of F & S began pouring into the room. "Stockton," said Mr. Fitweiler, "you and Fishbein will take Mrs. Barrows to her home. Mrs. Powell, you will go with them." Stockton, who had played a little football in high school, blocked Mrs. Barrows as she made for Mr. Martin. It took him and Fishbein together to force her out of the door into the hall, crowded with stenographers and office boys. She was still screaming imprecations at Mr. Martin, tangled and contradictory imprecations. The hubbub finally died out down the corridor.

"I regret that this has happened," said Mr. Fitweiler. "I shall ask you to dismiss it from your mind, Martin." "Yes sir," said Mr. Martin, anticipating his chief's "That will be all" by moving to the door. "I will dismiss it." He went out and shut the door, and his step was light and quick in the hall. When he entered his department he had slowed down to his customary gait, and he walked quietly across the room to the W20 file, wearing a look of studious concentration.

Suggestions for Discussion

1. How does the point of view contribute to the comic effects? How are contrast and suspense used to develop the action? How does the simulation of a court case contribute to suspense and plot development? At what point can the reader predict the resolution of the action? How is tension maintained until the very end?

2. Explain the ironic reversals in character and situation. How are they prepared for? To what extent are Mr. Martin and Mrs. Barrows types? Caricatures? How are they individualized?

3. Bergson has said that a character is "generally comic in proportion to his ignorance of himself. The comic person is unconscious." Apply this theory to the two principal characters.

4. Why was Mrs. Barrows particularly repugnant to Mr. Martin? Cite examples from the mock trial to support your answer.

5. What is ironical in the final choice of weapon? What finally defeats Mrs. Barrows? Why does he call her obscene?

6. Study the diction in the retrospective exposition of the advent of Mrs. Barrows and in the scene in her apartment. What words are repeated? How do the verbs in the description of Mrs. Barrows and her own use of clichés contribute to characterization and tone? How else is repetition used to achieve comic effects? How do legal and psychiatric terminology and animal imagery contribute to tone?

7. Although the primary tone is one of burlesque, how does seriousness impinge upon the comic elements?

Suggestions for Writing

1. Create a portrait of an obsessive–compulsive character.

2. Invent a fantasy in which you are finally situated in the catbird seat.

Raymond Carver

What We Talk About When We Talk About Love

Raymond Carver (b. 1939) was born in Clatskanie, Oregon, and still lives in the Pacific Northwest. He has received a number of honors including a Guggenheim Fellowship, National Endowment for the Arts grants, and the Mildred and Harold Strauss Living Award. Three collections of his short stories have been published: *Will You Please Be Quiet, Please* (1976), nominated for the National Book Award; *What We Talk About When We Talk About Love* (1981); and *Cathedral* (1984), nominated for the National Book Critics Circle Award. Although two couples are seated around the kitchen table drinking gin, the primary focus is upon Mel and to a lesser degree his second wife, Terri. In Mel's reminiscences about his personal and professional life and in his behavior he expresses differing and perhaps contradictory views of love.

My friend Mel McGinnis was talking. Mel McGinnis is a cardiologist, and sometimes that gives him the right.

The four of us were sitting around his kitchen table drinking gin. Sunlight filled the kitchen from the big window behind the sink. There were Mel and me and his second wife, Teresa—Terri, we called her—and my wife, Laura. We lived in Albuquerque then. But we were all from somewhere else.

There was an ice bucket on the table. The gin and the tonic water kept going around, and we somehow got on the subject of love. Mel thought real love was nothing less than spiritual love. He said he'd spent five years in a seminary before quitting to go to medical school. He said he still looked back on those years in the seminary as the most important years in his life.

Terri said the man she lived with before she lived with Mel loved her so much he tried to kill her. Then Terri said, "He beat me up one night. He dragged me around the living room by my ankles. He kept saying, 'I love you, I love you, you bitch.' He went on dragging me around the living room. My head kept knocking on things." Terri looked around the table. "What do you do with love like that?"

She was a bone-thin woman with a pretty face, dark eyes, and brown hair that hung down her back. She liked necklaces made of turquoise, and long pendant earrings.

"My God, don't be silly. That's not love, and you know it," Mel said. "I don't know what you'd call it, but I sure know you wouldn't call it love."

"Say what you want to, but I know it was," Terri said. "It may sound crazy to you, but it's true just the same. People are different, Mel. Sure, sometimes he may have acted crazy. Okay. But he loved me. In his own way maybe, but he loved me. There was love there, Mel. Don't say there wasn't."

Mel let out his breath. He held his glass and turned to Laura and me. "The man threatened to kill me," Mel said. He finished his drink and reached for the gin bottle. "Terri's a romantic. Terri's of the kick-me-so-I'll-know-you-love-me school. Terri, hon, don't look that way." Mel reached across the table and touched Terri's cheek with his fingers. He grinned at her.

"Now he wants to make up," Terri said.

"Make up what?" Mel said. "What is there to make up? I know what I know. That's all."

"How'd we get started on this subject, anyway?" Terri said. She raised her glass and drank from it. "Mel always has love on his mind," she said. "Don't you, honey?" She smiled, and I thought that was the last of it.

"I just wouldn't call Ed's behavior love. That's all I'm saying, honey," Mel said. "What about you guys?" Mel said to Laura and me. "Does that sound like love to you?"

"I'm the wrong person to ask," I said. "I didn't even know the man. I've only heard his name mentioned in passing. I wouldn't know. You'd have to know the particulars. But I think what you're saying is that love is an absolute."

Mel said. "The kind of love I'm talking about is. The kind of love I'm talking about, you don't try to kill people."

Laura said, "I don't know anything about Ed, or anything about the situation. But who can judge anyone else's situation?"

I touched the back of Laura's hand. She gave me a quick smile. I picked up Laura's hand. It was warm, the nails polished, perfectly manicured. I encircled the broad wrist with my fingers, and I held her.

"When I left, he drank rat poison," Terri said. She clasped her arms with her hands. "They took him to the hospital in Santa Fe. That's where we lived then, about ten miles out. They saved his life. But his gums went crazy from it. I mean they pulled away from his teeth. After that, his teeth stood out like fangs. My God," Terri said. She waited a minute, then let go of her arms and picked up her glass.

"What people won't do!" Laura said.

"He's out of the action now," Mel said. "He's dead."

Mel handed me the saucer of limes. I took a section, squeezed it over my drink, and stirred the ice cubes with my finger.

"It gets worse," Terri said. "He shot himself in the mouth. But he bungled that too. Poor Ed," she said. Terri shook her head.

"Poor Ed nothing," Mel said. "He was dangerous."

Mel was forty-five years old. He was tall and rangy with curly soft hair. His face and arms were brown from the tennis he played. When he was sober, his gestures, all his movements, were precise, very careful.

"He did love me though, Mel. Grant me that," Terri said. "That's all I'm asking. He didn't love me the way you love me. I'm not saying that. But he loved me. You can grant me that, can't you?"

"What do you mean, he bungled it?" I said.

Laura leaned forward with her glass. She put her elbows on the table and held her glass in both hands. She glanced from Mel to Terri and waited with a look of bewilderment on her open face, as if amazed that such things happened to people you were friendly with.

"How'd he bungle it when he killed himself?" I said.

"I'll tell you what happened," Mel said. "He took this twenty-two pistol he'd bought to threaten Terri and me with. Oh, I'm serious, the man was always threatening. You should have seen the way we lived in those days. Like fugitives. I even bought a gun myself. Can you believe it? A guy like me? But I did. I bought one for self-defense and carried it in the glove compartment. Sometimes I'd have to leave the apartment in the middle of the night. To go to the hospital, you know? Terri and I weren't married then, and my first wife had the house and kids, the dog, everything, and Terri and I were living in this apartment here. Sometimes, as I say, I'd get a call in the middle of the night and have to go in to the hospital at two or three in the morning. It'd be dark out there in the parking lot, and I'd break into a sweat before I could even get to my car. I never knew if he was going to come up out of the shrubbery or from behind a car and start shooting. I mean, the man was crazy. He was capable of wiring a bomb, anything. He used to call my service at all hours and say he needed to talk to the doctor, and when I'd return the call, he'd say, "Son of a bitch, your days are numbered.' Little things like that. It was scary, I'm telling you."

"I still feel sorry for him," Terri said.

"It sounds like a nightmare," Laura said. "But what exactly happened after he shot himself?"

Laura is a legal secretary. We'd met in a professional capacity. Before we knew it, it was a courtship. She's thirty-five, three years younger than I am. In addition to being in love, we like each other and enjoy one another's company. She's easy to be with.

"What happened?" Laura said.

Mel said, "He shot himself in the mouth in his room. Someone heard the shot and told the manager. They came in with a passkey, saw what had happened, and called an ambulance. I happened to be there when they brought him in, alive but past recall. The man lived for three days. His head swelled up to twice the size of a normal head. I'd never seen anything like it, and I hope I never do again. Terri wanted to go in and sit with him when she found out about it. We had a fight over it. I didn't think she should see him like that. I didn't think she should see him, and I still don't."

"Who won the fight?" Laura said.

"I was in the room with him when he died," Terri said. "He never came up out of it. But I sat with him. He didn't have anyone else."

"He was dangerous," Mel said. "If you call that love, you can have it."

"It was love," Terri said. "Sure, it's abnormal in most people's eyes. But he was willing to die for it. He did die for it."

"I sure as hell wouldn't call it love," Mel said. "I mean, no one knows what he did it for. I've seen a lot of suicides, and I couldn't say anyone ever knew what they did it for."

Mel put his hands behind his neck and tilted his chair back. "I'm not interested in that kind of love," he said. "If that's love, you can have it."

Terri said, "We were afraid. Mel even made a will out and wrote to his brother in California who used to be a Green Beret. Mel told him who to look for if something happened to him."

Terri drank from her glass. She said, "But Mel's right—we lived like fugitives. We were afraid. Mel was, weren't you, honey? I even called the police at one point, but they were no help. They said they couldn't do anything until Ed actually did something. Isn't that a laugh?" Terri said.

She poured the last of the gin into her glass and waggled the bottle. Mel got up from the table and went to the cupboard. He took down another bottle.

"Well, Nick and I know what love is," Laura said. "For us, I mean," Laura said. She bumped my knee with her knee. "You're supposed to say something now," Laura said, and turned her smile on me.

For an answer, I took Laura's hand and raised it to my lips. I made a big production out of kissing her hand. Everyone was amused.

"We're lucky," I said.

"You guys," Terri said. "Stop that now. You're making me sick. You're still on the honeymoon, for God's sake. You're still gaga, for crying out loud. Just wait. How long have you been together now? How long has it been? A year? Longer than a year?"

"Going on a year and a half," Laura said, flushed and smiling.

"Oh, now," Terri said. "Wait awhile."

She held her drink and gazed at Laura.

"I'm only kidding," Terri said.

Mel opened the gin and went around the table with the bottle.

"Here, you guys," he said. "Let's have a toast. I want to propose a toast. A toast to love. To true love," Mel said.

We touched glasses.

"To love," we said.

Outside in the backyard, one of the dogs began to bark. The leaves of the aspen that leaned past the window ticked against the glass. The afternoon sun was like a presence in this room, the spacious light of ease and generosity. We could have been anywhere, somewhere enchanted. We raised our glasses again and grinned at each other like children who had agreed on something forbidden.

"I'll tell you what real love is," Mel said. "I mean, I'll give you a good example. And then you can draw your own conclusions." He poured more gin into his glass. He added an ice cube and a sliver of lime. We waited and sipped our drinks. Laura and I touched knees again. I put a hand on her warm thigh and left it there.

"What do any of us really know about love?" Mel said. "It seems to me we're just beginners at love. We say we love each other and we do, I don't doubt it. I love Terri and Terri loves me, and you guys love each other too. You know the kind of love I'm talking about now. Physical love, that impulse that drives you to someone special, as well as love of the other person's being, his or her essence, as it were. Carnal love and, well, call it sentimental love, the day-to-day caring about the other person. But sometimes I have a hard time accounting for the fact that I must have loved my first wife too. But I did, I know I did. So I suppose I am like Terri in that regard. Terri and Ed." He thought about it and then he went on. "There was a time when I thought I loved my first wife more than life itself. But now I hate her guts. I do. How do you explain that? What happened to that love? What happened to it, is what I'd like to know. I wish someone could tell me. Then there's Ed. Okay, we're back to Ed. He loves Terri so much he tries to kill her and he winds up killing himself." Mel stopped talking and swallowed from his glass. "You guys have been together eighteen months and you love each other. It shows all over you. You glow with it. But you both loved other people before you met each other. You've both been married before, just like us. And you probably loved other people before that too, even. Terri and I have been together five years, been married for four. And the terrible thing, the terrible thing is, but the good thing too, the saving grace, you might say, is that if something happened to one of us—excuse me for saying this—but if something happened to one of us tomorrow, I think the other one, the other person, would grieve for a while, you know, but then the surviving party would go out and love again, have someone else soon enough. All this, all of this love we're talking about, it would just be a memory. Maybe not even a memory. Am I wrong? Am I way off base? Because I want you to set me straight if you think I'm wrong. I want to know. I mean, I don't know anything, and I'm the first one to admit it."

"Mel, for God's sake," Terri said. She reached out and took hold of his wrist. "Are you getting drunk? Honey? Are you drunk?"

"Honey, I'm just talking," Mel said. "All right? I don't have to be drunk to say what I think. I mean, we're all just talking, right?" Mel said. He fixed his eyes on her.

"Sweetie, I'm not criticizing," Terri said.

She picked up her glass.

"I'm not on call today," Mel said. "Let me remind you of that. I am not on call," he said.

"Mel, we love you," Laura said.

Mel looked at Laura. He looked at her as if he could not place her, as if she was not the woman she was.

"Love you too, Laura," Mel said. "And you, Nick, love you too. You know something?" Mel said. "You guys are our pals," Mel said.

He picked up his glass.

Mel said, "I was going to tell you about something. I mean, I was going to prove a point. You see, this happened a few months ago, but it's still going on right now, and it ought to make us feel ashamed when we talk like we know what we're talking about when we talk about love."

"Come on now," Terri said. "Don't talk like you're drunk if you're not drunk."

"Just shut up for once in your life," Mel said very quietly. "Will you do me a favor and do that for a minute? So as I was saying, there's this old couple who had this car wreck out on the interstate. A kid hit them and they were all torn to shit and nobody was giving them much chance to pull through."

Terri looked at us and then back at Mel. She seemed anxious, or maybe that's too strong a word.

Mel was handing the bottle around the table.

"I was on call that night," Mel said. "It was May or maybe it was June. Terri and I had just sat down to dinner when the hospital called. There'd been this thing out on the interstate. Drunk kid, teenager, plowed his dad's pickup into this camper with this old couple in it. They were up in their mid-seventies, that couple. The kid—eighteen, nineteen, something—he was DOA. Taken the steering wheel through his sternum. The old couple, they were alive, you understand. I mean, just barely. But they had everything. Multiple fractures, internal injuries, hemorrhaging, contusions, lacerations, the works, and they each of them had themselves concussions. They were in a bad way, believe me. And, of course, their age was two strikes against them. I'd say she was worse off than he was. Ruptured spleen along with everything else. Both kneecaps broken. But they'd been wearing their seatbelts and, God knows, that's what saved them for the time being."

"Folks, this is an advertisement for the National Safety Council," Terri said. "This is your spokesman, Dr. Melvin R. McGinnis, talking." Terri laughed. "Mel," she said, "sometimes you're just too much. But I love you, hon," she said.

"Honey, I love you," Mel said.

He leaned across the table. Terri met him halfway. They kissed.

"Terri's right," Mel said as he settled himself again. "Get those seatbelts on. But seriously, they were in some shape, those oldsters. By the time I got down there, the kid was dead, as I said. He was off in a corner, laid out on a gurney. I took one look at the old couple and told the ER nurse to get me a neurologist and an orthopedic man and a couple of surgeons down there right away."

He drank from his glass. "I'll try to keep this short," he said. "So we took the two of them up to the OR and worked like fuck on them most of the night. They had these incredible reserves, those two. You see that once in a while. So we did everything that could be done, and toward morning we're giving them a fifty–fifty chance, maybe less than that for her. So here they are, still alive the next morning. So, okay, we move them into the ICU, which is where they both kept plugging away at it for two weeks, hitting it better and better on all the scopes. So we transfer them out to their own room."

Mel stopped talking. "Here," he said, "let's drink this cheapo gin the hell up. Then we're going to dinner, right? Terri and I know a new place. That's where we'll go, to this new place we know about. But we're not going until we finish up this cut-rate, lousy gin."

Terri said, "We haven't actually eaten there yet. But it looks good. From the outside, you know."

"I like food," Mel said. "If I had it to do all over again, I'd be a chef, you know? Right, Terri?" Mel said.

He laughed. He fingered the ice in his glass.

"Terri knows," he said. "Terri can tell you. But let me say this. If I could come back again in a different life, a different time and all, you know what? I'd like to come back as a knight. You were pretty safe wearing all that armor. It was all right being a knight until gunpowder and muskets and pistols came along."

"Mel would like to ride a horse and carry a lance," Terri said.

"Carry a woman's scarf with you everywhere," Laura said.

"Or just a woman," Mel said.

"Shame on you," Laura said.

Terri said, "Suppose you came back as a serf. The serfs didn't have it so good in those days," Terri said.

"The serfs never had it good," Mel said. "But I guess even the knights were vessels to someone. Isn't that the way it worked? But then everyone is always a vessel to someone. Isn't that right? Terri? But what I liked about knights, besides their ladies, was that they had that suit of armor, you know, and they couldn't get hurt very easy. No cars in those days, you know? No drunk teenagers to tear into your ass."

"Vassals," Terri said.

"What?" Mel said.

"Vassals," Terri said. "They were called vassals, not vessels."

"Vassals, vessels," Mel said, "what the fuck's the difference? You knew what I meant anyway. All right," Mel said. "So I'm not educated. I learned my stuff. I'm a heart surgeon, sure, but I'm just a mechanic. I go in and I fuck around and I fix things. Shit," Mel said.

"Modesty doesn't become you," Terri said.

"He's just a humble sawbones," I said. "But sometimes they suffocated in all that armor, Mel. They'd even have heart attacks if it got too hot and they were too tired and worn out. I read somewhere that they'd fall off their horses and not be able to get up because they were too tired to stand with all that armor on them. They got trampled by their own horses sometimes."

"That's terrible," Mel said. "That's a terrible thing, Nicky. I guess they'd just lay there and wait until somebody came along and made a shish kebab out of them."

"Some other vessel," Terri said.

"That's right," Mel said. "Some vassal would come along and spear the bastard in the name of love. Or whatever the fuck it was they fought over in those days."

"Same things we fight over these days," Terri said.

Laura said, "Nothing's changed."

The color was still high in Laura's cheeks. Her eyes were bright. She brought her glass to her lips.

Mel poured himself another drink. He looked at the label closely as if studying a long row of numbers. Then he slowly put the bottle down on the table and slowly reached for the tonic water.

"What about the old couple?" Laura said. "You didn't finish that story you started."

Laura was having a hard time lighting her cigarette. Her matches kept going out.

The sunshine inside the room was different now, changing, getting thinner. But the leaves outside the window were still shimmering, and I stared at the pattern they made on the panes and on the Formica counter. They weren't the same patterns, of course.

"What about the old couple?" I said.

"Older but wiser," Terri said.

Mel stared at her.

Terri said, "Go on with your story, hon. I was only kidding. Then what happened?"

"Terri, sometimes," Mel said.

"Please, Mel," Terri said. "Don't always be so serious, sweetie. Can't you take a joke?"

"Where's the joke?" Mel said.

He held his glass and gazed steadily at his wife.

"What happened?" Laura said.

Mel fastened his eyes on Laura. He said, "Laura, if I didn't have Terri and if I didn't love her so much, and if Nick wasn't my best friend, I'd fall in love with you. I'd carry you off, honey," he said.

"Tell your story," Terri said. "Then we'll go to that new place, okay?"

"Okay," Mel said. "Where was I?" he said. He stared at the table and then he began again.

"I dropped in to see each of them every day, sometimes twice a day if I was up doing other calls anyway. Casts and bandages, head to foot, the both of them. You know, you've seen it in the movies. That's just the way they looked, just like in the movies. Little eye-holes and nose-holes and mouth-holes. And she had to have her legs slung up on top of it. Well, the husband was very depressed for the longest while. Even after he found out that his wife was going to pull through, he was still very depressed. Not about the accident, though. I mean, the accident was one thing, but it wasn't everything. I'd get up to his mouth-hole, you know, and he'd say no, it wasn't the accident exactly but it was because he couldn't see her through his eye-holes. He said that was what was making him feel so bad. Can you imagine? I'm telling you, the man's heart was breaking because he couldn't turn his goddamn head and *see* his goddamn wife."

Mel looked around the table and shook his head at what he was going to say.

"I mean, it was killing the old fart just because he couldn't *look* at the fucking woman."

We all looked at Mel.

"Do you see what I'm saying?" he said.

Maybe we were a little drunk by then. I know it was hard keeping things in focus. The light was draining out of the room, going back through the window where it had come from. Yet nobody made a move to get up from the table to turn on the overhead light.

"Listen," Mel said. "Let's finish this fucking gin. There's about enough left here for one shooter all around. Then let's go eat. Let's go to the new place."

"He's depressed," Terri said. "Mel, why don't you take a pill?"

Mel shook his head. "I've taken everything there is."

"We all need a pill now and then," I said.

"Some people are born needing them," Terri said.

She was using her finger to rub at something on the table. Then she stopped rubbing.

"I think I want to call my kids," Mel said. "Is that all right with everybody? I'll call my kids," he said.

Terri said, "What if Marjorie answers the phone? You guys, you've heard us on the subject of Marjorie? Honey, you know you don't want to talk to Marjorie. It'll make you feel even worse."

"I don't want to talk to Marjorie," Mel said. "But I want to talk to my kids."

"There isn't a day goes by that Mel doesn't say he wishes she'd get married again. Or else die," Terri said. "For one thing," Terri said, "she's bankrupting us. Mel says it's just to spite him that she won't get married again. She has a boyfriend who lives with her and the kids, so Mel is supporting the boyfriend too."

"She's allergic to bees," Mel said. "If I'm not praying she'll get married again, I'm praying she'll get herself stung to death by a swarm of fucking bees."

"Shame on you," Laura said.

"Bzzzzzzz," Mel said, turning his fingers into bees and buzzing them at Terri's throat. Then he let his hands drop all the way to his sides.

"She's vicious," Mel said. "Sometimes I think I'll go up there dressed like a beekeeper. You know, that hat that's like a helmet with the plate that comes down over your face, the big gloves, and the padded coat? I'll knock on the door and let loose a hive of bees in the house. But first I'd make sure the kids were out, of course."

He crossed one leg over the other. It seemed to take him a lot of time to do it. Then he put both feet on the floor and leaned forward, elbows on the table, his chin cupped in his hands.

"Maybe I won't call the kids, after all. Maybe it isn't such a hot idea. Maybe we'll just go eat. How does that sound?"

"Sounds fine to me," I said. "Eat or not eat. Or keep drinking. I could head right on out into the sunset."

"What does that mean, honey?" Laura said.

"It just means what I said," I said. "It means I could just keep going. That's all it means."

"I could eat something myself," Laura said. "I don't think I've ever been so hungry in my life. Is there something to nibble on?"

"I'll put out some cheese and crackers," Terri said.

But Terri just sat there. She did not get up to get anything.

Mel turned his glass over. He spilled it out on the table.

"Gin's gone," Mel said.

Terri said, "Now what?"

I could hear my heart beating. I could hear everyone's heart. I could hear the human noise we sat there making, not one of us moving, not even when the room went dark.

Suggestions for Discussion

1. In what respects does the setting for the discussion between the two couples affect the dialogue?

2. Characterize each of the participants by referring to their behavior, their expressions of love, and their attitudes toward love. For example, how do Terri and Mel differ in their views of love.

3. What to Mel is both the "terrible thing" and the "saving grace" about love?

4. What is the significance of Mel's story about the elderly couple whom he treated in the hospital? Why does he use vulgar language in describing their relationship? Mel has earlier described love as carnal and sentimental. How adequate are those adjectives in describing the love of the elderly couple?

5. Why is Mel's story of the elderly couple troubling to Nick and Laura? How do you know?

6. Note the changes in Mel's statements about love. To what extent are his differing statements of attitude affected by his drinking? By his earlier years in the seminary? By his profession as a cardiologist?

7. Are there discrepancies between Mel's views and his behavior? Why do you think he is a pill taker?

Suggestions for Writing

1. You have read a number of writers on the meaning of love. Drawing upon these readings, your experience and observation, develop in either narrative or expository form your feelings and thoughts about love.

2. Interview a number of your contemporaries. What appears to be their sense of the meaning of love? To what extent is their behavior consonant with their attitude?

Katherine Anne Porter
Rope

Katherine Anne Porter (1890–1980), American short-story writer, novelist, and critic, was born in Texas and educated in convent schools in Texas and New Orleans. She was a visiting lecturer at numerous colleges and universities and lived and traveled in Mexico, Germany, and France. Her books include *Flowering Judas* (1930), *Noon-Wine* (1937), *Pale Horse, Pale Rider* (1939), critical essays, *The Days Before* (1952), and a novel, *Ship of Fools* (1962). In "Rope," the frustration of husband and wife, expressed in displaced anger, is followed by an expression of the more enduring ties of a shared life.

On the third day after they moved to the country he came walking back from the village carrying a basket of groceries and a twenty-four-yard coil of rope. She came out to meet him, wiping her hands on her green smock. Her hair was tumbled, her nose was scarlet with sunburn; he told her that already she looked like a born country woman. His gray flannel shirt stuck to him, his heavy shoes were dusty. She assured him he looked like a rural character in a play.

Had he brought the coffee? She had been waiting all day long for coffee. They had forgot it when they ordered at the store the first day.

Gosh, no, he hadn't. Lord, now he'd have to go back. Yes, he would if it killed him. He thought, though, he had everything else. She reminded him it was only because he didn't drink coffee himself. If he did he would remember it quick enough. Suppose they ran out of cigarettes? Then she saw the rope. What was that for? Well, he thought it might do to hang clothes on, or something. Naturally, she asked him if he thought they were going to run a laundry. They already had a fifty-foot line hanging right before his eyes. Why, hadn't he noticed it, really? It was a blot on the landscape to her.

He thought there were a lot of things a rope might come in handy for. She wanted to know what, for instance. He thought a few seconds, but nothing occurred. They could wait and see, couldn't they? You need all sorts of strange odds and ends around a place in the country. She said, yes, that was so; but she thought just at that time when every penny counted, it seemed funny to buy more rope. That was all. She hadn't meant anything else. She hadn't just seen, not at first, why he felt it was necessary.

Well, thunder, he had bought it because he wanted to, and that was all there was to it. She thought that was reason enough, and couldn't understand why he hadn't said so, at first. Undoubtedly it would be useful, twenty-four yards of rope, there were hundreds of things, she couldn't think of any at the moment, but it would come in. Of course. As he had said, things always did in the country.

But she was a little disappointed about the coffee, and oh, look, look, look at the eggs! Oh, my, they're all running! What had he put on top of them? Hadn't he known eggs mustn't be squeezed? Squeezed, who had squeezed them, he wanted to know. What a silly thing to say. He had simply brought them along in the basket with the other things. If they got broke it was the grocer's fault. He should know better than to put heavy things on top of eggs.

She believed it was the rope. That was the heaviest thing in the pack, she saw him plainly when he came in from the road, the rope was a big package on top of everything. He desired the whole wide world to witness that this was not a fact. He had carried the rope in one hand and the basket in the other, and what was the use of her having eyes if that was the best they could do for her?

Well, anyhow, she could see one thing plain: no eggs for breakfast. They'd have to scramble them now, for supper. It was too damned bad. She had planned to have steak for supper. No ice, meat wouldn't keep. He wanted to know why she couldn't finish breaking the eggs in a bowl and set them in a cool place.

Cool place! if he could find one for her, she'd be glad to set them there. Well, then, it seemed to him they might very well cook the meat at the same time they cooked the eggs and then warm up the meat for tomorrow. The idea simply choked her. Warmed-over meat, when they might as well have had it fresh. Second best and scraps and makeshifts, even to the meat! He rubbed her shoulder a little. It doesn't really matter so much, does it, darling? Sometimes when they were playful, he would rub her shoulder and she would arch and purr. This time she hissed and almost clawed. He was getting ready to say that they could surely manage somehow when she turned on him and said, if he told her they could manage somehow she would certainly slap his face.

He swallowed the words red hot, his face burned. He picked up the rope and started to put it on the top shelf. She would not have it on the top shelf, the jars and tins belonged there; positively she would not have the top shelf cluttered up with a lot of rope. She had borne all the clutter she meant to bear in the flat in town, there was space here at least and she meant to keep things in order.

Well, in that case, he wanted to know what the hammer and nails were doing up there? And why had she put them there when she knew very well he needed that hammer and those nails upstairs to fix the window sashes? She simply slowed down everything and made double work on the place with her insane habit of changing things around and hiding them.

She was sure she begged his pardon, and if she had had any reason to believe he was going to fix the sashes this summer she would have left the hammer and nails right where he put them; in the middle of the bedroom floor where they could step on them in the dark. And now if he didn't clear the whole mess out of there she would throw them down the well.

Oh, all right, all right—could he put them in the closet? Naturally not, there were brooms and mops and dustpans in the closet, and why couldn't he find a place for his rope outside her kitchen? Had he stopped to consider there were seven God-forsaken rooms in the house, and only one kitchen?

He wanted to know what of it? And did she realize she was making a complete fool of herself? And what did she take him for, a three-year-old idiot? The whole trouble with her was she needed something weaker than she was to heckle and tyrannize over. He wished to God now they had a couple of children she could take it out on. Maybe he'd get some rest.

Her face changed at this, she reminded him he had forgot the coffee and had bought a worthless piece of rope. And when she thought of all the things they actually needed to make the place even decently fit to live in, well, she could cry, that was all. She looked so forlorn, so lost and despairing he couldn't believe it was only a piece of rope that was causing all the racket. What *was* the matter, for God's sake?

Oh, would he please hush and go away, and *stay* away, if he could, for five minutes? By all means, yes, he would. He'd stay away indefinitely if she wished. Lord, yes, there was nothing he'd like better than to clear out and never come back. She couldn't for the life of her see what was holding him, then. It was a swell time. Here she was, stuck, miles from a railroad, with a half-empty house on her hands, and not a penny in her pocket, and everything on earth to do; it seemed the God-sent moment for him to get out from under. She was surprised he hadn't stayed in town as it was until she had come out and done the work and got things straightened out. It was his usual trick.

It appeared to him that this was going a little far. Just a touch out of bounds, if she didn't mind his saying so. Why the hell had he stayed in town the summer before? To do a half-dozen extra jobs to get the money he had sent her. That was it. She knew perfectly well they couldn't have done it otherwise. She had agreed with him at the time. And that was the only time so help him he had ever left her to do anything by herself.

Oh, he could tell that to his great-grandmother. She had her notion of what had kept him in town. Considerably more than a notion, if he wanted to know. So, she was going to bring all that up again, was she? Well, she could just think what she pleased. He was tired of explaining. It may have looked funny but he had simply got hooked in, and what could he do? It was impossible to believe that she was going to take it seriously. Yes, yes, she knew how it was with a man: if he was left by himself a minute, some woman was certain to kidnap him. And naturally he couldn't hurt her feelings by refusing!

Well, what was she raving about? Did she forget she had told him those two weeks alone in the country were the happiest she had known for four years? And how long had they been married when she said that? All right, shut up! If she thought that hadn't stuck in his craw.

She hadn't meant she was happy because she was away from him. She meant she was happy getting the devilish house nice and ready for him. That was what she had meant, and now look! Bringing up something she had said a year ago simply to justify himself for forgetting her coffee and breaking the eggs and buying a wretched piece of rope they couldn't afford. She really thought it was time to drop the subject, and now she wanted only two things in the world. She wanted him to get that rope from underfoot, and go back to the village and get her coffee, and if he could remember it, he might bring a metal mitt for the skillets, and two more curtain rods, and if there were any rubber gloves in the village, her hands were simply raw, and a bottle of milk of magnesia from the drugstore.

He looked out at the dark blue afternoon sweltering on the slopes, and mopped his forehead and sighed heavily and said, if only she could wait a minute for *anything*, he was going back. He had said so, hadn't he, the very instant they found he had overlooked it?

Oh, yes, well . . . run along. She was going to wash windows. The country was so beautiful! She doubted they'd have a moment to enjoy it. He meant to go, but he could not until he had said that if she wasn't such a hopeless melancholiac she might see that this was only for a few days. Couldn't she remember anything pleasant about the other summers? Hadn't they ever had any fun? She hadn't time to talk about it, and now would he please not leave that rope lying around for her to trip on? He picked it up, somehow it had toppled off the table, and walked out with it under his arm.

Was he going this minute? He certainly was. She thought so. Sometimes it seemed to her he had second sight about the precisely perfect moment to leave her ditched. She had meant to put the mattresses out to sun, if they put them out this minute they would get at least three hours, he must have heard her say that morning she meant to put them out. So of course he would walk off and leave her to it. She supposed he thought the exercise would do her good.

Well, he was merely going to get her coffee. A four-mile walk for two pounds of coffee was ridiculous, but he was perfectly willing to do it. The habit was making a wreck of her, but if she wanted to wreck herself there was nothing he could do about it. If he thought it was coffee that was making a wreck of her, she congratulated him: he must have a damned easy conscience.

Conscience or no conscience, he didn't see why the mattresses couldn't very well wait until tomorrow. And anyhow, for God's sake, were they living in the house, or were they going to let the house ride them to death? She paled at this, her face grew livid about the mouth, she looked quite dangerous, and reminded him that housekeeping was no more her work than it was his: she had other work to do as well, and when did he think she was going to find time to do it at this rate?

Was she going to start on that again? She knew as well as he did that his work brought in the regular money, hers was only occasional, if they depended on what *she* made—and she might as well get straight on this question once for all!

That was positively not the point. The question was, when both of them were working on their own time, was there going to be a division of the housework, or wasn't there? She merely wanted to know, she had to make her plans. Why, he thought that was all arranged. It was understood that he was to help. Hadn't he always, in summers?

Hadn't he, though? Oh, just hadn't he? And when, and where, and doing what? Lord, what an uproarious joke!

It was such a very uproarious joke that her face turned slightly purple, and she screamed with laughter. She laughed so hard she had to sit down, and finally a rush of tears spurted from her eyes and poured down into the lifted corners of her mouth. He dashed towards her and dragged her up to her feet and tried to pour water on her head. The dipper hung by a string on a nail and he broke it loose. Then he tried to pump water with one hand while she struggled in the other. So he gave it up and shook her instead.

She wrenched away, crying for him to take his rope and go to hell, she had simply given him up: and ran. He heard her high-heeled bedroom slippers clattering and stumbling on the stairs.

He went out around the house into the lane; he suddenly realized he had a blister on his heel and his shirt felt as if it were on fire. Things broke so suddenly you didn't know where you were. She could work herself into a fury about simply nothing. She was terrible, damn it: not an ounce of reason. You might as well talk to a sieve as that woman when she got going. Damned if he'd spend his life humoring her! Well, what to do now? He would take back the rope and exchange it for something else. Things accumulated, things were mountainous, you couldn't move them or sort them out or get rid of them. They just lay around and rotted. He'd take it back. Hell, why should he? He wanted it. What was it anyhow? A piece of rope. Imagine anybody caring more about a piece of rope than about a man's feelings. What earthly right had she to say a word about it? He remembered all the useless, meaningless things she bought for herself: Why? because I wanted it; that's why! He stopped and selected a large stone by the road. He would put the rope behind it. He would put it in the tool-box when he got back. He'd heard enough about it to last him a life-time.

When he came back she was leaning against the post box beside the road waiting. It was pretty late, the smell of broiled steak floated nose high in the cooling air. Her face was young and smooth and fresh looking. Her unmanageable funny black hair was all on end. She waved to him from a distance, and he speeded up. She called out that supper was ready and waiting, was he starved?

You bet he was starved. Here was the coffee. He waved it at her. She looked at his other hand. What was that he had there?

Well, it was the rope again. He stopped short. He had meant to exchange it but forgot. She wanted to know why he should exchange it, if it was something he really wanted. Wasn't the air sweet now, and wasn't it fine to be here?

She walked beside him with one hand hooked into his leather belt. She pulled and jostled him a little as he walked, and leaned against him. He put his arm clear around her and patted her stomach. They exchanged wary smiles. Coffee, coffee for the Ootsum-Wootsums! He felt as if he were bringing her a beautiful present.

He was a love, she firmly believed, and if she had had her coffee in the morning, she wouldn't have behaved so funny . . . There was a whippoorwill still coming back, imagine, clear out of season, sitting in the crab-apple tree calling all by himself. Maybe his girl stood him up. Maybe she did. She hoped to hear him once more, she loved whippoorwills . . . He knew how she was, didn't he?

Sure, he knew how she was.

Suggestions for Discussion

1. Think of the multiple uses of rope and determine the ways in which the title serves as a metaphor for the quarrel and the bond between husband and wife. What does the phrase "enough rope" connote? How might it relate to the story?

2. What is the purpose of the indirect approach to the narrative through a third-person narrator? Is it more or less effective than if told from the point of view of husband or wife? Account for the frequent questions and their effect.

3. With what details are the character of husband and wife revealed?

4. What are the ostensible and real causes of the quarrel? Is the mechanism of displacement at work? Explain.

5. How do you learn of the husband and wife's economic situation?

6. How serious was the husband's threat to go away? How did the wife respond?

7. Account for the shift in tone on the husband's return. What other changes in tone do you find?

8. What does the introduction of the whippoorwill add to the resolution of the story?

9. Why was the wife particularly incensed at the time the husband asked if they were "going to let the house ride them to death"?

10. What effect is achieved by referring to the characters as husband and wife rather than as Dan and Mary or other proper names?

11. In what sense is this a story of affirmation?

Suggestions for Writing

1. Retell the story from the wife's or the husband's point of view.

2. Discuss the mechanism of displacement in human relationships. Account for it and illustrate it.

3. Argue for or against the idea that the title "Rope" is symbolic of the relationship. If you were to retitle the story what title would you give it and why?

Drama

Henrik Ibsen

Ghosts

A FAMILY-DRAMA IN THREE ACTS

Translated by William Archer

Henrik Ibsen (1828–1906), Norwegian dramatist, served as director of theaters in Bergen and Oslo. Among his plays are a poetic drama, *Peer Gynt* (1867), *A Doll's House* (1879), *The Wild Duck* (1884), *Hedda Gabler* (1890), and *The Master Builder* (1892). The interweaving of past and present emphasizes the theme of the play: that the ghosts of the past—"the sins of the fathers, old prejudices and beliefs, half-forgotten cruelties, and betrayals"—continue to haunt the living and forbid their achievement of freedom, joy, and truth.

Characters

MRS. ALVING (HELEN), *widow of Captain Alving, late Chamberlain*[1] *to the King.*
OSWALD ALVING, *her son, a painter.*

PASTOR MANDERS.
JACOB ENGSTRAND, *a carpenter.*
REGINA ENGSTRAND, *Mrs. Alving's maid.*

The action takes place at Mrs. Alving's country-house, beside one of the large fjords in Western Norway.

Act I

A spacious garden-room, with one door to the left, and two doors to the right. In the middle of the room a round table, with chairs about it. On the table

[1]Chamberlain (Kammerherre) is the only title of honour now existing in Norway. It is a distinction conferred by the King on men of wealth and position, and is not hereditary.

389

lie books, periodicals, and newspapers. In the foreground to the left a window, and by it a small sofa, with a work-table in front of it. In the background, the room is continued into a somewhat narrower conservatory, which is shut in by glass walls with large panes. In the right-hand wall of the conservatory is a door leading down into the garden. Through the glass wall one catches a glimpse of a gloomy fjord-landscape, veiled by steady rain.

Engstrand, the carpenter, stands by the garden-door. His left leg is somewhat bent; he has a clump of wood under the sole of his boot. Regina, with an empty garden syringe in her hand, hinders him from advancing.

REGINA [*in a low voice*]: What do you want? Stop where you are. You're positively dripping.

ENGSTRAND: It's the Lord's own rain, my girl.

REGINA: It's the devil's rain, *I* say.

ENGSTRAND: Lord! how you talk, Regina. [*Limps a few steps forward into the room.*] What I wanted to say was this——

REGINA: Don't clatter so with that foot of yours, I tell you! The young master's asleep upstairs.

ENGSTRAND: Asleep? In the middle of the day?

REGINA: It's no business of yours.

ENGSTRAND: I was out on the loose last night——

REGINA: I can quite believe that.

ENGSTRAND: Yes, we're weak vessels, we poor mortals, my girl——

REGINA: So it seems.

ENGSTRAND: ——and temptations are manifold in this world, you see; but all the same, I was hard at work, God knows, at half-past five this morning.

REGINA: Very well; only be off now. I won't stop here and have *rendezvous* with you.

ENGSTRAND: What is it you won't have?

REGINA: I won't have any one find you here; so just you go about your business.

ENGSTRAND [*advances a step or two*]: Blest if I go before I've had a talk with you. This afternoon I shall have finished my work at the school-house, and then I shall take to-night's boat and be off home to the town.

REGINA [*mutters*]: A pleasant journey to you.

ENGSTRAND: Thank you, my child. To-morrow the Asylum's to be opened, and then there'll be fine doings, no doubt, and plenty of intoxicating drink going, you know. And nobody shall say of Jacob Engstrand that he can't keep out of temptation's way.

REGINA: Oh!

ENGSTRAND: You see, there are to be any number of swells here to-morrow. Pastor Manders is expected from town, too.

REGINA: He's coming to-day.

ENGSTRAND: There you see! And I should be cursedly sorry if he found out anything to my disadvantage, don't you understand?

REGINA: Oh! is that your game?

ENGSTRAND: Is what my game?

REGINA [*looking hard at him*]:   What trick are you going to play on Pastor Manders?

ENGSTRAND: Hush! hush! Are you crazy? Do *I* want to play any trick on Pastor Manders? Oh no! Pastor Manders has been far too kind to me for that. But I just wanted to say, you know—that I mean to set off home again to-night.

REGINA: The sooner the better, say I.

ENGSTRAND: Yes, but I want to take you with me, Regina.

REGINA [*open-mouthed*]:   You want me——? What are you talking about?

ENGSTRAND: I want to take you home, I say.

REGINA [*scornfully*]:   Never in this world shall you get me home with you.

ENGSTRAND: We'll see about that.

REGINA: Yes, you may be sure we'll see about it! I, who have been brought up by a lady like Mrs. Alving! I, who am treated almost as a daughter here! Is it me you want to go home with you?—to a house like yours? For shame!

ENGSTRAND: What the devil do you mean? Do you set yourself up against your father, girl?

REGINA [*mutters without looking at him*]:   You've said often enough I was no child of yours.

ENGSTRAND: Stuff! Why should you trouble about that?

REGINA: Haven't you many a time sworn at me and called me a——? *Fi donc!*

ENGSTRAND: Curse me, now, if ever I used such an ugly word.

REGINA: Oh! I know quite well what word you used.

ENGSTRAND: Well, but that was only when I was a bit on, don't you know? H'm! Temptations are manifold in this world, Regina.

REGINA: Ugh!

ENGSTRAND: And besides, it was when your mother rode her high horse. I had to find something to twit her with, my child. She was always setting up for a fine lady. [*Mimics.*] "Let me go, Engstrand; let me be. Remember I've been three years in Chamberlain Alving's family at Rosenvold." [*Laughs.*] Mercy on us! She could never forget that the Captain was made a Chamberlain while she was in service here.

REGINA: Poor mother! You very soon worried her into her grave.

ENGSTRAND [*turns on his heel*]:   Oh, of course! I'm to be blamed for everything.

REGINA [*turns away; half aloud*]:   Ugh! And that leg too!

ENGSTRAND: What do you say, girl?

REGINA: *Pied de mouton.*

ENGSTRAND: Is that English, eh?

REGINA: Yes.

ENGSTRAND: Oh, ah; you've picked up some learning out here; and that may come in useful now, Regina.

REGINA [*after a short silence*]:   What do you want with me in town?

ENGSTRAND: Can you ask what a father wants with his only child? Am I not a lonely and forsaken widower?

REGINA: Oh! don't try on any nonsense like that! Why do you want me?

ENGSTRAND: Well, let me tell you, I've been thinking of starting a new line of business.

REGINA [*contemptuously*]:   You've tried that often enough, and never done any good.

ENGSTRAND: Yes, but this time you shall see, Regina! Devil take me——

REGINA [*stamps*]:   Don't swear!

ENGSTRAND: Hush, hush; you're right enough there, my girl. What I wanted to say was just this—I've laid by a very tidy pile from this Orphanage job.

REGINA: Have you? That's a good thing for you.

ENGSTRAND: What can a man spend his ha'pence on here in the country?

REGINA: Well, what then?

ENGSTRAND: Why, you see, I thought of putting the money into some paying speculation. I thought of a sort of sailors' tavern——

REGINA: Horrid!

ENGSTRAND: A regular high-class affair, of course; not a mere pigstye for common sailors. No! damn it! it would be for captains and mates, and—and—all those swells, you know.

REGINA: And I was to——?

ENGSTRAND: You were to help, to be sure. Only for appearance' sake, you understand. Devil a bit of hard work shall you have, my girl. You shall do exactly what you like.

REGINA: Oh, indeed!

ENGSTRAND: But there must be a petticoat in the house; that's as clear as daylight. For I want to have it a little lively in the evenings, with singing and dancing, and so forth. You must remember they're weary wanderers on the ocean of life. [*Nearer.*] Now don't be stupid and stand in your own light, Regina. What can become of you out here? Your mistress has given you a lot of learning; but what good is it to you? You're to look after the children at the new Orphanage, I hear. Is that the sort of thing for you, eh? Are you so desperately bent upon wearing yourself out for the sake of the dirty brats?

REGINA: No; if things go as I want them to, then—well, there's no saying—there's no saying.

ENGSTRAND: What do you mean by "there's no saying"?

REGINA: Never you mind. How much money have you saved up here?

ENGSTRAND: What with one thing and another, a matter of seven or eight hundred crowns.

REGINA: That's not so bad.

ENGSTRAND: It's enough to make a start with, my girl.

REGINA: Aren't you thinking of giving me any?

ENGSTRAND: No, I'm damned if I am!

REGINA: Not even of sending me a scrap of stuff for a new dress?

ENGSTRAND: If you'll come to town with me, you can get dresses enough.

REGINA: Pooh! I can do that on my own account if I want to.

ENGSTRAND: No, a father's guiding hand is what you want, Regina. Now, I've my eyes on a capital house in Little Harbour Street. It won't need much ready-money, and it could be a sort of sailors' home, you know.

REGINA: But I will *not* live with you. I have nothing whatever to do with you. Be off!

ENGSTRAND: You wouldn't remain long with me, my girl. No such luck! If you knew how to play your cards, such a fine girl as you've grown in the last year or two——

REGINA: Well?

ENGSTRAND: You'd soon get hold of some mate—or perhaps even a captain——

REGINA: I won't marry any one of that sort. Sailors have no *savoir vivre*.

ENGSTRAND: What haven't they got?

REGINA: I know what sailors are, I tell you. They're not the sort of people to marry.

ENGSTRAND: Then never mind about marrying them. You can make it pay all the same. [*More confidentially.*] He—the Englishman—the man with the yacht—he gave three hundred dollars, he did; and she wasn't a bit handsomer than you.

REGINA [*going towards him*]: Out you go!

ENGSTRAND [*falling back*]: Come, come! You're not going to strike me, I hope.

REGINA: Yes, if you begin to talk about mother I shall strike you. Get away with you, I say. [*Drives him back towards the garden door.*] And don't bang the doors. Young Mr. Alving——

ENGSTRAND: He's asleep; I know. It's curious how you're taken up about young Mr. Alving—[*more softly*] Oho! it surely can't be he that——?

REGINA: Be off at once! You're crazy, I tell you! No, not that way. There comes Pastor Manders. Down the kitchen stairs with you.

ENGSTRAND [*towards the right*]: Yes, yes, I'm going. But just you talk to him that's coming there. He's the man to tell you what a child owes its father. For I am your father all the same, you know. I can prove it from the church register.

[*He goes out through the second door to the right, which* REGINA *has opened, and fastens again after him.* REGINA *glances hastily at herself in the mirror, dusts herself with her pocket-handkerchief, and settles her collar; then she busies herself with the flowers.* PASTOR MANDERS, *in an overcoat, with an umbrella, and with a small travelling-bag on a strap over his shoulder, comes through the garden-door into the conservatory.*]

MANDERS: Good-morning, Miss Engstrand.

REGINA [*turning round, surprised and pleased*]: No, really! Good-morning, Pastor Manders. Is the steamer in already?

MANDERS: It's just in. [*Enters the sitting-room.*] Terrible weather we've been having lately.

REGINA [*follows him*]:   It's such blessed weather for the country, sir.

MANDERS: Yes, you're quite right. We townspeople think too little about that.   [*He begins to take off his overcoat.*]

REGINA: Oh, mayn't I help you? There! Why, how wet it is! I'll just hang it up in the hall. And your umbrella, too—I'll open it and let it dry.

[*She goes out with the things through the second door on the right. PASTOR MANDERS takes off his travelling-bag and lays it and his hat on a chair. Meanwhile REGINA comes in again.*]

MANDERS: Ah! it's a comfort to get safe under cover. Everything going on well here?

REGINA: Yes, thank you, sir.

MANDERS: You have your hands full, I suppose, in preparation for to-morrow?

REGINA: Yes, there's plenty to do, of course.

MANDERS: And Mrs. Alving is at home, I trust?

REGINA: Oh dear, yes. She's just upstairs looking after the young master's chocolate.

MANDERS: Yes, by-the-by—I heard down at the pier that Oswald had arrived.

REGINA: Yes, he came the day before yesterday. We didn't expect him before to-day.

MANDERS: Quite strong and well, I hope?

REGINA: Yes, thank you, quite; but dreadfully tired with the journey. He has made one rush all the way from Paris. I believe he came the whole way in one train. He's sleeping a little now, I think; so perhaps we'd better talk a little quietly.

MANDERS: Hush!—as quietly as you please.

REGINA [*arranging an armchair beside the table*]:   Now, do sit down, Pastor Manders, and make yourself comfortable. [*He sits down; she puts a footstool under his feet.*] There! are you comfortable now, sir?

MANDERS: Thanks, thanks, I'm most comfortable. [*Looks at her.*] Do you know, Miss Engstrand, I positively believe you've grown since I last saw you.

REGINA: Do you think so, sir? Mrs. Alving says my figure has developed too.

MANDERS: Developed? Well, perhaps a little; just enough.   [*Short pause.*]

REGINA: Shall I tell Mrs. Alving you are here?

MANDERS: Thanks, thanks, there's no hurry, my dear child. By-the-by, Regina, my good girl, just tell me: how is your father getting on out here?

REGINA: Oh, thank you, he's getting on well enough.

MANDERS: He called upon me last time he was in town.

REGINA: Did he, indeed? He's always so glad of a chance of talking to you, sir.

MANDERS: And you often look in upon him at his work, I daresay?

REGINA: I? Oh, of course, when I have time, I——

MANDERS: Your father is not a man of strong character, Miss Engstrand. He stands terribly in need of a guiding hand.

REGINA: Oh, yes; I daresay he does.

MANDERS: He needs to have some one near him whom he cares for, and whose judgment he respects. He frankly admitted that when he last came to see me.

REGINA: Yes, he mentioned something of the sort to me. But I don't know whether Mrs. Alving can spare me; especially now that we've got the new Orphanage to attend to. And then I should be so sorry to leave Mrs. Alving; she has always been so kind to me.

MANDERS: But a daughter's duty, my good girl—— Of course we must first get your mistress's consent.

REGINA: But I don't know whether it would be quite proper for me, at my age, to keep house for a single man.

MANDERS: What! My dear Miss Engstrand! When the man is your own father!

REGINA: Yes, that may be; but all the same—— Now if it were in a thoroughly respectable house, and with a real gentleman——

MANDERS: But, my dear Regina——

REGINA: ——one I could love and respect, and be a daughter to——

MANDERS: Yes, but my dear, good child——

REGINA: Then I should be glad to go to town. It's very lonely out here; you know yourself, sir, what it is to be alone in the world. And I can assure you I'm both quick and willing. Don't you know of any such place for me, sir?

MANDERS: I? No, certainly not.

REGINA: But, dear, dear sir, do remember me if——

MANDERS [*rising*]. Yes, yes, certainly, Miss Engstrand.

REGINA: For if I——

MANDERS: Will you be so good as to fetch your mistress?

REGINA: I will, at once, sir. [*She goes out to the left.*]

MANDERS [*paces the room two or three times, stands a moment in the background with his hands behind his back, and looks out over the garden. Then he returns to the table, takes up a book, and looks at the title-page; starts, and looks at several*]: H'm—indeed!

[MRS. ALVING *enters by the door on the left; she is followed by* REGINA, *who immediately goes out by the first door on the right.*]

MRS. ALVING [*holds out her hand*]: Welcome, my dear Pastor.

MANDERS: How do you do, Mrs. Alving? Here I am as I promised.

MRS. ALVING: Always punctual to the minute.

MANDERS: You may believe it wasn't so easy for me to get away. With all the Boards and Committees I belong to——

MRS. ALVING: That makes it all the kinder of you to come so early. Now we can get through our business before dinner. But where's your luggage?

MANDERS [*quickly*]: I left it down at the inn. I shall sleep there to-night.

MRS. ALVING [*suppressing a smile*]: Are you really not to be persuaded, even now, to pass the night under my roof?

MANDERS: No, no, Mrs. Alving; many thanks. I shall stay down there as usual. It's so convenient for starting again.

MRS. ALVING: Well, you must have your own way. But I really should have thought we two old people——

MANDERS: Now you're making fun of me. Ah! you're naturally in great spirits to-day—what between to-morrow's festival and Oswald's return.

MRS. ALVING: Yes; you can think what a delight it is to me! It's more than two years since he was home last. And now he has promised to stay with me all winter.

MANDERS: Has he really? That's very nice and dutiful of him. For I can well believe that life in Rome and Paris has far more attractions.

MRS. ALVING: True. But here he has his mother, you see. My own darling boy, he hasn't forgotten his old mother!

MANDERS: It would be grievous indeed, if absence and absorption in art and that sort of thing were to blunt his natural feelings.

MRS. ALVING: Yes, you may well say so. But there's nothing of that sort to fear in him. I'm quite curious to see whether you'll know him again. He'll be down presently; he's upstairs just now, resting a little on the sofa. But do sit down, my dear Pastor.

MANDERS: Thank you. Are you quite at liberty——?

MRS. ALVING: Certainly.   [*She sits by the table.*]

MANDERS: Very well. Then you shall see—— [*He goes to the chair where his travelling-bag lies, takes out a packet of papers, sits down on the opposite side of the table, and tries to find a clear space for the papers.*] Now, to begin with, here is——[*breaking off*]—Tell me, Mrs. Alving, how do these books come here?

MRS. ALVING: These books? They are books I am reading.

MANDERS: Do you read this sort of literature?

MRS. ALVING: Certainly I do.

MANDERS: Do you feel better or happier for reading of this kind?

MRS. ALVING: I feel, so to speak, more secure.

MANDERS: That's strange. How do you mean?

MRS. ALVING: Well, I seem to find explanation and confirmation of all sorts of things I myself have been thinking. For that's the wonderful part of it, Pastor Manders; there's really nothing new in these books, nothing but what most people think and believe. Only most people either don't formulate it to themselves, or else keep quiet about it.

MANDERS: Great heavens! Do you really believe that most people——?

MRS. ALVING: I do, indeed.

MANDERS: But surely not in this country? Not here, among us?

MRS. ALVING: Yes, certainly, among us too.

MANDERS: Well, I really must say——!

MRS. ALVING: For the rest, what do you object to in these books?

MANDERS: Object to in them? You surely don't suppose that I have nothing to do but study such productions as these?

MRS. ALVING: That is to say, you know nothing of what you are condemning.

MANDERS: I have read enough *about* these writings to disapprove of them.

MRS. ALVING: Yes; but your own opinion——

MANDERS: My dear Mrs. Alving, there are many occasions in life when one must rely upon others. Things are so ordered in this world; and it's well that they are. How could society get on otherwise?

MRS. ALVING: Well, I daresay you're right there.

MANDERS: Besides, I of course don't deny that there may be much that is interesting in such books. Nor can I blame you for wishing to keep up with the intellectual movements that are said to be going on in the great world, where you have let your son pass so much of his life. But——

MRS. ALVING: But?

MANDERS [*lowering his voice*]:   But one shouldn't talk about it, Mrs. Alving. One is certainly not bound to account to everybody for what one reads and thinks within one's own four walls.

MRS. ALVING: Of course not; I quite think so.

MANDERS: Only think, now, how you are bound to consider the interests of this Orphanage which you decided on founding at a time when you thought very differently on spiritual matters—so far as I can judge.

MRS. ALVING: Oh, yes; I quite admit that. But it was about the Orphanage——

MANDERS: It was about the Orphanage we were to speak; yes. All I say is: prudence, my dear lady! And now we'll get to business. [*Opens the packet, and takes out a number of papers.*] Do you see these?

MRS. ALVING: The documents?

MANDERS: All—and in perfect order. I can tell you it was hard work to get them in time. I had to put on strong pressure. The authorities are almost painfully scrupulous when you want them to come to the point. But here they are at last. [*Looks through the bundle.*] See! here is the formal deed of gift of the parcel of ground known as Solvik in the Manor of Rosenvold, with all the newly constructed buildings, schoolrooms, master's house, and chapel. And here is the legal fiat for the endowment and for the Regulations of the Institution. Will you look at them? [*Reads.*] "Regulations for the Children's Home to be known as 'Captain Alving's Foundation.' "

MRS. ALVING [*looks long at the paper*]:   So there it is.

MANDERS: I have chosen the designation "Captain" rather than "Chamberlain." "Captain" looks less pretentious.

MRS. ALVING: Oh, yes; just as you think best.

MANDERS: And here you have the Bank Account of the capital lying at interest to cover the current expenses of the Orphanage.

MRS. ALVING: Thank you; but please keep it—it will be more convenient.

MANDERS: With pleasure. I think we will leave the money in the Bank for the present. The interest is certainly not what we could wish—four per cent, and six months' notice of withdrawal. If a good mortgage could be found later on—of course it must be a first mortgage and an undoubted security—then we could consider the matter.

MRS. ALVING: Certainly, my dear Pastor Manders. You are the best judge in these things.

MANDERS: I will keep my eyes open at any rate. But now there's one thing more which I have several times been intending to ask you.

MRS. ALVING: And what's that?

MANDERS: Shall the Orphanage buildings be insured or not?

MRS. ALVING: Of course they must be insured.

MANDERS: Well, stop a minute, Mrs. Alving. Let us look into the matter a little more closely.

MRS. ALVING: I have everything insured; buildings and movables and stock and crops.

MANDERS: Of course you have—on your own estate. And so have I—of course. But here, you see, it's quite another matter. The Orphanage is to be consecrated, as it were, to a higher purpose.

MRS. ALVING: Yes, but that's no reason——

MANDERS: For my own part, I should not see the smallest impropriety in guarding against all contingencies——

MRS. ALVING: No, I should think not.

MANDERS: But what is the general feeling in the neighbourhood? You, of course, know better than I.

MRS. ALVING: H'm—the general feeling——

MANDERS: Is there any considerable number of people—really responsible people—who might be scandalised?

MRS. ALVING: What do you mean by "really responsible people"?

MANDERS: Well, I mean people in such independent and influential positions that one cannot help allowing some weight to their opinions.

MRS. ALVING: There are several people of that sort here, who would very likely be shocked if——

MANDERS: There, you see! In town we have many such people. Think of all my colleagues' adherents! People would be only too ready to interpret our action as a sign that neither you nor I had the right faith in a Higher Providence.

MRS. ALVING: But for your own part, my dear Pastor, you can at least tell yourself that——

MANDERS: Yes, I know—I know; my conscience would be quite easy, that is true enough. But nevertheless we should not escape grave misinterpretation; and that might very likely reflect unfavourably upon the Orphanage.

MRS. ALVING: Well, in that case, then——

MANDERS: Nor can I lose sight of the difficult—I may even say painful— position *I* might perhaps get into. In the leading circles of the town people are much taken up about this Orphanage. It is, of course, founded partly for the benefit of the town, as well; and it is to be hoped it will, to a considerable extent, result in lightening our Poor Rates. Now, as I have been your adviser, and have had the business matters in my hands, I cannot but fear that I may have to bear the brunt of fanaticism.

MRS. ALVING: Oh, you mustn't run the risk of that.

MANDERS: To say nothing of the attacks that would assuredly be made upon me in certain papers and periodicals, which——

MRS. ALVING: Enough, my dear Pastor Manders. That consideration is quite decisive.

MANDERS: Then you do not wish the Orphanage insured?

MRS. ALVING: No. We'll let it alone.

MANDERS [*leaning back in his chair*]:   But if a disaster were to happen?—one can never tell. Would you be able to make good the damage?

MRS. ALVING: No; I tell you plainly I should do nothing of the kind.

MANDERS: Then I must tell you, Mrs. Alving, we are taking no small responsibility upon ourselves.

MRS. ALVING: Do you think we can do otherwise?

MANDERS: No, that's just the thing; we really cannot do otherwise. We must not expose ourselves to misinterpretation; and we have no right whatever to give offence to our neighbours.

MRS. ALVING: You, as a clergyman, certainly should not.

MANDERS: I really think, too, we may trust that such an institution has fortune on its side; in fact, that it stands under a Special Providence.

MRS. ALVING: Let us hope so, Pastor Manders.

MANDERS: Then we'll let the matter alone.

MRS. ALVING: Yes, certainly.

MANDERS: Very well. Just as you think best. [*Makes a note.*] Then—no insurance.

MRS. ALVING: It's rather curious that you should just happen to mention the matter to-day.

MANDERS: I have often thought of asking you about it——

MRS. ALVING: ——for we very nearly had a fire down there yesterday.

MANDERS: You don't say so!

MRS. ALVING: Oh, it was of no importance. A heap of shavings had caught fire in the carpenter's workshop.

MANDERS: Where Engstrand works?

MRS. ALVING: Yes. The say he's often very careless with matches.

MANDERS: He has so many things in his head, that man—so many temptations. Thank God, he's now striving to lead a decent life, I hear.

MRS. ALVING: Indeed! Who says so?

MANDERS: He himself assures me of it. And he's certainly a capital workman.

MRS. ALVING: Oh, yes; so long as he's sober.

MANDERS: Yes, that's a sad weakness. But he's often driven to it by his bad leg, he says. Last time he was in town I was really touched by him. He came and thanked me so warmly for having got him work here, so that he might be near Regina.

MRS. ALVING: He doesn't see much of *her*.

MANDERS: Oh, yes; he has a talk with her every day. He told me so himself.

MRS. ALVING: Well, it may be so.

MANDERS: He feels so acutely that he needs some one to hold him back when temptation comes. That's what I can't help liking about Jacob Engstrand; he comes to you helplessly, accusing himself and confessing his own weakness. The last time he was talking to me—Believe me, Mrs. Alving, supposing it were a real necessity for him to have Regina home again——

MRS. ALVING [*rising hastily*]:   Regina!

MANDERS: ——you must not set yourself against it.

MRS. ALVING: Indeed I shall set myself against it! And besides—Regina is to have a position in the Orphanage.

MANDERS: But, after all, remember he's her father——

MRS. ALVING: Oh! I know best what sort of a father he has been to her. No! she shall never go to him with my goodwill.

MANDERS [*rising*]:   My dear lady, don't take the matter so warmly. You misjudge Engstrand sadly. You seem to be quite terrified——

MRS. ALVING [*more quietly*]:   It makes no difference. I have taken Regina into my house, and there she shall stay. [*Listens.*] Hush, my dear Mr. Manders; don't say any more about it. [*Her face lights up with gladness.*] Listen! there's Oswald coming downstairs. Now we'll think of no one but him.

[OSWALD ALVING, *in a light overcoat, hat in hand and smoking a large meerschaum, enters through the door on the left; he stops in the doorway.*]

OSWALD: Oh! I beg your pardon; I thought you were in the study. [*Comes forward.*] Good-morning, Pastor Manders.

MANDERS [*staring*]:   Ah——! How strange——!

MRS. ALVING: Well now, what do you think of him, Mr. Manders?

MANDERS: I—I—can it really be——?

OSWALD: Yes, it's really the Prodigal Son, sir.

MANDERS [*protesting*]:   My dear young friend——!

OSWALD: Well, then, the Reclaimed Son.

MRS. ALVING: Oswald remembers how much you were opposed to his becoming a painter.

MANDERS: To our human eyes many a step seems dubious which afterwards proves——[*wrings his hand*]. Anyhow, welcome, welcome home. Why, my dear Oswald—I suppose I may call you by your Christian name?

OSWALD: What else should you call me?

MANDERS: Very good. What I wanted to say was this, my dear Oswald— you mustn't believe that I utterly condemn the artist's calling. I have no doubt there are many who can keep their inner self unharmed in that profession, as in any other.

OSWALD: Let us hope so.

MRS. ALVING [*beaming with delight*]:   I know one who has kept both his inner and outer self unharmed. Just look at him, Mr. Manders.

OSWALD [*moves restlessly about the room*]:   Yes, yes, my dear mother; let's say no more about it.

MANDERS: Why, certainly—that's undeniable. And you have begun to make a name for yourself already. The newspapers have often spoken of you, most favourably. By-the-by, just lately they haven't mentioned you so often, I fancy.

OSWALD [*up in the conservatory*]:   I haven't been able to paint so much lately.

MRS. ALVING: Even a painter needs a little rest now and then.

MANDERS: I can quite believe it. And meanwhile he can be gathering his forces for some great work.

OSWALD: Yes.—Mother, will dinner soon be ready?

MRS. ALVING: In less than half an hour. He has a capital appetite, thank God.

MANDERS: And a taste for tobacco, too.

OSWALD: I found my father's pipe in my room and so——

MANDERS: Aha! then that accounts for it.

MRS. ALVING: For what?

MANDERS: When Oswald stood there, in the doorway, with the pipe in his mouth, I could have sworn I saw his father, large as life.

OSWALD: No, really?

MRS. ALVING: Oh! how can you say so? Oswald takes after me.

MANDERS: Yes, but there's an expression about the corners of the mouth— something about the lips that reminds one exactly of Alving; at any rate, now that he's smoking.

MRS. ALVING: Not in the least. Oswald has rather a clerical curve about his mouth, I think.

MANDERS: Yes, yes; some of my colleagues have much the same expression.

MRS. ALVING: But put your pipe away, my dear boy; I won't have smoking in here.

OSWALD [*does so*]:   By all means. I only wanted to try it; for I once smoked it when I was a child.

MRS. ALVING: You?

OSWALD: Yes. I was quite small at the time. I recollect I came up to father's room one evening when he was in great spirits.

MRS. ALVING: Oh, you can't recollect anything of those times.

OSWALD: Yes, I recollect distinctly. He took me up on his knees, and gave me the pipe. "Smoke, boy," he said; "smoke away, boy." And I smoked as hard as I could, until I felt I was growing quite pale, and the perspiration stood in great drops on my forehead. Then he burst out laughing heart-ily——

MANDERS: That was most extraordinary.

MRS. ALVING: My dear friend, it's only something Oswald has dreamt.

OSWALD: No, mother, I assure you I didn't dream it. For—don't you re-member this?—you came and carried me out into the nursery. Then I was sick, and I saw that you were crying.—Did father often play such pranks?

MANDERS: In his youth he overflowed with the joy of life——

OSWALD: And yet he managed to do so much in the world; so much that was good and useful; and he died so young, too.

MANDERS: Yes, you have inherited the name of an active and worthy man, my dear Oswald Alving. No doubt it will be an incentive to you——

OSWALD: It ought to, indeed.

MANDERS: It was good of you to come home for the ceremony in his honour.

OSWALD: I could do no less for my father.

MRS. ALVING: And I am to keep him so long! That's the best of all.

MANDERS: You're going to pass the winter at home, I hear.

OSWALD: My stay is indefinite, sir. But, oh! how delightful it is to be at home again!

MRS. ALVING [*beaming*]:   Yes, isn't it?

MANDERS [*looking sympathetically at him*]:   You went out into the world early, my dear Oswald.

OSWALD: I did. I sometimes wonder whether it wasn't *too* early.

MRS. ALVING: Oh, not at all. A healthy lad is all the better for it; especially when he's an only child. He oughtn't to hang on at home with his mother and father and get spoilt.

MANDERS: It's a very difficult question, Mrs. Alving. A child's proper place is, and must be, the home of his fathers.

OSWALD: There I quite agree with you, Pastor Manders.

MANDERS: Only look at your own son—there's no reason why we shouldn't say it in his presence—what has the consequence been for him? He's six or seven and twenty, and has never had the opportunity of learning what home life really is.

OSWALD: I beg your pardon, Pastor; there you're quite mistaken.

MANDERS: Indeed? I thought you had lived almost exclusively in artistic circles.

OSWALD: So I have.

MANDERS: And chiefly among the younger artists.

OSWALD: Yes, certainly.

MANDERS: But I thought few of these young fellows could afford to set up house and support a family.

OSWALD: There are many who can't afford to marry, sir.

MANDERS: Yes, that's just what I say.

OSWALD: But they can have a home for all that. And several of them have, as a matter of fact; and very pleasant, comfortable homes they are, too.

[MRS. ALVING *follows with breathless interest; nods, but says nothing.*]

MANDERS: But I am not talking of bachelors' quarters. By a "home" I understand the home of a family, where a man lives with his wife and children.

OSWALD: Yes; or with his children and his children's mother.

MANDERS [*starts; clasps his hands*]:   But, good heavens——!

OSWALD: Well?

MANDERS: Lives with—his children's mother!

OSWALD: Yes. Would you have him turn his children's mother out of doors?

MANDERS: Then it's illicit relations you are talking of! Irregular marriages, as people call them!

OSWALD: I have never noticed anything particularly irregular about the life these people lead.

MANDERS: But how is it possible that a—a young man or young woman with any decent principles can endure to live in that way?—in the eyes of all the world!

OSWALD: What are they to do? A poor young artist—a poor girl—it costs a lot to get married. What are they to do?

MANDERS: What are they to do? Let me tell you, Mr. Alving, what they ought to do. They ought to exercise self-restraint from the first; that's what they ought to do.

OSWALD: Such talk won't go far with warm-blooded young people, over head and ears in love.

MRS. ALVING: No, it wouldn't go far.

MANDERS [continuing]: How can the authorities tolerate such things? Allow them to go on in the light of day? [To MRS. ALVING.] Had I not cause to be deeply concerned about your son? In circles where open immorality prevails, and has even a sort of prestige——!

OSWALD: Let me tell you, sir, that I have been a constant Sunday-guest in one or two such irregular homes——

MANDERS: On Sunday of all days!

OSWALD: Isn't that the day to enjoy oneself? Well, never have I heard an offensive word, and still less have I witnessed anything that could be called immoral. No; do you know when and where I have come across immorality in artistic circles?

MANDERS: No, thank heaven, I don't!

OSWALD: Well, then, allow me to inform you. I have met with it when one or another of our pattern husbands and fathers has come to Paris to have a look round on his own account, and has done the artists the honour of visiting their humble haunts. *They* knew what was what. These gentlemen could tell us all about places and things we had never dreamt of.

MANDERS: What! Do you mean to say that respectable men from home here would——?

OSWALD: Have you never heard these respectable men, when they got home again, talking about the way in which immorality was running rampant abroad?

MANDERS: Yes, of course.

MRS. ALVING: I have too.

OSWALD: Well, you may take their word for it. They know what they're talking about! [Presses his hands to his head.] Oh! that that great, free, glorious life out there should be defiled in such a way!

MRS. ALVING: You mustn't get excited, Oswald. You will do yourself harm.

OSWALD: Yes; you're quite right, mother. It's not good for me. You see, I'm wretchedly worn out. I'll go for a little turn before dinner. Excuse me, Pastor; I know you can't take my point of view; but I couldn't help speaking out. [He goes out through the second door to the right.]

MRS. ALVING: My poor boy!

MANDERS: You may well say so. Then that's what he has come to!

[MRS. ALVING looks at him silently.]

MANDERS [*walking up and down*]:   He called himself the Prodigal Son—alas! alas!

[MRS. ALVING *continues looking at him.*]

MANDERS: And what do you say to all this?

MRS. ALVING: I say that Oswald was right in every word.

MANDERS [*stands still*]:   Right! Right! In such principles?

MRS. ALVING: Here, in my loneliness, I have come to the same way of thinking, Pastor Manders. But I've never dared to say anything. Well! now my boy shall speak for me.

MANDERS: You are much to be pitied, Mrs. Alving. But now I must speak seriously to you. And now it is no longer your business manager and adviser, your own and your late husband's early friend, who stands before you. It is the priest—the priest who stood before you in the moment of your life when you had gone most astray.

MRS. ALVING: And what has the priest to say to me?

MANDERS: I will first stir up your memory a little. The time is well chosen. To-morrow will be the tenth anniversary of your husband's death. To-morrow the memorial in his honour will be unveiled. To-morrow I shall have to speak to the whole assembled multitude. But to-day I will speak to you alone.

MRS. ALVING: Very well, Pastor Manders. Speak.

MANDERS: Do you remember that after less than a year of married life you stood on the verge of an abyss? That you forsook your house and home? That you fled from your husband? Yes, Mrs. Alving—fled, fled, and refused to return to him, however much he begged and prayed you?

MRS. ALVING: Have you forgotten how infinitely miserable I was in that first year?

MANDERS: It is only the spirit of rebellion that craves for happiness in this life. What right have we human beings to happiness? No, we have to do our duty! And your duty was to hold firmly to the man you had once chosen and to whom you were bound by a holy tie.

MRS. ALVING: You know very well what sort of life Alving was leading— what excesses he was guilty of.

MANDERS: I know very well what rumours there were about him, and I am the last to approve the life he led in his young days, if report did not wrong him. But a wife is not to be her husband's judge. It was your duty to bear with humility the cross which a Higher Power had, for your own good, laid upon you. But instead of that you rebelliously throw away the cross, desert the backslider whom you should have supported, go and risk your good name and reputation, and—nearly succeed in ruining other people's reputation into the bargain.

MRS. ALVING: Other people's? One other person's, you mean.

MANDERS: It was incredibly reckless of you to seek refuge with me.

MRS. ALVING: With our clergyman? With our intimate friend?

MANDERS: Just on that account. Yes, you may thank God that I possessed the necessary firmness; that I dissuaded you from your wild designs; and that it was vouchsafed me to lead you back to the path of duty, and home to your lawful husband.

MRS. ALVING: Yes, Pastor Manders, it was certainly your work.

MANDERS: I was but a poor instrument in a Higher Hand. And what a blessing has it not been to you, all the days of your life, that I got you to resume the yoke of duty and obedience! Did not everything happen as I foretold? Did not Alving turn his back on his errors, as a man should? Did he not live with you from that time, lovingly and blamelessly, all his days? Did he not become a benefactor to the whole district? And did he not raise you up to him, so that you little by little became his assistant in all his undertakings? And a capital assistant, too—Oh! I know, Mrs. Alving, that praise is due to you. But now I come to the next great error in your life.

MRS. ALVING: What do you mean?

MANDERS: Just as you once disowned a wife's duty, so you have since disowned a mother's.

MRS. ALVING: Ah!

MANDERS: You have been all your life under the dominion of a pestilent spirit of self-will. All your efforts have been bent towards emancipation and lawlessness. You have never known how to endure any bond. Everything that has weighed upon you in life you have cast away without care or conscience, like a burden you could throw off at will. It did not please you to be a wife any longer, and you left your husband. You found it troublesome to be a mother, and you sent your child forth among strangers.

MRS. ALVING: Yes. That is true. I did so.

MANDERS: And thus you have become a stranger to him.

MRS. ALVING: No! no! I am not.

MANDERS: Yes, you are; you must be. And how have you got him back again? Bethink yourself well, Mrs. Alving. You have sinned greatly against your husband;—that you recognise by raising yonder memorial to him. Recognise now, also, how you have sinned against your son. There may be time to lead him back from the paths of error. Turn back yourself, and save what may yet be saved in him. For [*with uplifted forefinger*] verily, Mrs. Alving, you are a guilt-laden mother!—This I have thought it my duty to say to you. [*Silence.*]

MRS. ALVING [*slowly and with self-control*]: You have now spoken out, Pastor Manders; and to-morrow you are to speak publicly in memory of my husband. I shall not speak to-morrow. But now I will speak frankly to you, as you have spoken to me.

MANDERS: To be sure; you will plead excuses for your conduct——

MRS. ALVING: No. I will only narrate.

MANDERS: Well?

MRS. ALVING: All that you have just said about me and my husband and our life after you had brought me back to the path of duty—as you called it— about all that you know nothing from personal observation. From that moment you, who had been our intimate friend, never set foot in our house again.

MANDERS: You and your husband left the town immediately after.

MRS. ALVING: Yes; and in my husband's lifetime you never came to see us.

It was business that forced you to visit me when you undertook the affairs of the Orphanage.

MANDERS [*softly and uncertainly*]: Helen—if that is meant as a reproach, I would beg you to bear in mind——

MRS. ALVING: ——the regard you owed to your position, yes; and that I was a runaway wife. One can never be too careful with such unprincipled creatures.

MANDERS: My dear—Mrs. Alving, you know that is an absurd exaggeration——

MRS. ALVING: Well, well, suppose it is. My point is that your judgment as to my married life is founded upon nothing but current gossip.

MANDERS: Well, I admit that. What then?

MRS. ALVING: Well, then, Mr. Manders—I will tell you the truth. I have sworn to myself that one day you should know it—you alone!

MANDERS: What is the truth, then?

MRS. ALVING: The truth is that my husband died just as dissolute as he had lived all his days.

MANDERS [*feeling after a chair*]: What do you say?

MRS. ALVING: After nineteen years of marriage, as dissolute—in his desires at any rate—as he was before you married us.

MANDERS: And those—those wild oats, those irregularities, those excesses, if you like, you call "a dissolute life"?

MRS. ALVING: Our doctor used the expression.

MANDERS: I don't understand you.

MRS. ALVING: You need not.

MANDERS: It almost makes me dizzy. Your whole married life, the seeming union of all these years, was nothing more than a hidden abyss!

MRS. ALVING: Nothing more. Now you know it.

MANDERS: This is—it will take me long to accustom myself to the thought. I can't grasp it! I can't realise it! But how was it possible to——? How could such a state of things be kept dark?

MRS. ALVING: That has been my ceaseless struggle, day after day. After Oswald's birth, I thought Alving seemed to be a little better. But it didn't last long. And then I had to struggle twice as hard, fighting for life or death, so that nobody should know what sort of a man my child's father was. And you know what power Alving had of winning people's hearts. Nobody seemed able to believe anything but good of him. He was one of those people whose life does not bide upon their reputation. But at last, Mr. Manders—for you must know the whole story—the most repulsive thing of all happened.

MANDERS: More repulsive than the rest?

MRS. ALVING: I had gone on bearing with him, although I knew very well the secrets of his life out of doors. But when he brought the scandal within our own walls——

MANDERS: Impossible! Here!

MRS. ALVING: Yes; here in our own home. It was there [*pointing towards the first door on the right*], in the dining-room, that I first got to know of it. I was busy with something in there, and the door was standing ajar. I heard our house-maid come up from the garden, with water for those flowers.

MANDERS: Well——?

MRS. ALVING: Soon after I heard Alving come too. I heard him say something softly to her. And then I heard—[*with a short laugh*]—oh! it still sounds in my ears, so hateful and yet so ludicrous—I heard my own servant-maid whisper, "Let me go, Mr. Alving! Let me be."

MANDERS: What unseemly levity on his part! But it cannot have been more than levity, Mrs. Alving; believe me, it cannot.

MRS. ALVING: I soon knew what to believe. Mr. Alving had his way with the girl; and that connection had consequences, Mr. Manders.

MANDERS [*as though petrified*]: Such things in this house! in this house!

MRS. ALVING: I had borne a great deal in this house. To keep him at home in the evenings—and at night—I had to make myself his boon companion in his secret orgies up in his room. There I have had to sit alone with him, to clink glasses and drink with him, and to listen to his ribald, silly talk. I have had to fight with him to get him dragged to bed——

MANDERS [*moved*]: And you were able to bear all that?

MRS. ALVING: I had to bear it for my little boy's sake. But when the last insult was added; when my own servant-maid—— Then I swore to myself: This shall come to an end. And so I took the reins into my own hand—the whole control over him and everything else. For now I had a weapon against him, you see; he dared not oppose me. It was then I sent Oswald from home. He was in his seventh year, and was beginning to observe and ask questions, as children do. That I could not bear. It seemed to me the child must be poisoned by merely breathing the air of this polluted home. That was why I sent him away. And now you can see, too, why he was never allowed to set foot inside his home so long as his father lived. No one knows what it has cost me.

MANDERS: You have indeed had a life of trial.

MRS. ALVING: I could never have borne it if I hadn't had my work. For I may truly say that I have worked! All those additions to the estate—all the improvements—all the useful appliances, that won Alving such general praise—do you suppose *he* had energy for anything of the sort?—he who lay all day on the sofa and read an old court guide! No; this I will tell you too: it was I who urged him on when he had his better intervals; it was I who had to drag the whole load when he relapsed into his evil ways, or sank into querulous wretchedness.

MANDERS: And to that man you raise a memorial?

MRS. ALVING: There you see the power of an evil conscience.

MANDERS: Evil——? What do you mean?

MRS. ALVING: It always seemed to me impossible but that the truth must come out and be believed. So the Asylum was to deaden all rumours and banish doubt.

MANDERS: In that you have certainly not missed your aim, Mrs. Alving.

MRS. ALVING: And besides, I had one other reason. I did not wish that Oswald, my own boy, should inherit anything whatever from his father.

MANDERS: Then it is Alving's fortune that——?

MRS. ALVING: Yes. The sums I have spent upon the Orphanage, year by year, make up the amount—I have reckoned it up precisely—the amount which made Lieutenant Alving a good match in his day.

MANDERS: I don't quite understand——

MRS. ALVING: It was my purchase-money. I do not choose that that money should pass into Oswald's hands. My son shall have everything from me— everything. [OSWALD ALVING *enters through the second door to the right; he has taken off his hat and overcoat in the hall.* MRS. ALVING *goes towards him.*] Are you back again already? my dear, dear boy!

OSWALD: Yes. What can a fellow do out of doors in this eternal rain? But I hear dinner's ready. That's capital!

REGINA [*with a parcel, from the dining-room*]:   A parcel has come for you, Mrs. Alving.   [*Hands it to her.*]

MRS. ALVING [*with a glance at* MR. MANDERS]:   No doubt copies of the ode for to-morrow's ceremony.

MANDERS: H'm——

REGINA: And dinner is ready.

MRS. ALVING: Very well. We'll come directly. I'll just——
                              [*Begins to open the parcel.*]

REGINA [*to* OSWALD]:   Would Mr. Alving like red or white wine?

OSWALD: Both, if you please.

REGINA: *Bien.* Very well, sir.   [*She goes into the dining-room.*]

OSWALD: I may as well help to uncork it.

[*He also goes into the dining-room, the door of which swings half-open behind him.*]

MRS. ALVING [*who has opened the parcel*]:   Yes, as I thought. Here is the Ceremonial Ode, Pastor Manders.

MANDERS [*with folded hands*]:   With what countenance I'm to deliver my discourse to-morrow——!

MRS. ALVING: Oh! you'll get through it somehow.

MANDERS [*softly, so as not to be heard in the dining-room*]:   Yes; it would not do to provoke scandal.

MRS. ALVING [*under her breath, but firmly*]:   No. But then this long, hateful comedy will be ended. From the day after to-morrow it shall be for me as though he who is dead had never lived in this house. No one shall be here but my boy and his mother.

[*From within the dining-room comes the noise of a chair overturned, and at the same moment is heard*]

REGINA [*sharply, but whispering*]:   Oswald! take care! are you mad? Let me go!

MRS. ALVING [*starts in terror*]:   Ah!

[*She stares wildly towards the half-opened door.* OSWALD *is heard coughing and humming. A bottle is uncorked.*]

MANDERS [*excited*]: What in the world is the matter? What is it, Mrs. Alving.

MRS. ALVING [*hoarsely*]: Ghosts! The couple from the conservatory—risen again!

MANDERS: What! Is it possible! Regina——? Is she——?

MRS. ALVING: Yes. Come. Not another word!

[*She seizes* MR. MANDERS *by the arm, and walks unsteadily towards the dining-room.*]

Act II

The same room. The mist still lies heavy over the landscape. MANDERS *and* MRS. ALVING *enter from the dining-room.*

MRS. ALVING [*still in the doorway*]: Velbekomme, Mr. Manders. [*Turns back towards the dining-room.*] Aren't you coming too, Oswald?

OSWALD [*from within*]: No, thank you. I think I shall go out a little.

MRS. ALVING: Yes, do. The weather seems brighter now. [*She shuts the dining-room door, goes to the hall door, and calls*] Regina!

REGINA [*outside*]: Yes, Mrs. Alving.

MRS. ALVING: Go down to the laundry, and help with the garlands.

REGINA: I'll go directly, Mrs. Alving.

[MRS. ALVING *assures herself that* REGINA *goes; then shuts the door.*]

MANDERS: I suppose he can't overhear us in there?

MRS. ALVING: Not when the door is shut. Besides, he's just going out.

MANDERS: I'm still quite upset. I can't think how I could get down a morsel of dinner.

MRS. ALVING [*controlling her nervousness, walks up and down*]: No more can I. But what's to be done now?

MANDERS: Yes; what's to be done? Upon my honour, I don't know. I'm so utterly without experience in matters of this sort.

MRS. ALVING: I'm quite convinced that, so far, no mischief has been done.

MANDERS: No; heaven forbid! But it's an unseemly state of things, nevertheless.

MRS. ALVING: The whole thing is an idle fancy of Oswald's; you may be sure of that.

MANDERS: Well, as I say, I'm not accustomed to affairs of the kind. But I should certainly think——

MRS. ALVING: Out of the house she must go, and that immediately. That's as clear as daylight.

MANDERS: Yes, of course she must.

MRS. ALVING: But where to? It would not be right to——

MANDERS: Where to? Home to her father, of course.

MRS. ALVING: To whom did you say?

MANDERS: To her—— But then, Engstrand is not——? Good God, Mrs. Alving, it's impossible! You must be mistaken after all.

MRS. ALVING: Alas! I'm mistaken in nothing. Johanna confessed all to me, and Alving could not deny it. So there was nothing to be done but to get the matter hushed up.

MANDERS: No, you could do nothing else.

MRS. ALVING: The girl left our service at once, and got a good sum of money to hold her tongue for the time. The rest she managed for herself when she got into the town. She renewed her old acquaintance with Engstrand, no doubt gave him to understand how much money she had received, and told him some tale about a foreigner who put in here with a yacht that summer. So she and Engstrand got married in hot haste. Why, you married them yourself.

MANDERS: But then, how to account for——? I recollect distinctly Engstrand coming to give notice of the marriage. He was broken down with contrition, and reproached himself so bitterly for the misbehaviour he and his sweetheart had been guilty of.

MRS. ALVING: Yes; of course he had to take the blame upon himself.

MANDERS: But such a piece of duplicity on his part! And towards me too! I never could have believed it of Jacob Engstrand. I shan't fail to give him a serious talking to; he may be sure of that. And then the immorality of such a connection! For money! How much did the girl receive?

MRS. ALVING: Three hundred dollars.

MANDERS: There! think of that! for a miserable three hundred dollars to go and marry a fallen woman!

MRS. ALVING: Then what have you to say of me? I went and married a fallen man.

MANDERS: But—good heavens!—what are you talking about? A fallen man?

MRS. ALVING: Do you think Alving was any purer when I went with him to the altar than Johanna was when Engstrand married her?

MANDERS: Well, but there's a world of difference between the two cases——

MRS. ALVING: Not so much difference after all, except in the price—a wretched three hundred dollars and a whole fortune.

MANDERS: How can you compare the two cases? You had taken counsel with your own heart and with your friends.

MRS. ALVING [*without looking at him*]:   I thought you understood where what you call my heart had strayed to at the time.

MANDERS [*distantly*]:   Had I understood anything of the kind, I should not have continued a daily guest in your husband's house.

MRS. ALVING: Well, the fact remains that with myself I took no counsel whatever.

MANDERS: Well then, with your nearest relatives—as your duty bade you— with your mother and both your aunts.

MRS. ALVING: Yes, that's true. Those three cast up the account for me. Oh! it's marvellous how clearly they made out that it would be downright madness to refuse such an offer. If mother could only see me now, and know what all that grandeur has come to!

MANDERS: Nobody can be held responsible for the result. This, at least, remains clear: your marriage was in accordance with law and order.

MRS. ALVING [*at the window*]: Oh! that perpetual law and order! I often think that's what does all the mischief here in the world.

MANDERS: Mrs. Alving, that is a sinful way of talking.

MRS. ALVING: Well, I can't help it; I can endure all this constraint and cowardice no longer. It's too much for me. I must work my way out to freedom.

MANDERS: What do you mean by that?

MRS. ALVING [*drumming on the window-sill*]: I ought never to have concealed the facts of Alving's life. But at that time I was afraid to do anything else—afraid on my own account. I was such a coward.

MANDERS: A coward?

MRS. ALVING: If people had come to know anything, they would have said—"Poor man! with a runaway wife, no wonder he kicks over the traces."

MANDERS: Such remarks might have been made with a certain show of right.

MRS. ALVING [*looking steadily at him*]: If I were what I ought to be, I should go to Oswald and say, "Listen, my boy; your father was self-indulgent and vicious——"

MANDERS: Merciful heavens——!

MRS. ALVING: ——and then I should tell him all I have told you—every word of it.

MANDERS: The idea is shocking, Mrs. Alving.

MRS. ALVING: Yes; I know that. I know that very well. I'm shocked at it myself. [*Goes away from the window.*] I'm such a coward.

MANDERS: You call it "cowardice" to do your plain duty? Have you forgotten that a son should love and honour his father and mother?

MRS. ALVING: Don't let us talk in such general terms. Let us ask: should Oswald love and honour Chamberlain Alving?

MANDERS: Is there no voice in your mother's heart that forbids you to destroy your son's ideals?

MRS. ALVING: But what about the truth?

MANDERS: But what about the ideals?

MRS. ALVING: Oh! Ideals! Ideals! If only I weren't such a coward!

MANDERS: Do not despise ideals, Mrs. Alving; they will avenge themselves cruelly. Take Oswald's case; he, unfortunately, seems to have few enough ideals as it is; but I can see that his father stands before him as an ideal.

MRS. ALVING: You're right there.

MANDERS: And this habit of mind you have yourself implanted and fostered by your letters.

MRS. ALVING: Yes; in my superstitious awe for Duty and Decency I lied to my boy, year after year. Oh! what a coward, what a coward I've been!

MANDERS: You have established a happy illusion in your son's heart, Mrs. Alving, and assuredly you ought not to under-value it.

MRS. ALVING: H'm; who knows whether it's so happy after all——? But, at any rate, I won't have any goings-on with Regina. He shan't go and ruin the poor girl.

MANDERS: No; good God! that would be dreadful!

MRS. ALVING: If I knew he was in earnest, and that it would be for his happiness——

MANDERS: What? What then?

MRS. ALVING: But it couldn't be; for I'm sorry to say Regina is not a girl to make him happy.

MANDERS: Well, what then? What do you mean?

MRS. ALVING: If I weren't such a pitiful coward I would say to him, "Marry her, or make what arrangement you please, only let us have nothing underhand about it."

MANDERS: Good heavens, would you let them *marry!* Anything so dreadful——! so unheard of——!

MRS. ALVING: Do you really mean "unheard-of"? Frankly, Pastor Manders, do you suppose that throughout the country there aren't plenty of married couples as closely akin as they?

MANDERS: I don't in the least understand you.

MRS. ALVING: Oh yes, indeed you do.

MANDERS: Ah, you are thinking of the possibility that—— Yes, alas! family life is certainly not always so pure as it ought to be. But in such a case as you point to, one can never know—at least with any certainty. Here, on the other hand—that you, a mother, can think of letting your son——!

MRS. ALVING: But I can't—I wouldn't for anything in the world; that's precisely what I am saying.

MANDERS: No, because you are a "coward," as you put it. But if you were not a "coward," then——? Good God! a connection so shocking.

MRS. ALVING: So far as that goes, they say we're all sprung from connections of that sort. And who is it that arranged the world so, Pastor Manders?

MANDERS: Questions of that kind I must decline to discuss with you, Mrs. Alving; you are far from being in the right frame of mind for them. But that you dare to call your scruples "cowardly"——!

MRS. ALVING: Let me tell you what I mean. I am timid and half-hearted because I cannot get rid of the Ghosts that haunt me.

MANDERS: What do you say haunts you?

MRS. ALVING: Ghosts! When I heard Regina and Oswald in there, I seemed to see Ghosts before me. I almost think we're all of us Ghosts, Pastor Manders. It's not only what we have inherited from our father and mother that "walks" in us. It's all sorts of dead ideas, and lifeless old beliefs, and so forth. They have no vitality, but they cling to us all the same, and we can't get rid of them. Whenever I take up a newspaper, I seem to see Ghosts gliding between the lines. There must be Ghosts all the country over, as thick as the sand of the sea. And then we are, one and all, so pitifully afraid of the light.

MANDERS: Ah! here we have the fruits of your reading! And pretty fruits they are, upon my word! Oh! those horrible, revolutionary, free-thinking books!

MRS. ALVING: You are mistaken, my dear Pastor. It was you yourself who set me thinking; and I thank you for it with all my heart.

MANDERS: I?

MRS. ALVING: Yes—when you forced me under the yoke you called Duty and Obligation; when you praised as right and proper what my whole soul rebelled against as something loathsome. It was then that I began to look into the seams of your doctrine. I wanted only to pick at a single knot; but when I had got that undone, the whole thing ravelled out. And then I understood that it was all machine-sewn.

MANDERS [*softly, with emotion*]: And was that the upshot of my life's hardest battle?

MRS. ALVING: Call it rather your most pitiful defeat.

MANDERS: It was my greatest victory, Helen—the victory over myself.

MRS. ALVING: It was a crime against us both.

MANDERS: When you went astray, and came to me crying, "Here I am; take me!" I commanded you, saying, "Woman, go home to your lawful husband." Was that a crime?

MRS. ALVING: Yes, I think so.

MANDERS: We two do not understand each other.

MRS. ALVING: Not now, at any rate.

MANDERS: Never—never in my most secret thoughts have I regarded you otherwise than as another's wife.

MRS. ALVING: Oh!—indeed?

MANDERS: Helen——!

MRS. ALVING: People so easily forget their past selves.

MANDERS: I do not. I am what I always was.

MRS. ALVING [*changing the subject*]: Well, well, well; don't let us talk of old times any longer. You are now over head and ears in Commissions and Boards of Direction, and I am fighting my battle with Ghosts both within me and without.

MANDERS: Those without I shall help you to lay. After all the shocking things I've heard from you to-day, I cannot in conscience permit an unprotected girl to remain in your house.

MRS. ALVING: Don't you think the best plan would be to get her provided for—I mean, by a good marriage.

MANDERS: No doubt. I think it would be desirable for her in every respect. Regina is now at the age when—— Of course I don't know much about these things, but——

MRS. ALVING: Regina matured very early.

MANDERS: Yes, did she not? I have an impression that she was remarkably well developed, physically, when I prepared her for confirmation. But in the meantime, she must go home, under her father's eye.—Ah! but Engstrand is not—— That he—that *he*—could so hide the truth from me!

[*A knock at the door into the hall.*]

MRS. ALVING: Who can that be? Come in!

ENGSTRAND [*in his Sunday clothes, in the doorway*]:   I beg your pardon humbly, but——

MANDERS: Ah! H'm——

MRS. ALVING: Is that you, Engstrand?

ENGSTRAND: ——there was none of the servants about, so I took the great liberty of just knocking.

MRS. ALVING: Oh! very well. Come in. Do you want to speak to me?

ENGSTRAND [*comes in*]:   No, I'm greatly obliged to you; it was with his Reverence I wanted to have a word or two.

MANDERS [*walking up and down the room*]:   H'm, indeed. You want to speak to me, do you?

ENGSTRAND: Yes, I should like so much to——

MANDERS [*stops in front of him*]:   Well; may I ask what you want?

ENGSTRAND: Well, it was just this, your Reverence; we've been paid off down yonder—my grateful thanks to you, ma'am,—and now everything's finished, I've been thinking it would be but right and proper if we, that have been working so honestly together all this time—well, I was thinking we ought to end up with a little prayer-meeting to-night.

MANDERS: A prayer-meeting? Down at the Orphanage?

ENGSTRAND: Oh, if your Reverence doesn't think it proper——

MANDERS: Oh yes! I do; but—h'm——

ENGSTRAND: I've been in the habit of offering up a little prayer in the evenings, myself.

MRS. ALVING: Have you?

ENGSTRAND: Yes, every now and then—just a little exercise, you might call it. But I'm a poor, common man, and have little enough gift, God help me! and so I thought, as the Reverend Mr. Manders happened to be here, I'd——

MANDERS: Well, you see, Engstrand, I must first ask you a question. Are you in the right frame of mind for such a meeting? Do you feel your conscience clear and at ease?

ENGSTRAND: Oh! God help us, your Reverence! we'd better not talk about conscience.

MANDERS: Yes, that's just what we must talk about. What have you to answer?

ENGSTRAND: Why—one's conscience—it can be bad enough now and then.

MANDERS: Ah, you admit that. Then will you make a clean breast of it, and tell the truth about Regina?

MRS. ALVING: [*quickly*]:   Mr. Manders!

MANDERS [*reassuringly*]:   Just let me——

ENGSTRAND: About Regina! Lord! how you frighten me! [*Looks at* MRS. ALVING.] There's nothing wrong about Regina, is there?

MANDERS: We'll hope not. But I mean, what is the truth about you and Regina? You pass for her father, eh!

ENGSTRAND [*uncertain*]: Well—h'm—your Reverence knows all about me and poor Johanna.

MANDERS: Come, no more prevarication! Your wife told Mrs. Alving the whole story before quitting her service.

ENGSTRAND: Well, then, may——! Now, did she really?

MANDERS: So you're found out, Engstrand.

ENGSTRAND: And she swore and took her Bible oath——

MANDERS: Did she take her Bible oath?

ENGSTRAND: No; she only swore; but she did it so earnestly.

MANDERS: And you have hidden the truth from me all these years? Hidden it from me! from me, who have trusted you without reserve, in everything.

ENGSTRAND: Well, I can't deny it.

MANDERS: Have I deserved this of you, Engstrand? Haven't I always been ready to help you in word and deed, so far as it stood in my power? Answer me. Have I not?

ENGSTRAND: It would have been a poor look-out for me many a time but for the Reverend Mr. Manders.

MANDERS: And you reward me thus! You cause me to enter falsehoods in the Church Register, and you withhold from me, year after year, the explanations you owed alike to me and to truth. Your conduct has been wholly inexcusable, Engstrand; and from this time forward all is over between us.

ENGSTRAND [*with a sigh*]: Yes! I suppose it must be.

MANDERS: How can you possibly justify yourself?

ENGSTRAND: How could I think she'd gone and made bad worse by talking about it? Will your Reverence just fancy yourself in the same trouble as poor Johanna——

MANDERS: I!

ENGSTRAND: Lord bless you! I don't mean just exactly the same. But I mean, if your Reverence had anything to be ashamed of in the eyes of the world, as the saying is—— We men oughtn't to judge a poor woman too hardly, your Reverence.

MANDERS: I am not doing so. It's you I am reproaching.

ENGSTRAND: Might I make so bold as to ask your Reverence a bit of a question?

MANDERS: Yes, ask away.

ENGSTRAND: Isn't it right and proper for a man to raise up the fallen?

MANDERS: Most certainly it is.

ENGSTRAND: And isn't a man bound to keep his sacred word?

MANDERS: Why, of course he is; but——

ENGSTRAND: When Johanna had got into trouble through that Englishman—or it might have been an American or a Russian, as they call them—well, you see, she came down into the town. Poor thing! she'd sent me about my business once or twice before: for she couldn't bear the sight of anything but what was handsome; and I'd got this damaged leg. Your Reverence recollects how I ventured up into a dancing-saloon, where seafaring people carried on with drink and devilry, as the saying goes. And then, when I was for giving them a bit of an admonition to lead a new life——

MRS. ALVING [*at the window*]:   H'm——

MANDERS: I know all about that, Engstrand; the ruffians threw you downstairs. You've told me of the affair already.

ENGSTRAND: I'm not puffed up about it, your Reverence. But what I wanted to say was, that then she came and confessed all to me, with weeping and gnashing of teeth. I can tell your Reverence I was sore at heart to hear it.

MANDERS: Were you indeed, Engstrand? Well, go on.

ENGSTRAND: So I said to her, "The American, he's sailing about on the boundless sea. And as for you, Johanna," said I, "you've committed a grievous sin and you're a fallen creature. But Jacob Engstrand," said I, "he's got two good legs to stand upon, *he* has——" You know, you Reverence, I was speaking figurative-like.

MANDERS: I understand quite well. Go on.

ENGSTRAND: Well, that was how I raised her up and made an honest woman of her, so that folks shouldn't get to know how she'd gone astray with foreigners.

MANDERS: All that was very good of you. Only I can't approve of your stooping to take money——

ENGSTRAND: Money? I? Not a farthing!

MANDERS [*inquiringly to* MRS. ALVING]:   But——

ENGSTRAND: Oh, wait a minute!—now I recollect. Johanna had a trifle of money. But I would have nothing to do with it. "No," said I, "that's mammon; that's the wages of sin. This dirty gold—or notes, or whatever it was—we'll just fling that back to the American," said I. But he was gone and away, over the stormy sea, your Reverence.

MANDERS: Was he really, my good fellow?

ENGSTRAND: Ay, sir. So Johanna and I, we agreed that the money should go to the child's education; and so it did, and I can account for every blessed farthing of it.

MANDERS: Why, this alters the case considerably.

ENGSTRAND: That's just how it stands, your Reverence. And I make so bold as to say I've been an honest father to Regina, so far as my poor strength went; for I'm but a poor creature, worse luck!

MANDERS: Well, well, my good fellow——

ENGSTRAND: But I may make bold to say that I've brought up the child, and lived kindly with poor Johanna, and ruled over my own house, as the Scripture has it. But I could never think of going up to your Reverence and puffing myself up and boasting because I too had done some good in the world. No, sir; when anything of that sort happens to Jacob Engstrand, he holds his tongue about it. It doesn't happen so very often, I daresay. And when I do come to see your Reverence, I find a mortal deal to say about what's wicked and weak. For I do say—as I was saying just now—one's conscience isn't always as clean as it might be.

MANDERS: Give me your hand, Jacob Engstrand.

ENGSTRAND: Oh, Lord! your Reverence——

MANDERS: Come, no nonsense [*wrings his hand*]. There we are!

ENGSTRAND: And if I might humbly beg your Reverence's pardon——

MANDERS: You? On the contrary, it's I who ought to beg your pardon——

ENGSTRAND: Lord, no, sir!

MANDERS: Yes, certainly. And I do it with all my heart. Forgive me for misunderstanding you. And I wish I could give you some proof of my hearty regret, and of my good-will towards you——

ENGSTRAND: Would your Reverence?

MANDERS: With the greatest pleasure.

ENGSTRAND: Well then, there's the very opportunity now. With the money I've saved here, I was thinking I might set up a Sailors' Home down in the town.

MRS. ALVING: You?

ENGSTRAND: Yes; it too might be a sort of Orphanage, in a manner of speaking. There are many temptations for seafaring folk ashore. But in this Home of mine, a man might feel as under a father's eye, I was thinking.

MANDERS: What do you say to this, Mrs. Alving?

ENGSTRAND: It isn't much I've got to start with, the Lord help me! But if I could only find a helping hand, why——

MANDERS: Yes, yes; we'll look into the matter. I entirely approve of your plan. But now, go before me and make everything ready, and get the candles lighted, so as to give the place an air of festivity. And then we'll pass an edifying hour together, my good fellow; for now I quite believe you're in the right frame of mind.

ENGSTRAND: Yes, I trust I am. And so I'll say good-bye, ma'am, and thank you kindly; and take good care of Regina for me—[*wipes a tear from his eye*]—poor Johanna's child; h'm, it's an odd thing, now; but it's just as if she'd grown into the very apple of my eye. It is indeed.

[*He bows and goes out through the hall*]

MANDERS: Well, what do you say of that man now, Mrs. Alving? That threw a totally different light on matters, didn't it?

MRS. ALVING: Yes, it certainly did.

MANDERS: It only shows how excessively careful one must be in judging one's fellow-creatures. But it's a great joy to ascertain that one has been mistaken. Don't you think so?

MRS. ALVING: I think you are, and will always be, a great baby, Manders.

MANDERS: I?

MRS. ALVING [*laying her two hands upon his shoulders*]: And I say that I've half a mind to put my arms round your neck, and kiss you.

MANDERS [*stepping hastily back*]: No, no! God bless me! What an idea!

MRS. ALVING [*with a smile*]: Oh! you needn't be afraid of me.

MANDERS [*by the table*]: You have sometimes such an exaggerated way of expressing yourself. Now, I'll just collect all the documents, and put them in my bag. [*He does so.*] There now. And now, good-bye for the present. Keep your eyes open when Oswald comes back. I shall look in again later.

[*He takes his hat and goes out through the hall door.*]

MRS. ALVING [*sighs, looks for a moment out of the window, sets the room in order a little, and is about to go into the dining-room, but stops at the door with a half-suppressed cry*]:   Oswald, are you still at table?

OSWALD [*in the dining-room*]:   I'm only finishing my cigar.

MRS. ALVING: I thought you'd gone for a little walk.

OSWALD: In such weather as this? [*A glass clinks.* MRS. ALVING *leaves the door open, and sits down with her knitting on the sofa by the window.*] Wasn't that Pastor Manders that went out just now?

MRS. ALVING: Yes; he went down to the Orphanage.

OSWALD: H'm.   [*The glass and decanter clink again.*]

MRS. ALVING [*with a troubled glance*]:   Dear Oswald, you should take care of that liqueur. It's strong.

OSWALD: It keeps out the damp.

MRS. ALVING: Wouldn't you rather come in to me?

OSWALD: I mayn't smoke in there.

MRS. ALVING: You know quite well you may smoke cigars.

OSWALD: Oh! all right, then; I'll come in. Just a tiny drop more first! There! [*He comes into the room with his cigar, and shuts the door after him. A short silence.*] Where's Manders gone to?

MRS. ALVING: I've just told you; he went down to the Orphanage.

OSWALD: Oh, ah; so you did.

MRS. ALVING: You shouldn't sit so long at table after dinner, Oswald.

OSWALD [*holding his cigar behind him*]:   But I find it so pleasant, mother. [*Strokes and pets her.*] Just think what it is for me to come home and sit at mother's own table, in mother's room, and eat mother's delicious dinners.

MRS. ALVING: My dear, dear boy!

OSWALD [*somewhat impatiently walks about and smokes*]:   And what else can I do with myself here? I can't set to work at anything.

MRS. ALVING: Why can't you?

OSWALD: In such weather as this? Without a single ray of sunlight the whole day? [*Walks up the room.*] Oh! not to be able to work!

MRS. ALVING: Perhaps it was not quite wise of you to come home?

OSWALD: Oh, yes, mother; I had to.

MRS. ALVING: Why? I would ten times rather forgo the joy of having you here than——

OSWALD [*stops beside the table*]:   Now just tell me, mother: does it really make you so very happy to have me home again?

MRS. ALVING: Does it make me happy!

OSWALD [*crumpling up a newspaper*]:   I should have thought it must be pretty much the same to you whether I was in existence or not.

MRS. ALVING: Have you the heart to say that to your mother, Oswald?

OSWALD: But you've got on very well without me all this time.

MRS. ALVING: Yes; I've got on without you. That's true.

[*A silence. Twilight gradually falls.* OSWALD *walks to and fro across the room. He has laid his cigar down.*]

OSWALD [*stops beside* MRS. ALVING]:   Mother, may I sit on the sofa beside you?

MRS. ALVING [*makes room for him*]:   Yes, do, my dear boy.

OSWALD [*sits down*]:   Now I'm going to tell you something, mother.

MRS. ALVING [*anxiously*]:   Well?

OSWALD [*looks fixedly before him*]:   For I can't go on hiding it any longer.

MRS. ALVING: Hiding what? What is it?

OSWALD [*as before*]:   I could never bring myself to write to you about it; and since I've come home——

MRS. ALVING [*seizes him by the arm*]:   Oswald, what *is* the matter?

OSWALD [*as before*]:   Both yesterday and to-day I've tried to put the thoughts away from me—to get free from them; but it won't do.

MRS. ALVING [*rising*]:   Now you must speak out, Oswald.

OSWALD [*draws her down to the sofa again*]:   Sit still; and then I'll try to tell you. I complained of fatigue after my journey——

MRS. ALVING: Well, what then?

OSWALD: But it isn't that that's the matter with me; it isn't any ordinary fatigue——

MRS. ALVING [*tries to jump up*]:   You're not ill, Oswald?

OSWALD [*draws her down again*]:   Do sit still, mother. Only take it quietly. I'm not downright ill, either; not what's commonly called "ill." [*Clasps his hands above his head.*] Mother, my mind is broken down—ruined—I shall never be able to work again.

[*With his hands before his face, he buries his head in her lap, and breaks into bitter sobbing.*]

MRS. ALVING [*white and trembling*]:   Oswald! Look at me! No, no; it isn't true.

OSWALD [*looks up with despair in his eyes*]:   Never to be able to work again! Never! never! It will be like living death! Mother, can you imagine anything so horrible?

MRS. ALVING: My poor boy! How has this horrible thing come over you?

OSWALD [*sits upright*]:   That's just what I can't possibly grasp or understand. I've never led a dissipated life—never, in any respect. You mustn't believe that of me, mother. I've never done that.

MRS. ALVING: I'm sure you haven't, Oswald.

OSWALD: And yet this has come over me just the same—this awful misfortune!

MRS. ALVING: Oh, but it will pass away, my dear, blessed boy. It's nothing but over-work. Trust me, I am right.

OSWALD [*sadly*]:   I thought so too at first; but it isn't so.

MRS. ALVING: Tell me the whole story from beginning to end.

OSWALD: Well, I will.

MRS. ALVING: When did you first notice it?

OSWALD: It was directly after I had been home last time, and had got back to Paris again. I began to feel the most violent pains in my head—chiefly in the back of my head, I thought. It was as though a tight iron ring was being screwed round my neck and upwards.

MRS. ALVING: Well, and then?

OSWALD: At first I thought it was nothing but the ordinary headache I had been so plagued with when I was growing up——

MRS. ALVING: Yes, yes——

OSWALD: But it wasn't that. I soon found that out. I couldn't work. I wanted to begin upon a big new picture, but my powers seemed to fail me; all my strength was crippled; I couldn't form any definite images; everything swam before me—whirling round and round. Oh! it was an awful state! At last I sent for a doctor, and from him I learned the truth.

MRS. ALVING: How do you mean?

OSWALD: He was one of the first doctors in Paris. I told him my symptoms, and then he set to work asking me a heap of questions which I thought had nothing to do with the matter. I couldn't imagine what the man was after——

MRS. ALVING: Well?

OSWALD: At last he said: "You have been worm-eaten from your birth." He used that very word—*vermoulu*.

MRS. ALVING [*breathlessly*]: What did he mean by that?

OSWALD: I didn't understand either, and begged him to explain himself more clearly. And then the old cynic said—[*clenching his fist*] Oh——!

MRS. ALVING: What did he say?

OSWALD: He said, "The sins of the fathers are visited upon the children."

MRS. ALVING [*rising slowly*]: The sins of the fathers——!

OSWALD: I very nearly struck him in the face——

MRS. ALVING [*walks away across the floor*]: The sins of the fathers——

OSWALD [*smiles sadly*]: Yes; what do you think of that? Of course I assured him that such a thing was out of the question. But do you think he gave in? No, he stuck to it; and it was only when I produced your letters and translated the passages relating to father——

MRS. ALVING: But then?

OSWALD: Then of course he was bound to admit that he was on the wrong track; and so I got to know the truth—the incomprehensible truth! I ought to have held aloof from my bright and happy life among my comrades. It had been too much for my strength. So I had brought it upon myself!

MRS. ALVING: Oswald! Oh no, don't believe it!

OSWALD: No other explanation was possible, he said. That's the awful part of it. Incurably ruined for life—by my own heedlessness! All that I meant to have done in the world—I never dare think of again—I'm not *able* to think of it. Oh! if I could but live over again, and undo all I've done! [*He buries his face in the sofa.* MRS. ALVING *wrings her hands and walks, in silent struggle, backwards and forwards.* OSWALD, *after a while, looks up and remains resting upon his elbow.*] If it had only been something inherited, something one wasn't responsible for! But this! To have thrown away so shamefully, thoughtlessly, recklessly, one's own happiness, one's own health, everything in the world—one's future, one's very life!

MRS. ALVING: No, no, my dear, darling boy! It's impossible. [*Bends over him.*] Things are not so desperate as you think.

OSWALD: Oh! you don't know—— [*Springs up.*] And then, mother, to cause you all this sorrow! Many a time I've almost wished and hoped that at bottom you didn't care so very much about me.

MRS. ALVING: I, Oswald? My only boy! You are all I have in the world! The only thing I care about!

OSWALD [*seizes both her hands and kisses them*]: Yes, mother dear, I see it well enough. When I'm at home, I see it, of course; and that's the hardest part for me. But now you know the whole story, and now we won't talk any more about it to-day. I daren't think of it for long together. [*Goes up the room.*] Get me something to drink, mother.

MRS. ALVING: Drink? What do you want to drink now?

OSWALD: Oh! anything you like. You have some cold punch in the house.

MRS. ALVING: Yes, but my dear Oswald——

OSWALD: Don't refuse me, mother. Do be nice, now! I must have something to wash down all these gnawing thoughts. [*Goes into the conservatory.*] And then—it's so dark here! [MRS. ALVING *pulls a bell-rope on the right.*] And this ceaseless rain! It may go on week after week for months together. Never to get a glimpse of the sun! I can't recollect ever having seen the sun shine all the times I've been at home.

MRS. ALVING: Oswald, you're thinking of going away from me.

OSWALD: H'm—[*drawing a deep breath*]—I'm not thinking of anything. I can't think of anything. [*In a low voice.*] I let thinking alone.

REGINA [*from the dining-room*]: Did you ring, ma'am?

MRS. ALVING: Yes; let us have the lamp in.

REGINA: I will, directly. It's ready lighted. [*Goes out.*]

MRS. ALVING [*goes across to* OSWALD]: Oswald, be frank with me.

OSWALD: Well, so I am, mother. [*Goes to the table.*] I think I've told you enough. [REGINA *brings the lamp and sets it upon the table.*]

MRS. ALVING: Regina, you might fetch us a half-bottle of champagne.

REGINA: Very well, ma'am. [*Goes out.*]

OSWALD [*puts his arm round* MRS. ALVING's *neck*]: That's just what I wanted. I knew mother wouldn't let her boy be thirsty.

MRS. ALVING: My own, poor, darling Oswald, how could I deny you anything now?

OSWALD [*eagerly*]: Is that true, mother? Do you mean it?

MRS. ALVING: How? What?

OSWALD: That you couldn't deny me anything.

MRS. ALVING: My dear Oswald——

OSWALD: Hush!

REGINA [*brings a tray with a half-bottle of champagne and two glasses, which she sets on the table*]: Shall I open it?

OSWALD: No, thanks. I'll do it myself. [REGINA *goes out again.*]

MRS. ALVING [*sits down by the table*]: What was it you meant, I mustn't deny you?

OSWALD [*busy opening the bottle*]: First let's have a glass—or two.

[*The cork pops; he pours wine into one glass, and is about to pour it into the other.*]

MRS. ALVING [*holding her hand over it*]:   Thanks; not for me.

OSWALD: Oh! won't you? Then I will!

[*He empties the glass, fills, and empties it again; then he sits down by the table.*]

MRS. ALVING [*in expectation*]:   Well?

OSWALD [*without looking at her*]:   Tell me—I thought you and Pastor Manders seemed so odd—so quiet—at dinner to-day.

MRS. ALVING: Did you notice it?

OSWALD: Yes. H'm—— [*After a short silence.*] Tell me: what do you think of Regina?

MRS. ALVING: What I think?

OSWALD: Yes; isn't she splendid?

MRS. ALVING: My dear Oswald, you don't know her as I do——

OSWALD: Well?

MRS. ALVING: Regina, unfortunately, was allowed to stay at home too long. I ought to have taken her earlier into my house.

OSWALD: Yes, but isn't she splendid to look at, mother? [*He fills his glass.*]

MRS. ALVING: Regina has many serious faults.

OSWALD: Oh, what does it matter?   [*He drinks again.*]

MRS. ALVING: But I'm fond of her, nevertheless, and I'm responsible for her. I wouldn't for all the world have any harm happen to her.

OSWALD [*springs up*]:   Mother! Regina is my only salvation.

MRS. ALVING [*rising*]:   What do you mean by that?

OSWALD: I can't go on bearing all this anguish of mind alone.

MRS. ALVING: Haven't you got your mother to share it with you?

OSWALD: Yes; that's what I thought; and so I came home to you. But that won't do. I see it won't do. I can't endure my life here.

MRS. ALVING: Oswald!

OSWALD: I must live differently, mother. That's why I must leave you. I won't have you looking on at it.

MRS. ALVING: My unhappy boy! But, Oswald, while you're so ill as this——

OSWALD: If it were only the illness, I should stay with you, mother, you may be sure; for you are the best friend I have in the world.

MRS. ALVING: Yes, indeed I am, Oswald; am I not?

OSWALD [*wanders restlessly about*]:   But it's all the torment, the remorse; and besides that, the great, killing dread. Oh! that awful dread!

MRS. ALVING [*walking after him*]:   Dread? What dread? What do you mean?

OSWALD: Oh, you mustn't ask me any more! I don't know. I can't describe it. [MRS. ALVING *goes over to the right and pulls the bell.*] What is it you want?

MRS. ALVING: I want my boy to be happy—that's what I want. He shan't go on racking his brains. [*To* REGINA, *who comes in at the door.*] More champagne—a whole bottle.   [REGINA *goes.*]

OSWALD: Mother!

MRS. ALVING: Do you think we don't know how to live here at home?

OSWALD: Isn't she splendid to look at? How beautifully she's built! And so thoroughly healthy!

MRS. ALVING [*sits by the table*]: Sit down, Oswald; let us talk quietly together.

OSWALD [*sits*]: I daresay you don't know, mother, that I owe Regina some reparation.

MRS. ALVING: You?

OSWALD: For a bit of thoughtlessness, or whatever you like to call it—very innocent, anyhow. When I was home last time——

MRS. ALVING: Well?

OSWALD: She used often to ask me about Paris, and I used to tell her one thing and another. Then I recollect I happened to say to her one day, "Wouldn't you like to go there yourself?"

MRS. ALVING: Well?

OSWALD: I saw her face flush, and then she said, "Yes, I should like it of all things." "Ah, well," I replied, "it might perhaps be managed"—or something like that.

MRS. ALVING: And then?

OSWALD: Of course I'd forgotten the whole thing; but the day before yesterday I happened to ask her whether she was glad I was to stay at home so long——

MRS. ALVING: Yes?

OSWALD: And then she looked so strangely at me and asked, "But what's to become of my trip to Paris?"

MRS. ALVING: Her trip!

OSWALD: And so I got out of her that she had taken the thing seriously; that she had been thinking of me the whole time, and had set to work to learn French——

MRS. ALVING: So that was why she did it!

OSWALD: Mother! when I saw that fresh, lovely, splendid girl standing there before me—till then I had hardly noticed her—but when she stood there as though with open arms ready to receive me——

MRS. ALVING: Oswald!

OSWALD: ——then it flashed upon me that my salvation lay in her; for I saw that she was full of the joy of life.

MRS. ALVING [*starts*]: The joy of life? Can there be salvation in that?

REGINA [*from the dining-room, with a bottle of champagne*]: I'm sorry to have been so long, but I had to go to the cellar.

[*Puts the bottle on the table.*]

OSWALD: And now fetch another glass.

REGINA [*looks at him in surprise*]: There is Mrs. Alving's glass, Mr. Alving.

OSWALD: Yes, but fetch one for yourself, Regina. [REGINA *starts and gives a lightning-like side glance at* MRS. ALVING.] Why do you wait?

REGINA [*softly and hesitatingly*]: Is it Mrs. Alving's wish?

MRS. ALVING: Fetch the glass, Regina.

[REGINA *goes out into the dining-room.*]

OSWALD [*follows her with his eyes*]:   Have you noticed how she walks?—so firmly and lightly!

MRS. ALVING: It can never be, Oswald!

OSWALD: It's a settled thing. Can't you see that? It's no use saying anything against it. [REGINA *enters with an empty glass, which she keeps in her hand.*] Sit down, Regina. [REGINA *looks inquiringly at* MRS. ALVING.]

MRS. ALVING: Sit down. [REGINA *sits on a chair by the dining-room door, still holding the empty glass in her hand.*] Oswald, what were you saying about the joy of life?

OSWALD: Ah! the joy of life, mother—that's a thing you don't know much about in these parts. I've never felt it here.

MRS. ALVING: Not when you're with me?

OSWALD: Not when I'm at home. But you don't understand that.

MRS. ALVING: Yes, yes; I think I almost understand it—now.

OSWALD: And then, too, the joy of work! At bottom, it's the same thing. But that, too, you know nothing about.

MRS. ALVING: Perhaps you're right, Oswald; tell me more about it.

OSWALD: Well, I only mean that here people are brought up to believe that work is a curse and a punishment for sin, and that life is something miserable, something we want to be done with, the sooner the better.

MRS. ALVING: "A vale of tears," yes; and we take care to make it one.

OSWALD: But in the great world people won't hear of such things. There, nobody really believes such doctrines any longer. There, you feel it bliss and ecstasy merely to draw the breath of life. Mother, have you noticed that everything I've painted has turned upon the joy of life?—always, always upon the joy of life?—light and sunshine and glorious air and faces radiant with happiness. That's why I'm afraid of remaining at home with you.

MRS. ALVING: Afraid? What are you afraid of here, with me?

OSWALD: I'm afraid lest all my instincts should be warped into ugliness.

MRS. ALVING [*looks steadily at him*]:   Do you think that would be the way of it?

OSWALD: I know it. You may live the same life here as there, and yet it won't be the same life.

MRS. ALVING [*who has been listening eagerly, rises, her eyes big with thought, and says*]:   Now I see the connection.

OSWALD: What is it you see?

MRS. ALVING: I see it now for the first time. And now I can speak.

OSWALD [*rising*]:   Mother, I don't understand you.

REGINA [*who has also risen*]:   Perhaps I ought to go?

MRS. ALVING: No. Stay here. Now I can speak. Now, my boy, you shall know the whole truth. And then you can choose. Oswald! Regina!

OSWALD: Hush! Here's Manders——

MANDERS [*comes in by the hall door*]:   There! We've had a most edifying time down there.

OSWALD: So have we.

MANDERS: We must stand by Engstrand and his Sailors' Home. Regina must go to him and help him——

REGINA: No, thank you, sir.

MANDERS [*noticing her for the first time*]: What? You here? and with a glass in your hand!

REGINA [*hastily putting the glass down*]: *Pardon!*

OSWALD: Regina is going with me, Mr. Manders.

MANDERS: Going with you!

OSWALD: Yes; as my wife—if she wishes it.

MANDERS: But, good God——!

REGINA: I can't help it, sir.

OSWALD: Or she'll stay here, if I stay.

REGINA [*involuntarily*]: Here!

MANDERS: I am thunderstruck at your conduct, Mrs. Alving.

MRS. ALVING: They will do neither one thing nor the other; for now I can speak out plainly.

MANDERS: You surely won't do that. No, no, no!

MRS. ALVING: Yes, I can speak and I will. And no ideal shall suffer after all.

OSWALD: Mother! What on earth are you hiding from me?

REGINA [*listening*]: Oh, ma'am! listen! Don't you hear shouts outside?

[*She goes into the conservatory and looks out.*]

OSWALD [*at the window on the left*]: What's going on? Where does that light come from?

REGINA [*cries out*]: The Orphanage is on fire!

MRS. ALVING [*rushing to the window*]: On fire?

MANDERS: On fire! Impossible! I've just come from there.

OSWALD: Where's my hat? Oh, never mind it—Father's Orphanage!

[*He rushes out through the garden door.*]

MRS. ALVING: My shawl, Regina! It's blazing!

MANDERS: Terrible! Mrs. Alving, it's a judgment upon this abode of sin.

MRS. ALVING: Yes, of course. Come, Regina.

[*She and* REGINA *hasten out through the hall.*]

MANDERS [*clasps his hands together*]: And uninsured too!

[*He goes out the same way.*]

Act III

The room as before. All the doors stand open. The lamp is still burning on the table. It is dark out of doors; there is only a faint glow from the conflagration in the background to the left.

MRS. ALVING, *with a shawl over her head, stands in the conservatory and looks out.* REGINA, *also with a shawl on, stands a little behind her.*

MRS. ALVING: All burnt!—burnt to the ground!

REGINA: The basement is still burning.

MRS. ALVING: How is it Oswald doesn't come home? There's nothing to be saved.

REGINA: Would you like me to take down his hat for him?

MRS. ALVING: Hasn't he even got his hat on?

REGINA [*pointing to the hall*]:   No; there it hangs.

MRS. ALVING: Let it be. He must come up now. I'll go and look for him myself.   [*She goes out through the garden door.*]

MANDERS [*comes in from the hall*]:   Isn't Mrs. Alving here?

REGINA: She's just gone down the garden.

MANDERS: This is the most terrible night I ever went through.

REGINA: Yes; isn't it a dreadful misfortune, sir?

MANDERS: Oh, don't talk about it! I can hardly bear to think of it.

REGINA: How can it have happened?

MANDERS: Don't ask me, Regina. How should *I* know? Do you, too——? Isn't it enough that your father——?

REGINA: What about him?

MANDERS: Oh! he has driven me clean out of my mind.——

ENGSTRAND [*comes through the hall*]:   Your Reverence!

MANDERS [*turns round in terror*]:   Are you after me here, too?

ENGSTRAND: Yes, strike me dead, but I must—— Oh, Lord! what am I saying? It's an awfully ugly business, your Reverence.

MANDERS [*walks to and fro*]:   Alas! alas!

REGINA: What's the matter?

ENGSTRAND: Why, it all came of that prayer-meeting, you see. [*Softly.*] The bird's limed, my girl. [*Aloud.*] And to think that it's my fault that it's his Reverence's fault!

MANDERS: But I assure you, Engstrand——

ENGSTRAND: There wasn't another soul except your Reverence that ever touched the candles down there.

MANDERS [*stops*]:   Ah! so you declare. But I certainly can't recollect that I ever had a candle in my hand.

ENGSTRAND: And I saw as clear as daylight how your Reverence took the candle and snuffed it with your fingers, and threw away the snuff among the shavings.

MANDERS: And you stood and looked on?

ENGSTRAND: Yes; I saw it as plain as a pike-staff.

MANDERS: It's quite beyond my comprehension. Besides, it's never been my habit to snuff candles with my fingers.

ENGSTRAND: And very risky it looked, that it did! But is there so much harm done after all, your Reverence?

MANDERS [*walks restlessly to and fro*]:   Oh, don't ask me!

ENGSTRAND [*walks with him*]:   And your Reverence hadn't insured it, neither?

MANDERS [*continuing to walk up and down*]:   No, no, no; you've heard that already.

ENGSTRAND [*following him*]:   Not insured! And then to go right down and set light to the whole thing. Lord! Lord! what a misfortune!

MANDERS [*wipes the sweat from his forehead*]: Ay, you may well say that, Engstrand.

ENGSTRAND: And to think that such a thing should happen to a benevolent Institution, that was to have been a blessing both to town and country, as the saying is! The newspapers won't handle your Reverence very gently, I expect.

MANDERS: No; that's just what I'm thinking of. That's almost the worst of it. All the malignant attacks and accusations———! Oh, it's terrible only to imagine it.

MRS. ALVING [*comes in from the garden*]: He can't be got away from the fire.

MANDERS: Ah! there you are, Mrs. Alving!

MRS. ALVING: So you've escaped your Inaugural Address, Pastor Manders.

MANDERS: Oh! I should so gladly———

MRS. ALVING [*in an undertone*]: It's all for the best. That Orphanage would have done no good to anybody.

MANDERS: Do you think not?

MRS. ALVING: Do you think it would?

MANDERS: It's a terrible misfortune, all the same.

MRS. ALVING: Let us speak plainly of it, as a piece of business. Are you waiting for Mr. Manders, Engstrand?

ENGSTRAND [*at the hall door*]: Ay, ma'am; indeed I am.

MRS. ALVING: Then sit down meanwhile.

ENGSTRAND: Thank you, ma'am; I'd rather stand.

MRS. ALVING [*to* MANDERS]: I suppose you're going by the steamer?

MANDERS: Yes; it starts in an hour.

MRS. ALVING: Be so good as to take all the papers with you. I won't hear another word about this affair. I have other things to think about.

MANDERS: Mrs. Alving———

MRS. ALVING: Later on I shall send you a Power of Attorney to settle everything as you please.

MANDERS: That I shall very readily undertake. The original destination of the endowment must now be completely changed, alas!

MRS. ALVING: Of course it must.

MANDERS: I think, first of all, I shall arrange that the Solvik property shall pass to the parish. The land is by no means without value. It can always be turned to account for some purpose or other. And the interest of the money in the Bank I could, perhaps, best apply for the benefit of some undertaking that has proved itself a blessing to the town.

MRS. ALVING: Do just as you please. The whole matter is now completely indifferent to me.

ENGSTRAND: Give a thought to my Sailors' Home, your Reverence.

MANDERS: Yes, that's not a bad suggestion. That must be considered.

ENGSTRAND: Oh, devil take considering—I beg your pardon!

MANDERS [*with a sigh*]: And I'm sorry to say I don't know how long I shall be able to retain control of these things—whether public opinion may not compel me to retire. It entirely depends upon the result of the official inquiry into the fire——

MRS. ALVING: What are you talking about?

MANDERS: And the result can by no means be foretold.

ENGSTRAND [*comes close to him*]:   Ay, but it can, though. For here stands Jacob Engstrand.

MANDERS: Well, well, but——?

ENGSTRAND [*more softly*]:   And Jacob Engstrand isn't the man to desert a noble benefactor in the hour of need, as the saying is.

MANDERS: Yes, but my good fellow—how——?

ENGSTRAND: Jacob Engstrand may be likened to a guardian angel, he may, your Reverence.

MANDERS: No, no; I can't accept that.

ENGSTRAND: Oh! you will though, all the same. I know a man that's taken others' sins upon himself before now, I do.

MANDERS: Jacob! [*Wrings his hand.*] You are a rare character. Well, you shall be helped with your Sailors' Home. That you may rely upon. [ENGSTRAND *tries to thank him, but cannot for emotion.* MR. MANDERS *hangs his travelling-bag over his shoulder.*] And now let's be off. We two go together.

ENGSTRAND [*at the dining-room door, softly to* REGINA]:   You come along too, girl. You shall live as snug as the yolk in an egg.

REGINA [*tosses her head*]:   Merci!

[*She goes out into the hall and fetches* MANDER'S *overcoat.*]

MANDERS: Good-bye, Mrs. Alving! and may the spirit of Law and Order descend upon this house, and that quickly.

MRS. ALVING: Good-bye, Manders.

[*She goes up towards the conservatory as she sees* OSWALD *coming in through the garden door.*]

ENGSTRAND [*while he and* REGINA *help* MANDERS *to get his coat on*]:   Good-bye, my child. And if any trouble should come to you, you know where Jacob Engstrand is to be found. [*Softly.*] Little Harbour Street, h'm——! [*To* MRS. ALVING *and* OSWALD.] And the refuge for wandering mariners shall be called "Captain Alving's Home," that it shall! And if I'm spared to carry on that house in my own way, I venture to promise that it shall be worthy of his memory.

MANDERS [*in the doorway*]:   H'm—h'm!—Now come, my dear Engstrand. Good-bye! Good-bye!   [*He and* ENGSTRAND *go out through the hall.*]

OSWALD [*goes towards the table*]:   What house was he talking about?

MRS. ALVING: Oh, a kind of Home that he and Manders want to set up.

OSWALD: It will burn down like the other.

MRS. ALVING: What makes you think so?

OSWALD: Everything will burn. All that recalls father's memory is doomed. Here am I, too, burning down.   [REGINA *starts and looks at him.*]

MRS. ALVING: Oswald! you oughtn't to have remained so long down there, my poor boy!

OSWALD [*sits down by the table*]: I almost think you're right.

MRS. ALVING: Let me dry your face, Oswald; you're quite wet.

> [*She dries his face with her pocket-handkerchief.*]

OSWALD [*stares indifferently in front of him*]: Thanks, mother.

MRS. ALVING: Aren't you tired, Oswald? Would you like to sleep?

OSWALD [*nervously*]: No, no—I can't sleep. I never sleep. I only pretend to. [*Sadly.*] That will come soon enough.

MRS. ALVING [*looking sorrowfully at him*]: Yes, you really are ill, my blessed boy.

REGINA [*eagerly*]: Is Mr. Alving ill?

OSWALD [*impatiently*]: Oh, do shut all the doors! This killing dread——

MRS. ALVING: Shut the doors, Regina.

[REGINA *shuts them and remains standing by the hall door.* MRS. ALVING *takes her shawl off.* REGINA *does the same.* MRS. ALVING *draws a chair across to* OSWALD'S, *and sits by him.*]

MRS. ALVING: There now! I'm going to sit beside you——

OSWALD: Ah! do. And Regina shall stay here, too. Regina shall be with me always. You'll come to the rescue, Regina, won't you?

REGINA: I don't understand——

MRS. ALVING: To the rescue?

OSWALD: Yes—in the hour of need.

MRS. ALVING: Oswald, have you not your mother to come to the rescue?

OSWALD: You? [*Smiles.*] No, mother; that rescue you will never bring me. [*Laughs sadly.*] You! ha ha! [*Looks earnestly at her.*] Though, after all, it lies nearest to you. [*Impetuously.*] Why don't you say "thou" to me, Regina? Why don't you call me "Oswald"?

REGINA [*softly*]: I don't think Mrs. Alving would like it.

MRS. ALVING: You shall soon have leave to do it. And sit over here beside us, won't you?

> [Regina *sits down quietly and hesitatingly at the other side of the table.*]

MRS. ALVING: And now, my poor suffering boy, I'm going to take the burden off your mind——

OSWALD: You, mother?

MRS. ALVING: ——All the gnawing remorse and self-reproach you speak of.

OSWALD: And you think you can do that?

MRS. ALVING: Yes, now I can, Oswald. You spoke of the joy of life; and at that word a new light burst for me over my life and all it had contained.

OSWALD [*shakes his head*]: I don't understand you.

MRS. ALVING: You ought to have known your father when he was a young lieutenant. He was brimming over with the joy of life!

OSWALD: Yes, I know he was.

MRS. ALVING: It was like a breezy day only to look at him. And what exuberant strength and vitality there was in him!

OSWALD: Well——?

MRS. ALVING: Well then, child of joy as he was—for he *was* like a child at that time—he had to live here at home in a half-grown town, which had no joys to offer him—only dissipations. He had no object in life—only an official position. He had no work into which he could throw himself heart and soul; he had only business. He had not a single comrade that knew what the joy of life meant—only loungers and boon-companions——

OSWALD: Mother!

MRS. ALVING: So the inevitable happened.

OSWALD: The inevitable?

MRS. ALVING: You said yourself, this evening, what would happen to you if you stayed at home.

OSWALD: Do you mean to say that father——?

MRS. ALVING: Your poor father found no outlet for the overpowering joy of life that was in him. And I brought no brightness into his home.

OSWALD: Not even you?

MRS. ALVING: They had taught me a lot about duties and so on, which I had taken to be true. Everything was marked out into duties—into my duties, and his duties, and—I'm afraid I made home intolerable for your poor father, Oswald.

OSWALD: Why did you never write me anything about all this?

MRS. ALVING: I have never before seen it in such a light that I could speak of it to you, his son.

OSWALD: In what light did you see it then?

MRS. ALVING [*slowly*]:   I saw only this one thing, that your father was a broken-down man before you were born.

OSWALD [*softly*]:   Ah!   [*He rises and walks away to the window.*]

MRS. ALVING: And then, day after day, I dwelt on the one thought that by rights Regina should be at home in this house—just like my own boy.

OSWALD [*turning round quickly*]:   Regina!

REGINA [*springs up and asks, with bated breath*]:   I?

MRS. ALVING: Yes, now you know it, both of you.

OSWALD: Regina!

REGINA [*to herself*]:   So mother was that kind of woman, after all.

MRS. ALVING: Your mother had many good qualities, Regina.

REGINA: Yes, but she was one of that sort, all the same. Oh! I've often suspected it; but—— And now, if you please, ma'am, may I be allowed to go away at once?

MRS. ALVING: Do you really wish it, Regina?

REGINA: Yes, indeed I do.

MRS. ALVING: Of course you can do as you like; but——

OSWALD [*goes towards* REGINA]:   Go away now? Isn't this your home?

REGINA: *Merci*, Mr. Alving!—or now, I suppose, I may say Oswald. But I can tell you this wasn't what I expected.

MRS. ALVING: Regina, I have not been frank with you——

REGINA: No, that you haven't, indeed. If I'd known that Oswald was ill, why—— And now, too, that it can never come to anything serious between us—— I really can't stop out here in the country and wear myself out nursing sick people.

OSWALD: Not even one who is so near to you?

REGINA: No, that I can't. A poor girl must make the best of her young days, or she'll be left out in the cold before she knows where she is. And I, too, have the joy of life in me, Mrs. Alving.

MRS. ALVING: Yes, I can see you have. But don't throw yourself away, Regina.

REGINA: Oh! what must be, must be. If Oswald takes after his father, I take after my mother, I daresay. May I ask, ma'am, if Mr. Manders knows all this about me?

MRS. ALVING: Mr. Manders knows all about it.

REGINA [*puts on her shawl hastily*]:   Well then, I'd better make haste and get away by this steamer. Pastor Manders is so nice to deal with; and I certainly think I've as much right to a little of that money as he has—that brute of a carpenter.

MRS. ALVING: You're heartily welcome to it, Regina.

REGINA [*looks hard at her*]:   I think you might have brought me up as a gentleman's daughter, ma'am; it would have suited me better. [*Tosses her head.*] But it's done now—it doesn't matter! [*With a bitter side glance at the corked bottle.*] All the same, I may come to drink champagne with gentlefolks yet.

MRS. ALVING: And if you ever need a home, Regina, come to me.

REGINA: No, thank you, ma'am. Mr. Manders will look after me, I know. And if the worst comes to the worst, I know of one house where I've every right to a place.

MRS. ALVING: Where is that?

REGINA: "Captain Alving's Home."

MRS. ALVING: Regina—now I see it—you're going to your ruin.

REGINA: Oh, stuff! Good-bye.   [*She nods and goes out through the hall.*]

OSWALD [*stands at the window and looks out*]:   Is she gone?

MRS. ALVING: Yes.

OSWALD [*murmuring aside to himself*]:   I think it's a great mistake, all this.

MRS. ALVING [*goes behind him and lays her hands on his shoulders*]:   Oswald, my dear boy; has it shaken you very much?

OSWALD [*turns his face towards her*]:   All that about father, do you mean?

MRS. ALVING: Yes, about your unhappy father. I'm so afraid it may have been too much for you.

OSWALD: Why should you fancy that? Of course it came upon me as a great surprise; but, after all, it can't matter much to me.

MRS. ALVING [*draws her hands away*]:   Can't matter! That your father was so infinitely miserable!

OSWALD: Of course I can pity him as I would anybody else; but——

MRS. ALVING: Nothing more? Your own father!

OSWALD [*impatiently*]:   Oh, there! "father," "father"! I never knew anything of father. I don't remember anything about him except that he once made me sick.

MRS. ALVING: That's a terrible way to speak! Should a son not love his father, all the same?

OSWALD: When a son has nothing to thank his father for? has never known him? Do you really cling to that old superstition?—you who are so enlightened in other ways?

MRS. ALVING: Is it only a superstition——?

OSWALD: Yes; can't you see it, mother? It's one of those notions that are current in the world, and so——

MRS. ALVING [*deeply moved*]:   Ghosts!

OSWALD [*crossing the room*]:   Yes; you may well call them Ghosts.

MRS. ALVING [*wildly*]:   Oswald!—then you don't love me, either!

OSWALD: You I know, at any rate.

MRS. ALVING: Yes, you know me; but is that all?

OSWALD: And of course I know how fond you are of me, and I can't but be grateful to you. And you can be so very useful to me, now that I'm ill.

MRS. ALVING: Yes, can't I, Oswald? Oh! I could almost bless the illness that has driven you home to me. For I can see very plainly you are not mine; I have to win you.

OSWALD [*impatiently*]:   Yes, yes, yes; all these are just so many phrases. You must recollect I'm a sick man, mother. I can't be much taken up with other people! I have enough to do thinking about myself.

MRS. ALVING [*in a low voice*]:   I shall be patient and easily satisfied.

OSWALD: And cheerful too, mother.

MRS. ALVING: Yes, my dear boy, you're quite right. [*Goes towards him.*] Have I relieved you of all remorse and self-reproach now?

OSWALD: Yes, you have. But who's to relieve me of the dread?

MRS. ALVING: The dread?

OSWALD [*walks across the room*]:   Regina could have been got to do it.

MRS. ALVING: I don't understand you. What is all this about dread—and Regina?

OSWALD: Is it very late, mother?

MRS. ALVING: It's early morning. [*She looks out through the conservatory.*] The day is dawning over the hills; and the weather is fine, Oswald. In a little while you shall see the sun.

OSWALD: I'm glad of that. Oh! I may still have much to rejoice in and live for——

MRS. ALVING: Yes, much—much, indeed!

OSWALD: Even if I can't work——

MRS. ALVING: Oh! you'll soon be able to work again, my dear boy, now that you haven't got all those gnawing and depressing thoughts to brood over any longer.

OSWALD: Yes, I'm glad you were able to rid me of all those fancies; and when I've got one thing more arranged—— [*Sits on the sofa.*] Now we'll have a little talk, mother.

MRS. ALVING: Yes, let us.

[*She pushes an armchair towards the sofa, and sits down close to him.*]

OSWALD: And meantime the sun will be rising. And then you'll know all. And then I shan't have that dread any longer.

MRS. ALVING: What am I to know?

OSWALD [*not listening to her*]: Mother, didn't you say, a little while ago, that there was nothing in the world you wouldn't do for me, if I asked you.

MRS. ALVING: Yes, to be sure I said it.

OSWALD: And you'll stick to it, mother?

MRS. ALVING: You may rely on that, my dear and only boy! I have nothing in the world to live for but you alone.

OSWALD: All right, then; now you shall hear. Mother, you have a strong, steadfast mind, I know. Now you're to sit quite still when you hear it.

MRS. ALVING: What dreadful thing can it be——?

OSWALD: You're not to scream out. Do you hear? Do you promise me that? We'll sit and talk about it quite quietly. Promise me, mother?

MRS. ALVING: Yes, yes; I promise. Only speak.

OSWALD: Well, you must know that all this fatigue, and my inability to think of work—all that is not the illness itself——

MRS. ALVING: Then what is the illness itself?

OSWALD: The disease I have as my birthright [*he points to his forehead and adds very softly*]—is seated here.

MRS. ALVING [*almost voiceless*]: Oswald! No, no!

OSWALD: Don't scream. I can't bear it. Yes, it's seated here—waiting. And it may break out any day—at any moment.

MRS. ALVING: Oh! what horror!

OSWALD: Now, do be quiet. That's how it stands with me——

MRS. ALVING [*jumps up*]: It's not true, Oswald. It's impossible. It can't be so.

OSWALD: I have had one attack down there already. It was soon over. But when I got to know what had been the matter with me, then the dread came upon me raging and tearing; and so I set off home to you as fast as I could.

MRS. ALVING: Then this is the dread——!

OSWALD: Yes, for it's so indescribably loathsome, you know. Oh! if it had only been an ordinary mortal disease——! For I'm not so afraid of death—though I should like to live as long as I can.

MRS. ALVING: Yes, yes, Oswald, you must!

OSWALD: But this is so unutterably loathsome! To become a little baby again! To have to be fed! To have to—— Oh, it's not to be spoken of!

MRS. ALVING: The child has his mother to nurse him.

OSWALD [*jumps up*]: No, never; that's just what I won't have. I can't endure to think that perhaps I should lie in that state for many years—get old and grey. And in the meantime you might die and leave me. [*Sits in* MRS. ALVING's *chair.*] For the doctor said it wouldn't necessarily prove fatal at once. He called it a sort of softening of the brain—or something of the kind. [*Smiles sadly.*] I think that expression sounds so nice. It always sets me thinking of cherry-coloured velvet—something soft and delicate to stroke.

MRS. ALVING [*screams*]: Oswald!

OSWALD [*springs up and paces the room*]: And now you have taken Regina from me. If I'd only had her! She would have come to the rescue, I know.

Mrs. Alving [*goes to him*]:   What do you mean by that, my darling boy? Is there any help in the world that I wouldn't give you?

Oswald: When I got over my attack in Paris, the doctor told me that when it came again—and it will come again—there would be no more hope.

Mrs. Alving: He was heartless enough to——

Oswald: I demanded it of him. I told him I had preparations to make. [*He smiles cunningly.*] And so I had. [*He takes a little box from his inner breast pocket and opens it.*] Mother, do you see this?

Mrs. Alving: What is that?

Oswald: Morphia.

Mrs. Alving [*looks horrified at him*]:   Oswald—my boy!

Oswald: I've scraped together twelve pilules——

Mrs. Alving [*snatches at it*]:   Give me the box, Oswald.

Oswald: Not yet, mother.   [*He hides the box again in his pocket.*]

Mrs. Alving: I shall never survive this!

Oswald: It must be survived. Now if I'd had Regina here, I should have told her how things stood with me, and begged her to come to the rescue at the last. She would have done it. I'm certain she would.

Mrs. Alving: Never!

Oswald: When the horror had come upon me, and she saw me lying there helpless, like a little new-born baby, impotent, lost, hopeless, past all saving——

Mrs. Alving: Never in all the world would Regina have done this.

Oswald: Regina would have done it. Regina was so splendidly light-hearted. And she would soon have wearied of nursing an invalid like me——

Mrs. Alving: Then heaven be praised that Regina is not here.

Oswald: Well then, it's you that must come to the rescue, mother.

Mrs. Alving [*screams aloud*]:   I!

Oswald: Who is nearer to it than you?

Mrs. Alving: I! your mother!

Oswald: For that very reason.

Mrs. Alving: I, who gave you life!

Oswald: I never asked you for life. And what sort of a life have you given me? I won't have it. You shall take it back again.

Mrs. Alving: Help! Help!   [*She runs out into the hall.*]

Oswald [*going after her*]:   Don't leave me. Where are you going?

Mrs. Alving [*in the hall*]:   To fetch the doctor, Oswald. Let me go.

Oswald [*also outside*]:   You shall not go. And no one shall come in.

[*The locking of a door is heard.*]

Mrs. Alving [*comes in again*]:   Oswald—Oswald!—my child!

Oswald [*follows her*]:   Have you a mother's heart for me, and yet can see me suffer from this unutterable dread?

Mrs. Alving [*after a moment's silence, commands herself, and says*]:   Here's my hand upon it.

OSWALD: Will you——?

MRS. ALVING: If it's ever necessary. But it will never be necessary. No, no; it's impossible.

OSWALD: Well, let us hope so, and let us live together as long as we can. Thank you, mother.

[*He seats himself in the armchair which* MRS. ALVING *has moved to the sofa. Day is breaking. The lamp is still burning on the table.*]

MRS. ALVING [*drawing near cautiously*]: Do you feel calm now?

OSWALD: Yes.

MRS. ALVING [*bending over him*]: It has been a dreadful fancy of yours, Oswald—nothing but a fancy. All this excitement has been too much for you. But now you shall have a long rest; at home with your mother, my own blessed boy. Everything you point to you shall have, just as when you were a little child. There now. That crisis is over now. You see how easily it passed. Oh! I was sure it would—— And do you see, Oswald, what a lovely day we're going to have? Brilliant sunshine! Now you'll be really be able to see your home.

[*She goes to the table and puts the lamp out. Sunrise. The glacier and the snow-peaks in the background glow in the morning light.*]

OSWALD [*sits in the armchair with his back towards the landscape, without moving. Suddenly he says*]: Mother, give me the sun.

MRS. ALVING [*by the table, starts and looks at him*]: What do you say?

OSWALD [*repeats, in a dull, toneless voice*]: The sun. The sun.

MRS. ALVING [*goes to him*]: Oswald, what's the matter with you? [OSWALD *seems to shrink together in the chair; all his muscles relax; his face is expressionless, his eyes have a glassy stare.* MRS. ALVING *is quivering with terror.*] What is this? [*Shrieks.*] Oswald, what's the matter with you? [*Falls on her knees beside him and shakes him.*] Oswald, Oswald! look at me! Don't you know me?

OSWALD [*tonelessly as before*]: The sun. The sun.

MRS. ALVING [*springs up in despair, entwines her hands in her hair and shrieks*]: I can't bear it! [*Whispers, as though petrified*] I can't bear it! Never! [*Suddenly.*] Where has he got them? [*Fumbles hastily in his breast.*] Here! [*Shrinks back a few steps and screams.*] No; no; no! Yes!—No; no!

[*She stands a few steps from him with her hands twisted in her hair, and stares at him in speechless terror.*]

OSWALD [*sits motionless as before and says*]: The sun. The sun.

Curtain

Suggestions for Discussion

1. What does each act contribute to the movement of the play if it is conceived as problem play? as tragedy?

2. Show how the central metaphor of the ghosts functions in each of the structural elements of the plot: retrospective exposition, inciting action, climax, and catastro-

phe. How do they affect the tone? Why is it appropriate to theme and plot that retrospective action should dominate?

3. Show how the interaction between Pastor Manders and Mrs. Alving, and between the mother and son, advances the movement of the play. In her efforts to exorcise the ghosts, at what points does Mrs. Alving revert to conventional responses to experience?

4. Does the play have verisimilitude? Is it in any important sense anachronistic? Does it transcend personal tragedy? In requiring Mrs. Alving to confront the possibilities of both incest and mercy killing, does the plot violate the reader's sense of probability?

5. Show how the characters of Regina and Engstrand are developed in ironic contrast with those of Oswald and Pastor Manders.

6. Although the focus of interest in the first act is Oswald's return from Paris and in the last act is his terror of being reduced to an imbecile, Mrs. Alving is the central protagonist and not Oswald. Support this statement with evidence.

7. How do you reconcile Oswald's preliminary denial that he has ever led a dissipated life with his subsequent placing of blame upon himself?

8. Discuss the setting with particular reference to the sun and light as contrasted with the gloom and ceaseless rain; the bourgeois parlor as contrasted with Parisian life. What other oppositions are developed? Show how the setting is related organically to tone and theme. What is the relation of the Alving living room to the other rooms of the house? of the Alving house to other houses in the community?

9. How do the following examples of irony advance the action and contribute to the tone: the uses to which money is put; Oswald's mocking reference to himself as the Prodigal Son; the contrast between Mrs. Alving's conception of the orphanage and Engstrand's scheme for the Seamen's Home; Oswald's view of Regina as possessing the "joy of life" that could save him; and the contrast in meaning between Manders' and Mrs. Alving's reaction to the fire? What other functions are served by the fire?

Suggestions for Writing

1. Develop Tertan's summation of *Ghosts*: "whoever kills the joy of living is responsible for the tragedy" or apply this aphorism to your observation of a contemporary situation.

2. Discuss some of the "ghosts" of the present that haunt the living.

3. What elements of the play seem dated and what seem to have contemporary significance?

Poetry

William Shakespeare

When in Disgrace with Fortune and Men's Eyes (Sonnet 29)
Let Me Not to the Marriage of True Minds (Sonnet 116)

William Shakespeare (1564–1616) is generally acknowledged to be the greatest playwright in the English language. He was born in Stratford-on-Avon, England. By 1592 he had become an actor and playwright in London, and in 1599 he helped establish the famous Globe Theater. In addition to the sonnets, his works include historical plays, comedies such as *A Midsummer Night's Dream* and tragedies such as *Macbeth, Hamlet, King Lear*, and *Othello*. The self-doubt in Sonnet 29 is resolved with the poet's thoughts of his love. In Sonnet 116 the poet attests to the inviolability and permanence of love.

Sonnet 29

When, in disgrace with fortune and men's eyes,
I all alone beweep my outcast state,
And trouble deaf heaven with my bootless cries,
And look upon myself and curse my fate;
Wishing me like to one more rich in hope,
Featured like him, like him with friends possessed,
Desiring this man's art, and that man's scope,
With what I most enjoy contented least;
Yet in these thoughts myself almost despising,
Haply I think on thee, and then my state,
Like to the lark at break of day arising
From sullen earth, sings hymns at heaven's gate;
For thy sweet love remembered such wealth brings
That then I scorn to change my state with kings.

Sonnet 116

Let me not to the marriage of true minds
Admit impediments. Love is not love
Which alters when it alteration finds,
Or bends with the remover to remove:
Oh, no! it is an ever-fixed mark,
That looks on tempests and is never shaken;
It is the star to every wandering bark,
Whose worth's unknown, although his height be taken.
Love's not Time's fool, though rosy lips and cheeks
Within his bending sickle's compass come;
Love alters not with his brief hours and weeks,
But bears it out even to the edge of doom.
If this be error and upon me proved,
I never writ, nor no man ever loved.

Suggestions for Discussion

1. How does the imagery in each of the sonnets contribute to its unity?

2. How does dramatic understatement at the end of the second of the two sonnets reinforce the theme?

William Blake

The Clod and the Pebble
The Garden of Love

William Blake (1757–1827), poet and artist, illustrated his poems with his own engravings. His works include *Songs of Innocence* (1789), *Songs of Experience* (1794), *The Marriage of Heaven and Hell* (1790), *The Gates of Paradise* (1793), and *Visions of the Daughters of Albion* (1793). The poems that follow suggest some of the contradictions inherent in concepts of love.

The Clod and the Pebble

"Love seeketh not Itself to please,
    Nor for itself hath any care,

But for another gives its ease,
 And builds a Heaven in Hell's despair."

So sung the Clod of Clay,
 Trodden with the cattle's feet,
But a Pebble in the brook
 Warbled out these metres meet:

"Love seeketh only Self to please,
 To bind another to its delight,
Joys in another's loss of ease,
 And builds a Hell in Heaven's Despite."

The Garden of Love

I went to the Garden of Love,
And I saw what I never had seen:
A Chapel was built in the midst,
Where I used to play on the green.

And the gates of this Chapel were shut,
And "Thou shalt not" writ over the door:
So I turned to the Garden of Love
That so many sweet flowers bore;

And I saw it was filled with graves,
And tomb-stones where flowers should be;
And Priests in black gowns were walking their rounds,
And binding with briars my joys and desires.

Suggestion for Discussion

Both of Blake's poems suggest some of the contradictions inherent in concepts of "love." What are they and what seems to be the poet's conclusion?

W. H. Auden

Lay Your Sleeping Head, My Love

Wystan Hugh Auden (1907–1973), English poet educated at Oxford University, was early recognized as a leader of the poets of his generation. His poetry collections include *The Orators* (1932), *The Double Man* (1941), *The Shield of Achilles* (1955), *Homage to Clio* (1960), *About the House* (1965), and *The Age of Anxiety* (1947), which won a Pulitzer Prize in 1948. His autobiography, *Certain World: A Commonplace Book*, was published in 1970. Auden also experimented with drama, and his criticism was collected in *The Dyer's Hand* in 1963. In 1967 he was made a fellow of Christ College, Oxford. The writer speaks of the threats to love in this poem that weaves back and forth between the present and future, the concrete and abstract.

Lay your sleeping head, my love,
Human on my faithless arm;
Time and fevers burn away
Individual beauty from
Thoughtful children, and the grave
Proves the child ephemeral:
But in my arms till break of day
Let the living creature lie,
Mortal, guilty, but to me
The entirely beautiful.

Soul and body have no bounds:
To lovers as they lie upon
Her tolerant enchanted slope
In their ordinary swoon,
Grave the vision Venus sends
Of supernatural sympathy,
Universal love and hope;
While an abstract insight wakes
Among the glaciers and the rocks
The hermit's sensual ecstasy.

Certainty, fidelity
On the stroke of midnight pass
Like vibrations of a bell,
And fashionable madmen raise
Their pedantic boring cry:
Every farthing of the cost,
All the dreaded cards foretell,
Shall be paid, but from this night
Not a whisper, not a thought,
Not a kiss nor look be lost.

Beauty, midnight, vision dies:
Let the winds of dawn that blow
Softly round your dreaming head
Such a day of sweetness show
Eye and knocking heart may bless,
Find the mortal world enough;
Noons of dryness see you fed
By the involuntary powers,
Nights of insult let you pass
Watched by every human love.

Suggestions for Discussion

1. What images are employed by the speaker to suggest the hazards of love?

2. Account for the movement from present to future and from particular to general.

Edna St. Vincent Millay

Love Is Not All

Edna St. Vincent Millay (1892–1950), American poet, wrote "Renascence," her first major poem, while she was still in college. Her early works such as *A Few Figs from Thistles* (1920) exhibited a cynical flippancy that deepened into bitter disillusionment in later works such as *The Harp-Weaver and Other Poems* (1923), a Pulitzer Prize selection, and *The Buck in the Snow* (1928). In this sonnet the poet exalts the power of love.

Love is not all; it is not meat nor drink
Nor slumber nor a roof against the rain,
Nor yet a floating spar to men that sink
And rise and sink and rise and sink again;
Love can not fill the thickened lung with breath,
Nor clean the blood, nor set the fractured bone;
Yet many a man is making friends with death
Even as I speak, for lack of love alone.
It well may be that in a difficult hour,
Pinned down by pain and moaning for release,
Or nagged by want past resolution's power,

I might be driven to sell your love for peace,
To trade the memory of this night for food.
It well may be. I do not think I would.

Denise Levertov

The Third Dimension

Denise Levertov (b. 1923), English-born poet who became a United States citizen in 1956, has written many collections of poetry, including *With Eyes at the Back of Our Heads* (1959), *O Taste and See* (1964), *The Sorrow Dance* (1966), *Relearning the Alphabet* (1970), and *Footprints* (1972). She has contributed to magazines and anthologies and has served as a visiting lecturer at several colleges. No words can express the depth and trauma of the speaker's love.

Who'd believe me if
I said, "They took and

split me open from
scalp to crotch, and

still I'm alive, and
walk around pleased with

the sun and all
the world's bounty." Honesty

isn't so simple:
a simple honesty is

nothing but a lie.
Don't the trees

hide the wind between
their leaves and

speak in whispers?
The third dimension

hides itself.
If the roadmen

crack stones, the
stones are stones:

but love
cracked me open

and I'm
alive to

tell the tale—but not
honestly:

the words
change it. Let it be—

here in the sweet sun
—a fiction, while I

breathe and
change pace.

Suggestions for Discussion

1. The poems by Millay and Levertov of a woman expressing her love are separated in time by approximately fifty years. What have they in common and how do they differ in mood, theme, style?

2. Millay's sonnet is Shakespearian in form. Compare her concluding couplet with that in "Let Me Not to the Marriage of True Minds."

3. How does Millay employ dramatic understatement? Compare her development of the love theme with that in the two sonnets by Shakespeare.

E. E. Cummings

I Like My Body When It Is with Your

E. E. Cummings (1894–1962) was an American whose book *The Enormous Room* (1922) and whose poetry *&* and *XLI Poems* (1925) established his reputation as an avant-garde writer interested in experimenting with stylistic techniques. Awarded several important prizes for poetry, he was also Charles Eliot Norton Lecturer at Harvard University in 1952 and wrote *i: six nonlectures* (1953). The repetitions and typography as well as the sensory detail contribute to Cummings's expression of joy in physical love.

i like my body when it is with your
body. It is so quite new a thing.

Muscles better and nerves more.
i like your body. i like what it does,
i like its hows. i like to feel the spine
of your body and its bones, and the trembling
-firm-smooth ness and which i will
again and again and again
kiss, i like kissing this and that of you,
i like, slowly stroking the, shocking fuzz
of your electric fur, and what-is-it comes
over parting flesh . . . . And eyes big love-crumbs,

and possibly i like the thrill

of under me you so quite new

Suggestions for Discussion

1. Account for the appeal of the poem.

2. How do the repetitions and the typography contribute to the poem's effectiveness? What distinguishes this poem from prose?

◇◇◇◇

Adrienne Rich

Living in Sin
Rape

Adrienne Rich (b. 1929), contemporary American poet, is the author of *A Change of World* (1951), *The Diamond Cutters*, (1955), *Snapshots of a Daughter-in-Law* (1963), *Necessities of Life* (1966), *Of Woman Born* (1976), and *Of Your Native Land, Your Life* (1986). She has contributed to such magazines as *Poetry*, *The Nation*, and *The New York Review of Books*. Her awards include a Guggenheim Fellowship, the National Book Award (1976), and the Ruth Lilly Poetry Prize (1986). The graphic physical images in "Living in Sin" suggest that the lovers are emerging from an illusory world into a world of reality. "Rape," published in *Diving Into the Wreck* (1973), reflects the poet's anger in her ironic attribution of the crime and the portrait of the cop who is pleased by the hysteria of the speaker's voice.

Living in Sin

She had thought the studio would keep itself;
no dust upon the furniture of love.

Half heresy, to wish the taps less vocal,
the panes relieved of grime. A plate of pears,
a piano with a Persian shawl, a cat
stalking the picturesque amusing mouse
had risen at his urging.
Not that at five each separate stair would writhe
under the milkman's tramp; that morning light
so coldly would delineate the scraps
of last night's cheese and three sepulchral bottles;
that on the kitchen shelf among the saucers
a pair of beetle-eyes would fix her own—
envoy from some black village in the mouldings . . .
Meanwhile he, with a yawn,
sounded a dozen notes upon the keyboard,
declared it out of tune, shrugged at the mirror,
rubbed at his beard, went out for cigarettes;
while she, jeered by the minor demons,
pulled back the sheets and made the bed and found
a towel to dust the table-top,
and let the coffee-pot boil over on the stove.
By evening she was back in love again,
though not so wholly but throughout the night
she woke sometimes to feel the daylight coming
like a relentless milkman up the stairs.

Suggestions for Discussion

1. What physical images in the studio scene imply that the lovers are emerging from an illusory world into a world of reality?

2. Comment on the irony of the title. Do you perceive an end or a beginning to the relationship? Consider the clues in the final lines.

Rape

There is a cop who is both prowler and father:
he comes from your block, grew up with your brothers,
had certain ideals.
You hardly know him in his boots and silver badge,
on horseback, one hand touching his gun.

You hardly know him but you have to get to know him:
he has access to machinery that could kill you.
He and his stallion clop like warlords among the trash,
his ideals stand in the air, a frozen cloud
from between his unsmiling lips.

And so, when the time comes, you have to turn to him,
the maniac's sperm still greasing your thighs,
your mind whirling like crazy. You have to confess
to him, you are guilty of the crime
of having been forced.

And you see his blue eyes, the blue eyes of all the family
whom you used to know, grow narrow and glisten,
his hand types out the details
and he wants them all
but the hysteria in your voice pleases him best.

You hardly know him but now he thinks he knows you:
he has taken down your worst moment
on a machine and filed it in a file.
He knows, or thinks he knows, how much you imagined;
he knows, or thinks he knows, what you secretly wanted.

He has access to machinery that could get you put away;
and if, in the sickening light of the precinct,
and if, in the sickening light of the precinct,
your details sound like a portrait of your confessor,
will you swallow, will you deny them. will you lie your way home?

Suggestions for Discussion

1. How do the lines "you are guilty of the crime of having been forced" convey the author's point of view? How do you know she is being ironic?

2. With what details do you learn of the cop's pleasure in the narrator's report? How does the narrator view the cop?

3. What does the last series of questions signify?

Suggestion for Writing

Discuss the changing attitudes of society and the law toward the victims of rape.

May Swenson

Women Should Be Pedestals

May Swenson (b. 1919) is an American poet best know for *Another Animal* (1954), *A Cage of Spines* (1958), *To Mix with Time* (1963), *Poems to Solve* (1966), and *Half Sun Half Sleep* (1967). She has won numerous prizes and grants, including Guggenheim, Ford Foundation, and Rockefeller Foundation fellowships, the National Institute of Arts and Letters Award, and the Shelley Award. The poet's anger is reflected in the pedestal and rocking horse metaphors.

```
Women                        Or they
   should be                    should be
      pedestals                    little horses
         moving                       those wooden
            pedestals                    sweet
               moving                       oldfashioned
                  to the                       painted
                     motions                     rocking
                        of men                      horses
            the gladdest things in the toyroom
                  The                               feelingly
                     pegs                        and then
                     of their                    unfeelingly
                  ears                        To be
               so familiar                 joyfully
            and dear                     ridden
         to the trusting              rockingly
      fists                        ridden until
To be chafed                    the restored
egos dismount and the legs stride away
Immobile                      willing
   sweetlipped                   to be set
      sturdy                        into motion
         and smiling                   Women
            women                         should be
               should always                 pedestals
                  be waiting                    to men
```

Suggestions for Discussion

1. How does the central metaphor define the author's point of view? How does it contribute to tone?

2. How does the second extended metaphor contribute to purpose and tone?

3. How do alliteration and repetition function in the poem?

4. Comment on the function of the verbs and adjectives in creating mood and tone.

Suggestion for Writing

Using the same title, write an ironic sketch or poem.

The Cultural Tradition: Popular Culture

◆◆◆

I wince when I'm called a former beauty queen or Miss U.S.A.

> —**Studs Terkel,** "Miss U.S.A."

"How can I go to work," I yelled, "when I've got so much leisure time on my hands?"

> —**Art Buchwald,** "Leisure Will Kill You"

. . . for this cherished and wishful idea of athletes as heroes and exemplars seems to lie too deep in our emotions and memories to be dislodged or altered by argument.

> —**Roger Angell,** "The Cheers for Keith"

And so the American family muddles on, dimly aware that something is amiss but distracted from an understanding of its plight by an endless stream of television images.

> —**Marie Winn,** "The Plug-In Drug: TV and the American Family"

"Kathie," I demanded, "why do you women in soap opera detest my sex?"

> —**S. J. Perelman,** "Meanness Rising from the Suds"

For James Bond is the Renaissance man in mid-century guise, lover, warrior, connoisseur.

> —**George Grella,** "James Bond: Culture Hero"

Pop songs can do more than chart changing attitudes toward love and romance; they can address topical issues and appeal to our social conscience.

—**Robert Palmer,** "What Pop Lyrics Say to Us Today"

Jazz may have established its cultural credentials, but the real rejuvenation of the music has a long way to go.

—**E. J. Hobsbawm,** "The Jazz Comeback"

"Oh, it's so horrible, it's so dreadful," Irene was sobbing. "I've been listening all day, and it's so depressing."

—**John Cheever,** "The Enormous Radio"

They was crying and crying and didn't even know what they was crying for. One day this is going to be a pitiful country, I thought.

—**Alice Walker,** "Nineteen Fifty-five"

Personal Reminiscence

◆◆◆◆

Studs Terkel

Miss U.S.A.

Studs Terkel (b. 1912) has been associated with radio station WFMT in Chicago for many years. He gained fame as an oral historian with the publication of *Division Street America* (1966), *Hard Times* (1970), *Working* (1974), and *American Dreams: Lost and Found* (1980), from which the following selection is taken.

Emma Knight, Miss U.S.A., 1973. She is twenty-nine.

I wince when I'm called a former beauty queen or Miss U.S.A. I keep thinking they're talking about someone else. There are certain images that come to mind when people talk about beauty queens. It's mostly what's known as t and a, tits and ass. No talent. For many girls who enter the contest, it's part of the American Dream. It was never mine.

You used to sit around the TV and watch Miss America and it was exciting, we thought, glamorous. Fun, we thought. But by the time I was eight or nine, I didn't feel comfortable. Soon I'm hitting my adolescence, like fourteen, but I'm not doing any dating and I'm feeling awkward and ugly. I'm much taller than most of the people in my class. I don't feel I can compete the way I see girls competing for guys. I was very much of a loner. I felt intimidated by the amount of competition females were supposed to go through with each other. I didn't like being told by *Seventeen* magazine: Subvert your interests if you have a crush on a guy, get interested in what he's interested in. If you play cards, be sure not to beat him. I was very bad at these social games.

After I went to the University of Colorado for three and a half years, I had it. This was 1968 through '71. I came home for the summer. An agent met me and wanted me to audition for commercials, modeling, acting jobs. Okay. I started auditioning and winning some.

I did things actors do when they're starting out. You pass out literature at conventions, you do print ads, you pound the pavements, you send out your resumés. I had come to a model agency one cold day, and an agent came out and said: "I want you to enter a beauty contest." I said: "No, uh-uh, never, never, never. I'll lose, how humiliating." She said: "I want some girls to represent the agency, might do you good." So I filled out the application blank: hobbies, measurements, blah, blah, blah. I got a letter: "Congratulations. You have been accepted as an entrant into the Miss Illinois-Universe contest." Now what do I do? I'm stuck.

You have to have a sponsor. Or you're gonna have to pay several hundred dollars. So I called up the lady who was running it. Terribly sorry, I can't do this. I don't have the money. She calls back a couple of days later: "We found you a sponsor, it's a lumber company."

It was in Decatur. There were sixty-some contestants from all over the place. I went as a lumberjack: blue jeans, hiking boots, a flannel shirt, a pair of suspenders, and carrying an axe. You come out first in your costume and you introduce yourself and say your astrological sign or whatever it is they want you to say. You're wearing a banner that has the sponsor's name on it. Then you come out and do your pirouettes in your one-piece bathing suit, and the judges look at you a lot. Then you come out in your evening gown and pirouette around for a while. That's the first night.

The second night, they're gonna pick fifteen people. In between, you had judges' interviews. For three minutes, they ask you anything they want. Can you answer questions? How do you handle yourself? Your poise, personality, blah, blah, blah. They're called personality judges.

I thought: This will soon be over, get on a plane tomorrow, and no one will be the wiser. Except that my name got called as one of the fifteen. You have to go through the whole thing all over again.

I'm thinking: I don't have a prayer. I'd come to feel a certain kind of distance, except that they called my name. I was the winner, Miss Illinois. All I could do was laugh. I'm twenty-two, standing up there in a borrowed evening gown, thinking: What am I doing here: This is like Tom Sawyer becomes an altar boy.

I was considered old for a beauty queen, which is a little horrifying when you're twenty-two. That's very much part of the beauty queen syndrome: the young, untouched, unthinking human being.

I had to go to this room and sign the Miss Illinois-Universe contract right away. Miss Universe, Incorporated, is the full name of the company. It's owned by Kayser-Roth, Incorporated, which was bought out by Gulf & Western. Big business.

I'm sitting there with my glass of champagne and I'm reading over this contract. They said: "Oh, you don't have to read it." And I said: "I never sign anything that I don't read." They're all waiting to take pictures, and I'm sitting there reading this long document. So I signed it and the phone rang and the guy was from a Chicago paper and said: "Tell me, is it Miss or Ms.?" I said: "It's Ms." He said: "You're kidding." I said: "No, I'm not." He wrote an article the next day saying something like it finally happened: a beauty queen, a feminist. I thought I was a feminist before I was a beauty queen, why should I stop now?

Then I got into the publicity and training and interviews. It was a throwback to another time where crossed ankles and white gloves and teacups were present. I was taught how to walk around with a book on my head, how to sit daintily, how to pose in a bathing suit, and how to frizz my hair. They wanted curly hair, which I hate.

One day the trainer asked me to shake hands. I shook hands. She said: "That's wrong. When you shake hands with a man, you always shake hands ring up." I said: "Like the pope? Where my hand is up, like he's gonna kiss it?" Right. I thought: Holy mackerel! It was a very long February and March and April and May.

I won the Miss U.S.A. pageant. I started to laugh. They tell me I'm the only beauty queen in history that didn't cry when she won. It was on network television. I said to myself: "You're kidding." Bob Barker, the host, said: "No, I'm not kidding." I didn't know what else to say at that moment. In the press releases, they call it the great American Dream. There she is, Miss America, your ideal. Well, not my ideal, kid.

The minute you're crowned, you become their property and subject to whatever they tell you. They wake you up at seven o'clock next morning and make you put on a negligee and serve you breakfast in bed, so that all the New York papers can come in and take your picture sitting in bed, while you're absolutely bleary-eyed from the night before. They put on the Kayser-Roth negligee, hand you the tray, you take three bites. The photographers leave, you whip off the negligee, they take the breakfast away, and that's it. I never did get any breakfast that day. (Laughs).

You immediately start making personal appearances. The Jaycees or the chamber of commerce says: "I want to book Miss U.S.A. for our Christmas Day parade." They pay, whatever it is, seven hundred fifty dollars a day, first-class air fare, round trip, expenses, so forth. If the United Fund calls and wants me to give a five-minute pitch on queens at a luncheon, they still have to pay a fee. Doesn't matter that it's a charity. It's one hundred percent to Miss Universe, Incorporated. You get your salary. That's your prize money for the year. I got fifteen thousand dollars, which is all taxed in New York. Maybe out of a check of three thousand dollars, I'd get fifteen hundred dollars.

From the day I won Miss U.S.A. to the day I left for Universe, almost two months, I got a day and a half off. I made about two hundred fifty appearances that year. Maybe three hundred. Parades, shopping centers, and things. Snip ribbons. What else do you do at a shopping center? Model clothes. The nice thing I got to do was public speaking. They said: "You want a ghost writer?" I said: "Hell, no, I know how to talk." I wrote my own speeches. They don't trust girls to go out and talk because most of them can't.

One of the big execs from General Motors asked me to do a speech in Washington, D.C., on the consumer and the energy crisis. It was the fiftieth anniversary of the National Management Association. The White House, for some reason, sent me some stuff on it. I read it over, it was nonsense. So I stood up and said: "The reason we have an energy crisis is because we are, industrially and personally, pigs. We have a short-term view of the resources available to us; and unless we wake up to what we're doing to our air and our water, we'll have a dearth, not just a crisis." Oh, they weren't real pleased. (Laughs.)

What I resent most is that a lot of people didn't expect me to live this version of the American Dream for myself. I was supposed to live it their way.

When it came out in a newspaper interview that I said Nixon should resign, that he was a crook, oh dear, the fur flew. They got very upset until I got an invitation to the White House. They wanted to shut me up. The Miss Universe corporation had been trying to establish some sort of liaison with the White House for several years. I make anti-Nixon speeches and get this invitation.

I figured they're either gonna take me down to the basement and beat me up with a rubber hose or they're gonna offer me a cabinet post. They had a list of fifteen or so people I was supposed to meet. I've never seen such a bunch of people with raw nerve endings. I was dying to bring a tape recorder but thought if you mention the word "Sony" in the Nixon White House, you're in trouble. They'd have cardiac arrest. But I'm gonna bring along a pad and paper. They were patronizing. And when one of 'em got me in his office and talked about all the journalists and television people being liberals, I brought up blacklisting, *Red Channels,* and the TV industry. He changed the subject.

Miss Universe took place in Athens, Greece. The junta was still in power. I saw a heck of a lot of jeeps and troops and machine guns. The Americans were supposed to keep a low profile. I had never been a great fan of the Greek junta, but I knew darn well I was gonna have to keep my mouth shut. I was still representing the United States, for better or for worse. Miss Philippines won. I ran second.

At the end of the year, you're run absolutely ragged. That final evening, they usually have several queens from past years come back. Before they crown the new Miss U.S.A., the current one is supposed to take what they call the farewell walk. They call over the PA: Time for the old queen's walk. I'm now twenty-three and I'm an old queen. And they have this idiot farewell speech playing over the airwaves as the old queen takes the walk. And you're sitting on the throne for about thirty seconds, then you come down and they announce the name of the new one and you put the crown on her head. And then you're old.

As the new one is crowned, the reporters and photographers rush on the stage. I've seen photographers shove the girl who has just given her reign up thirty seconds before, shove her physically. I was gone by that time. I had jumped off the stage in my evening gown. It is very difficult for girls who are terrified of this ending. All of a sudden (snaps fingers), you're out. Nobody gives a damn about the old one.

Miss U.S.A. and remnants thereof is the crown stored in the attic in my parents' home. I don't even know where the banners are. It wasn't me the fans of Miss U.S.A. thought was pretty. What they think is pretty is the banner and crown. If I could put the banner and crown on that lamp, I swear to God ten men would come in and ask it for a date. I'll think about committing an axe murder if I'm not called anything but a former beauty queen. I can't stand it any more.

Several times during my year as what's-her-face I had seen the movie *The Sting.* There's a gesture the characters use which means the con is on: they rub their nose. In my last fleeting moments as Miss U.S.A., as they were playing that silly farewell speech and I walked down the aisle and stood by the throne, I looked right into the camera and rubbed my finger across my nose. The next day, the pageant people spent all their time telling people that

I hadn't done it. I spent the time telling them that, of course, I had. I simply meant: the con is on. (Laughs.)

Miss U.S.A. is in the same graveyard that Emma Knight the twelve-year-old is. Where the sixteen-year-old is. All the past selves. There comes a time when you have to bury those selves because you've grown into another one. You don't keep exhuming the corpses.

If I could sit down with every young girl in America for the next fifty years, I could tell them what I liked about the pageant. I could tell them what I hated. It wouldn't make any difference. There're always gonna be girls who want to enter the beauty pageant. That's the fantasy: the American Dream.

Suggestions for Discussion

1. What sequence of events led Emma Knight to win the title of Miss U.S.A.?

2. Describe her life as Miss U.S.A.

3. What evidence does she show of her interest in politics? in women's rights?

4. For what reasons does she signal "the con is on" at the end of her reign?

Suggestions for Writing

1. Explain why Emma Knight believes there will always be "girls who want to enter the beauty pageant." Do you agree?

2. Describe a contest in which you were a participant. Use details that the casual observer would not know.

Bobbie Ann Mason

Reaching the Stars: My Life as a Fifties Groupie

Bobbie Ann Mason (b. 1942) is the author of *In Country,* a novel published in 1985, and of *Shiloh and Other Stories* (1982). In the reminiscence that follows, she describes her experiences as national president of the Hilltoppers' Fan Club in the 1950s.

In the late nineteen-fifties, when I was a teen-ager, I held a national office, published a journal, was interviewed on television and radio, and travelled widely to places like Cincinnati and Detroit and Blytheville, Arkansas. I was a shy, backward, antisocial country kid living on a farm near Mayfield, Kentucky, a hundred and fifty miles from the nearest city, Nashville, but I was ambitious and determined to hit the big time—or at least meet somebody famous. The first star I met was Gene Autry's dumpy sidekick in the floppy hat, Smiley Burnette. I was about thirteen when he came to town for a show at the Princess Theatre. You could buy a picture of him for a dollar or pay a dollar to have your picture taken with him. Smiley hooked his arm around my shoulders and posed me for the camera, but when I asked him to sign my autograph book he snarled, "I don't autograph nothing but the pictures for sale."

The second star on my life list was Tony Martin, the crooner who sang "There's No Tomorrow" and was married to Cyd Charisse. He came to town to publicize Tony Martin suits, which were manufactured by the Merit Clothing Company, the local factory where my mother worked. She and I went to the Hall Hotel and gawked at him as he got off the elevator. He was surprisingly short.

But from the time I was a child singers impressed me more than movie stars did. I listened to the radio constantly. Perry Como and Patti Page dominated the daytime airwaves in those days, but late on Saturday nights the radio blared out strange music: "John R here, way down South in Dixie, 1510 on the dial, fifty thousand watts of joy! WLAC, Nashville, Tennessee."

John R played raunchy, stomping-and-shouting blues numbers by black singers like Big Bill Broonzy and Memphis Slim and Little Junior Parker, Little Walter, T-Bone Walker, Elmore James, and Big Joe Turner. The theme song on John R's show was "Dig Those Blues," a slow, rolling piano blues. John R was white, but he sounded black. WLAC advertised mysterious products—Silky Strate, White Rose petroleum jelly, "lifetime" Bibles, and soul medallions. My parents and I stayed up late and turned the radio up loud, staring in amazement at our huge console, as big as a jukebox, as it blared out wild music. John R and another white disk jockey, Gene Nobles, who had a show earlier in the evening, played what they called "droopy-drawers songs" (the slow stuff) and "mean, low-down songs." The mean ones sounded dangerous. I could feel the power of big men stomping into their houses and dragging out their women when they'd been untrue. In the droopy-drawers songs, they cried their hearts out. John R talked through the songs: "Have mercy, baby! . . . Come on, honey. . . . Man, don't that tear you up?" Ruth Brown's "Mama, He Treats Your Daughter Mean" tore me up bad.

Gene Nobles specialized in bland white imitations of these risqué rhythm-and-blues songs—especially "cover" versions from Dot Records, owned by his sponsor, Randy's Record Shop in Gallatin, Tennessee. Randy's artists included Pat Boone and the Fontane Sisters. His star group was the Hilltoppers.

The Hilltoppers, I decided, represented everything I had ever felt and dreamed about my life. As I picked blackberries or hoed vegetables in the scorching morning sun, I longed to travel and see the world. The turbulent music on WLAC expressed my frustration, and the Hilltoppers made me feel there was an answer—some release from the cycle of the seasons, the planting and harvesting. (I didn't see the glamour in farm life then.) The Hilltoppers' style wasn't exactly Big Bill Broonzy and it wasn't rock and roll yet either—it was sort of like what would happen if Perry Como got hold of some

Big Bill Broonzy material—but it grabbed me and shook me up like a religious vision, a calling. This was mainly because the group was from Kentucky. The Hilltoppers were students at Western Kentucky State College, in Bowling Green, where the sports teams were called the Hilltoppers. A Kentucky singing quartet had achieved national fame! The only famous person from Kentucky I had ever heard of besides Abraham Lincoln was Arthur Lake, who played Dagwood in the Blondie-and-Dagwood movies.

The Hilltoppers' first hit was "Trying," a ballad written by one of the original members of the group, Billy Vaughn, and later on they were awarded a gold record for an old Johnny Mercer song, "P.S. I Love You." With the arrival of rock and roll, they started recording livelier imitations of black tunes—"The Door Is Still Open," "Only You," and Ruth Brown's "Teardrops from My Eyes." On some of the songs you could hear a rock-and-roll saxophone or a boogie piano, and even a bass vocal "bum-bum-bum" against the "do-do-do-do-do-do-do" background harmony. But their style was born in an earlier time. Jimmy Sacca, the lead singer, had a strong, distinctive baritone that strained to be a tenor—a cross between matinée-idol crooning and big-band swing. He was a dreamboat.

I started a Hilltoppers fan club, and the day that the package of membership cards, autographed glossy eight-by-ten photographs, and buttons ("I AM A HILLTOPPERS FAN") arrived was the turning point of my life. I advertised for members in Betty Burr's fan-club column in a New York fan magazine, and for a time my whole life revolved around the mailbox and the radio. I corresponded with a Hilltoppers fan on Long Island who monitored all of New York's radio stations, flipping the dial ceaselessly after school. She constructed elaborate charts, on graph paper, of Hilltoppers airplay. Over the next year, I diligently worked my way up through the Hilltoppers' power structure, mostly by pestering the Hilltoppers' secretary in Gallatin and trying to impress her and the Hilltoppers with my devotion so I could get to meet them, and at last became National President of the Hilltoppers Fan Clubs. As National President, I wrote and mailed a newsletter to three hundred fan-club chapters on an addressographed list—mostly addresses in the exotic environs of New York City. One of my jobs as National President was to conduct request campaigns to d.j.s. I wrote to d.j.s in all the big cities.

MEMO FROM THE NATIONAL HILLTOPPERS FAN CLUB
TO: ED BONNER, KXOK, ST. LOUIS
   Please play "Do the Bop," the new Hilltoppers record, on your show. It's a big hit! Thank you very much.
                                                        —"Till Then,"
                                        BOBBIE MASON, National President

("Till Then" was one of the Hilltoppers' early recordings.)

I prayed for their records to be hits. After reading Norman Vincent Peale, I applied the power of positive thinking to a tune called "Searching," so that the Hilltoppers might earn another gold record.

My memories of the Hilltoppers are vague. I actually got to know them very well, and if they walked into my house today they would be thoroughly familiar to me. I'm sure Jimmy Sacca would give me one of his big bear hugs and we would fall easily into joking conversation. We were friends. But even though I spent a lot of time with the Hilltoppers during my high-school years I knew very little about them. I didn't ask about their backgrounds—their parents, brothers and sisters, schooling, and the rest. Background had no meaning to me, because I hadn't been anywhere; where I was going was what counted. The Hilltoppers were stars, brilliant presences, and my function was to promote their fame, so that their glow would rub off on me, like the luminescent stuff from lightning bugs.

In *Hilltoppers Highlights*, the fan-club journal that I wrote and published, I reported what I knew of the Hilltoppers:

"Jimmy Sacca stands six-two and has black hair and brown eyes, loves steak, pizza, spaghetti (you can tell he's Italian!), and when time permits this ex-football player's hobby is miniature golf. He is also accomplished on the clarinet and saxophone. Jimmy comes from Lockport, N.Y.

"Blond, pug-nosed Don McGuire, the ladies' man of the Hilltoppers, surprises everybody with his deep bass voice. He went to Western Ky. on a basketball scholarship and became one of their star players. He planned to be a dentist until stardom beckoned. He hails from Hazard, Ky., is five-eleven, collects sports clothes, plays piano and drums.

"The clown of the Toppers, Seymour ('Sy') Spiegelman of Seneca Falls, N.Y., was Jimmy's roommate at college. He is five-eight, weighs 178, and has black hair and brown eyes. His hobbies are drawing and fishing, and he loves football, swimming, and tennis.

"Eddie Crowe, a friend of Jimmy's from Lockport, replaces Billy Vaughn, the original member of the group who penned their first hit, 'Trying.' Eddie lettered in four sports in high school. He's single, girls! In the Hilltoppers' show, he plays the trumpet and does comic impressions—James Cagney, James Stewart, Robert Mitchum."

In time, my mother and I travelled to Cincinnati to see the Hilltoppers perform. It was my first trip anywhere. The ride took sixteen hours, overnight, on a bus that jolted miserably around the curves along the Ohio River. I remember waking up at each stop and checking the town on the map, so I could say I had been there. I was so excited I couldn't eat, even though the group performing was not entirely the original Hilltoppers. While Don and Sy were in the Army (they'd been drafted, and this was just after the Korean War), Jimmy hired a series of replacements. The Hilltoppers were appearing with Barney Rapp's orchestra at the Castle Farms Ballroom in Cincinnati. It was a huge suburban dance hall that was packed with glamorous couples who drank liquor. Women smuggled in whiskey bottles under their wraps: I saw them do it. The Hilltoppers bounded onstage, wearing their red sweaters and beanies with "W" on them—the football sweaters and freshman beanies from their college. (I had ordered a beanie for myself from Western and had considered wearing it that evening, but it didn't go with my taffeta dress and borrowed rhinestone jewelry.) Their act was sensational. They sang all their hits, including "P.S. I Love You," "From the Vine Came the Grape," "I'd Rather Die Young," and my favorite, "Poor Butterfly." Their sound was principally Jimmy Sacca's lead backed up with a simple "doo-wah" harmony. In their sweaters and baggy gray flannels, they swayed from side to side in unison, sort of like cheerleaders. I learned later that their moves had been choreographed. At intermission, I was allowed to go backstage to meet my idols, and during their second show they introduced me proudly to the audience. In the second show, they wore tuxedos.

After the show, they bought my mother and me Cokes and potato chips. The Hilltoppers didn't drink, but they smoked and drove a Cadillac. They drove us back to the hotel in their sky-blue 1954 Fleetwood, and Jimmy Sacca gave me forty dollars to help operate the fan club.

At school, the Hilltoppers were my secret. I had few friends, because I lived out in the country, and also because I was shy and not interested in suntans and pajama parties. I read a lot: "The Search for Bridey Murphy," "The Practical Way to a Better Memory," "The Report on Unidentified Flying Objects."

The next time we saw the Hilltoppers was in Vincennes, Indiana. Mama and I were walking down the main street from Woolworth's to our hotel there when we spotted the Cadillac. It was the Hilltoppers, arriving in town for their show. I waved at them, and the Cadillac pulled over. Jimmy was driving.

"It's us again!" Mama cried.

Jimmy hopped out and hugged us. While the other members of the group—more replacements—checked into the hotel, Jimmy took us to eat at a grill down the street. We sat in a booth and ordered pork chops with apple-sauce and French fries.

"Well, what did you think when you heard the news?" Jimmy asked us worriedly.

"I was shocked," I said lamely. I didn't know what to say. I had seen the newspaper: one of the various substitute Hilltoppers has been arrested for possession of marijuana. My mother and I had never heard of marijuana, so the news didn't really faze us.

"I was at the racetrack," Jimmy said. "And the P.A. system called my name. I had no idea he was using the stuff. I fired him so fast he didn't know what hit him."

"He wasn't one of the real Hilltoppers," I said loyally. I longed for the day when Sy and Don would rejoin the group. I knew I would like them, because they looked like such cutups in their pictures. Jimmy and Don and Seymour and Billy, the original group, were all family men, with wives and children.

After we finished eating, Jimmy lit up a Pall Mall, and Mama said, "If y'all come to Mayfield, I'll get you some free Tony Martin suits from the Merit."

"How will you do that?" I asked, surprised.

"Willie Foster will let me have them," Mama said confidently.

Willie Foster was the president of the Merit Clothing Company. We had been to his farm for the annual employees' picnic—fried chicken and roasting ears and washtubs of cold drinks. His farm was like a plantation—a magnifi-cent place with acres of pasture and horses and a little lake with rowboats.

"We'd love to come to Mayfield," Jimmy said. "But you don't have to get us any suits."

"Well, you come, and I'll cook you up a big supper and get you some suits," Mama said. "I used to sew labels in coats, but the foreman told me to slow down because I was making more than the men. So I quit. I could make a dollar an hour, I was so fast." She laughed. "But with all the farm work I didn't have time to sew labels anyway."

"Well, since you quit, they won't let you have any free suits," I argued.

"Oh, Willie wasn't mad at me," Mama said. "Willie's good to his workers. And if the Hilltoppers wore his suits, that would be good publicity."

"Well, gee, Mrs. Mason," Jimmy said. "That would be swell."

He bought us strawberry sundaes and then we went to the show.

After that, Mama and I travelled many places to see the Hilltoppers. We went to Centralia, Illinois; Princeton, Indiana; Herrin, Illinois; Blytheville, Arkansas; and Cape Girardeau, Missouri, as well as St. Louis and Detroit. Daddy had to milk the cows and couldn't go. The Hilltoppers always welcomed us. Don and Sy got out of the Army and took their rightful places in the group. They were boyish, modest, and funny. I adored them. Being a groupie in the fifties was as innocent as the Girl Scouts. The Hilltoppers never even swore around me, except once—the day Jimmy forgot the words to "My Cabin of Dreams," which they lip-synced on Johnny Slagle's "Dance Matinée" on WXYZ in Detroit. They took a protective attitude toward me, and they were crazy about my mother, who didn't put on any airs just because she knew some stars. "I think it's nice they've got that Cadillac and ain't stuckup," Mama said. She still talked about those Tony Martin suits and how good the Hilltoppers would look in them.

During my years with the Hilltoppers, I met lots of stars: Buddy Morrow, Bill Haley and the Comets, Billy Ward and the Dominoes, the Fontane Sisters, the Four Lads, Ted Weems, Wink Martindale, Jaye P. Morgan, even Paul Hornung (the Green Bay Packer), and many others. In Memphis, I visited Vicki Woodall, the National President of Pat Boone's fan club, and a photo of me with Pat and Vicki appeared later in *16 Magazine*. (After she graduated, Vicki went to Hollywood to be Pat's secretary. Something like that was my ambition; the only alternative I could see was working at the Merit). When the Hilltoppers played the Michigan State Fair, in Detroit, I appeared with the Hilltoppers on Soupy Sales' original TV show, and I was also interviewed by Robin Seymour and Don McLeod, major d.j.s on my request list. Johnnie Ray, whose big hits were "Cry" and "The Little White Cloud That Cried," stopped by the Hilltoppers' trailer at the fair one day. He flirted with me and seemed a little reckless, but his show was terrific. On the same bill was Eydie Gormé—before she married Steve Lawrence and they became Steve and Eydie. Eydie told me she admired my pixie haircut. Some weeks later, I saw her on TV and she had had her hair pixied. And at the Cotton Ball in Blytheville, Arkansas, I met Narvel Felts, a guy with a slick pompadour who said he was a singer in the style of Elvis. He asked for my autograph because I was a National President. More than twenty years later, I heard his name again, on the radio. He had finally made it. He had a hit record.

The day my mother and I drove to Blytheville and met Narvel Felts was the day the Russians sent up Sputnik. After the Hilltoppers' show, Don McGuire drove back to Mayfield with us in our Nash Rambler and then caught a bus to his home in Owensboro. As we rode through the night, listening to Chuck Berry and Little Richard and Elvis Presley on an after-hours show from New Orleans, we were aware of Sputnik spying on us. I noted the Sputnik launch in my diary:

October 4. Blytheville, Ark. Cotton Ball. Hilltoppers and Jimmy Feather-stone Ork. Russian sattelite, Sputnik, launched.

November 3. Sputnik II.

November 7. 40th anniversary of Russian Revolution. President Eisenhower's address to the nation. Senior rings.

November 15. UFO sightings increase.

December 11. English theme, "National Security," A+.

That fall, when I was a senior, a girl named Janine Williams went with my mother and me to see the Hilltoppers at a ballroom in a little town in Tennessee. Janine was popular at school, and she made a great impression on the Hilltoppers with her teasing, flirtatious personality. All the crinolines she wore under her dress made her look ready for flight, for a trip into outer space. "My brother went to Louisville to the basketball tournament last year," she told the Hilltoppers. "He won the tickets, and he flew up there in an airplane. And he stayed in the same hotel as the teams."

This was an outright lie—I didn't know why she told it—but the Hilltoppers didn't know the difference, so I didn't know what to say. I was happy, though, showing off the Hilltoppers to my friend. Jimmy introduced both of us to the audience at a special moment in the show before they sang "To Be Alone," in which Don did an Ink Spots-style monologue in his surprising bass voice and caused girls to squeal. (He had cherubic looks.) The Hilltoppers had a new record, "Starry Eyes," backed with "You Sure Look Good to Me," but they didn't sing it. I was disappointed. I was afraid it wasn't going to be a hit, and I was getting frustrated with the power of positive thinking. I hadn't told the Hilltoppers about the ESP experiments I had been trying (they involved sending telepathic messages to d.j.s to play Hilltoppers tunes). I was afraid the Hilltoppers would laugh. I wanted them to think I was normal. One of the fan-club presidents I had visited in Cape Girardeau, Missouri, had a deformed back and didn't even go to school. Another one I knew weighed about three hundred pounds, and her ambition was to be an actress. It was depressing.

"What do you think of Elvis?" Janine asked the Hilltoppers later. Elvis was singing "All Shook Up" on the radio of the Cadillac as Jimmy drove us out to a café for hamburgers.

"He's great," said Sy. "He has a fine voice."

"If I could wiggle like that, we'd make a million dollars," Jimmy said.

Don laughed. "Our manager had a chance once to manage Elvis, but he turned it down. He said nobody with a name like 'Elvis' would get anywhere."

"I like Elvis," Mama said. "He can really carry a tune."

For me, there was something as familiar about Elvis as our farm, with the oak trees and the cows and the chickens. It was as though Elvis were me, listening to WLAC and then coming up with his own songs about the way he felt about the world. I tried not to think too hard about Elvis. Janine had said to me, "If I got Elvis in a dark corner, I'd tear his clothes off."

Janine grew impatient with me and my obsession, and we didn't stay friends. She was going steady with a basketball player I had once had a crush on, and she had no interest in things like flying saucers and reincarnation. I had read "Reincarnation: A Hope of the World," and it impressed me. I was filled with philosophical questions and I wrote a paper for English class on agnosticism. My teacher, Miss Florence, summoned me to her office and accused me of plagiarism. "Young lady, you have no business entertaining ideas like this," she said. "Where did you get such an idea?"

I quaked. "I read about it. I read lots of philosophy," I said, which was only partly a lie. Reincarnation was philosophy, sort of. I told her I had read John Locke, which *was* a lie. But I hadn't plagiarized. I really believed it was possible that God did not exist, and furthermore it seemed likely that there was no way to know whether he did or not.

Miss Florence had lavender hair, and she kept a handkerchief tucked in her sleeve. Now and then she daintily plucked it out and snuffled into it. She was a terrifying woman, much admired by the whole town. Everyone since the thirties had been in her English class.

"Take my advice," she said, growing softer. "Give up these strange ideas of yours. Your field is mathematics. That's what you're good at. Stay away from these peculiar questions, because they're destructive. And stick with the Bible. That's all the philosophy you'll ever need."

I was silent, rigid with fury—too intimidated to speak.

"You have a lot of big ideas, but they will lead you astray," Miss Florence said in dismissal.

I immersed myself in my presidential duties, publishing my bimonthly newsletter, *Hilltoppers Topics*. In Mayfield, I was an outcast, but in the greater world I was suave and self-important. When d.j.s interviewed me, I spoke glibly in *Billboard* lingo. "Well, Ed, this new platter is slated to be a chart-buster," I said to Ed Bonner on KXOK. I had my own stationery, with a Hilltoppers logo. Running a fan club was expensive, but the Hilltoppers sent me ten dollars a week for expenses and fifteen dollars a week for myself. I saved all my money for college. I started hating math.

My mother had been serious about those Tony Martin suits. Shortly before my graduation, the Hilltoppers came to Mayfield, and Mama whisked them off to the Merit and got them measured for the suits. They picked out an off-white material with a subtle gray stripe in it. (Later, when the suits were finished, Mama went to the Merit and personally sewed in the labels.) That spring, I was a soda jerk at the Rexall drugstore in Mayfield, making fifty cents an hour, and after school that day I was drawing a Coke from the fountain for one of the regulars when all four of the Hilltoppers strolled into the drugstore. It was my big moment: I could show them off. A classmate of mine, one of those popular cheerleaders—an uptown girl who had made me feel like a shabby bumpkin—was testing nail polish at the cosmetics counter. I rushed over and told her I would introduce her to the Hilltoppers. "They're here," I said, pointing to the end of the counter, where I had served them Cokes.

"Oh, I don't think so," she said, flashing her cheerleader smile. "I wouldn't know what to say." With two fingernails painted Persian Melon, she hurried out the back door of the drugstore. The Hilltoppers scared her.

It was a triumph, sort of. I got off work early, and the Hilltoppers drove me home in the Cadillac. Mama made a huge catfish supper, with hush puppies and slaw and blackberry pie, and that evening my family and I all went to Paducah and saw the Hilltoppers sing at the National Guard Armory with Blue Barron's orchestra. It was a perfect day. "Your mother is an amazing woman," Don said to me.

The Hilltoppers were so conventional, such nice guys. I didn't know how to talk to them about the crazy thoughts in my head. I had just received a reply to my letter to George Adamski, the man who claimed in his book about UFOs to have been on a spaceship to Venus. He thanked me for writing and assured me that he had indeed been to Venus, but he failed to answer my questions about the spacecraft's interior and the landscape of Venus.

That summer, I picked blackberries in the early-morning dew with rock-and-roll songs like "Get a Job" by the Silhouettes and Eddie Cochran's "Summertime Blues" blasting in my mind, and in the afternoons I trudged down the dusty lanes through the fields with the dog to round up the herd of cows. In the evenings, I worked at the Rexall. I went out with boys—boys who wanted to settle down and work in the new factories—but I wasn't impressed. I was always dreaming. Our house was close to Highway 45, which ran straight south to Tupelo, Mississippi, where Elvis was born. I knew he had dreamed the same dreams.

Miss Florence refused to write me a recommendation to Duke University, where I wanted to study parapsychology with the famous Dr. J. B. Rhine, so in the fall I went away to the University of Kentucky, in Lexington, where I fell in love with a boy who was interested in UFOs and mind expansion. He wrote a column for the college newspaper and had a sense of humor that reminded me of Max Shulman's "Rally Round the Flag, Boys!" I neglected my fan-club duties and failed to get *Hilltoppers Topics* out on schedule. All the mysteries of the universe lay before me, and I couldn't learn fast enough. I read "Brave New World" and "1984" and "On the Beach" and "Mandingo" and "Elmer Gantry." I studied French and psychology and philosophy and volleyball. After hours, I still listened to John R jive-talking along with Ruth Brown and Little Walter and Jimmy Reed. Buddy Holly died that winter. Elvis was in the Army.

Earlier in the school year, before I fell in love, the Hilltoppers played at homecoming, and I went to the dance without a date—an unheard-of thing for a girl to do in those days. But I wouldn't have missed their show. I never tired of seeing it—even the old comic bit when the guys rolled up Don's pantlegs without his knowledge while he was singing the solo of "Ka-Ding-Dong." They always opened with something fast-paced, like "I Can't Give You Anything but Love" or "I've Got the World on a String," and sometimes they followed up with "Toot Toot Tootsie (Goo' Bye)"—which Jimmy sang as "Toot Toot *Tootie*"—before launching into their own numbers. Jimmy was noted for his clumsy introductions: "Ladies and gentlemen, and now we want to do the song that you made possible our being here with by buying those . . ." That night, as he always did when I was at their show, Jimmy introduced me to the audience, and the spotlight hit my face, momentarily blinding me. This time, I was embarrassed, because I thought everyone there would know I didn't have a date and would think I was peculiar. I felt as though I had just arrived from the moon.

The curfew was extended to 2 A.M. that night, because the Hilltoppers' show was late, and Sy walked me to my dorm. We sat in the parlor, surrounded by sorority pledges and their anxious dates. Some of them stared at us. Sy was the only one in the room in a tuxedo. I was the only one in the room who seemed to have a date with a member of the famous singing group that had just performed at the big dance. The lights in the parlor were bright, and the elderly housemother patrolled nervously. I got a fit of giggles when she looked at Sy suspiciously, as though he might be secretly organizing a panty raid. She had drilled the dorm residents in the horrors of panty raids, making them seem something like acts of terrorism.

A year later, I saw the Hilltoppers for the last time, at a night club in Louisville, where they were performing with Mel Tormé. I had driven over with some girls from U.K. The Hilltoppers' popularity had declined drastically. It wasn't my fault, though. They were being eclipsed by rock and roll. In their tuxedos or in their Tony Martin suits, they never really got the hang of it. That night in Louisville, I remember Don and Sy sitting at a table in a corner with me. They were as kind as ever—funny and generous, the way I always remember them. I had on a black cocktail dress with a taffeta balloon hem. "Those U.K. boys better watch out," Don said, teasing me.

Shyly, I told them about my boyfriend. By then, he was going with some other girl and my life was in ruins, but I didn't go into detail. I apologized for letting my club work slip. The newsletter was two months late.

Don smiled. "It's about time you forgot about the fan club," he said.

"No, it's not," I said loyally.

"You'll have other interests," he said. "You'll get married, and have your own family."

"I don't know." I knew I could never love anyone but that boy with the sense of humor. I would never get married.

"People change and go on to something else," Don said. "We won't stay with this forever. It's no way to live—one dinky ballroom after another. Travelling around all the time isn't what it's cracked up to be."

"Even in a Cadillac?" I asked.

"Even in a Cadillac," Don said, smiling again. "By the way, we'll drop you off in Lexington tomorrow."

"Thank you," I said. It was my last chance to travel in their Cadillac, I thought—a good way to end my national presidency. They had traded in the blue Cadillac for a newer, black model. I imagine it even now, rushing through the night, unrestrained in its flight, charging across America.

It was after midnight that night when Mel Tormé finished his set, but the band wouldn't quit. The crowd was wild. Jimmy took the microphone again. He sang "I Can't Get Started," a droopy-drawers sort of song. He had had a couple of drinks, and he was in mellow spirits. Then he eased into "St. James Infirmary." As the deep sadness of the song emerged, he suddenly became real to me, not a star. "St. James Infirmary" was slow and bluesy, but it wasn't a droopy-drawers song. It was the meanest, low-downest, saddest song I ever heard. I thought I would die. It was after hours, way down South in Dixie. It was 1959.

The Hilltoppers rode their behemoth Cadillac and played one-night stands only a while longer. Sy worked in a tobacco warehouse for a time, and then he and Jimmy became sales representatives for Dot Records. Don settled in Lexington. I lost touch with them. In the seventies, during the nostalgia rage, I heard that Jimmy Sacca was on the road again with a new Hilltoppers group.

After college, in the sixties, I went to New York and got a job writing for a fan magazine—the same magazine that had once listed my fan club in its Betty Burr column. I found out that Betty Burr, who had once been an honorary member of my club, was only a name, like Miss Lonelyhearts. Part of my job at the fan mag was to write Betty Burr columns about fan clubs. I did that for about a year, and after that I left New York.

Suggestions for Discussion

1. Discuss Bobbie Ann's obligations as president of the fan club. What benefits did she derive from the position?

2. Why was her mother so supportive of Bobbie Ann's involvement?

3. Explain why Bobbie Ann eventually gave up the fan-club.

Suggestions for Writing

1. Describe your own or a friend's participation in a local or national fan club.

2. Bobbie Ann Mason wanted to "meet somebody famous." Tell about a famous person you have met or want to meet.

Essays
— ◆◆◆ —

Art Buchwald
Leisure Will Kill You

Art Buchwald (b. 1925), the nationally syndicated columnist, won the Pulitzer Prize for his humorous writings in 1982. Among his more than two dozen books are Washington Is Looking *(1976),* The Buchwald Stops Here *(1978),* While Reagan Slept *(1983), and* Laid Back in Washington *(1981), from which the following selection is taken.*

This country is producing so much leisure equipment for the home that nobody has any leisure time anymore to enjoy it. A few months ago I bought a television tape recorder to make copies of programs when I was out of the house.

Last week I recorded the Nebraska-Oklahoma football game. When I came home in the evening, I decided to play it back. But my son wanted to play "Baseball" on the TV screen with his Atari Computer. We finished four innings when my wife came in the room and asked me if I would like to listen to the Vienna Opera on our hi-fi stereo set. I told her I was waiting to finish the baseball match so I could watch the football game I had recorded.

She said if I watched the football game for three hours, I would miss *Love Boat*. I told her I would record *Love Boat* and we could watch it later in the evening. She protested that *Casablanca* was showing on Channel 5 at 11:30 and she wanted to see it again.

"Don't worry," I assured her, "we can watch *Love Boat* late Saturday and *Casablanca* on Sunday morning when we get up."

"But if we watch *Casablanca* tomorrow morning when can we see the instant Polaroid movies you took of Ben yesterday afternoon?"

"We'll see them after we play backgammon on the new table."

"If we do that," my daughter said, "we won't be able to see the Washington Redskins–New York Giants football game."

"I'll record the Redskins-Giants football game and we'll watch it while *60 Minutes* is on the air. We can see *60 Minutes* at 11 o'clock."

"But," my son said, "you promised to play the pinball machine with me at 11."

"Okay, we'll play pinball at 11 and watch *60 Minutes* at midnight."

My wife said, "Why don't we listen to the Vienna Opera while we're eating and then we can save an hour to play computer golf?"

"That's good thinking," I said. "The only problem is I've rented a TV tape for *Cleopatra* and that runs for three hours."

"You could show it on Monday night," she suggested.

"I can't do that. I have to return the tape Monday afternoon or be charged for it another week. I have an idea. I won't go to work Monday morning and we'll watch it then."

"I was hoping to use our Jacuzzi Monday morning," my wife said.

"Okay, then I'll tape *Cleopatra* and you can see it Monday afternoon."

"I'm using the set Monday afternoon," my son said, "to play digital hockey on the TV screen."

"You can't do that," I said. "I have to watch the *Today* show in the afternoon if I'm going to watch *Cleopatra* in the morning."

"Why can't you watch the *Today* show at dinnertime?" my wife asked.

"Because the Wolfingtons are coming over to hear me play 'Tea for Two' on the electric organ."

"I thought we might play computer bridge at dinner," my wife said.

"We'll play it after my encore," I assured her.

"Then when will we see *Monday Night Football?*" my son wanted to know.

"Tuesday," I said.

"Does that mean you're not going to work on Tuesday?" my wife asked.

"How can I go to work," I yelled, "when I've got so much leisure time on my hands?"

Suggestions for Discussion

1. Explain Buchwald's observation that our "country is producing so much leisure equipment for the home that nobody has any leisure time anymore to enjoy it." Do you agree? State your reasons.

2. Discuss whether or not the conflicts that Buchwald sets up in this short essay are realistic, believable, and resolvable.

3. Suggest solutions to the conflicts Buchwald identifies.

4. Discuss Buchwald's use of exaggeration and accumulated detail to give humor to his essay.

Suggestions for Writing

1. Identify and discuss dangers to the individual and to the family posed by excessive amounts of leisure.

2. Depict a busy scene in your own home.

Roger Angell

Reflections: The Cheers for Keith

Roger Angell (b. 1920) is senior fiction editor for *The New Yorker*. He is the author of several books about baseball, including *The Summer Game* (1972), *Five Seasons* (1977), and *Late Innings* (1982). In the essay that follows, he discusses the problems of drug abuse and compulsory drug testing in major league baseball.

A few weeks ago, I made a leisurely swing south and then west to watch the major-league ballplayers going through their familiar rituals in preparation for the long 1986 season, which is now under full steam and will occupy much of our sports attention through the summer months and on into the extravaganzas of the league playoffs and the World Series. Spring training is almost my favorite part of the baseball year, and the sunlit days I passed in Florida and Arizona this time around were exceptionally warming and hopeful, because of the presence on every side of a remarkable group of rising young pitchers and batters—just about the best rookie crop I can recall—whose various fortunes I will happily follow now in the box scores and daily doings of their teams. But even as I began to put these fresh names to memory— Jose Canseco, Bob Tewksbury, Pete Incaviglia, Wally Joyner, Will Clark, Bobby Witt, Dan Plesac, and the rest—and scribbled notes to myself about their unfamiliar mannerisms on the mound and in the batter's box, it occurred to me that there was a special reason for my optimism over the arrival of another freshman class of shining youngsters and for my pleasure in the evergreen renewals of still another baseball season: I hoped they would let me at last put aside my anger and confusion about the drug scandals that so altered the game last year. Sometime during this past winter, I suddenly realized that I didn't want to think about cocaine in baseball anymore. Most of my friends felt the same way, and so did a lot of the players I talked to about the matter during spring training. "Let's get it *over* with," one of them said. "Let's get on with the game." And the fans, I think, were more upset about drugs than anyone else. Like them, I was sick to death of the whole matter, and badly wished that those afflicted and now notorious stars and journeyman players had stayed away from the stuff in the first place, thus sparing me many anxieties and second thoughts about the nature of our sports infatuation in this country—about the realities of celebrity and big money and repeated, on-demand extraordinary athletic performance—and about the inflexibility of our old wish to keep the world of sports (no matter how artificial and commercial and exploitative it has plainly become) as a place of moral certitude and preserved values. I was also bored and wearied by the statements of position coming from the baseball commissioner and the players' union, and from lawyers and agents and sports columnists and editorial writers and drug therapists, and by speculation about the proper forms of drug detection and punishment and medical support that the game should now accept and endorse.

As a baseball writer, however, I dutifully did my work and tried to pay attention. I began to keep a file of drug stories, and annotations and reminders, and I interviewed a good many players and front-office people about drugs. But at the same time another part of me—the fan side—still felt aggrieved and bitter about the whole thing. None of this had anything much to do with *baseball*—the delectable and marvellously difficult old game that has brought me almost undiminished pleasure since I first began to take notice of it, more than fifty years ago. Like many other fans, of course, I could recall a previous inner clash of ideas and feelings—between baseball as I wanted it to be and baseball as it now inescapably and unhappily seemed to be in reality— during the seven-week baseball strike that brought the game to a halt during the summer of 1981. The same malaise has also afflicted me, in a creeping, fungoid fashion, during the gross inflation of salaries that followed the arrival of free agency for players in 1976, and raised the average major-league stipend from about forty-five thousand dollars in 1975 to the present four hundred and thirty thousand dollars—a swing that has taken these young athletes from the economic and social level of barkeepers and small farmers and veterinarians, say, to that of rock performers and Wall Street lawyers and corporate C.E.O.s. Now the presence of *drugs* in still another baseball crisis seemed almost too much. For the first time, I felt that I might be on the edge of turning away from baseball altogether, and consigning it in my mind to the inner forgettery, where I have tucked away so many other lost amenities and sweet, once-certain surroundings and institutions that most middle-class, middle-aged Americans have learned to do without. It was this horrid possibility—no more baseball for me, or else baseball seen with a distant, half-cynical, chilled attention—that shook me out of my self-pity, and forced me at last to try to sort out and set down some of the difficulties and angry conflicts that surround the matter, and even to venture some speculations about what has happened and why we feel so bad about it. Thinking about drugs and sports just now is probably not such a bad idea, in any case, because sooner or later the baseball owners and the Players Association (the major-leaguers' union) will compromise their differences and agree on a new drug program for the major leagues—and at that moment, of course, we fans will start to forget about the whole business as quickly as possible.

News about drug abuse turned up elsewhere in the media over this past winter: first when it was learned that some of the players for the New England Patriots, of the National Football League, who surprisingly played their way into the Super Bowl in January (and were there unmercifully demolished by the Chicago Bears), had been known by their coach to be struggling with drug problems during the regular season (the story was far less sensational in its details and implications than was first suggested in the Boston press); and then when Micheal Ray Richardson, a star guard with the New Jersey Nets, was incapacitated for a third time by his severe drug addiction and, under the rules of the National Basketball Association, was banned for life from play—a private tragedy that saddened and silenced everyone in the sport. Drugs are an inescapable presence in *all* sports, it seems, and I suspect that the whole mysterious, titillating, and scary subject is more on our minds than we care to admit. The widespread recent use of cocaine—research findings tell us that up to thirty per cent of the eighteen-to-twenty-five-year-olds in our society have been at least one-time users of the drug—is a disturbing matter: no one can be quite certain who among his friends or colleagues or relatives may now be trying the stuff, or is about to. Many of us already know a few young men or women whose lives and careers have been permanently damaged by cocaine; certainly anyone who has been involved with the sports world can easily bring to mind a particular athlete whose shining, wonderfully promising career was cut down by drug addiction. (For me, this will always be Mike Norris, the angular and elegant right-handed pitcher—he had a killing, over-the-top screwball—with the A's, who went twenty-two and nine with the young and dashing Oaklands in 1980, and deserved but did not win the American League's Cy Young Award for his work that summer. I can still see the unique little flourish of his trailing leg as he finished his delivery, and his comical, hot-dog mannerisms on the mound, and recall the charm and intelligence of his interviews. Injuries set him back after that season, but cocaine and alcohol finished the job, as he himself has admitted.) Cocaine addiction is a miserable illness, and there are peripheral risks to the innocent as well, who can conceivably fall victim to accidents at the hands of drug-affected vehicle drivers or pilots or surgeons. Work performance may be diminished in less critical places and professions, and the flow of enormous sums of money into the criminal substratum (where illicit dealers receive not only our cash but our tacit approval, since they are essential to the processes of the habit) inflicts cynicism and other psychic bruises on our society. Nothing much about cocaine use is known *for certain*, however, and the highly publicized trials of two accused drug dealers in Pittsburgh last September—when seven players, all but one of them still active in the majors, testified that they and many other players (seventeen were named) had been in-season cocaine users in the late nineteen-seventies and early eighties—provided a sudden focus for much free-floating concern. Previously, more than a dozen individual players—including established regulars like Tim Raines, Claudell Washington, Alan Wiggins, Steve Howe, and the aforementioned Mike Norris—had admitted to difficulties with the drug in recent years and had undergone therapy (and sometimes suspension by their clubs) while they attempted to deal with their problems. Four members of the Kansas City Royals—Willie Wilson, Vida Blue, Willie Aikens, and Jerry Martin—had even served jail terms for cocaine offenses. But the news from Pittsburgh was different, for it seemed to confirm some long-standing rumors about the prevalence of cocaine in the sport, and the September parade of testifying players, pale and unsmiling in their suits and ties (with some very familiar faces among them: Dale Berra, Dave Parker, Keith Hernandez), sent a seismic wave of dismay through the baseball world.

A bare four days after the Pittsburgh debacle, Commissioner Peter Ueberroth, whose understanding of the public-relations process is regarded with awe in the business world, came forward with a proposal, presented in dramatic fashion at simultaneous pregame clubhouse meetings around the leagues, that all major-leaguers should forthwith sign individual pledges to agree to a system of compulsory urine-testing for drugs, so that the good name of baseball could be restored "for us, our children, and for the generations to come." Mr. Ueberroth, who took office as commissioner in October of 1984, had come to baseball with a reputation as a swift, self-assured problem-solver. His achievements as president of the Los Angeles Olympic Organizing Committee had been dazzling, ultimately winning him *Time's* accolade as 1984's Man of the Year. In that post, he had supervised a system of compulsory drug-testing of Olympic competitors, although the screenings were not primarily for cocaine or marijuana but for performance-boosting amphetamines, steroids, and the like, and the athletes involved, of course, were amateurs. On taking over as baseball commissioner, he stated that the drug problem stood at the top of his agenda, and in the spring of 1985 he imposed a system of compulsory urine-testing for all minor-league players and for front-office workers throughout the sport (neither group has a union); he has since claimed that minor-league testing has been an unqualified success, although precise data about it have been hard to come by. Since Mr. Ueberroth did not present his sudden September testing plan to the Players Association, which had been a party to all such past discussions, he could not have been much surprised when the players balked, insisting that these matters should be resolved through their union. A charge of unfair labor practice in connection with this substantial issue has been filed by the Players Association, and a verdict is expected very soon. There were expressions of cynicism, and even bitterness, from many players about the Commissioner's motives in going public with his testing proposal directly after the Pittsburgh trials, since the whole tangled issue of drug abuse and drug-testing had been a matter of intense study by the owners and the union for several years. Discussions between the two sides had resulted in a Joint Drug Agreement, signed in May, 1984, which provided an essentially voluntary system of diagnosis, treatment, and rehabilitation for drug abusers, with many provisos—up to but not including compulsory testing—designed to involve even recalcitrant players in extended therapy without immediate penalty and with accompanying guarantees of privacy. The program, to be sure, had not been much used and was generally seen to be a tentative beginning to sorting out an obdurately difficult combination of social and medical and corporate issues, but the owners, in any case, announced during the World Series last fall that they were unanimously withdrawing from the Joint Drug Agreement, and they have since made it plain that their strategy would be to secure compulsory urine-testing from each player as part of his next contract. The Commissioner, I should add, has said that he regrets the owners' impetuosity in throwing away the Joint Drug Agreement, but it is hard for me to believe that he was not consulted about the matter, or that his advice, if presented, would not have had more effect. Drug-testing, we must conclude, has been suddenly perceived by the owners as a dramatic and politically useful simplification of an intractably complex private vice. (Mr. Ueberroth has also raised the spectre of cocaine-afflicted players' being blackmailed by their underworld suppliers and presumably forced to throw games at the behest of crooked gamblers, but this scare seems to have expired from unlikelihood; fixing the 1919 World Series required the mob to bribe seven or eight doltish, vastly underpaid members of the Chicago White Sox, and even then the trick almost misfired.)

The arguments against compulsory testing, some of which will be presented below, are of considerable weight, and they were much discussed among the players at the end of last season and over the winter. (I should explain that my own sampling of player opinion was always a narrow one, never encompassing more than three or four players on any one club, but the players I did consult always tried to offer a fair estimate of what others in their clubhouse believed. Most of the opinions summarized here, whether from players or from front-office people and executives, and even owners, must be unattributed, since individuals on both sides requested anonymity because of the pending grievance hearing—the Big Case, as it is sometimes called.) Players on different clubs, including several player representatives, who correspond roughly to shop stewards in the Players Association, told me that about half of their teammates had no objection to compulsory urine-testing—in fact, many of them were eager to see the plan in operation, so that the whole distracting issue could be forgotten and they could get on with their work—and others agreed with the notion that testing was a valid way for baseball to begin to set its house in order. A few of the players who had tried cocaine and run into difficulties with it (Rod Scurry, now of the Yankees, for one) said that compulsory testing was the only weapon that might deter habitual offenders. Players on the other side of the question, however, were vehement in their opposition to testing; most of *them* saw testing as a violation of their privacy, and a good many also saw it as an unsubtle scheme by the owners to drive a wedge between the players and their union. These fears were not unfounded, one would conclude, for by the time spring training came around about five hundred of the major-league players (of the one thousand and forty on the winter rosters) had agreed to testing clauses in their new contracts. In many cases (it's hard to say how many, since contract negotiations are kept private), an offer of more money in return for testing, and a threat of less money without testing, swung the balance. Compulsory testing seems to have carried the day, at least for the moment, and it is my belief that this conclusion to the issue has become very popular with the fans, not just because it appears to enhance, or even guarantee, the purity of the sport but also because it slightly but clearly demeans the players (who must produce a urine sample on demand, in the presence of a drug cop), and thus punishes them all for letting us down so badly, for damaging our dreams about the game.

Penalties for the cocaine users who had testified or had been named at the Pittsburgh trials were announced by the Commissioner at the beginning of the spring-training season. After private interviews with all the players involved, he divided them into three categories, with accompanying degrees of severity in their punishment. For seven prime offenders—including Joaquin Andujar, Dave Parker, and Keith Hernandez—he decreed a year's suspension from the game, with the accompanying provision that the suspension would be lifted in return for a fine of ten per cent of their salaries, plus two hundred hours' service in community programs to combat drug abuse, and compulsory drug testing for the remainder of their careers. Lesser penalties—sixty days' suspension or five-per-cent fines, fifty hours of community service, and compulsory testing—were imposed on four other players, and testing alone on the remaining ten. There may be some cogency to the Commissioner's expressed belief that this disposition of the very difficult matter of punishment might be of use in combatting drug abuse in and outside the game; and his determination of the cases—to judge by fans and friends I have heard from—has been popularly viewed as being fair and proper, although there remain a number of hard-line scribes and baseball executives who believe that the drug users, immunity or no immunity, should have been thrown out of the game for life, like the Chicago Black Sox. Mr. Ueberroth's tone toward the offenders has been regretful and conciliatory, but I have heard not a few coarse expressions of satisfaction from old-line coaches and front-office men, who surely speak for some of their employers in their belief that the wealthy, insufferably privileged young players of today have at last been cut down to size by the scandal, at least for the moment. There is a sense on the management side that the Players Association has lost some of its constituency over the issue of testing, and that, fairly or unfairly, the union is viewed by the public as having no plan or program of its own, and as standing stubbornly on the wrong side of the whole business.

Why not test? Here are some reasons presented to me by players, by officers of the Players Association, by a handful of front-office people, and by doctors and lawyers and friends and fans I talked to over the winter. The arguments are set forth in no special order.

● Compulsory testing is a violation of personal privacy. The embarrassment of a compulsory urine-test is not quite a constitutional issue, since the Fourth Amendment restrictions against unreasonable search and seizure apply only to measures imposed by the government, but testing clearly does harm to an individual's sense of self. Racehorses have their urine tested, to be sure, but, as one All-Star American League infielder put it to me last fall, "I am not a horse." Several of the more thoughtful front-office people I know explained to me this spring that compulsory testing is only a necessary small inconvenience, of exactly the same sort that we all accept when submitting ourselves to a metal detector at an airport—almost a convincing argument, I thought, until I began to envision lines of passengers at La-Guardia or O'Hare leading up to and into bathrooms occupied by waiting inspectors.

● It attaches a presumption of guilt to all the players. The easy little turnabout in our minds ("If they've done nothing wrong, they've got nothing to hide") when we seize upon the quick fix of compulsory testing damages *us* in the end, for it demolishes an essential premise of a free society.

● Urine-testing, up until now, has been an unreliable process, with a persistent error factor of from fifteen to twenty-five per cent, divided equally between false negative and false positive results. Follow-up tests, in the case of positives, may correct a mistake, but they, too, require great care, and afford further possibilities of error and misdiagnosis. A more accurate means of urine-testing is available, but it is so expensive—up to five hundred dollars a test—as to make its everyday use unlikely.

● Urine-testing makes no distinction between the occasional recreational use of a drug and habitual or addictive use.

● Compulsory testing is a two-class system: lightly or forgivingly applied to star players, rigorously applied to everyone else. (Many black players believe that the system will be employed against them in discriminatory fashion.) Examples of this disparity are easy to find. When Dwight Gooden was presented with his new 1.32-million-dollar contract by the Mets this winter, it contained a compulsory-drug-testing clause; he demurred, and the matter was dropped without further ado. Mike Armstrong, a borderline member of the Yankee pitching staff, similarly refused, on principle, a drug-testing clause in his two-hundred-and-ninety-five-thousand-dollar contract, and eventually was forced to settle for thirty thousand dollars less in order to get it dropped. Joel Youngblood, a veteran San Francisco outfielder who did not seem to fit into the Giants' plans for the coming season, was refused a three-year extension on his contract this winter unless he agreed to unspecified forms of drug testing; when he and his agent protested the vagueness of the terms in the testing clauses, he was told to take his wares elsewhere. No one had suggested or implied that Youngblood might be a drug user, but he was forced to carry the issue to a labor-grievance procedure before the ban was dropped. Then he made the team.

• Compulsory drug-testing in baseball has become a matter of public relations. Doctors and drug specialists I have consulted believe that, in practice, urine-testing is of limited use, and may even have a negative effect on therapy; the suggestion that it can help do away with the basic problem is illusory, and actually veils the stubborn nature of cocaine addiction and the difficulty of its cure.

• Compulsory testing in baseball, the national pastime, will become a symbolic, integral part of a national pattern of drug testing in industry and private business, in state and municipal governments, on newspapers, in schools, and so forth—part of a major alteration of our freedoms and priorities. This is a matter that has already produced very strong opinions on both sides. The recently presented findings of the President's Commission on Organized Crime recommended widespread testing in industry and compulsory testing of all federal employees, but this part of the report was immediately challenged by several members of the commission itself. The question of testing is being debated almost everywhere now, it seems (the National Football League is embroiled in much the same sort of wrangle as baseball), and may ultimately be resolved only in the courts. It should not come as an absolute surprise that proponents of a safer, more rigidly controlled society should turn up among the conservative businessmen and entrepreneurs who buy their way into sports franchises, and this larger issue—at its heart, an intergenerational conflict—has been visible just below the surface in the bitter labor and salary negotiations waged between the owners and the players over the past two decades. Regardless of our individual inclinations in this emotional subject, we should probably remind ourselves that if the practice of compulsory drug-testing is accepted by all professional sports organizations, it will only be a matter of time—a very short time, in my view—before it is required of all college athletes, and very soon thereafter, surely, we will be asking high-school boys and girls to subject themselves to the same process if they wish to try out for a team.

If there is any hope or certainty to be found in this sorry business, it must be searched out somewhere beyond or to one side of our wishes for a restored "image" of the game, and also beyond or to one side of the assumptions by the Commissioner and the owners that the fans' feelings about the drug issue are clear enough to constitute some kind of mandate. Confusions and contradictions crop up everywhere, and probably within most of us as well. Last September 10th, in a crucial game against the Cardinals at Shea Stadium, when Keith Hernandez came up to bat for the first time after his Pittsburgh court appearance, he received a sustained standing ovation from fifty thousand home-town fans (he had to step out of the batter's box to compose himself), and no one who was there—as I was—and no one I have talked to since has quite been able to decipher the full meaning of the outburst of feeling. Maybe the fans were expressing forgiveness for Keith's transgressions. Maybe they were hailing his extraordinary season's performance, afield and at the plate, and saying that this outweighed all. Maybe they were saying "It's O.K., Keith—we understand," or maybe they were only saying "Let's play ball!" or "Let's go, *Mets!*" Perhaps they were expressing their belief that some corner had been turned, and that drugs in baseball was over and done with at last. I just don't know. I've heard in dugouts and pressrooms and clubhouses that the use of cocaine in the majors is much reduced from what it was four or five years ago, but no one knows how many recreational or habitual users there were or are in baseball—an amazing vacuum at the very center of the controversy. Physicians employed under the Joint Drug Agreement were preparing a confidential medical survey on this question, but the survey expired when the owners abandoned the agreement in October.

The need for symbolic victory seems to outweigh every other consideration or sensible procedure. Many people would agree that Commissioner Ueberroth had to invoke *some* form of penalty against the cocaine users whose names had surfaced at Pittsburgh, but, as it happened, his system of suspension and forgiveness came down hardest on some players—Hernandez, for one, and Lonnie Smith, of the Royals, for another—who had recognized their own addiction and had voluntarily taken the necessary steps to cure it; they had broken the law, to be sure, and had been guilty of great and self-destructive foolishness (Hernandez had also lied about his cocaine habit before he was called to testify under oath and under immunity), but their turnabout, surely, was exactly the sort of difficult self-rehabilitation that the clubs and the leagues would hold up as an example to other afflicted players. Complexities and ironies abound, and in the end we can only respond to some of them with a dismissive shrug—the gesture of our times. Amphetamines, which probably affect game performance more than cocaine, are still in use in many clubs (there aren't as many clubhouse jokes about greenies—which are now sometimes called "beans"—as there once were), but amphetamines, when prescribed, are legal. So is alcohol, and drinking, of course, is an ancient and celebrated companion to big-time sports—a seatmate at the games, so to speak—with infinitely more widespread and destructive consequences than drugs. It sounds naïve to point out that the Commissioner and the clubs, to the best of my knowledge, have never imposed suspensions or other penalties on players or managers who have had their licenses revoked for drunk driving.

Mr. Ueberroth, it must be added, has put forward no over-all program of his own for the treatment and rehabilitation of drug-afflicted players, which further reinforces the suspicion that the *appearance* of a drug-free sport is his prime objective. I don't mean to suggest that he is indifferent to the problem of addiction or unconcerned about the welfare of the players—only that his peculiar office is, of its nature, symbolic, paternal, and much given to enforced optimism. On Opening Day last month, he announced a more detailed plan for the compulsory testing of all major-leaguers, with accompanying assurances of full confidentiality in the process, and with no penalty for an initial positive finding for any player, but at almost the same moment it became clear that testing has been little more than a gesture or a symbol all along. Barry Rona, the executive director of the Player Relations Committee (an owners' group), said at a hearing before baseball's impartial arbitrator that about four hundred and fifty of the new player contracts that included compulsory-testing clauses were of the non-guaranteed form—that is, the contract would no longer apply if the player was dropped before Opening Day—and he conceded that for technical legal reasons drug-tests could not be enforced upon their signers. If this sounds baffling, it's no wonder. According to the Players Association, the testing clauses in the contracts were only a suggestion of general intent and not a binding commitment; according to expert inside-the-game runes-readers, the turnabout was a strategic retreat by management's side—a strong suggestion that the owners would not, in the end, go to war over the issue of testing. Forty-three players have signed guaranteed contracts, with enforceable (according to Mr. Rona) testing clauses, but among these are some of the twenty-one players under drug penalty, including testing, by the Commissioner. Compulsory testing, if it ever comes, will thus involve perhaps five per cent of all major-leaguers, it now appears—a wholly unexpected turn of events, which seems to tell us that the great flap is about to die down at last.

The Players Association is quiet for the moment, as it awaits the impending grievance-procedure verdict on its fundamental argument that the drug-testing issue must be resolved, now as in the past, through collective bargaining. (The Association, it must be emphasized, has never flatly refused testing.) Whatever that verdict turns out to be, it seems clear that the owners and the Players Association will eventually have to agree upon an all-encompassing plan for drug education, therapy, and rehabilitation, which will be administered for the benefit of the players themselves, as individuals, rather than for any of the reasons that have inflamed and distracted us over the past year. This could happen almost any day, it appears, or it could be months away. The two sides were very close to an agreement about a week ago, but they have since receded from what looked like an ingenious solution to the bitterly divisive testing issue. When they do eventually come to terms, it will no doubt be over a plan very much like the Joint Drug Agreement, with some temporary acceptance of testing under limited conditions. (The Anti-Drug Program of the National Basketball Association, which has been in operation since September, 1983, empowers a single independent expert to determine whether there is reasonable cause to suspect that an individual player may be engaged in the use of illegal drugs, and this expert may then authorize the N.B.A. to test the player four times during a six-week period. Accommodations, in other words, are possible, and an accommodation, as I have said, will bring the two sides in baseball together once again.)

Several of the more progressive ball clubs—including the Baltimore Orioles, the Oakland A's, and the Milwaukee Brewers—have been working quietly on their own drug-rehabilitation programs while awaiting a resolution of the over-all testing issue. These anti-drug plans have been in place for several years now, and form part of the teams' larger Employee Assistance Programs. During the past winter, twenty-two members of the Orioles' major-league roster agreed to a drug plan devised by an agent, Ron Shapiro, which will be administered by the Johns Hopkins Hospital and School of Medicine, and which appears to guarantee player privacy, for the club would not know which players were in treatment unless the treatment should require their absence from the field; it also calls for testing. This year, the A's were able to obtain drug-testing agreements from a majority of their players on an individual basis *after* their contracts had been signed; the documents had no relation to each other, that is. Sal Bando, who administers the Employee Assistance Program for the Brewers, told me that programs dealing with cocaine abuse in baseball should be aimed specifically at the player who is at the edge of making the shift from being a social user to being one with a more habitual problem; the true addict, he said, would always come into the program automatically, out of need. He also said that among the Milwaukee players who have recourse to the Employee Assistance Program drug abuse is a much less common concern than everyday matters like stress, depression, divorce, child abuse, and alcohol.

Trust is what it comes down to, of course. Several players have told me that there are a handful of clubs with which they would readily sign drug-testing agreements, simply because they trusted the management there. The list was a small one, however, never exceeding five or six teams, and each of the players quickly added that he deeply suspected the ability or desire of most clubs to deal with their players in a non-punitive, consistent manner when it came to drugs. (Some clubs have shown a degree of compassion toward a player who has admitted to cocaine trouble for the first time, only to turn pious and punitive if he runs into further difficulties. The new edition of the *Bill James Baseball Abstract* has a chilling description of the Padres' self-righteousness last year when they decided to close the books on their second baseman and lead-off batter Alan Wiggins under such circumstances; he is now playing second and leading off for the Orioles.) "They've taken a very hard line on drugs and testing, and you've got to ask what they were after, when we already had an industry-wide agreement that had a real chance to work," one American League player said. "They wanted the monkey on our backs. We have this emotional pressure from the fans, and then here comes the Commissioner telling people there's nothing that shows up in the sport that he can't handle. It's not right. The atmosphere is still very hostile."

One general manager, speaking privately to me a few weeks ago, said, "In our business, we've gone from hero worship down to finding any excuse to blame and bloody the players. We're cynical, and we tend to despise them, and we invite the public to join us in that. Something must be done to turn that around soon. It's the Steinbrenner style, and it can destroy us in the end." That same week, an official of the Players Association made almost the same point in conversation. "All our assumptions about fairness and innocence have been changed by the drug scare," he said. "This is an ugly place for the national pastime to find itself, especially if it's being done in the name of morality and of role models for our children. It always comes down to the same set of assumptions: the players should be better than the rest of us— they should set an example, toe the line, and all that, because they're lucky to be playing ball and because they're getting all that money. It's pathetic stuff, if you think about it, and it's got nothing to do with the realities of drug addiction. I see the Steinbrenner world view in this. It's angry, and it seems to infect us all in the end."

What we fans and bystanders think about all this is what counts, of course, because baseball belongs to us in the end, rather than to its transient and impatient owners, and because drug abuse in society and the image of professional sports are matters of our own making—images of ourselves. Most of my friends who are also fans seemed extremely upset with the players whenever the matter of drugs came up in conversation in recent months. Now and then, I ventured to suggest that baseball is simply another slice of American society, after all, and that since drugs are an everyday reality now it probably shouldn't surprise us much if they also turn up in baseball. Sometimes I went farther and pointed out that the large salaries now paid to major-league players, combined with their youth and their sudden celebrity, and with the unceasing pressures on them to perform at a very high level of success in a restricted, highly competitive line of work, would almost seem to guarantee some use of cocaine among their numbers. But most of my friends were unconvinced. "They've got it made," I kept hearing. "And what about their responsibility to the fans and to families? Kids are looking up to them, you know. They're meant to be models."

And here I would shut up, most of the time, for this cherished and wishful idea of athletes as heroes and exemplars seems to lie too deep in our emotions and memories to be dislodged or altered by argument. It is there, all right— I recognize it in myself, even after years of association with the young men (they are now much younger than I am) who play ball for a living—but I don't believe it means much. Most children I have known, including my own, have made the switch from hero worship of some ballplayer (or movie star or rock musician) to a more restrained and knowledgeable and accepting view of that individual almost overnight, with few visible signs of shock or loss. I can no longer remember the exact moment when I stopped thinking of Babe Ruth as a demigod, having somehow learned—I was ten or twelve years old—that he was much given to drinking and gluttony (I could see that he was fat) and prostitutes, but the news somehow made him more interesting to me, rather than less, and it did not impel me to emulate his disreputable habits or to turn on him because he had somehow let me down. Last year, I mentioned this matter of lost image to the peerless Kansas City relief pitcher Dan Quisenberry (I was preparing to write an article about him), and he recalled the moment when he first read Jim Bouton's "Ball Four," a funny, raucously debunking account of daily life with the New York Yankees (for whom Bouton pitched from 1962 to '68), which depicted the lordly champions as a band of hard-drinking, girl-chasing boobs and overage adolescents. The book was roundly denounced by Commissioner Bowie Kuhn and the entire baseball establishment when it was published, in 1970. "I was about seventeen when I read 'Ball Four,' and all my friends and I *lived* for sports back then," Quisenberry said. "You could say I worshipped baseball, but when I read the book it only made the game and the players that much more exciting to me. I loved that book, but it didn't change me at all. I was a straight arrow back then, and I'm afraid I'm still a straight arrow today."

Last November, an acquaintance of mine came up to me at a party and produced a Polaroid photograph of his little daughter—I think she is about nine years old—dressed up in her Halloween costume. "She's Keith Hernandez," he said, and so she was, in perfect miniature: the blue-striped uniform, the orange interlocked "NY" on the cap, and the cap bill pulled low; the left-handed batting stance and the proudly upheld bat (it was painted papier-mâché); and a smudgy, painted-on Hernandez mustache. It was a captivating picture. "I just don't know what's going to happen to her when she grows up and hears about Keith and the cocaine," the father said. "She's a *total* fan of his. She's crazy about him. I don't know what I'll say."

I didn't know what to say, either, so I was startled when the same man came back over to me about half an hour later and said, "You know, I was thinking about what I said about Keith and Ada, and it just came to me that I'm crazy. It won't mean a thing to her when she finds out about Keith—I know that. She'll just grow up. I don't know why I've been so worried. She'll be fine."

Yes. I think a great many of us have begun to see how deeply we want baseball players and other athletes to be better than we are. We may wish this now more than ever before, because other heroes—in politics, in our daily lives—seem to be in short supply. We cared most for ballplayers, of course, back when they really were heroes to us and when we wanted to *be* them, if we could. We know better than that now, surely, but because we still wish to keep baseball, our old game, in some special place in our affections and our imagination we want the players to remain the same, too—to be good at the game and good at life as well. Good at heart. This is an image, all right, and there is no damage in it as long as we remind ourselves from time to time that it is a dream or a wish and that we really *do* know better. Ballplayers are not much different from the rest of us, except for their unforgivable skills when it comes to playing ball, and there is a sudden releasing pleasure for us that accompanies the realization that we need no longer patronize them by making them into heroes, and that they are not all of a kind. Not by a long shot. If you talk to them and listen to them talk on almost any subject, you will get a range of response that is almost impossible to summarize, especially if they're talking about something like drugs in sports. "Of *course* we're divided on this issue," one team rep said to me this spring. "It's right that we should be, because there's nothing easy about it. We're just trying to make up our minds."

Recently, I had the chance to talk with an old friend, Steve Garvey, the San Diego first baseman, who is baseball's acknowledged prince of straight arrows. We got around to drugs at one point, and he said, "I've known guys in baseball to get caught in drugs, and I could see how it happened, because this is such a tough game. I felt sorry for them, but I still think it's up to us players to do better than that, because of what we represent and who's watching us. That comes with the job and the good pay and the good life we've been given." Garvey takes this view somewhat farther in his recently published autobiography ("Garvey"), in which he says, "Baseball plays on its specialness to cultivate its position in the hearts and minds of the American people. We call ourselves the National Pastime and put ads on television dramatizing our importance as a tradition, even suggesting that going to games is the glue that keeps generations together. If we are going to tap those emotional veins to foster our own popularity, we in the game have an obligation to be clean—cleaner than the rest of society."

No surprise there, perhaps, but the very next morning, in Phoenix, I heard something rather different from Bruce Bochte, the Oakland A's first baseman. Bochte is an original. Three years ago, he took a sabbatical year off from baseball to live full time with his wife and two daughters in an economically and ecologically self-sufficient community on Whidbey Island, in Puget Sound. He is articulate and iconoclastic—but this sort of aside or explanation, it occurs to me, would not be necessary, or even acceptable, if he were employed in almost any other line of work. Bochte said, "Drugs—well, you know, drugs are around. We're just in a life style and at a salary level where drugs are going to come onto the scene. Sometimes I think the problem has been exaggerated, but if you're in a business where you're going to play a hundred and sixty-two games, travel all across the country, stay up late, be away from home, and all that, then drugs will come with the territory. The situation should be addressed, but most of our reactions to it are exaggerated.

"So much of all this comes down to image, just the way it did during the strike, when so many people were upset about what was really just basic stuff—negotiating over bargaining rights and the rest. The money came into it late. Why couldn't people understand that? I couldn't figure this out for the longest time. I think it came down to image. The baseball player still represents the image of the American hero. But what's happened in our country? What is this country really like? The journey or destiny of the American people now is just to make money. We're brought up with that, and it's what everybody judges his performance on and sets his values by. We have an over-preoccupation with making money in this country. Well, we ballplayers just picked up on that. The twenty-six owners in baseball are mostly millionaires. We watch them, and we have to work for them, and we're around them and other high-powered people all the time, so we just began to emulate them. The public has begun to see something different about the American hero, about major-league ballplayers, that they don't like at all. Now if anybody asks me about our image I say, 'Yeah, that's what we're about. We're Americans, so we're making a lot of money. We're exploited, we see drugs coming into the scene, we have antagonistic relationships with the people we work for'— well, *I* don't, not here with the A's, but most players sure do—'because that's what the American scene is like.' I don't want us to go around making out that we're a bunch of good guys. We're just the American thing.

"We have to work at the causes of drug abuse, I know, but you have to look at the basics, too. You can't convince me that people who spend all their time and energy trying to maximize the profits of their business—making deals, working their butts off—are not doing damage to themselves and their families and other people they're involved with. It's an extremist mode of being. It's stressful, and if we ballplayers sometimes get into drugs—well, those people are into stress and alcohol and heart attacks. So who are they to say we're destroying America? There are different ways of destroying America, and they're doing it. I know this runs against the old pastoral view of baseball and what it's about, but it's what I believe."

I don't think I can entirely accept this harsh, almost despairing view of things, but I can't say that I wholly disagree with any part of it. It doesn't matter much, either way, because I am not offering Bruce Bochte as a role model or as an image of anything but himself. He's just another ballplayer.

Suggestions for Discussion

1. What changes in baseball have contributed to wider drug use, according to Angell?

2. What arguments against compulsory testing does Angell present?

3. Explain the significance of the title, "The Cheers for Keith."

Suggestions for Writing

1. State and defend your position on compulsory drug testing for major league athletes.

2. Discuss the career of a favorite athlete who has overcome an alcohol or drug problem.

Marie Winn

The Plug-In Drug: TV and the American Family

Marie Winn is the author of *The Playground Book, The Sick Book, The Baby Reader,* and other books for parents and children. The following selection is taken from *The Plug-In Drug,* published in 1977.

A quarter of a century after the introduction of television into American society, a period that has seen the medium become so deeply ingrained in American life that in at least one state the television set has attained the rank of a legal necessity, safe from repossession in case of debt along with clothes, cooking utensils, and the like, television viewing has become an inevitable and ordinary part of daily life. Only in the early years of television did writers and commentators have sufficient perspective to separate the activity of watching television from the actual content it offers the viewer. In those early days writers frequently discussed the effects of television on family life. However, a curious myopia afflicted those early observers: almost without exception they regarded television as a favorable, beneficial, indeed, wondrous influence upon the family.

"Television is going to be a real asset in every home where there are children," predicts a writer in 1949.

"Television will take over your way of living and change your children's habits, but this change can be a wonderful improvement," claims another commentator.

"No survey's needed, of course, to establish that television has brought the family together in one room," writes *The New York Times* television critic in 1949.

Each of the early articles about television is invariably accompanied by a photograph or illustration showing a family cozily sitting together before the television set, Sis on Mom's lap, Buddy perched on the arm of Dad's chair, Dad with his arm around Mom's shoulder. Who could have guessed that twenty or so years later Mom would be watching a drama in the kitchen, the kids would be looking at cartoons in their room, while Dad would be taking in the ball game in the living room?

Of course television sets were enormously expensive in those early days. The idea that by 1975 more than 60 percent of American families would own two or more sets was preposterous. The splintering of the multiple-set family was something the early writers could not foresee. Nor did anyone imagine the number of hours children would eventually devote to television, the common use of television by parents as a child pacifier, the changes television would effect upon child-rearing methods, the increasing domination of family schedules by children's viewing requirements—in short, the *power* of the new medium to dominate family life.

After the first years, as children's consumption of the new medium increased, together with parental concern about the possible effects of so much television viewing, a steady refrain helped to soothe and reassure anxious parents. "Television always enters a pattern of influences that already exist: the home, the peer group, the school, the church, and culture generally," write the authors of an early and influential study of television's effects on children. In other words, if the child's home life is all right, parents need not worry about the effects of all that television watching.

But television does not merely influence the child; it deeply influences that "pattern of influences" that is meant to ameliorate its effects. Home and family life has changed in important ways since the advent of television. The peer group has become television-oriented, and much of the time children spend together is occupied by television viewing. Culture generally has been transformed by television. Therefore it is improper to assign to television the subsidiary role its many apologists (too often members of the television industry) insist it plays. Television is not merely one of a number of important influences upon today's child. Through the changes it has made in family life, television emerges as *the* important influence in children's lives today.

Television's contribution to family life has been an equivocal one. For while it has, indeed, kept the members of the family from dispersing, it has not served to bring them *together*. By its domination of the time families spend together, it destroys the special quality that distinguishes one family from another, a quality that depends to a great extent on what a family *does*, what special rituals, games, recurrent jokes, familiar songs, and shared activities it accumulates.

"Like the sorcerer of old," writs Urie Bronfenbrenner, "the television set casts its magic spell, freezing speech and action, turning the living into silent statues so long as the enchantment lasts. The primary danger of the television screen lies not so much in the behavior it produces—although there is danger there—as in the behavior it prevents: the talks, the games, the family festivities and arguments through which much of the child's learning takes place and through which his character is formed. Turning on the television set can turn off the process that transforms children into people."

Yet parents have accepted a television-dominated family life so completely that they cannot see how the medium is involved in whatever problems they might be having. A first-grade teacher reports:

"I have one child in the group who's an only child. I wanted to find out more about her family life because this little girl was quite isolated from the group, didn't make friends, so I talked to her mother. Well, they don't have time to do anything in the evening, the mother said. The parents come home after picking up the child at the baby-sitter's. Then the mother fixes dinner while the child watches TV. Then they have dinner and the child goes to bed. I said to this mother, 'Well, couldn't she help you fix dinner? That would be a nice time for the two of you to talk,' and the mother said, 'Oh, but I'd hate to have her miss "Zoom." It's such a good program!' "

Even when families make efforts to control television, too often its very presence counterbalances the positive features of family life. A writer and mother of two boys aged 3 and 7 described her family's television schedule in an article in *The New York Times:*

> We were in the midst of a full-scale War. Every day was a new battle and every program was a major skirmish. We agreed it was a bad scene all around and were ready to enter diplomatic negotiations . . . . In principle we have agreed on 2½ hours of TV a day, "Sesame Street," "Electric Company" (with dinner gobbled up in between) and two half-hour shows between 7 and 8:30 which enables the grown-ups to eat in peace and prevents the two boys from destroying one another. Their pre-bedtime choice is dreadful, because, as Josh recently admitted, "There's nothing much on I really like." So . . . it's "What's My Line" or "To Tell the Truth." . . . Clearly there is a need for first-rate children's shows at this time. . . .

Consider the "family life" described here: Presumably the father comes home from work during the "Sesame Street"–"Electric Company" stint. The children are either watching television, gobbling their dinner, or both. While the parents eat their dinner in peaceful privacy, the children watch another hour of television. Then there is only a half-hour left before bedtime, just enough time for baths, getting pajamas on, brushing teeth, and so on. The children's evening is regimented with an almost military precision. They watch their favorite programs, and when there is "nothing much on I really like," they watch whatever else is on—because *watching* is the important thing. Their mother does not see anything amiss with watching programs just for the sake of watching; she only wishes there were some first-rate children's shows on at those times.

Without conjuring up memories of the Victorian era with family games and long, leisurely meals, and large families, the question arises: isn't there a better family life available than this dismal, mechanized arrangement of children watching television for however long is allowed them, evening after evening?

Of course, families today still do *special* things together at times: go camping in the summer, go to the zoo on a nice Sunday, take various trips and expeditions. But their *ordinary* daily life together is diminished—that sitting around at the dinner table, that spontaneous taking up of an activity, those little games invented by children on the spur of the moment when there is nothing else to do, the scribbling, the chatting, and even the quarreling, all the things that form the fabric of a family, that define a childhood. Instead, the children have their regular schedule of television programs and bedtime, and the parents have their peaceful dinner together.

The author of the article in the *Times* notes that "keeping a family sane means mediating between the needs of both children and adults." But surely the needs of adults are being better met than the needs of the children, who are effectively shunted away and rendered untroublesome, while their parents enjoy a life as undemanding as that of any childless couple. In reality, it is those very demands that young children make upon a family that lead to growth, and it is the way parents accede to those demands that builds the relationships upon which the future of the family depends. If the family does not accumulate its backlog of shared experiences, shared *everyday* experiences that occur and recur and change and develop, then it is not likely to survive as anything other than a caretaking institution.

Family Rituals

Ritual is defined by sociologists as "that part of family life that the family likes about itself, is proud of, and wants formally to continue." Another text notes that "the development of a ritual by a family is an index of the common interest of its members in the family as a group."

What has happened to family rituals, those regular, dependable, recurrent happenings that gave members of a family a feeling of *belonging* to a home rather than living in it merely for the sake of convenience, those experiences that act as the adhesive of family unity far more than any material advantages?

Mealtime rituals, going-to-bed rituals, illness rituals, holiday rituals, how many of these have survived the inroads of the television set?

A young woman who grew up near Chicago reminisces about her childhood and gives an idea of the effects of television upon family rituals:

"As a child I had millions of relatives around—my parents both come from relatively large families. My father had nine brothers and sisters. And so every holiday there was this great swoop-down of aunts, uncles, and millions of cousins. I just remember how wonderful it used to be. These thousands of cousins would come and everyone would play and ultimately, after dinner, all the women would be in the front of the house, drinking coffee and talking, all the men would be in the back of the house, drinking and smoking, and all the kids would be all over the place, playing hide and seek. Christmas time was particularly nice because everyone always brought all their toys and games. Our house had a couple of rooms with go-through closets, so there were always kids running in a great circle route. I remember it was just wonderful.

"And then all of a sudden one year I remember becoming suddenly aware of how different everything had become. The kids were no longer playing Monopoly or Clue or the other games we used to play together. It was because we had a television set which had been turned on for a football game. All of that socializing that had gone on previously had ended. Now everyone was sitting in front of the television set, on a holiday, at a family party! I remember being stunned by how awful that was. Somehow the television had become more attractive."

As families have come to spend more and more of their time together engaged in the single activity of television watching, those rituals and pastimes that once gave family life its special quality have become more and more uncommon. Not since prehistoric times when cave families hunted, gathered, ate, and slept, with little time remaining to accumulate a culture of any significance, have families been reduced to such a sameness.

Real People

It is not only the activities that a family might engage in together that are diminished by the powerful presence of television in the home. The relationships of the family members to each other are also affected, in both obvious and subtle ways. The hours that the young child spends in a one-way relationship with television people, an involvement that allows for no communication or interaction, surely affect his relationships with real-life people.

Studies show the importance of eye-to-eye contact, for instance, in real-life relationships, and indicate that the nature of a person's eye-contact patterns, whether he looks another squarely in the eye or looks to the side or shifts his gaze from side to side, may play a significant role in his success or failure in human relationships. But no eye contact is possible in the child-television relationship, although in certain children's programs people purport to speak directly to the child and the camera fosters this illusion by focusing directly upon the person being filmed. (Mr. Rogers is an example, telling the child "I like you, you're special," etc.) How might such a distortion of real-life relationships affect a child's development of trust, of openness, of an ability to relate well to other *real* people?

Bruno Bettelheim writes:

> Children who have been taught, or conditioned, to listen passively most of the day to the warm verbal communications coming from the TV screen, to the deep emotional appeal of the so-called TV personality, are often unable to respond to real persons because they arouse so much less feeling than the skilled actor. Worse, they lose the ability to learn from reality because life experiences are much more complicated than the ones they see on the screen. . . .

A teacher makes a similar observation about her personal viewing experiences:

"I have trouble mobilizing myself and dealing with real people after watching a few hours of television. It's just hard to make that transition from watching television to a real relationship. I suppose it's because there was no effort necessary while I was watching, and dealing with real people always requires a bit of effort. Imagine, then, how much harder it might be to do the same thing for a small child, particularly one who watches a lot of television every day."

But more obviously damaging to family relationships is the elimination of opportunities to talk, and perhaps more important, to argue, to air grievances, between parents and children and brothers and sisters. Families frequently use television to avoid confronting their problems, problems that will not go away if they are ignored but will only fester and become less easily resolvable as time goes on.

A mother reports:

"I find myself, with three children, wanting to turn on the TV set when they're fighting. I really have to struggle not to do it because I feel that's telling them this is the solution to the quarrel—but it's so tempting that I often do it."

A family therapist discusses the use of television as an avoidance mechanism:

"In a family I know the father comes home from work and turns on the television set. The children come and watch with him and the wife serves them their meal in front of the set. He then goes and takes a shower, or works on the car or something. She then goes and has her own dinner in front of the television set. It's a symptom of a deeper-rooted problem, sure. But it would help them all to get rid of the set. It would be far easier to work on what the symptom really means without the television. The television simply encourages a double avoidance of each other. They'd find out more quickly what was going on if they weren't able to hide behind the TV. Things wouldn't necessarily be better, of course, but they wouldn't be anesthetized."

The decreased opportunities for simple conversation between parents and children in the television-centered home may help explain an observation made by an emergency room nurse at a Boston hospital. She reports that parents just seem to sit there these days when they come in with a sick or seriously injured child, although talking to the child would distract and comfort him. "They don't seem to know *how* to talk to their own children at any length," the nurse observes. Similarly, a television critic writes in *The New York Times:* "I had just a day ago taken my son to the emergency ward of a hospital for stitches above his left eye, and the occasion seemed no more real to me than Maalot or 54th Street, south-central Los Angeles. There was distance and numbness and an inability to turn off the total institution. I didn't behave at all; I just watched. . . ."

A number of research studies substantiate the assumption that television interferes with family activities and the formation of family relationships. One survey shows that 78 percent of the respondents indicated no conversation taking place during viewing except at specified times such as commercials. The study notes: "The television atmosphere in most households is one of quiet absorption on the part of family members who are present. The nature of the family social life during a program could be described as 'parallel' rather than interactive, and the set does seem to dominate family life when it is on." Thirty-six percent of the respondents in another study indicated that television viewing was the only family activity participated in during the week.

In a summary of research findings on television's effect on family interactions James Gabardino states: "The early findings suggest that television had a disruptive effect upon interaction and thus presumably human development. . . . It is not unreasonable to ask: 'Is the fact that the average American family during the 1950's came to include two parents, two children, and a television set somehow related to the psychosocial characteristics of the young adults of the 1970's?' "

Undermining the Family

In its effect on family relationships, in its facilitation of parental withdrawal from an active role in the socialization of their children, and in its replacement of family rituals and special events, television has played an important role in the disintegration of the American family. But of course it has not been the only contributing factor, perhaps not even the most important one. The steadily rising divorce rate, the increase in the number of working mothers, the decline of the extended family, the breakdown of neighborhoods and communities, the growing isolation of the nuclear family—all have seriously affected the family.

As Urie Bronfenbrenner suggests, the sources of family breakdown do not come from the family itself, but from the circumstances in which the family finds itself and the way of life imposed upon it by those circumstances. "When those circumstances and the way of life they generate undermine relationships of trust and emotional security between family members, when they make it difficult for parents to care for, educate and enjoy their children, when there is no support or recognition from the outside world for one's role as a parent and when time spent with one's family means frustration of career, personal fulfillment, and peace of mind, then the development of the child is adversely affected," he writes.

But while the roots of alienation go deep into the fabric of American social history, television's presence in the home fertilizes them, encourages their wild and unchecked growth. Perhaps it is true that America's commitment to the television experience masks a spiritual vacuum, an empty and barren way of life, a desert of materialism. But it is television's dominant role in the family that anesthetizes the family into accepting its unhappy state and prevents it from struggling to better its condition, to improve its relationships, and to regain some of the richness it once possessed.

Others have noted the role of mass media in perpetuating an unsatisfactory *status quo*. Leisure-time activity, writes Irving Howe, "must provide relief from work monotony without making the return to work too unbearable; it must provide amusement without insight and pleasure without disturbance— as distinct from art which gives pleasure through disturbance. Mass culture is thus oriented towards a central aspect of industrial society: the depersonalization of the individual." Similarly, Jacques Ellul rejects the idea that television is a legitimate means of educating the citizen: "Education . . . takes place only incidentally. The clouding of his consciousness is paramount. . . ."

And so the American family muddles on, dimly aware that something is amiss but distracted from an understanding of its plight by an endless stream of television images. As family ties grow weaker and vaguer, as children's lives become more separate from their parents', as parents' educational role in their children's lives is taken over by television and schools, family life becomes increasingly more unsatisfying for both parents and children. All that seems to be left is Love, an abstraction that family members *know* is necessary but find great difficulty giving each other because the traditional opportunities for expresssing love within the family have been reduced or destroyed.

For contemporary parents, love toward each other has increasingly come to mean successful sexual relations, as witnessed by the proliferation of sex manuals and sex therapists. The opportunities for manifesting other forms of love through mutual support, understanding, nurturing, even, to use an unpopular word, *serving* each other, are less and less available as mothers and fathers seek their independent destinies outisde the family.

As for love of children, this love is increasingly expressed through supplying material comforts, amusements, and educational opportunities. Parents show their love for their children by sending them to good schools and camps, by providing them with good food and good doctors, by buying them toys, books, games, and a television set of their very own. Parents will even go further and express their love by attending PTA meetings to improve their children's schools, or by joining groups that are acting to improve the quality of their children's television programs.

But this is love at a remove, and is rarely understood by children. The more direct forms of parental love require time and patience, steady, dependable, ungrudgingly given time actually spent *with* a child, reading to him, comforting him, playing, joking, and working with him. But even if a parent were eager and willing to demonstrate that sort of direct love to his children today, the opportunities are diminished. What with school and Little League and piano lessons and, of course, the inevitable television programs, a day seems to offer just enough time for a good-night kiss.

Suggestions for Discussion

1. Why did early critics regard television as a "favorable, beneficial, indeed, wondrous influence upon the family"?

2. Explain why television has not served to bring members of the family together.

3. Cite examples of the loss of social interaction in families described by Winn.

4. Explain Winn's belief that "television has played an important role in the disintegration of the American family." Do you agree? Explain.

Suggestions for Writing

1. Describe and comment on television viewing in your own home.

2. Compare and contrast Winn's depiction of family interaction with Art Buchwald's.

S. J. Perelman

Meanness Rising from the Suds

Sidney Joseph Perelman (1904–1979), distinguished American humorist, playwright, and screenwriter, is the author of many collections of essays and sketches, including *Crazy Like a Fox,* (1944), *The Swiss Family Perelman* (1950), and *The Last Laugh* (1981), from which the following selection is taken.

I used to pride myself on being impervious to the sentimentalities of soap opera, but when that loveliest of English actresses, Rachel Gurney, of *Up-*

stairs, *Downstairs*, perished on the *Titanic*, I wept so convulsively and developed such anorexia that I had to be force-fed. Hovering between life and death for weeks, I sat in a Bath chair on the great dappled lawns of my country house with my favorite collie at my feet and an alienist, until one of them—I can't recall which—recommended that I watch a few other soaps to palliate my anguish. So I did; I watched *Another World, Days of Our Lives, As the World Turns,* and *Somerset,* and in less time than you could say "Dr. Gregory Zilboorg" I was whole again. Compared to the torment their characters underwent, Rachel's fate was a piece of cake.

I usually avoid such personal revelations, reserving them for my diary and a few copies for friends, but not long ago a paragraph on this subject, in a periodical called *American Film,* horrified me anew. It said that *True* had examined the treatment of men in daytime soap opera and recoiled in shocked indignity. "Shows like 'Another World,' " it complained, "portrayed men as 'gutless and/or villainous boobs.' Moreover, [*True*] found that most male characters on daytime serials suffer from something, and listed the embarrassments that are visited on the stronger sex: 'sterility, stupidity, amnesia, alcoholism, impotence, night sweats, acne, acrophobia, senility, insecurity, and outright lunacy.' " The item continues, "An editor of a soap opera newsletter told *True* that some actors have quit in protest at the 'shambling fools' their characters were reduced to. Worse, some even found their characters so emasculated that their offscreen sex life was affected."

Hardly able to credit the evidence of my eyes, I swiftly dug up the relevant issue of *True* for confirmation. Every word was gospel. One actor, John Colenback, who has played Dr. Dan Stewart in *As the World Turns* for many years, charged, "The writers I worked with always managed to turn the men on the show into either evil or totally weak characters who were manipulated by women. . . . I was trapped in an extremely paranoid position. I was really vicious when I was working at the hospital, screaming at nurses and patients like a little Hitler. But at home I had to be the biggest of boobs, pushed around unmercilessly by my wife and my mother." (And, judging from that adverb, Colenback's travail also fractured his English.) Furthermore, *True* pointed out, these shows were not alone in their castrating complex, and gave more examples of male *faiblesse* gleaned from *Days of Our Lives:* "A man turns out to be the father of his brother's child. A husband ruins his wife's career by refusing to let her sing in public. . . . A man shaves off his mustache because a girl tells him that she doesn't trust men with face hair." All of them, I was forced to acknowledge, were unspeakable bounders—the husband in particular. Rather than wicked, actually he was a dolt. The craftier way to ruin his wife's career would have been to *compel* her to sing in public.

The second dent of soap opera on my consciousness had barely faded to a purplish bruise when out of left field came another—this time, though, more in the nature of a soft nudge. A ravishing friend of mine who, by a coincidence, had won her acting spurs on *Another World* and was now starred in a network show called *Millionaire Pauper* rang me up one evening from the Coast. Not for nothing had Kathleen been called the Zuleika Dobson of Hofstra University; in addition to green eyes, honey-colored hair, and a figure that capsized the senses, she had a brain stored with more knowledge than Chamber's Encyclopedia and a gaiety unequalled since Carole Lombard's. But tonight she was in a sombre mood. "Look, baby, I've got to come up for air," she confided. "I'm skying into town for a couple of nights. Do you know a real person that a person could spend an evening with—not a chauvinist pig or a garter-snapper?"

I tried to think of one, and, failing, timidly nominated myself.

There was a curious pause, and a crackling akin to chuckling, as though we were disconnected. Then I heard her voice. "You?" she asked dubiously. "Yes, you're sweet. But, frankly, dear, I've always felt there was—how shall I say—something lacking in you."

I bristled. "You mean that I'm kind of weak? Gutless? A boob?"

"No, just ineffectual—sort of Pre-Raphaelite. A bush-league Dante Gabriel Rossetti, so to speak. You're not really *evil*, like the men on my show. The trouble with you, darling—"

"Listen, this call is costing you an arm and a leg," I broke in, forgetting that she had reversed the charges. "I'll meet you at '21' tomorrow at eight. No, wait—you don't want to be bothered signing autographs. Let's make the corner of Fifty-eighth and Fifth, and if I'm late you can look in Bergdorf's windows."

The realization that Kathleen conceived of me as a sheep rankled throughout the night, and by morning I decided to change my image. Fie on the funereal lounge suit from Brooks I had worn hitherto, the discreet neckwear, the bespoke shoes; I would transform myself into a swinger, one of those breezy, jovial loudmouths around the Americana Hotel, and sweep her off her feet. At a quarter to seven, I stood aghast regarding my alter ego in the bathroom mirror. The peacock-blue safari suit, the Tibetan prayer beads encircling my neck were disastrous. All I needed was a little tin can on my head to look like Happy Hooligan. Eyes aplenty popped at the Golden Noodle subsequently as the headwaiter ushered Kathleen and me to our table, but they were riveted on her Celtic beauty rather than on me. Understated my old Brooks number may have been; still, it didn't glow in the dark.

Our faces were greasy with egg rolls and spareribs before I mustered up courage to pose the question gnawing at my subconscious. "Kathie," I demanded, "why do you women in soap opera detest my sex?"

"Hate your sex?" The widened eyes turned on me were as lambent as a jaguar's. "My dear, you talk like a sausage. We don't at all."

"You do, you do!" I drummed my fists on the table. "We're always being portrayed as drunkards and eunuchs and fatheads—greedy, lascivious morons without one redeeming virtue."

"But you *are* swine, you can't deny," she said, palms outspread. "Look at Verdun, the Huguenot massacre, the annual statistics on rape."

"And women are angels, I suppose," I retorted. "What about Messalina knocking off her lovers? And Catherine of Russia, Madame Defarge, and Lizzie Borden?"

"Oh, we've had a few hotheads, sure, but if you dig into it, you'll find men were usually to blame. Remember the breakfast Andrew Borden had served up that blazing Fall River morning? Warmed-over mutton soup, leftover mutton, and bananas. No wonder the poor thing went berserk."

"Don't try to squirm out of it," I said roughly. "You and your ilk are helping to perpetrate a lie. How can you accept money for blackening the opposite gender?"

"Well, money is the only thing they give us. I guess it's better than nothing."

"Really. I'm surprised you can sleep nights with that on your conscience."

"I did have trouble at first, until I switched to Compoz. You should, too—it's great for the kind of indignation you're suffering from." She shovelled in a second helping of subgum chow mein with water chestnuts. Typical feminine behavior. They eat a spoonful of yogurt when they're alone, but when you're buying, man, it's like Thanksgiving. "Now, shape up, honey—you know better than to bad-mouth my profession. We just speak the words you writers give us."

"Then we're traitors to our sex," I snapped. "We ought to be horsewhipped for maligning ourselves."

"Hyperbole," Kathleen dismissed. "Those scribes out there are merely using soap opera as a confessional. Believe me, I speak from experience—I lived with one a couple of months last year. He was a gorgeous animal. Body by Mark Spitz, hair like the raven's wing, pearly teeth, Byronic profile; the man was a veritable collage. And clever, too—not a speck of talent, but he knew exactly whose work to plagiarize. So we're in paradise as envisioned nowadays by Erica Jong—though, between you and me, I was brought up on Andrew Lang's *Orange Fairy Book* and I like to do a little sewing between-times."

"What ever attracted you to a bullock like that?" I asked, repressing a shudder. "Sheer physical perfection is abhorrent to me. Lacking nobility of mind, love is a barrel without hoops."

"You don't say," she commented. "Would you mind disengaging your foot from mine? There, that's better. . . . Well, one day I was seated in front of my checkbook, as Sir Arthur Sullivan's song has it, weary and ill at ease. Not only did it not balance but, chancing to glance through the cancelled checks, I discovered that, unbeknownst to me, I was supporting a household in Redondo Beach. I taxed Wolf, my lover, with it, and learned the place was tenanted by an orphan—a wistful, flaxen-haired call girl to whom, out of compassion, he had also given a charge account at I. Magnin."

"Whereupon I imagine you sent him packing."

"Yes, in my white Mercedes 450–SEL, which, blinded by tears of remorse, he drove into a stanchion on the San Diego Freeway. The shock to his psyche might have been irreparable, except that he embodied our idyll in his soap opera and then wrote it off as a deductible business expense."

"Kathleen mavourneen." I reached over and took her hand—the one that was not busy spooning up water chestnuts. "How can you allow yourself to be endlessly exploited by such parasites, trapped in an environment so alien to you? Need I remind you that with each passing day you grow older?"

"Oh, remind me, do," she begged. "That's why I flew three thousand miles—to be warned I was becoming a raddled old crone."

"Well, it isn't too apparent yet," I comforted her. "And anyway there are lots of old-crone parts you'll be able to play. No, what I'm trying to convey is that however stupid or clumsy your past has been, I'm big enough to overlook it."

"Then nothing else matters," she said warmly. "As long as you think I'm straight and clean and fine—"

"I didn't say that," I interrupted. "Let me finish. Now, I'm not very rich in this world's goods, but I know where there's a tiny cabin in a bee-loud glade just large enough for two. Can you guess what I see there?"

Like so many of your Hibernian persuasion, Kathleen is more than a bit psychic, and, after a moment's reflection, she told me. She saw herself bent over a washtub humming contentedly as several chubby youngsters played around her knees and I sat indoors writing paperbacks that I hoped to sell for four hundred thousand each so as to put meat on the table.

"Yes, yes, go on," I encouraged. "Is there anything else you want to tell me?"

"Just one thing, lambie," she said, and patted my hand. "Fearing you might become sleepy after these Chinese dinners you consistently feed me, I availed myself of a backup date with a person staying at the Americana."

"Some loudmouth in a safari suit and prayer beads, no doubt," I said, stung to the quick.

She nodded. "Poor in spirit but not in this world's goods—he owns forty-one percent of the Texas Panhandle. Hence," she said, rising, "that's why I'm rushing off precipitately, because he can't bear to be kept waiting at '21.' " She imprinted a light kiss on my ear and was gone in a rustle of silk.

Temperamentally, I'm an easygoing, philosophical chap stimulated by rejection, as I've often noted in my diary and a few copies for friends, and within a month the entire episode had faded from memory. Then, one afternoon, as I was watching *Millionaire Pauper*, the soap Kathleen appears on, I was taken aback by a new character introduced as comic relief—a bespectacled writer hopelessly besotted with a glamorous young actress. Torn between satyriasis and parsimony, he insists on conducting her to substandard Chinese restaurants, where he fondles her over the less expensive choices on the à la carte menu—but why should I compound the humiliations? The whole thing is a cowardly slur on the masculine sex, and any male voluntarily tuning in on the show should be horsewhipped. Still, don't let me influence you. That's just one viewer's opinion.

Suggestions for Discussion

1. According to Perelman, how do daytime soap operas portray men?

2. Describe the responses of some men who have played roles in these shows.

3. Characterize Kathleen.

4. Summarize the conversation in the Golden Noodle Restaurant.

5. Discuss Perelman's use of allusion as a source of humor in the essay.

Suggestions for Writing

1. Based on your observation of daytime soap opera, agree or disagree with Perelman's assertions about the depiction of men.

2. Write a humorous account of a date that went awry for you.

George Grella
James Bond: Culture Hero

George Grella (b. 1938), a member of the faculty at the University of Rochester, is the author of *Murders and Manners: The Formal Detective Novel* and of essays that have appeared in such journals as *Life,* the *New Republic,* and the *Kansas City Star.* The essay that follows (published in 1964) is a delightful exercise in ironic scholarship.

Ian Fleming's James Bond is the most famous spy since Mata Hari. The indomitable secret agent reaches every level of literacy: Presidents to popcorn chewers. Not only has the author become a kind of subliterary lion in *Time, The New Yorker,* and *The Saturday Review,* which have devoted interviews and articles to his work, but his opinion was solicited on a major network show about the U-2 affair, the producers seeming to consider Mr. Fleming something like the Walter Lippmann of espionage.

Yet there is no puzzle to solve, no criminal to discover, no brilliant method to reveal. Fleming has no view of a corrupt society in the manner of a Cain, a Hammett, or a Chandler; his style and outlook are facile and pedestrian. Unlike Mickey Spillane, he doesn't write pornographic thrillers. Unlike Graham Greene, he offers no metaphysical or psychological insight, no significant comment on the nature of good and evil. Eric Ambler, a genuine craftsman, gives us plausible incidents, people stumbling into affairs which are complex, ambiguous, and believable. Newer writers, such as John Le Carré in *The Spy Who Came in from the Cold* or Len Deighton in the largely unrecognized *Ipcress File,* portray the life of a professional spy as unglamorous, poverty-ridden, and full of odd danger—one never knows when his own organization may betray him, or how far a competing unit of his own government will go, or if he must kill someone on his side, or even what side he is on.

To put it plainly, James Bond, despite his lean good looks, his taste in food, wine, and women, his high standing in the British Secret Service, his license to kill, is stupid. He disobeys orders and blunders into situations he should have anticipated chapters in advance. He is almost always known to the enemy as soon as he arrives, undercover, on the scene of action. He usually flounders around long enough for his adversaries to disrupt his elaborate plans and capture him.

His only genius lies in an infinite capacity for taking pain. He has suffered (and survived) bombing, shooting, stabbing, poisoning, and automobile attack. He has managed to (barely) escape castration by carpet-beater; bisection by buzzsaw; rocket blast; shark, barracuda, and octopus attack; a near-fatal increase in height on a health farm stretching apparatus; and a dose of poison from the sex glands of a rare Eastern fish. Such bizarre punishment is oddly requited: Bond has enjoyed the charms of the expensive Tiffany Case; the Bahamian nature girl, Honeychile Rider; the mystic Solitaire; and the ineffable Pussy Galore.

No secret agent could behave with such incompetence and still achieve such high renown, such titillating rewards. Fleming's characters are grotesques, the much-publicized sex is chrome-plated, not at all shocking, and the plots are repetitive from book to book. The solution of the paradox of James Bond's popularity may be, not in considering the novels as thrillers, but as something very different, as historic epic and romance, based on the stuff of myth and legend.

Thus, the affectionate fondling of brand names, which readers cite as an example of authenticity, is a contemporary version of the conventional epic catalog. It is important for the reader to know that Bond wears Sea Island cotton shirts, smokes a Macedonian blend of cigarettes, tells time by a Rolex Oyster watch, fires a Walther PPK 7.65 automatic in a Berns-Martin Triple Draw holster, drives a Mark II Bentley Continental, and so on, just as it important for the reader of the *Iliad* to be told the immense detail of Achilles' shield. Instead of a catalog of ships, Fleming gives us a catalog of clothes, toilet accessories, or background material about some exotic place or some arcane field of knowledge. The catalogs reflect the culture: the long lists of brand names suggest the affluence of a capitalist civilization, just as Bond suggests the secure investment.

Bond fights epic battles, taking seriously what Pope used humorously in his mock epic, *The Rape of the Lock*—the epic game of cards. James Bond has won harrowing games of blackjack, baccarat, bridge, even canasta. Like Ulysses, he travels far, from Turkey to Las Vegas, the Mediterranean, the Caribbean, the Atlantic, even Miami Beach. He makes the obligatory trip to the underworld when he skindives in the Bahamas, travels through the sewers of Istanbul, visits the domain of Mr. Big in Harlem, negotiates Dr. No's cruel tunnel of terror. His name indicates further facets of his character: he is entrusted with the mammoth task of safeguarding an entire civilization; the free world depends on his actions.

In *Moonraker* the situation parallels the Perseus–St. George myth, an appropriate one for Bond's rescue of London from the great rocket of Sir Hugo Drax, the huge dragon menacing England. Drax has red hair, an ugly, burned face which even plastic surgery cannot mask, splayed "ogre's teeth"; the great burst of fire he hopes to turn on London is the modern equivalent of the dragon's flames. Fleming employs an ironic reversal of one aspect of the Perseus myth: instead of rescuing Andromeda from the cliff where she is chained, Bond and his Andromeda, Galatea Brand, are nearly killed when one of the Dover cliffs, with some urging from Drax, falls on them. Of course Bond survives and, after escaping steamhosing and the liftoff of the Moonraker rocket (more fire from the dragon's nostrils), saves London. Alone among Bond novels, the hero fails to get the girl at the end: as a modern St. George, it would scarcely be appropriate for him to win the fair maiden.

In *Live and Let Die*, Bond travels to New York to confront Mr. Big, a giant Negro who controls a black brotherhood of crime, gathering gold to aid the Soviet Union. With his Negro network, his voodoo cult, his clairvoyant mistress, Mr. Big is almost omnipotent; his followers believe he is Baron Samedi, the Devil himself. He even controls the fishes of the sea, summoning shark and barracuda to defend his island. But Bond hurls the epic boast, which we know will clinch his victory, "Big Man? Then let it be a giant, a homeric slaying." His boast is fulfilled; just as he and Solitaire are to be dragged over a coral reef and shredded, Bond's mine blows up Mr. Big's boat and Big is devoured by the fish he tamed, his immense head bobbing bodyless in the sea. Bond again saves Civilization, this time from the powers of blackness.

Goldfinger is probably the most obvious reworking of early myth. Auric Goldfinger, who drives a gold car, carries his money in solid gold, dreams of robbing Fort Knox, and likes his women gold-plated all over, is a reincarnation of King Midas. Midas was tone deaf and earned a pair of ass's ears for misjudging a music contest between Pan and Apollo; Goldfinger, when Bond first meets him, is wearing a hearing aid and sunning himself with a set of tin wings resembling a pair of long, slightly pointed ears. Midas' barber, unable to contain the secret of his master's aural adornment, whispered his message into a hole. Later a reed grew and told the secret to all passersby. James Bond, in Goldfinger's captivity, must foil the planned robbery of Fort Knox; he tapes his message to an airplane toilet seat, the only hole available, and thus transmits it to the outside world.

Fleming's best-known book, *Dr. No* (there's a movie version too), is the most purely mythic of his works. Dr. No is the archetypal monster who casts a blight on the land and who must be conquered by the unquenchable spirit of life. He inhabits a lavish underground fortress in a guano island in the Caribbean, from which he misguides American missiles with intricate electronic apparatus. He has come to the British government's attention through complaints of the Audubon Society about the deaths of thousands of roseate spoonbills. Dr. No intimidates the natives and scares off the birds with a fire-breathing tractor made to resemble a dragon; his dragon is devastating the island of dung, killing the birds, the game wardens, all natural life. For his violation of nature, Dr. No must be punished by the grand spirit of affirmation, James Bond. Naturally Bond's mission fails at first; he is detected and captured by the evil doctor. After a rich meal and an opportunity to enumerate and use the deluxe living accommodations of the island fortress, Bond is subjected to an agonizing series of tortures in a tunnel of horrors, including an ordeal by fire and by water. He manages to crawl through the bowels of the island (anthropomorphically, the bowels of the monster as well), and kill Dr. No's pet giant octopus, displaying all the while superhuman strength and stamina. He buries Dr. No alive in a small mountain of guano. He has brought back the fertility of the land by ridding nature of the destroyer. As his reward, he spends a night with Honeychile Rider, the nymph of the Bahamas, who knows the secrets of snakes, spiders, and seashells. His heroic reward is the possession of the nature spirit herself; it is richly deserved. James Bond has redeemed the Waste Land.

The much-touted background which distinguishes the Bond novel, the close attention to real places and real names, the bits of esoteric information, are all products of an expensive research organization. Aside from their epic function, the lists of names lend only a spurious authenticity which is negated by other lapses from realism. Not only do people like Dr. No and Mr. Big inhabit an unreal world, but even their surface reality is questionable. Fleming's painstaking tour of Manhattan with Bond in *Live and Let Die* proves only that he can read a New York City map. Mr. Fleming is maladroit at transcribing American English; his Negro dialect echoes *Porgy and Bess*. His Americans, from cabdrivers to CIA agents, speak like graduates of non-U public schools. In *Diamonds Are Forever,* Bond thinks the tails attached to automobile antennas are beaver tails. No one in America hunts beaver for their tails or for anything else and not even teenagers fly squirrel tails (which don't look at all like beaver tails) from their cars any more. It's been thirty years since jaded Cafe Society types slummed in Harlem; Fleming seems to think it's still fashionable.

But no matter; we are dealing with myths. Vivienne Michel, the breathless French-Canadian girl who narrates *The Spy Who Loved Me,* may be intended as a representation of the typical James Bond fan. Most of the book concentrates on her rather unexciting sexual reminiscences in an odd fusion of *True Confessions* and *McCall's.* She is rescued from a pair of gangsters in an Adirondack motel by the coincidental appearance of our agent. After first fumbling the job (he can't kill in cold blood, he explains, forgetting that he's hired for that job and in another book he's detailed a couple of these jobs), Bond triumphs. He and Vivienne couple hygienically (in air-conditioned comfort, on Beautyrest mattresses, with Sanitized toilet facilities), and Vivienne comments of the action, "He had come from nowhere like the prince in the fairy tales, and he had saved me from the dragon . . . and then, when the dragon was dead, he had taken me as his reward." Vivienne doesn't have Bond's powerful Bentley, she drives a "cute little Vespa." She lists a variety of brand names, but hers consist of clothes and motel appliances. Her comments about the dragon indicate that she, at least, recognizes what's up.

In Fleming's most recent novel, *On Her Majesty's Secret Service,* Bond saves England from biological warfare waged by Ernst Blofeld, the elusive chief of SPECTRE. He narrowly escapes death and matrimony. Blofeld murders Bond's bride of a few hours and escapes, no doubt to reappear in a future novel. Bond, though hardly chaste, still must be unmarried, celibate in his fight against evil. Since there can be no Son of Bond, Blofeld does agent 007 a great service.

Mr. Anthony Boucher, an astute and prolific critic of thrillers, complained in a *New York Times* review of the book that only bad shooting enabled Bond to escape his enemies. Mr. Boucher is correct, but he criticizes the book as a poor thriller, neglecting the myth: since Bond leads a charmed life, no one can ever shoot him dead.

Perhaps centuries from now, scholars will trace assiduously those references to Yardley soap, Kent brushes, Lanvin perfume, Sanitized toilet seats. Perhaps there will be a variorum Fleming, and "Fleming men" as there are "Milton men." Theses may be written on the epicene role of M, clearly a father figure (yet why unmarried? and that maternal sounding initial is rather damning). For James Bond is the Renaissance man in mid-century guise, lover, warrior, connoisseur. He fights the forces of darkness, speaks for the sanitary achievements of the age, enjoys hugely the fruits of the free enterprise economy. He lives the dreams of countless drab people, his gun ready, his honor intact, his morals loose: the hero of our anxiety-ridden, mythless age: the savior of our culture.

Suggestions for Discussion

1. In what ways is James Bond "stupid"?

2. What is the importance of brand names in the Bond stories?

3. Explain the mythic qualities Grella ascribes to the Bond novels. Which of the allusions made by Grella seem most convincing to you?

4. Discuss Bond as "the hero of our anxiety-ridden, mythless age: the savior of our culture."

Suggestions for Writing

1. To what extent can any of Grella's observations apply to the James Bond films that you have seen?

2. Discuss the use of violence in a Bond novel or film.

Robert Palmer

What Pop Lyrics Say to Us Today

Robert Palmer (b. 1945) is a musician, music critic and professor of American vernacular music at Brooklyn College. His books include *A Tale of Two Cities: Memphis Rock and New Orleans Roll* (1979), *Deep Blues* (1981), and *The Rolling Stones* (1983). In the essay that follows, he assesses the significance of rock lyrics in the 1980s.

Bruce Springsteen became the first rock lyricist to be courted by both of the major candidates in a Presidential election last fall. First Ronald Reagan singled him out as an artist whose songs instill pride in America. Walter Mondale retaliated, asserting that *he* had won the rock star's endorsement. "Bruce may have been born to run," Mr. Mondale quipped, quoting the title of a Springsteen hit, "but he wasn't born yesterday."

Rock is part of adult culture now, to an extent that would have been unthinkable as recently as a decade ago. It is no longer the exclusive reserve of young people sending messages to each other. But pop music has always reflected and responded to the currents of its own time, and today's pop music is no exception. What does it seem to be telling us about our own time? Part of the message is in the music itself—in the insistence of the beat, the shriek of heavily amplified guitars. But lyrics remain the most accurate barometer of what makes *these* times different from, for example, the 1960's and 70's.

Today's pop music is sending several dominant messages. Material values are on the ascendant, but idealism is by no means a spent force. Most pop songs are love songs, as always, but today's versions try to look at relationships without rose-colored glasses. Romantic notions are viewed with some suspicion; so are drugs. And important rock artists and rappers, while no longer anticipating radical change, are addressing issues, and challenging their listeners to actively confront the world around them. There have probably been more angry protest lyrics written and recorded in the last three or four years than in any comparable period of the 60's.

In the 60's, it would have been unthinkable for a politician to seek endorsements from rock musicians; rock was rebel music. Stars like Bob Dylan and the Rolling Stones wrote and recorded outspoken lyrics that urged sweeping social change and an end to war and flirted with the rhetoric of revolution. They sang openly about sex and drugs. The music was the voice of a new generation and a constant reminder of the generation gap. The battle lines were drawn.

The rock lyricists of the 60's were fond of talking about "love." To the Beatles, "love" was transcendent, an irresistible force for good that could accomplish practically anything.

> There's nothing you can do that can't be done
> There's nothing you can sing that can't be sung
> There's nothing you can say, but you can learn how to play the game
> It's easy. All you need is love.

Love is still something one hears a great deal about in pop lyrics, but the contemporary version is more hard-headed and down-to-earth than the cosmic, effulgent Love of the 60's. Many of today's songwriters argue that romance isn't as important as material values or sex. "What's love got to do with it?" Tina Turner asked in her recent heavy-breathing hit of the same title. And Madonna, whose come-hither pout and undulating style have made her pop's hottest video star, serves notice in her hit "Material Girl" (written by Peter Brown and Robert Rans) that she won't worry much about love as long as there's money in the bank.

> Only boys that save their pennies
> Make my rainy day . . .
> We're living in a material world
> And I'm a material girl

Madonna's carefully calculated image has struck a chord among many of today's more affluent young listeners, though she is perhaps too one-dimensional to be Queen of the Yuppies. And she will never be the darling of the feminists.

Nevertheless, during the past decade, the hue and cry against rock lyrics that demeaned women seemed to have a broad and salutary effect. One didn't hear many songs of the sort the Rolling Stones and other 60's bands used to perform, songs like the Stones' "Under My Thumb."

> Under my thumb her eyes are just kept to herself
> Under my thumb, well, I can still look at someone else
> It's down to me, the way she talks when she's spoken to
> Down to me, the change has come, she's under my thumb.

The title tune from Mick Jagger's new solo album, "She's the Boss," is sung like a taunt or a tease, but that doesn't disguise its message; Mr. Jagger seems to have experienced a shift in values since he wrote "Under My Thumb."

> She's the boss! She's the boss!
> She's the boss in bed, she's the boss in my head
> She's got the pants on, now she's the boss.

Still, many of today's pop lyrics continue to celebrate male dominance. Aggressively macho rock has been making a comeback. Heavy metal rock, which appeals almost exclusively to white male teen-agers and tends to treat women as either temptresses or chattel, is more popular than ever. Women like Tina Turner and Cyndi Lauper, who project a certain independence and strength, are helping to counter this trend, but sometimes one can't hear them very well over heavy metal's sexist thunder.

Amid these changes in attitude, the old-fashioned romantic love song, always the staple of pop lyrics, continues to flourish. Prince, another of today's biggest-selling artists, has progressed from early songs that dealt explicitly with various sexual situations and permutations to love lyrics of a more conventional sort. "Take Me With U" (sic), a song from his phenomenally successful album "Purple Rain," could have been written decades ago or yesterday.

> I don't care where we go
> I don't care what we do
> I don't care pretty baby
> Just take me with u

Pop songs can do more than chart changing attitudes toward love and romance; they can address topical issues and appeal to our social conscience. In the 60's, Bob Dylan and other songwriters composed anthems that were sung by civil rights workers as they headed south, and by hundreds of thousands demonstrating for peace and equal rights. "How many deaths will it take till we know that too many people have died," Dylan asked. "The answer, my friend, is blowin' in the wind." And, he added, in a line in another song that provided a name for the radical faction within Students for a Democratic Society, "You don't need a weatherman to tell which way the wind blows."

By the late 60's, the peace and civil rights movements were beginning to splinter. The assassinations of the Kennedys and Martin Luther King had robbed a generation of its heroes, the Vietnam war was escalating despite the protests, and at home, violence was on the rise. Young people turned to rock, expecting it to ask the right questions and come up with answers, hoping that the music's most visionary artists could somehow make sense of things. But rock's most influential artists—Bob Dylan, the Beatles, the Rolling Stones— were finding that serving as the conscience of a generation exacted a heavy toll. Mr. Dylan, for one, felt the pressures becoming unbearable, and wrote about his predicament in songs like "All Along the Watchtower."

> There must be some way out of here, said the joker to the thief.
> There's too much confusion, I can't get no relief.
> Businessmen they drink my wine, plowmen dig my earth.
> None of them along the line knows what any of it is worth.

Many rock artists of the 60's turned to drugs before the decade ended. For awhile, songs that were thought to be about drugs, whatever their original intentions (Bob Dylan's "Mr. Tambourine Man," the Byrds' "Eight Miles High," the Rolling Stones' "Get Off My Cloud"), were widely heard. Bob

Dylan sang that "everybody must get stoned," and many young people seemed to agree. But the fad for drug lyrics was shortlived. They were never again as prevalent as during that brief Indian summer of the counter-culture. One hears few drug references in today's pop lyrics, and when drugs *are* mentioned, listeners are usually advised to stay away from them; "Don't do it," Grandmaster Flash and the Furious Five cautioned listeners about to experiment with drugs in their rap hit "White Lines."

The mainstream rock of the 1970's produced little in the way of socially relevant lyrics. But toward the end of that decade a change began to be felt. The rise of punk rock in Britain brought to the country's pop charts angry songs about unemployment and nuclear Armageddon. In America, the issue of nuclear energy and the threat of nuclear war enlisted the sympathies of many prominent rock musicians. But attempts by Graham Nash, John Hall, and other anti-nuclear activists to turn their concerns into anthems were too self-conscious; the songs were quickly forgotten.

Rap, the new pop idiom that exploded out of New York's black and Latin neighborhoods in the late 70's, seemed to concern itself mostly with hedonism and verbal strutting—at first. Then, in the early 80's, came "The Message," the dance-single by Grandmaster Flash and the Furious Five that provided listeners with an angry, eye-witness account of inner-city neighborhoods and people abandoned to rot, prey to crime, poverty, and disease. "It's like a jungle/Sometimes it makes me wonder/How I keep from going under," chanted the group's champion rapper, Melle Mel.

The rap records of the last several years have confronted similar issues head-on, and they have been danceable enough to attract a sizable audience. Run-D.M.C.'s recent hit single "It's Like That" ticked off a list of some of the daily horrors many black Americans have to contend with. But you can't give up, Run-D.M.C. insisted to their young, predominately black and urban audience. You have to make something of yourself, to rise above "the way it is."

Bruce Springsteen's recent songs have also been topical and deeply felt. They have also been the most popular music of his career. He is writing for and about the America of his dreams and the America he sees around him, and his lyrics are followed closely by a huge audience, as last year's Presidential campaign references made abundantly clear.

The narrator of Mr. Springsteen's recent hit "Born in the U.S.A." is a Vietnam veteran who returns home to confront harsh realities.

> Went down to see my V.A. man
> He said 'Son don't you understand now'
> Had a brother at Khe Sanh fighting off the Viet Cong
> They're still there he's all gone

Other songs on Mr. Springsteen's most recent album suggest that there is a pervasive gloom hanging over the country's decaying inner cities and factory towns. But their message is a positive one. "Hold on," the songs seem to say, "you've got to have something to believe in." The laborer in "Working on the Highway" is certainly hanging on to *his* dream:

> I work for the county out on 95
> All day I hold a red flag and watch the traffic pass me by
> In my head I keep a picture of a pretty little miss
> Someday mister I'm gonna lead a better life than this.

Mr. Springsteen's songs look at America and find both despair and hope. And like Chuck Berry and so many other rock and roll lyricists, past and present, he finds a source of strength and inspiration in rock itself. Singing of his schooldays, he captures rock and roll's heart:

> We learned more from a three-minute record than we ever learned in school
> Tonight I hear the neighborhood drummer sound
> I can feel my heart begin to pound
> We made a promise we swore we'd always remember
> No retreat, no surrender.

Suggestions for Discussion

1. On what grounds does Palmer argue that rock is "part of adult culture now, to an extent that would have been unthinkable as recently as a decade ago"? Do you agree or disagree? Explain.

2. How do rock lyrics in the 1980s differ from those of the 1960s and 1970s?

3. How does Palmer characterize the recent songs of Bruce Springsteen?

Suggestions for Writing

1. What themes do you discover in the lyrics of a favorite contemporary song?

2. Palmer claims that contemporary rock is still often sexist. To what extent does your examination of the work of a contemporary performer support or modify Palmer's observation?

E. J. Hobsbawm

The Jazz Comeback

Eric John Hobsbawm (b. 1917) is University Professor of Politics and Society at the New School for Social Research. His books include *Primitive Rebels* (1959), *Bandits* (1969), *The Age of Capital* (1977), *The Age of Revolution* (1979), and most recently, *Workers* (1984). In the review essay that follows, he analyzes the current revival of public interest in jazz.

Sitting In:
Selected Writings on Jazz,
Blues and Related Topics
by Hayden Carruth.
University of Iowa Press, 192 pp.,
$22.50

His Way:
The Unauthorized Biography
of Frank Sinatra
by Kitty Kelley.
Bantam, 575 pp., $21.95

'Round Midnight
a film by Bernard Tavernier.

La Tristesse de Saint Louis:
Jazz Under the Nazis
by Mike Zwerin.
Beech Tree Books/William Morrow,
197 pp., $16.95

American Musicians:
Fifty-six Portraits in Jazz
by Whitney Balliett.
Oxford University Press, 415 pp., $22.95

In the Moment: Jazz in the 1980s
by Francis Davis.
Oxford University Press, 258 pp., $18.95

A Life in Jazz
by Danny Barker,
edited by Alyn Shipton.
Oxford University Press, 223 pp., $19.95

Up From the Cradle of Jazz:
New Orleans Music Since World War II
by Jason Berry, Jonathan Foose,
and Tad Jones.
University of Georgia Press,
272 pp., $35.00; $15.95 (paper)

Until recently jazz has occupied a curiously marginal position in the official culture of its native country, and even within the black community. The public for it has been tiny: far smaller than the public for classical music. Record producers, who probably contain a much higher proportion of jazz buffs than the American people at large, can hardly be expected to invest much in music that nowadays sells less than 4 percent of discs and tapes.[1]

The jazz public is enormously serious, even a public of connoisseurs. Since the 1930s it has certainly contained a considerable number of intellectuals with wide cultural interests. And yet official high culture in the US was extraordinarily slow to take note of what is probably the most serious homegrown American contribution to the twentieth-century arts. Hayden Carruth, poet, professor, and, since the early Thirties, an informed and thoughtful jazz enthusiast, observes that

> as a poet I never met another poet older than I who understood jazz as music
> . . . . Among poets of my own age I have met one or two who love and understand jazz, but none who has written intelligently about it. Most of my contemporaries have only a kind of nostalgic feeling for the "swing era." . . . Only when I come to poets whose musical education began after 1945, do I find any

[1]Francis Davis, *In the Moment*, p. ix.

number, though still comparatively few, who write about jazz with understanding . . . . For some in the baby-boom generation the beginning of jazz is the work of Charlie Parker. For most it is the work of Miles Davis.[2]

Not that jazz was hard to find for twentieth-century urban or, through radio, any, Americans. Its sound was familiar and not difficult of access, at any rate for those who first heard it in their teens. The problem was exactly the opposite. Jazz, or more generally the music of North American Negroes, was and is so deeply embedded in popular entertainment in the cities of the US that it was almost impossible to separate it out as a special kind of art.

Even in the black ghettos it had no separate existence, except for the communities of professional players who, like all professionals, whether physicists, economists, or musicians, live by and for peer judgment, even when they are being paid by people who cannot tell the difference between trumpet and trombone, or who think Kenneth Arrow makes shirts. As Carruth observes, even the late Malcolm X, who was a champion ballroom dancer in Boston and New York in the late 1930s, does not in his autobiography speak of the jazz to which he danced as music. He treats it as "a cultural adjunct."

A striking example of the impossibility of recognizing the jazz threads within American popular culture is Kitty Kelley's scandal-mongering biography of Frank Sinatra, who was in his day undeniably an excellent jazz singer. This is not surprising, since he learned his craft in the big-band "swing" era, when jazz briefly became the mainstream of youthful pop music, and began his career as a vocalist in the Harry James and Tommy Dorsey bands. In fact Ms. Kelley, though primarily interested in her subject's nonmusical activities, is sufficiently conscientious to record how Dorsey instructed him in jazz phrasing.

Yet it is evident that Sinatra, raised among New Jersey working-class Italian immigrants, came from a milieu that had about as little relation to black music as it was possible to have in urban America. He showed no interest in jazz as such: few jazz names appear in the ample index of *His Way*. He was simply a young Sicilian of some talent and boundless ambitions who wanted to make the big time as a singer of sentimental songs, and did so, thanks not least to a sexual magnetism that attracted audiences at all distances. Luckily for him (and for Sinatra's admirers) the jazz idiom, to which a young man in the Hoboken of the Forties took as naturally as he would to the company of Italian mobsters, gave sentimentality an interesting musical edge, and a sort of offhand distancing. Ten years older, and he might with equal conviction have sung "Sole Mio." Moreover, for all his immersion in jazz, for most of us Sinatra is no more primarily a jazz artist than was Bing Crosby, whose superb and relaxed jazz phrasing Dorsey urged Sinatra to imitate. His phrasing survived and protected him to some extent from the vocal erosion of age. He deservedly became and remains a star of show business, and his songs have probably accompanied and subsequently recalled more seductions than any other singer's. But his relation to jazz is peripheral.

The very omnipresence of the jazz element in American popular music, and especially dance and show music, after the First World War meant that

[2]Hayden Carruth, *Sitting In*, p. 176.

for most Americans it had no precise location or independent existence. It also meant that jazz was more easily recognized as an original form of art, and its practitioners as original artists of serious stature, by a public which came to it as to a foreign land: the Europeans.

The fact that jazz was thus taken seriously in Europe earlier than in the US has always rankled in its native country. It still does, if the American critical reception of Bernard Tavernier's moving film 'Round Midnight is anything to go by. Pauline Kael's grumpy reaction ("The French are pretty hard to take when they celebrate just how much they love American art") is not uncharacteristic. But what is hard for Americans to take is not the self-congratulation of Europeans, but that in this instance they have something to congratulate themselves about.

For it is undeniable that, from the early 1930s on, musicians who were seen by official high culture in their homeland as vaudeville acts or something to dance to were in Europe acclaimed by intellectuals, artists, and high society. Hitler destroyed the Central European avant-garde that was attracted by jazz, and the early links between Soviet culture and jazz have only lately been disinterred by the scholarly labors of the president of Oberlin College.[3] But nobody who knows anything about French culture will be surprised that Cocteau compared jazz to Stravinsky, while Stravinsky drew on jazz, that the man who started the world's first pure jazz magazine, Charles Delaunay, was the child of Cubist painters in the heyday of the Ecole de Paris, and that Jean-Paul Sartre, though seeming no more likely to tap his feet than his cousin Albert Schweitzer, knew that he ought to take jazz seriously. Perhaps because Boris Vian, as avant-garde as the next man, doubled as a Dixieland trumpeter in Paris clubs.

It is equally undeniable that the first book to survey and assess the leading jazz artists and "put jazz on the map in Europe and in its own country"[4] was written by a twenty-two-year-old Frenchman, Hugues Panassié, in 1934; or, for that matter, that then as now the European public, small as it was, could at times be the only public for which it was worth producing *American* jazz. A leading producer of the stateside jazz avant-garde's records today is in Milan, and 70 percent of his modest sales go outside the US.[5] For that matter, why did we have to wait for a Frenchman to make the first full-length feature film which takes a black musician seriously as a creative artist, and, what is more, casts a black jazz musician in this role—Dexter Gordon, whose performance in 'Round Midnight is astonishing, more moving than his music?

None of this alters the fact that, then as now, the US is where the action is, and where a jazz musician would want to be, appreciated or not, so long as he could earn a living there.

As it happens, Tavernier's film raises a more interesting question. Like almost all we know about jazz except the sounds themselves, it is jazz from the fan's point of view: naturally enough, cameras are not instruments through which musicians express themselves. Indeed, Gallophiles will recognize the

[3]S. Frederick Starr, *Red and Hot: The Fate of Jazz in the Soviet Union 1917–1980*, (Oxford University Press, 1983).
[4]Whitney Balliett, *American Musicians*, p. 3.
[5]Davis, *In the Moment*, pp. 206–213.

special flavor of the French intellectual jazz fan, always ready to discover a *poète maudit* even in blackface, loving jazz not only for itself but because it leads him to Rimbaud, and flattered by the proclaimed taste of older jazz musicians for Debussy.

No musician would make a film essentially about his relation with an admiring fan, but that is the central theme of 'Round Midnight. It is based on the case of a real Frenchman who did his best to protect the great but declining bebop pianist Bud Powell against himself in Paris. Tavernier's protagonist takes in a famous but alcoholic sax player, briefly nurses him back to respect and creativity through selfless care and immersion in the slow rhythms of French family life, perhaps seen here as unduly reticent and gentle; but he cannot prevent him from returning to New York where he dies. It is almost certainly the best feature film made about jazz, and illuminating both about the people and the music—for jazz fans are equally interested in both.

However, the fan sees his hero in a retrospective sentimental haze. Bud Powell in Paris was an altogether more frightening and inaccessible phenomenon than the gentle somnambulist self-destroyer whom Dexter Gordon plays so well. (The present writer, who saw Powell in Paris, speaks from personal memory.) The film combines the fans' resentment at the world's failure to accept the greatness of jazz with their reluctance to share it with outsiders. It is full of esoteric references—to Charlie Parker's wife, to Lester Young's tricks of language—whose very opaqueness confirms the aficionado's monopoly. Tavernier, justifiably, makes no attempt to distance himself from sentiment and cliché which are essential to fandom. (But then, neither did he do so in that other splendid film about art, artists, and, not incidentally, fathers and daughters, *A Sunday in the Country*.)

But the jazz fan, however knowledgeable, is fundamentally a lover. While old-style pop music, as everyone knows, crystallized and preserved the relation of human beings in love ("They're playing our song"), jazz, more often than not, is itself the love object for its devotees. The Czech novelist Josef Skvorecky has compared its initial impact to the first love of teen-agers in the era when such emotions, however fleeting, were still supposed to be unforgettable. "It had begun as a love affair like the others." This is the description of how jazz was discovered by Dr. Dietrich Schulz-Koehn, who occupies a small niche in the informal pantheon of jazz lovers' history as the German officer captured at St. Nazaire in 1944, whose first question to his American captors was: "Do you have any Count Basie records?"[6] The metaphor of love or falling in love keeps pushing its way into Mike Zwerin's enthusiastic but superficial account of jazz in Nazi-occupied Europe, itself a work of autobiography, sentiment, and piety rather than scholarship. ("Accuracy came first, but when there was a choice between poetry and journalism, I picked poetry."[7])

Few jazz fans are in a position to make films, though they have, in jazz photography, created a library of marvelous images. A number of young white men—and a small but growing number of women—also graduate from fans to players, though opinions about the musical interest of their activities have

---

[6]Mike Zwerin, *La tristesse de Saint Louis*, p. 3.
[7]*La tristesse de Saint Louis*, p. 1. For the metaphor, see e.g. pp. 19, 46, 61.

generally been divided. Fortunately a modest number have, over the years, compensated for the lack of commercial and institutional interest in jazz by turning themselves into impresarios or record producers. The recently repolished Blue Note label, founded and long maintained by two German refugee jazz fans, is a case in point. But what do they do with words?

Relatively few fans write poetry to or about the beloved, and when they do, it tends to rely excessively on the magic of names which vibrate only for other lovers. ("Oh I loved you Pete Brown. And you were a brother to me, Joe Marsala. And you too, sweet Billy Kyle."[8]) Rather more of them, belonging to the large underground of jazz lovers in academia, now write books of serious scholarship about the object of their passion. Characteristically, most of the books noted here are published by university presses. But very few indeed practice the extraordinarily difficult art of communicating in prose what musicians are and do.

Probably the only writer who has actually succeeded is Whitney Balliett of *The New Yorker*, whose *American Musicians* collects together twenty-four years of "jazz profiles." As a writer of *New Yorker* profiles he is distinguished but not exceptional. His unique strength as a descriptive writer on jazz lies in a musically informed combination of watchful, precise observation with ear and eye, a sort of Audubon-like impartiality, and an uncanny instinct for words which not only are but *sound* right. Very few listen and observe as exactly as he does, and nobody reports more exactly. Balliett's descriptions of solo improvisations—he is particularly good on drummers—are, as nearly as is possible, translations of the movement of music into language; as can be verified by checking his report of, say, Jess Stacy's famous 1938 piano solo at Carnegie Hall against the record.

> After a Goodman–Gene Krupa duet, there was a treading-water pause, and Stacy, suddenly given the nod by Goodman, took off. The solo lasted over two minutes, which was remarkable at a time when most solos were measured in seconds. One wonders how many people understood what they were hearing that night, for no one had ever played a piano solo like it. From the opening measures, it had an exalted, almost ecstatic quality, as if it were playing Stacy. It didn't, with its Debussy glints and ghosts, seem of its time and place. It was also revolutionary in that it was more of a cadenza than a series of improvised choruses. There were no divisions or seams, and it had a spiralling structure, an organic structure, in which each phrase evolved from its predecessor. Seesawing middle-register chords gave way to double-time runs, which gave way to dreaming rests, which gave way to singsong chords, which gave way to oblique runs. A climax would be reached only to recede before a still stronger one. Piling grace upon grace, the solo moved gradually but inexorably up the keyboard, at last ending in a superbly restrained cluster of upper-register single notes. There was an instant of stunned silence before Krupa came thundering back.

Unlike most jazz writers, he never gushes or conceals the weaknesses even of his favorites. His range of sympathy is unusually wide, from King Oliver to Cecil Taylor, though it does not entirely include Miles Davis and hard bop, about which (in this book) he is very reticent. In short, he is the ideal writer for the literate jazz lover who is forced to recollect emotion in tranquillity, far

---

[8]Carruth, *Sitting In*, p. 52.

from records and tapes. What, except admiration for a first-class craftsman in words, he communicates to those who do not like jazz, it is impossible for a jazz lover to say.

Since so much of what we know about jazz comes to us through the selfless but not unbiased devotion of the aficionados, not least as collectors, genealogists, chroniclers, or—as in Danny Barker's *A Life in Jazz*—translators of spoken reminiscence into print,[9] we ought to know a good deal more about the public for jazz and its evolution than we actually do. However, writers on jazz have tended to be as incurious about the listeners as they have been endlessly fascinated by the tiniest details about the musicians. The reception of jazz, especially in the US, still has to be seriously studied, although several of the books under review do provide incidental materials for such a study.

And yet, the future of jazz depends almost entirely on what happens to the public for it, as was clear during the fifteen or so years from the early 1960s on, when this public virtually vanished as the mass of the young stampeded to follow the rock fashions, in this as in several other respects a disaster decade for Western culture. (The rhythm-and-blues of the 1950s had still allowed a kind of amicable symbiosis between jazz and pop.[10]) The best that could be said about jazz in the early 1970s, even in New York—as usual it was said by Whitney Balliett—was that it had stopped collapsing. Its condition was "parlous but persuasive."[11] Once again, this is jazz as seen by fans or critics. For musicians who could no longer make a living by playing jazz it was the first rather than the second.

In spite of the (qualified) gloom of Francis Davis, whose *In the Moment* reports on the jazz scene of the 1980s, interest in jazz began to revive in the late 1970s with the visible exhaustion of rock music, and has been growing at an impressive pace recently. "The bins are bursting with reissues and clubs are suddenly doing record business," wrote a jazz journal at the end of 1986,[12] and the phenomenon appears to be international. It is once again becoming possible for more than a handful of musicians to earn a living playing jazz. Long-dissolved groups are reconstituted, musicians return from California studios and European exile and answer the question, "Where is jazz going right now?" with, "I don't know where it's going, but it's healthy."[13] Even if the revival lasts, jazz will certainly not be more than a minority taste, like reading poetry, as it has generally been; but it may once again be an economically workable one.

Given our ignorance of the public which is now turning to jazz, little can be said about it except that, as is obvious, "jazz audiences are generally upscale in income, well-educated and more white than black."[14] Nevertheless, the growing body of middle-class and professional blacks may now also con-

---

[9] The book has been put together by an English admirer. However, several of its most touching and instructive passages have long been available in that marvelous collage of the spoken jazzword, Nat Hentoff and Nat Shapiro's *Hear Me Talkin' to Ya'* (1955).

[10] *Up From the Cradle of Jazz*, is most instructive on this collapse of the market for jazz in New Orleans.

[11] Whitney Balliett, *New York Notes: A Journal of Jazz in the Seventies* (Da Capo Press, 1977), p. 3.

[12] *Jazz Times* (November 1986), p. 18.

[13] *Jazz Times*, interview with Benny Golson (November 1986), p. 19.

[14] *Jazz Times* (November 1986), p. 29.

sider, as their fathers did not, an educated admiration for jazz as a badge of race pride as well as of cultural status.[15]

Apart from the nucleus of gnarled long-time jazz buffs, this is a new and relatively young audience, often strikingly ignorant, but, in a peculiar way, highbrow. The one branch of jazz which seems to have been left out of the revival is the simple fun music that once appealed so powerfully, especially to white youth, and that resisted the decline of jazz longest: Dixieland. In New York itself, those strongholds of white middle-class males, recalling their youth, Eddie Condon's and Jimmy Ryan's, have now gone even as new locations for more advanced live jazz multiplied and flourished.

The decline of Dixieland is clearly not due to a lack of audience appeal, but to critics' and musicians' combined boredom with, and contempt for, "the same old ninety-three tunes in the standard early repertoire" of New Orleans and Chicago, played in unvarying versions by "fourth-rate musicians."[16] Moreover, to many young black musicians, traditional New Orleans music was uncomfortably close to Uncle Tom. Only perceptive and open-minded jazz lovers like Balliett and Carruth are today prepared to say a good word for Dixieland music, or rather for jazz played in pre-1940 style. Carruth (who incidentally suggests, with some exaggeration, that "the number of inferior imitators of post-bop jazz today is greater by far than the number of Dixielanders") reminds his

> younger friends that when they hear records . . . made by real jazz musicians trained in the modes that came before bop, whether black or white, northern or southern, they are hearing jazz, not Dixieland, and it makes no difference whether the opening and closing choruses are played in harmonic riffs or contrapuntal improvisations.

Nor does he exclude the possibility that even "work taken verbatim, so to speak, from old records" could be "done with such purity of musical devotion and such sensitivity to phrasing" that it could be taken for real jazz.

Indeed, Berry, Foose, and Jones's learned and instructive study of New Orleans music since 1945 goes so far as to omit all mention of what most of the world, including the tourists visiting the French Quarter, would regard as the typical sound of New Orleans. Theirs is New Orleans as represented by the Marsalis family (one of the clans of practitioners on which the popular musical life of the city is still based[17]) rather than the New Orleans of Buddy Bolden's ghost, Preservation Hall, and ceaseless clones of *South Ramparts Street Parade*. And the success of *'Round Midnight*, epic of be-bop, underlines the failure, a few months earlier, of *The Gig*, a charming film about that characteristic phenomenon of the older jazz scene, the white middle-class amateur Dixieland musicians enjoying themselves, a species still occasionally

---

[15]It is unthinkable that black intellectuals could today write a book like the late Franklin Frazier's *The Negro in the United States*, which, even in the revised edition of 1957, contained no reference to music, though sufficiently hip to include references to the novels of Chester Himes.

[16]Carruth, *Sitting in*, p. 173.

[17]*Up from the Cradle of Jazz*, pp. 10–16. Danny Barker, a member of one such family of mini-Bachs, throws much light on such kin groups in his *A Life in Jazz*.

represented by Woody Allen. It came and went, not of course silently, but rather unperceived. (It is mentioned in passing in Davis's book on page 86.)

The fact that the repertoire of the jazz revival now looks like including the noises people are told by the arbiters of jazz taste to enjoy, as well as some they actually do, may at last give a chance to the young avant-garde musicians who slogged their way despairingly through the darkness of the 1960s and 1970s, and to whom Francis Davis pays particular attention. It is at least possible that bookers will no longer give automatic priority to any of the diminishing band of veterans who can be associated with some remote and prestigious name of which even the johns have heard, even though their only obvious merit is physical survival. And it is certainly the case that jazz musicians like the pianist Ellis Marsalis, who brought up their sons in the true faith of Ornette Coleman and John Coltrane while unbelief raged all round them, are now indirectly coming into their own.

But it is also possible that the revival of some public interest in jazz has had the effect of leading some of the musicians who, in the dark years, made themselves even more inaccessible (to spite those who refused to listen to them anyway), back toward a mainstream music genuinely capable of appealing to audiences, or at least not actively alienating them. Such integration of musical revolutionaries in the mainstream was what created the last golden age of jazz between 1955 and 1960. Francis Davis notes, not without melancholy, that the flag carrier of the 1980s revival, the young trumpeter Wynton Marsalis, is a "resolutely conservative" musician. There are times today when the World Saxophone Quartet not only sounds like Ellington, but actually tries to. Some will welcome this development.

In these circumstances it is possible that jazz may finally be adopted into the postmodernist American establishment as part of the cultural ambiance of the new graduate professional classes. It has become intellectually respectable. Its players are likely to be formally trained in music, or even, like Wynton Marsalis, equally distinguished as classical and jazz performers. It can be readily combined with other consumer expenditures, as has been recognized in the now familiar bonding of jazz and cookery in Manhattan supper clubs and restaurants. Practicing gastronomy to the accompaniment of what good authorities claim to be the classical music of the twentieth-century US is culturally reassuring, even when one is not listening to it closely. It is even, in a modest way, a guarantee of economic exclusiveness, at least so long as the size of the jazz public and the capacity of clubs make it cheaper to buy a modest opera seat than to hear a live set in the Village.

However, among the many whom the new respectability of jazz excludes are those who made this music in the past, and on whom its creative future must rest: young men and women from the black ghetto. Not many of the very young have yet been drawn into the jazz revival in its native country. The degree in Jazz and Contemporary Music recently inaugurated at the New School in New York is now taught by a predominantly black faculty of distinguished older musicians to a largely white student body. For every black student who has joined the course so far there are six whites. Jazz may have established its cultural credentials, but the real rejuvenation of the music has a long way to go.

Suggestions for Discussion

1. How does the author document European interest in jazz?

2. Who are the audiences for jazz today? On what grounds are some audiences still excluded?

3. Discuss Hobsbawm's use of quotations from the works he is reviewing to support his arguments.

Suggestions for Writing

1. To what extent can you document an interest in jazz in your own community?

2. Discuss the work of a jazz performer you admire.

Fiction

John Cheever

The Enormous Radio

John Cheever (1912–1982), distinguished American novelist and short-story writer, won many awards including the Pulitzer Prize and the American Book Award. His books include *The Enormous Radio and Other Stories* (1954), *The Wapshot Chronicle* (1957), *The Wapshot Scandal* (1964), *Bullet Park* (1969), *Falconer* (1977), and *The Stories of John Cheever* (1979).

Jim and Irene Westcott were the kind of people who seem to strike that satisfactory average of income, endeavor, and respectability that is reached by the statistical reports in college alumni bulletins. They were the parents of two young children, they had been married nine years, they lived on the twelfth floor of an apartment house near Sutton Place, they went to the theatre on an average of 10.3 times a year, and they hoped someday to live in Westchester. Irene Westcott was a pleasant, rather plain girl with soft brown hair and a wide, fine forehead upon which nothing at all had been written, and in the cold weather she wore a coat of fitch skins dyed to resemble mink. You could not say that Jim Westcott looked younger than he was, but you could at least say of him that he seemed to feel younger. He wore his graying hair cut very short, he dressed in the kind of clothes his class had worn at Andover, and his manner was earnest, vehement, and intentionally naïve. The Westcotts differed from their friends, their classmates, and their neighbors only in an interest they shared in serious music. They went to a great many concerts—although they seldom mentioned this to anyone—and they spent a good deal of time listening to music on the radio.

Their radio was an old instrument, sensitive, unpredictable, and beyond repair. Neither of them understood the mechanics of radio—or of any of the other appliances that surrounded them—and when the instrument faltered, Jim would strike the side of the cabinet with his hand. This sometimes helped. One Sunday afternoon, in the middle of a Schubert quartet, the music faded away altogether. Jim struck the cabinet repeatedly, but there was no response; the Schubert was lost to them forever. He promised to buy Irene a new radio, and on Monday when he came home from work he told her that he had got one. He refused to describe it, and said it would be a surprise for her when it came.

The radio was delivered at the kitchen door the following afternoon, and with the assistance of her maid and the handyman Irene uncrated it and brought it into the living room. She was struck at once with the physical ugliness of the large gumwood cabinet. Irene was proud of her living room, she had chosen its furnishings and colors as carefully as she chose her clothes, and now it seemed to her that the new radio stood among her intimate possessions like an aggressive intruder. She was confounded by the number of dials and switches on the instrument panel, and she studied them thoroughly before she put the plug into a wall socket and turned the radio on. The dials flooded with a malevolent green light, and in the distance she heard the music of a piano quintet. The quintet was in the distance for only an instant; it bore down upon her with a speed greater than light and filled the apartment with the noise of music amplified so mightily that it knocked a china ornament from a table to the floor. She rushed to the instrument and reduced the volume. The violent forces that were snared in the ugly gumwood cabinet made her uneasy. Her children came home from school then, and she took them to the Park. It was not until later in the afternoon that she was able to return to the radio.

The maid had given the children their suppers and was supervising their baths when Irene turned on the radio, reduced the volume, and sat down to listen to a Mozart quintet that she knew and enjoyed. The music came through clearly. The new instrument had a much purer tone, she thought, than the old one. She decided that tone was most important and that she could conceal the cabinet behind a sofa. But as soon as she had made her peace with the radio, the interference began. A crackling sound like the noise of a burning powder fuse began to accompany the singing of the strings. Beyond the music, there was a rustling that reminded Irene unpleasantly of the sea, and as the quintet progressed, these noises were joined by many others. She tried all the dials and switches but nothing dimmed the interference, and she sat down, disappointed and bewildered, and tried to trace the flight of the melody. The elevator shaft in her building ran beside the living-room wall, and it was the noise of the elevator that gave her a clue to the character of the static. The rattling of the elevator cables and the opening and closing of the elevator doors were reproduced in her loudspeaker, and, realizing that the radio was sensitive to electrical currents of all sorts, she began to discern through the Mozart the ringing of telephone bells, the dialing of phones, and the lamentation of a vacuum cleaner. By listening more carefully, she was able to distinguish doorbells, elevator bells, electric razors, and Waring mixers, whose sounds had been picked up from the apartments that surrounded hers and transmitted through her loudspeaker. The powerful and ugly instrument, with its mistaken sensitivity to discord, was more than she could hope to master, so she turned the thing off and went into the nursery to see her children.

When Jim Westcott came home that night, he went to the radio confidently and worked the controls. He had the same sort of experience Irene had had. A man was speaking on the station Jim had chosen, and his voice swung instantly from the distance into a force so powerful that it shook the apartment. Jim turned the volume control and reduced the voice. Then, a minute or two later, the interference began. The ringing of telephones and doorbells set in, joined by the rasp of the elevator doors and the whir of cooking appliances. The character of the noise had changed since Irene had tried the radio earlier; the last of the electric razors was being unplugged, the vacuum cleaners had all been returned to their closets, and the static reflected that change in pace that overtakes the city after the sun goes down. He fiddled with the knobs but couldn't get rid of the noises, so he turned the radio off and told Irene that in the morning he'd call the people who had sold it to him and give them hell.

The following afternoon, when Irene returned to the apartment from a luncheon date, the maid told her that a man had come and fixed the radio. Irene went into the living room before she took off her hat or her furs and tried the instrument. From the loudspeaker came a recording of the "Missouri Waltz." It reminded her of the thin, scratchy music from an old-fashioned phonograph that she sometimes heard across the lake where she spent her summers. She waited until the waltz had finished, expecting an explanation of the recording, but there was none. The music was followed by silence, and then the plaintive and scratchy record was repeated. She turned the dial and got a satisfactory burst of Caucasian music—the thump of bare feet in the dust and the rattle of coin jewelry—but in the background she could hear the ringing of bells and a confusion of voices. Her children came home from school then, and she turned off the radio and went to the nursery.

When Jim came home that night, he was tired, and he took a bath and changed his clothes. Then he joined Irene in the living room. He had just turned on the radio when the maid announced dinner, so he left it on, and he and Irene went to the table.

Jim was too tired to make even a pretense of sociability, and there was nothing about the dinner to hold Irene's interest, so her attention wandered from the food to the deposits of silver polish on the candlesticks and from there to the music in the other room. She listened for a few moments to a Chopin prelude and then was surprised to hear a man's voice break in. "For Christ's sake, Kathy," he said, "do you always have to play the piano when I get home?" The music stopped abruptly. "It's the only chance I have," a woman said. "I'm at the office all day." "So am I," the man said. He added something obscene about an upright piano, and slammed a door. The passionate and melancholy music began again.

"Did you hear that?" Irene asked.

"What?" Jim was eating his dessert.

"The radio. A man said something while the music was still going on—something dirty."

"It's probably a play."

"I don't think it *is* a play," Irene said.

They left the table and took their coffee into the living room. Irene asked Jim to try another station. He turned the knob. "Have you seen my garters?" a man asked. "Button me up," a woman said. "Have you seen my garters?" the man said again. "Just button me up and I'll find your garters," the woman said. Jim shifted to another station. "I wish you wouldn't leave apple cores in the ashtrays," a man said. "I hate the smell."

"This is strange," Jim said.

"Isn't it?" Irene said.

Jim turned the knob again. " 'On the coast of Coromandel where the early pumpkins blow,' " a woman with a pronounced English accent said, " 'in the middle of the woods lived the Yonghy-Bonghy-Bò. Two old chairs, and a candle, one old jug without a handle . . .' "

"My God!" Irene cried. "That's the Sweeneys' nurse."

" 'These were all his worldly goods,' " the British voice continued.

"Turn that thing off," Irene said. "Maybe they can hear *us.*" Jim switched the radio off. "That was Miss Armstrong, the Sweeneys' nurse," Irene said. "She must be reading to the little girl. They live in 17-B. I've talked with Miss Armstrong in the Park. I know her voice very well. We must be getting other people's apartments."

"That's impossible," Jim said.

"Well, that was the Sweeneys' nurse," Irene said hotly. "I know her voice. I know it very well. I'm wondering if they can hear us."

Jim turned the switch. First from a distance and then nearer, nearer, as if borne on the wind, came the pure accents of the Sweeneys' nurse again: " '*Lady Jingly! Lady Jingly!* ' " she said, " '*Sitting where the pumpkins blow, will you come and be my wife,* said the Yonghy-Bonghy-Bò . . .' "

Jim went over to the radio and said "Hello" loudly into the speaker.

" '*I am tired of living singly,* ' " the nurse went on, " '*on this coast so wild and shingly, I'm a-weary of my life; if you'll come and be my wife, quite serene would be my life . . .* ' "

"I guess she can't hear us," Irene said. "Try something else."

Jim turned to another station, and the living room was filled with the uproar of a cocktail party that had overshot its mark. Someone was playing the piano and singing the Whiffenpoof Song, and the voices that surrounded the piano were vehement and happy. "Eat some more sandwiches," a woman shrieked. There were screams of laughter and a dish of some sort crashed to the floor.

"Those must be the Fullers, in 11-E," Irene said. "I knew they were giving a party this afternoon. I saw her in the liquor store. Isn't this too divine? Try something else. See if you can get those people in 18-C."

The Westcotts overheard that evening a monologue on salmon fishing in Canada, a bridge game, running comments on home movies of what had apparently been a fortnight at Sea Island, and a bitter family quarrel about an overdraft at the bank. They turned off their radio at midnight and went to bed, weak with laughter. Sometime in the night, their son began to call for a glass of water and Irene got one and took it to his room. It was very early. All the lights in the neighborhood were extinguished, and from the boy's window she could see the empty street. She went into the living room and tried the radio. There was some faint coughing, a moan, and then a man spoke. "Are you all right, darling?" he asked. "Yes," a woman said wearily. "Yes, I'm all right, I guess," and then she added with great feeling, "but, you know, Charlie, I don't feel like myself any more. Sometimes there are about fifteen or twenty minutes in the week when I feel like myself. I don't like to go to another doctor, because the doctor's bills are so awful already, but I just don't feel like myself, Charlie. I just never feel like myself." They were not young, Irene thought. She guessed from the timbre of their voices that they were middle-aged. The restrained melancholy of the dialogue and the draft from the bedroom window made her shiver, and she went back to bed.

The following morning, Irene cooked breakfast for the family—the maid didn't come up from her room in the basement until ten—braided her daughters' hair, and waited at the door until her children and her husband had been carried away in the elevator. Then she went into the living room and tried the radio. "I don't want to go to school," a child screamed. "I hate school. I won't go to school. I hate school." "You will go to school," an enraged woman said. "We paid eight hundred dollars to get you into that school and you'll go if it kills you." The next number on the dial produced the worn record of the "Missouri Waltz." Irene shifted the control and invaded the privacy of several breakfast tables. She overheard demonstrations of indigestion, carnal love, abysmal vanity, faith, and despair. Irene's life was nearly as simple and sheltered as it appeared to be, and the forthright and sometimes brutal language that came from the loudspeaker that morning astonished and troubled her. She continued to listen until her maid came in. Then she turned off the radio quickly, since this insight, she realized, was a furtive one.

Irene had a luncheon date with a friend that day, and she left her apartment at a little after twelve. There were a number of women in the elevator when it stopped at her floor. She stared at their handsome and impassive faces, their furs, and the cloth flowers in their hats. Which one of them had been to Sea Island, she wondered. Which one had overdrawn her bank account? The elevator stopped at the tenth floor and a woman with a pair of Skye terriers joined them. Her hair was rigged high on her head and she wore a mink cape. She was humming the "Missouri Waltz."

Irene had two Martinis at lunch, and she looked searchingly at her friend and wondered what her secrets were. They had intended to go shopping after lunch, but Irene excused herself and went home. She told the maid that she was not to be disturbed; then she went into the living room, closed the doors, and switched on the radio. She heard, in the course of the afternoon, the halting conversation of a woman entertaining her aunt, the hysterical conclusion of a luncheon party, and a hostess briefing her maid about some cocktail guests. "Don't give the best Scotch to anyone who hasn't white hair," the hostess said. "See if you can get rid of that liver paste before you pass those hot things, and could you lend me five dollars? I want to tip the elevator man."

As the afternoon waned, the conversations increased in intensity. From where Irene sat, she could see the open sky above the East River. There were hundreds of clouds in the sky, as though the south wind had broken the winter into pieces and were blowing it north, and on her radio she could hear the arrival of cocktail guests and the return of children and businessmen from their schools and offices. "I found a good-sized diamond on the bathroom floor this morning," a woman said. "It must have fallen out of that bracelet Mrs. Dunston was wearing last night." "We'll sell it," a man said. "Take it down to the jeweller on Madison Avenue and sell it. Mrs. Dunston won't know the difference, and we could use a couple of hundred bucks . . ." " 'Oranges and lemons, say the bells of St. Clement's,' " the Sweeneys' nurse sang. " 'Halfpence and farthings, say the bells of St. Martin's. When will you pay me? say the bells at old Bailey . . .' " "It's not a hat," a woman cried, and at her back roared a cocktail party. "It's not a hat, it's a love affair. That's what Walter Florell said. He said it's not a hat, it's a love affair," and then, in a lower voice, the same woman added, "Talk to somebody, for Christ's sake, honey, talk to somebody. If she catches you standing here not talking to anybody, she'll take us off her invitation list, and I love these parties."

The Westcotts were going out for dinner that night, and when Jim came home, Irene was dressing. She seemed sad and vague, and he brought her a drink. They were dining with friends in the neighborhood, and they walked to where they were going. The sky was broad and filled with light. It was one of those splendid spring evenings that excite memory and desire, and the air that touched their hands and faces felt very soft. A Salvation Army band was on the corner playing "Jesus Is Sweeter." Irene drew on her husband's arm and held him there for a minute, to hear the music. "They're really such nice people, aren't they?" she said. "They have such nice faces. Actually, they're so much nicer than a lot of the people we know." She took a bill from her purse and walked over and dropped it into the tambourine. There was in her face, when she returned to her husband, a look of radiant melancholy that he was not familiar with. And her conduct at the dinner party that night seemed strange to him, too. She interrupted her hostess rudely and stared at the people across the table from her with an intensity for which she would have punished her children.

It was still mild when they walked home from the party, and Irene looked up at the spring stars. " 'How far that little candle throws its beams,' " she exclaimed. " 'So shines a good deed in a naughty world.' " She waited that night until Jim had fallen asleep, and then went into the living room and turned on the radio.

Jim came home at about six the next night. Emma, the maid, let him in, and he had taken off his hat and was taking off his coat when Irene ran into the hall. Her face was shining with tears and her hair was disordered. "Go up to 16-C, Jim!" she screamed. "Don't take off your coat. Go up to 16-C. Mr. Osborn's beating his wife. They've been quarrelling since four o'clock, and now he's hitting her. Go up there and stop him."

From the radio in the living room, Jim heard screams, obscenities, and thuds. "You know you don't have to listen to this sort of thing," he said. He strode into the living room and turned the switch. "It's indecent," he said. "It's like looking in windows. You know you don't have to listen to this sort of thing. You can turn it off."

"Oh, it's so horrible, it's so dreadful," Irene was sobbing. "I've been listening all day, and it's so depressing."

"Well, if it's so depressing, why do you listen to it? I bought this damned radio to give you some pleasure," he said. "I paid a great deal of money for it. I thought it might make you happy. I wanted to make you happy."

"Don't, don't, don't, don't quarrel with me," she moaned, and laid her head on his shoulder. "All the others have been quarrelling all day. Everybody's been quarrelling. They're all worried about money. Mrs. Hutchinson's mother is dying of cancer in Florida and they don't have enough money to send her to the Mayo Clinic. At least, Mr. Hutchinson says they don't have enough money. And some woman in this building is having an affair with the handyman—with that hideous handyman. It's too disgusting. And Mrs. Melville has heart trouble and Mr. Hendricks is going to lose his job in April and

Mrs. Hendricks is horrid about the whole thing and that girl who plays the 'Missouri Waltz' is a whore, a common whore, and the elevator man has tuberculosis and Mr. Osborn has been beating Mrs. Osborn." She wailed, she trembled with grief and checked the stream of tears down her face with the heel of her palm.

"Well, why do you have to listen?" Jim asked again. "Why do you have to listen to this stuff if it makes you so miserable?"

"Oh, don't, don't, don't," she cried. "Life is too terrible, too sordid and awful. But we've never been like that, have we, darling? Have we? I mean we've always been good and decent and loving to one another, haven't we? And we have two children, two beautiful children. Our lives aren't sordid, are they, darling? Are they?" She flung her arms around his neck and drew his face down to hers. "We're happy, aren't we, darling? We are happy, aren't we?"

"Of course we're happy," he said tiredly. He began to surrender his resentment. "Of course we're happy. I'll have that damned radio fixed or taken away tomorrow." He stroked her soft hair. "My poor girl," he said.

"You love me, don't you?" she asked. "And we're not hypercritical or worried about money or dishonest, are we?"

"No, darling," he said.

A man came in the morning and fixed the radio. Irene turned it on cautiously and was happy to hear a California-wine commerical and a recording of Beethoven's Ninth Symphony, including Schiller's "Ode to Joy." She kept the radio on all day and nothing untoward came from the speaker.

A Spanish suite was being played when Jim came home. "Is everything all right?" he asked. His face was pale, she thought. They had some cocktails and went in to dinner to the "Anvil Chorus" from "Il Trovatore." This was followed by Debussy's "La Mer."

"I paid the bill for the radio today," Jim said. "It cost four hundred dollars. I hope you'll get some enjoyment out of it."

"Oh, I'm sure I will," Irene said.

"Four hundred dollars is a good deal more than I can afford," he went on. "I wanted to get something that you'd enjoy. It's the last extravagance we'll be able to indulge in this year. I see that you haven't paid your clothing bills yet. I saw them on your dressing table." He looked directly at her. "Why did you tell me you'd paid them? Why did you lie to me?"

"I just didn't want you to worry, Jim," she said. She drank some water. "I'll be able to pay my bills out of this month's allowance. There were the slipcovers last month, and that party."

"You've got to learn to handle the money I give you a little more intelligently, Irene," he said. "You've got to understand the we won't have as much money this year as we had last. I had a very sobering talk with Mitchell today. No one is buying anything. We're spending all our time promoting new issues, and you know how long that takes. I'm not getting any younger, you know. I'm thirty-seven. My hair will be gray next year. I haven't done as well as I'd hoped to do. And I don't suppose things will get any better."

"Yes, dear," she said.

"We've got to start cutting down," Jim said. "We've got to think of the children. To be perfectly frank with you, I worry about money a great deal. I'm not at all sure of the future. No one is. If anything should happen to me, there's the insurance, but that wouldn't go very far today. I've worked awfully hard to give you and the children a comfortable life," he said bitterly. "I don't like to see all of my energies, all of my youth, wasted in fur coats and radios and slipcovers and—"

"Please, Jim," she said. "Please. They'll hear us."

"*Who'll hear us?* Emma can't hear us."

"The radio."

"Oh, I'm sick!" he shouted. "I'm sick to death of your apprehensiveness. The radio can't hear us. Nobody can hear us. And what if they can hear us? Who cares?"

Irene got up from the table and went into the living room. Jim went to the door and shouted at her from there. "Why are you so Christly all of a sudden? What's turned you overnight into a convent girl? You stole your mother's jewelry before they probated her will. You never gave your sister a cent of that money that was intended for her—not even when she needed it. You made Grace Howland's life miserable, and where was all your piety and your virtue when you went to that abortionist? I'll never forget how cool you were. You packed your bag and went off to have that child murdered as if you were going to Nassau.. If you'd had any reasons, if you'd had any good reasons—"

Irene stood for a minute before the hideous cabinet, disgraced and sickened, but she held her hand on the switch before she extinguished the music and the voices, hoping that the instrument might speak to her kindly, that she might hear the Sweeneys' nurse. Jim continued to shout at her from the door. The voice on the radio was suave and noncommital. "An early-morning railroad disaster in Tokyo," the loudspeaker said, "killed twenty-nine people. A fire in a Catholic hospital near Buffalo for the care of blind children was extinguished early this morning by nuns. The temperature is forty-seven. The humidity is eighty-nine."

Suggestions for Discussion

1. Analyze the ways in which Cheever's characters deceive others and delude themselves.

2. Comment on the domestic life of the Westcotts and their neighbors. Discuss and evaluate their life styles and values.

3. What new insights do Jim or Irene gain during the story? Be specific.

4. Discuss the ways in which Cheever builds and maintains suspense.

Suggestions for Writing

1. Write a similar short story in which a television set plays the part of the radio. What differences might occur?

2. In what ways are the Westcotts typical of couples you know? In what ways do they differ? Compare and contrast them with a couple close to you.

Alice Walker

Nineteen Fifty-five

Alice Walker (b. 1944) has won the Pulitzer Prize and the American Book Award for her fiction. Her books include *Meridian* (1976), *The Color Purple* (1982), and *You Can't Keep a Good Woman Down* (1981), from which the following story is taken.

1955

The car is a brandnew red Thunderbird convertible, and it's passed the house more than once. It slows down real slow now, and stops at the curb. An older gentleman dressed like a Baptist deacon gets out on the side near the house, and a young fellow who looks about sixteen gets out on the driver's side. They are white, and I wonder what in the world they are doing in this neighborhood.

Well, I say to J. T., put your shirt on, anyway, and let me clean these glasses offa the table.

We had been watching the ballgame on TV. I wasn't actually watching, I was sort of daydreaming, with my foots up in J. T.'s lap.

I seen 'em coming on up the walk, brisk, like they coming to sell something, and then they rung the bell, and J. T. declined to put on a shirt but instead disappeared into the bedroom where the other television is. I turned down the one in the living room; I figured I'd be rid of these two double quick and J. T. could come back out again.

Are you Gracie Mae Still? asked the old guy, when I opened the door and put my hand on the lock inside the screen.

And I don't need to buy a thing, said I.

What makes you think we're sellin'? he asks, in that hearty Southern way that makes my eyeballs ache.

Well, one way or another and they're inside the house and the first thing the young fellow does is raise the TV a couple of decibels. He's about five feet nine, sort of womanish looking, with real dark white skin and a red pouting mouth. His hair is black and curly and he looks like a Loosianna creole.

About one of your songs, says the deacon. He is maybe sixty, with white hair and beard, white silk shirt, black linen suit, black tie, and black shoes. His cold gray eyes look like they're sweating.

One of my songs?

Traynor here just *loves* your songs. Don't you, Traynor? He nudges Traynor with his elbow. Traynor blinks, says something I can't catch in a pitch I don't register.

The boy learned to sing and dance livin' round you people out in the country. Practically cut his teeth on you.

Traynor looks up at me and bites his thumbnail.

I laugh.

Well, one way or another they leave with my agreement that they can record one of my songs. The deacon writes me a check for five hundred dollars, the boy grunts his awareness of the transaction, and I am laughing all over myself by the time I rejoin J. T.

Just as I am snuggling down beside him though I hear the front door bell going off again.

Forgit his hat? asks J. T.

I hope not, I say.

The deacon stands there leaning on the door frame and once again I'm thinking of those sweaty-looking eyeballs of his. I wonder if sweat makes your eyeballs pink because his are sure pink. Pink and gray and it strikes me that nobody I'd care to know is behind them.

I forgot one little thing, he says pleasantly. I forgot to tell you Traynor and I would like to buy up all of those records you made of the song. I tell you we sure do love it.

Well, love it or not, I'm not so stupid as to let them do that without making 'em pay. So I says, Well, that's gonna cost you. Because, really, that song never did sell all that good, so I was glad they was going to buy it up. But on the other hand, them two listening to my song by themselves, and nobody else getting to hear me sing it, give me a pause.

Well, one way or another the deacon showed me where I would come out ahead on any deal he had proposed so far. Didn't I give you five hundred dollars? he asked. What white man—and don't even mention colored—would give you more? We buy up all your records of that particular song: first, you git royalties. Let me ask you, how much you sell that song for in the first place? Fifty dollars? A hundred, I say. And no royalties from it yet, right? Right. Well, when we buy up all of them records you gonna git royalties. And that's gonna make all them race record shops sit up and take notice of Gracie Mae Still. And they gonna push all them other records of yourn they got. And you no doubt will become one of the big name colored recording artists. And then we can offer you another five hundred dollars for letting us do all this for you. And by God you'll be sittin' pretty! You can go out and buy you the kind of outfit a star should have. Plenty sequins and yards of red satin.

I had done unlocked the screen when I saw I could get some more money out of him. Now I held it wide open while he squeezed through the opening between me and the door. He whipped out another piece of paper and I signed it.

He sort of trotted out to the car and slid in beside Traynor, whose head was back against the seat. They swung around in a u-turn in front of the house and then they was gone.

J. T. was putting his shirt on when I got back to the bedroom. Yankees beat the Orioles 10 – 6, he said. I believe I'll drive out to Paschal's pond and go fishing. Wanta go?

While I was putting on my pants J. T. was holding the two checks.

I'm real proud of a woman that can make cash money without leavin' home, he said. And I said *Umph*. Because we met on the road with me singing in first one little low-life jook after another, making ten dollars a night for myself if I was lucky, and sometimes bringin' home nothing but my life. And J. T. just loved them times. The way I was fast and flashy and always on the go from one town to another. He loved the way my singin' made the dirt farmers cry like babies and the womens shout Honey, hush! But that's mens. They loves any style to which you can get 'em accustomed.

1956

My little grandbaby called me one night on the phone: Little Mama, Little Mama, there's a white man on the television singing one of your songs! Turn on channel 5.

Lord, if it wasn't Traynor. Still looking half asleep from the neck up, but kind of awake in a nasty way from the waist down. He wasn't doing too bad with my song either, but it wasn't just the song the people in the audience was screeching and screaming over, it was that nasty little jerk he was doing from the waist down.

Well, Lord have mercy, I said, listening to him. If I'da closed my eyes, it could have been me. He had followed every turning of my voice, side streets, avenues, red lights, train crossings and all. It give me a chill.

Everywhere I went I heard Traynor singing my song, and all the little white girls just eating it up. I never had so many ponytails switched across my line of vision in my life. They was so *proud*. He was a *genius*.

Well, all that year I was trying to lose weight anyway and that and high blood pressure and sugar kept me pretty well occupied. Traynor had made a smash from a song of mine, I still had seven hundred dollars of the original one thousand dollars in the bank, and I felt if I could just bring my weight down, life would be sweet.

1957

I lost ten pounds in 1956. That's what I give myself for Christmas. And J. T. and me and the children and their friends and grandkids of all description had just finished dinner—over which I had put on nine and a half of my lost ten—when who should appear at the front door but Traynor. Little Mama, Little Mama! It's that white man who sings _____.
The children didn't call it my song anymore. Nobody did. It was funny how that happened. Traynor and the deacon had bought up all my records, true, but on his record he had put "written by Gracie Mae Still." But that was just another name on the label, like "produced by Apex Records."

On the TV he was inclined to dress like the deacon told him. But now he looked presentable.

Merry Christmas, said he.

And same to you, Son.

I don't know why I called him Son. Well, one way or another they're all our sons. The only requirement is that they be younger than us. But then again, Traynor seemed to be aging by the minute.

You looks tired, I said. Come on in and have a glass of Christmas cheer.

J. T. ain't never in his life been able to act decent to a white man he wasn't working for, but he poured Traynor a glass of bourbon and water, then he took all the children and grandkids and friends and whatnot out to the den.

After while I heard Traynor's voice singing the song, coming from the stereo console. It was just the kind of Christmas present my kids would consider cute.

I looked at Traynor, complicit. But he looked like it was the last thing in the world he wanted to hear. His head was pitched forward over his lap, his hands holding his glass and his elbows on his knees.

I done sung that song seem like a million times this year, he said. I sung it on the Grand Ole Opry, I sung it on the Ed Sullivan show. I sung it on Mike Douglas, I sung it at the Cotton Bowl, the Orange Bowl. I sung it at Festivals. I sung it at Fairs. I sung it overseas in Rome, Italy, and once in a submarine *underseas.* I've sung it and sung it, and I'm making forty thousand dollars a day offa it, and you know what, I don't have the faintest notion what that song means.

Whatchumean, what do it mean? It mean what it says. All I could think was: These suckers is making forty thousand a *day* offa my song and now they gonna come back and try to swindle me out of the original thousand.

It's just a song, I said. Cagey. When you fool around with a lot of no count mens you sing a bunch of 'em. I shrugged.

Oh, he said. Well. He started brightening up. I just come by to tell you I think you are a great singer.

He didn't blush, saying that. Just said it straight out.

And I brought you a little Christmas present too. Now you take this little box and you hold it until I drive off. Then you take it outside under that first streetlight back up the street aways in front of that greenhouse. Then you open the box and see . . . Well, just *see.*

What had come over this boy, I wondered, holding the box. I looked out the window in time to see another white man come up and get in the car with him and then two more cars full of white mens start out behind him. They was all in long black cars that looked like a funeral procession.

Little Mama, Little Mama, what it is? One of my grandkids come running up and started pulling at the box. It was wrapped in gay Christmas paper— the thick, rich kind that's hard to picture folks making just to throw away.

J. T. and the rest of the crowd followed me out of the house, up the street to the streetlight and in front of the greenhouse. Nothing was there but some- body's gold-grilled white Cadillac. Brandnew and most distracting. We got to looking at it so till I almost forgot the little box in my hand. While the others were busy making 'miration I carefully took off the paper and ribbon and folded them up and put them in my pants pocket. What should I see but a pair of genuine solid gold caddy keys.

Dangling the keys in front of everybody's nose, I unlocked the caddy, mo- tioned for J. T. to git in on the other side, and us didn't come back home for two days.

1960

Well, the boy was sure nuff famous by now. He was still a mite shy of twenty but already they was calling him the Emperor of Rock and Roll.

Then what should happen but the draft.

Well, says J. T. There goes all the Emperor of Rock and Roll business.

But even in the army the womens was on him like white on rice. We watched it on the News.

Dear Gracie Mae [he wrote from Germany],

How you? Fine I hope as this leaves me doing real well. Before I come in the army I was gaining a lot of weight and gitting jittery from making all them dumb movies. But now I exercise and eat right and get plenty of rest. I'm more awake than I been in ten years.

I wonder if you are writing any more songs?

Sincerely,
Traynor

I wrote him back:

Dear Son,

We is all fine in the Lord's good grace and hope this finds you the same. J. T. and me be out all times of the day and night in that car you give me—which you know you didn't have to do. Oh, and I do appreciate the mink and the new self-cleaning oven. But if you send anymore stuff to eat from Germany I'm going to have to open up a store in the neighborhood just to get rid of it. Really, we have more than enough of everything. The Lord is good to us and we don't know Want.

Glad to here you is well and gitting your right rest. There ain't nothing like exercising to help that along. J. T. and me work some part of every day that we don't go fishing in the garden.

Well, so long Soldier.

Sincerely,
Gracie Mae

He wrote:

Dear Gracie Mae,

I hope you and J. T. like that automatic power tiller I had one of the stores back home send you. I went through a mountain of catalogs looking for it—I wanted something that even a woman could use.

I've been thinking about writing some songs of my own but every time I finish one it don't seem to be about nothing I've actually lived myself. My agent keeps sending me other people's songs but they just sound mooney. I can hardly git through 'em without gagging.

Everybody still loves that song of yours. They ask me all the time what do I think it means, really. I mean, they want to know just what I want to know. Where out of your life did it come from?

Sincerely,
Traynor

1968

I didn't see the boy for seven years. No. Eight. Because just about everybody was dead when I saw him again. Malcolm X, King, the president and
his brother, and even J. T. J. T. died of a head cold. It just settled in his
head like a block of ice, he said, and nothing we did moved it until one day
he just leaned out the bed and died.

His good friend Horace helped me put him away, and then about a year
later Horace and me started going together. We was sitting out on the front
porch swing one summer night, dusk-dark, and I saw this great procession of
lights winding to a stop.

Holy Toledo! said Horace. (He's got a real sexy voice like Ray Charles.)
Look *at* it. He meant the long line of flashy cars and the white men in white
summer suits jumping out on the drivers' sides and standing at attention.
With wings they could pass for angels, with hoods they could be the Klan.

Traynor comes waddling up the walk.

And suddenly I know what it is he could pass for. An Arab like the ones
you see in storybooks. Plump and soft and with never a care about weight.
Because with so much money, who cares? Traynor is almost dressed like
someone from a storybook too. He has on, I swear, about ten necklaces. Two
sets of bracelets on his arms, at least one ring on every finger, and some kind
of shining buckles on his shoes, so that when he walks you get a quite a few
twinkling lights.

Gracie Mae, he says, coming up to give me a hug. J. T.

I explain that J. T. passed. That this is Horace.

Horace, he says, puzzled but polite, sort of rocking back on his heels,
Horace.

That's it for Horace. He goes in the house and don't come back.

Looks like you and me is gained a few, I say.

He laughs. The first time I ever heard him laugh. It don't sound much like
a laugh and I can't swear that it's better than no laugh a'tall.

He's gitting fat for sure, but he's still slim compared to me. I'll never see
three hundred pounds again and I've just about said (excuse me) fuck it. I got
to thinking about it one day an' I thought: aside from the fact that they say
it's unhealthy, my fat ain't never been no trouble. Mens always have loved
me. My kids ain't never complained. Plus they's fat. And fat like I is I looks
distinguished. You see me coming and know somebody's *there*.

Gracie Mae, he says, I've come with a personal invitation to you to my
house tomorrow for dinner. He laughed. What did it sound like? I couldn't
place it. See them men out there? he asked me. I'm sick and tired of eating
with them. They don't never have nothing to talk about. That's why I eat so
much. But if you come to dinner tomorrow we can talk about the old days.
You can tell me about that farm I bought you.

I sold it, I said.

You did?

Yeah, I said, I did. Just cause I said I liked to exercise by working in a
garden didn't mean I wanted five hundred acres! Anyhow, I'm a city girl now.
Raised in the country it's true. Dirt poor—the whole bit—but that's all behind me now.

Oh well, he said, I didn't mean to offend you.

We sat a few minutes listening to the crickets.

Then he said: You wrote that song while you was still on the farm, didn't you, or was it right after you left?

You had somebody spying on me? I asked.

You and Bessie Smith got into a fight over it once, he said.

You *is* been spying on me!

But I don't know what the fight was about, he said. Just like I don't know what happened to your second husband. Your first one died in the Texas electric chair. Did you know that? Your third one beat you up, stole your touring costumes and your car and retired with a chorine to Tuskegee. He laughed. He's still there.

I had been mad, but suddenly I calmed down. Traynor was talking very dreamily. It was dark but seems like I could tell his eyes weren't right. It was like some*thing* was sitting there talking to me but not necessarily with a person behind it.

You gave up on marrying and seem happier for it. He laughed again. I married but it never went like it was supposed to. I never could squeeze any of my own life either into it or out of it. It was like singing somebody else's record. I copied the way it was sposed to be *exactly* but I never had a clue what marriage meant.

I bought her a diamond ring big as your fist. I bought her clothes. I built her a mansion. But right away she didn't want the boys to stay there. Said they smoked up the bottom floor. Hell, there were *five* floors.

No need to grieve, I said. No need to. Plenty more where she come from.

He perked up. That's part of what that song means, ain't it? No need to grieve. Whatever it is, there's plenty more down the line.

I never really believed that way back when I wrote that song, I said. It was all bluffing then. The trick is to live long enough to put your young bluffs to use. Now if I was to sing that song today I'd tear it up. 'Cause I done lived long enough to know it's *true*. Them words could hold me up.

I ain't lived that long, he said.

Look like you on your way, I said. I don't know why, but the boy seemed to need some encouraging. And I don't know, seem like one way or another you talk to rich white folks and you end up reassuring *them*. But what the hell, by now I feel something for the boy. I wouldn't be in his bed all alone in the middle of the night for nothing. Couldn't be nothing worse than being famous the world over for something you don't even understand. That's what I tried to tell Bessie. She wanted that same song. Overheard me practicing it one day, said, with her hands on her hips: Gracie Mae, I'ma sing your song tonight. I *likes* it.

Your lips be too swole to sing, I said. She was mean and she was strong, but I trounced her.

Ain't you famous enough with your own stuff? I said. Leave mine alone. Later on, she thanked me. By then she was Miss Bessie Smith to the World, and I was still Miss Gracie Mae Nobody from Notasulga.

The next day all these limousines arrived to pick me up. Five cars and twelve bodyguards. Horace picked that morning to start painting the kitchen.

Don't paint the kitchen, fool, I said. The only reason that dumb boy of ours is going to show me his mansion is because he intends to present us with a new house.

What you gonna do with it? he asked me, standing there in his shirtsleeves stirring the paint.

Sell it. Give it to the children. Live in it on weekends. It don't matter what I do. He sure don't care.

Horace just stood there shaking his head. Mama you sure looks *good*, he says. Wake me up when you git back.

Fool, I say, and pat my wig in front of the mirror.

The boy's house is something else. First you come to this mountain, and then you commence to drive and drive up this road that's lined with magnolias. Do magnolias grow on mountains? I was wondering. And you come to lakes and you come to ponds and you come to deer and you come up on some sheep. And I figure these two is sposed to represent England and Wales. Or something out of Europe. And you just keep on coming to stuff. And it's all pretty. Only the man driving my car don't look at nothing but the road. Fool. And then *finally*, after all this time, you begin to go up the driveway. And there's more magnolias—only they're not in such good shape. It's sort of cool up this high and I don't think they're gonna make it. And then I see this building that looks like if it had a name it would be The Tara Hotel. Columns and steps and outdoor chandeliers and rocking chairs. Rocking chairs? Well, and there's the boy on the steps dressed in a dark green satin jacket like you see folks wearing on TV late at night, and he looks sort of like a fat Dracula with all that house rising behind him, and standing beside him there's this little white vision of loveliness that he introduces as his wife.

He's nervous when he introduces us and he says to her: This is Gracie Mae Still, I want you to know me. I mean . . . and she gives him a look that would fry meat.

Won't you come in, Gracie Mae, she says, and that's the last I see of her.

He fishes around for something to say or do and decides to escort me to the kitchen. We go through the entry and the parlor and the breakfast room and the dining room and the servants' passage and finally get there. The first thing I notice is that, altogether, there are five stoves. He looks about to introduce me to one.

Wait a minute, I say. Kitchens don't do nothing for me. Let's go sit on the front porch.

Well, we hike back and we sit in the rocking chairs rocking until dinner.

Gracie Mae, he says down the table, taking a piece of fried chicken from the woman standing over him, I got a little surprise for you.

It's a house, ain't it? I ask, spearing a chitlin.

You're getting *spoiled*, he says. And the way he says *spoiled* sounds funny. He slurs it. It sounds like his tongue is too thick for his mouth. Just that quick he's finished the chicken and is now eating chitlins *and* a pork chop. *Me* spoiled, I'm thinking.

I already got a house. Horace is right this minute painting the kitchen. I bought that house. My kids feel comfortable in that house.

But this one I bought you is just like mine. Only a little smaller.

I still don't need no house. And anyway who would clean it?

He looks surprised.

Really, I think, some peoples advance *so* slowly.

I hadn't thought of that. But what the hell, I'll get you somebody to live in.

I don't want other folks living 'round me. Makes me nervous.

You *don't?* It *do?*

What I want to wake up and see folks I don't even know for?

He just sits there downtable staring at me. Some of that feeling is in the song, ain't it? Not the words, the *feeling*. What I want to wake up and see folks I don't even know for? But I see twenty folks a day I don't even know, including my wife.

This food wouldn't be bad to wake up to though, I said. The boy had found the genius of corn bread.

He looked at me real hard. He laughed. Short. They want what you got but they don't want you. They want what I got only it ain't mine. That's what makes 'em so hungry for me when I sing. They getting the flavor of something but they ain't getting the thing itself. They like a pack of hound dogs trying to gobble up a scent.

You talking 'bout your fans?

Right. Right. He says.

Don't worry 'bout your fans, I say. They don't know their asses from a hole in the ground. I doubt there's a honest one in the bunch.

That's the point. Dammit, that's the point! He hits the table with his fist. It's so solid it don't even quiver. You need a honest audience! You can't have folks that's just gonna lie right back to you.

Yeah, I say, it was small compared to yours, but I had one. It would have been worth my life to try to sing 'em somebody else's stuff that I didn't know nothing about.

He must have pressed a buzzer under the table. One of his flunkies zombies up.

Git Johnny Carson, he says.

On the phone? asks the zombie.

On the phone, says Traynor, what you think I mean, git him offa the front porch? Move your ass.

So two weeks later we's on the Johnny Carson show.

Traynor is all corseted down nice and looks a little bit fat but mostly good. And all the women that grew up on him and my song squeal and squeal. Traynor says: The lady who wrote my first hit record is here with us tonight, and she's agreed to sing it for all of us, just like she sung it forty-five years ago. Ladies and Gentlemen, the great Gracie Mae Still!

Well, I had tried to lose a couple of pounds my own self, but failing that I had me a very big dress made. So I sort of rolls over next to Traynor, who is dwarfted by me, so that when he puts his arm around back of me to try to hug me it looks funny to the audience and they laugh.

I can see this pisses him off. But I smile out there at 'em. Imagine squealing for twenty years and not knowing why you're squealing? No more sense of endings and beginnings than hogs.

It don't matter, Son, I say. Don't fret none over me.

I commence to sing. And I sound—wonderful. Being able to sing good ain't all about having a good singing voice a'tall. A good singing voice helps. But when you come up in the Hard Shell Baptist church like I did you understand early that the fellow that sings is the singer. Them that waits for programs and arrangements and letters from home is just good voices occupying body space.

So there I am singing my own song, my own way. And I give it all I got and enjoy every minute of it. When I finish Traynor is standing up clapping and clapping and beaming at first me and then the audience like I'm his mama for true. The audience claps politely for about two seconds.

Traynor looks disgusted.

He comes over and tries to hug me again. The audience laughs.

Johnny Carson looks at us like we both weird.

Traynor is mad as hell. He's supposed to sing something called a love ballad. But instead he takes the mike, turns to me and says: Now see if my imitation still holds up. He goes into the same song, *our song,* I think, looking out at his flaky audience. And he sings it just the way he always did. My voice, my tone, my inflection, everything. But he forgets a couple of lines. Even before he's finished the matronly squeals begin.

He sits down next to me looking whipped.

It don't matter, Son, I say, patting his hand. You don't even know those people. Try to make the people you know happy.

Is that in the song? he asks.

Maybe. I say.

1977

For a few years I hear from him, then nothing. But trying to lose weight takes all the attention I got to spare. I finally faced up to the fact that my fat is the hurt I don't admit, not even to myself, and that I been trying to bury it from the day I was born. But also when you git real old, to tell the truth, it ain't as pleasant. It gits lumpy and slack. Yuck. So one day I said to Horace, I'ma git this shit offa me.

And he fell in with the program like he always try to do and Lord such a procession of salads and cottage cheese and fruit juice!

One night I dreamed Traynor had split up with his fifteenth wife. He said: *You meet 'em for no reason. You date 'em for no reason. You marry 'em for no reason. I do it all but I swear it's just like somebody else doing it. I feel like I can't remember Life.*

The boy's in trouble, I said to Horace.

You've always said that, he said.

I have?

Yeah. You always said he looked asleep. You can't sleep through life if you wants to live it.

You not such a fool after all, I said, pushing myself up with my cane and hobbling over to where he was. Let me sit down on your lap, I said, while this salad I ate takes effect.

In the morning we heard Traynor was dead. Some said fat, some said heart, some said alcohol, some said drugs. One of the children called from

Detroit. Them dumb fans of his is on a crying rampage, she said. You just ought to turn on the t.v.

But I didn't want to see 'em. They was crying and crying and didn't even know what they was crying for. One day this is going to be a pitiful country, I thought.

Suggestions for Discussion

1. What parallels with the career of Elvis Presley does Walker suggest?

2. Describe the relationship between Traynor and Gracie Mae Still.

3. Characterize Gracie Mae.

4. Why does Traynor shower Gracie Mae with gifts?

5. How does Gracie Mae respond to Traynor's death?

Suggestions for Writing

1. Discuss loneliness as a theme in "Nineteen Fifty-five."

2. Discuss Walker's use of dialect to add color and develop characterization.

The Cultural Tradition: Art and Society

◆◆◆

I, too, dislike it: there are things that are important beyond
   all this fiddle,
  Reading it, however, with a perfect contempt for it, one
   discovers in
  it after all, a place for the genuine.
     —Marianne Moore, "Poetry"

The things of the poet are done to a man alone
As the things of love are done—or of death when he hears the
Step withdraw on the stair and the clock tick only.
     —Archibald MacLeish, "Invocation to the Social Muse"

Works of art, in my opinion, are the only objects in the material universe to possess internal order, and that is why,
though I don't believe that only art matters, I do believe in
Art for Art's sake.
     —E. M. Forster, "Art for Art's Sake"

Perhaps it will turn out that you are called to be an artist.
Then take that destiny upon yourself and bear it, its burdens and its greatness, without ever asking what recompense might come from outside.
     —Rainer Maria Rilke, "Letter to a Young Poet," 1903

But perhaps the voice of a great poet, the voice of the
Bible, the eternal voice of humanity that speaks clearly to
us from art, would give you the power of true sight and
hearing.
     —Hermann Hesse, "To a Cabinet Minister, August 1917"

Why do the arts in general lead such a precarious existence in America? Why is the audience for good music so limited, in spite of radio and records and all the other marvels of mass communication?

—**Christopher Lasch,** "The Degradation of Work and the Apotheosis of Art"

Letters and Personal Reminiscence

◆◆◆

Rainer Maria Rilke
Letter to a Young Poet
Translated by M. D. Herter Norton

Rainer Maria Rilke (1875–1926) was an Austrian writer born in Prague. He had an unhappy childhood, spent five years in a military academy, and attended the Universities of Prague, Munich, and Berlin. At the turn of the century he traveled to Russia where he met Tolstoi, who influenced him profoundly. For a time he was secretary to the sculptor Rodin. His early works reveal a deep association with mysticism and aestheticism. In *The Duino Elegies* (1930) and *Sonnets to Orpheus* (1936), both profound influences on all modern poetry, he saw the poet as mediator between God and man. In the following letter to a young poet, Rilke exhorts him to find his own voice and to base his writing on his own intimate experiences.

Paris, February 17th, 1903

My Dear Sir,

Your letter only reached me a few days ago. I want to thank you for its great and kind confidence. I can hardly do more. I cannot go into the nature of your verses; for all critical intention is too far from me. With nothing can one touch a work of art so little as with critical words: they always come down to more or less lucky misunderstandings. Things are not all so comprehensible and expressible as one would mostly have us believe; most events are inexpressible, take place in a realm which no word has ever entered, and more inexpressible than all else are works of art, mysterious existences, the life of which, while ours passes away, endures.

533

After these prefatory remarks, let me only tell you further that your verses have no individual style, although they do show a quiet and hidden incipience of the personal. I feel this most clearly in the last poem "My Soul." There something of your own wants to come through to expression. And in the lovely poem "To Leopardi" there does perhaps grow up a sort of kinship with that great solitary man. Nevertheless the poems are not yet anything on their own account, nothing independent, even the last and the one to Leopardi. Your kind letter, which accompanied them, does not fail to make clear to me various shortcomings which I felt in reading your verses without at the time being able particularly to name them.

You ask whether your verses are good. You ask me. You have asked others before. You send them to magazines. You compare them with other poems, and you are disturbed when certain editors reject your efforts. Now (since you have allowed me to advise you) I beg you to give up all that. You are looking outward, and that above all you should not now do. Nobody can counsel and help you, nobody. There is only one single way. Go into yourself. Investigate the reason that bids you write; find out whether it is spreading out its roots in the deepest places of your heart, acknowledge to yourself whether you would have to die if it were denied you to write. This above all: ask yourself in the stillest hour of your night: *must* I write? Delve into yourself for a deep answer. And if this should be affirmative, if you may meet this earnest question with a strong and simple "I must," then build your life according to this necessity; your life even into its most indifferent and slightest hour must be a sign of this urge and a testimony to it. Then draw near to Nature. Then try, as a first human being, to say what you see and experience and love and lose. Do not write love-poems; avoid at first those forms that are too hackneyed and commonplace: they are the most difficult, for it takes a great, fully matured power to give something of your own where good and even excellent traditions come to mind in quantity. Therefore save yourself from these general themes and seek those which your own everyday life offers you; describe your sorrows and desires, passing thoughts and the belief in some sort of beauty—describe all these with loving, quiet, humble sincerity and use, to express yourself, the things in your environment, the pictures from your dreams, and the subjects of your memory. If your daily life seems poor, do not blame it; blame yourself, tell yourself that you are not poet enough to call forth its riches; for to the creator there is no poverty and no poor indifferent place. And even if you were in some prison the walls of which let none of the sounds of the world come to your senses—would you not then still have your childhood, that precious, kingly possession, that treasure-house of memories? Turn your attention thither. Try to bring up the sunken sensations of that far past; your personality will grow more firm, your solitude will widen and will become a dusky dwelling by which the noise of others passes far away.—And if out of this turning inward, out of this sinking into your own world verses come, then it will not occur to you to ask any one whether they are good verses. Nor will you try to interest magazines in your poems: for you will see in them your fond natural possession, a fragment and a voice of your life. A work of art is good if it has sprung from necessity. In this nature of its origin lies its judgment: there is no other. Therefore, my dear sir, I have known no advice for you save this: to go into yourself and test the deeps in which your life takes rise; at its source you will find the answer to the question whether you *must* create. Accept it, just as it sounds, without trying to interpret it. Perhaps it will turn out that you are called to be an artist. Then take that destiny upon yourself and bear it, its burden and its greatness, without ever asking what recompense might come from outside. For the creator must be a world for himself and find everything in himself and in Nature with whom he has allied himself.

But perhaps after this descent into yourself and into your inner solitude you will have to give up becoming a poet (it is enough, as I have said, to feel that one could live without writing: then one should not be allowed to do it at all). But even then this inward searching which I ask of you will not have been in vain. Your life will in any case find its own ways thence, and that they may be good, rich and wide I wish you more than I can say.

What more shall I say to you? Everything seems to me to have its just emphasis; and after all I do only want to advise you to keep growing quietly and seriously throughout your development; you cannot disturb it more rudely than by looking outward and expecting from outside replies to questions that only your inmost feeling in your quietest hours can perhaps answer.

It was a pleasure to me to find in your letter the name of Professor Horaček; I keep for that lovable and learned man a great veneration and a gratitude that endures through the years. Will you, please, tell him how I feel; it is very good of him still to think of me, and I know how to appreciate it.

The verses which you kindly entrusted to me I am returning at the same time. And I thank you once more for your great and sincere confidence, of which I have tried, through this honest answer given to the best of my knowledge, to make myself a little worthier than, as a stranger, I really am.

Yours faithfully and with all sympathy:

RAINER MARIA RILKE

Suggestions for Discussion

1. What attitude toward art does Rilke express in the first paragraph of his letter?

2. What does Rilke seem to mean in the second paragraph by the term *individual style?* Is his use of the term a kind of criticism?

3. In the third paragraph Rilke analyzes the feelings that govern the life of a poet. How would you summarize his advice?

4. Explain Rilke's statement, "A work of art is good if it has sprung from necessity."

5. Rilke urges the young poet to "test the deeps in which your life takes rise." Is this advice pertinent to other aspects of life than the writing of poetry?

Suggestion for Writing

Read some of Rilke's poems in *Sonnets to Orpheus* or *Duino Elegies*. Write a paper in which you test some of his poems by the advice in this letter. Try to explain why Rilke's poems do have an individual voice.

Hermann Hesse

To a Cabinet Minister, August 1917

Translated by Ralph Manhelm

Hermann Hesse (1877–1962) received the Nobel Prize for Literature in 1946. He is ranked with Thomas Mann as one of the giants of modern German fiction. His best known works are *Magister Ludi* (1949), *Demian* (1919), *Siddhartha* (1923), and *Steppenwolf* (1927). The last three have achieved the status of cult novels for young readers throughout the world. This letter to a German cabinet minister, written during the First World War, states Hesse's belief in the power of art and thought to change people's lives, even in time of war.

This evening after a hard day's work I asked my wife to play me a Beethoven sonata. With its angelic voices the music recalled me from bustle and worry to the real world, to the one reality which we possess, which gives us joy and torment, the reality in which and for which we live.

Afterwards I read a few lines in the book containing the Sermon on the Mount and the sublime, age-old, and fundamental words: "Thou shalt not kill!"

But I found no peace, I could neither go to bed nor continue reading. I was filled with anxiety and unrest, and suddenly, Herr Minister, as I was searching my mind for their cause, I remembered a few sentences from one of your speeches that I read a few days ago.

Your speech was well constructed; otherwise, it was not particularly original, significant, or provocative. Reduced to the essentials, it said roughly what government officials have been saying in their speeches for a long time: that, generally speaking, "we" long for nothing so fervently as peace, as a new understanding among nations and fruitful collaboration in building the future, that we wish neither to enrich ourselves nor to satisfy homicidal lusts—but that the "time for negotiations" is not yet at hand and that for the present there is therefore no alternative but to go on bravely waging war. Just about every minister of any of the belligerent nations might have made such a speech, and probably will tomorrow or the day after.

If tonight your speech keeps me awake, although I have read many similar speeches with the same dreary conclusion and slept soundly afterwards, the fault, as I am now certain, lies with Beethoven's sonata and with that ancient book in which I afterwards read, that book which contains the wonderful commandments of Mount Sinai and the luminous words of the Savior.

Beethoven's music and the words of the Bible told me exactly the same thing; they were water from the same spring, the only spring from which man derives good. And then suddenly, Herr Minister, it came to me that your speech and the speeches of your governing colleagues in both camps do not flow from that spring, that they lack what can make human words important and valuable. They lack love, they lack humanity.

Your speech shows a profound feeling of concern and responsibility for your people, its army, and its honor. But it shows no feeling for mankind.

And, to put it bluntly, it implies hundreds of thousands more human sacrifices.

Perhaps you will call my reference to Beethoven sentimentality. I imagine, though, that you feel a certain respect for the Commandments and for the sayings of Jesus—at least in public. But if you believe in a single one of the ideals for which you are waging war, the freedom of nations, freedom of the seas, social progress, or the rights of small countries—if you truly, in your heart of hearts, believe in a single one of these generous ideals, you will have to recognize on rereading your speech that it does not serve that ideal or any other. It is not the expression and product of a faith, of any awareness of a human need, but, alas, the expression and product of a dilemma. An understandable dilemma, to be sure, for what could be more difficult at the present time than to acknowledge a certain disappointment with the course of the war and to start looking for the shortest way to peace?

But such a dilemma, even if it is shared by ten governments, cannot endure forever. Dilemmas are solved by necessities. One day it will become necessary for you and your enemy colleagues to face up to your dilemma and make decisions that will put an end to it.

The belligerents of both camps have long been disappointed with the course of the war. Regardless of who has won this battle or that battle, regardless of how much territory or how many prisoners have been taken or lost, the result has not been what one expects in a war. There has been no solution, no decision—and none is in sight.

You made your speech in order to hide this great dilemma from yourself and your people, in order to postpone vital decisions (which always call for sacrifices)—and other government officials make their speeches for the same reason. Which is understandable. It is easier for a revolutionary or even for a writer to see the human factor in a political situation and draw the proper inferences than for a responsible statesman. It is easier for one of us because he is under no obligation to feel personally responsible for the deep gloom that comes over a nation when it sees that it has not achieved its war aim and that many thousands of human lives and billions in wealth may well have been sacrificed in vain.

But that is not the only reason why it is harder for you to recognize the dilemma and make decisions that will put an end to the war. Another reason is that you hear too little music and read the Bible and the great authors too little.

You smile. Or perhaps you will say that you as a private citizen feel very close to Beethoven and to all that is noble and beautiful. And maybe you do. But my heartfelt wish is that one of these days, chancing to hear a piece of sublime music, you should suddenly recapture an awareness of those voices that well from a sacred spring. I wish that one of these days in a quiet moment you would read a parable of Jesus, a line of Goethe, or a saying of Lao-tzu.

That moment might be infinitely important to the world. You might find inner liberation. Your eyes and ears might suddenly be opened. For many years, Herr Minister, your eyes and ears have been attuned to theoretical aims rather than reality; they have long been accustomed—necessarily so!—to close themselves to much of what constitutes reality, to disregard it, to deny its existence. Do you know what I mean? Yes, you know. But perhaps the voice of a great poet, the voice of the Bible, the eternal voice of humanity that speaks clearly to us from art, would give you the power of true sight and hearing. What things you would see and hear! Nothing more about the labor shortage and the price of coal, nothing more about tonnages and alliances, loans, troop levies, and all the rest of what you have hitherto regarded as the sole reality. Instead, you would see the earth, our patient old earth, so littered with the dead and dying, so ravaged and shattered, so charred and desecrated. You would see soldiers lying for days in no-man's-land, unable with their mutilated hands to shoo the flies from their mortal wounds. You would hear the voices of the wounded, the screams of the mad, the accusing plaints of mothers and fathers, sweethearts and sisters, the people's cry of hunger.

If your ears should be opened once more to all these things that you have sedulously avoided hearing for months and years, then perhaps you would reexamine your aims, your ideals and theories, with a new mind and attempt to weigh their true worth against the misery of a single month, a single day, of war.

Oh, if this hour of music, this return to true reality, could somehow come your way! You would hear the voice of mankind, you would shut yourself up in your room and weep. And next day you would go out and do your duty toward mankind. You would sacrifice a few millions or billions in money, a trifling bit of prestige, and a thousand other things (all the things for which you are now prolonging the war), and, if need be, your minister's portfolio with them, and you would do what mankind, in untold fear and torment, is hoping and praying you will do. You would be the first among governing statesmen to condemn this wretched war, the first to tell his fellows what all feel secretly even now: that six months or even one month of war costs more than what anything it can achieve is worth.

If that were to happen, Herr Minister, your name would never be forgotten, your deed would stand higher in the eyes of mankind than the deeds of all those who have ever waged victorious wars.

Suggestions for Discussion

1. How does Hesse contrast Beethoven's music and Christ's Sermon on the Mount with the cabinet minister's speech?

2. How does this letter, written in 1917, speak to the world situation seventy years later?

3. What effect does Hesse believe the words of Christ or Goethe or Lao-tzu would have on the cabinet minister?

4. Discuss the tone of the letter writer. Is it respectful? How does he hope to persuade his reader?

Suggestion for Writing

The employment of the open letter as a vehicle of expressing opinion is an old custom. You may wish to write a paper comparing Hesse's letter with other statements in letter form by famous people. Or you may wish to write a paper analyzing the letters in your local newspaper that are written to express an opinion. How often are such letters carefully and calmly reasoned? What is the tone of most of these letters?

John Gardner
Learning from Disney and Dickens

John Champlin Gardner, Jr. (1933–1982) was a medieval and classical scholar, a professor of English Literature, head of the Creative Writing Program at the State University of New York at Binghamton, and author of novels, short stories, critical works, translations from Old and Middle English, and even opera librettos. In *On Moral Fiction* (1978), he calls upon the artist to act as a moral agent, saying, "I agree with Tolstoy. . . . The highest purpose of art is to make people good by choice." This essay from the *New York Times,* which he titled "Cartoons," is part of a book of essays by various writers, *In Praise of What Persists,* edited by Stephen Berg. Gardner wrote this memoir of his development as a writer shortly before his death in a motorcycle accident.

Trying to figure out the chief influences on my work as a writer turns out to be mainly a problem of deciding what not to include. I grew up in a family where literary influence was everywhere, including under the bridge on our dirt road, where I kept my comic books. My father is a memorizer of poetry and scripture, a magnificent performer in the old reciter tradition. (I once did a reading in Rochester, N.Y., near Batavia, where I grew up. After I'd finished several people remarked that I was a wonderful reader—"though not quite up to your father, of course.") He did readings of everything from Edgar Guest to Shakespeare and The Book of Job at the monthly Grange meetings, in schools, churches, hospitals. While he milked the cows, my mother (who'd once been his high school English teacher) would read Shakespeare's plays aloud to him from her three-legged stool behind the gutter, and he would take, yelling from the cow's flank, whatever part he'd decided on that night— Macbeth, King Lear, Hamlet, and so on.

My mother was a well-known performer too, except that she mainly sang. She had one of those honeysweet Welsh soprano voices and sang everything from anthems to the spirituals she'd learned from an old black woman who took care of her during her childhood in Missouri. Often my mother performed in blackface, with a red bandana, a practice that may sound distasteful unless you understand that she wasn't kidding; she was authentic, flatting, quarter-toning, belting it out: She was amazing. They frequently worked together, my mother and father, and were known all over western New York.

Sometimes they were in plays—my mother often directed—and wherever they went, riding around in the beat-up farm truck or just sitting in the kitchen, they sang, always in harmony, like crazy people.

The house was full of books, very few of them books that would now be thought fashionable aside from the Shakespeare and Dickens. My parents read aloud a lot—the narrative poems of Scott, miles of Longfellow, spooky stories by Edgar Allan Poe, the poems of Tennyson and Browning, also rather goofy religious writers (I loved them; what did I know?) like Lloyd C. Douglas and some woman whose name escapes me now, who wrote Jesus-filled love stories with titles like "A Patch of Blue." My grandmother, who was bedridden through much of my childhood, was especially fond of this religious lady, and one of my more pleasant chores was to read her these tender little novels. The climax was always the moment the boy shyly touched the girl's hand. I've never found anything more sexually arousing than that Jesus-filled, long-delayed touch. I mean it was smut, it nearly made me a pervert, and not a court in the land could nail her.

My favorite authors, at least when I was between the ages of 8 and 18, were in what might be described as the nonrealistic tradition: God, Dickens, and Disney. One of my less pleasant chores when I was young was to read the Bible from one end to the other. Reading the Bible straight through is at least 70 percent discipline, like learning Latin. But the good parts are, of course, simply amazing. God is an extremely uneven writer, but when He's good, nobody can touch him. I learned to find the good parts easily (some very sexy stuff here too), and both the poetry and the storytelling had a powerful effect on what I think good fiction ought to be!

Dickens I ran into when I was in my early teens, when I began to find the Hardy boys tiresome and unconvincing. I never liked realism much, but the irrealism of two boys having long conversations while riding on motorcycles (I was big on motorcycles myself) was more than I could put up with. Running across Dickens was like finding a secret door. I read book after book, and when I'd finished the last one I remember feeling a kind of horror, as if suddenly the color had gone out of the world; then luckily I discovered that when you went back to one of the ones you had read first, you couldn't remember half of it, you could read it again and find it even better, so life wasn't quite as disappointing as for a moment I'd thought.

For me at that time Disney and Dickens were practically indistinguishable. Both created wonderful cartoon images, told stories as direct as fairy tales, knew the value of broad comedy spiced up with a little weeping. I have since learned that Dickens is occasionally profound, as Disney never deigns to be; but that was never why I valued Dickens or have, now, a bust of him in my study to keep me honest. Unconsciously—without ever hearing the term, in fact—I learned about symbolism from Dickens and Disney, with the result that I would never learn to appreciate, as I suppose one should, those realistic writers who give you life data without resonance, things merely as they are. Dickens's symbolism may never be very deep—the disguised witches and fairy princesses, Uriah Heep and his mother flapping around like buzzards, or all the self-conscious folderol of "A Tale of Two Cities"—but in my experience, anyway, it spoils you forever for books that never go *oo-boom*.

There were other important influences during this period of my life, probably the most important of which was opera. The Eastman School of Music presented operas fairly often (and of course played host to traveling opera companies, including the Met). From Dickens and Disney (not to mention God) it took no adjustment to become opera-addicted. The plots of most operas (not all, heaven knows) are gloriously simple-minded or, to put it more favorably, elemental; the stage is nothing if not a grand cartoon (Wagner's mountainscapes and gnomes, Mozart's crazies, Humperdinck's angels, the weirdness and clowning that show up everywhere from "La Bohème" to "The Tales of Hoffmann"). I was by this time playing French horn, and of course I'd always been around singing. So I got hooked at once—hence my special fondness now for writing librettos.

By the time I reached college my taste was, I'm afraid, hopelessly set. Predictably I was ravished by Melville—all those splendid cartoon images, for instance Ahab and the Chinese coolies he's kept hidden until the first time he needs to lower away after whale—and of course by Milton, who must be considered one of the all-time great cartoonists, as when Satan

> Puts on swift wings, and toward the Gates of Hell
> Explores his solitary flight; sometimes
> He scours the right hand coast, sometimes the left,
> Now shaves with level wing the Deep, then soars
> Up the fiery concave touring high.

(It's true, Milton's a little boring now and then, and Milton teachers often don't properly value the cartoonist in him and want to know things about "Paradise Lost" that only some kind of crazy could get seriously interested in; but never mind.) I'm afraid the embarrassing truth is that the whole literary tradition opened out, for me, from Disney and his kind. I got caught up in the mighty cartoons of Homer and Dante, (much later Virgil and Apollonius), the less realistic 18th-and 19th-century novelists (Fielding, Smollett, Collins, and the rest), the glorious mad Russians (Tolstoy, Dostoyevsky, Bely), and those kinds of poets who fill one's head with strange, intense visions, like Blake, Coleridge, and Keats.

For me the whole world of literature was at this time one of grand cartoons. I thought of myself mainly as a chemistry major and took courses in English just for fun. I guess I thought literature was unserious, like going to the movies or playing in a dance band, even an orchestra. It did not seem to me that one ought to spend one's life on mere pleasure, like a butterfly or cricket. Beethoven, Shakespeare, Richard Strauss, Conan Doyle might be a delight, but to fritter away one's life in the arts seemed, well, not quite honest. Then I came across the New Criticism.

At the first college I went to (for two years) I'd read nearly all of the Modern Library, partly for fun, partly because I felt ignorant around my fellow students, people who could talk with seeming wisdom about Camus and Proust, Nietzsche and Plato—I soon discovered they hadn't really read what they claimed to have read, they'd just come from the right part of town—but I'd never in any serious sense "studied" literature. (I took a couple of courses where one was examined on what Carlyle and Cardinal Newman said, without much emphasis on why or to whom). But when I moved to Washington University in St. Louis I got a whole new vision of what literature was for—that is, the vision of the New Criticism. Like the fanatic I've always been, I fell to analyzing fiction, digging out symbols and structural subtleties, learning about "levels" and so on.

I don't say this was a foolish activity—in fact I think the New Critics were basically right: It's much more interesting and rewarding to talk about how literature "works" than to read biographies of the writer, which is mainly what the New Criticism replaced. Working with the famous books by Cleanth Brooks and Robert Penn Warren, I began to love things in fiction and poetry that I'd never before noticed, things like meaning and design, and, like all my generation, I made the great discovery that literature is worthwhile, not a thing to be scorned by serious puritans but a thing to be embraced and turned cunningly to advantage. I learned that literature is Good for you, and that writers who are not deeply philosophical should be scorned. I began to read realists—two of whom, Jane Austen and James Joyce, I actually liked— and I began to write "serious" fiction; that is, instead of writing pleasant jingles or stories I desperately hoped would be published in *The Saturday Evening Post* or maybe *Manhunt*, I began shyly eyeing *The Kenyon Review*. With a sigh of relief (though I'd enjoyed them, in a way) I quit math and science and signed up, instead, for courses in philosophy and sociology and psychology, which I knew would make me a better person and perhaps a famous writer so brilliant and difficult that to get through my books you would need a teacher.

This period lasted longer than I care to admit. On the basis of my earnestness and a more or less astonishing misreading of Nietzsche (I was convinced that he was saying that only fiction can be truly philosophical) I won a Woodrow Wilson Fellowship to the University of Iowa, where I meant to study in the famous Writers' Workshop but soon ended up taking medieval language and literature, the literature God had been nudging me toward all along: "Beowulf," "The Divine Comedy," the Gawain poet, and Chaucer. The scales fell from my eyes. My New Critical compulsion to figure out exactly how everything works, how every nuance plays against every other, had suddenly an immense field to plow. I continued to read and think about other literature—I went through a Thomas Mann phase, a Henry James phase, and so on—but I found myself spending more and more time trying to figure out medieval works.

It seems to me that when I began working on medieval literature, in the late 50's and early 60's, scholars knew very little about even the greatest works in that literature. No one had really figured out the structure of the works of the Gawain poet, not to mention "Beowulf" or the poetry of Chaucer. People were still arguing about whether or not "Beowulf" is a Christian poem; people were still trying to shuffle around "The Canterbury Tales." The usual New Critical method, which is to stare and stare at the work until it becomes clear, was useless on this material, because again and again you found yourself staring at something that felt like a symbol or an allusion, or felt that maybe it ought to be some kind of joke but you couldn't see the humor. To figure out the poem you had to figure out the world it came from—read the books the poets knew, try to understand esthetic principles abandoned and forgotten centuries ago. One had no choice but to become a sort of scholar.

Literary detective work is always fun, for a certain kind of mind at least, but the work I did on medieval literature, then on later classical literature,

Paul Gauguin
Self-Portrait (1889)

National Gallery of Art, Washington; Chester Dale Collection.

Suggestions for Discussion

1. Why does the painting appear to be divided in half? What are the symbols in each? How are the symbols interrelated? With which half does the painter seem to be more involved? What is the expression on his face?

(Continued on back)

2. What do the symbols in the painting tell you about Gauguin's sense of self? Describe the multiple symbols. What is the meaning of the position of the halo? Compare it with halos in other paintings.

3. What evidence is there that the portrait reflects an introspective, self-questioning person? How would you describe the features of the self-portrait?

4. Red and green are complementary colors. What is suggested to you by the fact that one apple is green and the other red and green?

5. What is Gauguin looking at? What is the relationship between the flowers and the snake? What does the direction of his glance suggest about his sense of self?

Suggestions for Writing

1. Assume that you know nothing about Gauguin's life and art. Write an essay in which you discuss his sense of self, his age, his health, and his values based on clues from the self-portrait.

2. Given what you know about Gauguin's life, write an essay in which you discuss what he reveals about himself in this painting.

Mary Cassatt
The Boating Party (1893–1894)

National Gallery of Art, Washington; Chester Dale Collection.

Suggestions for Discussion

1. The mother and child are the focal point of the painting. How does Cassatt achieve this through light and color, through the lines of the boat, the oar, and the sail? Why are these lines cut off by the border of the painting?

2. What is the relationship of the three figures? What suggests that the rower may be the father of the child? What is the symbol of his function? How do the figures contrast in color, shape, and feeling?

3. Compare the use of dark and light colors in the painting.

4. What gives a feeling of solidity and safey to the scene? Note the sail, the sea, the shore, the boat.

(Continued on back)

Suggestions for Writing

1. Write an essay in which you compare the feeling of this scene with that of Renoir's *The Luncheon of the Boating Party*. Consider the stillness of one, the liveliness of the other. What different kinds of relationships are suggested in each painting?

2. Examine the painting by Georges Seurat, *Sunday Afternoon on the Island of la Grande Jatte* (the source of the musical comedy *Sunday in the Park with George*). Compare and contrast the scene with Cassatt's.

3. Write a narrative about the people. What do you think happened before, during, and after the boating party?

Pierre Auguste Renoir

The Luncheon of the Boating Party (1881)

The Phillips Collection, Washington, D. C.

Suggestions for Discussion

1. It is Sunday (or a holiday). A group has left the city to row on the Seine and to dine on the terrace of a riverside cafe. What is the general ambiance of the painting? Consider the season and the weather, the dress of the people, their age, their class, their looks. What are they doing? What are their feelings?

2. In the central foreground of this crowded scene, there is a table and a man's back that appears to connect the two tables. How do the condition and contents of the table explain the moment (the last course of a French meal is fruit) and the state of the diners?

3. How many groups can you see? How do they differ in looks or activity? What is the relationship of the people in the painting? Does not the table also serve to call attention to the foreground figures? Are they similar to the other diners?

4. Is the euphoria described here real? complete? permanent?

(Continued on back)

Suggestions for Writing

1. What do young people do today in their leisure time? How similar or different might such a party be today? Write an essay in which you compare this scene with one in which you have participated.

2. Compare and contrast this painting with Georges Seurat's *Sunday Afternoon on the Island of La Grande Jatte* (not in this text). Consider the mood of each, the freedom and conviviality of one with the formality of the other.

3. Compare and contrast this painting with the one by Mary Cassatt in this text. Consider the intimacy of one with the comaraderie of the other, the depth of feeling of one with the lightness of the other.

Fernand Léger
La Grande Parade (1954)

Collection, Solomon R. Guggenheim Museum, New York.

Suggestions for Discussion

1. What gives a sense of unity to the painting? Consider the use of color.

2. Describe the figures and objects in the painting. How are they portrayed?

3. How does Legér project to the viewer the joy in the circus that he recalls? Consider the figures and the color and the relationship between the two.

4. How does the painting reveal Legér's interest in architecture?

(Continued on back)

Suggestions for Writing

1. Legér says of his art, "I have wanted to mark a return to simplicity by direct art without subtlety, which everyone can understand." How does this remark explain *La Grande Parade?* Write an essay in which you also relate this quotation to the theme of popular culture.

2. Legér's paintings illustrate the art movements of cubism and futurism. Look up these movements, and write a paper explaining how this painting illustrates these theories of art.

Robert-Victor-Félix Delaunay
Red Eiffel Tower (1911–1912)

Collection, Solomon R. Guggenheim Museum, New York. Photo: David Heald

Suggestions for Discussion

1. How does this painting express Delaunay's belief that the Eiffel Tower is an example of good technology? Consider color, form, the emotion aroused in the viewer. What prevents the Tower from appearing forbidding or mechanical? How does Delaunay create motion? What are his feelings about the future?

(Continued on back)

2. Look up a history of the construction of the Eiffel Tower and of the popular reaction to it at the time. How does Delaunay's response differ from the popular one?

3. Choose some contemporary technological construction, for example, a space shuttle, a nuclear power plant, or a multiple-level parking garage. Compare popular reactions to such a construction to reactions to the Tower. How could one describe them in painting or in writing so as to humanize them and to assert man's control over them?

4. In 1924 the poet Blaise Cendrar said of the Eiffel Tower, "No formula of art . . . can pretend to give plastic resolution to the Eiffel Tower. . . . The Tower rose over Paris, slender as a hat-pin. When we retreated from it, it dominated Paris, stark and perpendicular. When we came close, it tilted and leaned over us. Seen from the first platform it corkscrewed around its own axis, and seen from the top it collapsed into itself, doing the splits, its neck pulled in. . . ."

   Discuss this quotation in relation to the painting. Are Delaunay's and Cendrar's attitudes toward the Tower similar?

Suggestions for Writing

1. Write an imaginative essay in which you convert some construction into something either less ominous or more frivolous for the purpose of coming to terms with it.

2. Look up a painting by Legér, preferably *The Three Women (Le Grand Déjeuner)*, and compare Delaunay's treatment of technology with that of Legér's.

Honoré Daumier

The Uprising (1860)

The Phillips Collection, Washington, D. C.

Suggestions for Discussion

1. Probably inspired by popular demonstrations against the monarchy, Daumier is making a number of statements about people and power in this painting. How does Daumier see the people? Consider colors, shapes, faces, and posture. Notice the buildings and sky. What is their effect on the human subjects?

2. How does Daumier achieve the dominance of the central figure? Consider light, dress, expression. What is the effect of his gesture and the diagonal line formed by it?

3. Comment on the expression on the face of the central figure. Is he a romantic hero? What comment may Duamier be making as he compares the mass and the leader? Why is the leader strongly portrayed, the mass seen as blurred and inchoate?

4. What elements of caricature do you see in the painting?

(Continued on back)

Suggestions for Writing

1. One comment on this painting suggests that the streets can barely contain the mass depicted and that, except for the leader, the mass is totally undifferentiated. Write an essay in which you agree or disagree with these statements.

2. Write an essay characterizing the leader. What qualities do you see in his face and in his stance? Is he totally heroic?

3. For a brief research paper, examine the facts of the antimonarchical uprising in France in 1848. What in your reading may help account for the scene in the painting?

4. One critic has seen this painting as symbolic "of pent-up frustration of the waves of self-rule, of self-reliance, the epic moment in the history of freedom." Comment.

5. Choose some contemporary revolution—Central or South American, African, or Asian. Compare and contrast the newspaper photographs of these events with this painting.

George Grosz
Student (1922)

The Cleveland Museum of Art, Purchase, General Reserve Fund

Suggestions for Discussion

1. What elements in the costume and mask can you discern? What might they each serve to indicate?

(Continued on back)

2. Comment on the form and color. What emotional impact do they have?

3. Is Grosz making a comment on the nature of students? on higher education? Why is the student fractured?

4. What are the humorous and satirical elements in the portrait of the student?

5. The convention of the mask has long been used in drama. What might be the purpose for using a mask in this case? What emotions does the figure arouse in the viewer?

Suggestions for Writing

1. Could this sketch serve to describe yourself or students you know? Could it be a commentary on education as you have (or have not) experienced it? Describe a costume or mask that might fit you as a student, other students, or your professors, and explain the reasons for your design. Would the work created by your design be similar to that by Grosz?

2. How might you design costumes or masks for Mrs. Alving and other characters in *Ghosts?* Do you think they might add or detract from the impact of that play?

3. *Antigone* was written for the use of masks. What do you think was the purpose for the use of masks in Greek drama? Do some research on the function of the mask in Greek drama, and explain how it might increase your understanding of *Antigone* or *Ghosts.*

4. The playwright Ivan Goll said, "The new drama must have recourse to all technological props which are contemporary equivalents of the ancient mask. Such props are, for instance, the voice, the denatured masks and other accouterments which proclaim the character in a crudely typifying manner." Write a paper in which you relate these remarks to Grosz' sketch. How does the quotation help to explain Grosz' work?

Max Beckmann

Departure (1932—1933)

Oil on Canvas; tryptych, center panel 7' 3/4″ × 45 3/8″; side panels each 7 3/4′ × 39 1/4″. Collection, The Museum of Modern Art, New York. Given anonymously (by exchange).

Suggestions for Discussion

1. Examine the details of the left panel. Describe the four figures. What is each one doing?

2. What is the relation of the right panel to the left? What kind of carnival is suggested in the right panel? What is the role of the naked, dwarf-like figure? What kinds of violence are depicted in both these scenes?

3. Describe the scene in the central panel. Who are the figures? What are they doing? What do the sea and the limitless horizon symbolize in this scene, particularly as compared to the decor of the side panels?

4. Are the figures in this painting highly individual or types? Explain your answer by considering the style of the artist.

5. What is the function of color? How is it related to the theme?

6. Why are the images in the painting large and static instead of free and flowing?

(Continued on back)

Suggestions for Writing

1. A critic has suggested that the painting reflects Beckmann's view of the fundamental human condition. By referring to the details of the painting, write an essay in which you explain what you think that view is.

2. Beckmann painted *Departure* in 1932–1933. Although it may have reference to Nazi brutality, in what ways is it prophetic of the history of the twentieth century since that time? What contemporary events are suggested by the painting?

3. In an essay called "On My Painting," Beckmann describes a dream in which William Blake, the eighteenth-century English poet and painter, says to him, "Have confidence in objects, do not let yourself be intimidated by the horror of the world. Everything is ordered and correct and must fulfill its destiny in order to attain perfection. Seek this path and you will attain . . . increasing release from all that which now seems to you sad or terrible." Write an essay in which you discuss how this recorded dream helps explain the symbolism of the painting.

4. In 1920, Beckmann said of painters, "We must participate in the great misery to come. We have to lay our hearts and nerves bare to the deceived cries of people who have been lied to . . . the sole justification for our existence as artists, superfluous and egotistic though we are, is to confront people with the image of their destiny." What does this statement say about the role of the artist in society? For a research paper, compare and contrast the statements of several other artists with this one by Beckmann.

was for me the most exciting detective work I've ever done or heard of. The thing was, not only did you solve interesting puzzles, but when you got them solved you found you'd restored something magnificent, a work of art—in the case of "Beowulf" or "The Canterbury Tales"—supremely beautiful and noble. One unearthed tricks of the craft that nobody'd known or used for a long, long time—tricks one could turn on one's own work, making it different from anybody else's and yet not crazy, not merely novel.

I think every writer wants to sound like him- or herself; that's the main reason one sees so many experimental novels. And of course the risk in the pursuit of newness is that, in refusing to do what the so-called tradition does, one ends up doing exactly the same thing everybody else trying to get outside the tradition does. For better or worse (I'm no longer much concerned about whether it's better or worse), I joined up with an alternative tradition, one with which I felt almost eerily comfortable. My church-filled childhood delighted in discovering a Christianity distant enough—in fact, for all practical purposes, *dead* enough—to satisfy nostalgia without stirring embarrassment and annoyance, as modern Christianity does. For instance, when one reads about "ensoulment" in a medieval book—that is, when one reads arguments on precisely when the soul enters the fetus, and the argument comes from someone of the 13th century—one can read with interest; but when one hears a living Christian hotly debating ensoulment, hoping to be able to support abortion without feelings of guilt, one shrinks away, tries to get lost in the crowd.

I found in medieval culture and art, in other words, exactly what I needed as an instrument for looking at my own time and place. I of course never became for a moment a medieval Christian believer, but medieval ideas and attitudes gave me a means of triangulating, a place to stand. And, needless to say, medieval literature had built into it everything I'd liked best from the beginning, back in the days of God, Dickens, and Disney, of grotesques (cartoon people and places), noble feeling, humor (God was perhaps a little short on humor), and real storytelling.

I said earlier that I'm no longer much concerned about whether the work I've done and am doing is for better or worse. That is not quite as true as I might wish. Egoistic ambition is the kind of weed that grows out of dragon's blood: The more you chop it away the more it flourishes. But it's true that at a certain point in one's career one begins to face up to one's limitations, and the way to stay sane at such a moment is to soften one's standards a little— find good reasons for approving lumpy but well-intentioned work, one's own and everybody else's.

To put all this another way, when I think back now over the influences which have helped to shape the way I write, I notice with a touch of dismay that they were as much bad influences as good ones. I won't criticize God (anyway, He's almost certainly been misquoted), but clearly the influence of Dickens and Disney was not all to the good. Both of them incline one toward stylized gestures. Instead of looking very closely at the world and writing it down, the way James Joyce does, brilliantly getting down, say, the way an old man moves his tongue over his gums, or the way a beautiful woman idly plays with her bracelets, a writer like me, seduced by cartoon vision, tends to go again and again for the same gestural gimmicks, a consistent pattern of caricature (compare the way doors in Dostoyevsky are forever flying open or slamming).

I look over my fiction of 20 years and see it as one long frenzy of tics—endlessly repeated words like *merely* and *grotesque*, a disproportionate number of people with wooden fingers and a dreary penchant for frowning thoughtfully or darting their eyes around like maniacs. I seem incapable of writing a story in which people do not babble philosophically, not really because they're saying things I want to get said but because earnest babbling is one of the ways I habitually give vitality to my short-legged, overweight, twitching cartoon creations. And needless to say, from artists like Dickens and Disney I get my morbid habit of trying to make the reader fall into tender weeping.

The whole New Critical period I went through, and the scholarly period that followed it, betrayed me, I think, into an excessive concern with significance. It's probably the case that novels and stories are more interesting if, in some sense or another, they mean something. But it has begun to dawn on me that—in fiction, as in all the arts—a little meaning goes a long way. I think what chiefly made me notice this is the work of my creative writing students. Until about five years ago, I never taught creative writing, only medieval literature and now and then a little Greek. When I began to look hard and often at student writing, I soon discovered that one of the main mistakes in their writing is that students think (probably because they've taken too many English literature courses) that fiction is supposed to tell us things—instruct us, improve us, show us.

In a sense of course they're right, but only in a subtle and mysterious sense. When one has analyzed every symbolically neat detail in a story like "Death in Venice" or "Disorder and Early Sorrow"—when one has accounted for every verbal repetition, every pattern and relationship, and set down in alphabetical order every thought to be lifted or wrenched from the story—one discovers that, when you come right down to it, Mann has told us nothing we didn't know already. More by my writing students' early bad examples (they later get better) than by all the good literary examples I ever read, I've come to see that fiction simply dramatizes. It gives importance to ideas, it seems to me, pretty much in the way the string on which a handful of pearls have been strung gives a kind of importance to the pearls. When I read my earliest, most ingeniously constructed fictions ("The Resurrection" and "Grendel") I find I can no longer figure the damn things out—would that I'd kept all my charts! Insofar as such books are interesting, for me at least, they're interesting because I like the characters and hope, as I reread, that life (the rest of the book) won't treat them too badly.

I don't mean, of course, that I intend never again to use symbols or to design my stories so that the reader has the kind of experience William James described with such delight: "There goes the same thing I saw before again." What I do mean is that when I was 3 or 4, or 12 or 13, I understood fiction more profoundly than I understood it through most of my writing years. I understood that a story, like a painting, or like a symphony, is one of the most wonderful, one of the most useless, things in the world. The magnificence of a work of art lies precisely in the fact that nobody made the artist make it, he just did, and—except when one's in school—nobody makes the receiver read it, or look at it, or listen to it; he just does. The influence of my writing students has been to lead me to understand (or imagine I understand) that art's value is not that it expresses life's meaning (though presumably it does, as do butterflies and crickets) but that it is, simply, splendidly, *there*.

I think of the performances my mother and father would sometimes do at, for instance, the monthly meetings of the Grange. The way the night would go is this: First everybody would crowd into one immense room with trestle-tables and white-paper tablecloths, the tables all loaded down with food, all the redfaced farmers and their plump wives and children finding folding chairs near friends, and somebody would tap a water glass with the side of his spoon and would say a quick, self-conscious prayer, and then everybody would eat.

It was a wonderfully pleasant social time, lots of jokes and stories and abundant country food; but it wasn't a time they chose solely for its pleasantness: If you wanted to get farmers to come from all over the county late at night, after chores, you had to feed them. Then they'd all go into another room and have their business meeting—how much or how little they should organize, how to keep the feed-mills, the truckers, and the United States Congress in line. Nobody much cared for the business meeting, though sometimes somebody would "get off a good one," as they used to say.

Then, when the work was done my mother and father would stand there in the middle of the big, bright room and say poems or sing. How strange it seemed to me that all these serious, hard-working people should sit there grinning for an hour or more, listening, for instance, to my father telling them an endless, pointless story of a ghost in armor, or a ship rescued by pigeons, or somebody called Dangerous Dan McGrew. It was absurd. I wasn't just imagining it. The whole thing was deeply, weirdly absurd. Clearly if one is to devote a lifetime to doing something as crazy as that, one had better do it well—not necessarily because there is any great virtue in doing it well but only because, if one does it badly, people may wake up and notice that what one's doing is crazy.

Suggestions for Discussion

1. John Gardner, like Anne Tyler, describes his family and their influence on him. How are the two families different and similar?

2. Why did Gardner learn so much from Dickens and Disney? To what kind of writers does he contrast them? Explain his statement that when he was young, God, Dickens, and Disney were his favorite authors.

3. Explain how Gardner became interested first in literature as a serious occupation and then in the study of medieval literature. Why did medieval literature become so important to him? How did literary study influence his own writing?

4. How similar in tone is the memoir to the one by Anne Tyler?

5. What does Gardner mean by "cartoons" in literature?

6. Why does Gardner both begin and end the essay with an account of his parents?

Suggestions for Writing

1. In an essay, compare and contrast the memoirs by Gardner and Tyler. Discuss the structure and tone of each.

2. Write an essay explaining why Gardner lists Disney in the same breath as God and Dickens. How are Disney's cartoons related to art?

Essays

Aaron Copland

How We Listen to Music

Aaron Copland (b. 1900) studied music in the United States and France. His French teacher, Nadia Boulanger, was the first to conduct his Symphony for Organ and Orchestra in 1925. Much of Copland's work reflects the influence of American jazz and folk music: for example, in *John Henry* (1940) and in his well-known ballets *Billy the Kid* (1938), *Rodeo* (1942), and *Appalachian Spring* (1944). His major symphonic works are *El Salon Mexico* (1936) and *The Third Symphony;* he also has written music for films. Copland has remained a major influence in contemporary music and was awarded the National Medal for Arts in 1986. He has also written about music for the general public. This essay from *What to Listen for in Music* (1939, 1957) provides a defense for the difficulty of contemporary music and explains the obligations of the intelligent listener.

We all listen to music according to our separate capacities. But, for the sake of analysis, the whole listening process may become clearer if we break it up into its component parts, so to speak. In a certain sense we all listen to music on three separate planes. For lack of a better terminology, one might name these: (1) the sensuous plane, (2) the expressive plane, (3) the sheerly musical plane. The only advantage to be gained from mechanically splitting up the listening process into these hypothetical planes is the clearer view to be had of the way in which we listen.

The simplest way of listening to music is to listen for the sheer pleasure of the musical sound itself. That is the sensuous plane. It is the plane on which we hear music without thinking, without considering it in any way. One turns on the radio while doing something else and absent-mindedly bathes in the sound. A kind of brainless but attractive state of mind is engendered by the mere sound appeal of the music.

You may be sitting in a room reading this book. Imagine one note struck on the piano. Immediately that one note is enough to change the atmosphere of the room—providing that the sound element in music is a powerful and mysterious agent, which it would be foolish to deride or belittle.

The surprising thing is that many people who consider themselves qualified music lovers abuse that plane in listening. They go to concerts in order to lose themselves. They use music as a consolation or an escape. They enter an ideal world where one doesn't have to think of the realities of everyday life. Of course they aren't thinking about the music either. Music allows them to leave it, and they go off to a place to dream, dreaming because of and apropos of the music yet never quite listening to it.

Yes, the sound appeal of music is a potent and primitive force, but you must not allow it to usurp a disproportionate 'share of your interest. The sensuous plane is an important one in music, a very important one, but it does not constitute the whole story.

There is no need to digress further on the sensuous plane. Its appeal to every normal human being is self-evident. There is, however, such a thing as becoming more sensitive to the different kinds of sound stuff as used by various composers. For all composers do not use that sound stuff in the same way. Don't get the idea that the value of music is commensurate with its sensuous appeal or that the loveliest sounding music is made by the greatest composer. If that were so, Ravel would be a greater creator than Beethoven. The point is that the sound element varies with each composer, that his usage of sound forms an integral part of his style and must be taken into account when listening. The reader can see, therefore, that a more conscious approach is valuable even on this primary plane of music listening.

The second plane on which music exists is what I have called the expressive one. Here, immediately, we tread on controversial ground. Composers have a way of shying away from any discussion of music's expressive side. Did not Stravinsky himself proclaim that his music was an "object," a "thing," with a life of its own, and with no other meaning than its own purely musical existence? This intransigent attitude of Stravinsky's may be due to the fact that so many people have tried to read different meanings into so many pieces. Heaven knows it is difficult enough to say precisely what it is that a piece of music means, to say it definitely, to say it finally so that everyone is satisfied with your explanation. But that should not lead one to the other extreme of denying to music the right to be "expressive."

My own belief is that all music has an expressive power, some more and some less, but that all music has a certain meaning behind the notes and that the meaning behind the notes constitutes, after all, what the piece is saying, what the piece is about. The whole problem can be stated quite simply by asking, "Is there a meaning to music?" My answer to that would be, "Yes." And "Can you state in so many words what the meaning is?" My answer to that would be, "No." Therein lies the difficulty.

Simple-minded souls will never be satisfied with the answer to the second of these questions. They always want music to have a meaning, and the more concrete it is the better they like it. The more the music reminds them of a train, a storm, a funeral, or any other familiar conception the more expressive it appears to be to them. This popular idea of music's meaning—stimulated and abetted by the usual run of musical commentator—should be discouraged wherever and whenever it is met. One timid lady once confessed to me that she suspected something seriously lacking in her appreciation of music because of her inability to connect it with anything definite. That is getting the whole thing backward, of course.

Still, the question remains, How close should the intelligent music lover wish to come to pinning a definite meaning to any particular work? No closer than a general concept, I should say. Music expresses, at different moments, serenity or exuberance, regrets or triumph, fury or delight. It expresses each of these moods, and many others, in a numberless variety of subtle shadings and differences. It may even express a state of meaning for which there exists no adequate word in any language. In that case, musicians often like to say that it has only a purely musical meaning. They sometimes go further and say that *all* music has only a purely musical meaning. What they really mean is that no appropriate word can be found to express the music's meaning and that, even if it could, they do not feel the need of finding it.

But whatever the professional musician may hold, most musical novices still search for specific words with which to pin down their musical reactions. That is why they always find Tschaikovsky easier to "understand" than Beethoven. In the first place, it is easier to pin a meaning-word on a Tschaikovsky piece than on a Beethoven one. Much easier. Moreover, with the Russian composer, every time you come back to a piece of his it almost always says the same thing to you, whereas with Beethoven it is often quite difficult to put your finger right on what he is saying. And any musician will tell you that that is why Beethoven is the greater composer. Because music which always says the same thing to you will necessarily soon become dull music, but music whose meaning is slightly different with each hearing has a greater chance of remaining alive.

Listen, if you can, to the forty-eight fugue themes of Bach's *Well Tempered Clavichord*. Listen to each theme, one after another. You will soon realize that each theme mirrors a different world of feeling. You will also soon realize that the more beautiful a theme seems to you the harder it is to find any word that will describe it to your complete satisfaction. Yes, you will certainly know whether it is a gay theme or a sad one. You will be able, in other words, in your own mind, to draw a frame of emotional feeling around your theme. Now study the sad one a little closer. Try to pin down the exact quality of its sadness. Is it pessimistically sad or resignedly sad; is it fatefully sad or smilingly sad?

Let us suppose that you are fortunate and can describe to your own satisfaction in so many words the exact meaning of your chosen theme. There is still no guarantee that anyone else will be satisfied. Nor need they be. The important thing is that each one feel for himself the specific expressive quality of a theme or, similarly, an entire piece of music. And if it is a great work of art, don't expect it to mean exactly the same thing to you each time you return to it.

Themes or pieces need not express only one emotion, of course. Take such a theme as the first main one of the *Ninth Symphony*, for example. It is clearly made up of different elements. It does not say only one thing. Yet anyone hearing it immediately gets a feeling of strength, a feeling of power. It isn't a power that comes simply because the theme is played loudly. It is a power inherent in the theme itself. The extraordinary strength and vigor of the theme results in the listener's receiving an impression that a forceful statement has been made. But one should never try to boil it down to "the fateful hammer of life," etc. That is where the trouble begins. The musician, in his exasperation, says it means nothing but the notes themselves, whereas the nonprofessional is only too anxious to hang on to any explanation that gives him the illusion of getting closer to the music's meaning.

Now, perhaps, the reader will know better what I mean when I say that music does have an expressive meaning but that we cannot say in so many words what that meaning is.

The third plane on which music exists is the sheerly musical plane. Besides the pleasurable sound of music and the expressive feeling that it gives off, music does exist in terms of the notes themselves and of their manipulation. Most listeners are not sufficiently conscious of this third plane. . . .

Professional musicians, on the other hand, are, if anything, too conscious of the mere notes themselves. They often fall into the error of becoming so engrossed with their arpeggios and staccatos that they forget the deeper aspects of the music they are performing. But from the layman's standpoint, it is not so much a matter of getting over bad habits on the sheerly musical plane as of increasing one's awareness of what is going on, in so far as the notes are concerned.

When the man in the street listens to the "notes themselves" with any degree of concentration, he is most likely to make some mention of the melody. Either he hears a pretty melody or he does not, and he generally lets it go at that. Rhythm is likely to gain his attention next, particularly if it seems exciting. But harmony and tone color are generally taken for granted, if they are thought of consciously at all. As for music's having a definite form of some kind, that idea seems never to have occurred to him.

It is very important for all of us to become more alive to music on its sheerly musical plane. After all, an actual musical material is being used. The intelligent listener must be prepared to increase his awareness of the musical material and what happens to it. He must hear the melodies, the rhythms, the harmonies, the tone colors in a more conscious fashion. But above all he must, in order to follow the line of the composer's thought, know something of the principles of musical form. Listening to all of these elements is listening on the sheerly musical plane.

Let me repeat that I have split up mechanically the three separate planes on which we listen merely for the sake of greater clarity. Actually, we never listen on one or the other of these planes. What we do is to correlate them— listening in all three ways at the same time. It takes no mental effort, for we do it instinctively.

Perhaps an analogy with what happens to us when we visit the theater will make this instinctive correlation clearer. In the theater, you are aware of the actors and actresses, costumes and sets, sounds and movements. All these give one the sense that the theater is a pleasant place to be in. They constitute the sensuous plane in our theatrical reactions.

The expressive plane in the theater would be derived from the feeling that you get from what is happening on the stage. You are moved to pity, excitement, or gayety. It is this general feeling, generated aside from the particular words being spoken, a ceratin emotional something which exists on the stage, that is analogous to the expressive quality in music.

The plot and plot development is equivalent to our sheerly musical plane. The playwright creates and develops a character in just the same way that a composer creates and develops a theme. According to the degree of your awareness of the way in which the artist in either field handles his material you will become a more intelligent listener.

It is easy enough to see that the theatergoer never is conscious of any of these elements separately. He is aware of them all at the same time. The same is true of music listening. We simultaneously and without thinking listen on all three planes.

In a sense, the ideal listener is both inside and outside the music at the same moment, judging it and enjoying it, wishing it would go one way and watching it go another—almost like the composer at the moment he composes it; because in order to write his music, the composer must also be inside and outside his music, carried away by it and yet coldly critical of it. A subjective and objective attitude is implied in both creating and listening to music.

What the reader should strive for, then, is a more *active* kind of listening. Whether you listen to Mozart or Duke Ellington, you can deepen your understanding of music only by being a more conscious and aware listener—not someone who is just listening, but someone who is listening *for* something.

Suggestions for Discussion

1. According to Copland, on what different levels do we listen to music?

2. Why does Copland believe that listening to music as an escape is an inadequate response to it?

3. Does Copland believe that a musical composition can have meaning? Does he believe it possible to state that meaning easily?

4. How, according to Copland, is the meaning of a musical composition related to its expressive power? What boundaries does Copland place on the expressive power of music? Explain his use of Bach in this regard.

5. What for Copland are significant differences between Tschaikovsky and Beethoven? Why does he consider Beethoven the greater composer?

6. What are the elements of the third plane of music? How do professional musicians and listeners of music differ about this third plane? What criticism does Copland make of musicians? What obligation does the intelligent listener have to this plane?

7. Explain Copland's analogy between the elements in music and in drama. What important differences exist for the audience in its response to both forms of art?

8. Constrast Oscar Mandel's position with Copland's in the matter of meaning in the arts. Can you account for their different points of view?

Suggestions for Writing

1. Listen to a composition by Bach and to one by Duke Ellington and, insofar as you can, discuss the music on all three levels.

2. Summarize the arguments of Copland, Mandel, Mannes about the problems of responding to art. Which of these essays do you find most helpful for your own response? Explain your position in detail.

◇ ◇ ◇

Northrop Frye

The Keys to Dreamland

Northrop Frye (b. 1912), Distinguished Professor of English at the University of Toronto, is a leading literary critic. His essays have influenced generations of university English professors. Among his works are *Fearful Symmetry: A Study of William Blake* (1947), *Anatomy of Criticism* (1957), *The Well-Tempered Critic* (1963), and two collections of lectures, *A Natural Perspective* (1965) and *The Modern Century* (1967). In "The Keys to Dreamland" from *The Educated Imagination* (1964), Frye asserts that literature, which plays a significant role in our lives, is autonomous and must be judged on its own terms.

I have been trying to explain literature by putting you in a primitive situation on an uninhabited island, where you could see the imagination working in the most direct and simple way. Now let's start with our own society, and see where literature belongs in that, if it does. Suppose you're walking down the street of a North American city. All around you is a highly artificial society, but you don't think of it as artificial: you're so accustomed to it that you think of it as natural. But suppose your imagination plays a little trick on you of a kind that it often does play, and you suddenly feel like a complete outsider, someone who's just blown in from Mars on a flying saucer. Instantly you see how conventionalized everything is: the clothes, the shop windows, the movement of the cars in traffic, the cropped hair and shaved faces of the men, the red lips and blue eyelids that women put on because they want to conventionalize their faces, or "look nice," as they say, which means the same thing. All this convention is pressing toward uniformity or likeness. To be outside the convention makes a person look queer, or, if he's driving a car, a menace to life and limb. The only exceptions are people who have decided to conform to different conventions, like nuns or beatniks. There's clearly a strong force making toward conformity in society, so strong that it seems to have something to do with the stability of society itself. In ordinary life even the most splendid things we can think of, like goodness and truth and beauty, all mean essentially what we're accustomed to. As I hinted just now in speaking of female make-up, most of our ideas of beauty are pure convention, and even truth has been defined as whatever doesn't disturb the pattern of what we already know.

When we move on to literature, we again find conventions, but this time we notice that they are conventions, because we're not so used to them. These conventions seem to have something to do with making literature as unlike life as possible. Chaucer represents people as making up stories in ten-syllable couplets. Shakespeare uses dramatic conventions, which means, for instance, that Iago has to smash Othello's marriage and dreams of future happiness and get him ready to murder his wife in a few minutes. Milton has two nudes in a garden haranguing each other in set speeches beginning with such lines as "Daughter of God and Man, immortal Eve"—Eve being Adam's daughter because she's just been extracted from his ribcase. Almost every story we read demands that we accept as fact something that we know to be nonsense: that good people always win, especially in love; that murders are complicated and ingenious puzzles to be solved by logic, and so on. It isn't only popular literature that demands this: more highbrow stories are apt to be more ironic, but irony has its conventions too. If we go further back into literature, we run into such conventions as the king's rash promise, the enraged cuckold, the cruel mistress of love poetry—never anything that we now or any other time would recognize as the normal behavior of adult people, only the maddened ethics of fairyland.

Even the details of literature are equally perverse. Literature is a world where phoenixes and unicorns are quite as important as horses and dogs—and in literature some of the horses talk, like the ones in *Gulliver's Travels*. A random example is calling Shakespeare the "swan of Avon"—he was called that by Ben Jonson. The town of Stratford, Ontario, keeps swans in its river partly as a literary allusion. Poets of Shakespeare's day hated to admit that they were writing words on a page: they always insisted that they were producing music. In pastoral poetry they might be playing a flute (or more accurately an oboe), but every other kind of poetic effort was called song, with a harp, a lyre, or a lute in the background, depending on how highbrow the song was. Singing suggests birds, and so for their typical songbird and emblem of themselves, the poets chose the swan, a bird that can't sing. Because it can't sing, they made up a legend that it sang once before death, when nobody was listening. But Shakespeare didn't burst into song before his death: he wrote two plays a year until he'd made enough money to retire, and spend the last five years of his life counting his take.

So however useful literature may be in improving one's imagination or vocabulary, it would be the wildest kind of pedantry to use it directly as a guide to life. Perhaps here we see one reason why the poet is not only very seldom a person one would turn to for insight into the state of the world, but often seems even more gullible and simple-minded than the rest of us. For the poet, the particular literary conventions he adopts are likely to become, for him, facts of life. If he finds that the kind of writing he's best at has a good deal to do with fairies, like Yeats, or a white goddess, like Graves, or a life-force, like Bernard Shaw, or episcopal sermons, like T. S. Eliot, or bullfights, like Hemingway, or exasperation at social hypocrisies, as with the so-called angry school, these things are apt to take on a reality for him that seems badly out of proportion to his contemporaries. His life may imitate literature in a way that may warp or even destroy his social personality, as Byron wore himself out at thirty-four with the strain of being Byronic. Life and literature, then, are both conventionalized, and of the conventions of literature about all we can say is that they don't much resemble the conditions of life. It's when the two sets of conventions collide that we realize how different they are.

In fact, whenever literature gets too probable, too much like life, some self-defeating process, some mysterious law of diminishing returns, seems to set in. There's a vivid and expertly written novel by H. G. Wells called *Kipps*, about a lower-middle-class, inarticulate, very likeable Cockney, the kind of character we often find in Dickens. Kipps is carefully studied: he never sounds the "h" in home or head; nothing he does is out of line with what we expect such a person to be like. It's an admirable novel, well worth reading, and yet I have a nagging feeling that there's some inner secret in bringing him completely to life that Dickens would have and that Wells doesn't have.

All right, then, what would Dickens have done? Well, one of the things that Dickens often does do is write *badly*. He might have given Kipps sentimental speeches and false heroics and all sorts of inappropriate verbiage to say; and some readers would have clucked and tut-tutted over these passages and explained to each other how bad Dickens's taste was and how uncertain his hold on character could be. Perhaps they'd be right to. But we'd have had Kipps a few times the way he'd look to himself or the way he'd sometimes wish he could be: that's part of his reality, and the effect would remain with us however much we disapproved of it. Whether I'm right about this book or not, and I'm not at all sure I am, I think my general principle is right. What we'd never see except in a book is often what we go to books to find. Whatever is completely lifelike in literature is a bit of a laboratory specimen there. To bring anything really to life in literature we can't be lifelike: we have to be literaturelike.

The same thing is true even of the use of language. We're often taught that prose is the language of ordinary speech, which is usually true in literature. But in ordinary life prose is no more the language of ordinary speech than one's Sunday suit is a bathing suit. The people who actually speak prose are highly cultivated and articulate people, who've read a good many books, and even they can speak prose only to each other. If you read the beautiful sentences of Elizabeth Bennett's conversation in *Pride and Prejudice,* you can see how in that book they give a powerfully convincing impression of a sensible and intelligent girl. But any girl who talked as coherently as that on a street car would be stared at as though she had green hair. It isn't only the difference between 1813 and 1962 that's involved either, as you'll see if you compare her speech with her mother's. The poet Emily Dickinson complained that everybody said "What?" to her, until finally she practically gave up trying to talk altogether, and confined herself to writing notes.

All this is involved with the principle I've touched on before: the difference between literary and other kinds of writing. If we're writing to convey information, or for any practical reason, our writing is an act of will and intention: we mean what we say, and the words we use represent that meaning directly. It's different in literature, not because the poet doesn't mean what he says too, but because his real effort is one of putting words together. What's important is not what he may have meant to say, but what the words themselves say when they get fitted together. With a novelist it's rather the incidents in the story he tells that get fitted together—as D. H. Lawrence says, don't trust the novelist; trust his story. That's why so much of a writer's best writing is or seems to be involuntary. It's involuntary because the forms of literature itself are taking control of it, and these forms are what are embodied in the conventions of literature. Conventions, we see, have the same role in literature that they have in life: they impose certain patterns of order and stability on the writer. Only, if they're such different conventions, it seems clear that the order of words, or the structure of literature, is different from the social order.

The absence of any clear line of connection between literature and life comes out in the issues involved in censorship. Because of the large involuntary element in writing, works of literature can't be treated as embodiments of conscious will or intention, like people, and so no laws can be framed to control their behavior which assume a tendency to do this or an intention of doing that. Works of literature get into legal trouble because they offend some powerful religious or political interest, and this interest in its turn usually acquires or exploits the kind of social hysteria that's always revolving around sex. But it's impossible to give legal definitions of such terms as obscenity in relation to works of literature. What happens to the book depends mainly on the intelligence of the judge. It he's a sensible man we get a sensible decision; if he's an ass we get that sort of decision, but what we don't get is a legal decision, because the basis for one doesn't exist. The best we get is a precedent tending to discourage cranks and pressure groups from attacking serious books. If you read the casebook on the trial of *Lady Chatterley's Lover,* you may remember how bewildered the critics were when they were asked what the moral effect of the book would be. They weren't putting on an act: they didn't know. Novels can only be good or bad in their own categories. There's no such thing as a morally bad novel: its moral effect depends entirely on the moral quality of its reader, and nobody can predict what that will be. And if literature isn't morally bad it isn't morally good either. I suppose one reason why *Lady Chatterley's Lover* dramatized this question so vividly was that it's a rather preachy and self-conscious book: like the Sunday-school novels of my childhood, it bores me a little because it tries so hard to do me good.

So literature has no consistent connection with ordinary life, positive or negative. Here we touch on another important difference between structures of the imagination and structures of practical sense, which include the applied sciences. Imagination is certainly essential to science, applied or pure. Without a constructive power in the mind to make models of experience, get hunches and follow them out, play freely around with hypotheses, and so forth, no scientist could get anywhere. But all imaginative effort in practical fields has to meet the test of practicability, otherwise it's discarded. The imagination in literature has no such test to meet. You don't relate it directly to life or reality: you relate works of literature, as we've said earlier, to each other. Whatever value there is in studying literature, cultural or practical, comes from the total body of our reading, the castle of words we've built, and keep adding new wings to all the time.

So it's natural to swing to the opposite extreme and say that literature is really a refuge or escape from life, a self-contained world like the world of the dream, a world of play or make-believe to balance the world of work. Some literature is like that, and many people tell us that they only read to get away from reality for a bit. And I've suggested myself that the sense of escape, or at least detachment, does come into everybody's literary experience. But the real point of literature can hardly be that. Think of such writers as William Faulkner or François Mauriac, their great moral dignity, the intensity and compassion that they've studied the life around them with. Or think of James Joyce, spending seven years on one book and seventeen on another, and having them ridiculed or abused or banned by the customs when they did get published. Or of the poets Rilke and Valéry, waiting patiently for years in silence until what they had to say was ready to be said. There's a deadly seriousness in all this that even the most refined theories of fantasy or make-believe won't quite cover. Still, let's go along with the idea for a bit, because we're not getting on very fast with the relation of literature to life, or what we could call the horizontal perspective of literature. That seems to block us off on all sides.

The world of literature is a world where there is no reality except that of the human imagination. We see a great deal in it that reminds us vividly of the life we know. But in that very vividness there's something unreal. We can understand this more clearly with pictures, perhaps. There are trick-pictures—*trompe l'oeil,* the French call them—where the resemblance to life is very strong. An American painter of this school played a joke on his bitchy wife by painting one of her best napkins so expertly that she grabbed at the canvas trying to pull it off. But a painting as realistic as that isn't a reality but an illusion: it has the glittering unnatural clarity of a hallucination. The real realities, so to speak, are things that don't remind us directly of our own experience, but are such things as the wrath of Achilles or the jealousy of Othello, which are bigger and more intense experiences than anything we can reach—except in our imagination, which is what we're reaching with. Sometimes, as in the happy endings of comedies, or in the ideal world of romances, we seem to be looking at a pleasanter world than we ordinarily know. Sometimes, as in tragedy and satire, we seem to be looking at a world more devoted to suffering or absurdity than we ordinarily know. In literature we always seem to be looking either up or down. It's the vertical perspective that's important, not the horizontal one that looks out to life. Of course, in the greatest works of literature we get both the up and down views, often at the same time as different aspects of one event.

There are two halves to the literary experience, then. Imagination gives us both a better and a worse world than the one we usually live with, and demands that we keep looking steadily at them both. I said in my first talk that the arts follow the path of the emotions, and of the tendency of the emotions to separate the world into a half that we like and a half that we don't like. Literature is not a world of dreams, but it would be if we had only one half without the other. If we had nothing but romances and comedies with happy endings, literature would express only a wish-fulfillment dream. Some people ask why poets want to write tragedies when the world's so full of them anyway, and suggest that enjoying such things has something morbid or gloating about it. It doesn't, but it might if there were nothing else in literature.

This point is worth spending another minute on. You recall that terrible scene in *King Lear* where Gloucester's eyes are put out on the stage. That's part of a play, and a play is supposed to be entertaining. Now in what sense can a scene like that be entertaining? The fact that it's not really happening is certainly important. It would be degrading to watch a real blinding scene, and far more so to get any pleasure out of watching it. Consequently, the entertainment doesn't consist of its reminding us of a real blinding scene. If it did, one of the great scenes of drama would turn into a piece of repulsive pornography. We couldn't stop anyone from reading in this way, and it certainly wouldn't cure him, much less help the public, to start blaming or censoring Shakespeare for putting sadistic ideas in his head. But a reaction of that kind has nothing to do with drama. In a dramatic scene of cruelty and hatred we're seeing cruelty and hatred, which we know are permanently real things in human life, from the point of view of the imagination. What the imagination suggests is horror, not the paralyzing sickening horror of a real blinding scene, but an exuberant horror, full of the energy of repudiation. This is as powerful a rendering as we can ever get of life as we don't want it.

So we see that there are moral standards in literature after all, even though they have nothing to do with calling the police when we see a word in a book that's more familiar in sound than in print. One of the things Gloucester says in that scene is: "I am tied to the stake, and I must stand the course." In Shakespeare's day it was a favourite sport to tie a bear to a stake and set dogs on it until they killed it. The Puritans suppressed this sport, according to Macaulay, not because it gave pain to the bear but because it gave pleasure to the spectators. Macaulay may have intended his remark to be a sneer at the Puritans, but surely if the Puritans did feel this way they were one hundred percent right. What other reason is there for abolishing public hangings? Whatever their motives, the Puritans and Shakespeare were operating in the same direction. Literature keeps presenting the most vicious things to us as entertainment, but what it appeals to is not any pleasure in these things, but the exhilaration of standing apart from them and being able to see them for what they are because they aren't really happening. The more exposed we are to this, the less likely we are to find an unthinking pleasure in cruel or evil things. As the eighteenth century said in a fine mouth-filling phrase, literature refines our sensibilities.

The top half of literature is the world expressed by such words as sublime, inspiring, and the like, where what we feel is not detachment but absorption. This is the world of heroes and gods and titans and Rabelaisian giants, a world of powers and passions and moments of ecstasy far greater than anything we meet outside the imagination. Such forces would not only absorb but annihilate us if they entered ordinary life, but luckily the protecting wall of the imagination is here too. As the German poet Rilke says, we adore them because they disdain to destroy us. We seem to have got quite a long way from our emotions with their division of things into "I like this" and "I don't like this." Literature gives us an experience that stretches us vertically to the heights and depths of what the human mind can conceive, to what corresponds to the conceptions of heaven and hell in religion. In this perspective what I like or don't like disappears, because there's nothing left of me as a separate person: as a reader of literature I exist only as a representative of humanity as a whole. We'll see in the last talk how important this is.

No matter how much experience we may gather in life, we can never in life get the dimension of experience that the imagination gives us. Only the arts and sciences can do that, and of these, only literature gives us the whole sweep and range of human imagination as it sees itself. It seems to be very difficult for many people to understand the reality and intensity of literary experience. To give an example that you may think a bit irrelevant: why have so many people managed to convince themselves that Shakespeare did not write Shakespeare's plays, when there is not an atom of evidence that anybody else did? Apparently because they feel that poetry must be written out of personal experience, and that Shakespeare didn't have enough experience of the right kind. But Shakespeare's plays weren't produced by his experience: they were produced by his imagination, and the way to develop the imagination is to read a good book or two. As for us, we can't speak or think or comprehend even our own experience except within the limits of our own power over words, and those limits have been established for us by our great writers.

Literature, then, is not a dream-world: it's two dreams, a wish-fulfillment dream and an anxiety dream, that are focused together, like a pair of glasses, and become a fully conscious vision. Art, according to Plato, is a dream for awakened minds, a work of imagination withdrawn from ordinary life, dominated by the same forces that dominate the dream, and yet giving us a perspective and dimension on reality that we don't get from any other approach to reality. So the poet and the dreamer are distinct, as Keats says. Ordinary life forms a community, and literature is among other things an art of communication, so it forms a community too. In ordinary life we fall into a private and separate subconscious every night, where we reshape the world according to a private and separate imagination. Underneath literature there's another kind of subconscious, which is social and not private, a need for forming a community around certain symbols, like the Queen and the flag, or around certain gods that represent order and stability, or becoming and change, or death and rebirth to a new life. This is the mythmaking power of the human mind, which throws up and dissolves one civilization after another.

I've taken my title for this talk, "The Keys to Dreamland," from what is possibly the greatest single effort of the literary imagination in the twentieth century, Joyce's *Finnegans Wake*. In this book a man goes to sleep and falls, not into the Freudian separate or private subconscious, but into the deeper dream of man that creates and destroys his own societies. The entire book is written in the language of this dream. It's a subconscious language, mainly English, but connected by associations and puns with the eighteen or so other languages that Joyce knew. *Finnegans Wake* is not a book to read, but a book to decipher: as Joyce says, it's about a dreamer, but it's addressed to an ideal reader suffering from an ideal insomnia. The reader or critic, then, has a role complementing the poet's role. We need two powers in literature, a power to create and a power to understand.

In all our literary experience there are two kinds of response. There is the direct experience of the work itself, while we're reading a book or seeing a play, especially for the first time. This experience is uncritical, or rather precritical, so it's not infallible. If our experience is limited, we can be roused to enthusiasm or carried away by something that we can later see to have been second-rate or even phony. Then there is the conscious, critical response we make after we've finished reading or left the theatre, when we compare what we've experienced with other things of the same kind, and form a judgment of value and proportion on it. This critical response, with practice, gradually makes our pre-critical responses more sensitive and accurate, or improves our taste, as we say. But behind our responses to individual works, there's a bigger response to our literary experience as a whole, as a total possession.

The critic has always been called a judge of literature, which means, not that he's in a superior position to the poet, but that he ought to know something about literature, just as a judge's right to be on a bench depends on his knowledge of law. If he's up against something the size of Shakespeare, he's the one being judged. The critic's function is to interpret every work of literature in the light of all the literature he knows, to keep constantly struggling to understand what literature as a whole is about. Literature as a whole is not an aggregate of exhibits with red and blue ribbons attached to them, like a cat-show, but the range of articulate human imagination as it extends from the height of imaginative heaven to the depth of imaginative hell. Literature is a human apocalypse, man's revelation to man, and criticism is not a body of adjudications, but the awareness of that revelation, the last judgment of mankind.

Suggestions for Discussion

1. Explain Frye's belief in the power of conformity in society. What role does conformity play in the very life of society? How does it affect our habits and our ideas about beauty?

2. How does conformity, or convention, work in art? Frye says, "Almost every story we read demands that we accept as fact something that we know to be nonsense." What examples does Fry use to illustrate? Why is it important for Frye to establish the use of conventions in art?

3. What are Frye's objections to literature that is too much like real life? Are his objections valid? How does he relate Jane Austen and Emily Dickinson to his argument?

4. How does the use of imagination work differently in science and in literature?

5. Why is it important for the audience watching the scene in *King Lear* in which Gloucester's eyes are put out to know that the action is not real? What would happen to the audience if the action were really taking place?

6. What dimension of experience does the imagination (through art) give us that is unattainable in real life?

7. Frye says paradoxically that art is "dreamland" at the same time that it represents the greatest reality. Discuss the meaning of this paradox.

8. What is the style of this essay? What methods does Frye use to achieve it?

Suggestions for Writing

1. Investigate some of Shakespeare's plays with which you are familiar for additional examples of painful scenes that are, as we read or watch them, pleasurable. Write a paper in which you deal with the causes of this curious situation. A research project might explore literary critics, beginning with Aristotle, who have attempted to explain the relation of art to life.

2. Write a paper comparing Forster's "Art for Art's Sake" with Frye's essay. On what points do they seem to agree?

Mike Royko
The Virtue of Prurience

Mike Royko (b. 1932) is thoroughly a Chicagoan, having been born there and having worked on Chicago newspapers most of his life. He was for many years a columnist for the *Chicago Sun-Times,* is now a columnist for the *Chicago Tribune,* winner of a Pulitzer Prize for commentary, and author of four books. His essay on censorship provides a good example of how to treat a serious subject with wit.

My first right-wing endeavor—helping get a book banned—has failed miserably. I now can appreciate how frustrating life in our permissive society must be for such grim-lipped groups as the Moral Majority.

Normally, I don't favor censorship and have never before tried to get anything banned. But several months ago, I joined in a crusade that was being led by Bill and Barbara Younis of Hannibal, N.Y.

Bill and Barbara are parents of an 18-year-old high school senior, and they became alarmed when they discovered that their daughter was being required to read a book they considered vulgar.

They went to the school superintendent and demanded that the book be removed from the reading list. He refused.

So they asked friends and neighbors to sign petitions supporting them, and they demanded that the school board ban the book.

That's when I found out about it. A reporter from that part of New York called to ask me what I thought of the censorship efforts.

I responded by dropping the phone, shouting, "Hot damn, yowee!" and dancing gleefully around my office.

I reacted that way because it is a book that I wrote about 12 years ago. It is called "Boss" and is about Mayor Richard J. Daley, power, and Chicago politics.

Before long, there were news stories about the censorship efforts of the Younises, and my phone started ringing with calls from other writers.

One of them said:

"You slick devil, how did you ever pull that off?"

I'm just lucky, I guess.

"Well, I don't get it. My last book was so torrid and lurid that I blushed while writing it. And there hasn't even been a hint from anybody about banning it."

You're just unlucky, I guess.

Another writer called and said: "This is so unfair. In my last book, George did it with Lucy, Lucy did it with Wally, Wally did it with Evelyn, Evelyn did it with George, George did it with Wally, Lucy did it with Sally, and then they all did it together."

Sounds exhausting.

"What I don't understand, is why you, but not me. I mean, I could really use a break like that."

Maybe I just live right.

What they were talking about was the tremendous commercial value of being banned. By anyone, anywhere, just as long as you are banned. It works this way:

If you can get a book banned in, say, Minneapolis, and there is a great furor about it, the book will suddenly become a best-seller next door in St. Paul. Sure, you won't sell any books in Minneapolis. But for every book you don't sell in Minneapolis, you'll sell 10 in St. Paul.

That's all part of the forbidden-fruit syndrome. Tell people they can't have or do something, and they immediately want to do it.

With this in mind, I called my publisher and said: "Get those presses rolling. We're going to sell a ton."

He said: "Not yet. You haven't been banned yet. And just being threatened with censorship isn't enough. You've got to be tossed off the shelves."

So I got on the phone and called Mr. and Mrs. Younis.

"Your book is vulgar," they said. "It is filled with swear words."

I know. That's the way Chicago politicians talk, so I quoted them. But you're right. It's vulgar. Shocking.

"You agree?"

Hell . . . I mean, heck, yes. And I'm behind you 100 percent.

"You are?"

Of course I am. I think what you're doing is terrific. And if I were there, I'd sign your petition.

"You would?"

Darn right. I don't want 18-year-olds reading words like (bleep) and (censored) and (deleted). Who ever heard of 18-year-olds being exposed to such language?

"Would you send us a letter expressing your support?"

Of course. I'll do more than that. I'll write a column urging that my book be banned.

And I did.

Since then, I've been thumbing through travel folders, real-estate brochures for tropical hideaways, yachting magazines, and girlie magazines, anticipating life as a rich and censored author.

Nothing ever works out.

The school board set up a three-member committee to review the book and the Younises' complaint.

Then a hearing was held. Mr. and Mrs. Younis, bless them, came to the hearing and said things like: "It's got the kind of language you see painted on bridges. Books like this encourage young ladies to become prostitutes."

That's dynamite stuff. Would you want your daughter to read a book that would encourage her to enter the employ of a brothel? I should hope not.

Despite this, the committee ruled that the book would remain on the reading list.

Mr. and Mrs. Younis have now removed three of their four children from the school system and say they will send them to private schools.

A noble effort, but it doesn't do me much good. As the school superintendent said:

"We made our decision, and it was a good one. There is nothing wrong with that book."

Doggone busybody.

Suggestions for Discussion

1. What is the tone of Royko's essay? How does he achieve the right tone? Is it appropriate to the subject of the essay? Explain its title.

2. Why are fellow authors jealous of Royko? What examples of their works does he use? How are those works different from his? Should the book about George and Lucy and the others be banned? Explain.

3. What is "the forbidden-fruit syndrome"?

4. What serious issue does Royko suggest in his description of the Younis couple?

5. Why is censorship a danger to human freedom? Are there instances in which censorship might safely be imposed?

Suggestions for Writing

1. Royko says, "Tell people they can't have or do something, and they immediately want to do it." Write an essay illustrating this comment. Explain why you think Royko's observation about people may be accurate.

2. Write an essay in which you discuss a play, movie, poem, painting, or novel which you think should be banned. Explain your reasons. If you don't believe in banning anything, explain why, giving your reasons carefully.

E. M. Forster

Art for Art's Sake

Edward Morgan Forster (1879–1970) was a British novelist educated at King's College, Cambridge. He lived for a time in Italy, was a member of the Bloomsbury Group of writers and artists in London, and spent the major part of his life in Cambridge. His works include *Where Angels Fear to Tread* (1905), *A Room With a View* (1908), and *A Passage to India* (1924). In this essay from *Two Cheers for Democracy* (1951), Forster explains the importance of art as a source of comfort and order in a troubled society.

I believe in art for art's sake. It is an unfashionable belief, and some of my statements must be of the nature of an apology. Sixty years ago I should have faced you with more confidence. A writer or a speaker who chose "Art for Art's Sake" for his theme sixty years ago could be sure of being in the swim, and could feel so confident of success that he sometimes dressed himself in aesthetic costumes suitable to the occasion—in an embroidered dressing-gown, perhaps, or a blue velvet suit with a Lord Fauntleroy collar; or a toga, or a kimono, and carried a poppy or a lily or a long peacock's feather in his mediaeval hand. Times have changed. Not thus can I present either myself or my theme to-day. My aim rather is to ask you quietly to reconsider for a few minutes a phrase which has been much misused and much abused, but which has, I believe, great importance for us—has, indeed, eternal importance.

Now we can easily dismiss those peacock's feathers and other affectations— they are but trifles—but I want also to dismiss a more dangerous heresy, namely the silly idea that only art matters, an idea which has somehow got mixed up with the idea of art for art's sake, and has helped to discredit it. Many things besides art, matter. It is merely one of the things that matter, and high though the claims are that I make for it, I want to keep them in proportion. No one can spend his or her life entirely in the creation or the appreciation of masterpieces. Man lives, and ought to live, in a complex world, full of conflicting claims, and if we simplified them down into the aesthetic he would be sterilised. Art for art's sake does not mean that only art matters and I would also like to rule out such phrases as, "The Life of Art," "Living for Art," and "Art's High Mission." They confuse and mislead.

What does the phrase mean? Instead of generalising, let us take a specific instance—Shakespeare's *Macbeth*, for example, and pronounce the words, "*Macbeth* for *Macbeth's sake.*" What does that mean? Well, the play has several aspects—it is educational, it teaches us something about legendary Scotland, something about Jacobean England, and a good deal about human nature and its perils. We can study its origins, and study and enjoy its dramatic technique and the music of its diction. All that is true. But *Macbeth* is furthermore a world of its own, created by Shakespeare and existing in virtue of its own poetry. It is in this aspect *Macbeth* for *Macbeth*'s sake, and that is what I intend by the phrase "art for art's sake." A work of art—whatever else it may be—is a self-contained entity, with a life of its own imposed on it by its creator. It has internal order. It may have external form. That is how we recognise it.

Take for another example that picture of Seurat's which I saw two years ago in Chicago—"*La Grande Jatte.*" Here again there is much to study and to enjoy: the pointillism, the charming face of the seated girl, the nineteenth-century Parisian Sunday sunlight, the sense of motion in immobility. But here again there is something more; "*La Grande Jatte*" forms a world of its own, created by Seurat and existing by virtue of its own poetry: "*La Grande Jatte*" *pour "La Grande Jatte": l'art pour l'art.* Like *Macbeth* it has internal order and internal life.

It is to the conception of order that I would now turn. This is important to my argument, and I want to make a digression, and glance at order in daily life, before I come to order in art.

In the world of daily life, the world which we perforce inhabit, there is much talk about order, particularly from statesmen and politicians. They tend, however, to confuse order with orders, just as they confuse creation with regulations. Order, I suggest, is something evolved from within, not something imposed from without; it is an internal stability, a vital harmony, and in the social and political category, it has never existed except for the convenience of historians. Viewed realistically, the past is really a series of *disorders*, succeeding one another by discoverable laws, no doubt, and certainly marked by an increasing growth of human interference, but disorders all the same. So that, speaking as a writer, what I hope for today is a disorder which will be more favourable to artists than is the present one, and which will provide them with fuller inspirations and better material conditions. It will not last—nothing lasts—but there have been some advantageous disorders in the past—for instance, in ancient Athens, in Renaissance Italy, eighteenth-century France, periods in China and Persia—and we may do something to accelerate the next one. But let us not again fix our hearts where true joys are not to be found. We were promised a new order after the first world war through the League of Nations. It did not come, nor have I faith in present promises, by whomsoever endorsed. The implacable offensive of Science forbids. We cannot reach social and political stability for the reason that we continue to make scientific discoveries and to apply them, and thus to destroy the arrangements which were based on more elementary discoveries. If Science would discover rather than apply—if, in other words, men were more interested in knowledge than in power—mankind would be in a far safer position, the stability statesmen talk about would be a possibility, there could be a new order based on vital harmony, and the earthly millennium might approach. But Science shows no signs of doing this: she gave us the internal combustion engine, and before we had digested and assimilated it with terrible pains into our social system, she harnessed the atom, and destroyed any new order that seemed to be evolving. How can man get into harmony with his surroundings when he is constantly altering them? The future of our race is, in this direction, more unpleasant than we care to admit, and it has sometimes seemed to me that its best chance lies through apathy, uninventiveness, and inertia. Universal exhaustion might promote that Change of Heart which is at present so briskly recommended from a thousand pulpits. Universal exhaustion would certainly be a new experience. The human race has never undergone it, and is still too perky to admit that it may be coming and might result in a sprouting of new growth through the decay.

I must not pursue these speculations any further—they lead me too far from my terms of reference and maybe from yours. But I do want to emphasize that order in daily life and in history, order in the social and political category, is unattainable under our present psychology.

Where is it attainable? Not in the astronomical category, where it was for many years enthroned. The heavens and the earth have become terribly alike since Einstein. No longer can we find a reassuring contrast to chaos in the night sky and look up with George Meredith to the stars, the army of unalterable law, or listen for the music of the spheres. Order is not there. In the entire universe there seem to be only two possibilities for it. The first of them—which again lies outside my terms of reference—is the divine order, the mystic harmony, which according to all religions is available for those who can contemplate it. We much admit its possibility, on the evidence of the adepts, and we must believe them when they say that it is attained, if attainable, by prayer. "O thou who changest not, abide with me," said one of its poets. "*Ordina questo amor, o tu che m'ami,*" said another: "Set love in order thou who lovest me." The existence of a divine order, though it cannot be tested, has never been disproved.

The second possibility for order lies in the aesthetic category, which is my subject here: the order which an artist can create in his own work, and to that we must now return. A work of art, we are all agreed, is a unique product. But why? It is unique not because it is clever or noble or beautiful or enlightened or original or sincere or idealistic or useful or educational—it may embody any of those qualities—but because it is the only material object in the universe which may possess internal harmony. All the others have been pressed into shape from outside, and when their mold is removed they collapse. The work of art stands up by itself, and nothing else does. It achieves something which has often been promised by society, but always delusively. Ancient Athens made a mess—but the *Antigone* stands up. Renaissance Rome made a mess—but the ceiling of the Sistine got painted. James I made a mess—but there was *Macbeth*. Louis XIV—but there was *Phedre*. Art for art's sake? I should just think so, and more so than ever at the present time. It is the one orderly product which our muddling race has produced. It is the cry of a thousand sentinels, the echo from a thousand labyrinths; it is the lighthouse which cannot be hidden: *c'est le meilleur témoignage que nous puissions donner de notre dignité. Antigone* for *Antigone*'s sake, *Macbeth* for *Macbeth*'s, *"La Grande Jatte" pour "La Grande Jatte."*

If this line of argument is correct, it follows that the artist will tend to be an outsider in the society to which he has been born, and that the nineteenth century conception of him as a Bohemian was not inaccurate. The conception erred in three particulars: it postulated an economic system where art could be a full-time job, it introduced the fallacy that only art matters, and it overstressed idiosyncracy and waywardness—the peacock-feather aspect—rather than order. But it is a truer conception than the one which prevails in official circles on my side of the Atlantic—I don't know about yours: the conception which treats the artist as if he were a particularly bright government advertiser and encourages him to be friendly and matey with his fellow citizens, and not to give himself airs.

Estimable is mateyness, and the man who achieves it gives many a pleasant little drink to himself and to others. But it has no traceable connection with the creative impulse, and probably acts as an inhibition on it. The artist who is seduced by mateyness may stop himself from doing the one thing which he, and he alone, can do—the making of something out of words or sounds or paint or clay or marble or steel or film which has internal harmony and presents order to a permanently disarranged planet. This seems worth doing, even at the risk of being called uppish by journalists. I have in mind an article which was published some years ago in the London *Times*, an article called "The Eclipse of the Highbrow," in which the "Average Man" was exalted, and all contemporary literature was censured if it did not toe the line, the precise position of the line being naturally known to the writer of the article. Sir Kenneth Clark, who was at that time director of our National Gallery, commented on this pernicious doctrine in a letter which cannot be too often quoted. "The poet and the artist," wrote Clark, "are important precisely because they are not average men; because in sensibility, intelligence, and power of invention they far exceed the average." These memorable words, and particularly the words "power of invention," are the Bohemian's passport. Furnished with it, he slinks about society, saluted now by a brickbat and now by a penny, and accepting either of them with equanimity. He does not consider too anxiously what his relations with society may be, for he is aware of something more important than that—namely the invitation to invent, to create order, and he believes he will be better placed for doing this if he attempts detachment. So round and round he slouches, with his hat pulled over his eyes, and maybe with a louse in his beard, and—if he really wants one— a peacock's feather in his hand.

If our present society should disintegrate—and who dare prophesy that it won't?—this old-fashioned and démodé figure will become clearer: the Bohemian, the outsider, the parasite, the rat—one of those figures which have at present no function either in a warring or a peaceful world. It may not be dignified to be a rat, but many of the ships are sinking, which is not dignified either—the officials did not build them properly. Myself, I would sooner be a swimming rat than a sinking ship—at all events I can look around me for a little longer—and I remember how one of us, a rat with particularly bright eyes called Shelley, squeaked out, "Poets are the unacknowledged legislators of the world," before he vanished into the waters of the Mediterranean.

What laws did Shelley propose to pass? None. The legislation of the artist is never formulated at the time, though it is sometimes discerned by future generations. He legislates through creating. And he creates through his sensitiveness and power to impose form. Without form the sensitiveness vanishes. And form is as important today, when the human race is trying to ride the whirlwind, as it ever was in those less agitating days of the past, when the earth seemed solid and the stars fixed, and the discoveries of science were made slowly, slowly. Form is not tradition. It alters from generation to generation. Artists always seek a new technique, and will continue to do so as long as their work excites them. But form of some kind is imperative. It is the surface crust of the internal harmony, it is the outward evidence of order.

My remarks about society may have seemed too pessimistic, but I believe that society can only represent a fragment of the human spirit, and that another fragment can only get expressed through art. And I wanted to take this opportunity, this vantage ground, to assert not only the existence of art, but its pertinacity. Looking back into the past, it seems to me that that is all there has ever been: vantage grounds for discussion and creation, little vantage grounds in the changing chaos, where bubbles have been blown and webs spun, and the desire to create order has found temporary gratification, and the sentinels have managed to utter their challenges, and the huntsmen, though lost individually, have heard each other's calls through the impenetrable wood, and the lighthouses have never ceased sweeping the thankless seas. In this pertinacity there seems to me, as I grow older, something more and more profound, something which does in fact concern people who do not care about art at all.

In conclusion, let me summarise the various categories that have laid claim to the possession of Order.

(1) The social and political category. Claim disallowed on the evidence of history and of our own experience. If man altered psychologically, order here might be attainable: not otherwise.

(2) The astronomical category. Claim allowed up to the present century, but now disallowed on the evidence of the physicists.

(3) The religious category. Claim allowed on the evidence of the mystics.

(4) The aesthetic category. Claim allowed on the evidence of various works of art, and on the evidence of our own creative impulses, however weak these

may be or however imperfectly they may function. Works of art, in my opinion, are the only objects in the material universe to possess internal order, and that is why, though I don't believe that only art matters, I do believe in Art for Art's Sake.

Suggestions for Discussion

1. Why does Forster make clear that the belief in art for art's sake does not mean a belief that only art matters?

2. Where does art stand, for Forster, in the list of things that matter?

3. Explain Forster's phrase, "*Macbeth* for *Macbeth*'s sake." How does he use it to explain his main argument?

4. Explain Forster's comparison of the order of art with order in life. How does this comparison function in his argument?

5. What does Forster mean by claiming that a work of art is a unique product?

6. Examine Forster's categories that have laid claim to the possession of order. Why does he reject all but the religious and aesthetic categories?

Suggestions for Writing

1. Write a paper explaining Forster's defense of art.

2. Obviously, many people feel differently from Forster about the autonomy of art. In Marxist countries, for example, art is often considered to be a servant of the state. Write a paper in which you argue for or against Forster's position.

Oscar Mandel
Dissonant Music Sixty Years After

Oscar Mandel (b. 1926) is a professor in the Division of Humanities and Social Sciences at the California Institute of Technology. He is the author of numerous books and articles about drama, fiction, poetry, and literary criticism. He is also a playwright, poet, and fiction writer. In this extended essay, published in 1973, Mandel makes a strong argument against atonal music while defending experimentation in visual art and literature. Throughout, he shows his concern for the relation of art to society.

> *What will "vanguardism" leave to posterity? Nothing but smoldering cinders which its propagandists, shouting from the housetops, are trying to make us believe are a living forest.*
> —*Dmitri Shostakovitch*

> *Taking the "average" audience for major symphony concerts, and speaking personally, I can say that I care no more about them and their reactions than I do about the audience for jukeboxes in bars.*
> —*Charles Wuorinen*

I

There is no single musical term that neatly covers the multiple experiments and adventures in music launched in our century. We all know that the music of our epoch is impossible to confuse with that of the century before, whether it is composed by a moderate respectful of tradition or by an extremist sick of all precedent, and whether it is scored for a string quartet or issues from a formidable piece of electronic equipment. Yet how can one place a composer like Hindemith (for instance) in the company of the beep/blop magnetic-tape sound producers? Only by asserting that every age is endowed with a loose yet essential "philosophical" coherence which gives it identity. Thus, set off from a Beethoven or a Tchaikovsky, the most disparate and mutually hostile schools and individuals of our time keep company after all in the same cultural basket. In the following pages I will use the term "dissonant" as my unifying cultural concept for the simple reason that every layman recognizes it and himself applies it with a rough justice of his own to pretty nearly all serious music that has been composed since Schönberg. I might have preferred a term like "malsonant," because it has the merit of clearly including the breakdown of "beautiful melody" and cadence along with the collapse of traditional codes regarding harmony and tonality. But there are too many word-coins in circulation already. I merely ask that the reader accept the term "dissonant" for the purposes of this paper in an untechnically comprehensive sense.

Is it still possible, in the declining half of the twentieth century, to raise a sensible argument against dissonant music? Or is the question dead? In a recent issue of the *Columbia Forum* there appeared an article by a music critic, Joan Peyser, in praise of the "annihilation of tonality" which was carried out in the days of Schönberg and Alban Berg. That such an article should be printed in a serious journal suggests that the liquidation of *beauty* in music—because beauty is what it is finally all about—still needs defending. If so, all hope is not lost. Those of us who have sometimes felt like pitiable fossils because the experts and the professionals have been treating us like pitiable fossils for sixty or seventy years might try our voices again, take heart, and discover that we are still alive. Let us see therefore whether we can speak to our atonalists so sensibly that even if their very nursery ditties were dodecaphonic snatches, they might be willing to reconsider the foundations of their musical lives.

II

To begin at the beginning, we must come to an understanding about the aim of music. Why does music exist at all in an "advanced civilization"? Professionals are unlikely to trouble their minds with a "silly question" of this sort, but this is precisely where the appearance of an innocent outsider is important—someone who asks the unblushing primary questions. Leaving aside the practical uses of music—the bugle that wakes soldiers up, the band to which people dance, the organ helping a religious service along—we ask what is the purpose of music for the sake of which people sit down in large rooms and to which they listen for an hour, two hours, or three hours, with evident attention and satisfaction.

What if I propose that the aim of music (the aim, that is, of most music most of the time for most people in our civilization today) is to "refresh our spirits"? I take this modest phrase from the title page of Bach's *Clavier-Übung* of 1735. The idea of refreshing our spirits can be stated in many ways. Some ways will seem useless merely because the phrasing is archaic, or because certain words have been appropriated by groups of people we do not like to be associated with. Other ways will seem pertinent because the idioms are "in" with the experts. Furthermore, there is always a moderate "classical" approach and a titanic "romantic" attitude toward life and art: one person will say "Music must make me happy for a moment," another will say "Music must arouse my profoundest feelings," and neither may realize that the difference between them lies not in their feelings, but in their feelings about their feelings. I propose "refreshing our spirits," but I am willing to offer "a delight that goes to the roots of our being." Whichever phrase I choose, I am talking about pleasure.

Search as I will among all manner of possibilities, I cannot find another purpose to challenge that of refreshing our spirits. If we still believed in God, and especially in a Lutheran God, we might well make it an axiom that music exists to celebrate His glory. But even then, how would we know whether He felt celebrated or insulted, except by consulting our own delight first?

In the absence of God, what else can reasonably be proposed? That the purpose of music is to create knowledge about the world in the listener's or the composer's mind? I think it would be difficult to make this stick. This is a claim which we men of letters often assert for our poems, our novels, and our plays. Because literature uses words in common with philosophy, theology, history, journalism, and most sciences, a reasonable case can be made for the instructive value of literature. For many centuries now, literary critics and writers themselves have insisted that literature does, or at least ought to, inculcate. Inculcate what? Knowledge or Morality or both. Literature, the saying goes, is Interpretation of Life.

Even those of us who emphasize the primacy of pleasure in literature no less than in music would have to agree that if a child were brought up on nothing but poems, novels, and plays, he would acquire a tolerable view of life, not to mention an impressive battery of plain facts. A child brought up on nothing but music would grow up an idiot. If he were given a great deal of vocal music—songs, motets, masses, operas—the knowledge of life he would gain would come overwhelmingly from the separable texts. To say this is not to deny that instrumental music can accomplish *something* in the world of concepts and views of life. Ideas and images (along with feelings) of devotion, misery, enthusiasm, mockery, and the like can be induced by music, but they occur as random bobs on the surface, without logical integrations, and they cannot be marshaled into organized insights into the world. Music reminds us of ideas, while literature asserts them. Then again, when music carries a text, the composer occasionally uses his instruments to throw an idea, as it were, at the text. If a group of twittering flutes is brought in at the moment the text is expressing a "noble" thought, the music is being ironical: it flings a denial at the words. This is undoubtedly a thought. But how far does all this carry us? A few steps, and then we are back with "emotional power." Music creates emotion; and to say emotion (in this case) is to say pleasure.

If, however, I am told that my view is wrong, that atonal music, for example, is a commentary upon modern life, a way of grasping and understanding the quality of modern civilization, then I am forced to remove myself with my own axioms and to leave my dissenter with his. He will tell me, "Of course you reject atonal music; you insist on *enjoying* it, while I am showing you that it must interpret contemporary life for you." Our conversation founders on incompatible axioms for which there is no court of appeal.

It founders too when the professional musician claims that music exists primarily in order to further music—that music is an exploration of the endless possibilities of producing sounds, and as such is sufficient unto itself. This person considers the end of music achieved if he hears a new electronic sound-producer or if he creates a timbre never before heard by human ears. He might classify one of his products as irritating and another as gentle, but the two are equally successful in his mind. More: he strives as hard to obtain "intolerable" sounds as any other kind. The pleasure he creates in his listeners is defined most properly as a sense of satisfaction in invention: invention of sounds, combinations of sounds, and organizing principles for sounds. It is, in short, a professional's pleasure in the tools of his profession.

Two other avenues are open: Morality and Hygiene. Here discourse becomes easier. Music can be thought of as an aid to fervor in battle or success in love; its mission might be to assuage hatred and promote sympathy, to further digestion, or to tranquilize workers in a business office. Its therapeutic usefulness to the nervous may be stressed. Platonic warnings against seductive musical modes can be countered with case histories of recuperation under the influence of melody.

Those who subscribe to any of the moral or hygienic possibilities of music will agree that music "stirs our emotions," but for them stirring our emotions is never the end of the road. What is the good, they ask, of having our emotions stirred? Does the stirring make us better men, saner men, healthier men, or happier men? This is the real question.

The answer is yes: perhaps all of these together. And perhaps the expression "refreshing our spirits" amiably includes them all. If so, I would suggest that music cannot make us better, saner, or healthier unless it has first given us pleasure. Neither my digestion nor my humanity will be helped if I am actively hating what I hear. The pathway runs from the sounds of the instruments to our ears, thence to the stirring of emotions on the pleasurable side of the cerebral fence, and then finally, if at all, to moral or physical "refreshment." My own inclination is to call moral or physical amelioration an optional end (that is to say, music *can* do these things) and to insist that the only obligatory end is to give pleasure. For I can easily conceive of music that gives intense pleasure to a cheat, a terminal patient, or a psychotic, without mending any of them. Yet they will unhesitatingly call such music good. Fortunately, this particular doctrinal difference does not mean a parting of the ways. I do not care whether giving pleasure is the rigorously necessary means or the end itself. It is understood that if music fails to give sensuous delight, it will also fail to make us better, saner, or healthier.

III

The thorns become sharper as soon as we ask, Sensuous delight for whom? Artists are often irrational creatures. We hear them over and over again complaining about the lack of communication in our society; but the next moment they blithely recommend self-expression as the only genuine purpose of art. "I write to please myself." "I paint what I need to paint." "I compose in order to express my inner needs." Alas, there are as many platitudes for intellectuals in every age as there are saws for simple-minded burghers, and a young person can rise from the ranks of the average and take his place in the herd of the intellectual elite by means of a sincere exchange of commonplaces. From saying "I write in order to make lots of money," he ascends to "I write in order to obey an inner necessity."

Composers are not behindhand with these claims. "I do but sing because I must" is a favorite among them. And, like artists everywhere today, they leap easily from the idea that artistic creation arises from an inner need to express oneself to the notion that once the self has been expressed, the work of art is a success. This is in its way a fine notion. It admits no rebuttal. If the primary aim of a musical composition is to give satisfaction to its composer, all is well: thousands upon thousands of musical scores succeed every year; the world is rolling in masterpieces.

I take polite leave of the school of self-expression and turn to those who affirm as an axiomatic point that a piece of music must please "the public." But what public is "the public"? Let me cautiously accept the traditional distinction among three possible audiences. I know the drawbacks of these divisions and categories; reality keeps refuting them; reality insists on its own ambiguities. Yet reality does come in clusters, and I think we catch certain genuine clusters if we speak of (i) an audience of specialists (composers, performers, teachers, students, scholars, critics, and a few highly trained amateurs), (ii) a general educated audience with a taste for the arts, and (iii) the mass uneducated public whose aesthetic needs are satisfied by the jukebox.

Now if the aim of music is to satisfy the musicians themselves and a small band of believers at their side, we are almost as well off as under the axiom that music exists so that artists can express themselves, and we roundly declare this age of ours a great age of music. Dissonant music pleases not only each sound-maker by himself, it is also applauded by friends and allies. This music thrives especially in academic circles, where dissidence from intellectual commonplaces is quickly tamed by means of the well-placed snicker. Programs devoted exclusively to dissonant music are presented to small audiences of followers at infrequent intervals. Then again these refractory pieces are literally forced upon the general public by performers and conductors who feel that in good conscience they ought to promote the music of contemporary composers. Carefully cushioned by Mozart on one side of the program and Beethoven on the other, a grim little noise computed by Webern can dare scratch at the audience before retreating again to the academic nest. As Joan Peyser herself bluntly states: "The composer is alienated from his audience." But not from his audience of fellow technicians.

This is where I become uneasy. I cannot think of another period in history in which the primary aim of music—the music composed by nearly all the serious artists of a given time—was to please the musical group itself. Is this aim satisfactory? To whom? And why? Or is this one more instance of the "fragmentation" of our civilization? I am tempted to speak of sickness, of deterioration—somehow it would be better, I feel, if we all addressed each other, if a poet understood a physicist, if a chemist knew the secrets of convertible debentures, if a plumber could tell what makes his light bulb give light, and if a serious composer made music for himself, you and me, and congressmen from Indiana, all in one piece.

But these are axioms again. Once more the argument closes its doors. If Mr. Stockhausen were to tell me that he is perfectly satisfied with the audience he has—"let Puccini get the rest"—what could I say? Nothing. These considerations of "the health of civilization" are too distant. Who knows whether it is not a good thing that we should all be specialists in corners? Those of us who feel that dissonant music is an aberration must fall back on another axiom.

This axiom, of course, is that the primary aim of music is to delight a large audience of nonspecialists. There is nothing sacred about this axiom; nothing intrinsically superior to the axioms I have left behind. It is simply another yardstick. According to one yardstick, music is a success. According to another, it is a failure. Who decides which yardstick is the better one? Obviously the man who is doing the measuring. This leads me to the possibility of turning my axiom around. Instead of saying that the primary aim of music is to delight a large audience of nonspecialists, I can say, a little more humanely, that a great number of people who are not themselves musicians or critics *need* the pleasure of music, and *search* for it.

At this stage I dismiss the third audience I have mentioned: the mass audience. This audience is well served by contemporary music. It has the sweet violin music it needs for candlelight situations, it has trombone bands to dance by, it has crooners delivering simple love songs, it has the frenzies of acid rock for its orgiastic needs—in short, there is a vast supply of twentieth-century sound to delight the mass twentieth-century ear. One music in our time has satisfied the specialists, and another has satisfied the uneducated. There remains, in the vast middle, that class to which millions of us belong: the educated nonspecialists, to whom, *for sixty years*, fresh music has been denied.

I launch the exaggeration and then retreat from it—in order to recapture my ground and hold it. Stravinsky is practically a popular composer—through half a dozen of his works. Benjamin Britten, another moderate, has created intense beauty without lapsing into Victorian romanticism. Certain highly expressive works, like Bartók's quartets, which still play off discord against concord, attract the sophisticated wing of my second public. Besides, my argument concerns the Western world; it does not touch Soviet composers, who are not at liberty to manufacture any sounds they please and to express their "alienation." I could hedge, border, and clip in this vein for several pages. But when all the qualifying is done, the large truths stand unaltered: thoroughgoing dissonance dominates the field of "serious" music; all other styles are on the defensive; and thoroughgoing dissonance, according to the confession or the boast of our composers themselves, has been repelling the general public for the entire sixty-odd years of its existence.

IV

The claim that the future will love cacophony (or will no longer call it that) is beginning to sound as funny as the warnings of hopeful Christians, these two thousand years, that the end of the world is at hand. "In a few decades," Schönberg wrote a few decades ago, "audiences will recognize the *tonality* of this music today called atonal. . . . Atonal is what will be understood in the future." For Miss Peyser, this stale prophecy still has charm. "In time," she writes, "the strangeness will fade and men will embrace the great works that will appear." But in what time, may we ask? In the twentieth century sixty years is an epoch. Time is becoming more and more compressed; that is to say, more and more events are occurring in any given time span. Therefore, when we are told again and again that eventually dissonant music will seem normal, beautiful, inspiring, or what have you, we may be excused, we denizens of the twentieth century, for turning our backs at last.

Beethoven was a revolutionary composer; Wagner was a revolutionary composer; Debussy was a revolutionary composer. But did it take these men sixty years to persuade the educated thousands or millions? By no means. In their much slower times, they converted their thousands and millions in a decade or less. Dissonant composers clearly staged a revolution of a different order. They demolished the socioaesthetic foundations of art. From the revolutionary summons of a new music for society—which had given society Beethoven, Wagner, Debussy—they proceeded to organize a music *outside* of society. I do not assert that they intended this exit. But depart from society they did. And I add: any composer who dislikes the huddle of composers outdoors in exile must be ready as a rational being to declare the experiment of dissonance bankrupt.

This bankruptcy is clearest in the realm of vocal music. Since Puccini died in 1924, not a single opera has imposed itself as a permanent and reliable piece in the world's repertory. In agony are the mass, the oratorio, and the serious song. Instrumental music may hobble forward on its crutches without beauty, but the human voice clambering cheerlessly from sound to sound, forbidden on pain of death by ridicule to utter a melody, has absolutely nowhere to go. It seems never to occur to our experts and professionals that history offers no precedent for an entire epoch unable or unwilling to furnish singable music to the educated public. Nor that this fact is astounding. Nor that it proves that music is sick.

For the specialist it is not sick at all, I repeat. He and his friends in the trade congratulate themselves and one another in journals, congresses, at concerts, and in their correspondence on the unbelievable technical prowesses that have eliminated vulgar melodic expressiveness, that is to say, beauty. It is not sick for the masses, who go to their own sources; it is sick only for the millions who are the equivalent today of the audience in Prague that Mozart intoxicated with *Don Giovanni*. An entire age without serious music for itself! An entire age that must choose between the primitive structures of proletarian music and the utterly joyless constructions of specialists.

V

Music is the only bankrupt art. In the days when composers began killing beauty in music, painters and sculptors were scrapping the art of imitating beautiful nature. Everyone is agreed that this simultaneity was not a coincidence. A universal renovation of the arts was taking place, itself a portion of an even vaster movement of civilization into new areas of knowing, feeling, and judging. But when the same yardstick I have proposed for music is applied to the visual arts, the results are brutally different. In the visual arts, the time lag was no more and no less than what is to be expected. Nonrepresentational art, cubism, surrealism—the various modalities of the new age—all produced shock and outrage, and then were promptly integrated into the general sensibility. Today the same crowds that flock to their Philharmonic Halls to hear Beethoven's Seventh are interested and even avid supporters of contemporary artists, beginning of course with Picasso: not, I insist, five or six works by Picasso (as they will listen to five or six works by Stravinsky) but all of Picasso, down to his napkin doodles. Moreover, the same people who would not dream of buying a Boulez recording decorate their rooms with nonfigurative pictures. Very simply, the visual artists have succeeded, the composers have failed. If the composers assert, and many of them do, that the general public is benighted, they had better explain why this same public accepts modern painting.

But there is more. Another sign of success for the visual arts is that they have percolated down to the masses. I do not mean that in their popular forms they are at their best; this is not the point. The point is that an idiom meaningful to the large educated public of any given generation will inevitably influence the taste of the masses as well. Modern visualization is everywhere: the advertiser uses it; it appears in the work of church, bank, office, or restaurant decorators; it dominates the design of useful objects like airplanes, coffeepots, and chairs. Visual art lives; it speaks to the educated and the uneducated; it flows gracefully and normally from sophisticated specialist to naive layman. We do not have to say that "in time the strangeness will fade and men will embrace the great works that will appear." Let the future take care of itself. The visual artists and designers of our time have won their own time.

The failure of dissonant music to reach the popular consciousness, even in a debased and vulgarized form, is a remarkable symptom. One would expect that something of Alban Berg would have penetrated at least the music of the Beatles and their innumerable successors, whose appeal is to the supposedly sophisticated young. But not only is atonal music inaudible in the advertising jingle, in piped elevator music, and in dance music, it has not touched the folksingers who perform for undergraduates at Berkeley, or hairy quartets that pummel masses of young listeners into states of frenzy. They make odd sounds on odd instruments, to be sure; they use electronic equipment side by side with the academic composers; but their music is as lusciously harmonic and melodic as music can be; their effects are expressive and gorgeous. Are they forming the audience of the future that will applaud great atonal works? Far from it.

If we could raise a few hundred newborn infants in isolation from traditional classical music and contemporary popular music, and expose them to nothing but dissonant works, we would discover whether our revulsion is a judgment we make as prisoners of our culture or a result of basic physiological "lesions." But this we cannot do. Inevitably, our children hear the latest pop tune or Mozart. Obstinately, they grow up preferring either or both to dissonant music. I see no indication that the children of our grandchildren will make a different choice.

VI

Why has music failed, when the other arts have succeeded? Why have three generations of music lovers been compelled to turn for nearly all their musical experience to works of the past? It is hard to believe that the public has taken a mysterious plunge from the level of taste at which it operated in the days when, after certain difficulties, it managed to follow Beethoven or Wagner. Public taste has not degenerated with respect to the visual arts, and no one can show that it has collapsed vis-á-vis music. Music is "out in the cold" not because the house fell down on it, but because it vacated the house.

But why? The question is still unanswered. It is not enough to accuse modern composers of having deliberately declared war on humanity—of having invented poisonous sound combinations and sound sequences for the express purpose of pestering society. To be sure, in part they joined with other artists in the ever-enjoyable game of baiting-the-babbitt. But mostly they stumbled into a way by accident.

One explanation for this accident is to be found in the unequal vulnerability of our sight and hearing. Let me offer a simple example. We are more easily offended and hurt by a bawled or strident radio commercial than by a stupid advertising display in a newspaper. "At least the picture doesn't make noise!" Our hearing is more readily irritated than our sight, just as our sense of smell is more easily offended than either. It takes an extreme explosion of light to hurt us, whereas sound disturbs us all the time. There is no visual counterpart, for example, to the physical misery we feel when a knife is scraped against a plate. In sum, our sensory territory seems to have areas of tolerance of varying magnitudes. Because the area of tolerable sound experiences is relatively small, experiments in music reached and then crossed the boundary far more rapidly than parallel experiments in the visual arts.

I do not doubt that training or exposure can affect the extent and the precise contour of these areas of tolerance. But can they be stretched indefinitely? Partisans of dissonant music like Miss Peyser believe that time, training, and exposure will colonize new ground. A new generation will respond to Stockhausen and Boulez as we, laggards, adore Bach. However, two new generations have refused to budge, and Webern is still performed—sixty years later!—as "avant-garde music." I submit that our composers strayed into an area of aesthetic intolerance that will never be colonized—either, as I firmly believe, because this music inflicts physiological lesions on the human brain, or because it is kept at bay by the unavoidable presence and damaging otherness of traditional "beautiful sounds."

Those who like to speak of "the wonderful capacity of the human ear to adapt to new conditions"—I am quoting Professor Joseph Machlis—overestimate this capacity. The areas of tolerance do expand, contract, or simply alter in individuals and societies; and it is true that sounds which scraped at our nerves at one time may appear beautiful a year or a decade later. But to turn this limited flexibility and adaptability into a principle of infinite plasticity is mere recklessness.

How then is it that the first audience I have described—the audience of disciples and specialists—does exist, and does renew itself year after year? Are we dealing with special beings endowed by heredity with areas of tolerance distinct from our own? And if not, why can we not join this audience where it lives?

In the first place, we must keep in mind that an impassable gulf exists between this first audience and ourselves with regard to the aim of music itself. Much of this audience has lost interest in sensuous delight, in "refreshing the spirit," in beauty. Much of this audience, as I have noted earlier, is interested chiefly in refining the tools of the musical profession. Hence the complacency of this group, and its undeniable success. Success, that is, on the basis of an axiom which does not interest the second audience. Still, a few members of this audience will firmly state that atonal music, for example, is "beautiful." *They* experience none of the lesions I so mysteriously allude to; *they* feel the sensuous rapture that others feel in the presence of Bach. To those in this group whose training and exposure are no different in their essentials from ours, I reply that strong variations in the areas of tolerance—or, in other words, the physiology of beauty—do exist; that in sensing beauty in dissonant music they happen to lie at the far end of the curve; and that sixty years of dissonance have failed to move the center of that curve in any perceptible way.

To those in this group who claim that only extremes of training and discipline can reveal the beauty of dissonance and its ability to "refresh our spirits," I reply that life is short, we can all be trained in but a few disciplines, and the artist, like the engineer or the doctor, must take us as we are. Anyone who writes music that can be considered beautiful only by an audience which has, in effect, duplicated the composer's training, condemns himself to solitude. Less than anyone else can he hope that dissonant music will some day seem beautiful to the general intelligentsia.

Those who genuinely sense beauty in dissonant music, whether by natural endowment or through rigorous training, resemble nothing so much as the Hindu fakir lying on a bed of nails. Whether by nature or nurture, he too has a special area of tolerance. He despises us, perhaps, for feeling that sharp nails are unpleasant. To him they are kind. He argues that we are fusty conservatives. He believes the future is with beds of nails. He invites us to train ourselves to enjoy them. "In a few decades," he says, "men will recognize the softness of nails that today are called sharp." But we refuse to credit him. We say that beds of nails will be unpleasant to most people forever; we doubt that even of those who did train themselves like the fakir, more than a few would get to enjoy a bed of nails; we say that even if the effort succeeded, it would not be worth the time and energy expended: for is he happier on his bed of nails than we are on our spring mattresses? And finally we admire in and through him the curious diversity of human powers and sensibilities.

All in all, therefore, I maintain that dissonant music has taken us outside the general area of human tolerance. Most of those who "appreciate" this music do so without regard to tolerance or intolerance (I mean beauty or ugliness) because they are interested in sound organization—in the tools of their profession. The others are the fakirs of music; they are not harbingers of a new sensibility, but eccentrics of perception.

VII

The line of reasoning that tries to integrate dissonant music, now or in the future, for the untrained or the trained, into a system of "beautiful sounds" is better abandoned altogether. Theory is on much firmer ground if it proposes instead that music joined the other arts at the beginning of this century in a vast and exhaustive exploitation of ugliness (in the sensuous arts) and evil (in literature). This is the mainstream of twentieth-century art as a whole. By this double exploitation more than anything else it is marked off from the art that preceded it. As late as the 1890's, when the art-for-art's-sake movement was breaking with so much of the past and announcing so much of the future, the cult of beauty was still intact. A first liberation from bourgeois morality had yet to be followed by a second liberation from the cult of beauty. All the arts joined hands to carry out this revolution.

It so happens that music could not afford to make this revolution succeed. For literature and representational art, the exploitation of ugliness and evil left intact their moral, psychological, and philosophical interests—interests upon which writers and representational artists draw heavily for the aesthetic pleasure they create in their audience. But music, we have seen, is not Interpretation of Life. Music does not know the world, it surpasses the world. A string quartet does not tell us whether God is alive or dead, or what to do about the generation gap. For music, giving up beauty means rashly stripping itself naked. It had nothing else to fall back on.

At this point the arguments I have offered combine. As we glance at contemporary painting and sculpture, whether abstract or figurative, we discover that the dismissal of Renaissance standards of beauty did not lead instantly to ugliness. It turned out, instead, that the entire tradition of Western art, long and glorious though it was, had failed to occupy all the areas of possible beauty. The beauty of streamlining—to take one simple example—had yet to be exploited when the twentieth century opened. It became clear that the area of visual tolerance (to use the minimal term) was far larger than expected. Virgin land was available—room for exploration in effects of beauty.

This room for exploration did not exist for music because here the area of tolerance was and is much smaller. Music fell out of traditional areas of beauty and immediately lapsed into ugliness. But painters and sculptors did more than explore new areas of beauty: they also explored ugliness and evil as never before. However, the *figurative* painters and sculptors who did so retained their grasp on the worlds of moral, psychological, historical, and metaphysical interest. These worlds were closed to music. Music flung itself into ugliness, but found nothing outside the sensuous experience to relieve it. The artistic revolution of the twentieth century, so fruitful to the other arts, had spun music out of its proper orbit.[1] Composers who thought they would educate society to a new sense of beauty failed because they required either an aberrant physiological toleration or a peculiar discipline. Only those who aspired to confine their music to a minute public of professionals and disciples achieved the goal they had set for themselves and must therefore be called successful on their own axiomatic terms.

We who work from another axiom do not dismiss the ideals of these hermetic artists laboring for the few, or for themselves alone. Happy is the culture that can offer itself the luxury of art for all classes, including a class that savors esoterica. But here we see hermeticism excluding all else; dissonance monopolizing the field of serious music; an avant-garde, in short, without a main body in sight.

Every scientist knows that a hypothesis which refuses to work ought to be replaced by another one. The hypothesis of dissonance—it is fair to call it that—has refused to work for sixty years. It has refused to work, that is, for composers who have wanted to be, like Mozart and Beethoven, members of the general elite. If they are rational beings able to make fresh choices when old ones prove fruitless, they must now strike out in new directions. For let me assert as strongly as possible that I believe in change and in experiment, and that an arrest at the point reached by Brahms or Debussy or anyone else would simply have been another kind of death for music. But this does not mean that invention is good because it is invention, or that experiment is successful because it is experiment. In 1900 it was time for music, like the other arts, to move. By taking the same direction as the other arts, music

---

[1]Along with nonrepresentational painting that confined itself to the exploitation of ugliness. I discussed the catastrophe of ugly abstract visual art in the *Columbia Forum* in 1965. Ugly abstract art and ugly music are the two cripples of our culture.

happened to move into a climate refreshing for these others, but suffocating for itself.

What would have been the true direction, or what the true direction will be in the future, I do not even dream of knowing. If a composer eager to rejoin civilization were to ask my advice, I would underscore two points I have made: the first, that the sense of beauty is not quite as flexible a faculty as many think; and the second, that ugliness, like pepper, is an excellent condiment, but a wretched meal. I will not change history if I declare that for me, works like Benjamin Britten's *Rape of Lucrece* and *Les Illuminations* seem not only masterpieces in themselves but also sufficient explorations beyond Romantic territory. Perhaps this is the destined avenue; perhaps Britten is a dead end. Perhaps the solution will come from the world of electronics; perhaps from entirely unsuspected quarters. Perhaps there will be no solution at all. Every civilization has its obsessive failures.

For us, the large audience of men and women who are not, when all is said, hopeless cretins, a few contemporary works remain to be cherished, and the past keeps our spirits refreshed. Thank God for the past! For imagine the horror if all the sounds created before Schönberg suddenly disappeared and we were reduced to nothing but "avant-garde" music. Strong men would begin to rave in the streets. And yet every age but our own seems to have been cozy with its own music. Nineteenth-century music lovers felt little need to hear eighteenth-century scores; eighteenth-century music lovers lived peacefully with a minimum of Renaissance music; and so on down to the remotest past. Any generation of the past could have survived exclusively on its own music. Only for us is the past a life-need of the present.

Bereft of all that beauty, who would find comfort in the idea, even if he were simple enough to believe it, that sometime in the future the melodic fragments, the strident polychords, the atonalities that make his flesh crawl today will appear canorous? Even the Stockhausens and the Boulezes might take fright at their own noises. Perhaps it would occur to us that the cacophonists could afford to "realize musical structures" in their laboratories because they had the old masters to cover for them. They could say, "Beauty? That was taken care of long ago. Listen to Vivaldi. We have moved on to something else."

But there is nothing else.

Suggestions for Discussion

1. Why does Mandel settle on the term *dissonant*? Why is he unwilling to employ a coined word like *malsonant*?

2. What does Mandel consider the aim of music? How does this aim (or other aims he mentions) relate to his attack on dissonant music?

3. What important distinction does Mandel make between music on the one hand and visual art on the other? Is this a distinction with which you can agree?

4. What is Mandel's response to the assertion that music exists to interpret contemporary life, or to further music itself, or for moral or hygienic purposes? How does he dispose of such arguments?

5. Why does Mandel believe that music must please the public? How does he define *public?* Why does he confine his argument to the second group which makes up the term?

6. Mandel declares "the experiment of dissonance bankrupt." Explain. Why does he believe that music has failed?

7. Mandel says that "every age but our own seems to have been cozy with its own music." Relate this statement to his argument.

8. This essay is divided into seven parts. Explain the relation of the argument to each part.

Suggestions for Writing

1. People in the *second public* Mandel refers to don't seem to care for the music of either the *first* or the *third public*. Write an essay in which you explain the value or assert the worthlessness of "pop" music.

2. Assume that Mandel is wrong in his argument against atonal music. Write an essay defending atonal music as an important part of modern life. You should refer to specific composers and their work.

3. Write an essay in which you develop Mandel's statements about the success of modern painting. Do you agree with him? If not explain your position. Whether you agree or not, use specific examples of modern art to make your point. Are there examples of modern art which you might compare to atonal music—that is, bankrupt?

Anne Tyler

Still Just Writing

Anne Tyler (b. 1941) won creative writing awards while majoring in Russian at Duke, where she received her degree at 19. She went on to graduate study in Russian, worked as a librarian, and wrote her first novel at 22. She has written forty short stories situated in the contemporary South and seven novels, including *Searching for Caleb* (1975), *Earthly Possessions* (1977), and *The Dinner at Homesick Restaurant* (1982). This essay, published in 1980 in *The Writer and Her Work*, explains with understated wit how she has managed at the same time to be a successful writer, wife, and mother of two daughters.

While I was painting the downstairs hall I thought of a novel to write. Really I just thought of a character; he more or less wandered into my mind, wearing a beard and a broad-brimmed leather hat. I figured that if I sat down and organized this character on paper, a novel would grow up around him. But it was March and the children's spring vacation began the next day, so I waited.

After spring vacation the children went back to school, but the dog got worms. It was a little complicated at the vet's and I lost a day. By then it was Thursday; Friday is the only day I can buy the groceries, pick up new cedar chips for the gerbils, scrub the bathrooms. I waited till Monday. Still, that left me four good weeks in April to block out the novel.

By May I was ready to start actually writing, but I had to do it in patches. There was the follow-up treatment at the vet, and then a half-day spent trailing the dog with a specimen tin so the lab could be sure the treatment had really worked. There were visits from the washing machine repairman and the Davey tree man, not to mention briefer interruptions by the meter reader, five Jehovah's Witnesses, and two Mormons. People telephoned wanting to sell me permanent light bulbs and waterproof basements. An Iranian cousin of my husband's had a baby; the cousin's uncle died; then the cousin's mother decided to go home to Iran and needed to know where to buy a black American coat before she left. There *are* no black American coats; don't Americans wear mourning? I told her no, but I checked around at all the department stores anyway because she didn't speak English. Then I wrote chapters one and two. I had planned to work till 3:30 every day, but it was a month of early quittings: once for the children's dental appointment, once for the cat's rabies shot, once for our older daughter's orthopedist, and twice for her gymnastic meets. Sitting on the bleachers in the school gymnasium, I told myself I could always use this in a novel someplace, but I couldn't really picture writing a novel about 20 little girls in leotards trying to walk the length of a wooden beam without falling off. By the time I'd written chapter three, it was Memorial Day and the children were home again.

Characters on Hold

I knew I shouldn't expect anything from June. School was finished then and camp hadn't yet begun. I put the novel away. I closed down my mind and planted some herbs and played cribbage with the children. Then on the 25th, we drove one child to a sleepaway camp in Virginia and entered the other in a day camp, and I was ready to start work again. First I had to take my car in for repairs and the mechanics lost it, but I didn't get diverted. I sat in the garage on a folding chair while they hunted my car all one afternoon, and I hummed a calming tune and tried to remember what I'd planned to do next in my novel. Or even what the novel was about, for that matter. My character wandered in again in his beard and his broad-brimmed hat. He looked a little pale and knuckly, like someone scrabbling at a cliff edge so as not to fall away entirely.

I had high hopes for July, but it began with a four-day weekend, and on Monday night we had a long-distance call from our daughter's camp in Virginia. She was seriously ill in a Charlottesville hospital. We left our youngest with friends and drove three hours in a torrent of rain. We found our daughter frightened and crying, and another child (the only other child I knew in all of Virginia) equally frightened and crying down in the emergency room with possible appendicitis, so I spent that night alternating between a chair in the pediatraic wing and a chair in the emergency room. By morning, it had begun to seem that our daughter's illness was typhoid fever. We loaded her into the car and took her back to Baltimore, where her doctor put her on drugs and prescribed a long bed-rest. She lay in bed six days, looking wretched and calling for fluids and cold cloths. On the seventh day she got up her same old healthy self, and the illness was declared to be not typhoid fever after all but a simple virus, and we shipped her back to Virginia on the evening train. The next day I was free to start writing again but sat, instead, on the couch in my study, staring blankly at the wall.

Part-time Creativity

I could draw some conclusions here about the effect that being a woman/wife/mother has upon my writing, except that I am married to a writer who is also a man/husband/father. He published his first novel while he was a medical student in Iran; then he came to America to finish his training. His writing fell by the wayside, for a long while. You can't be on call in the emergency room for 20 hours and write a novel during the other four. Now he's a child psychiatrist, fulltime, and he writes his novels in the odd moments here and there—when he's not preparing a lecture, when he's not on the phone with a patient, when he's not attending classes at the psychoanalytic institute. He writes in Persian, still, in those black-and-white speckled composition books. Sometimes one of the children will interrupt him in English and he will answer in Persian, and they'll say, "What?" and he'll look up blankly, and it seems a sheet has to fall from in front of his eyes before he remembers where he is and switches to English. Often, I wonder what he would be doing now if he didn't have a family to support. He cares deeply about his writing and he's very good at it, but every morning at 5:30 he gets up and puts on a suit and tie and drives in the dark to the hospital. Both of us, in different ways, seem to be hewing our creative time in small, hard chips from our living time.

Drained and Drawn

Occasionally, I take a day off. I go to a friend's house for lunch, or weed the garden, or rearrange the linen closet. I notice that at the end of one of these days, when my husband asks me what I've been doing, I tend to exaggerate any hardships I may have encountered. ("A pickup nearly sideswiped me on Greenspring Avenue. I stood in line an hour just trying to buy the children some flip-flops.") It seems sinful to have lounged around so. Also, it seems sinful that I have more choice than my husband as to whether or not to undertake any given piece of work. I can refuse to do an article if it doesn't appeal to me, refuse to change a short story, refuse to hurry a book any faster than it wants to go—all luxuries. My husband, on the other hand, is forced to rise and go off to that hospital every blessed weekday of his life. *His* luxury is that no one expects him to drop all else for two weeks when a child has chicken pox. The only person who has no luxuries at all, it seems to me, is the woman writer who is the sole support of her children. I often think about how she must manage. I think that if I were in that position, I'd have to find a job involving manual labor. I have spent so long erecting partitions around the part of me that writes—learning how to close the door on it when ordinary life intervenes, how to close the door on ordinary life when it's time to start writing again—that I'm not sure I could fit the two parts of me back together now.

Before we had children I worked in a library. It was a boring job, but I tend to like doing boring things. I would sit on a stool alphabetizing Russian catalogue cards and listening to the other librarians talking around me. It made me think of my adolescence, which was spent listening to the tobacco stringers while I handled tobacco. At night I'd go home from the library and write. I never wrote what the librarians said, exactly, but having those voices in my ears all day helped me summon up my own characters' voices. Then our first baby came along—an insomniac. I quit work and stayed home all day with her and walked her all night. Even if I had found the time to write, I wouldn't have had the insides. I felt drained; too much care and feeling were being drawn out of me. And the only voices I heard now were by appointment—people who came to dinner, or invited us to dinner, and who therefore felt they had to make deliberate conversation. That's one thing writers never have, and I still miss it: the easy-going, on-again-off-again, gossipy murmurs of people working alongside each other all day.

Free and Useful

I enjoyed tending infants (though I've much preferred the later ages), but it was hard to be solely, continually in their company and not to be able to write. And I couldn't think of any alternative. I know it must be possible to have a child raised beautifully by a housekeeper, but every such child I've run into has seemed dulled and doesn't use words well. So I figured I'd better stick it out. As it happened, it wasn't that long—five years, from the time our first daughter was born till our second started nursery school and left me with my mornings free. But while I was going through it I thought it would be a lot longer. I couldn't imagine any end to it. I felt that everything I wanted to write was somehow coagulating in my veins and making me fidgety and slow. Then after a while I didn't have anything to write anyhow, but I still had the fidgets. I felt useless, no matter how many diapers I washed or strollers I pushed. The only way I could explain my life to myself was to imagine that I was living in a very small commune. I had spent my childhood in a commune, or what would nowadays be called a commune, and I was used to the idea of division of labor. What we had here, I told myself, was a perfectly sensible arrangement: One member was the liaison with the outside world, bringing in money; another was the caretaker, reading the Little Bear books to the children and repairing the electrical switches. This second member might have less physical freedom, but she had much more freedom to arrange her own work schedule. I must have sat down a dozen times a week and very carefully, consciously thought it all through. Often, I was merely trying to convince myself that I really did pull my own weight.

Strung Up

This Iranian cousin who just had the baby: She sits home now and cries a lot. She was working on her master's degree and is used to being out in the world more. "Never mind," I tell her, "you'll soon be out again. This stage doesn't last long."

"How long?" she asks.

"Oh . . . three years, if you just have the one."

"Three years!"

I can see she's appalled. Her baby is beautiful, very dark and Persian; and what's more, he sleeps—something I've rarely seen a baby do. What I'm trying to say to her (but of course, she'll agree without really hearing me) is that he's worth it. It seems to me that since I've had children, I've grown richer and deeper. They may have slowed down my writing for a while, but when I did write, I had more of a self to speak from. After all, who else in the world do you *have* to love, no matter what? Who else can you absolutely not give up on? My life seems more intricate. Also more dangerous.

After the children started school, I put up the partitions in my mind. I would rush around in the morning braiding their hair, packing their lunches; then the second they were gone I would grow quiet and climb the stairs to my study. Sometimes a child would come home early and I would feel a little tug between the two parts of me; I'd be absent-minded and short-tempered. Then gradually I learned to make the transition more easily. It feels like a sort of string that I tell myself to loosen. When the children come home, I drop the string and close the study door and that's the end of it. It doesn't always work perfectly, of course. There are times when it doesn't work at all: If a child is sick, for instance, I can't possibly drop the children's end of the string, and I've learned not to try. It's easier just to stop writing for a while. Or if they're home but otherwise occupied, I no longer attempt to sneak off to my study to finish that one last page; I know that instantly, as if by magic, assorted little people will be pounding on my door requiring Band-Aids, tetanus shots, and a complete summation of the facts of life.

Last spring, I bought a midget tape recorder to make notes on. I'd noticed that my best ideas came while I was running the vacuum cleaner, but I was always losing them. I thought this little recorder would help. I carried it around in my shirt pocket. But I was ignoring the partitions, is what it was; I was letting one half of my life intrude upon the other. A child would be talking about her day at school and suddenly I'd whip out the tape recorder and tell it, "Get Morgan out of that cocktail party; he's not the type to drink." "Huh?" the child would say. Both halves began to seem ludicrous, unsynchronized. I took the recorder back to Radio Shack.

Faith and Adaptation

A few years ago, my parents went to the Gaza Strip to work for the American Friends Service Committee. It was a lifelong dream of my father's to do something with the AFSC as soon as all his children were grown, and he'd been actively preparing for it for years. But almost as soon as they got there, my mother fell ill with a mysterious fever that neither the Arab nor the Israeli hospitals could diagnose. My parents had to come home for her treatment, and since they'd sublet their house in North Carolina, they had to live with us. For four months, they stayed here—but only on a week-to-week basis, not knowing when they were going back, or whether they were going back at all, or how serious my mother's illness was. It was hard for her, of course, but it should have been especially hard in another way for my father, who had simply to hang in suspended animation for four months while my mother was whisked in and out of hospitals. However, I believe he was as pleased with life as he always is. He whistled Mozart and puttered around insulating our windows. He went on long walks collecting firewood. He strolled over to the meetinghouse and gave a talk on the plight of the Arab refugees. "Now that we seem to have a little time," he told my mother, "why not visit the boys?" and during one of her outpatient periods he took her on a gigantic cross-country trip to see all my brothers and any other relatives they happened upon. Then my mother decided she ought to go to a faith healer. (She wouldn't usually do such a thing, but she was desperate.) "Oh. Okay," my father said, and he took her to a faith healer, whistling all the way. And when the faith healer didn't work, my mother said, "I think this is psychosomatic. Let's go back to Gaza." My father said, "Okay," and reserved two seats on the next plane over. The children and I went to see them the following summer: My mother's fever was utterly gone, and my father drove us down the Strip, weaving a little Renault among the tents and camels, cheerfully whistling Mozart.

I hold this entire, rambling set of events in my head at all times, and remind myself of it almost daily. It seems to me that the way my father lives (infinitely adapting, and looking around him with a smile to say, "Oh! So *this* is where I am!") is also the way to slip gracefully through a choppy life of writing novels, plastering the dining room ceiling, and presiding at slumber parties. I have learned, bit by bit, to accept a school snow-closing as an unexpected holiday, an excuse to play 17 rounds of Parcheesi instead of typing up a short story. When there's a midweek visitation of uncles from Iran (hordes of great, bald, yellow men calling for their glasses of tea, sleeping on guest beds, couches, two armchairs pushed together, and discarded crib mattresses), I have decided that I might as well listen to what they have to say, and work on my novel tomorrow instead. I smile at the uncles out of a kind of clear, swept space inside me. What this takes, of course, is a sense of limitless time, but I'm getting that. My life is beginning to seem unusually long. And there's a danger to it: I could wind up as passive as a piece of wood on a wave. But I try to walk a middle line.

Wait for Heaven

I was standing in the schoolyard waiting for a child when another mother came up to me. "Have you found work yet?" she asked. "Or are you still just writing?"

Now, how am I supposed to answer that?

I could take offense, come to think of it. Maybe the reason I didn't is that

I halfway share her attitude. They're *paying* me for this? For just writing down untruthful stories? I'd better look around for more permanent employment. For I do consider writing to be a finite job. I expect that any day now, I will have said all I have to say; I'll have used up all my characters, and then I'll be free to get on with my real life. When I make a note of new ideas on index cards, I imagine I'm clearing out my head, and that soon it will be empty and spacious. I file the cards in a little blue box, and I can picture myself using the final card one day—ah! through at last!—and throwing the blue box away. I'm like a dentist who continually fights tooth decay, working toward the time when he's conquered it altogether and done himself out of a job. But my head keeps loading up again; the little blue box stays crowded and messy. Even when I feel I have no ideas at all, and can't possibly start the next chapter, I have a sense of something still bottled in me, trying to get out.

People have always seemed funny and strange to me, and touching in unexpected ways. I can't shake off a sort of mist of irony that hangs over whatever I see. Probably that's what I'm trying to put across when I write; I may believe that I'm the one person who holds this view of things. And I'm always hurt when a reader says that I choose only bizarre or eccentric people to write about. It's not a matter of choice; it just seems to me that even the most ordinary person, in real life, will turn out to have something unusual at his center. I like to think that I might meet up with one of my past characters at the very next street corner. The odd thing is, sometimes I have. And if I were remotely religious, I'd believe that a little gathering of my characters would be waiting for me in heaven when I died. "*Then* what happened?" I'd ask them. "How have things worked out, since the last time I saw you?"

Eudora's Legacy

I think I was born with the impression that what happened in books was much more reasonable, and interesting, and *real*, in some ways, than what happened in life. I hated childhood, and spent it sitting behind a book waiting for adulthood to arrive. When I ran out of books I made up my own. At night, when I couldn't sleep, I made up stories in the dark. Most of my plots involved girls going west in covered wagons. I was truly furious that I'd been born too late to go west in a covered wagon.

I know a poet who says that in order to be a writer, you have to have had rheumatic fever in your childhood. I've never had rheumatic fever, but I believe that any kind of setting-apart situation will do as well. In my case, it was emerging from that commune—really an experimental Quaker community in the wilderness—and trying to fit into the outside world. I was eleven. I had never used a telephone and could strike a match on the soles of my bare feet. All the children in my new school looked very peculiar to me, and I certainly must have looked peculiar to them. I am still surprised, to this day, to find myself where I am. My life is so streamlined and full of modern conveniences. How did I get here? I have given up hope, by now, of ever losing my sense of distance; in fact, I seem to have come to cherish it. Neither I nor any of my brothers can stand being out among a crowd of people for any length of time at all.

I spent my adolescence planning to be an artist, not a writer. After all, books had to be about major events, and none had ever happened to me. All I knew were tobacco workers, stringing the leaves I handed them and talking up a storm. Then I found a book of Eudora Welty's short stories in the high school library. She was writing about Edna Earle, who was so slow-witted she could sit all day just pondering how the tail of the *C* got through the loop of the *L* on the Coca-Cola sign. Why, I knew Edna Earle. You mean you could *write* about such people? I have always meant to send Eudora Welty a thank-you note, but I imagine she would find it a little strange.

The Write of Passage

I wanted to go to Swarthmore College, but my parents suggested Duke instead, where I had a full scholarship, because my three brothers were coming along right behind me and it was more important for boys to get a good education than for girls. That was the first and last time that my being female was ever a serious issue. I still don't think it was just, but I can't say it ruined my life. After all, Duke had Reynolds Price, who turned out to be the only person I ever knew who could actually teach writing. It all worked out, in the end.

I believe that for many writers, the hardest time is that dead spot after college (where they're wonder-children. made much of) and before their first published work. Luckily, I didn't notice that part; I was so vague about what I wanted to do that I could hardly chafe at not yet doing it. I went to graduate school in Russian studies; I scrubbed decks on a boat in Maine; I got a job ordering books from the Soviet Union. Writing was something that crept in around the edges. For a while I lived in New York, where I became addicted to riding any kind of train or subway, and while I rode I often felt I was nothing but an enormous eye, taking things in and turning them over and sorting them out. But who would I tell them to, once I'd sorted them? I have never had more than three or four close friends, at any period of my life; and anyway, I don't talk well. I am the kind of person who wakes up at four in the morning and suddenly thinks of what she should have said yesterday at lunch. For me, writing something down was the only road out.

Rewarding Routines and Rituals

You would think, since I waited so long and so hopefully for adulthood, that it would prove to be a disappointment. Actually, I figure it was worth the wait. I like everything about it but the paperwork—the income tax and protesting the Sears bill and renewing the Triple-A membership. I always did count on having a husband and children, and here they are. I'm surprised to find myself a writer but have fitted it in fairly well, I think. The only real trouble that writing has ever brought me is an occasional sense of being invaded by the outside world. Why do people imagine that writers, having chosen the most private of professions, should be any good at performing in public, or should have the slightest desire to tell their secrets to interviewers from ladies' magazines? I feel I am only holding myself together by being extremely firm and decisive about what I will do and what I will not do. I will write my books and raise the children. Anything else just fritters me away. I know this makes me seem narrow, but in fact, I *am* narrow. I like routine and rituals and I hate leaving home; I have a sense of digging my heels in. I refuse to drive on freeways. I dread our annual vacation. Yet I'm continually prepared for travel: It is physically impossible for me to buy any necessity without buying a travel-sized version as well. I have a little toilet kit, with soap and a nightgown, forever packed and ready to go. How do you explain that?

As the outside world grows less dependable, I keep buttressing my inside world, where people go on meaning well and surprising other people with little touches of grace. There are days when I sink into my novel like a pool and emerge feeling blank and bemused and used up. Then I drift over to the schoolyard, and there's this mother wondering if I'm doing anything halfway useful yet. Am I working? Have I found a job? No, I tell her.

I'm still just writing.

Suggestions for Discussion

1. This essay is about a writer who is a woman, wife, and mother. Would a male writer have written a much different essay?

2. In what ways does the author keep her life compartmentalized? What advantages are there for her in doing so?

3. Anne Tyler writes about her difficulties objectively and without self-pity. What impact does this style of writing have?

4. Is this a formal or an informal essay? Explain your answer.

5. Explain the relevance of two incidents to the theme of the essay: her daughter's illness while at camp and her mother's illness which began on the Gaza strip.

6. Why does Tyler say she is not a good talker? In what way is the writer's job different from most others?

Suggestions for Writing

1. This essay explains a professional writer's methods of coping with the details of life from a woman's point of view. Write an essay showing how your gender shapes the way you meet your daily duties and imposes restraints on you.

2. Tyler presents her family as both loving and cohesive. Write an essay in which you explain how the love in this family is expressed. Is it supportive of the parents' lives?

Marya Mannes

How Do You Know It's Good?

Marya Mannes (b. 1904), although she has written fiction and poetry, has made her reputation as a tirelessly questioning essayist and journalist. Her essays have appeared in a variety of magazines from *Vogue,* on the one hand, to *The New Republic,* on the other. Her essays on euthanasia were collected in *Last Rights* (1974), and she wrote about television in *Who Owns the Air?* (1960). Her other essay collections include *More in Anger* (1958), *The New York I Know* (1961), and *But Will It Sell?* (1964), in which this essay appears. "How Do You Know It's Good?" challenges educated citizens to assert their independence of fads and trends in the arts and to question critics who popularize fads. She believes that all observers have an obligation to make intelligent judgments about art.

Suppose there were no critics to tell us how to react to a picture, a play, or a new composition of music. Suppose we wandered innocent as the dawn into an art exhibition of unsigned paintings. By what standards, by what values would we decide whether they were good or bad, talented or untalented, successes or failures? How can we ever know that what we think is right?

For the last fifteen or twenty years the fashion in criticism or appreciation of the arts has been to deny the existence of any valid criteria and to make the words "good" or "bad" irrelevant, immaterial, and inapplicable. There is no such thing, we are told, as a set of standards, first acquired through experience and knowledge and later imposed on the subject under discussion. This has been a popular approach, for it relieves the critic of the responsibility of judgment and the public of the necessity of knowledge. It pleases those resentful of disciplines, it flatters the empty-minded by calling them open-minded, it comforts the confused. Under the banner of democracy and the kind of equality which our forefathers did *not* mean, it says, in effect, "Who are you to tell us what *is* good or bad?" This is the same cry used so long and so effectively by the producers of mass media who insist that it is the public, not they, who decides what it wants to hear and see, and that for a critic to say that *this* program is bad and *this* program is good is purely a reflection of personal taste. Nobody recently has expressed this philosophy more succinctly than Dr. Frank Stanton, the highly intelligent president of CBS television. At a hearing before the Federal Communications Commission, this phrase escaped him under questioning: "One man's mediocrity is another man's good program."

There is no better way of saying "No values are absolute." There is another important aspect to this philosophy of *laissez faire:* It is the fear, in all observers of all forms of art, of guessing wrong. This fear is well come by, for who has not heard of the contemporary outcries against artists who later were called great? Every age has its arbiters who do not grow with their times, who cannot tell evolution from revolution or the difference between frivolous faddism, amateurish experimentation, and profound and necessary change. Who wants to be caught *flagrante delicto* with an error of judgment as serious as this? It is far safer, and certainly easier, to look at a picture or a play or a poem and to say "This is hard to understand, but it may be good," or simply to welcome it as a new form. The word "new"—in our country especially—has magical connotations. What is new must be good; what is old is probably bad. And if a critic can describe the new in language that nobody can understand, he's safer still. If he has mastered the art of saying nothing with exquisite complexity, nobody can quote him later as saying anything.

But all these, I maintain, are forms of abdication from the responsibility of judgment. In creating, the artist commits himself; in appreciating, you have a commitment of your own. For after all, it is the audience which makes the arts. A climate of appreciation is essential to its flowering, and the higher the expectations of the public, the better the performance of the artist. Conversely, only a public ill-served by its critics could have accepted as art and as literature so much in these last years that has been neither. If anything goes, everything goes; and at the bottom of the junkpile lie the discarded standards too.

But what are these standards? How do you get them? How do you know they're the right ones? How can you make a clear pattern out of so many intangibles, including that greatest one, the very private I?

Well for one thing, it's fairly obvious that the more you read and see and hear, the more equipped you'll be to practice that art of association which is at the basis of all understanding and judgment. The more you live and the more you look, the more aware you are of a consistent pattern—as universal as the stars, as the tides, as breathing, as night and day—underlying everything. I would call this pattern and this rhythm an order. Not order—*an* order. Within it exists an incredible diversity of forms. Without it lies chaos—the wild cells of destruction—sickness. It is in the end up to you to distinguish between the diversity that is health and the chaos that is sickness, and you can't do this without a process of association that can link a bar of Mozart with the corner of a Vermeer painting, or a Stravinsky score with a Picasso abstraction; or that can relate an aggressive act with a Franz Kline painting and a fit of coughing with a John Cage composition.

There is no accident in the fact that certain expressions of art live for all time and that others die with the moment, and although you may not always define the reasons, you can ask the questions. What does an artist say that is timeless; how does he say it? How much is fashion, how much is merely reflection? Why is Sir Walter Scott so hard to read now, and Jane Austen not? Why is baroque right for one age and too effulgent for another?

Can a standard of craftsmanship apply to art of all ages, or does each have its own, and different, definitions? You may have been aware, inadvertently, that craftsmanship has become a dirty word these years because, again, it implies standards—something done well or done badly. The result of this convenient avoidance is a plentitude of actors who can't project their voices, singers who can't phrase their songs, poets who can't communicate emotion, and writers who have no vocabulary—not to speak of painters who can't draw. The dogma now is that craftsmanship gets in the way of expression. You can do better if you don't know *how* you do it, let alone *what* you're doing.

I think it is time you helped reverse this trend by trying to rediscover craft: the command of the chosen instrument, whether it is a brush, a word, or a voice. When you begin to detect the difference between freedom and sloppiness, between serious experimentation and egotherapy, between skill and slickness, between strength and violence, you are on your way to separating the sheep from the goats, a form of segregation denied us for quite a while.

All you need to restore it is a small bundle of standards and a Geiger counter that detects fraud, and we might begin our tour of the arts in an area where both are urgently needed: contemporary painting.

I don't know what's worse: to have to look at acres of bad art to find the little good, or to read what the critics say about it all. In no other field of expression has so much double-talk flourished, so much confusion prevailed, and so much nonsense been circulated: further evidence of the close inter-dependence between the arts and the critical climate they inhabit. It will be my pleasure to share with you some of this double-talk so typical of our times.

Item one: preface for a catalogue of an abstract painter:

> "Time-bound meditation experiencing a life; sincere with plastic piety at the threshold of hallowed arcana; a striving for pure ideation giving shape to inner drive; formalized patterns where neural balances reach a fiction." End of quote. Know what this artist paints like now?

Item two: a review in the *Art News:*

> ". . . a weird and disparate assortment of material, but the monstrosity which bloomed into his most recent cancer of aggregations is present in some form everywhere. . . ." Then, later, "A gluttony of things and processes terminated by a glorious constipation."

Item three, same magazine, review of an artist who welds automobile frag-ments into abstract shapes:

> Each fragment . . . is made an extreme of human exasperation, torn at and fought all the way, and has its rightness of form as if by accident. *Any technique that requires order or discipline would just be the human ego.* No, these must be egoless, uncontrolled, undesigned and different enough to give you a bang— fifty miles an hour around a telephone pole. . . .

"Any technique that requires order of discipline would just be the human ego." What does he mean—"just be"? What are they really talking about? Is this journalism? Is it criticism? Or is it that other convenient abdication from standards of performance and judgment practiced by so many artists and crit-ics that they, like certain writers who deal only in sickness and depravity, "reflect the chaos about them"? Again, whose chaos? Whose depravity?

I had always thought that the prime function of art was to create order *out* of chaos—again, not the order of neatness or rigidity or convention or artifice, but the order of clarity by which one will and one vision could draw the essential truth out of apparent confusion. I still do. It is not enough to use parts of a car to convey the brutality of the machine. This is as slavishly rep-resentative, and just as easy, as arranging dried flowers under glass to convey nature.

Speaking of which, i.e., the use of real materials (burlap, old gloves, bot-tletops) in lieu of pigment, this is what one critic had to say about an exhibi-tion of Assemblage at the Museum of Modern Art last year:

> Spotted throughout the show are indisputable works of art, accounting for a quarter or even a half of the total display. But the remainder are works of non-art, anti-art, and art substitutes that are the aesthetic counterparts of the social deficiencies that land people in the clink on charges of vagrancy. These aesthetic bankrupts . . . have no legitimate ideological roof over their heads and not the price of a square intellectual meal, much less a spiritual sandwich, in their pockets.

I quote these words of John Canady of *The New York Times* as an example of the kind of criticism which puts responsibility to an intelligent public above popularity with an intellectual coterie. Canaday has the courage to say what he thinks and the capacity to say it clearly: two qualities notably absent from his profession.

Next to art, I would say that appreciation and evaluation in the field of music is the most difficult. For it is rarely possible to judge a new composition at one hearing only. What seems confusing or fragmented at first might well become clear and organic a third time. Or it might not. The only salvation here for the listener is, again, an instinct born of experience and association which allows him to separate intent from accident, design from experimentation, and pretense from conviction. Much of contemporary music is, like its sister art, merely a reflection of the composer's own fragmentation: an absorption in self and symbols at the expense of communication with others. The artist, in short, says to the public: If you don't understand this, it's because you're dumb. I maintain that you are not. You may have to go part way or even halfway to meet the artist, but if you must go the whole way, it's his fault, not yours. Hold fast to that. And remember it too when you read new poetry, that estranged sister of music.

> A multitude of causes, unknown to former times, are now acting with a combined force to blunt the discriminating powers of the mind, and, unfitting it for all voluntary exertion, to reduce it to a state of almost savage torpor. The most effective of these causes are the great national events which are daily taking place and the increasing accumulation of men in cities, where the uniformity of their occupations produces a craving for extraordinary incident, which the rapid communication of intelligence hourly gratifies. To this tendency of life and manners, the literature and theatrical exhibitions of the country have conformed themselves.

This startlingly applicable comment was written in the year 1800 by William Wordsworth in the preface to his "Lyrical Ballads"; and it has been cited by Edwin Muir in his recently published book "The Estate of Poetry." Muir states that poetry's effective range and influence have diminished alarmingly in the modern world. He believes in the inherent and indestructible qualities of the human mind and the great and permanent objects that act upon it, and suggests that the audience will increase when "poetry loses what obscurity is left in it by attempting greater themes, for great themes have to be stated clearly." If you keep that firmly in mind and resist, in Muir's words, "the vast dissemination of secondary objects that isolate us from the natural world," you have gone a long way toward equipping yourself for the examination of any work of art.

When you come to theatre, in this extremely hasty tour of the arts, you can approach it on two different levels. You can bring to it anticipation and innocence, giving yourself up, as it were, to the life on the stage and reacting to it emotionally, if the play is good, or listlessly, if the play is boring; a part of the audience organism that expresses its favor by silence or laughter and its disfavor by coughing and rustling. Or you can bring to it certain critical faculties that may heighten, rather than diminish, your enjoyment.

You can ask yourselves whether the actors are truly in their parts or merely projecting themselves; whether the scenery helps or hurts the mood; whether the playwright is honest with himself, his characters, and you. Somewhere along the line you can learn to distinguish between the true creative act and the false arbitrary gesture; between fresh observation and stale cliché; between the avant-garde play that is pretentious drivel and the avant-garde play that finds new ways to say old truths.

Purpose and craftsmanship—end and means—these are the keys to your judgment in all the arts. What is this painter trying to say when he slashes a broad band of black across a white canvas and lets the edges dribble down? Is it a statement of violence? Is it a self-portrait? If it is *one* of these, has he made you believe it? Or is this a gesture of the ego or a form of therapy? If it shocks you, what does it shock you into?

And what of this tight little painting of bright flowers in a vase? Is the painter saying anything new about flowers? Is it different from a million other canvases of flowers? Has it any life, any meaning, beyond its statement? Is there any pleasure in its forms or texture? The question is not whether a thing is abstract or representational, whether it is "modern" or conventional. The question, inexorably, is whether it is good. And this is a decision which only you, on the basis of instinct, experience, and association, can make for yourself. It takes independence and courage. It involves, moreover, the risk of wrong decision and the humility, after the passage of time, of recognizing it as such. As we grow and change and learn, our attitudes can change too, and what we once thought obscure or "difficult" can later emerge as coherent and illuminating. Entrenched prejudices, obdurate opinions are as sterile as no opinions at all.

Yet standards there are, timeless as the universe itself. And when you have committed yourself to them, you have acquired a passport to that elusive but immutable realm of truth. Keep it with you in the forests of bewilderment. And never be afraid to speak up.

Suggestions for Discussion

1. What is the problem posed in the first paragraph of this essay? How is this problem significant for the rest of the discussion?

2. How does Mannes relate Dr. Frank Stanton's remarks about television in the second paragraph to the issue of "good" and "bad" in high culture as well as popular culture?

3. What, according to Mannes, is a major cause of the philosophy of laissez faire in art criticism? What does she see as the dangers in the statement, "No values are absolute"? To what extent does she believe that values may be absolute?

4. How does Mannes believe we can achieve standards for judging art?

5. Why does Mannes object so strongly to the attack on craftsmanship in art? What is the argument in favor of ignoring craftsmanship? How do you respond to the conflict she describes?

6. Mannes gives some examples of what she calls double-talk in art criticism. Examine these examples. Can you make clear sense from them? How does Mannes attack these examples?

7. What is Mannes' definition of order in art? Is her definition one with which you agree?

8. Why does Mannes approve of her quotation from a review by John Canaday?

9. How do the author's criteria for judging painting and sculpture apply to music and theatre?

10. What is the tone of the essay? How is it achieved? What role does the pronoun *you* play in establishing the tone?

Suggestions for Writing

1. Examine a modern painting and explain why you think it is good. Remember Mannes' advice about what you must avoid in writing about art.

2. Collect some criticism of an art exhibition or gallery show in your area and go see the paintings or sculpture. Write an essay in which you evaluate the criticism based on your own experience of the work. You may want to write a comparable essay about a music performance or a play or a film.

3. Compare and contrast Mannes' arguments with those of Oscar Mandel.

Christopher Lasch

The Degradation of Work and the Apotheosis of Art

Christopher Lasch (b. 1932), born in Omaha, Nebraska, is the Don Alonzo Professor of History at the University of Rochester. His works include *The American Liberals and the Russian Revolution* (1962), *The Agony of the American Left* (1969), *The Culture of Narcissism* (1979), and *The Minimal Self* (1984). This essay from *Harper's Magazine* (February 1984) calls upon humanists to fight American indifference to the arts and to assert the significance of the arts to a fully democratic way of life.

Like many amateur musicians, I cherish enthusiasms and strong opinions—untested by professional experience or learned rebuttal—that I am always looking for a chance to inflict on anyone willing to listen. Beethoven's overuse of the diminished seventh; his addiction to chords in root position; the canard that Schumann couldn't orchestrate; the critical neglect of Ludwig Spohr; the Brahms-Wagner controversy (I am an anti-Wagnerian); the need for more compositions featuring prominent but easy parts for the viola: I am ready to expound on these topics whenever I can find a captive audience. Unfortunately no one needs to hear about these things from me, when there are so many authoritative commentators to choose from. Nor do they need to hear from me that music is the queen of the arts; that it combines the most immediate kind of sensuous pleasure with the most intellectual and abstract; that it provides the most compelling illustration of the possibility of disciplining feeling with form; that it uses the simplest and most economical means, an alphabet consisting of only twelve basic units, to achieve the most complex results; and that its capacity not merely to beguile time but to order experience and evoke its depths is inexhaustible.

How music does all these things is a mystery I will not attempt to elucidate. I will content myself with a more prosaic question on which, as a student of American society and culture, I can hope to shed some light: how does it happen that, in spite of all these riches, the great tradition of Western music remains so little understood and appreciated in this country? Why do the arts in general lead such a precarious existence in America? Why is the audience for good music so limited, in spite of radio and records and all the other marvels of mass communication?

The fiscal crisis in education reminds us, in case we had forgotten during the boom years after World War II, that the fine arts rank very low on the scale of American priorities. In the expansive educational climate of the Fifties and Sixties, the arts enjoyed a brief period of public favor. But the taxpayers' revolt, the shrinking tax base out of which education is supported, the end of the baby boom, and a series of deep cuts in federal spending have combined to force new economies on the schools; and in this climate of retrenchment, luxuries and frills are naturally the first to be dropped from the curriculum. It doesn't do much good for friends of the arts to protest that they are a necessity, not a frill. Such arguments are likely to make little impression on hard-pressed school boards hoping to rescue what they consider absolutely essential to the educational enterprise and confronted, moreover, with a powerful if misguided movement demanding a return to basics.

Even a cursory consideration of the current plight of music education leads to the conclusion that the school system, especially in times when funds are scarce, reflects the state of American culture as a whole. The crisis of music education forces us back to the question of why Americans continue to regard culture, with a capital "C," as a rather dubious and peripheral undertaking, something not quite serious, something incidental to the business of making a living and getting ahead in the world.

This way of posing the question is a little misleading, as I will try to show later on, but first let me outline some of the answers that have been offered and explain what is wrong with them. The stock answer is that Americans are a young and still somewhat crude people, preoccupied until recently with the conquest of a vast wilderness and with the establishment of the material foundations on which a future civilization could hope to rise. According to this view of things, the pioneer spirit lived on long after pioneering was completed, carrying with it the cultural prejudices that art is not quite manly, that real men don't eat quiche, and that although a real man may go to the opera occasionally to please his wife, he won't enjoy it and shouldn't enjoy it and certainly shouldn't admit to enjoying it even if he does.

Another explanation of American cultural backwardness stresses the commercial values long dominant in American society, themselves rooted in the pioneering ethic but endowed with the added prestige accorded in the twentieth century to business and everything connected with it. "The business of

America is business," said Calvin Coolidge, and Charles Wilson, Eisenhower's secretary of defense, added that what's good for General Motors is good for the country. Such wisdom still commands widespread, almost automatic agreement.

Another feature of American society that has allegedly inhibited the development of the arts is the country's cultural dependence on Europe, its cultural inferiority complex, its tendency to import culture instead of creating an indigenous culture of its own. The underdevelopment of American music offers a particularly good example of this cultural colonialism. Until recently, almost all of our conductors and opera singers came from Europe, American composers were held in very low esteem, and performing artists went to Europe for much of their training. Even today, the main tradition of Western music is for the most part a European tradition. American music may now be good enough to be judged by the highest standards, but the standards themselves, it can be argued, are still set in Europe.

The cultural legacy of Puritanism has been put forth as another influence inhibiting the growth of the fine arts in America. In the early years of this century, when American culture seemed to be on the verge of its coming-of-age, in the words of Van Wyck Brooks's famous manifesto, it was common to blame the underdevelopment of American culture on Puritanical repression and the Puritanical fear of beauty. According to Brooks, Puritanism represented the other side of pioneering, the spiritual equivalent of pioneering. Together they divided the American mind between them, the one "spectral and aloof," "sterile and inhuman," the other obsessed with practical results. Divided between two extremes, "bare facts and metaphysics, the machinery of self-preservation and the mystery of life," American culture lacked the "genial middle ground of human tradition" on which a vigorous development of art and intellect depends.

A final line of explanation makes democracy itself the source of America's failure to develop a tradition of high culture. American culture is the culture of the common man, in this view; it reflects a national commitment to social justice and to democratic standards of openness and sociability; and although it includes an adimiration of art, it cannot generate the great art that is inherently elitist and antisocial, "resistant to gregariousness," and dependent, in George Steiner's words, on a "cultivation of solitude verging on the pathological." In a 1980 essay in *Salmagundi*, "The Archives of Eden," Steiner maintains that the kind of culture that flourishes in the United States, in museums, concert halls, the record industry, the paperback-book industry, is a "custodial," not a creative or original culture: "Roger Sessions, Elliott Carter are composers of undoubted stature. Charles Ives is a most intriguing 'original.' Up to this point in its history, however, American music has been of an essentially provincial character. The great symphony of 'the new world' is by Dvořák."

The weakness of American music, according to Steiner, is the weakness of American high culture as a whole. Rejecting the argument that the country is still young, he attributes the meagerness of the American contribution to world culture to the preference, "thoroughly justifiable in itself," of "democratic endeavor over authoritarian caprice, of an open society over one of creative hermeticism and censorship, of a general dignity of mass status over the perpetuation of an elite" that is often "inhumane" in its conduct and outlook but remains essential to the production of original works of art. The cultural price of democracy, Steiner says, can be seen most clearly in the "disaster of pseudo-literacy and pseudo-numeracy in the American high school and in much of what passes for so-called 'higher education.'" Here Steiner's scorn for American culture overflows and finds its most appropriate object: "The pre-digested trivia, the prolix and pompous didacticism, the sheer dishonesty of presentation which characterize the curriculum, the teaching, the administrative politics of daily life in the high school, in the junior college, in the open-admission 'university' (how drastically America has devalued this proud term), constitute the fundamental scandal in American culture."

In one form or another, all these explanations of American cultural inferiority have been around for a long time, and all of them contain some truth. Yet all of them misconceive the problem by exaggerating the degree to which the plight of high culture is peculiar to the United States. In this respect, they are themselves symptoms of a national sense of cultural inferiority, which compares America unfavorably with Europe and ignores similar problems there. The crisis of high culture is not so much an American issue as a twentieth-century issue. The custodial attitude toward culture, the breakdown of the educational system, the attenuation of the creative spirit have now appeared in Europe as well, and not because Europe has been Americanized, as so many people complain, but because there is something intrinsic to industrial societies that is antagonistic to the fullest development of the artistic imagination.

If we look at contemporary music as a whole, what strikes us most forcefully is not the vitality of European music as compared with American music but the hostility of audiences to modern music, in Europe just as in the United States; the self-conscious, self-referential, and academic quality of most of the music now being written; and the endless recycling of masterpieces composed in the eighteenth and nineteenth centuries. The European musical tradition has become as custodial in its orientation as the American tradition. The passage of time has given the lie to the modernist dogma that great works of art find a popular audience in the fullness of time. Except for the early works of Stravinsky and a few other isolated favorites, many of them written in earlier styles, the products of musical modernism have not established themselves in the symphonic repertory, and the recent attempt to revive the Romantic style once again, precisely because it is such a self-conscious, often ironic undertaking, seems equally unlikely to generate a permanent body of acknowledged masterpieces. We have to face the possibility that the musical tradition in the West has arrived, at least temporarily, at a dead end, and that the crisis of music education therefore derives from its attempt to disseminate a tradition that no longer has much life. If the Western musical tradition has become a dead language, then music teachers, like Latin teachers, will find themselves engaged in a rear-guard action not to win a broader following for their subject but to save it from academic extinction.

I said at the outset that the question of why Americans don't show more interest in great art or support it more generously is misleading. It is misleading because it treats as a purely American problem what is actually a Western problem but also because it exaggerates society's indifference to art. The decline in the quality of artistic production has occurred at the very same time that art has come to be taken more seriously than ever before. In modern society, art is not an object of indifference. In some quarters, at least, it is an object of worship. It has come to enjoy the esteem formerly reserved for religion. Indeed, the difficulty may be not that art isn't taken seriously but that it is taken more seriously than is good for it. It has been cut off from the rest of life and put on a pedestal. It has been relegated to the museum and to the concert hall (and the concert hall, as has been pointed out, has become a museum in its own right), not because it is considered unimportant but because its adoration can best take place in an atmosphere uncontaminated by everyday concerns.

In earlier times, music often served as an accompaniment to other activities—dancing, socializing, religious worship. Only in the nineteenth century did music come to be segregated from ordinary life and surrounded with an aura of sanctity. This development coincided with the elevation of the performing artist and, above all, the composer to heroic status. Formerly, composers, like other musicians, had been regarded as craftsmen, as staff members of educational or religious institutions, even as superior household servants. In the nineteenth century, the artistic genius came to be seen as a heroic rebel, iconoclast, and pathbreaker. (The cult of Wagner and of his "music of the future" played a cental role in this glorification of the artist.) The flowering of music in the nineteenth century should not obscure the possibility that, in the long run, this deification of artistic genius had very bad effects, leading to the dead end of experimentation, the struggle for novelty and originality, and the defiance of established forms and constraints, or their reimposition in the most stifling manner, that characterize the musical scene today. It looks now as if nineteenth-century music represented the culmination of an earlier tradition rather than the dawn of a golden age. It looks as if it owed at least part of its glory to a dependence on its popular roots, to the persistence of dance forms and other reminders of the historic associations between music, popular recreation, and religious ritual. Nor is it a coincidence that it is the least pure of musical forms that have shown the most life in our own century: opera, ballet, even religious music, the continuing attraction of which, in an allegedly godless age, suggests that music is better off when the spirit of veneration is directed away from music itself and toward a more suitable object.

The best starting point for anyone who wants to understand the plight of modern music and the plight of the arts in general is the great Dutch historian Johan Huizinga's book *Homo Ludens*. Huizinga traces the decline of the "play-element" in culture, as he calls it. "The great archetypal activities of human society are all permeated with play from the start," he argues. Language, myth, and ritual, but also "law and order, commerce and profit, craft and art, poetry, wisdom and science," are "rooted in the primaeval soil of play." Even those activities that are carried on with an instrumental end in view, Huizinga says, have always contained an admixture of play, which enlists skill and intelligence, the utmost concentration of purpose, not in the service of utility but in the service of an arbitrary objective that has little importance in itself, compared with the arbitrary forms and conventions and rituals that define its pursuit.

The serious business of life, in other words, has always been colored by an attitude that is not serious in this sense and that finds more satisfaction in gratuitous difficulty than in the achievement of a given objective with a minimum of effort. The play-spirit, if you will, values maximum effort for minimal results. The futility of play, and nothing else, explains its appeal—its artificiality, the obstacles it sets up for no other purpose than to challenge the players to surmount them, the absence of any utilitarian or uplifting object. But the appeal of play is so basic that it has always pervaded other activities as well, lending to religion, to law, even to warfare an element of free fantasy without which they quickly degenerate into meaningless routine. This is precisely what has happened in our time, according to Huizinga. The rationalization of warfare, politics, and work has banished the play-element from the workaday world and forced it to take refuge in sports, games, and art, which are collapsing under the weight now imposed on them. Art has "lost rather than gained in playfulness," Huizinga says. It has become a "substitute for religion," and this "apotheosis of art" has had pernicious effects, on the whole: "It was a blessing for art to be largely unconscious of its high purpose and the beauty it creates. When art becomes self-conscious, that is, conscious of its own grace, it is apt to lose something of its eternal child-like innocence."

The most striking example of the process Huizinga was trying to analyze— the decline of the play-element in culture—is one he himself paid no attention to: the growing split between work and leisure. In most jobs, work long ago lost the qualities of playfulness and craftsmanship. It no longer satisfies what John Dewey called the "unconquerable impulse towards experiences enjoyable in themselves." Today work is strictly a means to an end—profits for the capitalist, wages for the worker. The taste for beauty and the instinct of workmanship no longer find satisfaction in the workplace and are therefore forced to seek other outlets. People who work at jobs deliberately divested of every challenge to ingenuity and imagination are encouraged to become consumers of beautiful objects, to cultivate an appreciation of great art and great music, to surround themselves with reproductions of great paintings and recordings of symphonic masterpeices. If they prefer the deadening drumbeat of rock-and-roll, this is not necessarily because serious music, so-called, is inherently unpopular but because it has become so closely identified not just with leisure but with the leisure class. Great works of art have increasingly taken on the quality of collectors' items, valued because they advertise the wealth and leisure necessary for their consumption.

The emergence of the institutions that preserve high culture today dates back, like the deification of art, to the nineteenth century. Opera houses, symphony orchestras, galleries, museums, the art market—these institutions monumentalized the wealth and social aspirations of the same industrial capitalists who were systematizing production, replacing skilled workers with machines, and redesigning the workplace as an environment conceived along strictly utilitarian lines and deeply opposed to the spirit of play. Having banished art from the factory, the captains of industry proceeded to glorify it and, incidentally, to display their own munificence and connoisseurship in a setting carefully sealed off from popular intrusion, uncontaminated by association with the workaday world.

In industrial societies, art is doubly segregated from everyday life, in the first place because it retains so few of its earlier associations with ritual, sociability, and work, and in the second place because the glorification of art has gone hand in hand with its definition as a leisure-time activity and specifically as an activity of the leisure class. "Culture in America," Thomas Hearn recently observed, "is dangerously close to becoming strictly a class matter. If you drink beer, you belong to the union and watch television. If you drink champagne, you belong to the country club and go to the symphony." The democratization of leisure has not democratized the consumption of high culture, and, even if it had, the creation of a broader audience for the arts would not restore the connections between art and everyday life, on which the vitality of art depends. Works of art, as Dewey put it, "idealize qualities found in common experience." When they lose touch with common experience, they become hermetic and self-referential, obsessed with originality at the expense of communicability, indifferent to anything beyond the artist's private, subjective, and idiosyncratic perception of reality.

Those who love the arts and deplore their marginal status in American society need to rethink the task confronting them. The task is not to broaden the market for the fine arts, not to create larger numbers of enlightened consumers of culture, but to end the segregation of art and to achieve a new integration of art and everyday life. Instead of encouraging people to make better use of their leisure time, friends of the arts should think about making the workplace more joyous and playful, even if this means challenging the basic premises of our society. I don't mean that employers should be encouraged to introduce free concerts during coffee breaks. I have in mind something more fundamental: the restoration of craftsmanship, the revival of the artistic dimension of practical activity, the unification of work and play.

In a period of fiscal retrenchment, justifying support for the arts assumes great urgency. Unfortunately, the issue tends to present itself to educators as a choice between a hardheaded appeal to practical arguments that practical men and women can allegedly understand and a more principled and dignified defense of art based on appeals to its intrinsic value. The *Music Educators Journal* devoted its March 1983 issue to just such a controversy: "utilitarian vs. aesthetic rationales for arts education." One side stressed the industrial, nationalistic, and therapeutic value of music. A proponent of the utilitarian position went so far as to argue that "music is one of the few remaining places in the curriculum in which a feeling of national pride is built up." Another utilitarian insisted that a discipline that "believes in its own lack of utility is doomed." The other side held that music is valuable precisely because it resists assimilation into the "instrumental values" that are dominant in American society.

Instead of continuing this debate, educators might reformulate the question. To state it as a choice between utilitarian and aesthetic defenses of the arts acquiesces in the divorce of art from practical life. This formulation accepts as the premise of debate the very condition that has led to the crisis of music and music education in the first place. Historically, the exaltation of art has been closely linked to the degradation of labor. Banished from the workplace, the artistic impulse has taken refuge in the rarefied realm of art for art's sake. It is no wonder that the fine arts have lost popular favor; nor are they likely to recover it by a last-minute attempt to make themselves useful. The issue is not how to make art useful but how to make useful activities artistic. This is not an issue that is likely to be settled in the schools. On the contrary, it will have to be settled in the workplace. But the schools will play an important part in its resolution, if only because they have the responsibility of training the work force and can therefore contribute to a public debate about the kind of work force that is needed. A debate on this issue is already taking shape, and it provides an opportunity to reexamine the relations between education and industry, culture and practical life.

The educational system has come under intense criticism, much of it justified. A number of recent reports have linked educational failure to the decline of American productivity and the weakening of America's position in the world market. The latest of these reports, issued by leaders of sixteen corporations and universities—including the presidents of Harvard, Radcliffe, Notre Dame, and the State University of New York—demands the integration of "domestic and foreign policies into aggressive, coordinated national strategies to meet the challenge of international competition." It calls for, among other things, a "displaced-worker program modeled after the GI Bill," improvements in the training of high-school mathematics and science teachers, "more competitive salaries for engineering faculties," and closer collaboration between industry and higher education in "problem-oriented research."

This is not a program likely to appeal to friends of the arts. But the debate over the connection between cultural decadence and economic decline creates an opportunity for those who reject this kind of program to offer a competing explanation of the crisis and a competing program for social and cultural renewal. They might point out, for example, that the schools are bad because our industrial system does not in fact need large numbers of skilled workers. As R. P. Blackmur once observed, it needs "only enough mind to create and tend the machines together with enough of the new illiteracy for other machines—those of our mass media—to exploit."

All the fashionable talk about the need to upgrade the work force through training in computer literacy, math, science, and engineering is based on a complete misreading of economic trends. The trend is toward a deskilled and degraded work force. The work force of the future will not consist of "information workers" and "data communicators." Skilled jobs will continue to be scarce. Already many industries dependent on skilled labor have exported production to places like Hong Kong and Taiwan, where skilled labor is cheap. Other industries are replacing skilled labor with capital. A careful student of employment patterns notes that the "major demand for workers in the next decade will not be for computer scientists and engineers but for janitors, nurses' aides, sales clerks, cashiers, nurses, fast-food preparers, secretaries, truck drivers, and kitchen helpers."

Since music educators have nothing to gain from the rage for computer literacy and the whole high-tech program, they ought to be the first to challenge it. But the best way to challenge it is to question its basic premises, not to conduct a halfhearted defense of music as an adjunct to a technical curriculum. I don't see why music educators, and all humanists, shouldn't be the first to point out that our society has little use for education in the arts, little use for education in general, because it provides most people with jobs that are repetitive, mechanical, and mindless. It gets the education system it deserves; indeed, it probably gets a better educational system than it needs to run the industrial machine. If Americans really believe in education, they had better think about changing the system of production so as to provide people with work that is challenging and artistic, work that demands an education.

I don't think there is much hope for the arts and the humanities unless they become serious critics of the educational system and the society behind it. We humanists won't get much of a hearing if we merely try to defend our own turf or seek to operate as one more pressure group in a political environment dominated by much stronger pressure groups. But if we join in a national debate on education and help give a clearer focus to the widespread public dissatisfaction, not just with education but with the industrial system in general, we can make our presence felt. Instead of debating on our adversaries' ground, we can force them to debate on ours. We know more about the good life than they do. We stand for the things America claims to believe in but disregards in practice: truth, beauty, the full development of human capacities. It is time we made our voices heard.

Suggestions for Discussion

1. After reading the essay, explain Lasch's subtitle "A Humanist Call to Arms."

2. What is the function of the first two paragraphs? How does Lasch move from questions about music to a question about art in general?

3. What case does Lasch make for art as a necessity rather than merely a frill?

4. What answers does Lasch provide to the question of why art possesses a low priority for most Americans? What examples does he use to explain the lack of esteem for art? Are the examples effective?

5. Lasch quotes George Steiner's comment on the causes for the weakness of American culture. What is his opinion of Steiner's remarks?

6. Lasch describes contemporary music as "self-referential" and "academic." Compare his judgment with Mandel's in his essay on dissonant music. Do you agree with their judgment?

7. According to Lasch, why has art been cut off from the rest of life? What role did the composer Wagner play in separating art from life? Explain.

8. Lasch discusses *Homo Ludens* by the Dutch historian Johan Huizinga in connection with his explanation for the isolation of art in modern society. Explain his use of Huizinga's ideas. How does Lasch add to them?

9. How would Lasch reinvigorate the arts and make them more meaningful to society? How does he relate this issue to the problems facing education?

Suggestions for Writing

1. Write an essay in which you compare and contrast the remarks about art and its audience in the essays by Mandel, Mannes, Copeland, and Lasch. This could be a miniature research paper. Exercise care in deciding what to quote and what to paraphrase. Try to evaluate their ideas and explain their significance to you.

2. What kind of music do you listen to? Explain why you like it and why you regard it as important to your life.

◇◇◇

Fiction

Willa Cather
The Sculptor's Funeral

Willa Cather (1873–1947) was born in Virginia and grew up in Nebraska. On leaving the University of Nebraska, where as an undergraduate she had written for a Lincoln newspaper, she worked in Pittsburgh as a reporter and then as a teacher, and wrote her first collection of stories, *The Troll Garden* (1905). Her works include *My Antonia* (1918), *A Lost Lady* (1923), *The Professor's House* (1925), *Death Comes for the Archbishop* (1927), and *Sapphira and the Slave Girl* (1940), which dealt with her native Virginia. She celebrated the frontier spirit, whether of art or of action. However, in this story, she shows how small-town intolerance and demands for conformity are inimical to artistic impulses and creativity.

A group of the townspeople stood on the station siding of a little Kansas town, awaiting the coming of the night train, which was already twenty minutes overdue. The snow had fallen thick over everything; in the pale starlight the line of bluffs across the wide, white meadows south of the town made soft, smoke-coloured curves against the clear sky. The men on the siding stood first on one foot and then on the other, their hands thrust deep into their trousers pockets, their overcoats open, their shoulders screwed up with the cold; and they glanced from time to time toward the southeast, where the railroad track wound along the river shore. They conversed in low tones and moved about restlessly, seeming uncertain as to what was expected of them. There was but one of the company who looked as though he knew exactly why he was there; and he kept conspicuously apart; walking to the far end of the platform, returning to the station door, then pacing up the track again, his chin sunk in the high collar of his overcoat, his burly shoulders drooping forward, his gait heavy and dogged. Presently he was approached by a tall, spare, grizzled man clad in a faded Grand Army suit, who shuffled out from the group and advanced with a certain deference, craning his neck forward until his back made the angle of a jackknife three-quarters open.

"I reckon she's a-goin' to be pretty late agin tonight, Jim," he remarked in a squeaky falsetto. "S'pose it's the snow?"

"I don't know," responded the other man with a shade of annoyance, speaking from out an astonishing cataract of red beard that grew fiercely and thickly in all directions.

The spare man shifted the quill toothpick he was chewing to the other side of his mouth. "It ain't likely that anybody from the East will come with the corpse, I s'pose," he went on reflectively.

"I don't know," responded the other, more curtly than before.

"It's too bad he didn't belong to some lodge or other. I like an order funeral myself. They seem more appropriate for people of some repytation," the spare man continued, with an ingratiating concession in his shrill voice, as he carefully placed his toothpick in his vest pocket. He always carried the flag at the G.A.R. funerals in the town.

The heavy man turned on his heel, without replying, and walked up the siding. The spare man shuffled back to the uneasy group. "Jim's ez full ez a tick, ez ushel," he commented commiseratingly.

Just then a distant whistle sounded, and there was a shuffling of feet on the platform. A number of lanky boys of all ages appeared as suddenly and slimily as eels wakened by the crack of thunder; some came from the waiting-room, where they had been warming themselves by the red stove, or half asleep on the slat benches; others uncoiled themselves from baggage trucks or slid out of express wagons. Two clambered down from the driver's seat of a hearse that stood backed up against the siding. They straightened their stooping shoulders and lifted their heads, and a flash of momentary animation kindled their dull eyes at that cold, vibrant scream, the worldwide call for men. It stirred them like the note of a trumpet; just as it had often stirred the man who was coming home to-night, in his boyhood.

The night express shot, red as a rocket, from out the eastward marsh lands and wound along the river shore under the long lines of shivering poplars that sentineled the meadows, the escaping steam hanging in grey masses against the pale sky and blotting out the Milky Way. In a moment the red glare from the headlight streamed up the snow-covered track before the siding and glittered on the wet, black rails. The burly man with the dishevelled red beard walked swiftly up the platform toward the approaching train, uncovering his head as he went. The group of men behind him hesitated, glanced questioningly at one another, and awkwardly followed his example. The train stopped, and the crowd shuffled up to the express car just as the door was thrown open, the spare man in the G.A.R. suit thrusting his head forward with curiosity. The express messenger appeared in the doorway, accompanied by a young man in a long ulster and traveling cap.

"Are Mr. Merrick's friends here?" inquired the young man.

The group of the platform swayed and shuffled uneasily. Philip Phelps, the banker, responded with dignity: "We have come to take charge of the body. Mr. Merrick's father is very feeble and can't be about."

"Send the agent out here," growled the express messenger, "and tell the operator to lend a hand."

The coffin was got out of its rough box and down on the snowy platform. The townspeople drew back enough to make room for it and then formed a close semicircle about it, looking curiously at the palm leaf which lay across the black cover. No one said anything. The baggage man stood by his truck, waiting to get at the trunks. The engine panted heavily, and the fireman dodged in and out among the wheels with his yellow torch and long oilcan, snapping the spindle boxes. The young Bostonian, one of the dead sculptor's pupils who had come with the body, looked about him helplessly. He turned to the banker, the only one of that black, uneasy, stoop-shouldered group who seemed enough of an individual to be addressed.

"None of Mr. Merrick's brothers are here?" he asked uncertainly.

The man with the red beard for the first time stepped up and joined the group. "No, they have not come yet: the family is scattered. The body will be taken directly to the house." He stooped and took hold of one of the handles of the coffin.

"Take the long hill road up, Thompson, it will be easier on the horses," called the liveryman as the undertaker snapped the door of the hearse and prepared to mount to the driver's seat.

Laird, the red-bearded lawyer, turned again to the stranger: "We didn't know whether there would be any one with him or not," he explained. "It's a long walk, so you'd better go up in the hack." He pointed to a single battered conveyance, but the young man replied stiffly: "Thank you, but I think I will go up with the hearse. If you don't object," turning to the undertaker, "I'll ride with you."

They clambered up over the wheels and drove off in the starlight up the long, white hill toward the town. The lamps in the still village were shining from under the low, snow-burdened roofs; and beyond, on every side, the plains reached out into emptiness, peaceful and wide as the soft sky itself, and wrapped in a tangible, white silence.

When the hearse backed up to a wooden sidewalk before a naked, weather-beaten frame house, the same composite, ill-defined group that had stood upon the station siding was huddled about the gate. The front yard was an icy swamp, and a couple of warped planks, extending from the sidewalk to the door, made a sort of rickety footbridge. The gate hung on one hinge, and was opened wide with difficulty. Steavens, the young stranger, noticed that something black was tied to the knob of the front door.

The grating sound made by the casket, as it was drawn from the hearse, was answered by a scream from the house; the front door was wrenched open, and a tall, corpulent woman rushed out bareheaded into the snow and flung herself upon the coffin, shrieking: "My boy, my boy! And this is how you've come home to me!"

As Steavens turned away and closed his eyes with a shudder of unutterable repulsion, another woman, also tall, but flat and angular, dressed entirely in black, darted out of the house and caught Mrs. Merrick by the shoulders, crying sharply: "Come, come, mother; you mustn't go on like this!" Her tone changed to one of obsequious solemnity as she turned to the banker: "The parlour is ready, Mr. Phelps."

The bearers carried the coffin along the narrow boards, while the under-taker ran ahead with the coffin rests. They bore it into a large, unheated room that smelled of dampness and disuse and furniture polish, and set it down under a hanging lamp ornamented with jingling glass prisms and before a "Rogers group" of John Alden and Priscilla, wreathed with smilax. Henry Steavens stared about him with the sickening conviction that there had been some horrible mistake, and that he had somehow arrived at the wrong destination. He looked painfully about over the clover-green Brussels, the fat plush upholstery; among the hand-painted china plaques and panels, and vases, for some mark of identification, for something that might once conceivably have belonged to Harvey Merrick. It was not until he recognized his friend in the crayon portrait of a little boy in kilts and curls hanging above the piano, that he felt willing to let any of these people approach the coffin.

"Take the lid off, Mr. Thompson; let me see my boy's face," wailed the elderly woman between her sobs. This time Steavens looked fearfully, almost beseechingly into her face, red and swollen under its masses of strong, black, shiny hair. He flushed, dropped his eyes, and then, almost incredulously, looked again. There was a kind of power about her face—a kind of brutal handsomeness, even, but it was scarred and furrowed by violence, and so coloured and coarsened by fiercer passions that grief seemed never to have laid a gentle finger there. The long nose was distended and knobbed at the end, and there were deep lines on either side of it; her heavy, black brows almost met across her forehead, her teeth were large and square, and set far apart—teeth that could tear. She filled the room; the men were obliterated, seemed tossed about like twigs in an angry water, and even Steavens felt himself being drawn into the whirlpool.

The daughter—the tall, raw-boned woman in crêpe, with a mourning comb in her hair which curiously lengthened her long face—sat stiffly upon the sofa, her hands, conspicuous for their large knuckles, folded in her lap, her mouth and eyes drawn down, solemnly awaiting the opening of the coffin. Near the door stood a mulatto woman, evidently a servant in the house, with a timid bearing and an emaciated face pitifully sad and gentle. She was weeping silently, the corner of her calico apron lifted to her eyes, occasionally suppressing a long, quivering sob. Steavens walked over and stood beside her.

Feeble steps were heard on the stairs, and an old man, tall and frail, odorous of pipe smoke, with shaggy, unkempt grey hair and a dingy beard, tobacco stained about the mouth, entered uncertainly. He went slowly up to the coffin and stood rolling a blue cotton handkerchief between his hands, seeming so pained and embarrassed by his wife's orgy of grief that he had no consciousness of anything else.

"There, there, Annie, dear, don't take on so," he quavered timidly, putting out a shaking hand and awkwardly patting her elbow. She turned with a cry, and sank upon his shoulder with such violence that he tottered a little. He did not even glance toward the coffin, but continued to look at her with a dull, frightened, appealing expression, as a spaniel looks at the whip. His sunken cheeks slowly reddened and burned with miserable shame. When his wife rushed from the room, her daughter strode after her with set lips. The servant stole up to the coffin, bent over it for a moment, and then slipped away to the kitchen, leaving Steavens, the lawyer, and the father to themselves. The old man stood trembling and looking down at his dead son's face. The sculptor's splendid head seemed even more noble in its rigid stillness than in life. The dark hair had crept down upon the wide forehead; the face seemed strangely long, but in it there was not that beautiful and chaste repose which we expect to find in the faces of the dead. The brows were so drawn that there were two deep lines above the beaked nose, and the chin was thrust forward defiantly. It was as though the strain of life had been so sharp and bitter that death could not at once wholly relax the tension and smooth the countenance into perfect peace—as though he were still guarding something precious and holy, which might even yet be wrested from him.

The old man's lips were working under his stained beard. He turned to the lawyer with timid deference: "Phelps and the rest are comin' back to set up with Harve, ain't they?" he asked. "Thank 'ee, Jim, thank 'ee." He brushed the hair back gently from his son's forehead. "He was a good boy, Jim; always a good boy. He was ez gentle ez a child and the kindest of 'em all—only we didn't none of us ever onderstand him." The tears trickled slowly down his beard and dropped upon the sculptor's coat.

"Martin, Martin. Oh, Martin! come here," his wife wailed from the top of the stairs. The old man started timorously: "Yes, Annie, I'm coming." He turned away, hesitated, stood for a moment in miserable indecision; then reached back and patted the dead man's hair softly, and stumbled from the room.

"Poor old man, I didn't think he had any tears left. Seems as if his eyes would have gone dry long ago. At his age nothing cuts very deep," remarked the lawyer.

Something in his tone made Steavens glance up. While the mother had been in the room, the young man had scarcely seen any one else; but now, from the moment he first glanced into Jim Laird's florid face and bloodshot eyes, he knew that he had found what he had been heartsick at not finding before—the feeling, the understanding that must exist in some one, even here.

The man was red as his beard, with features swollen and blurred by dissipation, and a hot, blazing blue eye. His face was strained—that of a man who is controlling himself with difficulty—and he kept plucking at his beard with a sort of fierce resentment. Steavens, sitting by the window, watched him turn down the glaring lamp, still its jangling pendants with an angry gesture, and then stand with his hands locked behind him, staring down into the master's face. He could not help wondering what link there could have been between the porcelain vessel and so sooty a lump of potter's clay.

From the kitchen an uproar was sounding; when the dining-room door opened, the import of it was clear. The mother was abusing the maid for having forgotten to make the dressing for the chicken salad which had been prepared for the watchers. Steavens had never heard anything in the least like it; it was injured, emotional, dramatic abuse, unique and masterly in its excruciating cruelty, as violent and unrestrained as had been her grief of twenty minutes before. With a shudder of disgust the lawyer went into the dining room and closed the door into the kitchen.

"Poor Roxy's getting it now," he remarked when he came back. "The Merricks took her out of the poorhouse years ago; and if her loyalty would let her, I guess the poor old thing could tell tales that would curdle your blood. She's the mulatto woman who was standing in here a while ago, with her apron to her eyes. The old woman is a fury; there never was anybody like her for demonstrative piety and ingenious cruelty. She made Harvey's life a hell for him when he lived at home; he was so sick ashamed of it. I never could see how he kept himself so sweet."

"He was wonderful," said Steavens slowly, "wonderful; but until tonight I have never known how wonderful."

"That is the true and eternal wonder of it, anyway; that it can come even from such a dung heap as this," the lawyer cried, with a sweeping gesture which seemed to indicate much more than the four walls within which they stood.

"I think I'll see whether I can get a little air. The room is so close I am beginning to feel rather faint," murmured Steavens, struggling with one of the windows. The sash was stuck, however, and would not yield, so he sat down dejectedly and began pulling at his collar. The lawyer came over, loosened the sash with one blow of his red fist and sent the window up a few inches. Steavens thanked him, but the nausea which had been gradually climbing into his throat for the last half hour left him with but one desire—a desperate feeling that he must get away from this place with what was left of Harvey Merrick. Oh, he comprehended well enough now the quiet bitterness of the smile that he had seen so often on his master's lips!

He remembered that once, when Merrick returned from a visit home, he brought with him a singularly feeling and suggestive bas-relief of a thin, faded old woman, sitting and sewing something pinned to her knee; while a full-lipped, full-blooded little urchin, his trousers held up by a single gallus, stood beside her, impatiently twitching her gown to call her attention to a butterfly he had caught. Steavens, impressed by the tender and delicate modelling of the thin, tired face, had asked him if it were his mother. He remembered the dull flush that had burned up in the sculptor's face.

The lawyer was sitting in a rocking-chair beside the coffin, his head thrown back and his eyes closed. Steavens looked at him earnestly, puzzled at the line of the chin, and wondering why a man should conceal a feature of such distinction under that disfiguring shock of beard. Suddenly, as though he felt the young sculptor's keen glance, he opened his eyes.

"Was he always a good deal of an oyster?" he asked abruptly. "He was terribly shy as a boy."

"Yes, he was an oyster, since you put it so," rejoined Steavens. "Although he could be very fond of people, he always gave one the impression of being detached. He disliked violent emotion; he was reflective, and rather distrustful of himself—except, of course, as regarded his work. He was surefooted enough there. He distrusted men pretty thoroughly and women even more, yet somehow without believing ill of them. He was determined, indeed, to believe the best, but he seemed afraid to investigate."

"A burnt dog dreads the fire," said the lawyer grimly, and closed his eyes.

Steavens went on and on, reconstructing that whole miserable boyhood. All this raw, biting ugliness had been the portion of the man whose tastes were refined beyond the limits of the reasonable—whose mind was an exhaustless gallery of beautiful impressions, and so sensitive that the mere shadow of a poplar leaf flickering against a sunny wall would be etched and held there forever. Surely, if ever a man had the magic word in his fingertips, it was Merrick. Whatever he touched, he revealed its holiest secret; liberated it from enchantment and restored to it its pristine loveliness, like the Arabian prince who fought the enchantress spell for spell. Upon whatever he had come in contact with, he had left a beautiful record of the experience—a sort of ethereal signature; a scent, a sound, a colour that was his own.

Steavens understood now the real tragedy of his master's life; neither love nor wine, as many had conjectured; but a blow which had fallen earlier and cut deeper than these could have done—a shame not his, and yet so unescapably his, to hide in his heart from his very boyhood. And without—the frontier warfare; the yearning of a boy, cast ashore upon a desert of newness and ugliness and sordidness, for all that is chastened and old, and noble with traditions.

At eleven o'clock the tall, flat woman in black crêpe entered and announced that the watchers were arriving, and asked them "to step into the dining-room." As Steavens rose, the lawyer said dryly: "You go on—it'll be a good experience for you, doubtless; as for me, I'm not equal to that crowd tonight; I've had twenty years of them."

As Steavens closed the door after him he glanced back at the lawyer, sitting by the coffin in the dim light, with his chin resting on his hand.

The same misty group that had stood before the door of the express car shuffled into the dining room. In the light of the kerosene lamp they separated and became individuals. The minister, a pale, feeble-looking man with white hair and blond chin-whiskers, took his seat beside a small side table and placed his Bible upon it. The Grand Army man sat down behind the stove and tilted his chair back comfortably against the wall, fishing his quill toothpick from his waistcoat pocket. The two bankers, Phelps and Elder, sat off in a corner behind the dinner table, where they could finish their discussion of the new usury law and its effect on chattel security loans. The real estate agent, an old man with a smiling, hypocritical face, soon joined them. The coal and lumber dealer and the cattle shipper sat on opposite sides of the hard coal-burner, their feet on the nickelwork. Steavens took a book from his pocket and began to read. The talk around him ranged through various topics of local interest while the house was quieting down. When it was clear that the members of the family were in bed, the Grand Army man hitched his shoulders and, untangling his long legs, caught his heels on the rounds of his chair.

"S'pose there'll be a will, Phelps?" he queried in his weak falsetto.

The banker laughed disagreeably, and began trimming his nails with a pearl-handled pocketknife.

"There'll scarcely be any need for one, will there?" he queried in his turn.

The restless Grand Army man shifted his position again, getting his knees still nearer his chin. "Why, the ole man says Harve's done right well lately," he chirped.

The other banker spoke up. "I reckon he means by that Harve ain't asked him to mortgage any more farms lately, so as he could go on with his education."

"Seems like my mind don't reach back to a time when Harve wasn't bein' edycated," tittered the Grand Army man.

There was a general chuckle. The minister took out his handkerchief and blew his nose sonorously. Banker Phelps closed his knife with a snap. "It's too bad the old man's sons didn't turn out better," he remarked with reflective authority. "They never hung together. He spent money enough on Harve to stock a dozen cattle farms and he might as well have poured it into Sand Creek. If Harve had stayed at home and helped nurse what little they had, and gone into stock on the old man's bottom farm, they might all have been well fixed. But the old man had to trust everything to tenants and was cheated right and left."

"Harve never could have handled stock none," interposed the cattleman. "He hadn't it in him to be sharp. Do you remember when he bought Sander's mules for eight-year olds, when everybody in town knew that Sander's father-in-law give 'em to his wife for a wedding present eighteen years before, an' they was full-grown mules then."

Every one chuckled, and the Grand Army man rubbed his knees with a spasm of childish delight.

"Harve never was much account for anything practical, and he shore was never fond of work," began the coal and lumber dealer. "I mind the last time he was home; the day he left, when the old man was out to the barn helpin' his hand hitch up to take Harve to the train, and Cal Moots was patchin' up the fence, Harve, he come out on the step and sings out, in his ladylike voice: 'Cal Moots, Cal Moots! please come cord my trunk.'"

"That's Harve for you," approved the Grand Army man gleefully. "I kin hear him howlin' yet when he was a big feller in long pants and his mother used to whale him with a rawhide in the barn for lettin' the cows get foundered in the cornfield when he was drivin' 'em home from pasture. He killed a cow of mine that-a-way onct—a pure Jersey and the best milker I had, an' the ole man had to put up for her. Harve, he was watchin' the sun set acrost the marshes when the anamile got away; he argued that sunset was oncommon fine."

"Where the old man made his mistake was in sending the boy East to school," said Phelps, stroking his goatee and speaking in a deliberate, judicial tone. "There was where he got his head full of trapesing to Paris and all such folly. What Harve needed, of all people, was a course in some first-class Kansas City business college."

The letters were swimming before Steavens's eyes. Was it possible that these men did not understand, that the palm of the coffin meant nothing to them? The very name of their town would have remained forever buried in the postal guide had it not been now and again mentioned in the world in connection with Harvey Merrick's. He remembered what his master had said to him on the day of his death, after the congestion of both lungs had shut off any probability of recovery, and the sculptor had asked his pupil to send his body home. "It's not a pleasant place to be lying while the world is moving and doing and bettering," he had said with a feeble smile, "but it rather seems as though we ought to go back to the place we came from in the end. The townspeople will come in for a look at me; and after they have had their say I shan't have much to fear from the judgment of God. The wings of the Victory, in there"—with a weak gesture toward his studio—"will not shelter me."

The cattleman took up the comment. "Forty's young for a Merrick to cash in; they usually hang on pretty well. Probably he helped it along with whisky."

"His mother's people were not long-lived, and Harvey never had a robust constitution," said the minister mildly. He would have liked to say more. He had been the boy's Sunday-school teacher, and had been fond of him; but he felt that he was not in a position to speak. His own sons had turned out badly, and it was not a year since one of them had made his last trip home in the express car, shot in a gambling house in the Black Hills.

"Nevertheless, there is no disputin' that Harvey frequently looked upon the wine when it was red, also variegated, and it shore made an oncommon fool of him," moralized the cattleman.

Just then the door leading into the parlor rattled loudly and everyone started involuntarily, looking relieved when only Jim Laird came out. His red face was convulsed with anger, and the Grand Army man ducked his head when he saw the spark in his blue, bloodshot eye. They were all afraid of Jim; he was a drunkard, but he could twist the law to suit his client's needs as no other man in all western Kansas could do; and there were many who tried. The lawyer closed the door gently behind him, leaned back against it and folded his arms, cocking his head a little to one side. When he assumed this attitude in the courtroom, ears were always pricked up, as it usually foretold a flood of withering sarcasm.

"I've been with you gentlemen before," he began in a dry, even tone, "when you've sat by the coffins of boys born and raised in this town; and, if I remember rightly, you were never any too well satisfied when you checked them up. What's the matter, anyhow? Why is it that reputable young men are as scarce as millionaires in Sand City? It might almost seem to a stranger that there was some way something the matter with your progressive town. Why did Ruben Sayer, the brightest young lawyer you ever turned out, after he had come home from the university as straight as a die, take to drinking and forge a check and shoot himself? Why did Bill Merrit's son die of the shakes in a saloon in Omaha? Why was Mr. Thomas's son, here, shot in a gambling-house? Why did young Adams burn his mill to beat the insurance companies and go to the pen?"

The lawyer paused and unfolded his arms, laying one clenched fist quietly on the table. "I'll tell you why. Because you drummed nothing but money and knavery into their ears from the time they wore knickerbockers; because you carped away at them as you've been carping here tonight, holding our friends Phelps and Elder up to them for their models, as our grandfathers held up George Washington and John Adams. But the boys, worse luck, were young and raw at the business you put them to; and how could they match coppers with such artists as Phelps and Elder? You wanted them to be successful rascals; they were only unsuccessful ones—that's all the difference. There was only one boy ever raised in this borderland between ruffianism and civilization, who didn't come to grief, and you hated Harvey Merrick more for winning out than you hated all the other boys who got under the wheels. Lord, Lord, how you did hate him! Phelps, here, is fond of saying that he could buy and sell us all out any time he's a mind to; but he knew Harve wouldn't have given a tinker's damn for his bank and all his cattle farms put together; and a lack of appreciation, that way, goes hard with Phelps.

"Old Nimrod, here, thinks Harve drank too much; and this from such as Nimrod and me!

"Brother Elder says Harve was too free with the old man's money—fell short in filial consideration, maybe. Well, we can all remember the very tone in which brother Elder swore his own father was a liar, in the county court; and we all know that the old man came out of that partnership with his son as bare as a sheared lamb. But maybe I'm getting personal, and I'd better be driving ahead at what I want to say."

The lawyer paused a moment, squared his heavy shoulders, and went on: "Harvey Merrick and I went to school together, back East. We were dead in earnest, and we wanted you all to be proud of us some day. We meant to be great men. Even I, and I haven't lost my sense of humour, gentlemen, I meant to be a great man. I came back here to practise, and I found you didn't in the least want me to be a great man. You wanted me to be a shrewd lawyer—oh, yes! Our veteran here wanted me to get him an increase of pension, because he had dyspepsia; Phelps wanted a new country survey that would put the widow Wilson's little bottom farm inside his south line; Elder wanted to lend money at 5 percent a month, and get it collected; old Stark here wanted to wheedle old women up in Vermont into investing their annuities in real-estate mortgages that are not worth the paper they are written on. Oh, you needed me hard enough, and you'll go on needing me; and that's why I'm not afraid to plug the truth home to you this once.

"Well, I came back here and became the damned shyster you wanted me to be. You pretend to have some sort of respect for me; and yet you'll stand up and throw mud at Harvey Merrick, whose soul you couldn't dirty and whose hands you couldn't tie. Oh, you're a discriminating lot of Christians! There have been times when the sight of Harvey's name in some Eastern paper has made me hang my head like a whipped dog; and, again, times when I liked to think of him off there in the world, away from all this hogwallow, doing his great work and climbing the big, clean up-grade he'd set for himself.

"And we? Now that we've fought and lied and sweated and stolen, and hated as only the disappointed strugglers in a bitter, dead little Western town know how to do, what have we got to show for it? Harvey Merrick wouldn't have given one sunset over your marshes for all you've got put together, and you know it. It's not for me to say why, in the inscrutable wisdom of God, a genius should ever have been called from his place of hatred and bitter waters; but I want this Boston man to know that the drivel he's been hearing here tonight is the only tribute any truly great man could ever have from such a lot of sick, side-tracked, burnt-dog, land-poor sharks as the here-present financiers of Sand City—upon which town may God have mercy!"

The lawyer thrust out his hand to Steavens as he passed him, caught up his overcoat in the hall, and had left the house before the Grand Army man had had time to lift his ducked head and crane his long neck about at his fellows.

Next day Jim Laird was drunk and unable to attend the funeral services. Steavens called twice at his office, but was compelled to start East without seeing him. He had a presentiment that he would hear from him again, and left his address on the lawyer's table; but if Laird found it, he never acknowledged it. The thing in him that Harvey Merrick had loved must have gone underground with Harvey Merrick's coffin; for it never spoke again, and Jim got the cold he died of driving across the Colorado mountains to defend one of Phelps's sons who had got into trouble out there by cutting government timber.

Suggestions for Discussion

1. Discuss the details Cather uses to characterize the small Kansas town to which the dead sculptor's body is brought for burial. Why is Steavens repelled by the furnishings in the house of Merrick's mother?

2. The sculptor's mother is overcome by grief. Steavens is repelled by her outburst of emotion. Why? How does Cather arrange details so that we will agree with Steavens?

3. How does Cather contrast Mrs. Merrick with her daughter? What function do both characters have in the story?

4. Why does Cather portray Jim Laird as a heavy drinker? What is his function in the story?

5. What was the real tragedy of the dead sculptor's life? How had it affected his work?

6. What is the theme of Cather's story? Why does she use the long speech by Laird to express it?

7. Contrast "The Sculptor's Funeral" with "Is He Living or Is He Dead?"

Suggestion for Writing

Cather's view of the artist as somehow alienated from his society is illustrated in this story. Write a paper dealing with the issue, using examples of well-known artists. You might make this a research project by investigating the life of Beethoven, Mozart, Baudelaire, or Poe. What about the relation of the artists to society in other cultures; for example, China, India, or Bali?

Poetry

William Blake

London

William Blake (1757–1827), one of the most innovative of English poets, was also a painter. A printer by trade, he printed and illustrated his own books of poetry, and also illustrated the Book of Job and Dante's *Divine Comedy.* He achieved some recognition for his painting, but none for his poetry, and lived in London an industrious and personally happy life of poverty. His *Songs of Innocence* and *Songs of Experience* are now viewed as significant events in the development of romanticism in English poetry. "London," which portrays the degradation of life in the great city, states with ironic power the gulf that lies between innocence and experience.

I wander thro' each charter'd street,
Near where the charter'd Thames does flow,
And mark in every face I meet
Marks of weakness, marks of woe.

In every cry of every Man,
In every Infant's cry of fear,
In every voice, in every ban,
The mind-forg'd manacles I hear.

How the Chimney-sweeper's cry
Every black'ning Church appalls;
And the hapless Soldier's sigh
Runs in blood down Palace walls.

But most thro' midnight streets I hear
How the youthful Harlot's curse
Blasts the new born Infant's tear,
And blights with plagues the Marriage hearse.

Suggestions for Discussion

1. What statement is Blake making about London?

2. Why does the poet use the word "charter'd" for both the streets of the city and the river that flows through it?

3. Why does the "Chimney-sweeper's cry" appall the "black'ning Church"?

4. Why does the "Harlot's curse" blast the "Infant's tear" and blight the "Marriage hearse"?

5. Is *hearse* the usual word associated with marriage? Why does Blake use it here?

6. The poem is filled with the poet's indignation. What is the cause of his feeling?

7. Is this a typical poem addressed to a city?

8. Does the social comment interfere in any way with the "art" of the poem? How are the two related?

Suggestion for Writing

Write an essay in which you relate "London" to several other poems of social protest.

Muriel Rukeyser

The Backside of the Academy

Muriel Rukeyser (b. 1913) is a member of the National Institute of Arts and Letters and an American poet whose works often center on social themes. She was educated at Vassar and received a Guggenheim Fellowship in 1943 and the Levinson Prize for Poetry in 1947. Her books include *Elegies* (1949), *The Green Wave* (1948), *Mazes* (1970), *The Gates* (1976), and *The Speed of Darkness* (1968), from which the following poem is taken. The speaker in the poem balances the "truths" printed over the doors of the Academy (for example, "Art Remains the One Way Possible of Speaking Truth") with the graffiti on the back of the building to create an ironic effect.

Five brick panels, three small windows, six lions' heads with rings in their
   mouths, five pairs of closed bronze doors—
the shut wall with the words carved across its head
ART REMAINS THE ONE WAY POSSIBLE OF SPEAKING TRUTH.—
On this May morning, light swimming in this street, the children running,
on the church beside the Academy the lines are flying

of little yellow-and-white plastic flags flapping in the light;
and on the great shut wall, the words are carved across:
WE ARE YOUNG AND WE ARE FRIENDS OF TIME.—
Below that, a light blue asterisk in chalk
and in white chalk, Hector, Joey, Lynn, Rudolfo.
A little up the street, a woman shakes a small dark boy,
she shouts What's wrong with you, ringing that bell!
In the street of rape and singing, poems, small robberies,
carved in an oblong panel of the stone:
CONSCIOUS UTTERANCE OF THOUGHT BY SPEECH OR ACTION
TO ANY END IS ART.—
On the lowest reach of the walls are chalked the words: Jack is a object,
Walter and Trina, Goo Goo, I love Trina,
and further along Viva Fidel now altered to Muera Fidel.
A deep blue marble is lodged against the curb.
A phone booth on one corner; on the other, the big mesh basket for trash.
Beyond them, the little park is always locked. For the two soldier brothers.
and past that goes on an eternal football game
which sometimes, as on this day in May, transforms to stickball
as, for one day in May,
five pairs of closed bronze doors will open
and the Academy of writers, sculptors, painters, composers, their guests and
    publishers will all roll in and
the wave of organ music come rolling out into
The street where light now blows and papers and little children and words,
    some breezes of Spanish blow and many colors of people.
A watch cap lies fallen against a cellophane which used to hold pistachio
nuts and here before me, on my street,
five brick panels, three small windows, six lions' heads with rings in their
    mouths, five pairs of closed bronze doors,
light flooding the street I live and write in; and across the river the one
word FREE against the ferris wheel and the roller coaster,
and here, painted upon the stones, Chino, Bobby, Joey, Fatmoma, Willy,
    Holy of God
and also Margaret is a shit and also fuck and shit;
far up, invisible at the side of the building:
WITHOUT VISION THE PEO
and on the other side, the church side,
where shadows of trees and branches, this day in May, are printed balanced
    on the church wall,
in-focus trunks and softened-focus branches
below the roof where the two structures stand,
bell and cross, antenna and weathervane,
I can see past the church the words of an ending line:
IVE BY BREAD ALONE.

Suggestions for Discussion

1. Explain the ironic meaning of the title. What does the word *backside* mean? Does
   it point to an ironic attitude in the poem?

2. Where is the Academy? Is its location important?

3. What is suggested by the change in the slogan "Viva Fidel" to "Muera Fidel"?

4. The speaker in the poem suggests that the Academy is comprised of writers, painters, sculptors, and composers. With what group are the members of the Academy contrasted? What is the point of the contrast?

5. Some of the capitalized phrases are fragmentary. Explain the fragmentary last line. How does it serve as a comment on the rest of the poem?

6. How would you summarize the poet's position in the debate over the commitment of the artist to a cause?

Suggestions for Writing

1. Write a paper comparing this poem to MacLeish's poem about the role of the poet. How do the two poets disagree?

2. *Theory of Flight* was Rukeyser's first collection. Many of its poems relate to social themes. You may wish to read them and compare them with the poem in this text. How much historical annotation do such poems require? Is such annotation, in your opinion, a negative aspect of the poetry? Write a paper carefully explaining your opinions.

Archibald MacLeish
Invocation to the Social Muse

Archibald MacLeish (1892–1982) was born in Glencoe, Illinois, and educated at Yale and Harvard. He practiced law briefly and lived most of the decade of the 1920's in France. He won the Pulitzer Prize for *Conquistador* in 1932. His volume *Frescoes for Mr. Rockefeller's City* (1933), his play in verse, *Panic* (1935), and the play written for radio, *The Fall of the City* (1937), all reveal his concern over the rise of fascism and his own move toward liberal politics. He was Librarian of Congress from 1939 to 1944 and Undersecretary of State during the Roosevelt administration. From 1949 to 1962 he was Boyleston Professor of Rhetoric at Harvard and won another Pulitzer Prize in 1958 for his verse drama *J. B.* "Invocation to the Social Muse" predates his poetry of social commitment and like his brief "Ars Poetica" expresses belief in art for art's sake.

Señora, it is true the Greeks are dead.

It is true also that we here are Americans:
That we use the machines: that a sight of the god is unusual:
That more people have more thoughts: that there are

Progress and science and tractors and revolutions and
Marx and the wars more antiseptic and murderous
And music in every home: there is also Hoover.

Does the lady suggest we should write it out in The Word?
Does Madame recall our responsibilities? We are
Whores, Fräulein: poets, Fräulein, are persons of

Known vocation following troops: they must sleep with
Stragglers from either prince and of both views.
The rules permit them to further the business of neither.

It is also strictly forbidden to mix in maneuvers.
Those that infringe are inflated with praise on the plazas—
Their bones are resultantly afterwards found under newspapers.

Preferring life with the sons to death with the fathers,
We also doubt on the record whether the sons
Will still be shouting around with the same huzzas—

For we hope Lady to live to lie with the youngest.
There are only a handful of things a man likes,
Generation to generation, hungry or

Well fed: the earth's one: life's
One: Mister Morgan is not one.
There is nothing worse for our trade than to be in style.

He that goes naked goes further at last than another.
Wrap the bard in a flag or a school and they'll jimmy his
Door down and be thick in his bed—for a month:

(Who recalls the address now of the Imagists?)
But the naked man has always his own nakedness.
People remember forever his live limbs.

They may drive him out of the camps but one will take him.
They may stop his tongue on his teeth with a rope's argument—
He will lie in a house and be warm when they are shaking.

Besides, Tovarishch, how to embrace an army?
How to take to one's chamber a million souls?
How to conceive in the name of a column of marchers?

The things of the poet are done to a man alone
As the things of love are done—or of death when he hears the
Step withdraw on the stair and the clock tick only.

Neither his class nor his kind nor his trade may come near him
There where he lies on his left arm and will die,
Nor his class nor his kind nor his trade when the blood is jeering

And his knee's in the soft of the bed where his love lies.
I remind you, Barinya, the life of the poet is hard—
A hardy life with a boot as quick as a fiver:

Is it just to demand of us also to bear arms?

Suggestions for Discussion

1. Whom does the poet address at various times in the poem? Explain his use of "Señora," "Lady," "Barinya."

2. Why does MacLeish say, "There is nothing worse for our trade than to be in style"? What "style" does he refer to in the context of the poem?

3. The invocation to the muse is a device of epic poetry. Why does MacLeish make use of the device in his title?

4. In the third from the last line, MacLeish asserts that "the life of the poet is hard." In what ways does he seem to argue that this is true?

5. Summarize the position in the poem about role of the poet.

Suggestion for Writing

Write an analysis of this poem in which you discuss MacLeish's concept of the poet and his role in society. In your paper explain whom the poet is addressing. What is the meaning of the four lines that begin, "There are only a handful of things a man likes"?

Marianne Moore

Poetry

Marianne Moore (1877–1972) was born in Missouri, graduated from Bryn Mawr College, taught at an Indian school, worked in the New York Public Library, edited *The Dial* between 1925 and 1929, and was a distinguished resident of Brooklyn Heights. Her first collection of poems was published in 1921, her *Collected Poems* in 1951. Among her works are *Predilection* (1955), a volume of critical essays, a poetic translation of La Fontaine's *Fables* (1954), and the volume of poetry *Tell Me, Tell Me* (1967). In the following poem, as she appears to put poetry in its place and dismisses high-flown theories about art, she affirms the power of the genuine article and the real significance of poetry.

I, too, dislike it: there are things that are important beyond all this fiddle,
   Reading it, however, with a perfect contempt for it, one discovers in
     it after all, a place for the genuine.
       Hands that can grasp, eyes
       that can dilate, hair that can rise
         if it must, these things are important not because a

high-sounding interpretation can be put upon them but because they are
useful. When they become so derivative as to become unintelligible,
the same thing may be said for all of us, that we
do not admire what
we cannot understand: the bat
holding on upside down or in quest of something to

eat, elephants pushing, a wild horse taking a roll, a tireless wolf under
a tree, the immovable critic twitching his skin like a horse that feels a flea,
the base-
ball fan, the statistician—
nor is it valid
to discriminate against "business documents and

school-books"; all these phenomena are important. One must make a
distinction
however: when dragged into prominence by half poets, the result is not
poetry,
nor till the poets among us can be
"literalists of
the imagination"—above
insolence and triviality and can present

for inspection, "imaginary gardens with real toads in them," shall we have
it. In the meantime, if you demand on the one hand,
the raw material of poetry in
all its rawness and
that which is on the other hand
genuine, you are interested in poetry.

Suggestions for Discussion

1. Why does the poet, on one hand, refer to poetry as "all this fiddle" and, on the
   other, find in it "a place for the genuine"?

2. What does the poet list as the important parts of poetry? Why does she dismiss the
   unintelligible in poetry?

3. Moore wants poets to become "'literalists of the imagination.'" Relate this phrase
   to her belief that the poets must create "'imaginary gardens with real toads in
   them.'"

Suggestions for Writing

1. Write a paper in which you compare the view of poetry in this poem with the view
   that poetry is a romantic outburst of pure emotion. What arguments would you use
   in defense of either position?

2. Rewrite the poem in prose sentences in a paragraph. Write a comment on what you have done with the poem. How have you changed it? Does your change effect a change in defining the piece as a poem?

Science, Technology, and the Future

◆◆◆

Science . . . is neither human nor inhuman. So far as the well-being of humanity is concerned, science needs guidance from other sources. Science in itself is not enough—or should not be.

    —**Karl Jaspers,** "Is Science Evil?"

The universe is vast and men are but tiny specks on an insignificant planet. But the more we realize our minuteness and our impotence in the face of cosmic forces, the more astonishing becomes what human beings have achieved.

    —**Bertrand Russell,** "If We are to Survive This Dark Time"

The power that man has over nature and himself, and that a dog lacks, lies in his command of imaginary experience. He alone has the symbols which fix the past and play with the future.

    —**Jacob Bronowski,** "The Reach of Imagination"

Nature's oddities are more than good stories. They are material for probing the limits of interesting theories about life's history and meaning.

    —**Stephen Jay Gould,** "Death Before Birth, or a Mite's *Nunc Dimittis*"

The direct societal effects of any pervasive technology are as nothing compared to its much more subtle and ultimately much more important side effects.

    —**Joseph Weizenbaum,** "On the Impact of the Computer on Society"

At the moment we are an ignorant species, flummoxed by the puzzles of who we are, where we came from, and what we are for. It is a gamble to bet on science for moving ahead, but it is, in my view, the only game in town.

—**Lewis Thomas,** "Making Science Work"

So the creationists distort. An attack on some parts of Darwin's views is equated with a rejection of evolution.

—**Niles Eldredge,** "Creation Isn't Science"

Essays

Francis Bacon

Idols of the Mind

Sir Francis Bacon (1561–1626) was a lawyer, essayist, philosopher, and states-man. Among his best known works are *The Advancement of Learning* (1605), *The New Organum* (1620), and *The New Atlantis* (1627). He is considered the originator of modern scientific induction because of his insistence on observa-tion and experimentation as a means to knowledge. In "Idols of the Mind," from *The New Organum*, Bacon illustrates those habits of thought which inhibit human understanding and the spirit of scientific inquiry.

XXIII

There is a great difference between the Idols of the human mind and the Ideals of the divine. That is to say, between certain empty dogmas, and the true signatures and marks set upon the works of creation as they are found in nature.

XXXVIII

The idols and false notions which are now in possession of the human under-standing, and have taken deep root therein, not only so beset men's minds that truth can hardly find entrance, but even after entrance obtained, they will again in the very instauration of the sciences meet and trouble us, unless men being forewarned of the danger fortify themselves as far as may be against their assaults.

XXXIX

There are four classes of Idols which beset men's minds. To these for distinction's sake I have assigned names,—calling the first class *Idols of the Tribe;* the second, *Idols of the Cave;* the third, *Idols of the Market Place;* the fourth, *Idols of the Theater.*

XL

The formation of ideas and axioms by true induction is no doubt the proper remedy to be applied for the keeping off and clearing away of idols. To point them out, however, is of great use; for the doctrine of Idols is to the Interpretation of Nature what the doctrine of the refutation of Sophisms is to common Logic.

XLI

The Idols of the Tribe have their foundation in human nature itself, and in the tribe or race of men. For it is a false assertion that the sense of man is the measure of things. On the contrary, all perceptions as well of the sense as of the mind are according to the measure of the individual and not according to the measure of the universe. And the human understanding is like a false mirror, which, receiving rays irregularly, distorts and discolors the nature of things by mingling its own nature with it.

XLII

The Idols of the Cave are the idols of the individual man. For everyone (besides the errors common to human nature in general) has a cave or den of his own, which refracts and discolours the light of nature; owing either to his own proper and peculiar nature; or to his education and conversation with others; or to the reading of books, and the authority of those whom he esteems and admires; or to the differences of impressions, accordingly as they take place in a mind preoccupied and predisposed or in a mind indifferent and settled; or the like. So that the spirit of man (according as it is meted out to different individuals) is in fact a thing variable and full of perturbation, and governed as it were by chance. Whence it was well observed by Heraclitus that men look for sciences in their own lesser worlds, and not in the greater or common world.

XLIII

There are also Idols formed by the intercourse and association of men with each other, which I call Idols of the Market Place, on account of the commerce and consort of men there. For it is by discourse that men associate; and words are imposed according to the apprehension of the vulgar. And therefore the ill and unfit choice of words wonderfully obstructs the under-standing. Nor do the definitions or explanations wherewith in some things learned men are wont to guard and defend themselves, by any means set the matter right. But words plainly force and overrule the understanding, and throw all into confusion, and lead men away into numberless empty contro-versies and idle fancies.

XLIV

Lastly, there are Idols which have immigrated into men's minds from the various dogmas of philosophies, and also from wrong laws of demonstration. These I call Idols of the Theater; because in my judgment all the received systems are but so many stage-plays, representing worlds of their own crea-tion after an unreal and scenic fashion. Nor is it only of the systems now in vogue, or only of the ancient sects and philosophies, that I speak; for many more plays of the same kind may yet be composed and in like artificial man-ner set forth; seeing that errors the most widely different have nevertheless causes for the most part alike. Neither again do I mean this only of entire systems, but also of many principles and axioms in science, which by tradi-tion, credulity, and negligence have come to be received.

But of these several kinds of Idols I must speak more largely and exactly, that the understanding may be duly cautioned.

XLV

The human understanding is of its own nature prone to suppose the existence of more order and regularity in the world than it finds. And though there be many things in nature which are singular and unmatched, yet it devises for them parallels and conjugates and relatives which do not exist. Hence the fiction that all celestial bodies move in perfect circles; spirals and dragons being (except in name) utterly rejected. Hence too the element of Fire with its orb is brought in, to make up the square with the other three which the sense perceives. Hence also the ratio of density of the so-called elements is arbitrarily fixed at ten to one. And so on of other dreams. And these fancies affect not dogmas only, but simple notions also.

XLVI

The human understanding when it has once adopted an opinion (either as being the received opinion or as being agreeable to itself) draws all things else to support and agree with it. And though there be a greater number and weight of instances to be found on the other side, yet these it either neglects and despises, or else by some distinction sets aside and rejects; in order that by this great and pernicious predetermination the authority of its former con-clusions may remain inviolate. And therefore it was a good answer that was made by one who when they showed him hanging in a temple a picture of those who had paid their vows as having escaped shipwreck, and would have him say whether he did not now acknowledge the power of the gods,—"Aye," asked he again, "but where are they painted that were drowned after their vows?" And such is the way of all superstition, whether in astrology, dreams, omens, divine judgments, or the like; wherein men, having a delight in such vanities, mark the events where they are fulfilled, but where they fail, though this happen much oftener, neglect and pass them by. But with far more subtlety does this mischief insinuate itself into philosophy and the sciences; in which the first conclusion colors and brings into conformity with itself all that come after, though far sounder and better. Besides, independently of that delight and vanity which I have described, it is the peculiar and perpetual error of the human intellect to be more moved and excited by affirmatives than by negatives; whereas it ought properly to hold itself indifferently disposed towards both alike. Indeed in the establishment of any true axiom, the negative instance is the more forcible of the two.

XLVII

The human understanding is moved by those things most which strike and enter the mind simultaneously and suddenly, and so fill the imagination; and then it feigns and supposes all other things to be somehow, though it cannot see how, similar to those few things by which it is surrounded. But for that going to and fro to remote and heterogeneous instances, by which axioms are tried as in the fire, the intellect is altogether slow and unfit, unless it be forced thereto by severe laws and overruling authority.

XLVIII

The human understanding is unquiet; it cannot stop or rest, and still presses onward, but in vain. Therefore it is that we cannot conceive of any end or limit to the world; but always as of necessity it occurs to us that there is something beyond. Neither again can it be conceived how eternity has flowed down to the present day; for that distinction which is commonly received of infinity in time past and in time to come can by no means hold; for it would thence follow that one infinity is greater than another, and that infinity is wasting away and tending to become finite. The like subtlety arises touching the infinite divisibility of lines, from the same inability of thought to stop. But this inability interferes more mischievously in the discovery of causes: for although the most general principles in nature ought to be held merely positive, as they are discovered, and cannot with truth be referred to a cause; nevertheless the human understanding being unable to rest still seeks something prior in the order of nature. And then it is that in struggling toward that which is further off it falls back upon that which is more nigh at hand; namely, on final causes: which have relation clearly to the nature of man rather than to the nature of the universe; and from this source have strangely defiled philosophy. But he is no less an unskilled and shallow philosopher who seeks causes of that which is most general, than he who in things subordinate and subaltern omits to do so.

XLIX

The human understanding is no dry light, but receives an infusion from the will and affections; whence proceed sciences which may be called "sciences as one would." For what a man had rather were true he more readily believes. Therefore he rejects difficult things from impatience of research; sober things, because they narrow hope; the deeper things of nature, from superstition; the light of experience, from arrogance and pride, lest his mind should seem to be occupied with things mean and transitory; things not commonly believed, out of deference to the opinion of the vulgar. Numberless in short are the ways, and sometimes imperceptible, in which the affections color and infect the understanding.

L

But by far the greatest hindrance and aberration of the human understanding proceeds from the dullness, incompetency, and deceptions of the senses; in that things which strike the sense outweight things which do not immediately strike it, though they be more important. Hence it is that speculation commonly ceases where sight ceases; insomuch that of things invisible there is little or no observation. Hence all the working of the spirits enclosed in tangible bodies lies hid and unobserved by men. So also all the more subtle changes of form in the parts of coarser substances (which they commonly call alteration, though it is in truth local motion through exceedingly small spaces) is in like manner unobserved. And yet unless these two things just mentioned be searched out and brought to light, nothing great can be achieved in nature, as far as the production of works is concerned. So again the essential nature of our common air, and of all bodies less dense than air (which are very many), is almost unknown. For the sense by itself is a thing infirm and erring; neither can instruments for enlarging or sharpening the senses do much; but all the truer kind of interpretation of nature is effected by instances and experiments fit and apposite; wherein the sense decides touching the experiment only, and the experiment touching the point in nature and the thing itself.

LI

The human understanding is of its own nature prone to abstractions and gives a substance and reality to things which are fleeting. But to resolve nature into abstractions is less to our purpose than to dissect her into parts; as did the school of Democritus, which went further into nature than the rest. Matter rather than forms should be the object of our attention, its configurations and changes of configuration, and simple action, and law of action or motion; for forms are figments of the human mind, unless you will call those laws of action forms.

LII

Such then are the idols which I call *Idols of the Tribe;* and which take their rise either from the homogeneity of the substance of the human spirit, or from its preoccupation, or from its narrowness, or from its restless motion, or from an infusion of the affections, or from the incompetency of the senses, or from the mode of impression.

LIII

The *Idols of the Cave* take their rise in the peculiar constitution, mental or bodily, of each individual; and also in education, habit, and accident. Of this kind there is a great number and variety; but I will instance those the pointing out of which contains the most important caution, and which have most effect in disturbing the clearness of the understanding.

LIV

Men become attached to certain particular sciences and speculations, either because they fancy themselves the authors and inventors thereof, or because they have bestowed the greatest pains upon them and become most habituated to them. But men of this kind, if they betake themselves to philosophy and contemplations of a general character, distort and color them in obedience to their former fancies; a thing especially to be noticed in Aristotle, who made his natural philosophy a mere bond-servant to his logic, thereby rendering it contentious and well nigh useless. The race of chemists again out of a few experiments of the furnace have built up a fantastic philosophy, framed with reference to a few things; and Gilbert also, after he had employed himself most laboriously in the study and observation of the lodestone, proceeded at once to construct an entire system in accordance with his favourite subject.

LVI

There are found some minds given to an extreme admiration of antiquity, others to an extreme love and appetite for novelty; but few so duly tempered that they can hold the mean, neither carping at what has been well laid down by the ancients, nor despising what is well introduced by the moderns. This however turns to the great injury of the sciences and philosophy; since these affectations of antiquity and novelty are the humors of partisans rather than judgments; and truth is to be sought for not in the felicity of any age, which is an unstable thing, but in the light of nature and experience, which is eternal. These factions therefore must be abjured, and care must be taken that the intellect be not hurried by them into assent.

LVIII

Let such then be our provision and contemplative prudence for keeping off and dislodging the *Idols of the Cave,* which grow for the most part either out of the predominance of a favourite subject, or out of an excessive tendency to compare or to distinguish, or out of partiality for particular ages, or out of the largeness or minuteness of the objects contemplated. And generally let every student of nature take this as a rule—that whatever his mind seizes and dwells upon with peculiar satisfaction is to be held in suspicion, and that so much the more care is to be taken in dealing with such questions to keep the understanding even and clear.

LIX

But the *Idols of the Market Place* are the most troublesome of all: idols which have crept into the understanding through the alliances of words and names. For men believe that their reason governs words; but it is also true that words react on the understanding; and this it is that had rendered philosophy and the sciences sophistical and inactive. Now words, being commonly framed and applied according to the capacity of the vulgar, follow those lines of division which are most obvious to the vulgar understanding. And whenever an understanding of greater acuteness or a more diligent observation would alter those lines to suit the true divisions of nature, words stand in the way and resist the change. Whence it comes to pass that the high and formal discussions of learned men end oftentimes in disputes about words and names; with which (according to the use and wisdom of the mathematicians) it would be more prudent to begin, and so by means of definitions reduce them to order. Yet even definitions cannot cure this evil in dealing with natural and material things; since the definitions themselves consist of words, and those words beget others: so that it is necessary to recur to individual instances, and those in due series and order; as I shall say presently when I come to the method and scheme for the formation of notions and axioms.

LX

The idols imposed by words on the understanding are of two kinds. They are either names of things which do not exist (for as there are things left unnamed through lack of observation, so likewise are there names which result from fantastic suppositions and to which nothing in reality corresponds), or they are names of things which exist, but yet confused and illdefined, and hastily and irregularly derived from realities. Of the former kind are Fortune, the Prime Mover, Planetary Orbits, Element of Fire, and like fictions which owe their origin to false and idle theories. And this class of idols is more easily expelled, because to get rid of them it is only necessary that all theories should be steadily rejected and dismissed as obsolete.

But the other class, which springs out of a faulty and unskillful abstraction, is intricate and deeply rooted. Let us take for example such a word as *humid;* and see how far the several things which the word is used to signify agree with each other; and we shall find the word *humid* to be nothing else than a mark loosely and confusedly applied to denote a variety of actions which will not bear to be reduced to any constant meaning. For it both signifies that which easily spreads itself round any other body; and that which in itself is indeterminate and cannot solidify; and that which readily yields in every direction; and that which easily divides and scatters itself; and that which easily unites and collects itself; and that which readily flows and is put in motion; and that which readily clings to another body and wets it; and that which is easily reduced to a liquid, or being solid easily melts. Accordingly when you come to apply the word—if you take it in one sense, flame is humid; if in another, air is not humid; if in another, fine dust is humid; if in another, glass is humid. So that it is easy to see that the notion is taken by abstraction only from water and common and ordinary liquids, without any due verification.

There are however in words certain degrees of distortion and error. One of the least faulty kinds is that of names of substances, especially of lowest species and well-deduced (for the notion of *chalk* and of *mud* is good, of *earth* bad); a more faulty kind is that of actions, as *to generate, to corrupt, to alter;* the most faulty is of qualities (except such as are the immediate objects of the sense) as *heavy, light, rare, dense,* and the like. Yet in all these cases some notions are of necessity a little better than others, in proportion to the greater variety of subjects that fall within the range of the human sense.

LXI

But the *Idols of the Theater* are not innate, nor do they steal into the understanding secretly, but are plainly impressed and received into the mind from the play-books of philosophical systems and the perverted rules of demonstration. To attempt refutations in this case would be merely inconsistent with what I have already said: for since we agree neither upon principles nor upon demonstrations there is no place for argument. And this is so far well, inasmuch as it leaves the honor of the ancients untouched. For they are no wise disparaged—the question between them and me being only as to the way. For as the saying is, the lame man who keeps the right road outstrips the runner who takes a wrong one. Nay it is obvious that when a man runs the wrong way, the more active and swift he is the further he will go astray.

But the course I propose for the discovery of sciences is such as leaves but little to the acuteness and strength of wits, but places all wits and understandings nearly on a level. For as in the drawing of a straight line or a perfect circle, much depends on the steadiness and practice of the hand, if it be done by aim of hand only, but if with the aid of rule or compass, little or nothing; so is it exactly with my plan. But though particular confutations would be of no avail, yet touching the sects and general divisions of such systems I must say something; something also touching the external signs which show that they are unsound; and finally something touching the causes of such great infelicity and of such lasting and general agreement in error; that so the access to truth may be made less difficult, and the human understanding may the more willingly submit to its purgation and dismiss its idols.

LXII

Idols of the Theater, or of Systems, are many, and there can be and perhaps will be yet many more. For were it not that now for many ages men's minds have been busied with religion and theology; and were it not that civil governments, especially monarchies, have been averse to such novelties, even in matters speculative; so that men labor therein to the peril and harming of their fortunes—not only unrewarded, but exposed also to contempt and envy; doubtless there would have arisen many other philosophical sects like to those which in great variety flourished once among the Greeks. For as on the phenomena of the heavens many hypotheses may be constructed, so likewise (and more also) many various dogmas may be set up and established on the phenomena of philosophy. And in the plays of this philosophical theater you may observe the same thing which is found in the theater of the poets, that stories invented for the stage are more compact and elegant, and more as one would wish them to be, than true stories out of history.

LXVII

A caution must also be given to the understanding against the intemperance which systems of philosophy manifest in giving or withholding assent; because intemperance of this kind seems to establish Idols and in some sort to perpetuate them, leaving no way open to reach and dislodge them.

This excess is of two kinds: the first being manifest in those who are ready in deciding, and render sciences dogmatic and magisterial: the other in those who deny that we can know anything, and so introduce a wandering kind of inquiry that leads to nothing: of which kinds the former subdues, the latter weakens the understanding. For the philosophy of Aristotle, after having by hostile confutations destroyed all the rest (as the Ottomans serve their brothers), has laid down the law on all points; which done, he proceeds himself to raise new questions of his own suggestion, and dispose of them likewise; so that nothing may remain that is not certain and decided: a practice which holds and is in use among his successors.

LXVIII

So much concerning the several classes of Idols, and their equipage: all of which must be renounced and put away with a fixed and solemn determination, and the understanding thoroughly freed and cleansed; the entrance into the kingdom of man, founded on the sciences, being not much other than the entrance into the kingdom of heaven, whereinto none may enter except as a little child.

Suggestions for Discussion

1. Bacon names the four idols he is going to discuss. They can be represented diagramatically as follows:

of Tribe	of Cave	of Market Place	of Theater

Relate each aphorism to one of the idols Bacon has named. How does each aphorism apply to or illustrate an idol?

2. In discussing the idols of the market place Bacon deals with nonexistent and ill-defined things. Why does he separate the two? He rapidly disposes of the first category with a number of short examples. The second he divides into three degrees of distortion. What are the degrees? Why does Bacon deal with ill-defined things more precisely than with nonexistent things?

3. For almost every division or subdivision Bacon provides an example or illustration. List at least one example for each. Which are the most important examples? Which divisions have no examples? Why?

4. The language of the aphorisms often has an archaic flavor. Examples: *instauration, whence*. What elements other than archaic words contribute to this flavor? What examples are no longer meaningful to a modern reader?

5. Bacon frequently uses vivid imagery. The concept of "idols of the mind" is imagistic. Discuss some of the images and show how they function to support his arguments in the aphorisms.

Suggestions for Writing

1. Select one of the idols and define it in your own words. Using contemporary illustrations, write an essay (approximately 500 words) to apply the idol to your own world.

2. You may wish to write a paper on some idols of the American mind. Follow Bacon's idols as a guide and try to classify your categories as Bacon does.

Bertrand Russell

If We Are to Survive This Dark Time

Bertrand Arthur William Russell (1872–1970), third Earl Russell, studied at Trinity College, Cambridge, where he later was lecturer and fellow. He lost his post because of his opposition to World War I. With Alfred North Whitehead he wrote *Principia Mathematica*, (1910–1913), a major contribution to symbolic logic which helped determine much of the course of modern philosophy. Among his many other works are *The Analysis of Mind* (1921), *Human Knowledge, Its Scope and Limits* (1948), and *The Impact of Science on Society* (1952). He was also an educator and a spokesman for many causes, popular and unpopular, all his life. He won the Nobel Prize for Literature in 1950. This essay (1961) clearly distinguishes between democratic and totalitarian concepts of man and society and projects hope for the future.

There is only too much reason to fear that Western civilization, if not the whole world, is likely in the near future to go through a period of immense sorrow and suffering and pain—a period during which, if we are not careful to remember them, the things that we are attempting to preserve may be forgotten in bitterness and poverty and disorder. Courage, hope, and unshakable conviction will be necessary if we are to emerge from the dark time spiritually undamaged. It is worthwhile, before the actual danger is upon us, to collect our thoughts, to marshal our hopes, and to plant in our hearts a firm belief in our ideals.

It is not the first time that such disasters have threatened the Western world. The fall of Rome was another such time, and in that time, as now, varying moods of despair, escape, and robust faith were exemplified in the writings of leading men. What emerged and became the kernel of the new civilization was the Christian Church. Many pagans were noble in their thoughts and admirable in their aspirations, but they lacked dynamic force.

Plotinus, the founder of neo-Platonism, was the most remarkable of the pagans of that time. In his youth he hoped to play some part in world affairs and accompanied the emperor in a campaign against Persia, but the Roman soldiers murdered the emperor and decided to go home. Plotinus found his way home as best he could, and decided to have done with practical affairs.

He then retired into meditation and wrote books full of beauty, extolling the eternal world and the inactive contemplation of it. Such philosophy, however admirable in itself, offered no cure for the ills from which the empire was suffering.

I think Plotinus was right in urging contemplation of eternal things, but he was wrong in thinking of this as enough to constitute a good life. Contemplation, if it is to be wholesome and valuable, must be married to practice; it must inspire action and ennoble the aims of practical statesmanship. While it remains secluded in the cloister it is only a means of escape.

Boethius, who represents the very last blossoming of Roman civilization, was a figure of more use to our age. After a lifetime spent in public administration and in trying to civilize a Gothic king, he fell into disfavour and was condemned to death. In prison he composed his great book, *The Consolations of Philosophy,* in which, with a combination of majestic calm and sweet reasonableness, he sets forth, as imperturbably as though he were still a powerful minister, the joys of contemplation, the delight in the beauty of the world and the hopes for mankind, which, even in that situation, did not desert him. Throughout the Dark Ages his book was studied and it transmitted to happier times the last purified legacy of the ancient world.

The sages of our times have a similar duty to perform. It is their duty to posterity to crystallize the achievements, the hopes, and the ideals which have made our time great—to study them with monumental simplicity, so they may shine like a beacon light through the coming darkness.

Two very different conceptions of human life are struggling for mastery of the world. In the West we see man's greatness in the individual life. A great society for us is one which is composed of individuals who, as far as is humanly possible, are happy, free, and creative. We do not think that individuals should be alike. We conceive society as like an orchestra, in which the different performers have different parts to play and different instruments upon which to perform, and in which cooperation results from a conscious common purpose. We believe that each individual should have his proper pride. He should have his personal conscience and his personal aims, which he should be free to develop except where they can be shown to cause injury to others. We attach importance to the diminution of suffering and poverty, to the increase of knowledge, and the production of beauty and art. The State for us is a convenience, not an object of worship.

The Russian government has a different conception of the ends of life. The individual is thought of no importance: he is expendable. What is important is the State, which is regarded as something almost divine and having a welfare of its own not consisting in the welfare of citizens. This view, which Marx took over from Hegel, is fundamentally opposed to the Christian ethic, which in the West is accepted by free-thinkers as much as by Christians. In the Soviet world human dignity counts for nothing.

It is thought right and proper that men should be groveling slaves, bowing down before the semidivine beings who embody the greatness of the State. When a man betrays his dearest friend and causes him, as a penalty for a moment's peevish indiscretion, to vanish into the mysterious horror of a Siberian labor camp; when a schoolchild, as a result of indoctrination by his teacher, causes his parents to be condemned to death; when a man of exceptional courage, after struggling against evils, is tried, convicted, and abjectly confesses that he has sinned in opposing the Moloch power of the authorities, neither the betrayal nor the confession brings any sense of shame to the perpetrator, for has he not been engaged in the service of his divinity?

It is this conception that we have to fight, a conception which, to my mind and to that of most men who appreciate what the Western world stands for, would, if it prevailed, take everything out of life that gives it value, leaving nothing but a regimented collection of grovelling animals. I cannot imagine a greater or more profound cause for which to fight. But if we are to win a victory—not only on the battlefield but in the hearts of men and in the institutions that they support—we must be clear in our own minds as to what it is that we value, and we must, like Boethius, fortify our courage against the threat of adversity.

While Russia underestimates the individual, there are those in the West who unduly magnify the separateness of separate persons. No man's ego should be enclosed in granite walls; its boundaries should be translucent. The first step in wisdom, as well as in morality, is to open the windows of the ego as wide as possible. Most people find little difficulty in including their children within the compass of their desires. In slightly lesser degree they include their friends, and in time of danger their country. Very many men feel that what hurts their country hurts them. In 1940 I knew Frenchmen living prosperously in America who suffered from the fall of France almost as they would have suffered from the loss of a leg. But it is not enough to enlarge our sympathies to embrace our own country. If the world is ever to have peace it will be necessary to learn to embrace the whole human race in the same kind of sympathy which we now feel toward our compatriots. And if we are to retain calm and sanity in difficult times, it is a great help if the furniture of our minds contains past and future ages.

Few things are more purifying to our conception of values than to contemplate the gradual rise of man from his obscure and difficult beginnings to his present eminence. Man, when he first emerged, was a rare and hunted species, not so fleet as the deer, not so nimble as the monkey, unable to defend himself against wild beasts, without the protection of warm fur against rain and cold, living precariously upon the food that he could gather, without weapons, without domestic animals, without agriculture.

The one advantage that he possessed—intelligence—gave him security. He learned the use of fire, of bows and arrows, of language, of domestic animals and, at last, of agriculture. He learned to co-operate in communities, to build great palaces and pyramids, to explore the world in all directions and, at last, to cope with disease and poverty. He studied the stars, he invented geometry, and he learned to substitute machines for muscles in necessary labour. Some of the most important of these advances are very recent and are as yet confined to Western nations.

In the former days most children died in infancy, mortality in adult life was very high, and in every country the great majority of the population endured abject poverty. Now certain nations have succeeded in preserving the lives of the overwhelming majority of infants, in lowering enormously the adult death rate, and in nearly eliminating abject poverty. Other nations, where disease and abject poverty are still the rule, could achieve the same level of well-being by adopting the same methods. There is, therefore, a new hope for mankind.

The hope cannot be realized unless the causes of present evils are understood. But it is the hope that needs to be emphasized. Modern man is master of his fate. What he suffers he suffers because he is stupid or wicked, not because it is nature's decree. Happiness is his if he will adopt the means that lie ready to his hands.

We of the Western world, faced with Communisms's hostile criticism, have been too modest and too defensive in our attitude. Throughout the long ages since life began the mechanism of evolution has involved cruel suffering, endless struggle for bare subsistence, and in the end, in most cases, death by starvation. This is the law in the animal kingdom, and it remained, until the present century, the law among human beings also. Now, at last, certain nations have discovered how to prevent abject poverty, how to prevent the pain and sorrow and waste of useless births condemned to premature death, and how to substitute intelligence and care for the blind ruthlessness of nature.

The nations that have made this discovery are trustees for the future of mankind. They must have the courage of their new way of life and not allow themselves to be bemused or bewildered by the slogans of the semicivilized. We have a right to hopes that are rational, that can be itemized and set forth in statistics. If we allow ourselves to be robbed of these hopes for the sake of irrational dreams, we shall be traitors to the human race.

If bad times lie ahead of us, we should remember while they last the slow march of man, chequered in the past by devastations and retrogressions, but always resuming the movement toward progress. Spinoza, who was one of the wisest of men and who lived consistently in accordance with his own wisdom, advised men to view passing events "under the aspect of eternity." Those who can learn to do this will find a painful present much more bearable than it would otherwise be. They can see it as a passing moment—a discord to be resolved, a tunnel to be traversed. The small child who has hurt himself weeps as if the world contained nothing but sorrow, because his mind is confined to the present. A man who has learned wisdom from Spinoza can see even a lifetime of suffering as a passing moment in the life of humanity. And the human race itself, from its obscure beginning to its unknown end, is only a minute episode in the life of the universe.

What may be happening elsewhere we do not know, but it is improbable that the universe contains nothing better than ourselves. With increase of wisdom our thoughts acquire a wider scope both in space and in time. The child lives in the minute, the boy in the day, the instinctive man in the year. The man imbued with history lives in the epoch. Spinoza would have us live not in the minute, the day, the year or the epoch but in eternity. Those who learn to do this will find that it takes away the frantic quality of misfortune and prevents the trend towards madness that comes with overwhelming disaster. He spent the last day of his life telling cheerful anecdotes to his host. He had written: "The wise man thinks less about death than about anything else," and he carried out this precept when it came to his own death.

I do not mean that the wise man will be destitute of emotion—on the contrary, he will feel friendship, benevolence, and compassion in a higher degree than the man who has not emancipated himself from personal anxieties. His ego will not be a wall between him and the rest of mankind. He will feel, like Buddha, that he cannot be completely happy while anybody is miserable. He will feel pain—a wider and more diffused pain than that of the egoist—but he will not find the pain unendurable. He will not be driven by it to invent comfortable fairy-tales which assure him that the sufferings of others are illusory. He will not lose poise and self-control. Like Milton's Satan, he will say:

> The mind is its own place, and in itself
> Can make a Heav'n of Hell, a Hell of Heav'n.

Above all, he will remember that each generation is trustee to future generations of the mental and moral treasure that man has accumulated through the ages. It is easy to forget the glory of man. When King Lear is going mad he meets Edgar, who pretends to be mad and wears only a blanket. King Lear moralizes: "Unaccommodated, man is no more but such a poor, bare, forked animal as thou art."

This is half of the truth. The other half is uttered by Hamlet:

"What a piece of work is a man! how noble in reason; how infinite in faculty! In form and moving how express and admirable; in action how like an angel! in apprehension how like a god!"

Soviet man, crawling on his knees to betray his friends and family to slow butchery, is hardly worthy of Hamlet's words, but it is possible to be worthy of them. It is possible for every one of us. Every one of us can enlarge his mind, release his imagination, and spread wide his affection and benevolence. And it is those who do this whom ultimately mankind reveres. The East reveres Buddha, the West reveres Christ. Both taught love as the secret of wisdom. The earthly life of Christ was contemporary with that of the Emperor Tiberius, who spent his life in cruelty and disgusting debauchery. Tiberius had pomp and power; in his day millions trembled at his nod. But he is forgotten by historians.

Those who live nobly, even if in their day they live obscurely, need not fear that they will have lived in vain. Something radiates from their lives, some light that shows the way to their friends, their neighbours—perhaps to long future ages. I find many men nowadays oppressed with a sense of impotence, with the feeling that in the vastness of modern societies there is nothing of importance that the individual can do. This is a mistake. The individual, if he is filled with love of mankind, with breadth of vision, with courage and with endurance, can do a great deal.

As geological time goes, it is but a moment since the human race began and only the twinkling of an eye since the arts of civilization were first invented. In spite of some alarmists, it is hardly likely that our species will completely exterminate itself. And so long as man continues to exist, we may be pretty sure that, whatever he may suffer for a time, and whatever brightness may be eclipsed, he will emerge sooner or later, perhaps strengthened and reinvigorated by a period of mental sleep. The universe is vast and men are but tiny specks on an insignificant planet. But the more we realize our minuteness and our impotence in the face of cosmic forces, the more astonishing becomes what human beings have achieved.

It is to the possible achievements of man that our ultimate loyalty is due, and in that thought the brief troubles of our unquiet epoch become endurable. Much wisdom remains to be learned, and if it is only to be learned through adversity, we must endeavour to endure adversity with what fortitude we can command. But if we can acquire wisdom soon enough, adversity may not be necessary and the future of man may be happier than any part of his past.

Suggestions for Discussion

1. How does the first paragraph summarize the concerns that Russell treats in the rest of the essay?

2. What is the function of Russell's references to Plotinus and Boethius?

3. Russell distinguishes between totalitarian and democratic governments in their attitude toward individual freedom. Explain his argument.

4. What is the tone of this essay? Why does Russell hold out promise of hope in "this dark time"?

Suggestion for Writing

Write an essay in which you define Russell's "dark time." Your essay should attempt to evaluate his optimism in face of the difficulties that he considers to lie ahead.

Karl Jaspers
Is Science Evil?

Karl Jaspers (1883–1969) was a German philosopher who deeply influenced the modern existentialist movement in philosophy and literature. His works include *Reason and Anti-Reason in Our Time* (1952), *Tragedy Is Not Enough* (1952), and *The Future of Man* (1961). In "Is Science Evil?" published in *Commentary* in 1950, Jaspers answers the accusation that modern science is responsible for the perverted experiments of Nazi doctors. Pointing out that crimes against humanity appeared long before science appeared, Jaspers defines the limits of science, but asserts its commitment to reason and truth.

No one questions the immense significance of modern science. Through industrial technology it has transformed our existence, and its insights have transformed our consciousness, all this to an extent hitherto unheard of. The human condition throughout the millennia appears relatively stable in comparison with the impetuous movement that has now caught up mankind as a result of science and technology, and is driving it no one knows where. Science has destroyed the substance of many old beliefs and has made others questionable. Its powerful authority has brought more and more men to the point where they wish to know and not believe, where they expect to be helped by science and only by science. The present faith is that scientific understanding can solve all problems and do away with all difficulties.

Such excessive expectations result inevitably in equally excessive disillusionment. Science has still given no answer to man's doubts and despair. Instead, it has created weapons able to destroy in a few moments that which science itself helped build up slowly over the years. Accordingly, there are today two conflicting viewpoints: first, the superstition of science, which holds scientific results to be as absolute as religious myths used to be, so that even religious movements are now dressed in the garments of pseudoscience. Second, the hatred of science, which sees it as a diabolical evil of mysterious origin that has befallen mankind.

These two attitudes—both nonscientific—are so closely linked that they are usually found together, either in alternation or in an amazing compound.

A very recent example of this situation can be found in the attack against science provoked by the trial in Nuremberg of those doctors who, under Nazi orders, performed deadly experiments on human beings. One of the most esteemed medical men among German university professors has accepted the verdict on these crimes as a verdict on science itself, as a stick with which to beat "purely scientific and biological" medicine, and even the modern science of man in general: "this invisible spirit sitting on the prisoner's bench in Nuremberg, this spirit that regards men merely as objects, is not present in Nuremberg alone—it pervades the entire world." And he adds, if this generalization may be viewed as an extenuation of the crime of the accused doctors, that is only a further indictment of purely scientific medicine.

Anyone convinced that true scientific knowledge is possible only of things that *can* be regarded as objects, and that knowledge of the subject is possible only when the subject attains a form of objectivity; anyone who sees science as the one great landmark on the road to truth, and sees the real achievements of modern physicians as derived exclusively from biological and scientific medicine—such a person will see in the above statements an attack on what he feels to be fundamental to human existence. And he may perhaps have a word to say in rebuttal.

In the special case of the crimes against humanity commited by Nazi doctors and now laid at the door of modern science, there is a simple enough argument. Science was not needed at all, but only a certain bent of mind for the perpetration of such outrages. Such crimes were already possible millennia ago. In the Buddhist Pali canon, there is the report of an Indian prince who had experiments performed on criminals in order to determine whether they had an immortal soul that survived their corpses: "You shall—it was ordered—put the living man in a tub, close the lid, cover it with a damp hide. lay on a thick layer of clay, put it in the oven, and make a fire. This was done. When we knew the man was dead, the tub was drawn forth, uncovered, the lid removed, and we looked carefully inside to see if we could perceive the escaping soul. But we saw no escaping soul." Similarly, criminals were slowly skinned alive to see if their souls could be observed leaving their bodies. Thus there were experiments on human beings before modern science.

Better than such a defense, however, would be a consideration of what modern science really genuinely is, and what its limits are.

Science, both ancient and modern, has, in the first place, three indispensable characteristics:

First, it is *methodical* knowledge. I know something scientifically only when I also know the method by which I have this knowledge, and am thus able to ground it and mark its limits.

Second, it is *compellingly certain*. Even the uncertain—i.e., the probable or improbable—I know scientifically only insofar as I know it clearly and compellingly as such, and know the degree of its uncertainly.

Third, it is *universally valid*. I know scientifically only what is identically valid for every inquirer. Thus scientific knowledge spreads over the world and remains the same. Unanimity is a sign of universal validity. When unanimity is not attained, when there is a conflict of schools, sects, and trends of fashion, then universal validity becomes problematic.

This notion of science as methodical knowledge, compellingly certain, and universally valid, was long ago possessed by the Greeks. Modern science has not only purified this notion; it has also transformed it: a transformation that can be described by saying that modern science is *indifferent to nothing*. Everything—the smallest and meanest, the furthest and strangest—that is in any way and at any time *actual*, is relevant to modern science, simply because it *is*. Modern science wants to be thoroughly universal, allowing nothing to escape it. Nothing shall be hidden, nothing shall be silent, nothing shall be a secret.

In contrast to the science of classical antiquity, modern science is *basically unfinished*. Whereas ancient science had the appearance of something completed, to which the notion of progress was not essential, modern science progresses into the infinite. Modern science has realized that a finished and total world-view is scientifically impossible. Only when scientific criticism is crippled by making particulars absolute can a closed view of the world pretend to scientific validity—and then it is a false validity. Those great new unified systems of knowledge—such as modern physics—that have grown up in the scientific era, deal only with single aspects of reality. And reality as a whole has been fragmented as never before; whence the openness of the modern world in contrast to the closed Greek cosmos.

However, while a total and finished world-view is no longer possible to modern science, the idea of a unity of the sciences has now come to replace it. Instead of the cosmos of the world, we have the cosmos of the sciences. Out of dissatisfaction with all the separate bits of knowledge is born the desire to unite all knowledge. The ancient sciences remained dispersed and without mutual relations. There was lacking to them the notion of a concrete totality of science. The modern sciences, however, seek to relate themselves to each other in every possible way.

At the same time the modern sciences have increased their claims. They put a low value on the possibilities of speculative thinking, they hold thought to be valid only as part of definite and concrete knowledge, only when it has stood the test of verification and thereby become infinitely modified. Only superficially do the modern and the ancient atomic theories seem to fit into the same theoretical mold. Ancient atomic theory was applied as a plausible interpretation of common experience; it was a statement complete in itself of what might possibly be the case. Modern atomic theory has developed through experiment, verification, refutation: that is, through an incessant transformation of itself in which theory is used not as an end in itself but as a tool of inquiry. Modern science, in its questioning, pushes to extremes. For example: the rational critique of appearance (as against reality) was begun in antiquity, as in the concept of perspective and its application to astronomy, but it still had some connection with immediate human experiences; today, however, this same critique, as in modern physics for instance, ventures to the very extremes of paradox, attaining a knowledge of the real that shatters any and every view of the world as a closed and complete whole.

So it is that in our day a scientific attitude has become possible that addresses itself inquisitively to everything it comes across, that is able to know what it knows in a clear and positive way, that can distinguish between the known and the unknown, and that has acquired an incredible mass of knowledge. How helpless was the Greek doctor or the Greek engineer! The ethos of modern science is the desire for reliable knowledge based on dispassionate investigation and criticism. When we enter its domain we feel as though we were breathing pure air, and seeing the dissolution of all vague talk, plausible opinions, haughty omniscience, blind faith.

But the greatness and the limitations of science are inseparable. It is a characteristic of the greatness of modern science that it comprehends its own limits:

(1) Scientific, objective knowledge is not a knowledge of Being. This means that scientific knowledge is particular, not general, that it is directed toward specific objects, and not toward Being itself. Through knowledge it-self, science arrives at the most positive recognition of what it does *not* know.

(2) Scientific knowledge or understanding cannot supply us with the aims of life. It cannot lead us. By virtue of its very clarity it directs us elsewhere for the sources of our life, our decisions, our love.

(3) Human freedom is not an object of science, but is the field of philosophy. Within the purview of science there is no such thing as liberty.

These are clear limits, and the person who is scientifically minded will not expect from science what it cannot give. Yet science has become, nevertheless, the indispensable element of all striving for truth, it has become the premise of philosophy and the basis in general for whatever clarity and candor are today possible. To the extent that it succeeds in penetrating all obscurities and unveiling all secrets, science directs to the most profound, the most genuine secret.

The unique phenomenon of modern science, so fundamentally different from anything in the past, including the science of the Greeks, owes its character to the many sources that were its origin; and these had to meet together in Western history in order to produce it.

One of these sources was Biblical religion. The rise of modern science is scarcely conceivable without its impetus. Three of the motives that have spurred research and inquiry seem to have come from it:

(1) The ethos of Biblical religion demanded truthfulness at all costs. As a result, truthfulness became a supreme value and at the same time was pushed to the point where it became a serious problem. The truthfulness demanded by God forbade making the search for knowledge a game or amusement, an aristocratic leisure activity. It was a serious affair, a calling in which everything was at stake.

(2) The world is the creation of God. The Greeks knew the cosmos as that which was complete and ordered, rational and regular, eternally subsisting. All else was nothing, merely material, not knowable and not worth knowing. But if the world is the creation of God, then everything that exists is worth knowing, just because it is God's creation; there is nothing that ought not to be known and comprehended. To know is to reflect upon God's thought. And God as creator is—in Luther's words—present even in the bowels of a louse.

The Greeks remained imprisoned in their closed world-view, in the beauty of their rational cosmos, in the logical transparency of the rational whole. Not only Aristotle and Democritus, but Thomas Aquinas and Descartes, too, obey this Greek urge, so paralyzing to the spirit of science, toward a closed universe. Entirely different is the new impulse to unveil the totality of creation. Out of this there arises the pursuit through knowledge of that reality which is not in accord with previously established laws. In the Logos itself [the Word, Reason] there is born the drive toward repeated self-destruction—not as self-immolation, but in order to arise again and ever again in a process that is to be continued infinitely. This science springs from a Logos that does not remain closed within itself, but is open to an anti-Logos which it permeates by the very act of subordinating itself to it. The continuous, unceasing reciprocal action of theory and experiment is the simple and great example and symbol of the universal process that is the dialectic between Logos and anti-Logos.

This new urge for knowledge sees the world no longer as simply beautiful. This knowledge ignores the beautiful and the ugly, the good and the wicked. It is true that in the end, *omne ens est bonum* [all Being is good], that is, as a creation of God. This goodness, however, is no longer the transparent and self-sufficient beauty of the Greeks. It is present only in the love of all existent things as created by God, and it is present therefore in our confidence in the significance of inquiry. The knowledge of the createdness of all worldly things replaces indifference in the face of the flux of reality with limitless questioning, an insatiable spirit of inquiry.

But the world that is known and knowable is, as created Being, Being of the second rank. For the world is unfathomable, it has its ground in another, a Creator, it is not self-contained and it is not containable by knowledge. The Being of the world cannot be comprehended as definitive, absolute reality but points always to another.

The idea of creation makes worthy of love whatever is, for it is God's creation; and it makes possible, by this, an intimacy with reality never before attained. But at the same time it gives evidence of the incalculable distance from that Being which is not merely created Being but Being itself, God.

(3) The reality of this world is full of cruelty and horror for men. "That's the way things are," is what man must truthfully say. If, however, God is the world's creator, then he is responsible for his creation. The question of justifying God's way becomes with Job a struggle with the divine for the knowledge of reality. It is a struggle against God, for God. God's existence is undisputed and just because of this the struggle arises. It would cease if faith were extinguished.

This God, with his unconditional demand for truthfulness, refuses to be grasped through illusions. In the Bible, he condemns the theologians who wish to console and comfort Job with dogmas and sophisms. This God insists upon science, whose content always seems to bring forth an indictment of him. Thus we have the adventure of knowledge, the furtherance of unrestricted knowledge—and at the same time, a timidity, an awe in the face of it. There was an inner tension to be observed in many scientists of the past century, as if they heard: God's will is unconfined inquiry, inquiry is in the service of God—and at the same time: it is an encroachment on God's domain, all shall not be revealed.

This struggle goes hand in hand with the struggle of the man of science against all that he holds most dear, his ideals, his beliefs; they must be proven, newly verified, or else transformed. Since God could not be believed in if he were not able to withstand all the questions arising from the facts of reality, and since the seeking of God involves the painful sacrifice of all illusions, so true inquiry is the struggle against all personal desires and expectations.

This struggle finds its final test in the struggle of the scientist with his own theses. It is the determining characteristic of the modern scientist that he seeks out the strongest points in the criticism of his opponents and exposes himself to them. What in appearance is self-destructiveness becomes, in this case, productive. And it is evidence of a degradation of science when discussion is shunned or condemned, when men imprison themselves and their ideas in a milieu of like-minded savants and become fanatically aggressive to all outside it.

That modern science, like all things, contains its own share of corruption, that men of science only too often fail to live up to its standards, that science can be used for violent and criminal ends, that man will steal, plunder, abuse, and kill to gain knowledge—all this is no argument against science.

To be sure, science as such sets up no barriers. As science, it is neither human nor inhuman. So far as the well-being of humanity is concerned, science needs guidance from other sources. Science in itself is not enough—or should not be. Even medicine is only a scientific means, serving an eternal ideal, the aid of the sick and the protection of the healthy.

When the spirit of a faithless age can become the cause of atrocities all over the world, then it can also influence the conduct of the scientist and the behavior of the physician, especially in those areas of activity where science itself is confused and unguided. It is not the spirit of science but the spirit of its vessels that is depraved. Count Keyserling's dictum—"The roots of truth-seeking lie in primitive aggression"—is as little valid for science as it is for any genuine truth seeking. The spirit of science is in no way primarily aggressive, but becomes so only when truth is prohibited; for men rebel against the glossing over of truth or its suppression.

In our present situation the task is to attain to that true science which knows what it knows at the same time that it knows what it cannot know. This science shows us the ways to the truth that are the indispensable precondition of every other truth. We know what Mephistopheles knew when he thought he had outwitted Faust:

> *Verachte nur Vernunft und Wissenschaft*
> *Des Menschen allerhöchste Kraft*
> *So habe ich Dich schon unbedingt.*

> (Do but scorn Reason and Science
> Man's supreme strength
> Then I'll have you for sure.)

Suggestions for Discussion

1. What is the function of the first two paragraphs of the essay? How is the third paragraph linked to the first two?

2. How does Jaspers use the Nuremberg trail to develop his ideas? Discuss Jasper's statement that there were experiments on human beings before science.

3. What role do the three characteristics of science play in Jaspers's defense of science?

4. Explain Jaspers's statement that "modern science is *basically unfinished.*" Is this statement part of his defense of science? How does it also serve as a definition of the limits of scientific knowledge? What are the limits?

5. How does Jaspers relate the limits of science to the area of what is unknowable scientifically? What is Jaspers' attitude toward this area?

Suggestions for Writing

1. Although Jaspers's essay is complex, is it difficult to read? If you think not, explain how the language and the organization of the essay contribute to its clarity.

2. Why does Jaspers close his essay with a quotation from Goethe's *Faust?* Write a paper in which you relate the quotation to the essay.

Jacob Bronowski

The Reach of the Imagination

Jacob Bronowski (1908–1974) was a Polish-born American scientist who has played a significant role in the scientific and cultural life of America. He has been particularly active in attempting to explain scientific concepts to humanists. He wrote *The Common Sense of Science* (1951), *Science and Human Values* (1959), and *William Blake, A Man with a Mask* (1965). His *Ascent of Man* (1974), a series of television essays that combined art, philosophy, and science, was a major effort to bridge the gap between the worlds of science and humanism. "The Reach of Imagination" argues that imagination is common to literature and science and inspires creativity in both.

For three thousand years, poets have been enchanted and moved and perplexed by the power of their own imagination. In a short and summary essay I can hope at most to lift one small corner of that mystery; and yet it is a critical corner. I shall ask, What goes on in the mind when we imagine? You will hear from me that one answer to this question is fairly specific: which is to say, that we can describe the working of the imagination. And when we describe it as I shall do, it becomes plain that imagination is a specifically *human* gift. To imagine is the characteristic act, not of the poet's mind, or the painter's, or the scientist's, but of the mind of man.

My stress here on the word *human* implies that there is a clear difference in this between the actions of men and those of other animals. Let me then start with a classical experiment with animals and children which Walter

Hunter thought out in Chicago about 1910. That was the time when scientists were agog with the success of Ivan Pavlov in forming and changing the reflex actions of dogs, which Pavlov had first announced in 1903. Pavlov had been given a Nobel Prize the next year, in 1904; although in fairness I should say that the award did not cite his work on the conditioned reflex, but on the digestive gland.

Hunter duly trained some dogs and other animals on Pavlov's lines. They were taught that when a light came on over one of three tunnels out of their cage, that tunnel would be open; they could escape down it, and were rewarded with food if they did. But once he had fixed that conditioned reflex, Hunter added to it a deeper idea: he gave the mechanical experiment a new dimension, literally—the dimension of time. Now he no longer let the dog go to the lighted tunnel at once; instead, he put out the light, and then kept the dog waiting a little while before he let him go. In this way Hunter timed how long an animal can remember where he has last seen the signal light to his escape route.

The results were and are staggering. A dog or a rat forgets which one of three tunnels has been lit up within a matter of seconds—in Hunter's experiment, ten seconds at most. If you want such an animal to do much better than this, you must make the task much simpler: you must face him with only two tunnels to choose from. Even so, the best that Hunter could do was to have a dog remember for five minutes which one of two tunnels had been lit up.

I am not quoting these times as if they were exact and universal: they surely are not. Hunter's experiment, more than fifty years old now, had many faults of detail. For example, there were too few animals, they were oddly picked, and they did not all behave consistently. It may be unfair to test a dog for what he *saw*, when he commonly follows his nose rather than his eyes. It may be unfair to test any animal in the unnatural setting of a laboratory cage. And there are higher animals, such as chimpanzees and other primates, which certainly have longer memories than the animals that Hunter tried.

Yet when all these provisos have been made (and met, by more modern experiments) the facts are still startling and characteristic. An animal cannot recall a signal from the past for even a short fraction of the time that a man can—for even a short fraction of the time that a child can. Hunter made comparable tests with six-year-old children, and found, of course, that they were incomparably better than the best of his animals. There is a striking and basic difference between a man's ability to imagine something that he saw or experienced, and an animal's failure.

Animals make up for this by other and extraordinary gifts. The salmon and the carrier pigeon can find their way home as we cannot: they have, as it were, a practical memory that man cannot match. But their actions always depend on some form of habit: on instinct or on learning, which reproduce by rote a train of known responses. They do not depend, as human memory does, on calling to mind the recollection of absent things.

Where is it that the animal falls short? We get a clue to the answer, I think, when Hunter tells us how the animals in his experiment tried to fix their recollection. They most often pointed themselves at the light before it went out, as some gun dogs point rigidly at the game they scent—and get the name *pointer* from the posture. The animal makes ready to act by building the signal into its action. There is a primitive imagery in its stance, it seems to me; it is as if the animal were trying to fix the light on its mind by fixing it in its body. And indeed, how else can a dog mark and (as it were) name one of the three tunnels, when he has no such words as *left* and *right*, and no such numbers as *one, two, three?* The directed gesture of attention and readiness is perhaps the only symbolic device that the dog commands to hold on to the past, and thereby to guide himself into the future.

I used the verb *to imagine* a moment ago, and now I have some ground for giving it a meaning. *To imagine* means to make images and to move them about inside one's head in new arrangements. When you and I recall the past, we imagine it in this direct and homely sense. The tool that puts the human mind ahead of the animal is imagery. For us, memory does not demand the preoccupation that it demands in animals, and it lasts immensely longer, because we fix it in images or other substitute symbols. With the same symbolic vocabulary we spell out the future—not one but many futures, which we weigh one against another.

I am using the word *image* in a wide meaning, which does not restrict it to the mind's eye as a visual organ. An image in my usage is what Charles Peirce called a *sign*, without regard for its sensory quality. Peirce distinguished between different forms of signs, but there is no reason to make his distinction here, for the imagination works equally with them all, and that is why I call them all images.

Indeed, the most important images for human beings are simply words, which are abstract symbols. Animals do not have words, in our sense: there is no specific center for language in the brain of any animal, as there is in the human being. In this respect at least we know that the human imagination depends on a configuration in the brain that has only evolved in the last one or two million years. In the same period, evolution has greatly enlarged the front lobes in the human brain, which govern the sense of the past and the future; and it is a fair guess that they are probably the seat of our other images. (Part of the evidence for this guess is that damage to the front lobes in primates reduces them to the state of Hunter's animals.) If the guess turns out to be right, we shall know why man has come to look like a highbrow or an egghead: because otherwise there would not be room in his head for his imagination.

The images play out for us events which are not present to our senses, and thereby guard the past and create the future—a future that does not yet exist, and may never come to exist in that form. By contrast, the lack of symbolic ideas, or their rudimentary poverty, cuts off an animal from the past and the future alike, and imprisons him in the present. Of all the distinctions between man and animal, the characteristic gift which makes us human is the power to work with symbolic images: the gift of imagination.

This is really a remarkable finding. When Philip Sidney in 1580 defended poets (and all unconventional thinkers) from the Puritan charge that they were liars, he said that a maker must imagine things that are not. Halfway between Sidney and us, William Blake said, "What is now proved was once only imagined." About the same time, in 1796, Samuel Taylor Coleridge for the first time distinguished between the passive fancy and the active imagination, "the living Power and prime Agent of all human Perception." Now we see that they were right, and precisely right: the human gift is the gift of imagination—and that is not just a literary phrase.

Nor is it just a literary gift; it is, I repeat, characteristically human. Almost everything that we do that is worth doing is done in the first place in the mind's eye. The richness of human life is that we have many lives; we live the events that do not happen (and some that cannot) as vividly as those that do; and if thereby we die a thousand deaths, that is the price we pay for living a thousand lives. (A cat, of course, has only nine.) Literature is alive to us because we live its images, but so is any play of the mind—so is chess: the lines of play that we foresee and try in our heads and dismiss are as much a part of the game as the moves that we make. John Keats said that the unheard melodies are sweeter, and all chess players sadly recall that the combinations that they planned and which never came to be played were the best.

I make this point to remind you, insistently, that imagination is the manipulation of images in one's head; and that the rational manipulation belongs to that, as well as the literary and artistic manipulation. When a child begins to play games with things that stand for other things, with chairs or chessmen, he enters the gateway to reason and imagination together. For the human reason discovers new relations between things not by deduction, but by that unpredictable blend of speculation and insight that scientists call induction, which—like other forms of imagination—cannot be formalized. We see it at work when Walter Hunter inquires into a child's memory, as much as when Blake and Coleridge do. Only a restless and original mind would have asked Hunter's questions and could have conceived his experiments, in a science that was dominated by Pavlov's reflex arcs and was heading toward the behaviorism of John Watson.

Let me find a spectacular example for you from history. What is the most famous experiment that you had described to you as a child? I will hazard that it is the experiment that Galileo is said to have made in Sidney's age, in Pisa about 1590, by dropping two unequal balls from the Leaning Tower. There, we say, is a man in the modern mold, a man after our own hearts: he insisted on questioning the authority of Aristotle and St. Thomas Aquinas, and seeing with his own eyes whether (as they said) the heavy ball would reach the ground before the light one. Seeing is believing.

Yet seeing is also imagining. Galileo did challenge the authority of Aristotle, and he did look at his mechanics. But the eye that Galileo used was the minds's eye. He did not drop balls from the Leaning Tower of Pisa—and if he had, he would have got a very doubtful answer. Instead, Galileo made an imaginary experiment in his head, which I will describe as he did years later in the book he wrote after the Holy Office silenced him: *Discorsi . . . intorno a due nuove scienze*, which was smuggled out to be printed in the Netherlands in 1638.

Suppose, said Galileo, that you drop two unequal balls from the tower at the same time. And suppose that Aristotle is right—suppose that the heavy ball falls faster, so that it steadily gains on the light ball, and hits the ground first. Very well. Now imagine the same experiment done again, with only one difference: this time the two unequal balls are joined by a string between them. The heavy ball will again move ahead, but now the light ball holds it back and acts as a drag or brake. So the light ball will be speeded up and the heavy ball will be slowed down; they must reach the ground together because they are tied together, but they cannot reach the ground as quickly as the heavy ball alone. Yet the string between them has turned the two balls into a single mass which is heavier than either ball—and surely (according to Aristotle) this mass should therefore move faster than either ball? Galileo's imaginary experiment has uncovered a contradiction; he says trenchantly, "You see how, from your assumption that a heavier body falls more rapidly than a lighter one, I infer that a (still) heavier body falls more slowly." There is only one way out of the contradiction: the heavy ball and the light ball must fall at the same rate, so that they go on falling at the same rate when they are tied together.

This argument is not conclusive, for nature might be more subtle (when the two balls are joined) than Galileo has allowed. And yet it is something more important: it is suggestive, it is stimulating, it opens a new view—in a word, it is imaginative. It cannot be settled without an actual experiment, because nothing that we imagine can become knowledge until we have translated it into, and backed it by, real experience. The test of imagination is experience. But then, that is as true of literature and the arts as it is of science. In science, the imaginary experiment is tested by confronting it with physical experience; and in literature, the imaginative conception is tested by confronting it with human experience. The superficial speculation in science is dismissed because it is found to falsify nature; and the shallow work of art is discarded because it is found to be untrue to our own nature. So when Ella Wheeler Wilcox died in 1919, more people were reading her verses than Shakespeare's; yet in a few years her work was dead. It had been buried by its poverty of emotion and its trivialness of thought: which is to say that it had been proved to be as false to the nature of man as, say, Jean Baptiste Lamarck and Trofim Lysenko were false to the nature of inheritance. The strength of the imagination, its enriching power and excitement, lies in its interplay with reality—physical and emotional.

I doubt if there is much to choose here between science and the arts: the imagination is not much more free, and not much less free, in one than in the other. All great scientists have used their imagination freely, and let it ride them to outrageous conclusions without crying "Halt!" Albert Einstein fiddled with imaginary experiments from boyhood, and was wonderfully ignorant of the facts that they were supposed to bear on. When he wrote the first of his beautiful papers on the random movement of atoms, he did not know that the Brownian motion which it predicted could be seen in any laboratory. He was sixteen when he invented the paradox that he resolved ten years later, in 1905, in the theory of relativity, and it bulked much larger in his mind than the experiment of Albert Michelson and Edward Morley which had upset every other physicist since 1881. All his life Einstein loved to make up teasing puzzles like Galileo's, about falling lifts and the detection of gravity; and they carry the nub of the problems of general relativity on which he was working.

Indeed, it could not be otherwise. The power that man has over nature and himself, and that a dog lacks, lies in his command of imaginary experience. He alone has the symbols which fix the past and play with the future, possible and impossible. In the Renaissance, the symbolism of memory was thought to be mystical, and devices that were invented as mnemonics (by Giordano Bruno, for example, and by Robert Fludd) were interpreted as magic signs. The symbol is the tool which gives man his power, and it is the same tool whether the symbols are images or words, mathematical signs or mesons. And the symbols have a reach and a roundness that goes beyond their literal and practical meaning. They are the rich concepts under which the mind gathers many particulars into one name, and many instances into one general induction. When a man says *left* and *right*, he is outdistancing the dog not only in looking for a light; he is setting in train all the shifts of meaning, the overtones and the ambiguities, between *gauche* and *adroit* and *dexterous*, between *sinister* and the sense of right. When a man counts *one, two, three*, he is not only doing mathematics; he is on the path to the mysticism of numbers in Pythagoras and Vitruvius and Kepler, to the Trinity and the signs of the Zodiac.

I have described imagination as the ability to make images and to move them about inside one's head in new arrangements. This is the faculty that is specifically human, and it is the common root from which science and literature both spring and grow and flourish together. For they do flourish (and languish) together; the great ages of science are the great ages of all the arts, because in them powerful minds have taken fire from one another breathless and higgledy-piggledy, without asking too nicely whether they ought to tie their imagination to falling balls or a haunted island. Galileo and Shakespeare, who were born in the same year, grew into greatness in the same age; when Galileo was looking through his telescope at the moon, Shakespeare was writing *The Tempest* and all Europe was in ferment, from Johannes Kepler to Peter Paul Rubens, and from the first table of logarithms by John Napier to the Authorized Version of the Bible.

Let me end with a last and spirited example of the common inspiration of literature and science, because it is as much alive today as it was three hundred years ago. What I have in mind is man's ageless fantasy, to fly to the moon. I do not display this to you as a high scientific enterprise; on the contrary, I think we have more important discoveries to make here on earth than wait for us, beckoning, at the horned surface of the moon. Yet I cannot belittle the fascination which that ice-blue journey has had for the imagination of men, long before it drew us to our television screens to watch the tumbling astronauts. Plutarch and Lucian, Ariosto and Ben Jonson wrote about it, before the days of Jules Verne and H. G. Wells and science fiction. The seventeenth century was heady with new dreams and fables about voyages to the moon. Kepler wrote one full of deep scientific ideas, which (alas) simply got his mother accused of witchcraft. In England, Francis Godwin wrote a wild and splendid work, *The Man in the Moone*, and the astronomer John Wilkins wrote a wild and learned one, *The Discovery of a New World*. They did not draw a line between science and fancy; for example, they all tried to guess just where in the journey the earth's gravity would stop. Only Kepler understood that gravity has no boundary, and put a law to it—which happened to be the wrong law.

All this was a few years before Isaac Newton was born, and it was all in his head that day in 1666 when he sat in his mother's garden, a young man of twenty-three, and thought about the reach of gravity. This was how he came to conceive his brilliant image, that the moon is like a ball which has been thrown so hard that it falls exactly as fast as the horizon, all the way round the earth. The image will do for any satellite, and Newton modestly calculated how long therefore an astronaut would take to fall round the earth once. He made it ninety minutes, and we have all seen now that he was right; but Newton had no way to check that. Instead he went on to calculate how long in that case the distant moon would take to round the earth, if indeed it behaves like a thrown ball that falls in the earth's gravity, and if gravity obeyed a law of inverse squares. He found that the answer would be twenty-eight days.

In that telling figure, the imagination that day chimed with nature, and made a harmony. We shall hear an echo of that harmony on the day when we land on the moon, because it will be not a technical but an imaginative triumph, that reaches back to the beginning of modern science and literature both. All great acts of imagination are like this, in the arts and in science, and convince us because they fill out reality with a deeper sense of rightness. We start with the simplest vocabulary of images, with *left* and *right* and *one, two, three,* and before we know how it happened the words and the numbers have conspired to make a match with nature: we catch in them the pattern of mind and matter as one.

Suggestions for Discussion

1. Although Bronowski proposes to discuss the imagination of man, he begins his essay by describing an experiment conducted on animals. How does Bronowski use the experiment to explore or define man's imagination?

2. Bronowski uses the metaphor of "reaching" in the essay. What objects does the imagination reach for? What is the function of the metaphor in the argument?

3. Explain how Bronowski uses Galileo and Newton in his argument.

Suggestion for Writing

Write a paper in which you compare Bronowski the scientist with Whitman the poet, based entirely on this essay and the poem by Whitman "When I Heard the Learn'd Astronomer." Might Whitman have been surprised at the poetic nature of Bronowski the scientist?

Joseph Weizenbaum

On the Impact of the Computer on Society

Joseph Weizenbaum (b. 1923) was born in Berlin but educated at Wayne State University. A professor of Computer Science and Engineering at MIT since 1979, he has done research in artificial intelligence and the structure of computer languages. He is concerned with the social impact of computers and cybernetics. His program ELIZA simulated the words of a nondirective psychological therapist. "On the Impact of the Computer on Society" (1972) asserts that if technology is a nightmare it is one of man's making, and that it is possible for man to formulate his own questions and find humane answers.

The direct societal effects of any pervasive new technology are as nothing compared to its much more subtle and ultimately much more important side effects. In that sense, the societal impact of the computer has not yet been felt.

To help firmly fix the idea of the importance of subtle indirect effects of technology, consider the impact on society of the invention of the microscope. When it was invented in the middle of the 17th century, the dominant commonsense theory of disease was fundamentally that disease was a punishment visited upon an individual by God. The sinner's body was thought to be inhabited by various so-called humors brought into disequilibrium in accordance with divine justice. The cure for disease was therefore to be found first in penance and second in the balancing of humors as, for example, by bleeding. Bleeding was, after all, both painful, hence punishment and penance, and potentially balancing in that it actually removed substance from the body. The microscope enabled man to see microorganisms and thus paved the way for the germ theory of disease. The enormously surprising discovery of extremely small living organisms also induced the idea of a continuous chain of life which, in turn, was a necessary intellectual precondition for the emergence of Darwinism. Both the germ theory of disease and the theory of evolution profoundly altered man's conception of his contract with God and consequently his self-image. Politically these ideas served to help diminish the power of the Church and, more generally, to legitimize the questioning of the basis of hitherto unchallenged authority. I do not say that the microscope alone was responsible for the enormous social changes that followed its invention. Only that it made possible the kind of paradigm shift, even on the commonsense level, without which these changes might have been impossible.

Is it reasonable to ask whether the computer will induce similar changes in man's image of himself and whether that influence will prove to be its most important effect on society? I think so, although I hasten to add that I don't believe the computer has yet told us much about man and his nature. To come to grips with the question, we must first ask in what way the computer is different from man's many other machines. Man has built two fundamentally different kinds of machines, nonautonomous and autonomous. An autonomous machine is one that operates for long periods of time, not on the basis of inputs from the real world, for example from sensors or from human drivers, but on the basis of internalized models of some aspects of the real world. Clocks are examples of autonomous machines in that they operate on the basis of an internalized model of the planetary system. The computer is, of course, the example par excellence. It is able to internalize models of essentially unlimited complexity and of a fidelity limited only by the genius of man.

It is the autonomy of the computer we value. When, for example, we speak of the power of computers as increasing with each new hardware and software development, we mean that, because of their increasing speed and storage capacity, and possibly thanks to new programming tricks, the new computers can internalize ever more complex and ever more faithful models of ever larger slices of reality. It seems strange then that, just when we exhibit virtually an idolatry of autonomy with respect to machines, serious thinkers in respected academies [I have in mind B. F. Skinner of Harvard University] can rise to question autonomy as a fact for man. I do not think that the appearance of this paradox at this time is accidental. To understand it, we must realize that man's commitment to science has always had a masochistic component.

Time after time science has led us to insights that, at least when seen superficially, diminish man. Thus Galileo removed man from the center of the universe, Darwin removed him from his place separate from the animals, and Freud showed his rationality to be an illusion. Yet man pushes his inquiries further and deeper. I cannot help but think that there is an analogy between man's pursuit of scientific knowledge and an individual's commitment to psychoanalytic therapy. Both are undertaken in the full realization that what the inquirer may find may well damage his self-esteem. Both may reflect his determination to find meaning in his existence through struggle in truth, however painful that may be, rather than to live without meaning in a world of ill-disguised illusion. However, I am also aware that sometimes people enter psychoanalysis unwilling to put their illusions at risk, not searching for a deeper reality but in order to convert the insights they hope to gain to personal power. The analogy to man's pursuit of science does not break down with that observation.

Each time a scientific discovery shatters a hitherto fundamental cornerstone of the edifice on which man's self-esteem is built, there is an enormous reaction, just as is the case under similar circumstances in psychoanalytic therapy. Powerful defense mechanisms, beginning with denial and usually terminating in rationalization, are brought to bear. Indeed, the psychoanalyst suspects that, when a patient appears to accept a soul-shattering insight without resistance, his very casualness may well mask his refusal to allow that insight truly operational status in his self-image. But what is the psychoanalyst to think about the patient who positively embraces tentatively proffered, profoundly humiliating self-knowledge, when he embraces it and instantly converts it to a new foundation of his life? Surely such an event is symptomatic of a major crisis in the mental life of the patient.

I believe we are now at the beginning of just such a crisis in the mental life of our civilization. The microscope, I have argued, brought in its train a revision of man's image of himself. But no one in the mid-17th century could have foreseen that. The possibility that the computer will, one way or another, demonstrate that, in the inimitable phrase of one of my esteemed colleagues, "the brain is merely a meat machine" is one that engages academicians, industrialists, and journalists in the here and now. How has the computer contributed to bringing about this very sad state of affairs? It must be said right away that the computer alone is not the chief causative agent. It is merely an extreme extrapolation of technology. When seen as an inducer of philosophical dogma, it is merely the reductio ad absurdum of a technological ideology. But how does it come to be regarded as a source of philosophic dogma?

I have suggested that the computer revolution need not and ought not to call man's dignity and autonomy into question, that it is a kind of pathology that moves men to wring from it unwarranted, enormously damaging interpretations. Is then the computer less threatening than we might have thought? Once we realize that our visions, possibly nightmarish visions, determine the effect of our own creations on us and on our society, their threat to us is surely diminished. But that is not to say that this realization alone will wipe out all danger. For example, apart from the erosive effect of a technological mentality on man's self-image, there are practical attacks on the freedom and dignity of man in which computer technology plays a critical role.

I mentioned earlier that computer science has come to recognize the importance of building knowledge into machines. We already have a machine—Dendral—that commands more chemistry than do many Ph.D. chemists, and another—Mathlab—that commands more applied mathematics than do many applied mathematicians. Both Dendral and Mathlab contain knowledge that can be evaluated in terms of the explicit theories from which it was derived. If the user believes that a result Mathlab delivers is wrong, then apart from possible program errors, he must be in disagreement, not with the machine or its programmer, but with a specific mathematical theory. But what about the many programs on which management, most particularly the government and the military, rely, programs which can in no sense be said to rest on explicable theories but are instead enormous patchworks of programming techniques strung together to make them work?

Incomprehensible Systems

In our eagerness to exploit every advance in technique we quickly incorporate the lessons learned from machine manipulation of knowledge in theory-based systems into such patchworks. They then "work" better. I have in mind systems like target selection systems used in Vietnam and war games used in the Pentagon, and so on. These often gigantic systems are put together by teams of programmers, often working over a time span of many years. But by the time the systems come into use, most of the original programmers have left or turned their attention to other pursuits. It is precisely when gigantic systems begin to be used that their inner workings can no longer be understood by any single person or by a small team of individuals. Norbert Wiener, the father of cybernetics, foretold of this phenomenon in a remarkably prescient article published more than a decade ago. He said there:

> It may well be that in principle we cannot make any machine the elements of whose behavior we cannot comprehend sooner or later. This does not mean in any way that we shall be able to comprehend these elements in substantially

less time than the time required for operation of the machine, or even within any given number of years or generations.

An intelligent understanding of [machines'] mode of performance may be delayed until long after the task which they have been set has been completed. This means that though machines are theoretically subject to human criticism, such criticism may be ineffective until long after it is relevant.

This situation, which is now upon us, has two consequences: first that decisions are made on the basis of rules and criteria no one knows explicitly, and second that the system of rules and criteria becomes immune to change. This is so because, in the absence of detailed understanding of the inner workings of a system, any substantial modification is very likely to render the system altogether inoperable. The threshold of complexity beyond which this phenomenon occurs has already been crossed by many existing systems, including some compiling and computer operating systems. For example, no one likes the operating systems for certain large computers, but they cannot be substantially changed nor can they be done away with. Too many people have become dependent on them.

An awkward operating system is inconvenient. That is not too bad. But the growing reliance on supersystems that were perhaps designed to help people make analyses and decisions, but which have since surpassed the understanding of their users while at the same time becoming indispensable to them is another matter. In modern war it is common for the soldier, say the bomber pilot, to operate at an enormous psychological distance from his victims. He is not responsible for burned children because he never sees their village, his bombs, and certainly not the flaming children themselves. Modern technological rationalizations of war, diplomacy, politics, and commerce such as computer games have an even more insidious effect on the making of policy. Not only have policy makers abdicated their decision-making responsibility to a technology they don't understand, all the while maintaining the illusion that they, the policy makers, are formulating policy questions and answering them, but responsibility has altogether evaporated. No human is any longer responsible for "what the machine says." Thus there can be neither right nor wrong, no question of justice, no theory with which one can agree or disagree, and finally no basis on which one can challenge "what the machine says." My father used to invoke the ultimate authority by saying to me, "it is written." But then I could read what was written, imagine a human author, infer his values, and finally agree or disagree. The systems in the Pentagon, and their counterparts elsewhere in our culture, have in a very real sense no authors. They therefore do not admit of exercises of imagination that may ultimately lead to human judgment. No wonder that men who live day in and out with such machines and become dependent on them begin to believe that men are merely machines. They are reflecting what they themselves have become.

The potentially tragic impact on society that may ensue from the use of systems such as I have just discussed is greater than might at first be imagined. Again it is side effects, not direct effects, that matter most. First, of course, there is the psychological impact on individuals living in a society in which anonymous, hence irresponsible, forces formulate the large questions of the day and circumscribe the range of possible answers. It cannot be surprising that large numbers of perceptive individuals living in such a society experience a kind of impotence and fall victim to the mindless rage that often accompanies such experiences. But even worse, since computer-based knowledge systems become essentially unmodifiable except in that they can grow, and since they induce dependence and cannot, after a certain threshold is crossed, be abandoned, there is an enormous risk that they will be passed from one generation to another, always growing. Man too passes knowledge from one generation to another. But because man is mortal, his transmission of knowledge over the generations is at once a process of filtering and accrual. Man doesn't merely pass knowledge, he rather regenerates it continuously. Much as we may mourn the crumbling of ancient civilizations, we know nevertheless that the glory of man resides as much in the evolution of his cultures as in that of his brain. The unwise use of ever larger and ever more complex computer systems may well bring this process to a halt. It could well replace the ebb and flow of culture with a world without values, a world in which what counts for a fact has long ago been determined and forever fixed.

Positive Effects

I've spoken of some potentially dangerous effects of present computing trends. Is there nothing positive to be said? Yes, but it must be said with caution. Again, side effects are more important than direct effects. In particular, the idea of computation and of programming languages is beginning to become an important metaphor which, in the long run, may well prove to be responsible for paradigm shifts in many fields. Most of the common-sense paradigms in terms of which much of mankind interprets the phenomena of the everyday world, both physical and social, are still deeply rooted in fundamentally mechanistic metaphors. Marx's dynamics as well as those of Freud are, for example, basically equilibrium systems. Any hydrodynamicist could come to understand them without leaving the jargon of his field. Languages capable of describing ongoing processes, particularly in terms of modular subprocesses, have already had an enormous effect on the way computer people think of every aspect of their worlds, not merely those directly related to their work. The information-processing view of the world so engendered qualifies as a genuine metaphor. This is attested to by the fact that it (i) constitutes an intellectual framework that permits new questions to be asked about a wide-ranging set of phenomena, and (ii) that it itself provides criteria for the adequacy of proffered answers. A new metaphor is important not in that it may be better than existing ones, but rather in that it may enlarge man's vision by giving him yet another perspective on his world. Indeed, the very effectiveness of a new metaphor may seduce lazy minds to adopt it as a basis for universal explanations and as a source of panaceas. Computer simulation of social processes has already been advanced by single-minded generalists as leading to general solutions of all of mankind's problems.

The metaphors given us by religion, the poets, and by thinkers like Darwin, Newton, Freud, and Einstein have rather quickly penetrated to the language of ordinary people. These metaphors have thus been instrumental in shaping our entire civilization's imaginative reconstruction of our world. The computing metaphor is as yet available to only an extremely small set of people. Its acquisition and internalization, hopefully as only one of many ways to see the world, seems to require experience in program composition, a kind of computing literacy. Perhaps such literacy will become very widespread in the advanced societal sectors of the advanced countries. But, should it become a dominant mode of thinking and be restricted to certain social classes, it will prove not merely repressive in the ordinary sense, but an enormously divisive societal force. For then classes which do and do not have access to the metaphor will, in an important sense, lose their ability to communicate with one another. We know already how difficult it is for the poor and the oppressed to communicate with the rest of the society in which they are embedded. We know how difficult it is for the world of science to communicate with that of the arts and of the humanities. In both instances the communication difficulties, which have grave consequences, are very largely due to the fact that the respective communities have unsharable experiences out of which unsharable metaphors have grown.

Responsibility

Given these dismal possibilities, what is the responsibility of the computer scientist? First I should say that most of the harm computers can potentially entrain is much more a function of properties people attribute to computers than of what a computer can or cannot actually be made to do. The nonprofessional has little choice but to make his attributions of properties to computers on the basis of the propaganda emanating from the computer community and amplified by the press. The computer professional therefore has an enormously important responsibility to be modest in his claims. This advice would not even have to be voiced if computer science had a tradition of scholarship and of self-criticism such as that which characterizes the established sciences. The mature scientist stands in awe before the depth of his subject matter. His very humility is the wellspring of his strength. I regard the instilling of just this kind of humility, chiefly by the example set by teachers, to be one of the most important missions of every university department of computer science.

The computer scientist must be aware constantly that his instruments are capable of having gigantic direct and indirect amplifying effects. An error in a program, for example, could have grievous direct results, including most certainly the loss of much human life. On 11 September 1971, to cite just one example, a computer programming error caused the simultaneous destruction of 117 high-altitude weather balloons whose instruments were being monitored by an earth satellite. A similar error in a military command and control system could launch a fleet of nuclear-tipped missiles. Only censorship prevents us from knowing how many such events involving nonnuclear weapons have already occurred. Clearly then, the computer scientist has a heavy responsibility to make the fallibility and limitations of the systems he is capable of designing brilliantly clear. The very power of his systems should serve to inhibit the advice he is ready to give and to constrain the range of work he is willing to undertake.

Of course, the computer scientist, like everyone else, is responsible for his actions and their consequences. Sometimes that responsibility is hard to accept because the corresponding authority to decide what is and what is not to be done appears to rest with distant and anonymous forces. That technology itself determines what is to be done by a process of extrapolation and that individuals are powerless to intervene in that determination is precisely the kind of self-fulfilling dream from which we must awaken.

Consider gigantic computer systems. They are, of course, natural extrapolations of the large systems we already have. Computer networks are another point on the same curve extrapolated once more. One may ask whether such systems can be used by anybody except by governments and very large corporations and whether such organizations will not use them mainly for anti-human purposes. Or consider speech recognition systems. Will they not be used primarily to spy on private communications? To answer such questions by saying that big computer systems, computer networks, and speech recognition systems are inevitable is to surrender one's humanity. For such an answer must be based either on one's profound conviction that society has already lost control over its technology or on the thoroughly immoral position that "if I don't do it, someone else will."

I don't say that systems such as I have mentioned are necessarily evil— only that they may be and, what is most important, that their inevitability cannot be accepted by individuals claiming autonomy, freedom, and dignity. The individual computer scientist can and must decide. The determination of what the impact of computers on society is to be is, at least in part, in his hands.

Finally, the fundamental question the computer scientist must ask himself is the one that every scientist, indeed every human, must ask. It is not "what shall I do?" but rather "what shall I be?" I cannot answer that for anyone save myself. But I will say again that if technology is a nightmare that appears to have its own inevitable logic, it is our nightmare. It is possible, given courage and insight, for man to deny technology the prerogative to formulate man's questions. It is possible to ask human questions and to find humane answers.

References

1. B. F. Skinner, *Beyond Freedom and Dignity* (Knopf, New York, 1971).
2. K. M. Colby, S. Weber, F. D. Hilf, *Artif. Intell.* **1**, 1 (1971).
3. N. Chomsky, *Aspects of the Theory of Syntax* (M.I.T. Press, Cambridge, Mass., 1965);—and M. Halle, *The Sound Pattern of English* (Harper & Row, New York, 1968).
4. L. Mumford, *The Pentagon of Power* (Harcourt Brace Jovanovich, New York, 1970).
5. H. A. Simon, *The Sciences of the Artificial* (M.I.T. Press, Cambridge, Mass., 1969), pp. 22–25.
6. B. Buchanan, G. Sutherland, E. A. Feigenbaum, in *Machine Intelligence*, B. Meltzer, Ed. (American Elsevier, New York, 1969).
7. W. A. Martin and R. J. Fateman, "The Macsyma system," in *Proceedings of the 2nd Symposium on Symbolic and Algebraic Manipulation* (Association for Computer Machines, New York, 1971); J. Moses, *Commun. Assoc. Computer March.* **14** (No. 8), 548 (1971).
8. N. Wiener, *Science* **131**, 1355 (1960).
9. R. Gillette, **174**, 477 (1971).

Suggestions for Discussion

1. Explain the meaning of the brief opening paragraph of this essay. How does Weizenbaum develop the ideas presented in this paragraph?

2. Why does Weizenbaum place so much importance on the invention of the microscope in the 17th century? What new developments in science did that invention make possible? What have been some consequences of those developments?

3. How does Weizenbaum define nonautonomous and autonomous machines? In what category does the computer fall? What does Weizenbaum mean when he speaks of the power of the computer?

4. Weizenbaum refers to B.F. Skinner's theories which question the autonomy of man. What is his reaction to Skinner's ideas?

5. Weizenbaum mentions the theories of Galileo, Darwin, and Freud. What do they have in common? Why, according to Weizenbaum, do men continue to be attracted to the theories of all three?

6. What positive effects on man and society does the author envision for the computer?

7. What are the responsibilities of the computer scientist in the future development of the computer?

8. How do we help determine the impact of the computer on society?

Suggestions for Writing

1. Weizenbaum is optimistic about the positive impact of computers on society. On what grounds does he base his optimism? Write an essay in which you agree or disagree with his conclusions. You might find it useful to compare this essay with those by Bronowski and Jaspers.

2. If you are able to use a computer or a word processor, write an essay in which you explain how you are positively aided by this ability. Have you found any negative results of your skill?

Lewis Thomas

A Trip Abroad

Lewis Thomas (b. 1913) is a physician whose medical career has centered on the Sloan Kettering Cancer Center in New York, the city of his birth. He has written for medical journals at the same time that he has written popular essays to present science and the scientist's view of the world to the lay public. He won the National Book Award in 1974 for *The Lives of a Cell: Notes of a Biology Watcher.* Other collections include *The Medusa and the Snail* (1979), *More Notes of a Biology Watcher* (1979) and *The Youngest Science: Notes of a Medicine-Watcher* (1983). "A Trip Abroad," from *The Medusa and the Snail,* glances irreverently at the accomplishments of science and longs for a simpler, less plastic life which, Lewis imagines, may soon be easier to find in space than here on earth.

I do not believe for a minute that we are nearing the end of human surprise, despite resonantly put arguments by wonderfully informed scientists who tell us that after molecular biology and astrophysics there is really very little more to learn of substance. Except, they always add, for the nature of human consciousness, and that, they always add, is placed beyond our reach by the principle of indeterminacy; that is, our thought is so much at the center of life that it cannot sit still while we examine it.

But there may be a way out of this; it may turn out that consciousness is a much more generalized mechanism, shared round not only among ourselves but with all the other conjoined things of the biosphere. Thus, since we are not, perhaps, so absolutely central, we may be able to get a look at it, but we will need a new technology for this kind of neurobiology; in which case we will likely find that we have a whole eternity of astonishment stretching out ahead of us. Always assuming, of course, that we're still here.

We must rely on our scientists to help us find the way through the near distance, but for the longer stretch of the future we are dependent on the poets. We should learn to question them more closely, and listen more carefully. A poet is, after all, a sort of scientist, but engaged in a qualitative science in which nothing is measurable. He lives with data that cannot be numbered, and his experiments can be done only once. The information in a poem is, by definition, not reproducible. His pilot runs involve a recognition of things that pop into his head. The skill consists in his capacity to decide quickly which things to retain, which to eject. He becomes an equivalent of a scientist, in the act of examining and sorting the things popping in, finding the marks of remote similarity, points of distant relationship, tiny irregularities that indicate that this one is really the same as that one over there only more important. Gauging the fit, he can meticulously place pieces of the universe together, in geometric configurations that are as beautiful and balanced as crystals. Musicians and painters listen, and copy down what they hear.

I wish that poets were able to give straight answers to straight questions, but that is like asking astrophysicists to make their calculations on their fingers, where we can watch the process. What I would like to know is: how should I feel about the earth, these days? Where has all the old nature gone? What became of the wild, writhing, unapproachable mass of the life of the world, and what happened to our old, panicky excitement about it? Just in fifty years, since I was a small boy in a suburban town, the world has become a structure of steel and plastic, intelligible and diminished. Mine was a puzzling maple grove of a village on the outskirts of New York City, and it vanished entirely, trees and all. It is now a syncytium of apartment houses, sprouting out of a matrix of cement flooded and jelled over an area that once contained 25,000 people who walked on grass. Now I live in another, more distant town, on a street with trees and lawns, and at night I can hear the soft sound of cement, moving like incoming tide, down the Sunrise Highway from New York.

If you fly around the earth and keep looking down, you will see that we have inserted ourselves everywhere. All fields are tilled. All mountains have been climbed and are being covered with concrete and plastic; some mountains, like the Appalachians, are simply cut down like trees. The fish are all trapped and domesticated, farmed in zoned undersea pastures. As for the animals, we will never have enough plastic bags for the bodies; soon the only survivors will be the cattle and sheep for the feeding of us, and the dogs and cats in our houses, fed while it lasts on the flesh of whales. And the rats and roaches, and a few reptiles.

The winged insects are vanishing, the calcium in the shells of eggs, and the birds.

We have dominated and overruled nature, and from now on the earth is ours, a kitchen garden until we learn to make our own chlorophyll and float it out in the sun inside plastic membranes. We will build Scarsdale on Mount Everest.

We will have everything under control, managed. Then what do we do? On long Sunday afternoons, what do we do, when there is nobody to talk to but ourselves?

It is because of these problems that we are now engaged in scrutinizing with such intensity the dark, bare flanks of Mars, hideous with lifelessness as it seems to be. We are like a family looking through travel brochures.

There is such a thing as too much of this. Because of our vast numbers and the rapidity with which we have developed prosthetic devices enabling us to hear and see each other, in person, all around the earth, we have become obsessed with ourselves. You'd think, to hear us think, that there was nothing else of significance on the earth except us.

Perhaps we should try to get away, for a while anyway. A change of scene might do us a world of good.

The trouble is, the barrenness of all the local planets. Perhaps we will be unlucky with our green thumbs, unable to create or maintain the faintest gasp of life on Mars or Titan. What's to stop us from looking elsewhere, farther on? If we can learn to navigate before the solar wind, we could, out there, hoist sail and tack our way out to where the wind fades off, practicing freefalls all the while, probing for gravity, trusting to luck, taking our chances. It would be like old times.

Suggestions for Discussion

1. Why does Thomas suggest that poets rather than scientists may be our source of comfort in the long run? Why are scientists good enough for the present? What limits does he see for science? for poets?

2. What are the differences between poets and scientists?

3. Summarize Thomas's dissatisfaction with modern suburbia. Why does he use the term *syncitium* to describe it?

4. What is the tone of this essay? What role does the last paragraph play in establishing that tone? the title of the essay?

5. What are the questions about life that, according to Thomas, need answering? Where will we get answers?

Suggestion for Writing

Write an essay describing the area in which you live. Is it different from Thomas's home? In what way? How is it similar? What is your attitude toward your hometown? Does it resemble Thomas's?

Stephen Jay Gould

Death Before Birth, or a Mite's *Nunc Dimittis*

Stephen Jay Gould (b. 1941), a New Yorker by birth, teaches geology, biology, and the history of science at Harvard and writes a column, "This View of Life," for *Natural History*. His books include *Ever Since Darwin* (1977), *Ontogeny and Phylogeny* (1977), and *Hen's Teeth and Horse's Toes* (1983). This selection from *The Panda's Thumb* (1980) explains how seemingly simple questions in science have amazingly complex answers. Exploring an answer to the question of why males and females are produced in approximately equal numbers in most familiar species, he leads us to consider the dramatic life of the male mite in the genus *Adactylidium*.

Can anything be more demoralizing than parental incompetence before the most obvious and innocent of children's questions: why is the sky blue, the grass green? Why does the moon have phases? Our embarrassment is all the more acute because we thought we knew the answer perfectly well, but hadn't rehearsed it since we ourselves had received a bumbled response in similar circumstances a generation earlier. It is the things we think we know—because they are so elementary, or because they surround us—that often present the greatest difficulties when we are actually challenged to explain them.

One such question, with an obvious and incorrect answer, lies close to our biological lives: why, in humans (and in most species familiar to us), are males and females produced in approximately equal numbers? (Actually, males are more common than females at birth in humans, but differential mortality of males leads to a female majority in later life. Still, the departures from a one to one ratio are never great.) At first glance, the answer seems to be, as in Rabelais's motto, "plain as the nose on a man's face." After all, sexual reproduction requires a mate; equal numbers imply universal mating—the happy Darwinian status of maximal reproductive capacity. At second glance, it isn't so clear at all, and we are drawn in confusion to Shakespeare's recasting of the simile: "A jest unseen, inscrutable, invisible, as a nose on a man's face." If maximal reproductive capacity is the optimal state for a species, then why make equal numbers of males and females? Females, after all, set the limit upon numbers of offspring, since eggs are invariably so much larger and less abundant than sperm in species familiar to us—that is, each egg can make an offspring, each sperm cannot. A male can impregnate several females. If a male can mate with nine females and the population contains a hundred individuals, why not make ten males and ninety females? Reproductive capacity will certainly exceed that of a population composed of fifty males and fifty females. Populations made predominantly of females should, by their more rapid rates of reproduction, win any evolutionary race with populations that maintain equality in numbers between the sexes.

What appeared obvious is therefore rendered problematical and the question remains: why do most sexual species contain approximately equal numbers of males and females? The answer, according to most evolutionary biologists, lies in a recognition that Darwin's theory of natural selection speaks only of struggle among *individuals* for reproductive success. It contains no statement about the good of populations, species, or ecosystems. The argument for ninety females and ten males was framed in terms of advantages for populations as a whole—the usual, congenial, and dead wrong, way in which most people think of evolution. If evolution worked for the good of populations as a whole, then sexual species would contain relatively few males.

The observed equality of males and females, in the face of obvious advantages for female predominance if evolution worked upon groups, stands as one of our most elegant demonstrations that Darwin was right—natural selection works by the struggle of individuals to maximize their own reproductive success. The Darwinian argument was first framed by the great British mathematical biologist R.A. Fisher. Suppose, Fisher argued, that either sex began to predominate. Let us say, for example, that fewer males than females are born. Males now begin to leave more offspring than females since their opportunities for mating increase as they become rarer—that is, they impregnate more than one female on average. Thus, if any genetic factors influence the relative proportion of males born to a parent (and such factors do exist), then parents with a genetic inclination to produce males will gain a Darwinian advantage—they will produce more than an average number of grandchildren thanks to the superior reproductive success of their predominantly male offspring. Thus, genes that favor the production of males will spread and male births will rise in frequency. But, this advantage for males fades out as male births increase and it disappears entirely when males equal females in number. Since the same argument works in reverse to favor female births when females are rare, the sex ratio is driven by Darwinian processes to its equilibrium value of one to one.

But how would a biologist go about testing Fisher's theory of sex ratio? Ironically, the species that confirm its predictions are no great help beyond the initial observation. Once we frame the basic argument and determine that the species we know best have approximately equal numbers of males and females, what do we achieve by finding that the next thousand species are similarly ordered? Sure, it all fits, but we do not gain an equal amount of confidence each time we add a new species. Perhaps the one to one ratio exists for another reason.

To test Fisher's theory, we must look for exceptions. We must seek unusual situations in which the premises of Fisher's theory are not met—situations that lead to a specific prediction about how sex ratio should depart from one to one. If change of premises leads to a definite and successful prediction of altered outcome, then we have an independent test that strongly boosts our confidence. This method is embodied in the old proverb that "the exception proves the rule," although many people misunderstand the proverb because it embodies the less common meaning of "prove." Prove comes from the Latin *probare*—to test or to try. Its usual, modern meaning refers to final and convincing demonstration and the motto would seem to say that exceptions establish indubitable validity. But in another sense, closer to its root, "prove" (as in "proving ground" or printer's "proof") is more like its cognate "probe"—a test or an exploration. It is the exception that probes the rule by testing and exploring its consequences in altered situations.

Here nature's rich diversity comes to our aid. The sterotyped image of a birder assiduously adding the rufous-crowned, peg-legged, speckle-backed, cross-billed, and cross-eyed towhee to his life list gives, in unwarranted ridicule, a perverted twist to the actual use made by naturalists of life's diversity. It is nature's richness that permits us to establish a science of natural history in the first place—for the variety virtually guarantees that appropriate exceptions can be found to probe any rule. Oddities and weirdnesses are tests of generality, not mere peculiarities to describe and greet with awe or a chuckle.

Fortunately, nature has been profligate in providing species and modes of life that violate the premises of Fisher's argument. In 1967, British biologist W. D. Hamilton (now at the University of Michigan) gathered the cases and arguments into an article entitled "Extraordinary sex ratios." I will discuss in this essay only the clearest and most important of these probing violations.

Nature rarely heeds our homilies in all cases. We are told, and with good reason, that mating of brothers and sisters should be avoided, lest too many unfavorable recessive genes gain an opportunity to express themselves in double dose. (Such genes tend to be rare, and chances are small that two unrelated parents will both carry them. But the probability that two sibs carry the same gene is usually fifty percent.) Nonetheless, some animals never heard the rule and indulge, perhaps exclusively, in sib mating.

Exclusive sib mating destroys the major premise of Fisher's argument for one to one sex ratios. If females are always fertilized by their brothers, then the same parents manufacture both partners of any mating. Fisher assumed that the males had different parents and that an undersupply of males awarded genetic advantages to those parents that could produce males preferentially. But if the same parents produce *both* the mothers and fathers of their grandchildren, then they have an equal genetic investment in each grandchild, no matter what percentage of males and females they produce among their children. In this case, the reason for an equal balance of males and females disappears and the previous argument for female predominance reasserts itself. If each pair of grandparents has a limited store of energy to invest in offspring, and if grandparents producing more offspring gain a Darwinian edge, then grandparents should make as many daughters as possible, and produce only enough sons to ensure that all their daughters will be fertilized. In fact, if their sons can muster sufficient sexual prowess, then parents should make just one son and use every bit of remaining energy to produce as many daughters as they can. As usual, bountiful nature comes to our aid with numerous exceptions to probe Fisher's rule: indeed, species with sib mating also tend to produce a minimal number of males.

Consider the curious life of a male mite in the genus *Adactylidium*, as described by E. A. Albadry and M. S. F. Tawfik in 1966. It emerges from its mother's body and promptly dies within a few hours, having done apparently nothing during its brief life. It attempts, while outside its mother, neither to feed nor to mate. We know about creatures with short adult lives—the mayfly's single day after a much lengthier larval life, for example. But the mayfly mates and insures the continuity of its kind during these few precious hours. The males of *Adactylidium* seem to do nothing at all but emerge and die.

To solve the mystery, we must study the entire life cycle and look inside the mother's body. The impregnated female of *Adactylidium* attaches to the egg of a thrips. That single egg provides the only source of nutrition for rearing all her offspring—for she will feed on nothing else before her death. This mite, so far as we know, engages exclusively in sib mating; thus, it should produce a minimal number of males. Moreover, since total reproductive energy is so strongly constrained by the nutritional resources of a single thrips' egg, progeny are strictly limited, and the more females the better. Indeed, *Adactylidium* matches our prediction by raising a brood of five to eight sisters accompanied by a single male who will serve as both brother and husband to them all. But producing a single male is chancy; if it dies, all sisters will remain virgins and their mother's evolutionary life is over.

If the mite takes a chance on producing but a single male, thus maximizing its potential brood of fertile females, two other adaptations might lessen the risk—providing both protection for the male and guaranteed proximity to his sisters. What better than to rear the brood entirely within a mother's body, feeding both larvae and adults within her, and even allowing copulation to occur inside her protective shell. Indeed, about forty-eight hours after she attaches to the thrips' egg, six to nine eggs hatch within the body of a female *Adactylidium*. The larvae feed on their mother's body, literally devouring her from inside. Two days later, the offspring reach maturity, and the single male copulates with all his sisters. By this time, the mother's tissues have disintegrated, and her body space is a mass of adult mites, their feces, and their discarded larval and nymphal skeletons. The offspring then cut holes through their mother's body wall and emerge. The females must now find a thrips' egg and begin the process again, but the males have already fulfilled their evolutionary role before "birth." They emerge, react however a mite does to the glories of the outside world, and promptly die.

But why not carry the process one stage further? Why should the male be born at all? After copulating with its sisters, its work is done, it is ready to chant the acarine version of Simeon's prayer, *Nunc dimittis*—Oh Lord, now lettest thou thy servant depart in peace. Indeed, since everything that is possible tends to occur at least once in the multifarious world of life, a close relative of *Adactylidium* does just this. *Acarophenax tribolii* also indulges exclusively in sib mating. Fifteen eggs, including but a single male, develop within the mother's body. The male emerges within his mother's shell, copulates with all his sisters, and dies before birth. It may not sound like much of a life, but the male *Acarophenax* does as much for its evolutionary continuity as Abraham did in fathering children into his tenth decade.

Nature's oddities are more than good stories. They are material for probing the limits of interesting theories about life's history and meaning.

Suggestions for Discussion

1. Gould begins his essay with children's questions which, while seemingly simple, are very difficult to answer. Explain why this is an effective introduction to his topic.

2. How does he answer the biological question of why in familiar species known to man, including our own, males and females are produced in approximately equal numbers? How does he show that an attempt to answer this question is much more complex than it first appears? How does he relate the question to Darwin's theory of natural selection?

3. Summarize R. A. Fisher's restatement of Darwin's theory that "natural selection works by the struggle of individuals to maximize their own reproductive success." How does Gould propose to test Fisher's theory?

4. How does Gould treat the history of the male mite of the genus *Adactylidium*? How does he make its history interesting and dramatic?

5. What is the role of the mite as chanted in Simeon's prayer, "*Nunc dimittis*—Oh Lord, now lettest thou thy servant depart in peace"?

Suggestion for Writing

Using Gould as a model, attempt to explore the implications of a scientific principle you have studied in one of your science courses. This attempt may lead you into further reading on the subject. Your purpose in this paper is to make clear, understandable—and interesting—to a common reader the complexities of scientific thought.

Aldous Huxley
Brave New World Revisited

Aldous Huxley (1894–1963) was born in England and educated at Oxford. He is the author of many novels including *Point Counter Point* (1928) and the anti-Utopian *Brave New World* (1932). He also wrote essays, short stories, poetry, and plays. After he moved to Southern California, he became increasingly interested in Hindu philosophy and mysticism. *The Doors of Perception* (1954) describes his experience with hallucenogenic drugs. In "Brave New World Revisited" he examined in 1956 the accuracy of his predictions. He admits that, in *1984*, Orwell (see Irving Howe's "The Enigmas of Power") foresaw political developments more preceptively than he. The essay concludes with a serious reflection on the difference between present-day attitudes toward drugs and those attitudes explored in *Brave New World*.

The most distressing thing that can happen to a prophet is to be proved wrong; the next most distressing thing is to be proved right. In the twenty-five years that have elapsed since *Brave New World* was written, I have undergone both these experiences. Events have proved me distressingly wrong; and events have proved me distressingly right.

Here are some of the points on which I was wrong. By the early Thirties Einstein had equated mass and energy, and there was already talk of chain reactions; but the Brave New Worlders knew nothing of nuclear fission. In the early Thirties, too, we knew all about conservation and irreplaceable resources; but their supply of metals and mineral fuel was just as copious in the seventh century After Ford as ours is today. In actual fact the raw-material situation will already be subcritical by A.F. 600 and the atom will be the principal source of industrial power. Again, the Brave New Worlders had solved the population problem and knew how to maintain a permanently favorable relationship between human numbers and natural resources. In actual fact, will our descendants achieve this happy consummation within the next six centuries? And if they *do* achieve it, will it be by dint of rational planning, or through the immemorial agencies of pestilence, famine, and internecine warfare? It is, of course, impossible to say. The only thing we can predict with a fair measure of certainty is that humanity (if its rulers decide to refrain from collective suicide) will be traveling at vertiginous speed along one of the most dangerous and congested stretches of its history.

The Brave New Worlders produced their children in biochemical factories. But though bottled babies are not completely out of the question, it is virtually certain that our descendants will in fact remain viviparous. Mother's Day is in no danger of being replaced by Bottle Day. My prediction was made for strictly literary purposes, and not as a reasoned forecast of future history. In this matter I knew in advance that I should be proved wrong.

From biology we now pass to politics. The dictatorship described in *Brave New World* was global and in its own peculiar way, benevolent. In the light of current events and developing tendencies, I sadly suspect that in this forecast, too, I may have been wrong. True, the seventh century After Ford is still a long way off, and it is possible that, by then, hard economic necessity, or the social chaos resulting from nuclear warfare, or military conquest by one Great Power, or some grisly combination of all three will have bludgeoned our descendants into doing what we ought to be doing now, from motives of enlightened self-interest and common humanity—namely, to collaborate for the common good. In time of peace, and when things are going tolerably well, people cannot be expected to vote for measures which, though ultimately beneficial, may be expected to have certain disagreeable consequences in the short run. Divisive forces are more powerful than those which make for union. Vested interests in languages, philosophies of life, table manners, sexual habits, political, ecclesiastical, and economic organizations are sufficiently powerful to block all attempts, by rational and peaceful methods, to unite mankind for its own good. And then there is nationalism. With its Fifty-Seven Varieties of tribal gods, nationalism is the religion of the twentieth century. We may be Christians, Jews, Moslems, Hindus, Buddhists, Confucians, or Atheists; but the fact remains that there is only one faith for which large masses of us are prepared to die and kill, and that faith is nationalism. That nationalism will remain the dominant religion of the human race for the next two or three centuries at the very least seems all too probable. If total nuclear war should be avoided, we may expect to see not the rise of a single world state but the continuance, in worsening conditions, of the present system, under which national states compete for markets and raw materials and prepare for partial wars. Most of these states will probably be dictatorships. Inevitably so; for the increasing pressure of population upon resources will make domestic conditions more difficult and international competition more intense. To prevent economic breakdown and to repress popular discontent, the governments of hungry countries will be tempted to enforce ever-stricter controls. Furthermore, chronic undernourishment reduces physical energy and disturbs the mind. Hunger and self-government are incompatible. Even where the average diet provides three thousand calories a day, it is hard enough to make democracy work. In a society in which most members are living on seventeen hundred to two thousand calories a day, it is simply impossible. The undernourished majority will always be ruled, from above, by the well-fed few. As population increases (twenty-seven hundred millions of us are now adding to our numbers at the rate of forty millions a year, and this increase is increasing according to the rules of compound interest); as geometrically increasing demands press more and more heavily on static or, at best, arithmetically increasing supplies; as standards of living are forced down and popular discontent is forced up; as the general scramble for diminishing resources becomes ever fiercer, these national dictatorships will tend to become more oppressive at home, more ruthlessly competitive abroad. "Government," says one of the Brave New Worlders, "is an affair of sitting, not hitting. You rule with the brains and the buttocks, not the fists." But where there are many competing national dictatorships, each in trouble at home and each preparing for total or partial war against its neighbors, hitting tends to be preferred to sitting, fists, as an instrument of policy, to brains, and the "masterly inactivity" (to cite Lord Salisbury's immortal phrase) of the hindquarters. In politics, the near future is likely to be closer to George Orwell's *1984* than to *Brave New World*.

Let me now consider a few of the points on which, I fear, I may have been right. The Brave New Worlders were the heirs and exploiters of a new kind of revolution, and this revolution was, in effect, the theme of my fable. Past revolutions have all been in fields external to the individual as a psycho-physical organism—in the field, for example, of ecclesiastical organization and religious dogma, in the field of economics, in the field of political organization, in the field of technology. The coming revolution—the revolution whose consequences are described in *Brave New World*—will affect men and women, not peripherally, but at the very core of their organic being. The older revolutionaries sought to change the social environment in the hope (if they were idealists and not mere power seekers) of changing human nature. The coming revolutionaries will make their assult directly on human nature as they find it, in the minds and bodies of their victims or, if you prefer, their beneficiaries.

Among the Brave New Worlders, the control of human nature was achieved by eugenic and dysgenic breeding, by systematic conditioning during infancy and, later on, by "hypnopaedia," or instruction during sleep. Infant conditioning is as old as Pavlov and hypnopaedia, though rudimentary, is already a well-established technique. Phonographs with built-in clocks, which turn them on and off at regular intervals during the night, are already on the market and are being used by students of foreign languages, by actors in a hurry to memorize their parts, by parents desirous of curing their children of bed-wetting and other troublesome habits, by self-helpers seeking moral and physical improvement through autosuggestion and "affirmations of positive thought." That the principles of selective breeding, infant conditioning, and hypnopaedia have not yet been applied by governments is due, in the democratic countries, to the lingering, liberal conviction that persons do not exist for the state, but that the state exists for the good of persons; and in the totalitarian countries to what may be called revolutionary conservatism—attachment to yesterday's revolution instead of the revolution of tomorrow. There is, however, no reason for complacently believing that this revolutionary conservatism will persist indefinitely. In totalitarian hands, applied psychology is already achieving notable results. One third of all the American prisoners captured in Korea succumbed, at least partially, to Chinese brainwashing, which broke down the convictions, installed by their education and childhood conditioning, and replaced these comforting axioms by doubt, anxiety, and a chronic sense of guilt. This was achieved by thoroughly old-fashioned procedures, which combined straight-forward instruction with what may be called conventional psychotherapy in reverse, and made no use of hypnosis, hypnopaedia, or mind-modifying drugs. If all or even some of these more powerful methods had been employed, brainwashing would probably have been successful with all the prisoners, and not with a mere thirty percent of them. In their vague, rhetorical way, speech-making politicians and sermon-preaching clergymen like to say that the current struggle is not material, but spiritual—an affair not of machines, but of ideas. They forget to add that the effectiveness of ideas depends very largely on the way in which they are inculcated. A true and beneficent idea may be so ineptly taught as to be without effect on the lives of individuals and societies. Conversely, grotesque and harmful notions may be so skillfully drummed into people's heads that, filled with faith, they will rush out and move mountains—to the glory of the devil and their own destruction. At the present time the dynamism of totalitarian ideas is greater than the dynamism of liberal, democratic ideas. This is not due, of course, to the intrinsic superiority of totalitarian ideas. It is due partly to the fact that, in a world where population is fast outrunning resources, ever larger measures of governmental control become necessary— and it is easier to exercise centralized control by totalitarian than by democratic methods. Partly, too, it is due to the fact that the means employed for the dissemination of totalitarian ideas are more effective, and are used more systematically, than the means employed for disseminating democratic and liberal ideas. These more effective methods of totalitarian propaganda, education, and brainwashing are, as we have seen, pretty old-fashioned. Sooner or later, however, the dictators will abandon their revolutionary conservatism and, along with it, the old-world procedures inherited from the prepsychological and palaeopharmacological past. After which, heaven help us all!

Among the legacies of the protopharmacological past must be numbered our habit, when we feel in need of a lift, a release from tension, a mental vacation from unpleasant reality, of drinking alcohol or, if we happen to belong to a non-Western culture, of smoking hashish or opium, of chewing coca leaves or betel or any one of scores of intoxicants. The Brave New Worlders did none of these things; they merely swallowed a tablet or two of a substance called Soma. This, needless to say, was not the same as the Soma mentioned in the ancient Hindu scriptures—a rather dangerous drug derived from some as yet unidentified plant native to South Central Asia—but a synthetic, possessing "all the virtues of alcohol and Christianity, none of their defects." In small doses the Soma of the Brave New Worlders was a relaxant, an inducer of euphoria, a fosterer of friendliness and social solidarity. In medium doses it transfigured the external world and acted as a mild hallucinant; and in large doses it was a narcotic. Virtually all the Brave New Worlders thought themselves happy. This was due in part to the fact that they had been bred and conditioned to take the place assigned to them in the social hierarchy, in part to the sleep-teaching which had made them content with their lot and in part to Soma and their ability, by its means, to take holidays from unpleasant circumstances and their unpleasant selves.

All the natural narcotics, stimulants, relaxants, and hallucinants known to the modern botanist and pharmacologist were discovered by primitive man and have been in use from time immemorial. One of the first things that Homo sapiens did with his newly devoloped rationality and self-consciousness was to set them to work finding out ways to bypass analytical thinking and to transcend or, in extreme cases, temporarily obliterate the isolating awareness of the self. Trying all things that grew in field or forest, they held fast to that which, in this context, seemed good—everything, that is to say, that would change the quality of consciousness, would make it different, no matter how, from everyday feeling, perceiving, and thinking. Among the Hindus, rhythmic breathing and mental concentration have, to some extent, taken the place of the mind-transforming drugs used elsewhere. But even in the land of yoga, even among the religious and even for specifically religious purposes, cannabis indica has been freely used to supplement the effects of spiritual exercises. The habit of taking vacations from the more-or-less purgatorial world, which we have created for ourselves, is universal. Moralists may denounce it; but, in the teeth of disapproving talk and repressive legislation, the habit persists, and mind-transforming drugs are everywhere available. The Marxian formula,

"Religion is the opium of the people," is reversible, and one can say, with even more truth, that "Opium is the religion of the people." In other words, mind-transformation, however induced (whether by devotional or ascetic or psychogymnastic or chemical means), has always been felt to be one of the highest, perhaps the very highest, of all attainable goods. Up to the present, governments have thought about the problem of mind-transforming chemicals only in terms of prohibition or, a little more realistically, of control and taxation. None, so far, has considered it in its relation to individual well-being and social stability; and very few (thank heaven!) have considered it in terms of Machiavellian statecraft. Because of vested interests and mental inertia, we persist in using alcohol as our main mind-transformer—just as our neolithic ancestors did. We know that alcohol is responsible for a high proportion of our traffic accidents, our crimes of violence, our domestic miseries; and yet we make no effort to replace this old-fashioned and extremely unsatisfactory drug by some new, less harmful, and more enlightening mind-transformer. Among the Brave New Worlders, Noah's prehistoric invention of fermented liquor has been made obsolete by a modern synthetic, specifically designed to contribute to social order and the happiness of the individual, and to do so at the minimum physiological cost.

In the society described in my fable, Soma was used as an instrument of statecraft. The tyrants were benevolent, but they were still tyrants. Their subjects were not bludgeoned into obedience; they were chemically coerced to love their servitude, to cooperate willingly and even enthusiastically in the preservation of the social hierarchy. By the malignant or the ignorant, anything and everything can be used badly. Alcohol, for example, has been used, in small doses, to facilitate the exchange of thought in a symposium (literally, a drinking party) of philosophers. It has also been used, as the slave traders used it, to facilitate kidnapping. Scopolamine may be used to induce "twilight sleep"; it may also be used to increase suggestibility and soften up political prisoners. Heroin may be used to control pain; it may also be used (as it is said to have been used by the Japanese during their occupation of China) to produce an incapacitating addiction in a dangerous adversary. Directed by the wrong people, the coming revolution could be as disastrous, in its own way, as a nuclear and bacteriological war. By systematically using the psychological, chemical, and electronic instruments already in existence (not to mention those new and better devices which the future holds in store), a tyrannical oligarchy could keep the majority in permanent and willing subjection. This is the prophecy I made in *Brave New World*. I hope I may be proved wrong, but am sorely afraid that I may be proved right.

Meanwhile it should be pointed out that Soma is not intrinsically evil. On the contrary, a harmless but effective mind-transforming drug might prove a major blessing. And anyhow (as history makes abundantly clear) there will never be any question of getting rid of chemical mind-transformers altogether. The choice confronting us is not a choice between Soma and nothing; it is a choice between Soma and alcohol, Soma and opium, Soma and hashish, ololiuqui, peyote, datura, agaric, and all the rest of the natural mind-transformers; between Soma and such products of scientific chemistry and pharmacology as ether, chloral, veronal, benzedrine, and the barbiturates. In a word, we have to choose between a more-or-less harmless all-around drug and a wide variety of more-or-less harmful and only partially effective drugs. And this choice will not be delayed until the seventh century After Ford. Phar-macology is on the march. The Soma of *Brave New World* is no longer a distant dream. Indeed, something possessing many of the characteristics of Soma is already with us. I refer to the most recent of the tranquilizing agents—the Happiness Pill, as its users affectionately call it, known in Amer-ica under the trade names of Miltown and Equanil. These Happiness Pills exert a double action; they relax the tension in striped muscle and so relax the associated tensions in the mind. At the same time they act on the enzyme system of the brain in such a way as to prevent disturbances arising in the hypothalamus from interfering with the workings of the cortex. On the mental level, the effect is a blessed release from anxiety and self-regarding emotivity.

In my fable the savage expresses his belief that the advantages of Soma must be paid for by losses on the highest human levels. Perhaps he was right. The universe is not in the habit of giving us something for nothing. And yet there is a great deal to be said for a pill which enables us to assume an atti-tude toward circumstances of detachment, ataraxia, "holy indifference." The moral worth of an action cannot be measured exclusively in terms of inten-tion. Hell is paved with good intentions, and we have to take some account of results. Rational and kindly behavior tends to produce good results, and these results remain good even when the behavior which produced them was itself produced by a pill. On the other hand, can we with impunity replace systematic self-discipline by a chemical? It remains to be seen.

Of all the consciousness-transforming drugs the most interesting, if not the most immediately useful, are those which, like lysergic acid and mescaline, open the door to what may be called the Other World of the mind. Many workers are already exploring the effects of these drugs, and we may be sure that other mind-transformers, with even more remarkable properties, will be produced in the near future. What man will ultimately do with these extraor-dinary elixirs, it is impossible to say. My own guess is that they are destined to play a part in human life at least as great as the part played, up till now, by alcohol, and incomparably more beneficent.

Suggestions for Discussion

1. Huxley reviews the predictions in his novel after twenty-five years. How does he regard his record of prediction?

2. How does Huxley use the occasion of "revisiting" his novel to discuss world prob-lems in 1956? In what ways is Huxley pessimistic about the future of the world?

3. What reasons does Huxley give for his belief that Orwell's predictions were politi-cally more accurate than his own?

4. What revolution does Huxley believe he has accurately predicted in his novel? Explain.

5. Huxley contends that the history of mankind involves various ways of bypassing thought, transcendence, or obliteration of self-awareness. Relate this contention to his discussion of historical problems.

6. What is Huxley's attitude toward "Soma" in the essay? What role does he think drugs will continue to play in society?

7. Explain the subtitle of the essay, "Proleptic meditations on Mother's Day."

Suggestions for Writing

1. Write an essay comparing the ideas in this piece with the selection from *Brave New World* in this anthology. How does the selection from the novel emphasize or explain Huxley's ideas in the essay?

2. Huxley analyzes the political role that nationalism now plays and may play in the future. Is his analysis correct? Write a paper which reflects your own ideas about nationalism. How would you define it? How is it related to patriotism?

Arthur C. Clarke

Broadway and the Satellites

Arthur C. Clarke (b. 1917) was born in England and served in the Royal Air Force during World War II. The originator of the idea of communications satellites, he has written about aeronautics, astronauts, astronomy, and underwater exploration. Among his best-known science fiction works are *Going into Space* (1954), *The Exploration of the Moon* (1954), and *The Lost Worlds of 2001* (1971). The following essay, taken from his *Voices from the Sky* (1965), discusses the emergence of a global communications network.

Sometime before the end of this century, a billion people will attend the same first night. They will do it, of course, not in person, but via the worldwide TV network foreshadowed by the Telstar satellite.

Before we consider the impact of communications satellites on the performing arts, let us see what technical developments may be expected. In a very few years, intercontinental TV will be commonplace. Viewers will think no more of being taken, live, from New York to New Delhi than they do today of being switched from one town to the next.

At first, however, ordinary viewers will still remain tuned to the local stations: unlike the short-wave ham, the TV viewer will not be able to roam at will over the world. The antennas needed to catch the feeble voices of today's satellites are so enormous, and must be backed by such elaborate receiving and tracking gear, that direct domestic reception is out of the question. We will be able to see only the foreign programs that our local networks decide to relay to us.

But this will not always be the case. Perhaps ten years from now, really high-powered TV transmitters will be put into orbit—and into the very special orbit that allows them to remain fixed in the sky (the so-called synchronous or stationary orbit). When that time comes, you will be able to tune in *directly* to European, Russian, or Chinese programs coming straight down from the sky; and there will be weeping and wailing on Madison Avenue.

And on Broadway? Not necessarily, though there will undoubtedly be profound changes, some for the better, some for the worse. Recently I had the interesting experience of seeing, while sitting in one midtown theater, a play being staged in another. The large-screen projection, the presence of the audience, and the usual intervals, gave a sense of immediacy and participation which home TV lacks. One can see a whole new art form springing up, with production techniques similar to those employed in studio TV and the movies, but quite different in other respects. Perhaps we may call it Teletheater.

TT, if it develops, will presumably move into the large number of surplus cinemas now threatened with conversion into bowling alleys or (as in England) legalized gambling dens. Every town or community of any size will have such a theater, and everyone from Alaska to Florida will be able to enjoy an identical performance. The show will be the same; only the audiences will be different. And the expression "Off Broadway" will start to look a little sick.

Now TT can obviously flourish without the use of communications satellites, but they will give it a tremendous boost. When the whole world can tune into the Comédie Française, Drury Lane, the Bolshoi, all the Stratfords, Lincoln Center, La Scala, the incentive to build teletheaters will be very great. And such theaters could, at least in principle, be independent of their own national networks: they could present foreign programs by direct pickup.

It is obvious that home TV, with its own widening frontiers, will compete to some extent with the new theaters; and the recent contest between cinema and TV may be repeated in a slightly different arena. The outcome may be much the same as before; the theaters will provide high definition, color, wide-screen, and stereo sound of a quality which home viewers will be unable to match. The aesthetic effect of all these gimmicks will doubtless be deplorable, at least until the producers learn to handle their new powers with moderation.

Any form of instantaneous, worldwide entertainment raises a whole host of problems—technical, cultural, and economic—only a few of which can be mentioned here. The first that comes to mind is the question of language.

This is not as important as might be thought, for it does not affect the majority of the performing arts. Ballet means as much (or as little) to an Eskimo as to a Basque. Even when there are words, the example of opera proves that the audience doesn't have to understand them; only for the play are they vital.

Time, I think, will take care of this difficulty. The development of truly global communications will accelerate, as nothing else has done, the adoption of a world language (almost certainly English) which will be spoken as a second tongue by all educated men. And the revolution in transport which is just getting underway may succeed in making even the English and the Americans bilingual. (I would like to think that the Peace Corps is the first step toward a world in which *all* men and women spend a couple of their formative years in a foreign country, which they will come to regard as their second home.)

Time zones present more fundamental difficulties. The Late, Late Show is already bad enough, but how many of us would get up in the middle of the night to watch anything short of a world heavyweight fight or the first landing on the Moon? Certainly, few people would enjoy "Hamlet" at 4 A.M.

I suspect (and fear) that this problem will also bring its own solutions. When everyone in the world is plugged into the same telephone exchange, and all calls are local ones, sleep is going to become impossible anyway. Physiologists and electronics experts are already at work on a "sleep compressor" which will allow two hours of artificial rest to be as effective as eight of the old-fashioned variety. When this dubious blessing is perfected, well in advance of 1984, the twenty-two-hour day will be upon us. We will need those pre-dawn premieres to occupy our copious leisure time.

And there is the intriguing problem of censorship. For the first time in history, no country will have any control over the entertainment sampled by its citizens. (At least in their own homes; the teletheaters will presumably have to watch their licenses.) Just what may happen if some really uninhibited client gets hold of a channel, I've described in *Tales of Ten Worlds*.

However, I must not raise false hopes. The global communications network will operate according to strict international rules, as all telecommunications have done for the last century. (A big UN-sponsored conference to lay down these regulations took place in 1963.) Nevertheless, there will be a lot of fun when the French beam raw Genet to the United States, and the U.S. aims the riper offerings of T. Williams at the U.S.S.R.

More seriously, it will be of great interest to watch the effects upon standards of performance when productions of all types can be exchanged freely over the whole Earth. Will there be a leveling down, or a leveling up? When I think that half the globe may soon be receiving instant soap opera from communications satellites, I sometimes feel more than a distant kinship to the late Dr. Frankenstein.

Before you get back for the second act, let me chill your blood a little further. Sooner or later, we are going to learn how to transmit electronically not only sights and sounds, but actual sensations, which will be fed directly into the nervous system. Then you will no longer look at pictures on an illuminated screen: the images will bypass your eyes and you will "experience" them inside your brain. The same thing would be true for sound, touch, smell, and all the other senses.

Many years ago, the "Feelies" of Aldous Huxley's *Brave New World* barely hinted at these possibilities, and for a much juicier treatment I refer you to Shepherd ("How To Succeed In Business . . .") Mead's novel *The Big Ball of Wax*. The ultimate development would be a world of dreamers, packed by their millions in the stately pleasure domes of Electro-sensory Entertainment, Inc. Here they would live vicarious lives that might be so much more vivid and exciting than mere reality that they would awake only with the utmost reluctance.

The French aristocrat who remarked haughtily "Life? I leave *that* to my servants," may have spoken for the future. Our descendants a hundred years hence may hand over the running of the world to their robots, while they themselves retire into a realm of electronically induced fantasies. And so they will pass away their lives, wired not merely for sound, but for everything.

I do hope you enjoy the rest of the performance.

Suggestions for Discussion

1. What technical developments does Clarke outline?

2. Explain what he means by Teletheater.

3. Discuss problems with any form of instantaneous worldwide entertainment.

4. Comment on his assertion that the ultimate development will be "a world of dreamers" living "vicarious lives."

Suggestions for Writing

1. To what extent does global Teletheater already exist? Explain and give examples.

2. Write a short story about a time when our descendants have retired "into a realm of electronically induced fantasies."

Grant Fjermedal

Artificial Intelligence

Grant Fjermedal has written *Magic Bullets: A Revolution in Cancer Treatment* (1984) and *The Tomorrow Makers: A Brave New World of Living Brain Machines* (1986). This essay, published in *Omni,* an excerpt from *The Tomorrow Makers,* presents in dramatic fashion the choice that people one day may be able to make between dying or continuing to live forever by transferring one's capacity for thinking from one's brain to a machine.

I'm sure that Hans Moravec is at least as sane as I am, but he certainly brought to mind the classic mad scientist as we sat in his fifth-floor office at Carnegie-Mellon University on a dark and stormy night. It was nearly midnight, and he mixed for each of us a bowl of chocolate milk and Cheerios, with slices of banana piled on top.

Then, with banana-slicing knife in hand, Moravec, the senior research scientist at Carnegie-Mellon's Mobile Robot Laboratory, outlined for me how he could create a robotic immortality for Everyman, a deathless universe in which life would go on forever. By creating computer copies of our minds and transferring, or downloading, this program into robotic bodies, Moravec explained, humans could survive for centuries.

"You are in an operating room. A robot brain surgeon is in attendance. . . . Your skull but not your brain is anesthetized. You are fully conscious. The surgeon opens you braincase and peers inside." This is how Moravec described the process in a paper he wrote called "Robots That Rove." The robotic surgeon's "attention is directed at a small clump of about one hundred neurons somewhere near the surface. Using high-resolution 3-D nuclear-magnetic-resonance holography, phased-array radio encephalography, and ultrasonic radar, the surgeon determines the three-dimensional structure and chemical makeup of that neural clump. It writes a program that models the behavior of the clump and starts it running on a small portion of the computer sitting next to you."

That computer sitting next to you in the operating room would in effect be your new brain. As each area of your brain was analyzed and simulated, the accuracy of the simulation would be tested as you pressed a button to shift between the area of the brain just copied and the simulation. When you couldn't tell the difference between the original and the copy, the surgeon would transfer the simulation of your brain into the new, computerized one and repeat the process on the next area of your biological brain.

"Though you have not lost consciousness or even your train of thought, your mind—some would say soul—has been removed from the brain and transferred to a machine," Moravec said, "In a final step your old body is disconnected. The computer is installed in a shiny new one, in the style, color, and material of your choice."

As we sat around Moravec's office I asked what would become of the original human body after the downloading. "You just don't bother waking it up again if the copying went successfully," he said. "It's so messy. Humans have got so many problems that you might just want to leave it retired. You don't take your junker car out if you've got a new one."

Moravec's idea is the ultimate in life insurance: Once one copy of the brain's contents has been made, it will be easy to make multiple backup copies, and these could be stashed in hiding places around the world, allowing you to embark on any sort of adventure without having to worry about aging or death. As decades pass into centuries you could travel the globe and then the solar system and beyond—always keeping an eye out for the latest in robotic bodies into which you could transfer your computer mind.

If living forever weren't enough, you could live forever several times over by activating some of your backup copies and sending different versions of yourself out to see the world. "You could have parallel experiences and merge the memories later," Moravec explained.

In the weeks and months that followed my stay at Carnegie-Mellon, I was intrigued by how many researchers seemed to believe downloading would come to pass. The only point of disagreement was *when*—certainly a big consideration to those of us still knocking around in mortal bodies. Although some of the researchers I spoke with at Carnegie-Mellon, MIT, and Stanford and in Japan thought that downloading was still generations away, there were others who believed achieving robotic immortality was imminent and seemed driven by private passions never to die.

The significance of the door Moravec is trying to open is not lost on others. Olin Shivers, a Carnegie-Mellon graduate student who works closely with Moravec as well as with Allen Newell, one of the founding fathers of artificial intelligence, told me, "Moravec wants to design a creature, and my professor Newell wants to design a creature. We are all, in a sense, trying to play God."

At MIT I was surprised to find Moravec's concept of downloading given consideration by Marvin Minsky, Donner Professor of Science and another father of artificial intelligence. Minsky is trying to learn how the billions of brain cells work together to allow a person to think and remember. If he succeeds, it will be a big step toward figuring out how to join perhaps billions of computer circuits together to allow a computer to receive the entire contents of the human mind.

"If a person is like a machine, once you get a wiring diagram of how he works, you can make copies," Minsky told me.

Although Minsky doesn't think he'll live long enough to download (he's fifty-seven now), he would consider it. "I think it would be a great thing to do," he said. "I've spent a long time learning things, and I'd hate to see it all go away."

Minsky also said he would have no qualms about waving good-bye to his human body and taking up residence within a robot. "Why not avoid getting sick and things like that?" he asked. "It's hard to see anything against it. I think people will get fed up with bodies after a while. Then you'll have another population problem: You'll have all the people of the past, as well as the new ones."

Another believer is Danny Hillis, one of Minsky's Ph.D. students and the founding scientist of Thinking Machines, a Cambridge-based company that is trying to create the kind of computer that might someday receive the contents of a brain. During my research several computer scientists would point to Hillis's connection machine as an example of a new order of computer architecture, one that's comparable to the human brain. (Hillis's connection machine doesn't have one large central processing unit as other computers do but a network of 64,000 small units—roughly analogous in concept, if not in size, to the brain's network of 40 billion neuronal processing units.)

"I've added up the things I want to do in my life, and it's about fifteen hundred years' worth of stuff," Hillis, now twenty-eight, told me one day as we stood out on the sixth-floor sun deck of the Thinking Machines building. "I enjoy having a body as much as anyone else does, but if it's a choice between downloading into a computer—even one that's stuck in a room someplace—and still being able to think versus just dying, I would certainly take that opportunity to think."

Gerald J. Sussman, a thirty-six-year-old MIT professor and a computer hacker of historic proportions, expressed similar sentiments. "Everyone would like to be immortal. I don't think the time is quite right, but it's close. I'm afraid, unfortunately, that I'm in the last generation to die."

"Do you really think that we're that close?" I asked.

"Yes," he answered, which reminded me of something Moravec had written not too long ago: "We are on a threshold of a change in the universe comparable to the transition from nonlife to life."

Suggestions for Discussion

1. Summarize the major thesis of this brief essay. Is it one that you take seriously? Explain your response.

2. What method does Fjermedal use to develop his essay? What is its tone? Is there an element of ambiguity in the tone?

3. Define the term *downloading*.

4. Explain the significance of the quotation in the last paragraph.

5. How close does this essay come to what we think of as science fiction?

Suggestions for Writing

1. Write an essay in which you describe a world inhabited by surrogate brains. What would be the advantages, disadvantages of such a world? Is it one that you would want to inhabit? Explain your response to this question.

2. Using this essay and others in this text, write a paper examining the directions of research in the fields of computer science.

Zenon W. Pylyshyn and Others
Artificial Intelligence Systems

The Computer Science and Engineering Research Study was initiated in 1974 and its findings published under the title *What Can Be Automated?* in 1984, edited by Bruce W. Arden. The special panel on Artificial Intelligence was headed by Zenon W. Pylyshyn of the University of Western Ontario, Canada. Professor Pylyshyn (b. 1937) has written *Perspectives on the Computer Tool* (1970), *Here and There in the Visual Field* (1985), *Computation and Cognition* (1984, 1986) and *Meaning and Cognitive Structure* (1986). He was responsible for the final draft of the chapter on Artificial Intelligence from which this essay is excerpted. The chapter provides a definition of *artificial intelligence* by the use of examples that illustrate clearly the variety of fields in which computers may be programmed to resemble human intelligence.

Using the term *artificial intelligence* gives recognition to the fact that studies of symbolic processes in computer science, and the attempts to understand that elusive quality known as "intelligence," are, at some level, inseparable. This recognition, which has indirectly been responsible for much misunderstanding and criticism, is, in fact, fundamental to the integrity of the field, since a pillar of the artificial intelligence field is the belief that tasks requiring what we would call "intelligent action," can, to some extent, be studied independently of such organisms as humans and the way in which they perform such tasks. In addition to shedding light on these tasks, as well as the class of processes capable of dealing effectively with them, research in A.I. has produced techniques and working systems for dealing with areas previously considered the sole province of human intelligence.

Although the discipline of artificial intelligence dates to the earliest speculation about the nature and limits of information-processing mechanisms, and although the early tools of nonnumerical computing—list-processing, time-sharing, graphics, and symbolic math systems—were developed in laboratories devoted to research in what would soon be known as artificial intelligence, the development of the science as we know it today began as recently as the mid-1950s when Newell, Shaw, Simon, and others recognized the potential of large-scale digital computers for this kind of non-numerical processing. Since that time, progress has been made, both in understanding the underlying technical issues, such as representing knowledge and controlling search and inference, and in developing practical systems. We begin our discussion by presenting some artificial intelligence systems that are currently in operation.

Working Artificial Intelligence Systems

A. A geologist dials a government data base on lunar rocks and types in a query.

User:	HOW MANY BRECCIAS CONTAIN OLIVINE?
Computer:	5.
User:	WHAT ARE THEY?
Computer:	S10019, S10059, S10065, S10067, S10073.
User:	LIST K/RB RATIOS FOR BRECCIAS.
Computer:	I HAVE 17 HITS. DO YOU WANT TO SEE THEM?
User:	YES.
Computer:	472.2222 S10018 D70-205
	... ...
	500.173 S10073 D70-215
User:	LIST MODAL FLAG ANALYSES FOR LUNAR SAMPLES THAT CONTAIN OLIV.
Computer:	I HAVE 13 HITS. DO YOU WANT TO SEE THEM?
User:	YES.

And so on.

At the Second Annual Lunar Science Confererce, held in January 1971, this system, described by Woods in 1973, answered 90 percent of the 110 requests put to it by geologists. To some extent, however, this results from the tendency of expert users to employ a narrower range of constructions than do nonexpert users, as well as the experts' tendency to tailor their questions to the perceived ability of the machine. Thus a linguistically less "fluent" system can be serviceable if it is intended for a particular community of specialist users.

B. A business executive specifies that he wishes to interact with GUS, a computerized travel consultant, on his personal terminal:

Client:	I want to go to San Diego May 28.
GUS:	What time do you want to leave?
Client:	I must be in San Diego before 10 AM.
GUS:	Would you like P.S.A. flight 102 that arrives at 9:15 AM?
Client:	What is the next flight?
GUS:	Air California flight 310 that leaves at 8:30 am and arrives at 10:00 AM.
Client:	I'll take the first one.

GUS: In what name should I make a reservation?
Client: Dan Bobrow.
GUS: I have confirmed the following flight: P.S.A. flight 102 on Wednesday May 28 from San Jose to San Diego which leaves at 7:30 AM and arrives at 9:15 AM. What date do you want to return on?
Client: On Friday in the evening.
GUS: Would you like the flight that leaves at 7:45 PM?
Client: That's fine.
GUS: I have confirmed the following flight: P.S.A. flight 307 on Friday May 30 from San Diego to San Jose which leaves at 7:45 PM and arrives at 9:30 PM. Thank you for calling. Goodbye.

Note that, to keep the conversation natural, complex inferences must be made. For example, the client answers the question about departure time indirectly. The system must infer the departure time from the client's statement that he must be at a certain place at a certain time. Similarly, it disambiguates various possible senses of "the first one" and "on Friday" (which Friday?) by the pragmatic context.

C. A physician calls up MYCIN, the computerized, interactive diagnostic assistant for infectious diseases. In response to questions from the machine, the physician types in a brief summary of the patient's medical records. MYCIN names specific infections (INFECTION-1) and cultures for later reference, continuing to ask questions about each infection until it has enough information for recommending treatment. A segment of the dialogue after the initial information entry follows.

Computer: My therapy recommendation will be based on the following probable infection(s) and potential causative organism(s): INFECTION-1 is PRIMARY BACTEREMIA
<Item 1> The identity of ORGANISM-1 may be PSEUDO-MONAS-AERUGINOSA
<Item 2> The identity of ORGANISM-1 may be KLEBSI-ELLA-PNEUMONIAE
<Item 3> The identity of ORGANISM-1 may be E.COLI
<Item 4> The identity of ORGANISM-1 may be BACTER-OIDES-FRAGILIS
<Item 5> The identity of ORGANISM-1 may be PROTEUS NON-MIRABILIS

On a scale of 0 to 4, where higher numbers indicate increasing severity, how would you rate Fred Smith's degree of sickness?

User: 3

Computer: Does Fred Smith have a clinically significant allergic reaction to any antimicrobial agent?

User: NO

Computer: Fred Smith's weight in kilograms (or <number> POUNDS):

User: 70

Computer: (Rec 1) My preferred therapy recommendation is as follows:
In order to cover for items < 1 2 3 5 6>:
Give: GENTAMICIN
Dose: 119 mg (1.7 mg/kg) q8h IV (or IM) for 10 days
Comments: Modify dose in renal failure
In order to cover for item <4>:
Give: CLINDAMYCIN
Dose: 595 mg (8.5 mg/kg) q6h IV (or IM) for 14 days
Comments: If diarrhea or other GI symptoms develop, patient should be evaluated for possible PSEUDOMEMBRANOUS COLITIS.

D. A student studying electronic circuit design and servicing consults his computerized tutor, SOPHIE.

Computer: THE PIECE OF EQUIPMENT YOU ARE STUDYING IS A REGULATED POWER SUPPLY. WOULD YOU LIKE TO START WITH A FAULTY INSTRUMENT WHICH NEEDS FIXING?

User: YES

Computer: THE INSTRUMENT HAS A FAULT AND ITS PRESENT CONTROL SETTING IS: [Gives settings of various currents, voltages, and variable resistances.]

User: WHAT IS THE OUTPUT?

Computer: THE OUTPUT VOLTAGE IS 11.7 VOLTS.

User: WHAT IS IT IN A WORKING INSTRUMENT?

Computer: IN A WORKING CIRCUIT THE OUTPUT VOLTAGE IS 19.9 VOLTS.

User: WHAT IS THE VOLTAGE BETWEEN R8 AND Q1?

Computer: THE VOLTAGE AT N1 IS 47.6 VOLTS.

User: WHAT IS THE BSE EMITTER VOLTAGE OF THE VOLT-AGE-LIMITING TRANSISTOR?

Computer: [corrects spelling] = BASE
THE BASE EMITTER VOLTAGE OF Q5 IS − .037 MILLI-VOLTS.

User: WHAT ABOUT FOR THE CURRENT LIMITING TRANSIS-
             TOR?

Computer: THE BASE EMITTER VOLTAGE OF Q6 IS .349 VOLTS.

User: WHAT SHOULD IT BE?

Computer: . . . .593 VOLTS.

User: REPLACE Q6.

In this brief excerpt it is clear that the computer thoroughly understands the circuit in question, that it can understand references to components by description and by name, and that it can understand clipped, incomplete sentences when the context makes the meaning clear.

.   .   .

E. A scientist types in simple English sentences to command a primitive robot vehicle. The commands mention only the end goal (for example, *push the orange pyramid off the platform in the hallway*). They say nothing about how to do this, nor about the order in which to carry out subtasks or any obstacles that might exist along the way. The computer converts the command to an internal propositional form and generates a plan for carrying out the command. The vehicle then moves a ramp up to the platform, ascends it, and completes the task.

None of the above systems is a production tool; they are all working experimental prototypes. MYCIN, SOPHIE, and the lunar rocks system are polished, high-performance systems. The lessons learned from them are being used in designing new systems such as GUS, the most embryonic of the examples above. GUS is being developed at the Xerox Corporation, primarily as a test bed for the newest generation of A.I. techniques relating to language, inference, and knowledge representation. The industrial-application example being developed as a practical application is primarily a demonstration of the applicability of machine-vision techniques. Although the Stanford Research Institute robot mentioned in (F), "Shakey," was used mainly to test ideas about the process of planning, various vision and theorem-proving systems have been incorporated for exploring the problems involved in making the systems work together. Other more practically-oriented robot systems have also been developed for use in space exploration.

In addition to these research tools, commercial artificial intelligence systems are being marketed for such jobs as interfacing natural languages, recognizing patterns, controlling robots, and designing and teaching symbolic mathematics with the help of computers. In all these areas, techniques are being explored that were developed during the past decade of research in artificial intelligence. Their performance is high enough that they are now considered commercial products. . . .

Of course, these are only a few examples of A.I. work; they were not chosen because they are particularly representative. Nonetheless, they illustrate better than any prescriptive definition the kind of systems that are being developed in artificial intelligence. . . .

The main areas covered are those of problem-solving, automatic theorem-proving, natural language-processing, the perception of speech and visual information, and such application areas as industrial production and "expert," or human-level, performance systems for medical and scientific applications.

Suggestions for Discussion

1. Discuss the function in the first paragraph of the claim that "intelligent action" is subject to study "independently of such organisms as human beings." How do computer scientists study artificial intelligence (A.I.)?

2. What is the importance of each of the examples of artificial intelligence systems that follow the second paragraph? How do the examples differ? What lessons may be learned from each example?

3. What other areas of intelligence were under development at the time this essay was written?

4. Why does the essay use examples instead of a prescriptive definition to explain artificial intelligence?

5. The conclusion states the kinds of artificial intelligence being studied. How do these areas differ?

6. How does this essay differ from that by Grant Fjermedal?

Suggestions for Writing

1. The essays in this text will provide you with material for a limited research paper on computer science. Examine the major functions of each essay and state a topic sentence and a proper subject for development into a 1,000-word paper.

2. Some people remain hostile to the increasing use of computers in everyday life. Explain the possible source of this hostility. If you share it, defend your position. If you approve of the use of computers, explain why.

3. Using the essays in this text, explain how artificial intelligence is different from other computer application or development.

Niles Eldredge

Creationism Isn't Science

Niles Eldredge, the curator of the Department of Invertebrates at the American Museum of Natural History in New York, is a scientist deeply concerned about Darwinian and other theories of evolution that derive from Charles Darwin's *On the Origin of Species* published in 1859. Following that date, a violent argument followed between science and religion which appeared to come to a close after the Scopes Trial in 1925. In recent years, however, with the rise of fundamentalist religion in the United States, an argument has flowered that creationism has as much validity as a theory as Darwin's theory of evolution. Eldredge attempts to show in this essay why the two theories are not equal and how the zeal of creationists is undermining the teaching of science in the schools.

Despite this country's apparent modernism, the creationist movement once again is growing. The news media proclaimed a juryless trial in California as "Scopes II" and those who cling to the myth of progress wonder how the country could revert to the primitive state it was in when Darrow and Bryan battled it out in the hot summer of 1925 in Dayton, Tennessee. But the sad truth is that we have not progressed. Creationism never completely disappeared as a political, religious, and educational issue. Scopes was convicted of violating the Tennessee statute forbidding the teaching of the evolutionary origins of mankind (although in fact he was ill and never really did teach the evolution segment of the curriculum). The result was a drastic cutback in serious discussion of evolution in many high school texts until it became respectable again in the 1960s.

Although technological advances since 1925 have been prodigious, and although science news magazines are springing up like toadstools, the American public appears to be as badly informed about the real nature of science as it ever was. Such undiluted ignorance, coupled with the strong anti-intellectual tradition in the US, provides a congenial climate for creationism to leap once more to the fore, along with school prayer, sex education, Proposition 13, and the other favorite issues of the populist, conservative movement. Much of the success of recent creationist efforts lies in a prior failure to educate our children about science—how it is done, by whom, and how its results are to be interpreted.

Today's creationists usually cry for "equal time" rather than for actually substituting the Genesis version of the origin of things for the explanations preferred by modern science. (The recent trial in California is an anachronism in this respect because the plaintiff simply affirmed that his rights of religious freedom were abrogated by teaching him that man "descended from apes"). At the heart of the creationists' contemporary political argument is an appeal to the time-honored American sense of fair play. "Look," they say, "evolution is only a theory. Scientists cannot agree on all details either of the exact course of evolutionary history, or how evolution actually takes place." True enough. Creationists then declare that many scientists have grave doubts that evolution actually has occurred—a charge echoed by Ronald Reagan during the campaign, and definitely false. They argue that since evolution is only a theory, why not, in the spirit of fair play, give equal time to equally plausible explanations of the origin of the cosmos, of life on earth, and of mankind? Why not indeed?

The creationist argument equates a biological, evolutionary system with a non-scientific system of explaining life's exuberant diversity. Both systems are presented as authoritarian, and here lies the real tragedy of American science education: the public is depressingly willing to see merit in the "fair play, equal time" argument precisely because it views science almost wholly in this authoritarian vein. The public is bombarded with a constant stream of oracular pronouncements of new discoveries, new truths, and medical and technological innovations, but the American education system gives most people no effective choice but to ignore, accept on faith, or reject out of hand each new scientific finding. Scientists themselves promote an Olympian status for their profession; it's small wonder that the public has a tough time deciding which set of authoritarian pronouncements to heed. So why not present them all and let each person choose his or her own set of beliefs?

Of course, there has to be some willingness to accept the expertise of specialists. Although most of us "believe" the earth is spherical, how many of us can design and perform an experiment to show that it must be so? But to stress the authoritarianism of science is to miss its essence. Science is the enterprise of comparing alternative ideas about what the cosmos is, how it works, and how it came to be. Some ideas are better than others, and the criterion for judging which are better is simply the relative power of different ideas to fit our observations. The goal is greater understanding of the natural universe. The method consists of constantly challenging received ideas, modifying them, or, best of all, replacing them with better ones.

So science is ideas, and the ideas are acknowledged to be merely approximations to the truth. Nothing could be further from authoritarianism—dogmatic assertions of what is true. Scientists deal with ideas that appear to be the best (the closest to the truth) given what they think they know about the universe at any given moment. If scientists frequently act as if their ideas *are* the truth, they are simply showing their humanity. But the human quest for a rational coming-to-grips with the cosmos recognizes imperfection in observation and thought, and incorporates the frailty into its method. Creationists disdain this quest, preferring the wholly authoritarian, allegedly "revealed" truth of divine creation as an understanding of our beginnings. At the same time they present disagreement among scientists as an expression of scientific failure in the realm of evolutionary biology.

To the charge that "evolution is *only* a theory," we say "all science is theory." Theories are ideas, or complex sets of ideas, which explain some aspect of the natural world. Competing theories sometimes coexist until one drives the other out, or until both are discarded in favor of yet another theory. But it is true that one major theory usually holds sway at any one time. All biologists, including biochemists, molecular geneticists, physiologists, behaviorists, and anatomists, see a pattern of similarity interlocking the spectrum of millions of species, from bacteria to timber wolves. Darwin finally convinced the world that this pattern of similarity is neatly explained by "descent with modification." If we imagine a genealogical system where an ancestor produces one or more descendants, we get a pattern of progressive similarity. The whole array of ancestors and descendants will share some feature inherited from the first ancestor; as each novelty appears, it is shared only with later descendants. All forms of life have the nucleic acid RNA. One major branch of life, the vertebrates, all share backbones. All mammals have three inner ear bones, hair, and mammary glands. All dogs share features not found in other carnivores, such as cats. In other words, dogs share similarities among themselves in addition to having general mammalian features, plus general vertebrate features, as well as anatomical and biochemical similarities shared with the rest of life.

How do we test the basic notion that life has evolved? The notion of evolution, like any scientific idea, should generate predictions about the natural world, which we can discover to be true or false. The grand prediction of evolution is that there should be one basic scheme of similarities interlocking all of life. This is what we have consistently found for over 100 years, as thousands of biologists daily compared different organisms. Medical experimentation depends upon the interrelatedness of life. We test drugs on rhesus monkeys and study the effects of caffeine on rats because we cannot experiment on ourselves. The physiological systems of monkeys are more similar to our own than to rats. Medical scientists know this and rely on this prediction to interpret the significance of their results in terms of human medicine. Very simply, were life not all interrelated, none of this would be possible. There would be chaos, not order, in the natural world. There is no competing, rational biological explanation for this order in nature, and there hasn't been for a long while.

Creationists, of course, have an alternative explanation for this order permeating life's diversity. It is simply the way the supernatural creator chose to pattern life. But any possible pattern could be there, including chaos—an absence of any similarity among the "kinds" of organisms on earth—and creationism would hold that it is just what the creator made. There is nothing about this view of life that smacks of prediction. It tells us nothing about what to expect if we begin to study organisms in detail. In short, there is nothing in this notion that allows us to go to nature to test it, to verify or reject it.

And there is the key difference. Creationism (and it comes in many guises, most of which do not stem from the Judeo-Christian tradition) is a belief system involving the supernatural. Testing an idea with our own experiences in the natural universe is simply out of bounds. The mystical revelation behind creationism is the opposite of science, which seeks rational understanding of the cosmos. Science thrives on alternative explanations, which must be equally subject to observational and experimental testing. No form of creationism even remotely qualifies for inclusion in a science curriculum.

Creationists have introduced equal-time bills in over 10 state legislatures, and recently met with success when Governor White of Arkansas signed such a bill into law on March 19 (reportedly without reading it). Creationists also have lobbied extensively at local school boards. The impact has been enormous. Just as the latest creationist bill is defeated in committee, and some of their more able spokesmen look silly on national TV, one hears of a local school district in the Philadelphia environs where some of the teachers have adopted the "equal time" or "dual model" approach to discussing "origins" in the biology curriculum on their own initiative. Each creationist "defeat" amounts to a Pyrrhic victory for their opponents. Increasingly, teachers are left to their own discretion, and whether out of personal conviction, a desire to be "fair," or fear of parental reprisal, they are teaching creationism along with evolution in their biology classes. It is simply the path of least resistance.

Acceptance of equal time for two alternative authoritarian explanations is a startling blow to the fabric of science education. The fundamental notion a student should get from high school science is that people can confront the universe and learn about it directly. Just one major inroad against this basic aspect of science threatens all of science education. Chemistry, physics, and geology—all of which spurn biblical revelation in favor of direct experience, as all science must—are jeopardized every bit as much as biology. That some creationists have explicitly attacked areas of geology, chemistry, and physics (in arguments over the age of the earth, for example) underscores the more general threat they pose to all science. We must remove science education from its role as authoritarian truthgiver. This view distorts the real nature of science and gives creationists their most potent argument.

The creationists' equal-time appeal maintains that evolution itself amounts to a religious belief (allied with a secular humanism) and should not be included in a science curriculum. But if it is included, goes the argument, it must appear along with other religious notions. Both are authoritarian belief systems, and neither is science, according to this creationist ploy.

The more common creationist approach these days avoids such sophistry and maintains that both creationism and evolution belong in the realm of science. But apart from some attempts to document the remains of Noah's Ark on the flanks of Mt. Ararat, creationists have been singularly unsuccessful in posing testable theories about the origin, diversity, and distribution of plants and animals. No such contributions have appeared to date either in creationism's voluminous literature or, more to the point, in the professional biological literature. "Science creationism" consists almost exclusively of a multipronged attack on evolutionary biology and historical geology. No evidence, for example, is presented in favor of the notion that the earth is only 20,000 years old, but many arguments attempt to poke holes in geochemists' and astronomers' reckoning of old Mother Earth's age at about 4.6 billion years. Analysis of the age of formation of rocks is based ultimately on the theories of radioactive decay in nuclear physics. (A body of rock is dated, often by several different means, in several different laboratories. The results consistently agree. And rocks shown to be roughly the same age on independent criteria (usually involving fossils) invariably check out to be roughly the same age when dated radiometrically. The system, although not without its flaws, works.) The supposed vast age of any particular rock can be shown to be false, but not by quoting Scripture.

All of the prodigious works of "scientific creationism" are of this nature. All can be refuted. However, before school boards or parent groups, creationists are fond of "debating" scientists by bombarding the typically ill-prepared biologist or geologist with a plethora of allegations, ranging from the second law of thermodynamics (said to falsify evolution outright) to the supposed absence of fossils intermediate between "major kinds." No scientist is equally at home in all realms of physics, chemistry, geology, and biology in this day of advanced specialization. Not all the proper retorts spring readily to mind. Retorts there are, but the game is usually lost anyway, as rebuttals strike an audience as simply another set of authoritarian statements they must take on faith.

Although creationists persist in depicting both science and creationism as two comparable, monolithic belief systems, perhaps the most insidious attack exploits free inquiry in science. Because we disagree on specifics, some of my colleagues and I are said now to have serious doubts that evolution has occurred. Distressing as this may be, the argument actually highlights the core issue raised by creationism. The creationists are acknowledging that science is no monolithic authoritarian belief system. But even though they recognize that there are competing ideas within contemporary biology, the creationists see scientific debate as a sign of weakness. Of course, it really is a sign of vitality.

Evolutionary theory since the 1940s (until comparatively recently) has focused on a single coherent view of the evolutionary process. Biologists of all disciplines agree to a remarkable degree on the outlines of this theory, the so-called "modern synthesis." In a nutshell, this was a vindication of Darwin's original position: that evolution is predominantly an affair of gradual progressive change. As environmental conditions changed, natural selection (a culling process similar to the "artificial" selection practiced by animal breeders) favored those variants best suited to the new conditions. Thus evolutionary change is fundamentally adaptive. The modern synthesis integrated the newly arisen science of genetics with the Darwinian view and held that the entire diversity of life could be explained in these simple terms.

Some biologists have attacked natural selection itself, but much of the current uproar in evolutionary biology is less radical in implication. Some critics see a greater role for random processes. Others, like me, see little evidence of gradual, progressive change in the fossil record. We maintain that the usual explanation—the inadequacy of the fossil record—is itself inadequate to explain the non-change, the maintenance of status quo which lasts in some cases for 10 million years or more in our fossil bones and shells. In this view, change (presumably by natural selection causing adaptive modifications) takes place in bursts of a few thousand years, followed usually by immensely longer periods of business as usual.

Arguments become heated. Charges of "straw man," "no evidence," and so on are flung about—which shows that scientists, like everyone, get their egos wrapped up in their work. They believe passionately in their own ideas, even if they are supposed to be calm, cool, dispassionate, and able to evaluate all possibilities evenly. (It is usually in the collective process of argument that the better ideas win out in science; seldom has anyone single-handedly evinced the open-mindedness necessary to drop a pet idea). But nowhere in this *sturm und drang* has any of the participants come close to denying that evolution has occurred.

So the creationists distort. An attack on some parts of Darwin's views is equated with a rejection of evolution. They conveniently ignore that Darwin merely proposed one of many sets of ideas on *how* evolution works. The only real defense against such tactics lies in a true appreciation of the scientific enterprise—the trial-and-error comparison of ideas and how they seem to fit the material universe. If the public were more aware that scientists are expected to disagree, that what a scientist writes today is not the last word, but a progress report on some very intensive thinking and investigation, creationists would be far less successful in injecting an authoritarian system of belief into curricula supposedly devoted to free, open rational inquiry into the nature of natural things.

Suggestions for Discussion

1. Eldredge refers to the Scopes II trial in California. What was the first Scopes trial in Tennessee about? What issues about evolution were raised in 1925 by the trial, and how are they relevant today?

2. What does Eldredge have to say about the relationship between the populist-conservative movement and creationism? How do you define *creationism?*

3. Explain Eldredge's response to the claim that since Darwinian evolution is only a theory, equal time in the schools should be given to the proponents of creationism.

4. For Eldredge, what are the dangers of accepting the authoritarianism of science? What does he believe the real function of the scientific enterprise to be? How do creationists, according to Eldredge, misunderstand the meaning of the constant debates raging in the scientific community?

5. What causes one major scientific theory to predominate for a given period of time? Summarize Eldredge's explanation of why Darwin's theory has held the support of scientists for such a long period.

6. Why does Eldredge believe that creationism does not lend itself to testing? What is the significance of testing theories?

7. For Eldredge, what is the most significant danger of the struggle by creationists for equal time in the schools? How do creationists take advantage, according to Eldredge, of scientific authoritarianism? Why does Eldredge believe that debates among scientists are a sign of vitality?

8. Summarize Eldredge's description of recent debates among evolutionists and his claim that these debates are distorted by creationists.

Suggestions for Writing

1. Write a paper in which you explain how one may believe in God without accepting the position of the creationists. Document your argument with examples.

2. Do you believe that creationists should be allowed equal time with biologists in the schools? If you do, explain your position.

3. Write a paper in which you summarize Eldredge's position and contrast it with arguments by a creationist. State why you agree with one side of the argument or the other.

Lewis Thomas

Making Science Work

Lewis Thomas (b. 1913), born in Flushing, New York, is a physician whose career has centered on the Sloan-Kettering Cancer Center in New York of which he is now President Emeritus. He has written scholarly articles for medical journals as well as popular essays that present science and the scientist's view of the world to the lay public. He won the National Book Award in 1974 for *The Lives of a Cell: Notes of a Biology Watcher.* Other collections include *The Medusa and the Snail* (1979), *More Notes of a Biology Watcher* (1979), *The Youngest Science: Notes of a Medicine-Watcher* (1983), and *Late Night Thoughts on Listening to Mahler's Ninth Symphony* (1983). This essay focuses on the remarkable advances in science in this century and suggests how society can maintain the momentum of scientific thought.

For about three centuries we have been doing science, trying science out, using science for the construction of what we call modern civilization. Every dispensable item of contemporary technology, from canal locks to dial telephones to penicillin to the Mars Lander, was pieced together from the analysis of data provided by one or another series of scientific experiments—also the technologies we fear the most for the threat they pose to civilization: radioactivity from the stored, stacked bombs or from leaking, flawed power plants, acid rain, pesticides, leached soil, depleted ozone, and increased carbon dioxide in the outer atmosphere.

Three hundred years seems a long time for testing a new approach to human interliving, long enough to settle back for critical appraisal of the scientific method, maybe even long enough to vote on whether to go on with it or not. There is an argument. Voices have been raised in protest since the beginning, rising in pitch and violence in the nineteenth century during the early stages of the industrial revolution, summoning urgent crowds into the streets any day these days on the issue of nuclear energy. Give it back, say some of the voices, it doesn't really work, we've tried it and it doesn't work, go back three hundred years and start again on something else less chancy for the race of man.

The scientists disagree, of course, partly out of occupational bias, but also from a different way of viewing the course and progress of science in the past fifty years. As they see it, science is just at its beginning. The principal discoveries in this century, taking all in all, are the glimpses of the depth of our ignorance about nature. Things that used to seem clear and rational, matters of absolute certainty—Newtonian mechanics, for example—have slipped through our fingers, and we are left with a new set of gigantic puzzles, cosmic uncertainties, ambiguities; some of the laws of physics are amended every few years, some are canceled outright, some undergo revised versions of legislative intent as if they were acts of Congress.

In biology, it is one stupefaction after another. Just thirty years ago we called it a biological revolution when the fantastic geometry of the DNA molecule was exposed to public view and the linear language of genetics was decoded. For a while things seemed simple and clear; the cell was a neat little machine, a mechanical device ready for taking to pieces and reassembling, like a tiny watch. But just in the last few years it has become almost imponderably complex, filled with strange parts whose functions are beyond today's imagining. DNA is itself no longer a straightforward set of instructions on a tape. There are long strips of what seem nonsense in between the genes, edited out for the assembly of proteins but essential nonetheless for the process of assembly; some genes are called jumping genes, moving from one segment of DNA to another, rearranging the messages, achieving instantly a degree of variability that we once thought would require eons of evolution. The cell membrane is no longer a simple skin for the cell; it is a fluid mosaic, a sea of essential mobile signals, an organ in itself. Cells communicate with one another, exchange messages like bees in a hive, regulate one another. Genes are switched on, switched off, by molecules from the outside whose nature is a mystery; somewhere inside are switches which, when thrown one way or the other, can transform any normal cell into a cancer cell, and sometimes back again.

It is not just that there is more to do, there is everything to do. Biological science, with medicine bobbing somewhere in its wake, is under way, but only just under way. What lies ahead, or what *can* lie ahead if the efforts in basic research are continued, is much more than the conquest of human disease or the amplification of agricultural technology or the cultivation of nutrients in the sea. As we learn more about the fundamental processes of living things in general we will learn more about ourselves, including perhaps the ways in which our brains, unmatched by any other neural structures on the planet, achieve the earth's awareness of itself. It may be too much to say that we will become wise through such endeavors, but we can at least come into possession of a level of information upon which a new kind of wisdom might be based. At the moment we are an ignorant species, flummoxed by the puzzles of who we are, where we came from, and what we are for. It is a gamble to bet on science for moving ahead, but it is, in my view, the only game in town.

The near views in our instruments of the dead soil of Mars, the bizarre rings of Saturn, and the strange surfaces of Saturn, Jupiter, Venus, and the rest, literally unearthly, are only brief glances at what is ahead for mankind in the exploration of our own solar system. In theory, there is no reason why human beings cannot make the same journeys in person, or out beyond into the galaxy.

We will solve our energy problems by the use of science, and in no other way. The sun is there, to be sure, ready for tapping, but we cannot sit back in the lounges of political lobbies and make guesses and wishes; it will take years, probably many years, of research. Meanwhile, there are other possibilities needing deeper exploration. Nuclear fission power, for all its present disadvantages, including where on earth to put the waste, can be made safer and more reliable by better research, while hydrogen fusion, inexhaustibly fueled from the oceans and much safer than fission, lies somewhere ahead. We may learn to produce vast amounts of hydrogen itself, alcohol or methane, when we have learned more about the changeable genes of single-celled microorganisms. If we are to continue to burn coal in large amounts, we will need research models for predicting how much more carbon dioxide we can inject into the planet's atmosphere before we run into the danger of melting the ice shelves of western Antarctica and flooding all our coasts. We will need science to protect us against ourselves.

It has become the fashion to express fear of computers—the machines will do our thinking, quicker and better than human thought, construct and replicate themselves, take over and eventually replace us—that sort of thing. I confess to apprehensions of my own, but I have a hunch that those are on my mind because I do not know enough about computers. Nor, perhaps, does anyone yet, not even the computer scientists themselves. For my comfort, I know for sure only one thing about the computer networks now being meshed together like interconnected ganglia around the earth: what they contain on their microchips are bits of information put there by human minds; perhaps they will do something like thinking on their own, but it will still be a cousin of human thought once removed and, because of newness, potentially of immense usefulness.

The relatively new term "earth science" is itself an encouragement. It is nice to know that our own dear planet has become an object of as much obsessive interest to large bodies of professional researchers as a living cell, and almost as approachable for discovering the details of how it works. Satellites scrutinize it all day and night, recording the patterns of its clouds, the temperatures at all parts of its surface, the distribution and condition of its forests, crops, waterways, cities, and barren places. Seismologists and geologists have already surprised themselves over and over again, probing the movement of crustal plates afloat on something or other, maybe methane, deep below the surface, meditating the evidences now coming in for the reality and continuing of continental drift, and calculating with increasing precision the data that describe the mechanisms involved in earthquakes. Their instruments are becoming as neat and informative as medicine's CAT scanners; the earth has deep secrets still, but they are there for penetrating.

The astronomers have long since become physicists, the physicists are astronomers; both are, as well, what we used to call chemists, examining the levels of ammonia or formaldehyde in clouds drifting billions of light-years away, measuring the concentrations of methane in the nearby atmosphere of Pluto, running into paradoxes. Contemporary physics lives off paradox. Niels Bohr said that a great truth is one for which the opposite is also a great truth. There are not so many neutrinos coming from our sun as there ought to be; something has gone wrong, not with the sun but with our knowledge. There are radioastronomical instruments for listening to the leftover sounds of the creation of the universe; the astronomers are dumbstruck, they can hardly hear themselves think.

The social scientists have a long way to go to catch up, but they may be up to the most important scientific business of all, if and when they finally get down to the right questions. Our behavior toward each other is the strangest, most unpredictable, and almost entirely unaccountable of all the phenomena with which we are obliged to live. In all of nature there is nothing so threatening to humanity as humanity itself. We need, for this most worrying of puzzles, the brightest and youngest of our most agile minds, capable of dreaming up ideas not dreamed before, ready to carry the imagination to great depths and, I should hope, handy with big computers but skeptical about long questionnaires and big numbers.

Fundamental science did not become a national endeavor in this country until the time of World War II, when it was pointed out by some influential and sagacious advisers to the government that whatever we needed for the technology of warfare could be achieved only after the laying of a solid foundation of basic research. During the Eisenhower administration a formal mechanism was created in the White House for the explicit purpose of furnishing scientific advice to the President, the President's Science Advisory Committee (PSAC), chaired by a new administration officer, the Science Adviser. The National Institutes of Health, which had existed before the war as a relatively small set of laboratories for research on cancer and infectious disease, expanded rapidly in the postwar period to encompass all disciplines of biomedical science. The National Science Foundation was organized specifically for the sponsorship of basic science. Each of the federal departments and agencies developed its own research capacity, relevant to its mission; the programs of largest scale were those in defense, agriculture, space, and atomic energy.

Most of the country's basic research has been carried out by the universities, which have as a result become increasingly dependent on the federal government for their sustenance, even their existence, to a degree now causing alarm signals from the whole academic community. The ever-rising costs of doing modern science, especially the prices of today's sophisticated and complex instruments, combined with the federal efforts to reduce all expenditures, are placing the universities in deep trouble. Meanwhile, the philanthropic foundations, which were the principal source of funds for university research before the war, are no longer capable of more than a minor contribution to science.

Besides the government's own national laboratories and the academic institutions there is a third resource for the country's scientific enterprise—industry. Up to very recently, industrial research has been conducted in relative isolation, unconnected with the other two. There are signs that this is beginning to change, and the change should be a source of encouragement for the future. Some of the corporations responsible for high technology, especially those involved in energy, have formed solid linkages with a few research universities—MIT and Cal Tech, for example—and are investing substantial sums in long-range research in physics and chemistry. Several pharmaceutical companies have been investing in fundamental biomedical research in association with medical schools and private research institutions.

There needs to be much more of this kind of partnership. The nation's future may well depend on whether we can set up within the private sector a new system for collaborative research. Although there are some promising partnership ventures now in operation, they are few in number; within industry the tendency remains to concentrate on applied research and development, excluding any consideration of basic science. The academic community tends, for its part, to stay out of fields closely related to the development of new products. Each side maintains adversarial and largely bogus images of the other, money-makers on one side and impractical academics on the other. Meanwhile, our competitors in Europe and Japan have long since found effective ways to link industrial research to government and academic science, and they may be outclassing this country before long. In some fields, most conspicuously the devising and production of new scientific instruments, they have already moved to the front.

There are obvious difficulties in the behavior of the traditional worlds of research in the United States. Corporate research is obliged by its nature to concentrate on profitable products and to maintain a high degree of secrecy during the process; academic science, by its nature, must be carried out in the open and depends for its progress on the free exchange of new information almost at the moment of finding. But these are not impossible barriers to collaboration. Industry already has a life-or-death stake in what will emerge from basic research in the years ahead; there can be no more prudent investment for the corporate world, and the immediate benefit for any corporation in simply having the "first look" at a piece of basic science would be benefit enough in the long run. The university science community, for all the talk of ivory towers, hankers day and night for its work to turn out useful; a close working connection with industrial researchers might well lead to an earlier perception of potential applicability than is now the case.

The age of science did not really begin three hundred years ago. That was simply the time when it was realized that human curiosity about the world represented a deep wish, perhaps embedded somewhere in the chromosomes of human beings, to learn more about nature by experiment and the confirmation of experiment. The doing of science on a scale appropriate to the problems at hand was launched only in the twentieth century and has been moving into high gear only within the last fifty years. We have not lacked explanations at any time in our recorded history, but now we must live and think with the new habit of requiring reproducible observations and solid facts for the explanations. It is not as easy a time for us as it used to be: we are raised through childhood in skepticism and disbelief; we feel the need of proofs all around, even for matters as deep as the working of our own consciousness, where there is as yet no clear prospect of proof about anything. Uncertainty, disillusion, and despair are prices to be paid for living in an age of science. Illumination is the product sought, but it comes in small bits, only from time to time, not ever in broad, bright flashes of public comprehension, and there can be no promise that we will ever emerge from the great depths of the mystery of being.

Nevertheless, we have started to do science on a world scale, and to rely on it, and hope for it. Not just the scientists, everyone, and not for the hope of illumination, but for the sure predictable prospect of new technologies, which have always come along, like spray in the wake of science. We need better ways of predicting how a piece of new technology is likely to turn out, better measures available on an international level to shut off the ones that carry hazard to the life of the planet (including, but perhaps not always so much *first of all*, as is usually the only consideration, our own species' life). We will have to go more warily with technology in the future, for the demands will be increasing and the stakes will be very high. Instead of coping, or trying to cope, with the wants of four billion people, we will very soon be facing the needs, probably desperate, of double that number and, soon thereafter, double again. The real challenge to human ingenuity, and to science, lies in the century to come.

I cannot guess at the things we will need to know from science to get through the time ahead, but I am willing to make one prediction about the method: we will not be able to call the shots in advance. We cannot say to ourselves, we need this or that sort of technology, therefore we should be doing this or that sort of science. It does not work that way. We will have to rely, as we have in the past, on science in general, and on basic, undifferentiated science at that, for the new insights that will open up the new opportunities for technological development. Science is useful, indispensable sometimes, but whenever it moves forward it does so by producing a surprise; you cannot specify the surprise you'd like. Technology should be watched closely, monitored, criticized, even voted in or out by the electorate, but science itself must be given its head if we want it to work.

Suggestions for Discussion

1. In the first paragraph, Thomas makes clear that scientific experimentation of the last three hundred years has had helpful as well as dangerous consequences. Why does he begin the essay this way?

2. What has been a popular negative response to science? What has caused this response? How do scientists view the record? Why is their response different from that of the general public?

3. How does Thomas use developments in DNA to illustrate the attitude of scientists toward science?

4. What are the positive consequences of scientific experimentation for Thomas? What positive use will come from advances in computer science?

5. In this brief essay, Thomas surveys advances and issues in a number of different sciences. How does he tie all of these together? How does he relate the social sciences to the "hard" sciences?

6. What bureaucratic structures has the government created to deal with scientific advances? What is the role of these bureaus in university research? How is industry a resource for scientific advancement? What argument does Thomas make for partnership among the three areas? What obstacles exist to prevent it? What are the incentives to achieve it?

7. What are the prices we pay for living in an age of science?

8. What distinctions does Thomas make between technology and science?

Suggestions for Writing

1. Choose one concrete example from the remarkable achievements in biology, physics, or astronomy mentioned in this essay and write a clear account of it. You will have to read additional material about DNA if you write about it, for example, but be certain that you give proper credit to your sources and paraphrase the material accurately.

2. Thomas asserts that the world of science is exciting, stimulating, and dangerous. Write an essay in which you explain this position. Use examples from sources other than this essay.

Fiction

Aldous Huxley
Conditioning the Children

Aldous Huxley (1894–1963) was born in England and educated at Oxford. He is the author of many novels including *Point Counter Point* (1928) and the anti-utopian *Brave New World* (1932). He also wrote essays, short stories, poetry, and plays. After he moved to Southern California, he became increasingly interested in Hindu philosophy and mysticism. *The Doors of Perception* (1954) describes his experience with hallucenogenic drugs. This brief selection from *Brave New World* describes without comment painful experiments to condition the minds of new-born infants.

The D.H.C.[1] and his students stepped into the nearest lift and were carried up to the fifth floor.

INFANT NURSERIES. NEO-PAVLOVIAN CONDITIONING ROOMS, announced the notice board.

The Director opened a door. They were in a large bare room, very bright and sunny; for the whole of the southern wall was a single window. Half a dozen nurses, trousered and jacketed in the regulation white viscose-linen uniform, their hair aseptically hidden under white caps, were engaged in setting out bowls of roses in a long row across the floor. Big bowls, packed tight with blossom. Thousands of petals, ripeblown and silkily smooth, like the cheeks of innumerable little cherubs, but of cherubs, in that bright light, not exclusively pink and Aryan, but also luminously Chinese, also Mexican, also apoplectic with too much blowing of celestial trumpets, also pale as death, pale with the posthumous whiteness of marble.

The nurses stiffened to attention as the D.H.C. came in.

"Set out the books," he said curtly.

In silence the nurses obeyed his command. Between the rose bowls the

---

[1]Director of Hatcheries and Conditioning.

books were duly set out—a row of nursery quartos opened invitingly each at some gaily coloured image of beast or fish or bird.

"Now bring in the children."

They hurried out of the room and returned in a minute or two, each pushing a kind of tall dumb-waiter laden, on all its four wire-netted shelves with eight-month-old babies, all exactly alike (a Bokanovsky Group, it was evident) and all (since their caste was Delta) dressed in khaki.

"Put them down on the floor."

The infants were unloaded.

"Now turn them so that they can see the flowers and books."

Turned, the babies at once fell silent, then began to crawl towards those clusters of sleek colors, those shapes so gay and brilliant on the white pages. As they approached, the sun came out of a momentary eclipse behind a cloud. The roses flamed up as though with a sudden passion from within; a new and profound significance seemed to suffuse the shining pages of the books. From the ranks of the crawling babies came little squeals of excitement, gurgles and twitterings of pleasure.

The Director rubbed his hands. "Excellent!" he said. "It might almost have been done on purpose."

The swiftest crawlers were already at their goal. Small hands reached out uncertainly, touched, grasped, unpetaling the transfigured roses, crumpling the illuminated pages of the books. The Director waited until all were happily busy. Then, "Watch carefully," he said. And, lifting his hand, he gave the signal.

The Head Nurse, who was standing by a switchboard at the other end of the room, pressed down a little lever.

There was a violent explosion. Shriller and ever shriller, a siren shrieked. Alarm bells maddeningly sounded.

The children started, screamed; their faces were distorted with terror.

"And now," the Director shouted (for the noise was deafening), "now we proceed to rub in the lesson with a mild electric shock."

He waved his hand again, and the Head Nurse pressed a second lever. The screaming of the babies suddenly changed its tone. There was something desperate, almost insane, about the sharp spasmodic yelps to which they now gave utterance. Their little bodies twitched and stiffened; their limbs moved jerkily as if to the tug of unseen wires.

"We can electrify that whole strip of floor," bawled the Director in explanation. "But that's enough," he signalled to the nurse.

The explosions ceased, the bells stopped ringing, the shriek of the siren died down from tone to tone into silence. The stiffly twitching bodies relaxed, and what had become the sob and yelp of infant maniacs broadened out once more into a normal howl of ordinary terror.

"Offer them the flowers and the books again."

The nurses obeyed; but at the approach of the roses, at the mere sight of those gaily-coloured images of pussy and cock-a-doodle-doo and baa-baa black sheep, the infants shrank away in horror; the volume of their howling suddenly increased.

"Observe," said the Director triumphantly, "observe."

Books and loud noises, flowers and electric shocks—already in the infant mind the couples were compromisingly linked; and after two hundred repetitions of the same or a similar lesson would be wedded indissolubly. What man has joined, nature is powerless to put asunder.

"They'll grow up with what the psychologists used to call an 'instinctive' hatred of books and flowers. Reflexes unalterably conditioned. They'll be safe from books and botany all their lives." The Director turned to his nurses. "Take them away again."

Still yelling, the khaki babies were loaded on to their dumb-waiters and wheeled out, leaving behind them the smell of sour milk and a most welcome silence.

Suggestions for Discussion

1. Summarize the Pavlovian experiment demonstrated on the children. Do the doctor and the student observers regard the experiment as cruel? Explain their attitude.

2. What details in the selection would you regard as contributing to the anti-utopian atmosphere? How does Huxley employ imagery in the details?

Suggestion for Writing

Write a story that describes a method of controlling human behavior. You may wish to place the events in a utopian, anti-utopian, or in a completely ordinary setting.

Poetry
— ◆◆◆ —

Walt Whitman
When I Heard the Learn'd Astronomer

Walt Whitman (1819–1892), regarded by many as the greatest American poet, was born on Long Island, New York. He was a printer, a journalist, and a nurse during the Civil War. Strongly influenced by Ralph Waldo Emerson, he published *Leaves of Grass* in 1855 at his own expense. He added sections to new editions over the years. By the time of his death, he had become a major influence on younger poets who were moved by his experiments in free verse and by his transcendental ideas. In "When I Heard the Learn'd Astronomer," impatient with explanations of abstract science, he turns instead to silent contemplation of nature which, he implies, provides a profounder insight than do the "charts and diagrams" of science.

When I heard the learn'd astronomer,
When the proofs, the figures, were ranged in columns before me,
When I was shown the charts and diagrams, to add, divide, and measure
    them,
When I sitting heard the astronomer where he lectured with much applause
    in the lecture-room,
How soon unaccountable I became tired and sick,
Till rising and gliding out I wander'd off by myself,
In the mystical moist night-air, and from time to time,
Look'd up in perfect silence at the stars.

Suggestions for Discussion

1. Notice that this poem is contained in one sentence. How does Whitman organize the sentence to lead to the climax of the last line?

2. What is the poet's attitude toward the scientist? Why does he reject the scientific method of looking at nature? Why is his response "unaccountable"?

3. What is the significance of the phrase *perfect silence* in the last line?

Suggestion for Writing

Write an essay in which you explain not only the idea in the poem but how the idea is developed. Your essay should consider how a prose statement of the idea would differ.

Freedom and Human Dignity

◆◆◆

The bureaucratization of life brings about its absolute decay in all orders. Wealth diminishes, births are few. Then the State, in order to attend to its own needs, forces on still more the bureaucratization of human existence. . . . The State's most urgent need is its apparatus of war, its army.

> —**José Ortega y Gasset,** "The Greatest Danger, the State"

"Liberty consists in being able to do anything which is not harmful to another or to others. . . ."

> —**"Declaration of the Rights of Man,"** Paris, August 27, 1789

I have a dream that my four little children will one day live in a nation where they will not be judged by the color of their skin but by the content of their character.

> —**Martin Luther King, Jr.,** "I Have a Dream", August 23, 1963

I believe that man will not merely endure: he will prevail. He is immortal, not because he alone among creatures has an inexhaustible voice but because he has a soul, a spirit capable of compassion and sacrifice and endurance."

> —**William Faulkner,** Nobel Prize Award Speech, 1949

Was he free? Was he happy? The question is absurd:
Had anything been wrong, we should certainly have heard.

> —**W. H. Auden,** "The Unknown Citizen"

Anti-Semitism does not fall within the category of ideas protected by the right of free opinion.

> —**Jean-Paul Sartre,** "The Passion of the Anti-Semite"

Tell me, then, whether you agree with and assent to my first principle, that neither injury nor retaliation nor warding off evil by evil is ever right.

> —**Plato,** The *Crito*

It is a terrible, and inexorable, law that one cannot deny the humanity of another without diminishing one's own: in the face of one's victim, one sees oneself.

> —**James Baldwin,** "Fifth Avenue, Uptown"

Personal Reminiscence

◆◆◆

W. E. B. Du Bois

On Being Crazy

William Edward Burghardt Du Bois (1868–1963) was born in Massachusetts. In the course of his life he became a major influence on American blacks. By 1903 he had written *The Souls of Black Folk* which stated his major objections to the attitudes found in the writings of Booker T. Washington, the most influential black figure in the early twentieth century. In 1909 he helped found the National Association for the Advancement of Colored People. He edited *Crisis,* the magazine of the NAACP, and also founded the influential quarterly *Phylon* at Atlanta University. In this brief sketch (1907), Du Bois, in a series of conversations, touches ironically on the insanity of the relations between blacks and whites in the early days of the twentieth century. It might be instructive to consider just how different the relations between the races are today.

It was one o'clock and I was hungry. I walked into a restaurant, seated myself, and reached for the bill of fare. My table companion rose.

"Sir," said he, "do you wish to force your company on those who do not want you?"

No, said I, I wish to eat.

"Are you aware, sir, that this is social equality?"

Nothing of the sort, sir, it is hunger—and I ate.

The day's work done, I sought the theatre. As I sank into my seat, the lady shrank and squirmed.

I beg pardon, I said.

"Do you enjoy being where you are not wanted?" she asked coldly.

Oh no, I said.

"Well you are not wanted here."

I was surprised. I fear you are mistaken, I said, I certainly want the music, and I like to think the music wants me to listen to it.

"Usher," said the lady, "this is social equality."

"No, madame," said the usher, "it is the second movement of Beethoven's Fifth Symphony."

After the theatre, I sought the hotel where I had sent my baggage. The clerk scowled.

"What do you want?"

Rest, I said.

"This is a white hotel," he said.

I looked around. Such a color scheme requires a great deal of cleaning, I said, but I don't know that I object.

"We object," said he.

Then why, I began, but he interrupted.

"We don't keep niggers," he said, "we don't want social equality."

Neither do I, I replied gently, I want a bed.

I walked thoughtfully to the train. I'll take a sleeper through Texas. I'm a little bit dissatisfied with this town.

"Can't sell you one."

I only want to hire it, said I, for a couple of nights.

"Can't sell you a sleeper in Texas," he maintained. "They consider that social equality."

I consider it barbarism, I said, and I think I'll walk.

Walking, I met another wayfarer, who immediately walked to the other side of the road, where it was muddy. I asked his reason.

"Niggers is dirty," he said.

So is mud, said I. Moreover, I am not as dirty as you—yet.

"But you're a nigger, ain't you?" he asked.

My grandfather was so called.

"Well then!" he answered triumphantly.

Do you live in the South? I persisted, pleasantly.

"Sure," he growled, "and starve there."

I should think you and the Negroes should get together and vote out starvation.

"We don't let them vote."

We? Why not? I said in surprise.

"Niggers is too ignorant to vote."

But, I said, I am not so ignorant as you.

"But you're a nigger."

Yes, I'm certainly what you mean by that.

"Well then!" he returned, with that curiously inconsequential note of triumph. "Moreover," he said, "I don't want my sister to marry a nigger."

I had not seen his sister, so I merely murmured, let her say no.

"By God, you shan't marry her, even if she said yes."

But—but I don't want to marry her, I answered, a little perturbed at the personal turn.

"Why not!" he yelled, angrier than ever.

Because I'm already married and I rather like my wife.

"Is she a nigger?" he asked suspiciously.

Well, I said again, her grandmother was called that.

"Well then!" he shouted in that oddly illogical way.

I gave up.

Go on, I said, either you are crazy or I am.
"We both are," he said as he trotted along in the mud.

Suggestions for Discussion

1. Why has Du Bois chosen these specific scenes for his conversations with white people?
2. In what way is the final conversation different from those preceding it?
3. Discuss some of the examples of Du Bois' use of irony.

Suggestion for Writing

Write an essay in which you examine the areas of racism dealt with in this selection from today's perspective. What significant differences would you find? What similarities? In what way is "On Being Crazy" relevant for our time?

Richard Wright

The Ethics of Living Jim Crow

A major American black writer, Richard Wright (1908–1960) wrote stories, novels, an autobiography, and other books about America's racial problems. His best-known works are *Native Son* (1940), *Black Boy* (1945), and *White Man, Listen* (1957). The following autobiographical account of his education in race relations in a totally segregated South is from *Uncle Tom's Children* (1938).

I

My first lesson in how to live as a Negro came when I was quite small. We were living in Arkansas. Our house stood behind the railroad tracks. Its skimpy yard was paved with black cinders. Nothing green ever grew in that yard. The only touch of green we could see was far away, beyond the tracks, over where the white folks lived. But cinders were good enough for me and I never missed the green growing things. And anyhow cinders were fine weapons. You could always have a nice hot war with huge black cinders. All you had to do was crouch behind the brick pillars of a house with your hands full of gritty ammunition. And the first woolly black head you saw pop out from behind another row of pillars was your target. You tried your very best to knock it off. It was great fun.

I never fully realized the appalling disadvantages of a cinder environment till one day the gang to which I belonged found itself engaged in a war with the white boys who lived beyond the tracks. As usual we laid down our cinder barrage, thinking that this would wipe the white boys out. But they replied with a steady bombardment of broken bottles. We doubled our cinder barrage, but they hid behind trees, hedges, and the sloping embankments of their lawns. Having no such fortifications, we retreated to the brick pillars of our homes. During the retreat a broken milk bottle caught me behind the ear, opening a deep gash which bled profusely. The sight of blood pouring over my face completely demoralized our ranks. My fellow-combatants left me standing paralyzed in the center of the yard, and scurried for their homes. A kind neighbor saw me and rushed me to a doctor, who took three stitches in my neck.

I sat brooding on my front steps, nursing my wound and waiting for my mother to come from work. I felt that a grave injustice had been done me. It was all right to throw cinders. The greatest harm a cinder could do was leave a bruise. But broken bottles were dangerous; they left you cut, bleeding, and helpless.

When night fell, my mother came from the white folks' kitchen. I raced down the street to meet her. I could just feel in my bones that she would understand. I knew she would tell me exactly what to do next time. I grabbed her hand and babbled out the whole story. She examined my wound, then slapped me.

"How come yuh didn't hide?" she asked me. "How come yuh awways fightin'?"

I was outraged, and bawled. Between sobs I told her that I didn't have any trees or hedges to hide behind. There wasn't a thing I could have used as a trench. And you couldn't throw very far when you were hiding behind the brick pillars of a house. She grabbed a barrel stave, dragged me home, stripped me naked, and beat me till I had a fever of one hundred and two. She would smack my rump with the stave, and, while the skin was still smarting, impart to me gems of Jim Crow wisdom. I was never to throw cinders any more. I was never to fight any more wars. I was never, never, under any conditions, to fight *white* folks again. And they were absolutely right in clouting me with the broken milk bottle. Didn't I know she was working hard every day in the hot kitchens of the white folks to make money to take care of me? When was I ever going to learn to be a good boy? She couldn't be bothered with my fights. She finished by telling me that I ought to be thankful to God as long as I lived that they didn't kill me.

All that night I was delirious and could not sleep. Each time I closed my eyes I saw monstrous white faces suspended from the ceiling, leering at me.

From that time on, the charm of my cinder yard was gone. The green trees, the trimmed hedges, the cropped lawns grew very meaningful, became a symbol. Even today when I think of white folks, the hard, sharp outlines of white houses surrounded by trees, lawns, and hedges are present somewhere in the background of my mind. Through the years they grew into an overreaching symbol of fear.

It was a long time before I came in close contact with white folks again.

We moved from Arkansas to Mississippi. Here we had the good fortune not to live behind the railroad tracks, or close to white neighborhoods. We lived in the very heart of the local Black belt. There were black churches and black preachers; there were black schools and black teachers; black groceries and black clerks. In fact, everything was so solidly black that for a long time I did not even think of white folks, save in remote and vague terms. But this could not last forever. As one grows older one eats more. One's clothing costs more. When I finished grammar school I had to go to work. My mother could no longer feed and clothe me on her cooking job.

There is but one place where a black boy who knows no trade can get a job, and that's where the houses and faces are white, where the trees, lawns, and hedges are green. My first job was with an optical company in Jackson, Mississippi. The morning I applied I stood straight and neat before the boss, answering all his questions with sharp yessirs and nosirs. I was very careful to pronounce my *sirs* distinctly, in order that he might know that I was polite, that I knew where I was, and that I knew he was a *white* man. I wanted that job badly.

He looked me over as though he were examining a prize poodle. He questioned me closely about my schooling, being particularly insistent about how much mathematics I had had. He seemed very pleased when I told him I had had two years of algebra.

"Boy, how would you like to try to learn something around here?" he asked me.

"I'd like it fine, sir," I said, happy. I had visions of "working my way up." Even Negroes have those visions.

"All right," he said. "Come on."

I followed him to the small factory.

"Pease," he said to a white man of about thirty-five, "this is Richard. He's going to work for us."

Pease looked at me and nodded.

I was then taken to a white boy of about seventeen.

"Morrie, this is Richard, who's going to work for us."

"Whut yuh sayin' there, boy!" Morrie boomed at me.

"Fine!" I answered.

The boss instructed these two to help me, teach me, give me jobs to do, and let me learn what I could in my spare time.

My wages were five dollars a week.

I worked hard, trying to please. For the first month I got along O.K. Both Pease and Morrie seemed to like me. But one thing was missing. And I kept thinking about it. I was not learning anything and nobody was volunteering to help me. Thinking they had forgotten that I was to learn something about the mechanics of grinding lenses, I asked Morrie one day to tell me about the work. He grew red.

"Whut yuh tryin' t' do, nigger, get smart?" he asked.

"Naw; I ain't tryin t' git smart," I said.

"Well, don't, if yuh know whut's good for yuh!"

I was puzzled. Maybe he just doesn't want to help me, I thought. I went to Pease.

"Say, are yuh crazy, you black bastard?" Pease asked me, his gray eyes growing hard.

I spoke out, reminding him that the boss had said I was to be given a chance to learn something.

"Nigger, you think you're *white*, don't you?"

"Naw, sir!"

"Well, you're acting mighty like it!"

"But, Mr. Pease, the boss said . . ."

Pease shook his fist in my face.

"This is a *white* man's work around here, and you better watch yourself!"

From then on they changed toward me. They said good-morning no more. When I was just a bit slow in performing some duty, I was called a lazy black son-of-a-bitch.

Once I thought of reporting all this to the boss. But the mere idea of what would happen to me if Pease and Morrie should learn that I had "snitched" stopped me. And after all the boss was a white man, too. What was the use?

The climax came at noon one summer day. Pease called me to his work-bench. To get to him I had to go between two narrow benches and stand with my back against a wall.

"Yes, sir," I said.

"Richard, I want to ask you something," Pease began pleasantly, not looking up from his work.

"Yes, sir," I said again.

Morrie came over, blocking the narrow passage between the benches. He folded his arms, staring at me solemnly.

I looked from one to the other, sensing that something was coming.

"Yes, sir," I said for the third time.

Pease looked up and spoke very slowly.

"Richard, *Mr.* Morrie here tells me you called me *Pease.*"

I stiffened. A void seemed to open up in me. I knew this was the showdown.

He meant that I had failed to call him Mr. Pease. I looked at Morrie. He was gripping a steel bar in his hands. I opened my mouth to speak, to protest, to assure Pease that I had never called him simply *Pease,* and that I had never had any intentions of doing so, when Morrie grabbed me by the collar, ramming my head against the wall.

"Now, be careful, nigger!" snarled Morrie, baring his teeth. "*I* heard yuh call 'im *Pease!*' 'N' if yuh say yuh didn't yuh're callin' me a *lie*, see?" He waved the steel bar threateningly.

If I had said: No, sir, Mr. Pease, I never called you *Pease*, I would have been automatically calling Morrie a liar. And if I had said: Yes, sir, Mr. Pease, I called you *Pease*, I would have been pleading guilty to having uttered the worst insult that a Negro can utter to a southern white man. I stood hesitating, trying to frame a neutral reply.

"Richard, I asked you a question!" said Pease. Anger was creeping into his voice.

"I don't remember calling you *Pease*, Mr. Pease," I said cautiously. "And if I did, I sure didn't mean . . ."

"You black son-of-a-bitch! You called me *Pease*, then!" he spat, slapping me till I bent sideways over a bench. Morrie was on top of me, demanding:

"Didn't yuh call 'im *Pease?* If yuh say yuh didn't, I'll rip yo' gut string loose with this bar, yuh black granny dodger! Yuh can't call a white man a liar 'n' git erway with it, you black son-of-a-bitch!"

I wilted. I begged them not to bother me. I knew what they wanted. They wanted me to leave.

"I'll leave," I promised. "I'll leave right *now.*"

They gave me a minute to get out of the factory. I was warned not to show up again, or tell the boss.

I went.

When I told the folks at home what had happened, they called me a fool. They told me that I must never again attempt to exceed my boundaries. When you are working for white folks, they said, you got to "stay in your place" if you want to keep working.

II

My Jim Crow education continued on my next job, which was portering in a clothing store. One morning, while polishing brass out front, the boss and his twenty-year-old son got out of their car and half dragged and half kicked a Negro woman into the store. A policeman standing at the corner looked on, twirling his night-stick. I watched out of the corner of my eye, never slackening the strokes of my chamois upon the brass. After a few minutes, I heard shrill screams coming from the rear of the store. Later the woman stumbled out, bleeding, crying, and holding her stomach. When she reached the end of the block, the policeman grabbed her and accused her of being drunk. Silently, I watched him throw her into a patrol wagon.

When I went to the rear of the store, the boss and his son were washing their hands at the sink. They were chuckling. The floor was bloody and strewn with wisps of hair and clothing. No doubt I must have appeared pretty shocked, for the boss slapped me reassuringly on the back.

"Boy, that's what we do to niggers when they don't want to pay their bills," he said, laughing.

His son looked at me and grinned.

"Here, hava cigarette," he said.

Not knowing what to do, I took it. He lit his and held the match for me. This was a gesture of kindness, indicating that even if they had beaten the poor old woman, they would not beat me if I knew enough to keep my mouth shut.

"Yes, sir," I said, and asked no questions.

After they had gone, I sat on the edge of a packing box and stared at the bloody floor till the cigarette went out.

That day at noon, while eating in a hamburger joint, I told my fellow Negro porters what had happened. No one seemed surprised. One fellow, after swallowing a huge bite, turned to me and asked:

"Huh! Is tha' all they did t' her?"

"Yeah. Wasn't tha' enough?" I asked.

"Shucks! Man, she's a lucky bitch!" he said, burying his lips deep into a juicy hamburger. "Hell, it's a wonder they didn't lay her when they got through."

III

I was learning fast, but not quite fast enough. One day, while I was delivering packages in the suburbs, my bicycle tire was punctured. I walked along the hot, dusty road, sweating and leading my bicycle by the handlebars.

A car slowed at my side.

"What's the matter, boy?" a white man called.

I told him my bicycle was broken and I was walking back to town.

"That's too bad," he said. "Hop on the running board."

He stopped the car. I clutched hard at my bicycle with one hand and clung to the side of the car with the other.

"All set?"

"Yes, sir," I answered. The car started.

It was full of young white men. They were drinking. I watched the flask pass from mouth to mouth.

"Wanna drink, boy?" one asked.

I laughed as the wind whipped my face. Instinctively obeying the freshly planted precepts of my mother, I said:

"Oh, no!"

The words were hardly out of my mouth before I felt something hard and cold smash me between the eyes. It was an empty whisky bottle. I saw stars, and fell backwards from the speeding car into the dust of the road, my feet becoming entangled in the steel spokes of my bicycle. The white men piled out and stood over me.

"Nigger, ain' yuh learned no better sense'n tha' yet?" asked the man who hit me. "Ain' yuh learned t' say *sir* t' a white man yet?"

Dazed, I pulled to my feet. My elbows and legs were bleeding. Fists doubled, the white man advanced, kicking my bicycle out of the way.

"Aw, leave the bastard alone. He's got enough," said one.

They stood looking at me. I rubbed my shins, trying to stop the flow of blood. No doubt they felt a sort of contemptuous pity, for one asked:

"Yuh wanna ride t' town now, nigger? Yuh reckon yuh know enough t' ride now?"

"I wanna walk," I said, simply.

Maybe it sounded funny. They laughed.

"Well, walk, yuh black son-of-a-bitch!"

When they left they comforted me with:

"Nigger, yuh sho better be damn glad it wuz us yuh talked t' tha' way. Yuh're a lucky bastard, 'cause if yuh'd said tha' t' somebody else, yuh might've been a dead nigger now."

IV

Negroes who had lived South know the dread of being caught alone upon the streets in white neighborhoods after the sun has set. In such a simple situation as this the plight of the Negro in America is graphically symbolized. While white strangers may be in these neighborhoods trying to get home, they can pass unmolested. But the color of a Negro's skin makes him easily recognizable, makes him suspect, converts him into a defenseless target.

Late one Saturday night I made some deliveries in a white neighborhood. I was pedaling my bicycle back to the store as fast as I could, when a police car, swerving toward me, jammed me into the curbing.

"Get down and put up your hands!" the policemen ordered.

I did. They climbed out of the car, guns drawn, faces set, and advanced slowly.

"Keep still!" they ordered.

I reached my hands higher. They searched my pockets and packages. They seemed dissatisfied when they could find nothing incriminating. Finally, one of them said:

"Boy, tell your boss not to send you out in white neighborhoods after sundown."

As usual, I said:

"Yes, sir."

V

My next job was a hall-boy in a hotel. Here my Jim Crow education broadened and deepened. When the bell-boys were busy, I was often called to assist them. As many of the rooms in the hotel were occupied by prostitutes, I was constantly called to carry them liquor and cigarettes. These women were nude most of the time. They did not bother about clothing, even for bell-boys. When you went into their rooms, you were supposed to take their nakedness for granted, as though it startled you no more than a blue vase or a red rug. Your presence awoke in them no sense of shame, for you were not regarded as human. If they were alone, you could steal sidelong glimpses at them. But if they were receiving men, not a flicker of your eyelids could show. I remember one incident vividly. A new woman, a huge, snowy-skinned blonde, took a room on my floor. I was sent to wait upon her. She was in bed with a thick-set man; both were nude and uncovered. She said she wanted some liquor and slid out of bed and waddled across the floor to get her money from a dresser drawer. I watched her.

"Nigger, what in hell you looking at?" the white man asked me, raising himself upon his elbows.

"Nothing," I answered, looking miles deep into the blank wall of the room.

"Keep your eyes where they belong, if you want to be healthy!" he said.

"Yes, sir."

VI

One of the bell-boys I knew in this hotel was keeping steady company with one of the Negro maids. Out of a clear sky the police descended upon his home and arrested him, accusing him of bastardy. The poor boy swore he had had no intimate relations with the girl. Nevertheless, they forced him to marry her. When the child arrived, it was found to be much lighter in complexion than either of the two supposedly legal parents. The white men around the hotel made a great joke of it. They spread the rumor that some white cow must have scared the poor girl while she was carrying the baby. If you were in their presence when this explanation was offered, you were supposed to laugh.

VII

One of the bell-boys was caught in bed with a white prostitute. He was castrated and run out of town. Immediately after this all the bell-boys and hall-boys were called together and warned. We were given to understand that the boy who had been castrated was a "mighty, mighty lucky bastard." We were impressed with the fact that next time the management of the hotel would not be responsible for the lives of "trouble-makin' niggers." We were silent.

VIII

One night, just as I was about to go home, I met one of the Negro maids. She lived in my direction, and we fell in to walk part of the way home together. As we passed the white night-watchman, he slapped the maid on her buttock. I turned around, amazed. The watchman looked at me with a long, hard, fixed-under stare. Suddenly he pulled his gun and asked:

"Nigger, don't yuh like it?"

I hesitated.

"I asked yuh don't yuh like it?" he asked again, stepping forward.

"Yes, sir." I mumbled.

"Talk like it, then!"

"Oh, yes, sir!" I said with as much heartiness as I could muster.

Outside, I walked ahead of the girl, ashamed to face her. She caught up with me and said:

"Don't be a fool! Yuh couldn't help it!"

This watchman boasted of having killed two Negroes in self-defense.

Yet, in spite of all this, the life of the hotel ran with an amazing smoothness. It would have been impossible for a stranger to detect anything. The maids, the hall-boys, and the bell-boys were all smiles. They had to be.

IX

I had learned my Jim Crow lessons so thoroughly that I kept the hotel job till I left Jackson for Memphis. It so happened that while in Memphis I applied for a job at a branch of the optical company. I was hired. And for some reason, as long as I worked there, they never brought my past against me.

Here my Jim Crow education assumed quite a different form. It was no longer brutally cruel, but subtly cruel. Here I learned to lie, to steal, to dissemble. I learned to play that dual role which every Negro must play if he wants to eat and live.

For example, it was almost impossible to get a book to read. It was assumed that after a Negro had imbibed what scanty schooling the state furnished he had no further need for books. I was always borrowing books from men on the job. One day I mustered enough courage to ask one of the men to let me get books from the library in his name. Surprisingly, he consented. I cannot help but think that he consented because he was a Roman Catholic and felt a vague sympathy for Negroes, being himself an object of hatred. Armed with a library card, I obtained books in the following manner: I would write a note to the librarian, saying: "Please let this nigger boy have the following books." I would then sign it with the white man's name.

When I went to the library, I would stand at the desk, hat in hand, looking as unbookish as possible. When I received the books desired I would take them home. If the books listed in the note happened to be out, I would sneak into the lobby and forge a new one. I never took any chances guessing with the white librarian about what the fictitious white man would want to read. No doubt if any of the white patrons had suspected that some of the volumes they enjoyed had been in the home of a Negro, they would not have tolerated it for an instant.

The factory force of the optical company in Memphis was much larger than that in Jackson, and more urbanized. At least they liked to talk, and would engage the Negro help in conversation whenever possible. By this means I found that many subjects were taboo from the white man's point of view. Among the topics they did not like to discuss with Negroes were the following: American white women; the Ku Klux Klan; France, and how Negro soldiers fared while there; French women; Jack Johnson; the entire northern part of the United States; the Civil War; Abraham Lincoln; U. S. Grant; General Sherman; Catholics; the Pope; Jews; the Republican Party; slavery; social equality; Communism; Socialism; the 13th and 14th Amendments to the Constitution; or any topic calling for positive knowledge or manly self-assertion on the part of the Negro. The most accepted topics were sex and religion.

There were many times when I had to exercise a great deal of ingenuity to keep out of trouble. It is a southern custom that all men must take off their hats when they enter an elevator. And especially did this apply to us blacks with rigid force. One day I stepped into an elevator with my arms full of packages. I was forced to ride with my hat on. Two white men stared at me coldly. Then one of them very kindly lifted my hat and placed it upon my armful of packages. Now the most accepted response for a Negro to make under such circumstances is to look at the white man out of the corner of his eye and grin. To have said: "Thank you!" would have made the white man *think* that you *thought* you were receiving from him a personal service. For such an act I have seen Negroes take a blow in the mouth. Finding the first alternative distasteful, and the second dangerous, I hit upon an acceptable course of action which fell safely between these two poles. I immediately— no sooner than my hat was lifted—pretended that my packages were about to spill, and appeared deeply distressed with keeping them in my arms. In this fashion I evaded having to acknowledge his service, and, in spite of adverse circumstances, salvaged a slender shred of personal pride.

How do Negroes feel about the way they have to live? How do they discuss it when alone among themselves? I think this question can be answered in a single sentence. A friend of mine who ran an elevator once told me:

"Lawd, man! Ef it wuzn't fer them polices 'n' them ol' lynch-mobs, there wouldn't be nothin' but uproar down here!"

Suggestions for Discussion

1. Analyze Wright's sketch in terms of (a) structure, (b) progression and unity in nine segments, (c) expository-narrative style, and/or (d) themes.

2. How does Wright's title contribute to the development of the major themes of the sketch? Why does he use *ethics* and *living*?

3. Discuss his use of personal experiences to illustrate his themes.

4. Discuss his use of violence in the sketch. Is it believable? significant? Explain.

Suggestions for Writing

1. Analyze the motivation behind an incident of discrimination that you have observed or experienced.

2. Analyze the dramatic irony in the last line and its climactic effect as the final comment on the whole sketch.

Kenneth B. Clark

An Interview with Martin Luther King

Kenneth B. Clark (b. 1914), an eminent educator and psychologist, was born in the Panama Canal Zone and graduated from Howard and Columbia Universities. He is a Distinguished Professor Emeritus of Psychology at the City University of New York. Described as the "scholar of the civil rights movement," he is the author of *Prejudice and Your Child* (1963), *Dark Ghetto* (1965), *Youth in the Ghetto*, and *Pathos of Power* (1974). His research was cited by the U. S. Supreme Court on *Brown vs. Board of Education* in its 1954 school desegregation ruling. This interview from *King, Malcolm, Baldwin, Three Interviews*, originally published in somewhat different form in 1963 in *The Negro Protest: James Baldwin, Malcom X, Martin Luther King Talk with Kenneth Clark*, explains King's acceptance of nonviolence as a way of life and as the most potent weapon people have in their struggle for freedom and human dignity.

CLARK: In December of 1955 an event in Montgomery, Alabama, catapulted a young man into national and international prominence. The Reverend Martin Luther King, Jr., led the effective Montgomery bus boycott wherein the Negro people of that city stated for the entire world the fact that they were no longer content with second-class citizenship. Since that time Doctor King has personified that dignity, that discipline, and that insistence upon the rights of an American citizen which the present thrust of the Negro people represents. Doctor King, I know that people throughout America have watched your leadership in the Birmingham situation. Before we talk about those problems which have gotten the headlines and coverage in all our mass media, I'd like to know a little about you as a person. Where were you born? Something about your family, brothers and sisters, and things of that sort.

KING: Yes. Well, I was born in the South, in Atlanta, Georgia, and I lived there all of my early years. In fact, I went to the public schools of Atlanta and I went to college in Atlanta. I left after college to attend theological school.

CLARK: What college did you go to?

KING: Morehouse College in Atlanta.

CLARK: Part of the Atlanta University System.

KING: That's right. And I was raised in the home of a minister; my father pastors the Ebenezer Church in Atlanta and has pastored this church for thirty-three years. I am now co-pastor of the same church with him. And we have—I mean there's a family of three children in the immediate family; I have one brother and one sister.

CLARK: Is your brother a pastor also?

KING: Yes, he is. He's the pastor of the First Baptist Church of Birmingham, Alabama.

CLARK: And you have a sister?

KING: Yes, she's in Atlanta, teaching at Spelman College.

CLARK: Now, about your own immediate family: I remember the last time we were together in Montgomery you had a son who had just been born before the Montgomery disturbances.

KING: Well, that was a daughter. The second child was a son, but our first child was a daughter. Since that time we've had two more, so we have four children now, two sons and two daughters, the most recent one being the daughter that came nine weeks ago.

CLARK: How wonderful. It seems as if you have children at times of major crises.

KING: Yes, that's right, and that brings new life to life.

CLARK: Very good. You went from Morehouse to Boston University to study philosophy, am I correct?

KING: Well, no, I went from Morehouse to Crozer Theological Seminary in Pennsylvania and then I went from Crozer to Boston University.

CLARK: In Boston you studied philosophy and, if I remember correctly, you have a Ph.D. in philosophy.

KING: Well, the actual field is philosophical theology.

CLARK: Now, if we could shift a little from the education within the academic halls to your education in the community. I look at our newspapers and see that you have not only engaged in and led many of these demonstrations, but have paid for this by seeing the inside of many jails. I've wondered—

how many jails have you been to as a result of your involvement in this direct-action, non-violent insistence upon the rights of Negroes?

KING: Well, I've been arrested fourteen times since we started out in Montgomery. Some have been in the same jail, that is, I've been in some jails more than once. I haven't calculated the number of different jails. I would say about eight of them were different jails. I remember once within eight days I transferred to three different jails within the state of Georgia. I think I've been to about eight different jails and I've been arrested about fourteen times.

CLARK: Have you attempted to make a study of these jails, for example, the type of jail, the type of individuals you've met in these jails as keepers, say, or wardens? What type of human beings are these or are they different types of human beings?

KING: Well, I have gone through the process of comparing the various jails. I guess this is one of those inevitable things that you find yourself doing to kind of lift yourself from the dull monotony of sameness when you're in jail and I find that they do differ. I've been in some new jails and I've been in some mighty old ones. In the recent jail experience in Birmingham I was in the new jail. The city jail is about a year old, I think, and in Albany, Georgia, last year I was in a very old jail. In Fulton County, Georgia, I was in a very new one.

CLARK: What about the human beings who are the jailkeepers? What about their attitude toward you as a person?

KING: Well, they vary also. I have been in jails where the jailers were exceptionally courteous and they went out of their way to see that everything went all right where I was concerned. On the other hand, I have been in jails where the jailers were extremely harsh and vitriolic in their words and in their manners. I haven't had any experience of physical violence from jailers, but I have had violence of words from them. Even in Birmingham, for the first few days, some of the jailers were extremely harsh in their statements.

CLARK: Have you ever been in an integrated jail? In the South?

KING: No, that's one experience I haven't had yet.

CLARK: Well, maybe after we get through integrating public accommodations the last thing will be to integrate the jailhouses.

KING: Yes.

CLARK: I am very much interested in the philosophy of non-violence and particularly I would like to understand more clearly for myself the relationship between the direct-action non-violence technique which you have used so effectively and your philosophy of, for want of better words I'll use, "love of the oppressor."

KING: All right.

CLARK: Doctor King, what do you see as the relationship between these two things, which could be seen as separate?

KING: Yes, I think so. One is a method of action: non-violent direct action is a method of acting to rectify a social situation that is unjust and it involves in engaging in a practical technique that nullifies the use of violence or calls for non-violence at every point. That is, you don't use physical violence against the opponent. Now, the love ethic is another dimension which goes into the realm of accepting non-violence as a way of life. There are many people who will accept non-violence as the most practical technique to be used in a social situation, but they would not go to the point of seeing the necessity of accepting non-violence as a way of life. Now, I accept both. I think that non-violent resistance is the most potent weapon available to oppressed people in their struggle for freedom and human dignity. It has a way of disarming the opponent. It exposes his moral defenses. It weakens his morale and at the same time it works on his conscience. He just doesn't know how to handle it and I have seen this over and over again in our struggle in the South. Now on the question of love or the love ethic, I think this is so important because hate is injurious to the hater as well as the hated. Many of the psychiatrists are telling us now that many of the strange things that happen in the subconscious and many of the inner conflicts are rooted in hate and so they are now saying "love or perish." Erich Fromm can write a book like *The Art of Loving* and make it very clear that love is the supreme unifying principle of life and I'm trying to say in this movement that it is necessary to follow the technique of non-violence as the most potent weapon available to us, but it is necessary also to follow the love ethic which becomes a force of personality integration.

CLARK: But is it not too much to expect that a group of human beings who have been the victims of cruelty and flagrant injustice could actually love those who have been associated with the perpetrators, if not the perpetrators themselves? How could you expect, for example, the Negroes in Birmingham who know Bull Connor to really love him in any meaningful sense?

KING: Well, I think one has to understand the meaning of "love" at this point. I'm certainly not speaking of an affectionate response. I think it is really nonsense to urge oppressed peoples to love their oppressors in an affectionate sense. And I often call on the Greek language to aid me at this point because there are three words in the Greek for "love." One is "eros," which is sort of an aesthetic or a romantic love. Another is "fileo," which is sort of an intimate affection between personal friends; this is friendship, it is a reciprocal love and on this level, you love those people that you like. And then the Greek language comes out with the word "agape," which is understanding, creative, redemptive good will for all men. It goes far beyond an affectionate response. Now when I say to you—

CLARK: That form means really understanding.

KING: Yes, that's right. And you come to the point of being able to love the person that does an evil deed in the sense of understanding and you can hate the deed that the person does. And I'm certainly not talking about "eros"; I'm not talking about friendship. I find it pretty difficult to like people like Bull Connor. I find it difficult to like Senator Eastman, but I think you can love where you can't like the person because life is an affectionate quality.

CLARK: Yes, I have admired your ability to feel this, and I must say to you also that as I read your expounding of the philosophy of love I found myself often feeling personally quite inadequate. Malcolm X, one of the most articulate exponents of the Black Muslim philosophy, has said of your movement and your philosophy that it plays into the hands of the white oppressors, that they are happy to hear you talk about love for the oppressor because this disarms the Negro and fits into the stereotype of the Negro as a meek, turning-the-other-cheek sort of creature. Would you care to comment on Mister X's beliefs?

KING: Well, I don't think of love, as in this context, as emotional bosh. I don't think of it as a weak force, but I think of love as something strong and that organizes itself into powerful direct action. Now, this is what I try to teach in this struggle in the South: that we are not engaged in a struggle that means we sit down and do nothing; that there is a great deal of difference between non-resistance to evil and non-violent resistance. Non-resistance leaves you in a state of stagnant passivity and deadly complacency where non-violent resistance means that you do resist in a very strong and determined manner and I think some of the criticisms of non-violence or some of the critics fail to realize that we are talking about something very strong and they confuse non-resistance with non-violent resistance.

CLARK: *He* goes beyond that in some of the things I've heard him say—to say that this is deliberately your philosophy of love of the oppressor which he identifies completely with the non-violent movement. He says this philosophy and this movement are actually encouraged by whites because it makes them comfortable. It makes them believe that Negroes are meek, supine creatures.

KING: Well, I don't think that's true. If anyone has ever lived with a non-violent movement in the South, from Montgomery on through the freedom rides and through the sit-in movement and the recent Birmingham movement and seen the reactions of many of the extremists and reactionaries in the white community, he wouldn't say that this movement makes—this philosophy makes them comfortable. I think it arouses a sense of shame within them often—in many instances. I think it does something to touch the conscience and establish a sense of guilt. Now so often people respond to guilt by engaging more in the guilt-evoking act in an attempt to drown the sense of guilt, but this approach certainly doesn't make the white man feel comfortable. I think it does the other thing. It disturbs his conscience and it disturbs this sense of contentment that he's had.

CLARK: James Baldwin raises still another point of the whole non-violent position, an approach. He does not reject it in the ways that Malcolm X does, but he raises the question of whether it will be possible to contain the Negro people within this framework of non-violence if we continue to have more of the kinds of demonstrations that we had in Birmingham, wherein police brought dogs to attack human beings. What is your reaction to Mr. Baldwin's anxiety?

KING: Well, I think these brutal methods used by the Birmingham police force and other police forces will naturally arouse the ire of Negroes and I think there is the danger that some will be so aroused that they will retaliate with violence. I think though that we can be sure that the vast majority of Negroes who engage in the demonstrations and who understand the non-violent philosophy will be able to face dogs and all of the other brutal methods that are used without retaliating with violence because they understand that one of the first principles of non-violence is the willingness to be the recipient of violence while never inflicting violence upon another. And none of the demonstrators in Birmingham engaged in aggressive or retaliatory violence. It was always someone on the sideline who had never been in the demonstrations and probably not in the mass meetings and had never been in a non-violent workshop. So I think it will depend on the extent to which we can extend the teaching of the philosophy of non-violence to the larger community rather than those who are engaged in the demonstrations.

CLARK: Well, how do you maintain this type of discipline, control and dignity in your followers who do participate in the demonstrations? You don't have a police force, you have no uniform, you're not an authoritarian organization, you're a group of people who are voluntarily associated. How do you account for this, I would say, beautiful dignity and discipline?

KING: Well, we do a great deal in terms of teaching both the theoretical aspects of non-violence as well as the practical application. We even have courses where we go through the experience of being roughed up and this kind of sociodrama has proved very helpful in preparing those who are engaged in demonstrations. The other thing is—

CLARK: Does this even include the children?

KING: Yes, it includes the children. In Birmingham where we had several young—we had some as young as seven years old to participate in the demonstrations, and they were in the workshops. In fact, none of them went out for a march, none of them engaged in any of the demonstrations before going through this kind of teaching session. So that through this method we are able to get the meaning of non-violence over, and I think there is a contagious quality in a movement like this when everybody talks about non-violence and being faithful to it and being dignified in your resistance. It tends to get over to the larger group because this becomes a part of the vocabulary of the movement.

CLARK: What is the relationship between your movement and such organizations as the N.A.A.C.P., C.O.R.E. and the Student Non-violent Coordinating Committee? They're separate organizations, but do you work together?

KING: Yes, we do. As you say, each of these organizations is autonomous, but we work together in many, many ways. Last year we started a voter-registration drive, an intensified voter-registration drive. And all of the organizations are working together, sometimes two or three are working together in the same community. The same thing is true with our direct-action programs. In Birmingham we had the support of Snick and C.O.R.E. and the N.A.A.C.P. C.O.R.E. sent some of its staff members in to assist us and

Snick sent some of its staff members. Roy Wilkins came down to speak in one of the mass meetings and to make it clear that even though the N.A.A.C.P. cannot operate in Alabama, we had the support of the N.A.A.C.P. So that we are all working together in a very significant way, and we are doing even more in the days ahead to co-ordinate our efforts.

CLARK: Is there any machinery—does machinery for coordination actually exist now?

KING: Well, we have had a sort of co-ordinating council where we get together as often as possible. Of course, we get involved in many of our programs in the various areas and can't make as many of these meetings as we would like but we often come together (I mean, the heads of all these organizations) to try to co-ordinate our various efforts.

CLARK: What about the Federal government? Have you made any direct appeal either in your own right or as part of this leadership group to have a more active involvement in the Federal government in the rights of Negroes?

KING: Yes, I have. I've made appeals and other members of the Southern Christian Leadership Conference have appealed to the President and the new administration generally to do more in dealing with the problem of racial injustice. I think Mister Kennedy has done some significant things in civil rights, but I do not feel that he has yet given the leadership that the enormity of the problem demands.

CLARK: By Mister Kennedy, now, do you mean the President?

KING: Yes, I'm speaking now of the President, mainly. And I would include the Attorney General. I think both of these men are men of genuine good will, but I think they must understand more about the depths and dimensions of the problem and I think there is a necessity now to see the urgency of the moment. There isn't a lot of time; time is running out, and the Negro is making it palpably clear that he wants all of his rights, that he wants them here, and that he wants them now.

CLARK: Is this not considered by some people an extremist position, that is, not really practical?

KING: Yes, I'm sure many people feel this, but I think they must see the truth of the situation. The shape of the world today does not afford us the luxury of slow movement and the Negro's quest for dignity and self-respect doesn't afford the nation this kind of slow movement.

CLARK: Doctor King, what do you think will be the outcome of the present confrontation, the present insistence of the Negroes for their rights as American citizens without equivocation and without qualification? Do you think this will be obtained?

KING: I do. Realism impels me to admit that there will be difficult days ahead. In some of the hard-core states in the South we will confront resistance. There will still be resistance and there will still be very real problems in the North as a result of the twin evils of employment and housing discrimination, but I think there are forces at work now that will somehow ward off all of these ominous possibilities. The rolling tide of world opinion will play a great part in this. I think the aroused conscience of many, many white people all over the country, the growing awareness of religious institutions that they have not done their job, and the determination of the Negro himself, and the growing industrialization in the South—all of these things, I believe—will conjoin to make it possible for us to move on toward the goal of integration.

CLARK: So you are hopeful?

KING: Yes, I am.

CLARK: And I thank you for your hope and I thank you for your actions.

KING: Thank you.

Suggestions for Discussion

1. Why does Clark elicit a number of biographical details from King in this interview? How do these facts relate to the position on nonviolent action that King espouses?

2. Summarize Malcolm X and James Baldwin's objections to King's beliefs. How does King answer their objections?

3. Examine King's distinctions between the kinds of love and explain why these distinctions are essential to his position that one must embrace the "love ethic" in dealing with one's oppressors.

4. Explain King's hope for integration. To what extent have his hopes been realized since his assassination.

Suggestions for Writing

1. Write a paper in which you summarize King's belief in "love of the oppressor" and agree or disagree with his position.

2. In this interview recorded for television in 1963, King says, "Time is running out, and the Negro is making it palpably clear that he wants all of his rights, that he wants them here, and that he wants them now." Write an essay in which you discuss the extent to which that wish has been achieved. What attitudes stand in the way of equal rights for blacks. Can you suggest some ways by which these attitudes can change?

Essays

Thomas Jefferson
The Declaration of Independence

The Continental Congress assembled in Philadelphia in 1776 delegated to Thomas Jefferson the task of writing a declaration of independence from Great Britain which the Congress amended and adopted on July 4. After the Revolution, Jefferson (1743–1826) became Governor of Virginia and in 1801 the third President of the United States. He was the father of what is called "Jeffersonian democracy," which exceeded the democracy then advocated by either Washington or Jefferson's rival, Alexander Hamilton. After leaving the presidency, he founded the University of Virginia as a place where truth could assert itself in free competition with other ideas. In its theory as well as in its style, the Declaration is a typical eighteenth-century view of man's place in society which included the right to overthrow a tyrannical ruler.

When in the course of human events, it becomes necessary for one people to dissolve the political bands which have connected them with another, and to assume among the powers of the earth, the separate and equal station to which the Laws of Nature and of Nature's God entitle them, a decent respect to the opinions of mankind requires that they should declare the causes which impel them to the separation.

We hold these truths to be self-evident, that all men are created equal, that they are endowed by their Creator with certain inalienable rights, that among these are life, liberty, and the pursuit of happiness. That to secure these rights, governments are instituted among men, deriving their just powers from the consent of the governed. That whenever any form of government becomes destructive of these ends, it is the right of the people to alter or to abolish it, and to institute new government, laying its foundation on such principles and organizing its powers in such form, as to them shall seem most likely to effect their safety and happiness. Prudence, indeed, will dictate that

724

governments long established should not be changed for light and transient causes; and accordingly all experience hath shown, that mankind are more disposed to suffer, while evils are sufferable, than to right themselves by abolishing the forms to which they are accustomed. But when a long train of abuses and usurpations, pursuing invariably the same object, evinces a design to reduce them under absolute despotism, it is their right, it is their duty, to throw off such government, and to provide new guards for their future security. Such has been the patient sufferance of these Colonies; and such is now the necessity which constrains them to alter their former systems of government. The history of the present King of Great Britain is a history of repeated injuries and usurpations, all having in direct object the establishment of an absolute tyranny over these States. To prove this, let facts be submitted to a candid world.

He has refused his assent to laws, the most wholesome and necessary for the public good.

He has forbidden his Governors to pass laws of immediate and pressing importance, unless suspended in their operation till his assent should be obtained; and when so suspended, he has utterly neglected to attend to them.

He has refused to pass other laws for the accommodation of large districts of people, unless those people would relinquish the right of representation in the legislature, a right inestimable to them and formidable to tyrants only.

He has called together legislative bodies at places unusual, uncomfortable, and distant from the depository of their public records, for the sole purpose of fatiguing them into compliance with his measures.

He has dissolved representative houses repeatedly, for opposing with manly firmness his invasions on the rights of the people.

He has refused for a long time, after such dissolutions, to cause others to be elected; whereby the legislative powers, incapable of annihilation, have returned to the people at large for their exercise; the State remaining in the meantime exposed to all the dangers of invasion from without and convulsions within.

He has endeavoured to prevent the population of these states; for that purpose obstructing the laws for naturalization of foreigners; refusing to pass others to encourage their migration hither, and raising the conditions of new appropriations of lands.

He has obstructed the administration of justice, by refusing his assent to laws for establishing judiciary powers.

He has made judges dependent on his will alone, for the tenure of their offices, and the amount and payment of their salaries.

He has erected a multitude of new offices, and sent hither swarms of officers to harass our people, and eat out their substance.

He has kept among us, in times of peace, standing armies without the consent of our legislatures.

He has affected to render the military independent of and superior to the civil power.

He has combined with others to subject us to a jurisdiction foreign of our constitution, and unacknowledged by our laws; giving his assent to their acts of pretended legislation:

For quartering large bodies of armed troops among us:

For protecting them, by a mock trial, from punishment for any murders which they should commit on the inhabitants of these States:

For cutting off our trade with all parts of the world:

For imposing taxes on us without our consent:

For depriving us in many cases of the benefits of trial by jury:

For transporting us beyond seas to be tried for pretended offences:

For abolishing the free system of English laws in a neighbouring Province, establishing therein an arbitrary government, and enlarging its boundaries so as to render it at once an example and fit instrument for introducing the same absolute rule into these Colonies:

For taking away our Charters, abolishing our most valuable laws, and altering fundamentally the forms of our governments:

For suspending our own legislatures, and declaring themselves invested with power to legislate for us in all cases whatsoever.

He has abdicated government here, by declaring us out of his protection and waging war against us.

He has plundered our seas, ravaged our coasts, burnt our towns, and destroyed the lives of our people.

He is at this time transporting large armies of foreign mercenaries to complete the works of death, desolation, and tyranny, already begun with circumstances of cruelty and perfidy scarcely paralleled in the most barbarous ages, and totally unworthy the head of a civilized nation.

He has constrained our fellow citizens taken captive on the high seas to bear arms against their country, to become the executioners of their friends and brethren, or to fall themselves by their hands.

He has excited domestic insurrections amongst us, and has endeavored to bring on the inhabitants of our frontiers, the merciless Indian savages, whose known rule of warfare, is an undistinguished destruction of all ages, sexes, and conditions.

In every stage of these oppressions we have petitioned for redress in the most humble terms: our repeated petitions have been answered only by repeated injury. A prince whose character is thus marked by every act which may define a tyrant is unfit to be the ruler of a free people.

Nor have we been wanting in attention to our British brethren. We have warned them from time to time of attempts by their legislature to extend an unwarrantable jurisdiction over us. We have reminded them of the circumstances of our emigration and settlement here. We have appealed to their native justice and magnanimity, and we have conjured them by the ties of our common kindred to disavow these usurpations, which would inevitably interrupt our connections and correspondence. They too have been deaf to the voice of justice and of consanguinity. We must, therefore, acquiesce in the necessity, which denounces our separation, and hold them, as we hold the rest of mankind, enemies in war, in peace friends.

We, therefore, the Representatives of the United States of America, in General Congress assembled, appealing to the Supreme Judge of the world for the rectitude of our intentions, do, in the name, and by authority of the good people of these Colonies, solemnly publish and declare, That these United Colonies are, and of right ought to be, Free and Independent States; that they are absolved from all allegiance to the British Crown, and that all political connection between them and the state of Great Britain, is and ought to be totally dissolved; and that as Free and Independent States, they have full power to levy war, conclude peace, contract alliances, establish commerce, and to do all other acts and things which Independent States may of right do. And for the support of this declaration, with a firm reliance on the protection of Divine Providence, we mutually pledge to each other our lives, our fortunes, and our sacred honor.

Suggestions for Discussion

1. What is the basis for Jefferson's belief that "all men are created equal"?

2. In the eighteenth century, the notion of the "divine right" of kings was still popular. How does Jefferson refute that notion?

3. Discuss the list of tyrannical actions which Jefferson attributes to the King of Great Britain. Account for the order in which he lists them.

4. This essay has been called a "model of clarity and precision." Explain your agreement with this statement. How does Jefferson balance strong feeling with logical argument?

Suggestion for Writing

Jefferson asserts that "all men are created equal," and yet he does not include black slaves as equals. In Jefferson's *Autobiography*, he wrote that a clause "reprobating the enslaving the inhabitants of Africa" was omitted in the final draft "in complaisance to South Carolina and Georgia." Was Jefferson merely opportunistic in agreeing to strike this clause? Write an essay in which you relate the ideas of the Declaration to the ideas in Lincoln's Gettysburg Address. Show how one set of ideas leads to the other.

◇◇◇◇

The Declaration of the Rights of Man

Soon after the fall of the Bastille on July 14, 1789, a day celebrated in France as July 4th is celebrated in the United States, the National Assembly was asked to provide a declaration which would correspond to the American Declaration of Independence. The Assembly appointed a committee of five to draft the document. After several weeks of debate and compromise, the completed declaration was approved and proclaimed on August 27, 1789. An analysis of the Declaration shows that while a number of phrases resemble the American model, it derived more particularly from the English Bill of Rights of 1689. Ironically, the basis for democratic government embodied in this document was to be subverted by a leader of the new republic who would declare himself Emperor.

The representatives of the French people, gathered in the National Assembly, believing that ignorance, neglect, and disdain of the rights of men are the sole causes of public misfortunes and of the corruption of governments, have resolved to set forth, in solemn declaration, the natural, inalienable, and sacred rights of men, in order that this Declaration, held always before the members of the body social, will forever remind them of their rights and duties; that the acts of legislative and executive power, always identifiable with the ends and purposes of the whole body politic, may be more fully respected; that the complaints of citizens, founded henceforth on simple and incontrovertible principles, may be turned always to the maintaining of the Constitution and to the happiness of all.

The National assembly therefore recognizes and declares, in the presence and under the auspices of the Supreme Being, the following rights of Man and of citizen:

1. Men are born and will remain free and endowed with equal rights. Social distinctions can be based only upon usefulness to the common weal.

2. The end and purpose of all political groups is the preservation of the natural and inalienable rights of Man. These rights are Liberty, the Possession of Property, Safety, and Resistance to Oppression.

3. The principle of all sovereignty will remain fundamentally in the State. No group and no individual can exercise authority which does not arise expressly from the State.

4. Liberty consists in being able to do anything which is not harmful to another or to others; therefore, the exercise of the natural rights of each individual has only such limits as will assure to other members of society the enjoyment of the same rights. These limits can be determined only by the Law.

5. The Law has the right to forbid only such actions as are harmful to society. Anything not forbidden by the Law can never be forbidden; and none can be forced to do what the Law does not prescribe.

6. The Law is the expression of the will of the people. All citizens have the right and the duty to concur in the formation of the Law, either in person or through their representatives. Whether it punishes or whether it protects, the Law must be the same for all. All citizens, being equal in the eyes of the Law, are to be admitted equally to all distinctions, ranks, and public employment, according to their capacities, and without any other discrimination than that established by their individual abilities and virtues.

7. No individual can be accused, arrested, or detained except in cases determined by the Law, and according to the forms which the Law has prescribed. Those who instigate, expedite, execute, or cause to be executed any arbitrary or extralegal prescriptions must be punished; but every citizen called or seized through the power of the Law must instantly obey. He will render himself culpable by resisting.

8. The Law should establish only those penalties which are absolutely and evidently necessary, and none can be punished except through the power of the Law, as already established and proclaimed for the public good and legally applied.

9. Every individual being presumed innocent until he has been proved guilty, if it is considered necessary to arrest him, the Law must repress with severity any force which is not required to secure his person.

10. None is to be persecuted for his opinions, even his religious beliefs, provided that his expression of them does not interfere with the order established by the Law.

11. Free communication of thought and opinion is one of the most precious rights of Man; therefore, every citizen can speak, write, or publish freely, except that he will be required to answer for the abuse of such freedom in cases determined by the Law.

12. The guarantee of the rights of Man and of the citizen makes necessary a Public Force and Administration; this Force and Administration has therefore been established for the good of all, and not for the particular benefit of those to whom it has been entrusted.

13. For the maintaining of this Public Force and Administration, and for the expense of administering it, a common tax is required; it must be distributed equally among the people, in accordance with their ability to pay.

14. All citizens have the right and duty to establish, by themselves or by their representatives, the requirements of a common tax, to consent to it freely, to indicate its use, and to determine its quota, its assessment, its collection, and its duration.

15. Society has the right and duty to demand from every public servant an accounting of his administration.

16. No society in which the guarantee of rights is not assured nor the distinction of legal powers determined can be said to have a constitution.

17. The possession of property being an inviolable and sacred right, none can be deprived of it, unless public necessity, legally proved, clearly requires the deprivation, and then only on the necessary condition of a previously established just reparation.

Suggestions for Discussion

1. What is the major purpose of setting forth the principles enunciated in this declaration?

2. The declaration refers to a Supreme Being. Why did not the writers of the declaration refer simply to God?

3. How do the seventeen "rights of the Man and of the citizen" define the relationship between the individual person and the State?

4. How does the declaration define the function of the Law and of the State?

5. How does the declaration propose to guarantee freedom of speech?

6. Can you explain why the declaration says that the possession of property is an "inviolable and sacred right"? How does this statement basically differ from modern revolutionary thought?

7. On what principles is this declaration based?

Suggestions for Writing

1. Write an essay about the similarities to and differences from this declaration with the American Declaration of Independence and with the Bill of Rights of the American Constitution.

2. Examine the English Bill of Rights of 1689 and write an essay in which you explain the close relationship between the French and English declarations.

Abraham Lincoln
The Gettysburg Address

Abraham Lincoln (1809–1865), the sixteenth President of the United States, is generally regarded, along with Thomas Jefferson, as one of the greatest American prose stylists. On November 19, 1863, he traveled to Gettysburg in southern Pennsylvania to dedicate the cemetery for the soldiers killed there the previous July. The simple words he composed form the most famous speech ever delivered in America. A close reading reveals why it continues to live for Americans today.

Four score and seven years ago our fathers brought forth on this continent, a new nation, conceived in Liberty, and dedicated to the proposition that all men are created equal.

Now we are engaged in a great civil war, testing whether that nation, or any nation so conceived and so dedicated, can long endure. We are met on a great battlefield of that war. We have come to dedicate a portion of that field, as a final resting place for those who here gave their lives that that nation might live. It is altogether fitting and proper that we should do this.

But, in a larger sense, we can not dedicate—we can not consecrate—we can not hallow—this ground. The brave men, living and dead, who struggled here, have consecrated it, far above our poor power to add or detract. The world will little note nor long remember what we say here, but it can never forget what they did here. It is for us the living, rather, to be dedicated here to the unfinished work which they who fought here have thus far so nobly advanced. It is rather for us to be here dedicated to the great task remaining before us—that from these honored dead we take increased devotion to that cause for which they gave the last full measure of devotion—that we here highly resolve that these dead shall not have died in vain—that this nation, under God, shall have a new birth of freedom—and that government of the people, by the people, for the people, shall not perish from the earth.

Suggestions for Discussion

1. How is the proposition "that all men are created equal" related to the issues of the Civil War?

2. Why does Lincoln not simply begin his essay "Eighty-seven years ago"? What would he lose in tone if he had done so?

3. In paragraph three, Lincoln says "The world will little note, nor long remember what we say here." How do you account for the fact that he was wrong? Why did he make this statement? What function does it serve?

4. How does Lincoln use the verbs *dedicate, consecrate, hallow?* Could one easily change the order of these words?

5. How does Lincoln connect the first paragraph of his speech to the last?

6. What was the "unfinished work" of the soldiers who died at the Battle of Gettysburg?

Suggestion for Writing

Write an essay in which you relate the power of this speech to the simplicity of its language.

Niccolò Machiavelli

Of Cruelty and Clemency, and Whether It Is Better to Be Loved or Feared

Niccolò Machiavelli (1469–1527) was a Florentine statesman. His best-known work, *The Prince,* written in 1513, is an astute analysis of the contemporary political scene. The work was first translated into English in 1640. This selection from *The Prince,* translated by Luigi Ricci and revised by E. R. P. Vincent, explains by examples from history why the prince must rely on the fear he creates rather than the love he might generate. Machiavelli explains also why the prince, though causing fear, must avoid incurring hatred.

Proceeding to the other qualities before named, I say that every prince must desire to be considered merciful and not cruel. He must, however, take care not to misuse this mercifulness. Cesare Borgia was considered cruel, but his cruelty had brought order to the Romagna, united it, and reduced it to peace and fealty. If this is considered well, it will be seen that he was really much more merciful than the Florentine people, who, to avoid the name of cruelty, allowed Pistoia to be destroyed. A prince, therefore, must not mind incurring the charge of cruelty for the purpose of keeping his subjects united and faithful; for, with a very few examples, he will be more merciful than those who, from excess of tenderness, allow disorders to arise, from whence spring bloodshed and rapine; for these as a rule injure the whole community, while the executions carried out by the prince injure only individuals. And of all princes, it is impossible for a new prince to escape the reputation of cruelty, new states being always full of dangers. Wherefore Virgil through the mouth of Dido says:

> Res dura, et regni novitas me talia cogunt
> Moliri, et late fines custode tueri.[1]

Nevertheless, he must be cautious in believing and acting, and must not be afraid of his own shadow, and must proceed in a temperate manner with prudence and humanity, so that too much confidence does not render him incautious, and too much diffidence does not render him intolerant.

From this arises the question whether it is better to be loved more than feared, or feared more than loved. The reply is, that one ought to be both feared and loved, but as it is difficult for the two to go together, it is much safer to be feared than loved, if one of the two has to be wanting. For it may be said of men in general that they are ungrateful, voluble dissemblers, anxious to avoid danger, and covetous of gain; as long as you benefit them, they are entirely yours; they offer you their blood, their goods, their life, and their children, as I have before said, when the necessity is remote; but when it approaches, they revolt. And the prince who has relied solely on their words, without making other preparations, is ruined; for the friendship which is gained by purchase and not through grandeur and nobility of spirit is bought but not secured, and at a pinch is not to be expended in your service. And men have less scruple in offending one who makes himself loved than one who makes himself feared; for love is held by a chain of obligation which, men being selfish, is broken whenever it serves their purpose; but fear is maintained by a dread of punishment which never fails.

Still, a prince should make himself feared in such a way that if he does not gain love, he at any rate avoids hatred; for fear and the absence of hatred may well go together, and will be always attained by one who abstains from interfering with the property of his citizens and subjects or with their women. And when he is obliged to take the life of anyone, let him do so when there is proper justification and manifest reason for it; but above all he must abstain from taking the property of others, for men forget more easily the death of their father than the loss of their patrimony. Then also pretexts for seizing property are never wanting, and one who begins to live by rapine will always find some reason for taking the goods of others, whereas causes for taking life are rarer and more fleeting.

But when the prince is with his army and has a large number of soldiers under his control, then it is extremely necessary that he should not mind being thought cruel; for without this reputation he could not keep an army united or disposed to any duty. Among the noteworthy actions of Hannibal is numbered this, that although he had an enormous army, composed of men of all nations and fighting in foreign countries, there never arose any dissension

---

[1] Our harsh situation and the newness of our kingdom compel me to contrive such measures and to guard our territory far and wide. (Dido offers this explanation to the newly landed Trojans of why her guards received them with hostile and suspicious measures.)

either among them or against the prince, either in good fortune or in bad. This could not be due to anything but his inhuman cruelty, which together with his infinite other virtues, made him always venerated and terrible in the sight of his soldiers, and without it his other virtues would not have sufficed to produce that effect. Thoughtless writers admire on the one hand his actions, and on the other blame the principal cause of them.

And that it is true that his other virtues would not have sufficed may be seen from the case of Scipio (famous not only in regard to his own times, but all times of which memory remains), whose armies rebelled against him in Spain, which arose from nothing but his excessive kindness, which allowed more licence to the soldiers than was consonant with military discipline. He was reproached with this in the senate by Fabius Maximus, who called him a corrupter of the Roman militia. Locri having been destroyed by one of Scipio's officers was not revenged by him, nor was the insolence of that officer punished, simply by reason of his easy nature; so much so, that some one wishing to excuse him in the senate, said that there were many men who knew rather how not to err, than how to correct the errors of others. This disposition would in time have tarnished the fame and glory of Scipio had he persevered in it under the empire, but living under the rule of the senate this harmful quality was not only concealed but became a glory to him.

I conclude, therefore, with regard to being feared and loved, that men love at their own free will, but fear at the will of the prince, and that a wise prince must rely on what is in his power and not on what is in the power of others, and he must only contrive to avoid incurring hatred, as has been explained.

Suggestions for Discussion

1. How does Machiavelli show that Cesare Borgia, known for his cruelty, was more merciful than the people of Florence?

2. Explain the use of the quotation from Virgil.

3. Explain Machiavelli's argument that the prince cannot rely on the love of his subjects.

4. What attitudes does Machiavelli express when he says that "men forget more easily the death of their father than the loss of their patrimony"?

5. Compare and contrast the actions of Scipio and Hannibal. How does Machiavelli explain their actions to prove his point about the need of the prince to inspire fear?

Suggestion for Writing

Write an essay in which you comment on the ideas in this selection which may be brilliant but not admirable. What aspects of life does the author ignore? Why? Why does this selection not express the concern for freedom and human dignity that characterizes most of the selections in this section?

José Ortega y Gasset
The Greatest Danger, the State
Anonymous Translation

José Ortega y Gasset (1883–1955) was a Spanish philosopher who wrote in opposition to authoritarianism in the late 1930s. His most accessible works are *The Revolt of the Masses* (1932) and *The Dehumanization of Art* (1948). This selection from *The Revolt of the Masses* clearly expresses his fear of the dangers of statism exemplified in fascist Italy and foreshadows the rise of fascism in Spain.

In a right ordering of public affairs, the mass is that part which does not act of itself. Such is its mission. It has come into the world in order to be directed, influenced, represented, organised—even in order to cease being mass, or at least to aspire to this. But it has not come into the world to do all this by itself. It needs to submit its life to a higher court, formed of the superior minorities. The question as to who are these superior individuals may be discussed *ad libitum*, but that without them, whoever they be, humanity would cease to preserve its essentials is something about which there can be no possible doubt, though Europe spend a century with its head under its wing, ostrich-fashion, trying if she can to avoid seeing such a plain truth. For we are not dealing with an opinion based on facts more or less frequent and probable, but on a law of social "physics," much more immovable than the laws of Newton's physics. The day when a genuine philosophy[1] once more holds sway in Europe—it is the one thing that can save her—that day she will once again realise that man, whether he like it or no, is a being forced by his nature to seek some higher authority. If he succeeds in finding it of himself, he is a superior man; if not, he is a mass-man and must receive it from his superiors.

For the mass to claim the right to act of itself is then a rebellion against its own destiny, and because that is what it is doing at present, I speak of the rebellion of the masses. For, after all, the one thing that can substantially and truthfully be called rebellion is that which consists in not accepting one's own destiny, in rebelling against one's self. The rebellion of the archangel Lucifer would not have been less if, instead of striving to be God—which was not his destiny—he had striven to be the lowest of the angels—equally not his destiny. (If Lucifer had been a Russian, like Tolstoi, he would perhaps have preferred this latter form of rebellion, none the less against God than the other more famous one.)

When the mass acts on its own, it does so only in one way, for it has no

---

[1] For philosophy to rule, it is not necessary that philosophers be the rulers—as Plato at first wished—nor even for rulers to be philosophers—as was his later, more modest wish. Both these things are, strictly speaking, most fatal. For philosophy to rule, it is sufficient for it to exist; that is to say, for the philosophers to be philosophers. For nearly a century past, philosophers have been everything but that—politicians, pedagogues, men of letters, and men of science.

other: it lynches. It is not altogether by chance that lynch law comes from America, for America is, in a fashion, the paradise of the masses. And it will cause less surprise, nowadays, when the masses triumph; that violence should triumph and be made the one *ratio*, the one doctrine. It is now some time since I called attention to this advance of violence as a normal condition.[2] Today it has reached its full development, and this is a good symptom, because it means that automatically the descent is about to begin. Today violence is the rhetoric of the period, the empty rhetorician has made it his own. When a reality of human existence has completed its historic course, has been shipwrecked and lies dead, the waves throw it up on the shores of rhetoric, where the corpse remains for a long time. Rhetoric is the cemetery of human realities, or at any rate a Home for the Aged. The reality itself is survived by its name, which, though only a word, is after all at least a word and preserves something of its magic power.

But though it is not impossible that the prestige of violence as a cynically established rule has entered on its decline, we shall still continue under that rule, though in another form. I refer to the gravest danger now threatening European civilization. Like all other dangers that threaten it, this one is born of civilization itself. More than that, it constitutes one of its glories: it is the State as we know it today. We are confronted with a replica of what we said in the previous chapter about science: the fertility of its principles brings about a fabulous progress, but this inevitably imposes specialization, and specialization threatens to strangle science.

The same thing is happening with the State. Call to mind what the State was at the end of the XVIIIth Century in all European nations. Quite a small affair! Early capitalism and its industrial organizations, in which the new, rationalised technique triumphs for the first time, had brought a commencement of increase in society. A new social class appeared, greater in numbers and power than the pre-existing: the middle class. This astute middle class possessed one thing, above and before all: talent, practical talent. It knew how to organize and discipline, how to give continuity and consistency to its efforts. In the midst of it, as in an ocean, the "ship of State" sailed its hazardous course. The ship of State is a metaphor reinvented by the bourgeoisie, which felt itself oceanic, omnipotent, pregnant with storms. That ship was, as we said, a very small affair: it had hardly any soldiers, bureaucrats, or money. It had been built in the Middle Ages by a class of men very different from the bourgeois—the nobles, a class admirable for their courage, their gifts of leadership, their sense of responsibility. Without them the nations of Europe would not now be in existence. But with all those virtues of the heart, the nobles were, and always have been, lacking in virtues of the head. Of limited intelligence, sentimental, instinctive, intuitive—in a word, "irrational." Hence they were unable to develop any technique, a thing which demands rationalization. They did not invent gunpowder. Incapable of inventing new arms, they allowed the bourgeois, who got it from the East or somewhere else, to utilize gunpowder and automatically to win the battle against the warrior noble, the "caballero," stupidly covered in iron so that he could hardly move in the fight, and who had never imagined that the eternal secret

[2]Vide *España Invertebrada*, 1912.

of warfare consists not so much in the methods of defense as in those of attack, a secret which was to be rediscovered by Napoleon.[3]

As the State is a matter of technique—of public order and administration—the "ancien régime" reaches the end of the XVIIIth Century with a very weak State, harassed on all sides by a widespread social revolt. The disproportion between State power and social power at this time is such that, comparing the situation then with that of the time of Charlemagne, the XVIIIth-Century State appears degenerate. The Carolingian State was of course much less powerful than the State of Louis XVI, but, on the other hand, the society surrounding it was entirely lacking in strength.[4] The enormous disproportion between social strength and the strength of public power made possible the Revolution, the revolutions—up to 1848.

But with the Revolution the middle class took possession of public power and applied their undeniable qualities to the State, and in little more than a generation created a powerful State, which brought revolution to an end. Since 1848, that is to say, since the beginning of the second generation of bourgeois governments, there have been no genuine revolutions in Europe. Not assuredly because there were not motives for them, but because there were no means. Public power was brought to the level of social power. *Good-bye forever to Revolutions!* The only thing now possible in Europe is their opposite: the *coup d'état*. Everything which in following years tried to look like a revolution was only a *coup d'état* in disguise.

In our days the State has come to be a formidable machine which works in marvelous fashion; of wonderful efficiency by reason of the quantity and precision of its means. Once it is set up in the midst of society, it is enough to touch a button for its enormous levers to start working and exercise their overwhelming power on any portion whatever of the social framework.

The contemporary State is the easiest seen and best-known product of civilization. And it is an interesting revelation when one takes note of the attitude that mass-man adopts before it. He sees it, admires it, knows that *there it is*, safeguarding his existence; but he is not conscious of the fact that it is a human creation invented by certain men and upheld by certain virtues and

---

[3]We owe to Ranke this simple picture of the great historic change by which for the supremacy of the nobles is substituted the predominance of the bourgeois; but of course its symbolic geometric outlines require no little filling-in in order to be completely true. Gunpowder was known from time immemorial. The invention by which a tube was charged with it was due to someone in Lombardy. Even then it was not efficacious until the invention of the cast cannonball. The "nobles" used firearms to a small extent, but they were too dear for them. It was only the bourgeois armies, with their better economic organisation, that could employ them on a large scale. It remains, however, literally true that the nobles, represented by the medieval type of army of the Burgundians, were definitely defeated by the new army, not professional but bourgeois, formed by the Swiss. Their primary force lay in the new discipline and the new rationalism of tactics.

[4]It would be worth while insisting on this point and making clear that the epoch of absolute monarchies in Europe has coincided with very weak States. How is this to be explained? Why, if the State was all-powerful, "absolute," did it not make itself stronger? One of the causes is that indicated, the incapacity—technical, organizing, bureaucratic—of the aristocracies of blood. But this is not enough. Besides that, it also happened that the absolute State and those aristocracies *did not want to aggrandize the State at the expense of society in general*. Contrary to the common belief, the absolute State instinctively respects society much more than our democratic State, which is more intelligent but has less sense of historic responsibility.

fundamental qualities which the men of yesterday had and which may vanish into air tomorrow. Furthermore, the mass-man sees in the State an anonymous power, and feeling himself, like it, anonymous, he believes that the State is something of his own. Suppose that in the public life of a country some difficulty, conflict, or problem presents itself, the mass-man will tend to demand that the State intervene immediately and undertake a solution directly with its immense and unassailable resources.

This is the gravest danger that today threatens civilization: State intervention; the absorption of all spontaneous social effort by the State, that is to say, of spontaneous historical action, which in the long run sustains, nourishes, and impels human destinies. When the mass suffers any ill-fortune or simply feels some strong appetite, its great temptation is that permanent, sure possibility of obtaining everything—without effort, struggle, doubt, or risk— merely by touching a button and setting the mighty machine in motion. The mass says to itself, *"L'Etat, c'est moi,"* which is a complete mistake. The state is the mass only in the sense in which it can be said of two men that they are identical because neither of them is named John. The contemporary State and the mass coincide only in being anonymous. But the mass-man does in fact believe that he is the State, and he will tend more and more to set its machinery working on whatsoever pretext, to crush beneath it any creative minority which disturbs it—disturbs it in any order of things: in politics, in ideas, in industry.

The result of this tendency will be fatal. Spontaneous social action will be broken up over and over again by State intervention; no new seed will be able to fructify. Society will have to live *for* the State, man *for* the governmental machine. And as, after all, it is only a machine whose existence and maintenance depend on the vital supports around it, the State, after sucking out the very marrow of society, will be left bloodless, a skeleton, dead with that rusty death of machinery, more gruesome than the death of a living organism.

Such was the lamentable fate of ancient civilization. No doubt the imperial State created by the Julii and the Claudii was an admirable machine, incomparably superior as a mere structure to the old republican State of the patrician families. But, by a curious coincidence, hardly had it reached full development when the social body began to decay.

Already in the times of the Antonines (IInd Century), the State overbears society with its anti-vital supremacy. Society begins to be enslaved, to be unable to live except *in the service of the State.* The whole of life is bureaucratized. What results? The bureaucratization of life brings about its absolute decay in all orders. Wealth diminishes, births are few. Then the State, in order to attend to its own needs, forces on still more the bureaucratization of human existence. This bureaucratization to the second power is the militarization of society. The State's most urgent need is its apparatus of war, its army. Before all the State is the producer of security (that security, be it remembered, of which the mass-man is born). Hence, above all, an army. The Severi, of African origin, militarize the world. Vain task! Misery increases, women are every day less fruitful, even soldiers are lacking. After the time of the Severi, the army had to be recruited from foreigners.

Is the paradoxical, tragic process of Statism now realized? Society, that it may live better, creates the State as an instrument. Then the State gets the upper hand and society has to begin to live for the State.[5] But for all that the State is still composed of the members of that society. But soon these do not suffice to support it, and it has to call in foreigners: first Dalmatians, then Germans. These foreigners take possession of the State, and the rest of society, the former populace, has to live as their slaves—slaves of people with whom they have nothing in common. That is what State intervention leads to: the people are converted into fuel to feed the mere machine which is the State. The skeleton eats up the flesh around it. The scaffolding becomes the owner and tenant of the house.

When this is realized, it rather confounds one to hear Mussolini heralding as an astounding discovery just made in Italy, the formula: "All for the State; nothing outside the State; nothing against the State." This alone would suffice to reveal in Fascism a typical movement of mass-men. Mussolini found a State admirably built up—not by him, but precisely by the ideas and the forces he is combating: by liberal democracy. He confines himself to using it ruthlessly, and, without entering now into a detailed examination of his work, it is indisputable that the results obtained up the present cannot be compared with those obtained in political and administrative working by the liberal State. If he has succeeded in anything it is so minute, so little visible, so lacking in substance as with difficulty to compensate for the accumulation of the abnormal powers which enable him to make use of that machine to its full extent.

Statism is the higher form taken by violence and direct action when these are set up as standards. Through and by means of the State, the anonymous machine, the masses act for themselves. The nations of Europe have before them a period of great difficulties in their internal life, supremely arduous problems of law, economics, and public order. Can we help feeling that under the rule of the masses the State will endeavor to crush the independence of the individual and the group, and thus definitely spoil the harvest of the future?

A concrete example of this mechanism is found in one of the most alarming phenomena of the last thirty years: the enormous increase in the police force of all countries. The increase of population has inevitably rendered it necessary. However accustomed we may be to it, the terrible paradox should not escape our minds that the population of a great modern city, in order to move about peaceably and attend to its business, necessarily requires a police force to regulate the circulation. But it is foolishness for the party of "law and order" to imagine that these "forces of public authority" created to preserve order are always going to be content to preserve the order that that party desires. Inevitably they will end by themselves defining and deciding on the order they are going to impose—which, naturally, will be that which suits them best.

It might be well to take advantage of our touching on this matter to observe the different reaction to a public need manifested by different types of society. When, about 1800, the new industry began to create a type of man—the industrial worker—more criminally inclined than traditional types, France hastened to create a numerous police force. Towards 1810 there occurs in England, for the same reasons, an increase in criminality, and the English

---

[5]Recall the last words of Septimus Severus to his sons: "Remain united, pay the soldiers, and take no heed of the rest."

suddenly realise that they have no police. The Conservatives are in power. What will they do? Will they establish a police force? Nothing of the kind. They prefer to put up with crime, as well as they can. "People are content to let disorder alone, considering it the price they pay for liberty." "In Paris," writes John William Ward, "they have an admirable police force, but they pay dear for its advantages. I prefer to see, every three or four years, half a dozen people getting their throats cut in the Ratcliffe Road, than to have to submit to domiciliary visits, to spying, and to all the machinations of Fouché."[6] Here we have two opposite ideas of the State. The Englishman demands that the State should have limits set to it.

[6]*Vide* Elie Halevy, *Historie du peuple anglais au XIX siècle*, Vol. I, p. 40 (1912).

Suggestions for Discussion

1. Why does a strong state emerge? What dangers does it pose for individual rights? Cite arguments from the text.

2. Explain why the state is so efficient a mechanism.

3. The author contrasts the attitudes of the British toward the rise of crime with those of the French. With whom does he sympathize? Why?

Suggestions for Writing

1. From your personal experience or from your reading or viewing demonstrate that the state can threaten individual freedoms.

2. Compare and contrast the ideas in this essay with those in Auden's poem, "The Unknown Citizen."

H. L. Mencken

The Nature of Liberty

Henry Louis Mencken (1880–1956), journalist, critic, and philologist, edited the magazines *The Smart Set* and *The American Mercury.* In addition to his auto-biography, he wrote six volumes of *Prejudices,* (1919–1927) containing his often irascible comments on American life and art, and the three-volume *The American Language,* (1918). The Sage of Baltimore was no admirer of democracy, and in this selection from *Prejudices* he wryly and outrageously pokes fun at police power and the invasion of the rights of the citizen in the United States.

Every time an officer of the constabulary, in the execution of his just and awful powers under American law, produces a compound fracture of the occiput of some citizen in his custody, with hemorrhage, shock, coma, and death, there comes a feeble, falsetto protest from specialists in human liberty. Is it a fact without significance that this protest is never supported by the great body of American freemen, setting aside the actual heirs and creditors of the victim? I think not. Here, as usual, public opinion is very realistic. It does not rise against the policeman for the plain and simple reason that it does not question his right to do what he has done. Policemen are not given nightsticks for ornament. They are given them for the purpose of cracking the skulls of the recalcitrant plain people, Democrats and Republicans alike. When they execute that high duty they are palpably within their rights.

The specialists aforesaid are the same fanatics who shake the air with sobs every time the Postmaster General of the United States bars a periodical from the mails because its ideas do not please him, and every time some poor Russian is deported for reading Karl Marx, and every time a Prohibition enforcement officer murders a bootlegger who resists his levies, and every time agents of the Department of Justice throw an Italian out of the window, and every time the Ku Klux Klan or the American Legion tars and feathers a Socialist evangelist. In brief, they are Radicals, and to scratch one with a pitchfork is to expose a Bolshevik. They are men standing in contempt of American institutions and in enmity to American idealism. And their evil principles are no less offensive to right-thinking and red-blooded Americans when they are United States Senators or editors of wealthy newspapers than when they are degraded I. W. W.'s throwing dead cats and infernal machines into meetings of the Rotary Club.

What ails them primarily is the ignorant and uncritical monomania that afflicts every sort of fanatic, at all times and everywhere. Having mastered with their limited faculties the theoretical principles set forth in the Bill of Rights, they work themselves into a passionate conviction that those principles are identical with the rules of law and justice, and ought to be enforced literally, and without the slightest regard for circumstance and expediency. It is precisely as if a High Church rector, accidentally looking into the Book of Chronicles and especially Chapter II, should suddenly issue a mandate from his pulpit ordering his parishioners, on penalty of excommunication and the fires of hell, to follow exactly the example set forth, to wit: "And Jesse begat his first born Eliab, and Abinadab the second, and Shimma the third, Netheneel the fourth, Raddai the fifth, Ozen the sixth, David the seventh," and so on. It might be very sound theoretical theology, but it would surely be out of harmony with modern ideas, and the rev. gentleman would be extremely lucky if the bishop did not give him 10 days in the diocesan hoosegow.

So with the Bill of Rights. As adopted by the Fathers of the Republic, it was gross, crude, inelastic, a bit fanciful and transcendental. It specified the rights of a citizen, but it said nothing whatever about his duties. Since then, by the orderly processes of legislative science and by the even more subtle and beautiful devices of juridic art, it has been kneaded and mellowed into a far greater pliability and reasonableness. On the one hand, the citizen still retains the great privilege of membership in the most superb free nation ever witnessed on this earth. On the other hand, as a result of countless shrewd enactments and sagacious decisions, his natural lusts and appetites are held in laudable check, and he is thus kept in order and decorum. No artificial impediment stands in the way of his highest aspiration. He may become anything, including even a policeman. But once a policeman, he is protected by the legislative and judicial arms in the peculiar rights and prerogatives that go with his high office, including especially the right to jug the laity at his will, to sweat and mug them, to subject them to the third degree, and to subdue their resistance by beating out their brains. Those who are unaware of this are simply ignorant of the basic principles of American jurisprudence, as they have been exposed times without number by the courts of first instance and ratified in lofty terms by the Supreme Court of the United States. The one aim of the controlling decisions, magnificently attained, is to safeguard public order and the public security, and to substitute a judicial process for the inchoate and dangerous interaction of discordant egos.

Let us imagine an example. You are, say, a peaceable citizen on your way home from your place of employment. A police sergeant, detecting you in the crowd, approaches you, lays his hand on your collar, and informs you that you are under arrest for killing a trolley conductor in Altoona, Pa., in 1917. Amazed by the accusation, you decide hastily that the officer has lost his wits, and take to your heels. He pursues you. You continue to run. He draws his revolver and fires at you. He misses you. He fires again and fetches you in the leg. You fall and he is upon you. You prepare to resist his apparently maniacal assault. He beats you into insensibility with his espantoon, and drags you to the patrol box.

Arrived at the watch house you are locked in a room with five detectives, and for six hours they question you with subtle art. You grow angry—perhaps robbed of your customary politeness by the throbbing in your head and leg—and answer tartly. They knock you down. Having failed to wring a confession from you, they lock you in a cell, and leave you there all night. The next day you are taken to police headquarters, your photograph is made for the Rogues' Gallery, and a print is duly deposited in the section labeled "Murderers." You are then carted to jail and locked up again. There you remain until the trolley conductor's wife comes down from Altoona to identify you. She astonishes the police by saying that you are not the man. The actual murderer, it appears, was an Italian. After holding you a day or two longer, to search your house for stills, audit your income tax returns, and investigate the premarital chastity of your wife, they let you go.

You are naturally somewhat irritated by your experience and perhaps your wife urges you to seek redress. Well, what are your remedies? If you are a firebrand, you reach out absurdly for those of a preposterous nature: the instant jailing of the sergeant, the dismissal of the Police Commissioner, the release of Mooney, a fair trial for Sacco and Vanzetti, free trade with Russia, One Big Union. But if you are a 100 per cent American and respect the laws and institutions of your country, you send for your solicitor—and at once he shows you just how far your rights go, and where they end. You cannot cause the arrest of the sergeant, for you resisted him when he attempted to arrest you, and when you resisted him he acquired an instant right to take you by force. You cannot proceed against him for accusing you falsely, for he has a right to make summary arrests for felony, and the courts have many times decided that a public officer, so long as he cannot be charged with corruption or malice, is not liable for errors of judgment made in the execution of his sworn duty. You cannot get the detectives on the mat, for when they questioned you you were a prisoner accused of murder, and it was their duty and their right to do so. You cannot sue the turnkey at the watch house or the warden at the jail for locking you up, for they received your body, as the law says, in a lawful and regular manner, and would have been liable to penalty if they had turned you loose.

But have you no redress whatever, no rights at all? Certainly you have a right, and the courts have jealously guarded it. You have a clear right, guaranteed to you under the Constitution, to go into a court of equity and apply for a mandamus requiring the *Polizei* to cease forthwith to expose your portrait in the Rogues' Gallery among the murderers. This is your inalienable right, and no man or men on earth can take it away from you. You cannot prevent them cherishing your portrait in their secret files, but you can get an order commanding them to refrain forever from exposing it to the gaze of idle visitors, and if you can introduce yourself unseen into their studio and prove that they disregard that order, you can have them haled into court for contempt and fined by the learned judge.

Thus the law, statute, common and case, protects the free American against injustice. It is ignorance of that subtle and perfect process and not any special love of liberty *per se* that causes radicals of anti-American kidney to rage every time an officer of the *gendarmerie,* in the simple execution of his duty, knocks a citizen in the head. The *gendarme* plainly has an inherent and inalienable right to knock him in the head: it is an essential part of his general prerogative as a sworn officer of the public peace and a representative of the sovereign power of the state. He may, true enough, exercise that prerogative in a manner liable to challenge on the ground that it is imprudent and lacking in sound judgment. On such questions reasonable men may differ. But it must be obvious that the sane and decorous way to settle differences of opinion of that sort is not by public outcry and florid appeals to sentimentality, not by ill-disguised playing to class consciousness and antisocial prejudice, but by an orderly resort to the checks and remedies superimposed upon the Bill of Rights by the calm deliberation and austere logic of the courts of equity.

The law protects the citizen. But to get its protection he must show due respect for its wise and delicate processes.

Suggestions for Discussion

1. Discuss the serious points about liberty that Mencken tries to make in this wry and ironic essay.

2. Analyze Mencken's use of irony. Identify specific examples.

3. Does Mencken choose his examples because they are true, amusing, or outrageous? Examine his motivation.

Suggestion for Writing

Write an ironic sketch about a local or national political situation.

William Faulkner
Nobel Prize Award Speech

William Faulkner (1897–1962) lived most of his life in Oxford, Mississippi. After a year at the university of his native state, he joined the Royal Canadian Air Force, eager to participate in World War I. His novels set in his imaginary Yoknapatawpha County include *The Sound and the Fury* (1929), *Light in August* (1932), *Absalom, Absalom!* (1936), and *The Hamlet* (1940). In his speech accepting the Nobel Prize for Literature in 1949, he states his belief in the significance and dignity of humankind and the need for the writer to reassert the universal truths of "love and honor and pity and pride and compassion and sacrifice."

I feel that this award was not made to me as a man but to my work—a life's work in the agony and sweat of the human spirit, not for glory and least of all for profit, but to create out of the materials of the human spirit something which did not exist before. So this award is only mine in trust. It will not be difficult to find a dedication for the money part of it commensurate with the purpose and significance of its origin. But I would like to do the same with the acclaim too, by using this moment as a pinnacle from which I might be listened to by the young men and women already dedicated to the same anguish and travail, among whom is already that one who will some day stand here where I am standing.

Our tragedy today is a general and universal physical fear so long sustained by now that we can even bear it. There are no longer problems of the spirit. There is only the question: When will I be blown up? Because of this, the young man or woman writing today has forgotten the problems of the human heart in conflict with itself which alone can make good writing because only that is worth writing about, worth the agony and the sweat.

He must learn them again. He must teach himself that the basest of all things is to be afraid; and, teaching himself that, forget it forever, leaving no room in his workshop for anything but the old verities and truths of the heart, the old universal truths lacking which any story is ephemeral and doomed—love and honor and pity and pride and compassion and sacrifice. Until he does so, he labors under a curse. He writes not of love but of lust, of defeats in which nobody loses anything of value, of victories without hope and, worst of all, without pity or compassion. His griefs grieve on no universal bones, leaving no scars. He writes not of the heart but of the glands.

Until he relearns these things, he will write as though he stood alone and watched the end of man. I decline to accept the end of man. It is easy enough to say that man is immortal simply because he will endure; that when the last ding-dong of doom has clanged and faded from the last worthless rock hanging tideless in the last red and dying evening, that even then there will still be one more sound: that of his puny inexhaustible voice, still talking. I refuse to accept this. I believe that man will not merely endure: he will prevail. He is immortal, not because he alone among creatures has an inexhaustible voice but because he has a soul, a spirit capable of compassion and sacrifice and endurance. The poet's, the writer's, duty is to write about these things. It is his privilege to help man endure by lifting his heart, by reminding him of the courage and honor and hope and pride and compassion and pity and sacrifice which have been the glory of his past. The poet's voice need not merely be the record of man, it can be one of the props, the pillars to help him endure and prevail.

Suggestions for Discussion

1. Do you agree with Faulkner's optimistic statement about man's ability to "endure and prevail"? Explain.

2. Do you think Faulkner's speech too brief for a major occasion such as the Nobel Prize Awards? Explain your answer.

3. Discuss whether or not man still lives in that state of general and universal physical fear to which Faulkner refers.

Suggestions for Writing

1. Summarize your own opinions about man's ability to survive the challenges of the next hundred years.

2. Prepare a formal speech in which you accept an international prize for literature or some other accomplishment.

Harriet Jacobs

The Women

Harriet Jacobs (1818–1896) describes the effects of Nat Turner's Rebellion in *Incidents in the Life of a Slave Girl* (1861). This selection from *Black Slave Narratives* pinpoints with simple clarity the moral dilemmas that face a young female slave caught between her owner's desires and his wife's jealousy.

I would ten thousand times rather that my children should be the half-starved paupers of Ireland than to be the most pampered among the slaves of America. I would rather drudge out my life on a cotton plantation, till the grave opened to give me rest, than to live with an unprincipled master and a jealous mistress. The felon's home in a penitentiary is preferable. He may repent, and turn from the error of his ways, and so find peace, but it is not so with a favorite slave. She is not allowed to have any pride of character. It is deemed a crime in her to wish to be virtuous.

Mrs. Flint possessed the key to her husband's character before I was born. She might have used this knowledge to counsel and to screen the young and the innocent among her slaves; but for them she had no sympathy. They were the objects of her constant suspicion and malevolence. She watched her husband with unceasing vigilance; but he was well practiced in means to evade it. What he could not find opportunity to say in words he manifested in signs. He invented more than were ever thought of in a deaf and dumb asylum. I let them pass, as if I did not understand what he meant; and many were the curses and threats bestowed on me for my stupidity. One day he caught me teaching myself to write. He frowned, as if he was not well pleased; but I suppose he came to the conclusion that such an accomplishment might help to advance his favorite scheme. Before long, notes were often slipped into my hand. I would return them, saying, "I can't read them, sir." "Can't you?" he replied; "then I must read them to you." He always finished the reading by asking, "Do you understand?" Sometimes he would complain of the heat of the tea room, and order his supper to be placed on a small table in the piazza. He would seat himself there with a well-satisfied smile, and tell me to stand by and brush away the flies. He would eat very slowly, pausing between the mouthfuls. These intervals were employed in describing the happiness I was so foolishly throwing away, and in threatening me with the penalty that finally awaited my stubborn disobedience. He boasted much of the forbearance he had exercised toward me, and reminded me that there was a limit to his patience. When I succeeded in avoiding opportunities for him to talk to me at home, I was ordered to come to his office, to do some errand. When there, I was obliged to stand and listen to such language as he saw fit to address to me. Sometimes I so openly expressed my contempt for him that he would become violently enraged, and I wondered why he did not strike me. Circumstanced as he was, he probably thought it was better policy to be forebearing. But the state of things grew worse and worse daily. In desperation I told him that I must and would apply to my grandmother for protection. He threatened me with death, and worse than death, if I made my complaint to her. Strange to say, I did not despair. I was naturally of a buoyant disposition, and always I had a hope of somehow getting out of his clutches. Like many a poor, simple slave before me, I trusted that some threads of joy would yet be woven into my dark destiny.

I had entered my sixteenth year, and every day it became more apparent that my presence was intolerable to Mrs. Flint. Angry words frequently passed between her and her husband. He had never punished me himself, and he would not allow anybody else to punish me. In that respect, she was never satisfied; but, in her angry moods, no terms were too vile for her to bestow upon me. Yet I, whom she detested so bitterly, had far more pity for her than he had, whose duty it was to make her life happy. I never wronged her, or wished to wrong her; and one word of kindness from her would have brought me to her feet.

After repeated quarrels between the doctor and his wife, he announced his intention to take his youngest daughter, then four years old, to sleep in his apartment. It was necessary that a servant should sleep in the same room, to be on hand if the child stirred. I was selected for that office, and informed for what purpose that arrangement had been made. By managing to keep within sight of people, as much as possible, during the daytime, I had hitherto succeeded in eluding my master, though a razor was often held to my throat to force me to change this line of policy. At night I slept by the side of my great aunt, where I felt safe. He was too prudent to come into her room. She was an old woman, and had been in the family many years. Moreover, as a married man, and a professional man, he deemed it necessary to save appearances in some degree. But he resolved to remove the obstacle in the way of his scheme; and he thought he had planned it so that he should evade suspicion. He was well aware how much I prized my refuge by the side of my old aunt, and he determined to dispossess me of it. The first night the doctor had the little child in his room alone. The next morning, I was ordered to take my station as nurse the following night. A kind Providence interposed in my favor. During the day Mrs. Flint heard of this new arrangement, and a storm followed. I rejoiced to hear it rage.

After a while my mistress sent for me to come to her room. Her first question was, "Did you know you were to sleep in the doctor's room?"

"Yes, ma'am."

"Who told you?"

"My master."

"Will you answer truly all the questions I ask?"

"Yes, ma'am."

"Tell me, then, as you hope to be forgiven, are you innocent of what I have accused you?"

"I am."

She handed me a Bible, and said, "Lay your hand on your heart, kiss this holy book, and swear before God that you tell me the truth."

I took the oath she required, and I did it with a clear conscience.

"You have taken God's holy word to testify your innocence," said she. "If you have deceived me, beware! Now take this stool, sit down, look me directly in the face, and tell me all that has passed between your master and you."

I did as she ordered. As I went on with my account her color changed frequently, she wept, and sometimes groaned. She spoke in tones so sad, that I was touched by her grief. The tears came to my eyes; but I was soon convinced that her emotions arose from anger and wounded pride. She felt that her marriage vows were desecrated, her dignity insulted; but she had no compassion for the poor victim of her husband's perfidy. She pitied herself as a martyr; but she was incapable of feeling for the condition of shame and misery in which her unfortunate, helpless slave was placed.

Yet perhaps she had some touch of feeling for me; for when the conference was ended, she spoke kindly, and promised to protect me. I should have been much comforted by this assurance if I could have had confidence in it; but my experiences in slavery had filled me with distrust. She was not a very refined woman, and had not much control over her passions. I was an object of her jealousy, and, consequently, of her hatred; and I knew I could not expect kindness or confidence from her under the circumstances in which I was placed. I could not blame her. Slaveholders' wives feel as other women would under similar circumstances. The fire of her temper kindled from small sparks, and now the flame became so intense that the doctor was obliged to give up his intended arrangement.

I knew I had ignited the torch, and I expected to suffer for it afterward; but I felt too thankful to my mistress for the timely aid she rendered me to care much about that. She now took me to sleep in a room adjoining her own. There I was an object of her especial care, though not of her especial comfort, for she spent many a sleepless night to watch over me. Sometimes I woke up, and found her bending over me. At other times she whispered in my ear, as though it was her husband who was speaking to me, and listened to hear what I would answer. If she startled me, on such occasions, she would glide stealthily away; and the next morning she would tell me I had been talking in my sleep, and ask who I was talking to. At last I began to be fearful for my life. It had been often threatened; and you can imagine, better than I can describe, what an unpleasant sensation it must produce to wake up in the dead of night and find a jealous woman bending over you. Terrible as this experience was, I had fears that it would give place to one more terrible.

My mistress grew weary of her vigils; they did not prove satisfactory. She changed her tactics. She now tried the trick of accusing my master of crime, in my presence, and gave my name as the author of the accusation. To my utter astonishment, he replied, "I don't believe it; but if she did acknowledge it, you tortured her into exposing me." Tortured into exposing him! Truly, Satan had no difficulty in distinguishing the color of his soul! I understood his object in making this false representation. It was to show me that I gained nothing by seeking the protection of my mistress; that the power was still all in his own hands. I pitied Mrs. Flint. She was a second wife, many years the junior of her husband; and the hoary-headed miscreant was enough to try the patience of a wiser and better woman. She was completely foiled, and knew not how to proceed. She would gladly have had me flogged for my supposed false oath; but, as I have already stated, the doctor never allowed anyone to whip me. The old sinner was politic. The application of the lash might have led to remarks that would have exposed him in the eyes of his children and grandchildren. How often did I rejoice that I lived in a town where all the inhabitants knew each other! If I had been on a remote plantation, or lost among the multitude of a crowded city, I should not be a living woman at this day.

The secrets of slavery are concealed like those of the Inquisition. My master was, to my knowledge, the father of eleven slaves. But did the mothers dare to tell who was the father of their children? Did the other slaves dare to allude to it, except in whispers among themselves? No, indeed! They knew too well the terrible consequences.

My grandmother could not avoid seeing things which excited her suspicions. She was uneasy about me, and tried various ways to buy me; but the never-changing answer was always repeated: "Linda does not belong to *me*. She is my daughter's property, and I have no legal right to sell her." The conscientious man! He was too scrupulous to *sell* me; but he had no scruples whatever about committing a much greater wrong against the helpless young girl placed under his guardianship, as his daughter's property. Sometimes my persecutor would ask me whether I would like to be sold. I told him I would rather be sold to anybody than to lead such a life as I did. On such occasions he would assume the air of a very injured individual, and reproach me for my ingratitude. "Did I not take you into the house, and make you the companion of my own children?" he would say. "Have I ever treated you like a Negro? I have never allowed you to be punished, not even to please your mistress. And this is the recompense I get, you ungrateful girl!" I answered that he had reasons of his own for screening me from punishment, and that the course he pursued made my mistress hate me and persecute me. If I wept, he would say, "Poor child! Don't cry! don't cry! I will make peace for you with your mistress. Only let me arrange matters in my own way. Poor, foolish girl! you don't know what is for your own good. I would cherish you. I would make a lady of you. Now go, and think of all I have promised you."

I did think of it.

Reader, I draw no imaginary pictures of southern homes. I am telling you the plain truth. Yet when victims make their escape from this wild beast of Slavery, northerners consent to act the part of bloodhounds, and hunt the poor fugitive back into his den, "full of dead men's bones, and all uncleanness." Nay, more, they are not only willing, but proud, to give their daughters in marriage to slaveholders. The poor girls have romantic notions of a sunny clime, and of the flowering vines that all the year round shade a happy home. To what disappointments are they destined! The young wife soon learns that the husband in whose hands she has placed her happiness pays no regard to his marriage vows. Children of every shade of complexion play with her own fair babies, and too well she knows that they are born unto him of his own household. Jealousy and hatred enter the flowery home, and it is ravaged of its loveliness.

Southern women often marry a man knowing that he is the father of many little slaves. They do not trouble themselves about it. They regard such children as property, as marketable as the pigs on the plantation; and it is seldom that they do not make them aware of this by passing them into the slavetrader's hands as soon as possible, and thus getting them out of their sight. I am glad to say there are some honorable exceptions.

I have myself known two southern wives who exhorted their husbands to free those slaves toward whom they stood in a "parental relation"; and their request was granted. These husbands blushed before the superior nobleness of their wives' natures. Though they had only counseled them to do that which it was their duty to do, it commanded their respect, and rendered their conduct more exemplary. Concealment was at an end, and confidence took the place of distrust.

Though this bad institution deadens the moral sense, even in white women, to a fearful extent, it is not altogether extinct. I have heard southern ladies say of Mr. Such-a-one, "He not only thinks it no disgrace to be the father of those little niggers, but he is not ashamed to call himself their master. I declare, such things ought not to be tolerated in any decent society!"

Suggestions for Discussion

1. Discuss the effectiveness of the author's narrative method. Compare it with that used by Richard Wright.

2. How successfully does she communicate her desperation? How does she do so?

Suggestion for Writing

Write a newspaper editorial commenting on the events reported by Harriet Jacobs.

Martin Luther King, Jr.

I Have a Dream

Martin Luther King, Jr. (1929–1968) was the most charismatic leader of the civil rights movement of the 1950s and 1960s until his assassination in 1968 in Memphis, Tennessee. He led sit-ins and demonstrations throughout the South and was president of the Southern Christian Leadership Conference as well as pastor of a large congregation in Atlanta. He followed the principles of Gandhi and Thoreau in all of his public actions and utterances. This speech, delivered in front of the Lincoln Memorial at a centennial celebration of the Emancipation Proclamation, moves us as deeply on paper today as it did when it was delivered with Martin Luther King's powerful skills of oratory. It points the way to a world free from the burden of racism.

Five score years ago, a great American, in whose symbolic shadow we stand, signed the Emancipation Proclamation. This momentous decree came as a great beacon light of hope to millions of Negro slaves who had been seared in the flames of withering injustice. It came as a joyous daybreak to end the long night of captivity.

But one hundred years later, we must face the tragic fact that the Negro is still not free. One hundred years later, the life of the Negro is still sadly crippled by the manacles of segregation and the chains of discrimination. One hundred years later, the Negro lives on a lonely island of poverty in the midst of a vast ocean of material prosperity. One hundred years later, the Negro is still languished in the corners of American society and finds himself an exile in his own land. So we have come here today to dramatize an appalling condition.

In a sense we have come to our nation's Capital to cash a check. When the architects of our republic wrote the magnificent words of the Constitution and the Declaration of Independence, they were signing a promissory note to which every American was to fall heir. This note was a promise that all men would be guaranteed the unalienable rights of life, liberty, and the pursuit of happiness.

It is obvious today that America has defaulted on this promissory note insofar as her citizens of color are concerned. Instead of honoring this sacred obligation, America has given the Negro people a bad check; a check which has come back marked "insufficient funds." But we refuse to believe that the bank of justice is bankrupt. We refuse to believe that there are insufficient funds in the great vaults of opportunity of this nation. So we have come to cash this check—a check that will give us upon demand the riches of freedom and the security of justice. We have also come to this hallowed spot to remind America of the fierce urgency of *now*. This is no time to engage in the luxury of cooling off or to take the tranquilizing drug of gradualism. *Now* is the time to make real the promises of Democracy. *Now* is the time to rise from the dark and desolate valley of segregation to the sunlit path of racial justice. *Now* is the time to open the doors of opportunity to all of God's children. *Now* is the time to lift our nation from the quicksands of racial injustice to the solid rock of brotherhood.

It would be fatal for the nation to overlook the urgency of the moment and to underestimate the determination of the Negro. This sweltering summer of the Negro's legitimate discontent will not pass until there is an invigorating autumn of freedom and equality. 1963 is not an end, but a beginning. Those who hope that the Negro needed to blow off steam and will now be content will have a rude awakening if the nation returns to business as usual. There will be neither rest nor tranquillity in America until the Negro is granted his citizenship rights. The whirlwinds of revolt will continue to shake the foundations of our nation until the bright day of justice emerges.

But there is something that I must say to my people who stand on the warm threshold which leads into the palace of justice. In the process of gaining our rightful place we must not be guilty of wrongful deeds. Let us not seek to satisfy our thirst for freedom by drinking from the cup of bitterness and hatred. We must forever conduct our struggle on the high plane of dignity and discipline. We must not allow our creative protest to degenerate into physical violence. Again and again we must rise to the majestic heights of meeting physical force with soul force. The marvelous new militancy which has engulfed the Negro community must not lead us to a distrust of all white people, for many of our white brothers, as evidenced by their presence here today, have come to realize that their destiny is tied up with our destiny and their freedom is inextricably bound to our freedom. We cannot walk alone.

And as we walk, we must make the pledge that we shall march ahead. We cannot turn back. There are those who are asking the devotees of civil rights, "When will you be satisfied?" We can never be satisfied as long as the Negro is the victim of the unspeakable horrors of police brutality. We can never be satisfied as long as our bodies, heavy with fatigue of travel, cannot gain lodging in the motels of the highways and the hotels of the cities. We cannot be satisfied as long as the Negro's basic mobility is from a smaller ghetto to a larger one. We can never be satisfied as long as a Negro in Mississippi cannot vote and a Negro in New York believes he has nothing for which to vote. No, no, we are not satisfied, and we will not be satisfied until justice rolls down like waters and righteousness like a mighty stream.

I am not unmindful that some of you have come here out of great trials and tribulations. Some of you have come fresh from narrow jail cells. Some of you have come from areas where your quest for freedom left you battered by the storms of persecution and staggered by the winds of police brutality. You have been the veterans of creative suffering. Continue to work with the faith that unearned suffering is redemptive.

Go back to Mississippi, go back to Alabama, go back to South Carolina, go back to Georgia, go back to Louisiana, go back to the slums and ghettos of our northern cities, knowing that somehow this situation can and will be changed. Let us not wallow in the valley of despair.

I say to you today, my friends, that in spite of the difficulties and frustrations of the moment I still have a dream. It is a dream deeply rooted in the American dream.

I have a dream that one day this nation will rise up and live out the true meaning of its creed: "We hold these truths to be self-evident; that all men are created equal."

I have a dream that one day on the red hills of Georgia the sons of former slaves and the sons of former slaveowners will be able to sit down together at the table of brotherhood.

I have a dream that one day even the state of Mississippi, a desert state sweltering with the heat of injustice and oppression, will be transformed into an oasis of freedom and justice.

I have a dream that my four little children will one day live in a nation where they will not be judged by the color of their skin but by the content of their character.

I have a dream today.

I have a dream that one day the state of Alabama, whose governor's lips are presently dripping with the words of interposition and nullification, will be transformed into a situation where little black boys and black girls will be able to join hands with little white boys and white girls and walk together as sisters and brothers.

I have a dream today.

I have a dream that one day every valley shall be exalted, every hill and mountain shall be made low, the rough places will be made plains, and the crooked places will be made straight, and the glory of the Lord shall be revealed, and all flesh shall see it together.

This is our hope. This is the faith with which I return to the South. With this faith we will be able to hew out of the mountain of despair a stone of hope. With this faith we will be able to transform the jangling discords of our nation into a beautiful symphony of brotherhood. With this faith we will be able to work together, to pray together, to struggle together, to go to jail together, to stand up for freedom together, knowing that we will be free one day.

This will be the day when all of God's children will be able to sing with new meaning

> My country, 'tis of thee,
> Sweet land of liberty,
>   Of thee I sing:
> Land where my fathers died,
> Land of the pilgrims' pride,
> From every mountainside
>   Let freedom ring.

And if America is to be a great nation this must become true. So let freedom ring from the prodigious hilltops of New Hampshire. Let freedom ring from the mighty mountains of New York. Let freedom ring from the heightening Alleghenies of Pennsylvania!

Let freedom ring from the snowcapped Rockies of Colorado!

Let freedom ring from the curvacious peaks of California!

But not only that; let freedom ring from Stone Mountain of Georgia.

Let freedom ring from Lookout Mountain of Tennessee!

Let freedom ring from every hill and molehill of Mississippi. From every mountainside, let freedom ring.

When we let freedom ring, when we let it ring from every village and every hamlet, from every state and every city, we will be able to speed up that day when all of God's children, black men and white men, Jews and Gentiles, Protestants and Catholics, will be able to join hands and sing in the words of the old Negro spiritual, "Free at last! free at last! thank God almighty, we are free at last!"

Suggestions for Discussion

1. What role does repetition play in this speech?

2. Discuss Reverend King's use of the Bible, the spiritual song, and the Declaration of Independence in this speech. How is each source dependent upon the other?

3. It is clear that this selection was designed as an oration. What are its oratorical qualities? Compare it with "Visible Man" by Andrew Hill as a statement on civil rights.

4. Why does King stress pacifism as a means in the struggle for civil rights?

Suggestions for Writing

1. What do you think has been the outcome of King's dream? Write an essay in which you discuss where the dream has been fulfilled and where it has remained unfulfilled.

2. Write a paragraph about the effective use of repetition in King's oration.

E. M. Forster

Jew-Consciousness

Edward Morgan Forster (1879–1970) was a British novelist educated at King's College, Cambridge. He lived for a time in Italy, was a member of the Blooms-bury Group of writers and artists in London, and spent the major part of his life in Cambridge. His works include *Where Angels Fear to Tread* (1905), *A Room With a View* (1908), *Howard's End* (1910), and *A Passage to India* (1924). In this selection (written in 1939) from *Two Cheers for Democracy* (1951) he tends to equate anti-Semitism with the nonsensical ideas which he says were prevalent in his public school days in the nineteenth century. His ironic stance was suitable for the English temperament of 1939. One wonders what he might have said had he known of the Holocaust that was soon to descend on Euro-pean Jewry.

Long, long ago, while Queen Victoria reigned, I attended two preparatory schools. At the first of these, it was held to be a disgrace to have a sister. Any little boy who possessed one was liable to get teased. The word would go round: "Oh, you men, have you seen the Picktoes' sister?" The men would then reel about with sideway motions, uttering cries of "sucks" and pretend-ing to faint with horror, while the Picktoes, who had hitherto held their own socially in spite of their name, found themselves banished into the wilderness, where they mourned. Major with Minor, in common shame. Naturally any-one who had a sister hid her as far as possible, and forbade her to sit with him at a Prizegiving or to speak to him except in passing and in a very formal manner. Public opinion was not bitter on the point, but it was quite definite. Sisters were disgraceful. I got through all right myself, because my conscience was clear, and though charges were brought against me from time to time they always fell through.

It was a very different story at my second school. Here, sisters were neg-ligible, but it was a disgrace to have a mother. Crabbe's mother, Gob's mother, eeugh! No words were too strong, no sounds too shrill. And since mothers at that time of life are commoner than sisters, and also less biddable, the atmosphere of this school was less pleasant, and the sense of guilt stronger. Nearly every little boy had a mother in a cupboard, and dreadful revelations occurred. A boy would fall ill and a mother would swoop and drive him away in a cab. A parcel would arrive with "From Mummy for her darling" branded upon it. Many tried to divert suspicion by being aggressive and fas-tening female parents upon the weak. One or two, who were good at games and had a large popularity-surplus, took up a really heroic line, acknowledged their mother brazenly, and would even be seen walking with her across the playing-field, like King Carol with Madame Lupescu. We admired such boys and envied them, but durst not imitate them. The margin of safety was too narrow. The convention was established that a mother spelt disgrace, and no individual triumph could reverse this.

Those preparatory schools prepared me for life better than I realised, for having passed through two imbecile societies, a sister-conscious and a mother-conscious, I am now invited to enter a third. I am asked to consider whether the people I meet and talk about are or are not Jews, and to form no opinion on them until this fundamental point has been settled. What revolting tosh! Neither science nor religion nor common sense has one word to say in its favour. All the same, Jew-consciousness is in the air, and it remains to be seen how far it will succeed in poisoning it. I don't think we shall ever reintroduce ghettos in England; I wouldn't say for certain, since no one knows what wickedness may not develop in his country or in himself if circumstances change. I don't think we shall go savage. But I do think we shall go silly. Many people have gone so already. Today, the average man suspects the people he dislikes of being Jews, and is surprised when the people he likes are Jews. Having been a Gentile at my first preparatory school and a Jew at my second, I know what I am talking about. I know how the poison works, and I know too that if the average man is anyone in particular he is a preparatory school boy. On the surface, things do not look too bad. Labour and Liberalism behave with their expected decency and denounce persecution, and respectability generally follows suit. But beneath the surface things are not so good, and anyone who keeps his ears open in railway carriages or pubs or country lanes can hear a very different story. A nasty side of our nation's character has been scratched up—the sniggering side. People who would not ill-treat Jews themselves, or even be rude to them, enjoy tittering over their misfortunes; they giggle when pogroms are instituted by someone else and synagogues defiled vicariously. "Serve them right really, Jews." This makes unpleasant reading, but anyone who cares to move out of his own enlightened little corner will discover that it is true. The grand Nordic argument, "He's a bloody capitalist so he must be a Jew, and as he's a Jew he must be a Red," has already taken root in our filling-stations and farms. Men employ it more frequently than women, and young men more frequently than old ones. The best way of confuting it is to say sneeringly, "That's propaganda." When "That's propaganda" has been repeated several times, the sniggering stops, for no goose likes to think that he has been got at. There is another reply which is more intellectual but which requires more courage. It is to say, "Are you sure you're not a Jew yourself? Do you know who your eight great-grand-parents were? Can you swear that all the eight are Aryan?" Cool reasonable-ness would be best of all, of course, but it does not work in the world of today any better than in my preparatory schools. The only effective check to silli-ness is silliness of a cleverer type.

Jew-mania was the one evil which no one foretold at the close of the last war. All sorts of troubles were discerned and discernible—nationalism, class-warfare, the split between the haves and the have-nots, the general lowering of cultural values. But no prophet, so far as I know, had foreseen this anti-Jew horror, whereas today no one can see the end of it. There had been warnings, of course, but they seemed no more ominous than a poem by Hi-laire Belloc. Back in India, in 1921, a Colonel lent me the Protocols of the Elders of Zion, and it was such an obvious fake that I did not worry. I had forgotten my preparatory schools, and did not see that they were about to come into their own. To me, anti-Semitism is now the most shocking of all things. It is destroying much more than the Jews; it is assailing the human mind at its source, and inviting it to create false categories before exercising judgment. I am sure we shall win through. But it will take a long time. Perhaps a hundred years must pass before men can think back to the mentality of 1918, or can say with the Prophet Malachi, "Have we not all one father? Hath not one God created us?" For the moment, all that we can do is to dig in our heels, and prevent silliness from sliding into insanity.

Suggestions for Discussion

1. Discuss the pictures of life in preparatory schools with which Forster opens his essay. What do his comments on "sister-consciousness" and "mother-consciousness" have to do with the rest of the essay?

2. Define what he calls the "grand Nordic argument" against the Jews. What does he mean by "Jew-mania"?

3. In this chapter from *Two Cheers for Democracy* (copyrighted in 1951), Forster refers to "the mentality of 1918." Define that mentality and discuss whether or not it still exists.

Suggestion for Writing

Write an essay discussing how widespread and how serious, in your experience, anti-Semitism is today.

Jonathan Schell

The Choice

Jonathan Schell was born in New York in 1943. His writings for *The New Yorker* have been expanded into books on international and domestic politics. In 1967 he wrote *The Village of Ben Suc* and in 1976 *The Time of Illusion*. In this excerpt from the concluding section of *The Fate of the Earth* (1982), Schell says that our present inaction in the face of possible annihilation is intolerable, and he proposes that we act now if we are to survive.

Four and a half billion years ago, the earth was formed. Perhaps a half billion years after that, life arose on the planet. For the next four billion years, life became steadily more complex, more varied, and more ingenious, until, around a million years ago, it produced mankind—the most complex and in-genious species of them all. Only six or seven thousand years ago—a period that is to the history of the earth as less than a minute is to a year—civilization emerged, enabling us to build up a human world, and to add to the marvels of evolution marvels of our own: marvels of art, of science, of social organization, of spiritual attainment. But, as we built higher and higher, the evolutionary foundation beneath our feet became more and more shaky, and now, in spite of all we have learned and achieved—or, rather, because of it—we hold this entire terrestrial creation hostage to nuclear destruction, threatening to hurl it back into the inanimate darkness from which it came. And this threat of self-destruction and planetary destruction is not something that we will pose one day in the future, if we fail to take certain precautions; it is here now, hanging over the heads of all of us at every moment. The machinery of destruction is complete, poised on a hair trigger, waiting for the "button" to be "pushed" by some misguided or deranged human being or for some faulty computer chip to send out the instruction to fire. That so much should be balanced on so fine a point—that the fruit of four and a half billion years can be undone in a careless moment—is a fact against which belief rebels. And there is another, even vaster measure of the loss, for stretching ahead from our present are more billions of years of life on earth, all of which can be filled not only with human life but with human civilization. The procession of generations that extends onward from our present leads far, far beyond the line of our sight, and, compared with these stretches of human time, which exceed the whole history of the earth up to now, our brief civilized moment is almost infinitesimal. And yet we threaten, in the name of our transient aims and fallible convictions, to foreclose it all. If our species does destroy itself, it will be a death in the cradle—a case of infant mortality. The disparity between the cause and the effect of our peril is so great that our minds seem all but powerless to encompass it. In addition, we are so fully enveloped by that which is menaced, and so deeply and passionately immersed in its events, which are the events of our lives, that we hardly know how to get far enough away from it to see it in its entirety. It is as though life itself were one huge distraction, diverting our attention from the peril to life. In its apparent durability, a world menaced with imminent doom is in a way deceptive. It is almost an illusion. Now we are sitting at the breakfast table drinking our coffee and reading the newspaper, but in a moment we may be inside a fireball whose temperature is tens of thousands of degrees. Now we are on our way to work, walking through the city streets, but in a moment we may be standing on an empty plain under a darkened sky looking for the charred remnants of our children. Now we are alive, but in a moment we may be dead. Now there is human life on earth, but in a moment it may be gone.

Once, there was time to reflect in a more leisurely way on our predicament. In August, 1945, when the invention of the bomb was made known through its first use on a human population, the people of Hiroshima, there lay ahead an interval of decades which might have been used to fashion a world that would be safe from extinction by nuclear arms, and some voices were in fact heard counseling deep reflection on the looming peril and calling for action to head it off. On November 28, 1945, less than four months after the bombing of Hiroshima, the English philosopher Bertrand Russell rose in the House of Lords and said:

> We do not want to look at this thing simply from the point of view of the next few years; we want to look at it from the point of view of the future of mankind. The question is a simple one: Is it possible for a scientific society to

continue to exist, or must such a society inevitably bring itself to destruction? It is a simple question but a very vital one. I do not think it is possible to exaggerate the gravity of the possibilities of evil that lie in the utilization of atomic energy. As I go about the streets and see St. Paul's, the British Museum, the Houses of Parliament, and the other monuments of our civilization, in my mind's eye I see a nightmare vision of those buildings as heaps of rubble with corpses all round them. That is a thing we have got to face, not only in our own country and cities, but throughout the civilized world.

Russell and others, including Albert Einstein, urged full, global disarmament, but the advice was disregarded. Instead, the world set about building the arsenals that we possess today. The period of grace we had in which to ward off the nuclear peril before it became a reality—the time between the moment of the invention of the weapons and the construction of the full-scale machinery for extinction—was squandered, and now the peril that Russell foresaw is upon us. Indeed, if we are honest with ourselves we have to admit that unless we rid ourselves of our nuclear arsenals a holocaust not only *might* occur but *will* occur—if not today, then tomorrow; if not this year, then the next. We have come to live on borrowed time: every year of continued human life on earth is a borrowed year, every day a borrowed day.

In the face of this unprecedented global emergency, we have so far had no better idea than to heap up more and more warheads, apparently in the hope of so thoroughly paralyzing ourselves with terror that we will hold back from taking the final, absurd step. Considering the wealth of our achievement as a species, this response is unworthy of us. Only by a process of gradual debasement of our self-esteem can we have lowered our expectations to this point. For, of all the "modest hopes of human beings," the hope that mankind will survive is the most modest, since it only brings us to the threshold of all the other hopes. In entertaining it, we do not yet ask for justice, or for freedom, or for happiness, or for any of the other things that we may want in life. We do not even necessarily ask for our personal survival; we ask only that we *be survived*. We ask for assurance that when we die as individuals, as we know we must, mankind will live on. Yet once the peril of extinction is present, as it is for us now, the hope for human survival becomes the most tremendous hope, just because it is the foundation for all the other hopes, and in its absence every other hope will gradually wither and die. Life without the hope for human survival is a life of despair.

The death of our species resembles the death of an individual in its boundlessness, its blankness, its removal beyond experience, and its tendency to baffle human thought and feeling, yet as soon as one mentions the hope of survival the similarities are clearly at an end. For while individual death is inevitable, extinction can be avoided; while every person must die, mankind can be saved. Therefore, while reflection on death may lead to resignation and acceptance, reflection on extinction must lead to exactly the opposite response: to arousal, rejection, indignation, and action. Extinction is not something to contemplate, it is something to rebel against. To point this out might seem like stating the obvious if it were not that on the whole the world's reaction to the peril of extinction has been one of numbness and inertia, much as though extinction were as inescapable as death is. Even today, the official response to the sickening reality before us is conditioned by a grim fatalism, in which the hope of ridding the world of nuclear weapons, and thus of surviving as a species, is all but ruled out of consideration as "utopian" or "extreme"—as though it were "radical" merely to want to go on living and to want one's descendants to be born. And yet if one gives up these aspirations one has given up on everything. As a species, we have as yet done nothing to save ourselves. The slate of action is blank. We have organizations for the preservation of almost everything in life that we want but no organization for the preservation of mankind. People seem to have decided that our collective will is too weak or flawed to rise to this occasion. They see the violence that has saturated human history, and conclude that to practice violence is innate in our species. They find the perennial hope that peace can be brought to the earth once and for all a delusion of the well-meaning who have refused to face the "harsh realities" of international life—the realities of self-interest, fear, hatred, and aggression. They have concluded that these realities are eternal ones, and this conclusion defeats at the outset any hope of taking the actions necessary for survival. Looking at the historical record, they ask what has changed to give anyone confidence that humanity can break with its violent past and act with greater restraint. The answer, of course, is that everything has changed. To the old "harsh realities" of international life has been added the immeasurably harsher new reality of the peril of extinction. To the old truth that all men are brothers has been added the inescapable new truth that not only on the moral but also on the physical plane the nation that practices aggression will itself die. This is the law of the doctrine of nuclear deterrence—the doctrine of "mutual assured destruction"—which "assures" the destruction of the society of the attacker. And it is also the law of the natural world, which, in its own version of deterrence, supplements the oneness of mankind with a oneness of nature, and guarantees that when the attack rises above a certain level the attacker will be engulfed in the general ruin of the global ecosphere. To the obligation to honor life is now added the sanction that if we fail in our obligation life will actually be taken away from us, individually and collectively. Each of us will die, and as we die we will see the world around us dying. Such imponderables as the sum of human life, the integrity of the terrestrial creation, and the meaning of time, of history, and of the development of life on earth, which were once left to contemplation and spiritual understanding, are now at stake in the political realm and demand a political response from every person. As political actors, we must, like the contemplatives before us, delve to the bottom of the world, and, Atlas-like, we must take the world on our shoulders.

The self-extinction of our species is not an act that anyone describes as sane or sensible; nevertheless, it is an act that, without quite admitting it to ourselves, we plan in certain circumstances to commit. Being impossible as a fully intentional act, unless the perpetrator has lost his mind, it can come about only through a kind of inadvertence—as a "side effect" of some action that we do intend, such as the defense of our nation, or the defense of liberty, or the defense of socialism, or the defense of whatever else we happen to believe in. To that extent, our failure to acknowledge the magnitude and significance of the peril is a necessary condition for doing the deed. We can do it only if we don't quite know what we're doing. If we did acknowledge the full dimensions of the peril, admitting clearly and without reservation that any use of nuclear arms is likely to touch off a holocaust in which the continuance of all human life would be put at risk, extinction would at that moment become not only "unthinkable" but also undoable. What is needed to make extinction possible, therefore, is some way of thinking about it that at least partly deflects our attention from what it is. And this way of thinking is supplied to us, unfortunately, by our political and military traditions, which, with the weight of almost all historical experience behind them, teach us that it is the way of the world for the earth to be divided up into independent, sovereign states, and for these states to employ war as the final arbiter for settling the disputes that arise among them. This arrangement of the political affairs of the world was not intentional. No one wrote a book proposing it; no parliament sat down to debate its merits and then voted it into existence. It was simply there, at the beginning of recorded history; and until the invention of nuclear weapons it remained there, with virtually no fundamental changes. Unplanned though this arrangement was, it had many remarkably durable features, and certain describable advantages and disadvantages; therefore, I shall refer to it as a "system"—the system of sovereignty. Perhaps the leading feature of this system, and certainly the most important one in the context of the nuclear predicament, was the apparently indissoluble connection between sovereignty and war. For without sovereignty, it appeared, peoples were not able to organize and launch wars against other peoples, and without war they were unable to preserve their sovereignty from destruction by armed enemies. (By "war" I here mean only international war, not revolutionary war, which I shall not discuss.) Indeed, the connection between sovereignty and war is almost a definitional one—a sovereign state being a state that enjoys the right and the power to go to war in defense or pursuit of its interests.

It was into the sovereignty system that nuclear bombs were born, as "weapons" for "war." As the years have passed, it has seemed less and less plausible that they have anything to do with war; they seem to break through its bounds. Nevertheless, they have gone on being fitted into military categories of thinking. One might say that they appeared in the world in a military disguise, for it has been traditional military thinking, itself an inseparable part of the traditional political thinking that belonged to the system of sovereignty, that has provided those intentional goals—namely, national interests—in the pursuit of which extinction may now be brought about unintentionally, or semi-intentionally, as a "side effect." The system of sovereignty is now to the earth and mankind what a polluting factory is to its local environment. The machine produces certain things that its users want—in this case, national sovereignty—and as unhappy side effect extinguishes the species.

The ambivalence resulting from the attempt to force nuclear weapons into the pre-existing military and political system has led to a situation in which, in the words of Einstein—who was farseeing in his political as well as in his scientific thought—"the unleashed power of the atom has changed everything save our modes of thinking, and we thus drift toward unparalleled catastrophes." As Einstein's observation suggests, the nuclear revolution has gone quite far but has not been completed. The question we have to answer is whether the completion will be extinction or a global political revolution—whether the "babies" that the scientists at Alamogordo brought forth will put an end to us or we will put an end to them. For it is not only our thoughts but also our actions and our institutions—our global political arrangements in their entirety—that we have failed to change. We live with one foot in each of two worlds. As scientists and technicians, we live in the nuclear world, in which whether we choose to acknowledge the fact or not, we possess instruments of violence that make it possible for us to extinguish ourselves as a species. But as citizens and statesmen we go on living in the prenuclear world, as though extinction were not possible and sovereign nations could still employ the instruments of violence as instruments of policy—as "a continuation of politics by other means," in the famous phrase of Karl von Clausewitz, the great philosopher of war. In effect, we try to make do with a Newtonian politics in an Einsteinian world. The combination is the source of our immediate peril. For governments, still acting within a system of independent nation-states, and formally representing no one but the people of their separate, sovereign nations, are driven to try to defend merely national interests with means of destruction that threaten not only international but intergenerational and planetary doom. In our present-day world, in the councils where the decisions are made there is no one to speak for man and for the earth, although both are threatened with annihilation.

The dilemma of the nation that in order to protect its national sovereignty finds that it must put the survival of mankind at risk is a trap from which there is no escape as long as nations possess arsenals of nuclear weapons. The deterrence doctrine seeks to rationalize this state of affairs, but it fails, because at the crucial moment it requires nations to sacrifice mankind for their own interests—an absurdity as well as a crime beyond reckoning. Indeed, the deterrence doctrine actually almost *compels* the world to live perpetually on the brink of doom, for any nation that took a step or two back would put its interests and, ultimately, its independence at the mercy of the military forces of its adversaries. And although, for any number of reasons, an adversary might not press its advantage (as, for example, the United States did not right after the Second World War, when it possessed a monopoly of nuclear weapons), no nation has yet volunteered to put itself at this competitive disadvantage. It appears that the only way to escape from the trap is to change the system, and take away from nuclear weapons the responsibility for defending nations. But unless one supposes that, in a global spread of quietism, nations and people in general are going to give up the pursuit of their interests and their ideals and become wholly inactive, this separation can be achieved only if a new way—a nonviolent way—of making and guaranteeing these decisions is found.

In the decades since nuclear arms first appeared in the world, the doctrine of nuclear deterrence has commanded the sincere respect and adherence of many people of good will—especially when they found themselves arguing, as they so often did, with the adherents of traditional military doctrine, who even today, in the face of extinction itself, go on arguing for "military superiority" and the like. And if one once accepts the existence of the doomsday machine, then deterrence theory, however flawed, does offer the hope of certain benefits, the main one being a degree of "stability." Therefore, the perpetual struggle of its adherents against the sheer lunacy of "fighting a nuclear war" is a creditable one. But the fundamental truth about the doctrine and about its role in the wider political—and, it must be added, biological—scheme of things also has to be recognized. For the doctrine's central claim—that it deploys nuclear weapons only in order to prevent their use—is simply not true. Actually, it deploys them to protect national sovereignty, and if this aim were not present they could be quickly dismantled. The doctrine, then, has been the intellectual screen behind which the doomsday machine was built. And its deceptive claim that only by building nuclear weapons can we save ourselves from nuclear weapons lent the doomsday machine a veneer of reason and of respectability—almost of benevolence—that it should never have been given. For to build this machine at all was a mistake of the hugest proportions ever known—without question the greatest ever made by our species. The only conceivable worse mistake would be to put the machine to use. Now deterrence, having rationalized the construction of the machine, weds us to it, and, at best, offers us, if we are lucky, a slightly extended term of residence on earth before the inevitable human or mechanical mistake occurs and we are annihilated.

Yet the deterrence policy in itself is clearly not the deepest source of our difficulty. Rather, as we have seen, it is only a piece of repair work on the immeasurably more deeply entrenched system of national sovereignty. People do not want deterrence for its own sake; indeed, they hardly know what it is, and tend to shun the whole subject. They want the national sovereignty that deterrence promises to preserve. National sovereignty lies at the very core of the political issues that the peril of extinction forces upon us. Sovereignty is the "reality" that the "realists" counsel us to accept as inevitable, referring to any alternative as "unrealistic" or "utopian." If the argument about nuclear weapons is to be conducted in good faith, then just as those who favor the deterrence policy (not to speak of traditional military doctrine) must in all honesty admit that their scheme contemplates the extinction of man in the name of protecting national sovereignty, so must those who favor complete nuclear and conventional disarmament, as I do, admit that their recommendation is inconsistent with national sovereignty; to pretend otherwise would be to evade the political question that is central to the nuclear predicament. The terms of the deal that the world has now struck with itself must be made clear. On the one side stand human life and the terrestrial creation. On the other side stands a particular organization of human life—the system of independent, sovereign nation-states. Our choice so far has been to preserve that political organization of human life at the cost of risking all human life. We are told that "realism" compels us to preserve the system of sovereignty. But that political realism is not biological realism; it is biological nihilism—and for that reason is, of course, political nihilism, too. Indeed, it is nihilism in every conceivable sense of that word. We are told that it is human fate—perhaps even "a law of human nature"—that, in obedience, perhaps, to some "territorial imperative," or to some dark and ineluctable truth in the bottom of our souls, we must preserve sovereignty and always settle our differences with violence. If this is our fate, then it is our fate to die. But must we embrace nihilism? Must we die? Is self-extermination a law of our nature? Is there nothing we can do? I do not believe so. Indeed, if we admit the reality of the basic terms of the nuclear predicament—that present levels of global armament are great enough to possibly extinguish the species if a holocaust should occur; that in extinction every human purpose would be lost; that because once the species has been extinguished there will be no second chance, and the game will be over for all time; that therefore this possibility must be dealt with morally and politically as though it were a certainty; and that either by accident or by design a holocaust can occur at any second—then, whatever political views we may hold on other matters, we are driven almost inescapably to take action to rid the world of nuclear arms. Just as we have chosen to make nuclear weapons, we can choose to unmake them. Just as we have chosen to live in the system of sovereign states, we can choose to live in some other system. To do so would, of course, be unprecedented, and in many ways frightening, even truly perilous, but it is by no means impossible. Our present system and the institutions that make it up are the debris of history. They have become inimical to life, and must be swept away. They constitute a noose around the neck of mankind, threatening to choke off the human future, but we can cut the noose and break free. To suppose otherwise would be to set up a false, fictitious fate, molded out of our own weaknesses and our own alterable decisions. We are indeed fated by our acquisition of the basic knowledge of physics to live for the rest of time with the knowledge of how to destroy ourselves. But we are not for that reason fated to destroy ourselves. We can choose to live.

Suggestions for Discussion

1. In the first paragraph, Schell says "that the fruit of four and a half billion years can be undone in a careless moment . . . is a fact against which belief rebels." How does this comment prepare us for what follows in the rest of the paragraph? in the rest of the essay?

2. Why, according to Schell, did Russell and Einstein urge full global disarmament? Why was their advice not followed? What have governments done instead?

3. Why does Schell say that merely wanting "to go on living" is regarded as "radical" or "extreme"?

4. Compare the point Schell makes about the dangers of sovereignty with the point made by Milton Mayer's essay, "A World Without Government."

5. What are the inherent difficulties and self-contradictions of trying to live in the prenuclear and the nuclear world at the same time?

6. Schell ends with the sentence, "We can choose to live." Is this an effective ending? What does choosing to live imply as a course of action?

Suggestions for Writing

1. Write an essay in which you discuss Schell's statement, "Life without hope for human survival is a life of despair." Relate the force of this statement to the alternatives which Schell offers.

2. Schell states that nuclear weapons are actually not military weapons. Write an essay agreeing or disagreeing with his position. You should entertain the notion of a limited nuclear war.

◇◇◇◇

George Orwell
The Principles of Newspeak

George Orwell (1903–1950), pseudonym of Eric Arthur Blair, a British writer with socialist sympathies, wrote essays and novels based on his experiences as a British imperial policeman in Burma, as an impoverished writer in Paris and London, and as a volunteer in the republican army in the Spanish Civil War. He was for a few years the editor of the magazine of the British Labour Party. Although his essays and letters are considered masterpieces of prose style, he is probably best known for the satirical anticommunist fable *Animal Farm* (1945) and for the novel *1984* published in 1949. Orwell conceived a terrifying vision of a future where mechanized language and thought have become the tools of a totalitarian society. This essay, written as an appendix to *1984*, presents "Newspeak," the official language of Oceania, as the logical outcome and instrument of a repressive government. It also suggests the Newspeak has its basis in what Orwell considered our degradation of the English language.

Newspeak was the official language of Oceania and had been devised to meet the ideological needs of Ingsoc, or English Socialism. In the year 1984 there was not as yet anyone who used Newspeak as his sole means of communication, either in speech or writing. The leading articles in the *Times* were written in it, but this was a tour de force which could only be carried out by a specialist. It was expected that Newspeak would have finally superseded Oldspeak (or Standard English, as we should call it) by about the year 2050. Meanwhile it gained ground steadily, all Party members tending to use Newspeak words and grammatical constructions more and more in their everyday speech. The version in use in 1984, and embodied in the Ninth and Tenth Editions of the Newspeak dictionary, was a provisional one, and contained many superfluous words and archaic formations which were due to be suppressed later. It is with the final, perfected version, as embodied in the Eleventh Edition of the dictionary, that we are concerned here.

The purpose of Newspeak was not only to provide a medium of expression for the world-view and mental habits proper to the devotees of Ingsoc, but to make all other modes of thought impossible. It was intended that when Newspeak had been adopted once and for all and Oldspeak forgotten, a heretical thought—that is, a thought diverging from the principles of Ingsoc—should be literally unthinkable, at least so far as thought is dependent on words. Its vocabulary was so constructed as to give exact and often very subtle expression to every meaning that a Party member could properly wish to express, while excluding all other meanings and also the possibility of arriving at them by indirect methods. This was done partly by the invention of new words, but chiefly by eliminating undesirable words and by stripping such words as remained of unorthodox meanings, and so far as possible of all secondary meanings whatever. To give a single example. The word *free* still existed in Newspeak, but it could only be used in such statements as "This dog is free from lice" or "This field is free from weeds." It could not be used in its old sense of "politically free" or "intellectually free," since political and intellectual freedom no longer existed even as concepts, and were therefore of necessity nameless. Quite apart from the suppression of definitely heretical works, reduction of vocabulary was regarded as an end in itself, and no word that could be dispensed with was allowed to survive. Newspeak was designed not to extend but to *diminish* the range of thought, and this purpose was indirectly assisted by cutting the choice of words down to a minimum.

Newspeak was founded on the English language as we now know it, though many Newspeak sentences, even when not containing newly created words, would be barely intelligible to an English-speaker of our own day. Newspeak words were divided into three distinct classes, known as the A vocabulary, the B vocabulary (also called compound words), and the C vocabulary. It will be simpler to discuss each class separately, but the grammatical peculiarities of the language can be dealt with in the section devoted to the A vocabulary, since the same rules held good for all three categories.

The A vocabulary. The A vocabulary consisted of the words needed for the business of everyday life—for such things as eating, drinking, working, putting on one's clothes, going up and down stairs, riding in vehicles, gardening, cooking, and the like. It was composed almost entirely of words that we already possess—words like *hit, run, dog, tree, sugar, house, field*—but in comparison with the present-day English vocabulary, their number was extremely small, while their meanings were far more rigidly defined. All ambiguities and shades of meaning had been purged out of them. So far as it could be achieved, a Newspeak word of this class was simply a staccato sound expressing *one* clearly understood concept. It would have been quite impossible to use the A vocabulary for literary purposes or for political or philosophical discussion. It was intended only to express simple, purposive thoughts, usually involving concrete objects or physical actions.

The grammar of Newspeak had two outstanding peculiarities. The first of these was an almost complete interchangeability between different parts of speech. Any word in the language (in principle this applied even to very abstract words such as *if* or *when*) could be used either as verb, noun, adjective, or adverb. Between the verb and the noun form, when they were of the same root, there was never any variation, this rule of itself involving the destruction of many archaic forms. The word *thought*, for example, did not exist in Newspeak. Its place was taken by *think*, which did duty for both noun and verb. No etymological principle was involved here; in some cases it was the original noun that was chosen for retention, in other cases the verb. Even where a noun and a verb of kindred meaning were not etymologically connected, one or other of them was frequently suppressed. There was, for example, no such word as *cut*, its meaning being sufficiently covered by the noun-verb *knife*. Adjectives were formed by adding the suffix *-ful* to the noun-verb, and adverbs by adding *-wise*. Thus, for example, *speedful* meant "rapid" and *speedwise* meant "quickly." Certain of our present-day adjectives, such as *good, strong, big, black, soft*, were retained, but their total number was very small. There was little need for them, since almost any adjectival meaning could be arrived at by adding *-ful* to a noun-verb. None of the now-existing adverbs was retained, except for a very few already ending in *-wise*; the *-wise* termination was invariable. The word *well*, for example, was replaced by *goodwise*.

In addition, any word—this again applied in principle to every word in the language—could be negatived by adding the affix *un-*, or could be strengthened by the affix *plus-*, or, for still greater emphasis, *doubleplus-*. Thus, for example, *uncold* meant "warm," while *pluscold* and *doublepluscold* meant, respectively, "very cold" and "superlatively cold." It was also possible, as in present-day English, to modify the meaning of almost any word by prepositional affixes such as *ante-*, *post-*, *up-*, *down-*, etc. By such methods it was found possible to bring about an enormous diminution of vocabulary. Given, for instance, the word *good*, there was no need for such a word as bad, since the required meaning was equally well—indeed, better—expressed by *ungood*. All that was necessary, in any case where two words formed a natural pair of opposites, was to decide which of them to suppress. *Dark*, for example, could be replaced by *unlight*, or *light* by *undark*, according to preference.

The second distinguishing mark of Newspeak grammar was its regularity. Subject to a few exceptions which are mentioned below, all inflections followed the same rules. Thus, in all verbs the preterite and the past participle were the same and ended in *-ed*. The preterite of *steal* was *stealed*, the preterite of *think* was *thinked*, and so on throughout the language, all such forms as *swam, gave, brought, spoke, taken*, etc., being abolished. All plurals were made by adding *-s* or *-es* as the case might be. The plurals of *man, ox, life* were *mans, oxes, lifes*. Comparison of adjectives was invariably made by adding *-er, -est* (*good, gooder, goodest*), irregular forms and the *more, most* formation being suppressed.

The only classes of words that were still allowed to inflect irregularly were the pronouns, the relatives, the demonstrative adjectives, and the auxiliary verbs. All of these followed their ancient usage, except that *whom* had been scrapped as unnecessary, and the *shall, should* tenses had been dropped, all their uses being covered by *will* and *would*. There were also certain irregularities in word-formation arising out of the need for rapid and easy speech. A word which was difficult to utter, or was liable to be incorrectly heard, was held to be ipso facto a bad word; occasionally therefore, for the sake of euphony, extra letters were inserted into a word or an archaic formation was retained. But this need made itself felt chiefly in connection with the B vocabulary. *Why* so great an importance was attached to ease of pronunciation will be made clear later in this essay.

The B vocabulary. The B vocabulary consisted of words which had been deliberately constructed for political purposes: words, that is to say, which not only had in every case a political implication, but were intended to impose a desirable mental attitude upon the person using them. Without a full understanding of the principles of Ingsoc it was difficult to use these words correctly. In some cases they could be translated into Oldspeak, or even into words taken from the A vocabulary, but this usually demanded a long paraphrase and always involved the loss of certain overtones. The B words were a sort of verbal shorthand, often packing whole ranges of ideas into a few syllables, and at the same time more accurate and forcible than ordinary language.

The B words were in all cases compound words.* They consisted of two or

---

*Compound words, such as *speakwrite*, were of course to be found in the A vocabulary, but these were merely convenient abbreviations and had no special ideological color.

more words, or portions of words, welded together in an easily pronounceable form. The resulting amalgam was always a noun-verb, and inflected according to the ordinary rules. To take a single example: the word *goodthink*, meaning, very roughly, "orthodoxy," or, if one chose to regard it as a verb, "to think in an orthodox manner." This inflected as follows: noun-verb, *goodthink;* past tense and past participle, *goodthinked;* present participle, *goodthinking;* adjective, *goodthinkful;* adverb, *goodthinkwise;* verbal noun, *goodthinker.*

The B words were not constructed on any etymological plan. The words of which they were made up could be any parts of speech, and could be placed in any order and mutilated in any way which made them easy to pronounce while indicating their derivation. In the word *crimethink* (thoughtcrime), for instance, the *think* came second, whereas in *thinkpol* (Thought Police) it came first, and in the latter word police had lost its second syllable. Because of the greater difficulty in securing euphony, irregular formations were commoner in the B vocabulary than in the A vocabulary. For example, the adjectival forms of *Minitrue, Minipax,* and *Miniluv* were, respectively, *Minitruthful, Minipeaceful,* and *Minilovely,* simply because *-trueful, paxful, and loveful* were slightly awkward to pronounce. In principle, however, all B words could inflect, and all inflected in exactly the same way.

Some of the B words had highly subtilized meanings, barely intellibible to anyone who had not mastered the language as a whole. Consider, for example, such a typical sentence from a *Times* leading article as *Oldthinkers unbellyfeel Ingsoc.* The shortest rendering that one could make of this in Oldspeak would be: "Those whose ideas were formed before the Revolution cannot have a full emotional understanding of the principles of English Socialism." But this is not an adequate translation. To begin with, in order to grasp the full meaning of the Newspeak sentence quoted above, one would have to have a clear idea of what is meant by *Ingsoc.* And, in addition, only a person thoroughly grounded in Ingsoc could appreciate the full force of the word *bellyfeel,* which implied a blind, enthusiastic acceptance difficult to imagine today; or of the word *oldthink,* which was inextricably mixed up with the idea of wickedness and decadence. But the special function of certain Newspeak words, of which *oldthink* was one, was not so much to express meanings as to destroy them. These words, necessarily few in number, had had their meanings extended until they contained within themselves whole batteries of words which, as they were sufficiently covered by a single comprehensive term, could now be scrapped and forgotten. The greatest difficulty facing the compilers of the Newspeak dictionary was not to invent new words, but, having invented them, to make sure what they meant: to make sure, that is to say, what ranges of words they canceled by their existence.

As we have already seen in the case of the word *free,* words which had once borne a heretical meaning were sometimes retained for the sake of convenience, but only with the undesirable meanings purged out of them. Countless other words such as *honor, justice, morality, internationalism, democracy, science,* and *religion* had simply ceased to exist. A few blanket words covered them, and, in covering them, abolished them. All words grouping themselves round the concepts of liberty and equality, for instance, were contained in the single word *crimethink,* while all words grouping themselves round the concepts of objectivity and rationalism were contained in the single word *oldthink.* Greater precision would have been dangerous. What was required in a Party member was an outlook similar to that of the ancient Hebrew who knew, without knowing much else, that all nations other than his own worshipped "false gods." He did not need to know that these gods were called Baal, Osiris, Moloch, Ashtaroth, and the like; probably the less he knew about them the better for his orthodoxy. He knew Jehovah and the commandments of Jehovah; he knew, therefore, that all gods with other names or other attributes were false gods. In somewhat the same way, the Party member knew what constituted right conduct, and in exceedingly vague, generalized terms he knew what kinds of departure from it were possible. His sexual life, for example, was entirely regulated by the two Newspeak words *sexcrime* (sexual immorality) and *goodsex* (chastity). *Sexcrime* covered all sexual misdeeds whatever. It covered fornication, adultery, homosexuality, and other perversions, and in addition, normal intercourse practiced for its own sake. There was no need to enumerate them separately, since they were all equally culpable, and, in principle, all punishable by death. In the C vocabulary, which consisted of scientific and technical words, it might be necessary to give specialized names to certain sexual aberrations, but the ordinary citizen had no need of them. He knew what was meant by *goodsex*—that is to say, normal intercourse between man and wife, for the sole purpose of begetting children, and without physical pleasure on the part of the woman; all else was *sexcrime*. In Newspeak it was seldom possible to follow a heretical thought further than the perception that it *was* heretical; beyond that point the necessary words were nonexistent.

No word in the B vocabulary was ideologically neutral. A great many were euphemisms. Such words, for instance, as *joycamp* (forced-labor camp) or *Minipax* (Ministry of Peace, i. e., Ministry of War) meant almost the exact opposite of what they appeared to mean. Some words, on the other hand, displayed a frank and contemptuous understanding of the real nature of Oceanic society. An example was *prolefeed*, meaning the rubbishy entertainment and spurious news which the Party handed out to the masses. Other words, again, were ambivalent, having the connotation "good" when applied to the Party and "bad" when applied to its enemies. But in addition there were great numbers of words which at first sight appeared to be mere abbreviations and which derived their ideological color not from their meaning but from their structure.

So far as it could be contrived, everything that had or might have political significance of any kind was fitted into the B vocabulary. The name of every organization, or body of people, or doctrine, or country, or institution, or public building, was invariably cut down into the familiar shape; that is, a single easily pronounced word with the smallest number of syllables that would preserve the original derivation. In the Ministry of Truth, for example, the Records Department, in which Winston Smith worked, was called *Recdep*, the Fiction Department was called *Ficdep*, the Teleprograms Department was called *Teledep*, and so on. This was not done solely with the object of saving time. Even in the early decades of the twentieth century, telescoped words and phrases had been one of the characteristic features of political language; and it had been noticed that the tendency to use abbreviations of this kind was most marked in totalitarian countries and totalitarian organizations. Examples were such words as *Nazi, Gestapo, Comintern, Inprecorr, Agitprop*. In the beginning the practice had been adopted as it were instinctively, but in Newspeak it was used with a conscious purpose. It was perceived that in thus abbreviating a name one narrowed and subtly altered its meaning, by cutting out most of the associations that would otherwise cling to it. The words *Communist International*, for instance, call up a composite picture of universal human brotherhood, red flags, barricades, Karl Marx, and the Paris Commune. The word Comintern, on the other hand, suggests merely a tightly knit organization and a well-defined body of doctrine. It refers to something almost as easily recognized, and as limited in purpose, as a chair or a table. *Comintern* is a word that can be uttered almost without taking thought, whereas *Comminust International* is a phrase over which one is obliged to linger at least momentarily. In the same way, the associations called up by a word like *Minitrue* are fewer and more controllable that those called up by *Ministry of Truth*. This accounted not only for the habit of ab-breviating whenever possible, but also for the almost exaggerated care that was taken to make every word easily pronounceable.

In Newspeak, euphony outweighed every consideration other than exacti-tude of meaning. Regularity of grammar was always sacrificed to it when it seemed necessary. And rightly so, since what was required, above all for po-litical purposes, were short clipped words of unmistakable meaning which could be uttered rapidly and which roused the minimum of echoes in the speaker's mind. The words of the B vocabulary even gained in force from the fact that nearly all of them were very much alike. Almost invariably these words—*goodthink, Minipax, prolefeed, sexcrime, joycamp, Ingsoc, bellyfeel, thinkpol,* and countless others—were words of two or three syllables, with the stress distributed equally between the first syllable and the last. The use of them encouraged a gabbling style of speech, at once staccato and monoto-nous. And this was exactly what was aimed at. The intention was to make speech, and especially speech on any subject not ideologically neutral, as nearly as possible independent of consciousness. For that purpose of everyday life it was no doubt necessary, or sometimes necessary, to reflect before speaking, but a Party member called upon to make a political or ethical judg-ment should be able to spray forth the correct opinions as automatically as a machine gun spraying forth bullets. His training fitted him to do this, the language gave him an almost foolproof instrument, and the texture of the words, with their harsh sound and a certain willful ugliness which was in accord with the spirit of Ingsoc, assisted the process still further.

So did the fact of having very few words to choose from. Relative to our own, the Newspeak vocabulary was tiny, and new ways of reducing it were constantly being devised. Newspeak, indeed, differed from almost all other languages in that its vocabulary grew smaller instead of larger every year. Each reduction was a gain, since the smaller the area of choice, the smaller the temptation to take thought. Ultimately it was hoped to make articulate speech issue from the larynx without involving the higher brain centers at all. This aim was frankly admitted in the Newspeak word *duckspeak,* meaning "to quack like a duck." Like various other words in the B vocabulary, *duckspeak* was ambivalent in meaning. Provided that the opinions which were quacked out were orthodox ones, it implied nothing but praise, and when the *Times* referred to one of the orators of the Party as a *double-plusgood duckspeaker* it was paying a warm and valued compliment.

The C vocabulary. The C vocabulary was supplementary to the others and consisted entirely of scientific and technical terms. These resembled the scientific terms in use today, and were constructed from the same roots, but the usual care was taken to define them rigidly and strip them of undesirable meanings. They followed the same grammatical rules as the words in the other two vocabularies. Very few of the C words had any currency either in everyday speech or in political speech. Any scientific worker or technician could find all the words he needed in the list devoted to his own speciality, but he seldom had more than a smattering of the words occurring in the other lists. Only a very few words were common to all lists, and there was no vocabulary expressing the function of Science as a habit of mind, or a method of thought, irrespective of its particular branches. There was, indeed, no word for "Science," any meaning that it could possibly bear being already sufficiently covered by the word *Ingsoc.*

From the foregoing account it will be seen that in Newspeak the expression of unorthodox opinions, above a very low level, was well-nigh impossible. It was of course possible to utter heresies of a very crude kind, a species of blasphemy. It would have been possible, for example, to say *Big Brother is ungood.* But this statement, which to an orthodox ear merely conveyed a self-evident absurdity, could not have been sustained by reasoned argument, because the necessary words were not available. Ideas inimical to Ingsoc could only be entertained in a vague wordless form, and could only be named in very broad terms which lumped together and condemned whole groups of heresies without defining them in doing so. One could, in fact, only use Newspeak for unorthodox purposes by illegitimately translating some of the words back into Oldspeak. For example, *All mans are equal* was a possible Newspeak sentence, but only in the same sense in which *All men are red-haired* is a possible Oldspeak sentence. It did not contain a grammatical error, but it expressed a palpable untruth, i.e., that all men are of equal size, weight, or strength. The concept of political equality no longer existed, and the secondary meaning had accordingly been purged out of the word *equal.* In 1984, when Oldspeak was still the normal means of communication, the danger theoretically existed that in using Newspeak words one might remember their original meanings. In practice it was not difficult for any person well grounded in *doublethink* to avoid doing this, but within a couple of generations even the possibility of such a lapse would have vanished. A person growing up with Newspeak as his sole language would no more know that *equal* had once had the secondary meaning of "politically equal," or that *free* had once meant "intellectually free," than, for instance, a person who had never heard of chess would be aware of the secondary meanings attaching to *queen* and *rook.* There would be many crimes and errors which it would be beyond his power to commit, simply because they were nameless and therefore unimaginable. And it was to be foreseen that with the passage of time the distinguishing characteristics of Newspeak would become more and more pronounced—its words growing fewer and fewer, their meanings more and more rigid, and the chance of putting them to improper uses always diminishing.

When Oldspeak had been once and for all superseded, the last link with the past would have been severed. History had already been rewritten, but fragments of the literature of the past survived here and there, imperfectly censored, and so long as one retained one's knowledge of Oldspeak it was possible to read them. In the future such fragments, even if they chanced to survive, would be unintelligible and untranslatable. It was impossible to translate any passage of Oldspeak into Newspeak unless it either referred to some techincal process or some very simple everyday action, or was already orthodox (*goodthinkful* would be the Newspeak expression) in tendency. In practice this meant that no book written before approximately 1960 could be translated as a whole. Prerevolutionary literature could only be subjected to ideological translation—that is, alteration in sense as well as language. Take for example the well-known passage from the Declaration of Independence:

> *We hold these truths to be self-evident, that all men are created equal, that they are endowed by their Creator with certain inalienable rights, that among these are life, liberty and the pursuit of happiness. That to secure these rights, Governments are instituted among men, deriving their powers from the consent of the governed. That whenever any form of Government becomes destructive of those ends, it is the right of the People to alter or abolish it, and to institute new Government . . .*

It would have been quite impossible to render this into Newspeak while keeping to the sense of the original. The nearest one could come to doing so would be to swallow the whole passage up in the single word *crimethink*. A full translation could only be an ideological translation, whereby Jefferson's words would be changed into a panegyric on absolute government.

A good deal of the literature of the past was, indeed, already being transformed in this way. Considerations of prestige made it desirable to preserve the memory of certain historical figures, while at the same time bringing their achievements into line with the philosophy of Ingsoc. Various writers, such as Shakespeare, Milton, Swift, Byron, Dickens, and some others were therefore in process of translation; when the task had been completed, their original writings, with all else that survived of the literature of the past, would be destroyed. These translations were a slow and difficult business, and it was not expected that they would be finished before the first or second decade of the twenty-first century. There were also large quantities of merely utilitarian literature—indispensable technical manuals and the like—that had to be treated in the same way. It was chiefly in order to allow time for the preliminary work of translation that the final adoption of Newspeak had been fixed for so late a date as 2050.

Suggestions for Discussion

1. Explain Orwell's statement that Newspeak was designed to "diminish the range of thought." How does he demonstrate this statement by the use of the word *free?*

2. Summarize the uses of the A Vocabulary. Contrast it with present-day English and discuss the former's use of the parts of speech. Why are verbs usually suppressed? Why were most existing adverbs abolished? Why were all noun plurals formed by adding *-s* or *-es?*

3. Define the B Vocabulary. What were its uses? Discuss the examples given, particularly the sentence, "Oldthinkers unbellyfeel Ingsoc."

4. What difficulties faced the compilers of the Newspeak dictionary?

5. What are the precedents for Newspeak word combinations such as *Recdep* and *Ficdep?* What comment on current standard English does Orwell make here?

6. How does the word *duckspeak* symbolize the purpose of Newspeak?

7. What are the uses of the C Vocabulary? Why did the word *science* cease to exist?

8. Discuss the sentences, "Big Brother is ungood" and "All mans are equal" as examples of Newspeak.

9. What is the Newspeak equivalent of the opening passage of the Declaration of Independence? Discuss Orwell's reasons for inventing this translation. Relate the translation to the entire essay.

Suggestions for Writing

1. Examine your local newspaper for examples of words that resemble Newspeak and write an essay discussing the reasons for your choice.

2. Write an essay explaining how Newspeak is an instrument of power. Why is it a necessary ideal of Oceania? Discuss some words or sentences from contemporary political speeches or essays which come close to Newspeak.

Rebecca West

The Meaning of Treason

Rebecca West (1892–1983) was born in Ireland. She was briefly an actress until she began to write on politics for the London press. She was the author of several novels, but her two most successful works were *Black Lamb and Gray Falcon*, a study of Jugoslavia published in 1941 and her penetrating account of the treason trials after the defeat of Germany in the second World War. The following essay from *Harper's Magazine*, October 1947, became the epilogue to her book *The Meaning of Treason* (1947). In it she explains how easy the descent was into treason when patriotism was undermined by prevailing attitudes of internationalism, and when commitment to one's own land became subservient to commitment to an idea or an ideal.

From time to time during my career as a journalist I have reported notable law cases, and I know that it is not only morbidity which makes the public enjoy following the trial of a serious crime. It is very difficult for those who study life to find a story that comes to its end under their eyes. When we select an individual whose course we want to trace, it is as likely as not that he covers his tracks with secrecy, or moves to a field outside our view, or delays his end until we ourselves have ended. That is why classical history is a valuable study; we can see the whole story, the beginning, the middle, and the end of Greece and Rome, Egypt and Persia. That is why the lives of great men in the past teach us more than knowledge of great men in the present; we know their remoter consequences. The dock brings a like illumination.

Here an individual story comes to its end in a collision with the community. Every case has its unique intellectual and spiritual significance. The appearance of the accused person, the changes in his face and voice, his agreement with society as disclosed by the witnesses who approve of him, his conflict with society as disclosed by the witnesses who disapprove of him, his relation to the crime of which he is truly or falsely accused, always reveal a special case. But the crime which he committed, if he was justly accused, or the other crime which was committed by the representatives of society if he was falsely accused, has always the same cause: refusal to respect the individuality of another or others. A world in which each man respected the soul of all other men, no matter how little they seemed to merit respect, would be crimeless.

There is an obvious political implication to be drawn from this. The authoritarian state is *ipso facto* criminal. When I covered the trial of William Joyce ("Lord Haw-Haw") for the *New Yorker* I saw a man in the dock who was doubly criminal. He had committed crimes against the law out of his desire to substitute a criminal state for a state which, if not completely innocent, aimed at the innocence of freedom. It was obviously doubtful if he would ever have been guilty of any offense had he not been tainted by this political guilt. But when his actual offense against the law was examined it was seen that he had acted in a manner which had long been extolled by many who were in theory pure of that guilt and firmly opposed to the authoritarian state.

Almost all contemporary left-wing writers of this generation and the last attacked the idea of nationalism. It was true that many of these attacks were made under the delusion that the words nationalism and imperialism mean the same thing, whereas nationalism—which means simply a special devotion of a people to its own material and spiritual achievements—implies no desire for the annexation of other territories and enslavement of other peoples. But a great many of these attacks were made under no such apprehension. It was genuinely felt that it was pure superstition which required a man to feel any warmer emotion about his own land, race, and people than about any other. Why then should any man feel a lump in his throat when he saw his flag or the statue at the harbor gate of his native land, or feel that in a dispute between his people and another he must obey the will of his kin and not aid their enemy?

I watched the trial of William Joyce, and of all traitors who were charged in courts which I could conveniently attend. They had all cleared their throats of that lump, they had all made that transit of frontiers recommended by the nationalists; and this had landed them in the service of the persecutors of reason, the fanatical believers in frontiers as the demarcation lines between the saved and the damned. But as their lives were unfolded it appeared that none of them had cast off their nationalist prejudice because of their strength, but had been divested of it by maladjusted ambition, by madness, by cowardice, by weakness. It seemed as if contemporary rationalists had been wrong, and I remembered that the trouble about man is twofold. He cannot learn truths which are too complicated; he forgets truths which are too simple. After I had seen twenty traitors tried it seemed to me that the reason why they were in the dock, why intellectuals preach against nationalism, is that we have forgotten certain simple truths.

We have forgotten that we live outward from the center of a circle and that what is nearest to the center is most real to us. If a man cut his hand, it hurts him more than if he cut some other man's hand; therefore he is more careful to guard his own. Even if he spend his whole life in teaching himself that we are all of one body, and that therefore his neighbor's pain is his also, he will still suffer more when his own hand is hurt, for the message then runs straight from his palm and fingers to his brain, traveling at a speed faster than light or sound, which bear the news of others' accidents. Throughout his life it remains true that what is nearest to his body is of greatest interest to his mind. When a baby is given food and held warmly by a certain woman, he grows up to feel a closer concern for her than for other women of her generation, and at her death will feel greatly disturbed. Should he be institution-bred and have no woman as his particular slave and tyrant, grievance will sour him till his last day.

If in his maturity he should live with a woman for any considerable period of time, he and she are apt, unless they are overtaken by certain obviously disagreeable circumstances, to behave as though there were a complete community of interest between them. There must have been some instinctive liking between them or they would never have been drawn together in the first place; they became involved in each other's prosperity; experience has taught each how the other will behave in most eventualities. Therefore they do better by one another than strangers would. Should he have children by this or any other woman, they will have great power over him, while other children will have little or none. He will know so much more about them. The veiled moment of their conception is his secret, and resemblances to him, to a familiar woman, or to his kin enable him to trace their inner lives, disguised though they be first by their inarticulateness and then by their articulateness. He can read them by the light of his own nature, and read his own nature by their light, and will have a sense of fusion between himself and those who are so inextricably tangled with that self.

If that man live in a house during the days of his childhood, he will know it better than any house he lives in later, though it shelter him forty years longer; and though the staircase wind as deviously as any in the world he will find his way down it in the darkness as surely as if it were straight. All his life long, when he hears talk of woods, he shall see beechwoods, if he come from a Buckinghamshire village, and a castle to him shall stand on Castle Rock, if Edinburgh was his home; and in the one case he shall know Southern English country folk, and in the other Lowland Scottish townsfolk, better than other Britons. Born and bred in England, he will find it easier to understand the English than the rest of men, not for any mystical reason, but because their language is his, because he is fully acquainted with their customs, and because he is the product of their common history. So also each continent enjoys a vague unity of self-comprehension, and is divided from the others by a sharp disunity; and even those who profess the closest familiarity with the next world speak with more robust certainty of this world and seem not to want to leave it.

This is not to say that a man loves what is nearest to him. He may hate his parents, his wife, and his children. Millions have done so. On the tables of the Law it was written "Honor thy father and thy mother, as the Lord God hath commanded thee; that thy days may be prolonged, and that it may go well with thee in the land which the Lord thy God giveth thee," and it is advice of almost gross practicality aimed at preventing the faithful from abandoning themselves to their natural impulses and wasting all their force on family rows. St. Paul, that great artist who perpetually betrayed his art because he was also a great man of action, and constantly abandoned the search for truth to seek instead a myth to inspire vigorous action, tried to gild the bondage of man to the familiar. "So ought men to love their own wives as their own body," he says. "He that loveth his wife loveth himself. For no man ever yet hated his own flesh, but nourisheth it and cherisheth it, even as the Lord the Church." But countless men have hated their own flesh. Everywhere and at all times men have carried such hatred to the point of slaying it, and still more have persecuted it by abstinence and mortification and debauchery. It has a value to them far above their loathing or their liking. It is their own flesh and they can have no direct experience of any other. Not with all the gold in the world or by incessant prayer can we obtain another instrument-case, packed with these our only instruments, the five senses, by which alone we can irradiate the universe that is a black void around us, and build a small irradiated platform in that darkness. A wife is someone who has stood on that irradiated platform long enough to be fully examined and to add the testimony of her own senses as to the nature of that encircling mystery. She may be loved or hated, or loved and hated, and serve in that research.

A child knows that what is near is easier for him to handle than what is far. All men took it for granted till recent times, when it was challenged, together with some other traditional assumptions, not because they had proved unsound, but because a number of urbanized populations from which the intellectual classes were largely drawn had lost their sense of spiritual as well as material process. They had lost their sense of material process owing to the development of the machine; goods which had formerly been produced by simple and comprehensible processes, often carried on where they could be witnessed by the consumer, were now produced by elaborate processes, not to be grasped by people without mechanical training, and carried on in the privacy of the large factories.

The reason for their ignorance of spiritual process was the urban lack of the long memory and the omniscient gossip enjoyed by the village. The townsman is surrounded by people whose circumstances he does not know and whose heredities are the secrets of other districts; and he is apt to take their dissimulating faces and their clothed bodies as the sum of them. People began to think of each other in a new way; as simple with a simplicity in fact unknown in organic life. They ignored the metabolism of human nature, by which experiences are absorbed into the mind and magically converted into personality, which rejects much of the material life brings to it and handles the rest to serve the interests of love or hate, good or evil, life or death, according to an inhabiting daemon, whose reasons are never given. Man conceived himself as living reasonably under the instruction of the five senses, which tell him to seek pleasure and avoid pain.

The first effect of this rational conception of life was cheerful vulgarity; and there are worse things than that. Man might well have felt this view of his destiny as a relief after the Christian philosophy, which abased his origin to criminality, and started him so low only to elevate him to the height, most disagreeable to most people, of company with godhead, after dragging him through all sorts of unpalatable experiences, including participation in a violent and apparently unnecessary death. In so far as a man adopted the new and rationalist philosophy he could be compared to an actor who, after spending a lifetime playing Hamlet and Othello and King Lear, retires to keep a country pub. All was thenceforward to go at a peaceable jog-trot. Children were to grow up straight striplings of light, undeformed by repression, unscarred by conflicts, because their parents would hand them over in their earliest years to the care of pedagogic experts. Divorce was not to be reckoned as a disgrace nor as a tragedy nor even as a failure, but as a pleasurable extension of experience, like travel. Furthermore—and this was considered as the sanest adjustment of all—the ardors of patriotism were to be abandoned, and replaced by a cool resolution to place one's country on a level with all others in one's affections, and to hand it over without concern to the dominion of any other power which could offer it greater material benefits. It was not out of cynicism that the benefits demanded were material: it was believed that the material automatically produced the intellectual and the spiritual. These reasonable steps having been taken, there was to follow harmony. The only peril was that it might become too sweet.

But the five senses had evidently not been rightly understood. Such children as were surrendered by their parents to expert treatment, complained against that surrender as if it had been any other kind of abandonment. They quarreled with the pedagogues as much as they would have quarreled with their parents; but, the bond of the flesh being absent, there was something sapless in their quarrels, and there was less energy engendered. Sexual life was not noticeably smoother than it had been. The epic love of marriage and the lyric love-song of the encounter both lost much by the pretense that they were the same. Nor, as patriotism was discredited, did peace come nearer. Indeed, the certainty of war now arched over the earth like a second sky, inimical to the first. If harmony had been our peril, we were preserved from it, both within and without. For it was plain that, as Christian philosophy had so harshly averred, the world was a stage on which an extraordinary drama, not yet fully comprehended by the intellect, was being performed; and its action was now an agony. But, owing to the adoption of the rationalist philosophy, some of the actors filling the most important parts were now incapable of speaking their lines. It appeared that *Hamlet* and *Othello* and *King Lear* would be no longer cathartic tragedies but repellent and distressing farces if the leading characters had, in the climactic scenes, been overtaken by the delusion that they had retired and were keeping country pubs.

So the evil moment came and was clear: not surpassed in evil since the days of the barbarian invasions. The devil of nationalism had been driven out of man, but he had not become the headquarters of the dove. Instead there had entered into him the seven devils of internationalism, and he was torn by their frenzies. Then what is against all devils came to his aid. The achievement (which, as yet, is unfinished, since peace does not reign) was accomplished by a continuance of the drama in spite of the difficulties created by the rationalist philosophy. Since the actors cast to play the leading parts would not speak, the action was carried on by the peoples who used to walk to and fro at the back of the scene, softly laughing or softly weeping, or simply quietly being. Now these people streamed across the continents, inscribing their beliefs on the surface of the earth by the course of their flights, and on the sites of their martyrdoms. They defeated fascism by not being fascist. They showed the contrast between fascism and nonfascism so clearly that the world, wishing to live, defended their side because it could be seen that they were the representatives of life. As they exorcised the devils from the body of Europe they seemed to affirm certain values. It was perhaps true that the origin of man was in criminality, for once a community refused to make the effort of seeking the company of godhead it certainly became criminal. It was perhaps true that hedonism is an impotent gospel, for now it could be seen that pleasure means nothing to many men. As fast as those who ran to save their lives ran those who ran to slay them, even if their pursuit, pressed too hard, might change them into fugitives, whose own lives were in danger. Now the scorned bonds of the flesh asserted their validity. It was the final and unbearable misery of these flights that husbands were separated from their wives, and parents lost sight of their children. The men who performed the cruelest surgery on these families, who threw the husband and wife into the gas chamber while the children traveled by train to an unknown destination, had themselves been brought up to condemn their own ties of blood. The anguish of the divided was obviously holy. The contentment of those who felt no reluctance to divide was plainly damned.

In this day of exposition those who made the other sacrifice of the near for the far, and preferred other countries to their own, proved also to be unholy. The relationship between a man and a fatherland is always disturbed by conflict, if either man or fatherland is highly developed. A man's demands for liberty must at some point challenge the limitations the state imposes on the individual for the sake of the mass. If he is to carry on the national tradition he must wrestle with those who, speaking in its name, desire to crystallize it at the point reached by the previous generation. In any case national life itself must frequently exasperate him, because it is the medium in which he is expressing himself, and every craftsman or artist is repelled by the resistance of his medium to his will. All men should have a drop or two of treason in their veins, if the nations are not to go soft like so many sleepy bears.

Yet to be a traitor is most miserable. All the men I saw in the prisoner's dock were sad as they stood their trials, not only because they were going to be punished. They would have been sad even if they had never been brought to justice. They had forsaken the familiar medium; they had trusted themselves to the mercies of those who had no reason to care for them; knowing their custodians' indifference they had lived for long in fear; and they were aware that they had thrown away their claim on those who might naturally have felt affection for them. Strangers, as King Solomon put it, were filled with their wealth, and their labors were in the house of a stranger, and they mourned at the last when their flesh and body were consumed. As a divorce sharply recalls what a happy marriage should be, so the treachery of these men recalled what a nation should be; a shelter where all talents are generously recognized, all forgivable oddities forgiven, all viciousness quietly frustrated, and those who lack talent honored for equivalent contributions of graciousness. Each of these men was as dependent on the good opinion of others as one is oneself; they needed a nation which was also a hearth, and their capacity for suffering made it tragic that they had gone out from their own hearth to suffer among strangers, because the intellectual leaders of their time had professed a philosophy which was scarcely more than a lapse of memory, and had forgotten, that a hearth gives out warmth.

Suggestions for Discussion

1. According to Rebecca West, how is the observation of a courtroom trial similar to the study of the history of the past?

2. How does West relate the act of treason to the life of crime? How is this relationship connected to the totalitarian state?

3. What does West see as the major dangerous consequences of the decline in nationalism before World War II? What led to the decline of nationalist feeling?

4. How does West connect feeling for home, parents, children, one's neighborhood, or one's town with nationalist feelings?

5. As you read the essay, does West's position seem blindly or narrowly patriotic? How does she achieve an objective and detached tone in her writing?

6. Explain the use of biblical references in the essay. What value do they have in establishing tone?

7. What does West see as an antidote or corrective to the attitudes which led to the treasonous acts of the people whose trials she observed?

Suggestions for Writing

1. Look up facts about "Lord Haw-Haw" and, based on what you discover, write an essay in which you show how his life illustrates the ideas advanced by Rebecca West in this essay.

2. Third World nationalism since World War II is very different from the nationalism examined in this essay. Try to discover through research some of the major differences and contrast the two. What have been some consequences of contemporary nationalism? What might be the consequences of a loss of such nationalist feeling?

Carol Tavris

Anger in an Unjust World

Carol Tavris is a social psychologist and magazine writer. She is author of *The Redbook Report on Female Sexuality* (1977) and of *Anger: The Misunderstood Emotion* (1982). This essay, excerpted from that book for *Ms. Magazine,* examines the reasons why most of us, in one way or another, contrive to tolerate injustice by suppressing our anger.

St. Thomas Aquinas imagined that people feel angry only when they are offended by their inferiors: "Thus a nobleman is angry if he be insulted by a peasant; a wise man, if by a fool; a master, if by a servant." If the nobleman insults the peasant, on the other hand, "anger does not ensue, but only sorrow." The irritating habit of modern peasants to react to insult with anger instead of sorrow, is, of course, the story of revolution.

Yet Aquinas was making an important point about the power of authority to establish legitimacy, and legitimacy is death to anger. For, in fact, most peasants, fools, and servants have not protested the injustices done them, nor even regarded them as injustices. The sense of injustice is made, not born, and although we think of anger as the handmaiden of justice, it is not its inevitable companion. Anger depends on our perceptions of a situation, perceptions of injustice included.

Many people believe that if they feel angry now about something, they must always have felt that way, although the anger may previously have been repressed, distorted, or displaced. A woman who, in 1975, feels angry with herself for having dropped out of medical school for marriage in 1955 wonders what she did with the anger she assumes she felt at the time. A man who, as an adult, feels angry with his parents for making him eat all the food on his plate when he was young thinks he felt as angry when he *was* young. The ex-medical student and the little boy may truly have felt angry in the past, but it's more likely that they were just going along with the times, following the rules, with perhaps a squawk or two of protest. Not only do people attribute their emotions backward to what they felt years ago, but they attribute them sideways, to what they think others should be feeling. Some attribute anger to women or minorities of previous generations and even centuries. When they wonder why a battered woman stays with a vicious husband, blaming herself instead of him for her abuse; or why a slave does not rebel; or why the Untouchables accept their caste of degradation; they are assuming that these sufferers interpret the situation as they do—and see a way out of it, as well.

The forces that keep people in their places, if not entirely contented then at least not angry, are not always as irrational as they seem. The decision that a particular situation is unjust must overcome a few psychological and practical hurdles, and so must the next decision: that the injustice merits anger instead of apathy. The question, therefore, is not simply "Why do people become angry?" but why they do not.

The Rationalizing Species

Golfer Tom Watson seemed to be cruising to an easy victory in the $300,000 Bryon Nelson Classic a few years ago when the weather and his luck turned suddenly against him. From a comfortable score of eight under par he dropped to four over par. "It doesn't upset me," Watson told a reporter. "Golf is not a fair game."

Life is not a fair game, either, but people have a curious capacity to behave as if it were. We tend to equate what is with what ought to be, and react with outrage to attacks on our way of doing things. We accept injustices more readily when they are built into the system, because the roles we play seem so normal and inevitable. For example, we take it for granted that it is within a boss's right to set working hours; but Eskimo workers in factories in Alaska found it hilarious that the white workers responded so obediently to the whistles summoning them to stop work or start it. To the Eskimo, the only authority that determines when people shall work is the tide. Yet American workers would find it just as hilarious, to say nothing of an infringement on their liberty, if they had to sing the company song in unison every morning, as many Japanese workers do, without question or anger.

What happens when people's faith in the legitimacy of the system is put to the test? Usually, it is the test that fails. The very organization of our mental faculties seems designed to screen out information we don't want to hear, information that is at odds with our basic beliefs. Psychologist Anthony G. Greenwald calls the self "The Totalitarian Ego," arguing that the ego organizes its knowledge, perceptions, and memory in predictably biased ways that are designed (like totalitarian governments) primarily to protect its organization.

The ego, says Greenwald, is a "self justifying historian," which seeks only that information that agrees with it, rewrites history when it needs to, and does not even see the evidence that threatens it. The organization of knowledge in the mind is like a library system: our built-in biases allow us to retrieve any specific information that we need rapidly; once we make a commitment to a particular cataloging system (say, a conservative ideology or a religious framework of belief), we spend more time maintaining the system than revising it. The biases of the mind persist because they work: they preserve self-confidence, they keep our mental organization in order, and they keep us persevering toward our goals, whatever those may be. The mind's cautiousness about accepting new ideas may seem foolhardy in a world bursting with innovation and discovery, but (at least until recently) it has been an adaptive success for our species. The flash of anger that people may feel when they are threatened with conflicting information is the mind's way of protecting its organization. "My mind's made up—don't confuse me with the facts" seems to have been an oddly successful strategy in the evolution of the brain. After all, if we kept "changing our minds" with each new bit of experience and observation, we would never know how to behave, what to think, or why we were working so hard for a future reward.

Many psychologists have by now posed theories of cognitive consistency to predict how people handle information that conflicts with their beliefs: we shall shift the belief slightly, or more likely the new information, to make the two coexist harmoniously.

Consistency theories all assume that human beings have a fundamental need to find meaning and order in life's experiences. Psychologist Melvin J. Lerner adds that we need to believe in a just world, one in which people get what they deserve, good is rewarded, the sinful punished. The Belief in a Just World, he argues, is "a fundamental delusion" that is central to the way we organize experience, making sense out of confusion, justice out of cruelty and unfairness, and orderliness out of random events. And it protects the legitimacy of the established order. Researchers have by now conducted dozens of experiments that show what happens when the belief in a just world clashes with an obvious fact of injustice. If you cannot do anything about the injustice, you will tend to denigrate the victim, deny the evidence, or reinterpret the event entirely. You will go to great lengths to protect the basic faith.

Denigrate the Victim

In a just world, innocent women are not raped. Women who are raped, therefore, must have "invited it"—by being seductive, or perhaps by merely being. In one experiment that simulated a jury trial, a defendant was depicted as having raped a married woman, a virgin, or a divorcee. The subjects in the study gave longer sentences to rapists of virgins than to rapists of divorcees, as you might expect, but, more interesting, they attributed more responsibility for the rape to the virgins and wives than to the divorcees. Apparently the knowledge that innocent, "respectable" women can be raped was too threatening to the jurors' belief in a just world, and so they found fault with the victims' behavior.

Similarly, many vehement antiabortionists cannot accept the statistics of rape, incest, poverty, contraceptive ignorance, and woman battering, preferring to believe that it is only immoral women who have abortions. Women are blamed for "getting themselves pregnant," as one Congressman put it, in that bizarre, anachronistic phrasing that exonerates the role of the male in conception. (The same Congressmen who advise that "the best contraceptive is the word no" would not take it kindly, I bet, if their women applied that word to them.)

Women are not the only objects of rationalizing denigration. The poor bring their suffering on themselves (say many of the well-to-do) because they are lazy, conniving, drunk, and violent. A man who is fired for trying to improve working conditions must have deserved it; he should have kept his mouth shut. Neoconservative Jews such as Norman Podhoretz and Irving Kristol must, to preserve their commitment to fascist but anticommunist nations such as Argentina, denigrate victims of Argentine anti-Semitism, most notably Jacobo Timerman; accepting his testimony threatens their political philosophy and their sense of religious security. Fighter pilots, on hearing that a buddy has been killed in a plane crash, will blame the buddy for having made a stupid error; if it was the plane that failed or the Air Force's error, the survivors are in danger too. All of these rationalizations help people avoid the panicky thought that poverty, job loss, anti-Semitism, or death could strike *them*.

Denial

Here's a familiar term for the psychoanalytic archives, this time referring not to an unconscious process but often a perfectly conscious one: screening out unpleasant information that might threaten one's convictions. Fundamentalist parents are fighting to have their children taught absolute values of right and wrong: they worry that schools are subjecting their children to information that might jeopardize their religious certainty. When writer Frances Fitz-Gerald asked one such mother whether she would consider sending her children to a nonfundamentalist school, the mother said, "No, because our eternal destiny is all-important, so you can't take a chance. College so often throws kids into confusion." To avoid confusion, many people prefer ignorance.

Denial seems to be at the heart of political philosophies. As a particularly depressing (if extreme) case, there are people who will tell you that the Holocaust never happened. But you can see garden-variety denial in the way individuals respond to the news that innocent people have been imprisoned or murdered by the Soviet Union, the United States, China, Vietnam, Argentina, Chile, France, Japan, South Africa, Haiti, Cuba . . . (fill in your choice for infamy). Depending on your politics, you will tend to deny the crimes committed by your favorite nations (for such crimes jeopardize your desire to believe in your allies' basic integrity and justice, and possibly jeopardize your economic interests as well), and emphasize those committed by your enemies (it is perfectly consistent to believe in the sins of your opponents). If you believe in the basic corruptibility of most political systems, however, you won't find it inconsistent evidence to be denied when one of them does something criminal or stupid.

Reinterpretation of the Injustice and Its Outcome

This mechanism to preserve faith in a world requires some flights of imagination: people "rewrite" the injustice they hear about so that it simply disappears, taking with it the need to be emotionally disturbed. For example, you might reinterpret the result of injustice, deciding that the victim wasn't such a victim after all; suffering is a good thing that builds moral character and makes the sufferer a better person. Or you might decide that the cause of the injustice was, let's say, not the government's decision to release Agent Orange on Vietnam, but a result of something the victim did or failed to do; perhaps those servicemen who now complain they were poisoned just forgot to take adequate precautions. Or might extend the time frame of the whole event to maintain your belief in ultimate justice: eventually, heroes and bastards will get their just deserts, but it may take a few years. Maybe a lifetime. Maybe in the afterlife . . .

So great is the need to believe in justice and order, says Lerner, that many people will even assume a large burden of anguish, blaming themselves, rather than yield the belief. Parents of terminally ill children, the most poignantly undeserving of victims, frequently berate themselves for their children's fate: "If I had only done this . . . " "If we'd never done that . . ."

This self-blame, paradoxically, allays the anxiety of the intolerable conclusion that no one is responsible.

In the laboratory, psychologists have watched before their very eyes as the belief in a just world "cools out" anger. Young adults observed a videotape of what they thought was a real experiment in learning (in fact, it was staged), in which another young woman suffered a series of severe shocks whenever she made "errors." At first the observers would flinch empathetically with each televised shock, and many expressed fury and indignation at the treatment they were watching: "I was really mad." "I felt like getting up and walking out." "I thought it was disgusting." In spite of these strong affirmations of anger, *not one* of the thousand people who have by now participated in this experiment have actually complained. Instead, most of them decided that the victim was a fool or a weakling for sitting still and allowing herself to be shocked. "I would never let anyone do that to me!" they asserted. Unable as they were to do anything about the injustice they observed, they condemned the victim and evaluated her critically. The more strongly the experimenters portrayed the innocent victim as a martyr, the more vehemently the observers condemned her.

Religion, of course, offers the ultimate just world, if not in this life then in the next. Religion and political ideology organize our angers as they legitimize our social systems. Indeed all the great religions have made the management of anger a central concern, with prescriptions designed to protect the social order and to generate anger, if at all, only on its behalf.

For instance, although the Old Testament itself is a veritable catalog of family squabbles, internecine wars, and the smiting of heathens, it continually reminds its readers that "He that is slow to anger is better than the mighty"— surely a sermon that would reassure the mighty. Jehovah of the Old Testament and Allah of Islam are angry gods, who require anger to be used freely in their service against enemies, infidels, and the wicked; but anger *within* the community is to be suppressed. This was a smart and successful philosophy for small nations surrounded by competing groups, the situation then and now in the Middle East.

In contrast, the religions of Taoism, Vishnuism, and Buddhism advocate the complete eradication of anger and any other emotion that serves a this-worldly desire (such as lust and greed). Because everything that happens in this world is predestined, according to these theologies, there is no point in getting riled up about evil, war, and sin. There is certainly no point in protesting one's caste; obedient behavior in this life will be rewarded with caste advancement in the next incarnation. (War and anger may be an occasional necessity, but they are not to be sought after or celebrated.)

Christianity stands between the martial religions and the pacifist ones: anger may be used to combat evil and injustice; anger is good or bad depending on its use, not its nature. Although in the New Testament divine vengeance has subsided in favor of divine forgiveness, human beings are still supposed to wait for forgiveness in heaven and not raise their voices too loudly for justice on earth. If we consider the secular results of Christianity, however, we see that those who turned the other cheek usually got a slap in return; and that the meek did indeed inherit the earth—to plow, to plant, and to harvest for their masters.

Ideas about justice are not all in the mind. Realistic, practical motives hold people in roles as victims of manipulation or injustice without their perceiving either. Sociologist Barrington Moore, Jr., calls their condition one of "exploitative reciprocity," and if revolutionaries emphasize the "exploitative," the people involved tend to emphasize the "reciprocity." Every social system, from the family to a nation, is based on a social contract of the rights and duties of its participants. The contract may be written or implicit, but the rules are usually clear to all, or become clear once they are broken.

Some feminists, for example, who feel angry about genital mutilation, such as circumcision or even excision of the clitoris that women in many Third World cultures endure, cannot understand why the women tolerate these practices and continue them. Yet these horrendous, painful customs are as essential to the women's security and survival—because they guarantee that the woman will continue to be protected by men—as a job contract is to a union worker here. (Many Third World feminists themselves put food, education and work at the top of their list of reforms for this reason.) In any relationship between authority and subordinate, the subordinate gives up something to get something: the benefits of the authority's protection, expertise, talent, access to the rain god, earnings.

The anger that fuels revolt does not arise, therefore, from objective conditions of deprivation or misery; as long as people regard those conditions as natural and inevitable, as God's law or man's way, they do not feel angry about them. So sociologists speak instead of "relative deprivation," the subjective comparisons that people make when they compare their actual lives to *what might be possible.* Alexis de Tocqueville observed that "evils which are patiently endured when they seem inevitable become intolerable when once the idea of escape from them is suggested," and the freed slave Frederick Douglass put the same idea more passionately: "Beat and cuff your slave," he wrote, "keep him hungry and spiritless, and he will follow the chain of his master like a dog, but feed and clothe him well, work him moderately, surround him with physical comfort, and dreams of freedom intrude."

In this country, the civil rights, women's rights, and human rights movements have been organized and sustained primarily by those who already had more education, opportunities, and success in the system than the less-fortunate members of their race, sex, or class.

Margaret Mead once said of liberals that they are "the yeast within the body politic upon which American society relies to keep its dream worth following. Without them, we should be lost. Yet with them, we are uncomfortable. For they draw their strength from the discrepancies in the very heart of American life." Rebels and dissidents challenge the complacent belief in a just world, and, as the theory would predict, they are usually denigrated for their efforts. While they are alive, they may be called "cantankerous," "crazy," "hysterical," "uppity," or "duped." Dead, some of them become saints and heroes, the sterling characters of history. It's a matter of proportion. One angry rebel is crazy, three is a conspiracy, 50 is a movement.

Suggestions for Discussion

1. Why does Tavris begin her discussion of anger with a reference to St. Thomas Aquinas? What important point did Aquinas make about the legitimacy of authority?

2. The author is concerned with the behavior of those who tolerate injustice by suppressing their anger. Does she believe this act is difficult? Natural? What does Tom Watson's statement, "Golf is not a fair game" mean in the context of this essay?

3. How does Tavris use the example of American, Eskimo, and Japanese workers to illustrate the way in which we learn to tolerate certain rules?

4. Tavris lists three categories of behavior that we use to protect our basic faith in existing order. Discuss these categories. How do they relate to each other to form a coherent system of acceptance?

5. What role does religion play in helping us suppress anger in an unjust world?

6. Tavris quotes from Frederick Douglass and Margaret Mead. Show how she uses their remarks.

Suggestions for Writing

1. Choose an example of your own tolerance of injustice. Examine the reasons for your tolerance. Can you explain them? Write an essay in which you analyze this example and either defend your actions or reject them.

2. This essay makes a significant statement about the modern feminist movement. Write an essay explaining the relation of the argument of the essay to the feminist position. Use some of Tavris's examples of how we tolerate injustice to illustrate your point. Relate the last two sentences of her essay to your discussion.

Jean-Paul Sartre

The Passion of the Anti-Semite

Translated by George J. Becker

Jean-Paul Sartre (1905–1980), existentialist philosopher, novelist, and playwright, played a leading role in post-World War II French intellectual life. His writings portray human beings as alone, responsible for their own acts, given the frightening need to choose their actions in a world without religious meaning. His fiction includes *Nausea, Intimacy,* and *The Age of Reason;* his plays *The Flies, No Exit,* and *The Respectful Prostitute;* his philosophy *Being and Nothingness.* However, all of his works reveal his philosophic ideas. Sartre refused the Nobel Prize for Literature believing that the award exaggerated a writer's influence. In this selection from *Anti-Semite and Jew,* he describes the irrational passion that governs the thoughts and behavior of the anti-Semite.

If a man attributes all or part of his own misfortunes and those of his country to the presence of Jewish elements in the community, if he proposes to remedy this state of affairs by depriving the Jews of certain of their rights, by keeping them out of certain economic and social activities, by expelling them from the country, by exterminating all of them, we say that he has anti-Semitic *opinions*.

This word *opinion* makes us stop and think. It is the word a hostess uses to bring to an end a discussion that threatens to become acrimonious. It suggests that all points of view are equal; it reassures us, for it gives an inoffensive appearance to ideas by reducing them to the level of tastes. All tastes are natural; all opinions are permitted. Tastes, colors, and opinions are not open to discussion. In the name of democratic institutions, in the name of freedom of opinion, the anti-Semite asserts the right to preach the anti-Jewish crusade everywhere.

At the same time, accustomed as we have been since the Revolution to look at every object in an analytic spirit, that is to say, as a composite whose elements can be separated, we look upon persons and characters as mosaics in which each stone coexists with the others without that coexistence affecting the nature of the whole. Thus anti-Semitic opinion appears to us to be a molecule that can enter into combination with other molecules of any origin whatsoever without undergoing any alteration. A man may be a good father and a good husband, a conscientious citizen, highly cultivated, philanthropic, *and* in addition an anti-Semite. He may like fishing and the pleasures of love, may be tolerant in matters of religion, full of generous notions on the condition of the natives in Central Africa, *and* in addition detest the Jews. If he does not like them, we say, it is because his experience has shown him that they are bad, because statistics have taught him that they are dangerous, because certain historical factors have influenced his judgment. Thus this opinion seems to be the result of external causes, and those who wish to study it are prone to neglect the personality of the anti-Semite in favor of a consideration of the percentage of Jews who were mobilized in 1914, the percentage of Jews who are bankers, industrialists, doctors, and lawyers, or an examination of the history of the Jews in France since early times. They succeed in revealing a strictly objective situation that determines an equally objective current of opinion, and this they call anti-Semitism, for which they can draw up charts and determine the variations from 1870 to 1944. In such wise anti-Semitism appears to be at once a subjective taste that enters into combination with other tastes to form a personality, and an impersonal and social phenomenon which can be expressed by figures and averages, one which is conditioned by economic, historical, and political constants.

I do not say that these two conceptions are necessarily contradictory. I do say that they are dangerous and false. I would admit, if necessary, that one may have an opinion on the government's policy in regard to the wine industry, that is, that one may decide, *for certain reasons*, either to approve or condemn the free importation of wine from Algeria: here we have a case of holding an opinion on the administration of things. But I refuse to characterize as opinion a doctrine that is aimed directly at particular persons and that seeks to suppress their rights or to exterminate them. The Jew whom the anti-Semite wishes to lay hands upon is not a schematic being defined solely by his function, as under administrative law; or by his status or his acts, as under the Code. He is a Jew, the son of Jews, recognizable by his physique, by the color of his hair, by his clothing perhaps, and, so they say, by his character. Anti-Semitism does not fall within the category of ideas protected by the right of free opinion.

Indeed, it is something quite other than an idea. It is first of all a *passion*. No doubt it can be set forth in the form of a theoretical proposition. The "moderate" anti-Semite is a courteous man who will tell you quietly: "Personally, I do not detest the Jews. I simply find it preferable, for various reasons, that they should play a lesser part in the activity of the nation." But a moment later, if you have gained his confidence, he will add with more abandon: "You see, there must be *something* about the Jews; they upset me physically."

This argument, which I have heard a hundred times, is worth examining. First of all, it derives from the logic of passion. For, really now, can we imagine anyone's saying seriously: "There must be something about tomatoes, for I have a horror of eating them"? In addition, it shows us that anti-Semitism in its most temperate and most evolved forms remains a syncretic whole which may be expressed by statements of reasonable tenor, but which can involve even bodily modifications. Some men are suddenly struck with impotence if they learn from the woman with whom they are making love that she is a Jewess. There is a disgust for the Jew, just as there is a disgust for the Chinese or the Negro among certain people. Thus it is not from the body that the sense of repulsion arises, since one may love a Jewess very well if one does not know what her race is; rather it is something that enters the body from the mind. It is an involvement of the mind, but one so deep-seated and complete that it extends to the physiological realm, as happens in cases of hysteria.

This involvement is not caused by experience. I have questioned a hundred people on the reasons for their anti-Semitism. Most of them have confined themselves to enumerating the defects with which tradition has endowed the Jews. "I detest them because they are selfish, intriguing, persistent, oily, tactless, etc."—"But, at any rate, you associate with some of them?"—"Not if I can help it!" A painter said to me: "I am hostile to the Jew because, with their critical habits, they encourage our servants to insubordination." Here are examples a little more precise. A young actor without talent insisted that the Jews had kept him from a successful career in the theatre by confining him to subordinate roles. A young woman said to me: "I have had the most horrible experiences with furriers; they robbed me, they burned the fur I entrusted to them. Well, they were all Jews." But why did she choose to hate Jews rather than furriers? Why Jews or furriers rather than such and such a Jew or such and such a furrier? Because she had in her a predisposition toward anti-Semitism.

A classmate of mine at the lycée told me that Jews "annoy" him because of the thousands of injustices that "Jew-ridden" social organizations commit in their favor. "A Jew passed his *agrégation*[1] the year I was failed, and you can't make me believe that that fellow, whose father came from Cracow or Lemberg, understood a poem by Ronsard or an eclogue by Virgil better than I." But he admitted that he disdained the *agrégation* as a mere academic exercise, and that he didn't study for it. Thus, to explain his failure, he made use

---

[1]Competitive state teachers' examination. [Translator's note.]

of two systems of interpretation, like those madmen who, when they are far gone in their madness, pretend to be the King of Hungary but, if questioned sharply, admit to being shoemakers. His thoughts moved on two planes without his being in the least embarrassed by it. As a matter of fact, he will in time manage to justify his past laziness on the grounds that it really would be too stupid to prepare for an examination in which Jews are passed in preference to good Frenchmen. Actually he ranked twenty-seventh on the official list. There were twenty-six ahead of him, twelve who passed and fourteen who failed. Suppose Jews had been excluded from the competition; would that have done him any good? And even if he had been at the top of the list of unsuccessful candidates, even if by eliminating one of the successful candidates he would have had a chance to pass, why should the Jew Weil have been eliminated rather than the Norman Mathieu or the Breton Arzell? To understand my classmate's indignation we must recognize that he had adopted in advance a certain idea of the Jew, of his nature and of his role in society. And to be able to decide that among twenty-six competitors who were more successful than himself, it was the Jew who robbed him of his place, he must a priori have given preference in the conduct of his life to reasoning based on passion. Far from experience producing his idea of the Jew, it was the latter which explained his experience. If the Jew did not exist, the anti-Semite would invent him.

That may be so, you will say, but leaving the question of experience to one side, must we not admit that anti-Semitism is explained by certain historical data? For after all it does not come out of the air. It would be easy for me to reply that the history of France tells us nothing about the Jews: they were oppressed right up to 1789; since then they have participated as best they could in the life of the nation, taking advantage, naturally, of freedom of competition to displace the weak, but no more and no less than other Frenchmen. They have committed no crimes against France, have engaged in no treason. And if people believe there is proof that the number of Jewish soldiers in 1914 was lower than it should have been, it is because someone had the curiosity to consult statistics. This is not one of those facts which have the power to strike the imagination by themselves; no soldier in the trenches was able on his own initiative to feel astonishment at not seeing any Jews in the narrow sector that constituted his universe. However, since the information that history gives on the role of Israel depends essentially on the conception one has of history, I think it would be better to borrow from a foreign country a manifest example of "Jewish treason" and to calculate the repercussions this "treason" may have had on contemporary anti-Semitism.

In the course of the bloody Polish revolts of the nineteenth century, the Warsaw Jews, whom the czars handled gently for reasons of policy, were very lukewarm toward the rebels. By not taking part in the insurrection they were able to maintain and improve their position in a country ruined by repression.

I don't know whether this is true or not. What is certain is that many Poles believe it, and this "historical fact" contributes not a little to their bitterness against the Jews. But if I examine the matter more closely, I discover a vicious circle: The czars, we are told, treated the Polish Jews well whereas they willingly ordered pogroms against those in Russia. These sharply different courses of action had the same cause. The Russian government considered the Jews in both Russia and Poland to be unassimiliable; according to the needs of their policy, they had them massacred at Moscow and Kiev because they were a danger to the Russian empire, but favored them at Warsaw as a means of stirring up discord among the Poles. The latter showed nothing but hate and scorn for the Jews of Poland, but the reason was the same: For them Israel could never become an integral part of the national collectivity. Treated as Jews by the czar and as Jews by the Poles, provided, quite in spite of themselves, with Jewish interests in the midst of a foreign community, is it any wonder that these members of a minority behaved in accordance with the representation made of them?

In short, the essential thing here is not an "historical fact" but the idea that the agents of history formed for themselves of the Jew. When the Poles of today harbor resentment against the Jews for their past conduct, they are incited to it by that same idea. If one is going to reproach little children for the sins of their grandfathers, one must first of all have a very primitive conception of what constitutes responsibility. Furthermore one must form his conception of the children on the basis of what the grandparents have been. One must believe that what their elders did the young are capable of doing. One must convince himself that Jewish character is inherited. Thus the Poles of 1940 treated the Israelites in the community as *Jews* because their ancestors in 1848 had done the same with their contemporaries. Perhaps this traditional representation would, under other circumstances, have disposed the Jews of today to act like those of 1848. It is therefore the *idea* of the Jew that one forms for himself which would seem to determine history, not the "historical fact" that produces the idea.

People speak to us also of "social facts," but if we look at this more closely we shall find the same vicious circle. There are too many Jewish lawyers, someone says. But is there any complaint that there are too many Norman lawyers? Even if all the Bretons were doctors would we say anything more than that "Brittany provides doctors for the whole of France"? Oh, someone will answer, it is not at all the same thing. No doubt, but that is precisely because we consider Normans as Normans and Jews as Jews. Thus wherever we turn it is the *idea of the Jew* which seems to be the essential thing.

It has become evident that no external factor can induce anti-Semitism in the anti-Semite. Anti-Semitism is a free and total choice of oneself, a comprehensive attitude that one adopts not only toward Jews but toward men in general, toward history and society; it is at one and the same time a passion and a conception of the world. No doubt in the case of a given anti-Semite certain characteristics will be more marked than in another. But they are always all present at the same time, and they influence each other. It is this syncretic totality which we must now attempt to describe.

I noted earlier that anti-Semitism is a passion. Everybody understands that emotions of hate or anger are involved. But ordinarily hate and anger have a *provocation:* I hate someone who has made me suffer, someone who contemns or insults me. We have just seen that anti-Semitic passion could not have such a character. It precedes the facts that are supposed to call it forth; it seeks them out to nourish itself upon them; it must even interpret them in a special way so that they may become truly offensive. Indeed, if you so much as mention a Jew to an anti-Semite, he will show all the signs of a lively irritation. If we recall that we must always *consent* to anger before it can manifest itself and that, as is indicated so accurately by the French idiom, we "put ourselves" into anger, we shall have to agree that the anti-Semite has *chosen* to live on the plane of passion. It is not unusual for people to elect to live a life of passion rather than one of reason. But ordinarily they love the *objects* of passion: women, glory, power, money. Since the anti-Semite has chosen hate, we are forced to conclude that it is the *state* of passion that he loves. Ordinarily this type of emotion is not very pleasant: a man who passionately desires a woman is impassioned because of the woman and in spite of his passion. We are wary of reasoning based on passion, seeking to support by all possible means opinions which love or jealousy or hate have dictated. We are wary of the aberrations of passion and of what is called monoideism. But that is just what the anti-Semite chooses right off.

How can one choose to reason falsely? It is because of a longing for impenetrability. The rational man groans as he gropes for the truth; he knows that his reasoning is no more than tentative, that other considerations may supervene to cast doubt on it. He never sees very clearly where he is going; he is "open"; he may even appear to be hesitant. But there are people who are attracted by the durability of a stone. They wish to be massive and impenetrable; they wish not to change. Where, indeed, would change take them? We have here a basic fear of oneself and of truth. What frightens them is not the content of truth, of which they have no conception, but the form itself of truth, that thing of indefinite approximation. It is as if their own existence were in continual suspension. But they wish to exist all at once and right away. They do not want any acquired opinions; they want them to be innate. Since they are afraid of reasoning, they wish to lead the kind of life wherein reasoning and research play only a subordinate role, wherein one seeks only what he has already found, wherein one becomes only what he already was. This is nothing but passion. Only a strong emotional bias can give a lightning-like certainty; it alone can hold reason in leash; it alone can remain impervious to experience and last for a whole lifetime.

The anti-Semite has chosen hate because hate is a faith; at the outset he has chosen to devaluate words and reasons. How entirely at ease he feels as a result. How futile and frivolous discussions about the rights of the Jews appear to him. He has placed himself on other ground from the beginning. If out of courtesy he consents for a moment to defend his point of view, he lends himself but does not give himself. He tries simply to project his intuitive certainty onto the plane of discourse. I mentioned awhile back some remarks by anti-Semites, all of them absurd: "I hate Jews because they make servants insubordinate, because a Jewish furrier robbed me, etc." Never believe that anti-Semites are completely unaware of the absurdity of their replies. They know that their remarks are frivolous, open to challenge. But they are amusing themselves, for it is their adversary who is obliged to use words responsibly, since he believes in words. The anti-Semites have the *right* to play. They even like to play with discourse for, by giving ridiculous reasons, they discredit the seriousness of their interlocutors. They delight in acting in bad faith, since they seek not to persuade by sound argument but to intimidate and disconcert. If you press them too closely, they will abruptly fall silent, loftily indicating by some phrase that the time for argument is past. It is not that they are afraid of being convinced. They fear only to appear ridiculous or to prejudice by their embarrassment their hope of winning over some third person to their side.

If then, as we have been able to observe, the anti-Semite is impervious to reason and to experience, it is not because his conviction is strong. Rather his conviction is strong because he has chosen first of all to be impervious.

He has chosen also to be terrifying. People are afraid of irritating him. No one knows to what lengths the aberrations of his passion will carry him—but he knows, for this passion is not provoked by something external. He has it well in hand; it is obedient to his will: now he lets go the reins and now he pulls back on them. He is not afraid of himself, but he sees in the eyes of others a disquieting image—his own—and he makes his words and gestures conform to it. Having this external model, he is under no necessity to look for his personality within himself. He has chosen to find his being entirely outside himself, never to look within, to be nothing save the fear he inspires in others. What he flees even more than Reason is his intimate awareness of himself. But someone will object: What if he is like that only with regard to the Jews? What if he otherwise conducts himself with good sense? I reply that that is impossible. There is the case of a fishmonger who, in 1942, annoyed by the competition of two Jewish fishmongers who were concealing their race, one fine day took pen in hand and denounced them. I have been assured that this fishmonger was in other respects a mild and jovial man, the best of sons. But I don't believe it. A man who finds it entirely natural to denounce other men cannot have our conception of humanity; he does not see even those whom he aids in the same light as we do. His generosity, his kindness are not like our kindness, our generosity. You cannot confine passion to one sphere.

The anti-Semite readily admits that the Jew is intelligent and hardworking; he will even confess himself inferior in these respects. This concession costs him nothing, for he has, as it were, put those qualities in parentheses. Or rather they derive their value from the one who possesses them: the more virtues the Jew has the more dangerous he will be. The anti-Semite has no illusions about what he is. He considers himself an average man, modestly average, basically mediocre. There is no example of an anti-Semite's claiming individual superiority over the Jews. But you must not think that he is ashamed of his mediocrity; he takes pleasure in it; I will even assert that he has chosen it. This man fears every kind of solitariness, that of the genius as much as that of the murderer; he is the man of the crowd. However small his stature, he takes every precaution to make it smaller, lest he stand out from the herd and find himself face to face with himself. He has made himself an anti-Semite because that is something one cannot be alone. The phrase, "I hate the Jews," is one that is uttered in chorus; in pronouncing it, one attaches himself to a tradition and to a community—the tradition and community of the mediocre.

We must remember that a man is not necessarily humble or even modest because he has consented to mediocrity. On the contrary, there is a passionate pride among the mediocre, and anti-Semitism is an attempt to give value to mediocrity as such, to create an elite of the ordinary. To the anti-Semite, intelligence is Jewish; he can thus disdain it in all tranquility, like all the other virtues which the Jew possesses. They are so many ersatz attributes that the Jew cultivates in place of that balanced mediocrity which he will never have. The true Frenchman, rooted in his province, in his country, borne along by a tradition twenty centuries old, benefiting from ancestral wisdom, guided by tried customs, does not *need* intelligence. His virtue depends upon the assimilation of the qualities which the work of a hundred generations has lent to the objects which surround him; it depends on property. It goes without saying that this is a matter of inherited property, not property one buys. The anti-Semite has a fundamental incomprehension of the various forms of modern property: money, securities, etc. These are abstractions, entities of reason related to the abstract intelligence of the Semite. A security belongs to no one because it can belong to everyone; moreover, it is a sign of wealth, not a concrete possession. The anti-Semite can conceive only of a type of primitive ownership of land based on a veritable magical rapport, in which the thing possessed and its possessor are united by a bond of mystical participation; he is the poet of real property. It transfigures the proprietor and endows him with a special and concrete sensibility. To be sure, this sensibility ignores eternal truths or universal values: the universal is Jewish, since it is an object of intelligence. What his subtle sense seizes upon is precisely that which the intelligence cannot perceive. To put it another way, the principle underlying anti-Semitism is that the concrete possession of a particular object gives as if by magic the meaning of that object. Maurras said the same thing when he declared a Jew to be forever incapable of understanding this line of Racine:

> Dans l'Orient désert, quel devint mon ennui.

But the way is open to me, mediocre me, to understand what the most subtle, the most cultivated intelligence has been unable to grasp. Why? Because I possess Racine—Racine and my country and my soil. Perhaps the Jew speaks a purer French than I do, perhaps he knows syntax and grammar better, perhaps he is even a writer. No matter; he has spoken this language for only twenty years, and I for a thousand years. The correctness of his style is abstract, acquired; my faults of French are in conformity with the genius of the language. We recognize here the reasoning that Barrès used against the holders of scholarships. There is no occasion for surprise. Don't the Jews have all the scholarships? All that intelligence, all that money can acquire one leaves to them, but it is as empty as the wind. The only things that count are irrational values, and it is just these things which are denied the Jews forever. Thus the anti-Semite takes his stand from the start on the ground of irrationalism. He is opposed to the Jew, just as sentiment is to intelligence, the particular to the universal, the past to the present, the concrete to the abstract, the owner of real property to the possessor of negotiable securities.

Besides this, many anti-Semites—the majority, perhaps—belong to the lower middle class of the towns; they are functionaries, office workers, small businessmen, who possess nothing. It is in opposing themselves to the Jew that they suddenly become conscious of being proprietors: in representing the Jew as a robber, they put themselves in the enviable position of people who could be robbed. Since the Jew wishes to take France from them, it follows that France must belong to them. Thus they have chosen anti-Semitism as a means of establishing their status as possessors. The Jew has more money than they? So much the better: money is Jewish, and they can despise it as they despise intelligence. They own less than the gentleman-farmer of Périgord or the large-scale farmer of the Beauce? That doesn't matter. All they have to do is nourish a vengeful anger against the robbers of Israel and they feel at once in possession of the entire country. True Frenchmen, good Frenchmen are all equal, for each of them possesses for himself alone France whole and indivisible.

Thus I would call anti-Semitism a poor man's snobbery. And in fact it would appear that the rich for the most part exploit this passion for their own uses rather than abandon themselves to it—they have better things to do. It is propagated mainly among the middle classes, because they possess neither land nor house nor castle, having only some ready cash and a few securities in the bank. It was not by chance that the petty bourgeoisie of Germany was anti-Semitic in 1925. The principal concern of this "white-collar proletariat" was to distinguish itself from the real proletariat. Ruined by big industry, bamboozled by the Junkers, it was nonetheless to the Junkers and the great industrialists that its whole heart went out. It went in for anti-Semitism with the same enthusiasm that it went in for wearing bourgeois dress: *because* the workers were internationalists, because the Junkers possessed Germany and it wished to possess it also. Anti-Semitism is not merely the joy of hating; it brings positive pleasures too. By treating the Jew as an inferior and pernicious being, I affirm at the same time that I belong to the elite. This elite, in contrast to those of modern times which are based on merit or labor, closely resembles an aristocracy of birth. There is nothing I have to do to merit my superiority, and neither can I lose it. It is given once and for all. It is a *thing*.

We must not confuse this precedence the anti-Semite enjoys by virtue of his principles with individual merit. The anti-Semite is not too anxious to possess individual merit. Merit has to be sought, just like truth; it is discovered with difficulty; one must deserve it. Once acquired, it is perpetually in question: a false step, an error, and it flies away. Without respite, from the beginning of our lives to the end, we are responsible for what merit we enjoy. Now the anti-Semite flees responsibility as he flees his own consciousness, and choosing for his personality the permanence of rock, he chooses for his morality a scale of petrified values. Whatever he does, he knows that he will remain at the top of the ladder; whatever the Jew does, he will never get any higher than the first rung.

We begin to perceive the meaning of the anti-Semite's choice of himself. He chooses the irremediable out of fear of being free; he chooses mediocrity out of fear of being alone, and out of pride he makes of this irremediable mediocrity a rigid aristocracy. To this end he finds the existence of the Jew absolutely necessary. Otherwise to whom would he be superior? Indeed, it is vis-à-vis the Jew and the Jew alone that the anti-Semite realizes that he has rights. If by some miracle all the Jews were exterminated as he wishes, he would find himself nothing but a concierge or a shopkeeper in a strongly hierarchical society in which the quality of "true Frenchman" would be at a low valuation, because everyone would possess it. He would lose his sense of rights over the country because no one would any longer contest them, and that profound equality which brings him close to the nobleman and the man of wealth would disappear all of a sudden, for it is primarily negative. His frustrations, which he has attributed to the disloyal competition of the Jew, would have to be imputed to some other cause, lest he be forced to look within himself. He would run the risk of falling into bitterness, into a melancholy hatred of the privileged classes. Thus the anti-Semite is in the unhappy position of having a vital need for the very enemy he wishes to destroy.

The equalitarianism that the anti-Semite seeks with so much ardor has nothing in common with that equality inscribed in the creed of the democracies. The latter is to be realized in a society that is economically hierarchical, and is to remain compatible with a diversity of functions. But it is in protest *against* the hierarchy of functions that the anti-Semite asserts the equality of Aryans. He does not understand anything about the division of labor and doesn't care about it. From his point of view each citizen can claim the title of Frenchman, not because he co-operates, in his place or in his occupation, with others in the economic, social, and cultural life of the nation, but because he has, in the same way as everybody else, an imprescriptible and inborn right to the indivisible totality of the country. Thus the society that the anti-Semite conceives of is a society of juxtaposition, as one can very well imagine, since his ideal of property is that of real and basic property. Since, in point of fact, anti-Semites are numerous, each of them does his part in constituting a community based on mechanical solidarity in the heart of organized society.

The degree of integration of each anti-Semite with this society, as well as the degree of his equality, is fixed by what I shall call the temperature of the community. Proust has shown, for example, how anti-Semitism brought the duke closer to his coachman, how, thanks to their hatred of Dreyfus, bourgeois families forced the doors of the aristocracy. The equalitarian society that the anti-Semite believes in is like that of mobs or those instantaneous societies which come into being at a lynching or during a scandal. Equality in them is the product of the non-differentiation of functions. The social bond is anger; the collectivity has no other goal than to exercise over certain individuals a diffused repressive sanction. Collective impulsions and stereotypes are imposed on individuals all the more strongly because none of them is defended by any specialized function. Thus the person is drowned in the crowd, and the ways of thinking and reacting of the group are of a purely primitive type. Of course, such collectivities do not spring solely from anti-Semitism; an uprising, a crime, an injustice can cause them to break out suddenly. But those are ephemeral formations which soon vanish without leaving any trace.

Since anti-Semitism survives the great crises of Jew-hatred, the society which the anti-Semites form remains in a latent state during normal periods, with every anti-Semite celebrating its existence. Incapable of understanding modern social organization, he has a nostalgia for periods of crisis in which the primitive community will suddenly reappear and attain its temperature of fusion. He wants his personality to melt suddenly into the group and be carried away by the collective torrent. He has this atmosphere of the pogrom in mind when he asserts "the union of all Frenchmen." In this sense anti-Semitism is, in a democracy, a covert form of what is called the struggle of the citizen against authority. Question any one of those turbulent young men who placidly break the law and band together to beat up a Jew in a deserted street: He will tell you that he wants a strong authority to take from him the crushing responsibility of thinking for himself. Since the Republic is weak, he is led to break the law out of love of obedience. But is it really strong authority that he wishes? In reality he demands rigorous order for others, and for himself disorder without responsibility. He wishes to place himself above the law, at the same time escaping from the consciousness of his liberty and his isolation. He therefore makes use of a subterfuge: The Jews take part in elections; there are Jews in the government; therefore the legal power is vitiated at its base. As a matter of fact, it no longer exists, so it is legitimate to ignore its decrees. Consequently there is no disobedience—one cannot disobey what does not exist. Thus for the anti-Semite there is a *real* France with a government *real* but diffused and without special organs, and an abstract France, official, Jew-ridden, against which it is proper to rebel.

Naturally this permanent rebellion is the act of a group; the anti-Semite would under no circumstances dare to act or think on his own. And the group would be unable to conceive of itself as a minority party, for a minority party is obliged to devise a program and to determine on a line of political action, all of which implies initiative, responsibility, and liberty. Anti-Semitic associations do not wish to invent anything; they refuse to assume responsibility; they would be horrified at setting themselves up as a certain fraction of French opinion, for then they would have to draw up a program and seek legal means of action. They prefer to represent themselves as expressing in all purity, in all passivity, the sentiments of the *real* country in its indivisible state.

Any anti-Semite is therefore, in varying degree, the enemy of constituted authority. He wishes to be the disciplined member of an undisciplined group; he adores order, but a *social* order. We might say that he wishes to provoke political disorder in order to restore social order, the social order in his eyes being a society that, by virtue of juxtaposition, is egalitarian and primitive, one with a heightened temperature, one from which Jews are excluded. These principles enable him to enjoy a strange sort of independence, which I shall call an inverted liberty. Authentic liberty assumes responsibilities, and the liberty of the anti-Semite comes from the fact that he escapes all of his. Floating between an authoritarian society which has not yet come into existence and an official and tolerant society which he disavows, he can do anything he pleases without appearing to be an anarchist, which would horrify him. The profound seriousness of his aims—which no word, no statement, no act can express—permits him a certain frivolity. He is a hooligan, he beats people up, he purges, he robs; it is all in a good cause. If the government is strong, anti-Semitism withers, unless it be a part of the program of the government itself, in which case it changes its nature. Enemy of the Jews, the anti-Semite has need of them. Anti-democratic, he is a natural product of democracies and can only manifest himself within the framework of the Republic.

We begin to understand that anti-Semitism is more than a mere "opinion" about the Jews and that it involves the entire personality of the anti-Semite.

Suggestions for Discussion

1. Why does Sartre call anti-Semitism "a poor man's snobbery"? Do you agree? Explain your point of view.

2. Why does Sartre reject the notion that anti-Semitism is simply a matter of opinion based on observation? How does he argue that not all opinions are equal?

3. Explain Sartre's observation that if the Jew did not exist, the anti-Semite would have to invent him.

4. Compare Sartre's essay with Forster's "Jew-Consciousness." How do the arguments, examples, and tone of the two essays differ?

Suggestions for Writing

1. Write an essay of 500 words in which you apply Sartre's attitude toward the anti-Semite to racist feelings toward another minority.

2. Write a defense of Sartre's assertion that "Anti-Semitism does not fall within the category of ideas protected by the rights of free opinion."

James Baldwin

Fifth Avenue, Uptown: A Letter from Harlem

James Baldwin (b. 1924) was born in New York of Southern, deeply religious and poor parents. At fourteen, he became a preacher in the Fireside Pentecostal Church in Harlem. His first novel *Go Tell It on the Mountain* (1953) reflects his experience as a preacher and, together with *Another Country* (1962), a novel about sex and race, established his reputation as a writer. Since the publication of a lengthy essay, *The Fire Next Time* (1962), he has taken a place as an important spokesman for blacks. He has written significant autobiographical essays and this essay from *Nobody Know My Name* (1961) examines the bitter distinctions that exist between privilege and poverty, between white and black.

There is a housing project standing now where the house in which we grew up once stood, and one of those stunted city trees is snarling where our doorway used to be. This is on the rehabilitated side of the avenue. The other side of the avenue—for progress takes time—has not been rehabilitated yet and it looks exactly as it looked in the days when we sat with our noses pressed against the windowpane, longing to be allowed to go "across the street." The grocery store which gave us credit is still there, and there can be no doubt that it is still giving credit. The people in the project certainly need it—far more, indeed, than they ever needed the project. The last time I passed by, the Jewish proprietor was still standing among his shelves, looking sadder and heavier but scarcely any older. Farther down the block stands the shoe-repair store in which our shoes were repaired until reparation became impossible and in which, then, we bought all our "new" ones. The Negro proprietor is still in the window, head down, working at the leather.

These two, I imagine, could tell a long tale if they would (perhaps they would be glad to if they could), having watched so many, for so long, struggling in the fishhooks, the barbed wire, of this avenue.

The avenue is elsewhere the renowned and elegant Fifth. The area I am describing, which, in today's gang parlance, would be called "the turf," is bounded by Lenox Avenue on the west, the Harlem River on the east, 135th Street on the north, and 130th Street on the south. We never lived beyond these boundaries; this is where we grew up. Walking along 145th Street—for example—familiar as it is, and similar, does not have the same impact because I do not know any of the people on the block. But when I turn east on 131st Street and Lenox Avenue, there is first a soda-pop joint, then a shoeshine "parlor," then a grocery store, then a dry cleaners', then the houses. All along the street there are people who watched me grow up, people who grew up with me, people I watched grow up along with my brothers and sisters; and, sometimes in my arms, sometimes underfoot, sometimes at my shoulder—or on it—their children, a riot, a forest of children, who include my nieces and nephews.

When we reach the end of this long block, we find ourselves on wide, filthy, hostile Fifth Avenue, facing that project which hangs over the avenue like a monument to the folly, and the cowardice, of good intentions. All along the block, for anyone who knows it, are immense human gaps, like craters. These gaps are not created merely by those who have moved away, inevitably into some other ghetto; or by those who have risen, almost always into a greater capacity for self-loathing and self-delusion; or yet by those who, by whatever means—War II, the Korean war, a policeman's gun or billy, a gang war, a brawl, madness, an overdose of heroin, or, simply, unnatural exhaustion—are dead. I am talking about those who are left, and I am talking principally about the young. What are they doing? Well, some, a minority, are fanatical churchgoers, members of the more extreme of the Holy Roller sects. Many, many more are "moslems," by affiliation or sympathy, that is to say that they are united by nothing more—and nothing less—than a hatred of the white world and all its works. They are present, for example, at every Buy Black street-corner meeting—meetings in which the speaker urges his hearers to cease trading with white men and establish a separate economy. Neither the speaker nor his hearers can possibly do this, of course, since Negroes do not own General Motors or RCA or the A & P, nor, indeed, do they own more than a wholly insufficient fraction of anything else in Harlem (those who *do* own anything are more interested in their profits than in their fellows). But these meetings nevertheless keep alive in the participators a certain pride of bitterness without which, however futile this bitterness may be, they could scarcely remain alive at all. Many have given up. They stay home and watch the TV screen, living on the earnings of their parents, cousins, brothers, or uncles, and only leave the house to go to the movies or to the nearest bar. "How're you making it?" one may ask, running into them along the block, or in the bar. "Oh, I'm TV-ing it"; with the saddest, sweetest, most shamefaced of smiles, and from a great distance. This distance one is compelled to respect; anyone who has traveled so far will not easily be dragged again into the world. There are further retreats, of course, than the TV screen or the bar. There are those who are simply sitting on their stoops, "stoned," animated for a moment only, and hideously, by the approach of someone who may lend them the money for a "fix." Or by the approach of someone from whom they can purchase it, one of the shrewd ones, on the way to prison or just coming out.

And the others, who have avoided all of these deaths, get up in the morning and go downtown to meet "the man." They work in the white man's world all day and come home in the evening to this fetid block. They struggle to instill in their children some private sense of honor or dignity which will help the child to survive. This means, of course, that they must struggle, stolidly, incessantly, to keep this sense alive in themselves, in spite of the insults, the indifference, and the cruelty they are certain to encounter in their working day. They patiently browbeat the landlord into fixing the heat, the plaster, the plumbing; this demands prodigious patience; nor is patience usually enough. In trying to make their hovels habitable, they are perpetually throwing good money after bad. Such frustration, so long endured, is driving many strong, admirable men and women whose only crime is color to the very gates of paranoia.

One remembers them from another time—playing handball in the playground, going to church, wondering if they were going to be promoted at school. One remembers them going off to war—gladly, to escape this block. One remembers their return. Perhaps one remembers their wedding day. And one sees where the girl is now—vainly looking for salvation from some other embittered, trussed, and struggling boy—and sees the all-but-abandoned children in the streets.

Now I am perfectly aware that there are other slums in which white men are fighting for their lives, and mainly losing. I know that blood is also flowing through those streets and that the human damage there is incalculable. People are continually pointing out to me the wretchedness of white people in order to console me for the wretchedness of blacks. But an itemized account of the American failure does not console me and it should not console anyone else. That hundreds of thousands of white people are living, in effect, no better than the "niggers" is not a fact to be regarded with complacency. The social and moral bankruptcy suggested by this fact is of the bitterest, most terrifying kind.

The people, however, who believe that this democratic anguish has some consoling value are always pointing out that So-and-So, white, and So-and-So, black, rose from the slums into the big time. The existence—the public existence—of, say, Frank Sinatra and Sammy Davis, Jr. proves to them that America is still the land of opportunity and that inequalities vanish before the determined will. It proves nothing of the sort. The determined will is rare—at the moment, in this country, it is unspeakably rare—and the inequalities suffered by the many are in no way justified by the rise of a few. A few have always risen—in every country, every era, and in the teeth of regimes which can by no stretch of the imagination be thought of as free. Not all of these people, it is worth remembering, left the world better than they found it. The determined will is rare, but it is not invariably benevolent. Furthermore, the American equation of success with the big times reveals an awful disrespect for human life and human achievement. This equation has placed our cities among the most dangerous in the world and has placed our youth among the most empty and most bewildered. The situation of our youth is not mysterious. Children have never been very good at listening to their elders, but they have never failed to imitate them. They must, they have no other models. That is exactly what our children are doing. They are imitating our immorality, our disrespect for the pain of others.

All other slum dwellers, when the bank account permits it, can move out of the slum and vanish altogether from the eye of persecution. No Negro in this country has ever made that much money and it will be a long time before any Negro does. The Negroes in Harlem, who have no money, spend what they have on such gimcracks as they are sold. These include "wider" TV screens, more "faithful" hi-fi sets, more "powerful" cars, all of which, of course, are obsolete long before they are paid for. Anyone who has ever struggled with poverty knows how extremely expensive it is to be poor; and if one is a member of a captive population, economically speaking, one's feet have simply been placed on the treadmill forever. One is victimized, economically, in a thousand ways—rent, for example, or car insurance. Go shopping one day in Harlem—for anything—and compare Harlem prices and quality with those downtown.

The people who have managed to get off this block have only got as far as a more respectable ghetto. This respectable ghetto does not even have the advantages of the disreputable one—friends, neighbors, a familiar church, and friendly tradesmen; and it is not, moreover, in the nature of any ghetto to remain respectable long. Every Sunday, people who have left the block take the lonely ride back, dragging their increasingly discontented children with them. They spend the day talking, not always with words, about the trouble they've seen and the trouble—one must watch their eyes as they watch their children—they are only too likely to see. For children do not like ghettos. It takes them nearly no time to discover exactly why they are there.

The projects in Harlem are hated. They are hated almost as much as policemen, and this is saying a great deal. And they are hated for the same reason: both reveal, unbearably, the real attitude of the white world, no matter how many liberal speeches are made, no matter how many lofty editorials are written, no matter how many civil-rights commissions are set up.

The projects are hideous, of course, there being a law, apparently respected throughout the world, that popular housing shall be as cheerless as a prison. They are lumped all over Harlem, colorless, bleak, high, and revolting. The wide windows look out on Harlem's invincible and indescribable squalor: the Park Avenue railroad tracks, around which, about forty years ago, the present dark community began; the unrehabilitated houses, bowed down, it would seem, under the great weight of frustration and bitterness they contain; the dark, the ominous schoolhouses from which the child may emerge maimed, blinded, hooked, or enraged for life; and the churches, churches, block upon block of churches, niched in the walls like cannon in the walls of a fortress. Even if the administration of the projects were not so insanely humiliating (for example: one must report raises in salary to the management, which will then eat up the profit by raising one's rent; the management has the right to know who is staying in your apartment; the management can ask you to leave, at their discretion), the projects would still be hated because they are an insult to the meanest intelligence.

Harlem got its first private project, Riverton*—which is now, naturally, a slum—about twelve years ago because at that time Negroes were not allowed to live in Stuyvesant Town. Harlem watched Riverton go up, therefore, in the most violent bitterness of spirit, and hated it long before the builders arrived. They began hating it at about the time people began moving out of their condemned houses to make room for this additional proof of how thoroughly the white world despised them. And they had scarcely moved in, naturally, before they began smashing windows, defacing walls, urinating in the elevators, and fornicating in the playgrounds. Liberals, both white and black, were appalled at the spectacle. I was appalled by the liberal innocence—or cynicism, which comes out in practice as much the same thing. Other people were delighted to be able to point to proof positive that nothing could be done to better the lot of the colored people. They were, and are, right in one respect: that nothing can be done as long as they are treated like colored people. The people in Harlem know they are living there because white people do not think they are good enough to live anywhere else. No amount of "improvement" can sweeten this fact. Whatever money is now being earmarked to improve this, or any other ghetto, might as well be burnt. A ghetto can be improved in one way only: out of existence.

Similarly, the only way to police a ghetto is to be oppressive. None of the Police Commissioner's men, even with the best will in the world, have any way of understanding the lives led by the people they swagger about in twos and threes controlling. Their very presence is an insult, and it would be, even if they spent their entire day feeding gumdrops to children. They represent the force of the white world, and that world's real intentions are, simply, for that world's criminal profit and ease, to keep the black man corraled up here, in his place. The badge, the gun in the holster, and the swinging club make vivid what will happen should his rebellion become overt. Rare, indeed, is the Harlem citizen, from the most circumspect church member to the most shiftless adolescent, who does not have a long tale to tell of police incompetence, injustice, or brutality. I myself have witnessed and endured it more than once. The businessmen and racketeers also have a story. And so do the prostitutes. (And this is not, perhaps, the place to discuss Harlem's very complex attitude toward black policemen, nor the reasons, according to Harlem, that they are nearly all downtown.)

It is hard, on the other hand, to blame the policeman, blank, good-natured, thoughtless, and insuperably innocent, for being such a perfect representative of the people he serves. He, too, believes in good intentions and is astounded and offended when they are not taken for the deed. He has never, himself, done anything for which to be hated—which of us has?—and

---

*The inhabitants of Riverton were much embittered by this description; they have, apparently, forgotten how their project came into being; and have repeatedly informed me that I cannot possibly be referring to Riverton, but to another housing project which is directly across the street. It is quite clear, I think, that I have no interest in accusing any individuals or families of the depredations herein described: but neither can I deny the evidence of my own eyes. Nor do I blame anyone in Harlem for making the best of a dreadful bargain. But anyone who lives in Harlem and imagines that he has *not* struck this bargain, or that what he takes to be his status (in whose eyes?) protects him against the common pain, demoralization, and danger, is simply self-deluded.

yet he is facing, daily and nightly, people who would gladly see him dead, and he knows it. There is no way for him not to know it: there are few things under heaven more unnerving than the silent, accumulating contempt and hatred of a people. He moves through Harlem, therefore, like an occupying soldier in a bitterly hostile country; which is precisely what, and where, he is, and is the reason he walks in twos and threes. And he is not the only one who knows why he is always in company: the people who are watching him know why, too. Any street meeting, sacred or secular, which he and his colleagues uneasily cover has as its explicit or implicit burden the cruelty and injustice of the white domination. And these days, of course, in terms increasingly vivid and jubilant, it speaks of the end of that domination. The white policeman standing on a Harlem street corner finds himself at the very center of the revolution now occurring in the world. He is not prepared for it—naturally, nobody is—and, what is possibly much more to the point, he is exposed, as few white people are, to the anguish of the black people around him. Even if he is gifted with the merest mustard grain of imagination, something must seep in. He cannot avoid observing that some of the children, in spite of their color, remind him of children he has known and loved, perhaps even of his own children. He knows that he certainly does not want *his* children living this way. He can retreat from his uneasiness in only one direction: into a callousness which very shortly becomes second nature. He becomes more callous, the population becomes more hostile, the situation grows more tense, and the police force is increased. One day, to everyone's astonishment, someone drops a match in the powder keg and everything blows up. Before the dust has settled or the blood congealed, editorials, speeches, and civil-rights commissions are loud in the land, demanding to know what happened. What happened is that Negroes want to be treated like men.

Negroes want to be treated like men: a perfectly straightforward statement, cointaining only seven words. People who have mastered Kant, Hegel, Shakespeare, Marx, Freud, and the Bible find this statement utterly impenetrable. The idea seems to threaten profound, barely conscious assumptions. A kind of panic paralyzes their features, as though they found themselves trapped on the edge of a steep place. I once tried to describe to a very well-known American intellectual the conditions among Negroes in the South. My recital disturbed him and made him indignant; and he asked me in perfect innocence, "Why don't all the Negroes in the South move North?" I tried to explain what *has* happened, unfailingly, whenever a significant body of Negroes move North. They do not escape Jim Crow: they merely encounter another, not-less-deadly variety. They do not move to Chicago, they move to the South Side; they do not move to New York, they move to Harlem. The pressure within the ghetto causes the ghetto walls to expand, and this expansion is always violent. White people hold the line as long as they can, and in as many ways as they can, from verbal intimidation to physical violence. But inevitably the border which has divided the ghetto from the rest of the world falls into the hands of the ghetto. The white people fall back bitterly before the black horde; the landlords make a tidy profit by raising the rent, chopping up the rooms, and all but dispensing with the upkeep; and what has once been a neighborhood turns into a "turf." This is precisely what happened when the Puerto Ricans arrived in their thousands—and the bitterness thus caused is, as I write, being fought out all up and down those streets.

Northerners indulge in an extremely dangerous luxury. They seem to feel that because they fought on the right side during the Civil War, and won, they have earned the right merely to deplore what is going on in the South, without taking any responsibility for it; and that they can ignore what is happening in Northern cities because what is happening in Little Rock or Birmingham is worse. Well, in the first place, it is not possible for anyone who has not endured both to know which is "worse." I know Negroes who prefer the South and white Southerners, because "At least there, you haven't got to play any guessing games!" The guessing games referred to have driven more than one Negro into the narcotics ward, the madhouse, or the river. I know another Negro, a man very dear to me, who says, with conviction and with truth, "The spirit of the South is the spirit of America." He was born in the North and did his military training in the South. He did not, as far as I can gather, find the South "worse"; he found it, if anything, all too familiar. In the second place, though, even if Birmingham *is* worse, no doubt Johannesburg, South Africa, beats it by several miles, and Buchenwald was one of the worst things that ever happened in the entire history of the world. The world has never lacked for horrifying examples; but I do not believe that these examples are meant to be used as justification for our own crimes. This perpetual justification empties the heart of all human feeling. The emptier our hearts become, the greater will be our crimes. Thirdly, the South is not merely an embarrassingly backward region, but a part of this country, and what happens there concerns every one of us.

As far as the color problem is concerned, there is but one great difference between the Southern white and the Northerner: the Southerner remembers, historically and in his own psyche, a kind of Eden in which he loved black people and they loved him. Historically, the flaming sword laid across this Eden is the Civil War. Personally, it is the Southerner's sexual coming of age, when, without any warning, unbreakable taboos are set up between himself and his past. Everything, thereafter, is permitted him except the love he remembers and has never ceased to need. The resulting, indescribable torment affects every Southern mind and is the basis of the Southern hysteria.

None of this is true for the Northerner. Negroes represent nothing to him personally, except, perhaps, the dangers of carnality. He never sees Negroes. Southerners see them all the time. Northerners never think about them whereas Southerners are never really thinking of anything else. Negroes are, therefore, ignored in the North and are under surveillance in the South, and suffer hideously in both places. Neither the Southerner nor the Northerner is able to look on the Negro simply as a man. It seems to be indispensable to the national self-esteem that the Negro be considered either as a kind of ward (in which case we are told how many Negroes, comparatively, bought Cadillacs last year and how few, comparatively, were lynched), or as a victim (in which case we are promised that he will never vote in our assemblies or go to school with our kids). They are two sides of the same coin and the South will not change—*cannot* change—until the North changes. The country will not change until it re-examines itself and discovers what it really means by freedom. In the meantime, generations keep being born, bitterness is increased by incompetence, pride, and folly, and the world shirinks around us.

It is a terrible, an inexorable, law that one cannot deny the humanity of another without diminishing one's own: in the face of one's victim, one sees oneself. Walk through the streets of Harlem and see what we, this nation, have become.

Suggestions for Discussion

1. Fifth Avenue from 48th to 95th streets in Manhattan has long been a symbol of wealth and elegance. In this essay Baldwin is describing Harlem. What is the effect of using this title and the comparison he develops?

2. What are the major arguments of this essay? How does Baldwin back up his assertions about mistreatment of blacks in Harlem and elsewhere?

3. Explain Baldwin's indictment of the housing developments in Harlem. Why were they hated by black people, according to Baldwin?

4. What, according to Baldwin, is the basic desire of black people in the United States? What inhibits the realization of this desire?

5. Discuss the tone of this essay. How does Baldwin achieve this tone? Your discussion should focus on an analysis of representative passages.

6. How does Baldwin compare the lives of black people in the North and the South?

Suggestions for Writing

1. Write an essay explaining Baldwin's comments about white policemen in Harlem. Are you familiar with attitudes towards the police in your own community? Are the attitudes similar or different from those Baldwin describes? Explain your statements.

2. Baldwin asserts that "one cannot deny the humanity of another without diminishing one's own: in the face of one's victim one sees oneself." Write an essay elaborating on this assertion and supporting your statements by examples with which you are familiar.

3. Baldwin relates the prevalence of crime in the ghetto to the basic problem of poverty and race relations. Write an essay commenting on his remarks. State your agreement or disagreement with his argument.

Plato

The *Crito*

Translated by Benjamin Jowett, revised by Peter White

Plato (428–348 B.C.), born of a noble family, lived in Athens during troubled political times. After the defeat of Athens in the Peloponnesian War, an autocratic and repressive government replaced the democracy, and it, in turn, was succeeded by a regime more demagogic than democratic. Under this government in 399 B.C., Socrates was prosecuted, tried, and condemned to death for subversive activities. In the *Apology* and the *Crito* (neither of them typical Platonic dialogues), Plato undertook the task of rehabilitating Socrates' reputation. Although the historian Xenophon has provided a somewhat different version of Socrates' trial, Plato's portrait of Socrates explains why he regarded him as the best of men. The *Crito* (and the *Phaedo*) presents Socrates in prison as he awaits execution. Crito, a wealthy Athenian, whose primary loyalty in this case is to his friend rather than to the state, urges Socrates to accept his help in escaping. In the course of the dialogue, Socrates leads Crito to agree that a respect for the law and a belief in personal integrity demand that Socrates accept his execution with dignity. Toward the end of the *Crito,* Plato personifies the laws of Athens to explain Socrates' decision to obey them.

Plato's *Republic,* written later than the *Crito,* and additional dialogues in which he uses Socrates to argue his own position on ethics, politics, and other philosophical issues, are Plato's versions of Socrates' conversations. He uses Socrates, however, as teacher of the Socratic method of discourse, which Plato employed in his dialogues, and so it is not surprising that soon after his fortieth year, Plato founded the Academy, the first institute for the purpose of educating suitable rulers for Athens, a school that became a model for many that followed.

SOCRATES: Why have you come at this hour, Crito? it must be quite early?

CRITO: Yes, certainly.

SOC: What is the exact time?

CR: The dawn is breaking.

SOC: I wonder that the keeper of the prison would let you in.

CR: He knows me, because I often come, Socrates; moreover, I have done him a kindness.

SOC: And are you only just arrived?

CR: I came some time ago.

SOC: Then why did you sit and say nothing instead of at once awakening me?

CR: That I could never have done, Socrates. I only wish I were not so sleepless and distressed myself. I have been looking at you, wondering how you can sleep so comfortably, and I didn't wake you on purpose, so that you could go on sleeping in perfect comfort. All through your life, I have often thought you were favored with a good disposition, but I have never been so impressed as in the present misfortune, seeing how easily and tranquilly you bear it.

Soc: Why, Crito, when a man has reached my age he ought not to be repining at the approach of death.

Cr: And yet other old men find themselves in similar misfortunes, and age does not prevent them from repining.

Soc: That is true. But you have not told me why you come at this early hour.

Cr: I come with a message which is painful—not, I expect, to you, but painful and oppressive for me and all your friends, and I think it weighs most heavily of all on me.

Soc: What? Has the ship come from Delos, on the arrival of which I am to die?[1]

Cr: No, the ship has not actually arrived, but she will probably be here today, as persons who have come from Sunium tell me that they left her there; and therefore tomorrow, Socrates, will be the last day of your life.

Soc: Very well, Crito; if such is the will of the gods, I am willing; but my belief is that there will be a day's delay.

Cr: Why do you think so?

Soc: I will tell you. I am to die on the day after the arrival of the ship.

Cr: Yes; that is what the authorities say.

Soc: But I do not think that the ship will be here until tomorrow; this I infer from a vision which I had last night, or rather only just now, when you fortunately allowed me to sleep.

Cr: And what was the nature of the vision?

Soc: There appeared to me the likeness of a woman, fair and comely, clothed in bright raiment, who called to me and said: O Socrates,

"The third day hence to fertile Phthia shalt thou come."[2]

Cr: What a singular dream, Socrates!

Soc: There can be no doubt about the meaning, Crito, I think.

Cr: Yes; the meaning is only too clear. But, oh! my beloved Socrates, let me entreat you once more to take my advice and escape. For if you die, I shall not only lose a friend who can never be replaced, but there is another evil: people who do not know you and me will believe that I might have saved you if I had been willing to give money but that I did not care. Now, can there be a worse disgrace than this—that I should be thought to value money more than the life of a friend? For the many will not be persuaded that I wanted you to escape and that you refused.

Soc: But why, my dear Crito, should we care about the opinion of the many? Good men, and they are the only persons who are worth considering, will think of these things truly as they occurred.

Cr: But you see, Socrates, that the opinion of the many must be regarded, for what is now happening shows that they can do the greatest evil to anyone who has lost their good opinion.

---

[1] Once every year Athens sent a state ship on a ceremonial pilgrimage to the island of Delos; no executions could be carried out between its departure and return.

[2] The apparition borrows the words in which Achilles contemplated a return from Troy to his home, *Iliad* 9.363.

Soc: I only wish it were so, Crito, and that the many could do the greatest evil; for then they would also be able to do the greatest good—and what a fine thing this would be! But in reality they can do neither; for they cannot make a man either wise or foolish, and whatever result they produce is the result of chance.

Cr: Well, I will not dispute with you; but please tell me, Socrates, whether you are not acting out of regard to me and your other friends: Are you not afraid that, if you escape from prison, we may get into trouble with the informers for having stolen you away and lose either the whole or a great part of our property—or that even a worse evil may happen to us? Now, if you fear on our account, be at ease; for in order to save you, we ought surely to run this or even a greater risk; be persuaded, then, and do as I say.

Soc: Yes, Crito, that is one fear which you mention, but by no means the only one.

Cr: Fear not—there are persons who are willing to get you out of prison at no great cost; and as for the informers, they are far from being exorbitant in their demands—a little money will satisfy them. My means, which are certainly ample, are at your service; and if, out of solicitude about me, you hesitate to use mine, there are non-Athenians here who will give you the use of theirs; and one of them, Simmias the Theban, has brought a large sum of money for this very purpose; and Cebes and many others are prepared to spend their money in helping you to escape. Therefore do not hesitate to save yourself because you are worried about this, and do not say, as you did in the court, that you will have difficulty in knowing what to do with yourself anywhere else. For men will love you in other places to which you may go, and not in Athens only; there are friends of mine in Thessaly, if you would like to go to them, who will value and protect you, and no Thessalian will give you any trouble. Nor can I think that you are at all justified, Socrates, in betraying your own life when you might be saved. You are only working to bring about what your enemies, who want to destroy you, would and did in fact work to accomplish. And further, I should say that you are deserting your own children; for you might bring them up and educate them, instead of which you go away and leave them, and they will have to take their chances; and if they do not meet with the usual fate of orphans, there will be small thanks to you. No man should bring children into the world who is unwilling to persevere to the end in their nurture and education. But you appear to be choosing the easier part, not the better and manlier, which would have been more becoming in one who has professed a life-long concern for virtue, like yourself. And indeed, I am ashamed not only of you but of us, who are your friends, when I reflect that the whole business will be attributed entirely to our want of courage. The trial need never have come on or might have been managed differently. And now it may seem that we have made a ridiculous bungle of this last chance, thanks to our lack of toughness and courage, since we failed to save you and you failed to save yourself, even though it was possible and practicable if we were good for anything at all. So, Socrates, you must not let this turn into a disgrace as well as a tragedy for yourself and us. Make up your mind then, or rather have your mind already made up; for the time of deliberation is over, and there is only one thing to be done, which must be done this very night, and, if we delay at all, it will be no longer practicable or possible; I beseech you therefore, Socrates, be persuaded by me, and do not be contrary.

Soc: My dear Crito, your solicitude is invaluable if it is rightly directed, but otherwise, the more intense, the more difficult it is to deal with. And so we should consider whether I ought to follow this course or not. You know it has always been true that I paid no heed to any consideration I was aware of except that argument which, on reflection, seemed best to me. I cannot throw over the arguments I used to make in times past just because this situation has arisen: they look the same to me as before, and I respect and honor them as much as ever. You must therefore understand that if, on the present occasion, we cannot make better arguments, I will not yield to you—not even if the power of the people conjures up the bugaboos of imprisonment and death and confiscation, as though we could be scared like little children. What will be the fairest way of considering the question? Shall I return to your old argument about the opinions of men? We were saying that some of them are to be regarded, and others not. Now were we right in maintaining this before I was condemned? And has the argument which was once good now proved to be talk for the sake of talking—mere childish nonsense? That is what I want to consider with your help, Crito: whether, under my present circumstances, the argument will appear to be in any way different or not, and whether we shall subscribe to it or let it go. That argument, which, as I believe, is maintained by many persons of authority, was to the effect, as I was saying, that the opinions of some men are to be regarded, and of other men not to be regarded. Now you, Crito, are not going to die tomorrow—at least, there is no human probability of this—and therefore you are disinterested and not liable to be deceived by the circumstances in which you are placed. Tell me, then, whether I am right in saying that some opinions, and the opinions of some men only, are to be valued and that other opinions, and the opinions of other men, are not to be valued. I ask you whether I was right in maintaining this?

Cr: Certainly.

Soc: The good opinions are to be regarded, and not the bad?

Cr: Yes.

Soc: And the opinions of the wise are good, and the opinions of the unwise are bad?

Cr: Certainly.

Soc: Now what was the argument about this: does the serious athlete attend to the praise and blame and opinion of every man or of one man only—his physician or trainer, whoever he may be?

CR: Of one man only.

SOC: And he ought to fear the censure and welcome the praise of that one only, and not of the many?

CR: Clearly so.

SOC: And he ought to act and train and eat and drink in the way which seems good to his single master, who has understanding, rather than according to the opinion of all other men put together?

CR: True.

SOC: And if he disobeys and disregards the opinion and approval of the one, and regards the opinion of the many who have no understanding, will he not suffer harm?

CR: Certainly he will.

SOC: And what will the harm be: where will it be localized, and what part of the disobedient person will it affect?

CR: Clearly, it will affect the body; that is what is destroyed.

SOC: Very good, and is not this true, Crito, of other things, which we need not separately enumerate? In questions of just and unjust, fair and foul, good and evil, which are the subjects of our present consultation, ought we to follow the opinion of the many, and to fear them, or the opinion of the one man who has understanding? Ought we not to fear and reverence him more than all the rest of the world, and, if we desert him, shall we not ruin and mutilate that principle in us which is improved by justice and deteriorated by injustice—there is such a principle?

CR: Certainly there is, Socrates.

SOC: Take a parallel instance: if, ignoring the advice of those who have understanding, we destroy that which is improved by health and is deteriorated by disease, would life be worth having? and that which has been destroyed is—the body?

CR: Yes.

SOC: Would life be worth living with an evil and corrupted body?

CR: Certainly not.

SOC: And will life be worth living if that faculty which injustice damages and justice improves is ruined? Do we suppose that principle—whatever it may be in man which has to do with justice and injustice—to be inferior to the body?

CR: Certainly not.

SOC: More honorable than the body?

CR: Far more.

SOC: Then, my friend, we must not regard what the many say of us but what he, the one man who has understanding of just and unjust, will say and what the truth will say. And therefore you begin in error when you advise that we should regard the opinion of the many about just and unjust, good and evil, honorable and dishonorable. "Well," someone will say, "but the many can kill us."

CR: That is plain, and a person might well say so. You are right, Socrates.

Soc: But dear Crito, the argument which we have gone over still seems as valid as before. And I should like to know whether I may say the same of another proposition—that not life, but a good life, is to be chiefly valued?

Cr: Yes, that also remains unshaken.

Soc: And a good life is equivalent to an honorable and just one—that holds also?

Cr: Yes, it does.

Soc: From these premises I proceed to argue the question whether I am justified in trying to escape without the consent of the Athenians; and if I am clearly right in escaping, then I will make the attempt, but, if not, I will abstain. The other considerations which you mention—of money and loss of character and the duty of educating one's children—are, I fear, only the doctrines of the multitude, who, if they could, would restore people to life as readily as they put them to death—and with as little reason. But since we have been forced this far by the logic of our argument, the only question which remains to be considered is whether we shall do right in giving money and thanks to those who will rescue me, and in taking a direct role in the rescue ourselves, or whether in fact we will be doing wrong. And if it appears that we will be doing wrong, then neither death nor any other calamity that follows from staying and doing nothing must be judged more important than that.

Cr: I think that you are right, Socrates. How then shall we proceed?

Soc: Let us consider the matter together, and you, either refute me if you can, and I will be convinced, or else cease, my dear friend, from repeating to me that I ought to escape against the wishes of the Athenians. It is most important to me that I act with your assent and not against your will. And now please consider whether my starting point is adequately stated, and also try to answer my questions as you think best.

Cr: I will.

Soc: Are we to say that we are never intentionally to do wrong, or that in one way we ought and in another we ought not to do wrong? Or is doing wrong always evil and dishonorable, as we often concluded in times past? Or have all those past conclusions been thrown overboard during the last few days? And have we, at our age, been earnestly discoursing with one another all our life long only to discover that we are no better than children? Or, in spite of the opinion of the many, and in spite of consequences, whether better or worse, shall we insist on the truth of what was then said, that injustice is always an evil and a dishonor to him who acts unjustly? Shall we say so or not?

Cr: Yes.

Soc: Then we must do no wrong?

Cr: Certainly not.

Soc: Nor, when injured, injure in return, as the many imagine; for we must injure no one at all?

Cr: Clearly not.

Soc: Again, Crito, may we do evil?

CR: Surely not, Socrates.

Soc: And what of doing evil in return for evil, which is the morality of the many—is that just or not?

CR: Not just.

Soc: For doing evil to another is the same as injuring him?

CR: Very true.

Soc: Then we ought not to retaliate or render evil for evil to anyone, whatever evil we may have suffered from him. But I would have you consider, Crito, whether you really mean what you are saying. For this opinion has never been held, and never will be held, by any considerable number of persons; and those who are agreed and those who are not agreed upon this point have no common ground and can only despise one another when they see how widely they differ. Tell me, then, whether you agree with and assent to my first principle, that neither injury nor retaliation nor warding off evil by evil is ever right. And shall that be the premise of our argument? Or do you decline and dissent from this? For so I have ever thought, and continue to think; but, if you are of another opinion, let me hear what you have to say. If, however, you remain of the same mind as formerly, I will proceed to the next step.

CR: You may proceed, for I have not changed my mind.

Soc: The next thing I have to say, or, rather, my next question, is this: Ought a man to do what he admits to be right, or ought he to betray the right?

CR: He ought to do what he thinks right.

Soc: In light of that, tell me whether or not there is some victim—a particularly undeserving victim—who is hurt if I go away without persuading the city. And do we abide by what we agree was just or not?

CR: I cannot answer your question, Socrates, because I do not see what you are getting at.

Soc: Then consider the matter in this way: imagine that I am about to run away (you may call the proceeding by any name which you like), and the laws and the government come and interrogate me: "Tell us, Socrates," they say; "what are you up to? are you not going by an act of yours to destroy us—the laws, and the whole state—as far as in you lies? Do you imagine that a state can subsist and not be overthrown in which the decisions of law have no power but are set aside and trampled upon by individuals?" What will be our answer, Crito, to questions like these? Anyone, and especially a rhetorician, would have a good deal to say against abrogation of the law that requires a sentence to be carried out. He will argue that this law should not be set aside. Or shall we retort, "Yes; but the state has injured us and given an unjust sentence." Suppose I say that?

CR: Very good, Socrates.

Soc: "And was that our agreement with you?" the laws would answer; "or were you to abide by the sentence of the state?" And if I were to express my astonishment at their talking this way, they would probably add: "Take control of your astonishment and answer, Socrates—you are in the habit of asking and answering questions. Tell us: What complaint have you to make against us which justifies you in attempting to destroy us and the state? In the first place, did we not bring you into existence? Your father married your mother by our aid and brought you into the world. Say whether you have any objection to urge against those of us who regulate marriage." None, I should reply. "Or against those of us who after birth regulate the nurture and education of children, in which you also were trained? Were not the laws, which have the charge of education, right in commanding your father to train you in music and athletics?" Right, I should reply. "Well then, since you were brought into the world and nurtured and educated by us, can you deny in the first place that you are our child and slave, as your fathers were before you? And if this is true, do you really think you have the same rights as we do and that you are entitled to do to us whatever we do to you? Would you have any right to strike or revile or do any other evil to your father or your master, if you had one, because you had been struck or reviled by him or received some other evil at his hands?— you would not say this? And because we think it right to destroy you, do you think that you have any right to destroy us in return, and your country, as far as in you lies? Will you, o professor of true virtue, pretend that you are justified in this? Has a philosopher like you failed to discover that our country is more to be valued and higher and holier far than mother or father or any ancestor, and more to be regarded in the eyes of the gods and of men of understanding? Also to be soothed and gently and reverently entreated when angry, even more than a father, and either to be persuaded or, if not persuaded, to be obeyed? And when we are punished by her, whether with imprisonment or beatings, the punishment is to be endured in silence; and if she leads us to wounds or death in battle, there we follow as is right; neither may anyone yield or retreat or leave his rank, but whether in battle, or in a court of law, or in any other place, he must do what his city and his country order him, or he must change their view of what is just; and if he may do no violence to his father or mother, much less may he do violence to his country." What answer shall we make to this, Crito? Do the laws speak truly, or do they not?

CR: I think that they do.

SOC: Then the laws will say, "Consider, Socrates, if we are speaking truly that in your present attempt you are going to do us an injury. For, having brought you into the world, and nurtured and educated you, and given you and every other citizen a share in every good which we had to give, we further proclaim to any Athenian, by the liberty which we allow him, that if he does not like us when he has come of age and has seen the ways of the city and made our acquaintance, he may go where he pleases and take his goods with him. None of us laws will stand in the way if any of you who are dissatisfied with us and the city want to go to a colony or to move anywhere else. None of us forbids anyone to go where he likes, taking his property with him. But he who has experience of the manner in which we order justice and administer the state, and still remains, has entered into an implied contract that he will do as we command him. And he who disobeys us is, as we maintain, thrice wrong: first, because in disobeying us he is disobeying his parents; secondly, because we are the authors of his education; thirdly, because he has made an agreement with us that he will duly obey our commands, but he neither obeys them nor convinces us that our commands are unjust. We show flexibility. We do not brutally demand his compliance but offer him the choice of obeying or persuading us; yet he does neither.

"These are the sorts of accusations to which, as we were saying, you, Socrates, will be exposed if you accomplish your intentions; you, above all other Athenians." Suppose now I ask, why I rather than anybody else? They might reasonably take me to task because I above all other men have acknowledged the agreement. "There is clear proof," they will say, "Socrates, that we and the city were not displeasing to you. Of all Athenians you have been the most constant resident in the city, which, as you never leave it, you may be supposed to love. For you never went out of the city either to see the games, except once, when you went to the Isthmus, or to any other place unless when you were on military service; nor did you travel as other men do. Nor had you any curiosity to know other states or their laws: your affections did not go beyond us and our state; we were your special favorites, and you acquiesced in our government of you; and here in this city you had your children, which is a proof of your satisfaction. Moreover, you might in the course of the trial, if you had liked, have fixed the penalty at banishment, and then you could have done with the city's consent what you now attempt against its will. But you pretended that you preferred death to exile and that you were not unwilling to die. And now you do not blush at the thought of your old arguments and pay no respect to us, the laws, of whom you are the destroyer, and are doing what only a miserable slave would do, running away and turning your back on the compacts and agreements by which you agreed to act as a citizen. And, first of all, answer this very question: Are we right in saying that by your actions if not in words you agreed to our terms of citizenship? Is that true or not?" How shall we answer, Crito? Must we not assent?

CR: We cannot help it, Socrates.

SOC: Then will they not say: "You, Socrates, are breaking the covenants and agreements which you made with us. You were not compelled to agree, or tricked, or forced to make up your mind in a moment, but had a period of seventy years during which you were free to depart if you were dissatisfied with us and the agreements did not seem fair. You did not pick Sparta or Crete, whose fine government you take every opportunity to praise, or any other state of the Greek or non-Greek world. You spent less time out of Athens than men who are crippled or blind or otherwise handicapped. That shows how much more than other Athenians you valued the city and us too, its laws (for who would value a city without laws?). And will you not now abide by your agreements? You will if you listen to us, Socrates, and you will not make yourself ridiculous by leaving the city.

"For just consider: if you transgress and err in this sort of way, what good will you do either to yourself or to your friends? That your friends will be driven into exile and deprived of citizenship or will lose their property is tolerably certain. And you yourself, if you go to one of the neighboring cities, like Thebes or Megara (both being well-ordered states, of course), will come as an enemy of their government, and all patriotic citizens will eye you suspiciously as a subverter of the laws, and you will confirm in the minds of the judges the justice of their own condemnation of you. For he who is a corrupter of the laws is more than likely to be a corrupter of the young and foolish portion of mankind. Will you then flee from well-ordered cities and law-abiding men? And will life be worth living if you do that? Or will you approach them and discourse unashamedly about—about what, Socrates? Will you discourse as you did here, about how virtue and justice and institutions and laws are the best things among men? Don't you think that such behavior coming from Socrates will seem disgusting? Surely one must think so. But if you go away from well-governed states to Crito's friends in Thessaly, where there is great disorder and license, they will be charmed to hear the tale of your escape from prison, set off with ludicrous particulars of the manner in which you were wrapped in a goatskin or some other disguise and metamorphosed in the usual manner of runaways. But will there be no one to comment that in your old age, when in all probability you had only a little time left to live, you were not ashamed to violate the most sacred laws from the greedy desire of a little more life? Perhaps not, if you keep them in good temper; but if they are out of temper, you will hear many degrading things. You will live as the flatterer and slave of all men, achieving what else but the chance to feast in Thessaly, as though you had gone abroad in order to get a meal? And where will the old arguments be, about justice and virtue? Say that you wish to live for the sake of your children—you want to bring them up and educate them—will you take them into Thessaly and deprive them of Athenian citizenship? Is this the benefit which you will confer upon them? Or are you under the impression that they will be better cared for and educated here if you are still alive, although absent from them; for your friends will take care of them? Do you fancy that, if you move to Thessaly, they will take care of them but that, if you move into the other world, they will not take care of them? No, if those who call themselves friends are good for anything, they will—to be sure, they will.

"Listen, then, Socrates, to us who have brought you up. Think not of life and children first and of justice afterwards but of justice first, so that you may defend your conduct to the rulers of the world below. For neither will you nor any that belong to you be happier or holier or juster in this life, or happier in another, if you do as Crito bids. Now you depart in innocence, a sufferer and not a doer of evil; a victim, not of the laws but of men. But if you escape, returning evil for evil and injury for injury, breaking the covenants and agreements which you have made with us and wronging those you ought least of all to wrong—that is to say, yourself, your friends, your country, and us—we shall be angry with you while you live, and our brethren, the laws in the world below, will receive you in no kindly spirit; for they will know that you have done your best to destroy us. Listen, then, to us and not to Crito."

This, dear Crito, is the voice I seem to hear murmuring in my ears, like the sound of the flute in the ears of the mystic; that voice, I say, is humming in my ears and prevents me from hearing any other. You must realize that you will be wasting your time if you speak against the convictions I hold at the moment. But if you think you will get anywhere, go ahead.

CR: No, Socrates, I have nothing to say.

SOC: Then be resigned, Crito, and let us follow this course, since this is the way the god points out.

Suggestions for Discussion

1. What arguments does Crito use to urge Socrates to escape? To what extent do you agree with his position? How does Socrates counter his arguments?

2. Why does Socrates say that one should only consider the opinion of good people?

3. What qualities of character does Plato create for both Crito and Socrates? Which of the two men is more like most of us?

4. Explain Socrates' use of the analogy of the athlete and his trainer and the parallel question of whether life is worth living in a corrupted body.

5. How does Socrates distinguish between the value of "life" and "a good life"?

6. Socrates persuades Crito that a good man should never intentionally commit a wrong act. How does he relate this assertion to the issue of whether he should attempt to escape from prison?

7. Why does Socrates summon up the laws of Athens to discuss his strict obedience to them? What arguments do they offer?

8. Why does Socrates say that he must listen to the voice of the god? How does he connect the laws of the state to the god?

Suggestions for Writing

1. Socrates' arguments for obeying the laws of the state have not always found universal agreement. How do you relate these arguments to those of Antigone in Sophocles' play? In modern times, civil disobedience has moved men like Henry David Thoreau, Mahatma Gandhi, and Martin Luther King. A research paper of five pages could compare and contrast the writings of Thoreau, Gandhi, and King with this dialogue by Plato.

2. Have you ever broken the law or been tempted to do so? What reasons have restrained you or otherwise guided your behavior? Write a paper of 500 words in which you analyze your own motives as Socrates analyzes his.

Ryszard Kapuściński

Fire on the Road

Translated by William Brand and Katarzyna Mroczkowska-Brand

Ryszard Kapuściński (b. 1932), a Polish writer who writes about Africa has written *The Emperor: Downfall of an Aristocrat* (1984), *The Shah of Shahs* (1985), and *Another Day of Life,* a book on Angola (1986), "Fire on the Road," which describes revolution in Nigeria in 1966, appeared in different form in *Wojna Futbolowa (The Football War),* published in Poland in 1986. The headnote to the essay makes clear that the actions in the current crisis facing whites and blacks in South Africa have a long history.

Introductory Note: Speaking in April at a rally in Soweto, Winnie Mandela was reported as saying, "Together, hand in hand, with our matches and our necklaces, we shall liberate this country."* In South Africa "necklaces" is the word used for tires filled with gasoline that are placed around the necks of collaborators and traitors to the cause of liberation, who are then doused with more gasoline and set on fire. Mrs. Mandela later said the press had distorted her speech and she repudiated the statement. But this kind of punishment and this kind of death have been practiced in South Africa for some time, to the horror of some and as a warning to others. Black policemen in flames in South Africa, like witches burning at the stake in Europe, and later, during World War II, Jews set on fire by Nazis in Warsaw and Bialystok, are victims of the same cruel myth, a belief deeply rooted among all fanatics, that fire is not only punishment but the only true purification—that all evil, if one wants to be really rid of it, has to be burned out in an absolutely literal sense.

The vision of fire as the highest agent of punishment and condemnation appears in many faiths and religions. It is one of the most suggestive images of the Apocalypse, a horrible sight, which from childhood admonishes us against temptation and sin—or else we will be hurled into the eternal flames of hell. But there is yet another, "educational," side of this phenomenon, well known to those who, by putting their opponents to the torch, treat suffering as a spectacle: by passively observing a man being burned alive we indirectly become participants in the crime, take part in it, have implicated ourselves.

What it feels like during the moments before one is set on fire I experienced myself when I was reporting on the first civil war in Nigeria in 1966 (the second war, which erupted soon thereafter, was over Biafra). The conflict I describe here touched off a series of internal clashes, coups, and upheavals in this most heavily populated of the African countries. They continue to this day and in two decades have claimed more than one million victims and caused enormous destruction. During the past twenty years only one Nigerian government came to power through elections (in 1979, the government of Shohu Shagari, now deposed). At all the other times, those who gained power gained it through coups (1966—Major General Johnson Aguiyi-Ironsi; 1966—Colonel [later General] Yakubu Gowon; 1975—Brigadier Murtala

*Quoted in the Sunday *Observer* (April 20, 1986), p. 10.

Muhammad; 1976—Lieutenant General Olusegun Obansanjo; 1983—Major General Muhammadu Buhari; 1985—Major General Ibrahim Babangida).

Most often these takeovers of power are bloody, and those who stage them either perish themselves soon thereafter at the hands of rivals (as did Aguiyi-Ironsi and Murtala Muhammad), or end up in exile (as has General Gowon). Over the last quarter-century the Nigerian officer corps, rent by tribal and political conflicts, obsessed by an implacable struggle for power, has been decimating itself at such a rate that few of those officers who were in the army when Nigeria gained independence in 1960 are alive today. Whoever wants to understand the history of those battles and the tensions and passions behind them should read Shakespeare's plays, and keep in his mind's eye the royal throne constantly dripping with blood.

—Translated by Klara Glowczewski

January 1966. In Nigeria a civil war is going on. I am a correspondent in that war. On a cloudy day I leave Lagos. In the outskirts police are stopping all cars. They are searching the trunks, looking for weapons. They rip open sacks of corn: Could there be ammunition in that corn?

Authority ends at the city limits.

Now the road leads through a green countryside of low hills covered with close, thick bush. This is a laterite road, rust colored, with a treacherous uneven surface.

These hills, this road, and these villages along the road are the country of the Yorubas, who inhabit southwestern Nigeria. They constitute one fourth of Nigeria's population. The heaven of the Yorubas is full of gods and their earth full of kings. The greatest god is called Oduduwa and he lives on high, higher than the stars, even higher than the sun. The kings, on the other hand, live close to the people. In every city and every village there is a king. The Yorubas are proud of this—they look down on the rest of the world, because no other nation has so many kings.

In 1962 the Yorubas split into two camps. The overwhelming majority belongs to the UPGA party; an insignificant minority belongs to the NNDP party. Thanks to the trickery of the Nigerian central government, the minority party rules the Yorubas' province. The central government, which is dominated by the NPC (National People's Congress) from the north, prefers a minority government in the province as a means of more easily controlling the Yorubas and curbing their separatist ambitions. In this situation the party of the majority—the UPGA—found itself in opposition. The deceived and embittered majority went on the warpath. In the fall of 1965 there were elections in the Yorubas' province. It was obvious that the majority party, UPGA, won. Nevertheless, the central government ignored the results and the mood of the Yorubas and announced the victory of the puppet NNDP, which went on to form a government. In protests against the official election results, the majority created a government of its own. For a time there were two governments. The members of the majority government were imprisoned in the end. At that point the UPGA launched an open war against the minority government.

And so we have misfortune, we have a war. It is an unjust, dirty, hooliganish war in which all methods are allowed—whatever it takes to knock out the opponent and gain control. This war needs a lot of fire so houses are burning, plantations are burning, and charred bodies lie in the streets and along the roads.

The whole land of the Yorubas is in flames.

I am driving along a road where they say no white man can come back alive. I am driving to see if a white man can, because I have to experience everything for myself. I know that a man shudders in the forest when he passes close to a lion. I got close to a lion so that I would know how it feels. I had to do it myself because I knew no one could describe it to me. And I cannot describe it myself. Nor can I describe a night in the Sahara. The stars over the Sahara are enormous. They sway above the sand like great chandeliers. The light of those stars is green. Night in the Sahara is as green as a Mazowsze meadow in Poland.

I might see the Sahara again and I might see the road that carried me through Yoruba country again. I drove that road up a hill and when I got to the crest I could see the first flaming roadblock down below.

It was too late to turn back.

Burning logs blocked the road. There was a big bonfire in the middle of the road. I slowed down, and then stopped, because it was impossible to keep going. I could see fifteen or twenty young people. Some of them had shotguns, some were holding knives, and the rest were armed with machetes. They were all dressed alike, in blue shirts with white sleeves. Those were the colors of the opposition, of the UPGA. On their heads they wore black and white caps with the letters UPGA. They had pictures of Chief Awolowo pinned to their shirts. Chief Awolowo was the leader of the opposition, the idol of the party.

I was in the hands of UPGA activists. They must have been smoking hashish because their eyes were unconscious, mad. They were soaked in sweat, possessed, berserk.

Now they descended on me and pulled me out of the car. I could hear them shouting, "UPGA! UPGA!" On this road, UPGA ruled. Now UPGA held me in its sway. I could feel three knife points against my back and I saw several machetes aimed at my head. Two activists stood a few steps away, pointing their guns at me in case I tried to get away. I was surrounded. Around me I could see sweaty faces, jumpy glances, I could see knives and gun barrels.

My African experience had taught me that the worst thing to do in such situations is to betray the moment of despair, the worst thing is to make some movement of self-defense, because that emboldens the people you face and unleashes a new wave of aggression in them.

In the Congo they poked machine guns in our bellies. We couldn't flinch. The most important thing was keeping still—to learn that keeping still takes practice and willpower, because everything inside screams to run for it or jump the other guy. But they are always in groups and that means certain death. This is a moment when he, the black, is testing me, looking for a weak point in me. He fears attacking my strong point, because he has too much fear of the white in him—that is why he looks for my weakness. So I have to cover all my weakness, hide it somewhere very deep within myself. This is Africa, I am in Africa. They do not know that I am not their enemy. They know that I am white, and the only white they have ever known is the colonizer who abased them, and now they want to make me pay for it.

The paradox of the situation is that I am to die out of responsibility for colonialism, I am to die in expiation of the slave merchants, I am to die to atone for the white planter's whip, I am to die because Lady Lugard ordered them to carry her in a litter.

The ones standing in the road wanted money. They wanted me to join the party, to become a member of UPGA, and to pay for it. I gave them five shillings. That was too little, because somebody hit me on the back of the head. I felt pain in my skull. In a moment another bomb went off in my head. After the third blow I felt enormous fatigue. Tired and sleepy, I asked how much they wanted.

They wanted five pounds.

Everything in Africa is getting more expensive. In the Congo soldiers were accepting people into the party for one pack of cigarettes and one blow with a rifle butt. But here I've already got it a couple of times and I'm still supposed to pay five pounds. I must have hesitated because the boss, who was supervising things, shouted to the activists, "Burn the car!" and that car, the Peugeot that was carrying me around Africa, was not mine. It belonged to the Polish state. One of them splashed gasoline onto the Peugeot.

I understood that the discussion had ended and I had no way out. I gave them the five pounds. They started fighting over it.

But they allowed me to drive on. Two boys moved the burning logs aside. I looked around. On both sides of the road there was a village and the village crowd was watching the action on the road. The people were silent; somebody in the crowd was holding up an UPGA banner. Most had photographs of Chief Awolowo pinned onto their shirts. I liked the girls best of all. Naked to the waist, they had the name of the party written on their full breasts: UP on the right breast, and GA on the left one.

I started off.

I could not turn back—they allowed me only to go forward. So I kept driving through a country at war, with a rooster tail of dust behind me. The landscape is beautiful there, all vivid colors, Africa the way I like it. Quiet, empty, with a bird taking flight in the path of the car every now and then. The roaring of a factory was only in my head. But an empty road and a car gradually restore calm.

Now I knew the price: UPGA had demanded five pounds of me. I only had four and a half pounds left, and fifty kilometers to go. I passed a burning village and an empty village where people were fleeing into the bush. Two goats were grazing by the roadside and smoke hung above the road.

Beyond the village was another flaming roadblock.

Activists in UPGA uniforms, knives in their hands, were kicking a driver who did not want to pay his membership fee. Nearby stood a bloody, beaten man—he hadn't been able to come up with the dues, either. Everything looked just as it had at the first roadblock. At this second roadblock I didn't even manage to announce my desire to join UPGA before I took a pair of hooks to the midsection and had my shirt torn. They turned my pockets inside out and took all my money.

I was waiting for them to set me on fire, because UPGA was burning a lot of people alive. I had seen many burned corpses. The boss at this roadblock popped me one in the face and I felt a warm sweetness in my mouth. Then he poured benzene on me, because here they burn people in benzene—it assures complete incineration.

I felt an animal fear, a fear that struck me like paralysis; I stood rooted to the ground, as if I were buried up to the neck. I could feel the sweat flowing over me, but under my skin I was as cold as if I were standing naked in subzero frost.

I wanted to live, but life was abandoning me. I wanted to live, but I did not know how to defend my life. My life was going to end in inhuman torment. I was going to go out in flames.

What did they want from me? They waved a knife before my eyes. They pointed the knife at my heart. The boss of the operation stuffed my money into his pocket and shouted at me, blasting me with his beery breath: "Power! UPGA must get power! We want power! UPGA is power!" He was shaking, swept up in the passion of power, he was mad about power, the very word "power" sent him into ecstasy, into the highest rapture. His face was covered with sweat, the veins on his forehead were bulging, and his eyes were shot with blood and madness. He was happy and he began to laugh in joy. They all started laughing. That laughter saved me.

They ordered me to drive on.

The little crowd around the roadblock shouted "UPGA!" and held up their hands with two fingers stretched out in the V sign: victory for UPGA on all fronts.

Some four kilometers down the road a third roadblock was burning. The road was straight here and I could see the smoke a long way off, and then the fire and the activists. I could not turn back. There were two barriers behind me. I could only go forward. I was trapped, falling out of one ambush and into another. But now I was out of money for ransom, and I knew that if I didn't pay up they would burn the car. Above all, I didn't want another beating. I was whipped, my shirt was in tatters, and I reeked of benzene.

There was only one way out: to run the roadblock. It was risky, because I might wreck the car or it might catch fire. But I had no choice.

I pressed the accelerator to the floor. The roadblock was a kilometer ahead. The speedometer needle jumped—110, 120, 140. The car shimmied and I gripped the wheel more tightly. I leaned on the horn. When I was right on top of it I could see that the bonfire stretched all the way across the road. The activists were waving their knives for me to stop. I saw that two of them were winding up to throw bottles of gasoline at the car and for a second I thought, *so this is the end, this is the end,* but there was no turning back. There was no turning. . . .

I smashed into the fire, the car jumped; there was a hammering against the belly pan, sparks showered over the windshield. And suddenly—the roadblock, the fire, and the shouting were behind me. The bottles had missed. The knives had missed. Hounded by terror, I drove another kilometer and then stopped to make sure the car wasn't on fire. It wasn't on fire. I was all wet. All my strength had left me, I was incapable of fighting, I was wide open, defenseless. I sat down on the sand and felt sick to my stomach.

Everything around me was alien. An alien sky and alien trees. Alien hills and manioc fields. I couldn't stay there, so I got back in and drove until I came to a town called Idiroko. On the way in, there was a police station and I stopped there. The policemen were sitting on a bench. They let me wash and straighten myself up.

I wanted to return to Lagos, but I couldn't go back alone. The commandant started organizing an escort. But the policemen were afraid to travel alone. They needed to borrow a car, so the commandant went into town. I sat on a bench reading the *Nigerian Tribune,* the UPGA paper. The whole paper was dedicated to party activities and the way the party was fighting for power. "Our furious battle," I read, "is continuing. For instance, our activists burned the eight-year-old pupil Janet Bosede Ojo of Ikere alive. The girl's father had voted for the NNDP." I read on: "In Ilesha the farmer Alek Aleke was burned alive. A group of activists used the 'Spray-and-Lite' method [also known as "UPGA candles"] on him. The farmer was returning from his fields when the activists grabbed him and commanded him to strip naked. The farmer undressed, fell to his knees, and begged for mercy. In this position he was sprayed with benzene and set afire." The paper was full of similar reports. UPGA was fighting for power, and the flames of that struggle were devouring people.

The commandant returned, but without a car. He designated three policemen to ride in my car. They were afraid to go. In the end they got in, pointed their rifles out the windows, and we drove off that way, like an armored car. At the first roadblock the fire was still burning but there was nobody in sight. The next two roadblocks were in full swing, but when they saw the police they let us through. The policemen weren't going to let anything stop the car; they didn't want to get into a fight with the activists. I understood them— they live here, and they want to survive. Today they had their rifles, but usually the police go unarmed here. Many policemen had been killed in the region.

At dusk we were in Lagos.

Suggestions for Discussion

1. The essay that describes an action in 1966 is preceded by an introductory note written in 1986. What is the relation of this note to the action described in the essay?

2. How are the incidents described in this essay organized? Is the organization effective? Might the author have arranged the narrative differently with similar effect?

3. Discuss the symbolic meaning of fire in the narrative. What is the author's attitude toward the use of fire as an instrument of terror?

4. Is the author brave? Give examples to illustrate your answer.

5. What is the tone of the essay? How does the author achieve this tone?

6. Where do the author's sympathies lie in the struggle for power in Nigeria in 1966? What is his attitude toward colonialism? How does he express this attitude?

7. What is the relation of the police to the activists?

Suggestions for Writing

1. Write an essay in which you analyze the causes of the terrorism described in this essay. You should explain the grounds by which some people may choose to justify the actions of the revolutionaries.

2. The power of this essay depends in large part on its language. Write an essay explaining the author's use of tone and how he achieves it.

Fiction

Franz Kafka

A Report to an Academy

Translated by Willa and Edwin Muir

Franz Kafka (1883–1924) portrayed alienated characters in an absurd world. He made little mark during his life, but is now considered a major modern writer. Many of his novels were published posthumously, including *The Trial, The Castle,* and *Amerika.* In his well-known story "Metamorphosis" he described the fate of an ordinary young man who awakens one morning to discover he has become a large bug. In the story before the reader, Kafka ironically describes how the need for freedom leads a captured ape to assume the characteristics of man.

Honored members of the Academy!

You have done me the honor of inviting me to give your Academy an account of the life I formerly led as an ape.

I regret that I cannot comply with your request to the extent you desire. It is now nearly five years since I was an ape, a short space of time, perhaps, according to the calendar, but an infinitely long time to gallop through at full speed, as I have done, more or less accompanied by excellent mentors, good advice, applause, and orchestral music, and yet essentially alone, since all my escorters, to keep the image, kept well off the course. I could never have achieved what I have done had I been stubbornly set on clinging to my origins, to the remembrances of my youth. In fact, to give up being stubborn was the supreme commandment I laid upon myself; free ape as I was, I submitted myself to that yoke. In revenge, however, my memory of the past has closed the door against me more and more. I could have returned at first, had human beings allowed it, through an archway as wide as the span of heaven over the earth, but as I spurred myself on in my forced career, the opening narrowed and shrank behind me; I felt more comfortable in the world of men and fitted it better; the strong wind that blew after me out of my past began to slacken; today it is only a gentle puff of air that plays around my heels; and the opening in the distance, through which it comes and through which I once came myself, has grown so small that, even if my strength and my will power sufficed to get me back to it, I should have to scrape the very skin from my body to crawl through. To put it plainly, much as I like expressing myself in images, your life as apes, gentlemen, insofar as something of that kind lies behind you, cannot be farther removed from you than mine is from me. Yet everyone on earth feels a tickling at the heels; the small chimpanzee and the great Achilles alike.

But to a lesser extent I can perhaps meet your demand, and indeed I do so with the greatest pleasure. The first thing I learned was to give a handshake; a handshake betokens frankness; well, today, now that I stand at the very peak of my career, I hope to add frankness in words to the frankness of that first handshake. What I have to tell the Academy will contribute nothing essentially new, and will fall far behind what you have asked of me and what with the best will in the world I cannot communicate—nonetheless, it should indicate the line an erstwhile ape has had to follow in entering and establishing himself in the world of men. Yet I could not risk putting into words even such insignificant information as I am going to give you if I were not quite sure of myself and if my position on all the great variety stages of the civilized world had not become quite unassailable.

I belong to the Gold Coast. For the story of my capture I must depend on the evidence of others. A hunting expedition sent out by the firm of Hagenbeck—by the way, I have drunk many a bottle of good red wine since then with the leader of that expedition—had taken up its position in the bushes by the shore when I came down for a drink at evening among a troop of apes. They shot at us; I was the only one that was hit; I was hit in two places.

Once in the cheek; a slight wound; but it left a large, naked, red scar which earned me the name of Red Peter, a horrible name, utterly inappropriate, which only some ape could have thought of, as if the only difference between me and the performing ape Peter, who died not so long ago and had some small local reputation, were the red mark on my cheek. This by the way.

The second shot hit me below the hip. It was a severe wound, it is the cause of my limping a little to this day. I read an article recently by one of the ten thousand windbags who vent themselves concerning me in the newspapers, saying: my ape nature is not yet quite under control; the proof being that when visitors come to see me, I have a predilection for taking down my trousers to show them where the shot went in. The hand which wrote that should have its fingers shot away one by one. As for me, I can take my trousers down before anyone if I like; you would find nothing but a well-groomed fur and the scar made—let me be particular in the choice of a word for this particular purpose, to avoid misunderstanding—the scar made by a wanton shot. Everything is open and aboveboard; there is nothing to conceal; when the plain truth is in question, great minds discard the niceties of refinement. But if the writer of the article were to take down his trousers before a visitor, that would be quite another story, and I will let it stand to his credit that he does not do it. In return, let him leave me alone with his delicacy!

After these two shots I came to myself—and this is where my own memories gradually begin—between decks in the Hagenbeck steamer, inside a cage. It was not a four-sided barred cage; it was only a three-sided cage nailed to a locker; the locker made the fourth side of it. The whole construction was too low for me to stand up in and too narrow to sit down in. So I had to squat with my knees bent and trembling all the time, and also, since probably for a time I wished to see no one, and to stay in the dark, my face was turned toward the locker while the bars of the cage cut into my flesh behind. Such a method of confining wild beasts is supposed to have its advantages during the first days of captivity, and out of my own experiences I cannot deny that from the human point of view this is really the case.

But that did not occur to me then. For the first time in my life I could see no way out; at least no direct way out; directly in front of me was the locker, board fitted close to board. True, there was a gap running right through the boards which I greeted with the blissful howl of ignorance when I first discovered it, but the hole was not even wide enough to stick one's tail through and not all the strength of an ape could enlarge it.

I am supposed to have made uncommonly little noise, as I was later informed, from which the conclusion was drawn that I would either soon die or if I managed to survive the first critical period would be very amenable to training. I did survive this period. Hopelessly sobbing, painfully hunting for fleas, apathetically licking a cocoanut, beating my skull against the locker, sticking out my tongue at anyone who came near me—that was how I filled in time at first in my new life. But over and above it all only the one feeling: no way out. Of course what I felt then as an ape I can represent now only in human terms, and therefore I misrepresent it, but although I cannot reach back to the truth of the old ape life, there is no doubt that it lies somewhere in the direction I have indicated.

Until then I had had so many ways out of everything, and now I had none. I was pinned down. Had I been nailed down, my right to free movement would not have been lessened. Why so? Scratch your flesh raw between your toes, but you won't find the answer. Press yourself against the bar behind you till it nearly cuts you in two, you won't find the answer. I had no way out but I had to devise one, for without it I could not live. All the time facing that locker—I should certainly have perished. Yet as far as Hagenbeck was concerned, the place for apes was in front of a locker—well then, I had to stop being an ape. A fine, clear train of thought, which I must have constructed somehow with my belly, since apes think with their bellies.

I fear that perhaps you do not quite understand what I mean by "way out." I use the expression in its fullest and most popular sense. I deliberately do not use the word "freedom." I do not mean the spacious feeling of freedom on all sides. As an ape, perhaps, I knew that, and I have met men who yearn for it. But for my part I desired such freedom neither then nor now. In passing: may I say that all too often men are betrayed by the word freedom. And as freedom is counted among the most sublime feelings, so the corresponding disillusionment can be also sublime. In variety theaters I have often watched, before my turn came on, a couple of acrobats performing on trapezes high in the roof. They swung themselves, they rocked to and fro, they sprang into the air, they floated into each other's arms, one hung by the hair from the teeth of the other. "And that too is human freedom," I thought, "self-controlled movement." What a mockery of holy Mother Nature! Were the apes to see such a spectacle, no theater walls could stand the shock of their laughter.

No, freedom was not what I wanted. Only a way out; right or left, or in any direction; I made no other demand; even should the way out prove to be an illusion; the demand was a small one, the disappointment could be no bigger. To get out somewhere, to get out! Only not to stay motionless with raised arms, crushed against a wooden wall.

Today I can see it clearly; without the most profound inward calm I could never have found my way out. And indeed perhaps I owe all that I have become to the calm that settled within me after my first few days in the ship. And again for that calmness it was the ship's crew I had to thank.

They were good creatures, in spite of everything. I find it still pleasant to remember the sound of their heavy footfalls which used to echo through my half-dreaming head. They had a habit of doing everything as slowly as possible. If one of them wanted to rub his eyes, he lifted a hand as if it were a drooping weight. Their jests were coarse, but hearty. Their laughter had always a gruff bark in it that sounded dangerous but meant nothing. They always had something in their mouths to spit out and did not care where they spat it. They always grumbled that they got fleas from me; yet they were not seriously angry about it; they knew that my fur fostered fleas, and that fleas jump; it was a simple matter of fact to them. When they were off duty some of them often used to sit down in a semicircle around me; they hardly spoke but only grunted to each other; smoked their pipes, stretched out on lockers; smacked their knees as soon as I made the slightest movement; and now and then one of them would take a stick and tickle me where I liked being tickled. If I were to be invited today to take a cruise on that ship I should certainly refuse the invitation, but just as certainly the memories I could recall between its decks would not all be hateful.

The calmness I acquired among these people kept me above all from trying to escape. As I looked back now, it seems to me I must have had at least an inkling that I had to find a way out or die, but that my way out could not be reached through flight. I cannot tell now whether escape was possible, but I believe it must have been; for an ape it must always be possible. With my teeth as they are today I have to be careful even in simply cracking nuts, but at that time I could certainly have managed by degrees to bite through the lock of my cage. I did not do it. What good would it have done me? As soon as I had poked out my head I should have been caught again and put in a worse cage; or I might have slipped among the other animals without being noticed, among the pythons, say, who were opposite me, and so breathed out my life in their embrace; or supposing I had actually succeeded in sneaking out as far as the deck and leaping overboard, I should have rocked for a little on the deep sea and then been drowned. Desperate remedies. I did not think it out in this human way, but under the influence of my surroundings I acted as if I had thought it out.

I did not think things out; but I observed everything quietly. I watched these men go to and fro, always the same faces, the same movements, often it seemed to me there was only the same man. So this man or these men walked about unimpeded. A lofty goal faintly dawned before me. No one promised me that if I became like them the bars of my cage would be taken away. Such promises for apparently impossible contingencies are not given. But if one achieves the impossible, the promises appear later retrospectively precisely where one had looked in vain for them before. Now, these men in themselves had no great attraction for me. Had I been devoted to the afore-mentioned idea of freedom, I should certainly have preferred the deep sea to the way out that suggested itself in the heavy faces of these men. At any rate, I watched them for a long time before I even thought of such things, indeed, it was only the mass weight of my observations that impelled me in the right direction.

It was so easy to imitate these people. I learned to spit in the very first days. We used to spit in each other's faces; the only difference was that I licked my face clean afterwards and they did not. I could soon smoke a pipe like an old hand; and if I also pressed my thumb into the bowl of the pipe, a roar of appreciation went up between decks; only it took me a very long time to understand the difference between a full pipe and an empty one.

My worst trouble came from the schnapps bottle. The smell of it revolted me; I forced myself to it as best I could; but it took weeks for me to master my repulsion. This inward conflict, strangely enough, was taken more seri-ously by the crew than anything else about me. I cannot distinguish the men from each other in my recollection, but there was one of them who came again and again, alone or with friends, by day, by night, at all kinds of hours; he would post himself before me with the bottle and give me instructions. He could not understand me, he wanted to solve the enigma of my being. He would slowly uncork the bottle and then look at me to see if I had followed him; I admit that I always watched him with wildly eager, too eager attention; such a student of humankind no human teacher ever found on earth. After the bottle was uncorked he lifted it to his mouth; I followed it with my eyes right up to his jaws; he would nod, pleased with me, and set the bottle to his lips; I, enchanted with my gradual enlightenment, squealed and scratched myself comprehensively wherever scratching was called for; he rejoiced, tilted the bottle, and took a drink; I, impatient and desperate to emulate him, be-fouled myself in my cage, which again gave him great satisfaction; and then, holding the bottle at arm's length and bringing it up with a swing, he would empty it at one draught, leaning back at an exaggerated angle for my better instruction. I, exhausted by too much effort, could follow him no farther and hung limply to the bars, while he ended his theoretical exposition by rubbing his belly and grinning.

After theory came practice. Was I not already quite exhausted by my the-oretical instruction? Indeed I was; utterly exhausted. That was part of my destiny. And yet I would take hold of the proffered bottle as well as I was able; uncork it, trembling; this successful action would gradually inspire me with new energy; I would lift the bottle, already following my original model almost exactly; put it to my lips and—and then throw it down in disgust, utter disgust, although it was empty and filled only with the smell of the spirit, throw it down on the floor in disgust. To the sorrow of my teacher, to the greater sorrow of myself, neither of us being really comforted by the fact that I did not forget, even though I had thrown away the bottle, to rub my belly most admirably and to grin.

Far too often my lesson ended in that way. And to the credit of my teacher, he was not angry; sometimes indeed he would hold his burning pipe against my fur, until it began to smolder in some place I could not easily reach, but then he would himself extinguish it with his own kind, enormous hand; he was not angry with me, he perceived that we were both fighting on the same side against the nature of apes and that I had the more difficult task.

What a triumph it was then both for him and for me, when one evening before a large circle of spectators—perhaps there was a celebration of some kind, a gramophone was playing, an officer was circulating among the crew— when on this evening, just as no one was looking, I took hold of a schnapps bottle that had been carelessly left standing before my cage, uncorked it in the best style, while the company began to watch me with mounting atten- tion, set it to my lips without hesitation, with no grimace, like a professional drinker, with rolling eyes and full throat, actually and truly drank it empty; then threw the bottle away, not this time in despair but as an artistic per- former; forgot, indeed, to rub my belly; but instead of that, because I could not help it, because my senses were reeling, called a brief and unmistakable "Hallo!" breaking into human speech, and with this outburst broke into the human community, and felt its echo: "Listen, he's talking!" like a caress over the whole of my sweat-drenched body.

I repeat: there was no attraction for me in imitating human beings; I imi- tated them because I needed a way out, and for no other reason. And even that triumph of mine did not achieve much. I lost my human voice again at once; it did not come back for months; my aversion for the schnapps bottle returned again with even greater force. But the line I was to follow had in any case been decided, once for all.

When I was handed over to my first trainer in Hamburg I soon realized that there were two alternatives before me: the Zoological Gardens or the variety stage. I did not hesitate. I said to myself: do your utmost to get onto the variety stage; the Zoological Gardens means only a new cage; once there, you are done for.

And so I learned things, gentlemen. Ah, one learns when one has to; one learns when one needs a way out; one learns at all costs. One stands over oneself with a whip; one flays oneself at the slightest opposition. My ape nature fled out of me, head over heels and away, so that my first teacher was almost himself turned into an ape by it, had soon to give up teaching and was taken away to a mental hospital. Fortunately he was soon let out again.

But I used up many teachers, indeed, several teachers at once. As I be- came more confident of my abilities, as the public took an interest in my progress and my future began to look bright, I engaged teachers for myself, established them in five communicating rooms, and took lessons from them all at once by dint of leaping from one room to the other.

That progress of mine! How the rays of knowledge penetrated from all sides into my awakening brain! I do not deny it: I found it exhilarating. But I must also confess: I did not overestimate it, not even then, much less now. With an effort which up till now has never been repeated I managed to reach the cultural level of an average European. In itself that might be nothing to speak of, but it is something insofar as it has helped me out of my cage and opened a special way out for me, the way of humanity. There is an excellent idiom: to fight one's way through the thick of things; that is what I have done, I have fought through the thick of things. There was nothing else for me to do, provided always that freedom was not to be my choice.

As I look back over my development and survey what I have achieved so far, I do not complain, but I am not complacent either. With my hands in my trouser pockets, my bottle of wine on the table, I half lie and half sit in my rocking chair and gaze out of the window: if a visitor arrives, I receive him with propriety. My manager sits in the anteroom; when I ring, he comes and listens to what I have to say. Nearly every evening I give a performance, and I have a success that could hardly be increased. When I come home late at night from banquets, from scientific receptions, from social gatherings, there sits waiting for me a half-trained little chimpanzee and I take comfort from her as apes do. By day I cannot bear to see her; for she has the insane look of the bewildered half-broken animal in her eye; no one else sees it, but I do, and I cannot bear it. On the whole, at any rate, I have achieved what I set out to achieve. But do not tell me that it was not worth the trouble. In any case, I am not appealing for any man's verdict, I am only imparting knowledge, I am only making a report. To you also, honored Members of the Academy, I have only made a report.

Suggestions for Discussion

1. Why is the speaker, an ape, addressing an academy? What tone does he use in his address?

2. How does Kafka contrast the life of the ape in Africa with the life of the human being in Europe? Who suffers from the contrast?

3. Kafka presents the story matter-of-factly and also ironically. Explain his use of irony in the story, referring to specific details during the ape's time of capture and after.

4. Why did the ape choose the variety stage over the Zoological Gardens as a way of life?

Suggestion for Writing

Write an essay in which you explain how the history of this ape is related to mankind's struggle for freedom. What is the ape's attitude toward freedom? How does it differ from man's?

William Faulkner
Dry September

William Faulkner (1897–1962) lived most of his life in Oxford, Mississippi. After a year at the university of his native state, he joined the Royal Canadian Air Force, eager to participate in World War I. His novels set in his imaginary Yoknapatawpha County include *The Sound and the Fury* (1929), *Light in August* (1932), *Absalom, Absalom!* (1936), and *The Hamlet* (1940). This story, taken from the section of Faulkner's *Collected Stories* (1950) called "The Village," offers an acute social and psychological analysis of life in a small Southern town after World War I. Notice how Faulkner focuses on the gentle barber, the hysterical spinster, and the brutal ex-soldier to provide social commentary.

I

Through the bloody September twilight, aftermath of sixty-two rainless days, it had gone like a fire in dry grass—the rumor, the story, whatever it was. Something about Miss Minnie Cooper and a Negro. Attacked, insulted, frightened: none of them, gathered in the barber shop on that Saturday evening where the ceiling fan stirred, without freshening it, the vitiated air, sending back upon them, in recurrent surges of stale pomade and lotion, their own stale breath and odors, knew exactly what had happened.

"Except it wasn't Will Mayes," a barber said. He was a man of middle age; a thin, sand-colored man with a mild face, who was shaving a client. "I know Will Mayes. He's a good nigger. And I know Minnie Cooper, too."

"What do you know about her?" a second barber said.

"Who is she?" the client said. "A young girl?"

"No," the barber said. "She's about forty, I reckon. She ain't married. That's why I dont believe—"

"Believe, hell!" a hulking youth in a sweat-stained silk shirt said. "Wont you take a white woman's word before a nigger's?"

"I dont believe Will Mayes did it," the barber said. "I know Will Mayes."

"Maybe you know who did it, then. Maybe you already got him out of town, you damn niggerlover."

"I dont believe anybody did anything. I dont believe anything happened. I leave it to you fellows if them ladies that get old without getting married dont have notions that a man cant—"

"Then you are a hell of a white man," the client said. He moved under the cloth. The youth had sprung to his feet.

"You dont?" he said. "Do you accuse a white woman of lying?"

The barber held the razor poised above the half-risen client. He did not look around.

"It's this durn weather," another said. "It's enough to make a man do anything. Even to her."

Nobody laughed. The barber said in his mild, stubborn tone: "I ain't accusing nobody of nothing. I just know and you fellows know how a woman that never—"

"You damn niggerlover!" the youth said.

"Shut up, Butch," another said. "We'll get the facts in plenty of time to act."

"Who is? Who's getting them?" the youth said. "Facts, hell! I—".

"You're a fine white man," the client said. "Aint you?" In his frothy beard he looked like a desert rat in the moving pictures. "You tell them, Jack," he said to the youth. "If there aint any white men in this town, you can count on me, even if I aint only a drummer and a stranger."

"That's right, boys," the barber said. "Find out the truth first. I know Will Mayes."

"Well, by God!" the youth shouted. "To think that a white man in this town—"

"Shut up, Butch," the second speaker said. "We got plenty of time."

The client sat up. He looked at the speaker. "Do you claim that anything excuses a nigger attacking a white woman? Do you mean to tell me you are a white man and you'll stand for it? You better go back North where you came from. The South dont want your kind here."

"North what?" the second said. "I was born and raised in this town."

"Well, by God!" the youth said. He looked about with a strained, baffled gaze, as if he was trying to remember what it was he wanted to say or to do. He drew his sleeve across his sweating face. "Damn if I'm going to let a white woman—"

"You tell them, Jack," the drummer said. "By God, if they—"

The screen door crashed open. A man stood in the floor, his feet apart and his heavy-set body poised easily. His white shirt was open at the throat; he wore a felt hat. His hot, bold glance swept the group. His name was McLendon. He had commanded troops at the front in France and had been decorated for valor.

"Well," he said, "are you going to sit there and let a black son rape a white woman on the streets of Jefferson?"

Butch sprang up again. The silk of his shirt clung flat to his heavy shoulders. At each armpit was a dark halfmoon. "That's what I been telling them! That's what I—"

"Did it really happen?" a third said. "This aint the first man scare she ever had, like Hawkshaw says. Wasn't there something about a man on the kitchen roof, watching her undress, about a year ago?"

"What?" the client said. "What's that?" The barber had been slowly forcing him back into the chair; he arrested himself reclining, his head lifted, the barber still pressing him down.

McLendon whirled on the third speaker. "Happen? What the hell difference does it make? Are you going to let the black sons get away with it until one really does it?"

"That's what I'm telling them!" Butch shouted. He cursed, long and steady, pointless.

"Here, here," a fourth said. "Not so loud. Dont talk so loud."

"Sure," McLendon said; "no talking necessary at all. I've done my talking. Who's with me?" He poised on the balls of his feet, roving his gaze.

The barber held the drummer's face down, the razor poised. "Find out the facts first, boys. I know Willy Mayes. It wasn't him. Let's get the sheriff and do this thing right."

McLendon whirled upon him his furious, rigid face. The barber did not look away. They looked like men of different races. The other barbers had ceased also above their prone clients. "You mean to tell me," McLendon said, "that you'd take a nigger's word before a white woman's? Why, you damn niggerloving—"

The third speaker rose and grasped McLendon's arm; he too had been a soldier. "Now, now. Let's figure this thing out. Who knows anything about what really happened?"

"Figure out hell!" McLendon jerked his arm free. "All that're with me get up from there. The ones that aint—" He roved his gaze, dragging his sleeve across his face.

Three men rose. The drummer in the chair sat up. "Here," he said, jerking at the cloth about his neck; "get this rag off me. I'm with him. I dont live here, but by God, if our mothers and wives and sisters—" He smeared the cloth over his face and flung it to the floor. McLendon stood in the floor and cursed the others. Another rose and moved toward him. The remainder sat uncomfortable, not looking at one another, then one by one they rose and joined him.

The barber picked the cloth from the floor. He began to fold it neatly. "Boys, dont do that. Will Mayes never done it. I know."

"Come on," McLendon said. He whirled. From his hip pocket protruded the butt of a heavy automatic pistol. They went out. The screen door crashed behind them reverberant in the dead air.

The barber wiped the razor carefully and swiftly, and put it away, and ran to the rear, and took his hat from the wall. "I'll be back as soon as I can," he said to the other barbers. "I cant let—" He went out, running, The two other barbers followed him to the door and caught it on the rebound, leaning out and looking up the street after him. The air was flat and dead. It had a metallic taste at the base of the tongue.

"What can he do?" the first said. The second one was saying "Jees Christ, Jees Christ" under his breath. "I'd just as lief be Will Mayes as Hawk, if he gets McLendon riled."

"Jees Christ, Jees Christ," the second whispered

"You reckon he really done it to her?" the first said.

II

She was thirty-eight or thirty-nine. She lived in a small frame house with her invalid mother and a thin, sallow, unflagging aunt, where each morning between ten and eleven she would appear on the porch in a lace-trimmed boudoir cap, to sit swinging in the porch swing until noon. After dinner she lay down for a while, until the afternoon began to cool. Then, in one of the three or four new voile dresses which she had each summer, she would go downtown to spend the afternoon in the stores with the other ladies, where they would handle the goods and haggle over the prices in cold, immediate voices, without any intention of buying.

She was of comfortable people—not the best in Jefferson, but good people enough—and she was still on the slender side of ordinary looking, with a bright, faintly haggard manner and dress. When she was young she had had a slender, nervous body and a sort of hard vivacity which had enabled her for a time to ride upon the crest of the town's social life as exemplified by the high school party and church social period of her contemporaries while still children enough to be unclassconscious.

She was the last to realize that she was losing ground; that those among whom she had been a little brighter and louder flame than any other were beginning to learn the pleasure of snobbery—male—and retaliation—female. That was when her face began to wear that bright, haggard look. She still carried it to parties on shadowy porticoes and summer lawns, like a mask or a flag, with that bafflement of furious repudiation of truth in her eyes. One evening at a party she heard a boy and two girls, all schoolmates, talking. She never accepted another invitation.

She watched the girls with whom she had grown up as they married and got homes and children, but no man ever called on her steadily until the children of the other girls had been calling her "aunty" for several years, the while their mothers told them in bright voices about how popular Aunt Minnie had been as a girl. Then the town began to see her driving on Sunday afternoons with the cashier in the bank. He was a widower of about forty—a high-colored man, smelling always faintly of the barber shop or of whisky. He owned the first automobile in town, a red runabout; Minnie had the first motoring bonnet and veil the town ever saw. Then the town began to say: "Poor Minnie." "But she is old enough to take care of herself," others said. That was when she began to ask her old schoolmates that their children call her "cousin" instead of "aunty."

It was twelve years now since she had been relegated into adultery by public opinion, and eight years since the cashier had gone to a Memphis bank, returning for one day each Christmas, which he spent at an annual bachelors' party at a hunting club on the river. From behind their curtains the neighbors would see the party pass, and during the over-the-way Christmas day visiting they would tell her about him, about how well he looked, and how they heard that he was prospering in the city, watching with bright, secret eyes her haggard, bright face. Usually by that hour there would be the scent of whisky on her breath. It was supplied her by a youth, a clerk at the soda fountain: "Sure; I buy it for the old gal. I reckon she's entitled to a little fun."

Her mother kept to her room altogether now; the gaunt aunt ran the house. Against that background Minnie's bright dresses, her idle and empty days, had a quality of furious unreality. She went out in the evenings only with women now, neighbors, to the moving pictures. Each afternoon she dressed in one of the new dresses and went downtown alone, where her young "cousins" were already strolling in the late afternoons with their delicate, silken heads and thin, awkward arms and conscious hips, clinging to one another or shrieking and giggling with paired boys in the soda fountain when she passed and went on along the serried store fronts, in the doors of which the sitting and lounging men did not even follow her with their eyes any more.

III

The barber went swiftly up the street where the sparse lights, insect-swirled, glared in rigid and violent suspension in the lifeless air. The day had died in a pall of dust; above the darkened square, shrouded by the spent dust, the sky was as clear as the inside of a brass bell. Below the east was a rumor of the twice-waxed moon.

When he overtook them McLendon and three others were getting into a car parked in an alley. McLendon stooped his thick head, peering out beneath the top. "Changed your mind, did you?" he said. "Damn good thing; by God, tomorrow when this town hears about how you talked tonight—"

"Now, now," the other ex-soldier said. "Hawkshaw's all right. Come on, Hawk; jump in."

"Will Mayes never done it, boys," the barber said. "If anybody done it. Why, you all know well as I do there ain't any town where they got better niggers than us. And you know how a lady will kind of think things about men when there aint any reason to, and Miss Minnie anyway—"

"Sure, sure," the soldier said. "We're just going to talk to him a little; that's all."

"Talk hell!" Butch said. "When we're through with the—"

"Shut up, for God's sake!" the soldier said. "Do you want everybody in town—"

"Tell them, by God!" McLendon said. "Tell every one of the sons that'll let a white woman—"

"Let's go; let's go: here's the other car." The second car slid squealing out of a cloud of dust at the alley mouth. McLendon started his car and took the lead. Dust lay like fog in the street. The street lights hung nimbused as in water. They drove on out of town.

A rutted lane turned at right angles. Dust hung above it too, and above all the land. The dark bulk of the ice plant, where the Negro Mayes was night watchman, rose against the sky. "Better stop here, hadn't we?" the soldier said. McLendon did not reply. He hurled the car up and slammed to a stop, the headlights glaring on the blank wall.

"Listen here, boys," the barber said, "if he's here, don't that prove he never done it? Don't it? If it was him, he would run. Don't you see he would?" The second car came up and stopped. McLendon got down; Butch sprang down beside him. "Listen, boys," the barber said.

"Cut the lights off!" McLendon said. The breathless dark rushed down. There was no sound in it save their lungs as they sought air in the parched dust in which for two months they had lived; then the diminishing crunch of McLendon's and Butch's feet, and a moment later McLendon's voice:

"Will! . . . Will!"

Below the east the wan hemorrhage of the moon increased. It heaved above the ridge, silvering the air, the dust, so that they seemed to breathe, live, in a bowl of molten lead. There was no sound of nightbird nor insect, no sound save their breathing and a faint ticking of contracting metal about the cars. Where their bodies touched one another they seemed to sweat dryly, for no more moisture came. "Christ!" a voice said; "let's get out of here."

But they didn't move until vague noises began to grow out of the darkness ahead; then they got out and waited tensely in the breathless dark. There was another sound: a blow, a hissing expulsion of breath and McLendon cursing in undertone. They stood a moment longer, then they ran forward. They ran in a stumbling clump, as though they were fleeing something. "Kill him, kill the son," a voice whispered. McLendon flung them back.

"Not here," he said. "Get him into the car." "Kill him, kill the black son!" the voice murmured. They dragged the Negro to the car. The barber had waited beside the car. He could feel himself sweating and he knew he was going to be sick at the stomach.

"What is it, captains?" the Negro said. "I ain't done nothing. 'Fore God, Mr. John." Someone produced handcuffs. They worked busily about the Negro as though he were a post, quiet, intent, getting in one another's way. He submitted to the handcuffs, looking swiftly and constantly from dim face to dim face. "Who's here, captains?" he said, leaning to peer into the faces until they could feel his breath and smell his sweaty reek. He spoke a name or two. "What you all say I done, Mr. John?"

McLendon jerked the car door open. "Get in!" he said.

The Negro did not move. "What you all going to do with me, Mr. John? I aint done nothing. White folks, captains, I aint done nothing: I swear 'fore God." He called another name.

"Get in!" McLendon said. He struck the Negro. The others expelled their breath in a dry hissing and struck him with random blows and he whirled and cursed them, and swept his manacled hands across their faces and slashed the barber upon the mouth, and the barber struck him also. "Get him in there," McLendon said. They pushed at him. He ceased struggling and got in and sat quietly as the others took their places. He sat between the barber and the soldier, drawing his limbs in so as not to touch them, his eyes going swiftly and constantly from face to face. Butch clung to the running board. The car moved on. The barber nursed his mouth with his handkerchief.

"What's the matter, Hawk?" the soldier said.

"Nothing," the barber said. They regained the highroad and turned away from town. The second car dropped back out of the dust. They went on, gaining speed; the final fringe of houses dropped behind.

"Goddamn, he stinks!" the soldier said.

"We'll fix that," the drummer in front beside McLendon said. On the running board Butch cursed into the hot rush of air. The barber leaned suddenly forward and touched McLendon's arm.

"Let me out, John," he said.

"Jump out, niggerlover," McLendon said without turning his head. He drove swiftly. Behind them the sourceless lights of the second car glared in the dust. Presently McLendon turned into a narrow road. It was rutted with disuse. It led back to an abandoned brick kiln—a series of reddish mounds and weed- and vine-choked vats without bottom. It had been used for pasture once, until one day the owner missed one of his mules. Although he prodded carefully in the vats with a long pole, he could not even find the bottom of them.

"John," the barber said.

"Jump out, then," McLendon said, hurling the car along the ruts. Beside the barber the Negro spoke:

"Mr. Henry."

The barber sat forward. The narrow tunnel of the road rushed up and past. Their motion was like an extinct furnace blast: cooler, but utterly dead. The car bounded from rut to rut.

"Mr. Henry," the Negro said.

The barber began to tug furiously at the door. "Look out, there!" the sol-

dier said, but the barber had already kicked the door open and swung onto
the running board. The soldier leaned across the Negro and grasped at him,
but he had already jumped. The car went on without checking speed.

The impetus hurled him crashing through dust-sheathed weeds, into the
ditch. Dust puffed about him, and in a thin, vicious crackling of sapless stems
he lay choking and retching until the second car passed and died away. Then
he rose and limped on until he reached the highroad and turned toward town,
brushing at his clothes with his hands. The moon was higher, riding high and
clear of the dust at last, and after a while the town began to glare beneath the
dust. He went on, limping. Presently he heard cars and the glow of them
grew in the dust behind him and he left the road and crouched again in the
weeds until they passed. McLendon's car came last now. There were four
people in it and Butch was not on the running board.

They went on; the dust swallowed them; the glare and the sound died
away. The dust of them hung for a while, but soon the eternal dust absorbed
it again. The barber climbed back onto the road and limped on toward town.

IV

As she dressed for supper on that Saturday evening, her own flesh felt like
fever. Her hands trembled among the hooks and eyes, and her eyes had a
feverish look, and her hair swirled crisp and crackling under the comb. While
she was still dressing the friends called for her and sat while she donned her
sheerest underthings and stockings and a new voile dress. "Do you feel strong
enough to go out?" they said, their eyes bright too, with a dark glitter. "When
you have had time to get over the shock, you must tell us what happened.
What he said and did; everything."

In the leafed darkness, as they walked toward the square, she began to
breathe deeply, something like a swimmer preparing to dive, until she ceased
trembling, the four of them walking slowly because of the terrible heat and
out of solicitude for her. But as they neared the square she began to tremble
again, walking with her head up, her hands clenched at her sides, their voices
about her murmurous, also with that feverish, glittering quality of their eyes.

They entered the square, she in the center of the group, fragile in her
fresh dress. She was trembling worse. She walked slower and slower, as children eat ice cream, her head up and her eyes bright in the haggard banner
of her face, passing the hotel and the coatless drummers in chairs along the
curb looking around at her: "That's the one: see? The one in pink in the
middle." "Is that her? What did they do with the nigger? Did they—?" "Sure.
He's all right." "All right, is he?" "Sure. He went on a little trip." Then the
drug store, where even the young men lounging in the doorway tipped their
hats and followed with their eyes the motions of her hips and legs when she
passed.

They went on, passing the lifted hats of the gentlemen, the suddenly
ceased voices, deferent, protective. "Do you see?" the friends said. Their
voices sounded like long, hovering sighs of hissing exultation. "There's not a
Negro on the square. Not one."

They reached the picture show. It was like a miniature fairyland with its
lighted lobby and colored lithographs of life caught in its terrible and beautiful

mutations. Her lips began to tingle. In the dark, when the picture began, it would be all right; she could hold back the laughing so it would not waste away so fast and so soon. So she hurried on before the turning faces, the undertones of low astonishment, and they took their accustomed places where she could see the aisle against the silver glare and the young men and girls coming in two and two against it.

The lights flicked away; the screen glowed silver, and soon life began to unfold, beautiful and passionate and sad, while still the young men and girls entered, scented and sibilant in the half dark, their paired backs in silhouette delicate and sleek, their slim, quick bodies awkward, divinely young, while beyond them the silver dream accumulated, inevitably on and on. She began to laugh. In trying to suppress it, it made more noise than ever; heads began to turn. Still laughing, her friends raised her and led her out, and she stood at the curb, laughing on a high, sustained note, until the taxi came up and they helped her in.

They removed the pink voile and the sheer underthings and the stockings, and put her to bed, and cracked ice for her temples, and sent for the doctor. He was hard to locate, so they ministered to her with hushed ejaculations, renewing the ice and fanning her. While the ice was fresh and cold she stopped laughing and lay still for a time, moaning only a little. But soon the laughing welled again and her voice rose screaming.

"Shhhhhhhhhhh! Shhhhhhhhhhhhhh!" they said, freshening the icepack, smoothing her hair, examining it for gray; "poor girl!" Then to one another: "Do you suppose anything really happened?" their eyes darkly aglitter, secret and passionate. "Shhhhhhhhhhh! Poor girl! Poor Minnie!"

V

It was midnight when McLendon drove up to his neat new house. It was trim and fresh as a birdcage and almost as small, with its clean, green-and-white paint. He locked the car and mounted the porch and entered. His wife rose from a chair beside the reading lamp. McLendon stopped in the floor and stared at her until she looked down.

"Look at that clock," he said, lifting his arm, pointing. She stood before him, her face lowered, a magazine in her hands. Her face was pale, strained, and weary-looking. "Haven't I told you about sitting up like this, waiting to see when I come in?"

"John," she said. She laid the magazine down. Poised on the balls of his feet, he glared at her with his hot eyes, his sweating face.

"Didn't I tell you?" He went toward her. She looked up then. He caught her shoulder. She stood passive, looking at him.

"Don't, John. I couldn't sleep . . . The heat; something. Please, John. You're hurting me."

"Didn't I tell you?" He released her and half struck, half flung her across the chair, and she lay there and watched him quietly as he left the room.

He went on through the house, ripping off his shirt, and on the dark, screened porch at the rear he stood and mopped his head and shoulders with the shirt and flung it away. He took the pistol from his hip and laid it on the table beside the bed, and sat on the bed and removed his shoes, and rose and slipped his trousers off. He was sweating again already, and he stooped and hunted furiously for the shirt. At last he found it and wiped his body again, and, with his body pressed against the dusty screen, he stood panting. There was no movement, no sound, not even an insect. The dark world seemed to lie stricken beneath the cold moon and the lidless stars.

Suggestions for Discussion

1. Faulkner tells this story of a lynching in five parts. Discuss the relation of the parts to each other.

2. What is the function of Hawkshaw? Why is it appropriate for the story to open in a barber shop? Explain the discussion between the barbers and the customers.

3. In what ways is John McLendon different from the other men? What explains his power over them?

4. Explain the significance of the scene in which Will Mayes hits Hawkshaw in the mouth.

5. How do you know that nothing has happened to Miss Minnie Cooper? What aspects of her character make clear that she has invented an affront?

6. Explain the title of the story. How does Faulkner use weather as a force in the story? What has weather to do with the lynching?

Suggestions for Writing

1. Write an essay in which you explain how this story is an eloquent attack on lynching. Does the author permit himself to comment on what has occurred?

2. Write an essay in which you explain how the characters in this story provide a comment on the relation between the races.

Ray Bradbury
Perhaps We Are Going Away

Ray Bradbury (b. 1920), who lives in Southern California, is among the most popular and prolific of science fiction writers. He is particularly well-known for *The Martian Chronicles* (1950), *The Illustrated Man* (1951), and *Dandelion Wine* (1957). In this brief and powerful story from *The Machineries of Joy* (1963), Bradbury imagines the sense of danger and of coming disaster which a young Indian boy feels as he gets his first glimpse of European soldiers in America.

It was a strange thing that could not be told. It touched along the hairs on his neck as he lay wakening. Eyes shut, he pressed his hands to the dirt.

Was the earth, shaking old fires under its crust, turning over in its sleep?

Were buffalo on the dust prairies, in the whistling grass, drumming the sod, moving this way like a dark weather?

No.

What? What, then?

He opened his eyes and was the boy Ho-Awi, of a tribe named for a bird, by the hills named for the shadows of owls, near the great ocean itself, on a day that was evil for no reason.

Ho-Awi stared at the tent flaps, which shivered like a great beast remembering winter.

Tell me, he thought, the terrible thing, where does it come from? Whom will it kill?

He lifted the flap and stepped out into his village.

He turned slowly, a boy with bones in his dark cheeks like the keels of small birds flying. His brown eyes saw god-filled, cloud-filled sky, his cupped ear heard thistles ticking the war drums, but still the greater mystery drew him to the edge of the village.

Here, legend said, the land went on like a tide to another sea. Between here and there was as much earth as there were stars across the night sky. Somewhere in all that land, storms of black buffalo harvested the grass. And here stood Ho-Awi, his stomach a fist, wondering, searching, waiting, afraid.

You too? said the shadow of a hawk.

Ho-Awi turned.

It was the shadow of his grandfather's hand that wrote on the wind.

No. The grandfather made the sign for silence. His tongue moved soft in a toothless mouth. His eyes were small creeks running behind the sunken flesh beds, the cracked sand washes of his face.

Now they stood on the edge of the day, drawn close by the unknown.

And Old Man did as the boy had done. His mummified ear turned, his nostril twitched. Old Man too ached for some answering growl from any direction that would tell them only a great timberfall of weather had dropped from a distant sky. But the wind gave no answer, spoke only to itself.

The Old Man made the sign which said they must go on the Great Hunt. This, said his hands like mouths, was a day for the rabbit young and the featherless old. Let no warrior come with them. The hare and the dying vulture must track together. For only the very young saw life ahead, and only the very old saw life behind; the others between were so busy with life they saw nothing.

The Old Man wheeled slowly in all directions.

Yes! He knew, he was certain, he was sure! To find this thing of darkness would take the innocence of the newborn and the innocence of the blind to see very clear.

Come! said the trembling fingers.

And snuffing rabbit and earthbound hawk shadowed out of the village into changing weather.

They searched the high hills to see if the stones lay atop each other, and they were so arranged. They scanned the prairies, but found only the winds which played there like tribal children all day. And found arrowheads from old wars.

No, the Old Man's hand drew on the sky, the men of this nation and that beyond smoke by the summer fires while the squaws cut wood. It is not arrows flying that we almost hear.

At last, when the sun sank into the nation of buffalo hunters, the Old Man looked up.

The birds, his hands cried suddenly, are flying south! Summer is over!

No, the boy's hands said, summer has just begun! I see no birds!

They are so high, said the Old Man's fingers, that only the blind can feel their passage. They shadow the heart more than the earth. I feel them pass south in my blood. Summer goes. We may go with it. Perhaps we are going away.

No! cried the boy aloud, suddenly afraid. Go where? Why? For what?

Who knows? said the Old Man, and perhaps we will not move. Still, even without moving, perhaps we are going away.

No! Go back! cried the boy, to the empty sky, the birds unseen, the unshadowed air. Summer, stay!

No use, said the Old One's single hand, moving by itself. Not you or me or our people can stay this weather. It is a season changed, come to live on the land for all time.

But from where does it come?

This way, said the Old Man at last.

And in the dusk they looked down at the great waters of the east that went over the edge of the world, where no one had ever gone.

There. The Old Man's hand clenched and thrust out. There *it* is.

Far ahead, a single light burned on the shore.

With the moon rising, the Old Man and the rabbit boy padded on the sands, heard strange voices in the sea, smelled wild burnings from the now suddenly close fire.

They crawled on their bellies. They lay looking in at the light.

And the more he looked, the colder Ho-Awi became, and he knew that all the Old Man had said was true.

For drawn to this fire built of sticks and moss, which flickered brightly in the soft evening wind which was cooler now, at the heart of summer, were such creatures as he had never seen.

These were men with faces like white-hot coals, with some eyes in these faces as blue as sky. All these men had glossy hair on their cheeks and chins, which grew to a point. One man stood with raised lightning in his hand and a great moon of sharp stuff on his head like the face of a fish. The others had bright round tinkling crusts of material cleaved to their chests which gonged slightly when they moved. As Ho-Awi watched, some men lifted the gonging bright things from their heads, unskinned the eye-blinding crab shells, the turtle casings from their chests, their arms, their legs, and tossed these discarded sheaths to the sand. Doing this, the creatures laughed, while out in the bay stood a black shape on the waters, a great dark canoe with things like torn clouds hung on poles over it.

After a long while of holding their breath, the Old Man and the boy went away.

From a hill, they watched the fire that was no bigger than a star now. You could wink it out with an eyelash. If you closed your eyes, it was destroyed.

Still, it remained.

Is this, asked the boy, the great happening?

The Old One's face was that of a fallen eagle, filled with dreadful years and unwanted wisdom. The eyes were resplendently bright, as if they welled with a rise of cold clear water in which all could be seen, like a river that drank the sky and earth and knew it, accepted silently and would not deny the accumulation of dust, time, shape, sound and destiny.

The Old Man nodded, once.

This was the terrible weather. This was how summer would end. This made the birds wheel south, shadowless, through a grieving land.

The worn hands stopped moving. The time of questions was done.

Far away, the fire leaped. One of the creatures moved. The bright stuff on his tortoise-shell body flashed. It was like an arrow cutting a wound in the night.

Then the boy vanished in darkness, following the eagle and the hawk that lived in the stone body of his grandfather.

Below, the sea reared up and poured another great salt wave in billions of pieces which crashed and hissed like knives swarming along the continental shores.

Suggestions for Discussion

1. Explain the power of this account of the advent of Western man in America.

2. Discuss Bradbury's characterizations. Are they as important to the story as the events that occur or the descriptions of the setting? Explain.

3. This story is extremely brief. Would you want it any longer? Explain.

Suggestions for Writing

1. Describe the first encounter between the Indians and the Europeans.

2. Write an essay in which you try to warn the Indians to be wary of the Europeans. Be as convincing as possible.

Poetry

Wilfred Owen
Dulce et Decorum Est

Wilfred Owen (1893–1918) was born in Shropshire, England, and educated at Birkenhead Institute. Among the most celebrated of the English war poets, he was killed in action in World War I. Another war poet, Siegfried Sassoon, collected Owen's poems which were first published in 1920. Other collections followed as did critical studies and memoirs. "Dulce et Decorum Est" (taken from Horace's statement, "It is sweet and fitting to die for one's country") opposes vivid and devastating images of the casualties of war with statements of sentimental patriotism. It shows war as the ultimate insult to human dignity.

Bent double, like old beggars under sacks,
Knock-kneed, coughing like hags, we cursed through sludge,
Till on the haunting flares we turned our backs,
And towards our distant rest began to trudge.
Men marched asleep. Many had lost their boots,
But limped on, blood-shod. All went lame, all blind;
Drunk with fatigue; deaf even to the hoots
Of gas-shells dropping softly behind.

Gas! Gas! Quick, boys!—An ecstasy of fumbling,
Fitting the clumsy helmets just in time,
But someone still was yelling out and stumbling
And flound'ring like a man in fire or lime.—
Dim through the misty panes and thick green light,
As under a green sea, I saw him drowning.
In all my dreams before my helpless sight
He plunges at me, guttering, choking, drowning.

If in some smothering dreams, you too could pace
Behind the wagon that we flung him in,
And watch the white eyes writhing in his face,
His hanging face, like a devil's sick of sin,
If you could hear, at every jolt, the blood
Come gargling from the froth-corrupted lungs
Bitter as the cud
Of vile, incurable sores on innocent tongues,—
My friend, you would not tell with such high zest
To children ardent for some desperate glory,
The old lie: *Dulce et decorum est*
Pro patria mori.

Suggestions for Discussion

1. In the first two stanzas, Owen presents two connected scenes of war. How are these two stanzas related to the final one?

2. Discuss the use of irony in the poem. Show why Owen uses the quotation from Horace.

3. Examine the series of images which Owen uses to describe war. Do they progress through the poem? Show why one cannot interchange the first two stanzas.

Suggestion for Writing

Owen's picture of the destruction of lives constitutes a poetic statement against war. Does this poem lead you to a belief in pacifism? Are there "just" and "unjust" wars? Try to sort out your attitudes and write an essay explaining under what conditions, if any, you might be willing to fight for your country. Support your statements with detailed arguments.

William Stafford

Freedom

William Edgar Stafford (b. 1914) was for many years a professor of English and humanities. His poetry has been published in such journals as *The Atlantic, Harper's,* and *The New Yorker.* His collections of poetry include *Traveling Through the Dark* (1963) and *The Rescued Years* (1966). In this brief reflection he shows how society limits our freedom and how ingenious we must be to enjoy it.

Freedom is not following a river.
Freedom is following a river,
   though, if you want to.
It is deciding now by what happens now.
It is knowing that luck makes a difference.

No leader is free; no follower is free—
   the rest of us can often be free.
Most of the world are living by
creeds too odd, chancey, and habit-forming
   to be worth arguing about by reason.

If you are oppressed, wake up about
four in the morning: most places,
you can usually be free some of the time
   if you wake up before other people.

Suggestions for Discussion

1. How would you characterize this poem: powerful, moving, provocative, disturbing, trivial? Explain your answer.

2. Discuss the significance of Stafford's title.

Suggestion for Writing

Compare and contrast this poem with "The Unknown Citizen" by Auden.

W. H. Auden

The Unknown Citizen

Wystan Hugh Auden (1907–1973), educated at Oxford University, was early recognized as a leader of the poets of his generation. His volumes of poetry include *The Orators* (1932), *The Double Man* (1941), and *The Age of Anxiety* (1947), which won a Pulitzer Prize in 1948. Born in England, he came to the United States at the outbreak of World War II. His autobiography, *Certain World: A Commonplace Book,* published in 1970, traces his return from leftist agnostic to the Church of England. In 1967 he was made a fellow of Christ Church, Oxford. In the following poem, published in 1940, Auden comments satirically on the behavior of a good citizen in a totalitarian state which resembles not only fascist Italy and Nazi Germany but democratic America and Britain as well.

The Unknown Citizen
(To JS/07/M/378 This Marble Monument Is Erected by the State)

He was found by the Bureau of Statistics to be
One against whom there was no official complaint,
And all the reports on his conduct agree
That, in the modern sense of an old-fashioned word, he was a saint,
For in everything he did he served the Greater Community.
Except for the War till the day he retired
He worked in a factory and never got fired,
But satisfied his employers, Fudge Motors Inc.
Yet he wasn't a scab or odd in his views,
For his Union reports that he paid his dues,
(Our report on his Union shows it was sound)
And our Social Psychology workers found
That he was popular with his mates and liked to drink.
The Press are convinced that he bought a paper every day
And that his reactions to advertisements were normal in every way.
Policies taken out in his name prove that he was fully insured,
And his Health-card shows he was once in a hospital but left it cured,
Both Producers Research and High-Grade Living declare
He was fully sensible to the advantages of the Installment Plan
And had everything necessary to the Modern Man,
A phonograph, a radio, a car and a frigidaire.
Our researchers into Public Opinion are content
That he held the proper opinions for the time of year;
When there was peace, he was for peace; when there was war, he went.
He was married and added five children to the population,
Which our Eugenist says was the right number for a parent of his generation,
And our teachers report that he never interfered with their education.
Was he free? Was he Happy? The question is absurd:
Had anything been wrong, we should certainly have heard.

Suggestions for Discussion

1. Discuss reasons for the state to bother erecting such a monument.

2. Analyze the strengths and weaknesses of the society described by Auden.

3. Discuss Auden's use of irony in the poem. Find specific examples.

Suggestions for Writing

1. Write a sketch describing and evaluating a typical day in the life of the unknown citizen.

2. Provide an alternative inscription for the monument.

◇◇◇◇

Robert Frost

Departmental

Robert Frost (1874–1963) was born in San Francisco, but of New England stock. At his father's death when Frost was eleven, he and his mother settled in Massachusetts. He studied for only seven weeks at Dartmouth and married two years later. After Frost's second unsuccessful attempt at college, this time at Harvard, his grandfather gave him a farm in Derry, New Hampshire, on the condition that he live there for ten years. When the ten years were up he left with his family for England where his first two books of poetry, *A Boy's Will* (1913) and *North of Boston* (1914) were published. He returned to America in 1915 to discover that he had a reputation as a poet. Eventually settling in Vermont, he traveled throughout America for many years giving lectures and public readings. He wrote many volumes of poetry and won four Pulitzer Prizes, many honorary degrees, and membership in distinguished academies. The United States Senate extended him greetings on his seventy-fifth and eighty-fifth birthdays, and he read one of his poems at the inauguration of President John F. Kennedy. "Departmental," from *A Further Range* (1936), reveals, with great irony, his commitment to a society that values human feelings and nourishes human dignity.

An ant on the tablecloth
Ran into a dormant moth
Of many times his size.
He showed not the least surprise.
His business wasn't with such.
He gave it scarcely a touch,
And was off on his duty run.
Yet if he encountered one
Of the hive's enquiry squad
Whose work is to find out God
And the nature of time and space,
He would put him onto the case.
Ants are a curious race;
One crossing with hurried tread
The body of one of their dead
Isn't given a moment's arrest—
Seems not even impressed.
But he no doubt reports to any
With whom he crosses antennae,
And they no doubt report
To the higher up at court.
Then word goes forth in Formic:
'Death's come to Jerry McCormic,
Our selfless forager Jerry.
Will the special Janizary
Whose office it is to bury
The dead of the commissary

Go bring him home to his people.
Lay him in state on a sepal.
Wrap him for shroud in a petal.
Embalm him with ichor of nettle.
This is the word of your Queen.'
And presently on the scene
Appears a solemn mortician;
And taking formal position
With feelers calmly atwiddle,
Seizes the dead by the middle,
And heaving him high in air,
Carries him out of there.
No one stands round to stare.
It is nobody else's affair.

It couldn't be called ungentle.
But how thoroughly departmental.

Suggestions for Discussion

1. What is the nature of the society of ants described in this poem?

2. Do the actions of the society of ants have relevance for human society?

3. What is the tone of the poem? Relate the line "Then word goes forth in Formic:" to the tone. What is "formic"?

4. What is the attitude of the speaker toward the "departmental" natures of the society of ants? How do we learn of his attitude?

5. How does the poet use meter to help establish the tone of the poem?

Suggestion for Writing

Compare the society depicted in "Departmental" with that of Auden's "The Unknown Citizen." How do both poets make use of irony in commenting on their world?

Drama
———— ◆◆◆◆ ————

Sophocles

Antigone
Translated by Dudley Fitts and Robert Fitzgerald

The Greek tragic playwright Sophocles (495?–406? B.C.) wrote a great number of plays, of which only seven have survived. He is best known for *Oedipus the King* whose name in our day, because of Sigmund Freud, has become synonymous with too close an attachment between mother and son. The play *Antigone* recounts the fate of the children of Oedipus and his wife-mother, particularly his older daughter Antigone, who gives her life choosing to obey the laws of the gods rather than those of men. This play counterpoises clearly the conflicting demands of government and religion or of government and individual conscience. A French translation and adaptation of the play by Jean Anouilh during the German occupation of France illustrated clearly to the French the relevance of *Antigone* to modern times. Beyond the pleasure and excitement of reading this fine translation by Dudley Fitts and Robert Fitzgerald, the student should keep in mind the significance of the play for his or her own life. The dilemmas that the characters face in *Antigone* are morally demanding whenever people choose to question the wisdom or legitimacy of the actions of the state.

Because of the curse that their father had laid upon them, ETEOCLES and POLYNEICES quarreled about the royal power, and POLYNEICES was finally driven from Thebes. He took refuge in Argos and married the daughter of KING ADRASTOS; then, as one of seven captains whose commander was ADRASTOS, he marched upon Thebes to recover his throne. In the assault, ETEOCLES and POLYNEICES met at the Seventh Gate and killed each other in combat. CREON became king, and his first official act was to forbid, on pain of death, the burial of POLYNEICES.

Dramatis Personæ

ANTIGONE	EURYDICE	HAIMON
ISMENE	CREON	TEIRESIAS
	A SENTRY	
	A MESSENGER	
	CHORUS	

SCENE: *Before the palace of* CREON, *King of Thebes. A central double door, and two lateral doors. A platform extends the length of the façade, and from this platform three steps lead down into the orchestra, or chorus-ground. Time: dawn of the day after the repulse of the Argive army from the assault on Thebes.*

Prologue

[ANTIGONE *and* ISMENE *enter from the central door of the Palace.*]

ANTIG: Ismenê, dear sister,
You would think that we had already suffered enough
For the curse on Oedipus:
I cannot imagine any grief
That you and I have not gone through. And now—
Have they told you the new decree of our King Creon?

ISMENE: I have heard nothing: I know
That two sisters lost two brothers, a double death
In a single hour; and I know that the Argive army
Fled in the night; but beyond this, nothing.

ANTIG: I thought so. And that is why I wanted you
To come out here with me. There is something we must do.

ISMENE: Why do you speak so strangely?

ANTIG: Listen, Ismenê:
Creon buried our brother Eteoclês
With military honours, gave him a soldier's funeral,
And it was right that he should; but Polyneicês,
Who fought as bravely and died as miserably,—
They say that Creon has sworn
No one shall bury him, no one mourn for him,
But his body must lie in the fields, a sweet treasure
For carrion birds to find as they search for food.
That is what they say, and our good Creon is coming here
To announce it publicly; and the penalty—
Stoning to death in the public square!
                    There it is,

And now you can prove what you are:
A true sister, or a traitor to your family.

ISMENE: Antigonê, you are mad! What could I possibly do?

ANTIG: You must decide whether you will help me or not.

ISMENE: I do not understand you. Help you in what?

ANTIG: Ismenê, I am going to bury him. Will you come?

ISMENE: Bury him! You have just said the new law forbids it.

ANTIG: He is my brother. And he is your brother, too.

ISMENE: But think of the danger! Think what Creon will do!

ANTIG: Creon is not strong enough to stand in my way.

ISMENE: Ah sister!
Oedipus died, everyone hating him
For what his own search brought to light, his eyes
Ripped out by his own hand; and Iocastê died,
His mother and wife at once: she twisted the cords
That strangled her life; and our two brothers died,
Each killed by the other's sword. And we are left:
But oh, Antigonê,
Think how much more terrible than these
Our own death would be if we should go against Creon
And do what he has forbidden! We are only women,
We cannot fight with men, Antigonê!
The law is strong, we must give in to the law
In this thing, and in worse. I beg the Dead
To forgive me, but I am helpless: I must yield
To those in authority. And I think it is dangerous business
To be always meddling.

ANTIG: If that is what you think,
I should not want you, even if you asked to come.
You have made your choice, you can be what you want to be.
But I will bury him; and if I must die,
I say that this crime is holy: I shall lie down
With him in death, and I shall be as dear
To him as he to me.
             It is the dead,
Not the living, who make the longest demands:
We die for ever . . .
                You may do as you like,
Since apparently the laws of the gods mean nothing to you.

ISMENE: They mean a great deal to me; but I have no strength
To break laws that were made for the public good.

ANTIG: That must be your excuse, I suppose. But as for me,
I will bury the brother I love.

ISMENE: Antigonê,
I am so afraid for you!

ANTIG: You need not be:
You have yourself to consider, after all.

ISMENE: But no one must hear of this, you must tell no one!
I will keep it a secret, I promise!

ANTIG: Oh tell it! Tell everyone!
Think how they'll hate you when it all comes out
If they learn that you knew about it all the time!

ISMENE: So fiery! You should be cold with fear.

ANTIG: Perhaps. But I am doing only what I must.

ISMENE: But can you do it? I say that you cannot.

ANTIG: Very well: when my strength gives out, I shall do no more.

ISMENE: Impossible things should not be tried at all.

ANTIG: Go away, Ismenê:
I shall be hating you soon, and the dead will too,
For your words are hateful. Leave me my foolish plan:
I am not afraid of the danger; if it means death,
It will not be the worst of deaths—death without honour.

ISMENE: Go then, if you feel that you must.
You are unwise,
But a loyal friend indeed to those who love you.

[*Exit into the Palace.* ANTIGONE *goes off, L. Enters the* CHORUS.]

Parodos

CHORUS: Now the long blade of the sun, lying [STROPHE 1]
Level east to west, touches with glory
Thebes of the Seven Gates. Open, unlidded
Eye of golden day! O marching light
Across the eddy and rush of Dircê's stream,*

---

*Dircê's stream: Dirce was the wife of King Lycus, King of Thebes when Oedipus' father Laios was a minor. Her sister-in-law, Antiope, who had loved Zeus and bore him twin sons, had fled Thebes to avoid her husband's wrath. Lycus punished Antiopê, but, after his death, Antiopê and her sons had Dircê killed by having her dragged to death on the horns of a bull. The two sons of Antiopê built the walls of Thebes with its seven gates, and one of them, Zethus, married the nymph Thebê from whose name came the name of the city.

Striking the white shields of the enemy
Thrown headlong backward from the blaze of morning!

CHORAG: Polyneicês their commander
Roused them with windy phrases,
He the wild eagle screaming
Insults above our land,
His wings their shields of snow,
His crest their marshalled helms.

CHORUS: Against our seven gates in a yawning ring   [ANTISTROPHE 1]
The famished spears came onward in the night;
But before his jaws were sated with our blood,
Or pinefire took the garland of our towers,
He was thrown back; and as he turned, great Thebes—
No tender victim for his noisy power—
Rose like a dragon behind him, shouting war.

CHORAG: For God hates utterly
The bray of bragging tongues;
And when he beheld their smiling,
Their swagger of golden helms,
The frown of his thunder blasted
Their first man from our walls.

CHORUS: We heard his shout of triumph high in the air   [STROPHE 2]
Turn to a scream; far out in a flaming arc
He fell with his windy torch, and the earth struck him.
And others storming in fury no less than his
Found shock of death in the dusty joy of battle.

CHORAG: Seven captains at seven gates
Yielded their clanging arms to the god
That bends the battle-line and breaks it.
These two only, brothers in blood,
Face to face in matchless rage,
Mirroring each the other's death,
Clashed in long combat.

CHORUS: But now in the beautiful morning of victory   [ANTISTROPHE 2]
Let Thebes of the many chariots sing for joy!
With hearts for dancing we'll take leave of war:
Our temples shall be sweet with hymns of praise,
And the long night shall echo with our chorus.

Scene I

CHORAG: But now at last our new King is coming:
Creon of Thebes, Menoiceus' son.
In this auspicious dawn of his reign
What are the new complexities
That shifting Fate has woven for him?
What is his counsel? Why has he summoned
The old men to hear him?

[*Enter* CREON *from the Palace. He addresses the* CHORUS *from the top step.*]

CREON: Gentlemen: I have the honour to inform you that our Ship of State, which recent storms have threatened to destroy, has come safely to harbour at last, guided by the merciful wisdom of Heaven. I have summoned you here this morning because I know that I can depend upon you: your devotion to King Laïos was absolute; you never hesitated in your duty to our late ruler Oedipus; and when Oedipus died, your loyalty was transferred to his children. Unfortunately, as you know, his two sons, the princes Eteoclês and Polyneicês, have killed each other in battle; and I, as the next in blood, have succeeded to the full power of the throne.

I am aware, of course, that no Ruler can expect complete loyalty from his subjects until he has been tested in office. Nevertheless, I say to you at the very outset that I have nothing but contempt for the kind of Governor who is afraid, for whatever reason, to follow the course that he knows is best for the State; and as for the man who sets private friendship above the public welfare, — I have no use for him, either. I call God to witness that if I saw my country headed for ruin, I should not be afraid to speak out plainly; and I need hardly remind you that I would never have any dealings with an enemy of the people. No one values friendship more highly than I; but we must remember that friends made at the risk of wrecking our Ship are not real friends at all.

These are my principles, at any rate, and that is why I have made the following decision concerning the sons of Oedipus: Eteoclês, who died as a man should die, fighting for his country, is to be buried with full military honours, with all the ceremony that is usual when the greatest heroes die; but his brother Polyneicês, who broke his exile to come back with fire and sword against his native city and the shrines of his fathers' gods, whose one idea was to spill the blood of his blood and sell his own people into slavery—Polyneicês, I say, is to have no burial: no man is to touch him or say the least prayer for him; he shall lie on the plain, unburied; and the birds and the scavenging dogs can do with him whatever they like.

This is my command, and you can see the wisdom behind it. As long as I am King, no traitor is going to be honoured with the loyal man. But whoever shows by word and deed that he is on the side of the State,—he shall have my respect while he is living, and my reverence when he is dead.

CHORAG: If that is your will, Creon son of Menoiceus,
You have the right to enforce it: we are yours.

CREON: That is my will. Take care that you do your part.

CHORAG: We are old men: let the younger ones carry it out.

CREON: I do not mean that: the sentries have been appointed.

CHORAG: Then what is it that you would have us do?

CREON: You will give no support to whoever breaks this law.

CHORAG: Only a crazy man is in love with death!

CREON: And death it is; yet money talks, and the wisest
Have sometimes been known to count a few coins too many.

[Enter SENTRY.]

SENTRY: I'll not say that I'm out of breath from running, King, because every time I stopped to think about what I have to tell you, I felt like going back. And all the time a voice kept saying, 'You fool, don't you know you're walking straight into trouble?'; and then another voice: 'Yes, but if you let somebody else get the news to Creon first, it will be even worse than that for you!' But good sense won out, at least I hope it was good sense, and here I am with a story that makes no sense at all; but I'll tell it anyhow, because, as they say, what's going to happen's going to happen, and—

CREON: Come to the point. What have you to say?

SENTRY: I did not do it. I did not see who did it. You must not punish me for what someone else has done.

CREON: A comprehensive defence! More effective, perhaps,
If I knew its purpose. Come: what is it?

SENTRY: A dreadful thing . . . I don't know how to put it—

CREON: Out with it!

SENTRY: Well, then;
The dead man—
                          Polyneicês—

[Pause. The SENTRY *is overcome, fumbles for words.* CREON *waits
impassively.*]

out there—

someone,—

New dust on the slimy flesh!

[*Pause. No sign from* CREON.]

Someone has given it burial that way, and
Gone . . .

[*Long pause.* CREON *finally speaks with deadly control:*]

CREON: And the man who dared do this?

SENTRY: I swear I
Do not know! You must believe me!

                                        Listen:
The ground was dry, not a sign of digging, no,
Not a wheeltrack in the dust, no trace of anyone.
It was when they relieved us this morning: and one of them,
The corporal, pointed to it.

                                        There it was,
The strangest—

            Look:
The body, just mounded over with light dust: you see?
Not buried really, but as if they'd covered it
Just enough for the ghost's peace. And no sign
Of dogs or any wild animal that had been there.

And then what a scene there was! Every man of us
Accusing the other: we all proved the other man did it,
We all had proof that we could not have done it.
We were ready to take hot iron in our hands,
Walk through fire, swear by all the gods,
It was not I!
I do not know who it was, but it was not I!

[CREON'S *rage has been mounting steadily, but the* SENTRY *is too
intent upon his story to notice it.*]

And then, when this came to nothing, someone said
A thing that silenced us and made us stare
Down at the ground: you had to be told the news,
And one of us had to do it! We threw the dice,
And the bad luck fell to me. So here I am,
No happier to be here than you are to have me:
Nobody likes the man who brings bad news.

CHORAG: I have been wondering, King: can it be that the gods have done
this?

[*Furiously.*]

CREON: Stop!
Must you doddering wrecks
Go out of your heads entirely? 'The gods!'
Intolerable!
The gods favour this corpse? Why? How had he served them?
Tried to loot their temples, burn their images,
Yes, and the whole State, and its laws with it!
Is it your senile opinion that the gods love to honour bad men?
A pious thought!—

No, from the very beginning
There have been those who have whispered together,
Stiff-necked anarchists, putting their heads together,
Scheming against me in alleys. These are the men,
And they have bribed my own guard to do this thing.

[Sententiously.]

Money!
There's nothing in the world so demoralising as money.
Down go your cities,
Homes gone, men gone, honest hearts corrupted,
Crookedness of all kinds, and all for money!

[To SENTRY:*]*

But you—!
I swear by God and by the throne of God,
The man who has done this thing shall pay for it!
Find that man, bring him here to me, or your death
Will be the least of your problems: I'll string you up
Alive, and there will be certain ways to make you
Discover your employer before you die;
And the process may teach you a lesson you seem to have missed:
The dearest profit is sometimes all too dear.
That depends on the source. Do you understand me?
A fortune won is often misfortune.

SENTRY: King, may I speak?

CREON: Your very voice distresses me.

SENTRY: Are you sure that it is my voice, and not your conscience?

CREON: By God, he wants to analyse me now!

SENTRY: It is not what I say, but what has been done, that hurts you.

CREON: You talk too much.

SENTRY: Maybe; but I've done nothing.

CREON: Sold your soul for some silver: that's all you've done.

SENTRY: How dreadful it is when the right judge judges wrong!

CREON: Your figures of speech
May entertain you now; but unless you bring me the man,
You will get little profit from them in the end.

[*Exit* CREON *into the Palace.*]

SENTRY: 'Bring me the man'—!
I'd like nothing better than bringing him the man!
But bring him or not, you have seen the last of me here.
At any rate, I am safe!

[*Exit* SENTRY.]

Ode I

CHORUS: Numberless are the world's wonders, but none   [STROPHE 1]
More wonderful than man; the stormgrey sea
Yields to his prows, the huge crests bear him high;
Earth, holy and inexhaustible, is graven
With shining furrows where his plows have gone
Year after year, the timeless labour of stallions.

[ANTISTROPHE 1]

The lightboned birds and beasts that cling to cover,
The lithe fish lighting their reaches of dim water,
All are taken, tamed in the net of his mind;
The lion on the hill, the wild horse windy-maned,
Resign to him; and his blunt yoke has broken
The sultry shoulders of the mountain bull.

Words also, and thought as rapid as air,   [STROPHE 2]
He fashions to his good use; statecraft is his,
And his the skill that deflects the arrows of snow,
The spears of winter rain: from every wind
He has made himself secure—from all but one:
In the late wind of death he cannot stand.

O clear intelligence, force beyond all measure!   [ANTISTROPHE 2]
O fate of man, working both good and evil!
When the laws are kept, how proudly his city stands!
When the laws are broken, what of his city then?
Never may the anarchic man find rest at my hearth,
Never be it said that my thoughts are his thoughts.

Scene II

[*Re-enter* SENTRY *leading* ANTIGONE.]

CHORAG: What does this mean? Surely this captive woman
Is the Princess, Antigonê. Why should she be taken?

SENTRY: Here is the one who did it! We caught her
In the very act of burying him.—Where is Creon?

CHORAG: Just coming from the house.

[*Enter* CREON, *C.*]

CREON: What has happened?
Why have you come back so soon?

[*Expansively.*]

SENTRY: O King,
A man should never be too sure of anything:
I would have sworn
That you'd not see me here again: your anger
Frightened me so, and the things you threatened me with;
But how could I tell then
That I'd be able to solve the case so soon?

No dice-throwing this time: I was only too glad to come!

Here is this woman. She is the guilty one:
We found her trying to bury him.

Take her, then; question her; judge her as you will.
I am through with the whole thing now, and glad of it.

CREON: But this is Antigonê! Why have you brought her here?

SENTRY: She was burying him, I tell you!

[*Severely.*]

CREON: Is this the truth?

SENTRY: I saw her with my own eyes. Can I say more?

CREON: The details: come, tell me quickly!

SENTRY: It was like this:
After those terrible threats of yours, King,
We went back and brushed the dust away from the body.
The flesh was soft by now, and stinking,
So we sat on a hill to windward and kept guard.
No napping this time! We kept each other awake.
But nothing happened until the white round sun

Whirled in the centre of the round sky over us:
Then, suddenly,
A storm of dust roared up from the earth, and the sky
Went out, the plain vanished with all its trees
In the stinging dark. We closed our eyes and endured it.
The whirlwind lasted a long time, but it passed;
And then we looked, and there was Antigonê!
I have seen
A mother bird come back to a stripped nest, heard
Her crying bitterly a broken note or two
For the young ones stolen. Just so, when this girl
Found the bare corpse, and all her love's work wasted,
She wept, and cried on heaven to damn the hands
That had done this thing
                       And then she brought more dust
And sprinkled wine three times for her brother's ghost.

We ran and took her at once. She was not afraid,
Not even when we charged her with what she had done.
She denied nothing.
                   And this was a comfort to me,
And some uneasiness: for it is a good thing
To escape from death, but it is no great pleasure
To bring death to a friend.
                   Yet I always say
There is nothing so comfortable as your own safe skin!

                   [*Slowly, dangerously.*]

CREON: And you, Antigonê,
          You with your head hanging,—do you confess this thing?

ANTIG: I do. I deny nothing.

          [*To* SENTRY:]

CREON: You may go.

                   [*Exit* SENTRY.]

          [*To* ANTIGONE:]

Tell me, tell me briefly:
Had you heard my proclamation touching this matter?

ANTIG: It was public. Could I help hearing it?

CREON: And yet you dared defy the law.

ANTIG: I dared.
          It was not God's proclamation. That final Justice
          That rules the world below makes no such laws.

> Your edict, King, was strong,
> But all your strength is weakness itself against
> The immortal unrecorded laws of God.
> They are not merely now: they were, and shall be,
> Operative for ever, beyond man utterly.
>
> I knew I must die, even without your decree:
> I am only mortal. And if I must die
> Now, before it is my time to die,
> Surely this is no hardship: can anyone
> Living, as I live, with evil all about me,
> Think Death less than a friend? This death of mine
> Is of no importance; but if I had left my brother
> Lying in death unburied, I should have suffered.
> Now I do not.
> You smile at me. Ah Creon,
> Think me a fool, if you like; but it may well be
> That a fool convicts me of folly.

CHORAG: Like father, like daughter: both headstrong, deaf to reason!
She has never learned to yield.

CREON: She has much to learn.
The inflexible heart breaks first, the toughest iron
Cracks first, and the wildest horses bend their necks
At the pull of the smallest curb.
Pride? In a slave?
This girl is guilty of a double insolence,
Breaking the given laws and boasting of it.
Who is the man here,
She or I, if this crime goes unpunished?
Sister's child, or more than sister's child,
Or closer yet in blood—she and her sister
Win bitter death for this!

[*To servants:*]

Go, some of you,
Arrest Ismenê. I accuse her equally.
Bring her: you will find her sniffling in the house there.

Her mind's a traitor: crimes kept in the dark
Cry for light, and the guardian brain shudders;
But how much worse than this
Is brazen boasting of barefaced anarchy!

ANTIG: Creon, what more do you want than my death?

CREON: Nothing.
That gives me everything.

ANTIG: Then I beg you: kill me.
This talking is a great weariness: your words
Are distasteful to me, and I am sure that mine
Seem so to you. And yet they should not seem so:
I should have praise and honour for what I have done.
All these men here would praise me
Were their lips not frozen shut with fear of you.

[Bitterly.]

Ah the good fortune of kings,
Licensed to say and do whatever they please!

CREON: You are alone here in that opinion.

ANTIG: No, they are with me. But they keep their tongues in leash.

CREON: Maybe. But you are guilty, and they are not.

ANTIG: There is no guilt in reverence for the dead.

CREON: But Eteoclês—was he not your brother too?

ANTIG: My brother too.

CREON: And you insult his memory?

[Softly.]

ANTIG: The dead man would not say that I insult it.

CREON: He would: for you honour a traitor as much as him.

ANTIG: His own brother, traitor or not, and equal in blood.

CREON: He made war on his country. Eteoclês defended it.

ANTIG: Nevertheless, there are honours due all the dead.

CREON: But not the same for the wicked as for the just.

ANTIG: Ah Creon, Creon,
Which of us can say what the gods hold wicked?

CREON: An enemy is an enemy, even dead.

ANTIG: It is my nature to join in love, not hate.

[Finally losing patience.]

CREON: Go join them, then; if you must have your love,
Find it in hell!

CHORAG: But see, Ismenê comes:

[Enter ISMENE, guarded.]

Those tears are sisterly, the cloud

That shadows her eyes rains down gentle sorrow.

CREON: You too, Ismenê,
Snake in my ordered house, sucking my blood
Stealthily—and all the time I never knew
That these two sisters were aiming at my throne!

                Ismenê,
Do you confess your share in this crime, or deny it?
Answer me.

ISMENE: Yes, if she will let me say so. I am guilty.

                       [*Coldly:*]

ANTIG: No, Ismenê. You have no right to say so.
You would not help me, and I will not have you help me.

ISMENE: But now I know what you meant; and I am here
To join you, to take my share of punishment.

ANTIG: The dead man and the gods who rule the dead
Know whose act this was. Words are not friends.

ISMENE: Do you refuse me, Antigonê? I want to die with you:
I too have a duty that I must discharge to the dead.

ANTIG: You shall not lessen my death by sharing it.

ISMENE: What do I care for life when you are dead?

ANTIG: Ask Creon. You're always hanging on his opinions.

ISMENE: You are laughing at me. Why, Antigonê?

ANTIG: It's a joyless laughter, Ismenê.

ISMENE: But can I do nothing?

ANTIG: Yes. Save yourself. I shall not envy you.
There are those who will praise you; I shall have honour, too.

ISMENE: But we are equally guilty!

ANTIG: No, more, Ismenê.
You are alive, but I belong to Death.

CREON: [*To the* CHORUS:]

Gentlemen, I beg you to observe these girls:
One has just now lost her mind; the other
It seems, has never had a mind at all.

ISMENE: Grief teaches the steadiest minds to waver, King.

CREON: Yours certainly did, when you assumed guilt with the guilty!

ISMENE: But how could I go on living without her?

CREON: You are.
            She is already dead.

ISMENE: But your own son's bride!

CREON: There are places enough for him to push his plow.
            I want no wicked women for my sons!

ISMENE: O dearest Haimon, how your father wrongs you!

CREON: I've had enough of your childish talk of marriage!

CHORAG: Do you really intend to steal this girl from your son?

CREON: No; Death will do that for me.

CHORAG: Then she must die?

CREON: You dazzle me.
                    —But enough of this talk!

                                        [*To* GUARDS:]

            You, there, take them away and guard them well:
            For they are but women, and even brave men run
            When they see Death coming.

                        [*Exeunt* ISMENE, ANTIGONE, and GUARDS.]

Ode II

                                        [STROPHE 1]

CHORUS: Fortunate is the man who has never tasted God's vengeance!
            Where once the anger of heaven has struck, that house is shaken
            For ever: damnation rises behind each child
            Like a wave cresting out of the black northeast,
            When the long darkness under sea roars up
            And bursts drumming death upon the windwhipped sand.

                                        [ANTISTROPHE 1]
            I have seen this gathering sorrow from time long past
            Loom upon Oedipus' children: generation from generation
            Takes the compulsive rage of the enemy god.
            So lately this last flower of Oedipus' line
            Drank the sunlight! but now a passionate word
            And a handful of dust have closed up all its beauty.

                What mortal arrogance   [STROPHE 2]

Transcends the wrath of Zeus?
Sleep cannot lull him, nor the effortless long months
Of the timeless gods: but he is young for ever,
And his house is the shining day of high Olympus.*
> All that is and shall be,
> And all the past, is his.
No pride on earth is free of the curse of heaven.

> The straying dreams of men   [ANTISTROPHE 2]
> May bring them ghosts of joy:
But as they drowse, the waking embers burn them;
Or they walk with fixed éyes, as blind men walk.
But the ancient wisdom speaks for our own time:
> *Fate works most for woe*
> *With Folly's fairest show.*
Man's little pleasure is the spring of sorrow.

Scene III

CHORAG: But here is Haimon, King, the last of all your sons.
Is it grief for Antigonê that brings him here,
And bitterness at being robbed of his bride?

[*Enter* HAIMON.]

CREON: We shall soon see, and no need of diviners.
—Son,
You have heard my final judgment on that girl:
Have you come here hating me, or have you come
With deference and with love, whatever I do?

HAIMON: I am your son, father. You are my guide.
You make things clear for me, and I obey you.
No marriage means more to me than your continuing wisdom.

CREON: Good. That is the way to behave: subordinate
Everything else, my son, to your father's will.
That is what a man prays for, that he may get
Sons attentive and dutiful in his house,
Each one hating his father's enemies,
Honouring his father's friends. But if his sons
Fail him, if they turn out unprofitably,
What has he fathered but trouble for himself
And amusement for the malicious?

Olympus: the summit of this mountain was regarded in Greek myth as the residence of the gods.

So you are right
Not to lose your head over this woman.
Your pleasure with her would soon grow cold, Haimon,
And then you'd have a hellcat in bed and elsewhere.
Let her find her husband in Hell!
Of all the people in this city, only she
Has had contempt for my law and broken it.

Do you want me to show myself weak before the people?
Or to break my sworn word? No, and I will not.
The woman dies.

I suppose she'll plead 'family ties.' Well, let her.
If I permit my own family to rebel,
How shall I earn the world's obedience?
Show me the man who keeps his house in hand,
He's fit for public authority.
                              I'll have no dealings
With law-breakers, critics of the government:
Whoever is chosen to govern should be obeyed—
Must be obeyed, in all things, great and small,
Just and unjust! O Haimon,
The man who knows how to obey, and that man only,
Knows how to give commands when the time comes.
You can depend on him, no matter how fast
The spears come: he's a good soldier, he'll stick it out.

Anarchy, anarchy! Show me a greater evil!
This is why cities tumble and the great houses rain down,
This is what scatters armies!

No, no: good lives are made so by discipline.
We keep the laws then, and the lawmakers,
And no woman shall seduce us. If we must lose,
Let's lose to a man, at least! Is a woman stronger than we?

CHORAG: Unless time has rusted my wits,
          What you say, King, is said with point and dignity.

                                        [*Boyishly earnest:*]

HAIMON: Father:
          Reason is God's crowning gift to man, and you are right
          To warn me against losing mine. I cannot say—
          I hope that I shall never want to say!—that you
          Have reasoned badly. Yet there are other men
          Who can reason, too; and their opinions might be helpful.
          You are not in a position to know everything
          That people say or do, or what they feel:

Your temper terrifies them—everyone
Will tell you only what you like to hear.
But I, at any rate, can listen; and I have heard them
Muttering and whispering in the dark about this girl.
They say no woman has ever, so unreasonably,
Died so shameful a death for a generous act:
'She covered her brother's body. Is this indecent?
'She kept him from dogs and vultures. Is this a crime?
'Death?—She should have all the honour that we can give her!'

This is the way they talk out there in the city.

You must believe me:
Nothing is closer to me than your happiness.
What could be closer? Must not any son
Value his father's fortune as his father does his?
I beg you, do not be unchangeable:
Do not believe that you alone can be right.
The man who thinks that,
The man who maintains that only he has the power
To reason correctly, the gift to speak, the soul—
A man like that, when you know him, turns out empty.

It is not reason never to yield to reason!

In flood time you can see how some trees bend,
And because they bend, even their twigs are safe,
While stubborn trees are torn up, roots and all.
And the same thing happens in sailing:
Make your sheet fast, never slacken,—and over you go,
Head over heels and under: and there's your voyage.
Forget you are angry! Let yourself be moved!
I know I am young; but please let me say this:
The ideal condition
Would be, I admit, that men should be right by instinct;
But since we are all too likely to go astray,
The reasonable thing is to learn from those who can teach.

CHORAG: You will do well to listen to him, King,
If what he says is sensible. And you, Haimon,
Must listen to your father.—Both speak well.

CREON: You consider it right for a man of my years and experience
To go to school to a boy?

HAIMON: It is not right
If I am wrong. But if I am young, and right,
What does my age matter?

CREON: You think it right to stand up for an anarchist?

HAIMON: Not at all. I pay no respect to criminals.

CREON: Then she is not a criminal?

HAIMON: The City would deny it, to a man.

CREON: And the City proposes to teach me how to rule?

HAIMON: Ah. Who is it that's talking like a boy now?

CREON: My voice is the one voice giving orders in this City!

HAIMON: It is no City if it takes orders from one voice.

CREON: The State is the King!

HAIMON: Yes, if the State is a desert.

                                                                    [*Pause.*]

CREON: This boy, it seems, has sold out to a woman.

HAIMON: If you are a woman: my concern is only for you.

CREON: So? Your 'concern'! In a public brawl with your father!

HAIMON: How about you, in a public brawl with justice?

CREON: With justice, when all that I do is within my rights?

HAIMON: You have no right to trample on God's right.

                                           [*Completely out of control:*]

CREON: Fool, adolescent fool! Taken in by a woman!

HAIMON: You'll never see me taken in by anything vile.

CREON: Every word you say is for her!

                                                   [*Quietly, darkly:*]

HAIMON: And for you.
            And for me. And for the gods under the earth.

CREON: You'll never marry her while she lives.

HAIMON: Then she must die.—But her death will cause another.

CREON: ·Another?
            Have you lost your senses? Is this an open threat?

HAIMON: There is no threat in speaking to emptiness.

CREON: I swear you'll regret this superior tone of yours!
            You are the empty one!

HAIMON: If you were not my father,
            I'd say you were perverse.

CREON: You girlstruck fool, don't play at words with me!

HAIMON: I am sorry. You prefer silence.

CREON: Now, by God—!
I swear, by all the gods in heaven above us,
You'll watch it, I swear you shall!

                                             [*To the* SERVANTS.]

                         Bring her out!
Bring the woman out! Let her die before his eyes,
Here, this instant, with her bridegroom beside her!

HAIMON: Not here, no; she will not die here, King.
And you will never see my face again.
Go on raving as long as you've a friend to endure you.

                                             [*Exit* HAIMON.]

CHORAG: Gone, gone.
Creon, a young man in a rage is dangerous!

CREON: Let him do, or dream to do, more than a man can.
He shall not save these girls from death.

CHORAG: These girls?
You have sentenced them both?

CREON: No, you are right.
I will not kill the one whose hands are clean.

CHORAG: But Antigonê?

                                             [*Sombrely:*]

CREON: I will carry her far away
Out there in the wilderness, and lock her
Living in a vault of stone. She shall have food,
As the custom is, to absolve the State of her death.
And there let her pray to the gods of Hell:
They are her only gods:
Perhaps they will show her an escape from death,
Or she may learn,
                         though late,
That piety shown the dead is pity in vain.

                                             [*Exit* CREON.]

Ode III

CHORUS: Love, unconquerable   [STROPHE]
Waster of rich men, keeper

Of warm lights and all-night vigil
In the soft face of a girl:
Sea-wanderer, forest-visitor!
Even the pure Immortals cannot escape you,
And mortal man, in his one day's dusk,
Trembles before your glory.

Surely you swerve upon ruin   [ANTISTROPHE]
The just man's consenting heart,
As here you have made bright anger
Strike between father and son—
And none has conquered but Love!
A girl's glánce wórking the will of heaven:
Pleasure to her alone who mocks us,
Merciless Aphroditê.*

Scene IV

[*As* ANTIGONE *enters guarded.*]

CHORAG: But I can no longer stand in awe of this,
Nor, seeing what I see, keep back my tears.
Here is Antigonê, passing to that chamber
Where all find sleep at last.

ANTIG: Look upon me, friends, and pity me   [STROPHE 1]
Turning back at the night's edge to say
Good-bye to the sun that shines for me no longer;
Now sleepy Death
Summons me down to Acheron,† that cold shore:
There is no bridesong there, nor any music.

CHORUS: Yet not unpraised, not without a kind of honour,
You walk at last into the underworld;
Untouched by sickness, broken by no sword.
What woman has ever found your way to death?

ANTIG: How often I have heard the story of Niobê,‡   [ANTISTROPHE 1]
Tantalos' wretched daughter, how the stone
Clung fast about her, ivy-close: and they say
The rain falls endlessly

*Aphroditê: Aphrodite was the Greek goddess of love.

†Acheron: in Greek myth, one of the rivers of the lower world, the other being Styx. The land of the living is separated from Hades by these rivers and the dead were rowed across them by Charon.

‡Niobê: the daughter of Tantalos (who was punished in Hades by the gods by being deprived of food and drink just as he reached for it or by pushing a large stone up a hill only to have it roll back). Niobê had seven children. Because she boasted that their number made her superior to Leto, the mother of Apollo and Artemis, the two gods killed them with arrows. Niobê wept for her children until she turned into a column of stone from which her tears flowed.

And sifting soft snow; her tears are never done.
I feel the loneliness of her death in mine.

CHORUS: But she was born of heaven, and you
Are woman, woman-born. If her death is yours,
A mortal woman's, is this not for you
Glory in our world and in the world beyond?

ANTIG: You laugh at me. Ah, friends, friends,   [STROPHE 2]
Can you not wait until I am dead? O Thebes,
O men many-charioted, in love with Fortune,
Dear springs of Dircê, sacred Theban grove,
Be witnesses for me, denied all pity,
Unjustly judged! and think a word of love
For her whose path turns
Under dark earth, where there are no more tears.

CHORUS: You have passed beyond human daring and come at last
Into a place of stone where Justice sits.
I cannot tell
What shape of your father's guilt appears in this.

ANTIG: You have touched it at last: that bridal bed   [ANTISTROPHE 2]
Unspeakable, horror of son and mother mingling:
Their crime, infection of all our family!
O Oedipus, father and brother!
Your marriage strikes from the grave to murder mine.
I have been a stranger here in my own land:
All my life
The blasphemy of my birth has followed me.

CHORUS: Reverence is a virtue, but strength
Lives in established law: that must prevail.
You have made your choice,
Your death is the doing of your conscious hand.

ANTIG: Then let me go, since all your words are bitter,   [EPODE]
And the very light of the sun is cold to me.
Lead me to my vigil, where I must have
Neither love nor lamentation; no song, but silence.

[CREON *interrupts impatiently.*]

CREON: If dirges and planned lamentations could put off death,
Men would be singing for ever.

[*To the* SERVANTS:]

Take her, go!
You know your orders: take her to the vault
And leave her alone there. And if she lives or dies,
That's her affair, not ours: our hands are clean.

ANTIG: O tomb, vaulted bride-bed in eternal rock,
          Soon I shall be with my own again
          Where Persephonê* welcomes the thin ghosts underground:
          And I shall see my father again, and you, mother,
          And dearest Polyneicês— dearest indeed
          To me, since it was my hand
          That washed him clean and poured the ritual wine:
          And my reward is death before my time!

          And yet, as men's hearts know, I have done no wrong,
          I have not sinned before God. Or if I have,
          I shall know the truth in death. But if the guilt
          Lies upon Creon who judged me, then, I pray,
          May his punishment equal my own.

CHORAG: O passionate heart,
          Unyielding, tormented still by the same winds!

CREON: Her guards shall have good cause to regret their delaying.

ANTIG: Ah! That voice is like the voice of death!

CREON: I can give you no reason to think you are mistaken.

ANTIG: Thebes, and you my fathers' gods,
          And rulers of Thebes, you see me now, the last
          Unhappy daughter of a line of kings,
          Your kings, led away to death. You will remember
          What things I suffer, and at what men's hands,
          Because I would not transgress the laws of heaven.

                                      [*To the* GUARDS, *simply*:]

          Come: let us wait no longer.

                                      [*Exit* ANTIGONE, *L., guarded.*]

Ode IV

CHORUS: All Danaê's beauty† was locked away   [STROPHE 1]
          In a brazen cell where the sunlight could not come:
          A small room, still as any grave, enclosed her.
          Yet she was a princess too,

Persephonê: the daughter of Zeus and Demeter, who was kidnapped by Hades and brought to the underworld to be his queen. Demeter demanded her return, and Zeus agreed, but because she had eaten of the forbidden pomegranate there, she was forced to spend half of each year with Hades.

†*Danaê's beauty:* Danaê was the daughter of Acrisius, the king of Artos, who locked her in a tower because of the prophecy that he would be killed by her son. Zeus, however, visited her in a shower of gold. She bore Zeus a son, Perseus, who unintentionally killed his grandfather.

And Zeus in a rain of gold poured love upon her.
O child, child,
No power in wealth or war
Or tough sea-blackened ships
Can prevail against untiring Destiny!

And Dryas' son‡ also, that furious king,   [ANTISTROPHE 1]
Bore the god's prisoning anger for his pride:
Sealed up by Dionysos in deaf stone,
His madness died among echoes.
So at the last he learned what dreadful power
His tongue had mocked:
For he had profaned the revels,
And fired the wrath of the nine
Implacable Sisters that love the sound of the flute.

And old men tell a half-remembered tale°   [STROPHE 2]
Of horror done where a dark ledge splits the sea
And a double surf beats on the grey shores:
How a king's new woman, sick
With hatred for the queen he had imprisoned,
Ripped out his two sons' eyes with her bloody hands
While grinning Arês watched the shuttle plunge
Four times: four blind wounds crying for revenge,

[ANTISTROPHE 2]

Crying, tears and blood mingled.—Piteously born,
Those sons whose mother was of heavenly birth!
Her father was the god of the North Wind
And she was cradled by gales,
She raced with young colts on the glittering hills
And walked untrammeled in the open light:
But in her marriage deathless Fate found means
To build a tomb like yours for all her joy.

Scene V

[*Enter blind* TEIRESIAS, *led by a boy. The opening speeches
of* TEIRESIAS *should be in singsong contrast to the
realistic lines of* CREON.]

TEIRES: This is the way the blind man comes, Princes, Princes,
           Lock-step, two heads lit by the eyes of one.

‡*Dryas' son:* Lycurgus, the king of Thrace, opposed the worship of Dionysus, who imprisoned
him and drove him mad.
°*And old men tell a half-remembered tale . . . for all her joy:* Strophe 2 refers to the story of
Phineus, king of Salmydessus, who had two children by his first wife, Cleopatra. His second wife,
Eidothea, put out the eyes of these two children. Antistrophe 2 refers to the sorrow of Cleopatra,
the daughter of the god Boreus, the North Wind. The tales of calamity and death in Ode IV
provide analogies of suffering for the fate of Antigone.

CREON: What new thing have you to tell us, old Teiresias?

TEIRES: I have much to tell you: listen to the prophet, Creon.

CREON: I am not aware that I have ever failed to listen.

TEIRES: Then you have done wisely, King, and ruled well.

CREON: I admit my debt to you. But what have you to say?

TEIRES: This, Creon: you stand once more on the edge of fate.

CREON: What do you mean? Your words are a kind of dread.

TEIRES: Listen, Creon:
I was sitting in my chair of augury, at the place
Where the birds gather about me. They were all a-chatter,
As is their habit, when suddenly I heard
A strange note in their jangling, a scream, a
Whirring fury; I knew that they were fighting,
Tearing each other, dying
In a whirlwind of wings clashing. And I was afraid.
I began the rites of burnt-offering at the altar,
But Hephaistos failed me: instead of bright flame,
There was only the sputtering slime of the fat thigh-flesh
Melting: the entrails dissolved in grey smoke,
The bare bone burst from the welter. And no blaze!

This was a sign from heaven. My boy described it,
Seeing for me as I see for others.

I tell you, Creon, you yourself have brought
This new calamity upon us. Our hearths and altars
Are stained with the corruption of dogs and carrion birds
That glut themselves on the corpse of Oedipus' son.
The gods are deaf when we pray to them, their fire
Recoils from our offering, their birds of omen
Have no cry of comfort, for they are gorged!
With the thick blood of the dead.
                                 O my son,
These are no trifles! Think: all men make mistakes,
But a good man yields when he knows his course is wrong.
And repairs the evil. The only crime is pride.

Give in to the dead man, then: do not fight with a corpse—
What glory is it to kill a man who is dead?
Think, I beg you:
It is for your own good that I speak as I do.
You should be able to yield for your own good.

CREON: It seems that prophets have made me their especial province.
All my life long.

> I have been a kind of butt for the dull arrows
> Of doddering fortune-tellers!
>   No, Teiresias:
> If your birds—if the great eagles of God himself
> Should carry him stinking bit by bit to heaven,
> I would not yield. I am not afraid of pollution:
> No man can defile the gods.
>   Do what you will,
> Go into business, make money, speculate
> In India gold or that synthetic gold from Sardis,
> Get rich otherwise than by my consent to bury him.
> Teiresias, it is a sorry thing when a wise man
> Sells his wisdom, lets out his words for hire!

TEIRES: Ah Creon! Is there no man left in the world—

CREON: To do what?—Come, let's have the aphorism!

TEIRES: No man who knows that wisdom outweighs any wealth?

CREON: As surely as bribes are baser than any baseness.

TEIRES: You are sick, Creon! You are deathly sick!

CREON: As you say: it is not my place to challenge a prophet.

TEIRES: Yet you have said my prophecy is for sale.

CREON: The generation of prophets has always loved gold.

TEIRES: The generation of kings has always loved brass.

CREON: You forget yourself! You are speaking to your King.

TEIRES: I know it. You are a king because of me.

CREON: You have a certain skill; but you have sold out.

TEIRES: King, you will drive me to words that—

CREON: Say them, say them!
Only remember: I will not pay you for them.

TEIRES: No, you will find them too costly.

CREON: No doubt. Speak:
Whatever you say, you will not change my will.

TEIRES: Then take this, and take it to heart!
The time is not far off when you shall pay back
Corpse for corpse, flesh of your own flesh.
You have thrust the child of this world into living night,
You have kept from the gods below the child that is theirs:
The one in a grave before her death, the other,

Dead, denied the grave. This is your crime:
And the Furies and the dark gods of Hell
Are swift with terrible punishment for you.

Do you want to buy me now, Creon?

                                   Not many days,
And your house will be full of men and women weeping,
And curses will be hurled at you from far
Cities grieving* for sons unburied, left to rot before the walls of
    Thebes.

These are my arrows, Creon: they are all for you.

                                        [*To* BOY:]

But come, child: lead me home.
Let him waste his fine anger upon younger men.
Maybe he will learn at last
To control a wiser tongue in a better head.

                                      [*Exit* TEIRESIAS.]

CHORAG: The old man has gone, King, but his words
        Remain to plague us. I am old, too,
        But I can not remember that he was ever false.

CREON: That is true. . . . It troubles me.
        Oh it is hard to give in! but it is worse
        To risk everything for stubborn pride.

CHORAG: Creon: take my advice.

CREON: What shall I do?

CHORAG: Go quickly: free Antigonê from her vault
        And build a tomb for the body of Polyneicês.

CREON: You would have me do this?

CHORAG: Creon, yes!
        And it must be done at once: God moves
        Swiftly to cancel the folly of stubborn men.

CREON: It is hard to deny the heart! But I
        Will do it: I will not fight with destiny.

CHORAG: You must go yourself, you cannot leave it to others.

Cities grieving: Creon had decreed that the corpses of Polyneices' allies also be left unburied.

CREON: I will go.

                  —Bring axes, servants:
Come with me to the tomb. I buried her, I
Will set her free.

               Oh quickly!
My mind misgives—
The laws of the gods are mighty, and a man must serve them
To the last day of his life!

                                    [*Exit* CREON.]

Pæan

CHORAG: God of many names   [STROPHE 1]

CHORUS: O Iacchos*
                          son
of Cadmeian Sémelê
                 O born of the Thunder!
Guardian of the West
               Regent
of Eleusis' plain
            O Prince of mænad Thebes
and the Dragon Field by rippling Ismenos:

CHORAG: God of many names   [ANTISTROPHE 1]
                 the flame of torches

CHORUS: flares on our hills
               the nymphs of Iacchos
dance at the spring of Castalia:†
from the vine-close mountain
                   come ah come in ivy:
Evohé evohé! sings through the streets of Thebes

CHORAG: God of many names   [STROPHE 2]

CHORUS: Iacchos of Thebes
    heavenly Child
            of Sémelê bride of the Thunderer!

Iacchos: Strophe 1, one of three deities (the others, Demeter and Persephone) at the Mysteries at Eleusis on the coast near Athens. These were rites revealed only to initiates and which celebrated life after death. The god Dionysus, son of Zeus and Sémelê, was also celebrated at these rites under the name of Iacchos. Dionysus was accompanied by possessed or intoxicated male and female Maenads, Satyrs, and Silenae. Cadmus, the father of Sémelê, was directed by the gods to the spot where he founded the citadel of the future city of Thebes. He was helped in this by the five surviving warriors, who sprang up from the dragon's teeth he had sown under Athenê's instructions. These five warriors were the ancestors of the noble families of Thebes.

†*spring of Castalia:* the spring at Delphi, sacred to Apollo and the nine Muses.

The shadow of plague is upon us:

come

with clement feet

oh come from Parnasos‡

down the long slopes

across the lamenting water

CHORAG: Iô Fire! Chorister of the throbbing stars!   [ANTISTROPHE 2]
O purest among the voices of the night!
Thou son of God, blaze for us!

CHORUS: Come with choric rapture of circling Mænads
Who cry *Iô Iacche!*

God of many names!

Exodos

[*Enter* MESSENGER.]

MESS: Men of the line of Cadmos, you who live
Near Amphion's citadel:

I cannot say
Of any condition of human life 'This is fixed,
This is clearly good, or bad.' Fate raises up,
And Fate casts down the happy and unhappy alike:
No man can foretell his Fate.

Take the case of Creon:
Creon was happy once, as I count happiness:
Victorious in battle, sole governor of the land,
Fortunate father of children nobly born.
And now it has all gone from him! Who can say
That a man is still alive when his life's joy fails?
He is a walking dead man. Grant him rich,
Let him live like a king in his great house:
If his pleasure is gone, I would not give
So much as the shadow of smoke for all he owns.

CHORAG: Your words hint at sorrow: what is your news for us?

MESS: They are dead. The living are guilty of their death.

CHORAG: Who is guilty? Who is dead? Speak!

MESS: Haimon.
Haimon is dead; and the hand that killed him
Is his own hand.

CHORAG: His father's? or his own?

‡*Parnasos:* the mountain above Delphi, sacred to Apollo and Dionysus.

MESS: His own, driven mad by the murder his father had done.

CHORAG: Teiresias, Teiresias, how clearly you saw it all!

MESS: This is my news: you must draw what conclusions you can from it.

CHORAG: But look: Eurydicê, our Queen:
               Has she overheard us?

               [*Enter* EURYDICE *from the Palace, C.*]

EURYD: I have heard something, friends:
               As I was unlocking the gate of Pallas' shrine,
               For I needed her help today, I heard a voice
               Telling of some new sorrow. And I fainted
               There at the temple with all my maidens about me.
               But speak again: whatever it is, I can bear it:
               Grief and I are no strangers.

MESS: Dearest Lady,
               I will tell you plainly all that I have seen.
               I shall not try to comfort you: what is the use,
               Since comfort could lie only in what is not true?
               The truth is always best.

                         I went with Creon
               To the outer plain where Polyneicês was lying,
               No friend to pity him, his body shredded by dogs.
               We made our prayers in that place to Hecatê*
               And Pluto*, that they would be merciful. And we bathed
               The corpse with holy water, and we brought
               Fresh-broken branches to burn what was left of it,
               And upon the urn we heaped up a towering barrow
               Of the earth of his own land.

                      When we were done, we ran
               To the vault where Antigonê lay on her couch of stone.
               One of the servants had gone ahead,
               And while he was yet far off he heard a voice
               Grieving within the chamber, and he came back
               And told Creon. And as the King went closer,
               The air was full of wailing, the words lost,
               And he begged us to make all haste. 'Am I a prophet?'
               He said, weeping, 'And must I walk this road,
               'The saddest of all that I have gone before?
               'My son's voice calls me on. Oh quickly, quickly!

Hecate and Pluto: gods of the underworld.

'Look through the crevice there, and tell me
'If it is Haimon, or some deception of the gods!'

We obeyed; and in the cavern's farthest corner
We saw her lying:
She had made a noose of her fine linen veil
And hanged herself. Haimon lay beside her,
His arms about her waist, lamenting her,
His love lost under ground, crying out
That his father had stolen her away from him.

When Creon saw him the tears rushed to his eyes
And he called to him: 'What have you done, child? Speak to me.
'What are you thinking that makes your eyes so strange?
'O my son, my son, I come to you on my knees!'
But Haimon spat in his face. He said not a word,
Staring—
                        And suddenly drew his sword
And lunged. Creon shrank back, the blade missed; and the boy,
Desperate against himself, drove it half its length
Into his own side, and fell. And as he died
He gathered Antigonê close in his arms again,
Choking, his blood bright red on her white cheek.
And now he lies dead with the dead, and she is his
At last, his bride in the houses of the dead.

> [*Exit* EURYDICE *into the Palace.*]

CHORAG: She has left us without a word. What can this mean?

MESS: It troubles me, too; yet she knows what is best,
                  Her grief is too great for public lamentation,
                  And doubtless she has gone to her chamber to weep
                  For her dead son, leading her maidens in his dirge.

CHORAG: It may be so: but I fear this deep silence.

> [*Pause.*]

MESS: I will see what she is doing. I will go in.

> [*Exit* MESSENGER *into the Palace.*]

> [*Enter* CREON *with attendants, bearing* HAIMON'S *body.*]

CHORAG: But here is the King himself: oh look at him,
                  Bearing his own damnation in his arms.

CREON: Nothing you say can touch me any more.
                  My own blind heart has brought me
                  From darkness to final darkness. Here you see

The father murdering, the murdered son—
And all my civic wisdom!
Haimon my son, so young, so young to die,
I was the fool, not you; and you died for me.

CHORAG: That is the truth; but you were late in learning it.

CREON: This truth is hard to bear. Surely a god
Has crushed me beneath the hugest weight of heaven,
And driven me headlong a barbaric way
To trample out the thing I held most dear.

The pains that men will take to come to pain!

[*Enter* MESSENGER *from the Palace.*]

MESS: The burden you carry in your hands is heavy,
But it is not all: you will find more in your house.

CREON: What burden worse than this shall I find there?

MESS: The Queen is dead.

CREON: O port of death, deaf world,
Is there no pity for me? And you, Angel of evil,
I was dead, and your words are death again.
Is it true, boy? Can it be true?
Is my wife dead? Has death bred death?

MESS: You can see for yourself.

[*The doors are opened, and the body of* EURYDICE *is
disclosed within.*]

CREON: Oh pity!
All true, all true, and more than I can bear!
O my wife, my son!

MESS: She stood before the altar, and her heart
Welcomed the knife her own hand guided,
And a great cry burst from her lips for Megareus dead,
And for Haimon dead, her sons; and her last breath
Was a curse for their father, the murderer of her sons.
And she fell, and the dark flowed in through her closing eyes.

CREON: O God, I am sick with fear.
Are there no swords here? Has no one a blow for me?

MESS: Her curse is upon you for the deaths of both.

CREON: It is right that it should be. I alone am guilty.
I know it, and I say it. Lead me in,

Quickly, friends.
I have neither life nor substance. Lead me in.

CHORAG: You are right, if there can be right in so much wrong.
The briefest way is best in a world of sorrow.

CREON: Let it come,
Let death come quickly, and be kind to me.
I would not ever see the sun again.

CHORAG: All that will come when it will; but we, meanwhile,
Have much to do. Leave the future to itself.

CREON: All my heart was in that prayer!

CHORAG: Then do not pray any more: the sky is deaf.

CREON: Lead me away. I have been rash and foolish.
I have killed my son and my wife.
I look for comfort; my comfort lies here dead.
Whatever my hands have touched has come to nothing.
Fate has brought all my pride to a thought of dust.

[As CREON *is being led into the house, the* CHORAGOS
advances and speaks directly to the audience.]

CHORAG: There is no happiness where there is no wisdom;
No wisdom but in submission to the gods.
Big words are always punished,
And proud men in old age learn to be wise.

Suggestions for Discussion

1. In the prologue, Ismenê states the argument for obeying authority. What is that argument? On what facts and feelings is it based?

2. What are Antigone's reasons for rejecting Creon's decree forbidding the burial of Polyneices? How do the characters of Ismene and Antigone correspond to the arguments they make for their differing actions?

3. What is the function of the Parados? How does it relate to the preceding Prologue? In what way are the speeches of the choragos different from those of the chorus?

4. In Scene I, Creon states the rationale for his decree. To what extent do you agree with his argument? What reason does the choragos give for obeying Creon?

5. Once Creon has learned that someone has performed burial rites for Polyneices, he suggests reasons. What are these reasons? Why does he reject at once the suggestion that the gods have intervened? How does Sophocles treat the sentry in Scenes I and II?

6. What is the function of the Odes in the play?

7. In Scene II, we have the first confrontation between Creon and Antigone. Who makes the better argument and how?

8. What does Creon's treatment of Ismene in Scene II tell us about his character? Why is the nature of Creon's character an important aspect of the play?

9. Scene III shows Creon with his son. How does this scene add to Creon's anger at being disobeyed? What do we learn about the king's attitude toward women? toward the difference between youth and age?

10. Discuss the difference between the speeches of the choragos in the first and fourth scenes.

11. How does Antigone face death? Do we remain totally sympathetic toward her suffering?

12. Discuss the confrontation between Creon and Teiresias in Scene V. How are Teiresias' prophecies borne out?

13. What are the functions of the last two parts of the play, the Paean and the Exodos? How does the final speech of the choragos at the end of the play summarize the tragedy that has occurred?

Suggestions for Writing

1. People have disagreed about who is the more important character, Creon or Antigone. Write a 500-word paper in which you state and explain your opinion on this issue.

2. Write a 500–750-word paper in which you discuss the laws of the state as opposed to either some higher authority or to individual conscience. Are you familiar with modern analogies of the conflict between two authorities? How would you behave in a situation in which you would have to choose as Antigone does? How would most people behave?

3. Write a 500-word paper in which you define tragic irony and elaborate on the definition by giving examples from *Antigone*.

The Examined Life: Education

◆◆◆

We survived. The depths had been icy and dark, but now a bright sun spoke to our souls. I was no longer simply a member of the proud graduating class of 1940; I was a proud member of the wonderful, beautiful Negro race.

    —Maya Angelou, "Graduation"

More than any other time in history, mankind faces a cross-roads. One path leads to despair and utter hopelessness. The other to total extinction. Let us hope that we have the wisdom to choose correctly.

    —Woody Allen, "My Speech to the Graduates"

The education of humanists cannot be regarded as complete, or even adequate, without exposure in some depth to where things stand in the various branches of science, and particularly, as I have said, in the areas of our ignorance.

    —Lewis Thomas, "Humanities and Science"

That man, I think, has had a liberal education, . . . who, no stunted ascetic, is full of life and fire, but whose passions are trained to come to heel by a vigorous will, the servant of a tender conscience; who has learned to love all beauty, whether of Nature or of art, to hate all vileness, and to respect others as himself.

    —T. H. Huxley, "A Liberal Education"

The challenge for the educational community is to figure out profiles of young people and then to help them find roles in which they can use their abilities in a productive way.

> —**Howard Gardner,** "Human Intelligence Isn't What We Think It Is"

If I intend for my life to matter to me, I had better read seriously, starting with newspapers and working up to philosophy and novels.

> —**Harold Brodkey,** "Reading, the Most Dangerous Game"

But beyond lies the great darkness of our ultimate Dreamer, who dreamed the light and the galaxies. Before act was, or substance existed, imagination grew in the dark. Man partakes of that ultimate wonder and creativeness.

> —**Loren Eiseley,** "The Hidden Teacher"

Personal Reminiscence

◆◆◆

Lincoln Steffens

I Go to College

Joseph Lincoln Steffens (1866–1936) was born in San Francisco and graduated from the University of California at Berkeley. After his return from three years of study in Europe, he became a well-known muckraker and journalist. As editor of *McClures, The American,* and *Everybody's* magazines he exposed corruption in business and government. His collections of essays include *The Shame of the Cities* (1904) and *The Struggle for Self-government* (1906). His *Autobiography* (1931) is a very personal account of the history not only of journalism in the United States but of the leftist movement as well. This selection from it recalls his carefree days as an undergraduate and the beginnings of his serious interest in learning, while it questions the connection between the search for knowledge and the baccalaureate degree.

Going to college is, to a boy, an adventure into a new world, and a very strange and complete world too. Part of his preparation for it is the stories he hears from those that have gone before; these feed his imagination, which cannot help trying to picture the college life. And the stories and the life are pretty much the same for any college. The University of California was a young, comparatively small institution when I was entered there in 1885 as a freshman. Berkeley, the beautiful, was not the developed villa community it is now; I used to shoot quail in the brush under the oaks along the edges of the college grounds. The quail and the brush are gone now, but the oaks are there and the same prospect down the hill over San Francisco Bay out through the Golden Gate between the low hills of the city and the high hills of Marin County. My class numbered about one hundred boys and girls, mostly boys, who came from all parts of the State and represented all sorts of people and occupations. There was, however, a significant uniformity of opinion and spirit among us, as there was, and still is, in other, older colleges. The American is molded to type early. And so are our college ways. We found already formed at Berkeley the typical undergraduate customs, rights, and privileged vices which we had to respect ourselves and defend against the faculty, regents, and the State government.

One evening, before I had matriculated, I was taken out by some upper classmen to teach the president a lesson. He had been the head of a private preparatory school and was trying to govern the private lives and the public morals of university "men" as he had those of his schoolboys. Fetching a long ladder, the upper classmen thrust it through a front window of Prexy's house and, to the chant of obscene songs, swung it back and forth, up and down, round and round, till everything breakable within sounded broken and the drunken indignation outside was satisfied or tired.

This turned out to be one of the last battles in the war for liberty against that president. He was allowed to resign soon thereafter and I noticed that not only the students but many of the faculty and regents rejoiced in his downfall and turned with us to face and fight the new president when, after a lot of politics, he was appointed and presented. We learned somehow a good deal about the considerations that governed our college government. They were not only academic. The government of a university was—like the State government and horse-racing and so many other things—not what I had been led to expect. And a college education wasn't, either, nor the student mind.

Years later, when I was a magazine editor, I proposed a series of articles to raise and answer the question: Is there any intellectual life in our colleges? My idea sprang from my remembered disappointment at what I found at Berkeley and some experiences I was having at the time with the faculties and undergraduates of the other colleges in the east. Berkeley, in my day, was an Athens compared with New Haven, for example, when I came to know Yale undergraduates.

My expectations of college life were raised too high by Nixon's Saturday nights. I thought, and he assumed, that at Berkeley I would be breathing in an atmosphere of thought, discussion, and some scholarship; working, reading, and studying for the answers to questions which would be threshed out in debate and conversation. There was nothing of the sort. I was primed with questions. My English friends never could agree on the answers to any of the many and various questions they disputed. They did not care; they enjoyed their talks and did not expect to settle anything. I was more earnest. I was not content to leave things all up in the air. Some of those questions were very present and personal to me, as some of those Englishmen meant them to be. William Owen was trying to convert me to the anarchistic communism in which he believed with all his sincere and beautiful being. I was considering his arguments. Another earnest man, who presented the case for the Roman Catholic Church, sent old Father Burchard and other Jesuits after me. Every conversation at Mr. Nixon's pointed some question, academic or scientific, and pointed them so sharp that they drove me to college with an intense desire to know. And as for communism or the Catholic Church, I was so torn that I could not answer myself. The Jesuits dropped me and so did Owen, in disgust, when I said I was going to wait for my answer till I had heard what the professors had to say and had learned what my university had to teach me upon the questions underlying the questions Oxford and Cambridge and Rome quarreled over and could not agree on. Berkeley would know.

There were no moot questions in Berkeley. There was work to do, knowledge and training to get, but not to answer questions. I found myself engaged, as my classmates were, in choosing courses. The choice was limited and, within the limits, had to be determined by the degree we were candidates for. My questions were philosophical, but I could not take philosophy, which fascinated me, till I had gone through a lot of higher mathematics which did not interest me at all. If I had been allowed to take philosophy, and so discovered the need and the relation of mathematics, I would have got the philosophy and I might have got the mathematics which I miss now more than I do the Hegelian metaphysics taught at Berkeley. Or, if the professor who put me off had taken the pains to show me the bearing of mathematical thought on theoretical logic, I would have undertaken the preparation intelligently. But no one ever developed for me the relation of any of my required subjects to those that attracted me; no one brought out for me the relation of anything I was studying to anything else, except, of course, to that wretched degree. Knowledge was absolute, not relative, and it was stored in compartments, categorical and independent. The relation of knowledge to life, even to student life, was ignored, and as for questions, the professors asked them, not the students; and the students, not the teachers, answered them—in examinations.

The unknown is the province of the student; it is the field for his life's adventure, and it is a wide field full of beckonings. Curiosity about it would drive a boy as well as a child to work through the known to get at the unknown. But it was not assumed that we had any curiosity or the potential love of skill, scholarship, and achievement or research. And so far as I can remember now, the professors' attitude was right for most of the students who had no intellectual curiosity. They wanted to be told not only what they had to learn, but what they had to want to learn—for the purpose of passing. That came out in the considerations which decided the choice among optional courses. Students selected subjects or teachers for a balance of easy and hard, to fit into their time and yet "get through." I was the only rebel of my kind, I think. The nearest to me in sympathy were the fellows who knew what they wanted to be: engineers, chemists, professional men, or statesmen. They grunted at some of the work required of them, studies that seemed useless to their future careers. They did not understand me very well, nor I them, because I preferred those very subjects which they called useless, highbrow, cultural. I did not tell them so; I did not realize it myself definitely; but I think now that I had had as a boy an exhausting experience of *being* something great. I did not want now to be but rather to know things.

And what I wanted to know was buried deep under all this "college stuff" which was called "shop." It had nothing to do with what really interested us in common. Having chosen our work and begun to do it as a duty, we turned to the socially important question: which fraternity to join. The upper classmen tried to force our answers. They laid aside their superiority to "rush" those of us whose antecedents were known and creditable. It was all snobbish, secret, and exclusive. I joined a fraternity out of curiosity: What were the secrets and the mystic rites? I went blindfold through the silly initiation to find that there were no secrets and no mysteries, only pretensions and bunk, which so disgusted me that I would not live at the clubhouse, preferring for a year the open doors of a boarding-house. The next great university question was as to athletics. My ex-athletes from Oxford and Cambridge, with their lung and other troubles, warned me; but it was a mistake that saved me. I went with the other freshmen to the campus to be tried out for football, baseball, running, jumping, etc. Caught by the college and class spirit, I hoped to give promise of some excellence. Baseball was impossible for me; I had been riding horses when the other boys were preparing for college on the diamond. I had learned to run at the military academy and in the first freshman tests I did one hundred yards enough under eleven seconds to be turned over to an athletic upper classman for instruction. Pointing up to Grizzly Peak, a high hill back of the college, he said: "All you need is wind and muscle. Climb that mountain every day for a year; then come back and we'll see."

I did not climb Grizzly Peak every day, but I went up so often that I was soon able to run up and back without a halt. At the end of the year I ran around the cinder track so long that my student instructor wearied of watching me, but, of course, I could not do a hundred yards much under twelve seconds. Muscle and wind I had, but all my physical reactions were so slow that I was of no social use in college athletics. I was out of the crowd as I had been as a boy.

I shone only in the military department. The commandant, a U.S. Army officer, seeing that I had had previous training, told me off to drill the awkward squad of my class, and when I had made of them the best-drilled company in college, he gave me the next freshman class to drill. In the following years I was always drillmaster of the freshmen and finally commanded the whole cadet corps. Thus I led my class in the most unpopular and meaningless of undergraduate activities. I despised it myself, prizing it only for the chances it gave me to swank and, once a week, to lord it over my fellow students, who nicknamed me the "D. S."—damn stinker.

My nickname was won not only as a disciplinarian, however; I rarely punished any one; I never abused my command. I could persuade the freshmen to drill by arguing that, since it was compulsory, they could have more fun doing it well than badly; and that it was the one exercise in which they could beat and shame the upper classmen whose carelessness was as affected as their superiority. That is to say, I engaged their enthusiasm. All other student enthusiasms, athletics, class and college politics, fashions, and traditions I laughed at and damned. I was a spoilsport. I was mean, as a horse is mean, because I was unhappy myself. I could be enthusiastic in a conversation about something we were learning, if it wasn't too cut and dried; we had such talks now and then at the clubhouse in my later years. But generally speaking we were discussing the news or some prank of our own.

One night, for example, we sallied forth to steal some chickens from Dr. Bonte, the popular treasurer of the university. I crawled into the coop and selected the chickens, wrung their necks, and passed them out with comments to the other fellows who held the bag.

"Here," I said, "is the rooster, Dr. Bonte himself; he's tough, but good enough for the freshmen. Next is a nice fat hen, old Mrs. Bonte. This one's a pullet, Miss Bonte," and so on, naming each of the Bonte girls, till we were interrupted.

There was a sound from the house, the lights flashed in the windows, and—some one was coming. The other fellows ran, and I—when I tore myself out—I ran too. Which was all right enough. But when I caught up with the other thieves I learned that they had left the sack of chickens behind! Our Sunday dinner was spoiled, we thought, but no: the next day the whole fraternity was invited to dinner at Dr. Bonte's on Sunday. We accepted with some suspicion, we went in some embarrassment, but we were well received and soon put at our ease by Dr. Bonte, who explained that some thieves had been frightened while robbing his roost. "They were not students, I take it," he said. "Students are not so easily frightened; they might have run away, but students would have taken the bag of chickens with them. I think they were niggers or Chinamen."

So seated hospitably at table we watched with deep interest the great platter of roasted chickens borne in and set down before Dr. Bonte, who rose, whetted his carving-knife, and turning first to me, said: "Well, Steffens, what will you have, a piece of this old cock, Dr. Bonte? Or is he too tough for any but a freshman? Perhaps you would prefer the old hen, Mrs. Bonte, or, say, one of the Bonte girls."

I couldn't speak. No one could; and no one laughed, least of all Dr. Bonte, who stood there, his knife and fork in the air, looking at me, at the others, and back at me. He wanted an answer; I must make my choice, but I saw a gleam of malicious humor in his eye; so I recovered and I chose the prettiest of the girls, pointing to the tenderest of the pullets. Dr. Bonte laughed, gave me my choice, and we had a jolly, ample dinner.

We talked about that, we and the students generally and the faculty—we discussed that incident long enough and hard enough to have solved it, if it had been a metaphysical problem. We might have threshed out the psychology of thieves, or gamblers, but no. We liked to steal, but we didn't care to think about it, not as stealing. And some of us gambled. We had to get money for theaters, operas, and other expenses in the city. I had only my board, lodging, and clothes paid for by my father, and others had not even that. We played cards, therefore, among ourselves, poker and whist, so that a lucky few got each month about all the money all of the other hard-ups had, and so had all the fun. We played long, late, and hard, and for money, not sport. The strain was too great.

One night my roommate, sunk low in his chair, felt a light kick on one of his extended legs; a second later there were two kicks against his other leg. Keeping still and watching the hands shown down, he soon had the signal system of two men playing partners, the better hand staying in the game. We said nothing but, watching, saw that others cheated, too. We knew well an old professional gambler from the mining-camps who was then in San Francisco. We told him all about it.

"Sure," he said, "cheating will sneak into any game that's played long enough. That's why you boys oughtn't to gamble. But if you do, play the game that's played. Cards is like horse-racing. I never bet a cent except I know, and know how, the game is crooked."

Having advised against it, he took us around to the gambling-houses and the race course and showed us many of the tricks of his trade, how to spot and profit by them—if we must play. "Now you won't need never to be suckers," he said. "And ye needn't be crooks either," he added after a pause. But we had it in for our opponents. We learned several ways to cheat; we practiced them till we were cool and sure. After that our "luck" was phenomenal. We had money, more than we needed. In my last two years at the university

I had a salary as military instructor at a preparatory school in the town, and my roommate, the adopted son of a rich goldminer, had a generous allowance. But we went on playing and cheating at cards for the excitement of it, we said, but really it was for the money. And afterward, when I was a student in Germany, I played on, fair but hard—and for money I did not need, till one night at the Café Bauer in Berlin, sitting in a poker game that had been running all night, an American who had long been playing in hard luck, lost a large amount, of which I carried away more than my share. The next day we read in the papers that when he got home he had shot himself. I have never gambled since—at cards.

I Become a Student

It is possible to get an education at a university. It has been done; not often, but the fact that a proportion, however small, of college students do get a start in interested, methodical study, proves my thesis, and the two personal experiences I have to offer illustrate it and show how to circumvent the faculty, the other students, and the whole college system of mind-fixing. My method might lose a boy his degree, but a degree is not worth so much as the capacity and the drive to learn, and the undergraduate desire for an empty baccalaureate is one of the holds the educational system has on students. Wise students some day will refuse to take degrees, as the best men (in England, for instance) give, but do not themselves accept, titles.

My method was hit on by accident and some instinct. I specialized. With several courses prescribed, I concentrated on the one or two that interested me most, and letting the others go, I worked intensively on my favorites. In my first two years, for example, I worked at English and political economy and read philosophy. At the beginning of my junior year I had several cinches in history. Now I liked history; I had neglected it partly because I rebelled at the way it was taught, as positive knowledge unrelated to politics, art, life, or anything else. The professors gave us chapters out of a few books to read, con, and be quizzed on. Blessed as I was with a "bad memory," I could not commit to it anything that I did not understand and intellectually need. The bare record of the story of man, with names, dates, and irrelative events, bored me. But I had discovered in my readings of literature, philosophy, and political economy that history had light to throw upon unhistorical questions. So I proposed in my junior and senior years to specialize in history, taking all the courses required and those also that I had flunked in. With this in mind I listened attentively to the first introductory talk of Professor William Cary Jones on American constitutional history. He was a dull lecturer, but I noticed that, after telling us what pages of what books we must be prepared in, he mumbled off some other references "for those that may care to dig deeper."

When the rest of the class rushed out into the sunshine, I went up to the professor and, to his surprise, asked for this memorandum. He gave it to me. Up in the library I ran through the required chapters in the two different books, and they differed on several points. Turning to the other authorities, I saw that they disagreed on the same facts and also on others. The librarian, appealed to, helped me search the book-shelves till the library closed, and then I called on Professor Jones for more references. He was astonished, invited me in, and began to approve my industry, which astonished me. I was not trying to be a good boy; I was better than that: I was a curious boy. He lent me a couple of his books, and I went off to my club to read them. They only deepened the mystery, clearing up the historical question, but leaving the answer to be dug for and written.

The historians did not know! History was not a science, but a field for research, a field for me, for any young man, to explore, to make discoveries in and write a scientific report about. I was fascinated. As I went on from chapter to chapter, day after day, finding frequently essential differences of opinion and of fact, I saw more and more work to do. In this course, American constitutional history, I hunted far enough to suspect that the Fathers of the Republic who wrote our sacred Constitution of the United States not only did not, but did not want to, establish a democratic government, and I dreamed for a while—as I used as a child to play I was Napoleon or a trapper—I promised myself to write a true history of the making of the American Constitution. I did not do it; that chapter has been done or well begun since by two men: Smith of the University of Washington and Beard (then) of Columbia (afterward forced out, perhaps for this very work). I found other events, men, and epochs waiting for students. In all my other courses, in ancient, in European, and in modern history, the disagreeing authorities carried me back to the need of a fresh search for (or of) the original documents or other clinching testimony. Of course I did well in my classes. The history professors soon knew me as a student and seldom put a question to me except when the class had flunked it. Then Professor Jones would say, "Well, Steffens, tell them about it."

Fine. But vanity wasn't my ruling passion then. What I had was a quickening sense that I was learning a method of studying history and that every chapter of it, from the beginning of the world to the end, is crying out to be rewritten. There was something for Youth to do; these superior old men had not done anything, finally.

Years afterward I came out of the graft prosecution office in San Francisco with Rudolph Spreckels, the banker and backer of the investigation. We were to go somewhere, quick, in his car, and we couldn't. The chauffeur was trying to repair something wrong. Mr. Spreckels smiled; he looked closely at the defective part, and to my silent, wondering inquiry he answered: "Always, when I see something badly done or not done at all, I see an opportunity to make a fortune. I never kick at bad work by my class: there's lots of it and we suffer from it. But our failures and neglects are chances for the young fellows coming along and looking for work."

Nothing is done. Everything in the world remains to be done or done over. "The greatest picture is not yet painted, the greatest play isn't written (not even by Shakespeare), the greatest poem is unsung. There isn't in all the world a perfect railroad, nor a good government, nor a sound law." Physics, mathematics, and especially the most advanced and exact of the sciences, are being fundamentally revised. Chemistry is just becoming a science; psychology, economics, and sociology are awaiting a Darwin, whose work in turn is awaiting an Einstein. If the rah-rah boys in our colleges could be told this, they might not all be such specialists in football, petting parties, and unearned degrees. They are not told it, however; they are told to learn what is known. This is nothing, philosophically speaking.

Somehow or other in my later years at Berkeley, two professors, Moses and Howison, representing opposite schools of thought, got into a controversy, probably about their classes. They brought together in the house of one of them a few of their picked students, with the evident intention of letting us show in conversation how much or how little we had understood of their respective teachings. I don't remember just what the subject was that they threw into the ring, but we wrestled with it till the professors could stand it no longer. Then they broke in, and while we sat silent and highly entertained, they went at each other hard and fast and long. It was after midnight when, the debate over, we went home. I asked the other fellows what they had got out of it, and their answers showed that they had seen nothing but a fine, fair fight. When I laughed, they asked me what I, the D.S., had seen that was so much more profound.

I said that I had seen two highly trained, well-educated Masters of Arts and Doctors of Philosophy disagreeing upon every essential point of thought and knowledge. They had all there was of the sciences; and yet they could not find any knowledge upon which they could base an acceptable conclusion. They had no test of knowledge; they didn't know what is and what is not. And they have no test of right and wrong; they have no basis for even an ethics.

Well, and what of it? They asked me that, and that I did not answer. I was stunned by the discovery that it was philosophically true, in a most literal sense, that nothing is known; that it is precisely the foundation that is lacking for science; that all we call knowledge rested upon assumptions which the scientists did not all accept; and that, likewise, there is no scientific reason for saying, for example, that stealing is wrong. In brief: there was no scientific basis for an ethics. No wonder men said one thing and did another; no wonder they could settle nothing either in life or in the academies.

I could hardly believe this. Maybe these professors, whom I greatly respected, did not know it all. I read the books over again with a fresh eye, with a real interest, and I could see that, as in history, so in other branches of knowledge, everything was in the air. And I was glad of it. Rebel though I was, I had got the religion of scholarship and science; I was in awe of the authorities in the academic world. It was a release to feel my worship cool and pass. But I could not be sure. I must go elsewhere, see and hear other professors, men these California professors quoted and looked up to as their high priests. I decided to go as a student to Europe when I was through Berkeley, and I would start with the German universities.

My father listened to my plan, and he was disappointed. He had hoped I would succeed him in his business; it was for that that he was staying in it. When I said that, whatever I might do, I would never go into business, he said, rather sadly, that he would sell out his interest and retire. And he did soon after our talk. But he wanted me to stay home and, to keep me, offered to buy an interest in a certain San Francisco daily paper. He had evidently had this in mind for some time. I had always done some writing, verse at the poetical age of puberty, then a novel which my mother alone treasured. Journalism was the business for a boy who liked to write, he thought, and he said

I had often spoken of a newspaper as my ambition. No doubt I had in the intervals between my campaigns as Napoleon. But no more. I was now going to be a scientist, a philosopher. He sighed; he thought it over, and with the approval of my mother, who was for every sort of education, he gave his consent.

Suggestions for Discussion

1. The first part of this reminiscence tells us about Steffens' carefree days as a student at Berkeley in the late nineteenth century. How does he describe student life? What was the main interest of most students at the university?

2. Why did Steffens fail to get ahead in athletics while achieving great success as a drillmaster? Why did military drill appeal to him?

3. What was Steffens' attitude toward money while he was a student? Why did he gamble? Explain how he learned to be a successful gambler. Explain why he gave up gambling.

4. Why was Steffens disappointed in his fraternity?

5. Explain the significance of the incident of the stealing of Dr. Bonte's chickens. Why is it included in this section?

6. What is the major difference between the first and second parts of the reminiscence?

7. How does Steffens get interested in the study of history? What determines his decision to continue his education in Germany?

8. Why were most of the students whom Steffens knew attending Berkeley? Does he respect their reasons? What does he think is the real reason for education?

9. How would you describe Steffens during his student days? Was he likeable? Explain your answer.

Suggestions for Writing

1. Using Steffens as a model, write an essay in which you attempt to summarize most of your classmates' reasons for going to college. Try to develop a questionnaire in which you sample opinion so that you have information to summarize. Write an opinion of the reasons you discover.

2. College life differs greatly from one institution to another. Write an essay in which you compare college life at your own college or university with that of another. You may wish to ask someone much older than yourself how his or her college life differed from yours. You may wish to contrast your own experiences with those of Steffens.

Maya Angelou

Graduation

Maya Angelou (b. 1928) was born in Stamps, Arkansas, to a childhood of poverty and pain. She has been a dancer and an actress, a coordinator of the Southern Christian Leadership Conference, a television writer and producer, and a poet. She is best known for her autobiographical works, *I Know Why the Caged Bird Sings* (1970), from which "Graduation" is taken, and *The Heart of a Woman* (1981). In "Graduation" the entire black community has prepared for graduation only to have its excitement destroyed by the white speaker who patronizingly offers them the prospect of servile jobs or, perhaps, athletic fame. While Angelou captures the pain of racial discrimination, she reaffirms finally the power of the blacks to survive.

The children in Stamps trembled visibly with anticipation. Some adults were excited too, but to be certain the whole young population had come down with graduation epidemic. Large classes were graduating from both the grammar school and the high school. Even those who were years removed from their own day of glorious release were anxious to help with preparations as a kind of dry run. The junior students who were moving into the vacating classes' chairs were tradition-bound to show their talents for leadership and management. They strutted through the school and around the campus exerting pressure on the lower grades. Their authority was so new that occasionally if they pressed a little too hard it had to be overlooked. After all, next term was coming, and it never hurt a sixth-grader to have a play sister in the eighth grade, or a tenth-year student to be able to call a twelfth-grader Bubba. So all was endured in a spirit of shared understanding. But the graduating classes themselves were the nobility. Like travelers with exotic destinations on their minds, the graduates were remarkably forgetful. They came to school without their books, or tablets or even pencils. Volunteers fell over themselves to secure replacements for the missing equipment. When accepted, the willing workers might or might not be thanked, and it was of no importance to the pregraduation rites. Even teachers were respectful of the now quiet and aging seniors, and tended to speak to them, if not as equals, as beings only slightly lower than themselves. After tests were returned and grades given, the student body, which acted like an extended family, knew who did well, who excelled, and what piteous ones had failed.

Unlike the white high school, Lafayette County Training School distinguished itself by having neither lawn, nor hedges, nor tennis court, nor climbing ivy. Its two buildings (main classrooms, the grade school and home economics) were set on a dirt hill with no fence to limit either its boundaries or those of bordering farms. There was a large expanse to the left of the school which was used alternately as a baseball diamond or a basketball court. Rusty hoops on the swaying poles represented the permanent recreational equipment, although bats and balls could be borrowed from the P.E. teacher if the borrower was qualified and if the diamond wasn't occupied.

Over this rocky area relieved by a few shady tall persimmon trees the graduating class walked. The girls often held hands and no longer bothered to speak to the lower students. There was a sadness about them, as if this old world was not their home and they were bound for higher ground. The boys, on the other hand, had become more friendly, more outgoing. A decided change from the closed attitude they projected while studying for finals. Now they seemed not ready to give up the old school, the familiar paths and class-rooms. Only a small percentage would be continuing on to college—one of the South's A & M (agricultural and mechanical) schools, which trained Negro youths to be carpenters, farmers, handymen, masons, maids, cooks and baby nurses. Their future rode heavily on their shoulders, and blinded them to the collective joy that had pervaded the lives of the boys and girls in the grammar school graduating class.

Parents who could afford it had ordered new shoes and ready-made clothes for themselves from Sears, Roebuck or Montgomery Ward. They also engaged the best seamstresses to make the floating graduating dresses and to cut down secondhand pants which would be pressed to a military slickness for the im-portant event.

Oh, it was important, all right. Whitefolks would attend the ceremony, and two or three would speak of God and home, and the Southern way of life, and Mrs. Parsons, the principal's wife, would play the graduation march while the lower-grade graduates paraded down the aisles and took their seats below the platform. The high school seniors would wait in empty classrooms to make their dramatic entrance.

In the Store I was the person of the moment. The birthday girl. The cen-ter. Bailey had graduated the year before, although to do so he had had to forfeit all pleasures to make up for his time lost in Baton Rouge.

My class was wearing butter-yellow piqué dresses, and Momma launched out on mine. She smocked the yoke into tiny crisscrossing puckers, then shirred the rest of the bodice. Her dark fingers ducked in and out of the lemony cloth as she embroidered raised daisies around the hem. Before she considered herself finished she had added a crocheted cuff on the puff sleeves, and a pointy crocheted collar.

I was going to be lovely. A walking model of all the various styles of fine hand sewing and it didn't worry me that I was only twelve years old and merely graduating from the eighth grade. Besides, many teachers in Arkansas Negro schools had only that diploma and were licensed to impart wisdom.

The days had become longer and more noticeable. The faded beige of for-mer times had been replaced with strong and sure colors. I began to see my classmates' clothes, their skin tones, and the dust that waved off pussy wil-lows. Clouds that lazed across the sky were objects of great concern to me. Their shiftier shapes might have held a message that in my new happiness and with a little bit of time I'd soon decipher. During that period I looked at the arch of heaven so religiously my neck kept a steady ache. I had taken to smiling more often, and my jaws hurt from the unaccustomed activity. Be-tween the two physical sore spots, I suppose I could have been uncomforta-ble, but that was not the case. As a member of the winning team (the gradu-ating class of 1940) I had outdistanced unpleasant sensations by miles. I was headed for the freedom of open fields.

Youth and social approval allied themselves with me and we trammeled memories of slights and insults. The wind of our swift passage remodeled my features. Lost tears were pounded to mud and then to dust. Years of withdrawal were brushed aside and left behind, as hanging ropes of parasitic moss.

My work alone had awarded me a top place and I was going to be one of the first called in the graduating ceremonies. On the classroom blackboard, as well as on the bulletin board in the auditorium, there were blue stars and white stars and red stars. No absences, no tardinesses, and my academic work was among the best of the year. I could say the preamble to the Constitution even faster than Bailey. We timed ourselves often: "Wethepeopleofthe-UnitedStatesinordertoformamoreperfectunion . . ." I had memorized the Presidents of the United States from Washington to Roosevelt in chronological as well as alphabetical order.

My hair pleased me too. Gradually the black mass had lengthened and thickened, so that it kept at last to its braided pattern, and I didn't have to yank my scalp off when I tried to comb it.

Louise and I had rehearsed the exercises until we tired out ourselves. Henry Reed was class valedictorian. He was a small, very black boy with hooded eyes, a long, broad nose and an oddly shaped head. I had admired him for years because each term he and I vied for the best grades in our class. Most often he bested me, but instead of being disappointed I was pleased that we shared top places between us. Like many Southern Black children, he lived with his grandmother, who was as strict as Momma and as kind as she knew how to be. IIe was courteous, respectful, and soft-spoken to elders, but on the playground he chose to play the roughest games. I admired him. Anyone, I reckoned, sufficiently afraid or sufficiently dull could be polite. But to be able to operate at a top level with both adults and children was admirable.

His valedictory speech was entitled "To Be or Not to Be." The rigid tenth-grade teacher had helped him write it. He'd been working on the dramatic stresses for months.

The weeks until graduation were filled with heady activities. A group of small children were to be presented in a play about buttercups and daisies and bunny rabbits. They could be heard throughout the building practicing their hops and their little songs that sounded like silver bells. The older girls (nongraduates, of course) were assigned the task of making refreshments for the night's festivities. A tangy scent of ginger, cinnamon, nutmeg and chocolate wafted around the home economics building as the budding cooks made samples for themselves and their teachers.

In every corner of the workshop, axes and saws split fresh timber as the woodshop boys made sets and stage scenery. Only the graduates were left out of the general bustle. We were free to sit in the library at the back of the building or look in quite detachedly, naturally, on the measures being taken for our event.

Even the minister preached on graduation the Sunday before. His subject was, "Let your light so shine that men will see your good works and praise your Father, Who is in Heaven." Although the sermon was purported to be addressed to us, he used the occasion to speak to backsliders, gamblers, and general ne'er-do-wells. But since he had called our names at the beginning of the service we were mollified.

Among Negroes the tradition was to give presents to children going only from one grade to another. How much more important this was when the person was graduating at the top of the class. Uncle Willie and Momma had sent away for a Mickey Mouse watch like Bailey's. Louise gave me four embroidered handkerchiefs. (I gave her three crocheted doilies.) Mrs. Sneed, the minister's wife, made me an underskirt to wear for graduation, and nearly every customer gave me a nickel or maybe even a dime with the instruction "Keep on moving to higher ground," or some such encouragement.

Amazingly the great day finally dawned and I was out of bed before I knew it. I threw open the back door to see it more clearly, but Momma said, "Sister, come away from that door and put your robe on."

I hoped the memory of that morning would never leave me. Sunlight was itself still young, and the day had none of the insistence maturity would bring it in a few hours. In my robe and barefoot in the backyard, under cover of going to see about my new beans, I gave myself up to the gentle warmth and thanked God that no matter what evil I had done in my life He had allowed me to live to see this day. Somewhere in my fatalism I had expected to die, accidentally, and never have the chance to walk up the stairs in the auditorium and gracefully receive my hard-earned diploma. Out of God's merciful bosom I had won reprieve.

Bailey came out in his robe and gave me a box wrapped in Christmas paper. He said he had saved his money for months to pay for it. It felt like a box of chocolates, but I knew Bailey wouldn't save money to buy candy when we had all we could want under our noses.

He was as proud of the gift as I. It was a soft-leatherbound copy of a collection of poems by Edgar Allan Poe, or, as Bailey and I called him, "Eap." I turned to "Annabel Lee" and we walked up and down the garden rows, the cool dirt between our toes, reciting the beautifully sad lines.

Momma made a Sunday breakfast although it was only Friday. After we finished the blessing, I opened my eyes to find the watch on my plate. It was a dream of a day. Everything went smoothly and to my credit. I didn't have to be reminded or scolded for anything. Near evening I was too jittery to attend to chores, so Bailey volunteered to do all before his bath.

Days before, we had made a sign for the Store, and as we turned out the lights Momma hung the cardboard over the doorknob. It read clearly: CLOSED. GRADUATION.

My dress fitted perfectly and everyone said that I looked like a sunbeam in it. On the hill, going toward the school, Bailey walked behind with Uncle Willie, who muttered, "Go on, Ju." He wanted him to walk ahead with us because it embarrassed him to have to walk so slowly. Bailey said he'd let the ladies walk together, and the men would bring up the rear. We all laughed, nicely.

Little children dashed by out of the dark like fireflies. Their crepe-paper dresses and butterfly wings were not made for running and we heard more than one rip, dryly, and the regretful "uh uh" that followed.

The school blazed without gaiety. The windows seemed cold and unfriendly from the lower hill. A sense of ill-fated timing crept over me, and if Momma hadn't reached for my hand I would have drifted back to Bailey and Uncle Willie, and possibly beyond. She made a few slow jokes about my feet getting cold, and tugged me along to the now-strange building.

Around the front steps, assurance came back. There were my fellow "greats," the graduating class. Hair brushed back, legs oiled, new dresses and pressed pleats, fresh pocket handkerchiefs and little handbags, all homesewn.

Oh, we were up to snuff, all right. I joined my comrades and didn't even see my family go in to find seats in the crowded auditorium.

The school band struck up a march and all classes filed in as had been rehearsed. We stood in front of our seats, as assigned, and on a signal from the choir director, we sat. No sooner had this been accomplished than the band started to play the national anthem. We rose again and sang the song, after which we recited the pledge of allegiance. We remained standing for a brief minute before the choir director and the principal signaled to us, rather desperately I thought, to take our seats. The command was so unusual that our carefully rehearsed and smooth-running machine was thrown off. For a full minute we fumbled for our chairs and bumped into each other awkwardly. Habits change or solidify under pressure, so in our state of nervous tension we had been ready to follow our usual assembly pattern: the American national anthem, then the pledge of allegiance, then the song every Black person I knew called the Negro National Anthem. All done in the same key, with the same passion and most often standing on the same foot.

Finding my seat at last, I was overcome with a presentiment of worse things to come. Something unrehearsed, unplanned, was going to happen, and we were going to be made to look bad. I distinctly remember being explicit in the choice of pronoun. It was "we," the graduating class, the unit, that concerned me then.

The principal welcomed "parents and friends" and asked the Baptist minister to lead us in prayer. His invocation was brief and punchy, and for a second I thought we were getting back on the high road to right action. When the principal came back to the dais, however, his voice had changed. Sounds always affected me profoundly and the principal's voice was one of my favorites. During assembly it melted and lowed weakly into the audience. It had not been in my plan to listen to him, but my curiosity was piqued and I straightened up to give him my attention.

He was talking about Booker T. Washington, our "late great leader," who said we can be as close as the fingers on the hand, etc. . . . Then he said a few vague things about friendship and the friendship of kindly people to those less fortunate than themselves. With that his voice nearly faded, thin, away. Like a river diminishing to a stream and then to a trickle. But he cleared his throat and said, "Our speaker tonight, who is also our friend, came from Texarkana to deliver the commencement address, but due to the irregularity of the train schedule, he's going to, as they say, 'speak and run.' " He said that we understood and wanted the man to know that we were most grateful for the time he was able to give us and then something about how we were willing always to adjust to another's program, and without more ado—"I give you Mr. Edward Donleavy."

Not one but two white men came through the door offstage. The shorter one walked to the speaker's platform, and the tall one moved over to the center seat and sat down. But that was our principal's seat, and already occupied. The dislodged gentleman bounced around for a long breath or two before the Baptist minister gave him his chair, then with more dignity than the situation deserved, the minister walked off the stage.

Donleavy looked at the audience once (on reflection, I'm sure that he wanted only to reassure himself that we were really there), adjusted his glasses and began to read from a sheaf of papers.

He was glad "to be here and to see the work going on just as it was in the other schools."

At the first "Amen" from the audience I willed the offender to immediate death by choking on the word. But Amens and Yes, sir's began to fall around the room like rain through a ragged umbrella.

He told us of the wonderful changes we children in Stamps had in store. The Central School (naturally, the white school was Central) had already been granted improvements that would be in use in the fall. A well-known artist was coming from Little Rock to teach art to them. They were going to have the newest microscopes and chemistry equipment for their laboratory. Mr. Donleavy didn't leave us long in the dark over who made these improvements available to Central High. Nor were we to be ignored in the general betterment scheme he had in mind.

He said that he had pointed out to people at a very high level that one of the first-line football tacklers at Arkansas Agricultural and Mechanical College had graduated from good old Lafayette County Training School. Here fewer Amen's were heard. Those few that did break through lay dully in the air with the heaviness of habit.

He went on to praise us. He went on to say how he had bragged that "one of the best basketball players at Fisk sank his first ball right here at Lafayette County Training School."

The white kids were going to have a chance to become Galileos and Madame Curies and Edisons and Gauguins, and our boys (the girls weren't even in on it) would try to be Jesse Owenses and Joe Louises.

Owens and the Brown Bomber were great heroes in our world, but what school official in the white-goddom of Little Rock had the right to decide that those two men must be our only heroes? Who decided that for Henry Reed to become a scientist he had to work like George Washington Carver, as a bootblack, to buy a lousy microscope? Bailey was obviously always going to be too small to be an athlete, so which concrete angel glued to what country seat had decided that if my brother wanted to become a lawyer he had to first pay penance for his skin by picking cotton and hoeing corn and studying correspondence books at night for twenty years?

The man's dead words fell like bricks around the auditorium and too many settled in my belly. Constrained by hard-learned manners I couldn't look behind me, but to my left and right the proud graduating class of 1940 had dropped their heads. Every girl in my row had found something new to do with her handkerchief. Some folded the tiny squares into love knots, some into triangles, but most were wadding them, then pressing them flat on their yellow laps.

On the dais, the ancient tragedy was being replayed. Professor Parsons sat, a sculptor's reject, rigid. His large, heavy body seemed devoid of will or willingness, and his eyes said he was no longer with us. The other teachers examined the flag (which was draped stage right) or their notes, or the windows which opened on our now-famous playing diamond.

Graduation, the hush-hush magic time of frills and gifts and congratulations and diplomas, was finished for me before my name was called. The accomplishment was nothing. The meticulous maps, drawn in three colors of ink, learning and spelling decasyllabic words, memorizing the whole of *The Rape of Lucrece*—it was for nothing. Donleavy had exposed us.

We were maids and farmers, handymen and washerwomen, and anything higher that we aspired to was farcical and presumptuous.

Then I wished that Gabriel Prosser and Nat Turner had killed all whitefolks in their beds and that Abraham Lincoln had been assassinated before the signing of the Emancipation Proclamation, and that Harriet Tubman had been killed by that blow on her head and Christopher Columbus had drowned in the *Santa María*.

It was awful to be Negro and have no control over my life. It was brutal to be young and already trained to sit quietly and listen to charges brought against my color with no chance of defense. We should all be dead. I thought I should like to see us all dead, one on top of the other. A pyramid of flesh with the whitefolks on the bottom, as the broad base, then the Indians with their silly tomahawks and teepees and wigwams and treaties, the Negroes with their mops and recipes and cotton sacks and spirituals sticking out of their mouths. The Dutch children should all stumble in their wooden shoes and break their necks. The French should choke to death on the Louisiana Purchase (1803) while silkworms ate all the Chinese with their stupid pigtails. As a species, we were an abomination. All of us.

Donleavy was running for election, and assured our parents that if he won we could count on having the only colored paved playing field in that part of Arkansas. Also—he never looked up to acknowledge the grunts of accep- tance—also, we were bound to get some new equipment for the home eco- nomics building and the workshop.

He finished, and since there was no need to give any more than the most perfunctory thank-you's, he nodded to the men on the stage, and the tall white man who was never introduced joined him at the door. They left with the attitude that now they were off to something really important. (The grad- uation ceremonies at Lafayette Country Training School had been a mere preliminary.)

The ugliness they left was palpable. An uninvited guest who wouldn't leave. The choir was summoned and sang a modern arrangement of "Onward, Christian Soldiers," with new words pertaining to graduates seeking their place in the world. But it didn't work. Elouise, the daughter of the Baptist minister, recited "Invictus," and I could have cried at the impertinence of "I am the master of my fate, I am the captain of my soul."

My name had lost its ring of familiarity and I had to be nudged to go and receive my diploma. All my preparations had fled. I neither marched up to the stage like a conquering Amazon, nor did I look in the audience for Bailey's nod of approval. Marguerite Johnson, I heard the name again, my honors were read, there were noises in the audience of appreciation, and I took my place on the stage as rehearsed.

I thought about colors I hated: ecru, puce, lavender, beige and black.

There was shuffling and rustling around me, then Henry Reed was giving his valedictory address, "To Be or Not to Be." Hadn't he heard the white- folks? We couldn't *be*, so the question was a waste of time. Henry's voice came out clear and strong. I feared to look at him. Hadn't he got the message? There was no "nobler in the mind" for Negroes because the world didn't think we had minds, and they let us know it. "Outrageous fortune"? Now, that was a joke. When the ceremony was over I had to tell Henry Reed some things. That is, if I still cared. Not "rub," Henry, "erase." "Ah, there's the erase." Us.

Henry had been a good student in elocution. His voice rose on tides of promise and fell on waves of warnings. The English teacher had helped him to create a sermon winging through Hamlet's soliloquy. To be a man, a doer, a builder, a leader, or to be a tool, an unfunny joke, a crusher of funky toadstools. I marveled that Henry could go through with the speech as if we had a choice.

I had been listening and silently rebutting each sentence with my eyes closed; then there was a hush, which in an audience warns that something unplanned is happening. I looked up and saw Henry Reed, the conservative, the proper, the A student, turn his back to the audience and turn to us (the proud graduating class of 1940) and sing, nearly speaking,

> "Lift ev'ry voice and sing[1]
> Till earth and heaven ring
> Ring with the harmonies of Liberty . . ."

It was the poem written by James Weldon Johnson. It was the music composed by J. Rosamond Johnson. It was the Negro national anthem. Out of habit we were singing it.

Our mothers and fathers stood in the dark hall and joined the hymn of encouragement. A kindergarten teacher led the small children onto the stage and the buttercups and daisies and bunny rabbits marked time and tried to follow:

> "Stony the road we trod
> Bitter the chastening rod
> Felt in the days when hope, unborn, had died.
> 'Yet with a steady beat
> Have not our weary feet
> Come to the place for which our fathers sighed?"

Every child I knew had learned that song with his ABC's and along with "Jesus Loves Me This I Know." But I personally had never heard it before. Never heard the words, despite the thousands of times I had sung them. Never thought they had anything to do with me.

On the other hand, the words of Patrick Henry had made such an impression on me that I had been able to stretch myself tall and trembling and say, "I know not what course others may take, but as for me, give me liberty or give me death."

And now I heard, really for the first time:

> "We have come over a way that with tears
> has been watered,
> We have come, treading our path through
> the blood of the slaughtered."

While echoes of the song shivered in the air, Henry Reed bowed his head, said "Thank you," and returned to his place in the line. The tears that slipped down many faces were not wiped away in shame.

We were on top again. As always, again. We survived. The depths had been icy and dark, but now a bright sun spoke to our souls. I was no longer

---

[1]"Lift Ev'ry Voice and Sing"—words by James Weldon Johnson and music by J. Rosamond Johnson. Copyright by Edward B. Marks Music Corporation. Used by permission.

simply a member of the proud graduating class of 1940; I was a proud member of the wonderful, beautiful Negro race.

Oh, Black known and unknown poets, how often have your auctioned pains sustained us? Who will compute the lonely nights made less lonely by your songs, or the empty pots made less tragic by your tales?

If we were a people much given to revealing secrets, we might raise monuments and sacrifice to the memories of our poets, but slavery cured us of that weakness. It may be enough, however, to have it said that we survive in exact relationship to the dedication of our poets (include preachers, musicians and blues singers).

Suggestions for Discussion

1. Describe the feeling that comes over the students and teachers at school at the prospect of graduation.

2. How does Angelou describe the feelings in her own family? How is she treated by her brother? her grandmother?

3. How does the black community become involved in the graduation? What special meaning does it have for them?

4. When do you begin to understand that something will go wrong? What details help you to understand? How do you know that the disappointment will come about from racial causes?

5. Summarize Donleavy's speech. How does Angelou make us feel its condescension and contempt?

6. How does the black community respond? What is the meaning of this response to Angelou? Explain.

Suggestions for Writing

1. Write an essay in which you contrast Angelou and Charles in the story "Expelled." Your paper should include an explanation of why school has such different significance for the two of them.

2. Angelou describes a situation once common in segregated Southern schools which were separate but "unequal." Since the 1960s that situation has presumably changed. Write a research paper of 1,000 words in which you report your findings about schools in the South since desegregation. What new problems may have replaced those that Angelou describes?

Essays

Lewis Thomas

Humanities and Science

Lewis Thomas (b. 1913) is a physician whose medical career has centered on the Sloan Kettering Cancer Care Center in New York, the city of his birth. He has written for medical journals at the same time that he has written popular essays to present science and the scientist's view of the world to the lay public. He won the National Book Award in 1974 for *The Lives of a Cell: Notes of a Biology Watcher.* Other collections include *The Medusa and the Snail* (1979), *More Notes of a Biology Watcher* (1979), *The Youngest Science: Notes of a Medicine-Watcher* (1983), and *Late Night Thoughts on Listening to Mahler's Ninth* (1984). In the following essay, Dr. Thomas advocates open discussion of what science does not yet know or understand.

Lord Kelvin was one of the great British physicists of the late nineteenth century, an extraordinarily influential figure in his time, and in some ways a paradigm of conventional, established scientific leadership. He did a lot of good and useful things, but once or twice he, like Homer, nodded. The instances are worth recalling today, for we have nodders among our scientific eminences still, from time to time, needing to have their elbows shaken.

On one occasion, Kelvin made a speech on the overarching importance of numbers. He maintained that no observation of nature was worth paying serious attention to unless it could be stated in precisely quantitative terms. The numbers were the final and only test, not only of truth but about meaning as well. He said, "When you can measure what you are speaking about, and express it in numbers, you know something about it. But when you cannot—your knowledge is of a meagre and unsatisfactory kind."

But, as at least one subsequent event showed, Kelvin may have had things exactly the wrong way round. The task of converting observations into numbers is the hardest of all, the last task rather than the first thing to be done, and it can be done only when you have learned, beforehand, a great deal about the observations themselves. You can, to be sure, achieve a very deep understanding of nature by quantitative measurement, but you must know what you are talking about before you can begin applying the numbers for making predictions. In Kelvin's case, the problem at hand was the age of the earth and solar system. Using what was then known about the sources of energy and the loss of energy from the physics of that day, he calculated that neither the earth nor the sun were older than several hundred million years. This caused a considerable stir in biological and geological circles, especially among the evolutionists. Darwin himself was distressed by the numbers; the time was much too short for the theory of evolution. Kelvin's figures were described by Darwin as one of his "sorest troubles."

T. H. Huxley had long been aware of the risks involved in premature extrapolations from mathematical treatment of biological problems. He said, in an 1869 speech to the Geological Society concerning numbers, "This seems to be one of the many cases in which the admitted accuracy of mathematical processes is allowed to throw a wholly inadmissible appearance of authority over the results obtained by them. . . . As the grandest mill in the world will not extract wheat flour from peascods, so pages of formulas will not get a definite result out of loose data."

The trouble was that the world of physics had not moved fast enough to allow for Kelvin's assumptions. Nuclear fusion and fission had not yet been dreamed of, and the true age of the earth could not even be guessed from the data in hand. It was not yet the time for mathematics in this subject.

There have been other examples, since those days, of the folly of using numbers and calculations uncritically. Kelvin's own strong conviction that science could not be genuine science without measuring things was catching. People in other fields of endeavor, hankering to turn their disciplines into exact sciences, beset by what has since been called "physics envy," set about converting whatever they knew into numbers and thence into equations with predictive pretensions. We have it with us still, in economics, sociology, psychology, history, even, I fear, in English-literature criticism and linguistics, and it frequently works, when it works at all, with indifferent success. The risks of untoward social consequences in work of this kind are considerable. It is as important—and as hard—to learn *when* to use mathematics as *how* to use it, and this matter should remain high on the agenda of consideration for education in the social and behavioral sciences.

Of course, Kelvin's difficulty with the age of the earth was an exceptional, almost isolated instance of failure in quantitative measurement in the nineteenth-century physics. The instruments devised for approaching nature by way of physics became increasingly precise and powerful, carrying the field through electromagnetic theory, triumph after triumph, and setting the stage for the great revolution of twentieth-century physics. There is no doubt about it: measurement works when the instruments work, and when you have a fairly clear idea of what it is that is being measured, and when you know what to do with the numbers when they tumble out. The system for gaining information and comprehension about nature works so well, indeed, that it carries another hazard: the risk of convincing yourself that you know everything.

Kelvin himself fell into this trap toward the end of the century. (I don't mean to keep picking on Kelvin, who was a very great scientist; it is just that he happened to say a couple of things I find useful for this discussion.) He stated, in a summary of the achievements of nineteenth-century physics, that it was an almost completed science; virtually everything that needed knowing about the material universe had been learned; there were still a few anomalies and inconsistencies in electromagnetic theory, a few loose ends to be tied up, but this would be done within the next several years. Physics, in these terms, was not a field any longer likely to attract, as it previously had, the brightest and most imaginative young brains. The most interesting part of the work had already been done. Then, within the next decade, came radiation, Planck, the quantum, Einstein, Rutherford, Bohr, and all the rest—quantum mechanics—and the whole field turned over and became a brand-new sort of human endeavor, still now, in the view of many physicists, almost a full century later, a field only at its beginnings.

But even today, despite the amazements that are turning up in physics each year, despite the jumps taken from the smallest parts of nature—particle physics—to the largest of all—the cosmos itself—the impression of science that the public gains is rather like the impression left in the nineteenth-century public mind by Kelvin. Science, in this view, is first of all a matter of simply getting all the numbers together. The numbers are sitting out there in nature, waiting to be found, sorted and totted up. If only they had enough robots and enough computers, the scientists could go off to the beach and wait for their papers to be written for them. Second of all, what we know about nature today is pretty much the whole story: we are very nearly home and dry. From here on, it is largely a problem of tying up loose ends, tidying nature up, getting the files in order. The only real surprises for the future— and it is about those that the public is becoming more concerned and apprehensive—are the technological applications that the scientists may be cooking up from today's knowledge.

I suggest that the scientific community is to blame. If there are disagreements between the world of the humanities and the scientific enterprise as to the place and importance of science in a liberal-arts education, and the role of science in twentieth-century culture, I believe that the scientists are themselves responsible for a general misunderstanding of what they are really up to.

Over the past half century, we have been teaching the sciences as though they were the same academic collection of cut-and-dried subjects as always, and—here is what has really gone wrong—as though they would always be the same. The teaching of today's biology, for example, is pretty much the same kind of exercise as the teaching of Latin was when I was in high school long ago. First of all, the fundamentals, the underlying laws, the essential grammar, and then the reading of texts. Once mastered, that is that: Latin is Latin and forever after will be Latin. And biology is precisely biology, a vast array of hard facts to be learned as fundamentals, followed by a reading of the texts.

Moreover, we have been teaching science as though its facts were somehow superior to the facts in all other scholarly disciplines, more fundamental, more solid, less subject to subjectivism, immutable. English literature is not just one way of thinking, it is all sorts of ways. Poetry is a moving target. The facts that underlie art, architecture, and music are not really hard facts, and you can change them any way you like by arguing about them, but science is treated as an altogether different kind of learning: an unambiguous, unalterable, and endlessly useful display of data needing only to be packaged and installed somewhere in one's temporal lobe in order to achieve a full understanding of the natural world.

And it is, of course, not like this at all. In real life, every field of science that I can think of is incomplete, and most of them—whatever the record of accomplishment over the past two hundred years—are still in the earliest stage of their starting point. In the fields I know best, among the life sciences, it is required that the most expert and sophisticated minds be capable of changing those minds, often with a great lurch, every few years. In some branches of biology the mind-changing is occurring with accelerating velocities. The next week's issue of any scientific journal can turn a whole field upside down, shaking out any number of immutable ideas and installing new bodies of dogma, and this is happening all the time. It is an almost everday event in physics, in chemistry, in materials research, in neurobiology, in genetics, in immunology. The hard facts tend to soften overnight, melt away, and vanish under the pressure of new hard facts, and the interpretations of what appear to be the most solid aspects of nature are subject to change, now more than at any other time in history. The conclusions reached in science are always, when looked at closely, far more provisional and tentative than are most of the assumptions arrived at by our colleagues in the humanities.

The running battle now in progress between the sociobiologists and the antisociobiologists is a marvel for students to behold, close up. To observe, in open-mouthed astonishment, the polarized extremes, one group of highly intelligent, beautifully trained, knowledgeable, and imaginative scientists maintaining that all sorts of behavior, animal and human, are governed exclusively by genes, and another group of equally talented scientists saying precisely the opposite and asserting that all behavior is set and determined by the environment, or by culture, and both sides brawling in the pages of periodicals such as *The New York Review of Books,* is an educational experience that no college student should be allowed to miss. The essential lesson to be learned has nothing to do with the relative validity of the facts underlying the argument, it is the argument itself that is the education: we do not yet know enough to settle such questions.

It is true that at any given moment there is the appearance of satisfaction, even self-satisfaction, within every scientific discipline. On any Tuesday morning, if asked, a good working scientist will gladly tell you that the affairs of the field are nicely in order, that things are finally looking clear and making sense, and all is well. But come back again, on another Tuesday, and he may let you know that the roof has just fallen in on his life's work, that all the old ideas—last week's ideas in some cases—are no longer good ideas, that something strange has happened.

It is the very strangeness of nature that makes science engrossing. That ought to be at the center of science teaching. There are more than seven-times-seven types of ambiguity in science, awaiting analysis. The poetry of Wallace Stevens is crystal-clear alongside the genetic code.

I prefer to turn things around in order to make precisely the opposite case. Science, especially twentieth-century science, has provided us with a glimpse of something we never really knew before, the revelation of human ignorance. We have been used to the belief, down one century after another, that we more or less comprehend everything bar one or two mysteries like the mental processes of our gods. Every age, not just the eighteenth century, regarded itself as the Age of Reason, and we have never lacked for explanations of the world and its ways. Now, we are being brought up short, and this has been the work of science. We have a wilderness of mystery to make our way through in the centuries ahead, and we will need science for this but not science alone. Science will, in its own time, produce the data and some of the meaning in the data, but never the full meaning. For getting a full grasp, for perceiving real significance when significance is at hand, we shall need minds at work from all sorts of brains outside the fields of science, most of all the brains of poets, of course, but also those of artists, musicians, philosophers, historians, writers in general.

It is primarily because of this need that I would press for changes in the way science is taught. There is a need to teach the young people who will be doing the science themselves, but this will always be a small minority among us. There is a deeper need to teach science to those who will be needed for thinking about it, and this means pretty nearly everyone else, in hopes that a few of these people—a much smaller minority than the scientific community and probably a lot harder to find—will, in the thinking, be able to imagine new levels of meaning that are likely to be lost on the rest of us.

In addition, it is time to develop a new group of professional thinkers, perhaps a somewhat larger group than the working scientists, who can create a discipline of scientific criticism. We have had good luck so far in the emergence of a few people ranking as philosophers of science and historians and journalists of science, and I hope more of these will be coming along, but we have not yet seen a Ruskin or a Leavis or an Edmund Wilson. Science needs critics of this sort, but the public at large needs them more urgently.

I suggest that the introductory courses in science, at all levels from grade school through college, be radically revised. Leave the fundamentals, the so-called basics, aside for a while, and concentrate the attention of all students on the things that are *not* known. You cannot possibly teach quantum mechanics without mathematics, to be sure, but you can describe the strangeness of the world opened up by quantum theory. Let it be known, early on, that there are deep mysteries, and profound paradoxes, revealed in their distant outlines, by the quantum. Let it be known that these can be approached more closely, and puzzled over, once the language of mathematics has been sufficiently mastered.

Teach at the outset, before any of the fundamentals, the still imponderable puzzles of cosmology. Let it be known, as clearly as possible, by the youngest minds, that there are some things going on in the universe that lie beyond comprehension, and make it plain how little is known.

Do not teach that biology is a useful and perhaps profitable science; that can come later. Teach instead that there are structures squirming inside all our cells, providing all the energy for living, that are essentially foreign creatures, brought in for symbiotic living a billion or so years ago, the lineal descendants of bacteria. Teach that we do not have the ghost of an idea how they got there, where they came from, or how they evolved to their present structure and function. The details of oxidative phosphorylation and photosynthesis can come later.

Teach ecology early on. Let it be understood that the earth's life is a system of interliving, interdependent creatures, and that we do not understand at all how it works. The earth's environment, from the range of atmospheric gases to the chemical constituents of the sea, has been held in an almost unbelievably improbable state of regulated balance since life began, and the regulation of stability and balance is accomplished solely by the life itself, like the internal environment of an immense organism, and we do not know how *that* one works, even less what it means. Teach that.

Go easy, I suggest, on the promises sometimes freely offered by science. Technology relies and depends on science these days, more than ever before, but technology is nothing like the first justification for doing research, nor is it necessarily an essential product to be expected from science. Public decisions about what to have in the way of technology are totally different problems from decisions about science, and the two enterprises should not be tangled together. The central task of science is to arrive, stage by stage, at a clearer comprehension of nature, but this does not mean, as it is sometimes claimed to mean, a search for mastery over nature. Science may provide us, one day, with a better understanding of ourselves, but never, I hope, with a set of technologies for doing something or other to improve ourselves. I am made nervous by assertions that human consciousness will someday be unraveled by research, laid out for close scrutiny like the workings of a computer, and then, *and then!* I hope with some fervor that we can learn a lot more than we now know about the human mind, and I see no reason why this strange puzzle should remain forever and entirely beyond us. But I would be deeply disturbed by any prospect that we might use the new knowledge in order to begin doing something about it, to improve it, say. This is a different matter from searching for information to use against schizophrenia or dementia, where we are badly in need of technologies, indeed likely one day to be sunk without them. But the ordinary, everyday, more or less normal human mind is too marvelous an instrument ever to be tampered with by anyone, science or no science.

The education of humanists cannot be regarded as complete, or even adequate, without exposure in some depth to where things stand in the various branches of science, and particularly, as I have said, in the areas of our ignorance. This does not mean that I know how to go about doing it, nor am I unaware of the difficulties involved. Physics professors, most of them, look with revulsion on assignments to teach their subject to poets. Biologists, caught up by the enchantment of their new power, armed with flawless instruments to tell the nucleotide sequences of the entire human genome, nearly matching the physicists in the precision of their measurements of living processes, will resist the prospect of broad survey courses; each biology professor will demand that any student in his path must master every fine detail within that professor's research program. The liberal-arts faculties, for their part, will continue to view the scientists with suspicion and apprehension. "What do the scientists want?" asked a Cambridge professor in Francis Cornford's wonderful *Microcosmographia Academica*. "Everything that's going," was the quick answer. That was back in 1912, and universities haven't much changed.

The worst thing that has happened to science education is that the great fun has gone out of it. A very large number of good students look at it as slogging work to be got through on the way to medical school. Others look closely at the premedical students themselves, embattled and bleeding for grades and class standing, and are turned off. Very few see science as the high adventure it really is, the wildest of all explorations ever undertaken by human beings, the chance to catch close views of things never seen before, the shrewdest maneuver for discovering how the world works. Instead, they become baffled early on, and they are misled into thinking that bafflement is simply the result of not having learned all the facts. They are not told, as they should be told, that everyone else—from the professor in his endowed chair down to the platoons of postdoctoral students in the laboratory all night—is baffled as well. Every important scientific advance that has come in looking like an answer has turned, sooner or later—usually sooner—into a question. And the game is just beginning.

An appreciation of what is happening in science today, and of how great a distance lies ahead for exploring, ought to be one of the rewards of a liberal-arts education. It ought to be a good in itself, not something to be acquired on the way to a professional career but part of the cast of thought needed for getting into the kind of century that is now just down the road. Part of the intellectual equipment of an educated person, however his or her time is to be spent, ought to be a feel for the queernesses of nature, the inexplicable things.

And maybe, just maybe, a new set of courses dealing systematically with ignorance in science might take hold. The scientists might discover in it a new and subversive technique for catching the attention of students driven by curiosity, delighted and surprised to learn that science is exactly as Bush described it: an "endless frontier." The humanists, for their part, might take considerable satisfaction watching their scientific colleagues confess openly to not knowing everything about everything. And the poets, on whose shoulders the future rests, might, late nights, thinking things over, begin to see some meanings that elude the rest of us. It is worth a try.

Suggestions for Discussion

1. Summarize Thomas's complaints about "the impression of science that the public gains."

2. How would he have science taught?

3. What advantages might there be in "a new set of courses dealing systematically with ignorance in science"?

Suggestions for Writing

1. Discuss one or more unanswered questions that you have encountered in your study of science.

2. Tell about an experience in which you had to change your mind because of new information.

Woody Allen

My Speech to the Graduates

Woody Allen (b. 1935) is an American actor, film maker, and writer, best known for such outstanding films as *Annie Hall* (1977), *Interiors* (1978), *Manhattan* (1979), and *Zelig* (1983). His humorous essays have appeared in *The New Yorker* and in the collections *Getting Even* (1971), *Without Feathers* (1975), and *The Floating Lightbulb. (1981).* In the following parody of a commencement address, Allen faces a world of gloom and chaos with humorous platitudes and endless good will as he displays his mastery of the anticlimax and the non sequitur.

More than any other time in history, mankind faces a crossroads. One path leads to despair and utter hopelessness. The other, to total extinction. Let us pray we have the wisdom to choose correctly. I speak, by the way, not with any sense of futility but with a panicky conviction of the absolute meaninglessness of existence which could easily be misinterpreted as pessimism. It is not. It is merely a healthy concern for the predicament of modern man. (Modern man is here defined as any person born after Nietzche's edict that "God is dead," but before the hit recording "I Wanna Hold Your Hand.") This "predicament" can be stated one of two ways, though certain linguistics philosophers prefer to reduce it to a mathematical equation where it can be easily solved and even carried around in the wallet.

Put in its simplest form, the problem is: How is it possible to find meaning in a finite world given my waist and shirt size? This is a very difficult question when we realize that science has failed us. True, it has conquered many diseases, broken the genetic code, and even placed human beings on the moon, and yet when a man of 80 is left in a room with two 18-year-old cocktail waitresses nothing happens. Because the real problems never change. After all, can the human soul be glimpsed through a microscope? Maybe—but you'd definitely need one of those very good ones with two eyepieces. We know that the most advanced computer in the world does not have a brain as sophisticated as that of an ant. True, we could say that of many of our relatives but we only have to put up with them at weddings or special occasions. Science is something we depend on all the time. If I develop a pain in the chest I must take an X-ray. But what if the radiation from the X-ray causes me deeper problems? Before I know it, I'm going in for surgery. Naturally, while they're giving me oxygen an intern decides to light up a cigarette. The next thing you know I'm rocketing over the World Trade Center in bed clothes. Is this science? True, science has taught us how to pasteurize cheese. And true, this can be fun in mixed company—but what of the H-bomb? Have you ever seen what happens when one of those things falls off a desk accidentally? And where is science when one ponders the eternal riddles? How did the cosmos originate? How long has it been around? Did matter begin with an explosion or by the word of God? And if by the latter, could He not have begun it just two weeks earlier to take advantage of some of the warmer weather? Exactly what do we mean when we say, man is mortal? Obviously it's not a compliment.

Religion too has unfortunately let us down. Miguel de Unamuno writes blithely of the "eternal persistence of consciousness," but this is no easy feat. Particularly when reading Thackeray. I often think how comforting life must have been for early man because he believed in a powerful, benevolent Creator who looked after all things. Imagine his disappointment when he saw his wife putting on weight. Contemporary man, of course, has no such peace of mind. He finds himself in the midst of a crisis of faith. He is what we fashionably call "alienated." He has seen the ravages of war, he has known natural catastrophes, he has been to singles bars. My good friend Jacques Monod spoke often of the randomness of the cosmos. He believed everything in existence occurred by pure chance with the possible exception of his breakfast, which he felt certain was made by his housekeeper. Naturally belief in a divine intelligence inspires tranquility. But this does not free us from our human responsibilities. Am I my brother's keeper? Yes. Interestingly, in my case I share that honor with the Prospect Park Zoo. Feeling godless then, what we have done is made technology God. And yet can technology really be the answer when a brand new Buick, driven by my close associate, Nat Persky, winds up in the window of Chicken Delight causing hundreds of customers to scatter? My toaster has never once worked properly in four years. I follow the instructions and push two slices of bread down in the slots and seconds later they rifle upward. Once they broke the nose of a woman I loved very dearly. Are we counting on nuts and bolts and electricity to solve our problems? Yes, the telephone is a good thing—and the refrigerator—and the air conditioner. But not every air conditioner. Not my sister Henny's, for instance. Hers makes a loud noise and still doesn't cool. When the man comes over to fix it, it gets worse. Either that or he tells her she needs a new one. When she complains, he says not to bother him. This man is truly alienated. Not only is he alienated but he can't stop smiling.

The trouble is, our leaders have not adequately prepared us for a mechanized society. Unfortunately our politicians are either incompetent or corrupt. Sometimes both on the same day. The Government is unresponsive to the needs of the little man. Under five-seven, it is impossible to get your Congressman on the phone. I am not denying that democracy is still the finest form of government. In a democracy at least, civil liberties are upheld. No citizen can be wantonly tortured, imprisoned, or made to sit through certain Broadway shows. And yet this is a far cry from what goes on in the Soviet Union. Under their form of totalitarianism, a person merely caught whistling is sentenced to 30 years in a labor camp. If, after 15 years, he still will not stop whistling they shoot him. Along with this brutal fascism we find its handmaiden, terrorism. At no other time in history has man been so afraid to cut his veal chop for fear that it will explode. Violence breeds more violence and it is predicted that by 1990 kidnapping will be the dominant mode of social interaction. Overpopulation will exacerbate problems to the breaking point. Figures tell us there are already more people on earth than we need to move even the heaviest piano. If we do not call a halt to breeding, by the year 2000 there will be no room to serve dinner unless one is willing to set the table on the heads of strangers. Then they must not move for an hour while we eat. Of course energy will be in short supply and each car owner will be allowed only enough gasoline to back up a few inches.

Instead of facing these challenges we turn instead to distractions like drugs and sex. We live in far too permissive a society. Never before has pornography been this rampant. And those films are lit so badly! We are a people who lack defined goals. We have never learned to love. We lack leaders and coherent programs. We have no spiritual center. We are adrift alone in the cosmos wreaking monstrous violence on one another out of frustration and pain. Fortunately, we have not lost our sense of proportion. Summing up, it is clear the future holds great opportunities. It also holds pitfalls. The trick will be to avoid the pitfalls, seize the opportunities, and get back home by six o'clock.

Suggestions for Discussion

1. Discuss Allen's use of exaggeration and understatement as sources of humor.

2. What real social problems does Allen address?

3. How does Allen's choice of allusion and vocabulary contribute to the effectiveness of his parody?

Suggestion for Writing

Write an essay in which, without diminishing Allen's skill as a comic writer, you consider why it is easy to parody a commencement address. Is it possible to compose an address that does not invite parody? What might be the content and tone of an effective address?

Anna Tuttle Villegas

The Teacher as Dragon

Anna Tuttle Villegas teaches English at the University of the Pacific in Stockton, California. "The Teacher as Dragon," which appeared in the San Francisco *Sunday Examiner and Chronicle* in 1983, describes the difficult task which faces the teacher of writing. It shows how easily students perceive the writing teacher as monster and how easily teachers assume that shape if they lose their optimism.

A few semesters ago, in fulfillment of a descriptive paper assignment, I received a student essay describing a high school English teacher. To this day I vividly recall the image it created. It was of a stout, ham-like body perched atop two trunkish legs that ended in toes having not toenails but yellow, calcified claws (which were always, the student noted, causing damage to hosiery). On top of this lumbering figure was planted a savage, baleful countenance fringed with sparse, kinky, red hair. Behind the inevitable thick-lensed spectacles glared beady porcine eyes whose sole purpose, it seems, was to seek out ne'er-do-wells and inflict on them stinging lashes of shame and guilt.

The indelible impression I have of the essay (and the woman) is the intricately painted relationship between appearance and character. True, I had emphasized to my students that they describe their subjects along thematic lines, but there was something supernaturally real and uncannily familiar to me about this fire-breathing dragon of an English teacher. I caught, in the reflections of her horn-rims, an image of myself.

In appearance I am nothing like her. Where she is short and stout, I am tall and leaning to the skinny side. Where she wears gaudy and sackish dresses, I wear informal pants and shirts, not unlike those of my students. The closest my hair comes to red are the few rusty strands left over from the chlorine bleach of last summer's daily swimming. I am blind as a bat, and my prescription is strong—but I don't wear horn-rimmed glasses. And my eyes are blue, not beady black.

Why, then, in the midst of midnight insomnia or the predawn stirrings of the soul, do I see myself in this red-haired vixen?

The teaching of writing, of good writing, is the teaching of thinking—not thinking presented in a general, abstracted, grandiose way, but thinking applied to the individual mind. When, as a writing teacher, I ask for an argumentative essay that springs from a student's interest in a subject, I am not asking for a legislative document or a psychological treatise. I am asking for reasonable thought on a limited topic conveyed from a unique perspective, the student's own.

To ask for reasonable thought—to ask for any individual thought—is a very risky business. It means that what will finally be evaluated by the teacher is a projection of the student's self, and, unless the student is that rare one who enters a writing class articulate, skilled and independently thoughtful, that part of the self tends to be particularly vulnerable.

No matter how often a writing teacher chants that "receiving a D grade doesn't mean you are a D person," students interpret a grade as a grade on their characters, and they react much like a calf whose flank is singed with a hot iron: bawling and kicking and protesting throatily against convention and authority, in their pained rage mistaking blue eyes for black ones.

No one likes to be told, or even have hinted at, that his mind is cluttered, untidy, disordered, lacking purpose. Yet when I comment that an essay fails to meet the objectives the writer has set for it, that it dawdles from point to point without developing any one idea, I have the unpleasant task of pointing a finger at the clutter.

I believe myself to be an expert at supportive tact, but it is in this aspect of my job and my relationship to my students that I find my kinship with the red-haired dragon. We are both concerned with the nurturing of creative thought, and in our attempts to bribe and cajole thought from our students we sometimes have to point out where it is wilting from the neglect of haste or lack of commitment. Then we become sisters: dragon ladies who bleed red ink instead of blood.

Our genealogy follows a long engagement in the profession. Although I don't yet resemble the red-haired teacher in person, in spirit I am beginning to. In her youth she, like me, must have entertained the belief that in teaching her students to write she was endowing them with an enduring tool for discovering themselves and their relationship to their world. She must have felt the thrill of discovery herself when she received papers that rewarded her with the richness of shared experience.

Unfortunately, long before I stood nervously before my first expository class, she must have encountered the disappointment of failed expectations. Subconsciously perhaps, she rallied by convincing herself that with gentle and persistent prodding of her students' minds she could extract from them substance for good essays and sustenance for her belief in their capacity to think. This, I speculate, may have delayed her eventual disenchantment with the human imagination for a few years. But as time and students passed by her, she was forced to accept the decay of her initial illusion about the rational animal's ability to communicate. It was at this time that her eyes got bad, her prescription thicker and her hair unruly. She was transforming herself into a person who was impervious to disappointment. She began to shield herself in her scales.

One doesn't have to count the dragon ladies one has known to realize that the constant failure of expectations creates bitterness, sours the appeal of meeting new minds, and physically transforms a person. The dragon teacher is an understandable product of many years of a gradual lowering of standards. Ultimately she found it easier to torment than to teach. With tormenting she could see at least an emotional response, while with teaching she despaired of ever finding an intellectual one.

I remember reading amid cheers that essay to my class. After reviewing the descriptive techniques the writer had used, we turned to a discussion of the relationship between thesis and descriptive detail. In a class of twenty students from widely varying geographic backgrounds, I found that fifteen of them had been taught high school English, if not by the dragon lady herself, by her identical sister. Her attitude and her appearance, even down to the fine detail of the calcified toenails, were those of an entire nation of English schoolmarms. And I am of the same breed.

I admit that I read the essay to my class with the intention of milking from it every ounce of humor that it had. In retrospect I see that what I was really doing, in a sneaky and lowdown way, was saying to my students: Look, here is what you might have had for a writing teacher. But you didn't. You have me—and aren't I different? Aren't I breaking the mold? Won't you write your hearts out for me?

I don't like the image of myself that I caught reflected in that essay. I don't like the image of my profession that appeared there, either. Writing well is the most powerful intellectual tool that a person—student or teacher or layman—can develop. I go to school every day, talk about conventions and rhetorical modes and ideas, drag home stacks of student essays, comment on conventions and modes and ideas and return to school the next day to begin again because I believe in the written word's power. And I refuse to succumb to the stereotype the outside world has of me.

I have great sympathy for the red-haired woman whom I have used so badly. I understand how she has evolved into her present state. But I am sorry she gave up. Our job is too important, our students' minds too precious, for me to give up too. My hair will not turn red.

Suggestions for Discussion

1. How does the student essay describe a high school English teacher? Why does the author begin her essay with this description? What use does she make of this description in the rest of the essay?

2. Why does the author believe it is difficult to teach writing? Do you agree with her analysis of student reaction to receiving a poor grade?

3. What does Villegas consider her primary function as a teacher of writing? Is she subject to frustration? Do you imagine that frustration will cause her to give up?

4. How does the author begin to identify with the high school teacher described in the student paper?

Suggestion for Writing

Have you had an English teacher who resembles the author of this essay or the high school teacher described by her student? Write an essay in which you discuss those qualities in your teacher that resemble those of either. Could you see qualities below the surface? Your essay should enable the reader to understand something about the character of your teacher as well as see him or her plainly.

T. H. Huxley

A Liberal Education

Thomas Henry Huxley (1825–1895), a biologist, was first of a line of important English scientists and writers bearing his name. He gave up his career in science to publicize Darwinism and to influence and change education in England. He was an agnostic and a believer in progress controlled by evolution. His works include *Evolution and Ethics* (1893) and nine volumes of collected essays and four volumes of memoirs. The following selection from *A Liberal Education* (1868) defines the goals of a liberal education and relates it to our need to learn the laws of nature.

Suppose it were perfectly certain that the life and fortune of every one of us would, one day or other, depend upon his winning or losing a game of chess. Don't you think that we should all consider it to be a primary duty to learn at least the names and the moves of the pieces; to have a notion of a gambit, and a keen eye for all the means of giving and getting out of check? Do you not think that we should look with a disapprobation amounting to scorn, upon the father who allowed his son, or the state which allowed its members, to grow up without knowing a pawn from a knight?

Yet it is a very plain and elementary truth, that the life, the fortune, and the happiness of every one of us, and, more or less, of those who are connected with us, do depend upon our knowing something of the rules of a game infinitely more difficult and complicated than chess. It is a game which has been played for untold ages, every man and woman of us being one of the two players in a game of his or her own. The chessboard is the world, the pieces are the phenomena of the universe, the rules of the game are what we call the laws of Nature. The player on the other side is hidden from us. We know that his play is always fair, just, and patient. But also we know, to our cost, that he never overlooks a mistake, or makes the smallest allowance for ignorance. To the man who plays well, the highest stakes are paid, with that sort of overflowing generosity with which the strong shows delight in strength. And one who plays ill is checkmated—without haste, but without remorse.

My metaphor will remind some of you of the famous picture in which Retzsch has depicted Satan playing at chess with man for his soul. Substitute for the mocking fiend in that picture, a calm, strong angel who is playing for love, as we say, and would rather lose than win—and I should accept it as an image of human life.

Well, what I mean by Education is learning the rules of this mighty game. In other words, education is the instruction of the intellect in the laws of Nature, under which name I include not merely things and their forces, but men and their ways; and the fashioning of the affections and of the will into an earnest and loving desire to move in harmony with those laws. For me education means neither more nor less than this. Anything which professes to call itself education must be tried by this standard, and if it fails to stand the test, I will not call it education, whatever may be the force of authority, or of numbers, upon the other side.

It is important to remember that, in strictness, there is no such thing as an uneducated man. Take an extreme case. Suppose that an adult man, in the full vigor of his faculties, could be suddenly placed in the world, as Adam is said to have been, and then left to do as he best might. How long would he be left uneducated? Not five minutes. Nature would begin to teach him, through the eye, the ear, the touch, the properties of objects. Pain and pleasure would be at his elbow telling him to do this and avoid that; and by slow degrees the man would receive an education, which, if narrow, would be thorough, real, and adequate to his circumstances, though there would be no extras and very few accomplishments.

And if to this solitary man entered a second Adam, or better still, an Eve, a new and greater world, that of social and moral phenomena, would be revealed. Joys and woes, compared with which all others might seem but faint shadows, would spring from the new relations. Happiness and sorrow would take the place of the coarser monitors, pleasure and pain; but conduct would still be shaped by the observation of the natural consequences of actions; or, in other words, by the laws of the nature of man.

To everyone of us the world was once as fresh and new as to Adam. And then, long before we were susceptible of any other mode of instruction, Nature took us in hand, and every minute of waking life brought its educational influence, shaping our actions into rough accordance with Nature's laws, so that we might not be ended untimely by too gross disobedience. Nor should I speak of this process of education as past for any one, be he as old as he may. For every man the world is as fresh as it was at the first day, and as full of untold novelties for him who has the eyes to see them. And Nature is still continuing her patient education of us in that great university, the universe, of which we are all members—Nature having no Test-Acts.

Those who take honors in Nature's university, who learn the laws which govern men and things and obey them, are the really great and successful men in this world. The great mass of mankind are the "Poll," who pick up just enough to get through without much discredit. Those who won't learn at all are plucked; and then you can't come up again. Nature's pluck means extermination.

Thus the question of compulsory education is settled so far as Nature is concerned. Her bill on that question was framed and passed long ago. But, like all compulsory legislation, that of Nature is harsh and wasteful in its operation. Ignorance is visited as sharply as willful disobedience—incapacity meets with the same punishment as crime. Nature's discipline is not even a word and a blow, and the blow first; but the blow without the word. It is left to you to find out why your ears are boxed.

The object of what we commonly call education—that education in which man intervenes and which I shall distinguish as artificial education—is to make good these defects in Nature's methods; to prepare the child to receive Nature's education, neither incapably nor ignorantly, nor with willful disobedience; and to understand the preliminary symptoms of her displeasure, without waiting for the box on the ear. In short, all artificial education ought to be an anticipation of natural education. And a liberal education is an artificial education, which has not only prepared a man to escape the great evils of disobedience to natural laws, but has trained him to appreciate and to seize upon the rewards, which Nature scatters with as free a hand as her penalties.

That man, I think, has had a liberal education, who has been so trained in youth that his body is the ready servant of his will, and does with ease and pleasure all the work that, as a mechanism, it is capable of; whose intellect is a clear, cold, logic engine, with all its parts of equal strength, and in smooth working order; ready, like a steam engine, to be turned to any kind of work, and spin the gossamers as well as forge the anchors of the mind; whose mind is stored with a knowledge of the great and fundamental truths of Nature and of the laws of her operations; one who, no stunted ascetic, is full of life and fire, but whose passions are trained to come to heel by a vigorous will, the servant of a tender conscience; who has learned to love all beauty, whether of Nature or of art, to hate all vileness, and to respect others as himself.

Such an one and no other, I conceive, has had a liberal education; for he is, as completely as a man can be, in harmony with Nature. He will make the best of her, and she of him. They will get on together rarely; she as his ever beneficent mother, he as her mouth-piece, her conscious self, her minister and interpreter.

Suggestions for Discussion

1. What is the function of the analogy of the rules of the game of chess and the laws of nature introduced in the first two paragraphs?

2. How does nature repay those who learn its rules? those who do not? What is Huxley's attitude toward nature?

3. How does Huxley define education? What does he regard as its major function? How is education related to the teachings of nature?

4. How does Huxley define liberal education? What qualities of life does a liberal education bestow on its recipients?

Suggestions for Writing

1. This essay dates from the mid-nineteenth century. What details in the writing reveal this fact to you? Write an essay in which you attempt to restate Huxley's major ideas in your own language.

2. Write an essay in which you comment on Huxley's ideas about the value of liberal education. Are they similar to your own? Do you believe that his ideas are necessarily dated? Explain.

Howard Gardner
Human Intelligence Isn't What We Think It Is

Howard Gardner (b. 1943), professor of psychology at Harvard University, also is research psychologist at the Boston Veterans Administration Medical Center and on the faculty of the Boston University School of Medicine. He is the author of *Frames of Mind: The Theory of Multiple Intelligences* (1985). In the essay that follows, he discusses the importance of recognizing and cultivating different kinds of intelligence.

"People Have Multiple Intelligences"

Intelligence is not an absolute such as height that can be measured simply, largely because people have multiple intelligences rather than one single intelligence.

In all, I have identified seven forms of intelligence. The two that are valued most highly in this society are linguistic and logical-mathematical intelligences. When people think of someone as smart, they are usually referring to those two, because individuals who possess linguistic and logical-mathematical abilities do well on tests that supposedly measure intelligence.

But there are five other kinds of intelligence that are every bit as important: Spatial, musical, bodily-kinesthetic and two forms of personal intelligence—interpersonal, knowing how to deal with others, and intrapersonal, knowledge of self. None of these ought to have a priority over others.

"Shifting Importance" of the Seven Varieties

The relative importance of these seven intelligences has shifted over time and varies from culture to culture. In a hunting society, for example, it is a lot more important to have extremely good control of your body and know your way around than to add or subtract quickly. In Japanese society, interpersonal intelligence—the ability to work well in groups and to arrive at joint decisions—is very important.

Historically, different systems of education have emphasized different blends of intelligence. In the old apprenticeship system, bodily, spatial and interpersonal abilities were valued. In old-fashioned religious schools, the focus was on linguistic and interpersonal abilities. The modern secular school emphasizes the linguistic and logical-mathematical, but in the school of the near future I think that linguistic will become much less crucial. For working with computers, logical-mathematical intelligence will be important for programing, and intrapersonal intelligence will be important for individual planning.

What I'm saying is that while both logical-mathematical and linguistic are important today, it won't always be that way. We need to be sensitive to the fact that blends of intelligences keep shifting so that in the future we don't get locked into a specific blend.

Secrets Unlocked by Biological Research

Research in biology has laid the foundation for the theory of multiple intelligences.

Studies show that when someone suffers damage to the nervous system through a stroke or tumor, all abilities do not break down equally. If you have an injury to areas of the left hemisphere of the brain, you will lose your language ability almost entirely, but that will not affect your musical, spatial or interpersonal skills to the same extent.

Conversely, you can have lesions in your right hemisphere that leave language capacity intact but that seriously compromise spatial, musical or interpersonal abilities. So we have a special capacity for language that is unconnected to our capacity for music or interpersonal skills, and vice versa.

I'm not suggesting that this analysis is the last word. I would like to think of it as the first word in a new way of looking at human abilities.

"America Wastes Potential!"

In America, we are wasting a lot of human potential by focusing on only linguistic and logical intelligence. If an individual doesn't happen to be good in these, he or she often gets thrown on society's scrap heap.

What happens is that a youngster takes an IQ test and doesn't do very well. He gets labeled as not very smart and the teacher treats him accordingly.

But there are many roles in society in which it is not important that a person have a high intelligence in language and logic so long as he or she can function at a basic level in these domains.

For example, somebody good at working with his hands and figuring out how machines function might find a responsible position in a science lab or working backstage in a theater. If kids with such abilities were encouraged— rather than discouraged because they can't figure out who wrote the *Iliad*— they could be extremely valuable to society.

IQ Tests "Have Destructive Social Effects"

I would like to get rid of intelligence and aptitude tests; they measure only two forms of intelligence and have destructive social effects. These tests have been successful because they serve as a good predictor of how people will do in school in the short run. But how much does doing well in school predict success outside of school? Very little.

Those of us who take a position against IQ tests have the burden of coming up with ways of assessing abilities that are not completely impractical. My notion is something between a report card and a test score.

I would assess intellectual propensities from an early age. I use the word *propensities* because I don't believe intelligences are fixed for many years. The earlier a strength is discovered, the more flexibility there is to develop it. Similarly, if a child has a low propensity, the earlier intervention begins, the easier it is to shore up the child. So early diagnosis is important.

Preschools Where "Children Can Do Exploring"

I would not assess abilities through traditional paper-and-pencil tests. Instead, we need learning environments—preschools—in which children can do a lot of exploring on their own or with help from adults.

All children play with blocks, for example, but what do they do with them? How complex are the structures they make? How well can they remember them? Can they revise them in various ways? All of these questions can be answered by adults observing and playing with the children.

The same environment could be equipped wth musical materials, and, again, children could explore on their own and with adults. If we had such environments, with periodic monitoring we could develop very good profiles of a child's propensities. This would give parents and teachers a better way of thinking about children than one or two test scores. Instead of looking at a child and saying, "He's smart" or "He's dumb," people would talk in terms of a child's strengths and weaknesses. It is a much more realistic view.

But no theory is going to tell people what to do once a child's propensities are assessed. That decision would depend on the value of those around the child. Some people would say, "Let's go with the child's strengths for all they are worth." Others would say, "It's very important to be good in language, so even though this kid isn't good in it, we're going to work on it."

"The Challenge for Education"

As children mature, the assessments would continue in a different vein. By the age of 10 or 11, the monitoring would shift to "domains," where you might come up with analyses such as "this person has the talent to be a doctor."

While having a high intelligence in an area doesn't predict exactly what you are going to do, it predicts the direction you are likely to move in. If somebody has a very highly developed bodily intelligence, he or she could become an athlete, dancer or surgeon. If somebody has a highly developed spatial intelligence, he or she might be at home in architecture, engineering, sculpture or painting.

The challenge for the educational community is to figure out profiles of young people and then to help them find roles in which they can use their abilities in a productive way.

Recognizing the Diversity of Our Capabilities

The Suzuki method of teaching music, developed in Japan, shows what can be done to foster a specific intelligence when the effort is undertaken intensively at an early age and a lot of energy is put into it. This method creates an environment that is rich with music; mothers play with the youngsters for 2 hours a day from the time they reach age 2. Within a few years, all participants become decent musicians.

In theory, we could "Suzuki" everything. The more time and energy invested early in life on a particular intelligence, the more you can buoy it up. I am not advocating this approach, merely pointing out the possibilities. But before we can make these kinds of decisions, we have to take a first step— recognizing the diverse intelligences of which human beings are capable.

Suggestions for Discussion

1. Name the seven forms of intelligence identified by Gardner.

2. What suggestions does he make for replacing traditional intelligence and aptitude tests?

3. How might the development of intelligence be enhanced?

Suggestions for Writing

1. Write about your strongest intelligence. Give examples from your experience.

2. Rank your own intelligences from strongest to least strong.

Harold Brodkey

Reading, the Most Dangerous Game

Harold Brodkey, educated at Harvard University, writes fiction for *The New Yorker*. He is the author of *First Love and Other Sorrows* (1957). In 1987 he was awarded a John Simon Guggenheim Memorial Foundation Fellowship. In the essay that follows, he explores the act of reading and advocates reading "seriously."

Reading is an intimate act, perhaps more intimate than any other human act. I say that because of the prolonged (or intense) exposure of one mind to another that is involved in it, and because it is the level of mind at which feelings and hopes are dealt in by consciousness and words.

Reading a good book is not much different from a love affair, from love, complete with shyness and odd assertions of power and of independence and with many sorts of incompleteness in the experience. One can marry the book: reread it, add it to one's life, live with it. Or it might be compared to pregnancy—serious reading even if you're reading trash: one is inside the experience and is about to be born; and one is carrying something, a sort of self inside oneself that one is about to give birth to, perhaps a monster. Of course, for men this is always verging on something else (part of which is a primitive rage with being masculine, a dismay felt toward women and the world, a reader's odd sense of women).

The act of reading as it really occurs is obscure: the decision to read a book in a real minute, how one selects the book, how one flirts with the choice, how one dawdles on the odd path of getting it read and then reread, the oddities of rereading, the extreme oddities of the procedures of continuing with or without interruptions to read, getting ready to read a middle chapter in its turn after going off for a while, then getting hold of the book physically, having it in one's hand, letting one's mind fill with thoughts in a sort of warm-up for the exercise of mind to come—one riffles through remembered scenes from this and other books, one diddles with half-memories of other pleasures and usefulnesses, one wonders if one can afford to read, one considers the limitations and possibilities of this book, one is humiliated in anticipation or superior or thrilled in anticipation, or nauseated in retrospect or as one reads. One has a sense of talk and of reviews and essays and of anticipation or dread and the will to be affected by the thing of reading, affected lightly or seriously. One settles one's body to some varying degree, and then one enters on the altered tempos of reading, the subjection to being played upon, one passes through phases, starting with reacting to or ignoring the cover of the book and the opening lines.

The piercing things, the stabbingly emotional stuff involved in reading, leads to envy, worse even than in sibling or neighborhood rivalry, and it leads to jealousy and possessiveness. If a book is not religious or trashy, the problem of salesmanship, always partly a con, arises in relation to it, to all the problems it presents. A good reader of Proust complains constantly as a man might complain of a wife or a woman of her husband. And Proust perhaps had such a marriage in mind with the reader. A good book, like pregnancy or a woman known to arouse love, or a man, is something you praise in the light of a general reluctance to risk the experience; and the quality of praise warns people against the book, warns them to take it seriously; you warn them about it, not wanting to be evangelical, a matchmaker or a malicious pimp for a troubled and troubling view of the world.

I can't imagine how a real text can be taught in a school. Even minor masterpieces, "Huckleberry Finn" or "The Catcher in the Rye," are too much for a classroom, too real an experience. No one *likes* a good book if they have actually read it. One is fanatically attached, restlessly attached, criminally attached, violently and criminally opposed, sickened, unable to bear it. In Europe, reading is known to be dangerous. Reading always leads to personal metamorphosis, sometimes irreversible, sometimes temporary, sometimes large-scale, sometimes less than that. A good book leads to alterations in one's sensibility and often becomes a premise in one's beliefs. One associates truth with texts, with impressive texts anyway; and when trashy books vanish from sight, it is because they lie too much and too badly and are not worth one's intimacy with them. Print has so much authority, however, that sometimes it is only at the beginning of an attempt at a second reading or at the end of it, and only then, if one is self-assured, that one can see whether a book was not really worth reading the first time; one tells by how alterable the truth in it seems in this more familiar light and how effective the book remains or, contrarily, how amazingly empty of meaning it now shows itself to be. It is a strange feeling to be a practiced enough reader and writer to see in some books that there is nothing there. It is eerie: why did the writer bother? What reward is there in being a fraud in one's language and in one's ideas? To believe they just didn't know is more unsettling than to doubt oneself or to claim to be superficial or prejudiced or to give up reading entirely, at least for a while.

Or, in our country, we deny what we see of this and even reverse it: fraud is presented as happiness; an empty book is said to be well constructed; a foolish argument is called innovative. This is a kind of bliss; but lying of that sort, when it is nearly universal, wrecks the possibility of our having a literary culture or even of our talking about books with each other with any real pleasure. It is like being phony yachtsmen who only know smooth water and who use their motors whenever they can. This guarantees an immense personal wretchedness, actually.

Of course, in Europe, cultural patterns exist which slow the rate of change in you as a reader (as well as supplying evidence to use in comprehending what happens and will happen to you if you change because of a book). Of course, such change is never entirely good or wise. In our country, we have nothing to hold us back from responding to any sort of idea. With us everything is for sale—everything is up for grabs, including ourselves—and we have very little tradition worth hanging onto except the antic.

The country is organized not by religion or political machinery but by what are seen as economic realities but which are fashions in making money and spending money. We are an army marching in the largest conceivable mass so entirely within cultural immediacy that it can be said this is new in the history in the world, emotionally new in that while this has been true of other cultures for brief periods in the past, it was never true as completely or for such a large part of the population or so continuously, with so few periods of stasis. We pretend to tradition but really, nothing prevents us changing.

And we do change. Divorce, born-again Christianity, the computer revolution, a return to the farm, a move to the city. In Boston, at college at Harvard, I first knew people who claimed to be cultivated to the degree they remained unchanged not only in spite of the reading they claimed to have done but with the help of it. They did not realize what an imbecile and provincial notion that was—it was simply untrue: you could see it, the untruth of it. A rule of thumb about culture is that personal or public yearning for a better time to come or one in the past and nostalgia of any sort are reliable signs of the counterfeit. The past is there to be studied in its reality, moment by moment, and the future can be discussed in its reality to come, which will be a reality moment by moment; but doing that means being honest just as doing it makes you too busy to yearn; and doing it shows you that nostalgia is a swindler's trick. A sense of the real is what is meant by good sense. And because of the nature of time and because of how relentlessly change occurs, good sense has to contain a good deal of the visionary as well as of ironic apology to cover the inevitable mistakes. And this is doubly so with us, in the United States. Reality here is special. And part of reality here or elsewhere is that novels, plays, essays, fact pieces, poems, through conversion or in the process of argument with them, change you or else—to use an idiom—you haven't listened.

If the reader is not at risk, he is not reading. And if the writer is not at risk, he is not writing. As a rule, a writer and a book or a poem are no good if the writer is essentially unchanged morally after having written it. If the work is really a holding operation, this will show in a closed or flat quality in the prose and in the scheme of the thing, a logiclessness, if you will pardon the neologism, in the writing. Writing always tends toward a kind of moral stance—this is because of the weight of logic and of truth in it—but judging the ways in which it is moral is hard for people who are not cultivated. Profoundly educated persons make the best judges.

The general risk in being a man or woman of cultivation is then very high, and this is so in any culture, and perhaps requires too much strength for even a small group to practice in ours. But should such a guerrilla group arise, it will have to say that cultivation and judgment issue from the mouths of books and can come from no other source. Over a period of centuries, ignorance has come, justifiably, to mean a state of booklessness. Movie-educated people are strained; they are decontextualized; they are cultivated in a lesser way. Television and contemporary music are haunted by the search for messiahs; the usual sign of mass inauthenticity is a false prophet (which usually means a war will shortly break out and be lost). The absence of good sense signals the decline of a people and of a civilization. Shrewdness without good sense is hell unleashed.

I would propose as a social cure that in fourth grade and in the first year at college, this society mandate that we undergo a year of reading with or without argument as the soul can bear, including argument with teachers and parents and local philosophers if there are any. Of course something like this happens anyway but we probably ought to institutionalize it in our faddish way.

After all, if you don't know what's in good books, how can your life not be utterly miserable all in all? Won't it fall apart with fearsome frequency? The best of what this species knows is in books. Without their help, how can you manage?

If I intend for my life to matter to me, I had better read seriously, starting with newspapers and working up to philosophy and novels. And a book in what it teaches, and in what it does in comforting and amusing us, in what it does in granting asylum to us for a while, had better be roughly equivalent to, or greater in worth than, an event involving other people in reality that teaches us or that grants us asylum for a while in some similar way, or there is no reason to bother with it. And I am careful toward books that offer refuge to my ego or my bad conscience. A writer who is opposed to notions of value and instruction is telling you he or she does not want to have to display loyalty or insight or sensitivity—to prose or to people: that would limit his or her maneuverability; and someone who does not believe that loyalty or insight or sensitivity or meaning has any meaning is hardly worth knowing in books or on the page although such people are unavoidable in an active life.

The procedures of real reading, if I may call it that, are not essentially shrewd, although certain writers, Twain and Proust for instance, often do play to the practice of shrewdness in their readers.

But the disappearance from the immediate world of one's attention, that infidelity to one's alertness toward outside attack, and then the gullibility required for a prolonged act of attention to something not directly inferior to one's own methods and experiences, something that emanates from someone else, that and the risk of conversion, the certainty that if the book is good, one will take on ideas and theories, a sense of style, a sense of things different from those one had before—if you think of those, you can see the elements of middle-class leisure and freedom, or upper-class insolence and power, or lower-class rebelliousness and hiddenness and disloyalty to one's surroundings, that are required for real reading.

And you can also see what the real nature of literature is—it is a matter of one's attention being removed from the real world and regarding nature and the world verbally: it is a messy mathematics in its way; it is a kind of science dealing in images and language, and it has to be right in the things it says; it has to be right about things.

I learned very early that when you were infatuated with someone, you read the same books the other person read or you read the books that had shaped the other person or you committed an infidelity and read for yourself and it was the beginning of trouble. I think reading and writing are the most dangerous human things because they operate on and from that part of the mind in which judgments of reality are made; and because of the authority language has from when we learn to speak and use its power as a family matter, as an immediate matter, and from when we learn to read and see its modern, middle-class power as a public matter establishing our rank in the world.

When a book is technically uninteresting, when such a book is not a kind of comically enraged protest against the pretensions of false technique and ludicrously misconceived subject matter, it is bound to be a phony. The democratic subversion of objects, of techniques, can never without real dishonesty stray far from its ostensible purpose, which is the democratic necessity of making our lives interesting to us. Folk art is, inevitably, a kind of baby talk in relation to high art—and this is shaming, but so is much in life, including one's odor giving one's secrets away (showing one's nervousness or one's lechery), but it is better to do that than live messageless and without nerves or desire. The moral extravagance of reading—its spiritual element and its class element—is bound to reflect both an absence of humility and a new kind of humility and both in odd ways. Two of our most conceited writers, Gertrude Stein and Ernest Hemingway, overtly wrote baby talk. Nowadays the young like financial reporting as a window on the world, and television and the interview. They are pursuing fact in the plethora of baby talk, and they are trying to exercise judgment in the middle of the overenthusiastic marketing of trash.

American colleges have taught our intellectuals to read politically in order to enter and stay in a group or on a track. One reads skimmingly then, and one keeps placing the authority for what one reads outside oneself. But actually people cannot read in a two-souled way, shrewdly, and with a capacity to feel and learn. Learning involves fear and sometimes awe and just plain factually is not shrewd—it is supershrewd if you like, it is a very grand speculation indeed; and graduate school stuff won't open out into awe and discovery or recognition or personal knowledge of events but only onto academic hustling. I mean when you stop theorizing and think about what is really there. Do I need to go on? One of the primary rules of language is that there must be a good reason for the listener to attend to a second sentence after the first one; to supply a good reason is called "being interesting." Not to attend to the second sentence is called "not listening." The reasons to listen are always selfish, but that does not mean they are only selfish.

It is hard to listen. It is also hard to write well and to think. These ought not to be unfamiliar statements. This ought not to be news.

See you in the bookstore soon.

Suggestions for Discussion

1. Discuss the significance of Brodkey's title.

2. Explain Brodkey's belief that the United States is organized by "fashion in making money and spending money."

3. Discuss the difficulties a reader encounters in Brodkey's lengthy, complex, and energetic sentences.

Suggestions for Writing

1. Analyze the reading that you do on a regular basis.

2. Discuss Brodkey's observation that "shrewdness without good sense is hell unleashed."

◇◇◇◇

Loren Eiseley

The Hidden Teacher

Loren Eiseley (1907–1977) was an anthropologist and academic administrator at the University of Pennsylvania. His publications include *Darwin's Century* (1958), which won the National Phi Beta Kappa Science Award, *The Mind as Nature* (1962), *The Unexpected Universe* (1969), *The Invisible Pyramid* (1970), and his autobiography, *All the Strange Hours: The Excavation of a Life* (1975). In the following essay, he emphasizes the importance of continuing exploration and discovery.

The putting of formidable riddles did not arise with today's philosophers. In fact, there is a sense in which the experimental method of science might be said merely to have widened the area of man's homelessness. Over two thousand years ago, a man named Job, crouching in the Judean desert, was moved to challenge what he felt to be the injustice of his God. The voice in the whirlwind, in turn, volleyed pitiless questions upon the supplicant— questions that have, in truth, precisely the ring of modern science. For the Lord asked of Job by whose wisdom the hawk soars, and who had fathered the rain, or entered the storehouses of the snow.

A youth standing by, one Elihu, also played a role in this drama, for he ventured diffidently to his protesting elder that it was not true that God failed to manifest Himself. He may speak in one way or another, though men do not perceive it. In consequence of this remark perhaps it would be well, whatever our individual beliefs, to consider what may be called the hidden teacher, lest we become too much concerned with the formalities of only one aspect of the education by which we learn.

We think we learn from teachers, and we sometimes do. But the teachers are not always to be found in school or in great laboratories. Sometimes what we learn depends upon our own powers of insight. Moreover, our teachers may be hidden, even the greatest teacher. And it was the young man Elihu who observed that if the old are not always wise, neither can the teacher's way be ordered by the young whom he would teach.

For example, I once received an unexpected lesson from a spider.

It happened far away on a rainy morning in the West. I had come up a long gulch looking for fossils, and there, just at eye level, lurked a huge yellow-and-black orb spider, whose web was moored to the tall spears of buffalo grass at the edge of the arroyo. It was her universe, and her senses did not extend beyond the lines and spokes of the great wheel she inhabited. Her extended claws could feel every vibration throughout that delicate structure. She knew the tug of wind, the fall of a raindrop, the flutter of a trapped moth's wing. Down one spoke of the web ran a stout ribbon of gossamer on which she could hurry out to investigate her prey.

Curious, I took a pencil from my pocket and touched a strand of the web. Immediately there was a response. The web, plucked by its menacing occupant, began to vibrate until it was a blur. Anything that had brushed claw or wing against that amazing snare would be thoroughly entrapped. As the vibrations slowed, I could see the owner fingering her guidelines for signs of struggle. A pencil point was an intrusion into this universe for which no precedent existed. Spider was circumscribed by spider ideas; its universe was spider universe. All outside was irrational, extraneous, at best, raw material for spider. As I proceeded on my way along the gully, like a vast impossible shadow, I realized that in the world of spider I did not exist.

Moreover, I considered, as I tramped along, that to the phagocytes, the white blood cells, clambering even now with some kind of elementary intelligence amid the thin pipes and tubing of my body—creatures without whose ministrations I could not exist—the conscious "I" of which I was aware had no significance to these amoeboid beings. I was, instead, a kind of chemical web that brought meaningful messages to them, a natural environment seemingly immortal if they could have thought about it, since generations of them had lived and perished, and would continue to so live and die, in that odd fabric which contained my intelligence—a misty light that was beginning to seem floating and tenuous even to me.

I began to see that among the many universes in which the world of living creatures existed, some were large, some small, but that all, including man's, were in some way limited or finite. We were creatures of many different dimensions passing through each other's lives like ghosts through doors.

In the years since, my mind has many times returned to that far moment of encounter with the orb spider. A message has arisen only now from the misty shreds of that webbed universe. What was it that had so troubled me about the incident? Was it that spidery indifference to the human triumph?

If so, that triumph was very real and could not be denied. I saw, had many times seen, both mentally and in the seams of exposed strata, the long backward stretch of time whose recovery is one of the great feats of modern science. I saw the drifting cells of the early seas from which all life, including our own, has arisen. The salt of those ancient seas is in our blood, its lime is in our bones. Every time we walk along a beach some ancient urge disturbs us so that we find ourselves shedding shoes and garments, or scavenging among seaweed and whitened timbers like the homesick refugees of a long war.

And war it has been indeed—the long war of life against its inhospitable environment, a war that has lasted for perhaps three billion years. It began with strange chemicals seething under a sky lacking in oxygen; it was waged through long ages until the first green plants learned to harness the light of the nearest star, our sun. The human brain, so frail, so perishable, so full of inexhaustible dreams and hungers, burns by the power of the leaf.

The hurrying blood cells charged with oxygen carry more of that element to the human brain than to any other part of the body. A few moments' loss of vital air and the phenomenon we know as consciousness goes down into the black night of inorganic things. The human body is a magical vessel, but its life is linked with an element it cannot produce. Only the green plant knows the secret of transforming the light that comes to us across the far reaches of space. There is no better illustration of the intricacy of man's relationship with other living things.

The student of fossil life would be forced to tell us that if we take the past into consideration the vast majority of earth's creatures—perhaps over ninety per cent—have vanished. Forms that flourished for a far longer time than man has existed upon earth have become either extinct or so transformed that their descendants are scarcely recognizable. The specialized perish with the environment that created them, the tooth of the tiger fails at last, the lances of men strike down the last mammoth.

In three billion years of slow change and groping effort only one living creature has succeeded in escaping the trap of specialization that has led in time to so much death and wasted endeavor. It is man, but the word should be uttered softly, for his story is not yet done.

With the rise of the human brain, with the appearance of a creature whose upright body enabled two limbs to be freed for the exploration and manipulation of his environment, there had at last emerged a creature with a specialization—the brain—that, paradoxically, offered escape from specialization. Many animals driven into the nooks and crannies of nature have achieved momentary survival only at the cost of later extinction.

Was it this that troubled me and brought my mind back to a tiny universe among the grass-blades, a spider's universe concerned with spider thought?

Perhaps.

The mind that once visualized animals on a cave wall is now engaged in a vast ramification of itself through time and space. Man has broken through the boundaries that control all other life. I saw, at last, the reason for my recollection of that great spider on the arroyo's rim, fingering its universe against the sky.

The spider was a symbol of man in miniature. The wheel of the web brought the analogy home clearly. Man, too, lies at the heart of a web, a web extending through the starry reaches of sidereal space, as well as backward into the dark realm of pre-history. His great eye upon Mount Palomar looks into a distance of millions of light-years, his radio ear hears the whisper of even more remote galaxies, he peers through the electron miscroscope upon the minute particles of his own being. It is a web no creature of earth has ever spun before. Like the orb spider, man lies at the heart of it, listening. Knowledge has given him the memory of earth's history beyond the time of his emergence. Like the spider's claw, a part of him touches a world he will never enter in the flesh. Even now, one can see him reaching forward into time with new machines, computing, analyzing, until elements of the shadowy future will also compose part of the invisible web he fingers.

Yet still my spider lingers in memory against the sunset sky. Spider thoughts in a spider universe—sensitive to raindrop and moth flutter, nothing beyond, nothing allowed for the unexpected, the inserted pencil from the world outside.

Is man at heart any different from the spider, I wonder: man thoughts, as limited as spider thoughts, contemplating now the nearest start with the threat of bringing with him the fungus rot from earth, wars, violence, the burden of a population he refuses to control, cherishing again his dream of the Adamic Eden he had pursued and lost in the green forests of America. Now it beckons again like a mirage from beyond the moon. Let man spin his web, I thought further; it is his nature. But I considered also the work of the phagocytes swarming in the rivers of my body, the unresting cells in their mortal universe. What is it we are a part of that we do not see, as the spider was not gifted to discern my face, or my little probe into her world?

We are too content with our sensory extensions, with the fulfillment of that ice age mind that began its journey amidst the cold of vast tundras and that pauses only briefly before its leap into space. It is no longer enough to see as a man sees—even to the ends of the universe. It is not enough to hold nuclear energy in one's hand like a spear, as a man would hold it, or to see the lightning, or times past, or time to come, as a man would see it. If we continue to do this, the great brain—the human brain—will be only a new version of the old trap, and nature is full of traps for the beast that cannot learn.

It is not sufficient any longer to listen at the end of a wire to the rustlings of galaxies; it is not enough even to examine the great coil of DNA in which is coded the very alphabet of life. These are our extended perceptions. But beyond lies the great darkness of the ultimate Dreamer, who dreamed the light and the galaxies. Before act was, or substance existed, imagination grew in the dark. Man partakes of that ultimate wonder and creativeness. As we turn from the galaxies to the swarming cells of our own being, which toil for something, some entity beyond their grasp, let us remember man, the self-fabricator who came across an ice age to look into the mirrors and the magic of science. Surely he did not come to see himself or his wild visage only. He came because he is at heart a listener and a searcher for some transcendent realm beyond himself. This he has worshiped by many names, even in the dismal caves of his beginning. Man, the self-fabricator, is so by reason of gifts he had no part in devising—and so he searches as the single living cell in the beginning must have sought the ghostly creature it was to serve.

Suggestions for Discussion

1. Discuss the rhetorical importance of the fourth paragraph, which introduces the "lesson from a spider."

2. In what sense is the "spider a symbol of man in miniature"?

3. Explain Eiseley's belief that man is "at heart a listener and a searcher."

Suggestions for Writing

1. Use your observations of the conduct of another creature to make generalizations about human behavior.

2. Speculate on Eiseley's notion that we are "a part of that we do not see."

What Should Michael Do?

In the selection that follows, sixteen writers and editors for *The New Republic* offer advice to Michael C. Sloan, who asks, "What should I do with my life?"

Two weeks ago we published the following letter from Michael C. Sloan of Bloomington, Indiana:

> I am a 22-year-old college graduate with a degree in English Lit from a "major, private university." I have noted with alarm your recent disparaging articles on

both the law and investment banking professions. So I ask you, what should I do with my life? The Placement Center has been no help, and—sorry, Mr. Barnes—I don't look good in uniform. Your speedy reply would be appreciated.

Michael deserved an answer. We know nothing about him except what's in his letter. But if he's a typical graduate of a major private university, we assume he's reasonably smart, reasonably ambitious, reasonably idealistic, not excessively anything except perhaps over-schooled and undereducated. What should Michael do? Here is enough advice to make him sorry he asked.

You're probably not going to want to hear this, Michael. The fact that you read TNR suggests you're interested in journalism. Forget it. There are too many scribblers already, and journalism's bad for your mental hygiene. I have two ideas. If you're of a secular bent, why not put together a chain of honest, nongouging auto repair shops? People like to go to places they can trust. That's why they like McDonald's: you can trust a Big Mac to taste the same every time and be reasonably priced. If word got around that a car repair place was honest, it would make a mint. As ridiculous as it sounds, honesty can pay. If you're more spiritually inclined, go to divinity school and become a minister. I'm not kidding. I might do this myself if I were in your shoes. The country is crawling with preachers who have a political agenda and modernist types who peddle a pinched, relativistic faith that inspires no one. What's needed are pastors (not just men, either) who haven't diluted their Christianity and don't have a political spiel. I know a few like this, and they are bright lights amid the darkness. And they truly help people.

FRED BARNES

That stretch of time from graduation day to day one of the first job of the rest of your life seems more precious in hindsight. Most people I know wish they had prolonged it. Almost everyone—those who followed it and, more likely, those who didn't—will provide the same excellent advice for the short term: don't be a lawyer, don't be an investment banker, and don't buy any heavy furniture. Go West or go East for a few months, or go even further in either direction for a year or so. Teach high school in a foreign country. Occasionally gaze out the window and ponder your real future, but keep these sessions to ten minutes per day during the first three months. There will still be some real jobs when you get back, and they may be better than the ones that were there just after graduation.

At some point you'll probably have to think about coming home. Take notes: examine the person.

JAMIE BAYLIS

Leave college.

1. Live at home and work for your hometown newspaper, or cut grass, or pump gas, but save money.

2. Travel on your savings. Concentrate on finding the city or town that pleases you most, especially the people in it.

3. Move to that city. Find a product or service in that place you can be enthusiastic about, whether it be a paper, a widget, a cause, a restaurant— whatever. Get a job representing that product—i.e., sales.

4. Take computer courses at night and pursue a hobby that you enjoy, such as flying, stamp collecting, or rare books.

5. Start a newsletter about your hobby using the computer to do all of the editing, layout, list mailing, etc. Sell it to other enthusiasts you encounter at fairs, through electronic bulletin boards, etc. If it takes off, do it full-time. Live happily ever after.

JEFFREY DEARTH

1. If you have to ask the price, you can't afford it, and if you have to ask what you should do, perhaps no advice is worth giving.

2. The possibilities in the letter appear to be limited to the professions. There is commerce—business—"trade." Liberal arts graduates are wanted in these, and often do well in them. Firms are looking for liberal arts graduates more and more, because they can handle more than one idea at the same time.

3. Behind the letter, I think, lurks a quite common attitude in the middle-class young now, that a career will be rewarding only if it is "literary" or "artistic," even in a marginal way. This is a trap. Not many are "literary" or "artistic" enough to do well.

4. Stop asking, and go out, look, and start doing. Almost any job away from academia will do. Twenty-two is young. You don't need to start now a career you'll follow for the rest of your life.

HENRY FAIRLIE

Did you read our editorial last week, "Teachers Go Pro"? Go spend a few years teaching or coaching or advising in a school somewhere. True, there are some big obstacles. Due to certification requirements, you'll have a hard time finding a public school that will take you. (New Jersey is one state that will.) But there are also good reasons to consider starting out as a teacher.

You know the many altruistic ones. There is also a half-selfish one that is often overlooked: time. A conscientious teacher's day is definitely as long as, or longer than, an average eight-hour workday. But thanks to summer vacations, you do have a quarter of a year to pursue other interests you may have and talents you may hope you have. Meanwhile your classmates in management intern programs, etc., never have a weekend, let alone a summer, to look up from their labors. Such an invitation to broad-mindedness is good for you, whatever you end up doing in life—and doing more than one thing isn't a bad idea at all. It's also good for our educational system, which can always use more energetic, curious teachers.

The salaries may not be great, but look at it this way. Investment bankers are addicted to their megabucks by age 25 and can't imagine trying some other line of work because it would mean a pay cut. In the freedom of your youthful penury, you can take whatever wild leap you want into another field and count on moving up. And who knows, thanks to the recent excellence-in-education drive, the pay scale for teachers may even improve in time to do you some good.

ANN HULBERT

First, don't panic. There's no need to march into a credentialed profession just yet. If you kick around for a few years, and then decide you want to be a doctor, lawyer, or MBA—hey, at least you gave yourself a chance. Second: even if you find yourself in law school, remember: *that doesn't mean you have to become a lawyer!* Third: don't just chase after the profession that happens to be paying the biggest bucks at the moment (currently investment banking). Such market signals often turn out to be wrong, for one thing, so this year's hot ticket is next year's labor glut. And $100,000 is no compensation for a job you don't like (well, not enough compensation anyway).

Charles Peters, my own mentor, always tells people to "do what you love to do and do best." Good advice. But what if what you love to do is not what you do best? What if you don't know what you love to do? Well, freedom to try and fail really is the distinct virtue of American capitalism. We pay a price for it—lack of the full measure of welfare state security of more "progressive" democracies. You might as well take advantage of it. The best way to do this is in some sort of entrepreneurial venture where you can create jobs, fill a need, and make a killing, too. But that takes special glands. Even as an employee, though, you can serve your country. What American needs now are smart people to rebuild our industry so we don't cede that whole economic sector to the Japanese and Southeast Asians.

We may not have souls, but it's useful when making job decisions to pretend that we do. And a job that costs you yours, be it lobbying or polluting or cheating, isn't worth it, even if there's nobody keeping score but you. Most of my friends who have sold out are now either trapped or so filled with concealed self-loathing that their lives are permanently distorted. Or so I like to imagine.

That's one advantage to being your own boss—you have the freedom *not* to do things, which employees don't have. But even employees usually have more leverage than they think, if they're careful to preserve their ability to walk out. Hence my final advice: if you really don't like it, it's O.K. to quit. Got me where I am today.

P.S. Mom, send another check.

MICKEY KAUS

Believe it or not, Michael, you should go into investment banking after all. Here's why. If you're like most talented people, you're torn between doing good and making good, the hunger for excitement and the hunger for security, the desire to go for it and the fear of failure. I'm not about to tell you that the latter emotions are ignoble. They aren't. Your problem is that, for rational economic reasons, the most morally and intellectually satisfying careers don't pay as well, except in "psychic income." Furthermore, many of the most exciting options are also the riskiest. If you knew for sure that you were a great poet, you wouldn't mind living like a poet. But who can be sure? Better a mediocre lawyer than a mediocre poet.

Many people think they aren't greedy, only to discover too late that they are. Or they take the big gamble, fail, and sulk. Washington is full of lobbyists and cynics and cynical lobbyists who used to be idealistic. New York has plenty of embittered middle-aged poets and actors.

The absurd incomes being "earned" [sic] by young investment bankers offer a chance to escape from this dilemma by reversing the usual pattern. Get your greed trip out of the way early. Then quit after a few years and spend the rest of your life doing good or having fun. Nothing bolsters idealism (or so I would imagine) like the knowledge that nothing you say or do will have any drastic effect on your own life-style. Or you can be a painter after all, and it doesn't matter if you're a lousy one. (In fact, if you've done really well early on, you'll be treated like a good painter whether you are one or not.)

The peril of this course is obvious: Will you really quit when you've socked away enough to guarantee a comfortable middle-class existence? Or will "enough" be an ever-receding concept, just beyond the next couple of deals? We have confidence in you, Michael. Don't let us down.

MICHAEL KINSLEY

Even though my field is politics, I think the area where you can advance society's interests is scientific and medical research. You don't have to believe that technology is a panacea to realize that scientific advances have dramatically improved the quality of life in America over the past few decades. A good second option is to use any entrepreneurial talent you have to figure out how to distribute the benefits of research equitably. But if you don't have a scientific or business-oriented bone in your body, then journalism is an honorable profession.

MORTON KONDRACKE

Try medicine. Even though you're a literature major, you can fulfill the prerequisites for med school in only one year. If you're moderately idealistic, practice psychiatry with sick people, say, in a state mental hospital. If you're extremely idealistic, join Doctors Without Frontiers or be a medic in a guerrilla war of your choice (Angola, El Salvador, Nicaragua: pick one). And even if you spend your days straightening noses in Scarsdale, you'll still be doing good.

CHARLES KRAUTHAMMER

Michael, investigative reporting—much out of style yet much needed—is your ticket. No experience is necessary. The pay isn't great, fame is unlikely, and the field is wide open, especially in Washington. Many mainstream journalists, in their eagerness to subscribe to the conventional wisdom that investigative reporting is dead, refuse to look into all sorts of interesting misdeeds. Other investigative reporters get bogged down in petty scandals about whether Senator Smith reported his two pet rabbits on his 1979 financial disclosure forms. Interesting investigative stories that explain how our government and economy actually work—about right-wing pork barrels, big-city political machines, new methods of political financing, and banks in trouble— just aren't being done. It takes only a reasonably intelligent, curious, and persistent person to begin to figure out what's going on and to tell the world about it. You're the guy.

JEFFERSON MORLEY

"Love and work," said Freud, are what make the good life. But the idea that we must love our work is a post-Freudian expectation. Unfortunately it's not enough to love your work: other people must love you for it. This is one reason why you are so mystified about what you should do with yourself. If you take the idealistic path, the cynics will say that you are from another era—an era which, in its deluded hopes, exacerbated our problems. If you go the way of the fleshpots, which on some readings is anything but the Peace Corps, there will always be someone with moral authority who will point the accusing finger and stigmatize: "yuppie." "If I am only for myself," as Rabbi Hillel once put it, "what am I?" But since there are always two positions, "If I am not for myself, who will be?"

There is a middle way: the life of art. Less and less is this the solitary life. The number of consumers for its products increases so fast that the uncertainty of success is, at the present moment, not greater in the arts than in other fields. And even in the one art, poetry, that has no body of consumers, its practitioners don't starve, as they used to. They teach. And get foundation grants, just like other writers and painters, sculptors, musicians, and filmmakers do. Still, to choose to be an artist is not to be moved by the pecuniary aspirations of the investment banker—though there are some who succeed beyond the wildest dreams of an investment banker. There is, of course, the objection that one doesn't choose to be an artist. One is or one isn't. One won't find this out, however, until the market for bad art declines, like the market for bad widgets. Unless the market for bad art won't decline, which is a distinct possibility.

MARTIN PERETZ

Look into yourself. Focus on your values, on what brings you satisfaction and gives you meaning. If you find nothing, consider plastics.

ROBERT B. REICH

Michael, your "degree in English Lit from a 'major, private university'" should have warned you off writing to a magazine for vocational advice, unless it be *Cosmopolitan*.

In our society there are other places to hear oracular voices. There are ladies in bandannas and dirndl skirts behind the dusty windows of run-down storefronts who are reputed to be good at this kind of work. Astrology has much to be said on its behalf. And those who attend Quaker meetings have on occasion heard the mighty voice from within speaking words of penetrating insight. Be warned, however, against guidance counselors or giving your money to the members of any profession whose name begins with a psy or a soc. Above all, if, in the future, you never again seek the advice of a collection of hacks and hackettes grown wizened staring at their computer terminals, you will die old, rich, respected by your neighbors, and the great-grandfather of many children.

NICHOLAS VON HOFFMAN

Forget everyone's dreary advice about career paths and corporate ladders. Why not experiment for the next few years? Liberal arts graduates have learned a little about thinking and writing and arguing, but don't know much about life outside school walls. Here's one approach.

Start off in California, with a low-level job in Silicon Valley, where you can pick up the essentials of the computer revolution. After you've had enough, head for Detroit and work in the auto industry for a while. If jobs are scarce, think about doing some volunteer work—say, at one of the churches that runs a shelter for the homeless. When you run out of savings, there's always the Sunbelt or rural America. You could try working on an oil rig or as a coal miner; as a farm hand or a cook in a roadside diner. Then move on to New York (perhaps as an assistant in an advertising agency or a publishing firm) or to Washington (as an aide on Capitol Hill).

By now you'll be three to five years out of school. You'll know how to program a computer, join a cause, brand a bull, make a good milk shake, and survive office politics. If you're still undecided about a career, you can always start up an employment agency for college graduates who don't know what to do with themselves. You'll make a killing.

DOROTHY WICKENDEN

Having been disabused of a career in law and a career in investment banking, Michael, you wonder whether there is a career in anything else. Your question is more confirmation of how much the militant materialism of present-day America has intimidated the imagination of its young people. After all, law and banking were *all* we ruled out. Of course money, power, and influence are certainly some things you could do with your life. And with these things, of course, you could also do good works. (Though "idealism" has a way of not surviving business school.) If you believe that your talents lie that way, I'd say go that way, directly. But first examine your talents carefully, to discover whether there are more primary contributions that you can make and more primary rewards that you can reap. Can you write? Can you dance? Can you see the end of a laboratory experiment in its beginning? Can you find things in paintings or poems that others cannot? Can you serve a parish? If you can do any of these things, it would be a shame to chase paper instead. (If these things disappoint you or if you disappoint them, you can chase paper later.) Such a self-examination, however, takes time. Above all, it takes experience. Since you don't feel a calling, I suggest that you exploit your state of suspension and head out toward the world. In an earlier era I might have recommended the Peace Corps. (Not least because "idealism" had a way of not surviving it, too.) These days I'd recommend a hardworking, wakeful sojourn in a foreign land. There you will be taught by strangeness about yourself and about things outside yourself. A more intelligent decision about your life is sure to result. I understand that this is demanding a late start, and a good deal of socioeconomic courage. But it is sad to watch people rush to surrender the fearlessness of their youth to the achievements and anxieties of a precocious middle age. "The institutions" aren't going away.

LEON WIESELTIER

What about graduate school? People have been frightened away from the life of the mind for almost two decades now by the legendary impossibility of finding a job as a university professor. But by the early 1990s—when you'll be getting your doctorate—universities will have more tenured positions open than at any time since the early 1960s, so there's a pretty good chance that you can actually get tenure somewhere. Since you live in Bloomington,

I take it that you don't have a fear of the Midwest (as many East Coast snobs do), so even if you do wind up in "America's heartland," you won't be too unhappy.

Jonathan Zasloff

Suggestions for Discussion

1. Discuss the range of opinions offered to Michael.

2. Discuss the humor in some of the responses.

3. In your opinion, is Michael offered any bad advice?

Suggestions for Writing

1. What advice can you offer Michael?

2. Write about what you plan to do with your own life.

Fiction

John Cheever

Expelled

John Cheever (1912–1982) was born in Massachusetts where he was expelled from a prep school, and thereby propelled into a literary career. He devoted himself primarily to writing novels and stories, and was published often in *The New Yorker*. He won the Pulitzer Prize in 1979 for the collection *The Stories of John Cheever*. His best known novels of suburban life are *The Wapshot Chronicle* (1957) and *The Wapshot Scandal* (1964). The prep school in "Expelled," which Cheever wrote at seventeen, exists to prepare the sons of the middle class for admission into acceptable Eastern colleges with little concern for aesthetic, moral, or intellectual values.

It didn't come all at once. It took a very long time. First I had a skirmish with the English department and then all the other departments. Pretty soon something had to be done. The first signs were cordialities on the part of the headmaster. He was never nice to anybody unless he was a football star, or hadn't paid his tuition, or was going to be expelled. That's how I knew.

He called me down to his office with the carved chairs arranged in a semicircle and the brocade curtains resting against the vacant windows. All about him were pictures of people who had got scholarships at Harvard. He asked me to sit down.

"Well, Charles," he said, "some of the teachers say you aren't getting very good marks."

"Yes," I said, "that's true." I didn't care about the marks.

"But Charles," he said, "you know the scholastic standard of this school is very high and we have to drop people when their work becomes unsatisfactory." I told him I knew that also. Then he said a lot of things about the traditions, and the elms, and the magnificent military heritage from our West Point founder.

It was very nice outside of his room. He had his window pushed open halfway and one could see the lawns pulling down to the road behind the trees and the bushes. The gravy-colored curtains were too heavy to move about in the wind, but some papers shifted around on his desk. In a little while I got up and walked out. He turned and started to work again. I went back to my next class.

The next day was very brilliant and the peach branches were full against the dry sky. I could hear people talking and a phonograph playing. The sounds came through the peach blossoms and crossed the room. I lay in bed and thought about a great many things. My dreams had been thick. I remembered two converging hills, some dry apple trees, and a broken blue egg cup. That is all I could remember.

I put on knickers and a soft sweater and headed toward school. My hands shook on the wheel. I was like that all over.

Through the cloudy trees I could see the protrusion of the new tower. It was going to be a beautiful new tower and it was going to cost a great deal of money. Some thought of buying new books for the library instead of putting up a tower, but no one would see the books. People would be able to see the tower five miles off when the leaves were off the trees. It would be done by fall.

When I went into the building the headmaster's secretary was standing in the corridor. She was a nice sort of person with brown funnels of hair furrowed about a round head. She smiled. I guess she must have known.

The Colonel

Every morning we went up into the black chapel. The brisk headmaster was there. Sometimes he had a member of the faculty with him. Sometimes it was a stranger.

He introduced the stranger, whose speech was always the same. In the spring life is like a baseball game. In the fall it is like football. That is what the speaker always said.

The hall is damp and ugly with skylights that rattle in the rain. The seats are hard and you have to hold a hymnbook in your lap. The hymnbook often slips off and that is embarrassing.

On Memorial Day they have the best speaker. They have a mayor or a Governor. Sometimes they have a Governor's second. There is very little preference.

The Governor will tell us what a magnificent country we have. He will tell us to beware of the Red menace. He will want to tell us that the goddam foreigners should have gone home a hell of a long time ago. That they should have stayed in their own goddam countries if they didn't like ours. He will not dare say this though.

If they have a mayor the speech will be longer. He will tell us that our country is beautiful and young and strong. That the War is over, but that if there is another war we must fight. He will tell us that war is a masculine trait that has brought present civilization to its fine condition. Then he will leave us and help stout women place lilacs on graves. He will tell them the same thing.

One Memorial Day they could not get a Governor or a mayor. There was a colonel in the same village who had been to war and who had a chest thick with medals. They asked him to speak. Of course he said he would like to speak.

He was a thin colonel with a soft nose that rested quietly on his face. He was nervous and pushed his wedding ring about his thin finger. When he was introduced he looked at the audience sitting in the uncomfortable chairs. There was silence and the dropping of hymnbooks like the water spouts in the aftermath of a heavy rain.

He spoke softly and quickly. He spoke of war and what he had seen. Then he had to stop. He stopped and looked at the boys. They were staring at their boots. He thought of the empty rooms in the other buildings. He thought of the rectangles of empty desks. He thought of the curtains on the stage and the four Windsor chairs behind him. Then he started to speak again.

He spoke as quickly as he could. He said war was bad. He said that there would never be another war. That he himself should stop it if he could. He swore. He looked at the young faces. They were all very clean. The boys' knees were crossed and their soft pants hung loosely. He thought of the empty desks and began to whimper.

The people sat very still. Some of them felt tight as though they wanted to giggle. Everybody looked serious as the clock struck. It was time for another class.

People began to talk about the colonel after lunch. They looked behind them. They were afraid he might hear them.

It took the school several weeks to get over all this. Nobody said anything, but the colonel was never asked again. If they could not get a Governor or a mayor they could get someone besides a colonel. They made sure of that.

Margaret Courtwright

Margaret Courtwright was very nice. She was slightly bald and pulled her pressed hair down across her forehead. People said that she was the best English teacher in this part of the country, and when boys came back from Harvard they thanked her for the preparation she had given them. She did not like Edgar Guest, but she did like Carl Sandburg. She couldn't seem to understand the similarity. When I told her people laughed at Galsworthy she said that people used to laugh at Wordsworth. She did not believe people were still laughing at Wordsworth. That was what made her so nice.

She came from the West a long time ago. She taught school for so long that people ceased to consider her age. After having seen twenty-seven performances of "Hamlet" and after having taught it for sixteen years, she became a sort of immortal. Her interpretation was the one accepted on college-board papers. That helped everyone a great deal. No one had to get a new interpretation.

When she asked me for tea I sat in a walnut armchair with grapes carved on the head and traced and retraced the arms on the tea caddy. One time I read her one of my plays. She thought it was wonderful. She thought it was wonderful because she did not understand it and because it took two hours to read. When I had finished, she said, "You know that thing just took right hold of me. Really it just swept me right along. I think it's fine that you like to write. I once had a Japanese pupil who liked to write. He was an awfully nice chap until one summer he went down to Provincetown. When he came back he was saying that he could express a complete abstraction. Fancy . . . a complete abstraction. Well, I wouldn't hear of it and told him how absurd it all was and tried to start him off with Galsworthy again, but I guess he had gone just too far. In a little while he left for New York and then Paris. It was really too bad. One summer in Provincetown just ruined him. His marks fell down . . . he cut classes to go to symphony. . . ." She went into the kitchen and got a tray of tarts.

The pastries were flaky and covered with a white coating that made them shine in the dead sunlight. I watched the red filling burst the thin shells and stain the triangles of bright damask. The tarts were good. I ate most of them.

She was afraid I would go the way of her Japanese pupil. She doubted anyone who disagreed with Heine on Shakespeare and Croce on expression.

One day she called me into her antiseptic office and spoke to me of reading Joyce. "You know, Charles," she said, "this sex reality can be quite as absurd as a hypercritical regard for such subjects. You know that, don't you? Of course, you do." Then she went out of the room. She had straight ankles and wore a gold band peppered with diamond chips on her ring finger. She seemed incapable of carrying the weight of the folds in her clothing. Her skirt was askew, either too long in front or hitching up on the side. Always one thing or the other.

When I left school she did not like it. She was afraid I might go too near Provincetown. She wished me good luck and moved the blotter back and forth on her desk. Then she returned to teaching "Hamlet."

Late in February Laura Driscoll got fired for telling her history pupils that Sacco and Vanzetti were innocent. In her farewell appearance the headmaster told everyone how sorry he was that she was going and made it all quite convincing. Then Laura stood up, told the headmaster that he was a damned liar, and waving her fan-spread fingers called the school a hell of a dump where everyone got into a rut.

Miss Courtwright sat closely in her chair and knew it was true. She didn't mind much. Professor Rogers with his anti-feminization movement bothered her a little, too. But she knew that she had been teaching school for a long time now and no movement was going to put her out of a job overnight— what with all the boys she had smuggled into Harvard and sixteen years of "Hamlet."

Laura Driscoll

History classes are always dead. This follows quite logically, for history is a dead subject. It has not the death of dead fruit or dead textiles or dead light. It has a different death. There is not the timeless quality of death about it. It is dead like scenery in the opera. It is on cracked canvas and the paint has faded and peeled and the lights are too bright. It is dead like old water in a zinc bathtub.

"We are going to study ancient history this year," the teacher will tell the pupils. "Yes, ancient history will be our field.

"Now of course, this class is not a class of children any longer. I expect the discipline to be the discipline of well-bred young people. We shall not have to waste any time on the scolding of younger children. No. We shall just be able to spend all our time on ancient history.

"Now about questions. I shall answer questions if they are important. If I do not think them important I shall not answer them, for the year is short, and we must cover a lot of ground in a short time. That is, if we all cooperate and behave and not ask too many questions we shall cover the subject and have enough time at the end of the year for review.

"You may be interested in the fact that a large percentage of this class was certified last year. I should like to have a larger number this year. Just think, boys: wouldn't it be fine if a very large number—a number larger than last year—was certified? Wouldn't that be fine? Well, there's no reason why we can't do it if we all cooperate and behave and don't ask too many questions.

"You must remember that I have twelve people to worry about and that you have only one. If each person will take care of his own work and pass in his notebook on time it will save me a lot of trouble. Time and trouble mean whether you get into college or not, and I want you all to get into college.

"If you will take care of your own little duties, doing what is assigned to you and doing it well, we shall all get along fine. You are a brilliant-looking group of young people, and I want to have you all certified. I want to get you into college with as little trouble as possible.

"Now about the books. . . ."

I do not know how long history classes have been like this. One time or another I suppose history was alive. That was before it died its horrible fly-dappled unquivering death.

Everyone seems to know that history is dead. No one is alarmed. The pupils and the teachers love dead history. They do not like it when it is alive. When Laura Driscoll dragged history into the classroom, squirming and smelling of something bitter, they fired Laura and strangled the history. It was too tumultuous. Too turbulent.

In history one's intellect is used for mechanical speculation on a probable century or background. One's memory is applied to a list of dead dates and names. When one begins to apply one's intellect to the mental scope of the period, to the emotional development of its inhabitants, one becomes dangerous. Laura Driscoll was terribly dangerous. That's why Laura was never a good history teacher.

She was not the first history teacher I had ever had. She is not the last I will have. But she is the only teacher I have ever had who could feel history with an emotional vibrance—or, if the person was too oblique, with a poetic understanding. She was five feet four inches tall, brown-haired, and bent-legged from horseback riding. All the boys thought Laura Driscoll was a swell teacher.

She was the only history teacher I have ever seen who was often ecstatical. She would stand by the boards and shout out her discoveries on the Egyptian cultures. She made the gargoylic churnings of Chartres in a heavy rain present an applicable meaning. She taught history as an interminable flood of events viewed through the distortion of our own immediacy. She taught history in the broad-handed rhythms of Hauptmann's drama, in the static melancholy of Egypt moving before its own shadow down the long sand, in the fluted symmetry of the Doric culture. She taught history as a hypothesis from which we could extract the evaluation of our own lives.

She was the only teacher who realized that, coming from the West, she had little business to be teaching these children of New England.

"I do not know what your reaction to the sea is," she would say. "For I have come from a land where there is no sea. My elements are the fields, the sun, the plastic cadence of the clouds and the cloudlessness. You have been brought up by the sea. You have been coached in the cadence of the breakers and the strength of the wind.

"My emotional viewpoints will differ from yours. Do not let me impose my perceptions upon you."

However, the college-board people didn't care about Chartres as long as you knew the date. They didn't care whether history was looked at from the mountains or the sea. Laura spent too much time on such trivia and all of her pupils didn't get into Harvard. In fact, very few of her pupils got into Harvard, and this didn't speak well for her.

While the other members of the faculty chattered over Hepplewhite legs and Duncan Phyfe embellishments, Laura was before five-handed Siva or the sexless compassion glorious in its faded polychrome. Laura didn't think much of America. Laura made this obvious and the faculty heard about it. The faculty all thought America was beautiful. They didn't like people to disagree.

However, the consummation did not occur until late in February. It was cold and clear and the snow was deep. Outside the windows there was the enormous roaring of broken ice. It was late in February that Laura Driscoll said Sacco and Vanzetti were undeserving of their treatment.

This got everyone all up in the air. Even the headmaster was disconcerted.

The faculty met.

The parents wrote letters.

Laura Driscoll was fired.

"Miss Driscoll," said the headmaster during her last chapel at the school, "has found it necessary to return to the West. In the few months that we have had her with us, she has been a staunch friend of the academy, a woman whom we all admire and love and who, we are sure, loves and admires the academy and its elms as we do. We are all sorry Miss Driscoll is leaving us. . . . ."

Then Laura got up, called him a damned liar, swore down the length of the platform and walked out of the building.

No one ever saw Laura Driscoll again. By the way everyone talked, no one wanted to. That was all late in February. By March the school was quiet again. The new history teacher taught dates. Everyone carefully forgot about Laura Driscoll.

"She was a nice girl," said the headmaster, "but she really wasn't made for teaching history. . . . No, she really wasn't a born history teacher."

Five Months Later

The spring of five months ago was the most beautiful spring I have ever lived in. The year before I had not known all about the trees and the heavy peach blossoms and the tea-colored brooks that shook down over the brown rocks. Five months ago it was spring and I was in school.

In school the white limbs beyond the study hall shook out a greenness, and the tennis courts became white and scalding. The air was empty and hard, and the vacant wind dragged shadows over the road. I knew all this only from the classrooms.

I knew about the trees from the window frames. I knew the rain only from the sounds on the roof. I was tired of seeing spring with walls and awnings to intercept the sweet sun and the hard fruit. I wanted to go outdoors and see the spring. I wanted to feel and taste the air and be among the shadows. That is perhaps why I left school.

In the spring I was glad to leave school. Everything outside was elegant and savage and fleshy. Everything inside was slow and cool and vacant. It seemed a shame to stay inside.

But in a little while the spring went. I was left outside and there was no spring. I did not want to go in again. I would not have gone in again for anything. I was sorry, but I was not sorry over the fact that I had gone out. I was sorry that the outside and the inside could not have been open to one another. I was sorry that there were roofs on the classrooms and trousers on the legs of the instructors to insulate their contacts. I was not sorry that I had left school. I was sorry that I left for the reasons that I did.

If I had left because I had to go to work or because I was sick it would not have been so bad. Leaving because you are angry and frustrated is different. It is not a good thing to do. It is bad for everyone.

Of course it was not the fault of the school. The headmaster and faculty were doing what they were supposed to do. It was just a preparatory school trying to please the colleges. A school that was doing everything the colleges asked it to do.

It was not the fault of the school at all. It was the fault of the system—the noneducational system, the college-preparatory system. That was what made the school so useless.

As a college-preparatory school it was a fine school. In five years they could make raw material look like college material. They could clothe it and breed it and make it say the right things when the colleges asked it to talk. That was its duty.

They weren't prepared to educate anybody. They were members of a college-preparatory system. No one around there wanted to be educated. No sir.

They presented the subjects the colleges required. They had math, English, history, languages, and music. They once had had an art department but it had been dropped. "We have enough to do," said the headmaster, "just to get all these people into college without trying to teach them art. Yes sir, we have quite enough to do as it is."

Of course there were literary appreciation and art appreciation and musical appreciation, but they didn't count for much. If you are young, there is very little in Thackeray that is parallel to your own world. Van Dyke's "Abbé Scaglia" and the fretwork of Mozart quartets are not for the focus of your ears and eyes. All the literature and art that holds a similarity to your life is forgotten. Some of it is even forbidden.

Our country is the best country in the world. We are swimming in prosperity and our President is the best president in the world. We have larger apples and better cotton and faster and more beautiful machines. This makes us the greatest country in the world. Unemployment is a myth. Dissatisfaction is a fable. In preparatory school America is beautiful. It is the gem of the ocean and it is too bad. It is bad because people believe it all. Because they become indifferent. Because they marry and reproduce and vote and they know nothing. Because the tempered newspaper keeps its eyes ceilingwards and does not see the dirty floor. Because all they know is the tempered newspaper.

But I will not say any more. I do not stand in a place where I can talk.

And now it is August. The orchards are stinking ripe. The tea-colored brooks run beneath the rocks. There is sediment on the stone and no wind in the willows. Everyone is preparing to go back to school. I have no school to go back to.

I am not sorry. I am not at all glad.

It is strange to be so very young and to have no place to report to at nine o'clock. That is what education has always been. It has been laced curtseys and perfumed punctualities.

But now it is nothing. It is symmetric with my life. I am lost in it. That is why I am not standing in a place where I can talk.

The school windows are being washed. The floors are thick with fresh oil.

Soon it will be time for the snow and the symphonies. It will be time for Brahms and the great dry winds.

Suggestions for Discussion

1. Why is Charles expelled from his school? How does he respond to his expulsion?

2. Explain the form the story takes as a series of short portraits. How do these portraits serve to express Charles's view of the school?

3. Compare Margaret Courtwright with Laura Driscoll. Which was the better teacher? Why?

4. How did the Colonel embarrass the school on Memorial Day? What is Charles's reaction to him? What does his reaction reveal about Charles?

5. Explain the function of the last section of the story.

Suggestion for Writing

What do you believe to be the primary purpose of education? Is it different from that described in the story? What do you expect from an education? Write an essay in which you explain your ideas.

Max Shulman

Love Is a Fallacy

Max Shulman (b. 1919) is the author of stories and novels as well as films and musical comedies. His works include *Barefoot Boy with Cheek* (1943), *Rally Round the Flag, Boys* (1957), and the TV series "Dobie Gillis." His amusing short story uses the classification of logical fallacies to document an ill-fated love affair.

Cool was I and logical. Keen, calculating, perspicacious, acute and astute—I was all of these. My brain was as powerful as a dynamo, as precise as a chemist's scales, as penetrating as a scalpel. And—think of it—I was only eighteen.

It is not often that one so young has such a giant intellect. Take, for example, Petey Burch, my roommate at the University of Minnesota. Same age, same background, but dumb as an ox. A nice enough fellow, you understand, but nothing upstairs. Emotional type. Unstable. Impressionable. Worst of all, a faddist. Fads, I submit, are the very negation of reason. To be swept up in every new craze that comes along, to surrender yourself to idiocy just because everybody else is doing it—this, to me, is the acme of mindlessness. Not, however, to Petey.

One afternoon I found Petey lying on his bed with an expression of such distress on his face that I immediately diagnosed appendicitis. "Don't move," I said. "Don't take a laxative. I'll get a doctor."

"Raccoon," he mumbled thickly.

"Raccoon?" I said, pausing in my flight.

"I want a raccoon coat," he wailed.

I perceived that his trouble was not physical, but mental. "Why do you want a raccoon coat?"

"I should have known it," he cried, pounding his temples. "I should have known they'd come back when the Charleston came back. Like a fool I spent all my money for textbooks, and now I can't get a raccoon coat."

"Can you mean," I said incredulously, "that people are actually wearing raccoon coats again?"

"All the Big Men on Campus are wearing them. Where've you been?"

"In the library," I said, naming a place not frequented by Big Men on Campus.

He leaped from the bed and paced the room. "I've got to have a raccoon coat," he said passionately. "I've got to!"

"Petey, why? Look at it rationally. Raccoon coats are unsanitary. They shed. They smell bad. They weigh too much. They're unsightly. They—"

"You don't understand," he interrupted impatiently. "It's the thing to do. Don't you want to be in the swim?"

"No," I said truthfully.

"Well, I do," he declared. "I'd give anything for a raccoon coat. Anything!"

My brain, that precision instrument, slipped into high gear. "Anything?" I asked, looking at him narrowly.

"Anything," he affirmed in ringing tones.

I stroked my chin thoughtfully. It so happened that I knew where to get my hands on a raccoon coat. My father had had one in his undergraduate days; it lay now in a trunk in the attic back home. It also happened that Petey had something I wanted. He didn't *have* it exactly, but at least he had first rights on it. I refer to his girl, Polly Espy.

I had long coveted Polly Espy. Let me emphasize that my desire for this young woman was not emotional in nature. She was, to be sure, a girl who excited the emotions, but I was not one to let my heart rule my head. I wanted Polly for a shrewdly calculated, entirely cerebral reason.

I was a freshman in law school. In a few years I would be out in practice. I was well aware of the importance of the right kind of wife in furthering a lawyer's career. The successful lawyers I had observed were, almost without exception, married to beautiful, gracious, intelligent women. With one omission, Polly fitted these specifications perfectly.

Beautiful she was. She was not yet of pin-up proportions, but I felt sure that time would supply the lack. She already had the makings.

Gracious she was. By gracious I mean full of graces. She had an erectness of carriage, an ease of bearing, a poise that clearly indicated the best of breeding. At table her manners were exquisite. I had seen her at the Kozy Kampus Korner eating the specialty of the house—a sandwich that contained scraps of pot roast, gravy, chopped nuts, and a dipper of sauerkraut—without even getting her fingers moist.

Intelligent she was not. In fact, she veered in the opposite direction. But I believed that under my guidance she would smarten up. At any rate, it was worth a try. It is, after all, easier to make a beautiful dumb girl smart than to make an ugly smart girl beautiful.

"Petey," I said, "are you in love with Polly Espy?"

"I think she's a keen kid," he replied, "but I don't know if you'd call it love. Why?"

"Do you," I asked, "have any kind of formal arrangement with her? I mean are you going steady or anything like that?"

"No. We see each other quite a bit, but we both have other dates. Why?"

"Is there," I asked, "any other man for whom she has a particular fondness?"

"Not that I know of. Why?"

I nodded with satisfaction. "In other words, if you were out of the picture, the field would be open. Is that right?"

"I guess so. What are you getting at?"

"Nothing, nothing," I said innocently, and took my suitcase out of the closet.

"Where are you going?" asked Petey.

"Home for the weekend." I threw a few things into the bag.

"Listen," he said, clutching my arm eagerly, "while you're home, you couldn't get some money from your old man, could you, and lend it to me so I can buy a raccoon coat?"

"I may do better than that," I said with a mysterious wink and closed my bag and left.

"Look," I said to Petey when I got back Monday morning. I threw open the suitcase and revealed the huge, hairy, gamy object that my father had worn in his Stutz Bearcat in 1925.

"Holy Toledo!" said Petey reverently. He plunged his hands into the raccoon coat and then his face. "Holy Toledo!" he repeated fifteen or twenty times.

"Would you like it?" I asked.

"Oh yes!" he cried, clutching the greasy pelt to him. Then a canny look came into his eyes. "What do you want for it?"

"Your girl," I said, mincing no words.

"Polly?" he said in a horrified whisper. "You want Polly?"

"That's right."

He flung the coat from him. "Never," he said stoutly.

I shrugged. "Okay. If you don't want to be in the swim, I guess it's your business."

I sat down in a chair and pretended to read a book, but out of the corner of my eye I kept watching Petey. He was a torn man. First he looked at the coat with the expression of a waif at a bakery window. Then he turned away and set his jaw resolutely. Then he looked back at the coat, with even more longing in his face. Then he turned away, but with not so much resolution this time. Back and forth his head swiveled, desire waxing, resolution waning. Finally he didn't turn away at all; he just stood and stared with mad lust at the coat.

"It isn't as though I was in love with Polly," he said thickly. "Or going steady or anything like that."

"That's right," I murmured.

"What's Polly to me, or me to Polly?"

"Not a thing," said I.

"It's just been a casual kick—just a few laughs, that's all."

"Try on the coat," said I.

He complied. The coat bunched high over his ears and dropped all the way down to his shoe tops. He looked like a mound of dead raccoons. "Fits fine," he said happily.

I rose from my chair. "Is it a deal?" I asked, extending my hand.

He swallowed. "It's a deal," he said and shook my hand.

I had my first date with Polly the following evening. This was in the nature of a survey; I wanted to find out just how much work I had to do to get her mind up to the standard I required. I took her first to dinner. "Gee, that was a delish dinner," she said as we left the restaurant. Then I took her to a movie. "Gee, that was a marvy movie," she said as we left the theater. And then I took her home. "Gee, I had a sensaysh time," she said as she bade me good night.

I went back to my room with a heavy heart. I had gravely underestimated the size of my task. This girl's lack of information was terrifying. Nor would it be enough merely to supply her with information. First she had to be taught to *think*. This loomed as a project of no small dimensions, and at first I was tempted to give her back to Petey. But then I got to thinking about her abundant physical charms and about the way she entered a room and the way she handled a knife and fork, and I decided to make an effort.

I went about it, as in all things, systematically. I gave her a course in logic. It happened that I, as a law student, was taking a course in logic myself, so I had all the facts at my finger tips. "Polly," I said to her when I picked her up on our next date, "tonight we are going over to the Knoll and talk."

"Oo, terrif," she replied. One thing I will say for this girl: you would go far to find another so agreeable.

We went to the Knoll, the campus trysting place, and we sat down under an old oak, and she looked at me expectantly. "What are we going to talk about?" she asked.

"Logic."

She thought this over for a minute and decided she liked it. "Magnif," she said.

"Logic," I said, clearing my throat, "is the science of thinking. Before we can think correctly, we must first learn to recognize the common fallacies of logic. These we will take up tonight."

"Wow-dow!" she cried, clapping her hands delightedly.

I winced, but went bravely on. "First, let us examine the fallacy called Dicto Simpliciter."

"By all means," she urged, batting her lashes eagerly.

"Dicto Simpliciter means an argument based on an unqualified generalization. For example: Exercise is good. Therefore everybody should exercise."

"I agree," said Polly earnestly. "I mean exercise is wonderful. I mean it builds the body and everything."

"Polly," I said gently, "the argument is a fallacy. *Exercise is good* is an unqualified generalization. For instance, if you have heart disease, exercise is bad, not good. Many people are ordered by their doctors *not* to exercise. You must *qualify* the generalization. You must say exercise is *usually* good, or exercise is good *for most people*. Otherwise you have committed a Dicto Simpliciter. Do you see?"

"No," she confessed. "But this is marvy. Do more! Do more!"

"It will be better if you stop tugging at my sleeve," I told her, and when she desisted, I continued. "Next we take up a fallacy called Hasty Generalization. Listen carefully: You can't speak French. I can't speak French. Petey Burch can't speak French. I must therefore conclude that nobody at the University of Minnesota can speak French."

"Really?" said Polly, amazed. "*Nobody?*"

I hid my exasperation. "Polly, it's a fallacy. The generalization is reached too hastily. There are too few instances to support such a conclusion."

"Know any more fallacies?" she asked breathlessly. "This is more fun than dancing even."

I fought off a wave of despair. I was getting nowhere with this girl, absolutely nowhere. Still, I am nothing if not persistent. I continued. "Next comes Post Hoc. Listen to this: Let's not take Bill on our picnic. Every time we take him out with us, it rains."

"I know somebody just like that," she exclaimed. "A girl back home—Eula Becker, her name is. It never fails. Every single time we take her on a picnic—"

"Polly," I said sharply, "it's a fallacy. Eula Becker doesn't *cause* the rain. She has no connection with the rain. You are guilty of Post Hoc if you blame Eula Becker."

"I'll never do it again," she promised contritely. "Are you mad at me?"

I sighed deeply. "No, Polly, I'm not mad."

"Then tell me some more fallacies."

"All right. Let's try Contradictory Premises."

"Yes, let's" she chirped, blinking her eyes happily.

I frowned, but plunged ahead. "Here's an example of Contradictory Premises: If God can do anything, can He make a stone so heavy that He won't be able to lift it?"

"Of course," she replied promptly.

"But if He can do anything, He can lift the stone," I pointed out.

"Yeah," she said thoughtfully. "Well, then I guess He can't make the stone."

"But He can do anything," I reminded her.

She scratched her pretty, empty head. "I'm all confused," she admitted.

"Of course you are. Because when the premises of an argument contradict each other, there can be no argument. If there is an irresistable force, there can be no immovable object. If there is an immovable object, there can be no irresistible force. Get it?"

"Tell me some more of this keen stuff," she said eagerly.

I consulted my watch. "I think we'd better call it a night. I'll take you home now, and you go over all the things you've learned. We'll have another session tomorrow night."

I deposited her at the girls' dormitory, where she assured me that she had had a perfectly terrif evening, and I went glumly home to my room. Petey lay snoring in his bed, the raccoon coat huddled like a great hairy beast at his feet. For a moment I considered waking him and telling him that he could have his girl back. It seemed clear that my project was doomed to failure. The girl simply had a logic-proof head.

But then I reconsidered. I had wasted one evening; I might as well waste another. Who knew? Maybe somewhere in the extinct crater of her mind, a few embers still smoldered. Maybe somehow I could fan them into flame. Admittedly it was not a prospect fraught with hope, but I decided to give it one more try.

Seated under the oak the next evening I said, "Our first fallacy tonight is called Ad Misericordiam."

She quivered with delight.

"Listen closely," I said. "A man applies for a job. When the boss asks him what his qualifications are, he replies that he has a wife and six children at home, the wife is a helpless cripple, the children have nothing to eat, no clothes to wear, no shoes on their feet, there are no beds in the house, no coal in the cellar, and winter is coming."

A tear rolled down each of Polly's pink cheeks. "Oh, this is awful, awful," she sobbed.

"Yes, it's awful," I agreed, "but it's no argument. The man never answered the boss's question about his qualifications. Instead he appealed to the boss's sympathy. He committed the fallacy of Ad Misericordiam. Do you understand?"

"Have you got a handkerchief?" she blubbered.

I handed her a handkerchief and tried to keep from screaming while she wiped her eyes. "Next," I said in a carefully controlled tone, "we will discuss False Analogy. Here is an example: Students should be allowed to look at their textbooks during examinations. After all, surgeons have X-rays to guide them during an operation, lawyers have briefs to guide them during a trial, carpenters have blueprints to guide them when they are building a house.

Why, then, shouldn't students be allowed to look at their textbooks during an examination?"

"There now," she said enthusiastically, "is the most marvy idea I've heard in years."

"Polly," I said testily, "the argument is all wrong. Doctors, lawyers, and carpenters aren't taking a test to see how much they have learned, but students are. The situations are altogether different, and you can't make an analogy between them."

"I still think it's a good idea," said Polly.

"Nuts," I muttered. Doggedly I pressed on. "Next we'll try Hypothesis Contrary to Fact."

"Sounds yummy," was Polly's reaction.

"Listen: If Madame Curie had not happened to leave a photographic plate in a drawer with a chunk of pitchblende, the world today would not know about radium."

"True, true," said Polly, nodding her head. "Did you see the movie? Oh, it just knocked me out. That Walter Pidgeon is so dreamy. I mean he fractures me."

"If you can forget Mr. Pidgeon for a moment," I said coldly, "I would like to point out that the statement is a fallacy. Maybe Madame Curie would have discovered radium at some later date. Maybe somebody else would have discovered it. Maybe any number of things would have happened. You can't start with a hypothesis that is not true and then draw any supportable conclusions from it."

"They ought to put Walter Pidgeon in more pictures," said Polly. "I hardly ever see him any more."

One more chance, I decided. But just one more. There is a limit to what flesh and blood can bear. "The next fallacy is called Poisoning the Well."

"How cute!" she gurgled.

"Two men are having a debate. The first one gets up and says, 'My opponent is a notorious liar. You can't believe a word that he is going to say.' . . . Now, Polly, think. Think hard. What's wrong?"

I watched her closely as she knit her creamy brow in concentration. Suddenly a glimmer of intelligence—the first I had seen—came into her eyes. "It's not fair," she said with indignation. "It's not a bit fair. What chance has the second man got if the first man calls him a liar before he even begins talking?"

"Right!" I cried exultantly. "One hundred percent right. It's not fair. The first man has *poisoned the well* before anybody could drink from it. He has hamstrung his opponent before he could even start. . . . Polly, I'm proud of you."

"Pshaw," she murmured, blushing with pleasure.

"You see, my dear, these things aren't so hard. All you have to do is concentrate. Think—examine—evaluate. Come now, let's review everything we have learned."

"Fire away," she said with an airy wave of her hand.

Heartened by the knowledge that Polly was not altogether a cretin, I began a long, patient review of all I had told her. Over and over and over again. I cited instances, pointed out flaws, kept hammering away without let-up. It was like digging a tunnel. At first everything was work, sweat, and darkness.

I had no idea when I would reach the light, or even *if* I would. But I persisted. I pounded and clawed and scraped, and finally I was rewarded. I saw a chink of light. And then the chink got bigger and the sun came pouring in and all was bright.

Five grueling nights this took, but it was worth it. I had made a logician out of Polly; I had taught her to think. My job was done. She was worthy of me at last. She was a fit wife for me, a proper hostess for many mansions, a suitable mother for my well-heeled children.

It must not be thought that I was without love for this girl. Quite the contrary. Just as Pygmalion loved the perfect woman he had fashioned, so I loved mine. I determined to acquaint her with my feelings at our very next meeting. The time had come to change our relationship from academic to romantic.

"Polly," I said when next we sat beneath our oak, "tonight we will not discuss fallacies."

"Aw, gee," she said, disappointed.

"My dear," I said, favoring her with a smile, "we have now spent five evenings together. We have gotten along splendidly. It is clear that we are well matched."

"Hasty Generalization," said Polly brightly.

"I beg your pardon," said I.

"Hasty Generalization," she repeated. "How can you say that we are well matched on the basis of only five dates?"

I chuckled with amusement. The dear child had learned her lessons well. "My dear," I said, patting her hand in a tolerant manner, "five dates is plenty. After all, you don't have to eat a whole cake to know that it's good."

"False Analogy," said Polly promptly. "I'm not a cake. I'm a girl."

I chuckled with somewhat less amusement. The dear child had learned her lessons perhaps too well. I decided to change tactics. Obviously the best approach was a simple, strong, direct declaration of love. I paused for a moment while my massive brain chose the proper words. Then I began:

"Polly, I love you. You are the whole world to me, and the moon and the stars and the constellations of outer space. Please, my darling, say that you will go steady with me, for if you will not, life will be meaningless. I will languish. I will refuse my meals. I will wander the face of the earth, a shambling, hollow-eyed hulk."

There, I thought, folding my arms, that ought to do it.

"Ad Misericordiam," said Polly.

I ground my teeth. I was no Pygmalion; I was Frankenstein, and my monster had me by the throat. Frantically I fought back the tide of panic surging through me. At all costs I had to keep cool.

"Well, Polly," I said, forcing a smile, "you certainly have learned your fallacies."

"You're darn right," she said with a vigorous nod.

"And who taught them to you, Polly?"

"You did."

"That's right. So you do owe me something, don't you, my dear? If I hadn't come along you never would have learned about fallacies."

"Hypothesis Contrary to Fact," she said instantly.

I dashed perspiration from my brow. "Polly," I croaked, "you mustn't take all these things so literally. I mean this is just classroom stuff. You know that the things you learn in school don't have anything to do with life."

"Dicto Simpliciter," she said, wagging her finger at me playfully.

That did it. I leaped to my feet, bellowing like a bull. "Will you or will you not go steady with me?"

"I will not," she replied.

"Why not?" I demanded.

"Because this afternoon I promised Petey Burch that I would go steady with him."

I reeled back, overcome with the infamy of it. After he promised, after he made a deal, after he shook my hand! "The rat!" I shrieked, kicking up great chunks of turf. "You can't go with him, Polly. He's a liar. He's a cheat. He's a rat."

"Poisoning the Well," said Polly, "and stop shouting. I think shouting must be a fallacy too."

With an immense effort of will, I modulated my voice. "All right," I said. "You're a logician. Let's look at this thing logically. How could you choose Petey Burch over me? Look at me—a brilliant student, a tremendous intellectual, a man with an assured future. Look at Petey—a knothead, a jitterbug, a guy who'll never know where his next meal is coming from. Can you give me one logical reason why you should go steady with Petey Burch?"

"I certainly can," declared Polly. "He's got a raccoon coat."

Suggestions for Discussion

1. Characterize the narrator, Petey, and Polly.

2. Demonstrate that Polly learns her logic. Does it ever fail her?

3. Explain why you do or do not feel satisfied with the conclusion of the story.

Suggestions for Writing

1. How might you use one of your school subjects to begin a relationship?

2. Describe a relationship that changed or ended unexpectedly.

Poetry

Langston Hughes
Theme for English B

Langston Hughes (1902–1962), a prominent black poet, was born in Missouri and educated at Lincoln University in Pennsylvania. Often using dialect and jazz rhythms, his work expresses the concerns and feelings of American blacks. His collections of poetry include *The Weary Blues* (1926) and *Shakespeare in Harlem* (1940); his novels include *Not Without Laughter* (1930) and *The Best of Simple* (1950). In "Theme for English B" he clearly expresses the chasm between the races which exists even in the college classroom.

> The instructor said,
> > *Go home and write*
> > *a page tonight.*
> > *And let that page come out of you—*
> > *Then, it will be true.*
>
> I wonder if it's that simple?
> I am twenty-two, colored, born in Winston-Salem.
> I went to school there, then Durham, then here
> to this college on the hill above Harlem.
> I am the only colored student in my class.
> The steps from the hill lead down into Harlem,
> through a park, then I cross St. Nicholas,
> Eighth Avenue, Seventh, and I come to the Y,
> the Harlem Branch Y, where I take the elevator
> up to my room, sit down, and write this page:
>
> It's not easy to know what is true for you or me
> at twenty-two, my age. But I guess I'm what

I feel and see and hear, Harlem, I hear you:
hear you, hear me—we two—you, me, talk on this page.
(I hear New York, too.) Me—who?

Well, I like to eat, sleep, drink, and be in love.
I like to work, read, learn, and understand life.
I like a pipe for a Christmas present,
or records—Bessie, bop, or Bach.
I guess being colored doesn't make me *not* like
the same things others folks like who are other races.
So will my page be colored that I write?

Being me, it will not be white.
But it will be
a part of you, instructor.
You are white—
yet a part of me, as I am a part of you.
That's American.
Sometimes perhaps you don't want to be a part of me.
Nor do I often want to be a part of you.
But we are, that's true!
As I learn from you,
I guess you learn from me—
Although you're older—and white—
and somewhat more free.

This is my page for English B.

Suggestions for Discussion

1. With what details does Hughes convey a strong sense of identity?

2. How does he reveal his feelings about composition, learning, Harlem, his racial background, and his instructor?

Suggestion for Writing

Write an essay in which you attempt to convey some of your feelings about your own background, your likes and dislikes. Try to focus on details as Hughes has done in his poem.

Theodore Roethke

Elegy for Jane: My Student, Thrown by a Horse

Theodore Roethke (1908–1963) was born in Michigan and educated at the University of Michigan and Harvard. His poetry celebrated human relationships, the land and all growing things with wit, an inventive verse form and, at times, an almost surrealist language. He taught poetry writing for many years at the University of Washington in Seattle, and won the Pulitzer Prize for *The Waking* (1953). His other collections include *The Lost Son and Other Poems* (1949) and *The Far Field* (1964). Essays and lectures are collected in *The Poet and His Craft* (1965). "Elegy for Jane" is a tender poem expressing grief at the death of one of his students. Like many other modern poems on death, it achieves its force through wit and understatement.

I remember the neckcurls, limp and damp as tendrils;
And her quick look, a sidelong pickerel smile;
And how, once startled into talk, the light syllables leaped for her,
And she balanced in the delight of her thought,
A wren, happy, tail into the wind,
Her song trembling the twigs and small branches.
The shade sang with her;
The leaves, their whispers turned to kissing;
And the mold sang in the bleached valleys under the rose.

Oh, when she was sad, she cast herself down into such a pure depth,
Even a father could not find her:
Scraping her cheek against straw;
Stirring the clearest water.

My sparrow, you are not here,
Waiting like a fern, making a spiny shadow.
The sides of wet stones cannot console me,
Nor the moss, wound with the last light.

If only I could nudge you from this sleep,
My maimed darling, my skittery pigeon.
Over this damp grave I speak the words of my love:
I, with no rights in this matter,
Neither father nor lover.

Suggestions for Discussion

1. What is the relation of the first two stanzas to the rest of the poem?

2. How does the poet remember his dead student? What is the effect of the details he recalls?

3. Why does he call his dead student "my maimed darling" or "my skittery pigeon"? How would you describe this language?

4. Discuss the feelings which the poem expresses. How do you relate these feelings to the poet's language?

5. Explain the last two lines of the poem.

Suggestion for Writing

This poem expresses the feelings of a teacher for a dead student. Does this expression of feeling come as a surprise to you? Write an essay in which you discuss, from your experience, the kinds of relationships which exist between teachers and students. Relate your comments to the feelings expressed in this poem.

Marianne Moore

The Student

Marianne Moore (1887–1972) was born in Missouri, was graduated from Bryn Mawr College, taught at an Indian school, worked in the New York Public Library, and edited *The Dial* (1925–1929). Her early poems were published in 1921, her *Collected Poems* in 1951. She also wrote *Predilections* (1955), a volume of critical essays, a poetic translation of La Fontaine's *Fables* (1954), and a collection of poetry, *Tell Me, Tell Me* (1967). The following poem, taken from *What Are Years?* (1941, 1969), analyzes and praises the student.

> "In America," began
> the lecturer, "everyone must have a
> degree. The French do not think that
> all can have it, they don't say everyone
>   must go to college." We
> do incline to feel
>   that although it may be unnecessary
>
> to know fifteen languages,
> one degree is not too much. With us, a
> school—like the singing tree of which
> the leaves were mouths singing in concert—is
>   both a tree of knowledge
> and of liberty,—
>   seen in the unanimity of college
> mottoes, *lux et veritas,*

Christo et ecclesiae, sapiet
felici. It may be that we
have not knowledge, just opinions, that we
    are undergraduates,
not students; we know
    we have been told with smiles, by expatriates

of whom we had asked "When will
your experiment be finished?" "Science
is never finished." Secluded
from domestic strife, Jack Bookworm led a
    college life, says Goldsmith;
and here also as
    in France or Oxford, study is beset with

dangers,—with bookworms, mildews,
and complaisancies. But someone in New
England has known enough to say
the student is patience personified,
    is a variety
of hero, "patient
    of neglect and of reproach,"—who can "hold by

himself." You can't beat hens to
make them lay. Wolf's wool is the best of wool,
but it cannot be sheared because
the wolf will not comply. With knowledge as
    with the wolf's surliness,
the student studies
    voluntarily refusing to be less

than individual. He
"gives his opinion and then rests on it;"
he renders service when there is
no reward, and is too reclusive for
    some things to seem to touch
him, not because he
    has no feeling but because he has so much.

Suggestions for Discussion

1. What significance do you find in quotations from Einstein, lines 23–24, and Emerson, lines 34–35?

2. Finally, what values does Moore find in the student?

Suggestion for Writing

Define the life of the student in your college.

◇◇◇◇

The Examined Life: Professional Values

◆◆◆

The memory is a living thing—it too is in transit. But during its moment, all that is remembered joins, and lives—the old and the young, the past and the present, the living and the dead.

—**Eudora Welty,** "Finding a Voice"

In this sense fiction became the agency of my efforts to answer the questions, Who am I, what am I, how did I come to be? What shall I make of the life around me, what celebrate, what reject, how confront the snarl of good and evil which is inevitable?

—**Ralph Ellison,** "On Becoming a Writer"

Maybe what I'm trying to get at is that my belief in some power outside of myself was there all along, but it was a belief that had little or no effect; it was of no use to me. But every now and then, though all too infrequently, while painting away in my studio, an event would occur that I couldn't explain, and which I called inspiration.

—**Jules Olitski,** "Wonder Is Sacred"

It has always seemed to me to constitute a fantastic notion that the social landscape of our large cities bears any direct relationship to that kind of stable, nurturing community which would support the fragile psyche of the mentally ill.

—**Gerald Weissmann,** "Foucault and the Bag Lady"

Today there are a number of issues involving life and death that raise questions of public morality. They are also questions of concern to most religions.

—**Mario Cuomo,** "Religious Belief and Public Morality"

If anthropological studies of the divine have no other value, they may suggest more sensitivity and more humility towards the different ways in which people understand God.

—**Raymond Firth,** "God and Anthropology"

Personal Reminiscence

◆◆◆◆

Eudora Welty

Finding a Voice

Eudora Welty (b. 1909), the preeminent Southern novelist and short-story writer, has published such works as *Delta Wedding* (1946), *Losing Battles* (1970), *The Optimist's Daughter* (1972), *Collected Stories* (1980), and *One Writer's Beginnings* (1985), from which the following excerpt is taken. In her reminiscence, she explores the source for the character she writes about.

What discoveries I've made in the course of writing stories all begin with the particular, never the general. They are mostly hindsight: arrows that I now find I myself have left behind me, which have shown me some right, or wrong, way I have come. What one story may have pointed out to me is of no avail in the writing of another. But "avail" is not what I want; freedom ahead is what each story promises—beginning anew. And all the while, as further hindsight has told me, certain patterns in my work repeat themselves without my realizing. There would be no way to know this, for during the writing of any single story, there is no other existing. Each writer must find out for himself, I imagine, on what strange basis he lives with his own stories.

I had been writing a number of stories, more or less one after the other, before it belatedly dawned on me that some of the characters in one story were, and had been all the time, the same characters who had appeared already in another story. Only I'd written about them originally under different names, at different periods in their lives, in situations not yet interlocking but ready for it. They touched on every side. These stories were all related (and the fact was buried in their inceptions) by the strongest ties—identities, kinships, relationships, or affinities already known or remembered or foreshadowed. From story to story, connections between the characters' lives, through their motives or actions, sometimes their dreams, already existed: there to be found. Now the whole assembly—some of it still in the future—fell, by stages, into place in one location already evoked, which I saw now was a focusing point for all the stories. What had drawn the characters together there was one strong strand in them all: they lived in one way or another in a dream or in romantic aspiration, or under an illusion of what their lives were coming to, about the meaning of their (now) related lives.

The stories were connected most provocatively of all to me, perhaps, through the entry into my story-telling mind of another sort of tie—a shadowing of Greek mythological figures, gods and heroes that wander in various guises, at various times, in and out, emblems of the characters' heady dreams.

Writing these stories, which eventually appeared joined together in the book called *The Golden Apples,* was an experience in a writer's own discovery of affinities. In writing, as in life, the connections of all sorts of relationships and kinds lie in wait of discovery, and give out their signals to the Geiger counter of the charged imagination, once it is drawn into the right field.

The characters who go to make up my stories and novels are not portraits. Characters I invent along with the story that carries them. Attached to them are what I've borrowed, perhaps unconsciously, bit by bit, of persons I have seen or noticed or remembered in the flesh—a cast of countenance here, a manner of walking there, that jump to the visualizing mind when a story is underway. (Elizabeth Bowen said, "Physical detail cannot be invented." It can only be chosen.) I don't write by invasion into the life of a real person: my own sense of privacy is too strong for that; and I also know instinctively that living people to whom you are close—those known to you in ways too deep, too overflowing, ever to be plumbed outside love—do not yield to, could never fit into, the demands of a story. On the other hand, what I do make my stories out of is the *whole* fund of my feelings, my responses to the real experiences of my own life, to the relationships that formed and changed it, that I have given most of myself to, and so learned my way toward a dramatic counterpart. Characters take on life sometimes by luck, but I suspect it is when you can write most entirely out of yourself, inside the skin, heart, mind, and soul of a person who is not yourself, that a character becomes in his own right another human being on the page.

It was not my intention—it never was—to invent a character who should speak for me, the author, in person. A character is in a story to fill a role there, and the character's life along with its expression of life is defined by that surrounding—indeed is created by his own story. Yet, it seems to me now, years after I wrote *The Golden Apples,* that I did bring forth a character with whom I came to feel oddly in touch. This is Miss Eckhart, a woman who has come from away to give piano lessons to the young of Morgana. She is formidable and eccentric in the eyes of everyone, is scarcely accepted in the town. But she persisted with me, as she persisted in spite of herself with the other characters in the stories.

Where did the character of Miss Eckhart come from? There was my own real-life piano teacher, "eligible" to the extent that she swatted my hands at the keyboard with a fly-swatter if I made a mistake; and when she wrote "Practice" on my page of sheet music she made her "P" as Miss Eckhart did— a cat's face with a long tail. She did indeed hold a recital of her pupils every June that was a fair model for Miss Eckhart's, and of many another as well, I suppose. But the character of Miss Eckhart was miles away from that of the teacher I knew as a child, or from that of anybody I did know. Nor was she like other teacher-characters I was responsible for: my stories and novels suddenly appear to me to be full of teachers, with Miss Eckhart different from them all.

What the story "June Recital" most acutely shows the reader lies in her inner life. I haven't the slightest idea what my real teacher's life was like inside. But I knew what Miss Eckhart's was, for it protruded itself well enough into the story.

As I looked longer and longer for the origins of this passionate and strange character, at last I realized that Miss Eckhart came from me. There wasn't any resemblance in her outward identity: I am not musical, not a teacher, nor foreign in birth; not humorless or ridiculed or missing out in love; nor have I yet let the world around me slip from my recognition. But none of that counts. What counts is only what lies at the solitary core. She derived from what I already knew for myself, even felt I had always known. What I have put into her is my passion for my own life work, my own art. Exposing yourself to risk is a truth Miss Eckhart and I had in common. What animates and possesses me is what drives Miss Eckhart, the love of her art and the love of giving it, the desire to give it until there is no more left. Even in the small and literal way, what I had done in assembling and connecting all the stories in *The Golden Apples,* and bringing them off as one, was not too unlike the June recital itself.

Not in Miss Eckhart as she stands solidly and almost opaquely in the surround of her story, but in the making of her character out of my most inward and most deeply feeling self, I would say I have found my voice in my fiction.

Of course any writer is in part all of his characters. How otherwise would they be known to him, occur to him, become what they are? I was also part Cassie in that same story, the girl who hung back, and indeed part of most of the main characters in the connected stories into whose minds I go. Except for Virgie, the heroine. She is right outside me. She is powerfully like Miss Eckhart, her co-equal in stubborn and passionate feeling, while more expressive of it—but fully apart from me. And as Miss Eckhart's powers shrink and fade away, the young Virgie grows up more rampant, and struggles into some sort of life independent from all the rest.

If somewhere in its course your work seems to you to have come into a life of its own, and you can stand back from it and leave it be, you are looking then at your subject—so I feel. This is how I came to regard the character of Virgie in *The Golden Apples.* She comes into her own in the last of the stories, "The Wanderers." Passionate, recalcitrant, stubbornly undefeated by failure or hurt or disgrace or bereavement, all the while heedlessly wasting of her gifts, she knows to the last that there is a world that remains out there, a world living and mysterious, and that she is of it.

Inasmuch as Miss Eckhart might have been said to come from me, the author, Virgie, at her moments, might have always been my subject.

Through learning at my later date things I hadn't known, or had escaped or possibly feared realizing, about my parents—and myself—I glimpse our whole family life as if it were freed of that clock time which spaces us apart so inhibitingly, divides young and old, keeps our living through the same experiences at separate distances.

It is our inward journey that leads us through time—forward or back, seldom in a straight line, most often spiraling. Each of us is moving, changing, with respect to others. As we discover, we remember; remembering, we discover; and most intensely do we experience this when our separate journeys converge. Our living experience at those meeting points is one of the charged dramatic fields of fiction.

I'm prepared now to use the wonderful word *confluence*, which of itself exists as a reality and a symbol in one. It is the only kind of symbol that for me as a writer has any weight, testifying to the pattern, one of the chief patterns, of human experience.

Here I am leading to the last scenes in my novel, *The Optimist's Daughter:*

> She had slept in the chair, like a passenger who had come on an emergency journey in a train. But she had rested deeply.
>
> She had dreamed that she *was* a passenger, and riding with Phil. They had ridden together over a long bridge.
>
> Awake, she recognized it: it was a dream of something that had really happened. When she and Phil were coming down from Chicago to Mount Salus to be married in the Presbyterian Church, they came on the train. Laurel, when she travelled back and forth between Mount Salus and Chicago, had always taken the sleeper. She and Phil followed the route on the day train, and she saw it for the first time.
>
> When they were climbing the long approach to a bridge after leaving Cairo, rising slowly higher until they rode above the tops of bare trees, she looked down and saw the pale light widening and the river bottoms opening out, and then the water appearing, reflecting the low, early sun. There were two rivers. Here was where they came together. This was the confluence of the waters, the Ohio and the Mississippi.
>
> They were looking down from a great elevation and all they saw was at the point of coming together, the bare trees marching in from the horizon, the rivers moving into one, and as he touched her arm she looked up with him and saw the long, ragged, pencil-faint line of birds within the crystal of the zenith, flying in a V of their own, following the same course down. All they could see was sky, water, birds, light, and confluence. It was the whole morning world.
>
> And they themselves were a part of the confluence. Their own joint act of faith had brought them here at the very moment and matched its occurrence, and proceeded as it proceeded. Direction itself was made beautiful, momentous. They were riding as one with it, right up front. It's our turn! she'd thought exultantly. And we're going to live forever.
>
> Left bodiless and graveless of a death made of water and fire in a year long gone, Phil could still tell her of her life. For her life, any life, she had to believe, was nothing but the continuity of its love.
>
> She believed it just as she believed that the confluence of the waters was still happening at Cairo. It would be there the same as it ever was when she went flying over it today on her way back—out of sight, for her, this time, thousands of feet below, but with nothing in between except thin air.

Of course the greatest confluence of all is that which makes up the human memory—the individual human memory. My own is the treasure most dearly regarded by me, in my life and in my work as a writer. Here time, also, is subject to confluence. The memory is a living thing—it too is in transit. But during its moment, all that is remembered joins, and lives—the old and the young, the past and the present, the living and the dead.

As you have seen, I am a writer who came of a sheltered life. A sheltered life can be a daring life as well. For all serious daring starts from within.

Suggestions for Discussion

1. Discuss her observation that the "characters who go to make up my stories and novels are not portraits. Characters I invent along with the story that carries them."

2. Why did she "come in touch" with the character of Miss Eckhart?

3. Explain her use of the word *confluence*.

Suggestions for Writing

1. Document her observation that "each of us is moving, changing, with respect to others."

2. Use your memory to recreate a scene or character of significance.

Ralph Ellison

On Becoming a Writer

Ralph Ellison (b. 1914), the distinguished American writer, is best known for *Invisible Man* (1952). *Shadow and Act* (1964), his collected essays, included the following reminiscence that explores his growing self-awareness as a "Negro-American."

In the beginning writing was far from a serious matter; it was a reflex of reading, an extension of a source of pleasure, escape, and instruction. In fact, I had become curious about writing by way of seeking to understand the aesthetic nature of literary power, the devices through which literature could command my mind and emotions. It was not, then, the *process* of writing which initially claimed my attention, but the finished creations, the artifacts, poems, plays, novels. The act of learning writing technique was, therefore, an amusing investigation of what seemed at best a secondary talent, an exploration, like dabbling in sculpture, of one's potentialities as a "Renaissance Man." This, surely, would seem a most unlikely and even comic concept to introduce here; and yet, it is precisely because I come from where I do (the Oklahoma of the years between World War I and the Great Depression) that I must introduce it, and with a straight face.

Anything and everything was to be found in the chaos of Oklahoma; thus the concept of the Renaissance Man has lurked long within the shadow of my past, and I shared it with at least a half dozen of my Negro friends. How we actually acquired it I have never learned, and since there is no true sociology of the dispersion of ideas within the American democracy, I doubt if I ever shall. Perhaps we breathed it in with the air of the Negro community of Oklahoma City, the capital of that state whose Negroes were often charged by exasperated white Texans with not knowing their "place." Perhaps we took it defiantly from one of them. Or perhaps I myself picked it up from some transplanted New Englander whose shoes I had shined of a Saturday afternoon. After all, the most meaningful tips do not always come in the form of money, nor are they intentionally extended. Most likely, however, my friends and I acquired the idea from some book or some idealistic Negro teacher, some dreamer seeking to function responsibly in an environment which at its most normal took on some of the mixed character of nightmare and of dream.

One thing is certain, ours was a chaotic community, still characterized by frontier attitudes and by that strange mixture of the naive and sophisticated, the benign and malignant, which makes the American past so puzzling and its present so confusing; that mixture which often affords the minds of the young who grow up in the far provinces such wide and unstructured latitude, and which encourages the individual's imagination—up to the moment "reality" closes in upon him—to range widely and, sometimes, even to soar.

We hear the effects of this in the Southwestern jazz of the 30's, that joint creation of artistically free and exuberantly creative adventurers, of artists who had stumbled upon the freedom lying within the restrictions of their musical tradition as within the limitations of their social background, and who in their own unconscious way have set an example for any Americans, Negro or white, who would find themselves in the arts. They accepted themselves and the complexity of life as they knew it, they loved their art and through it they celebrated American experience definitively in sound. Whatever others thought or felt, this was their own powerful statement, and only non-musical assaults upon their artistic integrity—mainly economically inspired changes of fashion—were able to compromise their vision.

Much of so-called Kansas City jazz was actually brought to perfection in Oklahoma by Oklahomans. It is an important circumstance for me as a writer to remember, because while these musicians and their fellows were busy creating out of tradition, imagination, and the sounds and emotions around them, a freer, more complex, and driving form of jazz, my friends and I were exploring an idea of human versatility and possibility which went against the barbs or over the palings of almost every fence which those who controlled social and political power had erected to restrict our roles in the life of the country. Looking back, one might say that the jazzmen, some of whom we idolized, were in their own way better examples for youth to follow than were most judges and ministers, legislators and governors (we were stuck with the notorious Alfalfa Bill Murray). For as we viewed these pillars of society from the confines of our segregated community we almost always saw crooks, clowns, or hypocrites. Even the best were revealed by their attitudes toward us as lacking the respectable qualities to which they pretended and for which they were accepted outside by others, while despite the outlaw nature of their art, the jazzmen were less torn and damaged by the moral compromises and insincerities which have so sickened the life of our country.

Be that as it may, our youthful sense of life, like that of many Negro children (though no one bothers to note it—especially the specialists and "friends of the Negro" who view our Negro-American life as essentially non-human) was very much like that of Huckleberry Finn, who is universally so praised and enjoyed for the clarity and courage of his moral vision. Like Huck, we observed, we judged, we imitated and evaded as we could the dullness, corruption, and blindness of "civilization." We were undoubtedly comic because, as the saying goes, we weren't supposed to know what it was all about. But to ourselves we were "boys," members of a wild, free, outlaw tribe which transcended the category of race. Rather we were Americans born into the forty-sixth state, and thus, into the context of Negro-American post-Civil War history, "frontiersmen." And isn't one of the implicit functions of the American frontier to encourage the individual to a kind of dreamy wakefulness, a state in which he makes—in all ignorance of the accepted limitations of the possible—rash efforts, quixotic gestures, hopeful testings of the complexity of the known and the given?

Spurring us on in our controlled and benign madness was the voracious reading of which most of us were guilty and the vicarious identification and empathetic adventuring which it encouraged. This was due, in part, perhaps to the fact that some of were fatherless—my own father had died when I was three—but most likely it was because boys are natural romantics. We were seeking examples, patterns to live by, out of a freedom which for all its being ignored by the sociologists and subtle thinkers, was implicit in the Negro situation. Father and mother substitutes also have a role to play in aiding the child to help create himself. Thus we fabricated our own heroes and ideals catch-as-catch-can; and with an outrageous and irreverent sense of freedom. Yes, and in complete disregard of ideas of respectability or the surreal incongruity of some of our projections. Gamblers and scholars, jazz musicians and scientists, Negro cowboys and soldiers from the Spanish-American and First World Wars, movie stars and stunt men, figures from the Italian Renaissance and literature, both classical and popular, were combined with the special virtues of some local bootlegger, the eloquence of some Negro preacher, the strength and grace of some local athlete, the ruthlessness of some businessman-physician, the elegance in dress and manners of some head-waiter or hotel doorman.

Looking back through the shadows upon this absurd activity, I realize now that we were projecting archetypes, recreating folk figures, legendary heroes, monsters even, most of which violated all ideas of social hierarchy and order and all accepted conceptions of the hero handed down by cultural, religious, and racist tradition. But we, remember, were under the intense spell of the early movies, the silents as well as the talkies; and in our community, life was not so tightly structured as it would have been in the traditional South—or even in deceptively "free" Harlem. And our imaginations processed reality and dream, natural man and traditional hero, literature and folklore, like maniacal editors turned loose in some frantic film-cutting room. Remember, too, that being boys, yet in the play-stage of our development, we were dream-serious in our efforts. But serious nevertheless, for *culturally* play is a preparation, and we felt that somehow the human ideal lay in the vague and constantly shifting figures—sometimes comic but always versatile, picaresque, and self-effacingly heroic—which evolved from our wildly improvisatory projections: figures neither white nor black. Christian nor Jewish, but representative of certain desirable essences, of skills and powers, physical, aesthetic, and moral.

The proper response to these figures was, we felt, to develop ourselves for the performance of many and diverse roles, and the fact that certain definite limitations had been imposed upon our freedom did not lessen our sense of obligation. Not only were we to prepare but we were to perform—not with mere competence but with an almost reckless verve; with, may we say (without evoking the quaint and questionable notion of *négritude*) Negro-American style? Behind each artist there stands a traditional sense of style, a sense of the felt tension indicative of expressive completeness; a mode of humanizing reality and of evoking a feeling of being at home in the world. It is something which the artist shares with the group, and part of our boyish activity expressed a yearning to make any and everything of quality *Negro-American;* to appropriate it, possess it, recreate it in our own group and individual images.

And we recognized and were proud of our group's own style wherever we discerned it, in jazzmen and prize-fighters, ballplayers, and tap dancers; in gesture, inflection, intonation, timbre, and phrasing. Indeed, in all those nuances of expression and attitude which reveal a culture. We did not fully understand the cost of that style, but we recognized within it an affirmation of life beyond all question of our difficulties as Negroes.

Contrary to the notion currently projected by certain specialists in the "Negro problem" which characterizes the Negro American as self-hating and defensive, we did not so regard ourselves. We felt, among ourselves at least, that we were supposed to be whoever we would and could be and do anything and everything which other boys did, and do it better. Not defensively, because we were ordered to do so; nor because it was held in the society at large that we were naturally, as Negroes, limited—but because we demanded it of ourselves. Because to measure up to our own standards was the only way of affirming our notion of manhood.

Hence it was no more incongruous, as seen from our own particular perspective in this land of incongruities, for young Negro Oklahomans to project themselves as Renaissance men than for white Mississippians to see themselves as ancient Greeks or noblemen out of Sir Walter Scott. Surely our fantasies have caused far less damage to the nation's sense of reality, if for no other reason than that ours were expressive of a more democratic ideal. Remember, too, as William Faulkner made us so vividly aware, that the slaves often took the essence of the aristocratic ideal (as they took Christianity) with far more seriousness than their masters, and that we, thanks to the tight telescoping of American history, were but two generations from that previous condition. Renaissance men, indeed!

I managed, by keeping quiet about it, to cling to our boyish ideal during three years in Alabama, and I brought it with me to New York, where it not only gave silent support to my explorations of what was then an unknown territory, but served to mock and caution me when I became interested in the Communist ideal. And when it was suggested that I try my hand at writing it was still with me.

The act of writing requires a constant plunging back into the shadow of the past where time hovers ghostlike. When I began writing in earnest I was forced, thus, to relate myself consciously and imaginatively to my mixed background as American, as Negro-American, and as a Negro from what in its own belated way was a pioneer background. More important, and inseparable from this particular effort, was the necessity of determining my true relationship to that body of American literature to which I was most attracted and through which, aided by what I could learn from the literatures of Europe, I would find my own voice and to which I was challenged, by way of achieving myself, to make some small contribution, and to whose composite picture of reality I was obligated to offer some necessary modifications.

This was no matter of sudden insight but of slow and blundering discovery, of a struggle to stare down the deadly and hypnotic temptation to interpret the world and all its devices in terms of race. To avoid this was very important to me, and in light of my background far from simple. Indeed, it was quite complex, involving as it did, a ceaseless questioning of all those formulas which historians, politicians, sociologists, and an older generation of Negro leaders and writers—those of the so-called "Negro Renaissance"—had evolved to describe my group's identity, its predicament, its fate, and its relation to the larger society and the culture which we share.

Here the question of reality and personal identity merge. Yes, and the question of the nature of the reality which underlies American fiction and thus the human truth which gives fiction viability. In this quest, for such it soon became, I learned that nothing could go unchallenged; especially that feverish industry dedicated to telling Negroes who and what they are, and which can usually be counted upon to deprive both humanity and culture of their complexity. I had undergone, not too many months before taking the path which led to writing, the humiliation of being taught in a class in sociology at a Negro college (from Park and Burgess, the leading textbook in the field) that Negroes represented the "lady of the races." This contention the Negro instructor passed blandly along to us without even bothering to wash his hands, much less his teeth. Well, I had no intention of being bound by any such humiliating definition of my relationship to American literature. Not even to those works which depicted Negroes negatively. Negro-Americans have a highly developed ability to abstract desirable qualities from those around them, even from their enemies, and my sense of reality could reject bias while appreciating the truth revealed by achieved art. The pleasure which I derived from reading had long been a necessity, and in the *act* of reading, that marvelous collaboration between the writer's artful vision and the reader's sense of life, I had become acquainted with other possible selves; freer, more courageous and ingenuous and, during the course of the narrative at least, even wise.

At the time I was under the influence of Ernest Hemingway, and his description, in *Death in the Afternoon*, of his thinking when he first went to Spain became very important as translated in my own naïve fashion. He was trying to write, he tells us,

> and I found the greatest difficulty aside from knowing truly what you really felt, rather than what you were supposed to feel, and had been taught to feel, was to put down what really happened in action; what the actual things were which produced the emotion that you experienced. . . .

His statement of moral and aesthetic purpose which followed focused my own search to relate myself to American life through literature. For I found the greatest difficulty for a Negro writer was the problem of revealing what he truly felt, rather than serving up what Negroes were supposed to feel, and were encouraged to feel. And linked to this was the difficulty, based upon our long habit of deception and evasion, of depicting what really happened within

our areas of American life, and putting down with honesty and without bowing to ideological expediencies the attitudes and values which give Negro-
American life its sense of wholeness and which render it bearable and human
and, when measured by our own terms, desirable.

I was forced to this awareness through my struggles with the craft of fiction;
yes, and by my attraction (soon rejected) to Marxist political theory, which
was my response to the inferior status which society sought to impose upon
me (I did not then, now, or ever *consider* myself inferior).

I did not know my true relationship to America—what citizen of the U.S.
really does?—but I did know and accept how I felt inside. And I also knew,
thanks to the old Renaissance Man, what I expected of myself in the matter
of personal discipline and creative quality. Since by the grace of the past and
the examples of manhood picked willy-nilly from the continuing-present of
my background, I rejected all negative definitions imposed upon me by others, there was nothing to do but search for those relationships which were
fundamental.

In this sense fiction became the agency of my efforts to answer the questions, Who am I, what am I, how did I come to be? What shall I make of the
life around me, what celebrate, what reject, how confront the snarl of good
and evil which is inevitable? What does American society *mean* when regarded out of my *own* eyes, when informed by my *own* sense of the past and
viewed by my *own* complex sense of the present? How, in other words,
should I think of myself and my pluralistic sense of the world, how express
my vision of the human predicament, without reducing it to a point which
would render it sterile before that necessary and tragic—though enhancing—
reduction which must occur before the fictive vision can come alive? It is
quite possible that much potential fiction by Negro-Americans fails precisely
at this point: through the writers' refusal (often through provincialism or lack
of courage or through opportunism) to achieve a vision of life and a resourcefulness of craft commensurate with the complexity of their actual situation.
Too often they fear to leave the uneasy sanctuary of race to take their chances
in the world of art.

Suggestions for Discussion

1. Discuss the significance of his Oklahoma experience to Ellison.

2. What distinction does Ellison make between "the process of writing" and "the finished creations, the artifacts, poems, plays, novels"?

3. Describe his use of literature to relate himself to American life.

Suggestions for Writing

1. Discuss a piece of fiction that has helped you "answer the questions, who am I,
   what am I, how did I come to be?"

2. Discuss the importance of where you "come from" to your understanding of yourself.

◇◇◇◇

Jules Olitski

Wonder Is Sacred

Jules Olitski (b. 1922) is a well-known painter and sculptor whose works are in the permanent collections of the Metropolitan Museum, the Museum of Modern Art, the Art Institute, and the Hirshhorn Museum and Sculpture Garden. In the reminiscence that follows, he writes about the events that have shaped him.

Wonder is sacred. It's what we begin with: childlike wonder, like seeing for the first time clouds swiftly moving across the moon. The sight leaves me chilled and wide-eyed still. One of my earliest memories, even before I learned to walk, is of being in the country and seeing smoke rise above a pile of burning leaves—and inhaling the wonderful fragrance of it all. To this day the sight and smell of burning leaves stops me in my tracks. I am almost overcome by a feeling of great joy, as if something loved and long, long gone had returned.

I've heard it said that a man never grows old if he keeps his childhood alive in memory. Maybe yes, maybe no; but surely he is done for if he loses all sense of wonder.

Many years ago, when I was eleven, I was reading late at night in the kitchen of our house in Patchogue, Long Island. I was eating a pear, cutting each slice with a knife. Raising the knife to my lips, I would take the slice from the blade. At one point my lips came away empty. Where was the slice of pear? The knife blade was clean. I looked in my lap, on the floor, between the pages of the book; no slice of pear to be seen. Wonder of wonders. God had eaten my slice of pear!

The book I was reading and had been reading night after night while my parents and brothers slept was the Old Testament. Somehow I had found my way to that book so full of wonders. I say somehow, because I had had no religious instruction—neither at home nor at school. Nonetheless, my belief in the God of the Old Testament was absolute. I dreamed of becoming a rabbi when I grew up. Naturally, at the age of eleven I considered myself abundantly qualified as far as goodness, righteousness, and wisdom were concerned. All I needed was a command of Hebrew and a Yeshiva diploma. All the same, from the age of four, I had also dreamed of growing up big and strong so that I could successfully commit murder: first my stepfather, after him my older stepbrother, and then, more than likely, the stepbrother my age. As to my poor dear mother—she had always remained mute while I was being bullied; only her eyes would speak: anxiously consoling and imploring—I never could quite decide what to do about her.

The evil I experienced in the cold bosom of my family was really of a low level: petty, sadistic acts accompanied by mocking laughter, jeers, or just callous indifference. Day in, day out, I was told I looked like a freak, had the mind of an idiot, and would die in the gutter if not in the electric chair. For a time, my mind numbed. I was left back in the second grade.

To understand the impact upon me of what was taking place in the kitchen that night, and my reaction upon the later reappearance of the slice of pear, I must backtrack further. I was born in the city of Snovsk in the U.S.S.R., a few months after my father, a commissar, had been tried by the state and executed in that city. My mother, grandmother, and I came to the U.S.A., and while my mother worked in a sweatshop to support us, my grandmother took care of me. When I was three and a half my mother remarried: a widower with two sons. At a stroke, it seemed warmth, love, and tenderness were replaced by cold, unrelenting malevolence. Where to turn for help? Each night I fantasized that my father was not dead: he wandered the earth searching for me; he would rescue me from my hell. He never came. In time I yielded up my hope, though in a sense, not entirely. God was watching. I had come to believe in the all-powerful, all-knowing and all-seeing God of my ancestors. A just God. When He got around to it He'd smite my enemies; they'd wish they'd never been born.

At the time, 1933 or thereabout, an evil, so horrible as to be beyond a child's comprehension, was making itself known to the world. I had a newspaper delivery route. Every now and then in a short paragraph on a back page of the newspaper, I read some words, rumors usually, that spoke of Jews being persecuted in Germany: beatings, disappearances, concentration camps, death camps. Was it possible? Something told me it was all too true. Why was everyone silent? Silence, at home, in the school, in our town—just a handful of words in a newspaper every now and then. Where was the good FDR, so beloved by the Jews? And God, the God of us all, surely He would not turn His face away from such a *schrecklichkeit*.

Oh, I believed! God was with me. He had eaten a slice of my pear. I had never felt such joy as at that moment; the kitchen had become a radiant and holy place. I was in a state of bliss, at least for a minute or more, until I came to my senses. What a poor host I was being! Quick, offer Him another slice. I turned the knife to make the cut, and *there*, clinging to the blade's underside, was the missing slice of pear! Stunned, I wondered, had it been there all along? No, impossible for me to have missed seeing it. No, I had been betrayed! God had tricked me. Like a cunning, cruel stepfather, God had made me play the fool. I raised a fist and shouted: I won't believe in you anymore!

Paul's words come to mind: "When I was a child, I spake as a child, I understood as a child, I thought as a child; but when I became a man, I put away childish things.

"For now we see through a glass, darkly. . . ."

Does God exist? My childish faith had not survived its first blow. And swiftly came horrors piled one upon the other: Hitler's and Stalin's and horrors that seem to come without end.

I long ago stopped believing in the God of my ancestors, but if He exists, this great and awful God who can look with equanimity or a tolerant smile upon horrors unspeakable—if He does exist, then I must not look upon His face.

I am convinced it was the love of my grandmother, a love given without stint and with no strings attached, that helped me survive with some degree of sanity those dreadful years of childhood. My grief at her death was to affect me most powerfully. My decision to become an artist was made as she was lowered into her grave.

Her death came at a time when I was in my last year of high school. My art teacher, a dear, good man, had taken me under his wing and was urging me to become a high-school art teacher like himself. The idea of securing my future in this way was tempting. How else could I make a living? I knew I had some talent for drawing and painting, but it never ocurred to me, even in fantasy, that I could ever make a living as an artist, or, for that matter, in any other line of work. I had so little confidence in myself. Even the idea of pursuing a teaching career was scary. But I was taken (literally) by the hand by my teacher and introduced to his professor friends at New York University as a prospective student. This was the closest I got to becoming a high-school art teacher.

When I decided to become an artist, I didn't know what making art really meant. Yes, I clearly had the talent. Even as a very young child I could draw accurately from the model. Since a talent for painting became evident during my high-school years, I wanted to continue the kind of work I felt suited for and in which I took considerable pleasure and satisfaction. But, I think what I most wanted in becoming an artist was to live a life utterly different from the kind of lives I saw being lived by my parents and their circle. Their lives seemed barren, without joy or purpose apart from getting rich. (How harshly I judged them! Youthful arrogance and dumbness.) I, to the contrary, would live a *really* meaningful life. At any rate, I told myself, I would be doing the kind of work I loved.

I tried not to think about my future. All I wanted out of art school was to learn to paint in the manner of the Old Masters and, who knows, maybe I could paint portraits to earn my living. This did happen. I went to art schools; I learned some Old Master techniques; I even had a brief career as a portrait painter. But it was to be ten years after the New York art schools before I had my first taste of what making art was about. It all began as one hell of an identity crisis.

1949. I was living in Paris, studying art on the GI Bill. I was away from family, friends, and my country. I spoke no French. But one afternoon many things suddenly seemed to come together, enough to make me question myself. What does the art I make have to do with me? Is it enough to make the kind of art I make? It seemed as if I had learned, from the art schools and museums and the art I saw in art galleries, to speak, as it were, in many voices—where was *my* voice? Had I a voice? How to find out? Surely this meant somehow connecting with the child I had once been. Was the child still alive? How to find out? I must look inside myself. But how? My eyes would have to be covered. If I couldn't look out, my vision would be forced inward. I squeezed out gobs of color from tubes of oil paint onto a wide plank of wood. That would be my palette. Brushes were placed close to hand where I could feel for them, as needed. A canvas was supported on a chair in front of me. I wrapped a towel around my head. I felt the tip of my brush sink into paint; I had a rough idea of where each color was, but I couldn't be sure. Was I in the yellow or orange? No matter. My brush found the canvas and moved on it. Another brush, another color, another brush, another color, another, another, another . . . I have no idea how long I worked before I peeked. Five minutes? An hour? I had to see!

What I saw were daubs of bright, flat colors that looked slap-dab rough and startingly alive. I forgot everything: who I was, the child, Grandma in her grave, everything but this crazy, alive-looking thing. A lot of raw canvas was still showing. Back to the blindfold and back to work. Except that it wasn't work. It was more like a child *playing:* completely playful and completely serious, both at the same time.

I painted blindfolded for I don't know how many months—in any case until I felt strong enough in myself that I could allow the work to take its course; to develop in time, I hoped, into good works of art. Through an odd, unanticipated route I had found my way into flat, bright, colored abstract painting. At a stroke the devices and techniques I had learned in the art schools were gone, as if I'd never gone to school. Before Paris, I had painted in the styles of certain Renaissance masters. I had also done work while under the influence of the Impressionists, Post-Impressionists, Nabis, Fauves, and Cubists. Though the "blindfold" paintings were not truly *realized* works of art, they were, I believe, my first true works. They had come out of play, and to me, at least, they looked alive. The kind of play I mean is serious play, inspired play, where imagination, intelligence, intuition, and experience all together and at once reconstruct reality into a vision (a unique vision, if we're talking about great works) of order and harmony.

In time, the methods and techniques I'd abandoned, such as underpainting, modeling, half-tones, impasto, chiaroscuro, tinting, glazing, and so forth found their way back into my work. Nothing is ever lost altogether, or so it seems.

Very well, the child spoke. A beginning. But a beginning, even an auspicious one, is not enough, does not take us very far. Now we must find out who we are as all the while external reality presses, testing us . . . we must find what we believe so that we may live in accord with our beliefs.

In *Poetry and Reality,* Goethe writes: "However much a man searches heaven and earth, the present and the future, for his higher destiny, he remains the victim of a perennial vacillation, of an external influence which perpetually troubles him until, once and for all, he makes up his mind to declare that right is that which accords with him."

In looking back, tracing how some of my beliefs got formed, I see I was fortunate from the start, in that there was always someone or something to endure, to go up against, to survive.

Obscurity and hard times are useful if they don't last forever and if they don't leave you crazy and suicidal. Because I could get no one interested in my work, and no one was watching (and try as I might, I could not get a one-man show; no art dealer was interested enough to take a chance), I felt I had nothing to lose. I could practice my art without much concern for the world and none for my face in it—the ideal situation for a young artist. I could fool around, try anything out. If I played the fool, no matter. I was unseen, and alone.

But I am leaving out the truth, the truth I almost dare not tell. Shaking my fist at God, that long ago night, by no means erased my belief that some kind of reality existed apart from the one I could see and touch. At times I had sensed a nearby presence. God who seeth? A higher Power? I don't know. A presence not necessarily Divine, but presence enough to convince me, as Hamlet puts it:

"There are more things in heaven and earth, Horatio, than are dreamt of in your philosophy."

I think of the time I looked in a mirror and saw a face, not mine. It was at a time I felt beset by problems: my marriage going sour, a job I minded going to, my frustration at not being able to get my work seen, agonizing over a troubled child, and guilt, lots of guilt.

I happened to catch a side glimpse of someone as I passed a hall mirror—but who? I stopped short. Was that me? I went back and looked. The more I looked, the more convinced I became: I was seeing someone else—granted, someone who looked like me, but wasn't me. Ghost of my father? I didn't think so. The eyes seemed ageless; they were without a trace of human feeling, certainly no pity or compassion . . . indeed, without any comprehension of my concerns; what were they saying? I stared and stared. I saw an image in his eyes: a long, long line of small gray ponies, without saddles or reins, ridden by men bundled in gray furs, hunched forward against a blinding snowstorm, moving ever so slowly across an unending plain. A half hour must have passed before I said, "You've come to tell me something. What?"

"You are not your concerns. Your concerns are not you." That's all he said. When I got back to the mirror after pouring myself a drink, all I saw was me.

Why resurrect my mirror spirit and put him in a book where he can be used against me by my enemies and make my friends embarrassed for me? Well, I'm damned if I know why. It's not as if I believe I have some special destiny and the image in the mirror came to remind me of it. Indeed the sense I have of my own destiny is merely of something unfolding and inevitable, something like the inevitability that the moment my mother-in-law arrives at our door for a visit, the plumbing will overflow.

Maybe what I'm trying to get at is that my belief in some power outside of myself was there all along, but it was a belief that had little or no effect; it was of no use to me. But every now and then, though all too infrequently, while painting away in my studio, an event would occur that I couldn't explain and which I called inspiration. It would feel as if I were being given over to something, to a force, working through me. Afterward, I never could remember the sequence of events. It was as if without knowing how or why, I had stepped from one level of consciousness into another and this other was powerfully charged with concentrated energy. All I needed to do was let it happen. When it did happen, that particular painting always appeared to me not only as singular, but also as an opening into new territory.

As we all know, inspiration, like love, can't be induced. If we are fortunate, it will happen, falling upon us like a gift from the gods. If we are very fortunate, it will happen more than once. The only thing I could hope for was that I would be at work when the miracle came about; so I worked all the time. And then some seven or eight years ago I came upon this sentence by Ralph Waldo Emerson: "Do the thing and you will have the power." I didn't know, and still don't, its exact meaning, but the words had for me a power in themselves, an incantatory power. It was as if, simply by saying the words and in that instant taking hold of the work, I had also taken hold of the power. Now here was a power I could induce. And what's more, the experience was similar to that which I had called inspiration. I believe I had tapped into some universal power. My experience is far from unique. Creative workers in many occupations and professions have experienced a communion with a divine source. It is maybe what Matisse had in mind when he asked himself if he believed in God and answered, yes, when at work.

Paul Klee wrote of ". . . works which are indications of the work of God," and of the artist as "merely a channel." And "Genesis eternal! Chosen are those artists who penetrate to the region of that secret place where primeval power nurtures all evolution."

Any further need I might have had for an open sesame into power was given me by William James: ". . . give up the feeling of responsibility, let go your hold, resign the care of your destiny to higher powers, be genuinely indifferent as to what becomes of it all . . . a greater self is there."

There is something of a paradox in all this. In order to be most truly myself, I must give myself up. In effect, it's winning through surrendering. I've come to believe that this power I can surrender to in my studio is indeed a higher power. I don't know its natural shape, nor do I need know it. Enough that I have found my way to it. What remains is to bring the power into all areas of my existence so that, in communing with the power, it may work on me as I believe it does on my art. Play, aliveness, openness, inquisitiveness, giving oneself, and all the rest are what being human should be about.

I believe in a Creator. My belief may well be simple-minded. It goes like this: Since creation exists, there had to be a Creator. We are told by astronomers and astrophysicists that creation continues. So I assume the Creator is still around. (It pleases me to imagine the Creator on some new and distant planet creating an utterly new gazelle.) "To me," says Isaac Bashevis Singer, "the most wonderful miracle is what Spinoza called the natural order of things. To me causality is more than a category of pure reason; it is the essence of creation." Of course, nothing can be proven about the existence of the Creator, one way or another. I can have no certainty, only belief.

I believe the Creator simply provided the creation. We have everything from which we choose: good, evil, everything. I am what I do. Behind another's conscience I cannot hide.

Suggestions for Discussion

1. Explain the significance of the missing slice of pear.
2. Explain his "belief in some power outside of myself."
3. Discuss Olitski's use of illustrative quotations.

Suggestions for Writing

1. Write about a person or event that significantly influenced your outlook or behavior.
2. Trace how some of your own beliefs have been formed.

◇ ◇ ◇ ◇

Essays and Addresses

◆◆◆

Saul Bellow
Adrienne Rich

From the National Book Award Acceptance Speeches

Each year since 1950, the American Book Awards have been presented for the best book of the year in two categories, fiction and nonfiction. Excerpts follow from the acceptance speeches of Saul Bellow (b. 1915), who won the award in 1965 for his novel *Herzog,* and Adrienne Rich (b. 1929), who won in 1974 for *Diving Into the Wreck: Poems, 1971–72.*

Saul Bellow

The fact that there are so many weak, poor and boring stories and novels written and published in America has been ascribed by our rebels to the horrible squareness of our institutions, the idiocy of power, the debasement of sexual instincts and the failure of writers to be alienated enough. The poems and novels of these same rebellious spirits, and their theoretical statements, are grimy and gritty and very boring too, besides being nonsensical, and it is evident now that polymorphous sexuality and vehement declarations of alienation are not going to produce great works of art either.

There is nothing left for us novelists to do but think. For unless we think, unless we make a clearer estimate of our condition, we will continue to write kid stuff, to fail in our function, we will lack serious interests and become truly irrelevant.

Here the critics must share the blame. They too have failed to describe the situation. Literature has for several generations been its own source, its own province, has lived upon its own traditions, and accepted a romantic separation or estrangement from the common world. This estrangement, though it produced some masterpieces, has by now enfeebled literature. The separatism of writers is accompanied by the more or less conscious acceptance of a theory of modern civilization. This theory says in effect that modern mass society is frightful, brutal, hostile to whatever is pure in the human spirit, a wasteland and a horror. To its ugliness, its bureaucratic regiments, its thefts, its lies, its wars and its unparalleled cruelties, the artist can never be reconciled. This is one of the traditions on which literature has lived uncritically. But it is the task of artists and critics in every generation to look with their own eyes. Perhaps they will see even worse evils, but they will at least be seeing for themselves. They will not, they cannot permit themselves, generation after generation, to hold views they have not examined for themselves.

By such willful blindness we lose the right to call ourselves artists; we have accepted what we ourselves condemn—narrow specialization, professionalism and snobbery and the formation of a caste. And unfortunately the postures of this caste, postures of liberation and independence and creativity, are attractive to poor souls dreaming everywhere of a fuller, freer life. The writer is admired, the writer is envied. But what has he to say for himself? Why, he says, just as writers have said for more than a century, that he is cut off from the life of his own society, despised by its overlords who are cynical and have nothing but contempt for the artist, without a true public, estranged. He dreams of ages when the poet or the painter expressed a perfect unit of time and place, had real acceptance, and enjoyed a vital harmony with his surroundings—he dreams of a golden age. In fact, without the golden age, there is no wasteland.

Well, this is no age of gold. It is only what it is. Can we do no more than complain about it? We writers have better choices. We can either shut up because the times are too bad, or continue because we have an instinct to make books, a talent to enjoy, which even these disfigured times cannot obliterate. Isolated professionalism is death. Without the common world the novelist is nothing but a curiosity and will find himself in a glass case along some dull museum corridor of the future.

We live in a technological age which seems insurmountably hostile to the artist. He must fight for his life, for his freedom, along with everyone else— for justice and equality, threatened by mechanization and bureaucracy. This is not to advise the novelist to rush immediately into the political sphere. But in the first stage he must begin to exert his intelligence, long unused. If he is to reject politics, he must understand what he is rejecting. He must begin to think, and to think not merely of his own narrower interests and needs.

Adrienne Rich

[This] statement . . . was prepared by three of the women nominated for the National Book Award for poetry, with the agreement that it would be read by whichever of us, if any, was chosen.

We, Audre Lord, Adrienne Rich and Alice Walker, together accept this award in the name of all the women whose voices have gone and still go unheard in a patriarchal world, and in the name of those who, like us, have been tolerated as token women in this culture, often at great cost and in great pain. We believe that we can enrich ourselves more in supporting and giving to each other than by competing against each other; and that poetry—if it *is* poetry—exists in a realm beyond ranking and comparison. We symbolically join together here in refusing the terms of patriarchal competition and declaring that we will share this prize among us, to be used as best we can for women. . . . We dedicate this occasion to the struggle for self-determination of all women, of every color, identification or derived class: the poet, the housewife, the lesbian, the mathematician, the mother, the dishwasher, the pregnant teen-ager, the teacher, the grandmother, the prostitute, the philosopher, the waitress, the women who will understand what we are doing here and those who will not understand yet; the silent women whose voices have been denied us, the articulate women who have given us strength.

Suggestions for Discussion

1. What advice does Bellow offer writers?

2. To what use did Rich put her opportunity to speak?

3. What common problems do both writers identify in modern society?

4. Explain what you perceive to be the principal difference between the speeches.

Suggestions for Writing

1. Write a brief address in which you identify an important issue for serious discussion.

2. Write a commentary on either of the excerpts.

Gerald Weissmann
Foucault and the Bag Lady

Gerald Weissmann is professor of medicine at the New York University Medical Center. He specializes in rheumatology, the diagnosis and treatment of arthritis and its connected disorders. A contributor to the *New York Times, Discover,* and *The Sciences,* he is the author of *The Woods Hole Cantata: Essays on Science and Society* (1985), and *They All Laughed at Christopher Columbus: Tales of Medicine and the Art of Discovery* (1987). In the following essay, Dr. Weissmann examines the care and treatment of the mentally ill in America's cities and argues for "the concept of asylum: a space where the mad and deranged can be protected not only from their internal demons but from the harsher brutalities of the street."

On cold Mondays in February the victims of winter cluster at Bellevue. Infarction and pneumonia, exposure and gangrene drive the inhabitants of street and park to its doors. It was therefore a routine event when police brought the woman we'll call Mrs. Kahaner to the emergency room. Suffering from apparent frostbite, she had been found at the side entrance of Lord & Taylor early on Sunday morning and was admitted with a temperature of 93 degrees Fahrenheit.

The nurse's notes described her belongings. She was evidently the prototypical bag lady. Her rags, pots, and jumbled impedimenta overflowed five shopping bags crammed into a wire cart. An unkept appointment slip found in her purse identified her as a former patient in one of the New York State mental hospitals from which she had been last discharged three years ago. A telephone call to that hospital yielded her provisional diagnosis (chronic schizophrenia), her medications on discharge (the usual phenothiazine derivatives), and her age (fifty-six). The nurse had guessed Mrs. Kahaner to be an unkempt forty-five or so. The telltale areas of black gangrene on her fingertips had almost directed her admission to the surgical service, but a more thorough examination by an astute medical resident brought her to the medical wards, where our Rheumatology Service was called to see her the next morning.

The resident had observed that the skin over Mrs. Kahaner's face was drawn so tightly that she seemed to be peering out from behind a mask of fine leather. Over her chest and extremities, patches of pearl white skin alternated with areas of café-au-lait pigmentation. Her digital gangrene was only an extreme sign of impaired circulation—even after she had been warmed to normal temperature, her hands and feet remained mottled purple and pink. Her hands were also deformed by pincerlike contractures, her mouth was dry, and her eyelids crusted. X-rays showed fibrosis of the lungs, an enlarged right side of the heart with a prominent pulmonary artery segment, and diffuse calcification of the soft tissues. The admitting diagnosis was scleroderma.

As we examined her, Mrs. Kahaner remained resolutely silent. Warmed, hydrated, with oxygen aboard, she slowly responded to those requests necessary for physical diagnosis, but not at all to questions of medical or personal history. Frightened and withdrawn, this thin woman with sparse, stringy hair looked at us as if ready to weep, but tears did not come. As we were quick to appreciate, her dry eyes were a consequence of the disease: the early engorgement and later exhaustion of salivary and lacrimal glands known as Sjögren's syndrome, which arises in the course of scleroderma. Indeed, so hidebound was the skin about her lids, that the lacrimal glands could not be expressed. And her relatively youthful appearance was due to the shiny reflection of her collagenous mask, which had lost its normal wrinkles and fissures. We fitted the known stigmata of her disease to the patient before us. It turned out that she displayed the characteristic involvement of skin, lungs, and blood vessels that results when normal connective tissue—a pliant web of complex sugars, tensile proteins, and clear capillaries—is replaced by a carapace of scar tissue: scleroderma.

Despite extensive research, we know next to nothing about the cause and care of this sometimes progressively fatal malady. We are unable to stop its major assaults on vital organs. And although we have learned to manage the crises of breathing, vessel spasm, and kidney failure that mark its progression, the underlying problem of scleroderma is as unsolved today as it was thirty years ago, when I first learned about the disease in medical school. Monographs have been published, hundreds of research reports have flowed into our journals, and clinical subsets and related syndromes have been described. But while we are now able to discuss with greater precision the effects of scleroderma on the major organs, we remain as helpless as the doctors who forty years ago watched a network of collagen fibers tighten inexorably about the hands of Paul Klee.

As the weeks progressed, our patient responded to symptomatic treatment: vasodilators, artificial tears, hydration, and a soft, palatable diet. A caring staff managed to enter into a kind of communication with Mrs. Kahaner. This enterprise was made difficult by her persistent belief that she was bedded in the municipal hospital of Reykjavik, and that the Icelandic police were monitoring her words and behavior. This delusional system and associated fantasies were elicited by the house staff and consulting psychiatrists, who with patience and a dram or two of the newer psychotropic drugs dampened her fears of the Arctic constabulary. She was put at vague mental ease for the first time in months.

Nevertheless, the further management of her psychiatric troubles eclipsed her somatic complaints when the time came to plan her disposition after discharge. It was clear to the medical staff that she required close, periodic monitoring of her scleroderma, and equally clear that she belonged in some sort of institution that would shelter and clothe her, and where her madness would be managed in such a fashion that she could avoid the injuries of weather and a violent city. She needed what she had never found, an asylum—in the original sense of that word: sanctuary, from the Greek word *asylon*, meaning "inviolable."

However ignorant our profession may be of the proper management of scleroderma, it is safe to say that we know less of the disorders we call schizophrenia. Mrs. Kahaner, it turned out, had been in and out of various mental hospitals for at least two decades; she was divorced, and no relatives could be traced. Her recent confinements had lasted only a month or two; her prompt discharges were attributed to "remissions" induced (so her keepers believed) by various combinations of a broadening pharmacopoeia. After each dis charge, she appeared with less regularity at follow-up clinics. For the past three years, interrupted only by two admissions to the emergency room of Roosevelt Hospital because she had been mugged, she divided her nights between the doorways of department stores and the rest rooms of Pennsylvania Station.

Mrs. Kahaner had joined that sublcass of "deinstitutionalized" mental patients who have congregated in our cities in a kind of behavioral mockery of the consumer society. These shopping-bag ladies follow trails of private acquisition not too dissimilar from those of their saner, middle-class sisters. From the avenues of the West Side to the doorway of Brooks Brothers, from the arcades of the subways to the entrance of B. Altman's, the sad battalions of mad ladies course our streets, loaded with possessions tucked in tattered paper bags. And the bags still carry their message of fashionable competition: *Bloomingdale's! Bonwit Teller! Bergdorf Goodman!* The bags, in anarchic disorder, are in turn stashed in that other symbol of our abundant life: a shopping cart from the supermarket. There is probably no other country in which the madmen and madwomen so neatly exhibit the claims of local enterprise. I cannot recall similar public displays of private goods among the cat ladies of Rome, the mendicants of Madrid, the down-and-out of London and Paris. Madness is surely as prevalent in those cities as in New York, but mockery of The Shopper in the person of the bag lady strikes me as pure Americana.

However, the disposition of poor Mrs. Kahaner after Bellevue will be governed by fashions in attitudes toward the mentally ill that know no borders. Motivated by the observation that the overt aberrancy of the badly disturbed can be managed by the wonders of psychopharmacology, our asylums have evolved over the past decades into homes of only temporary detainment. The therapeutic rescue fantasy—as current in Paris as in Glasgow, in London as in Albany—has been joined to the concept that the diagnostically insane will be more humanely treated, or achieve greater personal integration, if they are permitted freely to mix with the "community."

It has always seemed to me to constitute a fantastic notion that the social landscape of our large cities bears any direct relationship to that kind of stable, nurturing community which would support the fragile psyche of the mentally ill. Cast into an environment limited by the welfare hotel or park bench, lacking adequate outpatient services, prey to climatic extremes and urban criminals, the deinstitutionalized patients wind up as conscripts in an army of the homeless. Indeed, only this winter was the city of New York forced to open temporary shelters in church basements, armories, and lodging houses for thousands of half-frozen street dwellers. A psychiatrist of my acquaintance has summarized the experience of a generation in treating the mentally deranged: "In the nineteen-fifties, the mad people were warehoused in heated public hospitals with occasional access to trained professionals. In the sixties and seventies, they were released into the community and permitted to wander the streets without access to psychiatric care. In the eighties, we have made progress, however. When the mentally ill become too cold to wander the streets, we can warehouse them in heated church basements without supervision."

Clearly, what is lacking is the concept of asylum: a space where the mad and deranged can be protected not only from their internal demons but from the harsher brutalities of the street. Our loss of the asylum as an ideal can be traced to a number of social vectors, many of which take origin in the most altruistic of motives. Deinstitutionalization—a horrid word—became practical when the advent of palliative chemotherapy made possible the release of inmates whose overt behavior, on discharge, posed no immediate danger to patient or citizen. But despite the obvious fiscal and administrative relief afforded the state and local authorities, release would not have become widespread were it not for the vigorous efforts of well-meaning advocates of civil rights. These activists were rightfully convinced that commitment of the unwilling to mental institutions might represent the first step toward a Soviet-style incarceration for dissidents. Moreover, the return of the mad to the community was in accord not only with the rosy visions of fellowship and liberation that became prevalent in the sixties but also with a general distrust of arrangements made by any authority, be it juridical, governmental, or medical. And a prominent role was played in the attack upon the concept of asylum by radical sociologists, psychiatrists, and historians.

Absent any real knowledge of the nature of schizophrenia, one attractive path out of the forest of ignorance would be to deny that the term itself had meaning. It was not surprising, therefore, that the revisionist psychiatrist R. D. Laing seized the temper of the sixties and argued that those called "schizophrenic" were not sick in the medical sense. To Laing and his adherents, the schizophrenic—a soul more sensitive than the ordinary person—has made an entirely appropriate adjustment to an insane world. Since mental "disease" is only definable in relationship to a fractured, social framework of bourgeois values, *any* accommodation is acceptable, and the job of the healer is to adjust the discomfited to his level of accommodation. The Laingians argued that since a century of scientific inquiry had failed to prove that madness can be adequately described by the medical model, it was time to abandon the concept of schizophrenia as a disease. And if we can dispense with the therapeutic model, why not abandon those institutions that exist to treat this now nonexistent malady?

Most physicians, unlike other "mental health professionals," cannot be easily persuaded by this argument. For one reason, the argument suffers from what has been called the reification fallacy. This fallacy mistakes the *name* of a condition, or syndrome, for its *effects*. Were we to apply such flawed reasoning to the example of scleroderma, for instance, we would have to abandon the practice of making that diagnosis in Mrs. Kahaner's case. But by so doing, one would not alter in one sad, clinical detail the narrative of how our patient became trapped by collagen. Nor would her treatment, I daresay, be vastly improved by deinstitutionalizing Mrs. Kahaner before we had dilated her blood vessels, given her intravenous fluids, and helped her to breathe. In the example of scleroderma—a disease as enmeshed in mystery and as difficult to treat as schizophrenia—we are forced to resort to palliation, to support, and to clearheaded observation. I fail to see how our ignorance of the etiology of an illness gives us the right to assume that it is due to social maladjustment.

Indeed, the medical model may prove more effective. This model has already paid off in the case of lithium-sensitive, manic-depressive psychosis and in Alzheimer's disease. Until their basis in organic malfunction was identified, these conditions—like schizophrenia—were often attributed to social or familial wounds.

But the Laingian assault on the medical model and the modern response to that model—the asylum—has also been joined by the more urgent attack of historians and sociologists. They argue that mental hospitals subjugate and victimize the mad in the name of therapy, when what the mentally deranged require is liberation from the shame associated with the label of madness. Mental hospitals, so goes this charge, have since the seventeenth century served chiefly as schools for the brutal induction of shame; their obolition can only benefit the mad. This argument, in its most persuasive and scholarly form, is presented by the late Michel Foucault, the iconoclastic French historian of sexuality, prisons, and medicine.

In his major opus, *Madness and Civilization*, Foucault traces the history of mental institutions to the "Great Confinement" of the classical age. A royal edict of April 1656 led to the establishment of the Hôpital Général, a series of Parisian hospitals for the confinement of mendicants, fools, and other idle folk of the street. These institutions, some of which were founded as centers for the sequestration of lepers in medieval times (lazar houses), became depositories for beggars, the unemployable, and the mentally feeble. In keeping with the new commercial spirit of the age, the Hôpital General and its sister institutions of England and Germany set the inmates to productive work and small manufacture in order to prevent, in the words of the royal edict, "mendicancy and idleness as sources of disorder."

Foucault describes how the confined populace replaced the leper as an excommunicated class:

> The asylum was substituted for the lazar house—the old rites of excommunication were revived, but in the world of production and commerce. It is in this space invented by a society which had derived an ethical transcendence from the law of work that madness would appear and soon expand until it had annexed them [*sic*]—the nineteenth century would consent, would even insist that to the mad and to them alone be transferred these lands on which, a hundred and fifty years before, men had sought to pen the poor, the vagabond, the unemployed.

In these former lazar houses, the Age of Reason confined the socially undesirable: thief and demented, idler and aged, fool and madman. And so that strange mixture of the socially unwanted remained in chains or at forced labor until the advent of the French Revolution. It was at a branch of the Hôpital General, the Bicêtre, that Philippe Pinel struck these chains in an episode that signals the birth of liberal philanthropy. Pinel was confronted by an official of the Revolution, Georges Couthon, seeking suspects for trial. Pinel led him to the cells of the most seriously disturbed, where Citizen Couthon's attempts at interrogation were greeted with disjointed insults and loud obscenities.

It was useless to prolong the interviews. Couthon turned to Pinel and asked: "Now, Citizen, are you mad yourself to seek to unchain such beasts?" Pinel replied: "Citizen, I am convinced that these madmen are so intractable only because they have been deprived of air and liberty!"

"Well, do as you like with them, but I fear you may become victim of your own presumption." The official left, and Pinel removed the chains. The rest of the tale is the history of the modern mental hospital, at least until deinstitutionalization.

Now one would have thought that Foucault would come out cheering for Pinel. But no. In keeping with a tradition of radical criticism that includes the names of Herbert Marcuse and Ivan Illich, Foucault reserves his hardest blows for Pinel and the therapeutic reforms of bourgeois liberalism. Pinel stands accused by Foucault of substituting the psychological chains of the medical model for the iron shackles of the old lazar houses. The madman had become trapped in the birth of the asylum, and this new, therapeutic community confronted him with a new menace in the history of madness: guilt.

> The asylum no longer punished the madman's guilt, it is true, but it did more, it organized it for the man of reason as an awareness of the Other, a therapeutic intervention in the madman's existence.

Foucault, displaying that curious affinity of advanced French thought for the punitive tableaux of the Marquis de Sade, goes on to grieve for the unchained patients of the nineteenth century. He poses a very fashionable paradox:

> The dungeons, the chains, the continual spectacle, the sarcasms were, to the sufferer in his delirium, the very element of his liberation. . . . But the chains that fell, the indifference and silence of all those around him confined him in the limited use of an empty liberty. . . . Henceforth, more genuinely confined than he could have been in a dungeon and chains, a prisoner of nothing but himself, the sufferer was caught in relation to himself that was of the order of transgression, and in a non-relation to others that was of the same order of shame. . . . Delivered from his chains, he is now chained, by silence, to transgression and to shame.

Foucault's analysis of the relationship between keeper and inmate, between authority and the governed, extends to the interaction between doctor and patient. He points out that life in the asylum constituted a microcosm in which the values of a bourgeois state were symbolized: relationships between family and child, centering on authority; between transgression and punishment, centering on immediate justice; and between madness and disorder, centering on the social contract. Since the doctor stood *in loco parentis* for the whole society, Foucault suggested:

> It is from these [relationships] that the physician derives the power to cure, and it is to the degree that the patient finds himself, by so many old links, already alienated in the doctor, within *le couple médecin-malade*, that the doctor has the power to cure him.

This strikes me as a remarkable passage. To begin with, one can note that the French expression *le couple médecin-malade* has the same general meaning as the English "doctor-patient relationship," but in French it acquires a sexual overtone in its reference to the marriage couple. Secondly, Foucault adds the trendy spice of "alienation" to the principles of therapy: the madman, already alienated from the old bourgeois game of power and property, recapitulates that experience with his doctor. Finally, Foucault seems to equate alienation with the concept of transference. In psychoanalysis, transference—that strong bond between patient and therapist—is a positive element in self-discovery and possible cure. The only bond identified by Foucault is that of alienation, and this gives the doctor, as *locum tenens* of an alienating system, the "power to cure." But for Foucault, a cure is only a partial blessing, since it implies loss of freedom. Foucault has thus shifted the therapeutic setting from the Freudian one-on-one interview to the parade ground of the asylum, where the doctor as drillmaster instructs alienated conscripts in rules of the barracks.

In all aspects of his criticism of the asylum, Foucault uses as his point of reference a golden age of madness, which for him was the medieval age, where fools and crazies formed an integral part of the unregulated life of the street. Here, Foucault's vision of integration merges with that of the antiauthoritarian Left of the sixties. Foucault and the civil libertarians view the ameliorationist attitudes of mental health professionals as a destructive force in the battle for self-realization. They consider prisons, asylums, hospitals, and their squadrons of social workers, psychiatrists, and psychologists as the elements of a police state designed to censor the self-expression of the mad.

In the golden age of Foucault's medieval city, fools and madmen added to the richness of everyday life by their unique insights and startling behavior. The "reforms" of the Age of Reason destroyed this organic fabric and turned it into a straitjacket. That is the charge of Foucault, heard by the intellectuals of the West as the asylums have been emptied, mental health budgets cut, and the church basements filled.

But, I should have thought, there is little chance that poor, mad people find in our society even the glint of a golden age. In the cities of America, where the Mrs. Kahaners wander outside asylums in solitary danger, where violence is unchecked, and where the aggressive roam in quest of drugs and easy victims, we have, instead, partly reverted to the Hobbesian state of nature. I am frightened by that state and frightened for the army of fools and madmen we have let loose in it. To counter this condition, I, too, have a vision of a golden age, which by no means corresponds to the present-day treatment of the mentally ill. For me, it is the dream of the Age of Reason as articulated in the liberal philanthropy of Pinel. He gave us his vision of a true asylum for those shocked by the wars of the mind, an asylum that is, perhaps, more truly civil than that which Foucault presents. Pinel, in his 1801 treatise on the nature of madness, describes the hospital at Saragossa, where there was established

> a sort of counterpoise to the mind's extravagances by the charm inspired by cultivation of the fields, by the natural instinct that leads man to sow the earth and thus to satisfy his needs by the fruits of his labors. From morning on, you can see them—leaving gaily for the various parts of a vast enclosure . . . sharing with a sort of emulation the tasks appropriate to the seasons, cultivating wheat, vegetables, concerned in turn with the harvest, with trellises, with the vintage, with olive picking and finding in the evening, in their solitary asylum, calm and quiet sleep. The most constant experience has indicated, in this hospital, that this is the surest and most efficacious way to restore man to reason.

When we next meet Mrs. Kahaner, now lost in the shuffle between discharge from Bellevue and her unkept appointments at Creedmore, huddled in the closed doorways of Lord & Taylor, we might well ask whether her fate in our fractured city is better guided by the philanthropic vision of Pinel or the trendy critique of his dream by Foucault. Until reason and science unlock the shackles of her illness, we need, I believe, to give rest to this bag lady in a sanctuary, a therapeutic community—an asylum.

Suggestions for Discussion

1. From what medical and mental problems does Mrs. Kahaner suffer?

2. What arguments does Dr. Weissmann make against the ideas of Laing and Foucault?

3. What recommendations does he make for the care of the mentally ill?

Suggestions for Writing

1. Investigate and describe services in your community that might be mobilized to assist a person like Mrs. Kahaner.

2. Analyze Dr. Weissmann's use of specialized vocabulary, vivid illustration, and scholarly reading.

Studs Terkel

Carl Murray Bates, Mason

Studs Terkel (b. 1912) has long been associated with WFMT-FM in Chicago. He gained fame as an oral historian with the publication of *Division Street America* (1966), *Hard Times* (1970), *Working: People Talk About What They Do All Day and How They Feel About It* (1974), and *Talking to Myself: A Memoir of My Times* (1977). In the following selection, Terkel interviews a stonemason who is proud of his craft.

We're in a tavern no more than thirty yards from the banks of the Ohio. Toward the far side of the river, Alcoa smokestacks belch forth: an uneasy coupling of a bucolic past and an industrial present. The waters are polluted, yet the jobs out there offer the townspeople their daily bread.

He is fifty-seven years old. He's a stonemason who has pursued his craft since he was seventeen. None of his three sons is in his trade.

As far as I know, masonry is older than carpentry, which goes clear back to Bible times. Stone mason goes back way *before* Bible time: the pyramids of Egypt, things of that sort. Anybody that starts to build anything, stone, rock, or brick, start on the northeast corner. Because when they built King Solomon's Temple, they started on the northeast corner. To this day, you look at your courthouses, your big public buildings, you look at the cornerstone, when it was created, what year, it will be on the northeast corner. If I was gonna build a septic tank, I would start on the northeast corner. (Laughs.) Superstition, I suppose.

With stone we build just about anything. Stone is the oldest and best building material that ever was. Stone was being used even by the cavemen that put it together with mud. They built out of stone before they even used logs. He got him a cave, he built stone across the front. And he learned to use dirt, mud, to make the stones lay there without sliding around—which was the beginnings of mortar, which we still call mud. The Romans used mortar that's almost as good as we have today.

Everyone hears these things, they just don't remember 'em. But me being in the profession, when I hear something in that line, I remember it. Stone's my business. I, oh, sometimes talk to architects and engineers that have made a study and I pick up the stuff here and there.

Every piece of stone you pick up is different, the grain's a little different and this and that. It'll split one way and break the other. You pick up your stone and look at it and make an educated guess. It's a pretty good day layin' stone or brick. Not tiring. Anything you like to do isn't tiresome. It's hard work; stone is heavy. At the same time, you get interested in what you're doing and you usually fight the clock the other way. You're not lookin' for quittin'. You're wondering you haven't got enough done and it's almost quittin' time. (Laughs.) I ask the hod carrier what time it is and he says two thirty. I say, "Oh, my Lord, I was gonna get a whole lot more than this."

I pretty well work by myself. On houses, usually just one works. I've got the hod carrier there, but most of the time I talk to myself. "I'll get my hammer and I'll knock the chip off there." (Laughs.) A good hod carrier is half your day. He won't work as hard as a poor one. He knows what to do and make every move count makin' the mortar. It has to be so much water, so much sand. His skill is to see that you don't run out of anything. The hod carrier, he's above the laborer. He has a certain amount of prestige.

I think a laborer feels that he's the low man. Not so much that he works with his hands, it's that he's at the bottom of the scale. He always wants to get up to a skilled trade. Of course he'd make more money. The main thing is the common laborer—the word *common* laborer—sounds so common, he's at the bottom. Many that works with his hands takes pride in his work.

I get a lot of phone calls when I get home: how about showin' me how and I'll do it myself? I always wind up doin' it for 'em. (Laughs.) So I take a lot of pride in it and I do get, oh, I'd say, a lot of praise or whatever you want to call it. I don't suppose anybody, however much he's recognized, wouldn't like to be recognized a little more. I think I'm pretty well recognized.

One of my sons is an accountant and the other two are bankers. They're mathematicians, I suppose you'd call 'em that. Air-conditioned offices and all that. They always look at the house I build. They stop by and see me when I'm aworkin'. Always want me to come down and fix somethin' on their house, too. (Laughs.) They don't buy a house that I don't have to look at it first. Oh sure, I've got to crawl under it and look on the roof, you know . . .

I can't seem to think of any young masons. So many of 'em before, the man lays stone and his son follows his footsteps. Right now the only one of these sons I can think of is about forty, fifty years old.

I started back in the Depression times when there wasn't any apprenticeships. You just go out and if you could hold your job, that's it. I was just a kid then. Now I worked real hard and carried all the blocks I could. Then I'd get my trowel and I'd lay one or two. The second day the boss told me: I think you could lay enough blocks to earn your wages. So I guess I had only one day of apprenticeship. Usually it takes about three years of being a hod carrier to start. And it takes another ten or fifteen years to learn the skill.

I admired the men that we had at that time that were stonemasons. They knew their trade. So naturally I tried to pattern after them. There's been very little change in the work. Stone is still stone, mortar is still the same as it was fifty years ago. The style of stone has changed a little. We use a lot more, we call it golf. A stone as big as a baseball up to as big as a basketball. Just round balls and whatnot. We just fit 'em in the wall that way.

Automation has tried to get in the bricklayer. Set 'em with a crane. I've seen several put up that way. But you've always got in-between the windows and this and that. It just doesn't seem to pan out. We do have a power saw. We do have an electric power mix to mix the mortar, but the rest of it's done by hand as it always was.

In the old days they all seemed to want it cut out and smoothed. It's harder now because you have no way to use your tools. You have no way to use a string, you have no way to use a level or a plumb. You just have to look at it because it's so rough and many irregularities. You have to just back up and look at it.

All construction, there's always a certain amount of injuries. A scaffold will break and so on. But practically no real danger. All I ever did do was work on houses, so we don't get up very high—maybe two stories. Very seldom that any more. Most of 'em are one story. And so many of 'em use stone for a trim. They may go up four, five feet and then paneling or something. There's a lot of skinned fingers or you hit your finger with a hammer. Practically all stone is worked with hammers and chisels. I wouldn't call it dangerous at all.

Stone's my life. I daydream all the time, most times it's on stone. Oh, I'm gonna build me a stone cabin down on the Green River. I'm gonna build stone cabinets in the kitchen. That stone door's gonna be awful heavy and I don't know how to attach the hinges. I've got to figure out how to make a stone roof. That's the kind of thing. All my dreams, it seems like it's got to have a piece of rock mixed in it.

If I got some problem that's bothering me, I'll actually wake up in the night and think of it. I'll sit at the table and get a pencil and paper and go over it, makin' marks on paper or drawin' or however . . . this way or that way. Now I've got to work this and I've only got so much. Or they decided they want it that way when you already got it fixed this way. Anyone hates tearing his work down. It's all the same price but you still don't like to do it.

These fireplaces, you've got to figure how they'll throw out heat, the way you curve the fireboxes inside. You have to draw a line so they reflect heat. But if you throw out too much of a curve, you'll have them smoke. People in these fine houses don't want a puff of smoke coming out of the house.

The architect draws the picture and the plans, and the draftsman and the engineer, they help him. They figure the strength and so on. But when it comes to actually makin' the curves and doin' the work, you've got to do it with your hands. It comes right back to your hands.

When you get into stone, you're gettin' away from the prefabs, you're gettin' into the better homes. Usually at this day and age they'll start into sixty to seventy thousand and run up to about half a million. We've got one goin' now that's mighty close, three or four hundred thousand. That type of house is what we build.

The lumber is not near as good as it used to be. We have better fabricating material, such as plywood and sheet rock and things of that sort, but the lumber itself is definitely inferior. Thirty, forty years ago a house was almost entirely made of lumber, wood floors . . . Now they have vinyl, they have carpet, everything, and so on. The framework wood is getting to be of very poor quality.

But stone is still stone and the bricks are actually more uniform than they used to be. Originally they took a clay bank . . . I know a church been built that way. Went right on location, dug a hole in the ground and formed bricks with their hands. They made the bricks that built the building on the spot.

Now we've got modern kilns, modern heat, the temperature don't vary. They got better bricks now than they used to have. We've got machines that make brick, so they're made true. Where they used to, they were pretty rough. I'm buildin' a big fireplace now out of old brick. They run wide, long, and it's a headache. I've been two weeks on that one fireplace.

The toughest job I ever done was this house, a hundred years old plus. The lady wanted one room left just that way. And this doorway had to be closed. It had deteriorated and weathered for over a hundred years. The bricks was made out of broken pieces, none of 'em were straight. If you lay 'em crooked, it gets awful hard right there. You spend a lifetime tryin' to learn to lay bricks straight. And it took a half-day to measure with a spoon, to try to get the mortar to match. I'd have so much dirt, so much soot, so much lime, so when I got the recipe right I could make it in bigger quantity. Then I made it with a coffee cup. Half a cup of this, half a cup of that . . . I even used soot out of a chimney and sweepin's off the floor. I was two days layin' up a little doorway, mixin' the mortar and all. The boss told the lady it couldn't be done. I said, "Give me the time, I believe I can do it." I defy you to find where that door is right now. That's the best job I ever done.

There's not a house in this country that I haven't built that I don't look at every time I go by. (Laughs.) I can set here now and actually in my mind see so many that you wouldn't believe. If there's one stone in there crooked, I know where it's at and I'll never forget it. Maybe thirty years, I'll know a place where I should have took that stone out and redone it but I didn't. I still notice it. The people who live there might not notice it, but I notice it. I never pass that house that I don't think of it. I've got one house in mind right now. (Laughs.) That's the work of my hands. 'Cause you see, stone, you don't prepaint it, you don't camouflage it. It's there, just like I left it forty years ago.

I can't imagine a job where you go home and maybe go by a year later and you don't know what you've done. My work, I can see what I did the first day I started. All my work is set right out there in the open and I can look at it as I go by. It's something I can see the rest of my life. Forty years ago, the first blocks I ever laid in my life, when I was seventeen years old. I never go through Eureka—a little town down there on the river—that I don't look thataway. It's always there.

Immortality as far as we're concerned. Nothin' in this world lasts forever, but did you know that stone—Bedford limestone, they claim—deteriorates one-sixteenth of an inch every hundred years? And it's around four or five inches for a house. So that's gettin' awful close. (Laughs.)

Suggestions for Discussion

1. Describe the work that Bates does.

2. What details suggest his expert knowledge of his craft?

3. Discuss his pride in his work.

Suggestions for Writing

1. Write about a skill or talent that gives you pride in yourself.

2. Explain why you think his three sons have not followed in their father's craft.

Mario Cuomo

Religious Belief and Public Morality

Mario Matthew Cuomo (b. 1932) was elected Governor of New York in 1979. Educated at St. John's University, he served on the faculty of St. John's School of Law from 1963–1973. In this address to the Department of Theology at the University of Notre Dame, he discusses the challenges of applying religious belief to everyday life.

I speak here as a politician. And also as a Catholic, a lay person baptized and raised in the pre-Vatican II Church, educated in Catholic schools, attached to the Church first by birth, then by choice, now by love. An old-fashioned Catholic who sins, regrets, struggles, worries, gets confused, and most of the time feels better after confession. The Catholic Church is my spiritual home. My heart is there, and my hope.

There is, of course, more to being a Catholic than having a sense of spiritual and emotional resonance. Catholicism is a religion of the head as well as the heart, and to be a Catholic is to say "I believe" to the essential core of dogmas that distinguishes our faith. The acceptance of this faith requires a lifelong struggle to understand it more fully and to live it more truly, to translate truth into experience, to practice as well as to believe. That's not easy: applying religious belief to everyday life often presents difficult challenges.

It's always been that way. It certainly is today. The America of the late twentieth century is a consumer society, filled with endless distractions, where faith is more often dismissed than challenged, where the ethnic and other loyalties that once fastened us to our religion seem to be weakening.

In addition to all the weaknesses, dilemmas, and temptations that impede every pilgrim's progress, the Catholic who holds political office in a pluralistic democracy—who is elected to serve Jews and Moslems, atheists and Protestants, as well as Catholics—bears special responsibility. He or she undertakes to help create conditions under which *all* can live with a maximum of dignity and with a reasonable degree of freedom; where everyone who chooses may hold beliefs different from specifically Catholic ones—sometimes contradictory to them; where the laws protect people's right to divorce, to use birth control, and even to choose abortion.

In fact, Catholic public officials take an oath to preserve the Constitution that guarantees this freedom. And they do so gladly. Not because they love what others do with their freedom, but because they realize that in guaranteeing freedom for all, they guarantee *our* right to be Catholics; *our* right to pray, to use the sacraments, to refuse birth control devices, to reject abortion, not to divorce and remarry if we believe it to be wrong.

The Catholic public official lives the political truth most Catholics, throughout most of American history, have accepted and insisted on: the truth that to assure our freedom we must allow others the same freedom, even if occasionally it produces conduct by them that we would hold to be sinful.

I protect my right to be a Catholic by preserving your right to believe as a Jew, a Protestant, or nonbeliever, or as anything else you choose. We know that the price´ of seeking to force our beliefs on others is that they might someday force theirs on us. This freedom is the fundamental strength of our unique experiment in government. In the complex interplay of forces and considerations that go into the making of our laws and policies, its preservation must be a pervasive and dominant concern.

But insistence on freedom is easier to accept as a general proposition than in its applications to specific situations. There are other valid general principles firmly embedded in our Constitution, which, operating at the same time, create interesting and occasionally troubling problems. Thus the same amendment of the Constitution that forbids the establishment of a state church affirms my legal right to argue that my religious belief would serve well as an article of our universal public morality. I may use the prescribed processes of government—the legislative and executive and judicial processes—to convince my fellow citizens—Jews and Protestants and Buddhists and nonbelievers—that what I propose is as beneficial for them as I believe it is for me; that it is not just parochial or narrowly sectarian but fulfills a human desire for order, peace, justice, kindness, love, any of the values most of us agree are desirable even apart from their specific religious base or context.

I am free to argue for a governmental policy for a nuclear freeze not just to avoid sin but because I think my democracy should regard it as a desirable goal. I can, if I wish, argue that the state should not fund the use of contraceptive devices not because the pope demands it but because I think that the whole community—for the good of the whole community—should not sever sex from an openness to the creation of life.

And surely I can, if so inclined, demand some kind of law against abortion not because my bishops say it is wrong but because I think that the whole community, regardless of its religious beliefs, should agree on the importance of protecting life—including life in the womb, which is at the very least potentially human and should not be extinguished casually.

No law prevents us from advocating any of these things: I am free to do so. So are the bishops. And so is Reverend Falwell. In fact, the Constitution guarantees my right to try. And theirs. And his.

But should I? Is it helpful? Is it essential to human dignity? Does it promote harmony and understanding? Or does it divide us so fundamentally that it threatens our ability to function as a pluralistic community? When should I argue to make my religious value your morality? My rule of conduct your limitation? What are the rules and policies that should influence the exercise of this right to argue and promote?

I believe I have a salvific mission as a Catholic. Does that mean I am in conscience required to do everything I can as governor to translate *all* my religious values into the laws and regulations of the state of New York or the United States? Or be branded a hypocrite if I don't?

As a Catholic, I respect the teaching authority of the bishops. But must I agree with everything in the bishops' pastoral letter on peace and fight to include it in party platforms? And will I have to do the same for the forthcoming pastoral on economics even if I am an unrepentant supply-sider? Must I, having heard the pope renew the Church's ban on birth control devices, veto the funding of contraceptive programs for non-Catholics or dissenting Catholics in my state?

I accept the Church's teaching on abortion. Must I insist you do? By law? By denying you Medicaid funding? By a constitutional amendment? If so, which one? Would that be the best way to avoid abortions or to prevent them? These are only some of the questions for Catholics. People with other religious beliefs face similar problems.

Let me try some answers. Almost all Americans accept some religious values as a part of our public life. We are a religious people, many of us descended from ancestors who came here expressly to live their religious faith free from coercion or repression. But we are also a people of many religions, with no established church, who hold different beliefs on many matters.

Our public morality, then—the moral standards we maintain for everyone, not just the ones we insist on in our private lives—depends on a consensus view of right and wrong. The values derived from religious belief will not—and should not—be accepted as part of the public morality unless they are shared by the pluralistic community at large, by consensus.

That values happen to be religious values does not deny them acceptability as a part of this consensus. But it does not require their acceptability either. The agnostics who joined the civil rights struggle were not deterred because that crusade's values had been nurtured and sustained in black Christian churches. Those on the political left are not perturbed today by the religious basis of the clergy and lay people who join them in the protest against the arms race and hunger and exploitation.

The arguments start when religious values are used to support positions which would impose on other people restrictions they find unacceptable. Some people *do* object to Catholic demands for an end to abortion, seeing it as a violation of the separation of Church and State. And some others, while they have no compunction about invoking the authority of the Catholic bishops in regard to birth control and abortion, might reject out of hand their teaching on war and peace and social policy.

Ultimately, therefore, the question "whether or not we admit religious values into our public affairs" is too broad to yield a single answer. "Yes," we create our public morality through consensus and in this country that consensus reflects to some extent religious values of a great majority of Americans. But "no," all religiously based values don't have an a priori place in our public morality.

The community must decide if what is being proposed would be better left to private discretion than public policy; whether it restricts freedoms, and if so to what end, to whose benefit; whether it will produce a good or bad result; whether overall it will help the community or merely divide it. The right answers to these questions can be elusive. Some of the wrong answers, on the other hand, are quite clear. For example, there are those who say there is a simple answer to *all* these questions; they say that by history and practice of our people we were intended to be—and should be—a Christian country in law.

But where would that leave the nonbelievers? And whose Christianity would be law, yours or mine?

The "Christian nation" argument should concern—even frighten—two groups: non-Christians and thinking Christians. I believe it does. I think it's already apparent that a good part of this nation understands—if only instinctively—that anything which seems to suggest that God favors a political party or the establishment of a state church, is wrong and dangerous.

Way down deep the American people are afraid of an entangling relationship between formal religions—or whole bodies of religious belief—and government. Apart from constitutional law and religious doctrine, there is a sense that tells us it's wrong to presume to speak for God or to claim God's sanction of our particular legislation and His rejection of all other positions. Most of us are offended when we see religion being trivialized by its appearance in political throwaway pamphlets.

The American people need no course in philosophy or political science or church history to know that God should not be made into a celestial party chairman. To most of us, the manipulative invoking of religion to advance a politician or a party is frightening and divisive. The American people will tolerate religious leaders taking positions for or against candidates, although I think the Catholic bishops are right in avoiding that position. But the American people are leery about large religious organizations, powerful churches or synagogue groups, engaging in such activities—again, not as a matter of law or doctrine, but because our innate wisdom and democratic instinct teaches us that these things are dangerous.

Today there are a number of issues involving life and death that raise questions of public morality. They are also questions of concern to most religions. Pick up a newspaper and you are almost certain to find a bitter controversy over any one of them: Baby Jane Doe, the right to die, artificial insemination, embryos in vitro, abortion, birth control . . . not to mention nuclear war and the shadow it throws across all existence. Some of these issues touch the most intimate recesses of our lives, our roles as someone's mother or child or husband; some affect women in a unique way. But they are also public questions, for all of us.

Put aside what God expects—assume if you like that there is no God—then the greatest thing still left to us is life. Even a radically secular world must struggle with the questions of when life begins, under what circumstances it can be ended, when it must be protected, by what authority; it too must decide what protection to extend to the helpless and the dying, to the aged and the unborn, to life in all its phases.

As a Catholic, I have accepted certain answers as the right ones for myself and my family, and because I have, they have influenced me in special ways, as Matilda's husband, as a father of five children, as a son who stood next to his own father's deathbed trying to decide if the tubes and needles no longer served a purpose. As a governor, however, I am involved in defining policies that determine *other* people's rights in these same areas of life and death. Abortion is one of these issues, and while it is one issue among many, it is one of the most controversial and affects me in a special way as a Catholic public official. So let me spend some time considering it.

I should start, I believe, by noting that the Catholic Church's actions with respect to the interplay of religious values and public policy make clear that there is no inflexible moral principle that determines what our *political* conduct should be. For example, on divorce and birth control, without changing its moral teaching, the Church abides the civil law as it now stands, thereby accepting—without making much of a point of it—that in our pluralistic society we are not required to insist that *all* our religious values be the law of the land.

Abortion is treated differently. Of course there are differences both in degree and quality between abortion and some of the other religious positions the Church takes: abortion is a "matter of life and death," and degree counts. But the differences in approach reveal a truth, I think, that is not well enough perceived by Catholics and therefore still further complicates the process for us. That is, while we always owe our bishops' words respectful attention and careful consideration, the question whether to engage the political system in a struggle to have it adopt certain articles of our belief as part of public morality is not a matter of doctrine: it is a matter of prudential political judgment.

Recently, Michael Novak put it succinctly: "Religious judgment and political judgment are both needed," he wrote. "But they are not identical." My Church and my conscience require me to believe certain things about divorce, birth control, and abortion. My Church does not order me—under pain of sin or expulsion—to pursue my salvific mission according to a precisely defined political plan.

As a Catholic I accept the Church's teaching authority. While in the past some Catholic theologians may appear to have disagreed on the morality of some abortions (it wasn't, I think, until 1869 that excommunication was attached to all abortions without distinction), and while some theologians still do, I accept the bishops' position that abortion is to be avoided.

As Catholics, my wife and I were enjoined never to use abortion to destroy the life we created, and we never have. We thought Church doctrine was clear on this, and—more than that—both of us felt it in full agreement with what our hearts and our consciences told us. For me life or fetal life in the womb should be protected, even if five of nine justices of the Supreme Court and my neighbor disagree with me. A fetus is different from an appendix or a set of tonsils. At the very least, even if the argument is made by some scientists or some theologians that in the early stages of fetal development we can't discern human life, the full potential of human life is indisputably there. That—to my less subtle mind—by itself should demand respect, caution, indeed . . . reverence. But not everyone in our society agrees with Matilda and me.

And those who don't—those who endorse legalized abortions—aren't a ruthless, callous alliance of anti-Christians determined to overthrow our moral standards. In many cases, the proponents of legal abortion are the very people who have worked with Catholics to realize the goals of social justice set out in papal encyclicals: the American Lutheran Church, the Central Conference of American Rabbis, the Presbyterian Church in the United States, B'nai B'rith Women, the Women of the Episcopal Church. These are just a few of the religious organizations that don't share the Church's position on abortion.

Certainly, we should not be forced to mold Catholic morality to conform to disagreement by non-Catholics however sincere or severe their disagreement. Our bishops should be teachers, not pollsters. They should not change what we Catholics believe in order to ease our consciences or please our friends or protect the Church from criticism. But if the breadth, intensity, and sincerity of opposition to Church teaching shouldn't be allowed to shape our Catholic morality, it can't help but determine our ability—our realistic, political ability—to translate our Catholic morality into civil law, a law not for the believers who don't need it but for the disbelievers who reject it. And it is here, in our attempt to find a political answer to abortion—an answer beyond our private observance of Catholic morality—that we encounter controversy within and without the Church over how and in what degree to press the case that our morality should be everybody else's, and to what effect.

I repeat, there is no Church teaching that mandates the best political course for making our belief everyone's rule, for spreading this part of our Catholicism. There is neither an encyclical or a catechism that spells out a political strategy for achieving legislative goals. And so the Catholic trying to make moral and prudent judgments in the political realm must discern which, if any, of the actions one could take would be best.

This latitude of judgment is not something new in the Church, not a development that has arisen only with the abortion issue. Take, for example, the question of slavery. It has been argued that the failure to endorse a legal ban on abortions is equivalent to refusing to support the cause of abolition before the Civil War. This analogy has been advanced by the bishops of my own state.

But the truth of the matter is, few if any Catholic bishops spoke for abolition in the years before the Civil War. It wasn't, I believe, that the bishops endorsed the idea of some humans owning and exploiting other humans; Pope Gregory XVI, in 1840, had condemned the slave trade. Instead it was a practical political judgment that the bishops made. They weren't hypocrites; they were realists. At the time, Catholics were a small minority, mostly immigrants, despised by much of the population, often vilified and the object of sporadic violence. In the face of a public controversy that aroused tremendous passions and threatened to break the country apart, the bishops made a pragmatic decision. They believed their opinion would not change people's minds. Moreover they knew that there were southern Catholics, even some priests, who owned slaves. They concluded that under the circumstances arguing for a constitutional amendment against slavery would do more harm than good, so they were silent. As they have been, generally, in recent years, on the question of birth control. And as the Church has been on even more controversial issues in the past, even ones that dealt with life and death.

What is relevant to this discussion is that the bishops were making judgments about translating Catholic teachings into public policy, not about the moral validity of the teachings. In so doing they grappled with the unique political complexities of their time. The decision they made to remain silent on a constitutional amendment to abolish slavery or on the repeal of the Fugitive Slave Law wasn't a mark of their moral indifference: it was a measured attempt to balance moral truths against political realities. Their decision reflected their sense of complexity, not their diffidence. As history reveals, Lincoln behaved with similar discretion.

The parallel I want to draw here is not between or among what we Catholics believe to be moral wrongs. It is in the Catholic response to those wrongs. Church teaching on slavery and abortion is clear. But in the application of those teachings—the exact way we translate them into action, the specific laws we propose, the exact legal sanctions we seek—there was and is no one, clear, absolute route that the Church says, as a matter of doctrine, we must follow.

The bishops' pastoral letter, "The Challenge of Peace," speaks directly to this point. "We recognize," the bishops wrote,

> that the Church's teaching authority does not carry the same force when it deals with technical solutions involving particular means as it does when it speaks of principles or ends. People may agree in abhorring an injustice, for instance, yet sincerely disagree as to what practical approach will achieve justice. Religious groups are entitled as others to their opinion in such cases, but they should not claim that their opinions are the only ones that people of good will may hold.

With regard to abortion, the American bishops have had to weigh Catholic moral teaching against the fact of a pluralistic country where our view is in the minority, acknowledging that what is ideally desirable isn't always feasible, that there can be different political approaches to abortion besides unyielding adherence to an absolute prohibition. This is in the American-Catholic tradition of political realism. In supporting or opposing specific legislation the Church in this country has never retreated into a moral fundamentalism that will settle for nothing less than total acceptance of its views.

Indeed, the bishops have already confronted the fact that an absolute ban on abortion doesn't have the support necessary to be placed in our Constitution. In 1981, they put aside earlier efforts to describe a law they could accept and get passed, and supported the Hatch amendment instead. Some Catholics felt the bishops had gone too far with that action, some not far enough. Such judgments were not a rejection of the bishops' teaching authority: the bishops even disagreed among themselves. Catholics are allowed to disagree on these technical political questions without having to confess.

Respectfully, and after careful consideration of the position and arguments of the bishops, I have concluded that the approach of a constitutional amendment is not the best way for us to seek to deal with abortion.

I believe that legally interdicting abortion by either the federal government or the individual states is not a plausible possibility and even if it could be obtained, it wouldn't work. Given present attitudes, it would be "Prohibition" revisited, legislating what couldn't be enforced and in the process creating a disrespect for law in general. And as much as I admire the bishops' hope that a constitutional amendment against abortion would be the basis for a full, new bill of rights for mothers and children, I disagree that this would be the result.

I believe that, more likely, a constitutional prohibition would allow people to ignore the causes of many abortions instead of addressing them, much the way the death penalty is used to escape dealing more fundamentally and more rationally with the problem of violent crime.

Other legal options that have been proposed are, in my view, equally ineffective. The Hatch amendment, by returning the question of abortion to the states, would have given us a checkerboard of permissive and restrictive jurisdictions. In some cases people might have been forced to go elsewhere to have abortions and that might have eased a few consciences but it wouldn't have done what the Church wants to do—it wouldn't have created a deep-seated respect for life. Abortions would have gone on, millions of them.

Nor would a denial of Medicaid funding for abortion achieve our objectives. Given *Roe* v. *Wade*, it would be nothing more than an attempt to do indirectly what the law says cannot be done directly; worse, it would do it in a way that would burden only the already disadvantaged. Removing funding for the Medicaid program would not prevent the rich and middle classes from having abortions. It would not even assure that the disadvantaged wouldn't have them; it would only impose financial burdens on poor women who want abortions.

Apart from that unevenness, there is a more basic question. Medicaid is designed to deal with health and medical needs. But the arguments for the cutoff of Medicaid abortion funds are not related to those needs. They are moral arguments. If we assume health and medical needs exist, our personal view of morality ought not to be considered a relevant basis for discrimination.

We must keep in mind always that we are a nation of laws—when we like those laws, and when we don't. The Supreme Court has established a woman's constitutional right to abortion. The Congress has decided the federal government should not provide federal funding in the Medicaid program for abortion. That, of course, does not bind states in the allocation of their own state funds. Under the law, individual states need not follow the federal lead, and in New York I believe we *cannot* follow that lead. The equal protection clause in New York's constitution has been interpreted by the courts as a standard of fairness that would preclude us from denying only the poor— indirectly, by a cutoff of funds—the practical use of the constitutional right given by *Roe* v. *Wade*.

In the end, even if after a long and divisive struggle we were able to remove all Medicaid funding for abortion and restore the law to what it was— if we could put most abortions out of our sight, return them to the back rooms where they were performed for so long—I don't believe our responsibility as Catholics would be any closer to being fulfilled than it is now, with abortion guaranteed by the law as a woman's right.

The hard truth is that abortion isn't a failure of government. No agency or department of government forces women to have abortions, but abortion goes on. Catholics, the statistics show, support the right to abortion in equal proportion to the rest of the population. Despite the teaching in our homes and schools and pulpits, despite the sermons and pleadings of parents and priests and prelates, despite all the effort at defining our opposition to the sin of abortion, collectively we Catholics apparently believe—and perhaps act—little differently from those who don't share our commitment.

Are we asking government to make criminal what we believe to be sinful because we ourselves can't stop committing the sin? The failure here is not Caesar's. This failure is our failure, the failure of the entire people of God.

Nobody has expressed this better than a bishop in my own state, Joseph Sullivan, a man who works with the poor in New York City, is resolutely opposed to abortion, and argues, with his fellow bishops, for a change of law. "The major problem the Church has is internal," the bishop said last month in reference to abortion. "How do we teach? As much as I think we're responsible for advocating public policy issues, our primary responsibility is to teach our own people. We haven't done that. We're asking politicians to do what we haven't done effectively ourselves."

I agree with the bishop. I think our moral and social mission as Catholics must begin with the wisdom contained in the words "Physician, heal thyself." Unless we Catholics educate ourselves better to the values that define—and can ennoble—our lives, following those teachings better than we do now, unless we set an example that is clear and compelling then we will never convince this society to change the civil laws to protect what we preach is precious human life.

Better than any law or rule or threat of punishment would be the moving strength of our own good example, demonstrating our lack of hypocrisy, proving the beauty and worth of our instruction. We must work to find ways to avoid abortions without otherwise violating our faith. We should provide funds and opportunities for young women to bring their child to term, knowing both of them will be taken care of if that is necessary; we should teach our young men better than we do now their responsibilities in creating and caring for human life.

It is this duty of the Church to teach through its practice of love what Pope John Paul II has proclaimed so magnificently to all peoples. "The Church," he wrote in *Redemptor Hominis* (1979),

> which has no weapons at her disposal apart from those of the spirit, of the word and of love, cannot renounce her proclamation of "the word . . . in season and out of season." For this reason she does not cease to implore . . . everybody in the name of God and in the name of man: Do not kill! Do not prepare destruction and extermination for each other! Think of your brothers and sisters who are suffering hunger and misery! Respect each one's dignity and freedom!

The weapons of the word and of love are already available to us: we need no statute to provide them. I am not implying that we should stand by and pretend indifference to whether a woman takes a pregnancy to its conclusion or aborts it. I believe we should in all cases try to teach a respect for life. And I believe with regard to abortion that, despite *Roe* v. *Wade*, we can, in practical ways. Here, in fact, it seems to me that all of us can agree.

Without lessening their insistence on a woman's right to an abortion, the people who call themselves "pro-choice" can support the development of government programs that present an impoverished mother with the full range of support she needs to bear and raise her children, to have a real choice. Without dropping their campaign to ban abortion, those who gather under the banner of "pro-life" can join in developing and enacting a legislative bill of rights for mothers and children, as the bishops have already proposed.

While we argue over abortion, the United States' infant mortality rate places us sixteenth among the nations of the world. Thousands of infants die each year because of inadequate medical care. Some are born with birth defects that, with proper treatment, could be prevented. Some are stunted in their physical and mental growth because of improper nutrition. If we want to prove our regard for life in the womb, for the helpless infant—if we care about women having real choices in their lives and not being driven to abortions by a sense of helplessness and despair about the future of their child—then there is work enough for all of us. Lifetimes of it.

In New York, we have put in place a number of programs to begin this work, assisting women in giving birth to healthy babies. This year we doubled Medicaid funding to private-care physicians for prenatal and delivery services. The state already spends $20 million a year for prenatal care in out-patient clinics and for in-patient hospital care. One program in particular we believe holds a great deal of promise. It's called "new avenues to dignity," and it seeks to provide a teen-age mother with the special service she needs to continue with her education, to train for a job, to become capable of standing on her own, to provide for herself and the child she is bringing into the world.

My dissent, then, from the contention that we can have effective and enforceable legal prohibitions on abortion is by no means an argument for religious quietism, for accepting the world's wrongs because that is our fate as "the poor banished children of Eve."

Let me make another point. Abortion has a unique significance but not a preemptive significance. Apart from the question of the efficacy of using legal weapons to make people stop having abortions, we know our Christian responsibility doesn't end with any one law or amendment. That it doesn't end with abortion. Because it involves life and death, abortion will always be a central concern of Catholics. But so will nuclear weapons. And hunger and homelessness and joblessness, all the forces diminishing human life and threatening to destroy it. The "seamless garment" that Cardinal Bernardin has spoken of is a challenge to all Catholics in public office, conservatives as well as liberals.

We cannot justify our aspiration to goodness simply on the basis of the vigor of our demand for an elusive and questionable civil law declaring what we already know, that abortion is wrong. Approval or rejection of legal restrictions on abortion should not be the exclusive litmus test of Catholic loyalty. We should understand that whether abortion is outlawed or not, our work has barely begun: the work of creating a society where the right to life doesn't end at the moment of birth; where an infant isn't helped into a world that doesn't care if it's fed properly, housed decently, educated adequately; where the blind or retarded child isn't condemned to exist rather than empowered to live.

The bishops stated this duty clearly in 1974, in their statement to the Senate subcommittee considering a proposed amendment to restrict abortions. They maintained such an amendment could not be seen as an end in itself. "We do not see a constitutional amendment as the final product of our commitment or of our legislative activity," they said.

> It is instead the constitutional base on which to provide support and assistance to pregnant women and their unborn children. This would include nutritional,

prenatal, childbirth and postnatal care for the mother, and also nutritional and pediatric care for the child through the first year of life. . . . We believe that all of these should be available as a matter of right to all pregnant women and their children.

The bishops reaffirmed that view in 1976, in 1980, and again this year when the United States Catholic Committee asked Catholics to judge candidates on a wide range of issues—on abortion, yes; but also on food policy, the arms race, human rights, education, social justice, and military expenditures. The bishops have been consistently "pro-life" in the full meaning of that term, and I respect them for that.

The problems created by the matter of abortion are complex and confounding. Nothing is clearer to me than my inadequacy to find compelling solutions to all of their moral, legal, and social implications. I—and many others like me—am eager for enlightenment, eager to learn new and better ways to manifest respect for the deep reverence for life that is our religion and our instinct. I hope that this public attempt to describe the problems as I understand them will give impetus to the dialogue in the Catholic community and beyond, a dialogue that could show me a better wisdom than I've been able to find so far. It would be tragic if we let that dialogue become a prolonged, divisive argument that destroys or impairs our ability to practice any part of the morality given us in the Sermon on the Mount, to touch, heal, and affirm the human life that surrounds us.

We Catholic citizens of the richest, most powerful nation that has ever existed are like the stewards made responsible over a great household: from those to whom so much has been given, much shall be required. It is worth repeating that ours is not a faith that encourages its believers to stand apart from the world, seeking their salvation alone, separate from the salvation of those around them. We speak of ourselves as a body. We come together in worship as companions, in the ancient sense of that word, those who break bread together, and who are obliged by the commitment we share to help one another, everywhere, in all we do, and in the process, to help the whole human family. We see our mission to be "the completion of the work of creation."

This is difficult work today. It presents us with many hard choices. The Catholic Church has come of age in America. The ghetto walls are gone, our religion no longer a badge of irredeemable foreignness. This new-found status is both an opportunity and a temptation. If we choose, we can give in to the temptation to become more and more assimilated into a larger, blander culture, abandoning the practice of the specific values that made us different, worshiping whatever gods the marketplace has to sell while we seek to rationalize our own laxity by urging the political system to legislate on others a morality we no longer practice ourselves.

Or we can remember where we come from, the journey of two millennia, clinging to our personal faith, to its insistence on constancy and service and on hope. We can live and practice the morality Christ gave us, maintaining His truth in this world, struggling to embody His love, practicing it especially where that love is most needed, among the poor and the weak and the dispossessed. Not just by trying to make laws for others to live by, but by living the laws already written for us by God, in our hearts and our minds.

We can be fully Catholic; proudly, totally at ease with ourselves, a people in the world, transforming it, a light to this nation. Appealing to the best in our people not the worst. Persuading not coercing. Leading people to truth by love. And still, all the while, respecting and enjoying our unique pluralistic democracy. And we can do it even as politicians.

Suggestions for Discussion

1. Discuss the historical illustrations used by Governor Cuomo.

2. Summarize his discussion of the abortion issue.

3. Explain his assertion that an "insistence on freedom is easier to accept as a general proposition than in its applications to specific situations."

Suggestions for Writing

1. Discuss one of the "issues involving life and death that raise questions of public morality."

2. Using your own beliefs, comment on Governor Cuomo's position on abortion.

Raymond Firth

God and Anthropology

Raymond Firth (b. 1901), Emeritus Professor of Anthropology at the University of London, has written widely on the anthropology of New Guinea. His books include *Art and Life in New Guinea* (1936), *Elements of Social Organization* (1951), *Primitive Polynesian Economy* (1975), *We, the Tikopia* (1963), and *Human Types* (1983). In the essay that follows, Firth discuss anthropological studies of the divine.

Anthropologists have been a bit wary of God, even without a capital letter. Ever since the days of Edward Burnett Tylor more than a century ago, we have recognized that there is no society, as we ordinarily define it, which is without some form of religion. But the conceptual forms by reference to which the religion is described, manifested, impelled to action and validated, are of an immense range. Tylor encapsulated them for his "minimum definition" of religion under the general head of "spiritual beings". But to this was soon added a concept of impersonal mystical forces, far removed from any idea of voluntary action such as a spirit being might be thought to engage in.

In all the societies they have studied, modern social anthropologists have been led to perceive what may be called the essential human drama. People everywhere, in all kinds of technical and social conditions, have been preoccupied with the ultimate problems of living: relation to nature and to one another; reasons for variation in skill and endeavour; competing claims of loyalty and self-interest, generosity and greed, love and hate, self-denial and ambition; the anguish of pain, suffering and fear of death; ideas of the definition of the self and the relation between initiative and the operations of chance or fate. Every human society has had answers to the questions so posed, or at least has worked out ways of alleviating or preventing the worst misfortunes and promoting success.

Myths, creeds and rituals, in all societies, show how people try to locate responsibility for human affairs to some degree outside the human sphere. But major themes such as the creation of the world, of man and human institutions, the source of knowledge, the moral law, good and evil in the life of man, are very differently envisaged in different societies. An essential attribute of divinity is power—extra-human, extra-physical power—and associated with this is some notion of the sacred. When power and the sacred are interpreted at ultimate or utmost level, then divinity is God. Many societies have no such image of God as a unique ultimate being. While a monotheist might see here a fragmented conception of divinity, adherents of other religious systems see their own pantheon or analogous set of concepts as positively fitted to their problems.

In exposing religious ideas held in a range of societies, the modern anthropologist has set out a vast array of formulations about guardian spirits, powers, gods, deities, creator beings, demiurges, culture heroes. And since inferences about belief are derived from study of non-verbal rites and practices as well as from speech, an anthropologist's accounts of a religion can be deeply infused with analysis of worship, offering, libation, sacrifice, consecration, prayer, communion, prophecy, divination, spirit mediumship.

Problems familiar to us from the classical Greek philosophers appear in exotic context. When I investigated notions of the fate of the soul in so-called "primitive" communities, I found that while the health of the soul in life was a matter of critical interest, the future of the soul after death of the body was not a matter of deep concern to many peoples. They rarely believed the soul to be immortal, they often had no belief in its dependence upon any God, and had few notions of rewards and punishments in the afterlife. On the other hand, their eschatology has been more dynamic than ours, with the souls of the dead believed to be in frequent social intercourse with one another, those of the ancestors and those of the living. In Western belief, by contrast, the souls of the dead have very little to do and have almost no volition.

The problem of the relation of impersonal fate to personal responsibility was examined by the late Meyer Fortes, in his striking *Oedipus and Job in West African Religion* (1959), analysing beliefs of the Tallensi. Fortes pointed out that the Tallensi in their traditional beliefs handled the idea of man's fate as a combination of two elements of destiny, an initial endowment and a subsequent protective supervision by ancestral spirit guardians. These represented symbolically innate disposition and concrete parental upbringing on the one hand, and the more abstract forces of society on the other. The extent of a man's success in life was then a figurative expression of his ability to control his innate drives by the proper performance of ritual to his ancestors. Any failure—including his eventual death—was interpreted as a result of his unwitting neglect of obligation. Such religious conceptions are closely linked with basic ideas of family structure and kinship ties. They are given a sacred value, but this does not derive from any idea of God. In such a context, the outcome of any divine will is highly socialized, and is seen in definitely personal human terms.

The recurrent problem of evil has also received anthropological attention. In a recent collection of essays edited by David Parkin, *The Anthropology of Evil* (reviewed in the *TLS*, July 19, 1985), it is suggested that there is something inherently ambiguous in many peoples' understanding of evil. Accordingly there is great diversity in the reasons given for the existence of evil, and in the classification of what actions and persons may be labelled under this head. In theistic systems, where evil may be isolated as a principle, even personified, anthropologists recognize distinctions already made by theologians. In some Hindu and Sufi Muslim systems, evil becomes an aspect of God. In the Semitic religions there is a qualified semi-dualism, with God opposed by Satan but capable of mastering him and willing to help mortals in their struggle against evil. And full dualistic systems such as Manichaeism recognize good and evil as two opposed cosmic principles, eternally in antagonism. But for anthropologists the religious problem is not just one of theodicy in any narrow sense. Studies of Buddhism show that while there may be no belief in God, the concept of evil occurs at a folk level, though in a relatively weak form, consonant with the idea that the roots of wrongdoing lie within the individual himself. In many "pagan" religions, both man and his gods are conceived as naturally embodying a range of impulses which may lead to good or evil actions, judged by their results. In such a pagan system, creation is commonly believed to have been devoid of moral purpose, and evil is accepted as part of the constitution of the world. The problem is the power of evil, not its ultimate origin. Much effort may be spent, as it is in divination or spirit mediumship, to ascertain an immediate source of evil— for example, in witchcraft—but the controlling powers of the religious system may be neutral or indifferent unless they are stirred to intervention by propitiatory offering or sacrifice. In revealing the variations in the concept of evil in many societies, anthropologists have emphasized its human, pragmatic dimensions in a social context, and by implication have reinforced ideas of theodicy as a still open question.

In considering the ways in which anthropologists have dealt explicitly with the expression "God", three important points should be borne in mind. The first is that God rarely figures as a universal concept, with abstract connotation such as theologians commonly use. In an anthropological analysis, God is culturally located, and described in terms which translate what the people of a given society say and do in his regard. Secondly, while anthropologists may occasionally express propositions about God which arise from their own beliefs, for the most part they are citing the opinions of other people, produced in an alien society, and so are making a report, an interpretation at some remove from the actual experience that is being described and discussed. (The exact status of a theologian's assertions about God raises some interesting questions for anthropologists—how far, for instance, theological utterances about the existence and nature of God are made in awareness of the complex social parameters of any such general statements?) Thirdly, anthropological statements about God are essentially heuristic and exploratory. They are not concerned primarily with questions of truth or falsity or with moral qualities, but with the understanding of social concepts and relationships, with the way in which ideas of symbolic value relate to the structure of societies and the operations of people in them.

Ethnographically, interpretations of what may be thought to be specific apprehensions or images of God, among people of different cultures, fall into three broad categories. Colloquially, these may be seen as God among the "pagans", God in the mainstream theistic religions and God in the offshoot cults.

Of high significance in the first category are the findings of anthropologists in some—though not many—African societies, where a spiritual entity of supreme quality has been recognized. A classic example is that given by Jomo Kenyatta in his anthropological study of his own people, whom he called the Gikuyu, in *Facing Mount Kenya* (1938). Kenyatta stated, "The Gikuyu believe in one God, Ngai, the creator and giver of all things." He went on to say that Ngai had no father, mother or companion of any kind, lived in the sky but had temporary homes on earth, in the mountains, where he might rest when he brought blessings and punishments to the people. In prayers and sacrifices the Gikuyu turn towards Mount Kenya, which is believed to be Ngai's official residence and is accordingly known as "mountain of brightness" and thought to be holy. Ngai, invisible to ordinary mortal eyes, is called upon at the birth, initiation, marriage and death of a person. He is thus plausibly, from his combination of supreme qualities, described as God. But Ngai is a distant being and takes but little interest in people in their daily walks of life and must never be pestered by frequent appeal. And he is not accessible to individual prayer. Only a family group with the father at its head may supplicate him.

In other words, he is God for social units, not for persons. It may be asked whether Kenyatta, in his desire to represent the Kikuyu with dignity in the face of Western pressure and proselytization, did not exaggerate the role of Ngai as God. But Kenyatta's position is supported by comparable evidence from other African peoples—from E. E. Evans-Pritchard on the Nuer, S. F. Nadel on the Nupe, Godfrey Lienhardt on the Dinka and John Middleton on the Lugbara.

The picture of a supreme being thus presented is not a conventional Western one. It is a deist rather than a theist picture, that is, the supreme being is regarded as the ultimate source of reality, including humanity and human institutions, but one who does not often intervene in natural and human processes by way of voluntary acts of care or salvation. God may be the ground of moral value, but there is no general expression equivalent to "God is love". God is either otiose and indifferent or has a general benevolence which must be sharpened into supportive action for men, not by right thoughts but by rituals of propitiation. The location of God is vague. He is usually thought to be not in the terrestrial world, though the Lugbara speak of a transcendent God in the sky, and immanent other half on earth, with wives and many children, who is responsible for the inspiration of diviners, for the power of rainmakers and for all death. Even God's personality is in question. Most accounts are in anthropomorphic terms, but the syntax of some African languages, being genderless, leaves it open whether God is being referred to as "He", "She", or "It". Such a problem may not disturb modern Western theologians, for whom a concept of "modes of being" may cater for such difficulties.

But a semantic problem remains over God's name. In an African context, what is presented as a "pagan" religious concept may have been influenced by ideas from Islam—as with the Nupe. Then an anthropologist's own experience may have predisposed him to accept a theistic labelling—as perhaps Evans-Pritchard did with the Nuer *kwoth*. But the issue is a delicate one. Lienhardt, a sensitive interpreter of African religious thought, has described how the Dinka of the Sudan claim to encounter spirits of various kinds, which he glossed as "powers". A common Dinka term *nhialic* is used in some contexts where Lienhardt says it could be suitably translated as God, with reference to prayers and sacrifices offered to a father and creator. Yet the connotation of *nhialic* is much wider than this, embracing notions of the sky above, and of a collectivity of spirits. So Lienhardt concluded that to use the word God for such Dinka concepts would raise difficult metaphysical and semantic problems for which there is no Dinka parallel. His solution was to use the term Divinity: he argued that this, with a capital letter, can convey the idea not only of a being but also of a nature and existence with less personal meaning. Lienhardt's major study of Dinka religion is entitled *Divinity and Experience* (1961).

Anthropologists have shown growing boldness in tackling the concept of God in the mainstream theistic religions. Their studies have tended to refer to the divine in two ways: how concepts of God are formulated at the folk level rather than at the level of scholarly exegesis, and how the pragmatic experiences of a congregational worshipper relate to the theological pattern of ideas. Contributions to an understanding of the idea of God in the Christian faith have been fairly restricted. Long ago, there was a path-breaking study, *Christian Myth and Ritual* (1933), by E. O. James, who was both an anthropologist and in holy orders as a Professor of the Philosophy and History of Religion. In *The Family of God* (1959), W. Lloyd Walmer, an anthropologically trained sociologist, produced a lively analysis of the meaning and functions of the symbolism of Christian life in the United States. Recently, there have been intriguing studies, by the late Victor Turner and Edith Turner, of pilgrimage as a means of securing a closer relation to God's grace (*Image and Pilgrimage in Christian Culture: Anthropological perspectives*, 1978). Much comparative analysis of ideas of spirit and divinity in complex faiths appears in *Religious Organization and Religious Experience* (1982), edited by John Davis. And going to the roots of assertions about the divine, there has been anthropological inquiry into what is meant by such expressions as "I believe . . .". But direct analysis of the concept of God has been rare, though I myself have made some comment from a comparative humanist point of view upon the notions of gods and God. In the Islamic field, anthropologists have reflected upon the way in which a pious Muslim must try to lead a virtuous life in an imperfect world. The religious obligations of the Faithful to Allah, as interpreted with finality by the Prophet, are mandatory and all-embracing. They involve a tussle between the faculty of reason implanted by Allah and the passions and interests which animate every man and woman. Anthropologists have explored the varying interpretations of the notion of God's will in relation to the actions of men, and the meaning of prayer as an aid to carrying out God's will. To a pious Muslim villager, prayer is not the means of making ritual requests to God, but a sacred duty, and an instrument of self-control in the battle of reason against passion in the desired "surrender to God".

A marked feature of religious movement during the last four centuries or so has been the spread of major "universal" faiths through much of a "pagan" world. Anthropologists have seen this not as a simple conversion from darkness to light, the replacement of gods by God, but as a complex process of transfer of belief and ritual. They have studied strategies of the transfer, why people convert, how the new doctrines relate to the old, and what changes in the social structure are associated with an acknowledgement of a new divine Father and Lord. The anthropology of folk religion presents a kaleidoscopic picture of many different combinations of ideas of God and indigenous beliefs, when the data are interpreted in sociological rather than in theological terms.

Particularly striking have been the many anthropological studies of religious cults outside the established mainstream Churches—cults called, not too accurately, chiliastic or millenarian. These range from the independent Bantu Churches of South Africa to the voodoo cults of the Caribbean and the "cargo cults" of the Melanesia. Such cults are often marked by a theological tolerance in which God is assisted by local spirits of varying power, and they interpret the divine in terms of personal experience, very closely, in dreams, ecstasy, glossolalia. Social parameters of the cults are much in evidence. There are European and Asian analogies, but in Africa, the Caribbean and Melanesia the congregations are black, they retain many indigenous elements in their ritual, such as dancing or healing techniques, and traditional values such as the propriety of polygamy may still remain. Essentially, they are asserting a cultural appropriation of God. Their members can feel God personally—sometimes their prophet leader claims to *be* God. "Jehovah is ours, our very own" has been one cry. Long before the recognition of "indigenous theology" or a "black liberation theology", just as the poet Countee Cullen wrote of the "Black Christ", so these cults were presenting God in a new light. He was not the God of the Europeans, with their economic and political domination, but a God who could help the repressed people to an independent life of their own. (Analogies with the rise of Christianity are not far to seek.) Shot through with racial tension, the "cargo cults" in particular have been presented by some anthropologists, perhaps over-dramatically, as incipient revolutionary movements. On the other hand, they have sometimes seemed to be trying to lift themselves by their religious bootstraps, seeking by cultic means to get what they could not achieve on the pragmatic economic and political plane. But what in effect the cults have been saying is that self-help is an essential part of the redemptive process, even if it means a radical reinterpretation of God's nature and role.

For those who believe in God in any conventional way, much anthropological analysis of the idea of the divine may seem like a kind of cosmic *chutzpah*, a gigantic impertinence which might move the Almighty to amusement or compassion. But whether one believes in God as the ultimate reality, or in him as a political power-source, or as the final principle of love, or thinks as I do that God is a product of human imagination and yearning to provide some solution to the problems of existence, the findings of anthropologists can be of service. Anthropological enquiry has broadened our knowledge of the concept of God, and of the approaches made to God. Independently of "indigenous theology" and perhaps more forcefully, it has studied the meaning of God over a great social range, and explored the way in which these meanings relate to the different structures of society. It has also shown the inadequacy of an ethnocentric understanding of God. Many Christian missionaries and other servants of God have discovered that their message is truly meaningful only when the idea of the deity can be seen to have direct relevance to local community conditions. If anthropological studies of the divine have no other value, they may suggest more sensitivity and more humility towards the different ways in which people understand God.

Suggestions for Discussion

1. What three points should be considered when anthropologists deal explicitly with the expression *God?*

2. Give examples from Firth's discussion of anthropological interpretations of God among the "pagans," God in the mainstream theistic religions, and God in the offshoot cults.

3. Discuss his observation that anthropological studies "suggest more sensitivity and more humility towards the different ways in which people understand God."

Suggestions for Writing

1. Analyze Firth's use of the writings of others to illustrate his points. To what extent does he succeed in interesting you in reading further?

2. Analyze the ways in which Firth organizes and illustrates his material in order to make it accessible to the reader.

Brian Pippard

God and the Physical Scientist

Brian Pippard is the author of *An Introduction to Physical Theory* (1985) and two volumes of *The Physics of Vibration* (1978, 1983). In the essay that follows, he states his personal religious beliefs and examines the limitations of scientific models.

I am a physicist and an agnostic, neither believing nor disbelieving in a supreme being, lacking indeed any personal experience which might allow me to attach a meaning to the idea. To make this state of ignorance an excuse or even an incentive to attack the beliefs of others, as some do, seems to me indefensible. It is as if a tone-deaf man were to deride the pretensions of those who find in music an expression of realities which lie beyond the power of words. When the scientist can explain convincingly to a musician the origin and mechanism of musical feeling he may care to try his hand at religious belief. The true believer, however, need not fear—his citadel is impregnable to scientific assult because it occupies territory which is closed to science.

The domain of science is vast, comprising in principle all experiences and observations which can be agreed on by an overwhelming consensus. Where consensus fails, and discussion is fruitless, is in such matters as whether roses smell the same to you as to me. The inner world of individual consciousness is wholly private even to the psychologist, whose scientific concern is not to explain what Mind is, but to construct theories which help one to believe one understands why people act as they do. To use the musical analogy again, the science of psychology is something like the theories of harmony and counterpoint, in that analysis of the practice of the great masters enables a set of rules to be drawn up well enough to programme a computer. One does not expect the output to be great music; at best it may pass as the production of a competent hack. If something more exciting emerges it will only be by chance, and will require a human listener to recognize its worth. All attempts to model the brain as a super-computer are in principle scientific theories, concerned with mechanisms which can be described in words and assented to by any who care to understand. No such theory can jump the gap between a mechanism that has been designed to simulate a thinking creature, and the genuine article, the thinker I know myself to be and, for courtesy's sake (though without the same direct knowledge), I assume you are also.

The classic dichotomy of Mind and Matter remains as absolute as ever, and much of the controversy between religion and science could have been avoided if both sides had agreed on this. But scientists, in the enthusiasm of their success in interpreting the material world, have thoughtlessly extended their arguments into the mental and spiritual domains; conversely, some theologians and priests, traditionally the guardians of cosmological theories, have clung to their primitive accounts in the face of conflicting scientific evidence, fearing for their faith and moral standards, or those of their flock.

I have deliberately begun a discussion of scientific evidence concerning the existence and nature of God at the point where scientific method is called in doubt. By emphasizing our inability to include consciousness in the programme we scientists are forced to wonder whether what we study is reality itself or only a distorted view of reality—an invention of our minds, whatever those words may mean. That they do mean something, I think we all agree— we cannot believe that the collective efforts of a million minds can result in an agreed fiction concerning an illusion. But it is all too easy for us to accept uncritically a simplistic materialism which assumes the world of the senses to be essentially the same as what is "out there", as if God (if he existed) could look down and see something very like what we see, only presumably rather more clearly. Reacting from this, Niels Bohr led the way, among physicists, to the doctrine that the scientist has no concern with "reality"—his job is to construct a model to relate as exactly as possible the various observations on which all reasonable people can agree.

I intend the word "model" to convey the rather precise sense of an intellectual construction with carefully stated assumptions and rules for logical manipulation. Newton's *Principia* presented the first great model of the universe, which has since been extended and modified into something that is now immensely versatile. It includes not only the objects of everyday life that we think we perceive directly, but the atoms and molecules, themselves made up of fundamental particles, and the hypothetical forces by which they interact. The rules for manipulating the model include the non-Euclidean geometry of relativity theory and the equations of quantum mechanics. Applied to situations of such simplicity that the mathematical problems are soluble, or computers powerful enough to deal with them, they have led, on countless occasions, to solutions agreeing with observation in a way that rules out the possibility of mere accident. When theory and observation disagree the normal reaction is to seek for an error in calculation or experiment; failing which, the basic assumptions of the particular calculation are scrutinized to make sure a significant point has not been overlooked. In sixty years the model has been extended but not basically changed, and anyone who, without meticulous scrutiny, makes discrepancies an excuse for trying to overthrow it is dismissed as a crank.

Nevertheless the model is still a model, not reality itself, if only because its elementary units, electrons and protons, say, have to be assigned extraordinary properties unlike anything we can touch or see. There have always been physicists who like to think that underlying the apparent strangeness is a more sensible substructure that the grossness of our senses precludes from being observed directly. In their view the equations of quantum mechanics are derivative from something which is, apart from its tiny dimensions, much more like the world we know. However, as long ago as 1930 it was proved that no system involving "hidden variables" could yield the mathematical structure of quantum mechanics. Various attempts to get round this limitation have indeed resulted in what their authors think are plausible instances of the true reality—only the properties which have to be postulated are even more grotesquely unimaginable than those they sought to replace. In practice, most physicists accept quantum mechanics and the other basic postulates for what they are, a gloriously successful programme for describing consistently, and with great economy, the whole of the world of observation.

One aspect of this model which has perturbed scientists, theologians and laymen equally is the element of chance in quantum mechanics, closely linked to Heisenberg's uncertainty principle. There is no way of predicting precisely the outcome of an experiment—an electron emitted from a point on a hot filament may go here or there, and all we can do is calculate how many out of crowd of electrons leaving the same way will finish up at various places, never which one will go where. "God does not play dice" expressed Einstein's revulsion at the whole notion, which he could never bring himself to accept. And some theologians have seen in an apparent breakdown of causality the collapse of one of their strongest arguments for the existence of God. On the other hand, a few welcomed the intrusion of a chance element as a mechanism whereby God could fiddle the accounts without being detected. But can one really believe in a God who has gone to such trouble to create a marvellously consistent and fertile universe, leaving himself the option of interfering with it (but not too often, and only when no one is looking)? It is too much like cheating at Patience.

A better answer to these worries is to remember that at the level of human experience it is extremely hard to devise a convincing demonstration of the chance element of quantum mechanics. Normally, so many particles are involved in the processes we observe that the elementary caprices average out. This is why the rules of quantum mechanics, when applied to large collections of atoms, yield the simpler rules of classical mechanics, lacking any element of indeterminacy. Thus we have no examples from everyday life to make such randomness intuitively comprehensible. In any case, when we say we can't imagine how electrons or protons could behave so strangely we fall into the very trap we should have known to avoid—we are ascribing reality to the elements of a model. That even Einstein made this mistake shows how strong is the temptation. Whatever the ultimate reality is that underlies the sensory impressions we interpret as material objects, and explain in terms of fundamental particles and mathematical equations, it has so far eluded imagination; we must not expect to discover or deny God by comparing any model we have managed to construct for ourselves with a futile preconception of what it ought to have been.

All the same, the search for evidence of God's existence in the material world is not lightly abandoned. Why does the universe exist at all, if it was not created? The evidence that it all started with a Big Bang hangs together pretty well, better than any other hypothesis. The trouble is that we can talk about the beginning but not of a time before the beginning; nor, when we imagine the start as an inconceivably hot fireball, are we allowed to picture it situated somewhere in space. Space and time as we know them are aspects of the universe itself, not, as Newton supposed, a divine absolute framework and a divine clock within which our universe came into being at God's command. It is hard enough to imagine space and time as linked in the way demanded by relativity theory, let alone anything that transcends these primary concepts. No human meaning can be attached to the idea of God "outside the universe" nor, in a timeless nowhere, to words like "act of creation" or "God's purpose". To labour the point once again, our notion of the universe is part of the model we have built, and if we are to find God it will not be by looking within the model, or outside it, but in the no-place and no-time where we cannot look, the reality beyond our grasp. I think the majority of scientists accept that no explicit revelation of God's presence is to be expected in the faultless mechanics of the lifeless material world. There may be implicit (teleological, say) evidence, however, as well as arguments derived from the existence of living creatures.

When it comes to the point, the fact of Life itself turns out to be a rather useless clue. The same fundamental laws appear to govern living and non-living alike. Quantum mechanics accounts for the structure of atoms and the forces that hold them together in molecules, however large and complex they are. If a long double-helix of DNA has the potential, given the right environment, of dividing into two and thence rebuilding itself into two replicas of the original, this is still entirely in accordance with physical laws; and the more one investigates such matters the less probable does any departure from the laws seem. The behaviour of DNA underlies the process of reproduction in all life-forms, and follows from the architecture assumed by the molecule in response to the straightforward physical forces between its constituent parts.

Taking DNA as a typical, if primitive, sample of living matter, one must recognize that the difference between living and non-living resides in complexity of structure, not in additional forces of nature. New structures have new properties that the scientist's imagination cannot usefully foresee from what he already understands; yet when he observes something new he expects to find (though not always easily) that it is indeed one of the myriad potentialities of that deceptively simple fundamental model. It is the strength of the reductionist method in science that it distinguishes between basic principles which govern every element of a structure, and properties which emerge from the complexity of the structure as a whole and which are to be understood only by studying the whole, in the confidence that the basic principles need not be queried. The well-understood behaviour of semiconductors is all the physics one needs, in principle, to grasp how a large computer works, but between the textbook of solid-state physics and the working computer lies the steady evolution of complexity at the hands of computer scientists; and to follow the details is a most intricate task. How much more so with Life, which began and has since evolved, despite the wilfully ignorant claims of Creationists, by natural law and chance to a degree of complexity very far exceeding any conceivable computer.

Up to the present, scientists who have examined living creatures either as complete entities, or by taking them to pieces, have found nothing that cannot be ascribed to purposeless mechanism. Nor will they find more from the most delicate probing of a thinking brain; the biochemical and electrical processes may come to light but nothing that they will recognize as conscious thought, for there is not objective test for this.

Before proceeding beyond this critical point in the argument, let us pause to ask whether there is anything implicit in the physicist's model of the material world to indicate that it was set up in such a way that a high degree of complexity could evolve. For this might suggest a creative purpose in the universe. The question has been much discussed recently under the general heading of Anthropism and, as one has come to expect, the answer is ambiguous. It is true that the numbers occurring in the basic laws (for example, the empirical fact that the proton is 1,836 times more massive than the electron) have values which permit the development and survival of conditions like those on the Earth, giving time enough for chemical complexity to evolve. Very small changes in these numbers would stop the stars forming or make them burn out quickly, and if God had not given a lot of thought to the problem he might well have created a sterile universe. What we can't know is whether all possible universes may not exist in the mind of God, only some of which can support rational creatures who are able to imagine themselves unique. We may also have misinterpreted God's purpose in assuming that it was our eventual appearance that he had in mind at the moment of creation. But we have left the realm of physicists' models and taken refuge in metaphor. Let us simply note that those who are so disposed may find here proof of God's purpose, but like all such proofs it will not convince the unbeliever.

Having contemplated, however desultorily, the idea that God might have created a different universe, we should take note of a widespread barrier to belief, the problem of evil. How could God have allowed a world in which such cruelty and suffering are possible? The scientific rationalist answers that the world shows every sign of being a consistent mechanism operating according to inexorable laws, any departure from which would represent the denial of a basic principle of non-intervention. God cannot prevent the fall of a sparrow without unmaking the world, and if it was designed so that intelligent creatures could exercise free will we must take the rough with the smooth, working out our own salvation so far as it lies within our power. As for what is not within our power to change or control, we might as well blame God because pi is not equal to 3 as for permitting an earthquake to overwhelm a city.

But wait a moment—who is this scientific rationalist who will allow the possibility of free will in a strictly mechanical universe? I for one, and surely not alone. Since we have not the smallest inkling of the relationship between the material world and our capacity for thought, we must accept that it may, indeed is likely to, carry with it other equally mysterious properties, just as the computer is more than the sum of its parts. This does not mean that anything goes. Claims that the mind has power over matter are very much more frequent than successful demonstrations, and those who pray for rain when the wind is in the east are likely to be disappointed. Like Dr. Johnson in the matter of ghosts, or Father Brown on miracles, we must allow the possibility while probing every instance most sceptically. Thus we may doubt whether genuine free will is often exercised, seeing how automatic our responses are to an emergency, and even how, faced with the need for careful decision, we usually choose what we know in our hearts we always intended. Yet the desires which govern choice may well have been formed by the conscious exercise of will. And how many would allow that the genius of Mozart or Michelangelo was mere automatism? We should not attach too much weight to the arguments of behaviourists, Behaviorism is fine for flatworms and, I am prepared to concede, for rats in mazes; for thinking creatures it is baseless scientism.

The same applies to the efforts of the professional atheist, who must produce better arguments than bluff common sense to laugh away the certainty of those who are convinced of God's presence within them. To be sure, the varieties of belief are so many and so contradictory as to give the unbeliever every opportunity for scorn; not everyone that saith Lord, Lord, shall enter into the kingdom of heaven. But when scepticism has done its worst there remain those of transparent integrity against whom scientific materialism cannot prevail. And the honest scientist must admit that his own code provides no sanction for ignoring inconvenient evidence.

The agnostics among us, however, may doubt whether the gifts of rational thought and of divine indwelling are coextensive. Intellectual powers themselves are diverse enough to resist simple categorization—quite a number of literary people wholly lack the ability to appreciate mathematics or music, and conversely one of the most distinguished of recent physicists confessed (as was obvious to his friends) that poetry held no meaning for him. I have no difficulty in accepting, without envy, that some of my friends have inherited or acquired by experience a faculty that is not mine, which has given them an unshakeable assurance of God's purpose and their part in it. It may seem to them that my life must be drab and pointless, but there are compensations. The kaleidoscopic material world gives joy to those who have not learnt to despise it, and even if they cannot discern a controlling purpose they may still find confidence in its grand order to believe that, however insignificant their own part, ultimately all shall be well and all manner of thing shall be well.

Suggestions for Discussion

1. Discuss the rhetorical impact of Pippard's statement of his personal beliefs in the opening and closing lines of his essay.

2. On what grounds does Pippard argue that "the search for God's existence in the material world is not lightly abandoned"?

3. Analyze his discussion of "models."

Suggestions for Writing

1. How has your own study of science helped you formulate and resolve specific religious and/or ethical convictions?

2. Develop three questions about the relationship between science and religion that you would like to pose to Pippard.

The Examined Life: Personal Values

◆◆◆

It is a living system, an immense organism, still developing, regulating itself, making its own oxygen, maintaining its own temperature, keeping all its infinite living parts connected and interdependent, including us. It is the strangest of all places, and there is everything in the world to learn about it. It can keep us awake and jubilant with questions for millennia ahead, if we can learn not to meddle and not to destroy. Our great hope is in being such a young species, thinking in language only a short while, still learning, still growing up.

We are not like the social insects. They have only the one way of doing things and they will do it forever, coded for that way. We are coded differently, not just for binary choices, *go* or *no-go.* We can go four ways at once, depending on how the air feels: *go, no-go,* but also *maybe,* plus *what the hell let's give it a try.* We are in for one surprise after another if we keep at it and keep alive. We can build structures for human society never seen before, thoughts never thought before, music never heard before.

 —Lewis Thomas, "Seven Wonders"

I who am blind can give one hint to those who see—one admonition to those who would make full use of the gift of sight: Use your eyes as if tomorrow you would be stricken blind. And the same method can be applied to the other senses. Hear the music of voices, the song of a bird, the mighty strains of an orchestra, as if you would be stricken deaf tomorrow. Touch each object you want to touch as if tomorrow your tactile sense would fail. Smell the perfume of flowers, taste with relish each morsel, as if tomorrow you could never smell and taste again. Make the most of every sense; glory in all the facts of pleasure and beauty which the world reveals to you through the several means of contact which Nature provides. But of all the senses, I am sure that sight must be the most delightful.

—**Helen Keller,** "Three Days to See"

The secret of seeing, then, is the pearl of great price. If I thought he could teach me to find it and keep it forever, I would stagger barefoot across a hundred deserts after any lunatic at all. But although the pearl may be found, it may not be sought. The literature of illumination reveals this above all: although it comes to those who wait for it, it is always even to the most practiced and adept, a gift and a total surprise.

—**Annie Dillard,** "Sight into Insight"

Four hundred years ago a young poet and potential rival of Shakespeare had written of the knowledge-hungry Faust of legend:

Thou are still but Faustus and a man.

In that phrase Christopher Marlowe had epitomized the human tragedy: We were world eaters and knowledge seekers but we were also men. It was a well-nigh fatal flaw. Whether we, like the makers of stone spearpoints in Wyoming, are a fleeting illusion of the autumn light depends upon whether any remain to decipher Marlowe's words one thousand years in the future.

The events of my century had placed the next millennium as far off as a star. All the elaborate mechanisms of communication we have devised have not ennobled, nor brought closer, individual men to men. The means exist. It is Faustus who remains a man. Beyond this dark, I, who was also a man, could not penetrate.

—**Loren Eiseley,** "Man in the Autumn Light"

I went to the woods because I wished to live deliberately, to confront only the essential facts of life, and see if I could not learn what it had to teach, and not, when I came to die, discover that I had not lived. I did not wish to live what was not life, living is so dear; nor did I wish to practise resignation, unless it was quite necessary. I wanted to live deep and suck out all the marrow of life, to live so sturdily and Spartan-like as to put to rout all that was not life, to cut a broad swath and shave close, to drive life into a corner, and reduce it to its lowest terms, and, if it proved to be mean, why then to get the whole and genuine meanness of it, and publish its meanness to the world; or if it were sublime, to know it by experience, and be able to give a true account of it in my next excursion.

—**Henry David Thoreau,** "Why I Went to the Woods"

Personal Reminiscence

◆◆◆◆

Annie Dillard

Sight into Insight

Annie Dillard (b. 1945), a contributing editor to *Harper's,* won a Pulitzer Prize in 1974 for *Pilgrim at Tinker Creek.* Her more recent books are *Living by Fiction* and *Teaching a Stone to Talk: Expeditions and Encounters* both published in 1982. There are people of dull vision who don't really see and those like the writer for whom the effort truly to see is "a discipline requiring a lifetime of dedicated struggle."

When I was six or seven years old, growing up Pittsburgh, I used to take a precious penny of my own and hide it for someone else to find. It was a curious compulsion; sadly, I've never been seized by it since. For some reason I always "hid" the penny along the same stretch of sidewalk up the street. I'd cradle it at the roots of a maple, say, or in a hole left by a chipped-off piece of sidewalk. Then I'd take a piece of chalk and, starting at either end of the block, draw hugh arrows leading up to the penny from both directions. After I learned to write I labeled the arrows "SURPRISE AHEAD" or "MONEY THIS WAY." I was greatly excited, during all this arrow-drawing, at the thought of the first lucky passerby who would receive in this way, regardless of merit, a free gift from the universe. But I never lurked about. I'd go straight home and not give the matter another thought, until, some months later, I would be gripped by the impulse to hide another penny.

There are lots of things to see, unwrapped gifts and free surprises. The world is fairly studded and strewn with pennies cast broadside from a generous hand. But—and this is the point—who gets excited by a mere penny? If you follow one arrow, if you crouch motionless on a bank to watch a tremulous ripple thrill on the water, and are rewarded by the sight of a muskrat kit paddling from its den, will you count that sight a chip of copper only, and go your rueful way? It is a very dire poverty indeed for a man to be so malnourished and fatigued that he won't stoop to pick up a penny. But if you cultivate a healthy poverty and simplicity, so that finding a penny will make your day, then, since the world is in fact planted in pennies, you have with your poverty bought a lifetime of days. What you see is what you get.

Unfortunately, nature is very much a now-you-see-it, now-you-don't affair. A fish flashes, then dissolves in the water before my eyes like so much salt. Deer apparently ascend bodily into heaven; the brightest oriole fades into leaves. These disappearances stun me into stillness and concentration; they say of nature that it conceals with a grand nonchalance, and they say of vision that it is a deliberate gift, the revelation of a dancer who for my eyes only flings away her seven veils.

For nature does reveal as well as conceal: now-you-don't-see-it, now-you-do. For a week this September migrating red-winged blackbirds were feeding heavily down by Tinker Creek at the back of the house. One day I went out to investigate the racket; I walked up to a tree, an Osage orange, and a hundred birds flew away. They simply materialized out of the tree. I saw a tree, then a whisk of color, then a tree again. I walked closer and another hundred blackbirds took flight. Not a branch, not a twig budged: the birds were apparently weightless as well as invisible. Or, it was as if the leaves of the Osage orange had been freed from a spell in the form of red-winged blackbirds; they flew from the tree, caught my eye in the sky, and vanished. When I looked again at the tree, the leaves had reassembled as if nothing had happened. Finally I walked directly to the trunk of the tree and a final hundred, the real diehards, appeared, spread, and vanished. How could so many hide in the tree without my seeing them? The Osage orange, unruffled, looked just as it had looked from the house, when three hundred red-winged blackbirds cried from its crown. I looked upstream where they flew, and they were gone. Searching, I couldn't spot one. I wandered upstream to force them to play their hand, but they'd crossed the creek and scattered. One show to a customer. These appearances catch at my throat: they are the free gifts, the bright coppers at the roots of trees.

It's all a matter of keeping my eyes open. Nature is like one of those line drawings that are puzzles for children: Can you find hidden in the tree a duck, a house, a boy, a bucket, a giraffe, and a boot? Specialists can find the most incredibly hidden things. A book I read when I was young recommended an easy way to find caterpillars: you simply find some fresh caterpillar droppings, look up, and there's your caterpillar. More recently an author advised me to set my mind at ease about those piles of cut stems on the ground in grassy fields. Field mice make them; they cut the grass down by degrees to reach the seeds at the head. It seems that when the grass is tightly packed, as in a field of ripe grain, the blade won't topple at a single cut through the stem; instead, the cut stem simply drops vertically, held in the crush of grain. The mouse severs the bottom again and again, the stem keeps dropping an inch at a time, and finally the head is low enough for the mouse to reach the seeds. Meanwhile the mouse is positively littering the field with its little piles of cut stems into which, presumably, the author is constantly stumbling.

If I can't see this minutiae, I still try to keep my eyes open. I'm always on the lookout for ant lion traps in sandy soil, monarch pupae near milkweed, skipper larvae in locust leaves. These things are utterly common, and I've not seen one. I bang on hollow trees near water, but so far no flying squirrels have appeared. In flat country I watch every sunset in hopes of seeing the green ray. The green ray is a seldom-seen streak of light that rises from the sun like a spurting fountain at the moment of sunset; it throbs into the sky for two seconds and disappears. One more reason to keep my eyes open. A photography professor at the University of Florida just happened to see a bird die in midflight; it jerked, died, dropped, and smashed on the ground.

I squint at the wind because I read Stewart Edward White: "I have always maintained that if you looked closely enough you could *see* the wind—the dim, hardly-made-out, fine débris fleeing high in the air." White was an excellent observer, and devoted an entire chapter of *The Mountains* to the subject of seeing deer: "As soon as you can forget the naturally obvious and construct an artificial obvious, then you too will see deer."

But the artificial obvious is hard to see. My eyes account for less than 1 percent of the weight of my head; I'm bony and dense; I see what I expect. I just don't know what the lover knows; I can't see the artificial obvious that those in the know construct. The herpetologist asks the native, "Are there snakes in that ravine?" "No, sir." And the herpetologist comes home with, yessir, three bags full. Are there butterflies on that mountain? Are the bluets in bloom? Are there arrowheads here, or fossil ferns in the shale?

Peeping through my keyhole I see within the range of only about 30 percent of the light that comes from the sun; the rest is infrared and some little ultraviolet, perfectly apparent to many animals, but invisible to me. A nightmare network of ganglia, charged and firing without my knowledge, cuts and splices what I do see, editing it for my brain. Donald E. Carr points out that the sense impressions of one-celled animals are *not* edited for the brain: "This is philosophically interesting in a rather mournful way, since it means that only the simplest animals perceive the universe as it is."

A fog that won't burn away drifts and flows across my field of vision. When you see fog move against a backdrop of deep pines, you don't see the fog itself, but streaks of clearness floating across the air in dark shreds. So I see only tatters of clearness through a pervading obscurity. I can't distinguish the fog from the overcast sky; I can't be sure if the light is direct or reflected. Everywhere darkness and the presence of the unseen appalls. We estimate now that only one atom dances alone in every cubic meter of intergalactic space. I blink and squint. What planet or power yanks Halley's Comet out of orbit? We haven't seen it yet; it's a question of distance, density, and the pallor of reflected light. We rock, cradled in the swaddling band of darkness. Even the simple darkness of night whispers suggestions to the mind. This summer, in August, I stayed at the creek too late.

Strangers to Darkness

Where Tinker Creek flows under the sycamore log bridge to the tear-shaped island, it is slow and shallow, fringed thinly in cattail marsh. At this spot an astonishing bloom of life supports vast breeding populations of insects, fish, reptiles, birds, and mammals. On windless summer evenings I stalk along the creek bank or straddle the sycamore log in absolute stillness, watching for muskrats. The night I stayed too late I was hunched on the lawn staring spellbound at spreading, reflected stains of lilac on the water. A cloud in the sky suddenly lighted as if turned on by a switch; its reflection just as suddenly materialized on the water upstream, flat and floating, so that I couldn't see the creek bottom, or life in the water under the cloud. Downstream, away from the cloud on the water, water turtles smooth as beans were gliding down with the current in a series of easy, weightless push-offs, as men bound on the moon. I didn't know whether to trace the progress of one turtle I was sure of, risking sticking my face in one of the bridge's spider webs made invisible by the gathering dark, or take a chance on seeing the carp, or scan the mudbank in hope of seeing a muskrat, or follow the last of the swallows who caught at my heart and trailed it after them like streamers as they appeared from directly below, under the log, flying upstream with their tails forked, so fast.

But shadows spread and deepened and stayed. After thousands of years we're still strangers to darkness, fearful aliens in an enemy camp with our arms crossed over our chests. I stirred. A land turtle on the bank, startled, hissed the air from its lungs and withdrew to its shell. An uneasy pink here, an unfathomable blue there, gave great suggestion of lurking beings. Things were going on. I couldn't see whether that rustle I heard was a distant rattlesnake, slit-eyed, or a nearby sparrow kicking in the dry flood debris slung at the foot of a willow. Tremendous action roiled the water everywhere I looked, big action, inexplicable. A tremor welled up beside a gaping muskrat burrow in the bank and I caught my breath, but no muskrat appeared. The ripples continued to fan upstream with a steady, powerful thrust. Night was knitting an eyeless mask over my face, and I still sat transfixed. A distant airplane, a delta wing out of a nightmare, made a gliding shadow on the creek's bottom that looked like a stingray cruising upstream. At once a black fin slit the pink cloud on the water, shearing it in two. The two halves merged together and seemed to dissolve before my eyes. Darkness pooled in the cleft of the creek and rose, as water collects in a well. Untamed, dreaming lights flickered over the sky. I saw hints of hulking underwater shadows, two pale splashes out of the water, and round ripples rolling close together from a blackened center.

At last I stared upstream where only the deepest violet remained of the cloud, a cloud so high its underbelly still glowed, its feeble color reflected from a hidden sky lighted in turn by a sun halfway to China. And out of that violet, a sudden enormous black body arched over the water. Head and tail, if there was a head and tail, were both submerged in cloud. I saw only one ebony fling, a headlong dive to darkness; then the waters closed, and the lights went out.

I walked home in a shivering daze, up hill and down. Later I lay openmouthed in bed, my arms flung wide at my sides to steady the whirling darkness. At this latitude I'm spinning 836 miles an hour round the earth's axis; I feel my sweeping fall as a breakneck arch like the dive of dolphins, and the hollow rushing of wind raises the hairs on my neck and the side of my face. In orbit around the sun I'm moving 64,800 miles an hour. The solar system as a whole, like a merry-go-round unhinged, spins, bobs, and blinks at the speed of 43,200 miles an hour along a course set east of Hercules. Someone has piped, and we are dancing a tarantella until the sweat pours. I open my eyes and I see dark, muscled forms curl out of water, with flapping gills and flattened eyes. I close my eyes and I see stars, deep stars giving way to deeper stars, deeper stars bowing to deepest stars at the crown of an infinite cone.

"Still," wrote Van Gogh in a letter, "a great deal of light falls on everything." If we were blinded by darkness, we are also blinded by light. Sometimes here in Virginia at sunset low clouds on the southern or northern horizon are completely invisible in the lighted sky. I only know one is there because I can see its reflection in still water. The first time I discovered this mystery I looked from cloud to no-cloud in bewilderment, checking my bearings over and over, thinking maybe the ark of the covenant was just passing by south of Dead Man Mountain. Only much later did I learn the explanation: polarized light from the sky is very much weakened by reflection, but the light in clouds isn't polarized. So invisible clouds pass among visible clouds, till all slide over the mountains; so a greater light extinguishes a lesser as though it didn't exist.

In the great meteor shower of August, the Perseid, I wail all day for the shooting stars I miss. They're out there showering down, committing hara-kiri in a flame of fatal attraction, and hissing perhaps at last into the ocean. But at dawn what looks like a blue dome clamps down over me like a lid on a pot. The stars and planets could smash and I'd never know. Only a piece of ashen moon occasionally climbs up or down the inside of the dome, and our local star without surcease explodes on our heads. We have really only that one light, one source for all power, and yet we must turn away from it by universal decree. Nobody here on the planet seems aware of this strange, powerful taboo, that we all walk about carefully averting our faces, this way and that, lest our eyes be blasted forever.

Darkness appalls and light dazzles; the scrap of visible light that doesn't hurt my eyes hurts my brain. What I see sets me swaying. Size and distance and the sudden swelling of meanings confuse me, bowl me over. I straddle the sycamore log bridge over Tinker Creek in the summer. I look at the lighted creek bottom: snail tracks tunnel the mud in quavering curves. A crayfish jerks, but by the time I absorb what has happened, he's gone in a billowing smoke screen of silt. I look at the water: minnows and shiners. If I'm thinking minnows, a carp will fill my brain till I scream. I look at the water's surface: skaters, bubbles, and leaves sliding down. Suddenly, my own face, reflected, startles me witless. Those snails have been tracking my face! Finally, with a shuddering wrench of the will, I see clouds, cirrus clouds. I'm dizzy, I fall in.

This looking business is risky. Once I stood on a humped rock on nearby Purgatory Mountain, watching through binoculars the great autumn hawk migration below, until I discovered that I was in danger of joining the hawks on a vertical migration of my own. I was used to binoculars, but not, apparently, to balancing on humped rocks while looking through them. I reeled. Everything advanced and receded by turns; the world was full of unexplained foreshortenings and depths. A distant huge object, a hawk the size of an elephant, turned out to be the browned bough of a nearby loblolly pine. I followed a sharp-skinned hawk against a featureless sky, rotating my head unawares as it flew, and when I lowered the glass a glimpse of my own looming shoulder sent me staggering. What prevents the men on Palomar from falling, voiceless and blinded, from their tiny, vaulted chairs?

I reel in confusion; I don't understand what I see. With the naked eye I can see two million light-years to the Andromeda galaxy. Often I slop some creek water in a jar, and when I get home I dump it in a white china bowl. After the silt settles I return and see tracings of minute snails on the bottom, a planarian or two winding round the rim of water, roundworms shimmying frantically, and finally, when my eyes have adjusted to these dimensions, amoebae. At first the amoebae look like *muscae volitantes*, those curled moving spots you seem to see in your eyes when you stare at a distant wall. Then I see the amoebae as drops of water congealed, bluish, translucent, like chips of sky in the bowl. At length I choose one individual and give myself over to its idea of an evening. I see it dribble a grainy foot before it on its wet, unfathomable way. Do its unedited sense impressions include the fierce focus of my eyes? Shall I take it outside and show it Andromeda, and blow its little endoplasm? I stir the water with a finger, in case it's running out of oxygen. Maybe I should get a tropical aquarium with motorized bubblers and lights, and keep this one for a pet. Yes, it would tell its fissioned descendants, the universe is two feet by five, and if you listen closely you can hear the buzzing music of the spheres.

Oh, it's mysterious, lamplit evenings here in the galaxy, one after the other. It's one of those nights when I wander from window to window, looking for a sign. But I can't see. Terror and a beauty insoluble are a riband of blue woven into the fringes of garments of things both great and small. No culture explains, no bivouac offers real haven or rest. But it could be that we are not seeing something. Galileo thought comets were an optical illusion. This is fertile ground: since we are certain that they're not, we can look at what our scientists have been saying with fresh hope. What if there are *really* gleaming, castellated cities hung upside-down over the desert sand? What limpid lakes and cool date palms have our caravans always passed untried? Until, one by one, by the blindest of leaps, we light on the road to these places, we must stumble in darkness and hunger. I turn from the window. I'm blind as a bat, sensing only from every direction the echo of my own thin cries.

Learning to See

I chanced on a wonderful book called *Space and Sight*, by Marius Von Senden. When Western surgeons discovered how to perform safe cataract operations, they ranged across Europe and America operating on dozens of men and women of all ages who had been blinded by cataracts since birth. Von Senden collected accounts of such cases; the histories are fascinating. Many doctors had tested their patients' sense perceptions and ideas of space both before and after the operations. The vast majority of patients, of both sexes and all ages, had, in Von Senden's opinion, no idea of space whatsoever. Form, distance, and size were so many meaningless syllables. A patient "had no idea of depth, confusing it with roundness." Before the operation a doctor would give a blind patient a cube and a sphere; the patient would tongue it or feel it with his hands, and name it correctly. After the operation the doctor would show the same objects to the patient without letting him touch them; now he had no clue whatsoever to what he was seeing. One patient called lemonade "square" because it pricked on his tongue as a square shape pricked on the touch of his hands. Of another postoperative patient the doctor writes, "I have found in her no notion of size, for example, not even within the narrow limits which she might have encompassed with the aid of touch. Thus when I asked her to show me how big her mother was, she did not stretch out her hands, but set her two index fingers a few inches apart."

For the newly sighted, vision is pure sensation unencumbered by meaning. When a newly sighted girl saw photographs and paintings, she asked, "'Why do they put those dark marks all over them?' 'Those aren't dark marks,' her mother explained, 'those are shadows. That is one of the ways the eye knows that things have shape. If it were not for shadows, many things would look flat.' 'Well, that's how things do look,' Joan answered. 'Everything looks flat with dark patches.'"

In general the newly sighted see the world as a dazzle of "color-patches." They are pleased by the sensation of color, and learn quickly to name the colors, but the rest of seeing is tormentingly difficult. Soon after his operation, a patient "generally bumps into one of these color-patches and observes them to be substantial, since they resist him as tactual objects do. In walking about it also strikes him—or can if he pays attention—that he is continually passing in between the colors he sees, that he can go past a visual object, that a part of it then steadily disappears from view; and that in spite of this, however he twists and turns—whether entering the room from the door, for example, or returning back to it—he always has a visual space in front of him. Thus he gradually comes to realize that there is also space behind him, which he does not see."

The mental effort involved in these reasonings proves overwhelming for many patients. It oppresses them to realize, if they ever do at all, the tremendous size of the world, which they had previously conceived of as something touchingly manageable. It oppresses them to realize that they have been visible to people all along, perhaps unattractively so, without their knowledge or consent. A disheartening number of them refuse to use their new vision, continuing to go over objects with their tongues, and lapsing into apathy and despair.

On the other hand, many newly sighted people speak well of the world, and teach us how dull our own vision is. To one patient, a human hand, unrecognized, is "something bright and then holes." Shown a bunch of grapes, a boy calls out, "It is dark, blue and shiny. . . . It isn't smooth, it has bumps and hollows." A little girl visits a garden. "She is greatly astonished, and can scarcely be persuaded to answer, stands speechless in front of the tree, which she only names on taking hold of it, and then as 'the tree with the lights in it.'" Another patient, a twenty-two-year-old girl, was dazzled by the world's brightness and kept her eyes shut for two weeks. When at the end of that time she opened her eyes again, she did not recognize any objects, but "the more she now directed her gaze upon everything about her, the more it could be seen how an expression of gratification and astonishment overspread her features; she repeatedly exclaimed: 'Oh God! How beautiful!'"

I saw color-patches for weeks after I read this wonderful book. It was summer; the peaches were ripe in the valley orchards. When I woke in the morning, color-patches wrapped round my eyes, intricately, leaving not one unfilled spot. All day long I walked among shifting color-patches that parted before me like the Red Sea and closed again in silence, transfigured, wherever I looked back. Some patches swelled and loomed, while others vanished utterly, and dark marks flitted at random over the whole dazzling sweep. But I couldn't sustain the illusion of flatness. I've been around for too long. Form is condemned to an eternal danse macabre with meaning: I couldn't unpeach the peaches. Nor can I remember ever having seen without understanding; the color-patches of infancy are lost. My brain then must have been smooth as any balloon. I'm told I reached for the moon; many babies do. But the color-patches of infancy swelled as meaning filled them; they arrayed themselves in solemn ranks down distance which unrolled and stretched before me like a plain. The moon rocketed away. I live now in a world of shadows that shape and distance color, a world where space makes a kind of terrible sense. What Gnosticism is this, and what physics? The fluttering patch I saw in my nursery window—silver and green and shape-shifting blue—is gone; a row of Lombardy poplars takes its place, mute, across the distant lawn. That humming oblong creature pale as light that stole along the walls of my room at night, stretching exhilaratingly around the corners, is gone, too, gone the night I ate of the bittersweet fruit, put two and two together, and puckered forever my brain. Martin Buber tells this tale: "Rabbi Mendel once boasted to his teacher Rabbi Elimelekh that evenings he saw the angel who rolls away the light before the darkness, and mornings the angel who rolls away the darkness before the light. 'Yes,' said Rabbi Elimelekh, 'in my youth I saw that too. Later on you don't see these things anymore.'"

Why didn't someone hand these newly sighted people paints and brushes from the start, when they still didn't know what anything was? Then maybe we all could see color-patches too, the world unraveled from reason, Eden before Adam gave names. The scales would drop from my eyes; I'd see trees like men walking; I'd run down the road against all orders, hallooing and leaping.

Silver Flashes

Seeing is of course very much a matter of verbalization. Unless I call my attention to what passes before my eyes, I simply won't see it. If Tinker Mountain erupted, I'd be likely to notice. But if I want to notice the lesser cataclysms of valley life, I have to maintain in my head a running description of the present. It's not that I'm observant; it's just that I talk too much. Otherwise, especially in a strange place, I'll never know what's happening. Like a blind man at the ball game, I need a radio.

When I see this way I analyze and pry. I hurl over logs and roll away stones; I study the bank a square foot at a time, probing and tilting my head. Some days when a mist covers the mountains, when the muskrats won't show and the microscope's mirror shatters, I want to climb up the blank blue dome as a man would storm the inside of a circus tent, wildly, dangling, and with a steel knife claw a rent in the top, peep, and, if I must, fall.

But there is another kind of seeing that involves a letting go. When I see this way I sway transfixed and emptied. The difference between the two ways of seeing is the difference between walking with and without a camera. When

I walk with a camera I walk from shot to shot, reading the light on a calibrated meter. When I walk without a camera, my own shutter opens, and the moment's light prints on my own silver gut. When I see this second way I am above all an unscrupulous observer.

It was sunny one evening last summer at Tinker Creek; the sun was low in the sky, upstream. I was sitting on the sycamore log bridge with the sunset at my back, watching the shiners the size of minnows who were feeding over the muddy sand in skittery schools. Again and again, one fish, then another, turned for a split second across the current and flash! the sun shot out from its silver side. I couldn't watch for it. It was always just happening somewhere else, and it drew my vision just as it disappeared: flash! like a sudden dazzle of the thinnest blade, a sparking over a dun and olive ground at chance intervals from every direction. Then I noticed white specks, some sort of pale petals, small, floating from under my feet on the creek's surface, very slow and steady. So I blurred my eyes and gazed toward the brim of my hat and saw a new world. I saw the pale white circles roll up, roll up, like the world's turning, mute and perfect, and I saw the linear flashes, gleaming silver, like stars being born at random down a rolling scroll of time. Something broke and something opened. I filled up like a new wineskin. I breathed an air like light; I saw a light like water. I was the lip of a fountain the creek filled forever; I was ether, the leaf in the zephyr; I was flesh-flake, feather, bone.

When I see this way I see truly. As Thoreau says, I return to my senses. I am the man who watches the baseball game in silence in an empty stadium. I see the game purely; I'm abstracted and dazed. When it's all over and the white-suited players lope off the green field to their shadowed dugouts, I leap to my feet, I cheer and cheer.

But I can't go out and try to see this way. I'll fail, I'll go mad. All I can do is try to gag the commentator, to hush the noise of useless interior babble that keeps me from seeing just as surely as a newspaper dangled before my eyes. The effort is really a discipline requiring a lifetime of dedicated struggle; it marks the literature of saints and monks of every order east and west, under every rule and no rule, discalced and shod. The world's spiritual geniuses seem to discover universally that the mind's muddy river, this ceaseless flow of trivia and trash, cannot be dammed, and that trying to dam it is a waste of effect that might lead to madness. Instead you must allow the muddy river to flow unheeded in the dim channels of consciousness; you raise your sights; you look along it, mildly, acknowledging its presence without interest and gazing beyond it into the realm of the real where subjects and objects act and rest purely, without utterance. "Launch into the deep," says Jacques Ellul, "and you shall see."

The secret of seeing, then, is the pearl of great price. If I thought he could teach me to find it and keep it forever I would stagger barefoot across a hundred deserts after any lunatic at all. But although the pearl may be found, it may not be sought. The literature of illumination reveals this above all: although it comes to those who wait for it, it is always, even to the most practiced and adept, a gift and a total surprise. I return from one walk knowing where the killdeer nests in the field by the creek and the hour the laurel blooms. I return from the same walk a day later scarcely knowing my own name. Litanies hum in my ears; my tongue flaps in my mouth, *Alimonon,* alleluia! I cannot cause light; the most I can do is try to put myself in the path of its beam. It is possible, in deep space, to sail on solar wind. Light, be it particle or wave, has force: you rig a giant sail and go. The secret of seeing is to sail on solar wind. Hone and spread your spirit till you yourself are a sail, whetted, translucent, broadside to the merest puff.

When her doctor took her bandages off and led her into the garden, the girl who was no longer blind saw "the tree with the lights in it." It was for this tree I searched through the peach orchards of summer, in the forests of fall and down winter and spring for years. Then one day I was walking along Tinker Creek thinking of nothing at all and I saw the tree with the lights in it. I saw the backyard cedar where the mourning doves roost charged and transfigured, each cell buzzing with flame. I stood on the grass with the lights in it, grass that was wholly fire, utterly focused and utterly dreamed. It was less like seeing than like being for the first time seen, knocked breathless by a powerful glance. The flood of fire abated, but I'm still spending the power. Gradually the lights went out in the cedar, the colors died, the cells unflamed and disappeared. I was still ringing. I had been my whole life a bell, and never knew it until at that moment I was lifted and struck. I have since only very rarely seen the tree with the lights in it. The vision comes and goes, mostly goes, but I live for it, for the moment when the mountains open and a new light roars in spate through the crack, and the mountains slam.

Suggestions for Discussion

1. What is the central point of this essay?

2. How does the author's story about hiding pennies as a child relate to the thesis of the piece?

3. Discuss the tone of Dillard's description of observations of nature. How honest do you feel her reactions to nature are? Compare her reaction to nature with those of other naturalists you have read.

Suggestions for Writing

1. Recall a scene, either natural or social, to which you reacted strongly. Write about it.

2. Write a piece in which you analyze your attitude toward the natural world.

3. With wax crayons, magic markers, or water colors, attempt to represent a sight common to you as "patches of color." Then write a paper in which you describe the difficulties or pleasures you found in your attempt.

John Reed

Almost Thirty

John Reed (1887–1920), born in Portland, Oregon, was called by Upton Sinclair "the playboy of the social revolution." He worked on the *American Magazine,* became managing editor of *The Masses,* and when Villa's revolt broke out in Mexico, he reported for the *World* and sent graphic sketches to *Metropolitan.* After the Russian Revolution he wrote his most famed book, *Ten Days That Shook the World* (1919). In these reflections, Reed reviews significant events in his past and his failure to discover any final answers to sustain him.

In 1906 I went up to Harvard almost alone, knowing hardly a soul in the university. My college class entered over seven hundred strong, and, for the three months it seemed to me, going around to lectures and meetings, as if every one of the seven hundred had friends but me. I was thrilled with the immensity of Harvard, its infinite opportunities, its august history and traditions—but desperately lonely. I didn't know which way to turn, how to meet people. Fellows passed me in the Yard, shouting gaily to one another; I saw parties off to Boston Saturday night, whooping and yelling on the back platform of the street car, and they passed hilariously singing under my window in the early dawn. Athletes and musicians and writers and statesmen were emerging from the ranks of the class. The freshman clubs were forming.

And I was out of it all. I "went out" for the college papers, and tried to make the freshman crew, even staying in Cambridge vacations to go down to the empty boat-house and plug away at the machines—and was the last man kicked off the squad before they went to New London. I got to know many fellows to nod to, and a very few intimately; but most of my friends were whirled off and up into prominence, and came to see me no more. One of them said he'd room with me sophomore year—but he was tipped off that I wasn't "the right sort" and openly drew away from me. And I, too, hurt a boy who was my friend. He was a Jew, a shy, rather melancholy person. We were always together, we two outsiders. I became irritated and morbid about it— it seemed I would never be part of the rich splendor of college life with him around—so I drew away from him. . . . It hurt him very much, and it taught me better. Since then he has forgiven it, and done wonderful things for me, and we are friends.

My second year was better. I was elected an editor of two of the papers, and knew more fellows. The fortunate and splendid youths, the aristocrats who filled the clubs and dominated college society, didn't seem so attractive. In two open contests, the trial for editor of the college daily paper and that for assistant manager of the varsity crew, I qualified easily for election; but the aristocrats blackballed me. However, that mattered less. During my freshman year I used to *pray* to be liked, to have friends, to be popular with the crowd. Now I had friends, plenty of them; and I have found that when I am working hard at something I love, friends come without my trying, and stay; and fear goes, and that sense of being lost which is so horrible.

From that time on I never felt out of it. I was never popular with the aristocrats; I was never elected to any clubs but one, and that one largely because of a dearth of members who could write lyrics for the annual show. But I was on the papers, was elected president of the Cosmopolitan Club, where forty-three nationalities met, became manager of the Musical Clubs, captain of the water-polo team, and an officer in many undergraduate activities. As song-leader of the cheering section, I had the supreme blissful sensation of swaying two thousand voices in great crashing choruses during the big football games. The more I met the college aristocrats, the more their cold, cruel stupidity repelled me. I began to pity them for their lack of imagination, and the narrowness of their glittering lives—clubs, athletics, society. College is like the world; outside there is the same class of people, dull and sated and blind.

Harvard University under President Eliot was unique. Individualism was carried to the point where a man who came for a good time could get through and graduate without having learned anything; but on the other hand, anyone could find there anything he wanted from all the world's store of learning. The undergraduates were practically free from control; they could live pretty much where they pleased, and do as they pleased—so long as they attended lectures. There was no attempt made by the authorities to weld the student body together, or to enforce any kind of uniformity. Some men came with allowances of fifteen thousand dollars a year pocket money, with automobiles and servants, living in gorgeous suites in palatial apartment houses; others in the same class starved in attic bedrooms.

All sorts of strange characters, of every race and mind, poets, philosophers, cranks of every twist, were in our class. The very hugeness of it prevented any one man from knowing more than a few of his classmates, though I managed to make the acquaintance of about five hundred of them. The aristocrats controlled the places of pride and power, except when a democratic revolution, such as occurred in my senior year, swept them off their feet; but they were so exclusive that most of the real life went on outside their ranks—and all the intellectual life of the student body. So many fine men were outside the charmed circle that, unlike most colleges, there was no disgrace in not being a "club man." What is known as "college spirit" was not very powerful; no odium attached to those who didn't go to football games and cheer. There was talk of the world, and daring thought, and intellectual insurgency; heresy has always been a Harvard and a New England tradition. Students themselves criticized the faculty for not educating them, attacked the sacred institution of intercollegiate athletics, sneered at undergraduate clubs so holy that no one dared mention their names. No matter what you were or what you did—at Harvard you could find your kind. It wasn't a breeder for masses of mediocrely educated young men equipped with "business" psychology; out of each class came a few creative minds, a few scholars, a few "gentlemen" with insolent manners, and a ruck of nobodies. . . . Things have changed now. I liked Harvard better then.

Toward the end of my college course two influences came into my life, which had a good deal to do with shaping me. One was contact with Professor Copeland, who, under the pretense of teaching English composition, has stimulated generations of men to find color and strength and beauty in books and in the world, and to express it again. The other was what I call, for lack of a better name, the manifestation of the modern spirit. Some men, notably Walter Lippmann, had been reading and thinking and talking about politics and economics, not as dry theoretical studies, but as live forces acting on the world, on the University even. They formed the Socialist Club, to study and discuss all modern social and economic theories, and began to experiment with the community in which they lived.

Under their stimulus the college political clubs, which had formerly been quadrennial mushroom growths for the purpose of drinking beer, parading and burning red fire, took on a new significance. The Club drew up a platform for the Socialist Party in the city elections. It had social legislation introduced into the Massachusetts Legislature. Its members wrote articles in the college papers challenging undergraduate ideals, and muckraked the University for not paying its servants living wages, and so forth. Out of the agitation sprang the Harvard Men's League for Women's Suffrage, the Single Tax Club, an Anarchist group. The faculty was petitioned for a course in socialism. Prominent radicals were invited to Cambridge to lecture. An open forum was started, to debate college matters and the issues of the day. The result of this movement upon the undergraduate world was potent. All over the place radicals sprang up, in music, painting, poetry, the theatre. The more serious college papers took a socialistic or at least progressive tinge. Of course all this made no ostensible difference in the look of Harvard society, and probably the clubmen and the athletes, who represented us to the world, never even heard of it. But it made me, and many others, realize that there was something going on in the dull outside world more thrilling than college activities, and turned our attention to the writings of men like H. G. Wells and Graham Wallas, wrenching us away from the Oscar Wildean dilettantism that had possessed undergraduate littérateurs for generations.

After college Waldo Peirce and I went abroad as "bull-pushers" on a cattle-boat, for a year's happy-go-lucky wandering. Waldo rebelled at the smells and the ship's company, and jumped overboard off Boston Light, swimming back to shore and later taking the *Lusitania* to Liverpool; meanwhile, I was arrested for his murder, clapped in irons and brought before an Admiralty court at Manchester, where Waldo turned up in the nick of time. I tramped down across England alone, working on farms and sleeping in haymows, meeting Peirce in London again. Then we hoofed it to Dover and tried to stow away on a Channel streamer for France—and got arrested in Calais, of course. Separating, we went through northern France on foot, to Rouen and Paris, and started on a wild automobile trip through Touraine to the Spanish border, and across; and I proceeded into Spain alone, having adventures. I spent the winter in Paris, with excursions around the country, letting it soak in. Then I came home to America to settle down and make my living.

Lincoln Steffens recommended me for a job on *The American Magazine*, where I stayed three years, reading manuscripts and writing stories and verses. More than any other man Lincoln Steffens has influenced my mind. I met him first while I was at Harvard, where he came loving youth, full of understanding, with the breath of the world clinging to him. I was afraid of him then—afraid of his wisdom, his seriousness, and we didn't talk. But when

I came back from France I told him what I had seen and done, and he asked me what I wanted to do. I said I didn't know, except that I wanted to write. Steffens looked at me with that lovely smile: "You can do anything you want to," he said; and I believed him. Since then I have gone to him with my difficulties and troubles, and he has always listened while I solved them myself in the warmth of his understanding. Being with Steffens is to me like flashes of clear light; it is as if I see him, and myself, and the world, with new eyes. I tell him what I see and think, and it comes back to me beautiful, full of meaning. He does not judge or advise—he simply makes everything clear. There are two men who give me confidence in myself, who make me want to work, and to do nothing unworthy—Copeland and Steffens.

New York was an enchanted city to me. It was on an infinitely grander scale than Harvard. Everything was to be found there—it satisfied me utterly. I wandered about the streets, from the soaring imperial towers of down-town, along the East River docks, smelling of spices and the clipper ships of the past, through the swarming East Side—alien towns within towns—where the smoky flare of miles of clamorous pushcarts made a splendor of shabby streets; coming upon sudden shrill markets, dripping blood and fish-scales in the light of torches, the big Jewish women bawling their wares under the roaring great bridges; thrilling to the ebb and flow of human tides sweeping to work and back, west and east, south and north. I knew Chinatown, and Little Italy, and the quarter of the Syrians; the marionette theatre, Sharkey's and McSorley's saloons, the Bowery lodging houses and the places where the tramps gathered in winter; the Haymarket, the German Village, and all the dives of the Tenderloin. I spent all one summer night on top of a pier of the Williamsburg Bridge; I slept another night in a basket of squid in the Fulton Market, where the red and green and gold sea things glisten in the blue light of the sputtering arcs. The girls that walk the streets were friends of mine, and the drunken sailors off ships new-come from the world's end, and the Spanish longshoremen down on West Street.

I found wonderful obscure restaurants, where the foods of the whole world could be found. I knew how to get dope; where to go to hire a man to kill an enemy; what to do to get into gambling rooms, and secret dance halls. I knew well the parks, and streets of palaces, the theatres and hotels; the ugly growth of the city spreading like a disease, the decrepit places whence life was ebbing, and the squares and streets where an old, beautiful leisurely existence was drowned in the mounting roar of the slums. I knew Washington Square, and the artists and writers, the near-Bohemians, the radicals. I went to gangsters' balls at Tammany Hall, on excursions of the Tim Sullivan Association, to Coney Island on hot summer nights. . . . Within a block of my house was all the adventure of the world; within a mile was every foreign country.

In New York I first loved, and I first wrote of the things I saw, with a fierce joy of creation—and knew at last that I could write. There I got my first perceptions of the life of my time. The city and its people were an open book to me; everything had its story, dramatic, full of ironic tragedy and terrible humor. There I first saw that reality transcended all the fine poetic inventions of fastidiousness and medievalism. I was not happy or well long away from New York . . . I am not now, for that matter; but I cannot live continually in its heart any more. In the city I have no time for much but sensation and experience; but now I want some time of quiet, and leisure for thought,

so I can extract from the richness of my life something beautiful and strong. I
am living now in the country, within an hour of town, so I can go down
occasionally and plunge into the sea of people, the roaring and the lights—
and then come back here to write of it, in the quiet hills, in sunshine and
clean wind.

During this time I read a good deal of radical literature, attended meetings
of all sorts, met socialists, anarchists, single-taxers, labor-leaders, and besides,
all the hair-splitting Utopians and petty doctrine-mongers who cling to skirts
of Change. They interested me, so many different human types; and the liv-
ingness of theories which could dominate men and women captivated my
imagination. On the whole, ideas alone didn't mean much to me. I had to
see. In my rambles about the city I couldn't help but observe the ugliness of
poverty and all its train of evil, the cruel inequality between rich people who
had too many motor cars and poor people who didn't have enough to eat. It
didn't come to me from books that the workers produced all the wealth of the
world, which went to those who did not earn it.

The Lawrence strike of the textile workers had just ended, and the I.W.W.
dominated the social and industrial horizon like a portent of the rising of the
oppressed. That strike brought home to me hard the knowledge that the man-
ufacturers get all they can out of labor, pay as little as they must, and permit
the existence of great masses of the miserable unemployed in order to keep
wages down; that the forces of the State are on the side of property against
the propertyless. Our Socialist Party seemed to me duller than religion, and
almost as little in touch with labor. The Paterson strike broke out. I met Bill
Haywood, Elizabeth Gurley Flynn, Tresca, and the other leaders; they attracted me. I liked their understanding of the workers, their revolutionary
thought, the boldness of their dream, the way immense crowds of people took
fire and came alive under their leadership. Here was drama, change, democracy on the march and visible—a war of the people. I went to Paterson to
watch it, was mistaken for a striker while walking the public street, beaten by
the police, and jailed without any charge. In the jail I talked with exultant
men who had blithely defied the lawless brutality of the city government and
gone to prison laughing and singing. There were horrors in that jail too; men
and boys shut up for months without trial, men going mad and dying, bestial
cruelty and disease and filth—and all for the poor. When I came out I helped
to organize the Pageant of the Paterson Strike, in Madison Square Garden,
New York, drilling a thousand men and women in Paterson and bringing
them across New Jersey to act out, before an immensely moved audience of
twenty thousand people, the wretchedness of their lives and the glory of their
revolt.

Since then I have seen and reported many strikes, most of them desperate
struggles for the bare necessities of life; and all I have witnessed only confirms
my first idea of the class struggle and its inevitability. I wish with all my heart
that the proletariat would rise and take their rights—I don't see how else they
will get them. Political relief is so slow to come, and year by year the opportunities of peaceful protest and lawful action are curtailed. But I am not sure
any more that the working class is capable of revolution, peaceful or otherwise; the workers are so divided and bitterly hostile to each other, so badly

led, so blind to their class interest. The War has been a terrible shatterer of faith in economic and political idealism. And yet I cannot give up the idea that out of democracy will be born the new world—richer, braver, freer, more beautiful. As for me, I don't know what I can do to help—I don't know yet. All I know is that my happiness is built on the misery of other people, that I eat because others go hungry, that I am clothed when other people go almost naked through the frozen cities in winter; and that fact poisons me, disturbs my serenity, makes me write propaganda when I would rather play— though not so much as it once did.

I quit my job to work on the Pageant, and when it was all over I went to pieces nervously, and friends took me abroad for the summer. The strike was starved and lost, the men went back to work dispirited and disillusioned, and the leaders, too, broke down under the long strain of the fight. The I.W.W. itself seemed smashed—indeed it has never recovered its old prestige. I got diphtheria in Italy, and came back to New York weak and despondent. For six months I did almost nothing. And then, through the interest of Lincoln Steffens, *The Metropolitan Magazine* asked me to go to Mexico as a war correspondent, and I knew that I must do it.

Villa had just captured Chihuahua when I got to the border, and was getting ready to move on Torreón. I made straight for Chihuahua, and there got a chance to accompany an American mining man down into the mountains of Durango. Hearing that an old half-bandit, half-general was moving to the front, I cut loose and joined him, riding with a wild troop of Mexican cavalry two weeks across the desert, seeing battle at close range, in which my companions were defeated and killed, and fleeing for my life across the desert. I joined Villa then in his march on Torreón, and was in at the fall of that stronghold.

Altogether I was four months with the Constitutionalist armies in Mexico. When I first crossed the border deadliest fear gripped me. I was afraid of death, of mutilation, of a strange land and strange people whose speech and thought I did not know. But a terrible curiosity urged me on; I felt I *had to know* how I would act under fire, how I would get along with these primitive folks at war. And I discovered that bullets are not very terrifying, that the fear of death is not such a great thing, and that the Mexicans are wonderfully congenial. That four months of riding hundreds of miles across the blazing plains, sleeping on the ground with the *hombres,* dancing and carousing in looted haciendas all night after an all-day ride, being with them intimately in play, in battle, was perhaps the most satisfactory period of my life. I made good with these wild fighting men, and with myself. I loved them and I loved the life. I found myself again. I wrote better than I have ever written.

Then came the European War, to which I went as correspondent, spending a year and a half traveling in all the belligerent countries and on the front of five nations in battle. In Europe I found none of the spontaneity, none of the idealism of the Mexican revolution. It was a war of the workshops, and the trenches were factories turning out ruin—ruin of the spirit as well as of the body, the real and only death. Everything had halted but the engines of hate and destruction. European life, that flashed so many vital facets, ran in one channel, and runs in it now. There seems to me little to choose between the sides; both are horrible to me. The whole Great War is to me just a stoppage of the life and ferment of human evolution. I am waiting, waiting for it all to end, for life to resume so I can find my work.

In thinking it over, I find little in my thirty years that I can hold to. I haven't any God and don't want one; faith is only another word for finding oneself. In my life as in most lives, I guess, love plays a tremendous part. I've had love affairs, passionate happiness, wretched maladjustments; hurt deeply and been deeply hurt. But at last I have found my friend and lover, thrilling and satisfying, closer to me than anyone has ever been. And now I don't care what comes.

Suggestions for Discussion

1. What were Reed's most significant experiences at Harvard? How does he contrast the dominant groups of students?

2. What was the nature of Steffens's influence on Reed?

3. How would you sum up what living in New York meant to him?

4. What are the sources of Reed's pessimism? Of his affirmation?

Suggestions for Writing

1. "The end of a part of my life . . . the beginning of a new phase of life." What are some of your thoughts as you review your high school years and begin your work in college?

2. Have you had any great teacher or any subject at school so far that caught your imagination?

3. Describe your life at college or university, commenting upon its traditions, student body, activities, educational ideals, and faculty or focusing on a single aspect of college life.

4. Describe a mentor or teacher who has influenced your life.

Essays
—◆◆◆—

Lewis Thomas
Seven Wonders

Lewis Thomas (b. 1913) is a physician whose medical career has centered on the Sloan Kettering Cancer Center in New York, the city of his birth. He has written for medical journals at the same time that he has written popular essays to present science and the scientist's view of the world to the lay public. He won the National Book Award in 1974 for *The Lives of a Cell: Notes of a Biology Watcher*. Other collections include *The Medusa and the Snail* (1979), *More Notes of a Biology Watcher* (1979), *The Youngest Science: Notes of a Medicine-Watcher* (1983), and *Late Night Thoughts on Listening to Mahler's Ninth Symphony* (1983). In this essay, Thomas regards our own planet earth as the first of all Wonders of the modern world; it is a living system from which we can learn continuously, if we do not kill ourselves off and if we can learn to relate to others with affection and respect.

A while ago I received a letter from a magazine editor inviting me to join six other people at dinner to make a list of the Seven Wonders of the Modern World, to replace the seven old, out-of-date Wonders. I replied that I couldn't manage it, not on short order anyway, but still the question keeps hanging around in the lobby of my mind. I had to look up the old biodegradable Wonders, the Hanging Gardens of Babylon and all the rest, and then I had to look up that word "wonder" to make sure I understood what it meant. It occurred to me that if the magazine could get any seven people to agree on a list of any such seven things you'd have the modern Seven Wonders right there at the dinner table.

Wonder is a word to wonder about. It contains a mixture of messages: something marvelous and miraculous, surprising, raising unanswerable questions about itself, making the observer wonder, even raising skeptical questions like, "I *wonder* about that." Miraculous and marvelous are clues; both words come from an ancient Indo-European root meaning simply to smile or to laugh. Anything wonderful is something to smile in the presence of, in admiration (which, by the way, comes from the same root, along with, of all telling words, "mirror").

I decided to try making a list, not for the magazine's dinner party but for this occasion: seven things I wonder about the most.

I shall hold the first for the last, and move along.

My Number Two Wonder is a bacterial species never seen on the face of the earth until 1982, creatures never dreamed of before, living violation of what we used to regard as the laws of nature, things literally straight out of Hell. Or anyway what we used to think of as Hell, the hot unlivable interior of the earth. Such regions have recently come into scientific view from the research submarines designed to descend twenty-five hundred meters or more to the edge of deep holes in the sea bottom, where open vents spew superheated seawater in plumes from chimneys in the earth's crust, known to oceanographic scientists as "black smokers." This is not just hot water, or steam, or even steam under pressure as exists in a laboratory autoclave (which we have relied upon for decades as the surest way to destroy all microbial life). This is extremely hot water under extremely high pressure, with temperatures in excess of 300 degrees centigrade. At such heat, the existence of life as we know it would be simply inconceivable. Proteins and DNA would fall apart, enzymes would melt away, anything alive would die instantaneously. We have long since rules out the possibility of life on Venus because of that planet's comparable temperature; we have ruled out the possibility of life in the earliest years of this planet, four billion or so years ago, on the same ground.

B. J. A. Baross and J. W. Deming have recently discovered the presence of thriving colonies of bacteria in water fished directly from these deep-sea vents. Moreover, when brought to the surface, encased in titanium syringes and sealed in pressurized chambers heated to 250 degrees centigrade, the bacteria not only survive but reproduce themselves enthusiastically. They can be killed only by chilling them down in boiling water.

And yet they look just like ordinary bacteria. Under the electron microscope they have the same essential structure—cell walls, ribosomes, and all. If they were, as is now being suggested, the original archebacteria, ancestors of us all, how did they or their progeny ever learn to cool down? I cannot think of a more wonderful trick.

My Number Three Wonder is *oncideres*, a species of beetle encountered by a pathologist friend of mine who lives in Houston and has a lot of mimosa trees in his backyard. This beetle is not new, but it qualifies as a Modern Wonder because of the exceedingly modern questions raised for evolutionary biologists about the three consecutive things on the mind of the female of the species. Her first thought is for a mimosa tree, which she finds and climbs, ignoring all other kinds of trees in the vicinity. Her second thought is for the laying of eggs, which she does by crawling out on a limb, cutting a longitudinal slit with her mandible and depositing her eggs beneath the slit. Her third and last thought concerns the welfare of her offspring; beetle larvae cannot survive in live wood, so she backs up a foot or so and cuts a neat circular girdle all around the limb, through the bark and down into the cambium. It takes her eight hours to finish this cabinetwork. Then she leaves and where she goes I do not know. The limb dies from the girdling, falls to the ground in the next breeze, the larvae feed and grow into the next generation, and the questions lie there unanswered. How on earth did these three linked thoughts in her mind evolve together in evolution? How could any one of the three become fixed as beetle behavior by itself, without the other two? What are the odds favoring three totally separate bits of behavior—liking a particular tree, cutting a slit for eggs, and then girdling the limb—happening together by random chance among a beetle's genes? Does this smart beetle know what she is doing? And how did the mimosa tree enter the picture in its evolution? Left to themselves, unpruned, mimosa trees have a life expectancy of twenty-five to thirty years. Pruned each year, which is what the beetle's girdling labor accomplishes, the tree can flourish for a century. The mimosa-beetle relationship is an elegant example of symbiotic partnership, a phenomenon now recognized as pervasive in nature. It is good for us to have around on our intellectual mantelpiece such creatures as this insect and its friend the tree, for they keep reminding us how little we know about nature.

The Fourth Wonder on my list is an infectious agent known as the scrapie virus, which causes a fatal disease of the brain in sheep, goats, and several laboratory animals. A close cousin of scrapie is the C-J virus, the cause of some cases of senile dementia in human beings. These are called "slow viruses," for the excellent reason that an animal exposed to infection today will not become ill until a year and a half or two years from today. The agent, whatever it is, can propagate itself in abundance from a few infectious units today to more than a billion next year. I use the phrase "whatever it is" advisedly. Nobody has yet been able to find any DNA or RNA in the scrapie or C-J viruses. It may be there, but if so it exists in amounts too small to detect. Meanwhile, there is plenty of protein, leading to a serious proposal that the virus may indeed be *all* protein. But protein, so far as we know, does not replicate itself all by itself, not on this planet anyway. Looked at this way, the scrapie agent seems the strangest thing in all biology and, until someone in some laboratory figures out what it is, a candidate for Modern Wonder.

My Fifth Wonder is the olfactory receptor cell, located in the epithelial tissue high in the nose, sniffing the air for clues to the environment, the fragrance of friends, the smell of leaf smoke, breakfast, nighttime and bedtime, and a rose, even, it is said, the odor of sanctity. The cell that does all these things, firing off urgent messages into the deepest part of the brain, switching on one strange unacccountable memory after another, is itself a proper brain cell, a certified neuron belonging to the brain but miles away out in the open air, nosing around the world. How it manages to make sense of what it senses, discriminating between jasmine and anything else non-jasmine with infallibility, is one of the deep secrets of neurobiology. This would be wonder enough, but there is more. This population of brain cells, unlike any other neurons of the vertebrate central nervous system, turns itself over every few weeks; cells wear out, die and are replaced by brand-new cells rewired to the same deep centers miles back in the brain, sensing and remembering the same wonderful smells. If and when we reach an understanding of these cells and their functions, including the moods and whims under their governance, we will know a lot more about the mind than we do now, a world away.

Sixth on my list is, I hesitate to say, another insect, the termite. This time, though, it is not the single insect that is the Wonder, it is the collectivity. There is nothing at all wonderful about a single, solitary termite, indeed there is really no such creature, functionally speaking, as a lone termite, any more than we can imagine a genuinely solitary human being; no such thing. Two or three termites gathered together on a dish are not much better; they may move about and touch each other nervously, but nothing happens. But keep adding more termites until they reach a critical mass, and then the miracle begins. As though they had suddenly received a piece of extraordinary news, they organize in platoons and begin stacking up pellets to precisely the right height, then turning the arches to connect the columns, constructing the cathedral and its chambers in which the colony will live out its life for the decades ahead, air-conditioned and humidity-controlled, following the chemical blueprint coded in their genes, flawlessly, stone-blind. They are not the dense mass of individual insects they appear to be; they are an organism, a thoughtful, meditative brain on a million legs. All we really know about this new thing is that it does its architecture and engineering by a complex system of chemical signals.

The Seventh Wonder of the modern world is a human child, any child. I used to wonder about childhood and the evolution of our species. It seemed to me unparsimonious to keep expending all that energy on such a long period of vulnerability and defenselessness, with nothing to show for it, in biological terms, beyond the feckless, irresponsible pleasure of childhood. After all, I used to think, it is one sixth of a whole human life span! Why didn't our evolution take care of that, allowing us to jump catlike from our juvenile to our adult (and, as I thought) productive stage of life? I had forgotten about language, the single human trait that marks us out as specifically human, the property that enables our survival as the most compulsively, biologically, obsessively social of all creatures on earth, more interdependent and interconnected even than the famous social insects. I had forgotten that, and forgotten that children *do* that in childhood. Language is what childhood is for.

There is another related but different creature, nothing like so wonderful as a human child, nothing like so hopeful, something to worry about all day and all night. It is *us*, aggregated together in our collective, critical masses. So far, we have learned how to be useful to each other only when we collect in small groups—families, circles of friends, once in a while (although still rarely) committees. The drive to be useful is encoded in our genes. But when we gather in very large numbers, as in the modern nation-state, we seem capable of levels of folly and self-destruction to be found nowhere else in all of Nature.

As a species, taking all in all, we are still too young, too juvenile, to be trusted. We have spread across the face of the earth in just a few thousand years, no time at all as evolution clocks time, covering all livable parts of the planet, endangering other forms of life, and now threatening ourselves. As a species, we have everything in the world to learn about living, but we may be running out of time. Provisionally, but only provisionally, we are a Wonder.

And now the first on my list, the one I put off at the beginning of making a list, the first of all Wonders of the modern world. To name this one, you have to redefine the world as it has indeed been redefined in this most scientic of all centuries. We named the place we live in the *world* long ago, from the Indo-European root *wiros,* which meant man. We now live in the whole universe, that stupefying piece of expanding geometry. Our suburbs are the local solar system, into which, sooner or later, we will spread life, and then, likely, beyond into the galaxy. Of all celestial bodies within reach or view, as far as we can see, out to the edge, the most wonderful and marvelous and mysterious is turning out to be our own planet earth. There is nothing to match it anywhere, not yet anyway.

It is a living system, an immense organism, still developing, regulating itself, making its own oxygen, maintaining its own temperature, keeping all its infinite living parts connected and interdependent, including us. It is the strangest of all places, and there is everything in the world to learn about it. It can keep us awake and jubilant with questions for millennia ahead, if we can learn not to meddle and not to destroy. Our great hope is in being such a young species, thinking in language only a short while, still learning, still growing up.

We are not like the social insects. They have only the one way of doing things and they will do it forever, coded for that way. We are coded differently, not just for binary choices, *go* or *no-go*. We can go four ways at once, depending on how the air feels: *go*, *no-go*, but also *maybe*, plus *what the hell let's give it a try*. We are in for one surprise after another if we keep at it and keep alive. We can build structures for human society never seen before, music never heard before.

Provided we do not kill ourselves off, and provided we can connect ourselves by the affection and respect for which I believe our genes are also coded, there is no end to what we might do on or off this planet.

At this early stage in our evolution, now through our infancy and into our childhood and then, with luck, our growing up, what our species needs most of all, right now, is simply a future.

Suggestions for Discussion

1. Explain the source of wonder in Thomas's second, third, fourth, and sixth Wonders. What do they have in common?

2. Why is the fifth Wonder so remarkable?

3. Why did Thomas change his mind about the Wonder of childhood?

4. What does Thomas mean when he says that "language is what childhood is for"?

5. How does Thomas account for humanity's capability of levels of folly and self-destruction found nowhere else in Nature?

6. With what specific details does Thomas explain his feeling that the planet earth is the most wonderful, marvelous, and mysterious Wonder?

7. Wherein lies his hope for the future of the earth?

Suggestions for Writing

1. Describe the Wonders of the modern world from your perspective and discuss the reasons for your choice.

2. Develop in an essay your view of Thomas's hope for the future. What does it mean to you to "build structures for human society never seen before, thoughts never thought before, music never heard before"?

Rollo May

The Man Who Was Put in a Cage

Rollo May (b. 1909) is a practicing psychotherapist in New York. He is a member of the William Alanson White Institute of Psychiatry, Psychoanalysis, and Psychology. In addition to *Man's Search for Himself* (1953), he is author of *The Meaning of Anxiety* (1950), *Love and Will* (1969), and *Power and Innocence* (1972). In this parable from *Psychology and the Human Dilemma* (1966) the psychologist is impelled to act on the man's impassioned cry in the dream: when any man's freedom is taken away, the freedom of everyone is also taken away.

> *What a piece of work is man! how noble in reason! how infinite in faculty! in form and moving how express and admirable! . . . The paragon of animals!*
> —*Shakespeare*, Hamlet

We have quite a few discrete pieces of information these days about what happens to a person when he is deprived of this or that element of freedom. We have our studies of sensory deprivation and of how a person reacts when put in different kinds of authoritarian atmosphere, and so on. But recently I have been wondering what pattern would emerge if we put these various pieces of knowledge together. In short, what would happen to a living, whole person if his total freedom—or as nearly total as we can imagine—were taken away? In the course of these reflections, a parable took form in my mind.

The story begins with a king who, while standing in reverie at the window of his palace one evening, happened to notice a man in the town square below. He was apparently an average man, walking home at night, who had taken the same route five nights a week for many years. The king followed this man in his imagination—pictured him arriving home, perfunctorily kissing his wife, eating his late meal, inquiring whether everything was all right with the children, reading the paper, going to bed, perhaps engaging in the sex relation with his wife or perhaps not, sleeping, and getting up and going off to work again the next day.

And a sudden curiosity seized the king, which for a moment banished his fatigue: "I wonder what would happen if a man were kept in a cage, like the animals at the zoo?" His curiosity was perhaps in some ways not unlike that of the first surgeons who wondered what it would be like to perform a lobotomy on the human brain.

So the next day the king called in a psychologist, told him of his idea, and invited him to observe the experiment. When the psychologist demurred saying, "It's an unthinkable thing to keep a man in a cage," the monarch replied that many rulers had in effect, if not literally, done so, from the time of the Romans through Genghis Khan down to Hitler and the totalitarian leaders; so why not find out scientifically what would happen? Furthermore, added the king, he had made up his mind to do it whether the psychologist took part or not; he had already gotten the Greater Social Research Foundation to give a large sum of money for the experiment, and why let that money go to waste? By this time the psychologist also was feeling within himself a great curiosity about what would happen if a man were kept in a cage.

And so the next day the king caused a cage to be brought from the zoo—a large cage that had been occupied by a lion when it was new, then later by a tiger; just recently it had been the home of a hyena who died the previous week. The cage was put in an inner private court in the palace grounds, and the average man whom the king had seen from the window was brought and placed therein. The psychologist, with his Rorschach and Wechsler-Bellevue tests in his brief case to administer at some appropriate moment, sat down outside the cage.

At first the man was simply bewildered, and he kept saying to the psychologist, "I have to catch the tram, I have to get to work, look what time it is, I'll be late for work!" but later on in the afternoon the man began soberly to realize what was up, and then he protested vehemently, "The king can't do this to me! It is unjust! It's against the law." His voice was strong, and his eyes full of anger. The psychologist liked the man for his anger, and he became vaguely aware that this was a mood he had encountered often in people he worked with in his clinic. "Yes," he realized, "this anger is the attitude of people who—like the healthy adolescents of any era—want to fight what's wrong, who protest directly against it. When people come to the clinic in this mood, it is good—they can be helped."

During the rest of the week the man continued his vehement protests. When the king walked by the cage, as he did every day, the man made his protests directly to the monarch.

But the king answered, "Look here, you are getting plenty of food, you have a good bed, and you don't have to work. We take good care of you; so why are you objecting?"

After some days had passed, the man's protests lessened and then ceased. He was silent in his cage, generally refusing to talk. But the psychologist could see hatred glowing in his eyes. When he did exchange a few words, they were short, definite words uttered in the strong, vibrant, but calm voice of the person who hates and knows whom he hates.

Whenever the king walked into the courtyard, there was a deep fire in the man's eyes. The psychologist thought, "This must be the way people act when they are first conquered." He remembered that he had also seen that expression of the eyes and heard that tone of voice in many patients at his clinic: the adolescent who had been unjustly accused at home or in school and could do nothing about it; the college student who was required by public and campus opinion to be a star on the gridiron, but was required by his professors to pass courses he could not prepare for if he were to be successful in football—and who was then expelled from college for the cheating that resulted. And the psychologist, looking at the active hatred in the man's eyes, thought, "It is still good; a person who has this fight in him can be helped."

Every day the king, as he walked through the courtyard, kept reminding the man in the cage that he was given food and shelter and taken good care of, so why did he not like it? And the psychologist noticed that, whereas at first the man had been entirely impervious to the king's statements, it now seemed more and more that he was pausing for a moment after the king's speech—for a second the hatred was postponed from returning to his eyes—as though he were asking himself if what the king said were possibly true.

And after a few weeks more, the man began to discuss with the psychologist how it was a useful thing that a man is given food and shelter; and how man had to live by his fate in any case, and the part of wisdom was to accept fate. He soon was developing an extensive theory about security and the acceptance of fate, which sounded to the psychologist very much like the philosophical theories that Rosenberg and others worked out for the fascists in Germany. He was very voluble during this period, talking at length, although the talk was mostly a monologue. The psychologist noticed that his voice was flat and hollow as he talked, like the voice of people in TV previews who make an effort to look you in the eye and try hard to sound sincere as they tell you that you should see the program they are advertising, or the announcers on the radio who are paid to persuade you that you should like high-brow music.

And the psychologist also noticed that now the corners of the man's mouth always turned down, as though he were in some gigantic pout. Then the psychologist suddenly remembered: this was like the middle-aged, middle-class people who came to his clinic, the respectable bourgeois people who went to church and lived morally but were always full of resentment, as though everything they did was conceived, born, and nursed in resentment. It reminded the psychologist of Nietzsche's saying that the middle class was consumed with resentment. He then for the first time began to be seriously worried about the man in the cage, for he knew that once resentment gets a firm start and becomes well rationalized and structuralized, it may become like cancer. When the person no longer knows whom he hates, he is much harder to help.

During this period the Greater Social Research Foundation had a board of trustees meeting, and they decided that since they were expending a fund to keep a man supported in a cage, it would look better if representatives of the Foundation at least visited the experiment. So a group of people, consisting of two professors and a few graduate students, came in one day to look at the man in the cage. One of the professors then proceeded to lecture to the group about the relation of the autonomic nervous system and the secretions of the ductless glands to human existence in a cage. But it occurred to the other professor that the verbal communications of the victim himself might just possibly be interesting, so he asked the man how he felt about living in a cage. The man was friendly toward the professors and students and explained to them that he had chosen this way of life, that there were great values in security and in being taken care of, that they would of course see how sensible this course was, and so on.

"How strange!" thought the psychologist, "and how pathetic; why is it he struggles so hard to get them to approve his way of life?"

In the succeeding days when the king walked through the courtyard, the man fawned upon him from behind the bars in his cage and thanked him for the food and shelter. But when the king was not in the yard and the man was not aware that the psychologist was present, his expression was quite different—sullen and morose. When his food was handed to him through the bars by the keeper, the man would often drop the dishes or dump over the water and then would be embarrassed because of his stupidity and clumsiness. His conversation became increasingly one-tracked; and instead of the involved philosophical theories about the value of being taken care of, he had gotten down to simple sentences such as "It is fate," which he would say over and over again, or he would just mumble to himself, "It is." The psychologist was surprised to find that the man should now be so clumsy as to drop his food, or so stupid as to talk in those barren sentences, for he knew from his tests that the man had originally been of good average intelligence. Then it dawned upon the psychologist that this was the kind of behavior he had observed in some anthropological studies among the Negroes in the South—people who had been forced to kiss the hand that fed and enslaved them, who could no longer either hate or rebel. The man in the cage took more and more to simply sitting all day long in the sun as it came through the bars, his only movement being to shift his position from time to time from morning through the afternoon.

It was hard to say just when the last phase set in. But the psychologist became aware that the man's face now seemed to have no particular expression; his smile was no longer fawning, but simply empty and meaningless, like the grimace a baby makes when there is gas on its stomach. The man ate his food and exchanged a few sentences with the psychologist from time to time; but his eyes were distant and vague, and though he looked at the psychologist, it seemed that he never really *saw* him.

And now the man, in his desultory conversations, never used the word "I" any more. He had accepted the cage. He had no anger, no hate, no rationalizations. But he was now insane.

The night the psychologist realized this, he sat in his apartment trying to write a concluding report. But it was very difficult for him to summon up words, for he felt within himself a great emptiness. He kept trying to reassure himself with the words, "They say that nothing is ever lost, that matter is merely changed to energy and back again." But he could not help feeling that something *had* been lost, that something had gone out of the universe in this experiment.

He finally went to bed with his report unfinished. But he could not sleep; there was a gnawing within him which, in less rational and scientific ages, would have been called a conscience. Why didn't I tell the king that this is the one experiment that no man can do—or at least why didn't I shout that I would have nothing to do with the whole bloody business? Of course, the king would have dismissed me, the foundations would never have granted me any more money, and at the clinic they would have said that I was not a real scientist. But maybe one could farm in the mountains and make a living, and maybe one could paint or write something that would make future men happier and more free. . . .

But he realized that these musings were, at least at the moment, unrealistic, and he tried to pull himself back to reality. All he could get, however, was this feeling of emptiness within himself, and the words, "Something has been taken out of the universe, and there is left only a void."

Finally he dropped off to sleep. Some time later, in the small hours of the morning, he was awakened by a startling dream. A crowd of people had gathered, in the dream, in front of the cage in the courtyard, and the man in the cage—no longer inert and vacuous—was shouting through the bars of the cage in impassioned oratory. "It is not only I whose freedom is taken away!" he was crying. "When the king puts me or any man in a cage, the freedom of each of you is taken away also. The king must go!" The people began to chant, "The king must go!" and they seized and broke out the iron bars of the cage, and wielded them for weapons as they charged the palace.

The psychologist awoke, filled by the dream with a great feeling of hope and joy—an experience of hope and joy probably not unlike that experienced by the free men of England when they forced King John to sign the Magna Charta. But not for nothing had the psychologist had an orthodox analysis in the course of his training, and as he lay surrounded by this aura of happiness, a voice spoke within him: "Aha, you had this dream to make yourself feel better; it's just a wish fulfillment."

"The hell it is!" said the psychologist as he climbed out of bed. "Maybe some dreams are to be acted on."

Suggestions for Discussion

1. What possible implicit judgment of the average man is evident in the king's imaginative recreation of his life? What is the significance of the king's selection of an average man for his experiment?

2. Formulate a plausible explanation of the fact that the anger and subsequent hate manifested by the man in the cage signified that he could be helped.

3. Define the various phases of the victim's response to his imprisonment and account for each of them. Include an analysis of the changes in his conversations with the several observers. How did the analogies cited contribute to your understanding of his metamorphosis?

4. Account for the reactions of the psychologist after his realization that the man was no longer sane, especially his feeling of emptiness within himself, the sense that "there is left only a void." Account for his final postdream resolution.

Suggestions for Writing

1. What does the form of the parable contribute to May's thesis? Write a paragraph elaborating on May's thesis. What is lost when you state it directly?

2. Using a vital subject like freedom of choice or love or the dignity of man, write a parable of your own in which you place it in fresh perspective.

3. Read one of the works that depicts man as prisoner and victim by Robert Lifton, Bruno Bettleheim, Charles Frankl, or Hannah Arendt. Write an analysis of the effects of incarceration on the human spirit, paying special attention to what qualities and activities of the mind distinguish one man from another under such adverse circumstances.

4. Relate the opening lines from *Hamlet* to the parable. Or develop an essay on the most difficult or the most crucial choices you have ever made, or are currently contemplating, and the factors you regard as central in arriving at a resolution.

5. May attributes the man's capitulation largely to the fact of his security. Defend or criticize this thesis. What if the victim were not an average man but a bright mem-

ber of a youth commune, a poet, or a mystic? Rewrite the parable using one of the latter or any other victim as your protagonist.

Helen Keller

Three Days to See

Helen Keller (1880–1968) was deaf and blind from the age of nineteen months. Through her teacher, Annie Sullivan, she learned to communicate by using sign language and later through voice lessons. She graduated from Radcliffe College with honors and wrote a critically acclaimed autobiography, *Story of My Life* (1902). Other books are *Optimism* (1903), *The World I Live In* (1908), and *Out of the Dark* (1913). In this essay Keller movingly describes the delights she would experience were she to be given *Three Days to See*.

All of us have read thrilling stories in which the hero had only a limited and specified time to live. Sometimes it was as long as a year; sometimes as short as twenty-four hours. But always we were interested in discovering just how the doomed man chose to spend his last days or his last hours. I speak, of course, of free men who have a choice, not condemned criminals whose sphere of activities is strictly delimited.

Such stories set us thinking, wondering what we should do under similar circumstances. What events, what experiences, what associations should we crowd into those last hours as mortal beings? What happiness should we find in reviewing the past, what regrets?

Sometimes I have thought it would be an excellent rule to live each day as if we should die tomorrow. Such an attitude would emphasize sharply the values of life. We should live each day with a gentleness, a vigor, and a keenness of appreciation which are often lost when time stretches before us in the constant panorama of more days and months and years to come. There are those, of course, who would adopt the epicurean motto of "Eat, drink, and be merry," but most people would be chastened by the certainty of impending death.

In stories, the doomed hero is usually saved at the last minute by some stroke of fortune, but almost always his sense of values is changed. He becomes more appreciative of the meaning of life and its permanent spiritual values. It has often been noted that those who live, or have lived, in the shadow of death bring a mellow sweetness to everything they do.

Most of us, however, take life for granted. We know that one day we must die, but usually we picture that day as far in the future. When we are in buoyant health, death is all but unimaginable. We seldom think of it. The days stretch out in an endless vista. So we go about our petty tasks, hardly aware of our listless attitude toward life.

The same lethargy, I am afraid, characterizes the use of all our faculties and senses. Only the deaf appreciate hearing, only the blind realize the manifold blessings that lie in sight. Particularly does this observation apply to those who have lost sight and hearing in adult life. But those who have never suffered impairment of sight or hearing seldom make the fullest use of these blessed faculties. Their eyes and ears take in all sights and sounds hazily, without concentration and with little appreciation. It is the same old story of not being grateful for what we have until we lose it, of not being conscious of health until we are ill.

I have often thought it would be a blessing if each human being were stricken blind and deaf for a few days at some time during his early adult life. Darkness would make him more appreciative of sight; silence would teach him the joys of sound.

Now and then I have tested my seeing friends to discover what they see. Recently I was visited by a very good friend who had just returned from a long walk in the woods, and I asked her what she had observed. "Nothing in particular," she replied. I might have been incredulous had I not been accustomed to such responses, for long ago I became convinced that the seeing see little.

How was it possible, I asked myself, to walk for an hour through the woods and see nothing worthy of note? I who cannot see find hundreds of things to interest me through mere touch. I feel the delicate symmetry of a leaf. I pass my hands lovingly about the smooth skin of a silver birch, or the rough shaggy bark of a pine. In spring I touch the branches of trees hopefully in search of a bud, the first sign of awakening Nature after her winter's sleep. I feel the delightful, velvety texture of a flower, and discover its remarkable convolutions; and something of the miracle of Nature is revealed to me. Occasionally, if I am fortunate, I place my hand gently on a small tree and feel the happy quiver of a bird in full song. I am delighted to have the cool waters of a brook rush through my open fingers. To me a lush carpet of pine needles or spongy grass is more welcome than the most luxurious Persian rug. To me the pageant of seasons is a thrilling and unending drama, the action of which streams through my finger tips.

At times my heart cries out with longing to see all these things. If I can get so much pleasure from mere touch, how much more beauty must be revealed by sight. Yet, those who have eyes apparently see little. The panorama of color and action which fills the world is taken for granted. It is human, perhaps, to appreciate little that which we have and to long for that which we have not, but it is a great pity that in the world of light the gift of sight is used only as a mere convenience rather than as a means of adding fullness to life.

If I were the president of a university I should establish a compulsory course in "How to Use Your Eyes." The professor would try to show his pupils how they could add joy to their lives by really seeing what passes unnoticed before them. He would try to awake their dormant and sluggish faculties.

Perhaps I can best illustrate by imagining what I should most like to see if I were given the use of my eyes, say, for just three days. And while I am imagining, suppose you, too, set your mind to work on the problem of how you would use your own eyes if you had only three more days to see. If with the oncoming darkness of the third night you knew that the sun would never rise for you again, how would you spend those three precious intervening days? What would you most want to let your gaze rest upon?

I, naturally, should want most to see the things which have become dear to me through my years of darkness. You, too, would want to let your eyes rest long on the things that have become dear to you so that you could take the memory of them with you into the night that loomed before you.

If by some miracle I were granted three seeing days, to be followed by a relapse into darkness, I should divide the period into three parts.

On the first day, I should want to see the people whose kindness and gentleness and companionship have made my life worth living. First I should like to gaze long upon the face of my dear teacher, Mrs. Anne Sullivan Macy, who came to me when I was a child and opened the outer world to me. I should want not merely to see the outline of her face, so that I could cherish it in my memory, but to study that face and find in it the living evidence of the sympathetic tenderness and patience with which she accomplished the difficult task of my education. I should like to see in her eyes that strength of character which has enabled her to stand firm in the face of difficulties, and that compassion for all humanity which she has revealed to me so often.

I do not know what it is to see into the heart of a friend through that "window of the soul," the eye. I can only "see" through my finger tips the outline of a face. I can detect laughter, sorrow, and many other obvious emotions. I know my friends from the feel of their faces. But I cannot really picture their personalities by touch. I know their personalities, of course, through other means, through the thoughts they express to me, through whatever of their actions are revealed to me. But I am denied that deeper understanding of them which I am sure would come through sight of them, through watching their reactions to various expressed thoughts and circumstances, through noting the immediate and fleeting reactions of their eyes and countenance.

Friends who are near to me I know well, because through the months and years they reveal themselves to me in all their phases; but of casual friends I have only an incomplete impression, an impression gained from a handclasp, from spoken words which I take from their lips with my finger tips, or which they tap into the palm of my hand.

How much easier, how much more satisfying it is for you who can see to grasp quickly the essential qualities of another person by watching the subtleties of expression, the quiver of a muscle, the flutter of a hand. But does it ever occur to you to use your sight to see into the inner nature of a friend or acquaintance? Do not most of you seeing people grasp casually the outward features of a face and let it go at that?

For instance, can you describe accurately the faces of five good friends? Some of you can, but many cannot. As an experiment, I have questioned husbands of long standing about the color of their wives' eyes, and often they express embarrassed confusion and admit that they do not know. And, incidentally, it is a chronic complaint of wives that their husbands do not notice new dresses, new hats, and changes in household arrangements.

The eyes of seeing persons soon become accustomed to the routine of their surroundings, and they actually see only the startling and spectacular. But even in viewing the most spectacular sights the eyes are lazy. Court records reveal every day how inaccurately "eyewitnesses" see. A given event will be "seen" in several different ways by as many witnesses. Some see more than others, but few see everything that is within the range of their vision.

Oh, the things that I should see if I had the power of sight for just three days!

The first day would be a busy one. I should call to me all my dear friends and look long into their faces, imprinting upon my mind the outward evidences of the beauty that is within them. I should let my eyes rest, too, on the face of a baby, so that I could catch a vision of the eager, innocent beauty which precedes the individual's consciousness of the conflicts which life develops.

And I should like to look into the loyal, trusting eyes of my dogs—the grave, canny little Scottie, Darkie, and the stalwart, understanding Great Dane, Helga, whose warm, tender, and playful friendships are so comforting to me.

On that busy first day I should also view the small simple things of my home. I want to see the warm colors in the rugs under my feet, the pictures on the walls, the intimate trifles that transform a house into home. My eyes would rest respectfully on the books in raised type which I have read, but they would be more eagerly interested in the printed books which seeing people can read, for during the long night of my life the books I have read and those which have been read to me have built themselves into a great shining lighthouse, revealing to me the deepest channels of human life and the human spirit.

In the afternoon of that first seeing day, I should take a long walk in the woods and intoxicate my eyes on the beauties of the world of Nature, trying desperately to absorb in a few hours the vast splendor which is constantly unfolding itself to those who can see. On the way home from my woodland jaunt my path would lie near a farm so that I might see the patient horses plowing in the field (perhaps I should see only a tractor!) and the serene content of men living close to the soil. And I should pray for the glory of a colorful sunset.

When dusk had fallen, I should experience the double delight of being able to see by artificial light, which the genius of man has created to extend the power of his sight when Nature decrees darkness.

In the night of that first day of sight, I should not be able to sleep, so full would be my mind of the memories of the day.

The next day—the second day of sight—I should arise with the dawn and see the thrilling miracle by which night is transformed into day. I should behold with awe the magnificent panorama of light with which the sun awakens the sleeping earth.

This day I should devote to a hasty glimpse of the world, past and present. I should want to see the pageant of man's progress, the kaleidoscope of the ages. How can so much be compressed into one day? Through the museums, of course. Often I have visited the New York Museum of Natural History to touch with my hands many of the objects there exhibited, but I have longed to see with my eyes the condensed history of the earth and its inhabitants displayed there—animals and the races of men pictured in their native environment; gigantic carcasses of dinosaurs and mastodons which roamed the earth long before man appeared, with his tiny stature and powerful brain, to conquer the animal kingdom; realistic presentations of the processes of evolution in animals, in man, and in the implements which man has used to fashion for himself a secure home on this planet; and a thousand and one other aspects of natural history.

I wonder how many readers of this article have viewed this panorama of the face of living things as pictured in that inspiring museum. Many, of course, have not had the opportunity, but I am sure that many who *have* had the opportunity have not made use of it. There, indeed, is a place to use your eyes. You who see can spend many fruitful days there, but I, with my imaginary three days of sight, could only take a hasty glimpse, and pass on.

My next stop would be the Metropolitan Museum of Art, for just as the Museum of Natural History reveals the material aspects of the world, so does the Metropolitan show the myriad facets of the human spirit. Throughout the history of humanity the urge to artistic expression has been almost as powerful as the urge for food, shelter, and procreation. And here, in the vast chambers of the Metropolitan Museum, is unfolded before me the spirit of Egypt, Greece, and Rome, as expressed in their art. I know well through my hands the sculptured gods and goddesses of the ancient Nile-land. I have felt copies of Parthenon friezes, and I have sensed the rhythmic beauty of charging Athenian warriors. Apollos and Venuses and the Winged Victory of Samothrace are friends of my finger tips. The gnarled, bearded features of Homer are dear to me, for he, too, knew blindness.

My hands have lingered upon the living marble of Roman sculpture as well as that of later generations. I have passed my hands over a plaster cast of Michelangelo's inspiring and heroic Moses; I have sensed the power of Rodin; I have been awed by the devoted spirit of Gothic wood carving. These arts which can be touched have meaning for me, but even they were meant to be seen rather than felt, and I can only guess at the beauty which remains hidden from me. I can admire the simple lines of a Greek vase, but its figured decorations are lost to me.

So on this, my second day of sight, I should try to probe into the soul of man through his art. The things I knew through touch I should now see. More splendid still, the whole magnificent world of painting would be opened to me, from the Italian Primitives, with their serene religious devotion, to the Moderns, with their feverish visions. I should look deep into the canvases of Raphael, Leonardo dá Vinci, Titian, Rembrandt. I should want to feast my eyes upon the warm colors of Veronese, study the mysteries of El Greco, catch a new vision of Nature from Corot. Oh, there is so much rich meaning and beauty in the art of the ages for you who have eyes to see!

Upon my short visit to this temple of art I should not be able to review a fraction of that great world of art which is open to you. I should be able to get only a superficial impression. Artists tell me that for a deep and true appreciation of art one must educate the eye. One must learn through experience to weigh the merits of line, of composition, of form and color. If I had eyes, how happily would I embark upon so fascinating a study! Yet I am told that, to many of you who have eyes to see, the world of art is a dark night, unexplored and unilluminated.

It would be with extreme reluctance that I should leave the Metropolitan Museum, which contains the key to beauty—a beauty so neglected. Seeing persons, however, do not need a Metropolitan to find this key to beauty. The same key lies waiting in smaller museums, and in books on the shelves of even small libraries. But naturally, in my limited time of imaginary sight, I should choose the place where the key unlocks the greatest treasures in the shortest time.

The evening of my second day of sight I should spend at a theater or at the movies. Even now I often attend theatrical performances of all sorts, but the action of the play must be spelled into my hand by a companion. But how I should like to see with my own eyes the fascinating figure of Hamlet, or the gusty Falstaff amid colorful Elizabethan trappings! How I should like to follow each movement of the graceful Hamlet, each strut of the hearty Falstaff! And since I could see only one play, I should be confronted by a many-horned dilemma, for there are scores of plays I should want to see. You who have eyes can see any you like. How many of you, I wonder, when you gaze at a play, a movie, or any spectacle, realize and give thanks for the miracle of sight which enables you to enjoy its color, grace, and movement?

I cannot enjoy the beauty of rhythmic movement except in a sphere restricted to the touch of my hands. I can envision only dimly the grace of a Pavlova, although I know something of the delight of rhythm, for often I can sense the beat of music as it vibrates through the floor. I can well imagine that cadenced motion must be one of the most pleasing sights in the world. I have been able to gather something of this by tracing with my fingers the lines in sculptured marble; if this static grace can be so lovely, how much more acute must be the thrill of seeing grace in motion.

One of my dearest memories is of the time when Joseph Jefferson allowed me to touch his face and hands as he went through some of the gestures and speeches of his beloved Rip Van Winkle. I was able to catch thus a meager glimpse of the world of drama, and I shall never forget the delight of that moment. But, oh, how much I must miss, and how much pleasure you seeing ones can derive from watching and hearing the interplay of speech and movement in the unfolding of a dramatic performance! If I could see only one play, I should know how to picture in my mind the action of a hundred plays which I have read or had transferred to me through the medium of the manual alphabet.

So, through the evening of my second imaginary day of sight, the great figures of dramatic literature would crowd sleep from my eyes.

The following morning, I should again greet the dawn, anxious to discover new delights, for I am sure that, for those who have eyes which really see, the dawn of each day must be a perpetually new revelation of beauty.

This, according to the terms of my imagined miracle, is to be my third and last day of sight. I shall have no time to waste in regrets or longings; there is too much to see. The first day I devoted to my friends, animate and inanimate. The second revealed to me the history of man and Nature. Today I shall spend in the workaday world of the present, amid the haunts of men going about the business of life. And where can one find so many activities and conditions of men as in New York? So the city becomes my destination.

I start from my home in the quiet little suburb of Forest Hills, Long Island. Here, surrounded by green lawns, trees, and flowers, are neat little houses, happy with the voices and movements of wives and children, havens of peaceful rest for men who toil in the city. I drive across the lacy structure of steel which spans the East River, and I get a new and startling vision of the power and ingenuity of the mind of man. Busy boats chug and scurry about the river—racy speed boats, stolid, snorting tugs. If I had long days of sight ahead, I should spend many of them watching the delightful activity upon the river.

I look ahead, and before me rise the fantastic towers of New York, a city that seems to have stepped from the pages of a fairy story. What an awe-inspiring sight, these glittering spires, these vast banks of stone and steel—structures such as the gods might build for themselves! This animated picture is a part of the lives of millions of people every day. How many, I wonder, give it so much as a second glance? Very few, I fear. Their eyes are blind to this magnificent sight because it is so familiar to them.

I hurry to the top of one of those gigantic structures, the Empire State Building, for there, a short time ago, I "saw" the city below through the eyes of my secretary. I am anxious to compare my fancy with reality. I am sure I should not be disappointed in the panorama spread out before me, for to me it would be a vision of another world.

Now I begin my rounds of the city. First, I stand at a busy corner, merely looking at people, trying by sight of them to understand something of their lives. I see smiles, and I am happy. I see serious determination, and I am proud. I see suffering, and I am compassionate.

I stroll down Fifth Avenue. I throw my eyes out of focus so that I see no particular object but only a seething kaleidoscope of color. I am certain that the colors of women's dresses moving in a throng must be a gorgeous spectacle of which I should never tire. But perhaps if I had sight I should be like most other women—too interested in styles and the cut of individual dresses to give much attention to the splendor of color in the mass. And I am convinced, too, that I should become an inveterate window shopper, for it must be a delight to the eye to view the myriad articles of beauty on display.

From Fifth Avenue, I make a tour of the city—to Park Avenue, to the slums, to factories, to parks where children play. I take a stay-at-home trip abroad by visiting the foreign quarters. Always my eyes are open wide to all the sights of both happiness and misery so that I may probe deep and add to my understanding of how people work and live. My heart is full of the images of people and things. My eye passes lightly over no single trifle; it strives to touch and hold closely each thing its gaze rests upon. Some sights are pleasant, filling the heart with happiness; but some are miserably pathetic. To these latter I do not shut my eyes, for they, too, are part of life. To close the eye on them is to close the heart and mind.

My third day of sight is drawing to an end. Perhaps there are many serious pursuits to which I should devote the few remaining hours, but I am afraid that on the evening of that last day I should again run away to the theater, to a hilariously funny play, so that I might appreciate the overtones of comedy in the human spirit.

At midnight my temporary respite from blindness would cease, and permanent night would close in on me again. Naturally in those three short days I should not have seen all I wanted to see. Only when darkness had again descended upon me should I realize how much I had left unseen. But my mind would be so crowded with glorious memories that I should have little time for regrets. Thereafter the touch of every object would bring a glowing memory of how that object looked.

Perhaps this short outline of how I should spend three days of sight does not agree with the program you would set for yourself if you knew that you were about to be sticken blind. I am, however, sure that if you actually faced that fate your eyes would open to things you had never seen before, storing up memories for the long night ahead. You would use your eyes as never before. Everything you saw would become dear to you. Your eyes would touch and embrace every object that came within your range of vision. Then, at last, you would really see, and a new world of beauty would open itself before you.

I who am blind can give one hint to those who see—one admonition to those who would make full use of the gift of sight: Use your eyes as if tomorrow you would be stricken blind. And the same method can be applied to the other senses. Hear the music of voices, the song of a bird, the mighty strains of an orchestra, as if you would be stricken deaf tomorrow. Touch each object you want to touch as if tomorrow your tactile sense would fail. Smell the perfume of flowers, taste with relish each morsel, as if tomorrow you could never smell and taste again. Make the most of every sense; glory in the facts of pleasure and beauty which the world reveals to you through the several means of contact which Nature provides. But of all the senses, I am sure that sight must be the most delightful.

Suggestions for Discussion

1. With what details does Keller suggest the manifold things she observes, feels, and touches after an hour's walk through the woods?

2. What were Keller's criteria for her choices for the first day of seeing? What does she feel she loses in her understanding of her friends because of her lack of sight?

3. What desires and curiosities would be satisfied on Keller's second day?

4. What aspects of the theater does Keller miss in not being able to see?

5. What are Keller's goals in her visit to New York City?

6. What is significant about her plan for the evening of the last day?

7. How would you sum up Keller's values as reflected in her priorities for the three days of seeing?

8. Compare what Keller would expect to see in nature with what Annie Dillard sees. What do the two writers have in common?

Suggestions for Writing

1. How would you live each day (or a particular day) as if you were to die tomorrow?

2. Things I take (or don't take) for granted.

3. If you were creating a compulsory course on "How to Use your Eyes," what assignments would you make?

4. Should you have only three more days to see, how would you spend them?

Loren Eiseley
Man in the Autumn Light

Loren Eiseley (1907–1977) was an anthropologist and an academic administrator at the University of Pennsylvania. His publications include *Darwin's Century* (1958), which won the National Phi Beta Kappa Science Award and the Atheneum of Philadelphia Literature Award, *The Mind as Nature* (1962), *Francis Bacon and the Modern Dilemma* (1962), and *The Unexpected Universe* (1969). His last book *All the Strange Hours: The Excavation of a Life* (1975) was an autobiography. In the essay that follows, from *The Invisible Pyramid* (1970), Eiseley reflects his concern for preserving the natural environment as well as his deep respect for the poets whose power in his view exceeds that of molecular biologists.

The French dramatist Jean Cocteau has argued persuasively about the magic light of the theatre. People must remember, he contended, that "the theatre is a trick factory where the truth has no currency, where anything natural has no value, where the only things that convince us are card tricks and sleights of hand of a difficulty unsuspected by the audience."

The cosmos itself gives evidence, on an infinitely greater scale, of being just such a trick factory, a set of lights forever changing, and the actors themselves shape shifters, elongated shadows of something above or without. Perhaps in the sense men use the word natural, there is really nothing at all natural in the universe or, at best, that the world is natural only in being unnatural, like some variegated, color-shifting chameleon.

In Brazilian rivers there exists a fish, one of the cyprinodonts, which sees with a two-lensed eye, a kind of bifocal adjustment that permits the creature to examine the upper world of sunlight and air, while with the lower half of the lens he can survey the watery depths in which he lives. In this quality the fish resembles Blake, the English poet who asserted he saw with a double vision into a farther world than the natural. Now the fish, we might say, looks simultaneously into two worlds of reality, though what he makes of this divided knowledge we do not know. In the case of man, although there are degrees of seeing, we can observe that the individual has always possessed the ability to escape beyond naked reality into some other dimension, some place outside the realm of what might be called "facts."

Man is no more natural than the world. In reality he is, as we have seen, the creator of a phantom universe, the universe we call culture—a formidable realm of cloud shapes, ideas, potentialities, gods, and cities, which with man's death will collapse into dust and vanish back into "expected" nature.

Some landscapes, one learns, refuse history; some efface it so completely it is never found; in others the thronging memories of the past subdue the living. In my time I have experienced all these regions, but only in one place has the looming future overwhelmed my sense of the present. This happened in a man-made crater on the planet earth, but to reach that point it is necessary to take the long way round and to begin where time had lost its meaning. As near as I can pinpoint the place, it was somewhere at the edge of the Absaroka range along the headwaters of the Bighorn years ago in Wyoming. I had come down across a fierce land of crags and upland short-grass meadows, past aspens shivering in the mountain autumn. It was the season of the golden light. I was younger then and a hardened foot traveler. But youth had little to do with what I felt. In that country time did not exist. There was only the sound of water hurrying over pebbles to an unknown destination—water that made a tumult drowning the sound of human voices.

Somewhere along a creek bank I stumbled on an old archaeological site whose beautifully flaked spearpoints of jasper represented a time level remote from me by something like ten thousand years. Yet, I repeat, this was a country in which time had no power because the sky did not know it, the aspens had not heard it passing, the river had been talking to itself since before man arose, and in that country it would talk on after man had departed.

I was alone with the silvery aspens in the mountain light, looking upon time thousands of years remote, yet so meaningless that at any moment flame might spurt from the ash of a dead campfire and the hunters come slipping through the trees. My own race had no role in these mountains and would never have.

I felt the light again, the light that was falling across the void on other worlds. No bird sang, no beast stirred. To the west the high ranges with their snows rose pure and cold. It was a place to meet the future quite as readily as the past. The fluttering aspens expressed no choice, and I, a youngster with but few memories, chose to leave them there. The place was of no true season, any more than the indifferent torrent that poured among the boulders through summer and deep snow alike.

I camped in a little grove as though waiting, filled with a sense of incompleteness, alert for some intangible message that was never uttered. The philosopher Jacques Maritain once remarked that there is no future thing for God. I had come upon what seemed to be a hidden fragment of the days before creation. Because I was mortal and not an omniscient creature, I lingered beside the stream with a growing restlessness. I had brought time in my perishable body into a place where, to all intents, it could not exist. I was moving in a realm outside of time and yet dragging time with me in an increasingly excruciating effort. If man was a creature obliged to choose, then choice was here denied me. I was forced to wait because a message from the future could not enter this domain. Here was pure, timeless nature—sequences as incomprehensible as pebbles—dropped like the shaped stones of the red men who had no history. The world eaters, by contrast, with their insatiable hunger for energy, quickly ran through nature; they felt it was exhaustible. They had, like all the spore-bearing organisms, an instinctive hunger for flight. They wanted more from the dark storehouse of a single planet than a panther's skin or a buffalo robe could offer. They wanted a greater novelty, only to be found far off in the orchard of the worlds.

Eventually, because the message never came, I went on. I could, I suppose, have been safe there. I could have continued to hesitate among the stones and been forgotten, or, because one came to know it was possible, I could simply have dissolved in the light that was of no season but eternity. In the end, I pursued my way downstream and out into the sagebrush of ordinary lands. Time reasserted its hold upon me but not quite in the usual way. Sometimes I could almost hear the thing for which I had waited in vain, or almost remember it. It was as though I carried the scar of some unusual psychical encounter.

A physician once described to me in detail the body's need to rectify its injuries, to restore, insofar as possible, mangled bones and tissues. A precisely arranged veil of skin is drawn over ancient wounds. Similarly the injured mind struggles, even in a delusory way, to reassemble and make sense of its shattered world. Whatever I had been exposed to among the snow crests and the autumn light still penetrated my being. Mine was the wound of a finite creature seeking to establish its own reality against eternity.

I am all that I have striven to describe of the strangest organism on the planet. I am one of the world eaters in the time when that species has despoiled the earth and is about to loose its spores into space. As an archaeologist I also know that our planet-effacing qualities extend to time itself. When the swarming phase of our existence commences, we struggle both against the remembered enchantment of childhood and the desire to extinguish it under layers of concrete and giant stones. Like some few persons in the days of the final urban concentrations, I am an anachronism, a child of the dying light. By those destined to create the future, my voice may not, perhaps, be trusted. I know only that I speak from the timeless country revisited, from the cold of vast tundras and the original dispersals, not from the indrawings of men.

II

The nineteenth-century novelist Thomas Love Peacock once remarked critically that "a poet in our times is a semibarbarian in a civilized community. . . . The march of his intellect is like that of a crab, backward." It is my suspicion that though many moderns would applaud what Peacock probably meant only ironically, there is a certain virtue in the sidelong retreat of the crab. He never runs, he never ceases to face what menaces him, and he always keeps his pincers well to the fore. He is a creature adapted by nature for rearguard action and withdrawal, but never rout.

The true poet is just such a fortunate creation as the elusive crab. He is born wary and is frequently in retreat because he is a protector of the human spirit. In the fruition time of the world eaters he is threatened, not with obsolescence, but with being hunted to extinction. I rather fancy such creatures—poets, I mean—as lurking about the the edge of all our activities, testing with a probing eye, if not claw, our thoughts as well as our machines.

Blake was right about the double vision of poets. There is no substitute, in a future-oriented society, for eyes on stalks, or the ability to move suddenly at right angles from some dimly imminent catastrophe. The spore bearers, once they have reached the departure stage, are impatient of any but acceptable prophets—prophets, that is, of the swarming time. These are the men who uncritically proclaim our powers over the cosmic prison and who dangle before us ill-assorted keys to the gate.

By contrast, one of the most perceptive minds in American literature, Ralph Waldo Emerson, once maintained stubbornly: "The soul is no traveler." Emerson spoke in an era when it was a passion with American writers to go abroad, just as today many people yearn for the experience of space. He was not engaged in deriding the benefits of travel. The wary poet merely persisted in the recognition that the soul in its creative expression is genuinely *not* a traveler, that the great writer is peculiarly a product of his native environment. As an untraveled traveler, he picks up selectively from his surroundings a fiery train of dissimilar memory particles—"unlike things" which are woven at last into the likeness of truth.

Man's urge toward transcendence manifests itself even in his outward inventions. However, crudely conceived, his rockets, his cyborgs, are intended to leap some void, some recently discovered chasm before him, even as long ago he cunningly devised language to reach across the light-year distances between individual minds. The spore bearers of thought have a longer flight history than today's astronauts. They found, fantastic though it now seems, the keys to what originally appeared to be the impregnable prison of selfhood.

But these ancient word-flight specialists the poets have another skill that enhances their power beyond even the contemporary ability they have always had to sway minds. They have, in addition, a preternatural sensitivity to the backward and forward reaches of time. They probe into life as far as, if not farther than, the molecular biologist does, because they touch life itself and not its particulate structure. The latter is a recent scientific disclosure, and hence we acclaim the individual discoverers. The poets, on the other hand, have been talking across the ages until we have come to take their art for granted. It is useless to characterize them as dealers in the obsolete, because this venerable, word-loving trait in man is what enables him to transmit his eternal hunger—his yearning for the country of the unchanging autumn light. Words are man's domain, from his beginning to his fall.

Many years ago I chanced to read a story by Don Stuart entitled "Twilight." It is an account of the further history of humanity many millions of years in the future. The story is told by a man a few centuries beyond our time, who in the course of an experiment had been accidentally projected forward into the evening of the race. He had then escaped through his own powers, but in doing so had overleaped his own era and reached our particular century. The time voyager sings an unbearably sad song learned in that remote future—a song that called and sought and searched in hopelessness. It was the song of man in his own twilight, a song of the final autumn when hope had gone and man's fertility with it, though he continued to linger on in the shadow of the perfect machines which he had created and which would long outlast him.

What lifts this story beyond ordinary science fiction is its compassionate insight into the basic nature of the race—the hunger that had accompanied man to his final intellectual triumph in earth's garden cities. There he had lost the will and curiosity to seek any further to transcend himself. Instead, that passion had been lavished upon his great machines. But the songs wept and searched for something that had been forgotten—something that could never be found again. The man from the open noonday of the human triumph, the scientist of the thirty-first century, before seeking his own return down the time channel, carries out one final act that is symbolic of man's yearning and sense of inadequacy before the universe, even though he had wished, like Emerson, "to climb the steps of paradise." Man had failed in the end to sanctify his own being.

The indomitable time voyager standing before the deathless machines performs the last great act of the human twilight. He programs the instruments to work toward the creation of a machine which would incorporate what man by then had lost: curiosity and hope. In dying, man had transmitted his hunger to the devices which had contributed to his death. Is this act to be labeled triumph or defeat? We do not learn; we are too far down in time's dim morning. The poet speaks with man's own Delphic ambiguity. We are left wondering whether the time voyager had produced the only possible solution to the final decay of humanity—that is, the transference of human values to the world of imperishable machines—or, on the other hand, whether less reliance upon the machine might have prevented the decay of the race. These are questions that only the long future will answer, but "Twilight" is a magnificent evocation of man's ending that only a poet of this century could have adequately foreseen—that man in the end forgets the message that started him upon his journey.

III

On a planet where snow falls, the light changes, and when the light changes all is changed, including life. I am not speaking now of daytime things but of the first snows of winter that always leave an intimation in each drifting flake of a thousand-year turn toward a world in which summer may sometime forget to come back. The world has known such episodes: it has not always been the world it is. Ice like a vast white amoeba has descended at intervals from the mountains and crept over the hills and valleys of the continents, ingesting forests and spewing forth boulders.

Something still touches me from that vanished world as remote from us in years as an earth rocket would be from Alpha Centauri. Certainly Cocteau spoke the truth: to add to all the cosmic prisons that surround us there is the prison of the golden light that changes in the head of man—the light that cries to memory out of vanished worlds, the leaf-fall light of the earth's eternally changing theatre. And then comes the night snow that in some late hour transports us into that other, that vanished but unvanquished, world of the frost.

Near my house in the suburbs is a remaining fragment of woodland. It once formed part of a wealthy man's estate, and in one corner of the wood a huge castle created by imported workmen still looms among the trees that have long outlasted their original owner. A path runs through these woods and the people of multiplying suburbia hurry past upon it. For a long time I had feared for the trees.

One night it snowed and then a drop in temperature brought on the clear night sky. Dressed in a heavy sheepskin coat and galoshes, I had ventured out toward midnight upon the path through the wood. Out of old habit I studied the tracks upon the snow. People had crunched by on their way to the train station, but no human trace ran into the woods. Many little animals had ventured about the margin of the trees, perhaps timidly watching; none had descended to the path. On impulse, for I had never done so before in this spot, I swung aside into the world of no human tracks. At first it pleased me that the domain of the wood had remained so far untouched and undesecrated. Did man, still, after all his ravages, possess some fear of the midnight forest or some unconscious reverence toward the source of his origins? It seemed hardly likely in so accessible a spot, but I trudged on, watching the pole star through the naked branches. Here, I tried to convince myself, was a fragment of the older world, something that had momently escaped the eye of the world eaters.

After a time I came to a snow-shrouded clearing, and because my blood is, after all, that of the spore bearers, I sheltered my back against an enormous oak and continued to watch for a long time the circling of remote constellations above my head. Perhaps somewhere across the void another plotting eye on a similar midnight errand might be searching this arm of the galaxy. Would our eyes meet? I smiled a little uncomfortably and let my eyes drop, still unseeing and lost in contemplation, to the snow about me. The cold continued to deepen.

We were a very young race, I meditated, and of civilizations that had yet reached the swarming stage there had been but few. They had all been lacking in some aspect of the necessary technology, and their doom had come swift upon them before they had grasped the nature of the cosmos toward which they unconsciously yearned.

Egypt, which had planted in the pyramids man's mightiest challenge to effacing time, had conceived long millennia ago the dream of a sky-traveling boat that might reach the pole star. The Maya of the New World rain forests had also watched the drift of the constellations from their temples situated above the crawling vegetational sea about them. But of what their dreamers thought, the remaining hieroglyphs tell us little. We know only that the Maya were able to grope with mathematical accuracy through unlimited millions of years of which Christian Europe had no contemporary comprehension. The lost culture had remarkably accurate eclipse tables and precise time-commemorating monuments.

Ironically the fragments of those great stelae with all their learned calculations were, in the end, to be dragged about and worshiped upside down by a surviving peasantry who had forgotten their true significance. I, in this wintry clime under the shifting of the Bear, would no more be able to enter the mythology of that world of vertical time than to confront whatever eye might roam the dust clouds at this obscure corner of the galaxy. So it was, in turning, that I gazed in full consciousness at last upon the starlit clearing that surrounded me.

Except for the snow, I might as well have been standing upon the ruins that had thronged my mind. The clearing was artificial, a swath slashed by instruments of war through the center of the wood. Shorn trees toppled by bulldozers lay beneath the snow. Piles of rusted machinery were cast indiscriminately among the fallen trees. I came forward, groping like the last man out of a shell hole in some giant, unseen conflict. Iron, rust, timbers—the place was like the graveyard of an unseen, incessant war.

In the starlight my eye caught a last glimpse of living green. I waded toward the object but it lay upon its side. I rolled it over. It was a still-living Christmas tree hurled out with everything dispensable from an apartment house at the corner of the wood. I stroked it in wordless apology. Like others, I had taken the thin screen remaining from the original wood for reality. Only the snow, only the tiny footprints of the last surviving wood creatures, had led me to this unmasking. Behind this little stand of trees the world eaters had all the time been assiduously at work.

Well, and why not, countered my deviant slime-mold mind? The sooner men finished the planet, the sooner the spores would have to fly. I kicked vaguely at some geared piece of mechanism under its cover of snow. I thought of the last Mayan peasants worshiping the upended mathematical tablets of their forerunners. The supposition persisted in the best scientific circles that the astronomer priests had in the end proved too great a burden, they and their temples and observatories too expensive a luxury for their society to maintain—that revolt had cut them down.

But what if, a voice whispered at the back of my mind, as though the indistinct cosmic figure I had earlier conjured up had just spoken, what if during all that thousand years of computing among heavy unnatural numbers they had found a way to clamber through some hidden galactic doorway? Would it not have been necessary to abandon these monumental cities and leave their illiterate worshipers behind?

I turned over a snow-covered cogwheel. Who, after all, among such ruins could be sure that we were the first of the planet viruses to depart? Perhaps in the numbers and the hieroglyphs of long ago there had been hidden some other formula than that based upon the mathematics of rocket travel—some key to a doorway of air, leaving behind only the empty seedpods of the fallen cities. Slowly my mind continued to circle that dead crater under the winter sky.

Suppose, my thought persisted, there is still another answer to the ruins in the rain forests of Yucatan, or to the incised brick tablets baking under the Mesopotamian sun. Suppose that greater than all these, vaster and more impressive, an invisible pyramid lies at the heart of every civilization man has created, that for every visible brick or corbeled vault or upthrust skyscraper or giant rocket we bear a burden in the mind to excess, that we have a biological urge to complete what is actually uncompletable.

Every civilization, born like an animal body, has just so much energy to expend. In its birth throes it chooses a path, the pathway perhaps of a great religion as in the time when Christianity arose. Or an empire of thought is built among the Greeks, or a great power extends its roads, and governs as did the Romans. Or again, its wealth is poured out upon science, and science endows the culture with great energy, so that far goals seem attainable and yet grow illusory. Space and time widen to weariness. In the midst of triumph disenchantment sets in among the young. It is as though with the growth of cities an implosion took place, a final unseen structure, a spore-bearing structure, towering upward toward its final release.

Men talked much of progress and enlightenment on the path behind the thin screen of trees. I myself had walked there in the cool mornings awaiting my train to the city. All the time this concealed gash in the naked earth had been growing. I was wrong in just one thing in my estimate of civilization. I have said it is born like an animal and so, in a sense, it is. But an animal is whole. The secret tides of its body balance and sustain it until death. They draw it to its destiny. The great cultures, by contrast, have no final homeostatic feedback like that of the organism. They appear to have no destiny unless it is that of the slime mold's destiny to spore and depart. Too often they grow like a malignancy, in one direction only. The Maya had calculated the drifting eons like gods but they did not devise a single wheeled vehicle. So distinguished an authority as Eric Thompson has compared them to an overspecialized Jurassic monster.

A monster? My eyes swept slowly over the midnight clearing and its hidden refuse of fallen trunks and cogwheels. This was the pyramid that our particular culture was in the process of creating. It represented energy beyond anything the world of man had previously known. Our first spore flight had burst against the moon and reached, even now, toward Mars, but its base was a slime-mold base—the spore base of the world eaters. They fed upon the world, and the resources they consumed would never be duplicable again because their base was finite. Neither would the planet long sustain this tottering pyramid thrust upward from what had once been the soil of a consumed forest.

A rising wind began to volley snow across the clearing, burying deeper the rusted wheels and shrieking over the cast-off tree of Christmas. There was a hint in the chill air of a growing implacable winter, like that which finally descends upon an outworn planet—a planet from which life and oxygen are long since gone.

I returned to the shelter of the oak, my gaze sweeping as I did so the night sky of earth, now dark and overcast. It came to me then, in a lonely surge of feeling, that I was childless and my destiny not bound to my kind. With the tough oak at my back I remembered the feel of my father's face against my own on the night I had seen Halley's star. The comet had marked me. I was a citizen and a scientist of that nation which had first reached the moon. There in the ruined wood, remembering the shrunken seedpods of dead cities, I yearned silently toward those who would come after me if the race survived.

Four hundred years ago a young poet and potential rival of Shakespeare had written of the knowledge-hungry Faust of legend:

Thou art still but Faustus and a man.

In that phrase Christopher Marlowe had epitomized the human tragedy; We were world eaters and knowledge seekers but we were also men. It was a well-nigh fatal flaw. Whether we, like the makers of stone spearpoints in Wyoming, are a fleeting illusion of the autumn light depends upon whether any remain to decipher Marlowe's words one thousand years in the future.

The events of my century had placed the next millennium as far off as a star. All the elaborate mechanisms of communication we have devised have not ennobled, nor brought closer, individual men to men. The means exist. It is Faustus who remains a man. Beyond this dark, I, who was also a man, could not penetrate.

In the deepening snow I made a final obeisance to the living world. I took the still green, everlasting tree home to my living room for Christmas rites that had not been properly accorded it. I suppose the act was blindly compulsive. It was the sort of thing that Peacock in his time would have termed the barbarism of poets.

Suggestions for Discussion

1. How does the theater analogy pertain to the cosmos?

2. In what sense is man "the creator of a phantom universe"?

3. How does Eiseley contrast what he calls "the world eaters" and "pure, timeless nature"?

4. How does the simile of the crab relate to Eiseley's thesis? Why is there virtue in the retreat of the crab?

5. Why does the author admire the poets? Why does he feel their power exceeds that of the molecular biologist?

6. How does Eiseley interpret Emerson's belief that the great writer is peculiarly a product of his native environment?

7. How is the story "Twilight" invoked to advance Eiseley's philosophy? What is its theme? Its resolution or irresolution?

8. How does the metaphor of the autumn light relate to Eiseley's thesis?

9. How do the words *world eaters* convey Eiseley's tone and attitudes? Select other figures of speech and relate them to substance and tone.

10. When Eiseley ventured out on his midnight walk, what were his thoughts of past and present? What do his rhetorical questions signify?

11. On what historical basis does Eiseley suggest that the great cultures appear to have no destiny "unless it is that of the slime mold's destiny to spore and depart. Too often they grow like a malignancy, in one direction only"?

12. What is the meaning of the Marlowe quotation and its relationship to Eiseley's thesis?

13. Discuss the irony in Eiseley's gesture of providing Christmas rites for the tree.

Suggestions for Writing

1. What "degrees of seeing" have you observed among your acquaintances?

2. What steps do you feel should be taken to protect our environment?

3. Speculate on whether humanity's machines rob life of its human values, or whether they are capable of enhancing them.

Ellen Goodman

It's Failure, Not Success

Ellen Goodman (b. 1941) is a journalist whose columns for *The Boston Globe* are syndicated in over two hundred newspapers in the United States. She graduated from Radcliffe College and was a Nieman Fellow at Harvard University. Among her publications are *Turning Points* (1979) and collections of essays, *Close to Home* (1979) and *At Large* (1981). She won a Pulitzer Prize in 1980 and distinguished writing awards from the American Society of Newspaper Editors, also in 1980. With both wit and moral indignation Goodman assails the cynical, unethical, and antisocial philosophy of a best selling "How to Make It" book.

I knew a man who went into therapy about three years ago because, as he put it, he couldn't live with himself any longer. I didn't blame him. The guy was a bigot, a tyrant and a creep.

In any case, I ran into him again after he'd finished therapy. He was still a bigot, a tyrant and a creep, *but* . . . he had learned to live with himself.

Now, I suppose this was an accomplishment of sorts. I mean, nobody else could live with him. But it seems to me that there are an awful lot of people running around and writing around these days encouraging us to feel good about what we should feel terrible about, and to accept in ourselves what we should change.

The only thing they seem to disapprove of is disapproval. The only judgement they make is against being judgmental, and they assure us that we have nothing to feel guilty about except guilt itself. It seems to me that they are all intent on proving that I'm OK and You're OK, when in fact, I may be perfectly dreadful and you may be unforgivably dreary, and it may be— gasp!—*wrong.*

What brings on my sudden attack of judgmentitis is success, or rather, *Success!*—the latest in a series of exclamation-point books all concerned with How to Make it.

In this one, Michael Korda is writing a recipe book for success. Like the other authors, he leapfrogs right over the "Shoulds" and into the "Hows." He eliminates value judgments and edits out moral questions as if he were Fanny Farmer and the subject was the making of a blueberry pie.

It's not that I have any reason to doubt Mr. Korda's advice on the way to achieve success. It may very well be that successful men wear handkerchiefs stuffed neatly in their breast pockets, and that successful single women should carry suitcases to the office on Fridays whether or not they are going away for the weekend.

He may be realistic when he says that "successful people generally have very low expectations of others." And he may be only slightly cynical when he writes: "One of the best ways to ensure success is to develop expensive tastes or marry someone who has them."

And he may be helpful with his handy hints on how to sit next to someone you are about to overpower.

But he simply finesses the issues of right and wrong—silly words, embarrassing words that have been excised like warts from the shiny surface of the new how-to books. To Korda, guilt is not a prod, but an enemy that he slays on page four. Right off the bat, he tells the would-be successful reader that:

- It's OK to be greedy.
- It's OK to look out for Number One.
- It's OK to be Machiavellian (if you can get away with it).
- It's OK to recognize that honesty is not always the best policy (provided you don't go around saying so).
- And it's always OK to be rich.

Well, in fact, it's not OK. It's not OK to be greedy, Machiavellian, dishonest. It's not always OK to be rich. There is a qualitative difference between succeeding by making napalm or by making penicillin. There is a difference between climbing the ladder of success, and machete-ing a path to the top.

Only someone with the moral perspective of a mushroom could assure us that this was all OK. It seems to me that most Americans harbor ambivalence toward success, not for neurotic reasons, but out of a realistic perception of what it demands.

Success is expensive in terms of time and energy and altered behavior—the sort of behavior he describes in the grossest of terms: "If you can undermine your boss and replace him, fine, do so, but never express anything but respect and loyalty for him while you're doing it."

This author—whose *Power!* topped the best-seller list last year—is intent on helping rid us of that ambivalence which is a signal from our conscience. He is like the other "Win!" "Me First!" writers, who try to make us comfortable when we should be uncomfortable.

They are all Doctor Feelgoods, offering us placebo prescriptions instead of strong medicine. They give us a way to live with ourselves, perhaps, but not a way to live with each other. They teach us a whole lot more about "Failure!" than about success.

Suggestions for Discussion

1. How do you explain that the writers of the "How to Make It" books disapprove only of disapproval and that they make judgment only against being judgmental?

2. What do Goodman's metaphor, "he leapfrogs over the 'Shoulds' and into the 'Hows' " and her allusion to Fanny Farmer and the making of a blueberry pie convey to you about her view of Mr. Korda?

3. Does the fact that Goodman makes certain concessions about Korda's point of view suggest that she agrees with his philosophy?

4. Implicit and often explicit in her attack on Korda's view of success is Goodman's own view of success and failure. Discuss it by drawing upon specific passages.

5. How do the phrase, "finesses the issues of right and wrong" and the subsequent comment, "embarrassing words that have been excised like warts from the shiny surface of the new how-to books" contribute to the tone of Goodman's essay? How would you describe the tone?

6. Find other phrases and metaphors that communicate Goodman's disgust with the Korda best seller.

Suggestions for Writing

1. Select one of the following statements in Goodman's essay and challenge or defend it by drawing upon your observation and experience: "There is a qualitative difference between succeeding by making napalm or by making penicillin" or "There is a difference between climbing the ladder of success, and machete-ing a path to the top."

2. Select one of Korda's statements and defend or challenge it.

3. What is your conception of success and how to achieve it?

4. Write a review of one of the How To or Self Help books on the market.

Tom Wolfe

Mauve Gloves & Madmen, Clutter & Vine

Tom Wolfe (b. 1931) has been called "supercontemporary," "parajournalistic," and the "poet laureate of pop." Probably the most famous of the "new journalists," he is the author of *The Kandy-Kolored Tangerine-Flake Streamline Baby* (1965), *The Electric Kool-Aid Acid Test* (1968), *The Pump House Gang* (1968), *Radical Chic and Mau-Mauing the Flak Catchers* (1970), and *The Right Stuff* (1979). Wolfe's portrait of a writer, *Mauve Gloves & Madmen, Clutter & Vine* (1976), is a satiric commentary on superficial and materialistic values as well as those of the culture.

The well-known American writer . . . but perhaps it's best not to say exactly which well-known American writer . . . they're a sensitive breed! The most ordinary comments they take personally! And why would the gentleman we're about to surprise be any exception? He's in his apartment, a seven-room apartment on Riverside Drive, on the West Side of Manhattan, in his study, seated at his desk. As we approach from the rear, we notice a bald spot on the crown of his head. It's about the size of a Sunshine Chip-a-Roo cookie, this bald spot, freckled and toasty brown. Gloriously suntanned, in fact. Around this bald spot swirls a corona of dark-brown hair that becomes quite thick by the time it completes its mad Byronic rush down the back over his turtleneck and out to the side in great bushes over his ears. He knows the days of covered ears are numbered, because this particular look has become somewhat *Low Rent*. When he was coming back from his father's funeral, half the salesmen lined up at O'Hare for the commuter flights, in their pajama-striped shirts and diamond-print double-knit suits, had groovy hair much like his. And to think that just six years ago such a hairdo seemed . . . so defiant!

Meeting his sideburns at mid-jowl is the neck of his turtleneck sweater, an authentic Navy turtleneck, and the sweater tucks into his Levi's, which are the authentic Original XX Levi's, the original straight stovepipes made for wearing over boots. He got them in a bona fide cowhand's store in La Porte, Texas, during his trip to Houston to be the keynote speaker in a lecture series on "The American Dream: Myth and Reality." No small part of the latter was a fee of two thousand dollars plus expenses. This outfit, the Navy turtleneck and the double-X Levi's, means work & discipline. *Discipline!* as he says to himself every day. When he puts on these clothes, it means that he intends to write, and do nothing else, for at least four hours. *Discipline*, Mr. Wonderful!

But on the desk in front of him—that's not a manuscript or even the beginnings of one . . . that's *last month's bank statement*, which just arrived in the mail. And those are his canceled checks in a pile on top of it. In that big ledger-style checkbook there (the old-fashioned kind, serious-looking, with no crazy Peter Max designs on the checks) are his check stubs. And those slips of paper in the promiscuous heap are all unpaid bills, and he's taking the nylon cover off his Texas Instruments desk calculator, and he is about to measure the flow, the tide, the mad sluice, the crazy current of the money that pours through his fingers every month and which is now running against him in the most catastrophic manner, like an undertow, a riptide, pulling him under—

—him and this apartment, which cost him $75,000 in 1972; $20,000 cash, which came out of the $25,000 he got as a paperback advance for his fourth book, *Under Uncle's Thumb*, and $536.36 a month in bank-loan payments (on the $55,000 he borrowed) ever since, plus another $390 a month in so-called maintenance, which has steadily increased until it is now $460 a month . . . and although he already knows the answer, the round number, he begins punching the figures into the calculator . . . 536.36 plus . . . 460 . . . times 12 . . . and the calculator keys go *chuck chuck chuck chuck* and the curious little orange numbers, broken up like stencil figures, go trucking across the black path of the display panel at the top of the machine, giving a little orange shudder every time he hits the *plus* button, until there it is, stretching out seven digits long—11956.32—$12,000 a year! One thousand dollars a month—this is what he spends on his apartment alone! and by May he will have to come up with another $6,000 so he can rent the house on Martha's Vineyard again *chuck chuck chuck chuck* and by September another $6,750— $3,750 to send his daughter, Amy, to Dalton and $3,000 to send his son, Jonathan, to Collegiate (on those marvelous frog-and-cricket evenings up on the Vineyard he and Bill and Julie and Scott and Henry and Herman and Leon and Shelly and the rest, all Media & Lit. people from New York, have discussed why they send their children to private schools, and they have pretty well decided that it is the educational turmoil in the New York public schools that is the problem—the kids just wouldn't be educated!—plus some considerations of their children's personal safety—but—needless to say!—it has nothing to do with the matter of . . . well, *race*) and he punches that in . . . 6750 . . . *chuck chuck chuck chuck* . . . and hits the *plus* button . . . an orange shimmer . . . and beautiful! there's the figure—the three items, the apartment in town, the summer place, and the children's schooling—

$24,706.32!—almost $25,000 a year in fixed costs, just for a starter! for lodging and schooling! nothing else included! A grim nut!

It's appalling, and he's drowning, and this is only the beginning of it, just the basic grim nut—and yet in his secret heart he loves these little sessions with the calculator and the checks and the stubs and the bills and the marching orange numbers that stretch on and on . . . into such magnificently huge figures. It's like an electric diagram of his infinitely expanding life, a scoreboard showing the big league he's now in. Far from throwing him into a panic, as they well might, these tote sessions are one of the most satisfying habits he has. A regular vice! Like barbiturates! Calming the heart and slowing the respiration! Because it seems *practical*, going over expenses, his conscience sanctions it as a permissible way to avoid the only thing that can possibly keep him afloat: namely, more writing . . . He's deep into his calculator trance now . . . The orange has him enthralled. Think of it! He has now reached a stage in his life when not only a $1,000-a-month apartment but also a summer house on an island in the Atlantic is an absolute necessity—precisely that, absolute necessity . . . It's appalling!—and yet it's the most inexplicable bliss!—nothing less.

As for the apartment, even at $1,000 a month it is not elegant. Elegance would cost at least twice that. No, his is an apartment of a sort known as West Side Married Intellectual. The rooms are big, the layout is good, but the moldings, cornices, covings, and chair rails seem to be corroding. Actually, they are merely lumpy from too many coats of paint over the decades, and the parquet sections in the floor have dried out and are sprung loose from one another. It has been a long time since this apartment has had an owner who could both meet the down-payment nut *and* have the woodwork stripped and the flooring replaced. The building has a doorman but no elevator man, and on Sundays the door is manned by a janitor in gray khaki work clothes. But what's he supposed to do? He needs seven rooms. His son and daughter now require separate bedrooms. He and his wife require a third one (a third and fourth if the truth be known, but he has had to settle for three). He now needs, not just likes, this study he's in, a workroom that is his exclusively. He now *needs* the dining room, which is a real dining room, not a dogleg off the living room. Even if he is giving only a cocktail party, it is . . . *necessary* that they (one & all) note—however unconsciously—that he *does* have a dining room!

Right here on his desk are the canceled checks that have come in hung over from the cocktail party he gave six weeks ago. They're right in front of him now . . . $209.60 to the florists, Clutter & Vine, for flowers for the hallway, the living room, the dining room, and the study, although part of that, $100, was for a bowl of tightly clustered silk poppies that will become a permanent part of the living-room decor . . . $138.18 to the liquor store (quite a bit was left over however, meaning that the bar will be stocked for a while) . . . $257.50 to Mauve Gloves & Madmen, the caterers, even though he had chosen some of the cheaper hors d'oeuvres. He also tipped the two butlers $10 each, which made him feel a little foolish later when he learned that one of them was co-owner of Mauve Gloves & Madmen . . . $23.91 to the grocery store for he couldn't remember what . . . $173.95 to the Russian Tea Room for dinner afterward with Henry and Mavis (the guests of honor) and six other stragglers . . . $12.84 for a serving bowl from Bloomingdale's

. . . $20 extra to the maid for staying on late . . . and he's chucking all these figures into the calculator *chuck chuck chuck chuck* blink blink blink blink *truck truck truck truck* the slanted orange numbers go trucking and winking across the panel . . . 855.98 . . . $855.98 for a cocktail party!—not even a dinner party!—appalling!—and how slyly sweet . . .

Should he throw in the library stairs as a party expense, too? Perhaps, he thought, if he were honest, he would. The checks were right here: $420 to Lum B. Lee Ltd. for the stairs themselves, and another $95 to the customs broker to get the thing through customs and $45 to the trucker to deliver it making a total of $560! In any event, they're terrific . . . Mayfair heaven . . . the classic English type, stairs to nowhere, going up in a spiral around a central column, carved in the ancient bamboo style, rising up almost seven feet, so he can reach books on his highest shelf . . . He had had it made extra high by a cabinetmaking firm in Hong Kong, the aforementioned Lum B. Lee . . . Now, if the truth be known, the stairs are the result of a habit he has: he goes around the apartment after giving a party and stands where he saw particular guests standing, people who stuck in his mind, and tries to see what they saw from that position; in other words, how the apartment looked in their eyes. About a year ago he has seen Lenny Johns of the *Times* standing in the doorway of his study and looking in, so afterward, after Lenny and everyone else had gone, he took up the same position and looked in . . . and what he saw did not please him. In fact, it looked sad. Through Lenny Johns's eyes it must have looked like the basic writer's workroom out of *Writer's Digest:* a plain Danish-style desk (The Door Store) with dowel legs (dowel legs!), a modernistic (modernistic!) metal-and-upholstery office swivel chair, a low-slung (more Modernismus!) couch, a bank of undistinguished-looking file cabinets, a bookcase covering one entire wall but made of plain white-painted boards and using the wall itself as its back. The solution, as he saw it—without going into huge costs—was the library stairs—the stairs to nowhere!—an object indisputably useful and yet with an air of elegant folly!

It was after that same party that his wife had said to him: "Who was that weepy-looking little man you were talking to so much?"

"I don't know who you're talking about."

"The one with the three strands of hair pulled up from the side and draped over his scalp."

He knew she was talking about Johns. And he knew *she* knew Johns's name. She had met him before, on the Vineyard.

Meeting Lenny Johns socially was one of the many dividends of Martha's Vineyard. They have been going there for three summers now, renting a house on a hill on Chilmark . . . until it has become, well a *necessity!* It's no longer possible to stay in New York over the summer. It's not fair to the children. They shouldn't have to grow up that way. As for himself, he's gotten to know Lenny and Bill and Scott and Julie and Bob and Dick and Jody and Gillian and Frank and Shelly and the rest in a way that wouldn't be possible in New York. But quite aside from all that . . . just that clear sparkling late-August solitude, when you can smell the pine and the sea . . . heading down the piney path from the house on the hill . . . walking two hundred yards across the marshes on the pedestrian dock, just one plank wide, so that you have to keep staring down at it . . . it's hypnotic . . . the board, the marsh grass, your own tread, the sound of the frogs and the crickets . . . and then getting into the rowboat and rowing across the inlet to . . . the *dune* . . . the great swelling dune, with the dune grass waving against the sky on top . . . and then over the lip of it—to the beach! the most pristine white beach in the world! and the open sea . . . all spread out before you—yours! Just that! the sand, the sea, the sky—and solitude! No gates, no lifeguard stands, no concessions, no sprawling multitudes of transistor radios and plaid plastic beach chairs . . .

It is chiefly for these summers on the Vineyard that he has bought a car, a BMW sedan—$7,200—but very lively! It costs him $76 a month to keep it in a garage in the city for nine months of the year, another $674 in all, so that the hard nut for Martha's Vineyard is really $6,684—but it's a necessity, and one sacrifices for necessities. After three years on the Vineyard he feels very possessive about the place, even though he's a renter, and he immediately joined in with the move to publish a protest against "that little Albanian with a pickup truck," as he was (wrongly) called, some character named Zarno or something who had assembled a block of fifty acres on the Vineyard and was going to develop it into 150 building lots—one third of an acre each! (Only dimly did he recall that the house he grew up in, in Chicago, had been on about one fifth of an acre and hadn't seemed terribly hemmed in.) Bill T— wrote a terrific manifesto in which he talked about "these Snopes-like little men with their pickup trucks"—Snopes-like!—and all sorts of people signed it.

This campaign against the developers also brought the New York Media & Lit. people into contact for the first time with the Boston people. Until the Media & Lit. people began going there about ten years before, Martha's Vineyard had always been a Boston resort, "Boston" in the most proper social sense of the word. There wasn't much the Boston people could do about the New York people except not associate with them. When they said "New York people," they no doubt meant "Jews & Others," he figured. So when he was first invited to a Boston party, thanks to his interest in the antidevelopers campaign, he went with some trepidation and with his resentment tucked into his waistband like a .38. His mood darkened still more when he arrived in white ducks and an embroidered white cotton shirt, yoke-shouldered and open to the sternum—a little eccentric (actually a harmless sort of shirt known in Arizona as Fruit Western) but perfectly in the mood of standard New York People Seaside Funk—and found that the Boston men, to a man, had on jackets and ties. Not only that, they had on their own tribal colors. The jackets were mostly navy blazers, and the ties were mostly striped ties or ties with little jacquard emblems on them, but the pants had a go-to-hell air: checks and plaids of the loudest possible sort, madras plaids, yellow-on-orange windowpane checks, crazy-quilt plaids, giant houndstooth checks, or else they were a solid airmail red or taxi yellow or some other implausible go-to-hell color. They finished that off with loafers and white crew socks or no socks at all. The pants were their note of Haitian abandon . . . weekends by the sea. At the same time the jackets and ties showed they had not forgotten for a moment where the power came from. He felt desolate. He slipped the loaded resentment out of his waistband and cocked it. And then the most amazing thing happened—

His hostess came up and made a fuss over him! Exactly! She had read *Under Uncle's Thumb!* So had quite a few of the men, infernal pants and all! Lawyers and investment counselors! They were all interested in him! Quite a stream—he hardly had to move from the one spot all evening! And as the sun went down over the ocean, and the alcohol rose, and all of their basted teeth glistened—he could almost see something . . . *presque vu!* . . . a glimmer of the future . . . something he could barely make out . . . a vision in which America's best minds, her intellectuals, found a common ground, a natural unity, with the enlightened segments of her old aristocracy, her old money . . . the two groups bound together by . . . but by what? . . . he could *almost* see it, but not quite . . . it was *presque vu* . . . it was somehow a matter of taste . . . of sensibility . . . of grace, natural grace . . . just as he himself had a natural feel for the best British styles, which were after all the source of the Boston manners . . . What were the library stairs, if they weren't that? What were the Lobb shoes?

For here, now, surfacing to the top of the pile, is the check for $248 to John Lobb & Sons Ltd. Boot Makers—that was the way he wrote it out, Boot Makers, two words, the way it was on their bosky florid London letterhead—$248!—for one pair of shoes!—from England!—handmade! And now, all at once, even as *chuck chuck chuck* he punches it into the calculator, he is swept by a wave of sentiment, of sadness, sweet misery—guilt! Two hundred and forty-eight dollars for a pair of handmade shoes from England . . . He thinks of his father. He wore his first pair of Lobb shoes to his father's funeral. Black cap toes they were, the most formal daytime shoes made, and it was pouring that day in Chicago and his incomparable new shoes from England were caked with mud when he got back to his father's house. He took the shoes off, but then he froze—he couldn't bring himself to remove the mud. His father had come to the United States from Russia as a young man in 1922. He had to go to work at once, and in no time, it seemed, came the Depression, and he struggled through it as a tailor, although in the forties he acquired a dry-cleaning establishment and, later, a second one, plus a diaper-service business and a hotel-linen service. But this brilliant man—oh, how many times had his mother assured him of that!—had had to spend all those years as a tailor. This cultivated man!—more assurances—oh, how many yards of Goethe and Dante had he heard him quote in an accent that gripped the English language like a full nelson! And now his son, the son of this brilliant, cultivated but uneducated and thwarted man—now his son, his son with his education and his literary career, his son who had never had to work with his hands more than half an hour at a stretch in his life—his son had turned up at his funeral in a pair of handmade shoes from England! . . . Well, he let the mud dry on them. He didn't touch them for six months. He didn't even put the shoe trees (another $47) in. Perhaps the goddamned boots would curl up and die.

The number . . . 248 . . . is sitting right up there in slanted orange digits on the face of the calculator. That seems to end the reverie. He doesn't want to continue it just now. He doesn't want to see the 6684 for Martha's Vineyard up there again for a while. He doesn't want to see the seven digits of his debts (counting the ones after the decimal point) glowing in their full, magnificent, intoxicating length. It's time to get serious! *Discipline!* Only one thing will pull him out of all this: work . . . writing . . . and there's no way to put it off any longer. *Discipline,* Mr. Wonderful! This is the most difficult day of all, the day when it falls to his lot to put a piece of paper in the typewriter and start on page 1 of a new book, with that horrible arthritic siege—writing a book!—stretching out ahead of him (a tubercular blue glow, as his mind comprehends it) . . . although it lifts his spirits a bit to know that both *The Atlantic* and *Playboy* have expressed an interest in running chapters as he goes along, and *Penthouse* would pay even more, although he doesn't want it to appear in a one-hand magazine, a household aid, as literary penicillin to help quell the spirochetes oozing from all the virulent vulvas . . . Nevertheless! help is on the way! Hell!—there's not a magazine in America that wouldn't publish something from this book!

So he feeds a sheet of paper into his typewriter, and in the center, one third of the way down from the top, he takes care of the easy part first—the working title, in capital letters:

RECESSION AND REPRESSION
POLICE STATE AMERICA
AND THE SPIRIT OF '76

Suggestions for Discussion

1. How do the details of the writer's hair and clothes give you a sense of his personality? What do they tell you of Wolfe's view of him?

2. What is the tone conveyed in the paragraphs on the writer's finances?

3. How do you explain the writer's sense that his expenses are appalling and at the same time provide "inexplicable bliss"?

4. With what details do you learn that what others think is important to the writer?

5. What purpose is served by the repetition of the phrase "needs, not just likes"?

6. What does the importing of the library stairs contribute to your understanding of the writer's character?

7. With what details do you learn why Martha's Vineyard was "a necessity"?

8. How does Wolfe regard the Boston people? How does the writer view them?

9. Identify ironical and satiric elements in the essay.

10. Discuss the ways in which Wolfe's figurative language affects the tone and substance of the essay.

11. How does the sentence structure reflect the writer's state of mind?

12. What is the significance of the title?

13. What are the writer's values?

14. Why is the writer never named?

Suggestions for Writing

1. Discuss the shifts in your purchases from mere *likes* to *needs*.

2. Analyze the values of the writer as portrayed in this essay. What is your attitude toward them?

 ◇◇◇◇

May Sarton

The Rewards of Living a Solitary Life

May Sarton (b. 1912) is the author of several volumes of poetry, a number of novels, including *Faithful are the Wounds, Mrs. Stevens Hears the Mermaids Singing, Kinds of Love,* and a number of books of nonfiction. The author finds that a strong sense of self allows her to find happiness in a solitary life.

The other day an acquaintance of mine, a gregarious and charming man, told me he had found himself unexpectedly alone in New York for an hour or two between appointments. He went to the Whitney and spent the "empty" time looking at things in solitary bliss. For him it proved to be a shock nearly as great as falling in love to discover that he could enjoy himself so much alone.

What had he been afraid of, I asked myself? That, suddenly alone, he would discover that he bored himself, or that there was, quite simply, no self there to meet? But having taken the plunge, he is now on the brink of adventure; he is about to be launched into his own inner space, space as immense, unexplored, and sometimes frightening as outer space to the astronaut. His every perception will come to him with a new freshness and, for a time, seem startlingly original. For anyone who can see things for himself with a naked eye becomes, for a moment or two, something of a genius. With another human being present vision becomes double vision, inevitably. We are busy wondering, what does my companion see or think of this, and what do I think of it? The original impact gets lost, or diffused.

"Music I heard with you was more than music." Exactly. And therefore music *itself* can only be heard alone. Solitude is the salt of personhood. It brings out the authentic flavor of every experience.

"Alone one is never lonely: the spirit adventures, walking/In a quiet garden, in a cool house, abiding single there."

Loneliness is most acutely felt with other people, for with others, even with a lover sometimes, we suffer from our differences of taste, temperament, mood. Human intercourse often demands that we soften the edge of perception, or withdraw at the very instant of personal truth for fear of hurting, or of being inappropriately present, which is to say naked, in a social situation. Alone we can afford to be wholly whatever we are, and to feel whatever we feel absolutely. That is a great luxury!

For me the most interesting thing about a solitary life, and mine has been that for the last twenty years, is that it becomes increasingly rewarding. When I can wake up and watch the sun rise over the ocean, as I do most days, and know that I have an entire day ahead, uninterrupted, in which to write a few pages, take a walk with my dog, lie down in the afternoon for a long think (why does one think better in a horizontal position?), read and listen to music, I am flooded with happiness.

I am lonely only when I am overtired, when I have worked too long without a break, when for the time being I feel empty and need filling up. And I am lonely sometimes when I come back home after a lecture trip, when I have seen a lot of people and talked a lot, and am full to the brim with experience that needs to be sorted out.

Then for a little while the house feels huge and empty, and I wonder where my self is hiding. It has be recaptured slowly by watering the plants, perhaps, and looking again at each one as though it were a person, by feeding the two cats, by cooking a meal.

It takes a while, as I watch the surf blowing up in fountains at the end of the field, but the moment comes when the world falls away, and the self emerges again from the deep unconscious, bringing back all I have recently experienced to be explored and slowly understood, when I can converse again with my hidden powers, and so grow, and so be renewed, till death do us part.

Suggestions for Discussion

1. In asking herself what her friend had been afraid of when he finally found himself alone at a museum, Sarton speculates as to whether he was afraid he would be bored or whether there was no self to meet. How does the presence or absence of a self relate to her thesis?

2. Why does vision become double vision in the presence of another human being?

3. How does the author distinguish between loneliness and solitude? Why does she feel that loneliness is felt most acutely with other people?

4. What details does Sarton offer to explain her happiness in leading a solitary life? What role does the self play in her satisfaction?

Suggestions for Writing

1. Are you persuaded by Sarton of the joys of the solitary life?

2. Defend or challenge her position that loneliness is most acutely felt in the presence of other people.

E. M. Forster

What I Believe

E. M. Forster (1879–1970) was a British novelist, educated at Kings College, Cambridge. He lived for a time in Italy, was a member of the Bloomsbury group in London, composed of writers and artists, and spent the major part of his life at Cambridge. His works include *A Passage to India* (1924), *Where Angels Fear to Tread* (1905), and *A Room with a View* (1908). His last novel, *Maurice,* and a collection of short stories, *The Life to Come,* were published posthumously. Forster describes himself as an individualist and a liberal who has found his liberalism crumbling beneath him; at the same time he concludes with an affirmation of the importance of the individual and of sensitive people.

I do not believe in belief. But this is an age of faith, where one is surrounded by so many militant creeds that, in self-defense, one has to formulate a creed of one's own. Tolerance, good temper, and sympathy are no longer enough in a world which is rent by religious and racial persecution, in a world where ignorance rules, and science, who ought to have ruled, plays the subservient pimp. Tolerance, good temper, and sympathy—well, they are what matter really, and if the human race is not to collapse they must come to the front before long. But for the moment they don't seem enough, their action is no stronger than a flower, battered beneath a military jack boot. They want stiffening, even if the process coarsens them. Faith, to my mind, is a stiffening process, a sort of mental starch, which ought to be applied as sparingly as possible. I dislike the stuff. I do not believe in it, for its own sake, at all. Herein I probably differ from most of the contributors to this volume, who believe in belief, and are only sorry they can't swallow even more than they do. My lawgivers are Erasmus and Montaigne, not Moses and St. Paul. My temple stands not upon Mount Moriah but in the Elysian Field where even the immoral are admitted. My motto is "Lord, I disbelieve—help thou my unbelief."

I have, however, to live in an age of Faith—the sort of thing I used to hear praised and recommended when I was a boy. It is damned unpleasant, really. It is bloody in every sense of the word. And I have to keep my end up in it. Where do I start?

With personal relationships. Here is something comparatively solid in a world full of violence and cruelty. Not absolutely solid, for psychology has split and shattered the idea of a "person," and has shown that there is something incalculable in each of us, which may at any moment rise to the surface and destroy our normal balance. We don't know what we're like. We can't know what other people are like. How then can we put any trust in personal relationships, or cling to them in the gathering political storm? In theory we can't. But in practice we can and do. Though A isn't unchangeably A or B unchangeably B, there can still be love and loyalty between the two. For the purpose of living one has to assume that the personality is solid, and the "self" is an entity, and to ignore all contrary evidence. And since to ignore evidence is one of the characteristics of faith, I certainly can proclaim that I believe in personal relationships.

Starting from them, I get a little order into the contemporary chaos. One must be fond of people and trust them if one isn't to make a mess of life, and it is therefore essential that they shouldn't let one down. They often do. The moral of which is that I must myself be as reliable as possible, and this I try to be. But reliability isn't a matter of contract—that is the main difference between the world of personal relationships and the world of business relationships. It is a matter for the heart, which signs no documents. In other words, reliability is impossible unless there is a natural warmth. Most men possess this warmth, though they often have badluck and get chilled. Most of them, even when they are politicians, *want* to keep faith. And one can, at all events, show one's own little light here, one's own poor little trembling flame, with the knowledge that it's not the only light that is shining in the darkness, and not the only one which the darkness doesn't comprehend. Personal relations are despised today. They are regarded as bourgeois luxuries, as products of a time of fair weather which has now passed, and we are urged to get rid of them, and to dedicate ourselves to some movement or cause instead. I hate the idea of dying for a cause, and if I had to choose between betraying my country and betraying my friend, I hope I should have the guts to betray my country. Such a choice may scandalize the modern reader, and he may stretch out his patriotic hand to the telephone at once, and ring up the police. It wouldn't have shocked Dante, though. Dante places Brutus and Cassius in the lowest circle of ell because they had chosen to betray their friend Julius Caesar rather than their country Rome. Probably one won't be asked to make such an agonizing choice. Still there lies at the back of every creed something terrible and hard for which the worshiper may one day be required to suffer, and there is even a terror and a hardness in this creed of personal relationships, urbane and mild though it sounds. Love and loyalty to an individual can run counter to the claims of the state. When they do—down with the state, say I, which means that the state will down me.

This brings me along to democracy, "even Love, the Beloved Republic, which feeds upon Freedom and lives." Democracy isn't a beloved republic really, and never will be. But it is less hateful than other contemporary forms of government, and to that extent it deserves our support. It does start from the assumption that the individual is important, and that all types are needed to make a civilization. It doesn't divide its citizens into the bossers and the bossed, as an efficiency regime tends to do. The people I admire most are those who are sensitive and want to create something or discover something, and don't see life in terms of power, and such people get more of a chance under a democracy than elsewhere. They found religions, great or small, or they produce literature and art, or they do disinterested scientific research, or they may be what is called "ordinary people," who are creative in their private lives, bring out their children decently, for instance, or help their neighbors. All these people need to express themselves, they can't do so unless society allows them liberty to do so, and the society which allows them most liberty is a democracy.

Democracy has another merit. It allows criticism, and if there isn't public criticism there are bound to be hushed-up scandals. That is why I believe in the press, despite all its lies and vulgarity, and why I believe in Parliament.

The British Parliament is often sneered at because it's a talking shop. Well, I believe in it because it is a talking shop. I believe in the private member who makes himself a nuisance. He gets snubbed and is told that he is cranky or ill-formed, but he exposes abuses which would otherwise never have been mentioned, and very often an abuse gets put right just by being mentioned. Occasionally, too, in my country, a well-meaning public official loses his head in the cause of efficiency, and thinks himself God Almighty. Such officials are particularly frequent in the Home Office. Well, there will be questions about them in Parliament sooner or later, and then they'll have to mend their steps. Whether Parliament is either a representative body or an efficient one is very doubtful, but I value it because it criticizes and talks, and because its chatter gets widely reported.

So two cheers for democracy: one because it admits variety and two because it permits criticism. Two cheers are quite enough: there is no occasion to give three. Only Love, the Beloved Republic deserves that.

What about force, though? While we are trying to be sensitive and advanced and affectionate and tolerant, an unpleasant question pops up: Doesn't all society rest upon force? If a government can't count upon the police and the army, how can it hope to rule? And if an individual gets knocked on the head or sent to a labor camp, of what significance are his opinions?

This dilemma doesn't worry me as much as it does some. I realize that all society rests upon force. But all the great creative actions, all the decent human relations, occur during the intervals when force has not managed to come to the front. These intervals are what matter. I want them to be as frequent and as lengthy as possible and I call them "civilization." Some people idealize force and pull it into the foreground and worship it, instead of keeping it in the background as long as possible. I think they make a mistake, and I think that their opposites, the mystics, err even more when they declare that force doesn't exist. I believe that it does exist, and that one of our jobs is to prevent it from getting out of its box. It gets out sooner or later, and then it destroys us and all the lovely things which we have made. But it isn't out all the time, for the fortunate reason that the strong are so stupid. Consider their conduct for a moment in the Nibelung's *Ring*. The giants there have the guns, or in other words the gold; but they do nothing with it, they do not realize that they are all-powerful, with the result that the catastrophe is delayed and the castle of Walhalla, insecure but glorious, fronts the storms for generations. Fafnir, coiled around his hoard, grumbles and grunts; we can hear him under Europe today; the leaves of the wood already tremble, and the Bird calls its warnings uselessly. Fafnir will destroy us, but by a blessed dispensation he is stupid and slow, and creation goes on just outside the poisonous blast of his breath. The Nietzschean would hurry the monster up, the mystic would say he didn't exist, but Wotan, wiser than either, hastens to create warriors before doom declares itself. The Valkyries are symbols not only of courage but of intelligence; they represent the human spirit snatching its opportunity while the going is good, and one of them even finds time to love. Brunhilde's last song hymns the recurrence of love, and since it is the privilege of art to exaggerate she goes even further, and proclaims the love which is eternally triumphant and feeds upon freedom, and lives.

So that is what I feel about force and violence. It is, alas! the ultimate reality, on this earth, but—hooray!—it doesn't always get to the front. Some people call its absences "decadence"; I call them "civilization" and find in such interludes the chief justification for the human experiment. I look the other way until fate strikes me. Whether this is due to courage or to cowardice in my own case I cannot be sure. But I know that if men hadn't looked the other way in the past nothing of any value would survive. The people I respect most behave as if they were immortal and as if society were eternal. Both assumptions are false: both of them must be accepted as true if we are to go on eating and working and loving, and are to keep open a few breathing holes for the human spirit. No millennium seems likely to descend upon humanity; no better and stronger League of Nations will be instituted; no form of Christianity and no alternative to Christianity will bring peace to the world or integrity to the individual; no "change of heart" will occur. And yet we needn't despair, indeed we cannot despair; the evidence of history shows us that men have always insisted on behaving creatively under the shadow of the sword; that they have done their artistic and scientific and domestic stuff for the sake of doing it, and that we had better follow their example under the shadow of the airplanes. Others, with more vision or courage than myself, see the salvation of humanity ahead, and will dismiss my conception of civilization as paltry, a sort of tip-and-run game. Certainly it is presumptuous to say that we *can't* improve, and that man, who has only been in power for a few thousand years, will never learn to make use of his power. All I mean is that, if people continue to kill one another at the rate they do, the world cannot get better than it is, and that since there are more people than formerly, and their means for destroying one another more diabolic, the world may well get worse. What's good in people—and consequently in the world—is their insistence on creation, their belief in friendship, in loyalty, for its own sake; and though violence remains and is indeed the major partner in this muddled establishment, I believe that creativeness remains too, and will always assume direction when violence sleeps. So, though I am not an optimist, I cannot agree with Sophocles that it were better never to have been born. And although I see no evidence that each batch of births is superior to the last, I leave the field open for this happier view. This is such a difficult time to live in, especially for a European, one can't help getting gloomy and also a bit rattled.

There is of course hero worship, fervently recommended as a panacea in some quarters. But here we shall get no help. Hero worship is a dangerous vice, and one of the minor merits of a democracy is that it does not encourage it, or produce that unmanageable type of citizen known as the Great Man. It produces instead different kinds of small men, and that's a much finer achievement. But people who can't get interested in the variety of life and can't make up their own minds get discontented over this, and they long for a hero to bow down before and to follow blindly. It's significant that a hero is an integral part of the authoritarian stock in trade today. An efficiency regime can't be run without a few heroes stuck about to carry off the dullness—much as plums have to be put into a bad pudding to make it palatable. One hero at the top and a smaller one each side of him is a favorite arrangement, and the timid and the bored are comforted by such a trinity, and, bowing down, feel exalted by it.

No, I distrust Great Men. They produce a desert of uniformity around them and often a pool of blood, too, and I always feel a little man's pleasure when they come a cropper. Every now and then one reads in the newspapers some such statement as, "The *coup d'etat* appears to have failed and Admiral Boga's whereabouts is at the present unknown." Admiral Boga had probably every qualification for being a great man—an iron will, personal magnetism, dash, flair—but fate was against him, so he retires to unknown whereabouts instead of parading history with his peers. He fails with a completeness that no artist and no lover can experience, because with them the process of creation is itself an achievement, whereas with him the only possible achievement is success. I believe in aristocracy though—if that's the right word, and if a democrat may use it. Not an aristocracy of power, based upon rank and influence, but an aristocracy of the sensitive, the considerate, and the plucky. Its members are to be found in all nations and classes, and all through the ages, and there is a secret understanding between them when they meet. They represent the true human tradition, the one permanent victory of our queer race over cruelty and chaos. Thousands of them perish in obscurity; a few are great names. They are sensitive for others as well as for themselves, they are considerate without being fussy, their pluck is not swankiness but the power to endure, and they can take a joke. I give no examples—it is risky to do that—but the reader may as well consider whether this is the type of person he would like to meet and to be, and whether (going further with me) he would prefer that the type should *not* be an ascetic one. I'm against asceticism myself. I'm with the old Scotchman who wanted less chastity and more delicacy. I don't feel that my aristocrats are a real aristocracy if they thwart their bodies, since bodies are the instruments through which we register and enjoy the world. Still I don't insist here. This isn't a major point. It's clearly possible to be sensitive, considerate, and plucky and yet be an ascetic too, and if anyone possesses the first three qualities, I'll let him in! On they go— an invincible army, yet not a victorious one. The aristocrats, the elect, the chosen, the best people—all the words that describe them are false, and all attempts to organize them fail. Again and again authority, seeing their value, has tried to net them and to utilize them as the Egyptian priesthood or the Christian Church or the Chinese civil service or the Group Movement, or some other worthy stunt. But they slip through the net and are gone; when the door is shut they are no longer in the room; their temple, as one of them remarked, is the holiness of the heart's imagination, and their kingdom, though they never possess it, is the wide open world.

With this type of person knocking about, and constantly crossing one's path if one has eyes to see or hands to feel, the experiment of earthly life cannot be dismissed as a failure. But it may well be hailed as a tragedy, the tragedy being that no device has been found by which these private decencies can be transferred to public affairs. As soon as people have power they go crooked and sometimes dotty, too, because the possession of power lifts them into a region where normal honesty never pays. For instance, the man who is selling newspapers outside the Houses of Parliament can safely leave his papers to go for a drink, and his cap beside them: anyone who takes a paper is sure to drop a copper into the cap. But the men who are inside the Houses of Parliament—they can't trust one another like that; still less can the government they compose trust other governments. No caps upon the pavement here, but suspicion, treachery, and armaments. The more highly public life is organized the lower does its morality sink; the nations of today behave to each other worse than they ever did in the past, they cheat, rob, bully, and bluff, make war without notice, and kill as many women and children as possible; whereas primitive tribes were at all events restrained by taboos. It's a humiliating outlook—though the greater the darkness, the brighter shine the little lights, reassuring one another, signaling, "Well, at all events I'm still here. I don't like it very much, but how are you?" Unquenchable lights of my aristocracy! Signals of the invincible army! "Come along—anyway let's have a good time while we can." I think they signal that too.

The savior of the future—if ever he comes—will not preach a new gospel. He will merely utilize my aristocracy; he will make effective the good will and the good temper which are already existing. In other words he will introduce a new technique. In economics, we are told that if there was a new technique of distribution, there need be no poverty, and people would not starve in one place while crops were dug under in another. A similar change is needed in the sphere of morals and politics. The desire for it is by no means new; it was expressed, for example, in theological terms of Jacopone da Todi over six hundred years ago. "*Ordina questo amore, O tu che m'ami,*" he said. "O thou who lovest me—set this love in order." His prayer was not granted and I do not myself believe that it ever will be, but here, and not through a change of heart, is our probable route. Not by becoming better, but by ordering and distributing his native goodness, will man shut up force into his box, and so gain time to explore the universe and to set his work upon it worthily. At present he only explores it at odd moments, when force is looking the other way, and his divine creativeness appears as a trivial by-product, to be scrapped as soon as the drums beat and the bombers hum.

Such a change, claim the orthodox, can only be made by Christianity, and will be made by it in God's good time: man always has failed and always will fail to organize his own goodness, and it is presumptuous of him to try. This claim—solemn as it is—leaves me cold. I cannot believe that Christianity will ever cope with the present world-wide mess, and I think that such influence as it retains in modern society is due to its financial backing rather than to its spiritual appeal. It was a spiritual force once, but the indwelling spirit will have to be restated if it is to calm the water again, and probably restated in a non-Christian form. Naturally a great many people, and people who are not only good but able and intelligent, will disagree with me here; they will vehemently deny that Christianity has failed, or they will argue that its failure proceeds from the wickedness of men, and really proves its ultimate success. They have Faith, with a large F. My faith has a very small one, and I only bring it into the open because these are strenuous and serious days, and one likes to say what one thinks while speech is still free: it may not be free much longer.

These are the reflections of an individualist and a liberal who has found his liberalism crumbling beneath him and at first felt ashamed. Then, looking around, he decided there was no special reason for shame, since other people, whatever they felt, were equally insecure. And as for individualism—there seems no way out of this, even if one wants to find one. The dictator-hero can grind down his citizens till they are all alike, but he can't melt them into a single man. That is beyond his power. He can order them to merge, he can incite them to mass antics, but they are obliged to be born separately and to die separately and, owing to these unavoidable termini, will always be running off the totalitarian rails. The memory of birth and the expectation of death always lurk within the human being, making him separate from his fellows and consequently capable of intercourse with them. Naked I came into the world, naked I shall go out of it! And a very good thing too, for it reminds me that I am naked under my shirt. Until psychologists and biologists have done much more tinkering than seems likely, the individual remains firm and each of us must consent to be one, and to make the best of the difficult job.

Suggestions for Discussion

1. Considering Forster's title, his first sentence is unexpected. Is it the thesis of his essay? Would it be logical to end the essay with the first sentence? What is the function of the first paragraph? Argue for or against the effectiveness of the first sentence.

2. Forster proclaims that he, too, has faith. Is he inconsistent? What is his persuasive purpose in referring to "one of the characteristics of faith"?

3. Forster argues for a kind of "reliability." What is the argument based on? Can the loyal citizen show this reliability toward his state?

4. Is Forster inconsistent in stating there is "terror and hardness in this creed of personal relationships"?

5. Forster looks "the other way until fate strikes" him. Why? Does it matter whether this is due to courage or cowardice?

6. Forster argues for false assumptions. Why? Is his argument persuasive?

7. Admiral Boga "fails with a completeness that no artist and no lover can experience." Of what is Forster trying to persuade the reader?

8. Does Forster withdraw his criticism of Christianity? Is he weakening his argument against Christianity by ending it so softly? Explain.

9. Forster begins the last paragraph by referring to himself as "a liberal who has found his liberalism crumbling beneath him and at first felt ashamed." How did he lose his shame?

10. Forster says that individualism will remain because we are born separately and we die separately. Reconcile this view with his belief that we should behave as if we were immortal.

11. Are you persuaded that one could live by Forster's beliefs? Is Forster such a man as he presents himself in the essay?

12. Why does Forster believe that the aristocracy has a better chance of saving the world than Christianity? How does he define aristocracy?

Suggestions for Writing

1. Discuss the difficulties and inconsistencies of Forster's beliefs.

2. Describe your convictions and suggest the degree to which you are able to act on them.

3. Write on question 11 in the suggestions for discussion.

4. Write a persuasive argument in favor of an action you regard as crucial to your life in a democracy.

Henry David Thoreau

Why I Went to the Woods

Henry David Thoreau (1817–1862) was a philosopher and poet-naturalist whose independent spirit led him to the famous experiment recorded in *Walden, or Life in the Woods* (1854). Thoreau's passion for freedom and his lifetime resistance to conformity in thought and manners are forcefully present in his famous essay, "On the Duty of Civil Disobedience." Thoreau states that he went to the woods in order to encounter only the essential facts of life and avoid all that is petty, trivial, and unnecessary.

I went to the woods because I wished to live deliberately, to front only the essential facts of life, and see if I could not learn what it had to teach, and not, when I came to die, discover that I had not lived. I did not wish to live what was not life, living is so dear; nor did I wish to practise resignation, unless it was quite necessary. I wanted to live deep and suck out all the marrow of life, to live so sturdily and Spartan-like as to put to rout all that was not life, to cut a broad swath and shave close, to drive life into a corner, and reduce it to its lowest terms, and, if it proved to be mean, why then to get the whole and genuine meanness of it, and publish its meanness to the world; or if it were sublime, to know it by experience, and be able to give a true account of it in my next excursion. For most men, it appears to me, are in a strange uncertainty about it, whether it is of the devil or of God, and have *somewhat hastily* concluded that it is the chief end of man here to "glorify God and enjoy him forever."

Still we live meanly, like ants; though the fable tells us that we were long ago changed into men; like pygmies we fight with cranes; it is error upon error, and clout upon clout, and our best virtue has for its occasion a superfluous and evitable wretchedness. Our life is frittered away by detail. An honest man has hardly need to count more than his ten fingers, or in extreme cases he may add his ten toes, and lump the rest. Simplicity, simplicity, simplicity! I say, let your affairs be as two or three, and not a hundred or a thousand; instead of a million count half a dozen, and keep your accounts on your thumb-nail. In the midst of this chopping sea of civilized life, such are the clouds and storms and quicksands and thousand-and-one items to be allowed for, that a man has to live, if he would not founder and go to the bottom and not make his port at all, by dead reckoning, and he must be a great calculator indeed who succeeds. Simplify, simplify. Instead of three meals a day, if it be necessary eat but one; instead of a hundred dishes, five; and reduce other things in proportion. Our life is like a German Confederacy, made of up petty states, with its boundary forever fluctuating, so that even a German cannot tell you how it is bounded at any moment. The nation itself, with all its so-called internal improvements, which, by the way are all external and superficial, is just such an unwieldy and overgrown establishment, cluttered with furniture and tripped up by its own traps, ruined by luxury and heedless expense, by want of calculation and a worthy aim, as the million households in the lands; and the only cure for it, as for them, is in a rigid economy, a stern and more than Spartan simplicity of life and elevation of purpose. It lives too fast. Men think that it is essential that the *Nation* have commerce, and export ice, and talk through a telegraph, and ride thirty miles an hour, without a doubt, whether *they* do or not; but whether we should live like baboons or like men, is a little uncertain. If we do not get our sleepers, and forge rails, and devote days and nights to the work, but go to tinkering upon our *lives* to improve *them*, who will build railroads? And if railroads are not built, how shall we get to heaven in season? But if we stay at home and mind our business, who will want railroads? We do not ride on the railroad; it rides upon us. Did you ever think what those sleepers are that underlie the railroad? Each one is a man, an Irishman, or a Yankee man. The rails are laid on them, and they are covered with sand, and the cars run smoothly over them. They are sound sleepers, I assure you. And every few years a new lot is laid down and run over; so that, if some have the pleasure of riding on a rail, others have the misfortune to be ridden upon. And when they run over a man that is walking in his sleep, a supernumerary sleeper in the wrong position, and wake him up, they suddenly stop the cars, and make a hue and cry about it, as if this were an exception. I am glad to know that it takes a gang of men for every five miles to keep the sleepers down and level in their beds as it is, for this is a sign that they may sometimes get up again.

Why should we live with such hurry and waste of life? We are determined to be starved before we are hungry. Men say that a stitch in time saves nine, and so they take a thousand stitches to-day to save nine tomorrow. As for *work*, we haven't any of any consequence. We have the Saint Vitus' dance, and cannot possibly keep our heads still. If I should only give a few pulls at the parish bell-rope, as for a fire, that is, without setting the bell, there is hardly a man on his farm in the outskirts of Concord, notwithstanding that press of engagements which was his excuse so many times this morning, nor a boy, nor a woman, I might almost say, but would foresake all and follow that sound, not mainly to save property from the flames, but, if we will confess the truth, much more to see it burn, since burn it must, and we, be it known, did not set it on fire—or to see it put out, and have a hand in it, if that is done as handsomely; yes, even if it were the parish church itself. Hardly a man takes a half-hour's nap after dinner, but when he wakes he holds up his head and asks, "What's the news?" as if the rest of mankind had stood his sentinels. Some give directions to be waked every half-hour, doubtless for no other purpose; and then, to pay for it, they tell what they have dreamed. After a night's sleep the news is as indispensable as the breakfast.

"Pray tell me anything new that has happened to a man anywhere on this globe"—and he reads it over his coffee and rolls, that a man has had his eyes gouged out this morning on the Wachito River; never dreaming the while that he lives in the dark unfathomed mammoth cave of this world, and has but the rudiment of an eye himself.

For my part, I could easily do without the post-office. I think that there are very few important communications made through it. To speak critically, I never received more than one or two letters in my life—I wrote this some years ago—that were worth the postage. The penny-post is, commonly, an institution through which you seriously offer a man that penny for his thoughts which is so often safely offered in jest. And I am sure that I never read any memorable news in a newspaper. If we read of one man robbed, or murdered, or killed by accident, or one house burned, or one vessel wrecked, or one steamboat blown up, or one cow run over on the Western Railroad, or one mad dog killed, or one lot of grasshoppers in the winter—we never need read of another. One is enough. If you are acquainted with the principle, what do you care for a myriad instances and applications? To a philosopher all *news*, as it is called, is gossip, and they who edit and read it are old women over their tea. Yet not a few are greedy after this gossip. There was such a rush, as I hear, the other day at one of the offices to learn the foreign news by the last arrival, that several large squares of plate glass belonging to the establishment were broken by the pressure—news which I seriously think a ready wit might write a twelvemonth, or twelve years, beforehand with sufficient accuracy. As for Spain, for instance, if you know how to throw in Don Carlos and the Infanta, and Don Pedro and Seville and Granada, from time to time in the right proportions—they may have changed the names a little since I saw the papers—and serve up a bullfight when other entertainments fail, it will be true to the letter, and give us as good an idea of the exact state or ruin of things in Spain as the most succinct and lucid reports under this head in the newspapers; and as for England, almost the last significant scrap of news from that quarter was the revolution of 1649; and if you have learned the history of her crops for an average year, you never need attend to that thing again, unless your speculations are of a merely pecuniary character. If one may judge who rarely looks into the newspapers, nothing new does ever happen in foreign parts, a French revolution not excepted.

What news! how much more important to know what that is which was never old! "Kieou-he-yu (great dignitary of the state of Wei) sent a man to Khoung-tseu to know his news. Khoung-tseu caused the messenger to be seated near him, and questioned him in these terms: What is your master doing? The messenger answered with respect: My master desires to diminish the number of his faults, but he cannot come to the end of them. The messenger being gone, the philosopher remarked: What a worthy messenger! What a worthy messenger!" The preacher, instead of vexing the ears of drowsy farmers on their day of rest at the end of the week—for Sunday is the fit conclusion of an ill-spent week, and not the fresh and brave beginning of a new one—with this one other draggle-tail of a sermon, should shout with thundering voice, "Pause! Avast! Why so seeming fast, but deadly slow?"

Shams and delusions are esteemed for soundless truths, while reality is fabulous. If men would steadily observe realities only, and not allow themselves to be deluded, life, to compare it with such things as we know, would be like a fairy tale and the Arabian Nights' Entertainments. If we respected only what is inevitable and has a right to be, music and poetry would resound along the streets. When we are unhurried and wise, we perceive that only great and worthy things have any permanent and absolute existence, that petty fears and petty pleasures are but the shadow of the reality. This is always exhilarating and sublime. By closing the eyes and slumbering, and consenting to be deceived by shows, men establish and confirm their daily life of routine and habit everywhere, which still is built on purely illusory foundations. Children, who play life, discern its true law and relations more clearly than men, who fail to live it worthily, but who think that they are wiser by experience, that is, by failure. I have read in a Hindoo book, that "there was a king's son, who, being expelled in infancy from his native city, was brought up by a forester, and, growing up to maturity in that state, imagined himself to belong to the barbarous race with which he lived. One of his father's ministers having discovered him, revealed to him what he was, and the misconception of his character was removed, and he knew himself to be a prince. So soul," continues the Hindoo philosopher, "from the circumstances in which it is placed, mistakes its own character, until the truth is revealed to it by some holy teacher and then it knows itself to be *Brahme*." I perceive that we inhabitants of New England live this mean life that we do because our vision does not penetrate the surface of things. We think that that *is* which *appears* to be. If a man should walk through this town and see only the reality, where, think you, would the "Milldam" go to? If he should give us an account of the realities he beheld there, we should not recognize the place in his description. Look at the meetinghouse, or a courthouse, or a jail, or a shop, or a dwelling-house, and say what that thing really is before a true gaze, and they would all go to pieces in your account of them. Men esteem truth remote, in the outskirts of the system, behind the farthest star, before Adam and after the last man. In eternity there is indeed something true and sublime. But all these times and places and occasions are now and here. God himself culminates in the present moment, and will never be more divine in the lapse of all the ages. And we are enabled to apprehend at all what is sublime and noble only by the perpetual instilling and drenching of the reality that surrounds us. The universe constantly and obediently answers to our conceptions; whether we travel fast or slow, the track is laid for us. Let us spend our lives in conceiving then. The poet or the artist never yet had so fair and noble a design but some of his posterity at least could accomplish it.

Let us spend one day as deliberately as Nature, and not be thrown off the track by every nutshell and mosquito's wing that falls on the rails. Let us rise early and fast, or breakfast, gently and without perturbation; let company come and let company go, let the bells ring and the children cry—determined to make a day of it. Why should we knock under and go with the stream? Let us not be upset and overwhelmed in that terrible rapid and whirlpool called a dinner, situated in the meridian shallows. Weather this danger and you are safe, for the rest of the way is downhill. With unrelaxed nerves, with morning vigor, sail by it, looking another way, tied to the mast like Ulysses. If the engine whistles, let it whistle till it is hoarse for its pains. If the bell rings, why should we run? We will consider what kind of music they are like. Let us settle ourselves and work and wedge our feet downward through the mud and slush of opinion, and prejudice, and tradition, and delusion, and appearance, that alluvion which covers the globe, through Paris and London, through New York and Boston and Concord, through Church and State, through poetry and philosophy and religion, till we come to a hard bottom and rocks in place, which we can call *reality*, and say, This is, and no mistake; and then begin, having a *point d'appui*, below freshet and frost and fire, a place where you might found a wall or a state, or set a lamppost safely, or perhaps a gauge, not a Nilometer, but a Realometer, that future ages might know how deep a freshet of shams and appearances had gathered from time to time. If you stand right fronting and face to face to a fact, you will see the sun glimmer on both its surfaces, as if it were a cimeter, and feel its sweet edge dividing you through the heart and marrow, and so you will happily conclude your mortal career. Be it life or death, we crave only reality. If we are really dying, let us hear the rattle in our throats and feel cold in the extremities; if we are alive, let us go about our business.

Time is but the stream I go afishing in. I drink at it; but while I drink I see the sandy bottom and detect how shallow it is. Its thin current slides away but eternity remains. I would drink deeper; fish in the sky, whose bottom is pebbly with stars. I cannot count one. I know not the first letter of the alphabet. I have always been regretting that I was not as wise as the day I was born. The intellect is a cleaver; it discerns and rifts its way into the secret of things. I do not wish to be any more busy with my hands than is necessary. My head is hands and feet. I feel all my best faculties concentrated in it. My instinct tells me that my head is an organ for burrowing, as some creatures use their snout and fore paws, and with it I would mine and burrow my way through these hills. I think that the richest vein is somewhere hereabouts; so by the divining-rod and thin rising vapors, I judge; and here I will begin to mine.

Suggestions for Discussion

1. Why did Thoreau go to the woods?

2. With what details does Thoreau support his statement that "we live meanly like ants"?

3. Interpret Thoreau's rhetorical question in the context of his philosophy: "If you are acquainted with the principle, what do you care for a myriad instances and applications"?

4. With what details does Thoreau illustrate his impatience with man's proclivity for being deluded?

5. How do Thoreau's rhetorical questions, metaphors, and allusions contribute to substance and tone?

6. What aspects of American life does Thoreau repudiate and why?

7. What does he affirm? Paraphrase his last two paragraphs.

Suggestions for Writing

1. Discuss what you have learned from your observations of nature.

2. "Our life is frittered away by detail."

3. "Shams and delusions are esteemed for soundless truths, while reality is fabulous."

4. What would Thoreau's impressions be of our current preoccupations?

Jeffrey H. Goldstein

The Healing Power of Laughter

<blockquote>Jeffrey H. Goldstein (b. 1942) received his Ph.D. from Ohio State University and teaches psychology at Temple University. He has been a consultant to the National Science Foundation and the U.S. Department of Labor. He has co-edited *The Psychology of Humor* (1972) and written *Aggression and Crimes of Violence* (1975). He has contributed to a number of psychology, sociology, and anthropology journals. He traces the historical roots of the theory that laughter is conducive to healing and concludes that a sense of humor at least improves the quality of life.</blockquote>

There are fads in medicine and psychiatry just as surely as there are in art, literature, and styles of dress. Today it is fashionable to attribute healing and restorative powers to laughter, a claim that only 30 or 40 years ago would itself have been laughable.

Only since the end of the Second World War have Westerners come to think that stress and anxiety might lead to disease. To suggest the opposite— that laughter, relaxation, and joy could be therapeutic—was nearly unthinkable.

The notion that laughter is healthy owes much of its current popularity to Norman Cousins's "Anatomy of an Illness," published in the *New England Journal of Medicine* in 1976 and expanded into a best-selling book in 1979.

Cousins, then editor of the *Saturday Review*, described his bout with ankylosing spondylitis, a chronic, progressive disease inflaming the joints of the spine; and he attributed his rather remarkable recovery to self-treatment with vitamin C and laughter. The vitamin C, he believed, could combat inflammation, and the laughter could have positive effects on the body—since negative emotions, he had read, could produce negative effects.

Cousins's account was praised by many in the medical community, but others were skeptical. The late Sidney Kahn, of Mount Sinai School of Medicine, for instance, noted in the *Mount Sinai Journal of Medicine* that Cousins drew some arbitrary conclusions from the medical literature, and that spontaneous remissions of ankylosing spondylitis do occur. In other words, Cousins may have recovered naturally; he did not necessarily laugh his way back to health.

But despite some criticism, Cousins's influence has remained strong (indeed, after leaving *Saturday Review*, he became a senior lecturer in medical

humanities at the University of California at Los Angeles School of Medicine).
Partly as a result of his book, physicians are more likely than ever to think of
humor and other sources of emotional comfort as part of treatment.

A worrisome consequence of this is that the patient may be held responsible for his or her failure to recover; that by not having the will to live, the
proper outlook on life, or a sufficient sense of humor, the patient will be seen
to suffer willfully.

Though Cousins's suggestions will require serious scientific investigation, the
idea that laughter is therapeutic does have a long history. From the time of
Aristotle, a few scholars have recommended laughter as a means of strengthening the lungs and of furthering the health of the organism as a whole.

In the 13th century, Henri de Mondeville, a surgeon, proposed that laughter be used as an aid to recovery from surgery. Foreshadowing Cousins, de
Mondeville also noted that negative emotions might interfere with recovery:
"The surgeon must forbid anger, hatred, and sadness in the patient, and remind him that the body grows fat from joy and thin from sadness."

And Richard Mulcaster, a 16th-century physician, believed that laughter
was a physical exercise and, as such, was healthy. He wrote that laughter
could help those who have cold hands and cold chests and are troubled with
melancholia, since "it moveth much aire in the breast, and sendeth the
warmer spirites outward."

In one of the most thoughtful and complete analyses of laughter ever written, the 16th-century physician Laurent Joubert presented several views on
its origin and function that are still accepted, though in slightly different form.
Like Aristotle, Joubert saw laughter as arising from "a defect or ugliness that
is not painful or destructive." In this view, the ugliness incited sadness while
its relative painlessness incited joy. These contrary emotions were said to stir
the heart in alternating contractions and expansions, sadness causing the contractions and joy the expansions. The to-and-fro movement was transferred to
the diaphragm, leading to the rapid breathing we call "hearty laughter." To
Joubert, the consequences of laughter were manifestly beneficial, and could
be seen in the face and eyes. He wrote:

> Is it not in the face, and especially in the eyes which [laughter] moves so freely
> that nothing surpasses it? . . . Certainly there is nothing that gives more plea-
> sure and recreation than a laughing face, with its wide, shining, clear, and se-
> rene forehead, eyes shining, resplendent from any vantage point, and casting
> fire as do diamonds; cheeks vermillion and incarnate, mouth flush with the face,
> lips handsomely drawn back . . . chin drawn in, widened, and a bit recessed.

References to laughter's healthful effects are scattered through the philosophical and medical literature of the 18th and 19th centuries as well. Laughter was thought to be good exercise and more. Gottlieb Huçeland, a 19th-
century German professor, said, "Laughter is one of the most important helps
to digestion with which we are acquainted; the custom in vogue among our
ancestors, of exciting it by jesters and buffoons, was founded on true medical
principles. Cheerful and joyous companions are invaluable at meals."

Herbert Spencer proposed, in 1860, that laughter was a way of releasing
excess tension, and, therefore, is an important restorative mechanism—a view
of laughter influential even today.

Spencer's idea was taken up and elaborated, in 1928, by James Walsh, an

American physician, who wrote that the beneficial physical effects of laughter are mediated by psychological effects:

> The best formula for the health of the individual is contained in the mathematical expression: health varies as the amount of laughter. The effect of laughter upon the mind not only brings relaxation with it, so far as mental tension is concerned, but makes it also less prone to dreads and less solicitous about the future. This favorable effect on the mind influences various functions of the body and makes them healthier than would otherwise be the case.

Despite these statements extolling laughter's medical benefits, the moral view of laughter has usually been negative—decidedly so. It is only within the last hundred years or so that laughter in public has even been socially acceptable.

For much of Western history, laughter was considered impolite at best, satanic at worst. Medieval physicians tended to locate each emotion in some organ of the body. The seat of love, for instance, was the heart (and a good thing, too, or who knows what shapes we'd be sending on Valentine's Day). The seat of laughter was the spleen—an assignment apparently meant to assure that laughter was viewed as a "low" form of behavior.

In 1676, Robert Barclay wrote in "Apology for the True Christian Divinity":

> It is not lawful to use games, sports, plays, nor among other things comedies among Christians, under the notion of recreations, since they do not agree with Christian silence, gravity, and sobriety; for laughing, sporting, gaming, mocking, jesting, vain talking, etc., is not Christian liberty, nor harmless mirth.

The pilgrim settlers to America likewise looked upon laughter with disdain and permitted it only when it would serve to illustrate a moral lesson.

Victorian England, not surprisingly, frowned on laughter as well. While girls and women were permitted to smile in deference or to giggle at the slightest suggestion of impropriety, they were not to laugh with glee. They could be embarrassed but not happy. (Today, of course, they may be happy, but not embarrassed.) George Vasey, a philosopher of that era, argued in "The Philosophy of Laughter and Smiling" that children laugh, not out of any sense of joy or humor, but because they were tickled as infants.

In our century, the negative view of laughter received some support from the new field of psychology. Once Sigmund Freud had written on humor and laughter, in 1905, it was increasingly credible that humor reflected bitterness, underlying anxiety, or unspoken hostility. In "Jokes and Their Relation to the Unconscious," he discussed the functions and techniques of "tendentious wit," humor with an underlying motive, or tendency. Joking, he argued, can provide an outlet—though not a conscious one—for underlying sexual and aggressive impulses.

But Freud was careful to distinguish between hostile wit and benign humor, and recognized that some laughter, at least, might indicate the absence of underlying pathology. He wrote, in 1928:

> Humor . . . has also something fine and elevating . . . the triumph of narcissism, the ego's victorious assertion of its own vulnerability. It refuses to be hurt by the arrows of reality or be compelled to suffer. It insists that it is impervious to wounds dealt by the outside world, in fact, that these are merely occasions for affording it pleasure.

That is, a person in an unfortunate or unpleasant situation can become its master (at least temporarily) by turning it around and making a joke of it.

When opinions vacillate from one extreme to another—between the belief that laughter is evil and symptomatic of disease, and the belief that it is health giving and beneficial—there is likely to be some validity in each position.

It is true that laughter can indicate underlying, and perhaps unconscious, hostility and conflict. It is also true that laughter can express self-acceptance, joy, inner strength, and adjustment. There is considerable evidence on both sides, but we do not yet know enough about laughter and humor to evaluate its meaning with confidence. Nor do we know how to distinguish reliably between "healthy" and "malevolent" laughter. In short, laughter cannot be treated as a single, undifferentiated phenomenon.

Current evidence, more psychological than physiological suggests that laughter does not always reflect a state of adjustment or physical well-being. Psychologically, it may indicate self-deprecation, hostility toward others—as in racist joking—defensiveness, closed mindedness, or a preoccupation with scatology or sex. Socially, humor may be used to break the ice; but it may also be used defensively as a barrier to communication. Filling a conversation with jokes and witty remarks can be a way to avoid participation, to close oneself off from the proceedings.

Laughter and humor also may drive a wedge between people, as when a hostile or pointed remark makes another person or group the butt of a joke. Or humor may serve as a tactic of ingratiation, a way to manipulate others.

Physically, we now know that there are any number of conditions in which laughter indicates underlying pathology. In three neurological disorders— pseudobulbar palsy, amyotrophic lateral sclerosis (Lou Gehrig's disease), and multiple sclerosis—there is a distinctive type of "aberrant" laughter. Sudden outbursts occur often, but the laughter is beyond the control of the patient and does not reflect any sense of elation.

Similarly, a form of epilepsy, called gelastic epilepsy, involves dull, hollow, and clearly inappropriate laughter.

A change in the sense of humor often accompanies Alzheimer's disease and Pick's disease, also known as presenile dementias (early senility). Sufferers of these disorders tend to crack silly jokes, and cannot take serious matters seriously. There are also acute conditions, such as ethyl alcohol poisoning, that can result in inappropriate, excessive, or uncontrollable laughter.

It is clear that pathological laughter generally does not reflect an underlying sense of joy or elation, is not under the patient's conscious control, and is inappropriate to the social situation in which it occurs. But this suggests that the converse is also true: that healthy or normal laughter does reflect a sense of mirth, is to some degree under conscious control, and is appropriate to the situation.

The best-documented studies of healthy laughter examine those of its correlates that can be measured most readily: variations in heart rate, respiration, and the skin's electrical conductance, just prior to, during, and after laughter. In most of these studies, tension or arousal is found to increase during the telling of a joke, to increase further during laughter, and then to decrease following laughter.

Studies that combine psychological and physiological measures typically find that, over the short term, laughter may reduce arousal from whatever source, supporting the theory that laughter is sometimes effective for reducing stress. It is conceivable, too, that laughter or spontaneous joking can be used to indicate a person's general level of stress or anxiety, though the content and social nature of joking in these cases needs to be taken into account. For instance, if a person chronically jokes about a particular subject such as sex, it may indicate an area of conflict that the person cannot express in any other way. And the failure to laugh about certain subjects may convey as much information as laughter itself.

In these studies, laughter was examined only in experimental settings, and only for brief periods. To my knowledge, no one has ever studied the long-term consequences of chronic and repeated laughter. Though it has been argued for centuries that laughter is good exercise, and we do know that laughter does not deplete the amount of oxygen in peripheral blood, we still do not know whether those who laugh regularly—many times a day, for example—are really healthier and better adjusted than those who do not.

It is not too farfetched to speculate, however, that laughter is related in several ways to longevity. Of the major heart attack risks that have been identified (cigaret smoking, obesity, diabetes, hypertension, high blood levels of cholesterol, stress, and lack of exercise), laughter is clearly related to the reduction of stress and to physical exercise, and may be related to hypertension. We know that someone with a "Type A" personality, characterized by seriousness, stress, concern with time, impatience, and hostility, has a greater risk of heart attack than the "Type B" person, in whom a sense of humor may displace anger, anxiety, and hostility. We know, too, that people who are in a good mood, stimulated by epinephrine, are more apt to experience laughter and mirth than those who are unaroused or depressed, as by a tranquilizer such as chlorpromazine.

Cousins, and the late Rene Dubos, in his introduction to Cousins's book, have speculated that the newly discovered pituitary secretions called endorphins are related to laughter and its beneficial effects.

Endorphins are chemically related to opiates, such as heroin and morphine, and act to reduce pain and instill feelings of elation. Many long-distance runners, for instance, experience a state of euphoria that is related to the amount of betaendorphin in their bloodstreams. Laughter may act on the endocrine system, the pituitary gland in particular, to produce not only a reduction in physical stress and pain, but a sense of euphoria as well.

Of course, from reading some of the recent popular books on humor and health, one might think that all the research needed to support these speculations had already been conducted—that laughter has already been categorically proven to promote a long and healthy life. Cousins, for example, notes approvingly the sense of humor, love of baroque music, and longevity of Albert Schweitzer and Pablo Casals. But it is well to remember that the connections between laughter and long life, if any, have yet to be demonstrated. Indeed, as far as I can determine from a cursory reading of biographies and recent necrologies, comedians and comic writers do not live any longer than other people—they do not dramatically survive those of their contemporaries who have chosen the graver specialties of law, medicine, and investment banking.

It would be surprising if they did. At this point, one can say with confidence only that a sense of humor enhances the quality of life—but not necessarily its duration.

Suggestions for Discussion

1. What are the historical roots of Cousins's theory that laughter is conducive to healing?

2. What is one unfortunate consequence of Cousins's theory?

3. How do you explain the fact that the moral view of laughter has usually been negative in the light of the medical benefits that have been extolled?

4. How did Freud distinguish between hostile and benign humor and the sources of each? Explain his statement that humor represents "the triumph of narcissism, the ego's victorious assertion of its own vulnerability."

5. How does Goldstein's essay support his view that "laughter cannot be treated as a single, undifferentiated phenomenon"? Cite examples of the several rhetorical devises he uses to develop his thesis.

6. What evidence is brought to bear to suggest that laughter does not always reflect a state of adjustment or physical well being?

7. What studies give support to the view that laughter can be healing?

8. On what evidence does the author speculate that laughter may be related to longevity? What is the role of endorphins?

Suggestions for Writing

1. Analyze the nature of the humor in a favorite comedian or in a humorous writer.

2. Think of the demeanor and conversations of one or more of your friends or acquaintances. What role does humor or laughter seem to play in their lives? To what do you attribute its source?

3. Characterize a person whose humor seems pathological or one whose humor appears to be an outlet for aggressive impulses.

Stuart Chase

A Very Private Utopia

Stuart Chase (1888–1985) was a lifelong critic of social conditions in the United States. Among his published works are *The Tragedy of Waste* (1925), *Men and Machines* (1931), *The Economy of Abundance* (1934), and *Rich Land, Poor Land* (1936). Although Chase mentions very personal attributes of the good life, his essay transcends the personal; the ultimate goal is not what would make one happy but rather what would make one more alive.

Lewis Mumford in the *Golden Day* has given us a brilliant review of American culture as reflected in American literature from Jonathan Edwards to John Dewey. It is on the whole an exceedingly critical review. He tells us frequently, passionately, and beautifully what he is against, but only rarely does he let it be known what he is for. Modern industrial civilization has nourished a great array of critics. Few of them are as competent or as penetrating as Mr. Mumford, but all of them—save possibly the Utopians—follow his general method. They are indefatigable in pointing out the shortcomings of society, but they are vague as to the precise nature of available substitutes. They seldom define their standards. Yet standards they must have; otherwise it would be impossible to criticize. They either take it for granted that the reader shares their inward knowledge, or else, and more probably, the standards have never been formulated in the critic's conscious processes at all. They have grown in the back of his mind, darkly.

From the artists, the dramatists, the socialists, the poets, the uplifters of all varieties, has poured forth in never-ending flood the challenge that *homo sapiens* is only half alive.

What does he look like when he is alive?

The question would seem to be a fair one, but it is seldom answered. The writers of Utopia have struggled with it, but their canvases are usually so great that we are seldom able to see ourselves or our neighbors living or behaving in that world. There is a strange chill about all Utopias; they are inhabited by gods, not men. Even when a critical play of modern manners, the "Beggar on Horseback," forsook its role of satire for a moment and gave us a picture of happiness about a sun-drenched breakfast table, we stared unconvinced at such very yellow bliss. The negatives stretch to the horizon, but the positives are either lacking entirely or, when focused before us, appear cold or a little absurd. Indeed to seek to describe with clearness and precision the specific target at which programs for ushering in the good life should aim can only be an adventure tinged with absurdity. But a possible approach may be to delimit the kind of life one personally would like to live. Will this remove the Utopian chill and at the same time furnish the beginnings of a standard? We can but test it.

I have thrown my arrows with the rest at the sweating corpus of the world as it is. I have called it ugly, machine-minded, dull, ignorant, and cruel. I have said that the few live, and they precariously, while the many exist, half-dead in their frustrations and blind alleys. Before hurling another quiver it would seem only fair—however dubious the result—to define rather specifically what I mean, or think I mean, when I mark off the quick from the dead.

The hours roll into days, the days into years. Down this funnel of time one drifts, now easily, now painfully. One is happy, one is miserable. There are days of the most intense blue; days of a terrible black; with perhaps the majority of days an all-pervading mauve-gray. The causes for the color of these days are far from clear; one takes life as it comes. Modern psychology is groping for causes, but it has not as yet brought much that is genuinely helpful into the light. It cannot tell you where the good life has been competently analyzed or even adequately described. Science has perhaps even less to report than the poets and the critics. And so about all the data is oneself.

I note that the following things or conditions do, by and large, kill the juices of zestful living, and reduce me to mere existing, I state the negative first, the positive to follow shortly:

> Ill health.
> Monotonous work with no discernible goal—such as auditing, indexing, dishwashing.
> Eating poor food; eating in ugly places.
> The sensation of living in ugly or uncomfortable houses.
> All transit, whether by foot or on wheels, about New York City.
> Being looked down upon, or laughed at (save for very minor foibles).
> The bulk of all business interviews, conferences, talks—the juicelessness of the personal contact.
> The defacement of natural beauty with billboards, pop stands, suburban lots, gas tanks, shacks, factories. (A factory can be made to respond to architecture as well as a skyscraper.)
> Reading newspapers—save for perhaps one one-hundredth of the surface of not more than three of them.
> Going to formal entertainments—particularly dinners devoted to the raising of funds for worthy causes.
> Treating relatives as preferred creditors.
> Wearing ugly or uncomfortable clothes as decreed by the *mores,* e.g., coats and hats for men in summer.
> Shopping—with rare exceptions.
> Worrying about money.
> Being bored with bad plays, concerts, lectures, radios, meetings, conversations—especially the last.
> Being everlastingly hustled around.
> Seeing other people bored, unhappy, or in pain. Looking down mean streets and into frowsy windows.

My notebooks show scores of other conditions which take the joy out of life, but the above are the chief ones in the daily run of my activity. They consume, on the basis of a rough estimate, upwards of two thirds of my waking hours, though the ratio shifts with the seasons, being noticeably worse in winter. The average annual ratio, furthermore, is better when living in the country the year around than in the city. I am dead, I conclude, about two thirds of the time. I am alive, by and large, under the following conditions:

> On encountering a vivid awareness of health.
> In pursuing creative work, intellectual or manual. There are definite time limits to both.

Eating good food, drinking good wine, in comfortable places.
The sensation of living in well-designed and sunny houses.
Being looked up to and praised—but the butter must not be spread too thick.
Being with my friends.
Looking at beautiful scenery, beautiful pictures, beautiful things.
Reading great books; reading of new and stimulating ideas.
Looking at Charlie Chaplin's feet.
Swimming, diving, playing tennis, dancing, skiing, mountain climbing. Watching good sport at not too frequent intervals.
Daydreaming.
Going on spontaneous and amusing parties.
Making love spontaneously.
Wearing beautiful—not fashionable—clothes.
Collecting things. For me, certain sorts of information.
Listening to good music—especially Russian gypsy songs.
The sensation of being some paces in front of the wolf.
Home life—in fits and starts.
Kindly casual contacts with strangers.
Travel, other than for business reasons.
Keen discussion.
A good fight, not necessarily sanguinary, in what seems to be a decent cause.
The sense of being in bodily danger.

So runs the major classification of what seem to constitute the good life for me. To hold that the list is applicable to all is, of course, ridiculous. Yet it must serve as a starting-point for the thing we have set ourselves to define. I do not know how other people feel. Logic declares that, conditioned by the same forces that have conditioned me, other people would feel much the same, but logic is not an infallible guide in human affairs.

What kind of a community would I build to increase the count of the hours that live as against the count of the hours that die? God knows. The difficulty is that the pluses and the minuses are never clean-cut emotional states, registering faithfully at every exposure to a given condition. When one is in abounding health, even filling-station architecture is tolerable if not positively enjoyable. When one sits, like Mr. Polly, athwart a stile, with civil war in his interior, the sunset itself becomes a flat and overestimated spectacle. There are times when the best of friends becomes a bore, when one wishes all printing presses would stop forever. Indeed, the whole concept is in the curved grip of relativity.

Nevertheless, I think that I would be appreciably more alive in a community that deliberately fostered the sorts of things enumerated on the second list, of which good health is probably the most important single factor. If it be objected that the animals are mostly healthy, I would reply that they appear to get more out of life than the majority of human beings. Fortunately the laws underlying the promotion of health are beginning to be understood. We already have the technical knowledge available to increase immeasurably bodily well-being. Here and there it is being applied, as the declining death-rate and the lengthening age span show.

Secondly, I would like to live in a community where beauty abounded; where cities were nobly planned, industrial areas segregated; where great stretches of forest, lake, and mountain were left wild and free and close at hand; where houses and their furnishings were spare and fine and colorful, and there was not a single billboard in a day's march. Cities and houses have been so built; nature over great (but distant) areas is still free; advertising is only a century old, despite the pious historical labors of Bruce Barton. Surely a community rich in natural beauty, rich in architecture, is no Utopia. It has been repeatedly achieved, and without the vast potential assistance of mechanical power.

Thirdly, I would like to live, and to have my neighbors live, free from the fear of want. Such communities there have been, but not many of them. Peru under the Incas is said to have achieved this goal; Denmark is not far from it today. Not only is it the release of the individual which is desirable, but, vastly more important, the release of the whole group. As things are in America today I never know how far my own actions are ignoble by economic considerations, nor how far my neighbors and associates regard me on my own merits or as a means to a hopefully profitable end. All human relationships are poisoned with this suspicion; or cut and bruised with the frank brutality of elbowing one's way above the line of economic insecurity. This is the more lamentable in that the industrial arts have already demonstrated how utterly to abolish poverty, double—aye treble—the standard of living, produce more than enough to go around.

Fourthly, I would like to live in a community where I could do the kind of work that is the most fun. Fun for me is economic research and writing about it. If there should prove a plethora of better men in this field, I would have a lot of fun as an anthropologist, a psychologist, or a biologist. Or I might go back to my boyhood dreams of architecture. In exchange for the fun, the giving of an hour or two on the average day to the necessary manual work of the world would seem, in anticipation at least, the merest justice. Furthermore, digging ditches, painting walls, simple carpentry would both preserve the sense of reality and serve by contrast to heighten the fun of the chosen occupation.

I would like to be able to dress as I pleased, or indeed not to dress at all when the sun was high and the water blue. I should like to experiment with colors and combinations now rigidly proscribed for males by the folkways—save at fancy-dress balls. I should like to be able to dance more, sing more, let myself go more. Here New England dogs me like an iron shroud. I should like ampler and less hurried opportunities to play the games I enjoy. I should like to travel more; to visit the lost cities of which I dream; to climb in the Andes and the Himalayas. It does not do to turn one's back for long on the bright face of danger.

I should like to be a more compelling and less self-conscious lover, but just how a community would proceed to organize great lovers escapes me. (Here we hover at once on absurdity and on what, following health, is probably the most important factor in the good life—a balanced sexual rhythm.)

I would like to live is a world where many good books were being published—fiction, poetry, science, history, philosophy; where good plays and good music were just around the corner—without too much standing in line and too little ventilation; where good pictures were being hung; where the arts and crafts were flourishing on indigenous rather than imitative material; and particularly and especially, where good conversation abounded, together with the leisure to pursue it. Of all the joys which life has to offer none, for me, can exceed that of keen stimulating talk; and nothing is rarer in America today.

Finally, I would like to live in a community that held a genuine sense of its uniqueness; where one could take pride in community achievements, match one's art and craftsmanship and sport against a neighbor group; where one could contribute in person to the local theater, the local schools; help to plan a beautiful region, and see that plan grow before one's eyes—and so take root in one's own soil, a part of the earth, earthy, as well as a dreamer in the clouds. So the Greeks must have looked back to the plains and hills and cedar trees of Attica and Laconia. Here one might have the leisure to play with children as they should be played with; here one might bring the carnival and the pageant—with color and wine and flowers—back to meaning and to life.

Above all, leisure, leisure, a break in the remorseless and meaningless urgencies of the twentieth-century pace.

This—if you will—Utopia may be cold to you, but it is not cold to me. I can see it, feel it, aye, long for it. How would you change it to include the things for which you long? Anthropologists, you say, have yet to find a people without a well-marked religion; that need is indigenous, cardinal, and necessary to you. Good. Let us have a church with a great nave and a great organ and the sound of vespers across the evening fields. You dislike my games and want other games. Again good. The more games the better so long as we play them ourselves. You want to paint or design or build bridges. Each to his own desire, so long as the necessary work is done. You do not want to do anything. There will be a nice, forest-circled, psychopathic hospital until sanity returns. You do not want roots, you want to keep on the move. Would you object to moving through communities which had abolished squalor and striven to individualize and beautify themselves?

Add what you please, so long as it does not make for ugliness or drabness or cruelty; so long as it does not quench life that the lives of a few may burn with a spurious brightness. I do not know what your desires may be, but if they make you happy and others not too unhappy they are welcome. The question is not what is good for other people but good for you.

The preliminary definition of the good life which I have tried to outline is crude enough, but it can be used. Swing it as a searchlight where you will— on Mr. Calvin Coolidge or on Mr. Bernard Shaw; on Miss Jane Addams or on Mrs. Peaches Browning; on a soap factory, a department store, an iron mine, an advertising campaign, a prize fight, a laboratory, a best seller; swing it upon Wall Street or Main Street or Downing Street; on Denmark or on Pittsburgh—it can give basis for judgment. Would this person, or thing, or area, be out of place in such a community? Would it clash, jar, disintegrate; or would it be welcomed and at home? The architecture of Beacon Hill would, the architecture of South Chicago would not; the Lincoln Memorial would, Park Avenue would not; Mr. Chaliapin would, Mr. Shubert would not; the Olympic games would, professional baseball would not; Mr. H. G. Wells would (very much at home he would be), Dr. Frank Crane would not. Mark for yourself the quick from the dead.

The question is not primarily what would make you happy, but rather what would make you more alive. Perhaps complete Nirvana is the happiest conceivable state, but it remains at the opposite pole from vivid life. Pain, heartache, failure in achievement, failure in love, the shock of physical danger, even envy, must remain so long as we behave like human beings. Only the surplus of pain and confusion induced by stupidity would tend to disappear.

It would seem that the end of human effort upon this planet should be to give a maximum of living and a minimum of existing—the life more abundant. Against such an end, those who regard life as a gateway of mortification to a Utopia beyond the grave make their sincere protest. But it is doubtful how far that protest can continue effective in an era of wide knowledge and unlimited possibilities for technical control over nature.

Even if we can win to life ourselves, the contemplation of the existing of those over the brink about us takes, in a sensitive heart, most of the joy out of personal salvation here below. Even if democracy is not sound doctrine, and biological inferiority can be definitely established, there is no particular reason why those handicapped from the germ plasm—and who will perforce have to do most of the dirty work of the world—should not be given surroundings from which they can take the maximum of what life holds for them. Lafcadio Hearn can tell you about the ancient Japanese communities and how extraordinarily high in the sense of beauty and appreciation it has been proved possible for the mass to go.

Granting for the time being—until coal is gone, and the Ice Cap moves south again—granting that a beautiful life here and now should be the major goal of human effort, of what strands shall it be woven? How shall Mr. Mumford and his fellow-critics be appeased? The above is, if you will, a feeble and absurd beginning. But perhaps it will serve as a point of departure for the speculations of wise men and women.

Suggestions for Discussion

1. Although Chase entitles his essay *A Very Private Utopia*, his vision transcends the personal. Cite evidence to support this view.

2. Chase equates the good life with being fully alive. With what illustrations does he establish this definition? Under what general categories do they fall?

3. How does Chase distinguish being fully alive from being happy?

4. How does Chase indirectly define the self? Relate his concept to that of other writers in this book.

Suggestions for Writing

1. What is your personal conception of Utopia? Define its elements by means of a generalization and particulars to support it.

2. Describe your community as it fosters and/or impedes living the good life.

Joyce Carol Oates
New Heaven and Earth

Joyce Carol Oates (b. 1938) is an American novelist, who was awarded a Guggenheim Fellowship in 1967, and a professor of English at Princeton University. Her novels include the prize-winning *Them* (1969), and *With Shuddering Fall* (1964), *Upon the Sweeping Flood* (1966), *Garden of Earthly Delights* (1967), and *Expensive People* (1968). She was also the O. Henry Prize Story winner in 1967–1968 and contributes fiction to national magazines. In this essay she affirms that our old "objective, valueless philosophies" that have always worked to preserve the status quo will be replaced by a new, higher humanism or pantheism.

In spite of current free-roaming terrors in this country, it is really not the case that we are approaching some apocalyptic close. Both those who seem to be awaiting it with excitement and dread and those who are trying heroically to comprehend it in terms of recent American history are mistaking a crisis of transition for a violent end. Even Charles Reich's much maligned and much misinterpreted *The Greening of America*, which was the first systematic attempt to indicate the direction we are surely moving in, focuses much too narrowly upon a single decade in a single nation and, in spite of its occasional stunning accuracy, is a curiously American product—that is, it imagines all of history as running up into and somehow culminating in the United States. Consider Reich's last two sentences:

> . . . For one almost convinced that it was necessary to accept ugliness and evil, that it was necessary to be a miser of dreams, it is an invitation to cry or laugh. For one who thought the world was irretrievably encased in metal and plastic and sterile stone, it seems a veritable greening of America.

Compare that with the following passage from Teilhard de Chardin's *The Phenomenon of Man*, a less historical-nationalistic vision:

> In every domain, when anything exceeds a certain measurement, it suddenly changes its aspect, condition, or nature. The curve doubles back, the surface contracts to a point, the solid disintegrates, the liquid boils, the germ cell divides, intuition suddenly bursts on the piled up facts. . . . Critical points have been reached, rungs on the ladder, involving a change of state—jumps of all sorts *in the course* of development.

Or consider these lines from D. H. Lawrence's poem "Nullus," in which he is speaking of the private "self" that is Lawrence but also of the epoch in which this self exists:

> There are said to be creative pauses,
> pauses that are as good as death, empty and dead as death itself.
> And in these awful pauses the evolutionary change takes place.

What appears to be a breaking-down of civilization may well be simply the breaking-up of old forms by life itself (not an eruption of madness or self-destruction), a process that is entirely natural and inevitable. Perhaps we are in the tumultuous but exciting close of a centuries-old kind of consciousness—

a few of us like theologians of the medieval church encountering the unstoppable energy of the Renaissance. What we must avoid is the paranoia of history's "true believers," who have always misinterpreted a natural, evolutionary transformation of consciousness as being the violent conclusion of all of history.

The God-centered, God-directed world of the Middle Ages was transformed into the complex era we call the Renaissance, but the transition was as terrifying as it was inevitable, if the innumerable prophecies of doom that were made at the time are any accurate indication. Shakespeare's most disturbing tragedies—*King Lear* and *Troilus and Cressida*—reflect that communal anxiety, as do the various expressions of anxiety over the "New Science" later in the seventeenth century. When we look back into history, we are amazed, not at the distance that separates one century from another, but at their closeness, the almost poetic intimacy.

As I see it, the United States is the first nation—though so complex and unclassifiable an entity almost resists definition as a single unit—to suffer/enjoy the death throes of the Renaissance. How could it be otherwise, since our nation is sensitive, energetic, swarming with life, and, beyond any other developed nation in the world, the most obsessed with its own history and its own destiny? Approaching a kind of manic stage, in which suppressed voices are at last being heard, in which *no extreme viewpoint is any longer "extreme,"* the United States is preparing itself for a transformation of "being" similar to that experienced by individuals as they approach the end of one segment of their lives and must rapidly, and perhaps desperately, sum up everything that has gone before.

It is easy to misread the immediate crises, to be frightened by the spontaneous eruptions into consciousness of disparate groups (blacks, women, youth, "the backlash of the middle class"); it is possible to overlook how the collective voices of many of our best poets and writers serve to dramatize and exorcise current American nightmares. Though some of our most brilliant creative artists are obsessed with disintegration and with the isolated ego, it is clear by now that they are all, with varying degrees of terror, saying the same thing—that we are helpless, unconnected with any social or cultural unit, unable to direct the flow of history, that we cannot effectively communicate. The effect is almost that of a single voice, as if a communal psychoanalytic process were taking place. But there does come a time in an individual writer's experience when he realizes, perhaps against his will, that his voice is one of many, his fiction one of many fictions, and that all serious fictions are half-conscious dramatizations of what is going on in the world.

Here is a simple test to indicate whether you are ready for the new vision of man or whether you will fear and resist it: Imagine you are high in the air, looking down on a crowded street scene from a height so great that you cannot make out individual faces but can see only shapes, scurrying figures rather like insects. Your imagination projects you suddenly down into that mass. You respond with what emotion—dread or joy?

In many of us the Renaissance ideal is still powerful, its voice tyrannical. It declares: *I will, I want, I demand, I think, I am.* This voice tells us that we are not quite omnipotent but must act as if we were, pushing out into a world of other people or of nature that will necessarily resist us, that will try to destroy us, and that we must conquer. *I will exist* has meant only *I will im-*

pose my will on others. To that end man has developed his intellect and has extended his physical strength by any means possible because, indeed, at one time the world did have to be conquered. The Renaissance leapt ahead into its own necessary future, into the development and near perfection of machines. Machines are not evil, or even "unnatural," but simply extensions of the human brain. The designs for our machines are no less the product of our creative imaginations than are works of art, though it might be difficult for most people—especially artists—to acknowledge this. But a great deal that is difficult, even outrageous, will have to be acknowledged.

If technology appears to have dehumanized civilization, that is a temporary failing or error—for the purpose of technology is the furthering of the "human," the bringing to perfection of all the staggering potentialities in each individual, which are nearly always lost, layered over with biological or social or cultural crusts. Anyone who imagines that a glorious pastoral world has been lost, through machines, identifies himself as a child of the city, perhaps a second- or third-generation child of the city. An individual who has lived close to nature, on a farm, for instance, knows that "natural" man was never *in* nature; he had to fight nature, at the cost of his own spontaneity and, indeed, his humanity. It is only through the conscious control of the "machine" (i.e., through man's brain) that man can transcend the miserable struggle with nature, whether in the form of sudden devastating hailstorms that annihilate an entire crop, or minute deadly bacteria in the bloodstream, or simply the commonplace (but potentially tragic) condition of poor eyesight. It is only through the machine that man can become more human, more spiritual. Understandably, only a handful of Americans have realized this obvious fact, since technology seems at present to be villainous. Had our earliest ancestors been gifted with a box of matches, their first actions would probably have been destructive—or self-destructive. But we know how beneficial fire has been to civilization.

The Renaissance man invented and brought to near perfection the civilization of the machine. In doing this, he was simply acting out the conscious and unconscious demand of his time—the demand that man (whether man-in-the-world or man supposedly superior to worldly interests) master everything about him, including his own private nature, his own "ego," redefining himself in terms of a conqueror whose territory should be as vast as his own desire to conquer. The man who "masters" every aspect of his own being, subduing or obliterating his own natural instincts, leaving nothing to be unknown, uninvestigated, is the ideal of our culture, whether he is an industrialist or a "disinterested" scientist or a literary man. In other words, I see no difference between the maniacal acquisitiveness of traditional American capitalists and the meticulous, joyless, ironic manner of many scholars and writers.

It is certainly time to stop accusing "industry" or "science" or the "Corporate State" or "Amerika" of being inhuman or antihuman. The exaggerated and suprahuman potency attributed to machines, investing them with the power of the long-vanquished Devil himself, is amazing. It is also rather disheartening, if we observe the example of one of our most brilliant writers, Norman Mailer, who argues—with all the doomed, manic intensity of a late-medieval churchman resisting the future even when it is upon him—that the universe can still sensibly be divided into God and Devil, that there can be an "inorganic" product of the obviously organic mind of man. Mailer (and many others) exemplifies the old, losing, pitiful Last Stand of the Ego, the Self-Against-All-Others, the Conqueror, the Highest of all Protoplasms, Namer and Begetter of all Fictions.

What will the next phase of human experience be? A simple evolution into a higher humanism, perhaps a kind of intelligent pantheism, in which all substance in the universe (including the substance fortunate enough to perceive it) is there by equal right.

We have come to the end of, we are satiated with, the "objective," valueless philosophies that have always worked to preserve a status quo, however archaic. We are tired of the old dichotomies: Sane/Insane, Normal/Sick, Black/White, Man/Nature, Victor/Vanquished, and—above all this Cartesian dualism—I/It. Although once absolutely necessary to get us through the exploratory, analytical phase of our development as human beings, they are no longer useful or pragmatic. They are no longer *true*. Far from being locked inside our own skins, inside the "dungeons" of ourselves, we are now able to recognize that our minds belong, quite naturally, to a collective "mind," a mind in which we share everything that is mental, most obviously language itself, and that the old boundary of the skin is no boundary at all but a membrane connecting the inner and outer experiences of existence. Our intelligence, our wit, our cleverness, our unique personalities—all are simultaneously "our own" possessions and the world's. This has always been a mystical vision, but more and more in our time it is becoming a rational truth. It is no longer the private possession of a Blake, a Whitman, or a Lawrence, but the public, articulate offering of a Claude Lévi-Strauss, to whom anthropology is "part of a cosmology" and whose humanism is one that sees everything in the universe, including man, in its own place. It is the lifelong accumulative statement of Abraham Maslow, the humanist psychologist who extended the study of psychology from the realm of the disordered into that of the normal and the "more-than-normal," including people who would once have been termed mystics and been dismissed as irrational. It is the unique, fascinating voice of Buckminster Fuller, who believes that "human minds and brains may be essential in the total design" of the universe. And it is the abrasive argument of R. D. Laing, the Freudian/post-Freudian mystic, who has denied the medical and legal distinctions between "normal" and "abnormal" and has set out not only to experience but to articulate a metaphysical "illumination" whereby self and other become joined. All these are men of genius, whose training has been rigorously scientific. That they are expressing views once considered the exclusive property of mystics proves that the old dichotomy of Reason/Intuition has vanished or is vanishing.

As with all dichotomies, it will be transcended—not argued away, not battered into silence. The energies wasted on the old debates—Are we rational? Are we 90 percent Unconscious Impulses?—will be utilized for higher and more worthy human pursuits. Instead of hiding our most amazing, mysterious, and inexplicable experiences, we will learn to articulate and share them; instead of insisting upon rigid academic or intellectual categories (for instance, that "science fiction" is different from other fiction, or less traditional than the very recent "realistic novel"), we will see how naturally they flow into one another, supporting and explaining each other. Yesterday's wildly ornate, obscure, poetic prophecies evolve into today's calm statements of fact.

The vision of a new, higher humanism or pantheism is not irrational but is a logical extension of what we now know. It may frighten some of us because it challenges the unquestioned assumptions that we have always held. But these assumptions were never *ours*. We never figured them out, never discovered them for ourselves; we inherited them from the body of knowledge created by our men of genius. Now men of genius, such as British physicist/philosopher Sir James Jeans, are saying newer, deeper things:

> Today there is a wide measure of agreement, which on the physical side of science approaches almost to unanimity, that the stream of knowledge is heading toward a nonmechanical reality; the universe begins to look more like a great thought than like a great machine. Mind no longer appears as an accidental intruder into the realm of matter; we are beginning to suspect that we ought rather to hail it as the creator and governor of the realm of matter. . . .

Everywhere, suddenly, we hear the prophetic voice of Nietzsche once again, saying that man must overcome himself, that he must interpret and create the universe. (Nietzsche was never understood until now, until the world caught up with him, or approached him.) In such a world, which belongs to consciousness, there can be no distracting of energies from the need to push forward, to synthesize, to converge, to make a unity out of ostensible diversity. But too facile optimism is as ultimately distracting as the repetitive nihilism and despair we have inherited from the early part of this century. An absolutely honest literature, whether fiction or nonfiction, must dramatize for us the complexities of this epoch, showing us how deeply related we are to one another, how deeply we act out, even in our apparently secret dreams, the communal crises of our world. If demons are reawakened and allowed to run loose across the landscape of suburban shopping malls and parks, it is only so that their symbolic values—wasteful terror, despair, entropy—can be recognized. If all other dichotomies are ultimately transcended, there must still be the tension between a healthy acceptance of change and a frightened, morbid resistance to change.

The death throes of the old values are everywhere around us, but they are not at all the same thing as the death throes of particular human beings. We can transform ourselves, overleap ourselves beyond even our most flamboyant estimations. A conversion is always imminent; one cannot revert back to a lower level of consciousness. The "conversion" of the I-centered personality into a higher, or transcendental, personality cannot be an artifically, externally enforced event; it must be a natural event. It is surely as natural as the upward growth of a plant—if the plant's growth is not impeded. It has nothing to do with drugs, with the occult, with a fashionable cultivation of Eastern mysticism (not at all suitable for us in the West—far too passive, too life-denying, too ascetic); it has nothing to do with political beliefs. It is not Marxist, not Communist, not Socialist, not willing to align itself with any particular ideology. If anything, it is a flowering of the democratic ideal, a community of equals, but not a community mobilized against the rest of the world, not a unity arising out of primitive paranoia.

In the Sixties and at present we hear a very discordant music. We have got to stop screaming at one another. We have got to bring into harmony the various discordant demands, voices, stages of personality. Those more advanced must work to transform the rest, by being, themselves, models of sanity and integrity. The angriest of the ecologists must stop blaming industry for having brought to near perfection the implicit demands of society, as if anyone in our society—especially at the top—has ever behaved autonomously, unshaped by that society and its history. The optimism of *The Greening of America* seems to me a bit excessive or at least premature. There is no doubt that the future—the new consciousness—is imminent, but it may take generations to achieve it. The rapidly condensed vision, the demand for immediate gratification, is, once again, typically (and sadly) American. But, though the achievement of Reich's vision is much farther off than he seems to think, it is an inevitable one, and those of us who will probably not share personally in a transformed world can, in a way, anticipate it now, almost as if experiencing it now. If we are reasonably certain of the conclusion of a novel (especially one we have ourselves imagined), we can endure and even enjoy the intermediary chapters that move us toward that conclusion.

One of the unfortunate aspects of American intellectual life has been the nearly total divorce of academic philosophy from the issues of a fluid, psychic social reality. There are obvious reasons for this phenomenon, too complex to consider at the moment. But the book that needs to be written about the transformation of America cannot really be written by anyone lacking a thorough knowledge of where we have been and where we are right now, in terms of an intellectual development that begins and ends with the faculties of the mind. We require the meticulous genius of a Kant, a man of humility who is awakened from some epoch-induced "slumber" to synthesize vast exploratory fields of knowledge, to write the book that is the way into the future for us.

This essay, totally nonacademic in its lyric disorganization, in its bringing together of voices that, for all their differences, seem to be saying one thing, is intended only to suggest—no, really, to make a plea for—the awakening of that someone's slumber, the rejection of the positivist-linguist-"naming" asceticism that has made American philosophy so disappointing. We need a tradition similar to that in France, where the role of "philosopher" is taken naturally by men of genius who can address themselves to varied groups of people—scientists, writers, artists, and the public itself. Our highly educated and highly cultivated reading public is starved for books like *The Greening of America*. We have an amazingly fertile but somehow separate nation of writers and poets, living dreamily inside a culture but no more than symbiotically related to it. Yet these writers and poets are attempting to define that culture, to "act it out," to somehow make sense of it. The novel is the most human of all art forms—there are truths we can get nowhere else but in the novel—but now our crucial need is for something else. We need a large, generous, meticulous work that will synthesize our separate but deeply similar voices, one that will climb up out of the categories of "rational" and "irrational" to show why the consciousness of the future will feel joy, not dread, at the total rejection of the Renaissance ideal, the absorption into the psychic stream of the universe.

Lawrence asks in his strange poem "New Heaven and Earth" a question that seems to me parallel with Yeats's famous question in the sonnet "Leda and the Swan." In the Yeats poem mortal woman is raped by an immortal force, and, yes, this will and must happen; this cannot be escaped. But the point is: Did she put on his knowledge *with* his power, before the terrifying contact was broken? Lawrence speaks of mysterious "green streams" that flow from the new world (our everyday world—seen with new eyes) and asks, ". . . what are they?" What are the conversions that await us?

Suggestions for Discussion

1. Comment on Oates's observation that "Perhaps we are in the tumultuous but exciting close of a centuries-old kind of consciousness—a few of us like theologians of the medieval church encountering the unstoppable energy of the Renaissance."

2. Do you agree that contemporary crises often cause unwarranted fears because they are misread? Explain. Cite examples.

3. What does she believe to be the next phase of human experience? Do you agree? Explain.

4. Discuss her opinions about technology and industry.

5. Upon what assumptions about man and the universe is her optimism based? What personal values does she affirm?

Suggestions for Writing

1. Describe, in a speech or essay, your vision of man's future.

2. Examine Oates's use of literary references. How do they help to support her thesis?

Fiction
— ◆◆◆ —

Anton Chekhov

The Bet

Translated by Constance Garnett

Anton Chekhov (1860–1904), Russian short-story writer and playwright, practiced medicine briefly before devoting himself to literature. Among his plays are *The Sea Gull* (1896), *Uncle Vanya* (1900), *The Three Sisters* (1901), and *The Cherry Orchard* (1904). His stories, translated by Constance Garnett, were published as *The Tales of Chekhov* (1916–1923). The drama of the lawyer's solitary existence constitutes the central action of the story; it culminates in his walking out of the lodge a few hours before fulfilling the conditions of the bet; and it reaches its highest point of intensity, and its resolution, in the letter which passionately expresses his nihilism and supreme contempt for his fellow men.

I

It was a dark autumn night. The old banker was pacing from corner to corner of his study, recalling to his mind the party he gave in the autumn fifteen years before. There were many clever people at the party and much interesting conversation. They talked among other things of capital punishment. The guests, among them not a few scholars and journalists, for the most part disapproved of capital punishment. They found it obsolete as a means of punishment, unfitted to a Christian State and immoral. Some of them thought that capital punishment should be replaced universally by life imprisonment.

"I don't agree with you," said the host. "I myself have experienced neither capital punishment nor life imprisonment, but if one may judge *a priori*, then in my opinion capital punishment is more moral and more humane than imprisonment. Execution kills instantly, life imprisonment kills by degrees. Who is the more humane executioner, one who kills you in a few seconds or one who draws the life out of you incessantly, for years?"

"They're both equally immoral," remarked one of the guests, "because their purpose is the same, to take away life. The State is not God. It has no right to take away that which it cannot give back, if it should so desire."

Among the company was a lawyer, a young man of about twenty-five. On being asked his opinion, he said:

"Capital punishment and life imprisonment are equally immoral; but if I were offered the choice between them, I would certainly choose the second. It's better to live somehow than not to live at all."

There ensued a lively discussion. The banker who was then younger and more nervous suddenly lost his temper, banged his fist on the table, and turning to the young lawyer, cried out:

"It's a lie. I bet you two millions you wouldn't stick in a cell even for five years."

"If you mean it seriously," replied the lawyer, "then I bet I'll stay not five but fifteen."

"Fifteen! Done!" cried the banker. "Gentlemen, I stake two millions."

"Agreed. You stake two millions, I my freedom," said the lawyer.

So this wild, ridiculous bet came to pass. The banker, who at that time had too many millions to count, spoiled and capricious, was beside himself with rapture. During supper he said to the lawyer jokingly:

"Come to your senses, young man, before it's too late. Two millions are nothing to me, but you stand to lose three or four of the best years of your life. I say three or four, because you'll never stick it out any longer. Don't forget either, you unhappy man, that voluntary is much heavier than enforced imprisonment. The idea that you have the right to free yourself at any moment will poison the whole of your life in the cell. I pity you."

And now the banker, pacing from corner to corner, recalled all this and asked himself:

"Why did I make this bet? What's the good? The lawyer loses fifteen years of his life and I throw away two millions. Will it convince people that capital punishment is worse or better than imprisonment for life? No, no! all stuff and rubbish. On my part, it was the caprice of a well-fed man; on the lawyer's, pure greed of gold."

He recollected further what happened after the evening party. It was decided that the lawyer must undergo his imprisonment under the strictest observation, in a garden wing of the banker's house. It was agreed that during the period he would be deprived of the right to cross the threshold, to see living people, to hear human voices, and to receive letters and newspapers. He was permitted to have a musical instrument, to read books, to write letters, to drink wine, and smoke tobacco. By the agreement he could communicate, but only in silence, with the outside world through a little window specially constructed for this purpose. Everything necessary, books, music, wine, he could receive in any quantity by sending a note through the window. The agreement provided for all the minutest details, which made the confinement strictly solitary, and it obliged the lawyer to remain exactly fifteen years from twelve o'clock of November 14th, 1870 to twelve o'clock of November 14th, 1885. The least attempt on his part to violate the conditions, to escape if only for two minutes before the time freed the banker from the obligation to pay him the two millions.

During the first year of imprisonment, the lawyer, as far as it was possible to judge from his short notes, suffered terribly from loneliness and boredom. From his wing day and night came the sound of the piano. He rejected wine and tobacco. "Wine," he wrote, "excites desires, and desires are the chief foes of a prisoner; besides, nothing is more boring than to drink good wine alone, and tobacco spoils the air in his room." During the first year the lawyer was sent books of a light character; novels with a complicated love interest, stories of crime and fantasy, comedies, and so on.

In the second year the piano was heard no longer and the lawyer asked only for classics. In the fifth year, music was heard again, and the prisoner asked for wine. Those who watched him said that during the whole of that year he was only eating, drinking, and lying on his bed. He yawned often and talked angrily to himself. Books he did not read. Sometimes at nights he would sit down to write. He would write for a long time and tear it all up in the morning. More than once he was heard to weep.

In the second half of the sixth year, the prisoner began zealously to study languages, philosophy, and history. He fell on these subjects so hungrily that the banker hardly had time to get books enough for him. In the space of four years about six hundred volumes were brought at his request. It was while that passion lasted that the banker received the following letter from the prisoner: "My dear gaoler, I am writing these lines in six languages. Show them to experts. Let them read them. If they do not find one single mistake, I beg you to give orders to have a gun fired off in the garden. By the noise I shall know that my efforts have not been in vain. The geniuses of all ages and countries speak in different languages; but in them all burns the same flame. Oh, if you knew my heavenly happiness now that I can understand them!" The prisoner's desire was fulfilled. Two shots were fired in the garden by the banker's order.

Later on, after the tenth year, the lawyer sat immovable before his table and read only the New Testament. The banker found it strange that a man who in four years had mastered six hundred erudite volumes, should have spent nearly a year in reading one book, easy to understand and by no means thick. The New Testament was then replaced by the history of religions and theology.

During the last two years of his confinement the prisoner read an extraordinary amount, quite haphazard. Now he would apply himself to the natural sciences, then he would read Byron or Shakespeare. Notes used to come from him in which he asked to be sent at the same time a book on chemistry, a text-book of medicine, a novel, and some treatise on philosophy or theology. He read as though he were swimming in the sea among broken pieces of wreckage, and in his desire to save his life was eagerly grasping one piece after another.

II

The banker recalled all this, and thought:

"To-morrow at twelve o'clock he receives his freedom. Under the agreement, I shall have to pay him two millions. If I pay, it's all over with me. I am ruined for ever. . . ."

Fifteen years before he had too many millions to count, but now he was afraid to ask himself which he had more of, money or debts. Gambling on the Stock-Exchange, risky speculation, and the recklessness of which he could not rid himself even in old age, had gradually brought his business to decay; and the fearless, self-confident, proud man of business had become an ordinary banker, trembling at every rise and fall in the market.

"That cursed bet," murmured the old man clutching his head in despair. . . . "Why didn't the man die? He's only forty years old. He will take away my last farthing, marry, enjoy life, gamble on the Exchange, and I will look on like an envious beggar and hear the same words from him every day: 'I'm obliged to you for the happiness of my life. Let me help you.' No, it's too much! The only escape from bankruptcy and disgrace—is that the man should die."

The clock had just struck three. The banker was listening. In the house every one was asleep, and one could hear only the frozen trees whining outside the windows. Trying to make no sound, he took out of his safe the key of the door which had not been opened for fifteen years, put on his overcoat, and went out of the house. The garden was dark and cold. It was raining. A damp, penetrating wind howled in the garden and gave the trees no rest. Though he strained his eyes, the banker could see neither the ground, nor the white statues, nor the garden wing, nor the trees. Approaching the garden wing, he called the watchman twice. There was no answer. Evidently the watchman had taken shelter from the bad weather and was now asleep somewhere in the kitchen or the greenhouse.

"If I have the courage to fulfill my intention," thought the old man, "the suspicion will fall on the watchman first of all."

In the darkness he groped for the steps and the door and entered the hall of the garden-wing, then poked his way into a narrow passage and struck a match. Not a soul was there. Some one's bed, with no bedclothes on it, stood there, and an iron stove loomed dark in the corner. The seals on the door that led into the prisoner's room were unbroken.

When the match went out, the old man, trembling from agitation, peeped into the little window.

In the prisoner's room a candle was burning dimly. The prisoner himself sat by the table. Only his back, the hair on his head and his hands were visible. Open books were strewn about on the table, the two chairs, and on the carpet near the table.

Five minutes passed and the prisoner never once stirred. Fifteen years' confinement had taught him to sit motionless. The banker tapped on the window with his finger, but the prisoner made no movement in reply. Then the banker cautiously tore the seals from the door and put the key into the lock. The rusty lock gave a hoarse groan and the door creaked. The banker expected instantly to hear a cry of surprise and the sound of steps. Three minutes passed and it was as quiet inside as it had been before. He made up his mind to enter.

Before the table sat a man, unlike an ordinary human being. It was a skeleton, with tight-drawn skin, with long curly hair like a woman's, and a shaggy beard. The colour of his face was yellow, of an earthy shade; the cheeks were sunken, the back long and narrow, and the hand upon which he leaned his hairy head was so lean and skinny that it was painful to look upon. His hair was already silvering with grey, and no one who glanced at the senile emaciation of the face would have believed that he was only forty years old. On the table, before his bended head, lay a sheet of paper on which something was written in a tiny hand.

"Poor devil," thought the banker, "he's asleep and probably seeing millions in his dreams. I have only to take and throw this half-dead thing on the bed, smother him a moment with the pillow, and the most careful examination will find no trace of unnatural death. But, first, let us read what he has written here."

The banker took the sheet from the table and read:

"Tomorrow at twelve o'clock midnight, I shall obtain my freedom and the right to mix with people. But before I leave this room and see the sun I think it necessary to say a few words to you. On my own clear conscience and before God who sees me I declare to you that I despise freedom, life, health, and all that your books call the blessings of the world.

"For fifteen years I have diligently studied earthly life. True, I saw neither the earth nor the people, but in your books I drank fragrant wine, sang songs, hunted deer and wild boar in the forests, loved women. . . . And beautiful women, like clouds ethereal, created by the magic of your poets' genius, visited me by night, and whispered to me wonderful tales, which made my head drunken. In your books I climbed the summits of Elbruz and Mont Blanc and saw from there how the sun rose in the morning, and in the evening suffused the sky, the ocean and the mountain ridges with a purple gold. I saw from there how above me lightnings glimmered cleaving the clouds; I saw green forests, fields, rivers, lakes, cities; I heard sirens singing, and the playing of the pipes of Pan; I touched the wings of beautiful devils who came flying to me to speak of God. . . . In your books I cast myself into bottomless abysses, worked miracles, burned cities to the ground, preached new religions, conquered whole countries. . . .

"Your books gave me wisdom. All that unwearying human thought created in the centuries is compressed to a little lump in my skull. I know that I am cleverer than you all.

"And I despise your books, despise all worldly blessings and wisdom. Everything is void, frail, visionary and delusive as a mirage. Though you be proud and wise and beautiful, yet will death wipe you from the face of the earth like the mice underground; and your posterity, your history, and the immorality of your men of genius will be as frozen slag, burnt down together with the terrestrial globe.

"You are mad, and gone the wrong way. You take falsehood for truth and ugliness for beauty. You would marvel if suddenly apple and orange trees should bear frogs and lizards instead of fruit, and if roses should begin to breathe the odour of a sweating horse. So do I marvel at you, who have bartered heaven for earth. I do not want to understand you.

"That I may show you in deed my contempt for that by which you live, I waive the two millions of which I once dreamed as of paradise, and which I now despise. That I may deprive myself of my right to them, I shall come out from here five minutes before the stipulated term, and thus shall violate the agreement."

When he had read, the banker put the sheet on the table, kissed the head of the strange man, and began to weep. He went out of the wing. Never at any other time, not even after his terrible losses on the Exchange, had he felt such contempt for himself as now. Coming home, he lay down on his bed, but agitation and tears kept him a long time from sleeping. . . .

The next morning the poor watchman came running to him and told him that they had seen the man who lived in the wing climb through the window into the garden. He had gone to the gate and disappeared. The banker instantly went with his servants to the wing and established the escape of his prisoner. To avoid unnecessary rumours he took the paper with the renunciation from the table and, on his return, locked it in his safe.

Suggestions for Discussion

1. If you agree that "The Bet" is primarily the lawyer's story, why is our view of the lawyer filtered through the reminiscences and observations of the banker? Why are we permitted to see the lawyer directly only twice? What artistic purposes are served by the use of hearsay and notes and letters, and by the sparseness and flatness of the account of the lawyer's years of confinement?

2. Trace the changes in the lawyer's activities as they mark the development and resolution of the action. What are the implications as to his ultimate fate?

3. How do the shifts in time contribute to suspense and tone?

4. Find examples of irony and paradox.

5. How do you reconcile the lawyer's nihilism with his lyrical assertion that he has known the beauty of earth and love, has seen nature in her glory and tempestousness, and has achieved wisdom—"all that the unresting thought of man has created"? What evidence can you find that Chekhov's vision of life extends beyond negation of all values?

Suggestions for Writing

1. Chekhov has said, "When you depict sad or unlucky people and want to touch the reader's heart, try to be colder—it gives their grief, as it were, a background against which it stands out in greater relief. . . . You must be unconcerned when you write pathetic stories, . . . the more objective, the stronger will be the effect." Write an evaluation of Chekhov's theories in relation to the characters of the banker and the lawyer, the tone of the story, and its denouement.

2. Write a position paper on the lawyer's (banker's) "examined life."

3. Write your own preferred conclusion to "The Bet"; or describe the lawyer's next fifteen years; or recount a conversation in which the banker tells his story the next morning.

Walter Van Tilburg Clark

The Portable Phonograph

Walter Van Tilburg Clark (1909–1972) was an American short-story writer and novelist, many of whose works reflect his intense awareness of nature and of the relation between man and nature. His novels include *The Ox-Bow Incident* (1942), *The City of Trembling Leaves* (1945), and *The Track of the Cat* (1949). His collected stories have been published under the title *The Watchful Gods and Other Stories* (1950). In "The Portable Phonograph," survivors of war find momentary relief from their grim and threatened existence in the words of *The Tempest* and the music of Debussy.

The red sunset with narrow, black cloud strips like threads across it, lay on the curved horizon of the prairie. The air was still and cold, and in it settled the mute darkness and greater cold of night. High in the air there was wind, for through the veil of the dusk the clouds could be seen gliding rapidly south and changing shapes. A queer sensation of torment, of two-sided, unpredictable nature, arose from the stillness of the earth air beneath the violence of the upper air. Out of the sunset, through the dead, matted grass and isolated weed stalks of the prairie, crept the narrow and deeply rutted remains of a road. In the road, in places, there were crusts of shallow, brittle ice. There were little islands of an old oiled pavement in the road too, but most of it was mud, now frozen rigid. The frozen mud still bore the toothed impress of great tanks, and a wanderer on the neighboring undulations might have stumbled, in this light, into large, partially filled-in and weed-grown cavities, their banks channeled and beginning to spread into badlands. These pits were such as might have been made by falling meteors, but they were not. They were the scars of gigantic bombs, their rawness already made a little natural by rain, seed, and time. Along the road, there were rakish remnants of fence. There was also, just visible, one portion of tangled and multiple barbed wire still erect, behind which was a shelving ditch with small caves, now very quiet and empty, at intervals in its back wall. Otherwise there was no structure or remnant of a structure visible over the dome of the darkling earth, but only, in sheltered hollows, the darker shadows of young trees trying again.

Under the withering arch of the high wind a V of wild geese fled south. The rush of their pinions sounded briefly, and the faint, plaintive notes of their expeditionary talk. Then they left a still greater vacancy. There was the smell and expectation of snow, as there is likely to be when the wild geese fly south. From the remote distance, towards the red sky, came faintly the protracted howl and quick yap-yap of a prairie wolf.

North of the road, perhaps a hundred yards, lay the parallel and deeply intrenched course of a small creek, lined with leafless alders and willows. The creek was already silent under ice. Into the bank above it was dug a sort of cell, with a single opening, like the mouth of a mine tunnel. Within the cell there was a little red of fire, which showed dully through the opening, like a reflection or a deception of the imagination. The light came from the chary burning of four blocks of poorly aged peat, which gave off a petty warmth and much acrid smoke. But the precious remnants of wood, old fence posts and timbers from the long-deserted dugouts, had to be saved for the real cold, for the time when a man's breath blew white, the moisture in his nostrils stiffened at once when he stepped out, and the expansive blizzards paraded for days over the vast open, swirling and settling and thickening, till the dawn of the cleared day when the sky was thin blue-green and the terrible cold, in which a man could not live for three hours unwarmed, lay over the uniformly drifted swell of the plain.

Around the smoldering peat, four men were seated cross-legged. Behind them, traversed by their shadows, was the earth bench, with two old and dirty army blankets, where the owner of the cell slept. In a niche in the opposite wall were a few tin utensils which caught the glint of the coals. The host was rewrapping in a piece of daubed burlap four fine, leather-bound books. He worked slowly and very carefully, and at last tied the bundle securely with a piece of grass-woven cord. The other three looked intently upon the process, as if a great significance lay in it. As the host tied the cord, he spoke. He was an old man, his long, matted beard and hair gray to nearly white. The shadows made his brows and cheekbones appear gnarled, his eyes and cheeks deeply sunken. His big hands, rough with frost and swollen by rheumatism, were awkward but gentle at their task. He was like a prehistoric priest performing a fateful ceremonial rite. Also his voice had in it a suitable quality of deep, reverent despair, yet perhaps at the moment, a sharpness of selfish satisfaction.

"When I perceived what was happening," he said, "I told myself, 'It is the end. I cannot take much; I will take these.' "

"Perhaps I was impractical," he continued. "But for myself, I do not regret, and what do we know of those who will come after us? We are the doddering remnant of a race of mechanical fools. I have saved what I love; the soul of what was good in us is here; perhaps the new ones will make a strong enough beginning not to fall behind when they become clever."

He rose with slow pain and placed the wrapped volumes in the niche with his utensils. The others watched him with the same ritualistic gaze.

"Shakespeare, the Bible, *Moby Dick*, the *Divine Comedy*," one of them said softly. "You might have done worse, much worse."

"You will have a little soul left until you die," said another harshly. "That is more than is true of us. My brain becomes thick, like my hands." He held the big, battered hands, with their black nails, in the glow to be seen.

"I want paper to write on," he said. "And there is none."

The fourth man said nothing. He sat in the shadow farthest from the fire, and sometimes his body jerked in its rags from the cold. Although he was still young, he was sick and coughed often. Writing implied a greater future than he now felt able to consider.

The old man seated himself laboriously, and reached out, groaning at the movement, to put another block of peat on the fire. With bowed heads and averted eyes, his three guests acknowledged his magnanimity.

"We thank you, Doctor Jenkins, for the reading," said the man who had named the books.

They seemed then to be waiting for something. Doctor Jenkins understood, but was loath to comply. In an ordinary moment he would have said nothing. But the words of *The Tempest*, which he had been reading, and the religious attention of the three made this an unusual occasion.

"You wish to hear the phonograph," he said grudgingly.

The two middle-aged men stared into the fire, unable to formulate and expose the enormity of their desire.

The young man, however, said anxiously, between suppressed coughs, "Oh, please," like an excited child.

The old man rose again in his difficult way, and went to the back of the cell. He returned and placed tenderly upon the packed floor, where the firelight might fall upon it, an old portable phonograph in a black case. He smoothed the top with his hand, and then opened it. The lovely green-felt-covered disk became visible.

"I have been using thorns as needles," he said. "But tonight, because we have a musician among us"—he bent his head to the young man, almost invisible in the shadow—"I will use a steel needle. There are only three left."

The two middle-aged men stared at him in speechless adoration. The one with the big hands, who wanted to write, moved his lips, but the whisper was not audible.

"Oh, don't!" cried the young man, as if he were hurt. "The thorns will do beautifully."

"No," the old man said. "I have become accustomed to the thorns, but they are not really good. For you, my young friend, we will have good music tonight."

"After all," he added generously, and beginning to wind the phonograph, which creaked, "they can't last forever."

"No, nor we," the man who needed to write said harshly. "The needle, by all means."

"Oh, thanks," said the young man. "Thanks," he said again in a low, excited voice, and then stifled his coughing with a bowed head.

"The records, though," said the old man when he had finished winding, "are a different matter. Already they are very worn. I do not play them more than once a week. One, once a week, that is what I allow myself."

"More than a week I cannot stand it; not to hear them," he apologized.

"No, how could you?" cried the young man. "And with them here like this."

"A man can stand anything," said the man who wanted to write, in his harsh, antagonistic voice.

"Please, the music," said the young man.

"Only the one," said the old man. "In the long run, we will remember more that way."

He had a dozen records with luxuriant gold and red seals. Even in that light the others could see that the threads of the records were becoming worn. Slowly he read out the titles and the tremendous, dead names of the composers and the artists and the orchestras. The three worked upon the names in their minds, carefully. It was difficult to select from such a wealth what they would at once most like to remember. Finally, the man who wanted to write named Gershwin's "New York."

"Oh, no," cried the sick young man, and then could say nothing more because he had to cough. The others understood him, and the harsh man withdrew his selection and waited for the musician to choose.

The musician begged Doctor Jenkins to read the titles again, very slowly, so that he could remember the sounds. While they were read, he lay back against the wall, his eyes closed, his thin, horny hand pulling at his light beard, and listened to the voices and the orchestras and the single instruments in his mind.

When the reading was done he spoke despairingly. "I have forgotten," he complained; "I cannot hear them clearly."

"There are things missing," he explained.

"I know," said Doctor Jenkins. "I thought that I knew all of Shelley by heart. I should have brought Shelley."

"That's more soul than we can use," said the harsh man. "*Moby Dick* is better."

"By God, we can understand that," he emphasized.

The Doctor nodded.

"Still," said the man who had admired the books, "we need the absolute if we are to keep a grasp on anything."

"Anything but these sticks and peat clods and rabbit snares," he said bitterly.

"Shelley desired an ultimate absolute," said the harsh man. "It's too much," he said. "It's no good; no earthly good."

The musician selected a Debussy nocturne. The others considered and approved. They rose to their knees to watch the Doctor prepare for the playing, so that they appeared to be actually in an attitude of worship. The peat glow showed the thinness of their bearded faces, and the deep lines in them, and revealed the condition of their garments. The other two continued to kneel as the old man carefully lowered the needle onto the spinning disk, but the musician suddenly drew back against the wall again, with his knees up, and buried his face in his hands.

At the first notes of the piano the listeners were startled. They stared at each other. Even the musician lifted his head in amazement, but then quickly bowed it again, strainingly, as if he were suffering from a pain he might not be able to endure. They were all listening deeply, without movement. The wet, blue-green notes tinkled forth from the old machine, and were individual, delectable presences in the cell. The individual, delectable presences swept into a sudden tide of unbearably beautiful dissonance, and then continued fully the swelling and ebbing of that tide, the dissonant inpourings, and the resolutions, and the diminishments, and the little, quiet wavelets of interlude lapping between. Every sound was piercing and singularly sweet. In all the men except the musician, there occurred rapid sequences of tragically heightened recollection. He heard nothing but what was there. At the final, whispering disappearance, but moving quietly so that the others would not hear him and look at him, he let his head fall back in agony, as if it were drawn there by the hair, and clenched the fingers of one hand over his teeth. He sat that way while the others were silent, and until they began to breathe again normally. His drawn-up legs were trembling violently.

Quickly Doctor Jenkins lifted the needle off, to save it and not to spoil the recollection with scraping. When he had stopped the whirling of the sacred disk, he courteously left the phonograph open and by the fire, in sight.

The others, however, understood. The musician rose last, but then abruptly, and went quickly out at the door without saying anything. The others stopped at the door and gave their thanks in low voices. The Doctor nodded magnificently.

"Come again," he invited, "in a week. We will have the 'New York.' "

When the two had gone together, out towards the rimed road, he stood in the entrance, peering and listening. At first, there was only the resonant boom of the wind overhead, and then far over the dome of the dead, dark plain, the wolf cry lamenting. In the rifts of clouds the Doctor saw four stars flying. It impressed the Doctor that one of them had just been obscured by the beginning of a flying cloud at the very moment he heard what he had been listening for, a sound of suppressed coughing. It was not nearby, however. He believed that down against the pale alders he could see the moving shadow.

With nervous hands he lowered the piece of canvas which served as his door, and pegged it at the bottom. Then quickly and quietly, looking at the piece of canvas frequently, he slipped the records into the case, snapped the lid shut, and carried the phonograph to his couch. There, pausing often to stare at the canvas and listen, he dug earth from the wall and disclosed a piece of board. Behind this there was a deep hole in the wall, into which he put the phonograph. After a moment's consideration, he went over and reached down his bundle of books and inserted it also. Then, guardedly, he once more sealed up the hole with the board and the earth. He also changed his blankets, and the grass-stuffed sack which served as a pillow, so that he could lie facing the entrance. After carefully placing two more blocks of peat upon the fire, he stood for a long time watching the stretched canvas, but it seemed to billow naturally with the first gusts of a lowering wind. At last he prayed, and got in under his blankets, and closed his smoke-smarting eyes. On the inside of the bed, next the wall, he could feel with his hand the comfortable piece of lead pipe.

Suggestions for Discussion

1. What does the setting contribute to the tone of the story? What details prepare you for what follows? Describe the situation in which the four men find themselves.

2. The description of each man is restrained and sparse. With what details do you learn of the inner life and character of each? of what they have in common? of their differences?

3. Account for the old man's choice of books. Why would he take *The Tempest?* Explain the "harsh" man's allusion to Shelley with reference to the man's situation.

4. How does repetition contribute to tone and characterization?

5. How does the last sentence illuminate the action?

Suggestions for Writing

1. Compare "The Bet" and "The Portable Phonograph" as they portray their authors' respective structures of the world.

2. Place yourself in the host's position. What books or records would you have selected? Why?

E. B. White

The Second Tree from the Corner

E. B. White (1899–1985), perhaps America's best personal essayist, was a contributor of a monthly department to *Harper's* magazine (1938–1943), and was a contributing editor of *The New Yorker* magazine since 1926. His lightly satirical essays show great depth of feeling. They have been published under the titles *One Man's Meat* (1942), *The Second Tree from the Corner* (1947), and *The Points of My Compass* (1962). Among his other books are *Stuart Little* (1945), *The Wild Flag* (1946), *Charlotte's Web* (1952), and his revision, with additions, of William Strunk's *The Elements of Style* (1959, 1972, 1979). The second tree from the corner is a metaphor for what all men wanted, and Trexler was glad that "what he wanted, and what, in general, all men wanted . . . was both inexpressible and unattainable, and that it wasn't a wing."

"Ever had any bizarre thoughts?" asked the doctor.

Mr. Trexler failed to catch the word. "What kind?" he said.

"Bizarre," repeated the doctor, his voice steady. He watched his patient for any slight change of expression, any wince. It seemed to Trexler that the doctor was not only watching him closely but was creeping slowly toward him, like a lizard toward a bug. Trexler shoved his chair back an inch and gathered himself for a reply. He was about to say "Yes" when he realized that if he said yes the next question would be unanswerable. Bizarre thoughts, bizarre thoughts? Ever have any bizarre thoughts? What kind of thoughts *except* bizarre had he had since the age of two?

Trexler felt the time passing, the necessity for an answer. These psychiatrists were busy men, overloaded, not to be kept waiting. The next patient was probably already perched out there in the waiting room, lonely, worried, shifting around on the sofa, his mind stuffed with bizarre thoughts and amorphous fears. Poor bastard, thought Trexler. Out there all alone in that misshapen antechamber, staring at the filing cabinet and wondering whether to tell the doctor about that day on the Madison Avenue bus.

Let's see, bizarre thoughts. Trexler dodged back along the dreadful corridor of the years to see what he could find. He felt the doctor's eyes upon him and knew that time was running out. Don't be so conscientious, he said to himself. If a bizarre thought is indicated here, just reach into the bag and pick anything at all. A man as well supplied with bizarre thoughts as you are should have no difficulty producing one for the record. Trexler darted into the bag, hung for a moment before one of his thoughts, as a hummingbird pauses in the delphinium. No, he said, not that one. He darted to another (the one about the rhesus monkey), paused, considered. No, he said, not that.

Trexler knew he must hurry. He had already used up pretty nearly four seconds since the question had been put. But it was an impossible situation— just one more lousy, impossible situation such as he was always getting himself into. When, he asked himself, are you going to quit maneuvering yourself into a pocket? He made one more effort. This time he stopped at the asylum, only the bars were lucite—fluted, retractable. Not here, he said. Not this one.

He looked straight at the doctor. "No," he said quietly. "I never have any bizarre thoughts."

The doctor sucked in on his pipe, blew a plume of smoke toward the rows of medical books. Trexler's gaze followed the smoke. He managed to make out one of the titles, "The Genito-Urinary System." A bright wave of fear swept cleanly over him, and he winced under the first pain of kidney stones. He remembered when he was a child, the first time he ever entered a doctor's office, sneaking a look at the titles of the books—and the flush of fear, the shirt wet under the arms, the book on t.b., the sudden knowledge that he was in the advanced stages of consumption, the quick vision of the hemorrhage. Trexler sighed wearily. Forty years, he thought, and I still get thrown by the title of a medical book. Forty years and I still can't stay on life's little bucky horse. No wonder I'm sitting here in this dreary joint at the end of this woebegone afternoon, lying about my bizarre thoughts to a doctor who looks, come to think of it, rather tired.

The session dragged on. After about twenty minutes, the doctor rose and knocked his pipe out. Trexler got up, knocked the ashes out of his brain, and waited. The doctor smiled warmly and stuck out his hand. "There's nothing the matter with you—you're just scared. Want to know how I know you're scared?"

"How?" asked Trexler.

"Look at the chair you've been sitting in! See how it has moved back away from the desk? You kept inching away from me while I asked you questions. That means you're scared."

"Does it?" said Trexler, faking a grin. "Yeah, I suppose it does."

They finished shaking hands. Trexler turned and walked out uncertainly along the passage, then into the waiting room and out past the next patient, a ruddy pin-striped man who was seated on the sofa twirling his hat nervously and staring straight ahead at the files. Poor, frightened guy, thought Trexler, he's probably read in the *Times* that one American male out of every two is going to die of heart disease by twelve o'clock next Thursday. It says that in the paper almost every morning. And he's also probably thinking about that day on the Madison Avenue bus.

A week later, Trexler was back in the patient's chair. And for several weeks thereafter he continued to visit the doctor, always toward the end of the afternoon, when the vapors hung thick above the pool of the mind and darkened the whole region of the East Seventies. He felt no better as time went on, and he found it impossible to work. He discovered that the visits were becoming routine and that although the routine was one to which he certainly did not look forward, at least he could accept it with cool resignation, as once, years ago, he had accepted a long spell with a dentist who had settled down to a steady fooling with a couple of dead teeth. The visits, moreover, were now assuming a pattern recognizable to the patient.

Each session would begin with a résumé of symptoms—the dizziness in the streets, the constricting pain in the back of the neck, the apprehensions, the tightness of the scalp, the inability to concentrate, the despondency and the melancholy times, the feeling of pressure and tension, the anger at not being able to work, the anxiety over work not done, the gas on the stomach. Dullest set of neurotic symptoms in the world, Trexler would think, as he obediently trudged back over them for the doctor's benefit. And then, having listened attentively to the recital, the doctor would spring his question: "Have you ever found anything that gives you relief?" And Trexler would answer, "Yes. A drink." And the doctor would nod his head knowingly.

As he became familiar with the pattern Trexler found that he increasingly tended to identify himself with the doctor, transferring himself into the doctor's seat—probably (he thought) some rather slick form of escapism. At any rate, it was nothing new for Trexler to identify himself with other people. Whenever he got into a cab, he instantly became the driver, saw everything from the hackman's angle (and the reaching over with the right hand, the nudging of the flag, the pushing it down, all the way down along the side of the meter), saw everything—traffic, fare, everything—through the eyes of Anthony Rocco, or Isidore Freedman, or Matthew Scott. In a barbershop, Trexler was the barber, his fingers curled around the comb, his hand on the tonic. Perfectly natural, then, that Trexler should soon be occupying the doctor's chair, asking the questions, waiting for the answers. He got quite interested in the doctor, in this way. He liked him, and he found him a not too difficult patient.

It was on the fifth visit, about halfway through, that the doctor turned to Trexler and said, suddenly, "What do you want?" He gave the word "want" special emphasis.

"I d'know," replied Trexler uneasily. "I guess nobody knows the answer to that one."

"Sure they do," replied the doctor.

"Do you know what you want?" asked Trexler narrowly.

"Certainly," said the doctor. Trexler noticed that at this point the doctor's chair slid slightly backward, away from him. Trexler stifled a small, internal smile. Scared as a rabbit, he said to himself. Look at him scoot!

"What *do* you want?" continued Trexler, pressing his advantage, pressing it hard.

The doctor glided back another inch away from his inquisitor. "I want a wing on the small house I own in Westport. I want more money, and more leisure to do the things I want to do."

Trexler was just about to say, "And what are those things you want to do, Doctor?" when he caught himself. Better not go too far, he mused. Better not lose possession of the ball. And besides, he thought, what the hell goes on here, anyway—me paying fifteen bucks a throw for these séances and then doing the work myself, asking the questions, weighing the answers. So he wants a new wing! There's a fine piece of theatrical gauze for you! A new wing.

Trexler settled down again and resumed the role of patient for the rest of the visit. It ended on a kindly, friendly note. The doctor reassured him that his fears were the cause of his sickness, and that his fears were unsubstantial. They shook hands, smiling.

Trexler walked dizzily through the empty waiting room and the doctor followed along to let him out. It was late; the secretary had shut up shop and gone home. Another day over the dam. "Goodbye," said Trexler. He stepped into the street, turned west toward Madison, and thought of the doctor all alone there, after hours, in that desolate hole—a man who worked longer hours than his secretary. Poor, scared, overworked bastard, thought Trexler. And that new wing!

It was an evening of clearing weather, the Park showing green and desirable in the distance, the last daylight applying a high lacquer to the brick and brownstone walls and giving the street scene a luminous and intoxicating splendor. Trexler meditated, as he walked, on what he wanted. "What do you want?" he heard again. Trexler knew what he wanted, and what, in general, all men wanted; and he was glad, in a way, that it was both inexpressible and unattainable, and that it wasn't a wing. He was satisfied to remember that it was deep, formless, enduring, and impossible of fulfillment, and that it made men sick, and that when you sauntered along Third Avenue and looked through the doorways into the dim saloon, you could sometimes pick out from the unregenerate ranks the ones who had not forgotten, gazing steadily into the bottoms of the glasses on the long chance that they could get another little peek at it. Trexler found himself renewed by the rememberance that what he wanted was at once great and microscopic, and that although it borrowed from the nature of large deeds and of youthful love and of old songs and early intimations, it was not any one of these things, and that it had not been isolated or pinned down, and that a man who attempted to define it in the privacy of a doctor's office would fall flat on his face.

Trexler felt invigorated. Suddenly his sickness seemed health, his dizziness stability. A small tree, rising between him and the light, stood there saturated with the evening, each gilt-edged leaf perfectly drunk with excellence and delicacy. Trexler's spine registered an ever so slight tremor as it picked up this natural disturbance in the lovely scene. "I want the second tree from the corner, just as it stands," he said, answering an imaginary question from an imaginary physician. And he felt a slow pride in realizing that what he wanted none could bestow, and that what he had none could take away. He felt content to be sick, unembarrassed at being afraid; and in the jungle of his fear he glimpsed (as he had so often glimpsed them before) the flashy tail feathers of the bird courage.

Then he thought once again of the doctor, and of his being left there all alone, tired, frightened. (The poor, scared guy, thought Trexler.) Trexler began humming "Moonshine Lullaby," his spirit reacting instantly to the hypodermic of Merman's healthy voice. He crossed Madison, boarded a downtown bus, and rode all the way to Fifty-second Street before he had a thought that could rightly have been called bizarre.

Suggestions for Discussion

1. Each paragraph describes Mr. Trexler's sessions in the psychiatrist's office or his subsequent reflections about them. How does each sequence contribute to the resolution of the narrative? Describe the changes in Trexler's behavior and attitudes

toward the psychiatrist. State in your own words what Trexler wanted. What is he satirizing? What values is he affirming?

2. Discuss the appropriateness and effectiveness of the following images in relation to purpose and tone: "Trexler darted into the bag, hung for a moment before one of his thoughts, as a hummingbird pauses in the delphinium"; "he stopped at the asylum, only the bars were lucite—fluted, retractable"; "life's little bucky horse"; "the vapors hung thick above the pool of the mind"; "So he wants a new wing! There's a fine piece of theatrical gauze for you!"; "the flashy tail feathers of the bird courage"; "the hypodermic of Merman's healthy voice." In your analysis, generalize on the kinds of language represented by these quotations. What other contexts might you expect to contain such words as *hummingbird, bucky horse, theatrical gauze, tail feathers, hypodermic?* Why are the bars made of lucite and fluted and retractable? What is the effect on the reader of comparing Merman's voice to a hypodermic?

3. How does the use of specific details contribute to the illusion of reality? What sensory images do you find most vivid?

4. Characterize the humor. How does the diction, particularly the use of metaphor, contribute to the purpose and tone? Cite specific illustrations. How does the contrast between Trexler's unvoiced free associations and his actual statements in the psychiatrist's office contribute to the ironic tone?

5. From what point of view is the story written? What relationship does the narrator establish with the reader?

Suggestions for Writing

1. Write a narrative presenting your view of some aspect of our culture. Your feelings and attitudes should become apparent to the reader by implication rather than by explicit statement.

2. Write your own answer to the question "What do you want?" in the manner of the next to the last two paragraphs.

3. Recreate an imaginary session with one of your parents, your psychiatrist, your boss, your teacher, or your Congressman in which your feelings and attitudes are implicitly expressed.

Poetry
—◆◆◆—

Mattthew Arnold
Dover Beach

Matthew Arnold (1822–1888), son of the famous Headmaster of Rugby, Thomas Arnold, was first a poet but later abandoned poetry to become a lecturer, a critic of life and literature, and an inspector of schools. His *Collected Poems* appeared in 1869, *Essays in Criticism* in 1865 and 1888, *Culture and Anarchy* in 1869, *Friendship's Garland* in 1879, and *Mixed Essays* in 1879. In "Dover Beach," the speaker at a moment of emotional crisis, speaking to one he loves, raises the question of whether man can find any peace or joy or release from pain in a world of conflict.

The sea is calm tonight.
The tide is full, the moon lies fair
Upon the straits; on the French coast the light
Gleams and is gone; the cliffs of England stand,
Glimmering and vast, out in the tranquil bay.
Come to the window, sweet is the night-air!
Only, from the long line of spray
Where the sea meets the moon-blanched land,
Listen! you hear the grating roar
Of pebbles which the waves draw back, and fling,
At their return, up the high strand,
Begin, and cease, and then again begin,
With tremulous cadence slow, and bring
The eternal note of sadness in.

Sophocles long ago
Heard it on the Aegean, and it brought
Into his mind the turbid ebb and flow
Of human misery; we

Find also in the sound a thought,
Hearing it by this distant northern sea.
The Sea of Faith
Was once, too, at the full, and round earth's shore
Lay like the folds of a bright girdle furled.
But now I only hear
Its melancholy, long, withdrawing roar,
Retreating, to the breath
Of the night-wind, down the vast edges drear
And naked shingles of the world.

Ah, love, let us be true
To one another! for the world, which seems
To lie before us like a land of dreams,
So various, so beautiful, so new,
Hath really neither joy, nor love, nor light,
Nor certitude, nor peace, nor help for pain;
And we are here as on a darkling plain
Swept with confused alarms of struggle and flight,
Where ignorant armies clash by night.

Suggestions for Discussion

1. How does the sea symbolize modern life?
2. What is the speaker seeking and what values does he affirm?

Marianne Moore

The Mind Is an Enchanting Thing

Marianne Moore (1887–1972) was born in Missouri, was graduated from Bryn Mawr College, taught at an Indian school, worked in the New York Public Library, and edited *The Dial* (1925–1929). Her early poems were published in 1921, her *Collected Poems* in 1951. She is also the author of *Predilections* (1955), a volume of critical essays, a poetic translation of La Fontaine's *Fables* (1954), and a collection of poetry, *Tell Me, Tell Me* (1967). The symbols of enchantment are drawn from nature, science, and art.

is an enchanted thing
   like the glaze on a
katydid-wing
     subdivided by sun
     till the nettings are legion.
Like Gieseking playing Scarlatti;

like the apteryx-awl
   as a beak, or the
kiwi's rain-shawl
     of haired feathers, the mind
     feeling its way as though blind,
walks along with its eyes on the ground.

It has memory's ear
   that can hear without
having to hear.
     Like the gyroscope's fall,
     truly unequivocal
because trued by regnant certainty,

it is a power of
   strong enchantment. It
is like the dove-
     neck animated by
     sun; it is memory's eye;
it's conscientious inconsistency.

It tears off the veil; tears
   the temptation, the
mist the heart wears,
     from its eyes,—if the heart
     has a face; it takes apart
dejection. It's fire in the dove-neck's

iridescence; in the
   inconsistencies
of Scarlatti.
     Unconfusion submits
     its confusion to proof; it's
not a Herod's oath that cannot change.

Suggestions for Discussion

1. The symbols of the poem derive from nature, art, and science. Identify them.

2. How do the similes contribute to the theme of enchantment? What paradoxes do you find, and how do they underscore the central theme?

◇◇◇◇

Theodore Roethke
The Waking

Theodore Roethke (1908–1963), American poet, taught during the last years of his life at the University of Washington. *The Waking: Poems, 1933–1953* was the winner of the Pulitzer Prize for Poetry in 1953. He received the Bollingen Award for Poetry in 1958. A collected volume, *Words for the Wind,* appeared in 1958, and *The Far Field* was published posthumously in 1964. Among the many modes of learning, the poet learns "by going where I have to go".

I wake to sleep, and take my waking slow.
I feel my fate in what I cannot fear.
I learn by going where I have to go.

We think by feeling. What is there to know?
I hear my being dance from ear to ear.
I wake to sleep, and take my waking slow.

Of those so close beside me, which are you?
God bless the Ground! I shall walk softly there,
And learn by going where I have to go.

Light takes the Tree; but who can tell us how?
The lowly worm climbs up a winding stair;
I wake to sleep, and take my waking slow.

Great Nature has another thing to do
To you and me; so take the lively air,
And, lovely, learn by going where to go.

This shaking keeps me steady. I should know.
What falls away is always. And is near.
I wake to sleep, and take my waking slow.
I learn by going where I have to go.

Suggestions for Discussion

1. Relate the title to the substance of the poem.

2. What are the modes of learning? Cite specific passages.

3. How does the use of paradox contribute to tone and substance? Comment on the rhythm, rhyme scheme, repetition of refrain, imagery, and diction.

Suggestion for Writing

Examine your own processes of learning and comment on their relative effectiveness. Relate the mode of learning to the nature of what is to be learned.

Jorge Luís Borges

The Web

Translated from the Spanish by Alastair Reid

Jorge Luís Borges (1899–1986), Argentinian poet, short-story writer, essayist, critic, and university professor, was regarded until his death in 1986 as the greatest living man of letters writing in Spanish. Best known for his esoteric short fiction, Borges received little recognition in America until the publication in 1968 of English translations of *Ficciónes, Labyrinths,* and *The Aleph.* In this poem, which appeared shortly after Borges' death, he reviews a number of the key experiences of his life, anticipates his death, and wonders when it will occur, a death he faces with "impatient hope."

> Which of my cities
> am I doomed to die in?
> Geneva,
> where revelation reached me
> from Virgil and Tacitus
> (certainly not from Calvin)?
> Montevideo,
> where Luis Melián Lafinur,
> blind and heavy with years,
> died among the archives
> of that impartial
> history of Uruguay
> he never wrote?
> Nara,
> where in a Japanese inn
> I slept on the floor
> and dreamed the terrible
> image of the Buddha
> I had touched without seeing
> but saw in my dream?
> Buenos Aires,
> where I verge on being a foreigner?
> Austin, Texas,
> where my mother and I
> in the autumn of '61
> discovered America?
> What language
> am I doomed to die in?
> The Spanish my ancestors used
> to call for the charge, or to play *truco?*
> The English of the Bible
> my grandmother read from
> at the edges of the desert?

What time will it happen?
In the dove-colored twilight
when color drains away,
or in the twilight of the crow
when night abstracts and simplifies
all visible things?
Or at an inconsequential moment—
two in the afternoon?
These questions are
digressions that stem not from fear
but from impatient hope.
They form part of the fateful web
of cause and effect
that no man can foresee,
nor any god.

Suggestions for Discussion

1. Relate Borges' speculations to the title, "The Web."

2. Recall the earlier piece, *Borges and Myself.* What relationship, if any, do you perceive in the two pieces?

3. What is the nature of Borges' memories?

4. What personal values are expressed?

Suggestions for Writing

1. Drawing upon your observation and experience, discuss the "fateful web of cause and effect."

2. Relate a series of key experiences that has played a role in shaping your attitudes.

Glossary

◆◆◆

Abstraction, levels of Distinguished in two ways: in the range between the general and the specific and in the range between the abstract and the concrete.

A general word refers to a class, genus, or group; a specific word refers to a member of that group. *Ship* is a general word, but *ketch, schooner, liner,* and *tugboat* are specific. It must be remembered, however, that the terms *general* and *specific* are relative, not absolute. *Ketch,* for example, is more specific than *ship,* for a ketch is a kind of ship. But *ketch,* on the other hand, is more general than *Tahiti ketch,* for a Tahiti ketch is a kind of ketch.

The distinction between the abstract and the concrete also is relative. Ideas, qualities, and characteristics which do not exist by themselves may be called abstract; physical things such as *house, shoes,* and *horse* are concrete. Notice, however, that concrete words not only can range further into the specific (*bungalow, moccasin,* and *stallion*), but they also can range back toward the general (*domicile, clothing,* and *cattle*). In making these distinctions between the abstract and the concrete and between the general and the specific, there is no implication that good writing should be specific and concrete and that poor writing is general and abstract. Certainly most good writing is concrete and specific, but it is also general and abstract, constantly moving from the general to the specific and from the abstract to the concrete.

Allusion Reference to a familiar person, place, or thing, whether real or imaginary: Woodrow Wilson or Zeus, Siam or Atlantis, kangaroo or phoenix. The allusion is an economical way to evoke an atmosphere, a historical era, or an emotion.

Analogy In exposition, usually a comparison of some length in which the unknown is explained in terms of the known, the unfamiliar in terms of the familiar, the remote in terms of the immediate.

In argument, an analogy consists of a series of likenesses between two or more dissimilar things, demonstrating that they are either similar or identical in other respects also. The use of analogy in argument is open to criticism, for two things alike in many respects are not necessarily alike in all (for example, lampblack and diamonds are both pure carbon; they differ only in their crystal structure). Although analogy never *proves* anything, its dramatic quality, its assistance in establishing tone, its vividness make it one of the most valuable techniques of the writer.

Analysis A method of exposition by logical division, applicable to anything that can be divided into component parts: an object, such as an automobile or a watch; an institution, such as a college; or a process, such as mining coal or writing a poem. Parts or processes may be described technically and factually or impressionistically and selectively. In the latter method the parts are organized in relation to a single governing idea so that the mutually supporting function of each of the components in the total structure becomes clear to the reader. Parts may be explained in terms of their characteristic function. Analysis may also be concerned with the connection of events; given this condition or series of conditions, what effects will follow?

Argument Often contains the following parts: the *proposition,* that is, an assertion that leads to the issue; the *issue,* that is, the precise phase of the proposition which the writer is attempting to prove and the question on which the whole argument rests; the *evidence,* the facts and opinions which the author offers as testimony. He may order the evidence deductively by proceeding from certain premises to a *conclusion;* or *inductively* by generalizing from a number of instances and drawing a *conclusion.* Informal arguments frequently make greater use of the methods of exposition than they do of formal logic. See Deduction, Induction, Logic, and Analogy.

The attempt to distinguish between argument and persuasion is sometimes made by reference to means (Argument makes appeals to reason: persuasion, to emotions); sometimes to ends (Argument causes someone to change his mind; persuasion moves him to action). These distinctions, however, are more academic than functional, for in practice argument and persuasion are not discrete entities. Yet the proof in argument rests largely upon the objectivity of evidence; the proof in persuasion, upon the heightened use of language.

Assumption That part of an argument that is unstated because it is either taken for granted by the reader and writer or undetected by them. When the reader consciously disagrees with an assumption, the writer has misjudged his audience by assuming what the reader refuses to concede.

Attitude Toward subject, see Tone. Toward audience, see Audience.

Audience For the writer, his expected readers. When the audience is a general, unknown one, and the subject matter is closely related to the writer's opinions, preferences, attitudes, and tastes, then the writer's relationship to his audience is in a very real sense his relationship to himself. The writer who distrusts the intelligence of his audience or who adapts his material to what he assumes are the tastes and interests of his readers compromises his integrity.

On the other hand, if the audience is generally known (a college class, for example), and the subject matter is factual information, then the beginning writer may well consider the education, interests, and tastes of his audience. Unless he keeps a definite audience in mind, the beginner is apt to shift levels of usage, use inappropriate diction, and lose the reader by appealing to none of his interests.

"It is now necessary to warn the writer that his concern for the reader must be pure; he must sympathize with the reader's plight (most readers are in trouble about half the time) but never seek to know his wants. The whole duty of a writer is to please and satisfy himself, and the true writer always plays to an audience of one. Let him start sniffing the air, or glancing at the Trend Machine, and he is as good as dead although he may make a nice living." Strunk and White, *The Elements of Style* (Macmillan).

Cause and Effect   A seemingly simple method of development in which either the cause of a particular effect or the effects of a particular cause are investigated. However, because of the philosophical difficulties surrounding causality, the writer should be cautious in ascribing causes. For the explanation of most processes, it is probably safer to proceed in a sequential order, using transitional words to indicate the order of the process.

Classification   The division of a whole into the classes that compose it; or the placement of a subject into the whole of which it is a part. See Definition and Analysis.

Coherence   Literally, a sticking together, therefore, the joining or linking of one point to another. It is the writer's obligation to make clear to the reader the relationship of sentence to sentence and paragraph to paragraph. Sometimes coherence is simply a matter of putting the parts in a sequence that is meaningful and relevant—logical sequence, chronological order, order of importance. Other times it is helpful to underscore the relationship. An elementary but highly useful method of underscoring relationships is the use of transitional words; *but, however, yet* inform the reader that what is to follow contrasts with what went before; *furthermore, moreover, in addition to* continue or expand what went before.

Another elementary way of achieving coherence is the enumeration of ideas—*first, second, third*—so as to remind the reader of the development. A more subtle transition can be gained by repeating at the beginning of a paragraph a key word or idea from the end of the preceding paragraph. Such a transition reminds the reader of what has gone before and simultaneously prepares him for what is to come.

Comparison and Contrast   The presentation of a subject by indicating similarities between two or more things (comparison); by indicating differences (contrast). The basic elements in a comparative process, then, are (1) the terms of the comparison, or the various objects compared, and (2) the points of likeness or difference between the objects compared. Often comparison and contrast are used in definition and other methods of exposition.

Concreteness   See Abstraction, Levels of.

Connotation   All that the word suggests or implies in addition to its literal meaning. However, this definition is arbitrary and, from the standpoint of the writer, artificial, because the meaning of a word includes *all* that it suggests and implies.

Contrast   See Comparison.

Coordination   Elements of like importance in like grammatical construction. Less important elements should be placed in grammatically subordinate positions. See Parallelism and Subordination.

Deductive Reasoning   In logic, the application of a generalization to a particular; by analogy, in rhetoric, that development which moves from the general to the specific.

Definition   In logic, the placing of the word to be defined in a general class and then showing how it differs from other members of the class; in rhetoric, the meaningful extension (usually enriched by the use of detail, concrete illustration, anecdote, metaphor) of a logical definition in order to answer fully, clearly, and often implicitly the question, "What is——?"

Denotation   The literal meaning of a word. See Connotation.

Description   That form of discourse whose primary purpose is to present factual information about an object or experience (objective description); or to report the impression or evaluation of an object or experience (subjective description). Most description combines the two purposes. *It was a frightening night.* (An evaluation with which others might disagree.) *The wind blew the shingles off the north side of the house and drove the rain under the door.* (Two facts about which there can be little disagreement.)

Diction   Style as determined by choice of words. Good diction is characterized by accuracy and appropriateness to subject matter; weak diction, by the use of inappropriate, vague, or trite words. The relationship between the kinds of words a writer selects and his subject matter in large part determines tone. The deliberate use of inappropriate diction is a frequent device of satire.

Discourse, forms of   Traditionally, exposition, argument, description, and narration. See entries under each. These four kinds of traditional discourse are rarely found in a pure form. Argument and exposition may be interfused in the most complex fashion. Exposition often employs narration and description for purposes of illustration. It is important to remember, however, that in an effective piece of writing the use of more than one form of discourse is never accidental. It always serves the author's central purpose.

Emphasis   The arrangement of the elements of a composition so that the important meanings occur in structurally important parts of the composition. Repetition, order of increasing importance, exclamation points, rhetorical questions, and figures of speech are all devices to achieve emphasis.

Evidence   That part of argument or persuasion that involves proof. It usually takes the form of facts, particulars deduced from general principles, or opinions of authorities.

Exposition   That form of discourse which explains or informs. Most papers required of college students are expository. The *methods* of exposition presented in this text are identification, definition, classification, illustration, comparison and contrast, and analysis. See separate entries in glossary.

Figure of Speech   A form of expression in which the meanings of words are extended beyond the literal. The common figures of speech are metaphor, simile, analogy.

Generalization   A broad conception or principle derived from particulars. Often, simply a broad statement. See Abstraction.

Grammar   A systematic description of a language.

Identification   A process preliminary to definition of a subject. For the writer it is that vastly important period preliminary to writing when, wrestling with inchoate glimmerings, he begins to select and shape his materials. As a method of exposition, it brings the subject into focus by describing it.

Illustration   A particular member of a class used to explain or dramatize a class, a type, a thing, a person, a method, an idea, or a condition. The idea explained may be either stated or implied. For purposes of illustration, the individual member of a class must be a fair representation of the distinctive qualities of the class. The use of illustrations, examples, and specific instances adds to the concreteness and vividness of writing. See Narration.

Image   A word or statement which makes an appeal to the senses. Thus, there are visual images, auditory images, *etc.* As the most direct experience of the world is through the senses, writing which makes use of sense impressions (images) can be unusually effective.

Inductive Reasoning In logic, the formulation of a generalization after the observation of an adequate number of particular instances; by analogy, in rhetoric, that development which moves from the particular to the general.

Intention For the particular purpose or function of a single piece of writing, see Purpose. Intention determines the four forms of discourse. See Exposition, Argument, Description, Narration. These intentions may be explicitly or implicitly set forth by the writer.

Irony At its simplest, involves a discrepancy between literal and intended meaning; at its most complex, it involves an utterance more meaningful (and usually meaningful in a different way) to the listener than to the speaker. For example, Oedipus's remarks about discovering the murderer of the king are understood by the audience in a way Oedipus himself cannot understand them. The inability to grasp the full implications of his own remark is frequently feigned by the satirist.

Issue The limitation of a general proposition to the precise point on which the argument rests. Defeating the issue defeats the argument. Typically the main proposition of an argument will raise at least one issue for discussion and controversy.

Limitation of Subject Restriction of the subject to one that can be adequately developed with reference to audience and purpose.

Metaphor An implied comparison between two things that are seemingly different; a compressed analogy. Effectively used, metaphors increase clarity, interest, vividness, and concreteness.

Narration A form of discourse the purpose of which is to tell a story. If a story is significant in itself, the particulars appealing to the imagination, it is *narration*. If a story illustrates a point in exposition or argument, it may be called *illustrative narration*. If a story outlines a process step by step, the particulars appealing to the understanding, it is designated as *expository narration*.

Organization, methods of Vary with the form of discourse. Exposition uses in part, in whole, or in combination identification, definition, classification, illustration, comparison and contrast, and analysis. Argument and persuasion often use the method of organization of inductive or deductive reasoning, or analogy. Description is often organized either around a dominant impression or by means of a spatial arrangement. Narration, to give two examples, may be organized chronologically or in terms of point of view.

Paradox An assertion or sentiment seemingly self-contradictory, or opposed to common sense, which may yet be true.

Paragraph A division of writing that serves to discuss one topic or one aspect of a topic. The central thought is either implied or expressed in a topic sentence. Paragraphs have such a great variety of organization and function that it is almost impossible to generalize about them.

Parallelism Elements of similar rhetorical importance in similar grammatical patterns. See Coordination.

Parody Mimicking the language and style of another.

Perspective   The vantage point chosen by the writer to achieve his purpose, his strategy. It is reflected in his close scrutiny of, or distance from, his subject; his objective representation or subjective interpretation of it. See Diction, Purpose, Tone.

Persuasion   See Argument.

Point of View   In description, the position from which the observer looks at the object described; in narration, the person who sees the action, who tells the story; in exposition, the grammatical person of the composition. First person or the more impersonal third person is commonly used.

Proposition   See Argument.

Purpose   What the writer wants to accomplish with a particular piece of writing.

Rhetoric   The art of using language effectively.

Rhetorical Question   A question asked in order to induce thought and to provide emphasis rather than to evoke an answer.

Rhythm   In poetry and prose, patterned emphasis. Good prose is less regular in its rhythm than poetry.

Satire   The attempt to effect reform by exposing an object to laughter. Satire makes frequent recourse to irony, wit, ridicule, parody. It is usually classified under such categories as the following: social satire, personal satire, literary satire.

Style   "The essence of a sound style is that it cannot be reduced to rules—that it is a living and breathing thing, with something of the demoniacal in it—that it fits its proprietor tightly and yet ever so loosely, as his skin fits him. It is, in fact, quite as securely an integral part of him as that skin is . . . In brief, a style is always the outward and visible symbol of a man, and it cannot be anything else." H. L. Mencken, *On Style,* used with permission of Alfred A. Knopf, Inc.

"Young writers often suppose that style is a garnish for the meat of prose, a sauce by which a dull dish is made palatable. Style has no such separate entity; it is nondetachable, unfilterable. The beginner should approach style warily, realizing that it is himself he is approaching, no other; and he should begin by turning resolutely away from all devices that are popularly believed to indicate style—all mannerisms, tricks, adornments. The approach to style is by way of plainness, simplicity, orderliness, sincerity." E. B. White from *The Elements of Style* (Macmillan).

Subordination   Less important rhetorical elements in gramatically subordinate positions. See Parallelism and Coordination.

Syllogism   In formal logic, a deductive argument in three steps: a major premise, a minor premise, a conclusion. The major premise states a quality of a class (All men are mortal); the minor premise states that X is a member of the class (Socrates is a man); the conclusion states that the quality of a class is also a quality of a member of the class (Socrates is mortal). In rhetoric, the full syllogism is rarely used; instead, one of the premises is usually omitted. "You can rely on him; he is independent," is an abbreviated syllogism. Major premise: Independent people are reliable; minor premise: He is independent; conclusion: He is reliable. Constructing the full syllogism frequently reveals flaws in reasoning, such as the above, which has an error in the major premise.

Symbol A concrete image which suggests a meaning beyond itself.

Tone The manner in which the writer communicates his attitude toward the materials he is presenting. Diction is the most obvious means of establishing tone. See Diction.

Topic Sentence The thesis that the paragraph as a whole develops. Some paragraphs do not have topic sentences, but the thesis is implied.

Transition The linking together of sentences, paragraphs, and larger parts of the composition to achieve coherence. See Coherence.

Unity The relevance of selected material to the central theme of an essay. See Coherence.

Appendix: Art and Composition

◆◆◆

Discussion of art presents certain problems. It is difficult, sometimes impossible, to discover the thought processes of the visual artist or the "argument" of the painting; moreover, students may be unaware of how much the content of the painting derives from traditions of the form. The contemporary artist George Baselitz argues that painting projects no ideas and does not communicate or express publicly any statements, information, or opinions. A number of contemporary artists even find explication of their work repugnant. Nevertheless, the editors believe that painting can communicate and inspire not only emotions but ideas as well. They further believe that ideas relating to the themes of this text, while accounting for only a part of the total meaning or impact of these paintings, will provoke students to think and to write. Therefore, we offer these paintings in the expectation that students and instructors will find them exciting and will see even more in them for discussion or writing than we have suggested.

Paul Gauguin

Self-Portrait

Paul Gauguin (1848–1903) was born in Paris and died in the South Pacific on Hiva Oa, one of the Marquesas Islands. Having spent his early life as a sailor and a stockbroker, he began painting on the weekends. With the encouragement of Camille Pissaro, he began to devote himself exclusively to art and exhibited with the Impressionist painters from 1879 to 1886. Rebelling against the complexity of European civilization, he left Paris for Brittainy and Provence, and in 1891 he left France for Tahiti where he seemed to find a more spiritual house and where his paintings assumed the rich color and simple forms of native life. He returned to France in 1893 in an unsuccessful attempt to sell his paintings. Discouraged he returned to the South Pacific where he died of syphilis and in poverty. Gauguin's rejection of Western traditions in art and his use of abstract figures, symbols, and remarkable colors greatly influenced twentieth century painting. *Self-Portrait* (1889) reveals clues to his emotional state, presenting a moral dilemma represented by the halo and the snake.

Mary Cassatt
The Boating Party

Mary Cassatt (1845–1926) is generally regarded as the most important woman painter of her time. Born in Pittsburg, she spent most of her life in France identifying with the Impressionist movement of her close friends Manet and Degas and exhibiting with the Impressionists in Paris. She frequently painted tender scenes of motherhood and thoughtful portraits of women and young girls. Her work is marked by simplicity, vigor, and a remarkable sense of color.

Pierre August Renoir
The Luncheon of the Boating Party

Pierre August Renoir (1841–1919) was a French Impressionist painter. Born in Limoges, he began at 13 to work in a porcelain factory in Paris. In 1862, he began long lasting friendships with the painters Monet, Sisley, and Bazille; and over a period of time, they all strongly influenced each other. As Renoir began to be successful as a portrait painter, he developed the capacity for creating shimmering colors and dappled light in scenes of outdoor life. His style kept evolving, and after 1890 he began to paint voluptuous nude women, beautiful, radiant children, and rich summer landscapes. *The Luncheon of the Boating Party* (1881) is one of his most celebrated paintings.

Fernand Léger
La Grande Parade

Fernand Léger (1881–1955) was a French painter who studied architecture and painting before he became known as a cubist painter after 1910. He later taught in Paris and New York. His generally large canvases, with their energetic-looking figures and simplified forms in simple but vivid colors, evoke the spirit of the machine age and the pleasures of popular culture. His work appears in major museums in many countries and in the Léger Museum in Biot in southern France. *La Grande Parade* (1954) is a joyful depiction of a circus parade, a typical example of popular culture. Léger has described the meaning of the circus in the following terms, "I must tell you about the importance of the circus . . . around 1900 . . . What an event it was . . . We had no amusements in the provinces . . . At last the circus arrived with all its bustle . . . It was a lively event . . . colossal, weighty. And afterwards . . . the emotions remained . . . the circus was the event of my childhood. And so it's coming back in my paintings. . . ."

Robert-Victor-Félix Delaunay
Red Eiffel Tower

Robert-Victor-Félix Delaunay (1885–1941) was born in Paris. After finishing secondary school, he became an apprentice set designer. Although he began exhibiting with the Impressionists in 1904, first at the Salon d'Automne and then at the Salon des Indépendants, he became friends with the primitive painter Rousseau and studied the color theories of M. E. Chevreul. Later he came under the influence of the Cubists and painted his first *Eiffel Tower* in 1910. The next year he married the painter Sonia Terk with whom he frequently collaborated. In 1911 Kadinsky invited him to participate in the first Blue Rider exhibition in Munich. While living in Spain (1914–1920), he became a friend of the poet Guillaume Apollinaire who invented the term *Orphism* to describe the lyrical colors of Delaunay's paintings. Delaunay met members of the Ballets Russes for whom he designed a set. A major exhibition of his painting was held in 1922 in Paris, where he began his second Eiffel Tower Series and painted murals for the Paris World's Fair of 1937. He died in Montpelier.

Because he approved of what he regarded as benign rather than aggressive technology and because he found the Eiffel Tower the best example of that technology, Delaunay painted thirty different versions of the Tower.

Honoré Daumier
The Uprising

Honoré Daumier (1808–1879), French painter and caricaturist, was known as the greatest social satirist of his day. Having come with his family to Paris from Marseilles, he began to learn the art of lithography and to contribute to *Caricature.* His portrait of King Louis Phillipe as Gargantua led to his imprisonment for six months. After the government suppressed *Caricature,* Daumier contributed to *Charivari* with a series of cartoons that ridiculed the French bourgeois world. The 4,000 lithographs and 1,000 wood engravings, considered merely as cartoons in his lifetime, are now cherished as masterpieces. He also painted a number of small canvases and made many small sculptures. Increasing blindness caused him to suffer poverty, and he died in a cottage lent to him by the painter, Corot.

When Henry James, in an article on Daumier in 1890, stated that journalism was the greatest invention of the age, he did so in order to pay tribute to Daumier's lithographs, many of which he had found in a bookstore on the Left Bank in Paris. The French poet Paul Valery pointed out that Daumier was compared by many to Michelangelo and Rembrandt. Valery called Daumier the moralist of mankind. *The Uprising* (1860) is a good example of the power and intensity of his painting.

George Grosz
Student

George Grosz (1893–1959) was a German/American painter and caricaturist. Associated with the Dada movement before and during World War I, he achieved in post World War I Germany a reputation as a satirist of bourgeois society. He was brought to court three times for attacking traditional morality. With the advent of Hitler, he fled to New York where he taught at the Art Students League. He became a U. S. citizen in 1938. His autobiography, *A Little Yes and a Big No,* was translated into English in 1946. His work appears in major museums in Europe and the United States. The watercolor *Student* (1922) is a sketch of a costume Grosz designed for a play by Ivan Goll. The mask was to be made of odd pieces of junk and was to contain complicated equipment. The costume itself was also to be constructed.

Max Beckmann
Departure

Max Beckmann (1884–1950) was a German Expressionist painter who went into exile after the rise of Nazism. He went first to the Netherlands where he lived in Amsterdam and then to New York. During the last three years of his life, he taught at the Brooklyn Museum School. He is known for his large canvases with bold, highly stylized, symbolic figures which include circus performers, prostitutes, and torturers and their victims. The tryptic (three-part painting), *Departure,* depicts neither a beautiful nor pleasant scene. However, the viewer who contrasts the torture and horror of the side panels with the serenity of the middle panel experiences a purging of the emotions similar to that of the audience of classical tragedy.

Index